THE
GNB
Topical
CONCORDANCE

Bible Society

A

BIBLE SOCIETY
Stonehill Green, Westlea, Swindon SN5 7DG, England
© BFBS 1987

Bible text from the Good News Bible (Today's English Version), published by the
Bible Societies/Collins, © American Bible Society, New York, 1966, 1971, 1976.

Well-known passages of the Bible © Lion Publishing 1979

BFBS/1987/TEV 730
ISBN 0 564 077127

British Library Cataloguing in Publication Data

The GNB topical concordance.
1. Bible — concordances, English — Today's
English.
I. Robinson, David, *1940–* II. Bible.
English. Today's English. 1976
220.5'2 BS425

Printed in Great Britain by LR Printing Services Ltd, Crawley, England.

Bible Societies exist to provide resources for Bible distribution and use. Bible Society
in England and Wales (BFBS) is a member of the United Bible Societies, an
international partnership working in over 180 countries. Their common aim is to
reach all people with the Bible, or some part of it, in a language they can understand
and at a price they can afford. Parts of the Bible have now been translated into
approximately 1,800 languages. Bible Societies aim to help every church at every
point where it uses the Bible. You are invited to share in this work by your prayers
and gifts. Bible Society in your country will be very happy to provide details of its
activity.

Contents

Abbreviation of Bible books

Abbreviation		Abbreviation	
Acts	Acts	Judg	Judges
Amos	Amos	1 Kgs	1 Kings
1 Chr	1 Chronicles	2 Kgs	2 Kings
2 Chr	2 Chronicles	Lam	Lamentations
Col	Colossians	Lev	Leviticus
1 Cor	1 Corinthians	Lk	Luke
2 Cor	2 Corinthians	Mal	Malachi
Dan	Daniel	Mic	Micah
Deut	Deuteronomy	Mk	Mark
Ecc	Ecclesiastes	Mt	Matthew
Eph	Ephesians	Nah	Nahum
Esth	Esther	Neh	Nehemiah
Ex	Exodus	Num	Numbers
Ezek	Ezekiel	Obad	Obadiah
Ezra	Ezra	1 Pet	1 Peter
Gal	Galatians	2 Pet	2 Peter
Gen	Genesis	Phil	Philippians
Hab	Habakkuk	Phlm	Philemon
Hag	Haggai	Prov	Proverbs
Heb	Hebrews	Ps	Psalms
Hos	Hosea	Rev	Revelation
Is	Isaiah	Rom	Romans
Jas	James	Ruth	Ruth
Jer	Jeremiah	1 Sam	1 Samuel
Jn	John	2 Sam	2 Samuel
1 Jn	1 John	Song	Song of Songs
2 Jn	2 John	1 Thes	1 Thessalonians
3 Jn	3 John	2 Thes	2 Thessalonians
Job	Job	1 Tim	1 Timothy
Joel	Joel	2 Tim	2 Timothy
Jon	Jonah	Tit	Titus
Josh	Joshua	Zech	Zechariah
Jude	Jude	Zeph	Zephaniah

How to use the Topical Concordance

Welcome to the Topical Concordance. We hope that you will find this book a useful aid to your study of the Bible. It may be the first concordance you have seen, or you may have used several others. But the Topical Concordance is new and different, so it is important you should read this and find out how to get the most from your new Bible study "tool".

What is new and different about the Topical Concordance is that it lists verses containing *word-pairs* rather than individual words. If you look up **LOVE**, you'll find that instead of one long list of references it is divided into sections, such as **Love** and **Anger**, **Love** and **Children**, **Love** and **Christ**. This makes it easy to find passages relating to a particular theme.

Suppose you want to find the verses where **law** and **grace** are contrasted. In an ordinary concordance you would have to search through a long list of references to law, or to grace. With the Topical Concordance this is unnecessary. Under **LAW**, you will find:

Grace	
Jn	1.17 gives the **Law** through Moses, but **grace**
Rom	6.14 live under **law** but under God's **grace**.
	6.15 not under **law** but under God's **grace**?

Words of similar meaning (such as joyful and happy, evil and wicked, law and command) are often grouped together, to help you find all the passages on a particular theme:

FAITH	
.	
.	
.	
Abandon, Give up	
Mt	24.10 will **give up** their **faith** at that time;
Jn	16.1 so that you will not **give up** your **faith**.
1 Cor	13.7 Love never **gives up**; and its **faith**
1 Tim	4.1 some people will **abandon** the **faith**
Heb	6.4 how can those who **abandon** the **faith**
	6.6 And then they **abandoned** their **faith**!
2 Pet	1.10 you will never **abandon** your **faith**.
Rev	2.13 and you did not **abandon** your **faith**

We have listed the references for most word-pairs once only, so that we save space and can include a greater number of different words. **Eternal life**, for example, is listed under **LIFE**, not under **ETERNAL**. But at the back of the book is a complete **Word Index** which will tell you where every word-pair can be found. If you look up **ETERNAL** you will find:

ETERNAL
Believe see Believe–Life
Covenant see Eternal–Promise
Faithful see Faithful–Eternal
Glory
God
Kingdom
Last
Life see Life–Eternal
Light
Love see Love–Constant
Promise
Punishment
Sin
Son of God see Son of God–Life
Suffer see Eternal–Punishment
Word

The list includes all the words which are paired with **Eternal** in the Concordance. Words simply listed (**Glory, God, Kingdom,** and so on) can be found under the heading **ETERNAL** in the main part of the book. Cross-references tell you where to find all the other **Eternal** word-pairs. So to find the verses containing **eternal** and **believe**, you would turn to the heading **BELIEVE** and then look for **Life**:

BELIEVE	
.	
.	
.	
Life, Eternal, Raise, Rise	
Jn	3.15 **believes** in him may have **eternal life**
	3.16 **believes** in him may not die but have **eternal life**
	3.36 **believes** in the Son has **eternal life**

The **Word Index** is the best starting point for all study using the Topical Concordance. Here are a few examples

v

of how your study might work out in practice.

Finding passages on a particular topic

Suppose you want to know what the Bible has to say about the **forgiveness** of **sins.** You would look up either **SIN** or **FORGIVE** in the **Word Index.** In either case you will be directed to the main heading **FORGIVE** in the Concordance, where you will find this list:

Sin, Evil, Rebellion		
Ex	10.17	Now **forgive** my **sin** this once and pray
	29.36	so that **sin** may be **forgiven.**
	32.30	I can obtain **forgiveness** for your **sin.**
	32.32	Please **forgive** their **sin;**
	34.7	and **forgive evil** and **sin,**
	34.9	but **forgive** our **evil** and our **sin,**
Lev	4.20	people's **sin,** and they will be **forgiven.**

Note that the list includes references to the forgiveness of **Evil** and **Rebellion,** as well as **Sin.** In this way the Topical Concordance brings to your attention verses which relate to your theme, even though different words are used.

Making a complete study of a single word

Let us take **FAITH** for our example. First, look it up in the **Word Index.** (If you turn first to **FAITH** in the Concordance, you will miss some of the relevant word-pairs, because they will be listed the other way round, e.g. **Faith** and **Life** appears under **LIFE**.) Looking through the list of words paired with **FAITH** will help you decide which aspects of the subject to investigate. Or you may wish to do a really comprehensive study and look up all the word-pairs. The **Word Index** will tell you where to find every one.

When you turn to **FAITH** in the Concordance, you will find a list of Bible passages where it is mentioned at least three times. The first and last verse of the passage is given, and a following number (e.g. ×20) indicates how many times the word occurs in that passage:

FAITH			
Heb	10.22	– 13.7	×33
1 Tim	1.2	– 6.21	×22
Rom	3.22	– 5.2	×20
Gal	1.23	– 3.26	×16
Jas	1.3	– 2.26	×14
Mt	13.58	– 18.9	×10
Rom	14.1	– 16.25	×10
2 Tim	1.5	– 4.7	×9

A similar list can be found under all the main headings in the Concordance. It helps you to find the passages where faith is discussed rather than merely mentioned in passing. (Even when looking up an individual reference, it is better to read the whole passage from which the quotation comes. Isolated verses can give a false impression of the author's meaning.)

Finding an individual verse

You know that in the Bible it says "The Lord is my Shepherd". But *where* in the Bible? If you want to trace a reference, think of two important words in the verses and look for that word-pair in the **Word Index.** In this case, look for **Lord** under the heading **SHEPHERD**, or vice versa. This will tell you where to find the verses containing both **Shepherd** and **Lord.**

It may be that you want to find a verse but cannot remember the exact words. In that case, turn to the **Word Index** and look up the one key idea in the verse. A glance through the list of topics under that heading should indicate where the verse might be found.

Finding out about a person or place

Turn to the separate **Names Index** which follows the main Concordance. Under each name is a list of all the passages where that person or place is mentioned. If a name occurs several times within a chapter or series of chapters, the whole passage is listed rather than each individual verse. A following number (e.g. ×3) tells you how many times the name occurs within those chapters. So

the entry for Elisha looks like this:

ELISHA		
1 Kgs	19.16−21	×6
2 Kgs	2−9	×113
	13.14−21	×10
Lk	4.27	

In cases where two or more biblical characters share the same name, they are distinguished by a number following the name, e.g. **John (1)** is John the Baptist, **John (2)** is Jesus' disciple. If an individual man or woman is known by more than one name, cross-references help you to find all the relevant passages, e.g. **Simon (1)** see **Peter**.

Remembering the AV

As the language of the Authorized (King James) Version will be familiar to many readers, certain key words and phrases are listed with cross-references to their GNB equivalents, e.g. **AV ABOMINATION OF DESOLATION** see **AWFUL** − Horror.

We hope that the arrangement of the Topical Concordance will prove helpful, and that it will shed new light on the subjects you study.

The Editors

Key words are emboldened for ease of reference

Cross-references direct you to a heading where you will find a wide selection of references relating to your chosen theme

PUNISHMENT — Sin

Ps	39.11	You **punish** a man's **sins** by your
	58.10	when they see **sinners punished**,
	79.8	Do not **punish** us for the **sins**;
	89.32	then I will **punish** them for their **sins**;
	99.8	you **punished** them for their **sins**.
Prov	11.31	and **sinful** people will be **punished**.
Is	13.11	**punish** all wicked people for their **sins**.
	57.17	**sin** and greed, and so I **punished** them
Jer	1.16	I will **punish** my people because they have **sinned**;
	14.10	and **punish** them because of their **sins**."
	15.13	in order to **punish** them for the **sins**
	25.12	will **punish** Babylonia...for their **sin**
	30.14	your **punishment**...because your **sins**
	30.15	I **punished** you...because your **sins**
Lam	1.22	as you **punished** me for my **sins**.
	3.39	when we are **punished** for our **sin**?
Ezek	33.29	**punish** the people for their **sins**
	35.5	time of final **punishment** for her **sins**.
Hos	8.13	remember their **sin** and **punish** them
	9.9	remember their **sin** and **punish** them
	10.10	attack this **sinful** people and **punish**
	10.10	will be **punished** for their many **sins**.

Spare see **Mercy**

Wicked see **Evil**

PURE

Lev	14.2	—	16.34	x24
Ex	28.14	—	31.8	x10
Ex	37.2 − 29			x10
Heb	9.10	—	10.29	x10
Num	19.12 − 21			x9
Ex	25.11 − 39			x8
Num	8.6 − 21			x6
2 Chr	29.5	—	30.24	x6
Num	15.25	—	16.47	x5
Num	31.19 − 22			x5

Significant GNB words are listed in alphabetical order

PURPOSE

Acts	21.26	performed the **ceremony** of **purification**
	24.18	completed the **ceremony** of **purification**.
Heb	9.10	and various **purification ceremonies**.

Clean see **Holy**

Defile, Unclean

Lev	16.16	**purify** the Most Holy Place from the **uncleanness**
Num	19.13	does not **purify** himself remains **unclean**,
	19.19	water on the **unclean** person...to **purify**
	19.20	does not **purify** himself remains **unclean**,
Lam	4.7	were **undefiled** and **pure** as snow,
Ezek	24.13	to **purify** you, you remained **defiled**.
Tit	1.15	nothing is **pure** to those who are **defiled**
Heb	9.13	**unclean**, and this **purifies** them

Faultless see **Holy**

Forgive

Num	15.28	**purify** the man...and he will be **forgiven**.
Heb	9.22	**purified** by blood, and sins are **forgiven**
1 Jn	1.9	he will **forgive** us our sins and **purify** us

Holy, Clean, Faultless

Gen	35.2	**purify** yourselves and put on **clean**
Ex	30.35	Add salt to keep it **pure** and **holy**.
Lev	14.20	**purification**, and the man will be...**clean**.
Ezra	6.20	had **purified** themselves and were...**clean**.
Eph	5.27	in all its beauty — **pure** and **faultless**,
Col	1.22	**holy**, **pure**, and **faultless**,
1 Thes	2.10	was **pure**, right, and **without fault**.
2 Pet	3.14	to be **pure** and **faultless** in God's sight

Holy Place

Lev	16.16	to **purify** the Most Holy Place
	16.17	**Holy Place** to perform...**purification**
	16.20	ritual to **purify** the Most Holy Place,
	16.33	ritual to **purify** the Most Holy Place,

Sight

Job	11.4	claim you are **pure** in the **sight** of God.

Words of similar meaning are grouped together, to help you find all the references relevant to your topic

Important AV words are cross-referenced to their GNB equivalents

PURPOSE — God

God, Lord

2 Kgs	14.2	was not the Lord's purpose to destroy
Ps	33.1	The Lord frustrates the purposes
Lk	7.30	rejected God's purpose for themselves
	9.31	he would soon fulfil God's purpose
Acts	13.36	David served God's purposes
	20.27	the whole purpose of God.
Rom	9.11	the result of God's own purpose,
1 Cor	1.27	God purposely chose what the world
	2.10	the hidden depths of God's purposes.
Eph	1.9	God did what he had purposed,
	3.11	God...according to his eternal purpose
Jas	1.20	not achieve God's righteous purpose.
1 Pet	1.2	according to the purpose of God

AV QUICK see **ALIVE**

RAGE

2 Kgs	19.27 – 28	x2
Is	37.28 – 29	x2

Anger, Fury

Job	19.11	God is angry and rages against me;
Ps	50.3	raging fire is in front of him, a furious
	78.49	pouring out his anger and fierce rage,
	85.3	angry...and held back your furious rage.
Jer	23.19	His anger is a storm...that will rage
	30.23	Lord's anger is a storm...that will rage
Ezek	5.13	feel all the force of my anger and rage
	22.20	My anger and rage will melt them
Rev	11.18	rage, because the time for your anger

RAISE (RISE)

Cor	15.4	– 16.1	x23
Acts	2.24	– 5.31	x7
Rom	6.4	– 8.34	x7
Mt	26.32	– 28.7	x6
Mk	8.31	– 10.34	x6
Jn	5.21	– 7.39	x6

A table under the main heading directs you to passages where the word is frequently used

RAISE — Dead

1 Cor	15.16	neither has Christ been raised
	15.17	And if Christ has not been raised,
	15.20	the truth is that Christ has been raised
	15.22	be raised to life because of...Christ.
	15.23	each one will be raised...Christ, first
2 Cor	4.14	God, who raised the Lord Jesus to life,
	4.14	will also raise us up with Jesus
Eph	1.20	when he raised Christ from death
	2.6	union with Christ Jesus he raised us up
Col	1.18	the first-born Son, who was raised
	2.12	you were also raised with Christ
	3.1	You have been raised to life with Christ
1 Thes	1.10	his Son Jesus, whom he raised
	4.14	that Jesus died and rose again,
2 Tim	2.8	Jesus Christ, who was raised
Heb	13.20	God has raised from death our Lord Jesus.
1 Pet	1.3	he gave us new life by raising Jesus

Dead

Job	14.12	people die, never to rise.
Ps	88.10	miracles for the dead? Do they rise
Mt	17.9	Son of Man has been raised from death.
	22.23	that people will not rise from death.
	22.28	on the day when the dead rise to life,
	22.30	For when the dead rise to life
	22.31	as for the dead rising to life:
	27.53	and after Jesus rose from death,
	27.64	people that he was raised from death.
	28.7	He has been raised from death,
Mk	8.31	put to death, but...he will rise
	9.9	Son of Man has risen from death.
	9.10	What does this 'rising from death'
	12.18	that people will not rise from death,
	12.23	when all the dead rise to life
	12.25	For when the dead rise to life,
	12.26	as for the dead being raised:
	16.9	After Jesus rose from death
Lk	7.22	the dead are raised to life,
	14.14	the good people rise from death.

You don't need to look through all the **"Raise"** texts to find those referring to **"raising the dead"** — the Topical Concordance does it for you

Topical Concordance

ABANDON

Deut	31.6	—	32.30	x6
2 Chr	11.14	—	13.11	x5
Ps	37.25	—	38.21	x4
1 Kgs	8.57	—	9.9	x3
Ps	27.9 – 12			x3
Ps	71.9 – 18			x3
Ps	73.27	—	74.19	x3
Ps	88.5 – 18			x3
Jer	1.16	—	2.19	x3
Jer	16.11	—	17.13	x3

Darkness
Ps 44.19 you **abandoned** us in deepest **darkness**.
88.18 friends **abandon** me, and **darkness**
Prov 2.13 **abandoned**...life to live in the **darkness**

Enemies
1 Sam 28.16 **abandoned** you and become your **enemy**?
Ps 27.12 Don't **abandon** me to my **enemies**,
37.33 will not **abandon** him to his **enemy's**
41.2 will not **abandon** them to...their **enemies**.
74.19 **abandon** your...people to their...**enemies**;
119.121 don't **abandon** me to my **enemies**!
Mic 5.3 will **abandon** his people to their **enemies**

Faithful
Job 8.20 But God will never **abandon** the **faithful**
Ps 16.10 **faithfully**, and you will not **abandon** me
37.28 does not **abandon** his **faithful** people.

God, Lord
Lev 19.4 Do not **abandon** me and worship idols;
Deut 4.31 merciful **God**. He will not **abandon** you
32.15 They **abandoned God** their Creator
32.30 their **God**, had **abandoned** them;
Judg 6.13 The **Lord** has **abandoned** us
8.27 All the Israelites **abandoned God**
10.6 They **abandoned** the **Lord**
1 Sam 28.15 and **God** has **abandoned** me.
28.16 when the **Lord** has **abandoned** you
1 Kgs 9.9 they **abandoned** the **Lord** their **God**,
14.16 The **Lord** will **abandon** Israel
2 Kgs 17.21 Jeroboam made them **abandon** the **Lord**
2 Chr 7.22 they **abandoned** the **Lord** their **God**,
12.1 people **abandoned** the Law of the **Lord**.
13.11 We do what the **Lord** has commanded, but you have **abandoned** him.
21.10 had **abandoned** the **Lord**, the **God**
24.24 had **abandoned** him, the **Lord God**
Job 8.20 **God** will never **abandon** the faithful
Ps 9.10 **Lord**, will trust you; you do not **abandon** anyone who comes to you.
22.1 **God**, my **God**, why have you **abandoned**
27.9 don't **abandon** me, O **God**, my saviour.
37.25 good man **abandoned** by the **Lord**
37.28 for the **Lord** loves what is right and does not **abandon**
37.33 but the **Lord** will not **abandon** him
38.21 not **abandon** me, O **Lord**; do not stay away, my **God**!
71.11 They say, "**God** has **abandoned** him;
71.18 do not **abandon** me, O **God**!

Ps 74.1 you **abandoned** us like this, O **God**?
94.14 The **Lord** will not **abandon** his people;
Is 41.17 **God** of Israel, will never **abandon** them.
49.14 The **Lord** has **abandoned** us!
Jer 2.19 to **abandon** me, the **Lord** your **God**,
12.7 **Lord** says, "I have **abandoned** Israel;
17.13 **Lord**, you are Israel's hope; all who **abandon** you will be
22.9 you have **abandoned** your covenant with me, your **God**,
25.38 The **Lord** has **abandoned** his people
51.5 **God** Almighty, have not **abandoned**
Ezek 8.12 **Lord** doesn't see us! He has **abandoned**
9.9 the **Lord**, have **abandoned** their country
Mic 5.3 So the **Lord** will **abandon** his people
Mt 27.46 **God**, my **God**, why did you **abandon**
Mk 15.34 **God**, my **God**, why did you **abandon**

Temple
1 Kgs 9.7 I will also **abandon** this **Temple**
2 Chr 7.20 I will **abandon** this **Temple**
Lam 2.1 he **abandoned** even his **Temple**.
Mt 23.38 And so your **Temple** will be **abandoned**
Lk 13.35 And so your **Temple** will be **abandoned**

AV ABOMINATION OF DESOLATION
see **AWFUL — Horror**

ACCEPT

Rom	4.3 – 24			x9
Lev	22.19	—	23.11	x8
2 Kgs	5.15 – 26			x6
1 Cor	7.14 – 20			x6
Mal	1.10	—	2.14	x5
Rom	14.3	—	15.31	x5
Gen	33.10	—	34.17	x4
Lev	26.31	—	27.11	x3
1 Sam	10.4	—	12.3	x3
Jn	3.11 – 33			x3
Jn	12.48	—	14.21	x3
Rom	10.16	—	12.16	x3

Faith, Believe
Acts 6.7 number of priests **accepted** the **faith**.
Rom 4.3 because of his **faith God accepted** him
4.9 because of his **faith God accepted** him
4.11 of his **faith God** had **accepted** him
4.13 because he **believed** and was **accepted**
4.22 **faith**, "was **accepted** as righteous
4.24 **accepted** as righteous, who **believe** in
Gal 3.6 because of his **faith God accepted** him
1 Tim 1.15 to be completely **accepted** and **believed**:
4.9 to be completely **accepted** and **believed**.
Heb 4.2 they did not **accept** it with **faith**.
Jas 2.23 because of his **faith God accepted** him

Gift
Gen 33.10 **accept** my **gift**.
33.11 Please **accept** this **gift**
Num 7.5 **Accept** these **gifts** for use in the work
Deut 16.19 they are not to **accept** bribes, for **gifts**
2 Kgs 5.15 sir, **accept** a **gift** from me.
5.16 I swear that I will not **accept** a **gift**.
5.17 If you won't **accept** my **gift**,
Prov 6.35 **accept** any payment; no amount of **gifts**

1

Is	1.23	they are always **accepting gifts**
2 Cor	8.12	God will **accept** your **gift**
Rev	22.17	**accept** the water of life as a **gift**,

God's People

Ex	34.9	**accept** us as **your own people**.
Deut	26.18	has **accepted** you as **his own people**,
Jer	12.16	will **accept** the religion of **my people**
Rom	15.31	may be **acceptable** to **God's people**

Message see Word

Offering, Sacrifice

Ex	28.38	will **accept** all the **offerings**
Lev	1.4	and it will be **accepted** as a **sacrifice**
	7.18	God will not **accept** the man's **offering**.
	19.5	I will **accept** the **offering**.
	19.7	I will not **accept** the **offering**.
	23.11	**offering**...so that you may be **accepted**.
	26.31	and refuse to **accept** your **sacrifices**.
	27.9	animal that is **acceptable** as an **offering**
	27.11	which is not **acceptable** as an **offering**
Num	16.15	Do not **accept** any **offerings**
Judg	13.23	would not have **accepted** our **offerings**;
2 Sam	24.23	God **accept** your **offering**.
2 Chr	7.12	I **accept** this Temple...where **sacrifices**
Ezra	6.10	can **offer** sacrifices that are **acceptable**
Ps	20.3	May he **accept** all your **offerings**
Is	56.7	and **accept** the sacrifices you **offer**
Jer	6.20	I will not **accept** their **offerings**
Ezek	20.41	I will **accept** the **sacrifices**
Hos	14.2	**offering** to him: "Forgive...and **accept**
Amos	5.22	**grain-offerings**, I will not **accept** them;
Mal	1.10	I will not **accept** the **offerings**
	1.11	and **offer acceptable sacrifices**.
	2.13	he no longer **accepts** the **offerings**
Rom	15.16	an **offering acceptable** to God,
Phil	4.18	**offering** to God...which is **acceptable**
1 Pet	2.5	**offer** spiritual and **acceptable sacrifices**

Prayer

2 Chr	30.27	God heard their **prayers** and **accepted**
	33.13	God **accepted** Manasseh's **prayer**
Ps	119.108	**Accept** my **prayer** of thanks, O Lord,
Hos	14.2	Forgive all our sins and **accept** our **prayer**,
1 Tim	4.5	and the **prayer** make it **acceptable**

Righteous

Rom	4.3	God **accepted** him as **righteous**.
	4.6	whom God **accepts** as **righteous**,
	4.9	God **accepted** him as **righteous**.
	4.11	God had **accepted** him as **righteous**
	4.13	and was **accepted** as **righteous** by God.
	4.22	was **accepted** as **righteous** by God.
	4.23	words "he was **accepted** as **righteous**
	4.24	who are to be **accepted** as **righteous**,
Gal	3.6	God **accepted** him as **righteous**.
Jas	2.23	God **accepted** him as **righteous**.

Sacrifice see Offering

Teaching see Word

True

Job	5.27	It is **true**, so now **accept** it.
Lk	7.35	shown to be **true** by all who **accept** it.
1 Tim	1.15	a **true** saying, to be completely **accepted**
	4.9	a **true** saying, to be completely **accepted**

Word, Message, Teaching

2 Sam	16.23	was **accepted** as...the very **word** of God;
Job	17.3	**Accept** my **word**.
	22.22	**Accept** the **teaching**...keep his **words**
Ps	19.14	**words** and my thoughts be **acceptable**
Mt	19.12	Let him who can **accept** this **teaching**
Mk	4.20	They hear the **message**, **accept** it,
Jn	3.11	of you is willing to **accept** our **message**.

Jn	3.32	yet no one **accepts** his **message**.
	3.33	But whoever **accepts** his **message**
	8.37	you will not **accept** my **teaching**.
	12.48	me and does not **accept** my **message**
Eph	6.17	**accept** salvation...and the **word** of God
1 Thes	2.13	**message**, you heard it and **accepted** it,
1 Tim	4.5	**word**...and the prayer make it **acceptable**
Jas	1.21	Submit to God and **accept** the **word**

ACCUSE

Acts	22.30 — 26.7	x17
Mk	14.60 — 15.26	x5
Mt	26.62 — 27.37	x4
Gen	18.20 — 19.13	x3
Num	35.12 – 30	x3
Deut	19.16 – 19	x3
Dan	6.5 – 24	x3
Mt	12.10 – 42	x3
Lk	23.2 – 14	x3

Crime see Sin

Defend

| Acts | 25.16 | **defending** himself against the **accusation**. |
| Rom | 2.15 | **accuse** them and sometimes **defend** them. |

Evil see Sin

False

Ex	20.16	Do not **accuse** anyone **falsely**.
	23.7	Do not make **false accusations**
Deut	5.20	Do not **accuse** anyone **falsely**.
	19.16	by **falsely accusing** him of a crime,
	19.18	if the man has made a **false accusation**
	22.14	up **false** charges against her, **accusing**
Ps	119.78	be ashamed for **falsely accusing** me;
	140.11	May those who **accuse** others **falsely**
Prov	25.18	**false accusation** is as deadly as a sword
Mt	19.18	do not **accuse** anyone **falsely**;
Mk	10.19	do not **accuse** anyone **falsely**;
Lk	3.14	or **accuse** anyone **falsely**.
	18.20	do not **accuse** anyone **falsely**;

God, Lord

Job	13.19	Are you coming to **accuse** me, **God**?
	33.13	Why do you **accuse God** of never
	36.23	can tell **God** what to do or **accuse** him
Ps	32.2	man whom the **Lord** does not **accuse**
Jer	2.5	The **Lord** says: "What **accusation**
Hos	4.1	The **Lord** has an **accusation** to bring
	12.2	The **Lord** has an **accusation** to bring

God's People

Is	3.14	of **his people**...He makes this **accusation**:
	57.16	**people** life, and I will not...**accuse** them
Mic	6.2	**his people**...to bring an **accusation**
Rom	8.33	Who will **accuse God's** chosen **people**

Jesus

Mt	12.10	were there who wanted to **accuse Jesus**
	26.62	said to **Jesus**, "Have you no answer to ...this **accusation**
	27.37	notice of the **accusation**...'This is **Jesus**,
Mk	3.2	were there who wanted to **accuse Jesus**
	14.60	questioned **Jesus**, "Have you no answer to the **accusation**
	15.3	The chief priests were **accusing Jesus**
Lk	6.7	wanted a reason to **accuse Jesus**
	23.10	made strong **accusations** against **Jesus**.
Jn	8.6	**Jesus**, so that they could **accuse** him.

Jews

Acts	22.30	what the **Jews** were **accusing** Paul of;
	24.9	The **Jews** joined in the **accusation**
	26.2	all the things the **Jews accuse** me of,
	26.7	that I am being **accused** by the **Jews**!

Lord see God

Sin, Crime, Evil

Deut	19.16	by falsely **accusing** him of a **crime**,
Job	36.23	or **accuse** him of doing **evil**.
Ps	35.11	**Evil** men testify against me and **accuse** me of **crimes**
Is	59.12	Our **sins accuse** us.
Jer	14.7	Even though our **sins accuse** us,
Lk	23.14	of any of the **crimes** you **accuse** him of.
Acts	25.16	handing over any man **accused** of a **crime**
	25.18	**accuse** him of any of the **evil crimes**
1 Pet	2.12	when they **accuse** you of being **evildoers**,

ACKNOWLEDGE

	Hos	4.1 — 5.4	x5

God, Lord

Lev	22.32	Israel must **acknowledge** me to be holy. I am the **Lord**
Num	32.22	Then the **Lord** will **acknowledge**
Deut	26.3	now **acknowledge** to the **Lord** my **God**
	26.17	**acknowledged** the **Lord** as your **God**;
1 Chr	28.9	to **acknowledge** your father's **God**
Ps	83.16	**Lord**, and make them **acknowledge** your
	91.14	who **acknowledge** me as **Lord**.
	100.3	**Acknowledge** that the **Lord** is **God**.
Is	29.23	**acknowledge** that I am the holy **God**
	46.9	**acknowledge** that I alone am **God**
	52.6	you will **acknowledge** that I am **God**
Jer	9.3	do not **acknowledge** me as their **God**.
Ezek	6.7	will **acknowledge** that I am the **Lord**.
	12.16	will **acknowledge** that I am the **Lord**.
Dan	4.26	when you **acknowledge** that **God** rules
	4.32	**acknowledge** that the Supreme **God** has
Hos	2.20	and you will **acknowledge** me as **Lord**.
	4.1	people do not **acknowledge** me as **God**.
	5.4	and they do not **acknowledge** the **Lord**.
Zech	1.6	**acknowledged** that I, the **Lord**

Jesus

1 Jn	4.2	**acknowledges** that **Jesus** Christ came
2 Jn	.7	not **acknowledge** that **Jesus** Christ came

Lord see God

Power

Num	20.12	faith to **acknowledge** my holy **power**
	27.14	refused to **acknowledge** my holy **power**
Ps	83.16	make them **acknowledge** your **power**.
Is	33.13	have done and **acknowledge** my **power**.
Dan	4.32	will **acknowledge** that...**God** has **power**

ACTION

	Jas	2.14 – 26	x12
	Ezek	20.44 — 24.19	x6
	Ps	105.27 — 107.24	x5
	Is	31.3 — 33.10	x4
	Ps	145.4 – 17	x3
	Prov	13.16 — 14.31	x3
	Hos	12.1 – 6	x3
	2 Cor	12.7 – 18	x3

Disgusting

Ezra	9.11	the other with **disgusting**, filthy **actions**.
Ezek	12.16	how **disgusting** their **actions**
	16.27	are **disgusted** with your immoral **actions**.
	16.47	and copy their **disgusting actions**?
	33.26	Your **actions** are **disgusting**.

Evil see Sinful

God, Lord

1 Sam	12.7	the mighty **actions** the **Lord** did to save
Job	12.12	**God** has insight and power to **act**.
	24.22	**God acts** — and the wicked man dies.
Ps	37.7	and wait for the **Lord** to **act**;
	66.5	**God** has done, his wonderful **acts**
	92.5	How great are your **actions**, **Lord**!

Ps	105.27	They did **God's** mighty **acts**
	106.7	did not understand **God's** wonderful **acts**;
	106.21	**God** who had saved them by his mighty **acts**
	107.24	**Lord** can do, his wonderful **acts**
	111.4	The **Lord** does not let us forget his wonderful **actions**;
Prov	16.9	but **God** directs your **actions**.
Ecc	9.1	saw that **God** controls the **actions**
Is	31.3	When the **Lord acts**, the strong nation
	33.10	The **Lord** says to the nations, "Now I will **act**.
Ezek	30.3	the day when the **Lord** will **act**,
Dan	5.23	You **acted** against the **Lord** of heaven
	9.19	**Lord**, listen to us, and **act**!
Hos	12.6	and wait patiently for your **God** to **act**.
1 Pet	2.9	to proclaim the wonderful **acts** of **God**,

Mighty, Wonderful

Ex	15.11	Who can work miracles and **mighty acts**
1 Sam	12.7	the **mighty actions** the **Lord** did
Ps	66.5	his **wonderful acts** among men.
	71.17	and I still tell of your **wonderful acts**.
	77.12	I will meditate on all your **mighty acts**.
	78.43	performed his **mighty acts** and miracles
	105.27	They did **God's** mighty **acts**
	106.7	not understand **God's** wonderful **acts**;
	106.21	by his **mighty acts** in Egypt.
	107.24	his **wonderful acts** on the seas.
	111.4	not let us forget his **wonderful actions**
	145.4	they will proclaim your **mighty acts**.
1 Pet	2.9	to proclaim the **wonderful acts** of God,

Sinful, Evil, Wicked

Neh	1.7	We have **acted wickedly** against you
Job	31.5	I swear I have never **acted wickedly**
Ps	101.3	never tolerate **evil**. I hate the **actions**
Is	64.6	have been **sinful**; even our best **actions**
Ezek	20.44	your **wicked, evil actions** deserve.
	21.24	show your **sins** in your every **action**.
	22.15	will put an end to your **evil actions**.
	43.10	them ashamed of their **sinful actions**.
Dan	9.8	have **acted** shamefully and **sinned**
Jon	3.8	**wicked** behaviour and his **evil actions**.
Rom	8.13	you put to death your **sinful actions**,
2 Pet	2.8	as he saw and heard their **evil actions**.

Wonderful see Mighty

ADULTERY

	Ezek	22.11 — 23.48	x6
	Hos	2.2 — 4.13	x5
	Num	5.19 – 29	x4
	Mt	5.27 – 32	x4
	Ezek	16.17 – 38	x3
	Mk	10.11 – 19	x3

Commit

Ex	20.14	Do not **commit adultery**.
Lev	20.10	**commits adultery** with the wife
Num	5.19	If you have not **committed adultery**,
	5.20	if you have **committed adultery**
	5.27	If she has **committed adultery**, the
	5.29	that his wife has **committed adultery**.
Deut	5.18	Do not **commit adultery**.
Prov	6.32	a man who **commits adultery**
	30.20	she **commits adultery**, has a bath
Jer	3.9	**committed adultery** by worshipping
	5.7	but they **committed adultery**
	7.9	steal, murder, **commit adultery**,
	23.14	they **commit adultery** and tell lies;
	29.23	**committed adultery** and have told lies
Ezek	16.17	and **committed adultery** with them.
	16.32	are like a woman who **commits adultery**

Ezek	22.11	Some **commit adultery**...others seduce
	23.37	have **committed...adultery** with idols
	23.48	to every woman not to **commit adultery**
	33.26	Everyone **commits adultery**.
Hos	3.1	a woman who is **committing adultery**
	3.3	a prostitute or **committing adultery**;
	4.2	murder, steal, and **commit adultery**.
	4.13	your daughters-in-law **commit adultery**.
Mt	5.27	Do not **commit adultery**.
	5.28	is guilty of **committing adultery**
	5.32	is guilty of making her **commit adultery**
	15.19	lead him to kill, **commit adultery**,
	19.9	**commits adultery** if he marries some
	19.18	do not **commit adultery**;
Mk	7.22	**commit adultery**, be greedy, and do all
	10.11	**commits adultery** against his wife.
	10.12	marries another man **commits adultery**.
	10.19	do not **commit adultery**;
Lk	16.18	a divorced woman **commits adultery**.
	18.20	Do not **commit adultery**;
Jn	8.3	had been caught **committing adultery**,
	8.4	in the very act of **committing adultery**.
Rom	2.22	Do not **commit adultery**.
	2.22	but do you **commit adultery**?
	7.3	woman and does not **commit adultery**
	13.9	Do not **commit adultery**;
Heb	13.4	and those who **commit adultery**.
Jas	2.11	Do not **commit adultery**,
Rev	2.22	who **committed adultery** with her

Prostitute

Is	57.3	**adulterers**, and **prostitutes**.
Jer	5.7	committed **adultery**...with **prostitutes**.
Ezek	23.43	as a **prostitute**...worn out by **adultery**.
Hos	2.2	to stop her **adultery** and **prostitution**.
	3.3	a **prostitute** or committing **adultery**;

AFRAID

Deut	1.17	—	3.22	x8
Deut	17.13	—	21.21	x7
Lk	8.25	—	9.45	x6
Jer	38.19	—	42.11	x5
Mt	9.8	—	10.31	x5
Mk	4.41	—	6.50	x5
Mk	9.32	—	12.12	x5
Lk	1.12	—	2.10	x5
Lk	19.21	—	22.2	x5
Gen	42.4	—	43.23	x4
Judg	6.23	—	7.10	x4
1 Sam	17.32	—	18.29	x4
1 Sam	21.12	—	23.17	x4
1 Kgs	1.43	—	2.29	x4
Is	40.9	—	41.14	x4
Is	43.1	—	44.8	x4
Mt	28.4 — 10			x4
2 Cor	11.3	—	12.21	x4
Heb	11.23	—	13.6	x4
Ps	56.3 – 11			x3
Is	8.9 – 12			x3
Jer	1.8 – 17			x3
Zeph	3.13 – 16			x3
Mt	14.5 – 30			x3
Lk	12.4 – 32			x3
Acts	27.17 – 29			x3

Believe see **Trust**

Courage, Confident, Determined

Deut	20.3	**afraid** of your enemies, or lose **courage**,
	31.6	and **confident**. Do not be **afraid**
	31.8	so do not lose **courage** or be **afraid**.
Josh	1.9	to be **determined** and **confident**! Don't be **afraid**
	5.1	became **afraid** and lost their **courage**
	7.5	lost their **courage** and were afraid.

Josh	8.1	Don't be **afraid** or **discouraged**.
	10.25	**afraid** or **discouraged**. Be...**confident**
1 Chr	22.13	**confident**...don't let...make you **afraid**.
2 Chr	20.15	not be **discouraged** or be **afraid**
	32.7	and **confident**, and don't be **afraid**
Is	35.4	who is **discouraged**...don't be **afraid**!
Jer	51.46	Do not lose **courage** or be **afraid**
Zech	8.13	So have **courage** and don't be **afraid**.
Mt	14.27	**Courage!'**...'It is I. Don't be **afraid**!
Mk	6.50	**Courage!'**...'It is I. Don't be **afraid**!
Phil	1.28	Don't be **afraid**...always be **courageous**

Evil see **Sin**

Help, Protect

Is	41.13	Do not be **afraid**; I will **help** you.
	41.14	don't be **afraid**; I will **help** you.
	44.2	I have **helped** you. Do not be **afraid**;
Jer	1.8	**afraid**...I will be with you to **protect**
Heb	13.6	Lord is my **helper**, I will not be **afraid**.

Jews

Esth	8.17	became **Jews**, because they were **afraid**
	9.3	**Jews** because they were all **afraid** of
Mt	14.5	but he was **afraid** of the **Jewish** people,
Jn	7.13	were **afraid** of the **Jewish** authorities,
	9.22	were **afraid** of the **Jewish** authorities,
	19.38	he was **afraid** of the **Jewish** authorities.
	20.19	were **afraid** of the **Jewish** authorities.

Protect see **Help**

Save, Rescue

Gen	32.11	**Save** me...from...Esau. I am **afraid**
Deut	20.1	**afraid** of them. The Lord...**rescued** you
Ps	64.1	am **afraid** of my enemies — **save** my life!
Is	35.4	**afraid**! God is coming to your **rescue**,
	43.1	Do not be **afraid** — I will **save** you.

Sin, Evil

Rom	13.4	But if you do **evil**, then be **afraid**
1 Tim	5.20	commit **sins**...the rest may be **afraid**.

Suffer

Rev	2.10	be **afraid** of anything you are...to **suffer**
	18.10	are **afraid** of sharing in her **suffering**.
	18.15	are **afraid** of sharing in her **suffering**.

Trust, Believe

Ps	56.3	**afraid**, O Lord...I put my **trust** in you.
	56.4	I **trust** in God and am not **afraid**;
	56.11	In him I **trust**, and I will not be **afraid**.
Is	12.2	I will **trust** him and not be **afraid**.
Mk	5.36	Don't be **afraid**, only **believe**.
Lk	8.50	Don't be **afraid**; only **believe**,

Victory

Num	21.34	be **afraid** of him. I will give you **victory**
Josh	8.1	Don't be **afraid**...I will give you **victory**
1 Kgs	20.13	Don't be **afraid**...I will give you **victory**

ALTAR

Lev	1.5	—	10.12	x79
Ex	27.1	—	32.5	x31
2 Chr	28.24	—	35.16	x23
Ex	37.25	—	40.33	x21
2 Kgs	23.5 – 20			x15
Ezek	43.13	—	45.19	x14
2 Kgs	16.10	—	18.22	x11
Num	3.26	—	5.29	x10
Josh	22.10 – 34			x10
1 Kgs	12.32	—	13.33	x10
Lev	16.12	—	17.11	x9
Num	15.28	—	16.46	x9
1 Kgs	1.50	—	3.4	x9
Judg	6.24 – 32			x8
1 Kgs	6.20	—	9.25	x8
1 Kgs	18.26	—	19.14	x8

1 Chr	21.18 —	22.1	x8
2 Chr	4.1 —	8.12	x8
Num	23.1 – 30		x6
Num	7.1 – 84		x5
Num	18.3 – 17		x5
Ezek	6.4 – 13		x5
Mt	23.18 – 35		x5
Deut	12.3 – 31		x4
2 Sam	24.18 – 25		x4
Is	29.1 – 7		x4
Gen	35.1 – 7		x3
2 Kgs	21.3 – 5		x3
Hos	10.1 – 8		x3

Ashes

Lev 1.16 of the altar where the ashes are put.
6.10 the greasy ashes left on the altar
Num 4.13 remove the greasy ashes from the altar
1 Kgs 13.3 altar will fall apart, and the ashes on it
13.5 altar suddenly fell apart and the ashes
2 Kgs 25.14 ash containers used in cleaning the altar,
Jer 52.18 ash containers used in cleaning the altar,

Blood see Offering

Dedicate, Consecrate, Holy, Purify

Ex 29.36 This will purify the altar.
29.37 Then the altar will be completely holy,
29.44 I will make the Tent and the altar holy,
30.10 the ritual for purifying the altar
30.10 altar is to be completely holy, dedicated
40.10 dedicate the altar and all its equipment
Lev 8.15 of the altar, in order to dedicate it.
8.15 altar...he dedicated it and purified it.
10.12 altar, because this offering is very holy.
16.18 altar for burnt-offerings and purify it.
16.19 the altar seven times...he is to purify it
Num 7.10 to celebrate the dedication of the altar.
7.11 his gifts for the dedication of the altar
7.84 for the dedication of the altar
15.28 altar...perform the ritual of purification
16.38 holy when...presented at the...altar.
2 Kgs 16.14 bronze altar dedicated to the Lord
23.8 tore down the altars dedicated
2 Chr 7.9 for the dedication of the altar
Lam 2.7 his altar and deserted his holy Temple;
Ezek 43.18 the altar is built, you are to dedicate it
43.20 will purify the altar and consecrate it.
43.22 Purify the altar with its blood
43.26 priests are to consecrate the altar
Mt 23.19 or the altar which makes the gift holy?

Gift see Offering

Holy see Dedicate

Offering, Blood, Gift, Lamb, Present, Ram, Sacrifice, Sheep

Gen 8.20 as a sacrifice on the altar.
Ex 20.24 altar of earth for me, and on it sacrifice
29.12 bull's blood and...put it on the...altar.
29.13 them on the altar as an offering to me.
29.18 ram on the altar as a food offering.
29.20 blood against all four sides of the altar.
29.21 some of the blood that is on the altar
29.25 the altar, on top of the burnt-offering, as a food-offering
29.38 sacrifice on the altar two one-year-old lambs.
30.9 Do not offer on this altar any forbidden
30.20 or approach the altar to offer
30.28 the altar for burning offerings
31.9 the altar for burnt-offerings
35.16 the altar on which to burn offerings,
38.1 For burning offerings, he made an altar
40.6 the altar for burning offerings.
40.29 he placed the altar for burning offerings.

Lev 1.9 burn the whole sacrifice on the altar.
1.11 its blood on all four sides of the altar.
1.15 The priest shall present it at the altar,
1.15 Its blood...drained out against the...altar.
2.2 the altar...it has all been offered
2.9 offered...and...burn it on the altar.
3.2 blood against all four sides of the altar
3.5 the altar along with the burnt-offerings.
3.8 blood against all four sides of the altar
3.11 on the altar as a food-offering
3.13 blood against all four sides of the altar
3.16 on the altar as a food-offering
4.7 blood on...corners of the incense-altar
4.7 of the altar used for burning sacrifices,
4.10 the altar used for the burnt-offerings,
4.18 of the altar used for burning sacrifices,
4.24 altar, where the...burnt-offerings are
4.29 altar, where the...burnt-offerings are
4.33 altar, where the...burnt-offerings are
4.35 altar along with the food-offerings
5.9 its blood against the side of the altar.
5.12 burn it on the altar as a food-offering.
6.9 A burnt-offering...left on the altar
6.14 the grain-offering...in front of the altar.
6.15 altar...all of it has been offered
6.25 altar, where the animals for the burnt
7.2 offering is to be killed on the...altar,
7.3 be removed and offered on the altar:
7.5 the fat on the altar as a food-offering
8.15 the blood, and...put it on the...altar,
8.19 the blood on all four sides of the altar.
8.24 the blood on all four sides of the altar.
8.30 the blood that was on the altar
9.7 to the altar and offer the...burnt-offering
9.14 on the altar on...the burnt-offering.
9.24 the burnt-offering...on the altar.
10.12 beside the altar, because this offering
14.20 and offer it...on the altar.
16.18 altar for burnt-offerings and purify it.
16.19 sprinkle some of the blood on the altar
16.25 on the altar the fat...for the sin-offering.
17.6 the blood against the sides of the altar
17.11 all blood be poured out on the altar
22.22 not offer any such animals on the altar
Num 5.25 and present it on the altar.
5.26 token offering and burn it on the altar.
7.10 to present their gifts at the altar,
7.11 his gifts for the dedication of the altar.
16.17 and then present it at the altar.
16.38 they were presented at the Lord's altar.
18.9 sacred offerings not burnt on the altar,
18.17 Throw their blood against the altar ...their fat as a food-offering,
23.2 offered a bull and a ram on each altar.
23.4 built the seven altars and offered a bull
23.14 he built seven altars and offered a bull
23.30 offered a bull and a ram on each altar.
28.7 the first lamb, pour out at the altar
Deut 12.27 Offer...the sacrifices...on the...altar.
33.10 They will offer sacrifices on your altar.
Josh 13.14 share of the sacrifices burnt on the altar
22.23 own altar to burn sacrifices on
22.26 built an altar, not to...make offerings,
22.28 altar. It was not for burning offerings
22.29 an altar to burn offerings...or sacrifices.
Judg 13.19 and offered them on the rock altar
21.4 altar there, offered fellowship sacrifices
1 Sam 2.28 of the sacrifices burnt on the altar.
9.12 going to offer a sacrifice on the altar
2 Sam 24.22 to burn as an offering on the altar;
24.25 an altar to the Lord and offered
1 Kgs 3.2 still offering sacrifices at many...altars.
3.3 and offered them...on various altars.
3.4 offer sacrifices...where the...famous altar

1 Kgs	7.48	the altar, the table for the bread offered
	8.64	altar was too small for...offerings.
	9.25	offered burnt-offerings...on the altar
	12.32	the altar in Bethel he offered sacrifices
	12.33	and offered a sacrifice on the altar
	13.1	the altar to offer the sacrifice.
	13.2	serving at the pagan altars who offer
	18.36	sacrifice...Elijah approached the altar
2 Kgs	16.15	Use this large altar...for...burnt-offerings
	23.5	to offer sacrifices on the pagan altar
	23.8	altars where they had offered sacrifices.
1 Chr	6.49	sacrifices that were burnt on the altar
	16.40	burn sacrifices whole on the altar
	21.23	to burn as an offering on the altar,
	21.26	an altar...and offered burnt-offerings
	21.28	so he offered sacrifices on the altar
	21.29	the altar on which sacrifices were burnt
	22.1	altar where the people...are to offer
2 Chr	1.6	offering sacrifices on the bronze altar;
	4.19	the altar and the...bread offered to God;
	7.7	altar...was too small for...offerings.
	8.12	Solomon offered sacrifices...on the altar
	29.18	including the altar for burnt-offerings,
	29.21	to offer the animals...on the altar.
	29.22	the blood of each sacrifice on the altar.
	29.24	blood on the altar as a sacrifice
	30.14	altars...in Jerusalem for offering sacrifices
	33.16	altar...and he sacrificed
	35.11	priests sprinkled the blood on the altar.
	35.16	offering of burnt-offerings on the altar.
Ezra	7.17	and wine and offer them on the altar
Ps	40.6	You do not want sacrifices...on the altar
	51.19	bulls will be sacrificed on your altar.
	66.15	offer sheep to be burnt on the altar;
Is	29.2	will be like an altar covered with blood.
	56.7	the sacrifices you offer on my altar.
	60.7	offered on the altar as sacrifices
Jer	7.21	some sacrifices you burn...on the altar,
	7.31	altar called Topheth...they can sacrifice
	11.13	many altars for sacrifices
	32.35	built altars to Baal...to sacrifice
Ezek	43.22	offer it as a sacrifice...Purify the altar
	43.27	begin offering on the altar
Hos	12.11	are sacrificed in Gilgal, and the altars
Hag	2.14	they offer on the altar is defiled.
Zech	9.15	blood of a sacrifice poured on the altar
Mal	1.7	by offering worthless food on my altar.
	1.12	altar is worthless and when you offer on
Mt	5.23	to offer your gift to God at the altar
	5.24	your gift there in front of the altar,
	23.18	if he swears by the gift on the altar,
	23.19	gift or the altar which makes the gift
	23.20	swears by the altar...by it and...the gifts
1 Cor	9.13	who offer the sacrifices on the altar
	10.18	offered in sacrifice share in the altar's
	10.20	sacrificed on pagan altars is offered
Heb	10.6	whole on the altar or with sacrifices
	10.8	and offerings...animals burnt on the altar.
	13.10	to eat any of the sacrifice on our altar.
Jas	2.21	he offered his son Isaac on the altar.
Rev	8.3	and to offer it on the gold altar

Purify see **Dedicate**

Ram see **Offering**

Sacrifice see **Offering**

Serve

Ex	28.43	the altar to serve as priests
Lev	22.3	he can never again serve at the altar.
Num	4.14	used in the service at the altar:
1 Sam	2.28	to serve at the altar, to burne
	7.17	would serve as judge...he built an altar
1 Kgs	13.2	priests serving at the pagan altars
	13.33	ordinary families to serve at the altars

1 Kgs	22.46	prostitutes serving at the pagan altars
2 Kgs	23.20	on the altars where they served,
Ezek	40.46	for the priests who served at the altar.
	44.16	serve at my altar, and conduct
Joel	1.13	you priests who serve at the altar!
	2.17	serving the Lord between the altar
1 Cor	10.18	share in the altar's service to God.

Sheep see **Offering**

Sprinkle

Ex	29.21	altar and...anointing oil, and sprinkle it
Lev	8.11	sprinkled it seven times on the altar
	8.30	altar and sprinkled them on Aaron
	16.19	sprinkle some of the blood on the altar
2 Chr	30.16	who sprinkled it on the altar.
	35.11	priests sprinkled the blood on the altar.

Tent

Ex	28.43	the Tent...or approach the altar to serve
	29.44	I will make the Tent and the altar holy,
	30.18	Place it between the Tent and the altar,
	30.20	go into the Tent or approach the altar
	38.30	entrance of the Tent...the bronze altar
	40.6	Put in front of the Tent the altar
	40.7	between the Tent and the altar
	40.26	He put the gold altar in the Tent
	40.30	between the Tent and the altar
	40.32	they went into the Tent or to the altar,
	40.33	round the Tent and the altar
Lev	1.5	the altar...at the entrance of the Tent.
	4.7	corners of the incense-altar in the Tent.
	4.18	incense-altar inside the Tent
	16.20	the rest of the Tent...and the altar,
	16.33	Tent of the Lord's presence, the altar,
	17.6	the altar at the entrance of the Tent
Num	3.26	which is round the Tent and the altar,
	4.26	that is round the Tent and the altar,
	7.1	and dedicated the Tent...and the altar
1 Kgs	2.29	fled to the Tent and was by the altar,

Worship

Gen	12.8	also he built an altar and worshipped
	13.4	had built an altar. There he worshipped
	26.25	built an altar there and worshipped
1 Kgs	18.32	he rebuilt the altar for the worship
2 Kgs	18.22	to worship only at the altar
	21.3	he built altars for the worship
	21.5	altars for the worship of the stars.
2 Chr	32.12	worship and burn incense at one altar
	33.3	altars for the worship of Baal,
	33.5	altars for the worship of the stars.
	33.16	altar where the Lord was worshipped,
	34.4	the altars where Baal was worshipped
	34.5	the altars where they had worshipped.
Ps	26.6	and march in worship round your altar.
Is	36.7	to worship at one altar only.
Jer	17.2	Your people worship at the altars
Ezek	44.16	altar, and conduct the temple worship.
Acts	17.23	where you worship, I found an altar
Rev	11.1	the altar, and count those...worshipping

ANGEL

Rev	14.6	—	22.16	x44
Rev	7.1	—	12.9	x31
Zech	1.8	—	6.8	x26
Lk	1.11	—	2.21	x18
Acts	10.3	—	12.23	x15
Dan	10.11	—	12.7	x13
Heb	1.4	—	2.16	x12
Judg	13.3 – 20			x10
1 Chr	21.12 – 30			x10
Rev	1.1	—	3.14	x10
Num	22.22 – 35			x9
Judg	5.23	—	6.22	x9
Dan	3.25	—	4.35	x7

Acts	5.19 —	8.26		x7
Mt	24.31 —	26.53		x5
2 Sam	24.16 – 17			x4
Mt	1.20 —	2.19		x4
Jude	.6 – 14			x4
Gen	19.1 – 17			x3
Job	33.23 – 24			x3
Mt	13.39 – 49			x3

Announce

Rev	5.2	I saw a mighty **angel**, who **announced**
	22.16	sent my **angel** to **announce** these things

Church

Eph	3.10	means of the **church**, the **angelic** rulers
Rev	1.20	are the **angels** of the seven **churches**,
	2.1	**angel** of the **church** in Ephesus write:
	2.8	**angel** of the **church** in Smyrna write:
	2.12	**angel** of the **church** in Pergamum write:
	2.18	**angel** of the **church** in Thyatira write:
	3.1	the **angel** of the **church** in Sardis write:
	3.7	the **angel** of the **church** in Philadelphia
	3.14	**angel** of the **church** in Laodicea write:

Command

1 Kgs	13.18	**Lord's command** an **angel** told me
2 Kgs	1.3	an **angel** of the **Lord commanded** Elijah,
Ps	103.20	mighty **angels**, who obey his **commands**,
1 Thes	4.16	shout of **command**, the **archangel's** voice

Dead

Mt	22.30	**dead** rise...they will be like the **angels**
Mk	12.25	**dead** rise...they will be like the **angels**

Death, Destroy

Ex	12.23	**Angel** of **Death** enter your houses and
2 Sam	24.16	**Lord's angel** was about to **destroy**
1 Chr	21.12	using his **angel** to bring **death**
	21.15	sent an **angel** to **destroy** Jerusalem,
Rom	8.38	neither **death** nor life, neither **angels**
1 Cor	10.10	were destroyed by the **Angel** of **Death**.
Heb	11.28	that the **Angel** of **Death** would not kill

Devil, Satan

Zech	3.2	The **angel** of the **Lord** said to **Satan**,
Mt	4.11	the **Devil** left Jesus; and **angels** came
	25.41	prepared for the **Devil** and his **angels**!
Mk	1.13	tempted by **Satan**...but **angels** came
2 Cor	11.14	**Satan** can disguise himself...like an **angel**

Dream, Vision

Gen	31.11	**angel** of God spoke to me in the **dream**
Dan	4.13	**vision**, I saw...an **angel**, alert and
Mt	1.20	an **angel**...appeared to him in a **dream**
	2.13	**angel** of the **Lord** appeared in a **dream**
	2.19	**angel** of the **Lord** appeared in a **dream**
Lk	24.23	saying they had seen a **vision** of **angels**
Acts	10.3	**vision**, in which he clearly saw an **angel**

Father

Mt	16.27	the glory of his **Father** with his **angels**,
	24.36	**angels**...nor the Son; the **Father** alone
Mk	8.38	glory of his **Father** with the holy **angels**.
	13.32	**angels**...nor the Son; only the **Father**
Lk	9.26	of the **Father** and of the holy **angels**.
Rev	3.5	presence of my **Father** and of his **angels**

God

Gen	21.17	the **angel** of **God** spoke to Hagar,
	31.11	The **angel** of God spoke to me
Ex	14.19	The **angel** of **God**, who had been
Judg	13.6	as frightening as the **angel** of **God**.
	13.9	**God** did what Manoah asked, and his **angel** came
1 Sam	29.9	you as loyal as an **angel** of **God**.
2 Sam	14.17	because the king is like **God's angel**
	14.20	Majesty is as wise as the **angel** of **God**
	19.27	but you are like **God's angel**,

Job	15.15	**God** does not trust even his **angels**;
	33.23	one of **God's** thousands of **angels**,
Ps	91.11	**God** will put his **angels** in charge of
Dan	6.22	**God** sent his **angel** to shut the mouths
Zech	14.5	**God** will come, bringing all the **angels**
Mt	4.6	**God** will give orders to his **angels**
Lk	1.26	**God** sent the **angel** Gabriel to a town
	2.13	with the **angel**, singing praises to **God**:
	4.10	**God** will order his **angels** to take good
	12.8	same for him before the **angels** of **God**.
	12.9	reject him before the **angels** of **God**.
	15.10	**angels** of **God** rejoice over one sinner
Jn	1.51	heaven open and **God's angels** going up
Acts	10.3	which he clearly saw an **angel** of **God**
	10.22	An **angel** of **God** told him to invite
	27.23	an **angel** of the **God** to whom I belong
Heb	1.5	**God** never said to any of his **angels**,
	1.6	All **God's angels** must worship him.
	1.7	But about the **angels** God said,
	1.13	**God** never said to any of his **angels**:
	1.14	**angels**, then? They are spirits who serve **God**
	2.5	**God** has not placed the **angels** as rulers
2 Pet	2.4	**God** did not spare the **angels** who
Rev	8.2	the seven **angels** who stand before **God**,
	8.4	hands of the **angel** standing before **God**.

Help, Rescue

Gen	48.16	May the **angel**, who has **rescued** me
Num	20.16	to the **Lord** for **help**. He...sent an **angel**,
Ps	34.7	His **angel** guards...and **rescues** them
Dan	3.28	He sent his **angel** and **rescued**
	10.13	one of the chief **angels**, came to **help**
	10.20	**help** me except...Israel's guardian **angel**.
Mt	4.11	**angels** came and **helped** him.
Mk	1.13	but **angels** came and **helped** him.
Acts	7.35	set them free with the **help** of the **angel**
	12.11	**Lord** sent his **angel** to **rescue** me
Heb	2.16	that it is not the **angels** that he **helps**.

Holy

Mk	8.38	his Father with the **holy angels**.
Lk	9.26	of the Father and of the **holy angels**.
1 Tim	5.21	**holy angels** I solemnly call upon you
Jude	1.14	with many thousands of his **holy angels**
Rev	14.10	fire and sulphur before the **holy angels**

Jesus, Son of God, Son of Man

Mt	4.11	the Devil left **Jesus**; and **angels** came
	13.41	the **Son of Man** will send out his **angels**
	24.36	**angels** in heaven nor the **Son**;
	25.31	**Son of Man** comes...and all the **angels**
Mk	13.32	**angels** in heaven, nor the **Son**;
Lk	2.21	**Jesus**, the name which the **angel** had
	12.9	**Son of Man**...reject...before the **angels**
Jn	1.51	**angels** going up...on the **Son of Man**.
2 Thes	1.7	**Jesus** appears...with his mighty **angels**,
1 Tim	5.21	Christ **Jesus** and of the holy **angels**
Heb	1.4	**Son** was made greater than the **angels**
	1.5	to any of his **angels**, "You are my **Son**;
	1.6	**Son**...he said, "All **God's angels**
Rev	22.16	**Jesus**, have sent my **angel** to announce

Lord

Gen	16.7	The **angel** of the **Lord** met Hagar
	22.11	the **angel** of the **Lord** called to him
	22.15	**angel** of the **Lord** called to Abraham
Ex	3.2	the **angel** of the **Lord** appeared to him
Num	20.16	we cried to the **Lord** for help. He heard our cry and sent an **angel**,
	22.22	the **angel** of the **Lord** stood in the road
	22.31	Then the **Lord** let Balaam see the **angel**
Judg	2.1	The **angel** of the **Lord** went from Gilgal
	5.23	says the **angel** of the **Lord**,
	6.11	Then the **Lord's angel** came
	6.12	The **Lord's angel** appeared to him

Judg	6.19	brought them to the **Lord's angel**
	6.21	Then the **Lord's angel** reached out
	6.22	it was the **Lord's angel** he had seen,
	13.3	The **Lord's angel** appeared to her
	13.13	The **Lord's angel** answered
	13.15	not know that it was the **Lord's angel**
	13.20	and his wife saw the **Lord's angel** go up
2 Sam	24.16	the **Lord's angel** was about to destroy
1 Kgs	13.18	the **Lord's** command an **angel** told me
	19.7	**Lord's angel** returned and woke him
2 Kgs	1.3	an **angel** of the **Lord** commanded Elijah,
	1.15	The **angel** of the **Lord** said to Elijah
	19.35	**angel** of the **Lord** went to the Assyrian
1 Chr	21.18	The **angel** of the **Lord** told Gad
	21.27	**Lord** told the **angel** to put his sword
	21.30	afraid of the sword of the **Lord's angel**.
2 Chr	32.21	The **Lord** sent an **angel** that killed
Ps	34.7	**angel** guards those who honour the **Lord**
	35.5	as the **angel** of the **Lord** pursues them!
	35.6	**angel** of the **Lord** strikes them down!
	103.20	the **Lord**, you strong and mighty **angels**,
Is	37.36	**angel** of the **Lord** went to the Assyrian
	63.9	not an **angel**, but the **Lord** himself
Zech	1.8	I saw an **angel** of the **Lord** riding
	1.13	**Lord** answered the **angel** with
	3.1	standing before the **angel** of the **Lord**.
	3.2	The **angel** of the **Lord** said to Satan,
	3.5	the **angel** of the **Lord** stood there.
	12.8	lead them like the **angel** of the **Lord**,
	14.5	The **Lord** my God will come, bringing all the **angels** with him.
Lk	2.9	An **angel** of the **Lord** appeared
Acts	12.11	The **Lord** sent his **angel** to rescue me

Message, Words

Zech	1.13	the **angel** with comforting **words**,
Lk	1.29	deeply troubled by the **angel's message**
Heb	2.2	The **message** given...by the **angels**
Rev	14.6	another **angel**...with an eternal **message**
	19.9	**angel** added, "These are the true **words**
	22.6	**angel** said to me, "These **words** are true

Mighty, Strong

Ps	103.20	you **strong** and **mighty angels**,
2 Thes	1.7	from heaven with his **mighty angels**,
2 Pet	2.11	**angels**...so much **stronger** and **mightier**
Rev	5.2	And I saw a **mighty angel**
	10.1	Then I saw another **mighty angel**
	18.21	Then a **mighty angel** picked up a stone

Power

Acts	12.11	**angel** to rescue me from Herod's **power**
Rom	8.38	**angels** nor...heavenly rulers or **powers**,
Eph	3.10	**angelic** rulers and **powers** in the
1 Pet	3.22	ruling over all **angels** and...**powers**.
Rev	7.2	four **angels**...God had given the **power**

Praise see Worship

Presence

Zech	3.7	of the **angels** who are in my **presence**.
Lk	1.19	**angel** answered. "I stand in the **presence**
Rev	3.5	**presence** of my Father and of his **angels**

Rescue see Help

Satan see Devil

Servant

Num	22.22	by his two **servants**, the **angel**
Job	4.18	**servants**; he finds fault...with his **angels**.
Heb	1.7	his **angels** winds, and his **servants** flames
Rev	1.1	to his **servant** John by sending his **angel**
	22.6	sent his **angel** to show his **servants**

Sin

Lk	15.10	**angels** of God rejoice over one **sinner**
2 Pet	2.4	did not spare the **angels** who **sinned**

Son of God see Jesus

Son of Man see Jesus

Strong see Mighty

Throne

1 Kgs	22.19	his **throne** in heaven, with all his **angels**
2 Chr	18.18	his **throne** in heaven, with all his **angels**
Mt	25.31	**angels**...he will sit on his royal **throne**,
Rev	7.11	All the **angels** stood round the **throne**
	16.10	**angel** poured out his bowl on the **throne**

Vision see Dream

Words see Message

World

1 Cor	4.9	spectacle for the whole **world** of **angels**
Eph	3.10	the **angelic** rulers...in the heavenly **world**
Heb	2.5	**angels** as rulers over the new **world**

Worship, Praise

Ps	103.20	**Praise** the Lord, you...mighty **angels**,
	148.2	**Praise** him, all his **angels**,
Lk	2.13	appeared with the **angel**, singing **praises**
Col	2.18	false humility and the **worship** of **angels**.
	2.23	in their forced **worship** of **angels**,
Heb	1.6	All God's **angels** must **worship** him.

ANGER

Ezek	19.12	—	25.17	x22
Ps	74.1	—	80.16	x20
Is	63.3	—	66.15	x10
Ezek	5.13	—	9.8	x10
1 Kgs	14.9	—	16.33	x9
Ps	88.7	—	90.13	x9
Is	7.4	—	10.6	x9
2 Kgs	21.6	—	24.20	x8
Lam	1.12	—	3.43	x8
Deut	31.17	—	32.22	x7
2 Chr	28.9	—	30.8	x7
Job	18.4	—	21.30	x7
Is	12.1	—	14.6	x7
Jer	2.35	—	4.26	x7
Deut	9.7 — 22			x6
Deut	29.20 − 28			x6
Jer	6.11	—	8.19	x6
Jer	10.10	—	12.13	x6
Eph	4.26	—	6.4	x6
Rev	14.10	—	16.19	x6
Num	24.10	—	25.11	x5
Prov	19.12	—	22.14	x5
Jer	25.6 − 38			x5
Jer	32.29	—	33.5	x5
Jer	49.37	—	52.3	x5
Ezek	16.26 − 43			x5
Ex	32.10 − 22			x4
Ps	106.23 − 40			x4
Nah	1.2 − 6			x4
Zech	1.2 − 15			x4
Num	16.15 − 46			x3
2 Kgs	17.11 − 18			x3
Job	32.2 − 5			x3
Ps	85.3 − 5			x3
Is	2.10 − 21			x3
Is	51.17 − 22			x3
Jer	15.6 − 17			x3
Jer	44.3 − 8			x3
Hab	3.2 − 12			x3

Abandon, Reject

Deut	31.17	become **angry** with them; I will **abandon**
	32.19	he was **angry** and **rejected** his sons
1 Kgs	14.9	**rejected** me and have aroused my **anger**
Ps	74.1	you **abandoned** us...Will you be **angry**
	78.59	**angry** when he saw it, so he **rejected**

8

Jer	7.29	am **angry**, and have **rejected** my people.
Lam	2.1	On the day of his **anger** he **abandoned**

Bitter

2 Chr	25.10	**bitterly angry** with the people of Judah.
Job	7.11	I am **angry** and **bitter**.
Ezek	3.14	I felt **bitter** and **angry**.
Hos	12.14	made the Lord **bitterly angry**;
Eph	4.31	rid of all **bitterness**, passion, and **anger**.

Bow see **Worship**

Destroy, Death

Ex	32.10	**angry**...and I am going to **destroy** them.
	32.12	and **destroy** them...Stop being **angry**;
Num	25.11	did not **destroy** them in my **anger**.
Deut	7.4	will be **angry** with you and **destroy** you
	9.8	**angry** — **angry** enough to **destroy** you.
	9.19	**anger**...was furious enough to **destroy**
	29.23	**destroyed** when he was furiously **angry**.
2 Chr	12.12	Lord's **anger** did not completely **destroy**
Ezra	9.14	be so **angry** that you will **destroy** us
Job	4.9	God **destroys** them in his **anger**.
	9.5	and in **anger** he **destroys** them.
	20.28	**destroyed** in the flood of God's **anger**.
Ps	59.13	**destroy** them in your **anger**;
	78.38	**destroy** them...he held back his **anger**
	80.16	at them in **anger** and **destroy** them!
	88.16	**anger** crushes me; your...attacks **destroy**
	90.7	We are **destroyed** by your **anger**;
	106.23	his **anger** from **destroying** them.
Prov	27.4	**Anger** is cruel and **destructive**
Ecc	5.6	**angry** with you? Why let him **destroy**
Jer	25.36	his **anger** has **destroyed** your nation
	49.37	my great **anger** I will **destroy** the people
Ezek	16.38	my **anger**...I will punish you with **death**.
	20.13	**anger** there in the desert and **destroy**
	22.30	when my **anger** is about to **destroy** it,
	22.31	**anger** loose on them...I will **destroy**
	43.8	and so in my **anger** I **destroyed** them.
Hos	11.9	in my **anger**; I will not **destroy** Israel
	12.14	Lord bitterly **angry**; they deserve **death**
Zeph	1.18	be **destroyed** by the fire of his **anger**.
	3.8	**anger**. The whole earth will be **destroyed**
Rom	9.22	**anger**, who were doomed to **destruction**.

Enemies

2 Sam	22.16	**enemies** and roared at them in **anger**.
Ps	18.15	**enemies**...and roared at them in **anger**.
	74.23	forget the **angry** shouts of your **enemies**,
	119.139	My **anger** burns...because my **enemies**
	138.7	You oppose my **angry enemies**
Is	66.14	I show my **anger** against my **enemies**
Zech	8.2	has made me **angry** with her **enemies**.
Gal	5.20	**enemies**...they become jealous, **angry**,

Evil, Wicked

Deut	4.25	is **evil**...and it will make him **angry**.
	32.16	the **evil** they did made him **angry**.
1 Kgs	16.7	**anger** not only because of the **evil** he
2 Kgs	17.11	Lord's **anger** with all their **wicked** deeds
Ezra	9.14	**wicked** people...you will be so **angry**
Job	21.17	God ever punish the **wicked** in **anger**
Ps	55.3	the **wicked**...are **angry** with me
	75.8	**anger**. He pours it out, and...the **wicked**
	112.10	The **wicked** see this and are **angry**;
	119.53	I see the **wicked**...I am filled with **anger**.
Prov	11.23	when the **wicked** get...everyone is **angry**.
Jer	4.4	my **anger** will burn...because of the **evil**
	21.11	**evil** you are doing will make my **anger**
	44.3	had done **evil** and had made me **angry**.
Ezek	7.13	**anger** is on everyone...who are **evil**

Force

2 Chr	12.7	will not feel the full **force** of my **anger**,
	19.10	will feel the **force** of the Lord's **anger**.
Is	30.30	voice and feel the **force** of his **anger**.

Is	42.25	he made us feel the **force** of his **anger**
	51.20	They have felt the **force** of God's **anger**.
Lam	2.6	have felt the **force** of his **anger**.
Ezek	5.13	You will feel all the **force** of my **anger**
		Also: 6.12; 7.8; 8.18
	13.15	will feel the **force** of my **anger**.
	20.8	let them feel the full **force** of my **anger**
	20.13	to let them feel the **force** of my **anger**
	20.21	to let them feel the **force** of my **anger**
	24.13	you have felt the full **force** of my **anger**.
	36.18	I let them feel the **force** of my **anger**
Zeph	3.8	to let them feel the **force** of my **anger**.

Fury, Rage

Gen	4.5	**furious**, and he scowled in **anger**.
Deut	9.19	fierce **anger**, because he was **furious**
	29.23	destroyed when he was **furiously angry**.
	29.28	The Lord became **furiously angry**,
Job	19.11	God is **angry** and **rages** against me;
	20.23	God will punish him in **fury** and **anger**.
Ps	2.5	**anger** and terrifies them with his **fury**.
	7.6	your **anger**...Stand up against the **fury**
	78.38	back his **anger** and restrained his **fury**.
	78.49	pouring out his **anger** and fierce **rage**,
	85.3	**angry**...and held back your **furious rage**.
	88.16	Your **furious anger** crushes me;
	90.7	**anger**; we are terrified by your **fury**.
	90.11	**anger**? Who knows what fear your **fury**
	102.9	Because of your **anger** and **fury**,
	124.3	in their **furious anger** against us;
Is	13.9	cruel day of his fierce **anger** and **fury**.
Jer	21.5	my **anger**, my wrath, and my **fury**.
	23.19	His **anger** is a storm, a **furious** wind that will **rage**
	30.23	Lord's **anger** is a storm, a **furious** wind that will **rage**
	32.31	have made me **angry** and **furious**
	32.37	scattered them in my **anger** and **fury**,
	33.5	to strike down in my **anger** and **fury**.
	36.7	people with his terrible **anger** and **fury**.
	42.18	Just as my **anger** and **fury** were poured
	44.6	I poured out my **anger** and **fury**
Ezek	5.13	feel all the **force** of my **anger** and **rage**
	5.15	I am **angry** and **furious** with you
	16.38	in my **anger** and **fury** I will punish you
	22.20	My **anger** and **rage** will melt them
	25.14	will make Edom feel my **furious anger**.
Hos	13.11	**anger**...given you kings, and in my **fury**
Nah	1.6	**fury**? He pours out his flaming **anger**;
Hab	3.8	**angry**...the sea that made you **furious**?
	3.12	across the earth in **anger**; in **fury**
Acts	7.54	**furious** and ground their teeth...in **anger**.
Rom	2.8	God will pour out his **anger** and **fury**.
Rev	11.18	**rage**, because the time for your **anger**
	14.19	winepress of God's **furious anger**.
	16.19	his cup — the wine of his **furious anger**.
	19.15	the **furious anger** of the Almighty God.

God, Lord

Gen	18.30	Please don't be **angry**, **Lord**,
	18.32	Please don't be **angry**, **Lord**,
Ex	4.14	the **Lord** became **angry** with Moses
	32.11	**Lord**, why should you be so **angry**
Lev	10.6	and the **Lord** will be **angry**
Num	11.1	the **Lord** heard them, he was **angry**
	11.10	distressed because the **Lord** was **angry**
	11.33	the **Lord** became **angry** with the people
	12.9	The **Lord** was **angry** with them
	14.18	the **Lord**, am not easily **angered**;
	16.15	Moses was **angry** and said to the **Lord**
	16.46	**Lord's anger** has already broken out
	22.22	**God** was **angry** that Balaam was going
	25.3	So the **Lord** was **angry** with them
	32.10	The **Lord** was **angry** that day

Num	32.13	The **Lord** was **angry** with the people
	32.14	the fierce **anger** of the **Lord**
Deut	1.34	The **Lord** heard your complaints and became **anger**
	1.37	the **Lord** also became **angry** with me
	3.26	the **Lord** was **angry** with me
	4.21	the **Lord** your **God** was **angry**
	4.25	This is evil in the **Lord's** sight, and it will make him **angry**.
	6.15	the **Lord's anger** will come against you
	7.4	the **Lord** will be **angry** with you
	9.7	you made the **Lord** your **God angry**
	9.8	Sinai you made the **Lord angry**
	9.18	the **Lord** and had made him **angry**.
	9.19	I was afraid of the **Lord's** fierce **anger**,
	9.20	**Lord** was also **angry** enough with Aaron
	9.22	also made the **Lord** your **God angry**
	11.17	the **Lord** will become **angry** with you.
	13.17	the **Lord** will turn from his fierce **anger**
	29.20	the **Lord's** burning **anger** will flame
	29.23	which the **Lord** destroyed when he was furiously **angry**.
	29.27	the **Lord** became **angry** with his people
	31.29	they will have made the **Lord angry**
	32.16	made the **Lord** jealous; the evil they did made him **angry**.
	32.19	When the **Lord** saw this, he was **angry**
Josh	22.18	against the **Lord** today, he will be **angry**
	23.16	in **his anger** he will punish you,
Judg	2.12	to them and made the **Lord angry**.
	3.8	So the **Lord** became **angry** with Israel
	6.39	Gideon said to **God**, "Don't be **angry**
	10.7	**Lord** became **angry** with the Israelites
2 Sam	6.7	**Lord God** became **angry** with Uzzah
	6.8	the **Lord** had punished Uzzah in **anger**.
	22.8	quivered because **God** was **angry**!
	24.1	The **Lord** was **angry** with Israel
1 Kgs	11.9	the **Lord** was **angry** with Solomon
	14.22	**Lord** and did more to arouse his **anger**
	15.30	aroused the **anger** of the **Lord**,
	16.7	He aroused the **Lord's anger**
	16.13	had aroused the **anger** of the **Lord**,
	16.26	he aroused the **anger** of the **Lord**,
	16.33	more to arouse the **anger** of the **Lord**,
	22.53	he aroused the **anger** of the **Lord**,
2 Kgs	13.3	So the **Lord** was **angry** with Israel
	17.11	They aroused the **Lord's anger**
	17.17	**Lord's** sight, and so aroused his **anger**.
	17.18	The **Lord** was **angry** with the Israelites
	21.6	the **Lord** and stirred up his **anger**.
	22.13	The **Lord** is **angry** with us
	23.19	who thereby aroused the **Lord's anger**.
	23.26	the **Lord's** fierce **anger** had been aroused
	24.20	The **Lord** became so **angry** with the people
1 Chr	13.10	the **Lord** became **angry** with Uzzah
	13.11	the **Lord** had punished Uzzah in **anger**.
2 Chr	12.12	**Lord's anger** did not completely destroy
	19.2	brought the **Lord's anger** on you.
	19.10	feel the force of the **Lord's anger**.
	24.18	for these sins brought the **Lord's anger**
	25.15	This made the **Lord angry**
	28.9	**Lord God** of your ancestors was **angry**
	28.11	the **Lord** will punish you in his **anger**.
	28.13	against the **Lord** and made him **angry**
	28.25	on himself the **anger** of the **Lord**,
	29.8	the **Lord** has been **angry** with Judah
	29.10	the **God** of Israel, so that he will no longer be **angry** with us.
	33.6	the **Lord** and stirred up his **anger**.
	34.21	The **Lord** is **angry** with us
	36.16	the **Lord's anger** against his people
Ezra	5.12	made the **God** of Heaven **angry**,
	10.14	**God's anger** over this situation will be
Neh	13.18	bringing more of **God's anger** down

Job	4.9	**God** destroys them in his **anger**.
	9.13	**God's anger** is constant.
	15.13	are **angry** with **God** and denounce him.
	16.9	In **anger God** tears me limb from limb;
	19.11	**God** is **angry** and rages against me;
	20.23	**God** will punish him in fury and **anger**.
	20.28	in the flood of **God's anger**.
	21.17	**God** ever punish the wicked in **anger**
	21.30	On the day **God** is **angry** and punishes,
Ps	7.6	Rise in your **anger**, O **Lord**!
	18.7	because **God** was **angry**.
	21.9	The **Lord** will devour them in his **anger**,
	38.1	O **Lord**, don't punish me in your **anger**!
	58.9	fierce **anger God** will blow them away
	74.1	**God**? Will you be **angry** with your own
	77.9	**God** forgotten to be merciful? Has **anger**
	78.31	when **God** became **angry** with them
	78.59	**God** was **angry** when he saw it,
	80.4	**Lord God** Almighty, will you be **angry**
	90.13	will your **anger** last? Have pity, O **Lord**,
	94.1	a **God** who punishes; reveal your **anger**!
	103.8	The **Lord** is merciful and loving, slow to become **angry**
	106.23	against **God** and prevented his **anger**
	106.29	They stirred up the **Lord's anger**
	106.32	the people made the **Lord angry**,
	106.40	So the **Lord** was **angry** with his people;
	110.5	The **Lord** is at your right side; when he becomes **angry**,
	145.8	The **Lord** is loving and merciful, slow to become **angry**
Prov	22.14	those with whom the **Lord** is **angry**.
Ecc	5.6	Why make **God angry** with you?
Is	2.10	the **Lord's anger** and to hide
	2.19	the **Lord's anger** and to hide
	5.25	the **Lord's anger** will not be ended,
	9.12	even so the **Lord's anger** is not ended;
	9.17	the **Lord's anger** will not be ended,
	9.19	Because the **Lord** Almighty is **angry**
	9.21	even so the **Lord's anger** is not ended;
	10.4	so the **Lord's anger** will not be ended;
	12.1	**Lord**! You were **angry** with me,
	13.5	In his **anger** the **Lord** is coming
	13.13	the **Lord** Almighty, show my **anger**.
	26.20	a little while until **God's anger** is over.
	34.2	The **Lord** is **angry** with all the nations
	51.17	that the **Lord** in his **anger** gave you
	51.20	They have felt the force of **God's anger**.
	66.14	the **Lord**, help those who obey me, and I show my **anger**
Jer	2.35	surely the **Lord** is no longer **angry**
	4.8	because the fierce **anger** of the **Lord**
	4.26	because of the **Lord's** fierce **anger**.
	6.11	Your **anger** against them burns in me too, **Lord**,
	7.20	**Lord**, will pour out my fierce **anger**
	7.29	I, the **Lord**, am **angry**,
	25.6	not to make the **Lord angry**
	25.36	the **Lord** in his **anger** has destroyed
	25.38	war and the **Lord's** fierce **anger**
	30.23	The **Lord's anger** is a storm
	42.18	The **Lord**, the **God** of Israel, says, 'Just as my **anger**
	52.3	**Lord** became so **angry** with the people
Lam	1.12	Pain that the **Lord** brought on me in the time of his **anger**.
	2.1	The **Lord** in his **anger** has covered Zion
Ezek	7.13	because **God's anger** is on everyone.
	7.14	**God's anger** will fall on everyone
	9.8	Sovereign **Lord**, are you so **angry**
	13.13	Sovereign **Lord** says: "In my **anger**
	20.33	**God**, I warn you that in my **anger**
	21.17	**anger** will be over. I, the **Lord**, have
	22.22	feeling the **anger** of the **Lord**.

Ezek	25.17	will feel my **anger**. Then they will know that I am the **Lord**.
	35.11	the living **God**, I will pay you back for your **anger**,
	36.5	Sovereign **Lord**, have spoken out in the heat of my **anger**
	36.6	**Lord**, am saying in jealous **anger**
Dan	8.19	what the result of **God's anger** will be.
Hos	5.10	The **Lord** says, "I am **angry**
	12.14	have made the **Lord** bitterly **angry**;
Mic	7.9	**Lord**, so now we must endure his **anger**
Nah	1.3	The **Lord** does not easily become **angry**,
Hab	3.8	it the rivers that made you **angry**, **Lord**?
Zeph	2.2	before the burning **anger** of the **Lord**
	2.3	the day when the **Lord** shows his **anger**.
Zech	1.2	I, the **Lord**, was very **angry**
	1.12	**Lord**, you have been **angry** with
	6.8	have calmed down the **Lord's anger**.
	10.3	The **Lord** says, "I am **angry**
Mal	1.4	nation with whom the **Lord** is **angry**
Rom	1.18	**God's anger** is revealed from heaven
	2.5	**God's anger** and righteous judgements
	2.8	on them **God** will pour out his **anger**
	4.15	The Law brings down **God's anger**;
	5.9	we be saved by him from **God's anger**!
	9.22	is true of what **God** has done. He wanted to show his **anger**
	12.19	but instead let **God's anger** do it.
Eph	2.3	were destined to suffer **God's anger**.
	5.6	of these very things that **God's anger**
Col	3.6	of such things **God's anger** will come
1 Thes	1.10	and who rescues us from **God's anger**
	2.16	now **God's anger** has at last come down
	5.9	**God** did not choose us to suffer his **anger**,
Heb	3.17	whom was **God angry** for forty years?
Rev	14.19	the winepress of **God's** furious **anger**.
	15.1	are the final expression of **God's anger**.
	15.7	gold bowls full of the **anger** of **God**,
	16.1	out the seven bowls of **God's anger**
	19.15	the furious **anger** of the Almighty **God**.

God's People

Deut	29.27	the Lord became **angry** with **his people**
2 Chr	36.16	the Lord's **anger** against **his people**
Ps	74.1	you be **angry** with **your own people**
	78.21	**his people** with fire, and his **anger**
	78.59	was **angry**...so he rejected **his people**
	78.62	He was **angry** with **his own people**
	106.40	So the Lord was **angry** with **his people**;
Is	47.6	I was **angry** with **my people**;
Zech	1.15	back my **anger** against **my people**,
	10.3	**angry** with those...who rule **my people**,
Rom	10.19	I will make **my people angry**.

Gods, Idols

Deut	6.15	**gods**, the Lord's **anger** will come against
	7.4	other **gods**...the Lord will be **angry**
	32.21	their **idols** they have made me **angry**, jealous with their so-called **gods**,
Josh	23.16	worship other **gods**, then in his **anger**
1 Kgs	14.9	aroused my **anger** by making **idols**
	14.15	have aroused his **anger** by making **idols**
2 Kgs	22.17	**gods**, and so have stirred up my **anger**
2 Chr	28.25	**gods**...he brought on himself the **anger**
	34.25	**gods**, and so have stirred up my **anger**
Jer	8.19	me **angry** by worshipping your **idols**
	25.6	Lord **angry** by worshipping the **idols**
	25.7	you made him **angry** with your **idols**
	44.3	**angry**. They offered sacrifices to...**gods**
	44.8	make me **angry** by worshipping **idols**

Hate

Ps	55.3	they are **angry** with me and **hate** me.
	112.10	and are **angry**; they glare in **hate**

Ezek	35.11	**anger**, your jealousy, and your **hatred**
Eph	4.31	**anger**. No more shouting...no...**hateful**
Col	3.8	**anger**, passion, and **hateful** feelings.

Idols see Gods

Jesus

Mk	3.5	**Jesus** was **angry** as he looked round
	10.14	When **Jesus** noticed this, he was **angry**
Lk	13.14	was **angry** that **Jesus** had healed

Lord see God

Mercy

Deut	13.17	his fierce **anger** and show you **mercy**.
Neh	9.17	slow to be **angry**. Your **mercy**
Ps	77.9	God forgotten to be **merciful**? Has **anger**
	103.8	Lord is **merciful**...slow to become **angry**
	145.8	and **merciful**, slow to become **angry**
Jer	3.12	I am **merciful** and will not be **angry**;
Lam	2.21	**mercy** on the day of your **anger**.
	3.43	your **mercy** was hidden by your **anger**,
Hab	3.2	Be **merciful**, even when you are **angry**.

Offer, Sacrifice

Is	65.3	**angry**. They **offer** pagan **sacrifices**
Jer	11.17	made me **angry** by **offering sacrifices**
	44.3	me **angry**. They **offered sacrifices**
	44.8	**angry** by...**sacrificing** to other gods
Ezek	20.28	They made me **angry** by the **sacrifices**

Power

Ps	90.11	has felt the full **power** of your **anger**?
Is	2.10	**anger** and to hide from his **power**
	2.19	**anger** and to hide from his **power**
	2.21	**anger** and to hide from his **power** and
Ezek	20.34	will show you my **power** and my **anger**
Nah	1.3	easily become **angry**, but he is **powerful**

Promise

Num	32.10	**angry** that day and made a **promise**:
Ps	95.11	was **angry** and made a solemn **promise**:
Is	54.9	Now I **promise** not to be **angry**
Heb	3.11	was **angry** and made a solemn **promise**:
	4.3	was **angry** and made a solemn **promise**:

Rage see Fury

Reject see Abandon

Sacrifice see Offer

Save

Ps	138.7	You oppose my **angry** enemies and **save**
Rom	5.9	we be **saved** by him from God's **anger**!

Sin

Num	16.22	When one man **sins**, do you get **angry**
	32.14	**sinful** men ready to bring down the fierce **anger**
Deut	9.18	had **sinned**...and had made him **angry**.
1 Kgs	8.46	who does not **sin** — and in your **anger**
	16.2	Their **sins** have aroused my **anger**,
	21.22	up my **anger** by leading Israel into **sin**.
2 Kgs	21.15	have **sinned** against me and have stirred up my **anger**
2 Chr	6.36	who does not **sin** — and in your **anger**
	24.18	**sins** brought the Lord's **anger** on Judah
	28.13	**sinned** against the Lord and made him **angry**
Is	57.17	**angry** with them because of their **sin**
	64.5	**sinning**; in spite of your great **anger**
	64.9	be too **angry** with us or hold our **sins**
Eph	4.26	do not let your **anger** lead you into **sin**,
Heb	3.17	was God **angry**...the people who **sinned**,

Temple

Jer	7.20	out my fierce **anger** on this **Temple**.
Lam	2.1	**anger** he abandoned even his **Temple**.
Ezek	8.17	**Temple**...and make me even more **angry**.

11

Terrible

Jer	36.7	people with his **terrible anger** and fury.
Nah	1.6	his **terrible** fury...his flaming **anger**;
Rev	6.17	The **terrible** day of their **anger** is here,

Trouble

Ps	37.8	worry or **anger**; it only leads to **trouble**.
	55.3	bring **trouble** on me; they are **angry**
Prov	30.33	you stir up **anger**, you get into **trouble**.

Turn

Lev	26.28	then in my **anger** I will **turn** on you
Deut	13.17	Lord will **turn** from his fierce **anger**
1 Kgs	11.9	**turned** away...So the Lord was **angry**
Ezra	10.14	**anger** over this situation will be **turned**
Ps	60.1	**angry** with us — but now **turn** back
	79.6	**Turn** your **anger** on the nations
Is	54.8	I **turned** away **angry** for only a moment,
Jer	4.8	**anger** of the Lord has not **turned** away
	10.25	**Turn** your **anger** on the nations
	33.5	my **anger** and fury. I have **turned** away
Ezek	21.31	will feel my **anger** when I **turn** it loose
	22.31	So I will **turn** my **anger** loose on them

Wicked see Evil

Worship, Bow

Deut	6.15	do **worship** other gods, the Lord's **anger**
Josh	23.16	**worship** other gods, then in his **anger**
Judg	2.12	They **bowed**...and made the Lord **angry**.
1 Kgs	14.9	my **anger** by making idols...to **worship**.
2 Chr	30.8	and **worship**...he will no longer be **angry**
Ps	2.12	and **bow** down to him; or else his **anger**
	79.6	**anger** on...nations that do not **worship**
Jer	8.19	**angry** by **worshipping**...and by **bowing**
	10.25	**anger** on...nations that do not **worship**
	25.6	to make the Lord **angry** by **worshipping**
	44.8	make me **angry** by **worshipping** idols

ANNOUNCE

| | Is | 61.1 — 63.1 | x3 |
| | Acts | 3.18 – 24 | x3 |

Good News, Save

Ps	98.2	**announced** his victory...his **saving** power
Is	21.10	I have **announced** to you the **good news**
	40.9	Zion; **announce** the **good news**!
	52.7	**good news**...of peace! He **announces**
	63.1	powerful to **save**, coming to **announce**
Nah	1.15	**good news**! He is...to **announce** the
Acts	14.15	are here to **announce** the **Good News**,
	16.17	**announce** to you how you can be **saved**!
Gal	3.8	the scripture **announced** the **Good News**
Eph	6.15	readiness to **announce** the **Good News**
1 Tim	1.11	to me to **announce**, the **Good News**
1 Pet	1.12	who **announced** the **Good News**
Rev	14.6	message of **Good News** to **announce**

Servant, Prophet

Ezek	38.17	when I **announced** through my **servants**,
Acts	3.18	**announced**...through all the **prophets**
	3.21	**announced** through his holy **prophets**
	7.52	**announced** the coming of his...**Servant**.
	16.17	**servants** of...God! They **announce** to you
Rev	10.7	as he **announced** to his **servants**,

ANOINT

	Ex	28.41 — 31.11	x10
	Ex	39.38 — 40.15	x6
	1 Sam	15.1 — 16.13	x5
	Lev	8.2 – 30	x4
	Ex	35.8 – 28	x3
	1 Kgs	1.34 – 45	x3
	1 Kgs	19.15 – 16	x3
	2 Kgs	9.3 – 12	x3

Consecrate, Dedicate, Sacred

Ex	28.41	them and **dedicate** them by **anointing**
	30.25	and make a **sacred anointing** oil,
	37.29	He also made the **sacred anointing** oil
	40.9	Then **dedicate** the Tent...by **anointing** it
	40.10	**dedicate** the altar...by **anointing** it,
	40.13	**anoint** him, and in this way **consecrate**
Lev	10.7	have been **consecrated** by the **anointing**
Num	7.1	he **anointed** and **dedicated** the Tent

Holy

Ex	29.36	**anoint** it with olive-oil to make it **holy**.
	30.31	This **holy anointing** oil is to be used
	40.10	by **anointing** it, and it will be...**holy**.
Ps	89.20	by **anointing** him with **holy** oil.

King

1 Sam	15.1	to **anoint** you **king** of his people Israel.
	15.17	The Lord **anointed** you **king** of Israel,
	16.3	You will **anoint** as **king** the man I tell
2 Sam	2.4	and **anointed** David as **king** of Judah.
	2.7	have **anointed** me as their **king**.
	5.3	they **anointed** him, and he became **king**
	19.10	We **anointed** Absalom as our **king**,
1 Kgs	1.34	are to **anoint** him as **king**
	1.45	Nathan **anointed** him as **king**
	19.15	and **anoint** Hazael as **king** of Syria;
	19.16	**anoint** Jehu son of Nimshi as **king**
2 Kgs	9.3	proclaims that he **anoints** you **king**
	9.6	I **anoint** you **king** of my people Israel.
	9.12	I **anoint** you **king** of Israel.
	11.12	Joash was **anointed** and proclaimed **king**.
	23.30	son Joahaz and **anointed** him **king**.
1 Chr	11.3	they **anointed** him, and he became **king**
2 Chr	23.11	**anointed** Joash, and everyone shouted, "Long live the **king**!
	36.1	son Joahaz and **anointed** him **king**
Ps	89.20	my servant David **king** by **anointing** him

Sacred see Consecrate

Tent

Ex	30.26	Use it to **anoint** the **Tent**
	40.9	**Tent** and all its equipment by **anointing**
Lev	8.10	the **anointing** oil and put it on the **Tent**
Num	7.1	he **anointed** and dedicated the **Tent**

AV ANTICHRIST see ENEMY — Christ

APOSTLES

	Acts	4.2 — 6.6	x26
	Acts	13.43 — 16.4	x14
	Acts	1.2 — 2.43	x9
	2 Cor	11.5 — 12.12	x7
	1 Cor	15.5 – 10	x5
	Gal	1.1 — 2.8	x5
	Acts	8.1 — 9.27	x4
	1 Cor	9.1 – 5	x4
	Eph	1.1 — 4.11	x4

Believers

Acts	6.2	**apostles** called the...**believers** together
	8.1	All the **believers**, except the **apostles**,
	8.18	given to the **believers** when the **apostles**
	11.1	The **apostles** and the other **believers**
	16.4	**believers** the rules...by the **apostles**

Choose, Will

Mk	3.14	**chose** twelve, whom he named **apostles**
Lk	6.13	**chose** twelve...whom he named **apostles**:
Acts	1.2	the men he had **chosen** as his **apostles**.
Rom	1.1	an **apostle chosen** and called by God
1 Cor	1.1	by the **will** of God to be an **apostle**
2 Cor	1.1	**apostle** of Christ Jesus by God's **will**,
Eph	1.1	who by God's **will** is an **apostle**
Col	1.1	who by God's **will** is an **apostle**

2 Tim	1.1	**apostle** of Christ Jesus by God's **will,**	
Tit	1.1	**apostle** of Jesus Christ. I was **chosen**	

Christ see Jesus

Gentiles

Rom	11.13	I am an **apostle** to the **Gentiles,**
Gal	2.8	was made an **apostle** to the **Gentiles**
1 Tim	2.7	an **apostle** and teacher of the **Gentiles,**

God

Rom	1.1	an **apostle** chosen and called by **God**
	1.5	Through him **God** gave me the privilege of being an **apostle**
1 Cor	1.1	by the will of **God** to be an **apostle**
2 Cor	1.1	**apostle** of Christ Jesus by **God's** will,
Gal	2.8	by **God's** power I was made an **apostle**
Eph	1.1	by **God's** will is an **apostle** of Christ
Col	1.1	by **God's** will is an **apostle** of Christ
1 Tim	1.1	**apostle** of Christ Jesus by order of **God**
2 Tim	1.1	**apostle** of Christ Jesus by **God's** will,
	1.11	**God** has appointed me as an **apostle**
Tit	1.1	servant of **God** and an **apostle** of Jesus

Jesus, Christ

Mk	6.30	**apostles** returned and met with **Jesus**
Lk	6.17	**Jesus** had come down...with the **apostles**
	9.10	The **apostles**...told **Jesus** everything
	22.14	**Jesus** took his place...with the **apostles.**
Acts	1.6	the **apostles** met together with **Jesus**
	4.2	**apostles** were teaching...that **Jesus** had
Rom	1.1	a servant of **Christ Jesus** and an **apostle**
1 Cor	1.1	to be an **apostle** of **Christ Jesus,**
	9.1	I not an **apostle**? Haven't I seen **Jesus**
2 Cor	1.1	**apostle** of **Christ Jesus** by God's will,
Eph	1.1	will is an **apostle** of **Christ Jesus**
Col	1.1	God's will is an **apostle** of **Christ Jesus,**
1 Tim	1.1	From Paul, an **apostle** of **Christ Jesus**
2 Tim	1.1	**apostle** of **Christ Jesus** by God's will,
Tit	1.1	servant of God and an **apostle** of **Jesus**
1 Pet	1.1	**apostle** of **Jesus Christ**
2 Pet	1.1	a servant and **apostle** of **Jesus Christ**
Jude	.17	the **apostles** of our Lord **Jesus Christ.**

Jews

Acts	14.4	for the **Jews,** others for the **apostles.**
Gal	2.8	Peter was made an **apostle** to the **Jews.**

Power

Acts	4.33	great **power** the **apostles** gave witness
Gal	2.8	by God's **power** I was made an **apostle**

Prophets

1 Cor	12.28	**apostles,** in the second place **prophets,**
	12.29	They are not all **apostles** or **prophets**
Eph	2.20	laid by the **apostles** and **prophets,**
	3.5	to his holy **apostles** and **prophets.**
	4.11	to be **apostles,** others to be **prophets,**
Rev	18.20	people and the **apostles** and **prophets!**

Teachers

1 Cor	12.29	not all **apostles** or prophets or **teachers**
1 Tim	2.7	I was sent as an **apostle** and **teacher**
2 Tim	1.11	appointed me as an **apostle** and **teacher**

Will see Choose

APPROVAL

Heb	11.2 – 4		x3

God, Lord

Lev	10.19	would the **Lord** have **approved?**
2 Kgs	17.9	the **Lord** their **God disapproved** of.
Ps	101.6	will **approve** of those who are faithful to **God**
Mt	16.1	to show that **God approved** of him.
Mk	8.11	to show that **God approved** of him.
Lk	11.16	to show that **God approved** of him.

Jn	6.27	because **God,** the Father, has put his mark of **approval** on him.
	12.43	They loved the **approval** of men rather than the **approval** of God.
Rom	5.4	endurance brings **God's approval,**
	14.18	pleases **God** and is **approved** by others.
Gal	1.10	What I want is **God's approval!**
2 Tim	2.15	to win full **approval** in **God's** sight,
Heb	11.2	of ancient times won **God's approval.**
	11.4	his faith he won **God's approval**

ARGUE

Mk	8.11	—	9.34	x5
Job	13.3 – 12			x3
Prov	22.10	—	23.11	x3
Acts	23.10	—	25.19	x3
1 Tim	6.4 – 20			x3

Disciples

Mk	9.16	his **disciples,** "What are you **arguing**
	9.33	his **disciples,** "What were you **arguing**
Lk	9.46	**argument** broke out among the **disciples**
	22.24	**argument** broke out among the **disciples**
Jn	3.25	John's **disciples** began **arguing**

Quarrel

Prov	22.10	will be no more **arguments, quarrelling,**
Jer	15.10	have to **quarrel** and **argue** with everyone
1 Tim	6.4	an unhealthy desire to **argue** and **quarrel**
2 Tim	2.23	**arguments**...they end up in **quarrels.**
Tit	3.9	But avoid stupid **arguments...quarrels,**
Jude	.9	his **quarrel** with the Devil...they **argued**

AV ARK (OF THE COVENANT)
see COVENANT BOX

ARREST

Mk	12.12	—	14.51	x8
Mt	26.4 – 57			x5
Lk	20.19	—	22.54	x4
Acts	21.33	—	22.19	x4
Acts	9.2 – 21			x3

Jesus

Mt	26.4	and made plans to **arrest Jesus** secretly
	26.50	Then they came up, **arrested Jesus,**
	26.57	had **arrested Jesus** took him to the
Mk	12.12	The Jewish leaders tried to **arrest Jesus,**
	14.1	looking for a way to **arrest Jesus**
	14.46	So they **arrested Jesus** and held him
Lk	20.19	the chief priests tried to **arrest Jesus**
	22.54	They **arrested Jesus** and took him away
Jn	18.12	the Jewish guards **arrested Jesus,** bound
Acts	1.16	the guide for those who **arrested Jesus.**

Prison

Gen	39.20	Joseph **arrested** and put in the **prison**
2 Kgs	17.4	had Hoshea **arrested** and put in **prison.**
Mt	14.3	**arrest,** and he had him...put in **prison.**
Mk	6.17	**arrest,** and he had him...put in **prison.**
Acts	22.4	I **arrested**...and threw them into **prison.**

AUTHORITIES

Jn	7.1	—	9.22	x10
Jn	18.14	—	20.19	x6
Acts	16.19	—	17.9	x5
Jn	11.48	—	13.33	x4
Rom	13.1 – 6			x4
Jn	5.10 – 18			x3

Power

1 Cor	15.24	**authorities,** and **powers,**
Eph	1.21	**authorities, powers,** and lords;
	6.12	**authorities,** and cosmic **powers**
Col	1.16	**powers,** lords, rulers, and **authorities.**
	2.15	the **power** of the spiritual...**authorities;**
1 Pet	3.22	and heavenly **authorities** and **powers.**

AUTHORITY

Rev	11.6	—	13.12	x9
Mt	7.29	—	10.1	x5
Jn	7.17	—	8.42	x5
2 Chr	19.6 – 11			x4
Mk	1.22	—	3.15	x4
Rom	12.8	—	13.3	x4
Rev	16.9	—	18.1	x4
Dan	7.6 – 14			x3
Lk	4.32	—	5.24	x3
Jn	5.30 – 43			x3
Jude	.6 – 25			x3
Rev	1.18	—	2.26	x3

Father
Jn	5.43	I have come with my **Father's authority**
	8.28	**authority**, but...only what the **Father**
	10.25	things I do by my **Father's authority**
	12.49	on my own **authority**, but the **Father**
Acts	1.7	set by my **Father's** own **authority**,
Rev	2.26	**authority**...I received from my **Father**:

Forgive
Mt	9.6	has **authority** on earth to **forgive** sins.
Mk	2.10	has **authority** on earth to **forgive** sins.
Lk	5.24	has **authority** on earth to **forgive** sins.

God
Mt	9.8	praised **God** for giving such **authority**
Lk	12.5	fear **God**, who, after killing, has the **authority**
Jn	5.30	**authority**; I judge only as **God** tells me,
	7.17	comes from **God** or whether I speak on my own **authority**.
Rom	13.1	no **authority** exists without **God's**
	13.2	the existing **authority** opposes what **God**
2 Pet	2.10	and despise **God's authority**.
Jude	.8	they despise **God's authority**
Rev	16.9	the name of **authority**, who has **authority**

Jesus
Acts	2.22	**Jesus** of Nazareth...whose divine **authority**
1 Cor	1.10	the **authority** of our Lord **Jesus** Christ
1 Thes	4.2	by the **authority** of the Lord **Jesus**.

Lord
2 Chr	19.6	but on the **authority** of the **Lord**,
Jer	5.5	have rejected the **Lord's authority**
1 Cor	1.10	By the **authority** of our **Lord** Jesus
2 Cor	10.8	**authority** that the **Lord** has given
	13.10	**authority** that the **Lord** has given
1 Thes	4.2	by the **authority** of the **Lord** Jesus.
	5.27	by the **authority** of the **Lord**
Jude	.25	Christ our **Lord**, be glory, majesty, might, and **authority**,

AWE

God, Lord
Ex	14.31	they stood in **awe** of the **Lord**;
	15.6	**Lord**, is **awesome** in power;
Deut	28.58	**awesome** name of the **Lord** your **God**,
Job	22.4	is not because you stand in **awe** of **God**
	25.1	**God** is powerful; all must stand in **awe**
	37.22	and the glory of **God** fills us with **awe**.
Ps	68.35	How **awesome** is **God** as he comes
Ecc	3.14	**God** does is to make us stand in **awe**
	5.7	you must still stand in **awe** of **God**.
2 Cor	7.1	holy by living in **awe** of **God**.

AWFUL

Rev	18.10 – 19		x3

Horror
Dan	9.27	The **Awful Horror** will be placed

Dan	11.31	and set up The **Awful Horror**.
	12.11	from the time of The **Awful Horror**,
Mt	24.15	You will see 'The **Awful Horror**'
Mk	13.14	You will see 'The **Awful Horror**'

BAPTIZE

Acts	8.12	—	11.16	x11
Mt	3.6 – 16			x7
Lk	3.3 – 21			x7
Mk	1.4 – 9			x6
Jn	1.25 – 33			x6
Jn	3.22	—	4.2	x6
Acts	18.8	—	19.5	x6
1 Cor	1.13 – 17			x6
Acts	1.5	—	2.41	x5
Mk	10.38	—	11.30	x3
Rom	6.3 – 4			x3

Christ, Jesus
Mt	3.16	As soon as **Jesus** was **baptized**,
Mk	1.9	**Jesus**...was **baptized** by John
Lk	3.21	**Jesus** also was **baptized**.
Jn	4.1	**Jesus** was...**baptizing** more disciples
	4.2	**Jesus** himself did not **baptize** anyone;
Acts	2.38	be **baptized** in the name of **Jesus**
	8.16	**baptized** in the name of...**Jesus**.
	10.48	be **baptized** in the name of **Jesus**
Rom	6.3	**baptized** into union with **Christ Jesus**,
1 Cor	1.17	**Christ** did not send me to **baptize**.
Gal	3.27	were **baptized** into union with **Christ**
Col	2.12	**baptized**, you were buried with **Christ**,

Disciples
Mt	28.19	make them my **disciples**: **baptize** them
Jn	4.1	winning and **baptizing** more **disciples**
	4.2	**baptize** anyone; only his **disciples** did.
1 Cor	1.13	Were you **baptized** as Paul's **disciples**?
	1.15	that you were **baptized** as my **disciples**.

Jesus see Christ

Name
Mt	28.19	**baptize** them in the **name** of the Father,
Acts	2.38	be **baptized** in the **name** of Jesus Christ,
	8.16	been **baptized** in the **name** of the Lord
	10.48	to be **baptized** in the **name** of Jesus
	19.5	were **baptized** in the **name** of the Lord

Preach
Mk	1.4	in the desert, **baptizing** and **preaching**.
Acts	1.21	John **preached** his message of **baptism**
	10.37	John **preached** his message of **baptism**.

Sins
Mt	3.6	their **sins**, and he **baptized** them
Mk	1.4	away from your **sins** and be **baptized**,
	1.5	their **sins**, and he **baptized** them
Lk	3.3	away from your **sins** and be **baptized**,
Acts	2.38	turn away from his **sins** and be **baptized**
	13.24	turn from their **sins** and be **baptized**.
	19.4	The **baptism** of John was for those who turned from their **sins**
	22.16	be **baptized** and have your **sins** washed

Spirit of God
Mt	3.11	will **baptize** you with the **Holy Spirit**.
Mk	1.8	will **baptize** you with the **Holy Spirit**.
Lk	3.16	will **baptize** you with the **Holy Spirit**.
Jn	1.33	**baptize** with water, had said to me, 'You will see the **Spirit**
Acts	1.5	be **baptized** with the **Holy Spirit**.
	11.16	will be **baptized** with the **Holy Spirit**.
1 Cor	12.13	been **baptized** into the one body by the same **Spirit**,

BEAST

Rev	13.1	—	17.17	x39

Rev	19.19	—	20.10	x8

Authority

Rev	13.4	he had given his **authority** to the **beast**.
	13.12	used the vast **authority** of the first **beast**
	17.13	their power and **authority** to the **beast**.

Image

Rev	13.14	build an **image** in honour of the **beast**
	13.15	life into the **image** of the first **beast**,
	14.9	worships the **beast** and its **image**
	14.11	who worship the **beast** and its **image**,
	15.2	victory over the **beast** and its **image**
	16.2	the **beast** and on those who had worshipped its **image**.
	19.20	had worshipped the **image** of the **beast**.
	20.4	not worshipped the **beast** or its **image**,

Mark

Rev	13.17	this **mark**, that is, the **beast's** name
	14.9	**beast** and its image and receives the **mark**
	14.11	**beast** and its image, for anyone who has the **mark**
	16.2	who had the **mark** of the **beast**
	19.20	who had the **mark** of the **beast**
	20.4	had they received the **mark** of the **beast**

BEING

Gen	5.1	—	9.17	x16
Rom	6.6	—	9.5	x5
Gen	1.20	— 27		x3
1 Cor	15.39	— 45		x3
2 Cor	4.16	—	5.17	x3

Christ see Jesus

God

Ps	84.2	my whole **being**...to the living **God**.
	90.2	the world into **being**, you were...**God**.
Rom	7.22	inner **being** delights in the law of **God**.
	8.23	for **God** to...set our whole **being** free.
Col	3.10	This is the new **being** which **God**,
Heb	1.3	the exact likeness of **God's** own **being**,

Jesus, Christ

Rom	6.6	**being** has been put to death with **Christ**
	9.5	and **Christ**, as a human being, belongs
2 Cor	5.17	is joined to **Christ**, he is a new **being**
Phil	1.20	**being** I shall bring honour to **Christ**,
	2.10	honour of the name of **Jesus** all **beings**
1 Jn	4.2	**Jesus Christ** came as a human **being**
2 Jn	.7	**Jesus Christ** came as a human **being**.

Praise

Ps	29.1	**Praise** the Lord, you heavenly **beings**;
	103.1	All my **being**, **praise** his holy name!

BELIEVE

Jn	1.7	—	14.29	x82
Acts	13.12	—	20.21	x19
Rom	3.22	—	4.24	x12
1 Jn	3.23	—	5.13	x10
Rom	9.33	—	11.20	x9
1 Pet	1.8	—	4.17	x9
Jn	16.9	—	17.21	x7
Jn	19.35	—	20.31	x7
Acts	8.12	—	11.21	x7
Gal	2.16	—	3.22	x7
Mt	21.21	— 32		x6
Mk	15.32	—	16.16	x6
2 Thes	1.4	—	3.2	x6
Ex	4.1	— 31		x4
Acts	22.19	—	24.21	x4
1 Thes	4.14	— 16		x4
Jas	1.6	—	2.23	x4
Mt	8.13	—	9.29	x3

Mk	11.23	— 31		x3
Lk	1.20	— 45		x3
Lk	8.12	— 50		x3
Lk	24.11	— 41		x3
Rom	13.11	—	14.22	x3
1 Cor	15.2	— 14		x3
2 Cor	4.4	— 13		x3
1 Tim	3.16	—	4.10	x3
Heb	3.19	—	4.6	x3

Apostles

Acts	6.2	**apostles** called the...**believers** together
	8.1	All the **believers**, except the **apostles**,
	8.18	given to the **believers** when the **apostles**
	11.1	The **apostles** and the other **believers**
	16.4	**believers** the rules...by the **apostles**

Baptize

Mk	16.16	**believes** and is **baptized** will be saved
Acts	2.41	**believed** his message and were **baptized**
	8.13	also **believed**; and after being **baptized**,
	18.8	**believed**, and were **baptized**.

Christ see Jesus

Eternal see Life

Faith

Ps	78.22	no **faith** in him and did not believe
Mk	16.14	**faith** and because they were too stubborn to believe
Rom	4.3	**believed** God, and because of his **faith**
	4.5	**faith**, not on his deeds, and who **believes**
	4.9	**believed** God, and because of his **faith**
2 Cor	1.24	**believe**; we know that you stand firm in the **faith**.
	4.13	**faith**, we also speak because we **believe**.
Gal	3.6	**believed** God, and because of his **faith**
	3.22	**faith** in Jesus Christ is given to those who believe.
Jas	2.23	**believed** God, and because of his **faith**

God

2 Chr	20.20	Put your trust in...**God**, and...**Believe**
Job	22.17	rejected **God** and **believed** that he
Ps	106.24	they did not **believe** **God's** promise.
Jon	3.5	of Nineveh **believed** **God's** message
Jn	6.29	**God** wants you to do is to **believe**
	11.40	would see **God's** glory if you **believed**?
	14.1	**Believe** in God and **believe** also in me.
	16.27	have **believed** that I came from **God**.
	16.30	us **believe** that you came from **God**.
Acts	16.34	because they now **believed** in **God**.
	18.27	**God's** grace had become **believers**.
	20.21	to **God** and **believe** in our Lord Jesus.
	26.8	to **believe** that **God** raises the dead?
Rom	1.16	is **God's** power to save all who **believe**,
	3.22	**God** does this to all who **believe**
	4.3	Abraham **believed God**,
	4.5	who **believes** in the **God** who declares
	4.9	Abraham **believed God**,
	4.11	father of all who **believe** in **God**
	4.13	he **believed** and was accepted...by **God**.
	4.17	**God**, in whom Abraham **believed**
	10.4	who **believes** is put right with **God**.
	10.9	is Lord and **believe** that **God** raised him
1 Cor	1.21	**God** decided to save those who **believe**.
	3.5	simply **God's** servants, by whom you were led to **believe**.
	14.22	**God's** message is proof for **believers**,
Gal	3.6	**believed God**, and because of his faith
1 Thes	2.13	For **God** is at work in you who **believe**.
	4.14	so we **believe** that **God** will take back
Tit	3.8	who **believe** in **God** may be concerned
Heb	4.3	**believe**...receive that rest which **God**
	6.1	useless works and **believing** in **God**;
Jas	2.19	**believe** that there is only one **God**?

15

Jas   2.23 Abraham **believed** God,
1 Pet 1.21 Through him you **believe** in God
      2.17 love your **fellow-believers**, honour God,
      3.1   any of them do not **believe** God's word,
      4.17 not **believe** the Good News from God?
1 Jn 4.16 and **believe** the love which God has
      5.9   **believe** man's testimony; but God's

Good News see Message

Jesus, Christ, Son of God

Jn   2.22 and they **believed**...what Jesus had said.
      3.16 **Son**, so that everyone who **believes** in
      3.18 **believes** in the **Son** is not judged
      3.36 **believes** in the **Son** has eternal life
      4.39 of the Samaritans...**believed** in Jesus
      4.50 The man **believed** Jesus' words
      6.40 who see the **Son** and **believe** in him
      6.64 (Jesus knew...the ones that would not **believe**
      8.30 heard Jesus say these things **believed**
      9.22 he **believed** that Jesus was the Messiah
      11.27 I do **believe** that you are the Messiah, the **Son of God**,
      11.45 saw what Jesus did, and they **believed**
      12.11 rejecting them and **believing** in Jesus.
      12.42 the Jewish authorities **believed** in Jesus;
      20.31 may **believe** that Jesus is the Messiah,
Acts 11.17 we **believed** in the Lord Jesus Christ;
      15.11 We **believe** and are saved by the grace of the Lord Jesus
      16.31 **Believe** in the Lord Jesus,
      20.21 and **believe** in our Lord Jesus.
Rom   3.22 does this to all who **believe** in Christ,
      3.25 everyone who **believes** in Jesus.
      4.24 who **believe** in him who raised Jesus
      6.8   we have died with Christ, we **believe**
      10.9 confess that Jesus is Lord and **believe**
      16.5 of Asia to **believe** in Christ.
Gal   2.16 We, too, have **believed** in Christ Jesus
      3.22 in Jesus Christ...to those who **believe**.
Eph   1.13 You **believed** in Christ, and God
Phil 1.29 of serving Christ, not only by **believing**
1 Thes 4.14 We **believe** that Jesus died and rose
      4.16 Those who have died **believing** in Christ
1 Tim 1.15 accepted and **believed**: Christ Jesus came
Jas   2.1   as **believers** in our Lord Jesus Christ,
1 Jn 3.23 that we **believe** in his Son Jesus Christ
      5.1   **believe** that Jesus is the Messiah
      5.5   **believes** that Jesus is the Son of God.
      5.10 So whoever **believes** in the Son of God
      5.13 you that **believe** in the Son of God.

Lie

Prov 21.28 The testimony of a **liar** is not **believed**
Jer   28.15 are making these people **believe** a lie.
      29.31 and he made you **believe** lies.
Ezek 13.19 tell **lies** to my people, and they **believe**
1 Jn 5.10 does not **believe** God, has made him out to be a **liar**,

Life, Eternal, Raise, Rise

Jn   3.15 **believes** in him may have eternal life.
      3.16 **believe** in him may not die but have eternal life
      3.36 **believes** in the Son has eternal life
      5.24 and **believes** in him who sent me has eternal life.
      6.40 **believe** in him should have eternal life.
      6.47 he who **believes** has eternal life.
      7.38 **believes** in me, streams of life-giving
      11.25 and the life. Whoever **believes** in me
Acts 24.21 **believing** that the dead will rise to life.
      26.8 to **believe** that God raises the dead?
Rom   4.17 **believed** — the God who brings the dead to life

Rom   4.24 who **believe** in him who raised Jesus
      10.9 and **believe** that God raised him
1 Thes 4.16 **believing** in Christ will rise to life
1 Tim 1.16 **believe** in him and receive eternal life.
1 Pet 1.21 him you **believe** in God, who raised him
1 Jn 5.13 have eternal life — you that **believe**

Lord

Lk   1.45 **believe** that the Lord's message to you
Jn   9.38 I **believe**, Lord!" the man said,
      11.27 Lord!" she answered. "I do **believe**
      12.38 Lord, who **believed** the message we told?
Acts 5.14 and women who **believed** in the Lord.
      9.42 and many people **believed** in the Lord.
      11.21 people **believed** and turned to the Lord.
      15.40 by the **believers** to...the Lord's grace.
      16.15 I am a true **believer** in the Lord.
      18.8 Crispus...**believed** in the Lord,
Rom   10.16 Lord, who **believed** our message?
1 Thes 5.27 of the Lord to read this...to...**believers**.

Message, Good News, Word

Prov 21.28 a liar is not **believed**, but the word
Jer   7.4   Stop **believing** those deceitful words
Jon   3.5   of Nineveh **believed** God's message
Mt   11.14 you are willing to **believe** their message
Mk   1.15 your sins and **believe** the Good News!
Lk   1.20 But you have not **believed** my message,
      1.45 to **believe** that the Lord's message
Jn   1.7   all should hear the message and **believe**.
      4.41 more **believed** because of his message
      4.50 man **believed** Jesus' words and went.
      5.24 whoever hears my words and **believes**
      5.38 message in your hearts, for you do not **believe**
      12.38 who **believed** the message we told?
      17.20 **believe** in me because of their message.
Acts 2.41 Many of them **believed** his message
      4.4   many who heard the message **believed**
      8.12 But when they **believed** Philip's message about the good news
      14.9 Paul's words. Paul saw that he **believed**
      18.8 in Corinth heard the message, **believed**,
      28.24 his words, but others would not **believe**.
Rom   10.14 **believe** if they have not heard the message?
      10.16 who **believed** our message?
1 Cor 14.22 God's message is proof for **believers**,
2 Thes 1.10 because you have **believed** the message
      3.2   for not everyone **believes** the message.
1 Pet 2.8   they did not **believe** in the word;
      3.1   any of them do not **believe** God's word,
      4.17 who do not **believe** the Good News

Miracle

Ex   4.8   **believe** you or be convinced by the first miracle,
      4.9   **miracles** they still will not **believe** you,
Jn   2.23 **believed** in him as they saw the miracles
      4.48 will ever **believe** unless you see miracles
      12.37 miracles in their presence, they did not **believe**

Obey

Jn   8.31 those who **believed** in him, "If you obey
Rom   1.5   of all nations to **believe** and obey.
      3.27 obey the Law? No, but that we **believe**.
      4.13 obeyed the Law, but because he **believed**
      4.16 who obey the Law, but also to those who **believe**
      16.26 so that all may **believe** and obey.

Preach, Teach

Acts 13.38 is **preached** to you; and that everyone who **believes**
      15.1 and started **teaching** the **believers**

16

1 Cor   1.21   we **preach**, God decided to save those who **believe**.
       15.11   all **preach**, and this is what you **believe**.
       15.14   **preach** and you have nothing to **believe**.
1 Tim   3.16   He was **preached** among the nations, was **believed**

Raise see **Life**

Right With God see **Save**

Righteous
Rom   3.25   **righteous** and that he puts right everyone who **believes**
        4.11   who **believe** in God and are accepted as **righteous**
        4.13   **believed** and was accepted as **righteous**
        4.24   as **righteous**, who **believe** in him
Heb   10.38   **righteous** people, however, will **believe**

Rise see **Life**

Save, Right With God
Ps   78.22   not **believe** that he would **save** them.
Mk   16.16   **believes** and is baptized will be **saved**
Lk   8.12   them from **believing** and being **saved**.
Acts   15.11   We **believe** and are **saved**
       16.31   **Believe** in the Lord Jesus, and you will be **saved**
Rom   1.16   God's power to **save** all who **believe**,
        3.25   he puts **right** everyone who **believes**
       10.4   that everyone who **believes** is put **right**
1 Cor   1.21   God decided to **save** those who **believe**.
Gal   2.16   **believed** in Christ Jesus in order to be put **right**

Sin
Mk   1.15   Turn away from your **sins** and **believe**
Jn   8.24   die in your **sins** if you do not **believe**
       16.9   wrong about **sin**...they do not **believe**
Acts   10.43   **believes** in him will have his **sins**
       13.38   **believes** in him is set free from...**sins**
       15.9   forgave their **sins** because they **believed**.
       20.21   **sins** to God and **believe** in our Lord

Son of God see **Jesus**

Teach see **Preach**

Word see **Message**

BLESS

Gen	24.1	—	28.14	x36
Gen	47.7	—	49.26	x14
Deut	26.15	—	28.47	x12
Num	22.6	—	24.10	x10
Num	14.24	—	16.17	x10
Deut	33.1 – 24			x7
Zech	7.2	—	9.12	x7
Rom	10.12	—	12.14	x7
Deut	7.13	—	8.16	x6
Ruth	1.6	—	4.13	x6
Heb	6.7	—	7.7	x6
1 Pet	1.4	—	3.9	x6
Deut	10.8	—	12.7	x5
2 Sam	6.11	—	7.29	x5
Lk	1.28	—	2.40	x5
Gen	12.2 – 3			x4
Gen	17.16	—	18.18	x4
Num	6.23 – 27			x4
1 Sam	23.21	—	26.25	x4
Ps	115.12 – 15			x4
Prov	10.6	—	11.11	x4
Lk	6.28 – 34			x4
Gal	3.8 – 14			x4
Deut	30.1 – 19			x3
1 Sam	2.20 – 32			x3
1 Kgs	8.14 – 66			x3
Ps	67.1 – 7			x3
Is	19.24 – 25			x3
Is	65.9 – 23			x3
Lk	24.30 – 51			x3
Rom	15.27 – 29			x3
Eph	1.3 – 18			x3

Care see **Love**

Christ, Jesus
Rom   15.29   a full measure of the **blessing** of **Christ**.
2 Cor 11.31   Lord **Jesus** — **blessed** be his name
Gal   3.14   **Christ** did this in order that the **blessing**
Eph   1.3   our union with **Christ** he has **blessed** us

Curse
Gen   12.3   who **bless** you, But I will **curse** those
       27.12   a **curse** on myself instead of a **blessing**.
       27.29   be **cursed**, and may those who **bless**
Num   23.11   **curse** my enemies, but all you have done is **bless**
       24.9   will be **blessed**, And whoever **curses**
Deut   11.26   choice between a **blessing** and a **curse**
       11.29   **blessing** from Mount Gerizim and the **curse**
       23.5   he turned the **curse** into a **blessing**,
       30.1   a choice between a **blessing** and a **curse**
       30.19   between God's **blessing** and God's **curse**,
Josh   8.34   including the **blessings** and the **curses**,
2 Sam 16.12   **blessings** to take the place of his **curse**.
Neh   13.2   God turned the **curse** into a **blessing**.
Ps   62.4   **blessing**, but in your heart you **curse**
      109.17   be **cursed**! He hated to give **blessings**
      109.28   may **curse** me, but you will **bless** me.
Prov   3.33   **curse** on the homes of wicked men, but **blesses**
Lk   6.28   **bless** those who **curse** you
Rom   12.14   ask him to **bless**, not to **curse**.
1 Cor   4.12   When we are **cursed**, we **bless**;
1 Pet   3.9   with **cursing**; instead, pay back with a **blessing**,

God
Gen   9.1   **God blessed** Noah and his sons
       25.11   **God blessed** his son Isaac,
       28.3   May Almighty **God bless** your marriage
       35.9   **God** appeared to him again and **blessed**
       43.29   **God bless** you, my son.
       48.15   May the **God**...**bless** these boys!
       49.25   The Almighty **God** who **blesses** you
Ex   23.25   the **Lord** your **God**, I will **bless** you
Num   23.20   when **God blesses**, I cannot call it back.
Deut   2.7   how the **Lord** your **God** has **blessed** you
       12.7   **Lord** your **God**, who has **blessed** you,
       14.29   the **Lord** your **God** will **bless** you
       15.4   The **Lord** your **God** will **bless** you
       15.18   the **Lord** your **God** will **bless** you
       16.17   the **blessings** that...**God** has given him.
       23.20   your **God** will **bless** everything you do
       24.19   **God** will **bless** you in everything you
       28.2   Obey...**God** and all these **blessings**
       28.8   **God** will **bless** your work
       30.16   The **Lord** your **God** will **bless** you
       30.19   between God's **blessing** and God's curse,
Ruth   2.19   **God bless** the man who took an interest
1 Sam 26.25   **God bless** you, my son!
2 Sam   6.18   he **blessed**...in the name of...**Almighty**
       14.22   **bless** you, Your Majesty!
       23.5   how **God** will **bless** my descendants,
1 Kgs   8.14   and he asked **God's blessing** on them.
        8.55   In a loud voice he asked **God's blessing**
1 Chr   4.10   **Bless** me, **God**, and give me much land.
       26.4   **God blessed** by giving him eight sons,
2 Chr   1.1   and the **Lord** his **God blessed** him
        6.3   and asked **God's blessing** on them.
       26.5   and **God blessed** him.

2 Chr 26.18 the **Lord** God, and you no longer have his **blessing**.
Ezra 6.10 to the **God**...pray for his **blessing**
      7.6 Ezra had the **blessing** of...his **God**,
     8.22 **God blesses** everyone who trusts him,
Neh 13.2 **God** turned the curse into a **blessing**.
Ps 45.2 **God** has always **blessed** you.
    67.1 **God**, be merciful to us and **bless** us;
    67.6 **God**, our **God**, has **blessed** us.
    67.7 **God** has **blessed** us;
   72.15 may **God's blessings** be on him always!
   72.17 May all nations ask **God** to **bless** them
   84.9 **Bless** our king, O **God**,
   90.17 **God**, may your **blessings** be with us.
  118.26 May **God bless** the one who comes
Is   65.16 ask to be **blessed** by the Faithful **God**.
Joel 2.14 **God** will change his mind and **bless** you
Mt   21.9 **God bless** him who comes in the name
   23.39 **God bless** him who comes in the name
Mk   11.9 **God bless** him who comes in the name
  11.10 **God bless** the coming kingdom
Lk   2.40 and **God's blessings** were upon him.
  13.35 **God bless** him who comes in the name
  19.38 **God bless** the king who comes
Jn   12.13 **God bless** him who comes in the name
  12.13 **God bless** the King of Israel!
Acts 4.33 **God** poured rich **blessings** on them all.
   6.8 a man richly **blessed** by **God**
  11.23 saw how **God** had **blessed** the people,
  20.32 the **blessings God** has for all
Rom 10.12 **God**...richly **blesses** all who call to him.
  12.14 Ask **God** to **bless** those who persecute
2 Cor 1.11 and **God** will **bless** us;
  11.31 The **God**...**blessed** be his name
Gal   3.8 you **God** will **bless** all mankind.
  3.14 the **blessing** which **God** promised
Eph 3.6 with the Jews in **God's blessings**;
1 Tim 1.11 from the glorious and **blessed God**.
  6.15 by **God**, the **blessed** and only Ruler,
Heb 6.7 **God blesses** the soil which drinks in
  7.6 **blessed** him...who received **God's**
  9.15 eternal **blessings** that **God** has promised.
Jas   1.25 will be **blessed** by **God** in what he does.
  2.16 **God bless** you! Keep warm and eat well!
1 Pet 1.4 **blessings** that **God** keeps for his people.
  2.19 **God** will **bless** you for this
  2.20 **God** will **bless** you for it.
  3.9 a **blessing** is what **God** promised

Happy, Joyful
Deut 16.15 Be **joyful**, because the Lord has **blessed**
1 Kgs 8.66 home **happy** because of all the **blessings**
2 Chr 7.10 They were **happy** about all the **blessings**
Ps 92.10 you have **blessed** me with **happiness**.
Rev 20.6 **Happy** and greatly **blessed** are those

Honour
Ps 84.11 **blessing** us with kindness and **honour**.
 115.13 will **bless** everyone who **honours** him,
Jer 30.19 my **blessing** will bring them **honour**.

Jesus see Christ

Joyful see Happy

Kindness see Love

Life ·
Deut 30.19 **life** and death, between **God's blessing**
Ps 133.3 Lord has promised his **blessing** — **life**
Phlm .6 **blessing** which we have in our **life**

Lord, Name
see also **God**
Gen 21.1 The **Lord blessed** Sarah

Gen 22.16 **Lord** is speaking — that I will richly **bless** you.
  24.1 and the **Lord** had **blessed** him
  24.31 are a man whom the **Lord** has **blessed**.
  24.35 The **Lord** has greatly **blessed** my master
  26.12 because the **Lord blessed** him.
  26.29 is clear that the **Lord** has **blessed** you.
  27.2 a field which the **Lord** has **blessed**.
  30.27 the **Lord** has **blessed** me because of you.
  30.30 and the **Lord** has **blessed** you
  39.5 the **Lord blessed** the household
  39.21 **Lord** was with Joseph and **blessed** him,
Ex 20.11 I, the **Lord**, **blessed** the Sabbath
  32.29 so the **Lord** has given you his **blessing**.
Lev 25.21 The **Lord** will **bless** the land
Num 6.24 **Lord bless** you and take care of you;
  6.27 **Lord** said, "If they pronounce my **name** as a **blessing**
  10.32 all the **blessings** that the **Lord** gives
  24.1 knew that the **Lord** wanted him to **bless**
Deut 11.27 a **blessing**, if you obey the commands of the **Lord**
  14.24 the **Lord** has **blessed** you
  15.6 The **Lord** will **bless** you,
  15.10 and the **Lord** will **bless** you
  15.14 what the **Lord** has **blessed** you with
  16.15 the **Lord** has **blessed** your harvest
  28.3 The **Lord** will **bless** your towns
  28.4 **Lord** will **bless** you with many children
  28.5 The **Lord** will **bless** your corn crops
  28.6 The **Lord** will **bless** everything you do.
  28.47 The **Lord blessed** you in every way
  33.13 May the **Lord bless** their land with rain
  33.16 **Blessed** by the goodness of the **Lord**,
  33.23 **blessed** by the **Lord's** good favour;
Josh 17.14 because the **Lord** has **blessed** us.
Judg 13.24 child grew and the **Lord blessed** him.
  17.2 May the **Lord bless** you, my son!
Ruth 1.6 that the **Lord** had **blessed** his people
  2.4 The **Lord bless** you!" they answered.
  2.20 May the **Lord bless** Boaz!
  3.10 The **Lord bless** you," he said
  4.13 The **Lord blessed** her,
1 Sam 2.21 The **Lord** did **bless** Hannah
  15.13 saying, "The **Lord bless** you,
  23.21 the **Lord bless** you for being so kind
  24.19 **Lord bless** you for what you have done
  25.31 And when the **Lord** has **blessed** you,
2 Sam 2.5 **Lord bless** you for showing your loyalty
  6.11 and the **Lord blessed** Obed Edom
  6.12 **Lord** had **blessed** Obed Edom's family
  6.18 **blessed** the people in the **name** of the
  16.12 **Lord** will notice my misery and give me some **blessings**
1 Kgs 8.66 the **blessings** that the **Lord** had given
1 Chr 13.14 the **Lord blessed** Obed Edom's family
  16.2 **blessed** the people in the **name** of the
  17.27 You, **Lord**, have **blessed** them,
  23.13 to **bless** the people in his **name**.
2 Chr 7.10 the **blessings** that the **Lord** had given
  17.3 The **Lord blessed** Jehoshaphat
  30.27 asked the **Lord's blessing** on the people.
  31.10 because the **Lord** has **blessed** his people.
Ezra 7.6 Ezra had the **blessing** of the **Lord**
Job 42.12 **Lord blessed** the last part of Job's life
Ps 3.8 the **Lord** — may he **bless** his people.
  4.6 Give us more **blessings**, O **Lord**.
  5.12 You **bless** those who obey you, **Lord**;
  24.5 **Lord** will **bless** them and save them;
  28.9 **Lord**, and **bless** those who are yours.
  29.11 The **Lord** gives strength to his people and **blesses**
  37.22 Those who are **blessed** by the **Lord**

Ps	84.11	**Lord** is our protector and glorious king, **blessing** us
	115.12	**Lord** remembers us and will **bless** us;
	115.15	May you be **blessed** by the **Lord**,
	118.26	**bless** the one who comes in the **name**
	127.3	from the **Lord**; they are a real **blessing**.
	128.4	obeys the **Lord** will surely be **blessed**
	128.5	May the **Lord bless** you from Zion!
	129.8	We **bless** you in the **name** of the **Lord**.
	129.8	May the **Lord bless** you!
	133.3	the **Lord** has promised his **blessing**
	134.3	**Lord**, who made heaven and earth, **bless**
Prov	10.22	**Lord's blessing** that makes you wealthy.
	16.3	Ask the **Lord** to **bless** your plans
Is	19.25	The **Lord** Almighty will **bless** them
	45.7	both **blessing** and disaster. I, the **Lord**,
Jer	31.23	the **Lord bless** the sacred hill
Hos	10.12	**Lord**, and I will come and pour out **blessings**
Zech	7.2	to pray for the **Lord's blessing**
	8.21	**Lord** Almighty and pray for his **blessing**.
	8.22	**Lord** Almighty, and to pray for his **blessing**.
Lk	1.28	**Lord** is with you and has greatly **blessed**
	19.38	**bless** the king who comes in the **name**
Rom	10.12	same **Lord** of all and richly **blesses** all
1 Cor	1.7	**blessing**, as you wait for our **Lord** Jesus
2 Cor	11.31	of the **Lord** Jesus — **blessed** be his **name**

Love, Care, Kindness

Num	6.24	**Lord bless** you and take **care** of you;
Deut	7.13	He will **love** you and **bless** you
	23.5	into a **blessing**, because he **loved** you.
1 Sam	23.21	the **Lord bless** you for being so **kind**
Ps	4.6	more **blessings**, O Lord. Look on us with **kindness**!
	5.12	You **bless** those who obey you, Lord; your **love**
	67.1	and **bless** us; look on us with **kindness**,
	84.11	**blessing** us with **kindness** and honour.
	103.4	and **blesses** me with **love** and mercy.
Jer	16.5	**bless** my people with peace or show them **love**
Lk	6.32	**love** you, why should you receive a **blessing**?

Name see Lord

Obey, Prosper, Right

Gen	22.18	**blessed** your descendants — all because you **obeyed**
	26.5	**bless** you, because Abraham **obeyed** me
Deut	11.27	a **blessing**, if you **obey** the commands
	23.20	**Obey** this rule, and the Lord your God will **bless**
	28.2	**Obey** the Lord your God and all these **blessings**
	28.13	**prosper** and never fail if you **obey**
2 Sam	22.21	I do what is **right**; he **blesses** me
Ps	5.12	You **bless** those who **obey** you, Lord;
	18.20	I do what is **right**; he **blesses** me
	128.4	**obeys** the Lord will surely be **blessed**
1 Pet	2.20	you have done **right**, God will **bless** you

Offer, Sacrifice

Deut	16.10	**offering** in proportion to the **blessing**
1 Sam	9.12	he has to **bless** the **sacrifice**
2 Sam	6.18	**offering** the **sacrifices**, he **blessed**
1 Chr	16.2	**offering** the **sacrifices**, he **blessed**
Ezek	44.30	as an **offering**, and my **blessing** will rest
Joel	2.14	**bless** you with abundant crops. Then you can **offer**

Peace

Ps	29.11	and **blesses** them with **peace**
Jer	16.5	no longer **bless** my people with **peace**

Praise

Jer	4.2	to **bless** them, and they will **praise** me.
	30.19	**praise**; they will shout for joy. By my **blessing**
Mt	21.9	**Praise** to David's Son! God **bless** him
Mk	11.9	**Praise** God! God **bless** him who comes
Jn	12.13	**Praise** God! God **bless** him who comes

Pray

Ex	12.32	Also **pray** for a **blessing** on me.
1 Chr	4.10	**prayed** to the God of Israel, "**Bless** me,
Ezra	6.10	and **pray** for the **blessing** on me
Ps	4.6	who **pray**: "Give us more **blessings**,
Zech	7.2	to **pray** for the Lord's **blessing**
	8.21	and **pray** for his **blessing**.
	8.22	and to **pray** for his **blessing**.
Lk	6.28	**bless** those who curse you, and **pray**

Promise

Gen	21.1	Lord **blessed** Sarah, as he had **promised**
Deut	7.13	**blessings** in the land that he **promised**
	15.6	Lord will **bless** you, as he has **promised**.
Ps	133.3	the Lord has **promised** his **blessing**
Is	55.3	and give you the **blessings** I **promised**
Acts	13.34	sure **blessings** that I **promised** to David.
Gal	3.14	**blessing** which God **promised** to
Eph	1.18	are the wonderful **blessings** he **promises**
Heb	6.14	I **promise** you that I will **bless** you
	7.6	and **blessed** him, the man who received God's **promises**.
	9.15	eternal **blessings** that God has **promised**.
	11.20	faith that made Isaac **promise blessings**
1 Pet	3.9	because a **blessing** is what God **promised**

Prosper see Obey

Rich

Gen	22.16	I will **richly bless** you.
	24.35	**blessed** my master and made him a **rich**
Deut	7.14	in the world will be as **richly blessed**
	26.15	**bless** also the rich and fertile land
	33.14	**blessed** with sun-ripened fruit, **Rich**
	33.23	Naphtali is **richly blessed**
Is	63.7	has **richly blessed** the people of Israel
Acts	4.33	God poured **rich blessings** on them all.
	6.8	a man **richly blessed** by God
Rom	10.12	**richly blesses** all who call to him.
	11.12	brought **rich blessings** to the world,
Eph	1.18	how **rich** are the wonderful **blessings**
1 Pet	1.4	the **rich blessings** that God keeps

Right see Obey

Sacrifice see Offer

Words

Gen	24.60	their **blessing** in these **words**:
Num	6.23	to use the following **words** in **blessing**
Josh	22.6	with his **blessing** and with these **words**:
Ps	62.4	You speak **words** of **blessing**,

BLIND

Jn	9.1	—	12.40	x22
Is	42.7	—	44.9	x6
Mt	23.16 — 26			x5
Mt	15.14 — 31			x4
Deut	27.18	—	28.29	x3
1 Sam	2.33	—	4.15	x3
2 Sam	5.6 — 8			x3
Mk	10.46 — 51			x3
Lk	6.39	—	7.22	x3

Crippled

Lev	22.22	any animal that is **blind** or **crippled**
Deut	15.21	if they are **crippled** or **blind**
2 Sam	5.6	**blind** and the **crippled** could keep you
	5.8	attack those poor **blind cripples**.

Mt	15.30	the **blind**, the **crippled**,
	21.14	The **blind** and the **crippled** came to him
Lk	14.13	the **crippled**, the lame, and the **blind**;
	14.21	the **crippled**, the **blind**,

Cure see Sight

Darkness

Job	23.16	though the **darkness** has made me **blind**.
Is	29.18	**blind**, who have been living in **darkness**,
	42.7	**blind** and set free those who sit in **dark**
Rom	2.19	for the **blind**, a light for those who are in **darkness**,
1 Jn	2.11	the **darkness** has made him **blind**.

Poor

Lk	14.13	the **poor**, the crippled, the lame, and the **blind**;
	14.21	back the **poor**, the crippled, the **blind**,
Rev	3.17	You are **poor**, naked, and **blind**.

Sight, Cure

Ex	4.11	gives him **sight** or makes him **blind**?
Ps	146.8	and gives **sight** to the **blind**.
Lk	4.18	and recovery of **sight** to the **blind**;
	7.21	and gave **sight** to many **blind** people.
Jn	9.14	the mud and **cured** him of his **blindness**
	9.17	he **cured** you of your **blindness**
	9.21	know who **cured** him of his **blindness**.
	9.26	How did he **cure** you of your **blindness**?
	9.30	but he **cured** me of my **blindness**!
	9.32	giving **sight** to a person born **blind**.
	10.21	a demon give **sight** to **blind** people?
	11.37	He gave **sight** to the **blind** man,

Sin

Jn	9.2	whose **sin** caused him to be born **blind**?
	9.3	**blindness** has nothing to do with his **sins**

BLOOD

Lev	3.2	—	10.18	x32
Lev	14.6	—	17.14	x25
Heb	9.7	—	13.12	x20
Rev	16.3	—	19.13	x9
Ex	29.12	—	30.10	x7
Ezek	43.18	—	45.19	x6
Ex	7.17 — 21			x5
Ex	12.7 — 23			x5
Deut	12.16 — 27			x5
Is	34.3 — 7			x4
Ezek	16.6 — 22			x4
Ezek	38.22	—	39.19	x4
Zech	9.7 — 15			x4
Mt	26.28	—	27.8	x4
Jn	6.53 — 56			x4
Rev	6.12	—	8.8	x4
Ex	24.6 — 8			x3
Lev	1.5 — 15			x3
Num	18.17	—	19.5	x3
1 Sam	14.32 — 34			x3
1 Kgs	21.19	—	22.38	x3
2 Chr	29.22	—	30.16	x3
Ps	79.3 — 10			x3
Ezek	23.45	—	24.8	x3
Acts	1.19	—	2.20	x3
1 Cor	10.16. —		11.27	x3
1 Jn	5.6 — 8			x3

Flesh, Body

Gen	29.14	you are my own **flesh** and **blood**.
	37.27	our own **flesh** and **blood**.
Judg	9.2	Abimelech is your own **flesh** and **blood**.
2 Sam	5.1	We are your own **flesh** and **blood**.
	19.12	my own **flesh** and **blood**;
1 Chr	11.1	We are your own **flesh** and **blood**.
Ps	50.13	eat the **flesh** of bulls or drink the **blood**

Jn	6.53	eat the **flesh** of the Son of Man and drink his **blood**,
	6.54	eats my **flesh** and drinks my **blood**
	6.55	my **flesh** is the real food; my **blood**
	6.56	eats my **flesh** and drinks my **blood**
Rom	9.3	my own **flesh** and **blood**!
1 Cor	11.27	against the Lord's **body** and **blood**.
	15.50	**flesh** and **blood** cannot share
Heb	2.14	are people of **flesh** and **blood**,

High Priest see Priest

Lamb see Offer

Life

Gen	9.4	because the **life** is in the **blood**.
Lev	17.11	**life** of every living thing is in the **blood**,
	17.14	**life** of every living thing is in the **blood**,
Deut	12.23	for the **life** is in the **blood**.
Jn	6.53	drink his **blood**, you will not have **life**
	6.54	drinks my **blood** has eternal **life**,
Phil	2.17	my **life's blood** is to be poured out

Offer, Lamb, Sacrifice, Sheep

Ex	30.10	**blood** of the animal **sacrificed** for sin.
Lev	7.2	**burnt-offerings** are killed, and its **blood**
	7.33	to the priest who **offers** the **blood**
	14.14	take some of the **blood** of the **lamb**
	14.17	some of the **blood** of the **lamb**
	14.25	the **lamb** and take some of the **blood**
Num	18.17	be **sacrificed**. Throw their **blood**
2 Kgs	16.15	the **blood** of all the animals that are **sacrificed**
	25.14	catching the **blood** from the **sacrifices**,
2 Chr	29.22	then the **lambs**, and sprinkled the **blood**
	29.24	**blood** on the altar as a **sacrifice**
	30.16	Levites gave the **blood** of the **sacrifices**
Is	1.11	tired of the **blood** of bulls and **sheep**
	34.6	like the **blood** and fat of **lambs**
	66.3	a **grain-offering** or **offer** pigs' **blood**;
Jer	52.18	catching the **blood** from the **sacrifices**,
	52.19	holding the **blood** from the **sacrifices**,
Ezek	43.18	**blood** of the animals that were **sacrificed**.
	44.7	**blood** of the **sacrifices** are being **offered**
	44.15	to **offer** me the fat and the **blood**
Zech	9.11	sealed by the **blood** of **sacrifices**,
	9.15	will flow like the **blood** of a **sacrifice**
Phil	2.17	**blood** is to be poured out like an **offering**
Heb	9.7	with him **blood** which he **offers** to God
	9.12	the **blood** of goats and bulls to **offer**
	9.14	perfect **sacrifice** to God. His **blood**
Rev	7.14	them white with the **blood** of the **Lamb**.
	12.11	**blood** of the **Lamb** and by the truth

Priest, High Priest

Lev	1.5	Aaronite **priests** shall present the **blood**
	1.11	and the **priests** shall throw its **blood**
	3.2	Aaronite **priests** shall throw the **blood**
	3.8	The **priests** shall throw its **blood**
	3.13	The **priests** shall throw its **blood**
	4.5	**High Priest** shall take some of the bull's **blood**
	4.16	The **High Priest** shall take some of the bull's **blood**
	4.25	**priest** shall dip his finger in the **blood**
	4.30	**priest** shall dip his finger in the **blood**
	4.34	**priest** shall dip his finger in the **blood**
	7.14	to the **priest** who takes the **blood**
	7.33	to the **priest** who **offers** the **blood**
	14.14	The **priest** shall take some of the **blood**
	17.6	The **priest** shall throw the **blood**
2 Chr	29.24	**priests** killed the goats and poured their **blood**
	30.16	the **blood** of the sacrifices to the **priests**,
	35.11	and the **priests** sprinkled the **blood**

Ezek	45.19	The **priest** will take some of the **blood**
Heb	13.11	Jewish **High Priest** brings the **blood**

Sacrifice see **Offer**

Sheep see **Offer**

Sin

Ex	30.10	**blood** of the animal sacrificed for **sin**.
Lev	16.27	**blood** was brought...to take away **sin**,
	17.11	**blood**...to take away the people's **sins**.
1 Sam	14.34	**sin**...by eating meat with **blood** in it.
2 Chr	29.24	**blood** on the altar as a sacrifice to take away the **sin**
Zeph	1.17	have **sinned**... and now their **blood**
1 Cor	11.27	**sin** against the Lord's body and **blood**.
Heb	9.22	**sins** are forgiven only if **blood** is poured
	10.4	**blood** of bulls and goats can never take away **sins**
	13.12	to purify...from **sin** with his own **blood**.

Sprinkle

Lev	4.6	dip his finger in the **blood** and **sprinkle**
	5.9	and **sprinkle** some of its **blood**
	8.30	**blood** that was on the altar and **sprinkled**
	14.7	He shall **sprinkle** the **blood** seven times
	16.14	**blood** and with his finger **sprinkle** it
	16.15	**blood** into the Most Holy Place, and **sprinkle**
	16.19	he must **sprinkle** some of the **blood**
Num	19.4	**blood** and with his finger **sprinkle** it
2 Chr	29.22	and **sprinkled** the **blood** of each sacrifice
	30.16	**blood** of the sacrifices to the priests, who **sprinkled**
	35.11	and the priests **sprinkled** the **blood**
Ezek	43.18	by **sprinkling** on it the **blood**
Heb	9.21	**sprinkled** the **blood** on the Covenant
	11.28	order the **blood** to be **sprinkled**
	12.24	the **sprinkled blood** that promises

BODY

1 Cor	9.27	—	13.3	x26
1 Cor	5.3	—	7.34	x16
Eph	1.23	—	5.30	x16
1 Cor	15.35	—	44	x12
Lev	10.4	—	11.40	x11
2 Cor	4.10	—	5.10	x9
Mt	5.29	—	6.25	x8
Jn	19.31	—	20.12	x8
Rom	6.12	—	8.11	x8
Col	1.18	—	3.15	x8
1 Kgs	13.22	—	31	x7
2 Kgs	9.10	—	10.25	x7
Mk	14.8	—	16.1	x7
Lk	11.34	—	12.23	x7
Lk	22.19	—	24.23	x7
Job	18.13	—	21.33	x6
Mt	26.12	—	28.13	x6
2 Pet	1.14	—	3.12	x6
Deut	21.2	—	23	x5
Judg	19.28	—	20.36	x5
2 Sam	20.11	—	21.12	x5
Jer	14.16	—	16.4	x5
Heb	10.5	—	11.22	x5
Gen	50.2	—	26	x4
Job	6.4	—	7.15	x4
Phil	3.2	—	21	x4
1 Sam	31.8	—	12	x3
Job	33.19	—	25	x3
Jer	41.7	—	9	x3
Ezek	1.9	—	23	x3
Ezek	37.8	—	10	x3
Ezek	39.4	—	18	x3
Rom	12.4	—	5	x3

Dead, Destroy

Lev	11.8	or even touch their **dead bodies**;
	11.11	or even touch their **dead bodies**.
	11.24	Whoever touches the **dead bodies**
	11.31	touches them or their **dead bodies**
	11.32	if their **dead bodies** fall on anything
	11.35	Anything on which the **dead bodies** fall
	11.36	touches their **dead bodies** is unclean.
	11.40	who carries the **dead body** must wash
	26.30	your **dead bodies** on your fallen idols.
Num	19.18	the human bone or the **dead body**
Deut	14.8	or even touch their **dead bodies**.
	21.23	because a **dead body** hanging on a post
Judg	14.8	some honey inside the **dead body**.
	14.9	honey from the **dead body** of a lion.
Job	39.30	Around **dead bodies** the eagles gather,
Is	66.24	they will see the **dead bodies**
Jer	9.22	**Dead bodies** are scattered everywhere,
Ezek	37.9	to breathe into these **dead bodies**,
Dan	7.11	its **body** was thrown into the flames and **destroyed**.
Joel	2.20	Their **dead bodies** will stink.
Amos	4.10	nostrils with the stink of **dead bodies**
	8.3	There will be **dead bodies** everywhere,
Nah	3.3	**dead bodies** without number
Zeph	1.17	and their **dead bodies** will lie rotting
Hag	2.13	because he has touched a **dead body**
Mt	10.28	who can **destroy** both **body** and soul
	24.28	Wherever there is a **dead body**,
Lk	17.37	Wherever there is a **dead body**,
Acts	2.31	of the **dead**; his **body** did not rot
Rom	4.19	**body**, which was already practically **dead**,
	7.5	**bodies**, and all we did ended in **death**.
	7.24	this **body** that is taking me to **death**?
1 Cor	5.5	for his **body** to be **destroyed**,
	10.5	so their **dead bodies** were scattered
	15.35	**dead** be raised to life? What kind of **body**
2 Cor	4.10	in our mortal **bodies** the **death** of Jesus,
Jas	2.26	the **body** without the spirit is **dead**,
2 Pet	3.10	**bodies** will burn up and be **destroyed**,

Grave, Tomb

Num	19.18	or the dead **body** or the **grave**.
2 Sam	2.32	**body** and buried it in the family **tomb**
1 Kgs	13.22	your **body** will not be buried in your family **grave**.
	13.31	bury me in this **grave** and lay my **body**
Lk	23.55	saw the **tomb** and how Jesus' **body**
Jn	19.42	**tomb** was close by, they placed Jesus' **body** there.
Acts	2.31	his **body** did not rot in the **grave**.
	13.36	and his **body** rotted in the **grave**.

Hang

Gen	40.19	Then he will **hang** your **body** on a pole,
Deut	21.22	and his **body** is **hung** on a post,
	21.23	a dead **body hanging** on a post
Josh	10.26	**hanged** them on five trees, where their **bodies**
2 Sam	21.12	Philistines had **hanged** the **bodies**
Esth	9.13	**bodies** of Haman's ten sons to be **hung**

Heavenly

1 Cor	15.40	are **heavenly bodies** and earthly **bodies**
2 Cor	5.4	**body**, but that we want to have the **heavenly**
2 Pet	3.10	the **heavenly bodies** will burn up
	3.12	the **heavenly bodies** will be melted

Hell

Mt	5.29	your whole **body** thrown into **hell**.
	5.30	for your whole **body** to go to **hell**.
	10.28	can destroy both **body** and soul in **hell**.

Jesus

Mt	27.58	and asked for the **body** of **Jesus**.
Mk	15.42	asked him for the **body** of **Jesus**.
	15.47	where the **body** of **Jesus** was placed.
	16.1	to go and anoint the **body** of **Jesus**.
Lk	2.52	**Jesus** grew both in **body** and in wisdom,
	23.52	and asked for the **body** of **Jesus**.
	23.55	how **Jesus' body** was placed in it.
	24.3	did not find the **body** of...**Jesus**.
Jn	19.38	if he could take **Jesus' body**.
	19.40	The two men took **Jesus' body**
	19.42	they placed **Jesus' body** there.
	20.12	where the **body** of **Jesus** had been,

Life, Raise

Is	26.19	Their **bodies** will come back to **life**.
Ezek	37.9	**bodies**, and to bring them back to **life**
	37.10	the **bodies**, and they came to **life**
Mt	27.64	**body**, and then tell the people that he was **raised**
Rom	8.11	give **life** to your mortal **bodies**
1 Cor	15.35	be **raised** to **life**? What kind of **body**
	15.42	to **life**. When the **body** is buried,
	15.44	it is a physical **body**; when **raised**,
2 Cor	4.10	his **life** also may be seen in our **bodies**
	4.11	his **life** may be seen in this mortal **body**
	5.10	in his **bodily life**.
Col	1.18	the source of the **body's life**.

Love

1 Cor	13.3	give up my **body** to be burnt — but if I have no **love**,
Eph	4.16	**body** grows and builds itself up through **love**.
	5.28	just as they **love** their own **bodies**.

Raise see Life

Sin

Ps	38.3	**body** is diseased because of my **sins**.
Rom	6.12	**Sin** must no longer rule in your...**bodies**
	7.23	of **sin** which is at work in my **body**.
	8.10	**bodies** are going to die because of **sin**.
1 Cor	6.18	other **sin** a man commits does not affect his **body**;
	11.27	is guilty of **sin** against the Lord's **body**
Heb	10.10	all purified from **sin** by...his own **body**
1 Pet	2.24	Christ...carried our **sins** in his **body**
Jude	.8	make them **sin** against their own **bodies**;

Spirit

Mal	2.15	God make you one **body** and **spirit**
Lk	1.80	grew and developed in **body** and **spirit**
1 Cor	5.3	**body**, still I am there with you in **spirit**;
	5.5	**body** to be destroyed, so that his **spirit**
	7.34	to be dedicated both in **body** and **spirit**;
Col	2.5	in **body**, yet I am with you in **spirit**
1 Thes	5.23	being — **spirit**, soul, and **body** — free
Jas	2.26	as the **body** without the **spirit** is dead,

Spirit of God

Lk	3.22	**Spirit** came down upon him in **bodily**
Rom	8.11	**bodies** by the presence of his **Spirit**
1 Cor	6.19	**body** is the temple of the **Holy Spirit**,
	12.13	into the one **body** by the same **Spirit**,
Eph	4.4	There is one **body** and one **Spirit**,

Tomb see Grave

BOW

Dan	2.46	—	3.28	x11
1 Kgs	1.16	—	2.19	x6
Gen	17.3	—	19.1	x4
Gen	42.6	—	44.14	x4
Gen	48.12	—	50.18	x4
Is	44.17	—	46.6	x4
Gen	23.7	—	24.52	x3

Gen	33.3	—	7	x3
Gen	37.7	—	10	x3
2 Sam	14.4	—	15.5	x3
1 Kgs	18.7	—	19.18	x3
Esth	3.2	—	5	x3

Gods, Idols

Ex	20.5	Do not **bow** down to any **idol**
	23.24	Do not **bow** down to their **gods**
Deut	5.9	Do not **bow** down to any **idol**
Josh	23.7	or worship those **gods** or **bow** down
Judg	2.12	the **gods** of the peoples round them. They **bowed**
1 Kgs	19.18	not **bowed** to Baal or kissed his **idol**.
2 Kgs	17.35	worship other **gods**; do not **bow** down
Ps	97.7	all the **gods bow** down before the Lord.
Is	44.17	into an **idol**, and then he **bows** down
	44.19	into an **idol**. Here I am **bowing** down
	46.6	to make a **god**; then they **bow**
Jer	8.19	by **bowing** down to your useless foreign **gods**?
Dan	3.12	do not worship your **god** or **bow** down
	3.14	to worship my **god** and to **bow** down
	3.18	your **god**, and we will not **bow** down
	3.28	than **bow** down and worship any **god**

Worship, Praise, Temple

Gen	24.52	**bowed** down and **worshipped** the Lord.
Ex	4.31	they **bowed** down and **worshipped**.
	24.1	**bow** down in **worship**.
	34.8	**bowed** down to the ground and **worshipped**
1 Kgs	1.47	Then King David **bowed** in **worship**
1 Chr	16.29	offering and come into his **Temple**. **Bow**
2 Chr	20.18	people **bowed** with him and **worshipped**
Ezra	10.1	**bowing** in prayer in front of the **Temple**,
Neh	9.6	powers **bow** down and **worship** you.
Ps	5.7	**worship** in your holy **Temple** and **bow**
	29.2	**Praise** the Lord's glorious name; **bow**
	86.9	and **bow** down to you; they will **praise**
	95.6	let us **bow** down and **worship** him;
	138.2	**bow** down, and **praise** your name
Ezek	46.3	**bow** down and **worship** the Lord
1 Cor	14.25	he will **bow** down and **worship** God,

BREAD

Jn	6.7	—	58	x20
Ex	12.8	—	13.7	x10
Lev	23.6	—	24.9	x10
Lev	6.16	—	8.32	x8
1 Cor	10.3	—	11.29	x8
Judg	6.19	—	8.5	x6
Ezek	4.9	—	17	x6
Mt	15.34	—	16.12	x6
1 Sam	21.3	—	6	x5
Ex	29.2	—	34	x4
Ex	34.18	—	35.13	x4
Deut	16.3	—	8	x4
Mk	6.8	—	43	x4
Mk	8.5	—	17	x4
Jn	13.26	—	30	x4
Ex	23.15	—	18	x3
Lev	2.4	—	7	x3
Num	6.15	—	19	x3
1 Kgs	17.6	—	12	x3
2 Chr	29.18	—	30.21	x3
Lk	24.30	—	35	x3
1 Cor	5.8			x3

Body

Mt	26.26	took...**bread**...this is my **body**
Mk	14.22	took...**bread**...this is my **body**.
Lk	22.19	took...**bread**...This is my **body**,
1 Cor	10.17	**bread**, all of us, though many, are one **body**,

1 Cor 11.23 took...**bread**...This is my **body**,
       11.29 the Lord's **body** when he eats the **bread**

Cup
1 Cor 11.26 eat this **bread** and drink from this **cup**
       11.27 Lord's **bread** or drinks from his **cup**
       11.28 eat the **bread** and drink from the **cup**.
       11.29 eats the **bread** and drinks from the **cup**,

Heaven
Neh 9.15 you gave them **bread** from **heaven**,
Jn   6.31 He gave them **bread** from **heaven**
       6.32 was not the **bread** from **heaven**;
       6.41 the **bread** that came down from **heaven**.
       6.50 the **bread** that comes down from **heaven**.
       6.51 **bread** that came down from **heaven**.
       6.58 the **bread** that came down from **heaven**;

Life
Mt   4.4 cannot **live** on **bread** alone, but needs
Lk   4.4 Man cannot **live** on **bread** alone
Jn   6.35 I am the **bread** of **life**,
       6.48 I am the **bread** of **life**.
       6.51 I am the **living bread** that came down
       6.58 eats this **bread** will **live** for ever

Offer, Present
Ex   23.18 Do not **offer bread** made with yeast
       25.30 to be the sacred **bread offered** to me.
       29.23 basket of **bread** which has been **offered**
       34.25 Do not **offer bread** made with yeast
       35.13 the **bread offered** to God;
       39.36 and the **bread offered** to God;
       40.23 on it the **bread offered** to the Lord,
Lev   2.4 the **offering** is **bread** baked in an oven
       2.5 **offering** is **bread** cooked on a griddle
       2.7 If the **offering** is **bread** cooked in a pan
       7.12 an **offering** of **bread** made without yeast:
       7.13 **offer** loaves of **bread** baked without
       7.14 **present** one part of each kind of **bread**
       8.31 **bread** that is in the basket of ordination
            offerings,
     10.12 **offered** to the Lord, make unleavened **bread**
     23.14 **bread**, until you have brought this **offering**
     23.17 **bread** and **present** them to the Lord
     23.18 the **bread** the community is to **present**
     23.20 The priest shall **present** the **bread**
Num   4.7 for the **bread offered** to the Lord
       6.15 He shall also **offer** a basket of **bread**
       6.17 **offer** it with the basket of **bread**;
     15.20 **bread** made from the new corn is to be
            presented
1 Sam 21.6 **bread** he had was the loaves **offered**
1 Kgs 7.48 the table for the **bread offered** to God,
1 Chr 23.29 for the **bread offered** to God,
     28.16 the loaves of **bread offered** to God.
2 Chr 2.4 we will present **offerings** of sacred **bread**
     4.19 the tables for the **bread offered** to God;
     13.11 They present the **offerings** of **bread**
Neh 10.33 sacred **bread**, the daily **grain-offering**,
Amos 4.5 and **offer** your **bread** in thanksgiving
Mt   12.4 his men ate the **bread offered** to God,
Mk   2.26 and ate the **bread offered** to God.
Lk   6.4 took the **bread offered** to God,
Heb   9.2 the table with the **bread offered** to God.

Sacred
Ex   25.30 to be the **sacred bread** offered to me.
1 Sam 21.4 any ordinary **bread**, only **sacred bread**;
     21.6 the priest gave David the **sacred bread**
1 Chr 9.32 the **sacred bread** for the Temple
2 Chr 2.4 we will present offerings of **sacred bread**
     29.18 the table for the **sacred bread**,
Neh 10.33 **sacred bread**, the daily grain-offering

Thanks
Amos 4.5 and offer your **bread** in **thanksgiving**
Mt   26.26 **bread**, gave a prayer of **thanks**, broke
Mk   14.22 **bread**, gave a prayer of **thanks**, broke
Lk   22.19 he took a piece of **bread**, gave **thanks**
Jn   6.11 took the **bread**, gave **thanks** to God
       6.23 **bread** after the Lord had given **thanks**.
Acts 27.35 took some **bread**, gave **thanks** to God

Unleavened, Without Yeast
Ex   12.8 and with **bread** made **without yeast**.
     12.15 with yeast — eat only **unleavened bread**.
     12.39 baked **unleavened bread** from the dough
     13.6 **unleavened bread** and on the seventh
     23.15 the Festival of **Unleavened Bread**
     34.18 Keep the Festival of **Unleavened Bread**
Lev 6.16 be made into **bread** baked **without yeast**
     7.12 an offering of **bread** made **without yeast**:
     7.13 loaves of **bread** baked **without yeast**.
     8.2 and the basket of **unleavened bread**
     8.26 from the basket of **unleavened bread**
     10.12 make **unleavened bread** with it
     23.6 the Festival of **Unleavened Bread**
Num 6.15 a basket of **bread** made **without yeast**:
     9.11 Celebrate it with **unleavened bread**
     28.17 which only **bread** prepared **without yeast**
Deut 16.3 do not eat **bread** prepared **with yeast**.
     16.8 are to eat **bread** prepared **without yeast**,
Josh 5.11 grain and **bread** made **without yeast**.
1 Sam 28.24 and baked some **bread without yeast**.
2 Kgs 23.9 but they could eat the **unleavened bread**
2 Chr 8.13 the Festival of **Unleavened Bread**,
            Also: 30.13; 30.21; 35.17
Ezra 6.22 the Festival of **Unleavened Bread**.
Ezek 45.21 will eat **bread** made **without yeast**
Mt   26.17 of the Festival of **Unleavened Bread**
Mk   14.1 Passover and **Unleavened Bread**
     14.12 of the Festival of **Unleavened Bread**
Lk   22.1 the Festival of **Unleavened Bread**
     22.7 the Festival of **Unleavened Bread**
Acts 12.3 of the Festival of **Unleavened Bread**
     20.6 after the Festival of **Unleavened Bread**

BRIBE
         Prov   15.27 —   17.23   x3

Accept
Ex   23.8 Do not **accept** a **bribe**,
Deut 10.17 and he does not **accept bribes**.
     16.19 and they are not to **accept bribes**,
1 Sam 8.3 so they **accepted bribes**
     12.3 Have I **accepted** a **bribe** from anyone?
Prov 17.23 Corrupt judges **accept** secret **bribes**
Is   1.23 are always **accepting** gifts and **bribes**.
     33.15 cheat the poor and don't **accept bribes**.

BURDEN
1 Kgs	12.4 – 14		x5
2 Chr	10.4 – 14		x5
Jer	23.33 – 38		x5
Neh	4.10 –	5.18	x3

Sin
Ps   38.4 my **sins**...are a **burden** too heavy
Is   43.24 Instead you **burdened** me with your **sins**;
Ezek 33.10 We are **burdened** with our **sins**
2 Tim 3.6 are **burdened** by the guilt of their **sins**

CARE
Ezek	34.2 – 23			x7
1 Tim	5.5	–	6.20	x6
Gen	36.24	–	37.16	x5
1 Sam	16.11	–	17.34	x5
Jer	30.13	–	31.28	x5

Hos	11.3	—	14.8	x5
Acts	13.40	—	15.40	x5
Ruth	2.20	—	4.16	x4
1 Kgs	1.2	—	2.7	x4
Esth	2.3 – 20			x4
Gen	30.29 – 36			x3
Gen	45.11	—	46.34	x3
Prov	27.5 – 18			x3
Is	46.3 – 4			x3
Jer	23.2 – 4			x3
Lk	10.34 – 40			x3
Jn	21.15 – 17			x3
1 Pet	5.2 – 7			x3

Flock, Sheep, Shepherd

Gen	30.29	**flocks** have prospered under my **care.**
	30.31	I will...take **care** of your **flocks**
	30.36	Jacob took **care** of...Laban's **flocks.**
	37.2	took **care** of the **sheep** and goats
	37.12	to take **care** of their father's **flock,**
	37.13	brothers are taking **care** of the **flock.**
	37.16	who are taking **care** of their **flock,**
	46.32	are **shepherds** and take **care** of livestock
Ex	3.1	Moses was taking **care** of the **sheep**
1 Sam	16.11	but he is out taking **care** of the **sheep.**
	16.19	the one who takes **care** of the **sheep.**
	17.15	to take **care** of his father's **sheep.**
	17.28	Who is taking **care** of those **sheep**
	17.34	I take **care** of my father's **sheep.**
Ps	28.9	their **shepherd,** and take **care** of them
	95.7	the people he **cares** for, the **flock**
Is	40.11	He will take **care** of his **flock**
	61.5	They will take **care** of your **flocks**
Ezek	34.2	**care** of yourselves, but never tend the **sheep.**
	34.8	**care** of themselves and not the **sheep.**
	34.10	**shepherds;** never again will I let you take **care**
	34.11	will look for my **sheep** and take **care**
	34.12	**care** of his **sheep** that were scattered
	34.23	one **shepherd,** and he will take **care**
Hos	12.12	and took **care** of his **sheep.**
Zech	11.7	And I took **care** of the **flock.**
Lk	2.8	taking **care** of their **flocks.**
Jn	10.13	and does not **care** about the **sheep.**
	21.15	Take **care** of my **lambs**
	21.16	Take **care** of my **sheep.**
	21.17	Take **care** of my **sheep.**
Acts	20.28	**care.** Be **shepherds** of the church of
1 Pet	5.2	**shepherds** of the **flock** that God gave you and to take **care**
	5.3	your **care,** but be examples to the **flock.**

God

Gen	50.24	but **God** will...take **care** of you
Deut	11.12	Lord your **God** takes **care** of this land
Job	18.21	fate of those who **care** nothing for **God.**
Ps	10.11	The wicked man says to himself "**God** doesn't **care!**"
	54.3	men who do not **care** about **God.**
	68.5	**God**...**cares** for orphans
	95.7	**God;** we are the people he **cares** for,
Is	46.4	am your **God** and will take **care** of you
Lk	4.10	**God** will order his angels to take good **care** of you.
Acts	14.26	commended to the **care** of **God's** grace
	15.14	**God** first showed his **care** for the
	20.32	I commend you to the **care** of **God**

Lord

Num	6.24	**Lord** bless you and take **care** of you;
Deut	11.12	**Lord** your **God** takes **care** of this land
Judg	18.6	The **Lord** is taking **care** of you
Ps	10.4	man does not **care** about the **Lord;**
	18.35	O **Lord**...your **care** has made me great,

Ps	27.10	but the **Lord** will take **care** of me.
	31.5	in your **care.** You will save me, **Lord;**
	37.18	The **Lord** takes **care** of those who obey
Is	40.27	**Lord** doesn't know your troubles or **care**
Zech	10.3	**Lord** Almighty, will take **care** of them.
Lk	10.40	**Lord,** don't you **care** that my sister
Acts	15.40	to the **care** of the **Lord's** grace.

Sheep see **Flock**

Shepherd see **Flock**

CASE

Deut	17.8 – 9			x5
Job	13.3 – 18			x5
2 Chr	19.8 – 11			x4
Mic	6.1 – 2			x4
Acts	24.22	—	25.26	x3

Present, Argue

Num	27.5	Moses **presented** their **case** to the Lord
Deut	17.9	**present** your **case** to the...priests
Job	5.8	and **present** my **case** to him.
	13.3	I want to **argue** my **case** with him.
	13.8	Are you going to **argue** his **case**
	23.4	state my **case** before him and **present**
Prov	22.23	The Lord will **argue** their **case**
	23.11	and he will **argue** their **case**
Is	1.23	when widows **present** their **case.**
	41.1	Get ready to **present** your **case**
	41.21	gods of the nations, **present** your **case.**
	43.26	**Present** your **case** to prove
	45.21	Come and **present** your **case** in court;
Jer	12.1	if I **argued** my **case** with you,
Mic	6.1	Arise, O Lord, and **present** your **case;**

CELEBRATE

Ex	12.14	—	13.10	x8
2 Chr	30.1 – 23			x8
2 Chr	35.1 – 18			x5
Ex	23.14 – 16			x4
Deut	16.1 – 15			x4
Lk	15.6 – 32			x4
Lev	23.5 – 41			x3
2 Kgs	23.21 – 23			x3
Zech	14.16 – 19			x3

Festival, Honour, Passover, Shelters, Unleavened Bread

Ex	12.14	**celebrate** this day as a...**festival**
	12.17	must **celebrate** this day as a **festival.**
	12.21	your families can **celebrate Passover.**
	12.47	Israel must **celebrate** this **festival,**
	12.48	**celebrate Passover** to **honour** the Lord,
	13.5	you must **celebrate** this **festival**
	13.10	**Celebrate** this **festival**
	23.14	**Celebrate** three **festivals** a year to **honour**
	23.15	**celebrate** the **Festival** of **Unleavened**
	23.16	**Celebrate** the Harvest **Festival**
Lev	23.5	**Passover, celebrated** to **honour** the Lord
	23.39	**celebrate** this **festival** for seven days,
Num	9.11	**Celebrate** it with **unleavened bread**
	29.12	**Celebrate** this **festival** in **honour**
Deut	16.1	**Honour**...God by **celebrating Passover**
	16.10	then **celebrate** the Harvest **Festival** to **honour**
	16.13	**celebrate** the **Festival** of **Shelters**
	16.15	**Honour**...God by **celebrating** this **festival**
1 Kgs	8.65	Israel **celebrated** the **Festival** of **Shelters**
	12.33	in **celebration** of the **festival**
2 Kgs	23.21	to **celebrate** the **Passover** in **honour**
	23.22	No **Passover** like this one had ever been **celebrated**
	23.23	**Passover** was **celebrated** in Jerusalem.

2 Chr	7.8	Israel **celebrated** the **Festival** of **Shelters**
	30.1	**celebrate** the **Passover**...in **honour**
	30.5	and **celebrate** the **Passover**
	30.13	**celebrate** the **Festival** of **Unleavened**
	30.21	**celebrated** the **Festival** of **Unleavened**
	35.1	King Josiah **celebrated** the **Passover** ...in **honour**
	35.17	**celebrated** the **Passover** and the **Festival**
	35.18	the **Passover** had never been **celebrated**
Ezra	3.4	They **celebrated** the **Festival** of **Shelters**
	6.19	exile **celebrated Passover**
	6.22	**celebrated** the **Festival** of **Unleavened**
Is	33.20	we **celebrate** our religious **festivals**.
Ezek	45.21	the **celebration** of the **Passover Festival**.
Hos	2.11	**festivals** and her Sabbath **celebrations**
	9.1	**celebrating** your **festivals** like pagans.
Nah	1.15	**celebrate** your **festivals**
Zech	14.16	to **celebrate** the **Festival** of **Shelters**.
	14.18	Egyptians refuse to **celebrate** the **Festival**
	14.19	do not **celebrate** the **Festival** of **Shelters**.
Mt	26.18	and I will **celebrate** the **Passover**
1 Cor	5.8	Let us **celebrate** our **Passover**

CHEAT

Mal	3.5 – 9			x4
Deut	24.14	–	25.16	x3
Ezek	18.7 – 18			x3

Poor

Deut	24.14	Do not **cheat** a **poor**...servant
Is	33.15	Don't...**cheat** the **poor**
Ezek	18.12	He **cheats** the **poor**
	22.29	The wealthy **cheat**...the **poor**
Lk	19.8	to the **poor**, and if I have **cheated**

CHIEF PRIESTS

Mt	26.3	–	28.12	x13
Mk	14.1	–	15.31	x10
Lk	22.2	–	24.20	x8
Jn	18.3	–	19.21	x5
Mt	20.18	–	21.45	x4
Acts	25.2	–	26.12	x4
Mk	10.33	–	11.27	x3
Lk	19.47	–	20.19	x3
Jn	11.47	–	12.10	x3

Arrest

Lk	20.19	the **chief priests** tried to **arrest** Jesus
Jn	7.32	**chief priests** sent some guards to **arrest**
Acts	9.14	from the **chief priests** to **arrest** all

Council

Mt	26.59	**chief priests** and the whole **Council** tried
Mk	14.55	The **chief priests** and the whole **Council**
Jn	11.47	**chief priests** met with the **Council**
Acts	22.30	**chief priests** and the whole **Council**

Elders

Mt	16.21	from the **elders**, the **chief priests**,
	21.23	the **chief priests** and the **elders**
		Also: 26.3; 26.47; 27.1; 27.3
	27.12	the **chief priests** and **elders**.
	27.20	The **chief priests** and the **elders**
	28.12	The **chief priests** met with the **elders**
Mk	8.31	by the **elders**, the **chief priests**,
	14.53	where all the **chief priests**, the **elders**,
	15.1	**chief priests** met hurriedly with the **elders**
Lk	9.22	the **elders**, the **chief priests**,
	22.66	the **elders**, the **chief priests**,
Acts	4.23	the **chief priests** and the **elders**
	23.14	to the **chief priests** and **elders**
	25.15	**chief priests** and **elders** brought charges

Jesus

Mt	21.45	The **chief priests**...heard **Jesus'** parables
Mk	15.3	The **chief priests** were accusing **Jesus**
	15.10	the **chief priests** had handed **Jesus** over
Lk	20.19	and the **chief priests** tried to arrest **Jesus**
	22.52	Then **Jesus** said to the **chief priests**

Pharisees

Mt	21.45	The **chief priests** and the **Pharisees**
	27.62	the **chief priests** and the **Pharisees**
Jn	7.45	the **chief priests** and **Pharisees**
	11.47	So the **Pharisees** and the **chief priests**
	11.57	The **chief priests** and the **Pharisees**
	18.3	the **chief priests** and the **Pharisees**;

Teachers of the Law

Mt	2.4	**chief priests** and the **teachers of the**
		Also: 16.21; 20.18; 21.15; 27.41
Mk	8.31	the **chief priests**, and the **teachers**
		Also: 10.33; 11.18
	11.27	**chief priests**, the **teachers of the Law**,
	14.1	**chief priests** and the **teachers of the**
	14.43	**chief priests**, the **teachers of the Law**,
	14.53	**chief priests**...and the **teachers of the**
	15.31	**chief priests** and the **teachers of the**
Lk	9.22	**chief priests**, and the **teachers of the**
	19.47	**chief priests**, the **teachers of the Law**,
	20.1	**chief priests** and the **teachers of the**
	20.19	**teachers of the Law** and the **chief**
	22.2	**chief priests** and the **teachers of the**
		Also: 22.66; 23.10

CHILD OF GOD

Rom	8.14	—	9.26	x11
1 Jn	2.29	—	5.18	x11
Gal	3.26	—	4.28	x7
Heb	12.5 – 23			x6

Father

Mt	5.45	may become the **sons** of your **Father**
Jn	1.13	**children**...God himself was their **Father**.
2 Cor	6.18	your **father**, and you shall be my **sons**

CHOOSE

Is	40.20	—	45.4	x12
1 Chr	15.2	—	17.9	x11
Deut	9.29	—	12.18	x9
2 Chr	6.1	—	7.16	x8
1 Sam	16.1	—	17.8	x7
1 Kgs	8.12 – 53			x7
1 Kgs	11.32	—	14.21	x7
1 Chr	28.4	—	29.1	x7
Rom	11.2 – 29			x7
1 Pet	1.1	—	2.9	x7
Num	16.1	—	18.6	x6
Deut	30.1 – 19			x6
Gen	24.3 – 44			x5
Ps	89.3 – 51			x5
Acts	1.2 – 26			x5
Acts	15.7 – 40			x5
1 Sam	2.10 – 35			x4
1 Sam	12.3 – 13			x4
Ps	105.5 – 43			x4
1 Cor	1.27	—	2.7	x4
Ex	12.3 – 21			x3
Lev	16.9 – 20			x3
Josh	20.2 – 9			x3
1 Sam	24.6 – 10			x3
Ps	132.10 – 17			x3
Jer	12.7 – 9			x3
Jer	33.15 – 26			x3

Mt	24.22 – 31	x3
Mk	3.14 – 16	x3
Jn	15.16 – 19	x3

Blessing
Deut	11.26	giving you the **choice** between a **blessing**
	21.5	**chosen** them to serve him and to pronounce **blessings**
	30.1	given you a **choice** between a **blessing**
Ps	84.9	**Bless** our king, O God, the king you have **chosen**.
Rom	11.29	about whom he **chooses** and **blesses**.

Evil
Deut	30.15	a **choice** between good and **evil**
Is	65.12	You **chose** to disobey me and do **evil**.
	66.4	They **chose** to disobey me and do **evil**.
Rom	7.21	what is **evil** is the only **choice** I have.

God, Father
Deut	7.6	your **God**...**chose** you to be his
	12.18	**chosen** by the **Lord** your **God**.
	14.2	the **Lord** your **God**; he has **chosen** you
	14.23	**God** has **chosen** to be worshipped;
	17.8	**chosen** by the **Lord** your **God**.
	21.5	The **Lord** your **God** has **chosen** them
2 Sam	3.39	though I am the king **chosen** by **God**
	23.1	whom the **God** of Jacob **chose**
1 Kgs	14.7	**God**...says to him: 'I **chose** you
1 Chr	16.12	descendants of Israel, whom **God chose**,
	28.4	the **God** of Israel, **chose** me
	29.1	is the one whom **God** has **chosen**,
2 Chr	6.42	**Lord God**, do not reject the king you have **chosen**.
Ezra	6.12	the **God** who **chose** Jerusalem
Neh	9.7	**Lord God**, **chose** Abram
Ps	45.7	That is why **God**...has **chosen** you
	68.16	mountain on which **God chose** to live?
	69.13	**God**, at a time you **choose**.
	84.9	O **God**, the king you have **chosen**.
Ecc	3.1	happens at the time **God chooses**.
Is	4.3	whom **God** has **chosen** for survival,
Dan	9.25	until **God's chosen** leader comes.
	9.26	**God's chosen** leader will be killed
Hab	1.12	**God** and protector, you have **chosen**
Zech	4.14	are the two men whom **God** has **chosen**
Lk	2.34	This child is **chosen** by **God**
	23.35	the Messiah whom **God** has **chosen**!
Jn	10.36	the **Father** chose me and sent me
Acts	3.26	And so **God chose** his Servant
	10.41	witnesses that **God** had already **chosen**,
	13.17	**God**...**chose** our ancestors
	15.7	**God chose** me from among you
	22.14	**God** of our ancestors has **chosen** you
Rom	1.1	an apostle **chosen** and called by **God**
	5.6	the wicked at the time that **God chose**.
	8.29	Those whom **God** had already **chosen**
	9.11	**choice** of one son might be completely the result of **God's**
	11.5	left of those whom **God** has **chosen**
	11.6	For if **God's choice** were based
	11.7	only the small group that **God chose**
	11.28	But because of **God's choice**,
	11.29	For **God** does not change his mind about whom he **chooses**
1 Cor	1.27	**God** purposely **chose** what the world
Gal	1.15	But **God** in his grace **chose** me
Eph	1.4	**God** had already **chosen** us
	1.11	and **God chose** us to be his own
Col	3.12	of **God**; he loved you and **chose** you
1 Thes	1.4	that **God** loves you and has **chosen** you
	5.9	**God** did not **choose** us to suffer
2 Thes	2.13	For **God chose** you as the first
Heb	1.2	the one whom **God** has **chosen**
	1.9	is why **God**, your **God**, has **chosen** you

Heb	3.2	He was faithful to **God**, who **chose** him
Jas	2.5	**God chose** the poor people
1 Pet	1.2	**chosen** according to the purpose of **God**
	1.20	been **chosen** by **God** before the creation
	2.4	but **chosen** by **God** as valuable.
	5.13	in Babylon, also **chosen** by **God**,
2 Pet	1.10	to make **God's** call and his **choice**

Good News
Is	61.1	He has **chosen** me...To bring **good news**
Lk	4.18	he has **chosen** me to bring **good news**
Acts	15.7	**chose** me...to preach the **Good News**
Rom	1.1	**chosen**...to preach his **Good News**.

Grace see **Love**

Jesus, Son of God
Mt	11.27	the **Son chooses** to reveal him.
Lk	9.35	This is my **Son**, whom I have **chosen**
	10.22	the **Son chooses** to reveal him.
Acts	3.20	send **Jesus**...the Messiah he has...**chosen**
Rom	8.29	**chosen**...to become like his **Son**,

Life
Deut	30.15	**choice** between...**life** and death.
	30.19	the **choice** you make. **Choose life**.
Jer	1.5	I **chose** you before I gave you **life**.
	21.8	giving you a **choice** between...**life**
Acts	13.48	who had been **chosen** for eternal **life**

Lord

see also **God**
Ex	15.17	**Lord**, have **chosen** for your home,
	35.30	The **Lord** has **chosen** Bezalel,
Lev	16.9	the goat **chosen** by lot for the **Lord**
	16.20	to the **Lord** the live goat **chosen**
Num	16.6	see which of us the **Lord** has **chosen**.
	34.19	These are the men the **Lord chose**:
Deut	7.7	The **Lord** did not love you and **choose**
	12.5	the **Lord** will **choose** the one place
	12.11	The **Lord** will **choose** a single place
	12.14	the one place that the **Lord** will **choose**
	17.15	is the one whom the **Lord** has **chosen**.
	18.5	The **Lord chose** from all your tribes
	28.10	will see that the **Lord** has **chosen** you
Josh	9.27	in the place where the **Lord** has **chosen**
	24.22	that you have **chosen** to serve the **Lord**.
1 Sam	10.1	that the **Lord** has **chosen** you
	10.24	Here is the man the **Lord** has **chosen**!
	12.3	the **Lord** and the king he has **chosen**.
	12.5	The **Lord** and the king he has **chosen**
	12.6	The **Lord** is the one who **chose** Moses
	16.8	the **Lord** hasn't **chosen** him either.
	16.9	the **Lord** hasn't **chosen** him either,
	16.10	the **Lord** hasn't **chosen** any of these.
	24.6	whom the **Lord chose** as king!
	24.10	one whom the **Lord chose** to be king.
	26.9	The **Lord** will...punish whoever harms his **chosen**
2 Sam	1.14	dared to kill the **Lord's chosen** king?
	1.16	one whom the **Lord chose** to be king.
	6.21	**Lord**, who **chose** me instead of your
	16.18	the side of the one **chosen** by the **Lord**,
	19.21	the one whom the **Lord chose** as king.
	21.6	Saul, the **Lord's chosen** king.
1 Kgs	14.21	the city which the **Lord** had **chosen**
1 Chr	15.2	are the ones the **Lord chose** to carry it
	16.41	**chosen** to sing praises to the **Lord**
	28.5	**chose** Solomon to rule...the **Lord's**
	28.10	realize that the **Lord** has **chosen** you
2 Chr	6.1	**Lord**, you have **chosen** to live in clouds
	12.13	**Lord** had **chosen** from all the territory
	22.7	whom the **Lord** had **chosen** to destroy
	29.11	the **Lord** has **chosen** to burn incense
Ps	2.2	the **Lord** and against the king he **chose**.

Ps	4.3	that the **Lord** has **chosen** the righteous
	20.6	the **Lord** gives victory to his **chosen**
	33.12	**Lord**; happy are the people he has **chosen**
	89.18	O **Lord**, **chose** our protector;
	89.51	insult your **chosen** king, O **Lord**!
	132.10	do not reject your **chosen** king, **Lord**.
	132.13	The **Lord** has **chosen** Zion;
Is	45.1	The **Lord** has **chosen** Cyrus to be king!
	49.1	the **Lord** **chose** me
	49.7	because the **Lord** has **chosen** his servant;
	61.1	The Sovereign **Lord** has...**chosen** me
Jer	21.8	I, the **Lord**, am giving you a **choice**
	23.5	**Lord** says, "The time...when I will **choose**
Lam	4.20	the king the **Lord** had **chosen**,
Ezek	37.28	**Lord**, have **chosen** Israel to be my own
Mic	7.14	**Lord**, the people you have **chosen**.
Hag	2.23	I have **chosen**." The **Lord**...has spoken.
Lk	4.18	**Lord** is upon me, because he has **chosen**
	10.1	this the **Lord** **chose** another seventy-two
Acts	9.15	**Lord** said...'Go, because I have **chosen**

Love, Grace

Deut	4.37	he **loved** your ancestors, he **chose** you
	7.7	did not **love** you and **choose** you
2 Sam	22.51	constant **love** to the one he has **chosen**,
2 Chr	6.42	you have **chosen**. Remember the **love**
Ps	18.50	constant **love** to the one he has **chosen**,
Is	44.2	my **chosen** people whom I **love**
Jer	12.7	my **chosen** nation...the people I **love**
Mt	12.18	I have **chosen**, the one I **love**,
Rom	11.5	God has **chosen** because of his **grace**.
	11.6	His **choice** is based on his **grace**
Gal	1.15	But God in his **grace** **chose** me
Col	3.12	he **loved** you and **chose** you
1 Thes	1.4	God **loves** you and has **chosen** you

Priests

1 Sam	2.28	**chose** his family to be my **priests**,
	2.35	I will **choose** a **priest**
1 Kgs	12.31	and he **chose** **priests** from families
	13.33	to **choose** **priests** from ordinary families
1 Chr	15.23	**priests**...were **chosen** to blow trumpets
Ezra	8.24	From among the leading **priests** I **chose**
Lk	1.9	by the **priests**, he was **chosen** by lot
1 Pet	2.9	the **chosen** race, the King's **priests**

Right

2 Chr	1.11	You have made the **right** **choice**.
Lk	10.42	Mary has **chosen** the **right** thing,
Rom	2.18	from the Law to **choose** what is **right**;

Son of God see **Jesus**

CHRIST (JESUS)

see also **JESUS**

Eph	1.3	—	6.6	x43
1 Cor	1.5	—	12.27	x32
Col	1.2	—	4.3	x32
2 Cor	1.5	—	6.15	x25
Gal	1.4	—	6.12	x23
Rom	5.6	—	10.17	x22
1 Jn	2.2	—	4.21	x22
1 Cor	15.3 – 28			x17
Phil	1.13	—	4.13	x17
2 Cor	8.23	—	13.3	x16
Rom	14.9	—	16.18	x15
1 Pet	1.11	—	5.10	x14
Heb	9.11	—	10.12	x10
Phlm	.6 – 20			x5
1 Thes	2.7	—	4.16	x3

Blood see **Death**

Body, Church

Rom	7.4	you are part of the **body** of **Christ**;
	12.5	we are one **body** in union with **Christ**,
	16.16	**churches** of **Christ** send...greetings.
1 Cor	6.15	are parts of the **body** of **Christ**
	10.16	we are sharing in the **body** of **Christ**.
	12.12	**Christ** is like a single **body**,
	12.27	All of you are **Christ's** **body**,
2 Cor	8.23	the **churches** and bring glory to **Christ**.
Eph	1.22	**Christ's** feet and gave him to the **church**
	1.23	The **church** is **Christ's** **body**,
	4.12	to build up the **body** of **Christ**
	4.25	members together in the **body** of **Christ**.
	5.23	**Christ** has authority over the **church**;
	5.23	the Saviour of the **church**, his **body**.
	5.24	the **church** submits itself to **Christ**.
	5.25	just as **Christ** loved the **church**
	5.29	just as **Christ** does the **church**;
	5.32	applying to **Christ** and the **church**.
Col	1.18	He is the head of his **body**, the **church**
	1.24	**Christ's** sufferings on behalf of his **body**,
	2.19	**Christ**, who is the head of the **body**.
1 Pet	2.24	**Christ** himself carried our sins in his **body**

Death, Blood, Cross

Mt	26.4	arrest **Jesus**...and put him to **death**.
	26.59	against **Jesus** to put him to **death**;
	27.1	against **Jesus** to put him to **death**.
	27.20	and have **Jesus** put to **death**.
	27.53	after **Jesus** rose from **death**,
Mk	14.1	arrest **Jesus**...and put him to **death**.
	14.24	**Jesus** said, "This is my **blood**
	16.9	After **Jesus** rose from **death**
Lk	22.2	find a way of putting **Jesus** to **death**.
	23.32	to be put to **death** with **Jesus**.
Jn	12.9	whom **Jesus** had raised from **death**.
	19.34	into **Jesus'** side, and at once **blood**
	19.41	where **Jesus** had been put to **death**,
Acts	2.32	God has raised...**Jesus** from **death**,
	4.2	that **Jesus** had risen from **death**,
	5.30	God...raised **Jesus** from **death**,
Rom	4.24	raised **Jesus** our Lord from **death**.
	6.4	just as **Christ** was raised from **death**
	6.6	put to **death** with **Christ** on his **cross**
	6.9	**Christ** has been raised from **death**
	8.11	God, who raised **Jesus** from **death**,
	8.11	then he who raised **Christ** from **death**
	10.7	to bring **Christ** up from **death**).
1 Cor	1.17	to make sure that **Christ's** **death**
	1.18	For the message about **Christ's** **death**
	2.2	**Jesus** **Christ** and...his **death**
	2.2	and especially his **death** on the **cross**.
	10.16	we are sharing in the **blood** of **Christ**.
	15.12	**Christ** has been raised from **death**,
	15.14	**Christ** has not been raised from **death**,
	15.15	said that he raised **Christ** from **death**,
	15.20	**Christ** has been raised from **death**
2 Cor	4.10	in our...bodies the **death** of **Jesus**
	4.11	in danger of **death** for **Jesus'** sake,
Gal	2.19	put to **death** with **Christ** on his **cross**
	3.1	the **death** of **Jesus** **Christ** on the **cross**!
	5.11	my preaching about the **cross** of **Christ**
	6.12	be persecuted for the **cross** of **Christ**.
Eph	1.7	For by the sacrificial **death** of **Christ**
	1.20	when he raised **Christ** from **death**
	2.13	by the sacrificial **death** of **Christ**.
	2.16	his **death** on the **cross** **Christ** destroyed
	5.14	rise from **death**, and **Christ** will shine
Phil	2.8	to **death** — his **death** on the **cross**.
	3.18	make them enemies of **Christ's** **death**
Col	2.15	And on that **cross** **Christ** freed himself
1 Thes	1.10	**Jesus**, whom he raised from **death**
2 Tim	2.8	. **Jesus** **Christ**, who was raised from **death**,

Heb	9.14	is accomplished by the **blood** of **Christ**!
	10.19	by means of the **death** of **Jesus**.
	13.20	raised from **death** our Lord **Jesus**,
1 Pet	1.2	obey **Jesus Christ** and be purified by his **blood**.
	1.3	by raising **Jesus Christ** from **death**.
1 Jn	1.7	**blood** of **Jesus**...purifies us

Father see God

God, Father

Rom	3.22	**God** puts people right through...**Christ**.
	5.6	**Christ** died for the wicked at the time that **God** chose.
	8.17	possess with **Christ** what **God** has kept
	9.3	**God's** curse and separated from **Christ**.
	14.18	**Christ** in this way, he pleases **God**
	15.7	of **God**, as **Christ** has accepted you.
1 Cor	1.30	**God** has made **Christ**...our wisdom.
	3.23	and **Christ** belongs to **God**.
	11.3	and **God** is supreme over **Christ**.
	15.25	For **Christ** must rule until **God** defeats
2 Cor	1.5	through **Christ** we share in **God's**
	2.14	with **Christ** we are always led by **God**
	2.15	incense offered by **Christ** to **God**
	3.4	have confidence in **God** through **Christ**
	4.6	**God's** glory shining in the face of **Christ**
	5.18	by **God**, who through **Christ** changed us
	5.19	**God** was making all mankind his friends through **Christ**.
	5.20	for **Christ**, as though **God** himself
Gal	2.16	**God** only through faith in **Jesus Christ**,
	2.17	with **God** by our union with **Christ**,
Eph	1.3	and **Father** of our Lord **Jesus Christ**
	1.22	**God** put all things under **Christ's** feet
	4.32	as **God** has forgiven you through **Christ**.
	5.5	the Kingdom of **Christ** and of **God**.
	6.6	do what **God** wants, as slaves of **Christ**.
Col	2.2	**God's** secret, which is **Christ** himself.
	2.13	**God** has now brought you to life with **Christ**.
	3.3	your life is hidden with **Christ** in **God**.
Heb	3.6	**Christ** is faithful as the Son in charge of **God's** house.
1 Pet	4.16	thank **God** that you bear **Christ's** name.
Rev	20.6	shall be priests of **God** and of **Christ**,

Human

Rom	9.5	and **Christ**, as a **human** being,
2 Cor	5.16	we judged **Christ** according to **human**
Col	2.9	lives in **Christ**, in his **humanity**
Heb	2.14	**Jesus**...shared their **human** nature.
1 Jn	4.2	**Jesus Christ** came as a **human** being.
2 Jn	.7	**Jesus Christ** came as a **human** being.

Lord

Lk	2.11	Saviour was born — **Christ** the **Lord**!
Rom	16.18	are not serving **Christ** our **Lord**,
Eph	1.3	Father of our **Lord Jesus Christ**
Phil	3.8	the knowledge of **Christ Jesus** my **Lord**.
1 Pet	3.15	for **Christ**...and honour him as **Lord**.

Offer, Sacrifice

1 Cor	5.7	**Christ**, our...lamb, has been **sacrificed**.
2 Cor	2.15	incense **offered** by **Christ** to God
Eph	1.7	For by the **sacrificial** death of **Christ**
	2.13	by the **sacrificial** death of **Christ**.
Heb	9.14	**Christ**...**offered** himself as a perfect
	9.25	**Christ** did not go in to **offer** himself
	9.28	**Christ** also was **offered** in **sacrifice**
	10.9	puts the **sacrifice** of **Christ** in their
	10.12	**Christ**, however, **offered** one **sacrifice**
	13.15	as our **sacrifice** through **Jesus**,
1 Pet	1.19	it was the costly **sacrifice** of **Christ**,
	2.5	**sacrifices** to God through **Jesus**

Preach, Proclaim

Mt	4.17	**Jesus** began to **preach** his message:
Mk	1.14	**Jesus** went to Galilee and **preached**
	2.2	**Jesus** was **preaching** the message
	4.33	**Jesus preached** his message
Acts	5.42	**preach** the Good News about **Jesus**
	9.20	to **preach** that **Jesus** was the Son
	9.27	had **preached** in the name of **Jesus**
	17.18	Paul was **preaching** about **Jesus**
	19.13	of **Jesus**, whom Paul **preaches**.
Rom	10.17	message comes through **preaching Christ**.
	15.19	**proclaimed**...the Good News about **Christ**.
	15.20	**proclaim** the Good News...where **Christ**
	16.25	the Good News I **preach** about **Jesus**
1 Cor	1.23	we **proclaim** the crucified **Christ**,
2 Cor	2.12	to **preach** the Good News about **Christ**
	4.5	we **preach Jesus Christ** as Lord
	11.4	and **preaches** a different **Jesus**, not the **one** we **preached**;
Gal	5.11	my **preaching** about the cross of **Christ**
Eph	2.17	**Christ** came and **preached** the Good
Phil	1.15	**preach Christ** because they are jealous
	1.17	others do not **proclaim Christ** sincerely
	1.18	so long as **Christ** is **preached**
	2.11	**proclaim** that **Jesus Christ** is Lord.
Col	1.28	So we **preach Christ** to everyone
	4.3	to **preach**...about the secret of **Christ**.
1 Thes	3.2	**preaching** the Good News about **Christ**.
Rev	20.4	**proclaimed** the truth that **Jesus** revealed

Pure

1 Pet	1.2	obey **Jesus Christ** and be **purified**
1 Jn	1.7	blood of **Jesus**...**purifies** us
	3.3	**pure**, just as **Christ** is **pure**.

Real

Col	2.17	the **reality** is **Christ**.
	3.4	Your **real** life is **Christ**
	3.24	For **Christ** is the **real** Master you serve.

Sacrifice see Offer

Sake

Acts	5.41	suffer disgrace for the **sake** of **Jesus**.
	21.13	die there for the **sake** of...**Jesus**.
Rom	1.5	being an apostle for the **sake** of **Christ**,
1 Cor	4.10	For **Christ's sake** we are fools
2 Cor	4.5	as your servants for **Jesus' sake**
	4.11	in danger of death for **Jesus' sake**,
	5.21	**Christ** was without sin, but for our **sake**
	12.10	and difficulties for **Christ's sake**.
Phil	2.30	died for the **sake** of the work of **Christ**,
	3.7	now reckon as loss for **Christ's sake**.
	3.8	**sake** of...the knowledge of **Christ**
2 Tim	1.8	a prisoner for **Christ's sake**.
Phlm	.1	prisoner for the **sake** of **Christ Jesus**,
	.20	the Lord's **sake**; as a brother in **Christ**,
	.23	prison with me for the **sake** of...**Jesus**,
1 Jn	2.12	sins are forgiven for the **sake** of **Christ**.

Sin

Rom	5.8	were still **sinners** that **Christ** died for us!
1 Cor	8.12	you will be **sinning** against **Christ**
	15.3	that **Christ** died for our **sins**,
2 Cor	5.21	**Christ** was without **sin**
Gal	1.4	**Christ** gave himself for our **sins**,
	2.17	that **Christ** is serving the cause of **sin**?
Eph	1.7	death of **Christ**...our **sins** are forgiven.
Heb	10.12	**Christ**...offered one sacrifice for **sins**
1 Pet	2.24	**Christ** himself carried our **sin**
	3.18	For **Christ** died for **sins** once and for all
1 Jn	2.2	**Christ**...the means by which our **sins**
	2.12	**sins** are forgiven for the **sake** of **Christ**.
	3.5	that **Christ** appeared...to take away **sins**

1 Jn   3.6   lives in union with **Christ** does not...**sin;**

CHURCH

Rev	1.4	—	3.22	x19
Acts	11.22	—	16.5	x13
1 Cor	14.4	—	16.19	x12
Eph	5.23 – 32			x8
1 Tim	2.8	—	3.15	x8
Rom	15.26	—	16.23	x6
2 Cor	8.1 – 24			x5
1 Cor	10.32	—	12.28	x4
Acts	8.1	—	9.31	x3
Acts	20.17	—	21.18	x3
2 Cor	11.8	—	12.13	x3
Gal	1.2 – 22			x3
Col	1.18 – 25			x3
3 Jn	.6 – 10			x3

Christ, Jesus
Rom   16.16   **churches** of **Christ** send...greetings.
2 Cor   8.23   the **churches** and bring glory to **Christ.**
Eph   1.22   **Christ's** feet and gave him to the **church**
1.23   The **church** is **Christ's** body,
3.21   glory in the **church** and in **Christ Jesus**
5.23   **church** has authority over the **church;**
5.24   the **church** submits itself to **Christ.**
5.25   just as **Christ** loved the **church**
5.29   just as **Christ** does the **church;**
5.32   applying to **Christ** and the **church.**

God
Acts   20.28   Be shepherds of the **church** of **God,**
1 Cor   1.2   the **church** of **God** which is in Corinth,
10.32   or Gentiles or to the **church** of **God.**
11.16   **churches** of **God** have any other custom
11.22   you rather despise the **church** of **God**
12.28   In the **church God** has put all in place:
14.4   **God's** message helps the whole **church.**
14.33   in all the **churches** of **God's** people,
15.9   because I persecuted **God's church.**
2 Cor   1.1   To the **church** of **God** in Corinth,
8.1   know what **God's** grace has accomplished in the **churches**
Gal   1.13   without mercy the **church** of **God**
Eph   3.21   to **God** be the glory in the **church**
5.26   did this to dedicate the **church** to **God**
Col   1.25   made a servant of the **church** by **God,**
1 Thes   1.1   the **church** in Thessalonica, who belong to **God**
2.14   to the **churches** of **God** in Judaea,
2 Thes   1.1   the **church** in Thessalonica, who belong to **God**
1.4   about you in the **churches** of **God.**
1 Tim   3.5   can he take care of the **church** of **God?**
3.15   is the **church** of the living **God,**
1 Pet   5.13   **church** in Babylon, also chosen by **God**

Jesus see **Christ**

CIRCUMCISE

Rom	2.25	—	4.12	x19
Gal	5.2	—	6.15	x8
Gen	17.10 – 26			x7
Josh	5.2 – 8			x7
Ezek	32.24 – 32			x7
Gen	34.14 – 25			x6
1 Cor	7.18 – 19			x5
Acts	7.8			x4
Col	2.11	—	3.11	x4
Ex	12.44 – 48			x3
Jn	7.22 – 23			x3
Acts	15.1	—	16.3	x3

Covenant
Gen   17.13   must be **circumcised**...to show that my **covenant**

Jer   9.25   **circumcised**...not kept the **covenant**
Acts   7.8   **circumcision** as a sign of the **covenant.**

Gentiles
Acts   11.2   were in favour of **circumcising Gentiles**
11.3   in the home of **uncircumcised Gentiles**
15.5   The **Gentiles** must be **circumcised**
Rom   2.26   If the **Gentile,** who is not **circumcised,**
3.1   **Gentiles?** Or is there any value in being **circumcised?**
Col   3.11   between **Gentiles** and Jews, **circumcised**

Jews
Acts   16.3   **circumcised** him...because all the **Jews**
Rom   2.28   who is a real **Jew,** truly **circumcised?**
Eph   2.11   the **Jews,** who call themselves "the **circumcised**
Col   3.11   Gentiles and **Jews, circumcised**

Law, Obey
Gen   17.23   **obeyed** God and **circumcised** his son
Ezek   44.7   **uncircumcised** foreigners...who do not **obey**
Jn   7.23   boy is **circumcised**...so that Moses' **Law**
Acts   15.1   **circumcised** as the **Law** of Moses
15.5   **circumcised** and told to **obey** the **Law**
21.21   the **Law**...telling them not to **circumcise**
Rom   2.25   If you **obey** the **Law,** your **circumcision**
2.26   is not **circumcised, obeys** the...**Law,**
2.27   **Law,** even though you...are **circumcised;**
Gal   5.3   be **circumcised**...is obliged to **obey**
6.13   **circumcision** do not **obey** the **Law;**

CLEAN

Lev	10.10	—	17.15	x41
Num	18.11	—	19.19	x10
2 Chr	29.15	—	30.19	x9
Gen	7.2	—	8.20	x3
Lev	6.11	—	7.20	x3
Deut	14.11	—	15.22	x3
Is	1.6 – 18			x3
Ezek	36.25 – 33			x3
Ezek	39.12 – 16			x3
Mt	23.25 – 26			x3
Mk	1.40 – 42			x3
Lk	11.25 – 41			x3
Jn	13.10 – 11			x3

Sin
Lev   16.30   **sins,** so that they will be ritually **clean.**
Ps   51.2   and make me **clean** from my **sin!**
51.7   Remove my **sin,** and I will be **clean;**
Is   1.18   with **sin,** but I will wash you as **clean**
Ezek   36.33   I make you **clean** from all your **sins,**

Unclean
Gen   7.8   whether ritually **clean** or **unclean,**
Lev   10.10   is ritually **clean** and what is **unclean.**
11.47   what is ritually **clean** and **unclean,**
13.59   whether it is ritually **clean** or **unclean.**
14.57   is **unclean** and when it is **clean.**
20.25   **clean**...Do not eat **unclean** animals
22.4   **clean.** Any priest is **unclean** if he
Num   19.19   **clean** is to sprinkle...on the **unclean**
Deut   12.15   whether ritually **clean** or **unclean,**
12.22   ritually **clean** or **unclean,**
15.22   whether ritually **clean** or **unclean,**
Job   14.4   Nothing **clean**...from anything as **unclean**
Ezek   22.26   between **clean** and **unclean** things,
Acts   10.15   **unclean** that God has declared **clean.**
11.9   **unclean** that God has declared **clean.**

CLOUD

Num	9.15	—	12.10	x17
Job	35.5	—	38.37	x9
Ezek	30.3	—	32.7	x6

Ex	13.21	—	14.24	x5
Ex	24.15 – 18			x4
Ex	33.9	—	34.5	x4
Ex	40.34 – 38			x4
Rev	14.14 – 16			x4
Gen	9.13 – 16			x3
Ex	19.9	—	20.21	x3
2 Sam	22.10	—	23.4	x3
Ps	18.9 – 12			x3
Lk	9.34 – 35			x3

Dark

Ex	14.20	**cloud** made it **dark** for the Egyptians,
	20.21	Moses went near the **dark cloud**
Deut	4.11	thick **clouds** of **dark** smoke
2 Sam	22.10	with a **dark cloud** under his feet.
	22.12	with **darkness**; thick **clouds**,
1 Kgs	8.12	to live in **clouds** and **darkness**.
	18.45	the sky was covered with **dark clouds**
2 Chr	6.1	chosen to live in **clouds** and **darkness**.
Job	3.5	thick **darkness**; cover it with **clouds**,
	38.9	with **clouds** and wrapped it in **darkness**.
Ps	18.9	with a **dark cloud** under his feet.
	18.11	himself with **darkness**; thick **clouds**,
	18.12	and broke through the **dark clouds**.
	97.2	**Clouds** and **darkness** surround him;
Joel	2.2	**dark**...day, a black and **cloudy** day.
Zeph	1.15	of **darkness**...a black and **cloudy** day,

Heaven, Power, Son of Man

Mt	24.30	the **Son of Man** coming on the **clouds** of **heaven** with **power**
	26.64	and coming on the **clouds** of **heaven**!
Mk	13.26	**Son of Man** will appear, coming in the **clouds** with great **power**
	14.62	and coming with the **clouds** of **heaven**!
Lk	21.27	Then the **Son of Man** will appear, coming in a **cloud** with great **power**
Acts	1.9	to **heaven**...and a **cloud** hid him
Rev	10.1	down out of **heaven**...in a **cloud**
	11.12	they went up into **heaven** in a **cloud**.

COMFORT

Lam	1.2	—	2.13	x5
Job	15.11	—	16.5	x3
Ps	119.50 – 76			x3

God, Lord

Job	15.11	**God** offers you **comfort**
Ps	119.52	and they bring me **comfort**, O **Lord**.
Is	12.1	**Lord**...now you **comfort** me
	40.1	**Comfort** my people," says our **God**
	49.13	The **Lord** will **comfort** his people;
	52.9	The **Lord** will rescue...and **comfort**
Zech	1.13	**Lord** answered...with **comforting** words,
Mt	5.4	**God** will **comfort** them!

COMMAND

Ps	119.2 – 173			x39
Deut	4.2	—	13.18	x35
Lev	4.1	—	10.18	x32
Num	8.20	—	10.27	x20
Ex	38.22	—	40.32	x19
1 Kgs	11.2	—	15.5	x17
Ex	14.7	—	20.22	x16
Ex	31.6	—	36.6	x16
Lev	16.34	—	22.31	x16
Num	31.6	—	33.38	x16
Deut	28.1	—	34.9	x15
1 Jn	2.3	—	5.3	x14
Num	1.19	—	6.22	x13
Num	15.23	—	20.27	x13
Josh	19.50	—	24.26	x13
Josh	7.1	—	11.23	x11
2 Kgs	16.16	—	18.32	x11

2 Chr	32.6	—	36.23	x11
Lev	24.23	—	27.34	x10
Deut	15.5	—	19.9	x10
1 Chr	12.3	—	16.14	x10
Ezra	6.3	—	7.21	x9
Gen	1.3 – 24			x7
Ex	23.15	—	24.8	x7
Ezek	20.11 – 25			x7
Deut	26.13 – 18			x6
Jer	35.7 – 18			x6
Josh	4.3	—	5.3	x5
1 Sam	15.11 – 26			x5
Ps	105.7 – 45			x5
2 Jn	.4 – 6			x5
Num	36.2 – 10			x4
Jer	7.22 – 31			x4

Desire

1 Chr	29.19	**desire** to obey everything that you **command**
Job	23.12	God **commands**...not my own **desires**.
Ps	119.131	In my **desire** for your **commands**

Disobey, Rebel, Refuse, Reject

Ex	16.28	people **refuse** to obey my **commands**?
Lev	20.22	**commands**, so that you will not be **rejected**
	26.15	**refuse** to obey my laws and **commands**
	26.43	**rejected** my laws and my **commands**.
Num	20.24	of you **rebelled** against my **command**
	22.18	I could not **disobey** the **command**
	24.13	I could not **disobey** the **command**
	27.14	of you **rebelled** against my **command**
Deut	1.26	But you **rebelled** against the **command**
	5.32	has **commanded** you. Do not **disobey**
	9.16	you had already **disobeyed** the **command**
	11.28	if you **disobey** these **commands**
	17.20	from **disobeying** the **Lord's commands**
	26.13	not **disobeyed**...any of your **commands**
Josh	22.20	Achan...**refused** to obey the **command**
1 Sam	12.15	but **disobey** his **commands**,
	15.11	away...and **disobeyed** my **commands**.
	15.23	you **rejected** the Lord's **command**,
	15.24	I **disobeyed** the Lord's **command**
	15.26	You **rejected** the Lord's **command**
	28.18	You **disobeyed** the Lord's **command**
2 Sam	12.9	have you **disobeyed** my **commands**?
	22.23	I have not **disobeyed** his **commands**.
1 Kgs	2.43	promise and **disobeyed** my **command**?
	9.6	if you **disobey** the laws and **commands**
	11.11	with me and **disobeyed** my **commands**,
	13.21	**disobeyed** him and did not do what he **commanded**.
	13.26	who **disobeyed** the Lord's **command**!
	15.5	never **disobeyed** any of his **commands**,
	18.18	are **disobeying** the Lord's **commands**
	20.36	have **disobeyed** the Lord's **command**,
2 Kgs	17.12	and **disobeyed** the Lord's **commands**.
	17.15	**disobeying** the Lord's **command**
	18.6	never **disobeyed** him, but...kept all the **commands**
	21.22	and **disobeyed** the Lord's **commands**.
1 Chr	10.13	He **disobeyed** the Lord's **commands**;
2 Chr	7.19	ever **disobey** the laws and **commands**
	24.20	why you have **disobeyed** his **commands**
Ezra	6.11	further **command** that if anyone **disobeys**
	9.10	We have again **disobeyed** the **commands**
Neh	9.16	and **refused** to obey your **commands**.
Esth	1.12	king's **command**, she **refused** to come.
	1.15	Vashti with a **command**, and she **refused**
	3.3	he was **disobeying** the king's **command**;
Ps	18.22	I have not **disobeyed** his **commands**.
	44.18	we have not **disobeyed** your **commands**.
	50.17	You **refuse**...you **reject** my **commands**.
	95.10	They **refuse** to obey my **commands**.

Ps	107.11	they had **rebelled** against the **commands**
	119.21	are those who **disobey** your **commands**.
	119.110	I have not **disobeyed** your **commands**.
Jer	23.38	And if they **disobey** my **command**
	43.7	They **disobeyed** the **Lord's command**
Ezek	5.6	Jerusalem **rebelled** against my **commands**
	5.6	**rejected** my **commands** and **refused**
	11.12	and **disobeying** my **commands**.
	20.13	my laws and **rejected** my **commands**,
	20.16	because they had **rejected** my **commands**,
	20.24	because they had **rejected** my **commands**,
Dan	9.5	We have **rejected** what you **commanded**
Mt	15.3	why do you **disobey** God's **command**
Rom	5.14	did when he **disobeyed** God's **command**.
Heb	3.10	and **refuse** to obey my **commands**.

Father see God

Forget see Remember

God, Father

Gen	1.3	Then **God commanded**...light
	1.6	Then **God commanded**...sky
	1.9	Then **God commanded**...earth
	1.14	Then **God commanded**...sun
	1.20	Then **God commanded**...living beings
	1.24	Then **God commanded**...animal
	6.22	did everything that **God commanded**.
	7.9	with Noah, as **God** had **commanded**
	7.16	with Noah, as **God** had **commanded**
	21.4	circumcised...as **God** had **commanded**.
Ex	8.27	**Lord** our **God**, just as he **commanded**
	18.16	I tell them **God's commands** and laws.
	18.20	should teach them **God's commands**
	18.23	if you do this, as **God commands**,
	32.27	**Lord God** of Israel **commands** every one
Lev	18.4	I **command**. I am the **Lord** your **God**.
	19.3	**commanded**. I am the **Lord** your **God**.
	25.38	is the **command** of the **Lord** your **God**,
Num	22.18	the **command** of the **Lord** my **God**
Deut	1.19	what the **Lord** our **God commanded** us
	1.26	the **command** of the **Lord** your **God**
	1.41	as the **Lord** our **God commanded** us.
	2.37	our **God** had **commanded** us not to go.
	4.2	the **commands** of the **Lord** your **God**
	5.12	**Lord** your **God**, have **commanded** you.
	5.16	the **Lord** your **God**, **command** you,
	5.32	**Lord** your **God** has **commanded** you.
	6.1	the **Lord** your **God commanded** me
	6.20	the **Lord** our **God command** us to obey
	6.24	**Lord** our **God commanded** us to obey
	6.25	everything that **God** has **commanded** us,
	9.16	the **command** that the **Lord** your **God**
	11.22	your **God**, do everything he **commands**,
	11.27	the **commands** of the **Lord** your **God**
	26.16	**Lord** your **God commands** you to obey
	28.1	**God** and faithfully keep all his **commands**
	28.9	**God** and do everything he **commands**,
	28.15	**God** and do not...keep all his **commands**
	30.16	the **commands** of the **Lord** your **God**,
Josh	9.24	your **God** had **commanded** his servant
	10.40	**God** of Israel had **commanded**.
	22.3	the **commands** of the **Lord** your **God**.
	22.5	**commanded** you: love the **Lord** your **God**,
	23.16	your **God commanded** you to keep
	24.24	our **God**. We will obey his **commands**.
	24.26	wrote these **commands** in the book of the Law of **God**.
Judg	4.6	the **God** of Israel, has given you this **command**:
Sam	12.14	**God**, serve...and obey his **commands**,
	13.13	the **command** the **Lord** your **God**
Chr	14.16	David did what **God** had **commanded**

1 Chr	16.14	is our **God**; his **commands** are for all
	24.19	**commands** of the **Lord God** of Israel.
	28.8	**Lord** our **God** has **commanded** us,
2 Chr	2.4	our **God**. He has **commanded** Israel
	17.4	father's **God**, obeyed **God's commands**,
	24.20	The **Lord God** asks why you have disobeyed his **commands**
Ezra	6.14	been **commanded** by the **God** of Israel
	10.3	the others who honour **God's commands**
Neh	12.45	other rituals that **God** had **commanded**.
Job	6.10	**God** is holy; I have never opposed what he **commands**.
	23.12	I always do what **God commands**;
	37.5	**God's command** amazing things happen,
	37.12	They do all that **God commands**,
	37.15	you know how **God** gives the **command**
Ps	105.7	is our **God**; his **commands** are for all
	105.31	**God commanded**, and flies and gnats
	107.11	against the **commands** of Almighty **God**
	119.115	I will obey the **commands** of my **God**.
	149.9	the nations as **God** has **commanded**.
Ecc	12.13	for **God**, and obey his **commands**,
Jer	25.27	**God** of Israel, am **commanding** them
	27.4	**God** of Israel, told me to **command**
	42.5	**commands** that the **Lord** our **God** gives
Ezek	20.19	**God**. Obey my laws and my **commands**.
Jon	4.7	at **God's command**, a worm
Zech	6.15	the **commands** of the **Lord** your **God**.
Mt	15.3	why do you disobey **God's command**
	15.6	this way you disregard **God's command**,
Mk	7.8	You put aside **God's command**
Jn	10.18	is what my **Father** has **commanded** me
	12.49	**Father** who sent me has **commanded** me
	14.31	**Father**...I do everything as he **commands**
	15.10	as I have obeyed my **Father's commands**
Rom	4.17	**God**...whose **command** brings into being
	5.14	did when he disobeyed **God's command**.
	16.26	and by the **command** of the eternal **God**
Heb	9.20	that **God** has **commanded** you to obey.
2 Pet	3.5	long ago **God** gave a **command**,
	3.7	by the same **command** of **God**,
1 Jn	2.3	If we obey **God's commands**,
	3.24	obeys **God's commands** lives in union
	5.2	loving **God** and obeying his **commands**.
	5.3	**God** means that we obey his **commands**
2 Jn	.4	just as the **Father commanded** us.
	.6	live in obedience to **God's commands**.

Jesus

Mt	17.18	**Jesus** gave a **command** to the demon
Mk	4.39	**Jesus** stood up and **commanded** the
Lk	8.56	but **Jesus commanded** them not to tell
	9.42	**Jesus** gave a **command** to the evil spirit,
Acts	19.13	I **command** you in the name of **Jesus**,
2 Thes	3.6	we **command** you in the name of our Lord **Jesus** Christ
	3.12	**Jesus** Christ we **command** these people
1 Jn	3.23	What he **commands** is that we believe in his Son **Jesus** Christ

Just, Right

Ex	15.26	**right** and by keeping my **commands**,
	18.16	**right**, and I tell them **God's commands**
Ps	19.8	The **commands** of the Lord are **just**
	106.3	obey his **commands**...do what is **right**.
	111.7	faithful and **just**; all his **commands**
	119.172	because your **commands** are **just**.
Jer	22.3	**command** you to do what is **just**
Zeph	2.3	obey his **commands**. Do what is **right**,
Zech	7.9	**commands**...You must see that **justice**

Lord

see also **God**

Gen	7.5	everything that the **Lord commanded**.

Ex	6.13	The **Lord commanded** Moses and Aaron
	7.6	Aaron did what the **Lord commanded**.
	7.10	and did as the **Lord** had **commanded**.
	7.20	and Aaron did as the **Lord commanded**
	12.28	and did what the **Lord** had **commanded**
	12.50	and did what the **Lord** had **commanded**
	16.16	**Lord** has **commanded** that each of you
	16.23	**Lord** has **commanded** that tomorrow
	16.32	**Lord** has **commanded** us to save some
	16.34	As the **Lord** had **commanded** Moses,
	17.1	at the **command** of the **Lord**.
	19.7	the **Lord** had **commanded** him.
	20.22	The **Lord commanded** Moses to say
	24.3	**Lord's commands** and all the
	24.4	wrote down all the **Lord's commands**.
	24.7	the **Lord's commands** were written,
	31.12	The **Lord commanded** Moses
	33.5	the **Lord** had **commanded** Moses to say
	34.4	just as the **Lord** had **commanded**.
	35.1	This is what the **Lord** has **commanded**
	35.4	This is what the **Lord** has **commanded**:
	35.10	everything that the **Lord commanded**:
	36.1	just as the **Lord** has **commanded**.
	36.5	the work which the **Lord commanded**
	38.22	that the **Lord** had **commanded**.
	39.1	as the **Lord** had **commanded** Moses.
		Also: 39.5, 7, 21, 24, 29, 31, 32, 42
	39.43	it all just as the **Lord** had **commanded**.
		Also: 40.16, 19, 21, 23, 25, 27, 29, 32
Lev	4.1	The **Lord commanded** Moses
	4.2	and broke any of the **Lord's commands**
	4.13	the **Lord's commands** without intending
	4.22	the **Lord's commands** without intending
	4.27	the **Lord's commands** without intending
	5.17	breaking any of the **Lord's commands**,
	6.8	The **Lord commanded** Moses
	6.24	The **Lord commanded** Moses
	7.36	day the **Lord commanded** the people
	7.38	**Lord** gave these **commands** to Moses
	8.4	Moses did as the **Lord** had **commanded**
	8.5	is what the **Lord** has **commanded**.
	8.9	just as the **Lord** had **commanded** him.
	8.13	just as the **Lord** had **commanded**.
		Also: 8.17, 20; 29
	8.31	just as the **Lord** had **commanded**.
	8.34	**Lord commanded** us to do what we
	8.35	doing what the **Lord** has **commanded**.
	8.36	**Lord** had **commanded** through Moses.
	9.6	**Lord** has **commanded** you to do all
	9.7	just as the **Lord** has **commanded**.
	9.10	just as the **Lord** had **commanded** Moses.
	10.1	because the **Lord** had not **commanded**
	10.13	That is what the **Lord commanded** me.
	10.15	just as the **Lord** has **commanded**.
	16.34	Moses did as the **Lord** had **commanded**.
	17.1	The **Lord commanded** Moses
	17.11	the **Lord** has **commanded** that all blood
	18.26	keep the **Lord's** laws and **commands**,
	18.30	the **Lord** said, "Obey the **commands**
	19.37	my laws and **commands**. I am the **Lord**.
	20.22	**Lord** said, "Keep all my...**commands**
	21.1	The **Lord commanded** Moses to say
		Also: 21.16; 22.1; 22.17
	24.23	did what the **Lord** had **commanded**
	25.1	**Lord** spoke to Moses...and **commanded**
	25.18	Obey all the **Lord's** laws and **commands**
	26.46	**commands** that the **Lord** gave to Moses
	27.34	**commands** that the **Lord** gave Moses
Num	1.19	as the **Lord** had **commanded**
	1.54	that the **Lord** had **commanded**

Num	2.33	As the **Lord** had **commanded** Moses,
	2.34	did everything the **Lord** had **commanded**
	3.14	Desert the **Lord commanded** Moses
	3.39	by clans at the **command** of the **Lord**,
	4.34	Following the **Lord's command**
	4.49	registered as the **Lord** had **commanded**
	5.11	The **Lord commanded** Moses
		Also: 6.1, 22
	8.20	as the **Lord commanded** Moses.
	8.22	did everything the **Lord** had **commanded**
	9.5	just as the **Lord** had **commanded** Moses.
	9.18	camp at the **command** of the **Lord**,
	9.20	according to the **command** of the **Lord**.
	9.23	to the **commands** which the **Lord** gave
	10.13	to march at the **command** of the **Lord**
	15.23	do everything that the **Lord commanded**
	15.36	as the **Lord** had **commanded**.
	15.37	The **Lord commanded** Moses
	16.40	as the **Lord** had **commanded** Eleazar
	17.11	Moses did as the **Lord commanded**.
	18.25	The **Lord commanded** Moses
	19.1	The **Lord commanded** Moses and Aaron
	20.9	as the **Lord** had **commanded**.
	20.27	did what the **Lord** had **commanded**
	24.13	not disobey the **command** of the **Lord**
	25.16	The **Lord commanded** Moses
	27.11	the **Lord**, have **commanded** you.
	27.22	Moses did as the **Lord** had **commanded**
	27.23	As the **Lord** had **commanded**,
	28.1	The **Lord commanded** Moses
	29.40	that the **Lord** had **commanded**
	31.7	as the **Lord** had **commanded** Moses,
	31.31	Eleazar did what the **Lord commanded**.
	31.41	as the **Lord** had **commanded**.
	31.47	and as the **Lord** had **commanded**,
	32.21	**command** of the **Lord** they are to
	32.27	into battle under the **Lord's command**.
	32.29	**Lord's command** and if with their help
	32.31	we will do as the **Lord** has **commanded**.
	33.2	At the **command** of the **Lord**
	33.38	At the **command** of the **Lord**
	36.2	The **Lord commanded** you to distribute
	36.5	the following **command** from the **Lord**.
	36.10	did as the **Lord** had **commanded** Moses,
Deut	1.3	the **Lord** had **commanded** him
	2.1	as the **Lord** had **commanded**,
	4.23	the **Lord**...made with you. Obey his **command**
	8.6	do as the **Lord** has **commanded** you:
	10.5	just as the **Lord** had **commanded**,
	10.12	the **Lord** and do all that he **commands**.
	12.25	this **command**, the **Lord** will be pleased,
	13.4	Follow the **Lord**...keep his **commands**;
	13.5	the **Lord** has **commanded** you to live.
	17.3	contrary to the **Lord's command**.
	17.20	the **Lord's commands** in any way.
	26.14	O **Lord**; I have done everything you **commanded**
	29.1	the **Lord commanded** Moses to make
	33.21	They obeyed the **Lord's commands**
	34.9	kept the **commands** that the **Lord**
Josh	4.8	As the **Lord** had **commanded** Joshua,
	5.3	did as the **Lord** had **commanded**,
	7.1	The **Lord's command** to Israel
	8.8	just as the **Lord** has **commanded**.
	11.9	to them what the **Lord** had **commanded**:
	11.15	The **Lord** had given his **commands**
	11.20	what the **Lord** had **commanded** Moses.
	11.23	as the **Lord** had **commanded** Moses.
	14.2	As the **Lord** had **commanded** Moses,
	14.5	the land as the **Lord** had **commanded**
	15.13	As the **Lord commanded** Joshua
	17.4	The **Lord commanded** Moses to give us,

Josh 19.50 As the **Lord** had **commanded**
     21.2 The **Lord commanded** through Moses
     21.3 the **Lord's command** the people
     21.8 **Lord** had **commanded** through Moses.
     22.9 had taken as the **Lord** had **commanded**
Judg 2.17 had obeyed the **Lord's commands**,
     3.4 obey the **commands** that the **Lord**
     7.9 That night the **Lord commanded** Gideon
1 Sam 12.15 to the **Lord** but disobey his **commands**,
    15.13 I have obeyed the **Lord's command**.
    15.23 you rejected the **Lord's command**,
    15.24 I disobeyed the **Lord's command**
    15.26 You rejected the **Lord's command**,
    28.18 You disobeyed the **Lord's command**,
2 Sam 5.25 did what the **Lord** had **commanded**
    24.19 David obeyed the **Lord's command**
1 Kgs 11.2 even though the **Lord** had **commanded**
    12.24 They all obeyed the **Lord's command**
    13.1 **Lord's command** a prophet from Judah
    13.2 Following the **Lord's command**
    13.9 **Lord** has **commanded** me not to eat
    13.17 the **Lord** has **commanded** me not to eat
    13.18 and at the **Lord's command** an angel
    13.26 who disobeyed the **Lord's command**!
    13.32 the **Lord's command** against the altar
    17.5 Elijah obeyed the **Lord's command**
    18.18 are disobeying the **Lord's commands**
    20.35 **Lord's command** a member of a group
    20.36 have disobeyed the **Lord's command**,
2 Kgs 1.3 an angel of the **Lord commanded** Elijah,
     1.4 Elijah did as the **Lord commanded**,
    14.6 followed what the **Lord** had **commanded**
    17.12 and disobeyed the **Lord's command**
    17.15 disobeying the **Lord's command**
    18.6 kept all the **commands** that the **Lord**
    21.22 and disobeyed the **Lord's commands**.
    23.3 with the **Lord** to...keep his...**commands**
    24.3 This happened at the **Lord's command**
1 Chr 10.13 He disobeyed the **Lord's commands**;
    15.15 **Lord** had **commanded** through Moses.
    21.19 David obeyed the **Lord's command**
2 Chr 11.4 They obeyed the **Lord's command**
    13.11 We do what the **Lord** has **commanded**,
    25.4 followed what the **Lord** had **commanded**
    34.31 with the **Lord** to...keep his...**commands**
Ezra 7.11 **commands** which the **Lord** had given
Neh 10.29 obey all that the **Lord**...**commands** us;
Ps 19.7 **commands** of the **Lord** are trustworthy,
    19.8 The **commands** of the **Lord** are just
    33.6 The **Lord** created the heavens by his
         command,
    37.34 in the **Lord** and obey his **commands**;
    68.11 The **Lord** gave the **command**,
    106.34 the **Lord** had **commanded** them to do,
    112.1 the **Lord**...obeying his **commands**.
    119.108 O **Lord**, and teach me your **commands**.
    119.145 **Lord**, and I will obey your **commands**!
    119.151 **Lord**, and all your **commands** are
    119.166 **Lord**, and I do what you **command**.
    122.4 to the **Lord** according to his **command**.
    128.1 the **Lord**, who live by his **commands**.
    148.5 the name of the **Lord**! He **commanded**,
Is 34.16 The **Lord** has **commanded** it
    38.4 Then the **Lord commanded** Isaiah
Jer 4.12 wind that comes at the **Lord's command**
    14.17 **Lord commanded** me to tell the people
    22.3 **Lord, command** you to do what is just
    26.8 the **Lord** had **commanded** me to speak,
    43.4 **Lord's command** to remain in the land
    43.7 They disobeyed the **Lord's command**
    44.23 **Lord** by not obeying all his **commands**.
Ezek 10.6 When the **Lord commanded** the man
    28.10 **Lord**, have given the **command**.
    37.9 Tell the wind that the...**Lord commands**

Ezek 43.19 the Sovereign **Lord, command** this.
    45.13 the Sovereign **Lord, command** it.
    46.16 The Sovereign **Lord commands**
Joel 2.11 **Lord** thunders **commands** to his army.
Amos 6.11 When the **Lord** gives the **command**
     9.1 I saw the **Lord**...He gave the **command**
Jon 1.17 At the **Lord's command** a large fish
Mal 2.1 **Lord** Almighty says...'This **command**
Mt 27.10 as the **Lord** had **commanded** me.
Lk   1.6 obeyed fully all the **Lord's**...**commands**.
1 Cor 7.10 **command** which is not my own but the
         Lord's:
     7.25 do not have a **command** from the **Lord**,
    14.37 writing to you is the **Lord's command**.
2 Thes 3.6 **command** you in the name of our **Lord**
     3.12 **Lord** Jesus Christ we **command** these
2 Pet 3.2 **command** from the **Lord** and Saviour

New
1 Jn 2.7 this **command**...to you is not **new**;
      2.8 the **command**...to you is **new**,
2 Jn .5 This is no **new command** I am writing

Observe
Deut 5.15 I **command** you to **observe** the Sabbath.
    15.5 **observe** everything that I **command** you
Jer 17.22 they must **observe** it...as I **commanded**

Offerings see **Sacrifice**

Rebel see **Disobey**

Refuse see **Disobey**

Reject see **Disobey**

Remember, Forget
Num 15.39 you will **remember** all my **commands**
Deut 6.6 Never **forget** these **commands**
    11.18 **Remember** these **commands**
    16.12 obey these **commands**; do not **forget**
    26.13 or **forgotten** any of your **commands**
Josh 1.9 **Remember** that I have **commanded** you
Ps 119.16 your **commands** I will not **forget**.
    119.83 I have not **forgotten** your **commands**.

Rest see **Sabbath**

Right see **Just**

Sabbath, Rest
Ex 16.23 has **commanded**...a holy **day** of **rest**.
Lev 19.3 the Sabbath, as I have **commanded**.
Deut 5.15 I **command** you to observe the Sabbath.
Ezek 20.16 **commands**...and profaned the Sabbath
    20.24 my **commands**...profaned the Sabbath,
Lk 23.56 Sabbath they **rested**, as the Law **commanded**.

Sacrifice, Offerings
Ex   8.27 **sacrifices**...just as he **commanded** us.
Lev 10.18 the **sacrifice** there, as I **commanded**.
2 Chr 29.24 the king had **commanded** burnt-offerings
Jer 7.22 **commands** about burnt-offerings
    19.5 as **sacrifices**. I never **commanded** them

Turn
Deut 9.12 **turned** away from what I **commanded**
    11.28 disobey these **commands** and **turn** away
1 Sam 15.11 he has **turned** away...and disobeyed my
         commands.
Neh 1.9 if you **turn** back...and do what I have
         commanded
Ps 51.13 your **commands**, and they will **turn** back
Dan 9.5 you **command**...and have **turned** away
Acts 17.30 but now he **commands** all...to **turn** away
2 Pet 2.21 **turn** away from the sacred **command**

COMMANDMENT
Ex   20.1 – 17

Deut	5.1 – 21	
Ps	119.10 – 143	x10
Rom	7.8 – 13	x6
Mt	22.36 – 40	x4
Mk	12.28 – 33	x4
Jn	13.34 — 15.12	x4
Ex	31.18 — 32.16	x3
Deut	4.13 — 5.22	x3
Ps	78.5 – 56	x3
Mt	19.17 – 20	x3

God, Lord
Ex   31.18 on which **God** himself had written the **commandments**
Deut 5.22 **commandments** the **Lord** gave to all
Acts 13.47 the **commandment** that the **Lord** has
1 Cor 7.19 to obey **God's commandments.**
Rev 12.17 those who obey **God's commandments**
      14.12 those who obey **God's commandments**

Important
Mt   5.19 least **important** of the **commandments**
     22.38 and the most **important commandment.**
     22.39 second most **important commandment**
Mk 12.28 **commandment** is the most **important**
     12.31 second most **important commandment**
     12.33 It is more **important** to obey these two **commandments**

Lord see God

Sin
Rom 7.8 that **commandment sin** found its chance
      7.9 **commandment** came, **sin** sprang to life,
     7.11 **Sin** found its chance, and by means of the **commandment**
     7.13 of the **commandment sin** is shown

COMPASSION

Ex	33.19 — 34.6	x2
Is	63.9 – 15	x2

Lord
Ex   33.19 I am the **Lord**, and I show **compassion**
     34.6 I, the **Lord**, am...full of **compassion**
Ps 116.5 **Lord** is merciful and...**compassionate.**
  119.156But your **compassion**, **Lord**, is great;
Is   30.19 The **Lord** is **compassionate**,
Jas   5.11 **Lord** is full of mercy and **compassion.**

CONDEMN

Josh	7.11 – 22	x4
Ezek	20.35 — 21.24	x4
Jn	7.51 — 8.26	x4
Rom	2.1 — 3.8	x4
Rom	8.1 – 34	x4
Jude	.4 – 15	x4
Josh	9.23 — 11.20	x3
Jn	18.38 — 19.6	x3

Destruction
Deut 13.17 that was **condemned** to **destruction,**
Josh 7.11 the things **condemned** to **destruction.**
      7.12 now been **condemned** to **destruction!**
    10.37 **condemned** the city to total **destruction,**
    11.20 would be **condemned** to total **destruction**
    22.20 the things **condemned** to **destruction;**
Ps   9.5 **condemned** the heathen and **destroyed**
Is   34.2 He has **condemned** them to **destruction.**
    34.5 whom he has **condemned** to **destruction.**
2 Pet 2.6 **condemned**...Sodom and Gomorrah, **destroying** them

Evil see Sin

God, Lord
Josh 9.23 **God** has **condemned** you.
Ruth 1.21 the **Lord** Almighty has **condemned** me

2 Chr 21.12 **God** of your ancestor David, **condemns**
Job 10.2 Don't **condemn** me, **God.**
    34.17 Are you **condemning** the righteous **God?**
    34.18 **God condemns** kings and rulers
Ps   1.5 Sinners will be **condemned** by **God**
    5.10 **Condemn** and punish them, O **God;**
    7.11 **God**...always **condemns** the wicked
   36.2 thinks that **God** will not...**condemn** it.
   75.7 **God** who is the judge, **condemning** some
Prov 12.2 **Lord**...**condemns** those who plan evil.
Jer 8.14 The **Lord** our **God** has **condemned** us
   17.5 **Lord** says, "I will **condemn** the person
Zech 3.2 May the **Lord condemn** you, Satan!
Lk   6.37 and **God** will not **condemn** you;
Rom 8.3 **God** did. He **condemned** sin
  14.23 **God condemns** him when he eats it,
2 Pet 2.6 **God condemned** the cities of Sodom
1 Jn 3.20 **condemns** us, we know that **God**
   3.21 **condemn** us, we have courage in **God's**
Rev 18.20 For **God** has **condemned** her

Jesus, Lord
Mt   27.3 learnt that **Jesus** had been **condemned,**
Acts 13.27 words come true by **condemning Jesus.**
Rom 8.34 will **condemn** them? Not Christ **Jesus,**
1 Cor 11.32 by the **Lord**, so that we shall not be **condemned**

Righteous
Job 34.17 Are you **condemning** the **righteous God?**
Ps   7.11 **righteous** judge and...**condemns** the
Ezek 23.45 **Righteous** men will **condemn** them

Sin, Evil, Wicked
Ex   23.7 **condemn** anyone who does such an **evil**
Ps   1.5 **Sinners** will be **condemned** by God
    7.11 and always **condemns** the **wicked**
    9.5 **condemned** the heathen and...**wicked;**
   28.3 Do not **condemn** me with the **wicked,**
   36.2 not discover his **sin** and **condemn** it.
  130.3 **sins**, who could escape being **condemned?**
Prov 12.2 but **condemns** those who plan **evil.**
  17.15 **Condemning** the innocent or letting the **wicked**
Lam 1.22 **Condemn** them for all their **wickedness;**
Ezek 21.24 You show your **sins**...stand **condemned,**
Jn   5.29 done **evil** will rise and be **condemned.**
   8.11 not **condemn** you...do not **sin** again.
Rom 3.7 should I still be **condemned** as a **sinner?**
   5.18 as the one **sin condemned** all mankind,
   8.3 He **condemned sin** in human nature
2 Thes 2.12 pleasure in **sin**, will be **condemned.**
Jas   2.9 of **sin**, and the Law **condemns** you

CONFESS

Ezra	9.15 — 10.11	x3
Ps	32.3 – 5	x3

God
Josh 7.19 the **God** of Israel, and **confess.**
Ezra 10.11 **confess** your sins to...**God**
Job 34.31 have you **confessed** your sins to **God**
Is   45.14 and **confess**, 'God is with you
Dan 9.4 Lord my **God** and **confessed** the sins
Zech 13.9 they will **confess** that I am their **God.**
Rom 10.10 right with **God**; it is by our **confession**
  14.11 everyone will **confess** that **God** is **God.**
1 Cor 14.25 bow down and worship **God, confessing,**
1 Jn 1.9 But if we **confess** our sins to **God**

Jesus
Rom 10.9 If you **confess** that **Jesus** is Lord,
1 Cor 12.3 can **confess** "**Jesus** is Lord," unless

Lord
Josh 7.19 truth here before the **Lord**...and **confess.**
Ezra 10.11 **confess** your sins to the **Lord,**

Jer	14.20	**Lord**; we **confess** our own sins
Dan	9.4	to the **Lord** my God and **confessed**
Rom	10.9	If you **confess** that Jesus is **Lord**
1 Cor	12.3	one can **confess**."Jesus is **Lord**," unless
Heb	13.15	by lips that **confess** him as **Lord**.

Sin

Lev	5.5	he must **confess** the sin,
	16.21	and **confess** over it all the evils, **sins**,
	26.40	your descendants will **confess** their **sins**
Num	5.7	he must **confess** his sin
1 Kgs	8.47	**confessing** how sinful...they have been,
2 Chr	6.37	**confessing** how sinful...they have been,
Ezra	10.1	weeping and **confessing** these **sins**,
	10.11	**confess** your **sins** to the Lord,
Neh	1.6	I **confess** that we...have **sinned**.
	9.1	they stood and began to **confess** the sins
	9.3	they **confessed** their sins and worshipped
Job	34.31	have you **confessed** your sins to God
Ps	32.3	When I did not **confess** my sins,
	32.5	Then I **confessed** my sins to you;
	38.18	I **confess** my sins;
Prov	28.13	if you try to hide your sins. **Confess**
Jer	14.20	**confess** our own sins and the sins
Dan	9.4	and **confessed** the sins of my people.
	9.20	**confessing** my sins and the sins of my
Mt	3.6	They **confessed** their sins
Mk	1.5	They **confessed** their sins,
Jas	5.16	**confess** your sins to one another
1 Jn	1.9	But if we **confess** our sins to God

CONSCIENCE

1 Cor	10.25 – 29	x5
1 Cor	8.7 – 12	x3
1 Tim	1.5 – 19	x3
1 Jn	3.20 – 21	x3

Clear

Acts	23.1	My **conscience** is perfectly **clear**
	24.16	best always to have a **clear conscience**
1 Cor	4.4	My **conscience** is **clear**
1 Tim	1.5	a pure heart, a **clear conscience**,
	1.19	keep your faith and a **clear conscience**.
	3.9	of the faith with a **clear conscience**.
2 Tim	1.3	whom I serve with a **clear conscience**,
Heb	13.18	We are sure we have a **clear conscience**,
1 Pet	3.16	Keep your **conscience clear**,

CONSULT

2 Kgs	1.2 – 16	x5
Josh	18.6 — 19.51	x4
Ezek	14.1 – 10	x4
Lev	19.31 — 20.27	x3
1 Sam	22.13 — 23.4	x3
2 Kgs	3.11 – 13	x3
2 Kgs	21.6 — 22.14	x3
2 Chr	33.6 — 34.22	x3

Fortune-teller see Medium

Gods, Idols

2 Kgs	1.2	**consult** Baalzebub, the **god** of...Ekron,
	1.3	to **consult** Baalzebub, the **god** of Ekron?
	1.6	to **consult** Baalzebub, the **god** of Ekron?
	1.16	**consult** Baalzebub, the **god** of Ekron
	1.16	if there were no **god** in Israel to **consult**
	17.17	to pagan **gods**; they **consulted** mediums
Ezek	21.21	he **consults** his **idols**;
Zech	10.2	People **consult idols** and fortune-tellers,

Medium, Fortune-teller

1 Sam	28.7	**medium**, and I will go and **consult** her.
2 Kgs	17.17	**consulted mediums** and fortune-tellers,
	21.6	**consulted fortune-tellers** and **mediums**,
2 Chr	33.6	**consulted fortune-tellers** and **mediums**.
Is	19.3	and they will go and **consult mediums**

Zech	10.2	People **consult** idols and **fortune-tellers**,

Prophet

1 Kgs	22.7	**prophet** through whom we can **consult**
2 Kgs	3.11	Is there a **prophet**...we can **consult**
	3.13	**prophets** that your father...**consulted**.
	8.8	**prophet**, and ask him to **consult** the
	22.14	to **consult** a woman named Huldah, a **prophet**
2 Chr	18.6	**prophet** through whom we can **consult**
	34.22	to **consult** a woman named Huldah, a **prophet**
Ezek	14.4	who then comes to **consult** a **prophet**,
	14.7	and then goes to **consult** a **prophet**,
	14.10	**prophet** and the one who **consults** him

CONTROL

Rom	8.5 – 7		x5
1 Sam	18.10 — 19.23		x4
Dan	4.25 — 5.23		x4
1 Sam	10.6 — 11.6		x3

God, Lord

Num	24.2	The **spirit of God** took **control** of him,
Judg	6.34	of the **Lord** took **control** of Gideon
1 Sam	10.6	of the **Lord** will take **control** of you,
	10.10	the **spirit of God** took **control** of him,
	11.6	the **spirit of God** took **control** of him,
	16.13	the **spirit of the Lord** took **control**
	18.10	spirit from **God** suddenly took **control**
	19.9	evil spirit from the **Lord** took **control**
	19.20	Then the **spirit of God** took **control**
	19.23	the **spirit of God** took **control**
2 Sam	2.1	the **Lord**, "Shall I go and take **control**
1 Chr	10.14	the **Lord** killed him and gave **control**
	12.18	**God's** spirit took **control**
2 Chr	17.5	The **Lord** gave Jehoshaphat firm **control**
	24.20	Then the **spirit of God** took **control**
Prov	21.1	The **Lord controls** the mind of a king
Ecc	9.1	that **God controls** the actions
Ezek	11.5	spirit of the **Lord** took **control** of me
Dan	4.25	**God controls** all human kingdoms,
	5.21	**God controls** all human kingdoms
Rom	8.7	**God** when he is **controlled** by his
Eph	2.2	**controls** the people who disobey **God**.
1 Pet	4.2	earthly lives **controlled** by **God's** will

Human

Dan	4.25	God **controls** all **human** kingdoms,
	5.21	God **controls** all **human** kingdoms
Rom	8.5	minds **controlled** by what **human** nature
	8.6	To be **controlled** by **human** nature
	8.7	he is **controlled** by his **human** nature;
1 Pet	4.2	**controlled** by God's will and not by **human** desires.

Life

Jer	10.23	no person has **control** over his own **life**.
Ezek	13.20	your attempt to **control life** and death.
Rom	8.6	be **controlled** by the Spirit results in **life**
Gal	5.25	he must also **control** our **lives**.
Eph	5.2	Your **life** must be **controlled** by love,
1 Pet	4.2	earthly **lives controlled** by God's will
2 Pet	3.3	whose **lives** are **controlled** by...lusts.

Lord see God

Spirit of God

see also **God**

Rom	8.5	**controlled** by what the **Spirit** wants.
	8.6	to be **controlled** by the **Spirit**
Gal	5.25	The **Spirit**...must also **control** our lives.
2 Pet	1.21	under the **control** of the Holy **Spirit**
Rev	1.10	the **Spirit** took **control** of me,
	4.2	At once the **Spirit** took **control** of me
	17.3	The **Spirit** took **control** of me,

Rev   21.10 The **Spirit** took **control** of me

COURAGE

	1 Jn	2.28	—	5.14	x4
	Ezek	21.7	—	22.14	x3

Fail
Deut 31.8   He will not **fail**...so do not lose **courage**
Job   19.27 My **courage** failed because you said,
Is   13.7   and everyone's **courage** will **fail**.
Ezek 21.7   their **courage** will fail,

God, Lord
1 Sam 30.6   but the **Lord** his **God** gave him **courage**.
2 Sam 7.27   **God** of Israel! I have the **courage** to
1 Chr 17.25 I have the **courage** to pray this prayer to you, my **God**,
Ezra 7.28   **Lord** my **God** has given me **courage**,
Job   23.16 **God** has destroyed my **courage**.
Ps   31.24 be **courageous**, all you that hope in the **Lord**.
1 Thes 2.2   our **God** gave us **courage** to tell
1 Jn 3.21   we have **courage** in **God's** presence.
      5.14   We have **courage** in **God's** presence,

COVENANT

	Heb	7.22	—	10.29	x17
	Jer	31.31	—	34.18	x16
	Gen	17.2 – 21			x10
	Deut	29.1 – 25			x7
	Lev	26.9 – 45			x6
	Deut	7.9		9.15	x6
	Jer	11.2 – 10			x6
	Ezek	16.8 – 62			x6
	Gen	9.9 – 16			x5
	2 Kgs	23.2 – 21			x5
	2 Chr	34.30 – 32			x5
	Mal	2.4	—	3.1	x5
	Deut	4.13	—	5.2	x4
	2 Kgs	17.15	—	18.12	x4
	Ps	89.3 – 39			x4
	Gal	3.17	—	4.24	x4
	Ex	34.10 – 28			x3
	Judg	2.1 – 20			x3
	1 Kgs	8.9 – 23			x3
	1 Chr	16.15 – 17			x3
	2 Chr	15.12 – 15			x3

Blood, Sacrifice, Seal
Ex   24.8   This is the **blood** that **seals** the **covenant**
Ps   50.5   **covenant** with me by offering a **sacrifice**.
Zech 9.11   **covenant** with you...**sealed** by the **blood**
Mt   26.28 my **blood**, which **seals** God's **covenant**,
Mk   14.24 my **blood** which **seals** God's **covenant**.
Lk   22.20 new **covenant** sealed with my **blood**,
1 Cor 11.25 new **covenant**, **sealed** with my **blood**.
Heb   9.20 the **blood** which **seals** the **covenant**
      10.29 the **blood** of God's **covenant**
      12.24 **covenant**, and to the sprinkled **blood**
      13.20 his **sacrificial death**, by which the eternal **covenant** is **sealed**

Command
Ex   24.7   **covenant**, in which the Lord's **commands**
Lev   26.15 and **commands** and break the **covenant**
Deut 29.1   **covenant** that the Lord **commanded**
      33.9   obeyed your **commands**...your **covenant**.
Josh 23.16 **covenant** which the Lord...**commanded**
Judg   2.20 **covenant** that I **commanded** their
1 Kgs 11.11 **covenant**...and disobeyed my **commands**,
Ps   25.10 his **covenant** and obey his **commands**.
      103.18 **covenant** and who...obey his **commands**,
      132.12 **covenant** and to the **commands** I give
Jer   11.8   **commanded** them to keep the **covenant**,
Mal   2.4   you this **command**, so that my **covenant**
Heb   9.20 **covenant** that God has **commanded** you

Eternal, Everlasting, Last
Gen   9.12 As a sign of this **everlasting covenant**
       9.16 I will...remember the **everlasting covenant**
      17.7   as an **everlasting covenant**.
      17.13 my **covenant** with you is **everlasting**.
      17.19 It is an **everlasting covenant**.
2 Sam 23.5   he has made an **eternal covenant**
1 Chr 16.15 God's **covenant**, which he made to **last**
      16.17 **covenant** with Jacob, one that will **last**
Ps   89.28 and my **covenant**...will **last for ever**.
      105.10 a **covenant**...that will **last for ever**.
      111.9 and made an **eternal covenant**
Is   24.5   the **covenant** he made to **last for ever**.
      55.3   I will make a **lasting covenant** with you
      61.8   And make an **eternal covenant**
Jer   32.40 I will make an **eternal covenant**
      50.5   They will make an **eternal covenant**
Ezek 16.60 I will make a **covenant**...that will **last**
Heb   13.20 by which the **eternal covenant** is sealed.

Forget see **Remember**

God, Lord
Gen   15.18 the **Lord** made a **covenant** with Abram.
      17.7   everlasting **covenant**. I will be your **God**
Ex   24.7   **covenant**, in which the **Lord's**
      24.8   seals the **covenant** which the **Lord** made
      34.10 **Lord** said...'I now make a **covenant**
Lev   2.13 the **covenant** between you and **God**.
      26.44 my **covenant** with them, and I am the **Lord** their **God**.
Deut   4.23 **covenant** that the **Lord** your **God** made
       5.2   the **Lord** our **God** made a **covenant**,
       7.12 then the **Lord**...will...keep his **covenant**
       9.9   the **covenant** that the **Lord** had made
      17.2   the **Lord** and broken his **covenant**
      29.1   the **covenant** that the **Lord** commanded
      29.12 **covenant** that the **Lord** your **God** is
      29.14 whom the **Lord** is making this **covenant**
      29.25 the **Lord's** people broke the **covenant** they had made with him, the **God**
Josh 23.16 **covenant** which the **Lord** your **God**
1 Kgs 8.9   when the **Lord** made a **covenant**
       8.21 of the **covenant** which the **Lord** made
2 Kgs 11.17 enter into a **covenant** with the **Lord**
      17.35 **Lord** had made a **covenant** with them
      18.12 their **God**, but broke the **covenant**
      23.3   and made a **covenant** with the **Lord**
      23.21 their **God**, as written in the book of the **covenant**.
1 Chr 16.15 Never forget **God's covenant**,
      16.17 The **Lord** made a **covenant** with Jacob,
2 Chr 5.10 when the **Lord** made a **covenant**
       6.11 of the **covenant** which the **Lord** made
       6.14 **god** like you. You keep your **covenant**
      13.5   the **God** of Israel, made an unbreakable **covenant**
      29.10 a **covenant** with the **Lord**, the **God**
      34.31 and made a **covenant** with the **Lord**
      34.32 the **covenant**...made with the **God**
Ps   78.10 did not keep their **covenant** with **God**;
      105.10 The **Lord** made a **covenant** with Jacob,
Is   24.5   breaking **God's** laws and...the **covenant**
Jer   4.4   your **covenant** with me, your **Lord**,
      22.9   your **covenant** with me, your **God**,
      33.25 **Lord**, have a **covenant** with day and
Zech   9.11 **Lord** says, "Because of my **covenant**
      11.10 the **covenant** which the **Lord** had made
Mal   2.10 we despise the **covenant** that **God** made
Mt   26.28 which seals **God's covenant**, my **blood**
Mk   14.24 my **blood** which seals **God's covenant**.
Lk   22.20 This cup is **God's** new **covenant**
Acts   3.25 share in the **covenant** which **God** made
1 Cor 11.25 This cup is **God's** new **covenant**,

Gal	3.17	**God** made a **covenant** with Abraham
Heb	8.6	**covenant**...between **God** and his people
	8.8	says the **Lord**, when I will draw up a new **covenant**
	8.13	of a new **covenant**, **God** has made
	9.20	which seals the **covenant** that **God**
	10.29	thing the blood of **God's covenant**

Jesus

Heb	7.22	**Jesus** the guarantee of a better **covenant**.
	12.24	**Jesus**, who arranged the new **covenant**,

Keep see Obey

Last see Eternal

Lord see God

Obey, Keep

Gen	17.9	must agree to **keep** the **covenant** with
	17.14	he has not **kept** the **covenant** with me.
	17.19	I will **keep** my **covenant** with him
	17.21	I will **keep** my **covenant** with your son
Ex	19.5	**obey** me and **keep** my **covenant**,
Lev	26.9	will **keep** my part of the **covenant**
	26.15	refuse to **obey**...and break the **covenant**
Deut	4.13	to **keep** the **covenant** he made with you
	7.9	will **keep** his **covenant** and show his
	7.12	will continue to **keep** his **covenant**
	29.9	**Obey**...all the terms of this **covenant**,
Josh	23.16	do not **keep** the **covenant** which the
1 Kgs	8.23	You **keep** your **covenant** with your
2 Kgs	17.15	did not **keep** the **covenant** he had made
	18.12	**obey** the **Lord**...but broke the **covenant**
	23.3	a **covenant** with the Lord to **obey** him,
2 Chr	6.14	You **keep** your **covenant** with your
	15.14	that they would **keep** the **covenant**,
	34.31	a **covenant** with the Lord to **obey** him,
	34.32	promise to **keep** the **covenant**.
	34.32	**obeyed** the requirements of the **covenant**
Neh	1.5	You faithfully **keep** your **covenant**
	9.32	You faithfully **keep** your **covenant**
Ps	25.10	all who **keep** his **covenant** and **obey**
	25.14	**obey** him and he affirms his **covenant**
	78.10	They did not **keep** their **covenant** with God; they refused to **obey**
	103.18	**covenant** and who faithfully **obey**
	105.8	He will **keep** his **covenant** for ever,
Is	56.4	me and faithfully **keep** my **covenant**,
	56.6	and faithfully **keep** his **covenant**:
Jer	4.4	**Keep** your **covenant** with me,
	9.25	have not **kept** the **covenant** it
	9.25	people of Israel have **kept** my **covenant**.
	11.3	not **obey** the terms of this **covenant**.
	11.6	of the **covenant** and to **obey** them.
	11.8	I had commanded them to **keep** the **covenant**,
	31.32	they did not **keep** that **covenant**.
	34.18	the **covenant** and did not **keep** its terms.
Ezek	20.37	and make you **obey** my **covenant**.
Heb	9.20	the **covenant** that God has commanded you to **obey**.

Priests

Neh	13.29	the **covenant** you made with the **priests**
Jer	33.21	I have made a **covenant** with the **priests**
	34.18	the **priests**...made a **covenant** with me
Mal	2.4	so that my **covenant** with the **priests**,

Promise

Gen	9.11	make my **covenant** with you: I **promise**
	15.18	a **covenant** with Abram. He said, "I **promise**
	17.4	make this **covenant** with you: I **promise**
Ex	6.4	made my **covenant** with them, **promising**
2 Kgs	23.3	people **promised** to keep the **covenant**.
1 Chr	16.16	the **covenant** he made...the **promise**

2 Chr	21.7	a **covenant** with David and **promised**
	34.32	**promise** to keep the **covenant**.
Neh	9.8	a **covenant** with him. You **promised**
	9.32	faithfully keep your **covenant promises**.
Ps	89.3	have made a **covenant**...I have **promised**
	89.28	my **promise** to him, and my **covenant**
	89.34	not break my **covenant**...or...one **promise**
	105.8	He will keep his **covenant**...his **promises**
Ezek	16.59	your **promises** and broke the **covenant**.
Mal	2.5	In my **covenant** I **promised** them life
Gal	3.17	God made a **covenant**...and **promised**
Eph	2.12	the **covenants**...based on God's **promises**
Heb	12.24	new **covenant**, and...blood that **promises**

Remember, Forget

Gen	9.16	and **remember** the everlasting **covenant**
Ex	2.24	**remembered** his **covenant** with Abraham,
	6.5	and I have **remembered** my **covenant**.
Lev	26.42	I will **remember** my **covenant** with Jacob
Deut	4.23	do **not forget** the **covenant**
	4.31	and he will **not forget** the **covenant**
2 Kgs	17.38	and you shall **not forget** the **covenant**
1 Chr	16.15	**Never forget** God's **covenant**,
Ps	44.17	**forgotten** you or broken the **covenant**
	74.20	**Remember** the **covenant** you made
	106.45	he **remembered** his **covenant**,
	111.5	he **never forgets** his **covenant**.
Lk	1.72	and **remember** his sacred **covenant**.

Sacrifice see Blood

Seal see Blood

Sign

Gen	9.12	As a **sign** of this everlasting **covenant**
	9.13	It will be the **sign** of my **covenant**
	17.13	physical **sign** to show that my **covenant**
Ex	31.16	keep this day as a **sign** of the **covenant**.
Ezek	20.20	so that it will be a **sign** of the **covenant**
Acts	7.8	circumcision as a **sign** of the **covenant**.

COVENANT BOX

1 Sam	3.3	—	7.2	x34
1 Chr	15.1	—	17.1	x17
Josh	3.3	—	4.16	x13
2 Sam	6.2	—	7.2	x11
Ex	25.10	—	27.21	x8
Josh	6.4	—	8.33	x8
2 Chr	5.2	—	6.41	x8
Ex	39.35	—	40.21	x7
1 Kgs	8.1 – 21			x7
1 Chr	13.3 – 12			x7
Deut	10.1 – 8			x5
Ex	30.6	—	31.7	x4
Lev	16.2 – 15			x4
Num	17.4 – 10			x3
Deut	31.9 – 26			x3
2 Sam	15.24 – 29			x3

Holy Place see Tent

Levites

1 Sam	6.15	The **Levites** lifted off the **Covenant Box**
2 Sam	15.24	**Levites**, carrying the sacred **Covenant**
i Chr	15.2	**Levites** should carry the **Covenant Box**,
	15.12	fellow-**Levites**, so that you can bring the **Covenant Box**
	15.26	the **Levites**...carrying the **Covenant Box**.
	15.27	and the **Levites** who carried the **Box**.
2 Chr	5.4	then the **Levites** lifted the **Covenant Box**

Priests

Josh	3.3	the **priests** carrying the **Covenant Box**
	3.6	the **priests** to take the **Covenant Box**
	3.8	the **priests** carrying the **Covenant Box**
	3.13	the **priests** who carry the **Covenant Box**
	3.14	the **priests**...carrying the **Covenant Box**.

Josh	3.17	**priests** carrying the Lord's **Covenant**
	4.9	the **priests** carrying the **Covenant Box**
	4.11	**priests** with the Lord's **Covenant Box**
	4.16	the **priests** carrying the **Covenant Box**
	6.6	the **priests**...'Take the **Covenant Box**,
	6.8	the **priests**...carrying the **Covenant Box**,
	6.12	the **priests** carrying the...**Covenant Box**;
	8.33	**Covenant Box**, facing the levitical **priests**
1 Kgs	8.3	the **priests** lifted the **Covenant Box**
	8.6	the **priests** carried the **Covenant Box**
2 Chr	5.7	the **priests** carried the **Covenant Box**

Sacred

1 Sam	3.3	where the **sacred Covenant Box** was.
2 Sam	15.24	carrying the **sacred Covenant Box**.
2 Chr	35.3	the **sacred Covenant Box** in the Temple

Temple

1 Kgs	8.21	the **Temple** for the **Covenant Box**
2 Chr	6.11	placed in the **Temple** the **Covenant Box**,
	35.3	the sacred **Covenant Box** in the **Temple**
Ps	132.8	to the **Temple**...with the **Covenant Box**,
Rev	11.19	God's **temple** in heaven was opened, and the **Covenant Box**

Tent, Holy Place

Ex	26.33	**Tent**, and...put the **Covenant Box**
Lev	24.3	**Covenant Box**...in the **Most Holy Place**.
2 Sam	6.17	brought the **Box** and put it...in the **Tent**
	7.2	God's **Covenant Box** is kept in a **tent**!
1 Chr	15.1	God's **Covenant Box** and put up a **tent**
	16.1	They took the **Covenant Box** to the **tent**
	17.1	Lord's **Covenant Box** is kept in a **tent**!

CREATE

	Is	42.5 —	45.18	x10
	Gen	1.1 —	2.4	x6
	Rom	8.19 – 39		x6
	Gen	5.1 —	6.7	x3
	Is	64.8 —	66.2	x3
	1 Cor	11.8 – 9		x3
	Eph	1.10 —	2.15	x3
	Col	1.15 – 16		x3
	Heb	1.2 —	2.10	x3

Being

Gen	1.27	So God **created** human **beings**
	5.1	(When God **created** human **beings**,
Ps	90.2	**created**...or brought the world into **being**,
1 Cor	15.45	Adam, was **created** a living **being**";

Command

Ps	33.6	**created** the heavens by his **command**,
	33.9	the world was **created**; at his **command**
	148.5	He **commanded**, and they were **created**;
Ecc	12.13	**commands**...is all that man was **created**
2 Pet	3.5	**command**...heavens and earth were **created**.

God, Lord

Gen	1.21	So **God created** the great sea-monsters,
	1.27	So **God created** human beings
	2.4	When the **Lord God made** the universe
	5.1	(When **God created** human beings,
Deut	4.32	back to the time when **God created** man
	32.15	They abandoned **God** their **Creator**
1 Chr	16.26	but the **Lord created** the heavens.
2 Chr	2.12	**Lord God** of Israel, **Creator** of heaven
Job	4.17	in the sight of **God**...his **Creator**?
	31.15	The same **God** who **created** me
	35.10	they don't turn to **God**, their **Creator**,
	36.3	to show that **God**, my **Creator**, is just.
Ps	33.6	**Lord created** the heavens by his
	51.10	**Create** a pure heart in me, O **God**,
	96.5	but the **Lord created** the heavens.
	148.5	the **Lord**...commanded, and they were **created**;

Prov	3.19	**Lord created** the earth by his wisdom;
	8.22	The **Lord created** me first of all,
Is	17.7	for help to their **Creator**, the holy **God**
	27.11	**God** their **Creator** will not pity them
	40.28	**Lord** is the everlasting **God**; he **created**
	42.5	**God created** the heavens
	43.1	the **Lord** who **created** you says,
	43.15	your holy **God. I created** you,
	44.2	I am the **Lord** who **created** you;
	44.24	I am the **Lord**...who **created** you.
	45.18	The **Lord created** the heavens
	54.5	Your **Creator**...the **Lord** Almighty
Amos	4.13	**God** is the one who...**created** the winds.
	7.1	**Lord**. In it I saw him **create** a swarm
Zech	12.1	the **Lord** who...**created** the earth,
Mal	2.10	Didn't the same **God create** us all?
Mk	10.6	the time of **creation**, 'God made them
	13.19	beginning when **God created** the world
Jn	1.3	Through him **God** made...all **creation**
Acts	4.24	in prayer to **God**: "Master and **Creator**
Rom	1.20	Ever since **God created** the world
	1.25	**God** has **created** instead of the **Creator**
	8.19	All of **creation** waits with eager longing for **God**
1 Cor	8.6	**God**, the Father, who is the **Creator**
Eph	3.9	**God**, who is the **Creator** of all
	4.24	which is **created** in **God's** likeness
Col	1.16	For through him **God created** everything
	3.10	the new being which **God**, its **Creator**,
1 Tim	4.3	**God created** those foods to be eaten,
	4.4	Everything that **God** has **created** is good
Heb	1.2	through whom **God created** the universe
	1.10	**Lord**, in the beginning **created** the earth,
	2.10	It was only right that **God**, who **creates**
	4.13	from **God**; everything in all **creation**
	11.3	the universe was **created** by **God's** word,
Jas	1.17	it comes down from **God**, the **Creator**
	3.9	who is **created** in the likeness of **God**.
1 Pet	1.20	been chosen by **God** before the **creation**
Rev	3.14	the origin of all that **God** has **created**.
	10.6	the name of **God**...who **created** heaven,

Life

Ps	104.30	they are **created**; you give new **life**
Zech	12.1	**created** the earth, and gave **life**
Eph	2.10	he has **created** us for a **life**

Lord see God

New

Ps	51.10	**Create** a pure heart...a **new**...spirit
	104.30	they are **created**; you give **new life**
Is	65.18	in what I **create**. The **new** Jerusalem
Jer	31.22	I have **created** something **new**
Eph	2.15	in order to **create**...one **new** people
	4.24	put on the **new** self, which is **created**

World, Universe

Gen	1.1	when **God created** the **universe**,
	2.4	that is how the **universe** was **created**.
Ps	33.9	the **world** was **created**;
	90.2	**created** the hills or brought the **world**
Is	40.28	he **created** all the **world**.
	66.2	I myself **created** the whole **universe**
Jer	10.12	by his wisdom he **created** the **world**
	27.5	I **created** the **world**,
	51.15	by his wisdom he **created** the **world**
Mt	13.35	since the **creation** of the **world**.
	25.34	ever since the **creation** of the **world**.
Mk	13.19	when **God created** the **world**
Lk	11.50	the **creation** of the **world**,
Jn	1.1	Before the **world** was **created**,
Rom	1.20	Ever since **God created** the **world**
Col	1.16	**God created** the whole **universe**
Heb	1.2	through whom **God created** the **universe**,
	4.3	from the time he **created** the **world**.

Heb	9.11	it is not a part of this **created world**.
	9.26	ever since the **creation** of the **world**.
	11.3	the **universe** was **created** by God's word,
1 Pet	1.20	chosen...before the **creation** of the **world**
2 Pet	3.4	it was since the **creation** of the **world**!
Rev	13.8	before the **creation** of the **world**
	17.8	before the **creation** of the **world**

CREATURES

Ezek	9.3	—	11.22	x21
Ezek	1.5 – 23			x17
Rev	4.6	—	8.9	x15
1 Kgs	6.23	—	8.6	x9
Ex	25.18	—	26.31	x5
Ex	36.8	—	37.9	x4
Ezek	41.18 – 25			x4
2 Chr	3.7 – 14			x3
Is	6.2 – 6			x3
Rev	14.3	—	16.3	x3

Elders

Rev	5.6	the four living **creatures** and the **elders**.
	5.8	**creatures** and the twenty-four **elders**
	5.11	the four living **creatures**, and the **elders**,
	7.11	the **elders**, and...living **creatures**.
	14.3	the four living **creatures**, and the **elders**;
	19.4	**elders** and the four living **creatures**

Human

Ezek	1.5	like four living **creatures** in **human** form,
	1.10	living **creature** had four different faces: a **human** face
	10.8	**creature** had what looked like a **human**

Praise

Ps	103.22	**Praise** the Lord, all his **creatures**
	145.10	All your **creatures**...will **praise** you,
	145.21	let all his **creatures** **praise**
	150.6	**Praise** the Lord, all living **creatures**!
Is	42.10	**praise** him, all **creatures** of the sea!

Throne

1 Sam	4.4	is **enthroned** above the winged **creatures**.
2 Sam	6.2	is **enthroned** above the winged **creatures**.
2 Kgs	19.15	**enthroned** above the winged **creatures**,
1 Chr	13.6	**enthroned** above the winged **creatures**.
Ps	80.1	your **throne** above the winged **creatures**,
	99.1	is **enthroned** above the winged **creatures**
Is	37.16	**enthroned** above the winged **creatures**,
Rev	5.6	**throne**, surrounded by...living **creatures**
	5.11	the **throne**, the four living **creatures**,
	7.11	round the **throne**, the...living **creatures**.
	14.3	the **throne**, the four living **creatures**,

CRIME

Lk	22.37	—	23.39	x6
Deut	24.16	—	25.2	x4
2 Kgs	14.6			x3
2 Chr	25.4			x3
Ecc	8.11 – 12			x3
Acts	24.20	—	25.18	x3

Commit

Mt	27.23	What **crime** has he **committed**?
Mk	15.14	But what **crime** has he **committed**?
Lk	23.22	But what **crime** has he **committed**?
Jn	18.30	if he had not **committed** a **crime**.
Acts	18.14	**crime** or wrong that has been **committed**,

Evil see Sin

Punish

2 Sam	3.39	May the Lord **punish** these **criminals**
Ecc	8.11	Because **crime** is not **punished** quickly
Is	29.21	prevent the **punishment** of **criminals**,
Jer	16.10	**punish** them...They will ask what **crime**
Hos	12.14	their **crimes**. The Lord will **punish** them

Sin, Evil

Job	13.23	What are my **sins**...What **crimes**
Ps	58.2	**evil** you can do, and commit **crimes**
Prov	29.16	**evil** men are in power, **crime** increases
Ecc	8.12	A **sinner** may commit a hundred **crimes**
Is	50.1	because of your **sins**...your **crimes**.
	59.12	our **crimes** against you...Our **sins**
	59.15	**evil** finds himself the victim of **crime**.
Jer	16.10	what **crime**...and what **sin** they have
Amos	5.12	terrible your **sins**...how many **crimes**
Acts	18.14	If this were a matter of some **evil crime**
	25.18	not accuse him of any of the **evil crimes**
1 Tim	1.9	and **criminals**, for the godless and **sinful**,

CROSS

Mk	15.21 – 39			x5
Jn	19.17 – 31			x5
1 Cor	1.13	—	2.2	x4
Gal	5.11	—	6.14	x4
Mt	27.32 – 42			x3
Col	1.20	—	2.15	x3

Jesus, Christ, Death

Mt	27.32	soldiers forced him to carry **Jesus' cross**.
Mk	15.21	soldiers forced him to carry **Jesus' cross**.
	15.39	of the **cross** saw how **Jesus** had **died**.
Jn	19.25	close to **Jesus' cross** were his mother
Acts	10.39	to **death** by nailing him to a **cross**
Rom	6.6	put to **death** with **Christ** on his **cross**,
1 Cor	1.17	**Christ's death** on the **cross** is not robbed
	1.18	about **Christ's death** on the **cross**
	2.2	and especially his **death** on the **cross**
2 Cor	13.4	he was put to **death** on the **cross**
Gal	2.19	put to **death** with **Christ** on his **cross**,
	3.1	the **death** of **Jesus Christ** on the **cross**!
	5.11	my preaching about the **cross** of **Christ**
	6.12	be persecuted for the **cross** of **Christ**.
	6.14	only about the **cross** of our Lord **Jesus**
Eph	2.16	his **death** on the **cross Christ** destroyed
Phil	2.8	to **death** — his **death** on the **cross**.
	3.18	enemies of **Christ's death** on the **cross**.
Col	1.20	Son's sacrificial **death** on the **cross**
	2.15	And on that **cross Christ** freed himself

CROWN

Rev	12.1	—	14.14	x4

Glory

Ps	8.5	you **crowned** him with **glory**
Prov	4.9	She will be your **crowning glory**.
	16.31	grey hair is a **glorious crown**.
Is	28.1	Its **glory** is fading like the **crowns**
	28.5	will be like a **glorious crown** of flowers
Heb	2.7	you **crowned** him with **glory**
	2.9	We see him now **crowned** with **glory**
1 Pet	5.4	you will receive the **glorious crown**

Thorns

Mt	27.29	made a **crown** out of **thorny**
Mk	15.17	made a **crown** out of **thorny** branches,
Jn	19.2	The soldiers made a **crown** out of **thorny** branches
	19.5	**Jesus** came out, wearing the **crown** of **thorns**

CUP

1 Cor	10.16	—	11.29	x8
Gen	44.2 – 17			x6
Jer	25.15 – 28			x4
Ezek	23.31 – 33			x4
Lk	22.17 – 42			x4
Gen	40.11 – 13			x3
Dan	5.2 – 23			x3
Mt	26.27 – 42			x3
Rev	16.19	—	18.6	x3

Anger

Is	51.17	the cup...that the Lord in his anger
	51.22	the cup that I gave you in my anger.
Jer	25.15	is a wine cup filled with my anger.
Rev	14.10	full strength into the cup of his anger!
	16.19	his cup — the wine of his furious anger.

Punish

Is	51.17	You have drunk the cup of punishment
Jer	49.12	to drink from the cup of punishment
Ezek	23.31	give you the same cup of punishment
Obad	.16	have drunk a bitter cup of punishment
Hab	2.16	you drink your own cup of punishment,

Suffer

Mt	20.22	Can you drink the cup of suffering
	26.39	take this cup of suffering from me!
	26.42	cup of suffering cannot be taken away
Mk	10.38	Can you drink the cup of suffering
	14.36	this cup of suffering away from me.
Lk	22.42	this cup of suffering away from me.
Jn	18.11	I will not drink the cup of suffering

CURSE

Deut	27.13 —	30.19	x21
Num	22.6 —	24.10	x14
Job	1.11 —	3.10	x8
2 Sam	16.5 – 13		x7
Prov	26.2 —	30.11	x6
Num	5.18 – 27		x5
Mal	1.14 —	3.9	x5
Gal	3.10 – 13		x5
Gen	3.14 —	5.29	x4
Lev	24.10 – 16		x4
1 Sam	14.24 – 28		x4
Ps	109.17 – 28		x4
Jer	23.10 —	26.6	x4
Gen	27.12 – 29		x3
Deut	11.26 – 29		x3
Neh	13.2 – 25		x3
Jer	44.8 – 22		x3
Jer	48.10 —	49.13	x3
Rev	16.9 – 21		x3

Bitter

Num	5.18	the bitter water that brings a curse.
1 Kgs	2.8	He cursed me bitterly the day I went
Rom	3.14	their speech is filled with bitter curses.

God, Lord

Gen	5.29	ground on which the Lord put a curse,
Lev	24.10	During the quarrel he cursed God,
	24.15	anyone who curses God must suffer
	24.16	who curses the Lord shall be stoned
Num	5.21	may the Lord make your name a curse
	23.8	can I curse what God has not cursed,
	23.27	God will be willing to let you curse
Deut	7.26	because they are under the Lord's curse.
	21.23	hanging on a post brings God's curse
	27.15	God's curse on anyone who makes an
	27.16	God's curse on anyone who dishonours
	27.17	God's curse on anyone who moves a
	27.18	God's curse on anyone who leads a
	27.19	God's curse on anyone who deprives
	27.20	God's curse on anyone who disgraces
	27.21	God's curse on anyone who has sexual
	27.22	God's curse on anyone who has
	27.23	God's curse on anyone who has
	27.24	God's curse on anyone who secretly
	27.25	God's curse on anyone who accepts
	27.26	God's curse on anyone who does not
	28.16	The Lord will curse your towns
	28.17	The Lord will curse your corn crops
	28.18	The Lord will curse you
	28.19	The Lord will curse everything you do.

Deut	30.19	between God's blessing and God's curse,
Josh	6.26	will be under the Lord's curse.
1 Sam	26.19	may the Lord's curse fall on them.
2 Sam	16.10	curses me because the Lord told him to,
	16.11	The Lord told him to curse;
	19.21	he cursed the one whom the Lord chose
1 Kgs	21.10	accuse him to his face of cursing God
	21.13	publicly accused him of cursing God
2 Kgs	2.24	cursed them in the name of the Lord.
Neh	13.2	God turned the curse into a blessing.
Job	2.9	Why don't you curse God and die?
	3.2	God, put a curse on the day I was
	24.18	the land he owns is under God's curse;
Ps	10.3	greedy man curses and rejects the Lord.
Prov	3.33	Lord puts a curse on the homes of
	29.24	and God will curse him if he doesn't.
Is	8.21	they will curse their king and their God.
	24.6	God has pronounced a curse on the
Jer	11.3	God of Israel, have placed a curse on
	15.11	Lord, may all their curses come true
	23.10	Because of the Lord's curse
	48.10	(Curse the man who does not do the Lord's work
Zech	5.4	The Lord...will send this curse out,
Mt	25.41	you that are under God's curse!
Jn	7.49	so they are under God's curse!
Rom	9.3	that I myself were under God's curse
Gal	3.10	book of the Law is under God's curse!
	3.13	hanged on a tree is under God's curse.
Heb	6.8	it is in danger of being cursed by God
2 Pet	2.14	They are under God's curse!
Rev	13.6	It began to curse God,
	16.9	and they cursed the name of God,
	16.11	and they cursed the God of heaven
	16.21	cursed God on account of the plague
	22.3	Nothing that is under God's curse

Jesus, Lord

Mk	11.21	Jesus, "Look...the fig-tree you cursed
1 Cor	12.3	can say "A curse on Jesus!
	16.22	not love the Lord — a curse on him!
Jas	3.9	thanks to our Lord...and also to curse

DANGER

2 Cor	11.26		x4
Ps	18.4 – 19		x3
Jon	1.4 – 7		x3
Acts	19.27 – 40		x3

Afraid, Fear

Gen	15.1	be afraid...I will shield you from danger
Lev	26.6	afraid...I will get rid of the dangerous
Ps	27.1	from all danger; I will never be afraid.
	49.5	I am not afraid in times of danger
	91.5	You need not fear any dangers at night
Ecc	12.5	afraid...and walking will be dangerous.
Lam	3.47	we live in danger and fear.

Death

2 Sam	22.6	The danger of death was round me,
Ps	18.4	The danger of death was all round me,
	18.5	The danger of death was round me,
	116.3	The danger of death was all round me;
Rom	8.35	hunger or poverty or danger or death?
	8.36	we are in danger of death at all times;
2 Cor	1.10	From such terrible dangers of death
	4.11	we are always in danger of death

Fear see Afraid

DARKNESS

1 Jn	1.5 —	2.11	x6
Job	10.21 —	12.25	x5
Job	17.12 —	19.8	x5
Job	28.3 —	30.30	x5
Joel	2.2 —	3.15	x5

Gen	1.2 - 18			x4
Job	22.11	--	24.17	x4
Job	34.22	-	36.30	x4
Ps	18.9 - 28			x4
Is	58.10	-	60.2	x4
Lk	11.34	-	12.3	x4
Eph	4.18	-	6.12	x4
2 Sam	22.10 - 29			x3
Job	15.22 - 30			x3
Job	38.9 - 19			x3
Ps	88.6 - 18			x3
Ps	139.11 - 12			x3
Song	1.5	-	2.17	x3
Is	5.20 - 30			x3
Is	8.22	-	9.2	x3
Is	49.9	-	50.10	x3
Lam	2.1	-	3.6	x3
Ezek	12.6 - 12			x3
Amos	5.8 - 20			x3
Jn	12.35 - 46			x3
2 Pet	1.19	-	2.17	x3

Death

Job	12.22	He sends light to places dark as death.
Ps	49.19	death, where the darkness lasts for ever.
Lam	3.6	live in the stagnant darkness of death.
Mt	4.16	who live in the dark land of death
Lk	1.79	who live in the dark shadow of death.

Gloom

Job	3.5	it a day of gloom and thick darkness;
	10.21	to a land that is dark and gloomy,
Ps	107.10	were living in gloom and darkness,
	107.14	them out of their gloom and darkness
Joel	2.2	It will be a dark and gloomy day,
Amos	5.20	darkness...it will be a day of gloom.
Zeph	1.15	a day of darkness and gloom,
Heb	12.18	the darkness and the gloom,

Power

Lk	22.53	when the power of darkness rules.
Acts	26.18	darkness to the light and from the power of Satan
Eph	6.12	and cosmic powers of this dark age.
Col	1.13	rescued us from the power of darkness

DAY

Christ see Jesus

God

Rom	2.5	on the Day when God's anger and
	2.16	that Day when God through Jesus
Eph	4.30	the Day will come when God will set
1 Pet	2.12	and so praise God on the Day of his
2 Pet	3.12	wait for the Day of God and do your
Jude	.6	God is keeping them for that great Day
Rev	16.14	the great Day of Almighty God.

Jesus, Christ

1 Cor	1.8	on the Day of our Lord Jesus Christ.
	3.13	seen when the Day of Christ exposes it.
2 Cor	1.13	so that in the Day of our Lord Jesus
Phil	1.6	on the Day of Christ Jesus.
	1.10	blame on the Day of Christ.
	2.16	proud of you on the Day of Christ,
1 Tim	6.14	until the Day when our Lord Jesus
1 Pet	1.7	on the Day when Jesus Christ is

Judgement

Mt	7.22	When Judgement Day comes, many will
	10.15	Judgement Day God will show more
	11.22	Judgement Day God will show more
	11.24	Judgement Day God will show more
	12.36	Judgement Day everyone will have to
	12.41	On Judgement Day the people of
	12.42	On Judgement Day the Queen of Sheba
Lk	10.12	Judgement Day God will show more
	10.14	more mercy on Judgement Day
	11.31	On Judgement Day the Queen of Sheba
	11.32	On Judgement Day the people of
Acts	24.25	and the coming Day of Judgement,
2 Pet	2.4	waiting for the Day of Judgement.
	2.9	for the Day of Judgement,
1 Jn	4.17	have courage on Judgement Day;

Last

Jn	6.39	raise them all to life on the last day.
	6.40	raise them to life on the last day.
	6.44	raise him to life on the last day.
	6.54	raise him to life on the last day.
	11.24	will rise to life on the last day.
	12.48	will be his judge on the last day!
Acts	2.17	This is what I will do in the last days,
2 Tim	3.1	difficult times in the last days.
Heb	1.2	in these last days he has spoken to us
Jas	5.3	piled up riches in these last days.
1 Pet	1.20	revealed in these last days for your
2 Pet	3.3	in these last days some people will
Jude	.18	When the last days come, people will

Lord

see also **Jesus**

Is	13.6	The day of the Lord is near, the day
	13.9	The day of the Lord is coming
Ezek	13.5	on the day of the Lord.
Joel	1.15	The day of the Lord is near;
	2.1	The day of the Lord is coming soon.
	2.11	How terrible is the day of the Lord!
	2.31	the great and terrible day of the Lord
	3.14	the day of the Lord will soon come.
Amos	5.18	you who long for the day of the Lord!
	5.20	The day of the Lord will bring darkness
Zeph	1.14	The great day of the Lord is near
Mal	4.5	the great and terrible day of the Lord
Acts	2.20	the great and glorious Day of the Lord
1 Cor	5.5	may be saved in the Day of the Lord.
1 Thes	4.15	alive on the day the Lord comes
	5.2	the Day of the Lord will come as a
2 Thes	2.2	claim that the Day of the Lord has
2 Tim	1.18	the Lord grant him his mercy on that Day!
Heb	10.25	the Day of the Lord is coming nearer.
Jas	5.8	the day of the Lord's coming is near.
2 Pet	3.10	the Day of the Lord will come like a
Rev	1.10	On the Lord's day the Spirit took

DEAD

see also **DEATH**

1 Cor	15.12 - 51			x10
Lev	11.8 - 40			x9
2 Sam	1.5	-	3.35	x8
1 Kgs	1.5	-	3.23	x8
Rev	20.5 - 14			x8
2 Sam	12.18	-	14.14	x7
Lk	7.12	-	10.30	x7
Num	35.12 - 27			x6
Mk	11.20	-	12.27	x6
Lev	19.28	-	21.11	x5
Mt	22.24 - 32			x5
Deut	25.5	-	26.14	x4
1 Sam	17.51	-	20.13	x4
1 Kgs	19.2	-	21.15	x4
Ecc	9.4	-	11.8	x4
Mt	8.22	-	11.5	x4
Lk	20.28 - 38			x4
Gen	42.13 - 38			x3
Ex	21.34 - 36			x3
Judg	3.25	-	5.27	x3

1 Sam	24.14	—	25.34	x3
2 Sam	18.20	—	19.13	x3
Amos	4.10	—	6.10	x3
Jon	4.3 – 8			x3
Jn	5.21 – 28			x3
Acts	4.2	—	5.10	x3
Heb	11.4 – 35			x3
Jas	2.17 – 26			x3
Rev	1.17 – 18			x3

Alive

2 Sam	19.6	**alive** today and all of us were **dead**.
Jon	4.3	I am better off **dead** than **alive**.
	4.8	I am better off **dead** than **alive**,
Lk	15.24	of mine was **dead**, but now he is **alive**;
	15.32	brother was **dead**, but now he is **alive**;
	20.38	of the **dead**, for to him all are **alive**.
	24.5	among the **dead** for one who is **alive**?
1 Thes	5.10	we are **alive** or **dead** when he comes.
Rev	1.18	was **dead**, but now I am **alive** for ever
	3.1	being **alive**, even though you are **dead**!

God, Lord

2 Sam	14.14	**God** does not bring the **dead** back to
Ps	115.17	The **Lord** is not praised by the **dead**,
Is	26.19	the **Lord** will revive those who have long been **dead**.
Mt	22.32	the **God** of the living, not of the **dead**.
Mk	12.27	the **God** of the living, not of the **dead**.
Lk	20.38	the **God** of the living, not of the **dead**,
Acts	26.8	to believe that **God** raises the **dead**?·
Rom	4.17	**God** who brings the **dead** to life
2 Cor	1.9	but only on **God**, who raises the **dead**.

Jesus, Lord

Mk	15.44	to hear that **Jesus** was already **dead**.
Jn	19.33	came to **Jesus**...he was already **dead**,
Rom	14.9	the **Lord** of the living and of the **dead**.
2 Tim	4.1	Christ **Jesus**, who will judge the living and the **dead**,

Life

2 Sam	14.14	does not bring the **dead** back to **life**,
1 Kgs	19.4	away my **life**; I might as well be **dead**!
2 Kgs	8.5	had brought a **dead** person back to **life**,
Ezek	32.24	In **life** they spread terror, but now they lie **dead**
	32.25	In **life** they spread terror, but now they lie **dead**
	37.9	**dead** bodies...bring them back to **life**.
Mt	10.8	bring the **dead** back to **life**,
	11.5	the **dead** are brought back to **life**,
	22.28	on the day when the **dead** rise to **life**,
	22.30	For when the **dead** rise to **life**
	22.31	as for the **dead** rising to **life**:
Mk	12.23	all the **dead** rise to **life**
	12.25	For when the **dead** rise to **life**,
Lk	7.22	the **dead** are raised to **life**,
	20.33	on the day when the **dead** rise to **life**,
	20.37	proves that the **dead** are raised to **life**.
Jn	5.21	raises the **dead** and gives them **life**,
Acts	4.2	proved that the **dead** will rise to **life**.
	23.6	I have that the **dead** will rise to **life**!
	24.21	that the **dead** will rise to **life**.
Rom	4.17	The God who brings the **dead** to **life**
	11.15	It will be **life** for the **dead**!
1 Cor	15.12	that the **dead** will not be raised to **life**?
	15.15	that the **dead** are not raised to **life**,
	15.29	that the **dead** are not raised to **life**,
	15.32	if the **dead** are not raised to **life**,
	15.35	How can the **dead** be raised to **life**?
	15.42	when the **dead** are raised to **life**
Eph	2.5	spiritually **dead**...he brought us to **life**
Heb	11.35	their **dead** relatives raised back to **life**.
Rev	20.5	rest of the **dead** did not come to **life**

Lord see God, Jesus

Sin

Rom	6.11	as **dead**, so far as **sin** is concerned,
	7.8	Apart from law, **sin** is a **dead** thing.
Eph	2.1	**dead** because of your disobedience and **sins**.
Col	2.13	spiritually **dead** because of your **sins**
Heb	3.17	people who **sinned**, who fell down **dead**

DEATH

see also **DEAD**

Rom	5.9	—	8.38	x23
Lev	20.9	—	22.8	x8
Jer	50.35	—	51.50	x8
1 Cor	15.20 – 56			x8
Lam	1.20	—	4.13	x7
Prov	14.12	—	17.22	x6
2 Cor	3.6	—	5.14	x6
Rev	20.6	—	21.8	x6
Num	35.24 – 33			x5
Deut	30.15	—	32.25	x5
2 Kgs	13.24	—	15.18	x5
1 Jn	5.6 – 17			x5
Gen	25.11	—	27.41	x4
2 Sam	12.10	—	15.21	x4
Job	30.23	—	31.30	x4
Ecc	7.2	—	8.8	x4
Ezek	33.4 – 8			x4
1 Cor	1.17	—	3.22	x4
Phil	1.21	—	3.18	x4
Heb	2.9 – 15			x4
Heb	9.15	—	11.28	x4
Rev	1.5	—	2.11	x4
Ps	49.14 – 19			x3
Mt	27.4 – 25			x3
Jn	11.4	—	12.33	x3
Eph	1.7	—	2.16	x3

Alive

Josh	10.28	the city to **death**; no one was left **alive**;
	11.11	there to **death**; no one was left **alive**,
	11.14	person to **death**; no one was left **alive**.
Lam	4.9	**death**, with no food to keep them **alive**.
Heb	9.17	is **alive**; it comes...only after his **death**.
1 Pet	3.18	put to **death** physically, but made **alive**

Crime see Sin

Deserve

Hos	12.14	they **deserve death** for their crimes.
Lk	23.15	this man has done to **deserve death**.
	23.22	anything he has done to **deserve death**!
Acts	25.11	for which I **deserve** the **death** penalty,
	25.25	which he **deserved** the **death** sentence.
Rom	1.32	who live in this way **deserve death**.

Free see Rescue

Hurt

1 Cor	15.55	Where, **Death**, is your power to **hurt**?
	15.56	**Death** gets its power to **hurt** from sin
Rev	2.11	will not be **hurt** by the second **death**.

Punish, Sentence

Gen	9.5	I will **punish** with **death** any animal
Lev	19.20	will be **punished** but not put to **death**,
Num	16.29	natural **death** without some **punishment**
Ezra	7.26	he is to be **punished** promptly: by **death**
Job	31.11	wickedness should be **punished** by **death**.
	31.28	Such a sin should be **punished** by **death**;
Ps	94.21	and **sentence** the innocent to **death**.
Jer	26.11	deserves to be **sentenced** to **death**
Ezek	11.9	I have **sentenced** you to **death**,
	16.38	and fury I will **punish** you with **death**.
Hos	12.14	**death**...The Lord will **punish** them
Jon	1.14	don't **punish** us with **death**

Mt	24.9	to be **punished** and be put to **death**.
Acts	13.28	to pass the **death sentence** on him,

Rescue, Free, Save

2 Chr	22.11	she **saved** him from **death** at the hands
Job	5.15	But God **saves** the poor from **death**;
	33.18	he **saves** them from **death** itself.
Ps	6.4	in your mercy **rescue** me from **death**.
	9.13	**Rescue** me from **death**, O Lord,
	33.19	He **saves** them from **death**;
	49.12	greatness cannot **save** him from **death**;
	49.15	will **save** me from the power of **death**.
	49.20	greatness cannot **save** him from **death**;
	56.13	because you have **rescued** me from **death**
	68.20	who **rescues** us from **death**.
	86.2	**Save** me from **death**, because I am loyal
	116.8	The Lord **saved** me from **death**;
	116.16	You have **saved** me from **death**.
Prov	11.4	**death**, but honesty can **save** your life.
Lk	23.22	deserve **death**! I will...set him **free**.
Acts	2.24	raised him from **death**, setting him **free**
Rom	8.2	me **free** from the law of sin and **death**.
2 Cor	1.10	terrible dangers of **death** he **saved** us,
Eph	1.7	**death** of Christ are set **free**,
Heb	5.7	who could **save** him from **death**.
	9.15	a **death** which sets people **free**
Jas	5.20	will **save** that sinner's soul from **death**
Rev	1.5	by his sacrificial **death** he has **freed** us

Sacrifice

Is	53.10	**death** was a **sacrifice** to bring
Acts	20.28	through the **sacrificial death** of his Son.
Rom	3.25	by his **sacrificial death** we are now become
	5.9	**sacrificial death** we are now put right
Eph	1.7	For by the **sacrificial death** of Christ
	2.13	by the **sacrificial death** of Christ.
Col	1.20	peace through his Son's **sacrificial death**
Heb	13.20	as the result of his **sacrificial death**,
Rev	1.5	by his **sacrificial death** he has freed us
	5.9	**sacrificial death** you bought for God

Save see **Rescue**

Sentence see **Punish**

Sin, Crime, Wicked

Num	16.38	who were put to **death** for their **sin**,
Deut	21.22	man has been put to **death** for a **crime**
	22.26	not committed a **sin** worthy of **death**.
	24.16	are not to be put to **death** for **crimes**
1 Kgs	17.18	of my **sins** and so cause my son's **death**?
2 Kgs	14.6	are not to be put to **death** for **crimes**
2 Chr	25.4	are not to be put to **death** for **crimes**
Job	31.11	**wickedness** should be punished by **death**.
	31.28	Such a **sin** should be punished by **death**;
	31.30	never **sinned** by praying for their **death**.
Ps	9.17	**Death** is the destiny of all the **wicked**,
Prov	12.28	**wickedness** is the road to **death**.
	17.11	**Death** will come...to **wicked** people
Is	53.8	He was put to **death** for the **sins**
Mt	27.4	I have **sinned** by betraying an innocent man to **death**!
Lk	23.32	**criminals**...led out to be put to **death**
Rom	5.12	and his **sin** brought **death** with it.
	5.17	the **sin** of one man **death** began to rule
	5.21	just as **sin** ruled by means of **death**,
	6.16	either of **sin**, which results in **death**,
	6.23	For **sin** pays its wage — **death**
	7.13	caused my **death**...It was **sin** that did it;
	8.2	free from the law of **sin** and **death**.
	8.13	you put to **death** your **sinful** actions,
1 Cor	15.56	**Death** gets its power to hurt from **sin**
Jas	1.15	and **sin**...gives birth to **death**.
1 Jn	5.16	a **sin** that does not lead to **death**
	5.17	is **sin** which does not lead to **death**.
Rev	1.5	his...**death** he has freed us from our **sins**

DECEIVE

	Rev	18.23	—	20.10	x5
	Mt	24.4 – 24			x4
	Gen	31.20 – 27			x3
	1 Kgs	22.20 – 22			x3
	2 Chr	18.19 – 21			x3
	Dan	11.23 – 32			x3
	Mk	13.5 – 22			x3
	Eph	4.14	—	5.6	x3
	Jas	1.16 – 26			x3
	1 Jn	1.8	—	3.7	x3

Sin, Evil, Wicked

Num	25.18	**evil** they did to you when they **deceived**
Deut	32.5	a **sinful** and **deceitful** nation.
Job	15.35	**evil**; their hearts are...full of **deceit**.
	31.5	**wickedly** and never tried to **deceive**
Ps	7.14	think up **evil**; they...practise **deception**.
Prov	12.5	the **wicked** only want to **deceive** you.
Lam	2.14	**deceived** you by never exposing your **sin**.
Hos	7.3	**deceive** the king...by their **evil** plots.
	10.2	**deceitful** must now suffer for their **sins**.
Mk	7.22	and do all sorts of **evil** things; **deceit**,
Rom	3.13	full of deadly **deceit**; **wicked** lies roll
2 Thes	2.10	and use every kind of **wicked deceit**
Heb	3.13	that none of you be **deceived** by **sin**
1 Jn	1.8	we have no **sin**, we **deceive** ourselves

DEDICATE

	Ex	28.3	—	31.15	x15
	Num	5.25	—	8.21	x14
	Lev	27.14 – 29			x10
	Ex	38.24	—	40.11	x7
	Lev	8.9 – 26			x6
	1 Chr	26.20 – 28			x4
	2 Chr	29.19	—	31.6	x4
	Lev	21.11	—	22.3	x3
	1 Sam	1.11	—	2.20	x3
	Jn	17.17 – 19			x3

God see **Lord**

Holy, Pure, Sacred

Ex	16.23	a **holy** day of rest, **dedicated** to him.
	29.6	the **sacred** sign of **dedication**
	30.10	to be completely **holy**, **dedicated** to me,
	30.37	it as a **holy** thing **dedicated** to me.
	35.2	**sacred**, a solemn day of rest **dedicated**
	38.24	**dedicated** to the Lord for the **sacred**
	39.30	the **sacred** sign of **dedication**,
Lev	8.9	the **sacred** sign of **dedication**,
	8.15	this way he **dedicated** it and **purified** it.
	22.2	**sacred** offerings that the people...**dedicate**
Num	8.15	have **purified** and **dedicated** the Levites,
Dan	9.24	and the **holy** Temple will be **rededicated**
1 Cor	6.11	**purified** from sin...**dedicated** to God;
Eph	2.21	a **sacred** temple **dedicated** to the Lord.
2 Pet	3.11	Your lives should be **holy** and **dedicated**

Lord, God

Gen	28.18	olive-oil on it to **dedicate** it to **God**.
Ex	12.42	this same night is **dedicated** to the **Lord**
	16.25	a day of rest **dedicated** to the **Lord**,
	28.36	engrave on it '**Dedicated** to the **Lord**.
	29.6	engraved 'Dedicated to the **Lord**.
	30.10	**dedicated** to me, the **Lord**.
	35.2	day of rest **dedicated** to me, the **Lord**.
	35.22	and **dedicated** them to the **Lord**.
	38.24	that had been **dedicated** to the **Lord**
	38.29	bronze which was **dedicated** to the **Lord**
	39.30	engraved on it "**Dedicated** to the **Lord**.
Lev	8.9	sign of **dedication**, just as the **Lord**
	8.10	this way he **dedicated** it all to the **Lord**.
	8.11	in order to **dedicate** them to the **Lord**.
	8.26	unleavened bread **dedicated** to the **Lord**,

Lev	22.2	Israel **dedicate** to me. I am the **Lord**.
	25.4	a year **dedicated** to the **Lord**.
	27.14	someone **dedicates** his house to the **Lord**
	27.16	**dedicates** part of his land to the **Lord**,
	27.22	If a man **dedicates** to the **Lord** a field
	27.26	to the **Lord**, so no one may **dedicate** it
	27.28	unconditionally **dedicated** to the **Lord**,
Num	5.25	hold it out in **dedication** to the **Lord**,
	6.2	and **dedicates** himself to the **Lord**
	6.5	time that he is **dedicated** to the **Lord**
	6.6	is the sign of his **dedication** to **God**,
	6.12	and **rededicate** to the **Lord** his time
	8.21	and Aaron **dedicated** them...to the **Lord**.
Judg	13.5	will be **dedicated** to **God** as a Nazirite.
	13.7	the boy is to be **dedicated** to **God**
	16.17	been **dedicated** to **God** as a Nazirite
	17.3	**dedicating** the silver to the **Lord**.
1 Sam	1.28	So I am **dedicating** him to the **Lord**
	7.3	**Dedicate** yourselves completely to the **Lord**
1 Kgs	7.51	father David had **dedicated** to the **Lord**
	15.15	objects his father had **dedicated** to **God**,
2 Kgs	12.18	and Ahaziah had **dedicated** to the **Lord**
	16.14	The bronze altar **dedicated** to the **Lord**
1 Chr	26.20	storerooms for gifts **dedicated** to **God**.
	26.26	gifts **dedicated** to **God** by King David,
	28.12	and the gifts **dedicated** to the **Lord**.
	29.21	**dedicating** them to the **Lord**,
2 Chr	5.1	father David had **dedicated** to the **Lord**
	15.18	his father Abijah had **dedicated** to **God**,
	29.19	to **God**, and we have **rededicated** it.
	30.15	they **dedicated** themselves to the **Lord**,
	30.17	and **dedicated** the lambs to the **Lord**.
	31.6	they **dedicated** to the **Lord** their **God**.
	35.3	who were **dedicated** to the **Lord**:
Neh	10.36	**dedicate** him to **God**.
Is	23.18	commerce will be **dedicated** to the **Lord**.
Jer	4.4	**Lord**, and **dedicate** yourselves to me,
Ezek	45.1	one part is to be **dedicated** to the **Lord**.
	48.9	is to be **dedicated** to the **Lord**.
	48.14	The area **dedicated** to the **Lord**
Zech	14.20	with the words "**Dedicated** to the **Lord**"
Lk	2.23	male is to be **dedicated** to the **Lord**.
Acts	22.3	as **dedicated** to **God** as are all of you
Rom	12.1	as a living sacrifice to **God**, **dedicated**
	15.16	acceptable to **God**, **dedicated** to him
1 Cor	6.11	you have been **dedicated** to **God**;
	7.34	with the **Lord's** work, because she wants to be **dedicated**
Eph	2.21	a sacred temple **dedicated** to the **Lord**.
	5.26	did this to **dedicate** the church to **God**
1 Tim	2.8	men who are **dedicated** to **God**
	5.22	to **dedicate** him to the **Lord's** service.
2 Pet	3.11	should be holy and **dedicated** to **God**,

Nazirite

Num	6.2	vow to become a **Nazirite** and **dedicates**
	6.12	**rededicate**...his time as a **Nazirite**.
Judg	13.5	will be **dedicated** to **God** as a **Nazirite**.
	13.7	**dedicated** to **God** as a **Nazirite**
	16.17	been **dedicated** to **God** as a **Nazirite**

Pure see Holy

Sacred see Holy

DEFEND

	Acts	24.10	—	26.24	x6
	2 Sam	22.3	—	23.12	x5
	Ps	18.1 – 46			x5
	Deut	32.4	—	33.29	x3
	Judg	6.31 – 32			x3
	Ps	28.1 – 8			x3
	Ps	91.2 – 9			x3
	Is	1.8 – 23			x3

| | Is | 49.4 | — | 51.22 | x3 |
| | Nah | 2.1 | — | 3.13 | x3 |

Cause

Ps	35.23	**defend** me...and plead my **cause**.
	43.1	**defend** my **cause** against the ungodly;
	74.22	and **defend** your **cause**!
	119.154	**Defend** my **cause**, and set me free;
	140.12	you **defend** the **cause** of the poor
Is	49.4	can trust the **Lord** to **defend** my **cause**;

God, Lord

Ex	15.2	The **Lord** is my strong **defender**;
Deut	32.4	The **Lord** is your mighty **defender**,
	33.27	**God** has always been your **defender**,
1 Sam	2.25	**God** can **defend** him; but who can **defend** a man
2 Sam	22.3	**God** alone is our **defence**.
	22.47	The **Lord** lives! Praise my **defender**!
Ps	4.1	O **God**, my **defender**!
	18.1	**Lord**! You are my **defender**.
	18.31	**Lord** alone is **God**; **God** alone is our **defence**.
	18.46	my **defender**...the **God** who saves me.
	28.1	O **Lord**, my **defender**, I call to you.
	28.7	The **Lord** protects and **defends** me;
	28.8	The **Lord** protects...he **defends** and saves
	35.23	**defend** me; rise up, my **God**, and plead
	42.9	To **God**, my **defender**, I say,
	43.1	**God**, declare me innocent, and **defend**
	54.4	The **Lord** is my **defender**.
	55.22	with the **Lord**, and he will **defend** you;
	59.17	my **defender**. My Refuge is **God**,
	74.22	**God**, and **defend** your **cause**!
	81.1	Shout for joy to **God** our **defender**!
	91.2	You are my **defender**...You are my **God**;
	91.9	You have made the **Lord** your **defender**,
	94.22	**Lord** **defends** me; my **God** protects me.
	135.14	The **Lord** will **defend** his people;
	140.7	My Sovereign **Lord**, my strong **defender**,
	140.12	**Lord**, I know that you **defend** the cause
Prov	23.11	The **Lord** is their powerful **defender**,
Is	26.1	**God** himself **defends** its walls!
	30.29	the **Lord**, the **defender** of Israel.
	31.5	**Lord**...will protect Jerusalem and **defend**
	49.4	can trust the **Lord** to **defend** my cause;
	50.9	Sovereign **Lord** himself **defends** me
	51.22	**Lord** your **God** **defends** you and says,
Ezek	13.5	be **defended**...on the day of the **Lord**.
Phil	1.16	**God** has given me the work of **defending**

Poor, Rights

Ps	82.3	**Defend** the **rights** of the **poor**
	109.31	because he **defends** the **poor** man
	140.12	that you **defend** the cause of the **poor**
Prov	29.14	If a king **defends** the **rights** of the **poor**
Is	1.17	orphans their **rights**, and **defend** widows.
	11.4	he will judge the **poor** fairly and **defend**

DEFILE

	Ezek	22.3	—	24.13	x7
	Num	5.3	—	6.12	x5
	Jer	2.7	—	3.9	x5
	Ezek	36.17	—	37.23	x5
	Ezek	20.18 – 43			x4
	Num	35.33 – 34			x3
	Hag	2.13 – 14			x3
	Acts	10.14	—	11.8	x3

Idols

2 Chr	36.14	in worshipping **idols**, and so they **defiled**
Jer	7.30	**idols**...in my Temple and have **defiled**
	16.18	they have **defiled** my land with **idols**
Ezek	20.18	or **defile** yourselves with their **idols**.
	20.31	and **defile** yourselves with the same **idols**
	22.3	**defiled** yourself by worshipping **idols**,

Ezek	22.4	are **defiled** by the **idols** you made,
	23.7	**defile** herself by worshipping...**idols**.
	23.30	and **defiled** yourself with their **idols**.
	36.18	the **idols** by which they had **defiled** it.
	36.25	**idols** and everything else that has **defiled**
	37.23	**defile** themselves with disgusting **idols**
Hos	6.10	**defiled** themselves by worshipping **idols**.

Sin

Jer	16.18	their **sin** and wickedness, because they have **defiled** my land
Ezek	14.11	me and **defiling** themselves by their **sins**.

Unclean

Lev	15.31	**uncleanness**, so...they would not **defile**
	21.11	ritually **unclean** nor is he to **defile**
Num	5.3	**unclean** people out, so that they will not **defile** the camp,
Acts	10.14	anything ritually **unclean** or **defiled**.
	10.28	any person ritually **unclean** or **defiled**.
	11.8	No ritually **unclean** or **defiled** food

DEFY

	1 Sam	17.26 − 45	x3
	Ezek	20.8 − 21	x3

God, Lord

1 Sam	17.26	to **defy** the army of the living **God**?
	17.36	has **defied** the army of the living **God**.
	17.45	the **God**...which you have **defied**.
2 Chr	26.16	He **defied** the **Lord** his **God**
	28.19	of his people and had **defied** the **Lord**,
	32.17	**defied** the **Lord**, the **God** of Israel.
Job	15.25	who shakes his fist at **God** and **defies**
Ps	9.19	**Lord**! Do not let men **defy** you!

DEMAND

	1 Kgs	20.2 − 9	x4

God

Deut	10.12	the Lord your **God demands** of you:
Ezra	10.3	We will do what **God's Law demands**.
Job	27.8	the hour when **God demands** their life?
Ps	78.18	**God** to the test by **demanding** the food
Lk	7.29	obeyed **God's** righteous **demands**
Rom	8.4	**God** did this so that the righteous **demands** of the Law

DEMONS

	Lk	7.33 − 11.20	x18
	Mt	7.22 − 12.28	x15
	Mk	5.15 − 7.30	x7
	Mk	1.32 − 39	x4
	Lk	4.33 − 41	x4
	Jn	7.20 − 8.52	x4
	1 Cor	10.20 − 21	x4
	Jn	10.20 − 21	x3

Power, Name

Mt	7.22	your **name** we drove out many **demons**
	9.34	the **power** to drive out **demons**.
	12.27	drive out **demons** because Beelzebul gives me the **power**
	12.28	me the **power** to drive out **demons**,
Mk	3.22	of the **demons** who gives him the **power**
	9.38	was driving out **demons** in your **name**,
	16.17	they will drive out **demons** in my **name**;
Lk	9.1	**power**...to drive out all **demons**
	9.49	man driving out **demons** in your **name**,
	11.15	the **demons**, who gives him the **power**
	11.18	drive out **demons** because Beelzebul gives me the **power**
	11.20	**God's power** that I drive out **demons**,

Spirits

Jer	50.39	be haunted by **demons** and evil **spirits**,

Mt	8.16	who had **demons** in them. Jesus drove out the evil **spirits**
Lk	4.33	who had the **spirit** of an evil **demon**
1 Tim	4.1	obey lying **spirits** and follow...**demons**.
Rev	16.14	They are the **spirits** of **demons**
	18.2	haunted by **demons** and unclean **spirits**;

DEPEND

	Ps	62.1 − 10	x4
	Gal	3.10 − 18	x3

God, Lord

2 Sam	22.31	This **God** — how...**dependable** his words!
2 Chr	20.15	battle **depends** on **God**, not on you.
Ps	18.30	This **God** — how...**dependable** his words!
	52.7	is a man who did not **depend** on **God**
	62.1	for **God** to save me; I **depend** on him
	62.5	I **depend** on **God** alone;
	62.7	salvation and honour **depend** on **God**;
	118.8	in the **Lord** than to **depend** on man.
	118.9	to trust in the **Lord** than to **depend**
	146.5	and who **depends** on the **Lord** his **God**,
Is	48.2	and that you **depend** on Israel's **God**,
Mic	5.7	They will **depend** on **God**, not man.
Rom	2.17	you **depend** on the Law and boast about **God**;
Gal	3.18	For if **God's** gift **depends** on the Law

Jesus

Heb	12.2	on **Jesus**, on whom our faith **depends**

Lord see **God**

DESIRE

	Rom	6.12 − 7.18	x6
	Gal	5.13 − 6.8	x4
	Phil	1.20 − 3.19	x4
	Ezra	7.13 − 18	x3
	1 Tim	5.11 − 6.9	x3
	Jas	4.1 − 5	x3
	Jude	.16 − 19	x3

Evil see **Sin**

God, Lord

Ps	7.9	a righteous **God** and judge our...**desires**.
	26.2	**Lord**; judge my **desires** and thoughts.
	37.4	in the **Lord**, and he will give you your heart's **desire**.
Jer	24.7	the **desire** to know that I am the **Lord**.
Mt	5.6	**desire** is to do what **God** requires;
1 Pet	4.2	**God's** will and not by human **desires**.

Human, Natural

Prov	27.20	**Human desires** are like the world of the
Rom	6.12	obey the **desires** of your **natural** self.
	7.5	**human nature**, the sinful **desires** stirred
	7.18	**human nature**. For...though the **desire**
	13.14	sinful **nature** and satisfying its **desires**.
Gal	5.16	satisfy the **desires** of the **human nature**.
	5.24	**human nature** with all its...**desires**.
	6.8	sows in the field of his **natural desires**,
Eph	2.3	lived according to our **natural desires**,
1 Pet	4.2	**God's** will and not by **human desires**.
Jude	.19	controlled by their **natural desires**,

Lord see **God**

Natural see **Human**

Sin, Evil

Ps	7.9	and **desires**. Stop the wickedness of **evil**
	10.3	wicked man is proud of his **evil desires**;
	17.3	and found no **evil desire** in me.
Rom	7.5	the **sinful desires** stirred up by the Law
	7.8	**sin** found its chance to stir up all kinds of selfish **desires**
	13.14	**sinful** nature and satisfying its **desires**.

1 Cor	10.6	to warn us not to **desire evil** things,
2 Tim	3.6	**sins** and driven by all kinds of **desires**,
Jas	1.14	and trapped by his own **evil desire**.
	1.15	**desire** conceives and gives birth to **sin**;
1 Jn	2.16	the world — what the **sinful** self **desires**,
Jude	.16	they follow their own **evil desires**;

DESTROY

Jer	46.8	—	51.64	x57
Deut	2.12	—	10.10	x29
Jer	4.6	—	13.9	x26
Deut	28.20	—	33.27	x17
Gen	18.23	—	20.4	x15
Zeph	1.2	—	3.8	x14
2 Pet	1.4	—	3.16	x14
Is	9.5	—	10.25	x11
Is	28.17	—	34.5	x11
Dan	6.26	—	9.26	x10
Hos	10.2	—	13.14	x10
Josh	6.17	—	7.13	x9
Jer	25.9	—	27.10	x9
Jer	42.10	—	44.29	x9
Lam	1.15	—	3.48	x9
Mic	4.11	—	6.14	x9
Gen	6.13	—	9.15	x8
Is	13.6	—	16.8	x8
Nah	1.8	—	3.19	x8
Zech	11.2	—	12.9	x8
Lev	26.22 – 44			x6
1 Sam	15.3 – 18			x4
Is	23.1 – 14			x4
Ezek	30.6 – 15			x4
Ezek	32.7 – 15			x4
Num	16.21 – 45			x3
Judg	20.34 – 42			x3
Neh	2.3 – 17			x3
Ps	18.4 – 40			x3
Ps	73.18 – 27			x3
Ps	106.23 – 36			x3
Ps	118.10 – 12			x3
Dan	11.17 – 30			x3
Obad	.8 – 18			x3
Jude	.5 – 11			x3
Rev	11.5 – 18			x3

Abandon, Desolate

Lev	26.44	completely **abandon** or **destroy** them.
Deut	4.31	will not **abandon** you or **destroy** you,
	31.17	**abandon** them...they will be **destroyed**.
2 Kgs	19.17	**destroyed** many nations, made their lands **desolate**,
Ps	73.27	**abandon** you...perish; you will **destroy**
Is	37.18	**destroyed** many nations, made their lands **desolate**,
Ezek	32.15	Egypt a **desolate** waste and **destroy**
Hos	11.8	I **abandon** you? Could I ever **destroy**
Nah	2.10	Nineveh is **destroyed**, deserted, **desolate**!

Afraid, Terrified

Gen	32.11	**afraid** that he is coming to...**destroy** us
Ps	90.7	**destroyed** by your anger; we are **terrified**
Mt	10.28	be **afraid** of God, who can **destroy**

Altars

Ex	34.13	tear down their **altars**, **destroy**
2 Kgs	18.22	and **altars** that Hezekiah **destroyed**,
	21.3	**destroyed**; he built **altars** for the
2 Chr	31.1	and **destroyed** the **altars**
	32.12	**destroyed** the Lord's shrines and **altars**
	33.3	Hezekiah had **destroyed**. He built **altars**
Is	36.7	**altars** that Hezekiah **destroyed**
Ezek	6.6	will be **destroyed**, so that all their **altars**
Hos	10.2	will break down their **altars** and **destroy**
Amos	3.14	I will **destroy** the **altars** of Bethel.

Anger, Fury

Ex	32.10	**angry**...and I am going to **destroy** them.
	32.12	and **destroy** them...Stop being **angry**;
Num	25.11	did not **destroy** them in my **anger**.
Deut	7.4	will be **angry** with you and **destroy** you
	9.8	**angry** — **angry** enough to **destroy** you.
	9.19	**anger**...was **furious** enough to **destroy**
	29.23	**destroyed** when he was **furiously angry**.
2 Chr	12.12	Lord's **anger** did not completely **destroy**
Ezra	9.14	be so **angry** that you will **destroy** us
Job	4.9	God **destroys** them in his **anger**.
	9.5	and in **anger** he **destroys** them.
	20.28	**destroyed** in the flood of God's **anger**.
Ps	59.13	**destroy** them in your **anger**;
	78.38	**destroy** them...he held back his **anger**
	80.16	at them in **anger** and **destroy** them!
	88.16	**anger** crushes me; your...attacks **destroy**
	90.7	We are **destroyed** by your **anger**;
	106.23	his **anger** from **destroying** them.
Prov	27.4	**Anger** is cruel and **destructive**
Ecc	5.6	**angry** with you? Why let him **destroy**
Is	51.13	**fury** of those...ready to **destroy** you?
Jer	25.36	his **anger** has **destroyed** your nation
	49.37	my great **anger** I will **destroy** the people
Ezek	20.13	**anger** there in the desert and **destroy**
	22.30	when my **anger** is about to **destroy** it,
	22.31	**anger** loose on them...I will **destroy**
	30.15	feel my **fury**. I will **destroy** the wealth
	43.8	and so in my **anger** I **destroyed** them.
Hos	11.9	in my **anger**; I will not **destroy** Israel
Zeph	1.18	be **destroyed** by the fire of his **anger**.
	3.8	**anger**. The whole earth will be **destroyed**
Rom	9.22	**anger**, who were doomed to **destruction**.

Beings

Gen	6.17	the earth to **destroy** every living **being**.
	7.4	in order to **destroy** all the living **beings**
	7.23	**destroyed** all living **beings**
	8.21	again will I **destroy** all living **beings**,
	9.11	again will all living **beings** be **destroyed**
	9.15	will never again **destroy** all living **beings**.

Death

Deut	2.34	**destroyed** every town, and put everyone to **death**,
	3.6	**destroyed** all the towns and put to **death**
	5.25	risk **death** again? That...fire will **destroy**
2 Sam	22.5	of **death** were all round me...**destruction**
Job	28.22	Even **death** and **destruction**
Ps	18.4	of **death** was all round me...**destruction**
Is	25.8	The Sovereign Lord will **destroy death**
Jer	50.37	**Destroy** its horses and chariots! **Death**
Hos	13.14	**death**! Bring on your **destruction**,
Amos	9.4	to **death**. I am determined to **destroy**
Nah	1.8	**destroys** his enemies; he sends to their **death** those
1 Cor	10.10	were **destroyed** by the Angel of **Death**.
	15.54	**Death** is **destroyed**; victory is complete!
Eph	2.16	his **death** on the cross Christ **destroyed**
Heb	2.14	his **death** he might **destroy** the Devil,

Defend see Save

Desolate see Abandon

Disaster, Doom

Deut	28.22	**destroy** your crops. These **disasters** will
	31.17	be **destroyed**. Many terrible **disasters**
Prov	24.16	but **disaster destroys** the wicked.
Jer	4.6	is bringing **disaster** and great **destruction**
	6.1	**Disaster** and **destruction** are about
	46.21	**doom** had arrived...their **destruction**.
Mic	2.10	have **doomed** this place to **destruction**.
Rom	9.22	who were **doomed** to **destruction**.

Evil see Sin

Fury see **Anger**

God's People, Religion

Deut	9.26	don't **destroy** your own people,
Ps	78.38	to **his** people. He...did not **destroy** them.
	106.23	said that he would **destroy his** people,
Is	43.28	**destruction** on Israel; I let **my**...**people**
	65.8	Neither will I **destroy** all **my people**
Jer	5.18	I will not completely **destroy my** people.
	15.7	I **destroyed** you, **my** people,
	23.1	who **destroy** and scatter **his** people!
Lam	1.15	to **destroy** my young men. He crushed **my** **people** like grapes
	2.11	grief at the **destruction** of **my** people.
	3.48	tears at the **destruction** of **my** people.
Dan	11.28	to **destroy** the **religion** of God's **people**.
	11.30	to **destroy** the **religion** of God's **people**.
Hos	11.6	It will **destroy my people**
Zech	9.15	protect **his** people, and they will **destroy**
Acts	3.23	from **God's people** and **destroyed**.

Goddess see **Idols**

Gods see **Idols**

Grief see **Mourn**

Idols, Goddess, Gods

Ex	23.24	**Destroy** their **gods**
Num	33.52	**Destroy** all their stone and metal **idols**
2 Chr	34.33	Josiah **destroyed** all the disgusting **idols**
Ps	106.36	**idols**, and this caused their **destruction**.
Is	10.11	have **destroyed** Samaria and all its **idols**
Jer	7.6	other **gods**, for that will **destroy** you.
Ezek	6.3	a sword to **destroy** the places where people worship **idols**.
	30.13	I will **destroy** the **idols**
Hos	8.4	made **idols** — for their own **destruction**.
	10.8	Israel worship **idols**, will be **destroyed**.
Mic	5.13	**destroy** your **idols** and sacred stone
Nah	1.14	I will **destroy** the **idols**
Acts	19.27	be **destroyed** — the **goddess** worshipped

Innocent

Gen	18.23	you really going to **destroy** the **innocent**
	18.24	fifty **innocent** people...will you **destroy**
	18.28	**innocent** people...Will you **destroy**
	20.4	I am **innocent**! Would you **destroy** me
Job	9.21	**innocent** or guilty, God will **destroy** us.

Mourn, Grief

Jer	49.3	Ai is **destroyed**...go into **mourning**!
	51.8	suddenly fallen and is **destroyed**! **Mourn**
	51.54	of **mourning** for the **destruction**
Lam	2.11	exhausted with grief at the **destruction**
Joel	1.10	**mourns** because the corn is **destroyed**,
Zech	7.3	to **mourn** because of the **destruction**

Obey, Serve

Deut	8.20	If you do not **obey** the Lord, then you will be **destroyed**
	28.45	**destroyed**, because you did not **obey**
Josh	7.1	was to be **destroyed** was not **obeyed**.
2 Chr	17.6	in **serving** the Lord and **destroyed** all
Is	60.12	**serve** you Will be completely **destroyed**.
	65.8	**destroy** all my people — I will save those who **serve** me.
Jer	12.17	**obey**, then I will...uproot it and **destroy**

Place of Worship, Pagan, Sacred

Ex	23.24	**Destroy**...their **sacred** stone pillars.
	34.13	**destroy** their **sacred** pillars,
Lev	26.30	I will **destroy** your **places of worship**
	26.31	**destroy** your **places of worship**,
1 Kgs	15.14	**destroy** all the **pagan places of worship**,
	22.43	**places of worship** were not **destroyed**,
2 Kgs	10.27	So they **destroyed** the **sacred** pillar
	12.3	**places of worship** were not **destroyed**,
2 Kgs	15.4	**places of worship** were not **destroyed**,
	15.35	**places of worship** were not **destroyed**
	18.4	**destroyed** the **pagan places of worship**
2 Chr	15.17	**destroy** all the **pagan places of worship**
	17.6	**destroyed** all the **pagan places of**
	20.33	**places of worship** were not **destroyed**.
	31.1	**destroyed** the altars and the **pagan places**
	34.3	to **destroy** the **pagan places of worship**.
Jer	43.13	will **destroy** the **sacred** stone monuments
Hos	10.2	and **destroy** their **sacred** pillars.
Mic	5.13	will **destroy** your idols and **sacred** stone

Pride

2 Chr	17.6	**pride** in serving the Lord and **destroyed**
Prov	16.18	**Pride** leads to **destruction**
Is	2.11	human **pride** will be ended and human arrogance **destroyed**.
	2.17	human **pride** will be ended and human arrogance **destroyed**.
	26.5	those who were **proud**; he **destroyed**
Jer	13.9	I will **destroy** the **pride** of Judah
Ezek	30.6	Egypt's **proud** army will be **destroyed**.
	32.12	that you are **proud** of will be **destroyed**.
Dan	8.25	**proud** of himself and **destroy** many

Protect see **Save**

Religion see **God's People**

Rescue see **Save**

Sacred see **Place of Worship**

Save, Defend, Protect, Rescue

Deut	9.26	don't **destroy**...the people you **rescued**
2 Sam	21.2	to **protect**, but Saul had tried to **destroy**
Job	5.21	will **save** you when **destruction** comes.
	20.26	Everything he has **saved** is **destroyed**;
	29.17	I **destroyed**...cruel men and **rescued**
	33.18	let them be **destroyed**; he **saves** them
Ps	50.22	I will **destroy** you, and there will be no one to **save** you.
Prov	10.15	**protects** the rich; poverty **destroys**
	10.29	**protects** honest people, but **destroys**
	13.3	**protect** your life. A careless talker **destroys** himself.
	21.22	**defended** by strong men, and **destroy**
Is	16.4	**Protect** us from those who...**destroy** us.
	65.8	**destroy** all my people — I will **save**
Jer	11.12	**save** them when this **destruction** comes.
	30.11	to you and **save** you. I will **destroy**
	46.14	**defend** yourselves; all you have will be **destroyed** in war!
	46.28	to you and **save** you. I will **destroy**
Ezek	22.30	**defend** the land when my anger is about to **destroy** it,
Hos	7.13	be **destroyed**. I wanted to **save** them,
Amos	3.11	**destroy** their **defences**,
Mic	6.14	you do **save** I will **destroy** in war.
Nah	3.13	stands **defenceless**...Fire will **destroy**
Zeph	1.18	**save** them. The...earth will be **destroyed**
Zech	9.15	**protect** his people, and they will **destroy**
Mk	3.4	To **save** a man's life or to **destroy** it?
Lk	6.9	To **save** a man's life or **destroy** it?
1 Cor	5.5	be **destroyed**, so...his spirit may be **saved**
Jas	4.12	He alone can **save** and **destroy**.

Serve see **Obey**

Sin, Evil, Wicked

Deut	29.19	would **destroy** all of you, good and **evil**
1 Sam	12.25	continue to **sin**, you...will be **destroyed**.
	15.18	**destroy** those **wicked** people of Amalek
2 Chr	12.7	they admit their **sin**, I will not **destroy**
Job	22.20	All that the **wicked** own is **destroyed**,
	24.22	**destroys** the mighty...the **wicked** man
Ps	9.5	and **destroyed** the **wicked**;
	26.9	Do not **destroy** me with the **sinners**;

Ps	37.38	but **sinners** are completely **destroyed**,.
	54.5	their own **evil** to punish my enemies. He will **destroy** them
	78.38	He forgave their **sin** and did not **destroy**
	94.23	and **destroy** them for their **sins**;
	101.8	I will **destroy** the **wicked** in our land;
	104.35	**sinners** be **destroyed** from the earth;
	140.11	**evil** overtake violent men and **destroy**
	145.20	but he will **destroy** the **wicked**.
Prov	14.11	an **evil** man's house has been **destroyed**.
	16.4	the destiny of the **wicked** is **destruction**.
	24.16	but disaster **destroys** the **wicked**.
Is	1.31	be **destroyed** by their own **evil** deeds,
	13.9	and every **sinner** will be **destroyed**.
	29.20	Every **sinner** will be **destroyed**.
	30.28	**destruction** and puts an end to their **evil**
Jer	6.7	**evil** fresh. I hear violence and **destruction**
	25.12	their **sin**. I will **destroy** that country
Ezek	18.30	and don't let your **sin destroy** you.
Amos	3.14	for their **sins**, I will **destroy** the altars
	9.8	this **sinful** kingdom...I will **destroy** it
Mic	2.10	Your **sins** have doomed this place to **destruction**.
	6.13	and **destruction** because of your **sins**.
Hab	3.13	of the **wicked** and completely **destroyed**
Zeph	1.3	the **wicked**. I will **destroy** all mankind,
Rom	6.6	of the **sinful** self might be **destroyed**,

Temple

Ezra	5.12	The **Temple** was **destroyed**,
	6.12	and tries to **destroy** the **Temple** there.
Ps	74.3	have **destroyed** everything in the **Temple**.
Jer	51.11	for the **destruction** of his **Temple**.
Dan	9.17	your **Temple**, which has been **destroyed**;
	9.26	city and the **Temple** will be **destroyed**
Zech	7.3	of the **destruction** of the **Temple**,
Jn	11.48	will take action and **destroy** our **Temple**
1 Cor	3.17	So if anyone **destroys** God's **temple**

Terrified see **Afraid**

Violent

Ps	5.6	You **destroy** all liars and despise **violent**,
	140.11	overtake **violent** men and **destroy** them.
Is	10.7	**violent** plans in mind...to **destroy**
	60.18	**violence** will be...no more; **Destruction**
Jer	6.7	hear **violence** and **destruction** in the city;
	20.8	**Violence! Destruction!**
	48.3	**Violence! Destruction!**
Hos	12.1	**destructive**...acts of **violence** increase
Hab	1.3	**Destruction** and **violence** are all round
Rev	11.13	a **violent** earthquake; a tenth of the city was **destroyed**,

Wicked see **Sin**

Wisdom

1 Cor	1.19	I will **destroy** the **wisdom** of the wise

World

Gen	6.13	I will **destroy** them...because the **world**
Is	14.17	**destroyed** cities and turned the **world**
Jer	46.8	rise and cover the **world**; I will **destroy**
	51.25	mountain that **destroys** the whole **world**,
1 Cor	1.28	to **destroy** what the **world** thinks
2 Pet	1.4	the **destructive** lust that is in the **world**,
	3.6	that the old **world** was **destroyed**.

Worship

Deut	4.3	**destroyed** everyone who **worshipped** Baal
	12.2	**destroy** all the places where the people **worship** their gods
2 Kgs	21.3	**worship** that his father...had **destroyed**;
2 Chr	33.3	**worship** that his father...had **destroyed**.
Ps	106.36	**worshipped** idols, and this caused their **destruction**.

Jer	7.6	Stop **worshipping** other gods, for that will **destroy** you.
	48.46	people who **worshipped** Chemosh have been **destroyed**,
Ezek	6.3	**destroy** the places where people **worship**
Hos	10.8	Israel **worship** idols, will be **destroyed**.
Zeph	1.4	**destroy** the last trace of the **worship**
	1.5	**destroy** anyone who...**worships** the sun,
Acts	19.27	be **destroyed** — the goddess **worshipped**

DETERMINED

Deut	31.6	— 32.8	x4
Josh	1.6 — 18		x4
Lev	5.15 —	6.6	x3
1 Sam	20.7 — 33		x3
Ecc	6.10 —	7.25	x3
Is	14.13 — 27		x3

Confident

Deut	31.7	Be **determined** and **confident**;
	31.23	Be **confident** and **determined**.
Josh	1.6	Be **determined** and **confident**,
	1.7	Just be **determined**, be **confident**;
	1.18	Be **determined** and **confident**!
1 Kgs	2.2	Be **confident** and **determined**,
1 Chr	22.13	Be **determined** and **confident**,
	28.20	Be **confident** and **determined**.

DEVOTED

Rom	10.2 —	12.11	x3

Lord, God

2 Kgs	10.16	how **devoted** I am to the **Lord**.
1 Chr	2.7	loot that had been **devoted** to **God**.
2 Chr	31.21	loyalty and **devotion** to his **God**.
	32.32	his **devotion** to the **Lord** are recorded
	35.26	Josiah did — his **devotion** to the **Lord**
Ezra	7.10	**devoted** his life to studying the Law of the **Lord**,
Jn	2.17	**devotion** to your house, O **God**, burns
Rom	10.2	**devoted** to **God**; but their **devotion** is
	12.11	the **Lord** with a heart full of **devotion**.
2 Cor	7.12	**God's** sight, how deep your **devotion** to
Heb	5.7	humble and **devoted**, **God** heard him.

DISASTER

Jer	23.12 —	26.19	x8
Deut	28.20 —	29.27	x7
Is	28.15 —	31.2	x5
Lam	1.21 —	4.21	x5
Deut	31.17 —	32.23	x4
1 Kgs	21.21 —	22.23	x4
Jer	17.16 —	19.3	x4
Prov	24.16 — 22		x3
Is	45.7 —	47.11	x3
Jer	11.15 — 23		x3
Ezek	7.5 — 26		x3
Mic	1.12 —	2.4	x3

Punish

Lev	26.16	will **punish** you. I will bring **disaster**
2 Chr	20.9	any **disaster** struck them to **punish** them
Job	21.17	meet with **disaster**? Did God ever **punish**
Is	13.11	bring **disaster** on the earth and **punish**
	31.2	He sends **disaster**. He carries out his threats to **punish**
Jer	23.12	**disaster**...the time of their **punishment**
	25.13	**punish** Babylonia with all the **disasters**
Ezek	35.5	**disaster**, the time of final **punishment**

Strike

Num	8.19	from the **disaster** that would **strike** them
2 Chr	20.9	any **disaster** struck them to punish them
Ps	91.10	and so no **disaster** will **strike** you,
Prov	6.15	**disaster** will **strike** them without
Amos	3.6	**disaster strike** a city unless the Lord

Threat

Ex	32.14	people the **disaster** he had **threatened**.
Is	31.2	sends **disaster**. He carries out his **threats**
Jer	11.17	but now I **threaten** them with **disaster**.
	25.13	the **disasters** that I **threatened** to bring
	36.31	you the **disaster** that I have **threatened**.

Trouble

Deut	28.20	on you **disaster**, confusion, and **trouble**
2 Kgs	14.10	**trouble** that will only bring **disaster**
2 Chr	25.19	**trouble** that will only bring **disaster**
Jer	17.16	bring **disaster** on them; I did not wish a time of **trouble**

DISCIPLE

Mk	1.21	—	14.50	x86
Mt	8.18	—	24.3	x69
Lk	5.30	—	12.22	x43
Jn	18.1	—	21.24	x34
Mt	26.1	—	28.19	x23
Lk	16.1	—	22.49	x22
Jn	11.7	—	16.29	x19
Jn	1.35	—	4.33	x15
Jn	6.3 – 71			x9
Jn	8.31	—	9.28	x5
Mk	16.7 – 20			x4
Lk	14.26 – 33			x3

Afraid

Lk	9.34	the **disciples** were **afraid**

Amazed

Mt	19.25	the **disciples** heard...they were...**amazed**
Mk	6.51	The **disciples** were completely **amazed**,
	10.26	the **disciples** were completely **amazed**

Believe

Jn	2.11	and his **disciples believed** in him.
Acts	9.26	not **believe** that he was a **disciple**,

Betray

Jn	6.71	**disciples**, was going to **betray** him.

Cross

Lk	14.27	his own **cross**...cannot be my **disciple**.

Jesus

Mt	9.10	and joined **Jesus** and his **disciples**
	10.1	**Jesus** called his twelve **disciples** together
	13.10	Then the **disciples** came to **Jesus**
	14.22	**Jesus** made the **disciples** get into the
	14.25	**Jesus** came to the **disciples**,
	14.33	**disciples** in the boat worshipped **Jesus**.
	15.32	**Jesus** called his **disciples** to him
	16.20	**Jesus** ordered his **disciples** not to tell
	16.21	time on **Jesus** began to say plainly to his **disciples**
	17.3	the three **disciples** saw Moses and Elijah talking with **Jesus**.
	17.10	Then the **disciples** asked **Jesus**
	17.19	the **disciples** came to **Jesus** in private
	17.24	**Jesus** and his **disciples** came to
	18.1	At that time the **disciples** came to **Jesus**
	20.29	As **Jesus** and his **disciples** were leaving
	21.1	**Jesus** and his **disciples** approached
	21.6	**disciples**...did what **Jesus** had told them
	23.1	Then **Jesus** spoke to the crowds and to his **disciples**
	24.3	As **Jesus** sat on the Mount...the **disciples**
	26.17	the **disciples** came to **Jesus** and asked
	26.19	The **disciples** did as **Jesus** had told them
	26.20	**Jesus** and the twelve **disciples** sat down
	26.36	Then **Jesus** went with his **disciples**
	27.57	he also was a **disciple** of **Jesus**.
	28.16	**disciples** went...where **Jesus** had told
Mk	1.21	**Jesus** and his **disciples** came to the town
	1.29	**Jesus** and his **disciples**

Mk	3.7	**Jesus** and his **disciples** went away
	3.9	**Jesus** told his **disciples** to get a boat
	3.20	**Jesus** and his **disciples** had no time
	5.1	**Jesus** and his **disciples** arrived
	6.31	**Jesus** and his **disciples** didn't even have
	6.33	place ahead of **Jesus** and his **disciples**.
	6.39	**Jesus** then told his **disciples** to make all
	6.45	**Jesus** made his **disciples** get into the
	8.1	**Jesus** called the **disciples** to him
	8.7	**Jesus**...told the **disciples** to distribute
	8.27	Then **Jesus** and his **disciples** went away
	8.31	Then **Jesus** began to teach his **disciples**
	8.33	But **Jesus**...looked at his **disciples**,
	8.34	**Jesus** called the crowd and his **disciples**
	9.4	three **disciples** saw Elijah and Moses talking with **Jesus**.
	9.16	**Jesus** asked his **disciples**
	9.28	**Jesus** had gone indoors, his **disciples**
	9.30	**Jesus** and his **disciples** left that place
	9.33	going indoors **Jesus** asked his **disciples**,
	9.35	**Jesus** sat down, called the twelve **disciples**,
	10.10	**disciples** asked **Jesus** about this matter.
	10.23	**Jesus** looked round at his **disciples** and
	10.32	**Jesus** and his **disciples** were now on the
	10.46	as **Jesus** was leaving with his **disciples**
	11.1	**Jesus** sent two of his **disciples** on ahead
	11.19	**Jesus** and his **disciples** left the city.
	14.12	**Jesus**' **disciples** asked him,
	14.17	**Jesus** came with the twelve **disciples**.
	16.14	**Jesus** appeared to the eleven **disciples**
Lk	5.30	group complained to **Jesus**' **disciples**.
	6.20	**Jesus** looked at his **disciples** and said,
	8.3	resources to help **Jesus** and his **disciples**.
	8.9	**disciples** asked **Jesus** what this parable
	8.22	**Jesus** got into a boat with his **disciples**
	8.24	**disciples** went to **Jesus** and woke him
	8.26	**Jesus** and his **disciples** sailed on
	9.1	**Jesus** called the twelve **disciples** together
	9.18	**Jesus** was praying alone, the **disciples**
	9.36	**Jesus** all alone. The **disciples** kept quiet
	9.37	**Jesus** and the three **disciples** went down
	9.56	Then **Jesus** and his **disciples** went on
	10.23	**Jesus** turned to the **disciples** and said
	10.38	**Jesus** and his **disciples** went on their
	18.1	Then **Jesus** told his **disciples** a parable
	18.31	**Jesus** took the twelve **disciples** aside
	22.35	Then **Jesus** asked his **disciples**
	22.49	the **disciples** who were with **Jesus** saw
Jn	1.37	two **disciples** heard...and went with **Jesus**
	2.2	**Jesus** and his **disciples** had also been
	2.12	**Jesus** and his...**disciples** went to
	3.22	**Jesus** and his **disciples** went to the
	4.1	that **Jesus** was...baptizing more **disciples**
	4.27	At that moment **Jesus**' **disciples** returned
	4.31	the **disciples** were begging **Jesus**
	6.3	**Jesus**...sat down with his **disciples**.
	6.16	**Jesus**' **disciples** went down to the lake,
	6.22	knew that **Jesus** had not gone in it with his **disciples**,
	6.24	**Jesus** was not there, nor his **disciples**
	12.4	One of **Jesus**' **disciples**
	13.2	**Jesus** and his **disciples** were at supper
	13.23	the **disciples**, the one whom **Jesus** loved
	13.25	that **disciple** moved closer to **Jesus**' side
	13.29	**disciples** thought that **Jesus** had told
	18.1	**Jesus**...left with his **disciples**.
	18.2	**Jesus** had met there with his **disciples**.
	18.15	Peter and another **disciple** followed **Jesus**
	18.19	questioned **Jesus** about his **disciples**
	19.26	**Jesus** saw his mother and the **disciple** he
	20.2	the other **disciple**, whom **Jesus** loved,
	20.30	In his **disciples**' presence **Jesus** performed
	21.1	**Jesus** appeared once more to his **disciples**

Jn   21.2   and two other **disciples** of **Jesus**
     21.4   **disciples** did not know that it was **Jesus**.
     21.7   **disciple** whom **Jesus** loved said to Peter,
     21.14 time **Jesus** appeared to the **disciples**
     21.20 **disciple**, whom **Jesus** loved — the one
     21.23 of **Jesus** that this **disciple** would not die.

Love

Mt   10.37 **loves**...more than me is not fit to be my
            disciple;
Lk   14.26 be my **disciple** unless he **loves** me more
Jn   13.23 the **disciples**, the one whom Jesus **loved**
     19.26 his mother and the **disciple** he **loved**
     20.2   the other **disciple**, whom Jesus **loved**,
     21.7   **disciple** whom Jesus **loved** said to Peter,
     21.20 other **disciple**, whom Jesus **loved**

Pray

Mk   14.32 to his **disciples**, "Sit here while I **pray**.
Lk   5.33   **disciples** of John fast...and offer **prayers**,
     9.18   was **praying** alone, the **disciples** came
     11.1   **disciples** said...'Lord, teach us to **pray**
     22.45 his **prayer**, he went back to the **disciples**
Jn   18.1   this **prayer**, he left with his **disciples**

Preach

Mk   16.20 **disciples** went and **preached** everywhere,

Teach

Mt   13.52 every **teacher** of the Law who becomes a
            disciple
     15.2   that your **disciples** disobey the **teaching**
Mk   7.5   your **disciples** do not follow the **teaching**
     8.31   Then Jesus began to **teach** his **disciples**
     9.31   because he was **teaching** his **disciples**:
Lk   11.1   **disciples** said to him, "Lord, **teach** us
     18.1   his **disciples** a parable to **teach** them
Jn   8.31   my **teaching**, you are really my **disciples**;
     11.16 **disciples**, "Let us all go with the **Teacher**,
     18.19 his **disciples** and about his **teaching**.

Understand, Words

Mt   16.12 **disciples understood** that he was not
     17.13 **disciples understood** that he was talking
Mk   10.24 **disciples** were shocked at these **words**
Lk   18.34 But the **disciples** did not **understand**
Jn   12.16 His **disciples** did not **understand** this

DISEASE

Lev	13.2	—	14.54	x22
Lk	4.27	—	9.1	x10
2 Kgs	5.1	—	27	x7
Mt	8.2	—	11.5	x7
Deut	28.21	—	61	x5
Jer	27.8	—	29.18	x5
Jer	42.17	—	44.27	x5
2 Chr	26.19	—	23	x3
Jer	14.12	—	16.4	x3
Jer	21.6	—	9	x3
Zech	14.12	—	18	x3
Mk	1.34	—	42	x3

Clean see **Heal**

Cure see **Heal**

Demons, Spirits

Mt   4.24   kinds of **diseases**...people with **demons**,
     10.1   out evil **spirits** and to heal every **disease**
     10.8   **skin-diseases**, and drive out **demons**.
Mk   1.34   of **diseases** and drove out many **demons**.
Lk   6.18   their **diseases**. Those who were troubled by
            evil **spirits**
     7.21   **diseases**, and evil **spirits**, and gave sight
     8.2   been healed of evil **spirits** and **diseases**:
     9.1   out all **demons** and to cure **diseases**.

Acts 19.12 **diseases** were driven away, and the ...**spirits**

Famine

Jer   21.7   **famine**, and the **disease** — I will let all
Ezek 6.11   by **famine**, and by **disease**.
      12.16 the **famine**, and the **diseases**,
      14.21 **famine**, wild beasts, and **disease**
Rev   6.8   **famine**, **disease**, and wild animals.
      18.8   **disease**, grief, and **famine**.

Heal, Clean, Cure

Lev   14.2   person **cured** of a dreaded **skin-disease**.
      14.3   If the **disease** is **healed**,
      14.7   **disease**...he shall pronounce him **clean**.
2 Kgs 5.3   He would **cure** him of his **disease**.
      5.6   I want you to **cure** him of his **disease**.
      5.10   be completely **cured** of his **disease**.
      5.11   over the **diseased** spot, and **cure** me!
Ps   103.3 and **heals** all my **diseases**.
Mt   4.23   and **healing** people who had all kinds of
             disease
      8.3   once the man was **healed** of his **disease**.
      9.35   **healed** people with every kind of **disease**
      10.1   to **heal** every **disease** and every sickness.
      10.8   **heal** those who suffer from ...**skin-diseases**,
      11.5   dreaded **skin-diseases** are made **clean**,
Mk   1.34   **healed** many...with all kinds of **diseases**
      1.42   **disease** left the man, and he was **clean**.
Lk   5.13   Be **clean**!'...the **disease** left the man.
      5.15   and be **healed** from their **diseases**.
      6.18   and to be **healed** of their **diseases**.
      7.21   Jesus **cured** many people of...**diseases**,
      7.22   dreaded **skin-diseases** are made **clean**,
      8.2   been **healed** of evil spirits and **diseases**:
      9.1   out all demons and to **cure diseases**.
1 Cor 12.30 **heal diseases** or to speak in strange

Punish

Ex   9.3   **punish** you by sending a terrible **disease**
      15.26 not **punish** you with any of the **diseases**
Is   10.16 is going to send **disease** to **punish**
Jer   27.8   **punish** that nation by war...and **disease**
Ezek 38.22 **punish** him with **disease** and bloodshed.

Spirits see Demons

Strike

Ex   9.15   **strike** you and your people with **disease**,
Num   14.36 so the Lord **struck** them with a **disease**,
Deut 28.22 will **strike** you with infectious **diseases**,
2 Kgs 15.5   Lord **struck** Uzziah with a...**skin-disease**
Zech 14.18 they will be **struck** by the same **disease**
Rev   18.8   **struck** with plagues — **disease**, grief,

Terrible

Gen   12.17 the Lord sent **terrible diseases** on him
Ex   9.3   punish you by sending a **terrible disease**
Deut 32.24 they will die from **terrible diseases**.
Ps   106.15 also sent a **terrible disease** among them.
      106.29 **terrible disease** broke out among them.
Jer   16.4   They will die of **terrible diseases**
      21.6   alike will die of a **terrible disease**.
Zech 14.12 The Lord will bring a **terrible disease**
      14.15 A **terrible disease** will also fall on

DISGRACE

Lev	18.7	—	22.32	x17
Ezek	36.20	—	32	x6
Is	44.9	—	45.24	x5
Gen	34.5	—	27	x4
Jer	2.26	—	3.25	x4
Ezek	32.24	—	30	x4
Prov	10.5	—	11.16	x3
Prov	13.5	—	14.34	x3
Jer	20.11	—	18	x3

	Ezek	6.9 —	8.6	x3
	1 Cor	11.4 – 14		x3

Holy see Name

Honour

Is	9.1	once **disgraced**, but the future will bring **honour**
Dan	5.19	**honoured** or **disgraced** anyone he wanted
Hos	4.7	I will turn your **honour** into **disgrace**.
	4.18	preferring **disgrace** to **honour**.
Hab	2.16	your **honour** will be turned to **disgrace**.
2 Cor	6.8	We are **honoured** and **disgraced**;

Humiliate see Shame

Name, Holy

Lev	18.21	bring **disgrace** on the **name** of God
	20.3	unclean and **disgraces** my holy **name**,
	21.6	**holy** and must not **disgrace** my **name**.
	22.2	not bring **disgrace** on my holy **name**,
	22.32	not bring **disgrace** on my holy **name**;
Ezek	36.20	they brought **disgrace** on my **holy name**,
	36.21	my **holy name**, since the Israelites brought **disgrace** on it
	36.22	**holy name**, which you have **disgraced**
	36.23	great **name** — the **name** you **disgraced**
	39.7	and I will not let my **name** be **disgraced**
	43.7	**disgrace** my holy **name** by worshipping
	43.8	They **disgraced** my holy **name** by all

Shame, Humiliate

Ps	35.26	be covered with **shame** and **disgrace**.
	44.15	in **disgrace**; I am covered with **shame**
	71.13	be **shamed** and **disgraced**.
	109.29	**disgrace**; may they wear their **shame**
Prov	13.5	people are **shameful** and **disgraceful**.
	19.26	Only a **shameful**, **disgraceful** person
Is	2.9	will be **humiliated** and **disgraced**
	42.17	will be **humiliated** and **disgraced**.
	54.4	be **disgraced**...you will not be **humiliated**.
	61.7	Your **shame** and **disgrace** are ended.
Jer	3.25	in **shame** and let our **disgrace** cover us.
	22.22	your city **disgraced** and put to **shame**
	23.40	on them everlasting **shame** and **disgrace**
	50.12	city will be **humiliated** and **disgraced**.
Ezek	36.32	want you to feel the **shame** and **disgrace**
Hos	10.6	will be **disgraced** and put to **shame**
Hab	2.15	**humiliated** and **disgraced** your
2 Pet	2.13	they are a **shame** and a **disgrace**

DISOBEY

	Ps	119.10 – 126	x5
	Rom	10.21 — 11.32	x5
	2 Kgs	17.12 — 18.12	x4
	Jer	42.13 — 43.7	x3
	Rom	4.15 — 5.19	x3
	Eph	2.1 – 5	x3
	Heb	10.28 — 11.31	x3

Command see God

Evil see Sin

God, Command, Law, Lord

Num	14.41	why are you **disobeying** the Lord now?
	22.18	not **disobey** the **command** of...my **God**
	24.13	not **disobey** the **command** of the Lord
Deut	5.32	Lord your **God** has **commanded** you. Do not **disobey** any of his **laws**.
	9.16	**disobeyed** the **command**...your **God**
	11.28	if you **disobey** these **commands**
	17.20	from **disobeying** the **Lord's commands**
	26.13	not **disobeyed**...any of your **commands**
	28.15	But if you **disobey** the Lord your **God**
Josh	5.4	because they had **disobeyed** the Lord.
	22.23	**disobeyed** the Lord and built our own
Sam	12.15	do not listen to the Lord but **disobey**

1 Sam	13.14	have **disobeyed** him, the Lord will find
	15.11	away...and **disobeyed** my **commands**.
	15.24	I **disobeyed** the **Lord's command**
	28.18	You **disobeyed** the **Lord's command**
2 Sam	12.9	have you **disobeyed** my **commands**?
	22.23	all his **laws**; I have not **disobeyed**
1 Kgs	2.43	promise and **disobeyed** my **command**?
	9.6	**disobey** the **laws** and **commands** I have
	11.11	with me and **disobeyed** my **commands**,
	13.21	The Lord says that you **disobeyed** him
	13.26	who **disobeyed** the **Lord's command**!
	15.5	never **disobeyed** any of his **commands**.
	18.18	are **disobeying** the **Lord's commands**
	20.36	have **disobeyed** the **Lord's command**,
2 Kgs	17.12	and **disobeyed** the **Lord's command**
	17.15	**disobeying** the **Lord's command**
	18.6	faithful to the **Lord** and never **disobeyed**
	18.12	**disobeyed** all the **laws** given by Moses,
	21.22	and **disobeyed** the **Lord's commands**.
1 Chr	10.13	He **disobeyed** the **Lord's commands**;
2 Chr	7.19	and your people ever **disobey** the **laws**
	24.20	**Lord God** asks why you have **disobeyed**
Ezra	6.11	further **command** that if anyone **disobeys**
	7.26	anyone **disobeys** the **laws** of your **God**
	9.10	We have again **disobeyed** the **commands**
Neh	13.27	**disobey** our **God** by marrying foreign
Esth	3.3	he was **disobeying** the king's **command**;
Ps	18.22	all his **laws**; I have not **disobeyed**
	44.18	we have not **disobeyed** your **commands**,
	78.8	**disobedient** people, whose trust in **God**
	89.30	But if his descendants **disobey** my **law**
	119.21	are those who **disobey** your **commands**.
	119.110	I have not **disobeyed** your **commands**.
	119.118	reject everyone who **disobeys** your **laws**;
	119.126	because people are **disobeying** your **law**.
Jer	23.38	And if they **disobey** my **command**
	34.17	Lord, say that you have **disobeyed** me:
	40.3	against the Lord and **disobeyed** him.
	42.13	must not **disobey** the Lord your **God**
	42.21	you are **disobeying** everything that...**God**
	43.7	They **disobeyed** the **Lord's command**
Lam	1.18	the Lord is just, for I have **disobeyed**
Ezek	11.12	and **disobeying** my **commands**.
Mt	15.3	why do you **disobey** **God's command**
Rom	2.25	is of value; but if you **disobey** the **Law**,
	4.15	**law**, there is no **disobeying** of the **law**.
	5.14	did when he **disobeyed** **God's command**.
	11.30	you **disobeyed** **God** in the past;
	11.31	the Jews now **disobey** **God**,
	11.32	For **God** has made all people prisoners of **disobedience**.
Eph	2.2	controls the people who **disobey** **God**.
Heb	10.28	who **disobeys** the **Law** of Moses is put
	11.31	killed with those who **disobeyed** **God**,

Sin, Evil

1 Sam	15.24	have **sinned**," Saul replied. "I **disobeyed**
2 Sam	12.9	**disobeyed** my commands? Why did you do this **evil**
Is	65.12	You chose to **disobey** me and do **evil**.
	66.4	They chose to **disobey** me and do **evil**.
Jer	18.10	that nation **disobeys** me and does **evil**,
	40.3	**sinned** against the Lord and **disobeyed**
Rom	1.30	to do **evil**; they **disobey** their parents;
	5.14	did not **sin** in the same way that Adam did when he **disobeyed**
	5.19	**sinners** as the result of the **disobedience**
Eph	2.1	because of your **disobedience** and **sins**.

DISPLEASE

	Gen	38.7 – 10	x2

God, Lord

Gen	38.7	and it **displeased** the Lord,
	38.10	What he did **displeased** the Lord,

1 Sam	15.19	and so do what **displeases** the **Lord**?
1 Kgs	16.19	Jeroboam he **displeased** the **Lord**
1 Chr	21.7	**God** was **displeased** with what had been
2 Chr	29.6	our **God** and did what was **displeasing**
Ps	85.4	**God** our saviour...stop being **displeased**
Is	59.15	**Lord** has seen this, and he is **displeased**
1 Thes	2.15	How **displeasing** they are to **God**!

DISPUTE

	Ex	18.13 – 26		x6
	Deut	1.12 – 16		x3
	1 Cor	6.1 – 7		x3

Settle, Judge

Ex	18.13	was **settling disputes** among the people,
	18.23	can go home with their **disputes settled**.
	24.14	and so whoever has a **dispute** to **settle**
Deut	1.12	responsibility for **settling** your **disputes**?
	1.16	**Judge** every **dispute** fairly,
	25.1	Israelites go to court to **settle** a **dispute**
1 Sam	7.6	**settled disputes** among the Israelites.
	7.16	in these places he would **settle disputes**.
2 Sam	15.2	with a **dispute** that he wanted the king to **settle**,
	15.4	**judge**! Then anyone who had a **dispute**
1 Kgs	3.28	given him the wisdom to **settle disputes**
1 Chr	26.29	keeping records and **settling disputes**
Is	2.4	will **settle disputes** among great nations.
Mic	4.3	will **settle disputes** among the nations,
Mt	5.25	**settle** the **dispute** with him while there
Lk	12.58	**settle** the **dispute** with him before you
1 Cor	6.5	**settle** a **dispute** between

DOVE

	Gen	8.8 – 12		x4
	Lev	14.22 – 15.29		x4
	Song	5.2 – 6.9		x4

Heaven

| Lk | 3.22 | a **dove**. And a voice came from **heaven**, |
| Jn | 1.32 | come down like a **dove** from **heaven** |

Offering, Priest

Lev	1.14	**burnt-offering**, it must be a **dove** or a
	5.7	**doves** or...pigeons, one for a **sin-offering**
	12.6	a pigeon or a **dove** for a **sin-offering**.
	14.22	**doves** or...pigeons, one for the **sin-offering**
	15.29	two **doves** or two pigeons to the **priest**
Num	6.10	two **doves** or two pigeons to the **priest**

DREAM

	Gen	40.5 – 42.9		x22
	Dan	1.17 – 2.45		x20
	Gen	37.5 – 20		x9
	Dan	4.5 – 5.12		x9
	Jer	23.25 – 32		x6
	Mt	1.20 – 2.22		x5
	Gen	31.10 – 24		x3
	Judg	7.13 – 15		x3
	Is	29.7 – 8		x3

Interpret

Gen	40.8	gives the ability to **interpret dreams**,
	40.16	**interpretation** of the...steward's **dream**
	41.12	our **dreams**, and he **interpreted** them
	41.15	been told that you can **interpret dreams**.
Deut	13.1	A prophet or an **interpreter** of **dreams**
	13.5	put to death any **interpreter** of **dreams**
Dan	1.17	skill in **interpreting** visions and **dreams**.
	5.12	wise and skilful in **interpreting dreams**,
Zech	10.2	**interpret dreams**, but only mislead you;

Vision

| Num | 12.6 | in **visions** and speak to them in **dreams**. |
| Job | 7.14 | me with **dreams**; you send me **visions** |

Job	20.8	will vanish like a **dream**, like a **vision**
	33.15	**God** speaks in **dreams** and **visions**.
Dan	1.17	in interpreting **visions** and **dreams**.
	2.28	tell you the **dream**, the **vision** you had
	4.5	**dream** and saw terrifying **visions**
	7.1	a **dream** and saw a **vision** in the night.
Joel	2.28	**dreams**, and...young men will see **visions**.
Acts	2.17	**visions**, and...old men will have **dreams**.

DUTY

	1 Chr	23.5 – 28.21		x16
	2 Chr	23.4 – 19		x6
	Num	3.7 – 4.27		x5
	2 Kgs	11.5 – 12.9		x5
	Deut	24.5 – 25.7		x4
	2 Chr	31.2 – 18		x4
	Ezek	44.11 – 45.17		x4
	Num	8.24 – 26		x3
	2 Kgs	22.4 – 24.16		x3
	1 Chr	9.25 – 33		x3

Obey

Zech	3.7	**obey** my laws and perform the **duties**
Eph	6.1	Christian **duty** to **obey** your parents,
Col	3.20	Christian **duty** to **obey** your parents

Sabbath

2 Kgs	11.5	you come on **duty** on the **Sabbath**,
	11.7	groups that go off **duty** on the **Sabbath**
	11.9	those going off **duty** on the **Sabbath**
2 Chr	23.4	Levites come on **duty** on the **Sabbath**,
	23.8	they went off **duty** on the **Sabbath**,

ELDERS

	Mt	26.3 – 28.12		x9
	Acts	14.23 – 16.4		x7
	Rev	4.4 – 5.14		x7
	Acts	4.5 – 6.12		x5
	Mk	14.43 – 15.1		x3
	Acts	23.14 – 25.15		x3
	1 Tim	4.14 – 5.19		x3

Apostles

Acts	15.2	**apostles** and **elders** about this matter.
	15.4	the **apostles**, and the **elders**,
	15.6	The **apostles** and the **elders** met together
	15.22	Then the **apostles** and the **elders**
	15.23	the **apostles** and the **elders**,
	16.4	the **apostles** and **elders** in Jerusalem,

Church

Acts	11.30	sent the money to the **church elders**
	14.23	In each **church** they appointed **elders**,
	15.4	**church**, the apostles, and the **elders**,
	15.22	the **elders**...with the whole **church**
	20.17	the **elders** of the **church** to meet him.
	21.18	and all the **church elders** were present.
Tit	1.5	appoint **church elders** in every town.
Jas	5.14	He should send for the **church elders**,
1 Pet	5.1	appeal to the **church elders**

AV ELECT see **GOD'S PEOPLE**

AV ELECTION see **CHOOSE**

ENCOURAGE

	1 Thes	2.12 – 5.14		x6
	Acts	13.15 – 16.40		x5
	2 Cor	7.6 – 13		x5
	Is	40.2 – 41.7		x3

Cheer

Job	29.24	my **cheerful** face **encouraged** them.
2 Cor	7.7	**cheered** us, but also his report of how you **encouraged** him.
Phlm	.7	much **encouragement**! You have **cheered**

God

1 Sam	23.16	**encouraged** him with assurances of **God's**
Ps	69.32	who worship **God** will be **encouraged**.
Rom	15.5	may **God**, the source of...**encouragement**
2 Cor	7.6	**God**, who **encourages** the downhearted,
Heb	12.5	**encouraging** words which **God** speaks

Help

Is	41.6	**help** and **encourage** one another.
1 Cor	14.3	them **help**, **encouragement**, and comfort.
1 Thes	5.11	**encourage** one another and **help** one
	5.14	**encourage** the timid, **help** the weak,

Teach

2 Tim	4.2	and **encourage**, as you **teach**
Tit	1.9	**encourage** others with the true **teaching**

ENEMY

Lam	1.3	—	5.3	x22
Lev	26.7 – 44			x11
2 Sam	22.1 – 49			x11
Deut	32.27	—	33.29	x10
Esth	7.6	—	9.24	x10
Ps	18.3 – 48			x10
Jer	17.3	—	21.7	x10
Neh	4.11	—	6.16	x8
Jer	48.2	—	51.36	x8
Ezek	33.3	—	36.2	x8
Deut	19.4	—	20.19	x7
Deut	28.7 – 68			x7
Ps	74.3 – 23			x6
1 Kgs	8.33 – 50			x5
Ps	31.8 – 20			x5
Ps	55.3 – 18			x5
Ps	78.42 – 66			x5
Ps	109.6 – 29			x5
Ex	23.4 – 28			x4
1 Sam	14.24 – 47			x4
2 Chr	6.24 – 36			x4
Ps	27.3 – 12			x4
Ps	44.5 – 16			x4
Ps	69.4 – 19			x4
Ps	89.10 – 51			x4
Ps	106.10 – 42			x4
Ps	119.98 – 157			x4
Jer	15.9 – 14			x4
Mic	7.6 – 10			x4

Afraid, Terrified

Deut	20.3	Do not be **afraid** of your **enemies**,
1 Sam	18.29	**afraid** of David and was his **enemy**
Neh	4.14	Don't be **afraid** of our **enemies**.
Job	11.19	You won't be **afraid** of your **enemies**;
Ps	3.6	not **afraid** of the thousands of **enemies**
	27.3	not be **afraid**; even if **enemies** attack
	31.13	**enemies** whispering; **terror** is all round
	55.3	**terrified** by the threats of my **enemies**,
	64.1	I am **afraid** of my **enemies** — save
	78.53	**afraid**; but the sea came rolling over their **enemies**.
	112.8	**afraid**; he is certain to see his **enemies**
Jer	6.25	**enemies** are armed and **terror** is all
	32.21	and wonders that **terrified** our **enemies**,
	49.37	people of Elam **afraid** of their **enemies**,
Lam	2.22	my **enemies** to hold a carnival of **terror**
Phil	1.28	Don't be **afraid** of your **enemies**

Blood see Death

Christ

1 Cor	15.25	For **Christ** must rule until God defeats all **enemies**
2 Cor	5.18	through **Christ** changed us from **enemies**
Phil	3.18	make them **enemies** of **Christ's** death
1 Jn	2.18	that the **Enemy** of **Christ** would come;
	2.22	Such a person is the **Enemy** of **Christ**

1 Jn	4.3	he has is from the **Enemy** of **Christ**;
2 Jn	.7	a deceiver and the **Enemy** of **Christ**.

Conquer see Victory

Cruel, Violent

2 Sam	22.49	**enemies** and protect me from **violent**
2 Kgs	17.20	handing them over to **cruel enemies**
Ps	7.3	cause done **violence** to my **enemy**
	18.48	**enemies** and protect me from **violent**
	41.5	My **enemies** say **cruel** things
	42.9	from the **cruelty** of my **enemies**?
	43.2	from the **cruelty** of my **enemies**?
	55.9	of my **enemies**, O Lord! I see **violence**
	74.19	helpless people to their **cruel enemies**;
	129.2	my **enemies** have persecuted me **cruelly**,
	144.11	Save me from my **cruel enemies**;
Is	25.5	our **enemies**...the shouts of **cruel**
Ezek	25.15	taken **cruel** revenge on...**enemies**

Death, Blood

1 Kgs	3.11	or riches or the **death** of your **enemies**,
2 Chr	1.11	or fame or the **death** of your **enemies**
Nah	1.8	his **enemies**; he sends to their **death**
Zech	9.15	will shed the **blood** of their **enemies**;
1 Cor	15.26	last **enemy** to be defeated will be **death**.
Phil	3.18	make them **enemies** of Christ's **death**

Defend see Help

Destroy, Slaughter

Deut	33.27	your **enemies**...and told you to **destroy**
Josh	7.13	to **destroy**! You cannot stand against your **enemies**
1 Sam	2.10	The Lord's **enemies** will be **destroyed**;
	20.15	completely **destroyed** all your **enemies**,
2 Sam	22.41	my **enemies** run from me; I **destroy**
Esth	9.5	their **enemies**. They...**slaughtered** them.
	9.18	had **slaughtered** their **enemies**
Ps	9.6	**enemies** are finished...you have **destroyed**
	18.40	my **enemies** run from me; I **destroy**
	54.5	my **enemies**. He will **destroy** them
	74.3	our **enemies** have **destroyed** everything
	118.10	**enemies** were round me; but I **destroyed**
	124.6	who has not let our **enemies destroy** us.
	143.12	**enemies** and **destroy** all my oppressors,
Is	18.5	the **enemy** will **destroy** the Sudanese
Jer	8.16	Our **enemies** have come to **destroy**
	48.2	The **enemy**...plot to **destroy**
Lam	2.3	**enemy** came. He raged...like fire, **destroying**
	2.5	an **enemy**, the Lord has **destroyed** Israel;
	2.21	by **enemy** swords. You **slaughtered** them
Ezek	25.15	age-long **enemies** and **destroyed** them
	28.7	**enemies** to attack you. They will **destroy**
	35.5	**enemy** and let her people be **slaughtered**
Dan	11.17	order to **destroy** his **enemy's** kingdom,
Amos	3.11	**enemy** will surround their land, **destroy**
Mic	5.9	conquer her **enemies** and **destroy** them
Nah	1.8	flood he completely **destroys** his **enemies**;
Zech	9.15	and they will **destroy** their **enemies**.
Rev	11.5	their mouths and **destroys** their **enemies**;

Evil see Sinful

Help, Defend, Protect

Num	10.9	**defending** yourselves against an **enemy**
Deut	23.14	**protect** you and to give you victory over your **enemies**.
	28.31	**enemies**...there will be no one to **help**
	33.7	And **help** them against their **enemies**.
	33.29	to **defend** you...Your **enemies**
Judg	2.18	**help** him and would save the people from their **enemies**
1 Sam	2.1	at my **enemies**...God has **helped** me!
	10.1	and **protect** them from all their **enemies**.
2 Sam	22.30	**enemies** and...overcome their **defences**.

2 Sam	22.49	victory over my **enemies** and **protect** me
Ezra	8.31	us and **protected** us from **enemy** attacks
Job	9.13	crushed his **enemies** who **helped** Rahab,
	11.19	**enemies**...people will ask you for **help**.
Ps	7.6	my **enemies**; rouse yourself and **help** me!
	18.29	**enemies** and...overcome their **defences**.
	18.48	victory over my **enemies** and **protect** me
	59.1	from my **enemies**, my God; **protect** me
	60.11	**Help** us against the **enemy**;
	61.3	my **protector**, my...**defence** against my **enemies**.
	108.12	**Help** us against the **enemy**;
	118.7	**helps** me, and I will see my **enemies**
	143.9	**protection**...rescue me from my **enemies**.
Is	27.5	if the **enemies**...want my **protection**,
	47.12	some **help** to you; perhaps you can frighten
Lam	1.7	**enemy**, there was no one to **help** her;
	2.3	to **help** us when the **enemy** came.
Nah	3.13	stands **defenceless** before your **enemies**.

Persecute, Oppress

Deut	30.7	**enemies**, who hated you and **oppressed**
Esth	7.6	Our **enemy**, our **persecutor**,
Ps	31.15	**enemies**, from those who **persecute** me.
	55.3	my **enemies**, crushed by the **oppression**
	56.1	my **enemies** **persecute** me all the time.
	74.19	**enemies**; don't forget your **persecuted**
	106.42	They were **oppressed** by their **enemies**
	119.157	I have many **enemies** and **oppressors**,
	129.1	how your **enemies** have **persecuted** you
	129.2	my **enemies** have **persecuted** me cruelly,
	143.12	**enemies** and destroy all my **oppressors**,
Mt	5.44	your **enemies** and...those who **persecute**

Plot, Plan

2 Chr	24.25	**enemy** withdrew...his officials **plotted**
Neh	4.12	of the **plans** our **enemies** were making
Ps	71.10	My **enemies** want to kill me; they...**plot**
Is	30.16	you **plan** to escape from your **enemies**
Jer	11.18	me of the **plots** that my **enemies**
	48.2	**enemy** have captured Heshbon and **plot**
Lam	3.60	my **enemies** hate me and how they **plot**

Power

Ex	15.6	awesome in **power**; it breaks the **enemy**
Deut	7.23	will put your **enemies** in your **power**
1 Sam	24.4	he would put your **enemy** in your **power**
	26.8	God has put your **enemy** in your **power**
2 Sam	22.18	rescued me from my **powerful enemies**
	22.30	my **enemies** and **power** to overcome
Ps	3.7	all my **enemies** and leave them **powerless**
	18.17	rescued me from my **powerful enemies**
	18.29	to attack my **enemies** and **power**
	37.33	not abandon him to his **enemy's power**
	41.2	them to the **power** of their **enemies**.
	44.5	by your **power** we defeat our **enemies**.
	66.3	**power** is so great that your **enemies** bow
	106.41	**power** of the heathen, and their **enemies**
	110.2	royal **power**. "Rule over your **enemies**,
	138.7	**enemies** and save me by your **power**.
	144.11	cruel **enemies**; rescue me from the **power**
Is	42.13	he shows his **power** against his **enemies**.
	64.2	and reveal your **power** to your **enemies**,
Jer	12.7	into the **power** of their **enemies**.
	32.21	our **enemies**, you used your **power**
Lam	1.5	Her **enemies** succeeded; they hold her in their **power**.
Lk	1.71	from our **enemies**, from the **power** of all
	10.19	overcome all the **power** of the **Enemy**,

Protect see Help

Punish, Revenge

Deut	32.41	take **revenge** on my **enemies** and **punish**
	32.43	He takes **revenge** on his **enemies**

Judg	11.36	has given you **revenge** on your **enemies**,
1 Sam	14.24	before I take **revenge** on my **enemies**.
	18.25	as **revenge** on his **enemies**.
	25.26	taking **revenge** and killing your **enemies**.
Esth	8.13	ready to take **revenge** on their **enemies**
Ps	3.7	You **punish** all my **enemies**
	54.5	their own evil to **punish** my **enemies**.
	109.20	**punish** my **enemies** in that way
Prov	29.24	own worst **enemy**. He will be **punished**
Is	1.24	I will take **revenge** on you, my **enemies**,
	26.11	Your **enemies** do not know that you will **punish** them.
	27.7	**punished**...as severely as its **enemies**,
	35.4	coming to **punish** your **enemies**.
	59.18	He will **punish** his **enemies**
	63.4	it was time to **punish** their **enemies**.
	66.6	the Lord **punishing** his **enemies**!
Jer	20.12	me see you take **revenge** on my **enemies**,
	30.14	you like an **enemy**; your **punishment**
	46.10	today he will **punish** his **enemies**.
Ezek	25.15	cruel **revenge** on their age-long **enemies**
Mic	4.13	go and **punish** your **enemies**!
Zeph	3.15	your **punishment**; he has removed all your **enemies**.

Save, Rescue

Judg	2.18	**save** the people from their **enemies**
	8.34	had **saved** them from all their **enemies**
1 Sam	4.3	with us and **save** us from our **enemies**.
	12.10	**Rescue** us from our **enemies**, and we
	12.11	**rescued** you from your **enemies**, and you
2 Sam	18.19	Lord has **saved** him from his **enemies**.
	19.9	King David **saved** us from our **enemies**,
	22.1	**saved** David from...his other **enemies**,
	22.4	and he **saves** me from my **enemies**.
	22.18	**rescued** me from my powerful **enemies**
2 Kgs	17.39	I will **rescue** you from your **enemies**.
Job	6.23	to **save** me from some **enemy** or tyrant?
Ps	3.7	**Save** me...punish all my **enemies**
	9.13	my **enemies** cause me! **Rescue** me
	17.7	**save** me; at your side I am safe from my **enemies**.
	17.13	my **enemies** and defeat them! **Save** me
	18.3	and he **saves** me from my **enemies**.
	18.17	**rescued** me from my powerful **enemies**
	30.1	have **saved** me and kept my **enemies**
	31.15	**save** me from my **enemies**,
	44.7	but you have **saved** us from our **enemies**
	59.1	**Save** me from my **enemies**, my God;
	64.1	am afraid of my **enemies** — **save** my life!
	69.18	**save** me; rescue me from my **enemies**.
	78.42	when he **saved** them from their **enemies**
	106.10	he **rescued** them from their **enemies**.
	107.2	he has **saved**...you from your **enemies**
	109.27	my **enemies** know that you are the one who **saves** me.
	138.7	oppose my angry **enemies** and save me
	142.6	**Save** me from my **enemies**;
	143.9	**rescue** me from my **enemies**.
	144.11	**Save** me from my cruel **enemies**;
Is	34.8	will **rescue** Zion and take vengeance on her **enemies**.
	35.4	**rescue**, coming to punish your **enemies**.
	61.2	**save** his people And defeat their **enemies**.
Mic	4.10	will **save** you from your **enemies**.
Lk	1.71	he would **save** us from our **enemies**,
	1.73	promised to **rescue** us from our **enemies**

Sinful, Evil, Wicked

Esth	7.6	**enemy**, our persecutor, is this **evil** man
Ps	17.9	attacks of the **wicked**. Deadly **enemies**
	17.13	**enemies**...Save me from the **wicked**
	37.20	But the **wicked** will die; the **enemies**
	54.5	their own **evil** to punish my **enemies**.
	55.3	my **enemies**, crushed by...the **wicked**.

Ps	68.21	enemies...who persist in their sinful	
	89.22	enemies will never succeed...the wicked	
	92.9	enemies will die, and all the wicked	
	92.11	defeat of my enemies and heard the cries of the wicked.	
	109.20	punish my enemies...who say such evil	
Ezek	33.6	enemy will come and kill those sinners,	
Col	1.21	his enemies because of the evil things	
1 Tim	5.14	our enemies no chance of speaking evil	

Slaughter see Destroy

Suffer
Job	31.29	been glad when my enemies suffered,
Ps	9.13	See the sufferings of my enemies cause me!
	42.9	suffering from the cruelty of my enemies?
	43.2	go on suffering from...my enemies?
Lam	1.21	make my enemies suffer as I do.

Terrified see Afraid

Victory, Conquer, Triumph
Gen	14.20	gave you victory over your enemies.
	22.17	descendants will conquer their enemies.
	24.60	conquer the cities of their enemies!
Lev	26.7	will be victorious over your enemies;
	26.16	because your enemies will conquer you
Num	24.18	He will conquer his enemies in Edom
Deut	23.14	to give you victory over your enemies.
	28.25	The Lord will give your enemies victory
	33.29	you victory. Your enemies will come
Josh	10.13	the nation had conquered its enemies.
	21.44	the victory over all their enemies.
Judg	3.28	has given you victory over your enemies,
	16.23	god has given us victory over our enemy
	16.24	has given us victory over our enemy,
2 Sam	22.40	and victory over my enemies.
	22.48	He gives me victory over my enemies;
	22.49	you give me victory over my enemies
2 Kgs	21.14	their enemies, who will conquer them
2 Chr	20.27	triumph, because the Lord had defeated their enemies.
	25.8	victory...and he will let your enemies
Neh	9.27	let their enemies conquer and rule them.
	9.28	you let their enemies conquer them.
Ps	13.2	long will my enemies triumph over me?
	18.39	and victory over my enemies.
	18.47	He gives me victory over my enemies;
	18.48	you give me victory over my enemies
	27.6	So I will triumph over my enemies
	74.4	Your enemies have shouted in triumph
	81.14	quickly defeat their enemies and conquer
	89.42	have given the victory to his enemies;
	140.9	Don't let my enemies be victorious;
Jer	19.7	will let their enemies triumph over them
Lam	1.7	to the enemy...Her conquerors laughed
	1.16	The enemy has conquered me;
	2.17	He gave our enemies victory,
Mic	5.9	Israel will conquer her enemies

Violent see Cruel

Wicked see Sinful

ESCAPE
1 Kgs	19.17	—	20.42	x8
Num	35.6 ÷ 31			x6
Jer	38.2	—	39.18	x6
1 Sam	19.10 – 18			x5
Jer	44.14	—	46.16	x5
1 Kgs	11.17	—	12.18	x4
Job	1.15 – 19			x4
Is	23.6	—	24.18	x4
Jer	50.28	—	52.7	x4
Ex	14.5 – 27			x3
Deut	19.2 – 11			x3
1 Sam	22.20	—	23.13	x3

2 Kgs	10.24	—	11.2	x3
Is	2.10 – 21			x3
Lam	1.3	—	3.7	x3
Mt	2.13	—	3.9	x3
Acts	27.30	—	28.4	x3
Heb	11.34	—	12.25	x3
2 Pet	1.4	—	2.20	x3

Anger
Is	2.10	to escape from the Lord's anger
	2.19	to escape from the Lord's anger
	2.21	to try to escape from his anger
Lam	2.22	could escape on that day of your anger.

Death
Num	35.31	must be put to death. He cannot escape
1 Kgs	19.17	Anyone who escapes being put to death
1 Chr	29.15	and we cannot escape death.
Ecc	8.8	death. That is a battle we cannot escape;
Jer	31.2	to those people who had escaped death.
	39.18	not be put to death. You will escape
	44.28	But a few of you will escape death
	51.50	You have escaped death!
Ezek	35.6	living God — death is your fate, and you cannot escape it.
Acts	25.11	death penalty, I do not ask to escape

Destroy
Deut	7.20	and will destroy those who escape
1 Kgs	20.42	be destroyed for letting his army escape
2 Kgs	19.11	he decides to destroy. Do you think that you can escape?
Job	30.13	off my escape and try to destroy me;
Ps	60.4	so that they might escape destruction.
Is	37.11	he decides to destroy. Do you think that you can escape?
Jer	11.11	destruction...and they will not escape.
	48.8	Not a town will escape the destruction;
Ezek	24.26	someone who escapes the destruction
2 Pet	1.4	you may escape from the destructive lust

Punishment
Prov	11.21	punished, but righteous men will escape
	16.5	will never let them escape punishment.
	19.5	be punished — there will be no escape.
	19.9	tells lies in court can escape punishment
Zeph	2.3	you will escape punishment on the day
Mt	3.7	escape from the punishment God is
	3.9	don't think you can escape punishment
Lk	3.7	escape from the punishment God is
2 Cor	13.2	I come nobody will escape punishment.

Trap
Ps	124.7	escaped like a bird from a hunter's trap;
Prov	6.5	the trap like a bird or a deer escaping
Is	24.18	who escapes...will be caught in a trap.
2 Tim	2.26	and escape from the trap of the Devil,
2 Pet	2.18	trap those who are...beginning to escape

ETERNAL (EVERLASTING)
Jn	3.15	—	6.68	x12
Ps	118.1 – 29			x5
Ps	119.89 – 160			x3
Is	60.19	—	61.8	x3
Dan	12.2 – 7			x3
Mt	18.8	—	19.29	x3
Mt	25.41 – 46			x3
Rom	5.21	—	6.23	x3
Heb	9.12 – 15			x3
1 Jn	1.2	—	3.15	x3
1 Jn	5.11 – 20			x3
Jude	.6 – 21			x3

Covenant see Promise

Glory
Is	60.19	your eternal light; The light of my glory

c

2 Cor	4.17	a tremendous and **eternal glory**,
2 Tim	2.10	and brings **eternal glory**.
1 Pet	5.10	who calls you to share his **eternal glory**

God

Gen	21.33	the **Everlasting God**.
Deut	33.27	**God**...your defence; his **eternal** arms
Ps	52.1	**God's** faithfulness is **eternal**.
	55.19	**God**, who has ruled from **eternity**,
	90.2	you were **eternally God**,
Is	9.6	Mighty **God**," "**Eternal** Father,
	40.28	The Lord is the **everlasting God**;
Jer	10.10	are the living **God** and the **eternal** king.
Dan	12.7	in the name of the **Eternal God**.
Hab	1.12	You are my **God**, holy and **eternal**.
Rom	16.26	and by the command of the **eternal God**
Eph	3.11	**God** did this according to his **eternal**
Heb	9.15	**eternal** blessings that **God** has promised.
1 Jn	5.20	is the true **God**, and this is **eternal** life.

Kingdom

2 Pet	1.11	the **eternal Kingdom** of our Lord

Last

Ps	33.11	his purposes **last eternally**.
	100.5	love is **eternal** and his faithfulness **lasts**
	119.89	will **last** for ever; it is **eternal** in heaven.
Is	60.20	will be your **eternal** light, More **lasting**
Jn	6.27	for the food that **lasts** for **eternal** life.

Light

Is	60.19	I, the Lord, will be your **eternal light**;
	60.20	will be your **eternal light**,

Promise, Covenant

Gen	9.12	As a sign of this **everlasting covenant**
	9.16	I will...remember the **everlasting covenant**
	17.7	as an **everlasting covenant**.
	17.13	my **covenant** with you is **everlasting**.
	17.19	It is an **everlasting covenant**.
2 Sam	23.5	he has made an **eternal covenant**
Ps	111.9	and made an **eternal covenant**
Is	61.8	And make an **eternal covenant**
Jer	32.40	I will make an **eternal covenant**
	50.5	They will make an **eternal covenant**
Heb	9.15	**eternal** blessings that God has **promised**.
	13.20	by which the **eternal covenant** is sealed.
1 Jn	2.25	**promised** to give us — **eternal** life.

Punishment, Suffer

Dan	12.2	and some will **suffer eternal** disgrace.
Mt	25.46	will be sent off to **eternal punishment**,
2 Thes	1.9	**suffer** the **punishment** of **eternal**
Jude	.7	**suffer** the **punishment** of **eternal** fire

Sin

Mk	3.29	because he has committed an **eternal sin**.

Suffer see Punishment

Word

Ps	119.89	Your **word**, O Lord...is **eternal**
Jn	5.24	hears my **words**...has **eternal** life.
	6.68	have the **words** that give **eternal** life.
1 Pet	1.23	the living and **eternal word** of God

EVIL

	Prov	8.13	— 17.20	x29
	Jer	2.19	— 9.7	x15
	Ezek	18.8 — 31		x12
	1 Pet	2.1	— 3.17	x10
	Job	34.8	— 36.23	x8
	Hos	4.9	— 7.12	x8
	Rom	1.18	— 3.8	x8
	Jas	1.13	— 3.16	x8
	Job	1.1	— 5.6	x7
	Job	20.12	— 22.23	x7
	Jer	20.13	— 23.22	x7
	Ezek	33.8 — 19		x7
	Mt	12.31	— 13.49	x7
	Deut	28.15	— 32.16	x6
	Prov	24.1	— 26.26	x6
	Is	30.8	— 33.15	x6
	Is	56.2	— 59.15	x6
	Jer	11.8	— 13.23	x6
	Ezek	5.11	— 8.9	x6
	Mal	1.4	— 4.1	x6
	Rom	12.9	— 13.4	x6
	1 Sam	16.14 — 23		x5
	Jer	18.8 — 23		x5
	Gen	6.5 — 12		x4
	Deut	13.5 — 14		x4
	Ps	34.13 — 21		x4
	Ps	51.2 — 9		x4
	Ps	101.3 — 8		x4
	Ps	109.3 — 20		x4
	Ps	141.4 — 9		x4
	Is	1.4 — 31		x4
	Jer	44.3 — 22		x4

Actions, Deeds, Practices, Ways

Lev	20.23	disgusted me with all their **evil practices**.
Judg	2.19	refused to give up their own **evil ways**.
1 Kgs	13.33	still did not turn from his **evil ways**.
2 Kgs	8.18	the **evil ways** of the kings of Israel.
	13.2	he never gave up his **evil ways**.
	17.13	your **evil ways** and obey my commands.
2 Chr	36.8	**practices** and the **evil** he committed,
Job	21.28	the man who **practised evil**?
Ps	7.14	**evil**; they plan trouble and **practise**
	101.3	never tolerate **evil**. I hate the **actions**
Prov	8.13	I hate pride and arrogance, and **evil**
	15.9	The Lord hates the **ways** of **evil** people
Ecc	3.17	and the **evil** alike, because...every **action**,
Jer	15.7	you did not stop your **evil ways**.
	26.3	will listen and give up their **evil ways**.
	35.15	have told you to give up your **evil ways**
	36.3	they will turn from their **evil ways**.
	36.7	and turn from their **evil ways**,
	44.5	would not give up your **evil practice**
	44.22	endure your wicked and **evil practices**.
Ezek	20.44	your wicked, **evil actions** deserve.
	22.15	will put an end to your **evil actions**.
Jon	3.8	wicked behaviour and his **evil actions**.
Mic	6.16	followed the **evil practices** of King Omri
Jn	3.19	because their **deeds** are **evil**.
	3.20	not want his **evil deeds** to be shown up.
Acts	17.30	to turn away from their **evil ways**.
Rom	1.18	whose **evil ways** prevent the truth
Heb	10.17	not remember their sins and **evil deeds**.
2 Pet	2.8	as he saw and heard their **evil actions**.
Rev	16.11	they did not turn from their **evil ways**.

Deceive see False

Deeds see Actions

Destroy, Doom

Deut	29.19	would **destroy** all of you, good and **evil**
Ps	1.6	the **evil** are on the way to their **doom**.
	54.5	their own **evil** to punish my enemies. He will **destroy** them
	140.11	**evil** overtake violent men and **destroy**
Prov	14.11	an **evil** man's house has been **destroyed**.
Is	1.4	**doomed**, you sinful nation, you...**evil**
	1.31	be **destroyed** by their own **evil** deeds,
	3.11	But **evil** men are **doomed**;
	5.20	You are **doomed**! You call **evil** good
	30.28	**destruction** and puts an end to their **evil**
Jer	6.7	**evil** fresh. I hear violence and **destruction**
Ezek	16.23	**doomed**! Doomed! You did all that **evil**,
	18.30	**evil**...don't let your sin **destroy** you.

Disgusting

Lev	20.23	**disgusted** me with all their **evil** practices.
2 Chr	36.8	his **disgusting** practices and the **evil**
Ezek	5.11	the **evil, disgusting** things you did,
	6.9	will be **disgusted**...because of the **evil**
	6.11	because of all the **evil, disgusting** things
	8.9	in and look at the **evil, disgusting** things
	18.24	**evil, disgusting** things that **evil** men do,

Doom see Destroy

Example

2 Kgs	13.11	the **evil example** of King Jeroboam,
Ps	1.1	**evil** men...do not follow the **example** of
Prov	4.14	**evil** men go. Do not follow the **example**
1 Cor	10.6	**example** for us...not to desire **evil**

False, Deceive, Lie

Num	25.18	**evil** they did to you when they **deceived**
Job	15.35	**evil**; their hearts are...full of **deceit**.
	27.4	**evil**, my tongue will never tell a **lie**.
Ps	7.14	think up **evil**; they...practise **deception**.
	34.13	from speaking **evil** and from telling **lies**.
	43.1	deliver me from **lying** and **evil** men!
	50.19	**evil**; you never hesitate to tell **lies**.
	52.3	love **evil** more than good and **falsehood**
	140.11	**falsely** not succeed; may **evil** overtake
Prov	6.16	**evil**, a witness who tells one **lie** after
	8.13	arrogance, **evil** ways and **false** words.
	17.4	to **evil** ideas, and **liars** listen
Is	32.7	**evil** things...to ruin the poor with **lies**
Ezek	21.29	make are **lies**. You are wicked and **evil**,
Dan	11.27	motives will be **evil**, and they will **lie**
Hos	7.3	**deceive** the king...by their **evil** plots.
Mt	5.11	**evil lies** against you because you are my
Mk	7.22	and do all sorts of **evil** things; **deceit**,
1 Pet	2.1	of all **evil**; no more **lying** or hypocrisy
	3.10	from speaking **evil** and stop telling **lies**.

God see Lord

Justice

Prov	16.12	cannot tolerate **evil**, because **justice**
	21.15	**justice** is done, good people are happy, but **evil** people
	28.5	**Evil** people do not know what **justice** is
Amos	5.15	Hate what is **evil**...and see that **justice**
Hab	1.4	**justice** is never done. **Evil** men get the

Keep From see Prevent

Lie see False

Lord, God

Gen	6.11	everyone else was **evil** in **God's** sight,
	6.12	**God** looked at the world and saw that it was **evil**
	38.7	was **evil**, and it displeased the **Lord**,
Ex	20.7	name for **evil** purposes, for I, the **Lord**
	22.28	Do not speak **evil** of **God**
Deut	4.25	This is **evil** in the **Lord's** sight,
	5.11	name for **evil** purposes, for I, the **Lord**
	28.20	If you do **evil** and reject the **Lord**
	32.16	idolatry made the **Lord** jealous; the **evil**
Josh	22.16	you done this **evil** thing against the **God**
1 Sam	12.20	done such an **evil** thing, do not turn away from the **Lord**,
	25.39	**Lord** has punished Nabal for his **evil**.
1 Kgs	16.7	the **Lord's** anger...because of the **evil**
1 Chr	2.3	was so **evil** that the **Lord** killed him.
Job	16.11	**God** has handed me over to **evil** men.
	21.7	Why does **God** let **evil** men live,
	22.23	to **God** and put an end to all the **evil**
	34.12	Almighty **God** does not do **evil**;
	36.23	can tell **God** what to do or accuse him of doing **evil**.
Ps	54.5	May **God** use their own **evil** to punish

Ps	56.7	O **God**, for their **evil**;
	73.9	They speak **evil** of **God** in heaven
	97.10	The **Lord** loves those who hate **evil**;
	109.14	**Lord** remember the **evil** of his ancestors
	140.1	Save me, **Lord**, from **evil** men;
Prov	3.32	the **Lord** hates people who do **evil**,
	8.13	To honour the **Lord** is to hate **evil**;
	11.20	The **Lord** hates **evil-minded** people
	15.9	The **Lord** hates the ways of **evil** people
	15.26	The **Lord** hates **evil** thoughts
	15.29	**Lord** listens, but he ignores those who are **evil**.
	16.6	the **Lord** and nothing **evil** will happen
Ecc	3.17	**God** is going to judge the righteous and the **evil** alike,
Is	14.5	**Lord** has ended the power of the **evil**
Jer	36.7	the **Lord** and turn from their **evil** ways,
	44.22	the **Lord** could no longer endure your wicked and **evil** practices.
	51.56	I am a **God** who punishes **evil**,
Ezek	7.13	**God's** anger is on everyone. Those who are **evil** cannot survive.
Mal	2.17	**Lord** Almighty thinks all **evildoers** are
	3.15	**Evil** men...test **God's** patience
Acts	19.9	**evil** things about the Way of the **Lord**.
Rom	2.24	the Gentiles speak **evil** of **God**.
Col	1.21	far away from **God**...because of the **evil**
2 Thes	3.2	**God** will rescue us from...**evil** people;
1 Tim	6.1	one will speak **evil** of the name of **God**
2 Tim	4.18	the **Lord** will rescue me from all **evil**
Tit	2.5	no one will speak **evil** of the message that comes from **God**.
Jas	1.13	For **God** cannot be tempted by **evil**,
1 Pet	3.17	be **God's** will, than for doing **evil**.

Mind

Deut	15.9	such an **evil** thought enter your **mind**.
Ps	73.7	pour out **evil**, and their **minds** are busy
Prov	6.14	planning **evil** in their perverted **minds**,
Ecc	9.3	their **minds** are full of **evil** and madness,
2 Cor	4.4	**minds**...kept in the dark by the **evil** god

Practices see Actions

Prevent, Keep From

1 Chr	4.10	and **keep** me **from** anything **evil**
Job	36.21	**evil**; your suffering was sent to **keep**
Ezek	13.22	**prevent evil** people from giving up **evil**
Hos	5.4	**evil** that the people have done **prevents**
Rom	1.18	people whose **evil** ways **prevent** the truth
2 Cor	4.4	**evil** god of this world. He **keeps** them
1 Pet	3.10	must **keep from** speaking **evil**

Refuse, Reject

Deut	28.20	If you do **evil** and **reject** the Lord
Judg	2.19	**refused** to give up their own **evil** ways.
Ps	1.1	who **reject** the advice of **evil** men,
	10.3	**evil** desires; the greedy man...**rejects**
	36.4	and he never **rejects** anything **evil**.
Prov	4.15	**evil**! **Refuse** it and go on your way.
	13.19	people **refuse** to turn away from **evil**.
Jer	13.10	**evil** people have **refused** to obey me.
Ezek	18.8	**refuses** to do **evil** and gives an honest
	18.17	**refuses** to do **evil** and doesn't lend
Dan	9.5	been **evil**...We have **rejected**

Rid

Deut	13.5	in order to **rid** yourselves of this **evil**.
	17.7	in this way you will get **rid** of this **evil**.
	19.19	In this way you will get **rid** of this **evil**.
	21.21	and so you will get **rid** of this **evil**.
	22.21	In this way you will get **rid** of this **evil**. Also: 22.22, 24; 24.7
Ps	101.5	**rid** of anyone who whispers **evil** things
1 Pet	2.1	**Rid** yourselves, then, of all **evil**

Sin

Gen	4.7	you have done **evil**, **sin** is crouching
Ex	34.7	of generations and forgive **evil** and **sin**;
	34.9	but forgive our **evil** and our **sin**,
Lev	16.21	and confess over it all the **evils**, **sins**,
2 Chr	33.19	the **sins** he committed...the **evil** he did,
Neh	4.5	**evil** they do and don't forget their **sins**,
Job	22.5	you have **sinned**...because of all the **evil**
	34.8	the company of **evil** men and...**sinners**.
Ps	1.1	of **evil** men, who do not follow...**sinners**
	19.13	be perfect and free from the **evil** of **sin**.
	51.2	**evil** and make me clean from my **sin**!
	51.9	to my **sins** and wipe out all my **evil**.
	107.17	of their **sins** and because of their **evil**;
Prov	29.6	**Evil** people are trapped in their own **sins**
Is	1.4	**sinful** nation, you corrupt and **evil**
	53.5	**sins** he was wounded...because of the **evil**
	53.12	the fate of **evil** men...of many **sinners**
Jer	18.23	forgive their **evil** or pardon their **sin**.
Ezek	3.19	**evil** man and he doesn't stop **sinning**,
	18.21	If an **evil** man stops **sinning**
	18.27	When an **evil** man stops **sinning**
	18.30	from all the **evil**...don't let your **sin**
	33.9	**evil** man and he doesn't stop **sinning**,
	33.19	When an **evil** man gives up **sinning**
Dan	9.5	We have **sinned**, we have been **evil**,
	9.16	our **sins** and the **evil** our ancestors did.
	9.24	and your holy city from **sin** and **evil**.
Hos	7.2	will remember all this **evil**; but their **sins**
Zech	1.4	telling them not to live **evil**, **sinful** lives
Mt	12.31	be forgiven any **sin** and any **evil** thing
	13.41	to **sin** and all others who do **evil** things,
Mk	3.28	all their **sins** and all the **evil** things
Rom	1.18	**sin** and **evil** of the people whose **evil**
Gal	1.4	this present **evil** age, Christ gave himself for our **sins**,
Heb	10.17	not remember their **sins** and **evil** deeds
Jas	1.15	Then his **evil** desire conceives and gives birth to **sin**;

Spirit

1 Sam	16.14	Lord's spirit left Saul, and an **evil spirit**
	16.15	**evil spirit** sent by God is tormenting
	16.16	Then when the **evil spirit** comes on you,
	16.23	**evil spirit** sent by God came on Saul,
	18.10	**evil spirit** from God suddenly took
	19.9	**evil spirit** from the Lord took control
Jer	50.39	be haunted by demons and **evil spirits**,
Lk	4.33	had the **spirit** of an **evil** demon in him;

Ways see Actions

EXILE

Ezra	1.4	—	10.16	x26
Neh	7.6 – 66			x9
Ezek	11.15	—	12.4	x7
Ezek	29.1	—	33.21	x7
Amos	5.5	—	7.17	x5
Lev	26.34 – 41			x4
Jer	28.4	—	29.20	x4
Jer	48.7	—	49.3	x3
Ezek	24.1	—	26.1	x3
Mic	1.11	—	2.13	x3
Mt	1.6 – 17			x3

Enemies

Lev	26.34	are in **exile** in the land of your **enemies**.
	26.38	in **exile**...by the land of your **enemies**.
	26.41	into **exile** in the land of their **enemies**.

God's People

Ezra	1.4	If any of **his people** in **exile** need help
Is	27.8	**his people** by sending them into **exile**.
	56.8	**his people** Israel home from **exile**,

Punish, Sins

Ezra	7.26	**punished** promptly: by death or by **exile**
Is	27.8	The Lord **punished** his people by...**exile**.
Ezek	39.23	into **exile** because of the **sins**
Mic	4.6	I **punished**...who have suffered in **exile**.

Servants

Ezra	2.55	**servants** who returned from **exile**:
	2.58	**servants** who returned from **exile**
Neh	7.57	**servants** who returned from **exile**:
	7.60	**servants** who returned from **exile**

Sins see Punish

FAITH

	Heb	10.22	—	13.7	x33
	1 Tim	1.2	—	6.21	x22
	Rom	3.22	—	5.2	x20
	Gal	1.23	—	3.26	x16
	Jas	1.3	—	2.26	x14
	Mt	13.58	—	18.9	x10
	Rom	14.1	—	16.25	x10
	2 Tim	1.5 ,	—	4.7	x9
	Mk	9.23	—	11.22	x8
	Rom	9.30	—	10.17	x6
	Eph	1.15	—	4.13	x6
	Lk	17.5	—	18.42	x5
	Phil	1.25	—	3.9	x5
	Col	1.4	—	2.12	x5
	1 Thes	3.2 – 10			x5
	Tit	1.1	—	3.15	x5
	1 Pet	1.5 – 21			x5
	Mt	8.10	—	9.22	x4
	Lk	7.9	—	8.48	x4
	Rom	1.8 – 17			x4
	1 Cor	12.9	—	13.13	x4
	Heb	3.1	—	4.14	x4
	1 Cor	15.1	—	16.13	x3
	Gal	5.5	—	6.10	x3
	2 Thes	1.3	—	2.13	x3
	2 Pet	1.1 – 10			x3

Abandon, Give up

Mt	24.10	will **give up** their **faith** at that time;
Jn	16.1	so that you will not **give up** your **faith**.
1 Cor	13.7	Love never **gives up**; and its **faith**
1 Tim	4.1	some people will **abandon** the **faith**
Heb	6.4	how can those who **abandon** their **faith**
	6.6	And then they **abandoned** their **faith**!
2 Pet	1.10	you will never **abandon** your **faith**.
Rev	2.13	and you did not **abandon** your **faith**

Action

Rom	14.23	because his **action** is not based on **faith**.
1 Cor	8.9	**action** make those...weak in the **faith**
Jas	2.14	say that he has **faith** if his **actions**
	2.17	it is with **faith**: if it...includes no **actions**
	2.18	person has **faith**, another has **actions**.
	2.20	to be shown that **faith** without **actions**
	2.22	**faith** and his **actions** worked together;
	2.26	**faith** without **actions** is dead.

Basis, Means

Rom	3.30	on the **basis** of their **faith**,
	4.16	And so the promise was **based** on **faith**
	14.23	because his action is not **based** on **faith**.
	15.13	peace by **means** of your **faith** in him,
Gal	3.14	**means** of...Jesus, so that through **faith**
	3.22	promised on the **basis** of **faith** in Jesus
Phil	3.9	comes from God and is **based** on **faith**.
Col	1.5	**faith** and love are **based** on what you
Heb	11.4	By **means** of his **faith** Abel still speaks,
1 Jn	5.4	over the world by **means** of our **faith**.

Christ see Jesus

Endurance
Is   7.9 If your **faith** is not **enduring**,
1 Tim 6.11 **faith**, love, **endurance**, and gentleness.
2 Tim 3.10 my **faith**, my patience...my **endurance**,
Tit   2.2 in their **faith**, love, and **endurance**.
Rev 13.10 This calls for **endurance** and **faith**

Fail
Lk 22.32 that your **faith** will not **fail**.
1 Cor 13.7 its **faith**, hope, and patience never **fail**.
2 Tim 3.8 and who are **failures** in the **faith**.
Heb 4.11 **fail**...because of their lack of **faith**.

Forgive see **Right With God**

Give Up see **Abandon**

God
Ezra 10.2 have broken **faith** with **God** by marrying
Mk 11.22 Have **faith** in **God**.
Rom 1.17 how **God** puts people right with himself: it is
          through **faith**
    3.22 **God** puts people right through their **faith** in
          Jesus
    3.28 put right with **God** only through **faith**,
    4.3 believed **God**, and because of his **faith**
    4.5 his **faith**...and who believes in the **God**
    4.9 believed **God**, and because of his **faith**
    4.11 of his **faith** **God** had accepted him
    4.14 **faith** means nothing and **God's** promise
    4.20 **faith** did not leave him, and he did not doubt
          God's promise;
    4.22 through **faith**, "was accepted as righteous by
          God.
    5.1 been put right with **God** through **faith**
    5.2 **faith** into this experience of **God's** grace,
    9.30 right with **God**, were put right with him
          through **faith**;
    10.6 being put right with **God** through **faith**
    10.10 **faith** that we are put right with **God**
    12.3 the amount of **faith** that **God** has given
Gal 2.16 put right with **God** only through **faith**
    3.6 believed **God**, and because of his **faith**
    3.11 who is put right with **God** through **faith**
    3.24 be put right with **God** through **faith**.
    3.26 **faith** that all of you are **God's** sons
    5.5 **God's** Spirit working through our **faith**.
Phil 2.17 sacrifice that your **faith** offers to **God**.
    3.9 comes from **God** and is based on **faith**.
1 Thes 1.3 **God** and Father how you put your **faith**
    1.8 the news about your **faith** in **God**
1 Tim 1.4 **God's** plan, which is known by **faith**.
    6.11 Strive for righteousness, **godliness**, **faith**,
Tit   1.1 sent to help the **faith** of **God's** chosen
Heb 10.22 come near to **God** with a sincere heart and a
          sure **faith**,
    11.2 by their **faith** that people of ancient times won
          God's approval.
    11.4 was **faith** that made Abel offer to **God**
    11.6 No one can please **God** without **faith**,
    11.7 **faith** that made Noah hear **God's**
    11.8 **faith** that made Abraham obey when **God**
    11.39 **faith**! Yet they did not receive what **God**
Jas 2.23 believed **God**, and because of his **faith**
    2.24 with **God**, and not by his **faith** alone.
1 Pet 1.5 **faith** are kept safe by **God's** power
    1.21 your **faith** and hope are fixed on **God**.
Jude .3 **faith** which once and for all **God** has

Grace
Rom 5.2 **faith** into this experience of **God's** grace,
Eph 2.8 **God's** grace...you have been saved through
          faith.

Hope
1 Cor 13.7 and its **faith**, **hope**,

1 Cor 13.13 **faith**, **hope**, and love;
2 Cor 10.15 we **hope** that your **faith** may grow
Col 1.5 your **faith**...based on what you **hope** for,
1 Thes 5.8 **faith**...as a breastplate, and our **hope**
Heb 11.1 **faith** is to be sure of the things we **hope**
1 Pet 1.21 your **faith** and **hope** are fixed on God.

Jesus, Christ, Son of God
Mt 9.2 **Jesus** saw how much **faith** they had,
    17.20 haven't enough **faith**," answered **Jesus**
Mk 10.52 **Jesus** told him, "your **faith** has made
Lk 5.20 **Jesus** saw how much **faith** they had
Jn 20.31 **Son of God**, and that through your **faith**
Acts 3.16 **faith** in **Jesus** that has made him well,
    24.24 as he talked about **faith** in **Christ Jesus**.
Rom 3.22 people right through their **faith** in **Jesus**
1 Cor 15.17 And if **Christ** has not been raised, then your
          faith
Gal 2.16 **God** only through **faith** in **Jesus Christ**,
    2.20 I live by **faith** in the **Son of God**,
    3.14 of **Christ Jesus**, so that through **faith**
    3.22 promised on the basis of **faith** in **Jesus**
Eph 1.15 I heard of your **faith** in the Lord **Jesus**
    3.12 union with **Christ** and through our **faith**
    4.13 **faith** and in our knowledge of the **Son**
Phil 3.9 is given through **faith** in **Christ**,
Col 1.4 have heard of your **faith** in **Christ Jesus**
    2.5 stand together in your **faith** in **Christ**.
    2.12 raised with **Christ** through your **faith**
1 Tim 3.13 their **faith** in **Christ Jesus**.
    6.13 **Jesus**, who firmly professed his **faith**
2 Tim 3.15 salvation through **faith** in **Christ Jesus**.
Phlm .5 the **faith** you have in the Lord **Jesus**.
Heb 12.2 on **Jesus**, on whom our **faith** depends
2 Pet 1.1 through...**Jesus**...have been given a **faith**

Lord
Ex 14.31 and they had **faith** in the **Lord**
Josh 22.22 and did not keep **faith** with the **Lord**,
Ps 27.14 Trust in the **Lord**. Have **faith**,
    112.7 his **faith** is strong, and he trusts in the **Lord**.
Eph 1.15 I heard of your **faith** in the **Lord** Jesus
    4.5 is one **Lord**, one **faith**, one baptism
Phlm .5 the **faith** you have in the **Lord** Jesus.

Means see **Basis**

Message, Preach
Rom 10.8 the **message** of **faith** that we **preach**
    10.17 **faith** comes from hearing the **message**,
    12.6 **God's** **message**...according to the **faith**
    16.25 your **faith**, according to the Good News I
          preach
Gal 1.23 **preaching** the **faith** that he once tried to
1 Tim 2.7 proclaim the **message** of **faith** and truth.

Peace
Mk 5.34 **faith** has made you well. Go in **peace**.
Lk 7.50 Your **faith** has saved you; go in **peace**.
    8.48 **faith** has made you well. Go in **peace**.
Rom 5.1 with **God** through **faith**, we have **peace**
    15.13 **peace** by means of your **faith** in him,
Eph 6.23 brothers **peace** and love with **faith**.
2 Tim 2.22 **faith**, love, and **peace**,

Please
Heb 11.6 No one can **please** God without **faith**,

Preach see **Message**

Right With God, Forgive
Acts 26.18 **faith**...they will have their sins **forgiven**
Rom 1.17 put **right with God** through **faith**
    3.22 people **right** through their **faith** in Jesus
    3.25 are **forgiven** through their **faith** in him.
    3.28 put **right with God** only through **faith**
    3.30 Jews **right**...on the basis of their **faith**,

Rom	5.1	been put **right with God** through faith
	9.30	were put **right with him** through faith;
	10.6	being put **right with God** through faith
	10.10	it is by our faith that we are put right
Gal	2.16	**right with God**...through faith in Jesus
	3.8	Gentiles **right with himself** through faith.
	3.11	who is put **right with God** through faith
	3.24	be put **right with God** through faith.
Jas	2.24	**right with God**, and not by his faith

Righteous

Rom	4.3	his faith God accepted him as **righteous**.
	4.9	his faith God accepted him as **righteous**.
	4.11	faith God had accepted him as **righteous**
	4.22	faith, "was accepted as **righteous**
Gal	3.6	his faith God accepted him as **righteous**.
Phil	3.9	through faith in Christ, the **righteousness**
1 Tim	6.11	for **righteousness**, godliness, faith, love,
2 Tim	2.22	and strive for **righteousness**, faith,
Heb	11.4	faith he won...approval as a **righteous**
	11.7	the **righteousness** that comes by faith.
Jas	2.23	his faith God accepted him as **righteous**.

Sin

Rom	3.25	**sins** are forgiven through their faith
	14.23	that is not based on faith is **sin**.
1 Cor	8.9	who are weak in the faith fall into **sin**.

Son of God see Jesus

Strong

Ps	112.7	faith is **strong**, and he trusts in the
Acts	16.5	churches were made **stronger** in the faith
Rom	15.1	are **strong** in the faith ought to help
1 Cor	16.13	firm in the faith, be brave, be **strong**.
Col	2.7	and become **stronger** in your faith,

Sure

Heb	10.22	with a sincere heart and a **sure** faith,
	11.1	have faith is to be **sure** of the things

Teaching

Rom	16.17	faith and go against the **teaching**
Col	2.7	in your faith, as you were **taught**.
1 Tim	4.6	words of faith and of the true **teaching**

Truth

2 Thes	2.13	and by your faith in the **truth**.
1 Tim	2.7	proclaim the message of faith and **truth**.
	3.9	hold to the revealed **truth** of the faith
2 Tim	2.18	way of **truth** and are upsetting the faith

FAITHFUL

Deut	28.1	—	33.9	x11
Ps	89.1 – 37			x7
Jer	2.2	—	5.3	x6
Rev	1.5	—	3.14	x6
Deut	6.25	—	8.18	x5
Deut	10.20	—	13.4	x5
Job	1.1	—	2.9	x5
Mt	24.45	—	25.23	x5
Heb	2.17	—	3.6	x5
Neh	9.8 – 33			x4
Ps	119.4 – 90			x4
Josh	22.5	—	24.14	x3
Ps	31.5 – 23			x3
Is	38.3 – 19			x3
Is	65.16	—	66.5	x3
Lk	16.10 – 12			x3
Col	1.2 – 23			x3

Command see Obey

Covenant

Deut	7.9	is **faithful**. He will keep his **covenant**
	8.18	still **faithful** today to the **covenant**
	29.9	Obey **faithfully** all...this **covenant**,
	33.9	And were **faithful** to your **covenant**.

Neh	1.5	You **faithfully** keep your **covenant**
	9.32	**faithfully** keep your **covenant promises**.
Ps	50.5	**faithful** people...who made a **covenant**
	78.37	they were not **faithful** to their **covenant**
	103.18	to his **covenant** and who **faithfully** obey
Is	56.4	and **faithfully** keep my **covenant**,
	56.6	and **faithfully** keep his **covenant**:
Dan	9.4	You are **faithful** to your **covenant**
Heb	8.9	They were not **faithful** to the **covenant**

Eternal

Ps	52.1	God's **faithfulness** is **eternal**.
	100.5	love is **eternal** and his **faithfulness** lasts
	117.2	and his **faithfulness** is **eternal**.
Is	61.8	**faithfully** reward my people And make an **eternal** covenant

God

Gen	24.27	the **God** of my master Abraham, who has **faithfully** kept
Deut	4.4	who were **faithful** to the **Lord** your **God**
	6.25	we **faithfully** obey everything that **God**
	7.9	the **Lord** your **God** is the only **God** and that he is **faithful**.
	7.12	them **faithfully**, then the **Lord** your **God**
	10.20	**God** and worship only him. Be **faithful**
	28.1	the **Lord** your **God** and **faithfully** keep
	28.15	your **God** and do not **faithfully** keep
	28.58	obey **faithfully** all **God's** teachings
	30.20	your **God**, obey him and be **faithful**
	31.12	**God** and to obey his teachings **faithfully**.
	32.4	Your **God** is **faithful** and true;
	32.46	may **faithfully** obey all **God's** teachings.
Josh	14.8	I **faithfully** obeyed the **Lord** my **God**.
	14.14	he **faithfully** obeyed the **Lord**, the **God**
	22.5	love the **Lord** your **God**...be **faithful**
1 Kgs	8.61	always be **faithful** to the **Lord** our **God**,
	11.4	was not **faithful** to the **Lord** his **God**,
2 Chr	26.5	the **Lord** **faithfully**, and **God** blessed
	27.6	he **faithfully** obeyed the **Lord** his **God**.
Job	1.1	**God** and was **faithful** to him.
	8.20	But **God** will never abandon the **faithful**
Ps	31.5	you are a **faithful** **God**.
	52.1	**God's faithfulness** is eternal.
	57.3	**God** will show me his constant love and **faithfulness**.
	71.22	I will praise your **faithfulness**, my **God**.
	78.8	trust in **God** was never firm and who did not remain **faithful**
	86.15	loving **God**...always kind and **faithful**.
	101.6	of those who are **faithful** to **God**
Prov	16.6	loyal and **faithful**, and **God** will forgive
Is	65.16	ask to be blessed by the **Faithful God**.
Jer	5.1	and tries to be **faithful** to **God**?
Hos	11.12	the **faithful** and holy **God**.
Hab	2.4	live because they are **faithful** to **God**.
Zech	8.8	be their **God**, ruling over them **faithfully**
Mal	2.14	before **God** that you would be **faithful**
Rom	3.3	this mean that **God** will not be **faithful**?
	15.8	to show that **God** is **faithful**,
Heb	3.2	He was **faithful** to **God**
	3.5	Moses was **faithful** in **God's** house
	3.6	**faithful** as the Son in charge of **God's**
Rev	6.9	**God's** word and had been **faithful**
	12.17	**God's** commandments and are **faithful**
	14.12	**God's** commandments and are **faithful**

Jesus

Eph	1.1	who are **faithful** in their life in union with Christ **Jesus**:
1 Tim	6.14	keep them **faithfully** until the Day when our Lord **Jesus**
Rev	1.5	from **Jesus** Christ, the **faithful** witness,
	12.17	**faithful** to the truth revealed by **Jesus**.
	14.12	commandments and are **faithful** to **Jesus**.

Just, Right

Deut	32.4	perfect and **just**...Your God is **faithful**
Neh	9.33	You have done **right** to punish us; you have been **faithful**,
Ps	37.28	**right** and does not abandon his **faithful**
	89.14	**justice**; love and **faithfulness** are shown
	111.7	In all he does he is **faithful** and **just**;
Jer	5.1	what is **right** and tries to be **faithful**
Zech	8.8	ruling over them **faithfully** and **justly**.
Rev	19.11	**Faithful** and True; it is with **justice**

Law see Obey

Life

1 Sam	2.9	protects the **lives** of his **faithful** people,
1 Kgs	15.14	**faithful** to the Lord all his **life**.
2 Chr	15.17	**faithful** to the Lord all his **life**.
1 Cor	4.17	and **faithful** son in the Christian **life**.
Eph	1.1	**faithful** in their **life** in union with Christ

Lord

see also **God**

Deut	17.19	honour the **Lord** and to obey **faithfully**
	18.13	Be completely **faithful** to the **Lord**.
Josh	23.8	be **faithful** to the **Lord**,
	24.14	honour the **Lord** and serve him sincerely and **faithfully**.
1 Sam	12.24	Obey the **Lord** and serve him **faithfully**
	26.23	The **Lord** rewards those who are **faithful**
2 Sam	2.6	now may the **Lord** be kind and **faithful**
	15.20	the **Lord** be kind and **faithful** to you.
	22.26	O **Lord**, you are **faithful** to those who are **faithful** to you,
1 Kgs	15.14	he remained **faithful** to the **Lord**
2 Kgs	18.6	He was **faithful** to the **Lord**
	20.3	**Lord**, that I have served you **faithfully**
2 Chr	15.17	he remained **faithful** to the **Lord**
	19.9	for the **Lord**, **faithfully** obeying
	32.1	Hezekiah served the **Lord faithfully**,
Ps	16.3	excellent are the **Lord's faithful** people!
	18.25	O **Lord**, you are **faithful** to those who are **faithful** to you;
	30.4	to the **Lord**, all his **faithful** people!
	31.23	Love the **Lord**, all his **faithful** people.
	89.5	ones sing of your **faithfulness**, **Lord**.
	89.8	in all things you are **faithful**, O **Lord**.
	100.5	The **Lord** is good...his **faithfulness** lasts
	145.13	The **Lord** is **faithful** to his promises,
Is	38.3	**Lord**, that I have served you **faithfully**
Jer	3.22	away from the **Lord**; he will heal you and make you **faithful**.
	5.3	Surely the **Lord** looks for **faithfulness**.
	42.5	the **Lord** be a true and **faithful** witness
Acts	11.23	to be **faithful** and true to the **Lord**
2 Thes	3.3	But the **Lord** is **faithful**

Loyal, True

Deut	32.4	Your God is **faithful** and **true**;
2 Kgs	20.3	I have served you **faithfully** and **loyally**,
Ps	78.37	not **loyal** to him; they were not **faithful**
	103.18	**true** to his covenant and who **faithfully**
Prov	3.3	Never let go of **loyalty** and **faithfulness**.
	16.6	Be **loyal** and **faithful**
	20.6	talks about how **loyal** and **faithful** he is,
Is	38.3	I have served you **faithfully** and **loyally**,
Jer	42.5	a **true** and **faithful** witness against us
Hos	2.19	I will be **true** and **faithful**,
Acts	11.23	to be **faithful** and **true** to the Lord
Rev	2.13	**true**...and you did not abandon your **faith**
	3.14	the **faithful** and **true** witness,
	19.11	Its rider is called **Faithful** and **True**;

Obey, Command, Law, Teaching

Deut	4.6	**Obey** them **faithfully**
Deut	6.25	we **faithfully** obey everything that God
	7.12	**commands** and obey them **faithfully**
	8.1	**Obey faithfully** all the **laws** that I have
	11.22	**Obey faithfully** all the **laws** that I have
	11.22	everything he **commands**, and be **faithful**
	12.28	**Obey faithfully** everything that I have
	13.4	**commands**; worship him and be **faithful**
	17.19	obey **faithfully** everything that is
	26.16	obey all his **laws**; so obey them **faithfully**
	28.1	obey the Lord your God and **faithfully**
	28.13	if you obey **faithfully** all his **commands**
	28.15	do not **faithfully** keep all his **commands**
	28.58	not obey **faithfully** all God's **teachings**
	29.9	**Obey faithfully** all the terms of this
	30.20	obey him and be **faithful** to him,
	31.12	and to obey his **teachings faithfully**.
	32.46	so that they may **faithfully** obey
	33.9	**obeyed** your **commands**...were **faithful**
Josh	14.8	I **faithfully** obeyed the Lord my God.
	14.14	because he **faithfully** obeyed the Lord,
	22.5	**obey** his **commandments**, be **faithful** to
1 Sam	12.24	**Obey** the Lord and serve him **faithfully**
1 Kgs	2.4	careful to **obey** his **commands faithfully**
	8.61	**faithful** to the Lord our God, **obeying**
2 Chr	7.17	**faithfully** as...David did, **obeying** my
	19.9	**faithfully** obeying him in everything you
	27.6	powerful because he **faithfully obeyed**
Ps	86.11	and I will **obey** you **faithfully**;
	103.18	and who **faithfully** obey his **commands**.
	119.4	and told us to **obey** them **faithfully**.
Prov	16.6	**faithful**, and God will forgive...**Obey**
Is	66.5	**obey** him: "Because you are **faithful** to
Jer	42.5	and **faithful** witness against us if we do not **obey**
Ezek	11.20	and **faithfully obey** all my **commands**.
	37.24	ruler and will **obey** my **laws faithfully**.
1 Tim	6.14	**obey** your orders...keep them **faithfully**
Tit	2.10	**faithful**...to bring credit to the **teaching**
Heb	10.1	**Law** is not a full and **faithful** model
Rev	3.8	**teaching** and have been **faithful** to me.
	12.17	**obey** God's **commandments**...are **faithful**
	14.12	**obey** God's **commandments**...are **faithful**

Praise

Ps	30.4	**praise** to the Lord, all his **faithful**
	71.22	I will **praise** your **faithfulness**, my God.
	149.1	**praise** him in the assembly of his **faithful**

Proclaim

Ps	89.1	will **proclaim** your **faithfulness** for ever.
Jer	23.28	should **proclaim** that message **faithfully**.
Rev	6.9	they had **proclaimed** God's word and had been **faithful**

Punish

Neh	9.33	to **punish** us; you have been **faithful**,
Ps	31.23	the **faithful**, but **punishes** the proud
	119.75	**punished** me because you are **faithful**.

Right see Just

Sin

Num	14.18	love and **faithfulness** and forgive **sin**
Neh	9.33	**faithful**, even though we have **sinned**.
Prov	16.6	**faithful**, and God will forgive your **sin**.

Teaching see Obey

True see Loyal

FALSE

Ezek	12.24	—	14.9	x7
2 Pet	2.1	—	3.16	x6
1 Jn	4.1	—	5.21	x4
Rev	18.23	—	20.10	x4
Ex	23.1 – 7			x3
Ezek	20.7	—	22.28	x3

2 Cor	10.4	—	11.26	x3
Col	2.4 – 23			x3

Deceive, Cheat, Lie

Lev	19.35	**cheat** anyone by using **false** measures
Prov	29.12	**false** information...officials will be **liars**.
Is	59.13	thoughts are **false**; our words are **lies**.
Ezek	13.6	are **false**, and their predictions are **lies**.
	13.7	are **false**, and the predictions...are **lies**.
	13.8	are **false**, and your visions are **lies**.
	14.9	is **deceived** into giving a **false** answer,
	21.29	are **false**, and the predictions...are **lies**.
Hos	12.7	**cheat** their customers with **false** scales.
Zech	8.17	**false** testimony under oath. I hate **lying**,
Mal	3.5	give **false** testimony, those who **cheat**
Mt	24.11	**false** prophets will appear and **deceive**
Mk	10.19	not accuse anyone **falsely**; do not **cheat**;
2 Cor	4.2	not act with **deceit**, nor do we **falsify**
	11.13	**false** apostles, who **lie** about their work
Col	2.4	do not let anyone **deceive** you with **false**
1 Tim	1.10	those who **lie** and give **false** testimony
Rev	18.23	and with your **false** magic you **deceived**

Predictions

Ezek	13.6	are **false**, and their **predictions** are lies.
	13.7	are **false**, and the **predictions** you make
	13.9	**false** visions and...misleading **predictions**.
	13.23	**false** visions and misleading **predictions**
	21.29	are **false**, and the **predictions** you make
	22.28	**false** visions and make **false predictions**.

FAST

Is	58.3 – 6			x7
Esth	4.3	—	5.1	x3
Jer	36.6 – 9			x3
Joel	1.14	—	2.15	x3
Zech	7.3	—	8.19	x3
Mt	6.16 – 18			x3
Mk	2.18 – 20			x3
Acts	13.2	—	14.23	x3

Mourn

2 Sam	1.12	and **mourned** and **fasted** until evening
Esth	4.3	**mourning** among the Jews. They **fasted**,
	9.31	of **fasts** and times of **mourning**.
Joel	2.12	with **fasting** and weeping and **mourning**.
Zech	7.5	they **fasted** and **mourned** in the fifth

Pray

Ezra	8.23	**fasted** and **prayed** for God to protect
Esth	4.16	hold a **fast** and **pray** for me.
Lk	2.36	worshipped God, **fasting** and **praying**.
Acts	13.3	They **fasted** and **prayed**

FATHER

Jn	10.14	—	18.11	x66
Jn	1.13	—	6.65	x32
Mt	5.16	—	7.21	x17
1 Jn	1.2	—	4.14	x13
Mt	10.20	—	13.43	x11
Jn	8.16 – 54			x11
Lk	9.26	—	12.32	x10
Eph	1.2	—	6.23	x8
Mt	23.9	—	26.53	x7
Lk	22.29	—	24.49	x5
Mt	18.10 – 35			x4
Is	63.16	—	64.8	x3
Jn	20.17 – 21			x3
2 Cor	1.2 – 3			x3
Gal	1.1 – 4			x3
Col	1.2 – 11			x3
1 Pet	1.2 – 17			x3
2 Jn	.3 – 9			x3

Forgive see **Mercy**

God

Ps	89.26	You are my **father** and my **God**;
Mal	2.10	**father**? Didn't the same **God** create us
Jn	1.18	as **God** and is at the **Father's** side,
	5.18	had said that **God** was his own **Father**
	6.27	because **God**, the **Father**,
	6.46	he who is from **God** is the only one who has seen the **Father**.
	8.41	**God** himself is the only **Father** we have,
	8.42	If **God** really were your **Father**,
	8.54	my **Father** — the very one you say is your **God**.
	15.26	**God** and who comes from the **Father**.
	20.17	who is my **Father** and their **Father**, my **God** and their **God**.
Acts	2.33	the right-hand side of **God**, his **Father**,
Rom	1.7	**God** our **Father** and the Lord Jesus
	8.15	we cry out to **God**, "**Father**!
	15.6	with one voice the **God** and **Father**
1 Cor	1.3	**God** our **Father** and the Lord Jesus
	8.6	is for us only one **God**, the **Father**
	15.24	over the Kingdom to **God** the **Father**.
2 Cor	1.2	**God** our **Father** and the Lord Jesus
	1.3	us give thanks to the **God** and **Father**
	11.31	The **God** and **Father** of the Lord Jesus
Gal	1.1	from Jesus Christ and **God** the **Father**,
	1.3	**God** our **Father** and the Lord Jesus
	1.4	to the will of our **God** and **Father**.
Eph	1.2	**God** our **Father** and the Lord Jesus
	1.3	us give thanks to the **God** and **Father**
	1.17	the **God** of our Lord Jesus Christ, the glorious **Father**,
	4.6	is one **God** and **Father** of all mankind,
	5.20	for everything to **God** the **Father**.
	6.23	**God** the **Father** and the Lord Jesus
Phil	1.2	**God** our **Father** and the Lord Jesus
	2.11	to the glory of **God** the **Father**.
	4.20	To our **God** and **Father** be the glory
Col	1.2	May **God** our **Father** give you grace
	1.3	always give thanks to **God**, the **Father**
	3.17	thanks through him to **God** the **Father**.
1 Thes	1.1	belong to **God** the **Father** and the Lord
	1.3	remember before our **God** and **Father**
	3.11	**God** and **Father** himself and our **Lord**
	3.13	in the presence of our **God** and **Father**
2 Thes	1.1	belong to **God** our **Father** and the Lord
	1.2	**God** our **Father** and the Lord Jesus
	2.16	Christ himself and **God** our **Father**
1 Tim	1.2	**God** the **Father** and Christ Jesus our
2 Tim	1.2	**God** the **Father** and Christ Jesus our
Tit	1.4	**God** the **Father** and Christ Jesus our
Phlm	.3	**God** our **Father** and the Lord Jesus
Jas	1.27	**God** the **Father** considers to be pure
1 Pet	1.2	to the purpose of **God** the **Father**
	1.3	us give thanks to the **God** and **Father**
	1.17	call him **Father**, when you pray to **God**
2 Pet	1.17	honour and glory by **God** the **Father**,
1 Jn	3.9	and because **God** is his **Father**,
2 Jn	1.3	May **God** the **Father** and Jesus Christ
Jude	.1	who live in the love of **God** the **Father**
Rev	1.6	of priests to serve his **God** and **Father**.

Grace

Rom	1.7	our **Father**...give you **grace**
1 Cor	1.3	our **Father**...give you **grace**
2 Cor	1.2	our **Father**...give you **grace**
Gal	1.3	our **Father**...give you **grace**
Eph	1.2	our **Father**...give you **grace**
Phil	1.2	our **Father**...give you **grace**
Col	1.2	our **Father** give you **grace** and peace.
1 Thes	1.1	to God the **Father**...May **grace**
2 Thes	1.2	our **Father**...give you **grace**
	2.16	**Father**, who loved us and in his **grace**
1 Tim	1.2	**Father** and Christ Jesus...give you **grace**,

2 Tim	1.2	**Father** and Christ Jesus...give you **grace**,
Phlm	.3	our **Father**...give you **grace**
2 Jn	.3	**Father** and Jesus Christ...give us **grace**

Jesus, Son of God
see also **God**

Mt	11.27	knows the **Son** except the **Father**,
	24.36	nor the **Son**; the **Father** alone knows.
	26.42	**Jesus** went away and prayed, "My **Father**
	28.19	in the name of the **Father**, the **Son**,
Mk	13.32	nor the **Son**; only the **Father** knows.
Lk	10.22	who the **Son** is except the **Father**,
	23.46	**Jesus** cried out in a loud voice, "**Father**!
Jn	1.14	he received as the **Father's** only **Son**.
	1.18	only **Son**, who is...at the **Father's** side,
	3.35	**Father** loves his **Son** and has put
	5.19	the **Father** does, the **Son** also does.
	5.20	**Father** loves the **Son** and shows him all
	5.23	the **Son**...as they honour the **Father**.
	6.40	**Father** wants is that all who see the **Son**
	8.27	that **Jesus** was talking to them about the **Father**.
	13.3	**Jesus** knew that the **Father** had given
	14.13	the **Father's** glory will be shown through the **Son**.
Acts	13.32	**Son**; today I have become your **Father**.
Heb	1.5	**Son**; today I have become your **Father**.
	1.5	be his **Father**, and he will be my **Son**.
	5.5	**Son**; today I have become your **Father**.
1 Jn	1.3	**Father** and with his **Son** Jesus Christ.
	2.1	the **Father** on our behalf — **Jesus** Christ,
	2.22	rejects both the **Father** and the **Son**.
	2.23	rejects the **Son** also rejects the **Father**;
	2.24	in union with the **Son** and the **Father**.
	4.14	**Father** sent his **Son** to be the Saviour
2 Jn	.9	has both the **Father** and the **Son**.

Life, Raise

Jn	5.21	as the **Father raises** the dead and gives them **life**,
	5.26	the **Father** is himself the source of **life**.
	14.6	and the **life**; no one goes to the **Father**
Acts	2.33	**raised** to the right-hand side of God, his **Father**,
Gal	1.1	the **Father**, who **raised** him from death.
1 Jn	1.2	eternal **life** which was with the **Father**

Lord

Mt	11.25	**Father**, **Lord** of heaven and earth!
Lk	10.21	**Father**, **Lord** of heaven and earth!
Jn	14.8	**Lord**, show us the **Father**;
Jas	3.9	to give thanks to our **Lord** and **Father**

Love

Jer	3.4	are my **father**, and you have **loved** me
Jn	3.35	**Father** loves his **Son** and has put
	5.20	**Father** loves the **Son** and shows him all
	8.42	were your **Father**, you would **love** me,
	10.17	**Father** loves me because I am willing
	14.21	My **Father** will **love** whoever loves me;
	14.23	my teaching. My **Father** will **love** him,
	14.31	**love** the **Father**; that is why I do
	15.9	I **love** you just as the **Father** loves me
	15.10	obeyed my **Father's** commands and remain in his **love**.
	16.27	for the **Father** himself **loves** you
2 Thes	2.16	**Father**, who **loved** us and in his grace
1 Jn	2.15	the world, you do not **love** the **Father**.
	3.1	See how much the **Father** has **loved** us
Jude	.1	who live in the **love** of God the **Father**

Mercy, Forgive

Mt	6.14	**Father** in heaven will also **forgive** you.
	6.15	then your **Father** will not **forgive**
Mk	11.25	**Father** in heaven will **forgive** the wrongs
Lk	6.36	**merciful** just as your **Father** is **merciful**.
	23.34	**Forgive** them, **Father**! They don't know
2 Cor	1.3	the **merciful Father**, the God
2 Jn	.3	God the **Father**...give us...**mercy**,

Power

Jn	13.3	**Father** had given him complete **power**;
	17.11	**Father**! Keep them safe by the **power**
Rom	6.4	by the glorious **power** of the **Father**,
	8.15	**power** we cry out to God, "**Father**!

Raise see Life

Son of God see Jesus

Spirit of God

Mt	10.20	come from the **Spirit** of your **Father**
	28.19	**Father**, the **Son**, and the **Holy Spirit**,
Lk	11.13	**Father** in heaven give the **Holy Spirit**
Jn	4.23	**Spirit** people will worship the **Father**
	14.26	**Holy Spirit**, whom the **Father** will send
Acts	2.33	**Father**, and...received...the **Holy Spirit**,
Rom	8.15	**Spirit's** power we cry...to God, "**Father**!
Gal	4.6	the **Spirit** who cries out, "**Father**, my **Father**.
Eph	1.17	glorious **Father**, to give you the **Spirit**,
	2.18	**Spirit** into the presence of the **Father**.
1 Pet	1.2	the **Father** and were made a holy people by his **Spirit**,

World

Jn	10.36	the **Father**...sent me into the **world**.
	13.1	leave this **world** and go to the **Father**.
	14.31	**world** must know that I love the **Father**;
	16.28	the **Father**, and I came into the **world**;
	17.25	**Father**! The **world** does not know you,
1 Jn	2.15	the **world**, you do not love the **Father**.
	2.16	the **Father**; it all comes from the **world**.

FAULT

1 Sam	29.3 – 8		x3

God

Job	34.32	asked **God** to show you your **faults**,
Rom	9.19	how can **God** find **fault** with anyone?
Heb	8.8	But **God** finds **fault** with his people
2 Pet	3.14	to be pure and **faultless** in **God's** sight

Lord

Ps	19.12	Deliver me, **Lord**, from hidden **faults**!
	59.4	because of any **fault** of mine, O **Lord**,
1 Cor	1.8	**faultless** on the Day of our **Lord** Jesus
1 Thes	5.23	**fault** at the coming of our **Lord** Jesus

Sin

Job	10.6	all my **sins** and hunt down every **fault**
Ps	51.3	I recognize my **faults**...my **sins**.
Heb	7.26	he has no **fault** or **sin** in him;

FAVOUR

Gen	32.5	—	34.11	x5
Prov	18.5	—	19.12	x5
Acts	24.27	—	25.9	x3

Lord, God

Gen	30.6	**God** has judged in my **favour**.
Num	6.26	May the **Lord** look on you with **favour**
Deut	33.23	blessed by the **Lord's** good **favour**;
1 Sam	2.26	**favour** both with the **Lord** and with
	13.12	have not tried to win the **Lord's favour**.
2 Sam	7.29	enjoy your **favour**. You, Sovereign **Lord**,
1 Kgs	8.52	**Lord**, may you always look with **favour**
1 Chr	17.27	to enjoy your **favour**. You, **Lord**,
Ezra	7.28	By **God's** grace I have won the **favour**
Ps	7.8	Judge in my **favour**, O **Lord**;
	103.6	**Lord** judges in **favour** of the oppressed
Jer	26.19	the **Lord** and tried to win his **favour**.

Jer	36.9	people fasted to gain the **Lord's favour**.
Dan	7.22	in **favour** of the people of the Supreme **God**.
Lk	2.52	gaining **favour** with **God** and men.
	18.7	**God** not judge in **favour** of his own
Acts	7.46	He won **God's favour**
2 Cor	6.2	**God** says: "When the time came for me to show you **favour**
Phlm	.20	do me this **favour** for the **Lord's** sake;
1 Pet	5.5	**God**...shows **favour** to the humble.

FEAR

Mal	1.14 —	3.16	x4
Ex	1.12 – 20		x3
1 Sam	13.7 —	15.32	x3
Job	22.10 —	24.17	x3
Job	31.23 – 34		x3
Job	41.24 – 33		x3
Is	8.9 – 13		x3
Lk	12.5		x3
1 Jn	4.18		x3

Afraid, Terrified, Terror, Tremble

Gen	15.12	and **fear** and **terror** came over him.
Ex	15.14	and they **tremble** with **fear**;
	19.16	people in the camp **trembled** with **fear**.
	20.18	they **trembled** with **fear** and stood
Deut	2.25	**afraid**...Everyone will **tremble** with **fear**
	28.66	**terror**, and you will live in constant **fear**
Josh	9.24	**terrified** of you; we were in **fear** of our
1 Sam	13.7	with him were **trembling** with **fear**.
	14.15	soldiers in the camp **trembled** with **fear**;
	15.32	Agag came...**trembling** with **fear**,
2 Sam	17.10	as **fearless** as lions, will be **afraid**
Job	18.20	shudder and **tremble** with **fear**
	23.15	I **tremble** with **fear** before him.
	26.11	they shake and **tremble** with **fear**.
Ps	4.4	**Tremble** with **fear** and stop sinning;
	55.5	I am gripped by **fear** and **trembling**;
	119.120	I am **afraid**; I am filled with **fear**
Is	8.12	be **afraid** of the things that they **fear**.
	21.4	and I am **trembling** with **fear**.
	32.11	**tremble** with **fear**!
	41.5	are frightened and **tremble** with **fear**.
Jer	5.22	you **fear** me? Why don't you **tremble**
	30.5	I heard a cry of **terror**, a cry of **fear**
	33.9	**fear** and **tremble** when they hear about
Ezek	12.18	**tremble**...and shake with **fear**
	12.19	They will **tremble**...and shake with **fear**
	27.35	kings are **terrified**, and **fear** is written
	32.10	will **tremble** in **fear** for their own lives.
	38.20	of the earth will **tremble** for **fear** of me.
Mic	7.17	**trembling** and **afraid**. They will turn in **fear**
Nah	2.10	Hearts melt with **fear**; knees **tremble**,
Hab	1.7	They spread **fear** and **terror**,
	3.16	and I **tremble**; my lips quiver with **fear**.
Mk	5.33	so she came, **trembling** with **fear**,
Acts	7.32	**trembled** with **fear** and dared not look.
1 Cor	2.3	weak and **trembled** all over with **fear**,
2 Cor	7.15	welcomed him with **fear** and **trembling**.
Eph	6.5	human masters with **fear** and **trembling**;
Phil	2.12	with **fear** and **trembling** to complete
Jas	2.19	also believe — and **tremble** with **fear**.
1 Jn	4.18	in anyone who is **afraid**, because **fear**

God, Lord

Ex	1.17	But the midwives **feared God**
	1.20	Because the midwives **feared God**
	9.30	officials do not yet **fear** the **Lord God**.
	15.16	O **Lord**, and stand helpless with **fear**
Deut	7.21	he is a great **God** and one to be **feared**.
	11.25	**God** will make the people **fear** you,
	25.18	They had no **fear** of **God**
Job	15.4	no one would **fear God**;

Job	31.23	Because I **fear God's** punishment,
Ps	2.11	Serve the **Lord** with **fear**;
	47.2	**Lord**, the Most High, is to be **feared**;
	76.7	you, **Lord**, are **feared** by all.
	76.11	**God** makes men **fear** him;
	102.15	The nations will **fear** the **Lord**;
Prov	2.5	know what it means to **fear** the **Lord**
	15.16	Better to be poor and **fear** the **Lord**
Is	66.5	what the **Lord** says, you that **fear** him
Jer	5.22	I am the **Lord**; why don't you **fear** me?
Dan	6.26	should **fear** and respect Daniel's **God**.
Hos	3.5	Then they will **fear** the **Lord**
	10.3	king because we did not **fear** the **Lord**.
Mic	6.9	It is wise to **fear** the **Lord**
	7.17	will turn in **fear** to the **Lord** our **God**.
Mal	3.16	the people who **feared** the **Lord** spoke
Lk	5.26	Full of **fear**, they praised **God**,
	7.16	were filled with **fear** and praised **God**
	12.5	will show you whom to **fear**: **fear God**,
	18.2	was a judge who neither **feared God**
	18.4	I don't **fear God** or respect man,
	23.40	saying, " Don't you **fear God**?
2 Cor	5.11	know what it means to **fear** the **Lord**

Heart

Gen	42.28	**hearts** sank, and in **fear** they asked
Deut	28.67	**hearts** will pound with **fear** at everything
Job	41.24	His stony **heart** is without **fear**,
Jer	32.40	make them **fear** me with all their **heart**,
Ezek	21.7	their **hearts** will be filled with **fear**.
Nah	2.10	**Hearts** melt with **fear**;
2 Cor	7.5	**fears** in our **hearts**.

Judgement, Punish

Job	31.23	Because I **fear God's** punishment,
Ps	81.15	**fear** before me; their **punishment** would
	119.120	with **fear** because of your **judgements**.
Ezek	7.27	will shake with **fear**. I will **punish**
Heb	10.27	wait in **fear** for the coming **Judgement**
1 Jn	4.18	because **fear** has to do with **punishment**.

Lives

Josh	9.24	we were in **fear** of our **lives**.
Ezek	32.10	will tremble in **fear** for their own **lives**.
Heb	2.15	their **lives** because of their **fear** of death.

Lord see God

Obey see Respect

Praise

Ps	139.14	**praise** you because you are to be **feared**;
Is	25.3	will **praise** you; you will be **feared**
Lk	5.26	Full of **fear**, they **praised God**,
	7.16	were filled with **fear** and **praised God**

Punish see Judgement

Respect, Obey

Ex	1.17	**feared God** and so did not **obey**
Is	66.2	who **fear** me and **obey** me.
	66.5	you that **fear** him and **obey** him:
Dan	6.26	should **fear** and **respect** Daniel's **God**.
Mal	2.5	those days they did **respect** and **fear** me.
	3.16	who **feared** the **Lord** and **respected** him.
Lk	18.2	neither **feared God** nor **respected** man.
	18.4	I don't **fear God** or **respect** man,
Eph	6.5	**obey** your human masters with **fear** and

Terrified see Afraid

Terror see Afraid

Tremble see Afraid

FEAST

Lk	12.36 —	16.22	x11
Mt	22.2 —	23.6	x7
1 Kgs	1.9 – 41		x4

Esth	8.17	—	9.22	x4
Job	1.4 – 18			x4

Happy, Joyful

Esth	8.17	holiday with **feasting** and **happiness**.
	9.17	they made it a **joyful** day of **feasting**.
	9.19	as a **joyous** holiday, a time for **feasting**
Ecc	10.19	**Feasting** makes you **happy** and wine
Jer	7.34	the **happy** sounds of wedding **feasts**.
		Also: 16.9; 25.10; 33.11
	51.39	**feast** and make them drunk and **happy**.
Lk	14.15	How **happy** are those who will...**feast**

Servant

1 Kgs	10.5	**servants** who waited on him at **feasts**,
2 Chr	9.4	**servants** who waited on him at **feasts**,
Mt	22.8	**servants** and said to them, 'My...**feast**
Lk	14.17	time for the **feast**, he sent his **servant**

Wedding

Gen	29.22	a **wedding-feast** and invited everyone.
Judg	14.12	days of the **wedding feast** are over.
Jer	7.34	the happy sounds of **wedding feasts**.
		Also: 16.9; 25.10; 33.11
Mt	22.2	a king who prepared a **wedding feast**
	22.4	is ready. Come to the **wedding feast!**
	22.8	My **wedding feast** is ready,
	25.10	went in with him to the **wedding feast**,
Lk	12.36	to come back from a **wedding feast**.
	14.8	someone invites you to a **wedding feast**,
Rev	19.9	to the **wedding-feast** of the Lamb.

FELLOWSHIP-OFFERING

Lev	3.1	—	4.35	x6
Lev	6.12	—	7.37	x6
Num	6.14	—	7.84	x5
Ezek	45.13	—	46.12	x4
Lev	9.4	—	10.14	x3
1 Kgs	8.63	—	9.25	x3

Present

Lev	7.11	for the **fellowship-offerings presented**
	22.21	anyone **presents** a **fellowship-offering**
Num	10.10	**present** your...**fellowship-offerings**.
Josh	8.31	also **presented** their **fellowship-offerings**.

Sacrifice

Ex	24.5	**sacrificed**...cattle as **fellowship-offerings**.
	32.6	burn as **sacrifices** and others to eat as **fellowship-offerings**.
Lev	9.4	**fellowship-offering**. They are to **sacrifice**
Num	6.17	**sacrifice** the ram to the Lord as a **fellowship-offering**,
	15.8	**sacrifice** in fulfilment of a vow or as a **fellowship-offering**,
Deut	27.7	**sacrifice** and eat your **fellowship-offerings**
Josh	22.27	with **sacrifices** and **fellowship-offerings**.
Judg	20.26	They **offered fellowship sacrifices**
	21.4	**offered fellowship sacrifices**
1 Sam	10.8	and **offer...fellowship-sacrifices**.
	11.15	They **offered fellowship-sacrifices**,
2 Sam	6.17	**offered sacrifices** and **fellowship-offerings**
1 Chr	16.1	**sacrifices** and **fellowship-offerings** to
2 Chr	33.16	and he **sacrificed fellowship-offerings**
Ezek	46.2	burn his **sacrifices** whole and offer his **fellowship-offerings**.

FESTIVAL

Ezek	44.24	—	46.11	x11
Jn	4.45	—	7.37	x11
Ex	12.11	—	13.10	x10
Lev	23.2 – 44			x9
Jn	10.22	—	13.29	x8
Ex	23.14 – 18			x7

Num	28.16	—	29.39	x6
2 Chr	30.1	—	31.3	x6
Ex	34.18 – 25			x5
1 Sam	20.5 – 34			x5
2 Chr	7.8	—	8.13	x5
Deut	16.10 – 16			x4
2 Chr	35.1 – 17			x4
Mt	26.2	—	27.15	x4
Mk	14.1	—	15.6	x4
1 Kgs	12.32 – 33			x3
Zech	14.16 – 19			x3
Lk	2.41 – 43			x3

Dedication

Jn	10.22	**Festival** of the **Dedication** of the Temple

Holy

2 Chr	2.4	**Festivals**, and other **holy** days honouring
	8.13	for each **holy** day: Sabbaths, New Moon **Festivals**,
Is	1.14	your New Moon **Festivals** and **holy** days
Col	2.16	**holy** days or the New Moon **Festival** or

Honour, Worship

Ex	5.1	a **festival** in the desert to **honour** me.
	10.9	hold a **festival** to **honour** the Lord.
	12.11	is the Passover **Festival** to **honour** me,
	13.6	a **festival** to **honour** the Lord.
	23.14	three **festivals** a year to **honour** me.
	23.17	**festivals** all your men must...**worship** me,
	32.5	will be a **festival** to **honour** the Lord.
Lev	23.37	**festivals** on which you **honour** the Lord
	23.40	a religious **festival** to **honour** the Lord
	23.44	religious **festivals** to **honour** the Lord.
	26.2	religious **festivals** and **honour** the place
Num	28.16	Passover **Festival** in **honour** of the Lord
	28.18	**festival** you are to gather for **worship**,
	29.12	this **festival** in **honour** of the Lord
Deut	16.10	Harvest **Festival**, to **honour** the Lord
2 Chr	2.4	**Festivals**, and other holy days **honouring**
Ezek	46.9	to **worship** the Lord at any **festival**,
Hos	9.5	**festivals** in **honour** of the Lord,
Jn	12.20	Jerusalem to **worship** during the **festival**.

Lamb see Offer

Law, Regulations

Lev	23.2	**regulations** for the religious **festivals**,
	23.44	**regulations** for...the religious **festivals**
2 Chr	31.3	**festivals** which are required by the **Law**
Ezra	3.4	the **Festival** of Shelters according to the **regulations**;
Ezek	44.24	**festivals** according to my...**regulations**,
Dan	7.25	change their religious **laws** and **festivals**,

Offer, Lamb, Sacrifice

Ex	23.18	**sacrificed** to me during these **festivals**
Num	15.3	as an **offering** at your regular religious **festivals**;
	28.26	**Festival**, when you present the **offering**
2 Chr	35.8	bulls for **sacrifices** during the **festival**.
	35.16	Passover **Festival**, and the **offering**
Ezek	36.38	were **offered** as **sacrifices** at a **festival**.
	45.22	the **festival** the ruling prince must **offer**
	45.23	the **festival** he is to **sacrifice** to the Lord
	46.9	the **festival** he will **offer**...six **lambs**,
Mk	14.12	**Festival** of Unleavened Bread, the day the **lambs**
Lk	22.7	the **Festival** of Unleavened Bread when the **lambs**

Regulations see Law

Religious

Gen	1.14	and **religious festivals** begin;
Ex	12.14	celebrate this day as a **religious festival**
Lev	23.2	regulations for the **religious festivals**,
	23.37	are the **religious festivals** on which you

Lev	23.40	a **religious festival** to honour the Lord
	23.44	**religious festivals** to honour the Lord.
	26.2	**religious festivals** and honour the place
Num	10.10	and your other **religious festivals**
	15.3	at your regular **religious festivals**;
	28.17	fifteenth day a **religious festival** begins
1 Kgs	12.32	a **religious festival** on the fifteenth day
Is	33.20	we celebrate our **religious festivals**.
Ezek	44.24	They are to keep the **religious festivals**
Dan	7.25	change their **religious** laws and **festivals**,
Amos	5.21	I hate your **religious festivals**;
Jn	5.1	to Jerusalem for a **religious festival**.

Sacrifice see **Offer**

Unleavened Bread

Ex	23.15	the **Festival** of **Unleavened Bread**
	34.18	Keep the **Festival** of **Unleavened Bread**
Lev	23.6	the **Festival** of **Unleavened Bread** begins,
2 Chr	8.13	**festivals** — the **Festival** of **Unleavened Bread**,
	30.13	the **Festival** of **Unleavened Bread**.
	30.21	the **Festival** of **Unleavened Bread**.
	35.17	and the **Festival** of **Unleavened Bread**.
Ezra	6.22	the **Festival** of **Unleavened Bread**.

Worship see **Honour**

FLOCK

Gen	29.2	—	31.43	x26
Gen	37.12	—	38.17	x5
Zech	11.4 – 17			x5
Song	1.7	—	2.16	x4
Song	6.2 – 6			x4
Gen	46.32	—	47.4	x3
Ezek	34.17 – 31			x3

Sheep, Shepherd

Gen	12.16	gave him **flocks** of **sheep** and goats,
	24.35	has given him **flocks** of **sheep** and goats,
	29.2	three **flocks** of **sheep** lying round it.
	29.3	**flocks** came together there, the **shepherds**
Judg	5.16	with the **sheep**? to listen to **shepherds** calling
		the **flocks**?
2 Chr	35.7	herds and **flocks** thirty thousand **sheep**,
Job	24.2	**sheep** and put them with their...**flocks**.
	31.20	had come from my own **flock** of **sheep**
Ps	78.71	**flocks**, and he made him...the **shepherd**
	79.13	the **sheep** of your **flock**,
	80.1	**Shepherd** of Israel...leader of your **flock**.
Song	1.7	among the **flocks** of the other **shepherds**?
	6.6	teeth are as white as a **flock** of **sheep**
Is	13.20	no **shepherd** will ever pasture his **flock**
	40.11	take care of his **flock** like a **shepherd**;
Jer	31.10	them as a **shepherd** guards his **flock**.
	31.24	and **shepherds** with their **flocks**.
	51.23	to slaughter **shepherds** and their **flocks**,
Ezek	34.31	my **sheep**, the **flock** that I feed,
	36.37	in numbers like a **flock** of **sheep**.
Joel	1.18	the **flocks** of **sheep** also suffer.
Zech	9.16	a **shepherd** saves his **flock** from danger.
	11.4	part of the **shepherd** of a **flock** of **sheep**
	11.9	the **flock**, "I will not be your **shepherd**
	11.16	**flock**, but he does not help the **sheep**
	11.17	**shepherd** is doomed! He has abandoned his
		flock.
Mt	26.31	the **sheep** of the **flock** will be scattered.
Jn	10.16	become one **flock** with one **shepherd**.
1 Pet	5.2	**shepherds** of the **flock** that God gave

FLOOD

Gen	6.17	—	11.10	x12
Jer	46.7	—	47.2	x3

Destroy, Drown, Fall

Gen	6.17	to send a **flood** on the earth to **destroy**

Gen	9.11	living beings be **destroyed** by a **flood**;
	9.15	that a **flood** will never again **destroy**
Job	20.28	his wealth will be **destroyed** in the **flood**
Song	8.7	no **flood** can **drown** it.
Is	28.17	and **floods** will **destroy** your security.
Dan	9.26	like a **flood**, bringing...**destruction**
Nah	1.8	rushing **flood** he completely **destroys**
Lk	6.49	the **flood** hit that house it **fell**
2 Pet	3.6	**flood**, that the old world was **destroyed**.

FOOD-OFFERING

Lev	1.9	—	8.28	x21
Lev	21.6	—	24.7	x16
Num	28.2	—	29.36	x10
Ex	29.18	—	30.20	x4
Num	15.3 – 25			x4

Holy

Lev	21.6	**food-offerings** to me...he must be **holy**.
	21.8	**holy**, because he presents the **food-offerings**
		to me.
	21.22	and the very **holy food-offering**,

Pleasing

Lev	1.9	smell of this **food-offering** is **pleasing**
		Also: 1.13; 17; 2.2, 9; 3.5
	3.16	as a **food-offering pleasing** to the Lord.
	8.20	**food-offering**, and the smell was **pleasing**
	8.28	**food-offering**, and the smell was **pleasing**
Num	15.3	smell of these **food-offerings** is **pleasing**
	15.13	**food-offering**, a smell **pleasing** to the
	15.14	**food-offering**, a smell that **pleases** the
	18.17	a **food-offering**, a smell **pleasing** to me.
	28.2	**food-offerings** that are **pleasing** to him.
	28.6	as a **food-offering**, a smell **pleasing**
	28.8	also is a **food-offering**, a smell **pleasing**
	28.13	**food-offering**, a smell **pleasing** to the
	28.24	Lord a **food-offering**, a smell **pleasing**
	29.6	These **food-offerings** are a smell **pleasing**
	29.13	a **food-offering**...a smell **pleasing** to him:
	29.36	a **food-offering**...a smell **pleasing** to him:

Present

Lev	3.14	**present** the following...as a **food-offering**
	10.15	**presented** as a **food-offering** to the
	21.8	he **presents** the **food-offerings** to me.
	21.17	may **present** the **food-offering** to me.
	21.21	may **present** the **food-offering** to me.
	23.25	**Present** a **food-offering** to the Lord
	23.26	and **present** a **food-offering** to the Lord.
	23.36	you shall **present** a **food-offering**.
	23.37	worship and **presenting food-offerings**,
Num	15.13	this when he **presents** a **food-offering**,
	28.3	**food-offerings** that are to be **presented**

FOOLISH

Prov	17.7	—	20.3	x16
Prov	26.1	—	30.32	x16
Prov	14.1	—	15.21	x14
Prov	7.7	—	12.16	x12
Ecc	4.5	—	7.25	x12
Ecc	1.17	—	2.19	x9
2 Cor	11.1	—	12.11	x8
Ecc	9.17	—	10.14	x5
Mt	25.2 – 10			x4
Judg	16.10 – 15			x3
Job	5.2 – 5			x3
Job	12.17	—	13.9	x3
Is	44.20 – 25			x3
Jer	4.22	—	5.21	x3
1 Cor	1.20 – 25			x3
1 Cor	3.18	—	4.10	x3

Act

2 Sam	24.10	I have **acted foolishly**.

1 Chr	21.8	I have **acted foolishly**.
2 Chr	16.9	You have **acted foolishly**,
Job	12.17	and makes leaders **act** like **fools**.
Ecc	7.7	he is **acting** like a **fool**.
Ezek	28.17	your fame made you **act** like a **fool**.
2 Cor	12.11	I am **acting** like a **fool**

Evil

Job	15.31	If he is **foolish** enough to trust in **evil**,
Prov	30.32	**foolish** enough to...plan **evil**,
Is	32.6	**fool** speaks **foolishly** and thinks up **evil**

Idol

Jer	10.8	**foolish**. What can they learn from...**idols**?
	50.38	**idols**, that have made **fools** of the

Ignorant

Prov	9.4	**ignorant** people!" And to the **foolish**
	9.16	**ignorant** people!" To the **foolish** man
	14.18	**Ignorant** people get what...**foolishness**
Jer	5.4	and **ignorant**. They behave **foolishly**;
Rom	2.20	**foolish**, and a teacher for the **ignorant**.
2 Tim	2.23	from **foolish** and **ignorant** arguments;
1 Pet	2.15	the **ignorant** talk of **foolish** people

Intelligent see Wise

Knowledge see Wise

Right

Prov	15.21	**foolishness**, but the wise will do...**right**.
Ecc	5.1	as **foolish** people do, people who don't know **right**
	10.2	the **right** thing and for a **fool** to do

Sense

Deut	32.6	you **foolish**, **senseless** people?
Job	5.2	be a **foolish**, **senseless** thing to do.
Prov	8.5	Are you **foolish**? Learn to have **sense**.
	14.15	**fool** will believe anything; **sensible**
	23.9	Don't try to talk **sense** to a **fool**
Is	44.20	**sense** as eating ashes. His **foolish** ideas

Sin

Num	12.11	this punishment for our **foolish sin**.
Ps	39.8	all my **sins**, and don't let **fools** laugh
	107.11	**fools**, suffering because of their **sins**
Prov	14.9	**Foolish** people don't care if they **sin**
	24.9	Any scheme a **fool** thinks up is **sinful**.

Stupid

Ps	49.10	as well as **foolish** and **stupid** men.
	92.6	**fool** cannot know; a **stupid** man cannot
	94.8	how can you be such **stupid fools**?
Prov	14.8	Why is a **stupid** person **foolish**?
	15.21	**Stupid** people are happy with...**foolishness**
	17.12	some **fool** busy with a **stupid** project.
	20.1	and **foolish**. It's **stupid** to get drunk.
	26.11	**fool** doing some **stupid** thing a second
	26.12	**stupid fool** is better off than someone
	29.20	There is more hope for a **stupid fool**
Ecc	7.25	how wicked and **foolish stupidity** is.
Is	19.11	**fools**! Egypt's wisest men give **stupid**
Jer	4.22	people are **stupid**...They are like **foolish**
	5.21	you **foolish** and **stupid** people,
	10.8	All of them are **stupid** and **foolish**.

Wise, Intelligent, Knowledge, Understand

Job	12.17	**wisdom** of rulers and makes leaders act like **fools**.
	26.3	your **knowledge** with a **fool** like me!
	39.17	**foolish** and did not give her **wisdom**.
Ps	49.10	even **wise** men die, as well as **foolish**
	92.6	something a **fool** cannot...**understand**:
Prov	10.1	A **wise** son makes his father proud of him; a **foolish** one
	10.14	**knowledge** they can, but when **fools**
	10.23	**foolish** to enjoy doing wrong. **Intelligent**

Prov	11.29	**Foolish** men will always be servants to the **wise**.
	14.1	**wisdom** of women, but are destroyed by **foolishness**.
	14.3	**fool's** pride makes him talk...a **wise**
	14.17	temper do **foolish** things; **wiser** people
	14.24	**Wise** people are rewarded...but **fools**
	14.33	**fools** know nothing about **wisdom**.
	15.7	by people who are **wise**, not by **fools**.
	15.20	A **wise** son makes his father happy. Only a **fool** despises
	15.21	their **foolishness**, but the **wise** will do
	17.24	at **wise** action, but a **fool** starts off
	17.28	**fool** may be thought **wise** and intelligent
	18.2	A **fool** does not care whether he **understands** a thing
	26.9	**fool** quoting a **wise** saying reminds you
	29.9	an **intelligent** man brings a lawsuit against a **fool**,
Ecc	1.17	between **knowledge** and **foolishness**, **wisdom** and madness.
	2.12	meant to be **wise** or reckless or **foolish**.
	2.13	**Wisdom** is better than **foolishness**,
	2.14	**Wise** men can see where they are going, and **fools** cannot.
	2.15	fate as **fools**. So what have I gained from being so **wise**?
	2.16	**wise** men, and no one remembers **fools**.
	2.16	must all die — **wise** and **foolish** alike.
	2.19	might be **wise**, or he might be **foolish**
	6.8	is a **wise** man better off than a **fool**?
	7.4	**fool**. A **wise** person thinks about death.
	10.2	**wise** man to do the right...and for a **fool**
	10.12	**wise** man says brings...honour, but a **fool**
Is	19.11	**fools**! Egypt's **wisest** men give stupid
	29.14	who are **wise** will turn out to be **fools**,
	29.24	**Foolish** people will learn to **understand**,
	44.25	show that their **wisdom** is **foolishness**.
Jer	4.22	**foolish** children...have no **understanding**.
Mt	25.2	**foolish**, and the other five were **wise**
	25.8	the **foolish** ones said to the **wise** ones
Rom	1.22	say they are **wise**, but they are **fools**;
1 Cor	1.20	that this world's **wisdom** is **foolishness**!
	1.25	**foolishness** is **wiser** than human **wisdom**,
	3.18	a **fool**, in order to be really **wise**
	4.10	sake we are **fools**; but you are **wise**
2 Cor	11.19	**wise**, and so you gladly tolerate **fools**!

Words

Ecc	10.12	a **fool** is destroyed by his own **words**.
Eph	5.6	anyone deceive you with **foolish words**

FORGET

Prov	2.1	—	7.1	x8
Deut	6.6	—	9.7	x7
Gen	40.23	—	41.51	x4
Deut	4.9 – 39			x4
Ps	119.16 – 109			x4
Is	49.14 – 16			x4
Deut	24.22	—	26.13	x3
Job	7.9	—	9.27	x3
Ps	78.7 – 42			x3
Ps	106.7 – 21			x3
Jer	2.32	—	3.21	x3
Jer	20.9 – 14			x3

Commands see Law

God, Lord

Gen	8.1	**God** had not **forgotten** Noah
	41.51	**God** has made me **forget** all my
Deut	4.39	and never **forget**: the **Lord** is **God**
	6.12	certain that you do not **forget** the **Lord**
	8.11	you do not **forget** the **Lord** your **God**
	8.14	proud and **forget** the **Lord** your **God**

Deut	8.19	Never **forget** the **Lord** your **God**
	9.7	Never **forget** how you made the **Lord** your **God** angry
	32.18	**forgot** their **God**, their mighty saviour,
Judg	2.10	and the next generation **forgot** the **Lord**
	3.7	of Israel **forgot** the **Lord** their **God**
1 Sam	6.6	**forget** how **God** made fools of them
	12.9	the people **forgot** the **Lord** their **God**
1 Chr	16.15	Never **forget** **God's** covenant,
Job	8.13	hope is gone, once **God** is **forgotten**.
Ps	9.12	**God** remembers those who suffer; he does not **forget** their cry,
	13.1	much longer will you **forget** me, **Lord**
	40.17	you have not **forgotten** me...my **God**
	42.9	**God**...I say, "Why have you **forgotten**
	59.11	O **God**, or my people may **forget**.
	69.33	The **Lord** listens to those in need and does not **forget**
	77.9	Has **God forgotten** to be merciful?
	78.7	put their trust in **God** and not **forget**
	103.2	the **Lord**, my soul, and do not **forget**
	106.7	**God's** wonderful acts; they **forgot**
	106.21	**forgot** the **God** who had saved them
	111.4	The **Lord** does not let us **forget**
	132.1	**Lord**, do not **forget** David
Is	17.10	have **forgotten** the **God** who rescues you
	49.14	The **Lord** has abandoned us! He has **forgotten** us.
	51.13	you **forgotten** the **Lord** who made you,
	62.6	remind the **Lord** of his promises And never let him **forget** them.
Jer	3.21	and have **forgotten** the **Lord** their **God**.
	20.9	I will **forget** the **Lord**
	44.21	the **Lord** did not know about them or that he **forgot** them?
Ezek	22.12	have **forgotten** me." The Sovereign **Lord**
	23.35	**Lord** is saying: "Because you **forgot** me
Amos	8.7	the **God** of Israel, has sworn, "I will never **forget**
Lk	12.6	not one sparrow is **forgotten** by **God**.
Heb	6.10	**God** is not unfair. He will not **forget**
	12.5	Have you **forgotten** the encouraging words which **God** speaks

Law, Commands

Deut	6.6	Never **forget** these **commands**
	16.12	obey these **commands**; do not **forget**
	26.13	or **forgotten** any of your **commands**
Ps	119.16	**laws**; your **commands** I will not **forget**.
	119.61	but I do not **forget** your **law**.
	119.83	I have not **forgotten** your **commands**.
	119.109	I have not **forgotten** your **law**.
Prov	31.5	**forget** the **laws** and ignore the rights

Lord see **God**

Mercy

| Ps | 77.9 | Has **God forgotten** to be **merciful**? |

Suffering

Gen	41.51	has made me **forget** all my **sufferings**
Job	9.27	**forget** my pain, all my **suffering** comes
Ps	9.12	those who **suffer**; he does not **forget**
	42.9	**forgotten** me...must I go on **suffering**
	44.24	Don't **forget** our **suffering** and trouble!
Jn	16.21	baby is born, she **forgets** her **suffering**,

FORGIVE

Lk	5.20	—	7.49	x10
Lev	4.20	—	6.7	x9
Mk	1.4	—	4.12	x8
Num	14.18	—	15.28	x7
2 Chr	6.21	—	7.14	x7
1 Kgs	8.30 – 50			x6
Mt	6.12 – 15			x6
Mt	12.31 – 32			x4

Mt	18.21 – 35			x4
Col	1.14	—	3.13	x4
Heb	8.12	—	10.18	x4
Num	30.5 – 12			x3
Ps	25.7 – 18			x3
Is	53.10 – 12			x3
Dan	9.9 – 24			x3
Mt	9.2 – 6			x3
Lk	11.4	—	12.10	x3
2 Cor	2.7 – 10			x3
1 Jn	1.9	—	2.12	x3

Christ see **Jesus**

Evil see **Sin**

God, Father, Heaven

Lev	19.22	and **God** will **forgive** him.
Josh	24.19	He is a holy **God** and will not **forgive**
1 Kgs	8.30	home in **heaven** hear us and **forgive** us.
	8.34	to them in **heaven**. **Forgive** the sins
	8.36	to them in **heaven**. **Forgive** the sins
	8.39	in your home in **heaven**, **forgive** them,
1 Chr	6.49	for the sacrifices by which **God forgives**
2 Chr	6.21	home in **heaven** hear us and **forgive** us.
	6.25	to them in **heaven**. **Forgive** the sins
	6.27	to them in **heaven** and **forgive** the sins
	6.30	your home in **heaven** and **forgive** them.
	7.14	hear them in **heaven**, **forgive** their sins,
	30.19	the **God** of our ancestors, in your goodness **forgive**
Neh	9.17	But you are a **God** who **forgives**;
Ps	78.38	But **God** was merciful to his people. He **forgave**
	79.9	**God**, and save us; rescue us and **forgive**
	99.8	them that you are a **God** who **forgives**,
Prov	16.6	and **God** will **forgive** your sin.
Is	43.25	I am the **God** who **forgives** your sins,
	55.7	our **God**; he is...quick to **forgive**.
Mt	6.14	**Father** in **heaven** will also **forgive** you.
	6.15	then your **Father** will not **forgive**
Mk	1.4	and **God** will **forgive** your sins.
	2.7	**God** is the only one who can **forgive**
	4.12	turn to **God**, and he would **forgive**
	11.25	**Father** in **heaven** will **forgive** the wrongs
Lk	3.3	and **God** will **forgive** your sins.
	5.21	**God** is the only one who can **forgive**
	6.37	**forgive** others, and **God** will **forgive**
	23.34	**Forgive** them, **Father**! They don't know
Acts	3.19	and turn to **God**, so that he will **forgive**
Eph	4.32	**forgive** one another, as **God** has **forgiven**
Col	2.13	**God forgave** us all our sins;
Heb	2.17	to **God**, so that the people's sins would be **forgiven**.

Heart

| Mt | 18.35 | **forgive** your brother from your **heart**. |

Heaven see **God**

Jesus, Christ, Son of Man

Mt	9.6	**Son of Man** has authority...to **forgive**
	12.32	against the **Son of Man** can be **forgiven**;
Mk	2.10	**Son of Man** has authority...to **forgive**
Lk	5.24	**Son of Man** has authority...to **forgive**
	12.10	against the **Son of Man** can be **forgiven**
Acts	2.38	of **Jesus Christ**, so that your sins will be **forgiven**;
	13.38	**Jesus** that the message about **forgiveness**
2 Cor	2.10	to **forgive** anything — I do it in **Christ's**
Eph	4.32	**God** has **forgiven** you through **Christ**.
1 Jn	2.12	sins are **forgiven** for the sake of **Christ**.

Lord

Ex	32.30	**Lord**; perhaps I can obtain **forgiveness**
Num	14.20	The **Lord** answered, "I will **forgive** them
	30.5	The **Lord** will **forgive** her,

Num	30.8	The **Lord** will **forgive** her.
	30.12	The **Lord** will **forgive** her,
Deut	21.8	**Lord**, **forgive** your people Israel
	29.20	The **Lord** will not **forgive** such a man.
2 Sam	12.13	The **Lord forgives** you;
2 Kgs	5.18	I hope that the **Lord** will **forgive** me
	24.4	The **Lord** could not **forgive** Manasseh
2 Chr	6.27	O **Lord**, listen to them in heaven and **forgive** the sins .
	30.20	The **Lord**...**forgave** the people
Ps	25.11	**Lord**, and **forgive** my sins,
Is	2.9	Do not **forgive** them, **Lord**!
	55.7	to the **Lord**, our God; he is merciful and quick to **forgive**.
Jer	5.1	the **Lord** will **forgive** Jerusalem.
	5.7	**Lord** asked, "Why should I **forgive** the
Lam	3.42	O **Lord**, have not **forgiven** us.
Ezek	45.13	will be **forgiven**. I, the Sovereign **Lord**,
Dan	9.19	**Lord**, hear us. **Lord**, **forgive** us
Amos	7.2	Sovereign **Lord**, **forgive** your people!
Mic	7.18	**Lord**; you **forgive** the sins of your
Acts	8.22	to the **Lord** that he will **forgive** you
Col	3.13	just as the **Lord** has **forgiven** you.

Offer see Sacrifice

Pray

Ex	10.17	Now **forgive** my sin this once and **pray**
Num	14.19	**forgive**, I **pray**, the sin of these
1 Kgs	8.33	humbly **praying** to you for **forgiveness**,
2 Chr	6.24	humbly **praying** to you for **forgiveness**,
	30.20	Hezekiah's **prayer**; he **forgave** the people
Is	53.12	and **prayed** that they might be **forgiven**.
Hos	14.2	**Forgive**...our sins...accept our **prayer**,
Mk	11.25	And when you stand and **pray**, **forgive**
Acts	8.22	**pray** to the Lord that he will **forgive**

Promise

Ex	34.7	my **promise** for...generations and **forgive**
Ps	25.11	**promise**, Lord, and **forgive** my sins,
Joel	2.13	**promise**; he is always ready to **forgive**
1 Jn	1.9	he will keep his **promise**...he will **forgive**

Rebellion see Sin

Repent, Turn

Jer	36.3	**turn** from their evil ways...I will **forgive**
Mk	4.12	**turn** to God, and he would **forgive**
Lk	17.3	and if he **repents**, **forgive** him.
	17.4	I **repent**,' you must **forgive** him.
	24.47	**repentance** and the **forgiveness** of sins
Acts	3.19	**turn** to God, so that he will **forgive**
	5.31	to **repent** and have their sins **forgiven**.

Sacrifice, Offer

Ex	29.36	a **sacrifice**, so that sin may be **forgiven**.
Lev	4.31	**sacrifice**...and he will be **forgiven**.
		Also: 4.35; 5.10, 13, 16; 6.7
1 Chr	6.49	for the **sacrifices** by which God **forgives**
Is	53.10	was a **sacrifice** to bring **forgiveness**.
Ezek	45.13	-**offerings**, so...your sins will be **forgiven**.
Heb	10.18	these have been **forgiven**, an **offering**

Sin, Evil, Rebellion

Ex	10.17	Now **forgive** my **sin** this once and pray
	29.36	so that **sin** may be **forgiven**.
	32.30	I can obtain **forgiveness** for your **sin**.
	32.32	Please **forgive** their **sin**;
	34.7	and **forgive** **evil** and sin;
	34.9	but **forgive** our **evil** and our **sin**,
Lev	4.20	people's **sin**, and they will be **forgiven**.
	4.26	**sin** of the ruler, and he will be **forgiven**.
	4.31	the man's **sin**, and he will be **forgiven**.
		Also: 4.35; 5.10, 13, 16; 6.7
	19.22	man's **sin**, and God will **forgive** him.

Num	14.18	**forgive** **sin** and **rebellion**
	14.19	**forgive**, I pray, the **sin** of these people,
	15.28	from his **sin**, and he will be **forgiven**.
	25.13	about **forgiveness** for the people's **sin**.
Deut	32.43	and **forgives** the **sins** of his people.
Josh	24.19	and will not **forgive** your **sins**.
1 Sam	15.25	**forgive** my **sin** and go back with me,
2 Sam	24.10	**sin** in doing this! Please **forgive** me.
1 Kgs	8.34	**Forgive** the **sins** of your people,
	8.36	**Forgive** the **sins** of the king
	8.50	**Forgive** all their **sins** and their **rebellion**
1 Chr	6.49	by which God **forgives** Israel's **sins**.
	21.8	**sin** in doing this! Please **forgive** me.
	28.11	where **sins** are **forgiven**.
2 Chr	6.25	**Forgive** the **sins** of your people
	6.27	to them in heaven and **forgive** the **sins**
	6.39	merciful to them and **forgive** all the **sins**
	7.14	**forgive** their **sins**,
Neh	4.5	Don't **forgive** the **evil** they do
Job	7.21	Can't you ever **forgive** my **sin**?
	10.14	**sin**, so that you could refuse to **forgive**
Ps	25.7	**Forgive** the **sins** and errors of my
	25.11	and **forgive** my **sins**,
	25.18	and **forgive** all my **sins**.
	32.1	are those whose **sins** are **forgiven**,
	32.5	and you **forgave** all my **sins**.
	78.38	He **forgave** their **sin**
	79.9	rescue us and **forgive** our **sins**
	85.2	You have **forgiven** your people's **sins**
	103.3	He **forgives** all my **sins**
	109.14	and never **forgive** his mother's **sins**.
Prov	14.9	don't care if they **sin**, but good people want to be **forgiven**.
	16.6	and God will **forgive** your **sin**.
Is	6.7	and your **sins** are **forgiven**.
	22.14	This **evil** will never be **forgiven** them
	27.9	Israel's **sins** will be **forgiven** only when
	33.24	and all **sins** will be **forgiven**.
	38.17	You **forgive** all my **sins**.
	40.2	and their **sins** are now **forgiven**.
	43.25	I am the God who **forgives** your **sins**,
	53.12	place of many **sinners** and prayed that they might be **forgiven**.
Jer	5.7	should I **forgive** the **sins** of my people?
	18.23	Do not **forgive**...or pardon their **sin**.
	31.34	I will **forgive** their **sins**
	33.8	**forgive** their **sins** and...**rebellion**
	36.3	Then I will **forgive**...their **sins**.
Lam	3.42	**rebelled**, and you...have not **forgiven** us.
Ezek	18.22	All his **sins** will be **forgiven**,
	33.16	I will **forgive** the **sins** he has committed
	45.13	so that your **sins** will be **forgiven**.
Dan	9.9	**forgiving**, although he has **rebelled**
	9.24	**Sin** will be **forgiven** and eternal justice
Hos	14.2	**Forgive** all our **sins** and accept our
Mic	7.18	you **forgive** the **sins** of your people
Mt	9.2	Your **sins** are **forgiven**.
	9.5	Your **sins** are **forgiven**,
	9.6	has authority on earth to **forgive** **sins**.
	12.31	you that people can be **forgiven** any **sin**
	26.28	out for many for the **forgiveness** of **sins**.
Mk	1.4	and God will **forgive** your **sins**.
	2.5	your **sins** are **forgiven**.
	2.7	is the only one who can **forgive** **sins**!
	2.9	Your **sins** are **forgiven**',
	2.10	has authority on earth to **forgive** **sins**.
	3.28	that people can be **forgiven** all their **sins**
Lk	1.77	by having their **sins** **forgiven**.
	3.3	and God will **forgive** your **sins**.
	5.20	Your **sins** are **forgiven**, my friend.
	5.21	is the only one who can **forgive** **sins**!
	5.23	Your **sins** are **forgiven** you,
	5.24	has authority on earth to **forgive** **sins**.
	7.47	that her many **sins** have been **forgiven**.

Lk	7.48	Your **sins** are **forgiven**.	
	7.49	who even **forgives sins**?	
	11.4	**Forgive** us our **sins**, for we **forgive**	
	12.10	**evil** things against the **Holy Spirit** will not be **forgiven**.	
	17.3	If your brother **sins**, rebuke him, and if he repents, **forgive** him.	
	24.47	the **forgiveness** of **sins** must be preached	
Jn	20.23	**forgive** people's **sins**, they are **forgiven**	
Acts	2.38	so that your **sins** will be **forgiven**;	
	3.19	so that he will **forgive** your **sins**.	
	5.31	to repent and have their **sins forgiven**.	
	10.43	in him will have his **sins forgiven**	
	13.38	the message about **forgiveness** of **sins**	
	15.9	**forgave** their **sins** because they believed.	
	26.18	they will have their **sins forgiven**	
Rom	3.25	**sins** are **forgiven** through their faith	
	4.7	are **forgiven**, whose **sins** are pardoned!	
Eph	1.7	our **sins** are **forgiven**.	
Col	1.14	our **sins** are **forgiven**.	
	2.13	God **forgave** us all our **sins**;	
Heb	1.3	**forgiveness** for the **sins** of mankind,	
	2.17	that the people's **sins** would be **forgiven**.	
	8.12	I will **forgive** their **sins**	
	9.5	over the place where **sins** were **forgiven**.	
	9.22	**sins** are **forgiven** only if blood is poured	
	10.18	**forgiven**, and offering to take away **sins**	
Jas	5.15	**sins** he has committed will be **forgiven**.	
	5.20	about the **forgiveness** of many **sins**.	
1 Jn	1.9	he will **forgive** us our **sins**	
	2.2	means by which our **sins** are **forgiven**,	
	2.12	because your **sins** are **forgiven**	
	4.10	means by which our **sins** are **forgiven**.	

Son of Man see **Jesus**

Spirit of God

Mt	12.31	**evil** things against the **Holy Spirit** will not be **forgiven**.
	12.32	says something against the **Holy Spirit** will not be **forgiven**
Mk	3.29	**evil** things against the **Holy Spirit** will never be **forgiven**,
Lk	12.10	**evil** things against the **Holy Spirit** will not be **forgiven**.

Turn see **Repent**

FORTUNE-TELLER

Dan	1.20	—	2.27	x4
Dan	4.7	—	5.11	x3

Magic

2 Kgs	21.6	and **magic** and consulted **fortune-tellers**
2 Chr	33.6	and **magic** and consulted **fortune-tellers**
Dan	1.20	**fortune-teller** or **magician** in his whole
	2.2	he sent for his **fortune-tellers**, **magicians**,
	2.10	**fortune-tellers**, **magicians**, and wizards.
	2.27	**magician**, **fortune-teller**, or astrologer
	4.7	Then all the **fortune-tellers**, **magicians**
	5.11	chief of the **fortune-tellers**, **magicians**,

Medium

1 Sam	28.3	all the **fortune-tellers** and **mediums**
	28.9	forced the **fortune-tellers** and **mediums**
2 Kgs	17.17	consulted **mediums** and **fortune-tellers**,
	21.6	consulted **fortune-tellers** and **mediums**.
	23.24	all the **mediums** and **fortune-tellers**,
2 Chr	33.6	consulted **fortune-tellers** and **mediums**.
Is	8.19	**fortune-tellers** and **mediums**, who chirp

FREE

Rom	3.24	—	8.32	x20
1 Cor	7.15	—	10.29	x13
Gal	1.4	—	5.13	x13
Jer	34.8	—	17	x10

Ex	21.2	—	27	x6
Deut	15.10	—	18	x5
Is	51.11	—	52.4	x5
Mt	27.15	—	26	x5
Lk	23.18	—	24.21	x5
Jn	18.39	—	19.12	x5
Acts	2.24	—	5.40	x5
Col	1.14	—	3.11	x5
Lev	25.10	—	54	x4
Mk	15.6	—	15	x4
Phil	1.7	—	2.7	x4
Gen	24.8	—	41	x3
Ex	6.6	—	27	x3
Is	32.9	—	18	x3
Jn	8.32	—	36	x3
Acts	7.25	—	35	x3
Eph	1.6	—	14	x3

Captives see **Prisoners**

Christ

Rom	3.24	**Christ** Jesus, who sets them **free**
1 Cor	7.22	**free** man who has been called by **Christ**
Gal	1.4	**free** from this present evil age, **Christ**
	5.1	**Freedom** is what we have — **Christ** has set us **free**
Eph	1.7	death of **Christ** we are set **free**,
Col	2.11	by **Christ**, which consists of being **freed**
	2.15	And on that cross **Christ freed** himself
	2.20	have died with **Christ** and are set **free**

Evil see **Sin**

Fear

Ps	34.4	he **freed** me from all my **fears**.

Happy

Ps	68.6	leads prisoners out into **happy freedom**,
Prov	29.6	while honest people are **happy** and **free**.
Is	35.10	will be **happy** for ever, for ever **free**
	51.11	will be **happy** for ever, for ever **free**
Mal	4.2	be as **free** and **happy** as calves let out

Help

Lk	1.68	**help** of his people and has set them **free**.
Acts	7.35	set them **free** with the **help** of the angel
Rom	15.26	**freely** decided to give an offering to **help**
2 Cor	8.17	eager to **help** that of his own **free** will

Holy

Is	47.4	The **holy** God of Israel sets us **free**
Dan	9.24	**freeing** your people and your **holy** city
1 Thes	4.3	you to be **holy** and completely **free** from

Jews

Mk	15.9	to set **free** for you the king of the **Jews**?
Jn	18.39	set **free** for you the King of the **Jews**?
1 Cor	12.13	**Jews** or Gentiles, whether slaves or **free**,
Gal	3.28	**Jews** and Gentiles...slaves and **free** men,

Life

Ezra	9.8	have **freed** us...and given us new **life**.
Is	32.9	who live an easy **life**, **free** from worries
	32.11	living an easy **life**, **free** from worries;
	51.14	be set **free**; they will live a long **life**
Rom	5.17	**freely** put right with him will rule in **life**
	5.18	all mankind **free** and gives them **life**.
	6.23	but God's **free** gift is eternal **life**
	8.2	**life** in union with Christ...has set me **free**
Heb	2.15	**free** those who were slaves all their **lives**
	13.5	your **lives free** from the love of money
1 Pet	1.18	**free** from the worthless manner of **life**

Power, Might

Deut	7.8	**might** and set you **free** from slavery
Ps	54.1	me by your **power**, O God; set me **free**
	79.11	**power free** those who are condemned to
Is	10.27	will **free** you from the **power** of Assyria,

Is	49.26	free. They will know that I am Israel's **powerful** God.
	60.16	the **mighty** God of Israel sets you **free**.
Jer	31.11	**free** and have saved them from a **mighty**
Acts	2.24	setting him **free** from its **power**,
Rom	6.7	he is set **free** from the **power** of sin.
Col	2.11	**freed** from the **power** of this sinful self.
	2.15	**freed** himself from the **power** of the

Prisoners, Captives

Job	3.18	**prisoners** enjoy peace, **free** from shouts
	12.14	who can **free** the man God **imprisons**?
Ps	68.6	leads **prisoners** out into happy **freedom**,
	79.11	**prisoners**, and by your great power **free**
	102.20	the groans of **prisoners** and set **free**
	146.7	The Lord sets **prisoners** free
Is	14.17	the man who never **freed** his **prisoners**
	42.7	set **free** those who sit in dark **prisons**.
	45.13	and set my **captive** people **free**.
	49.9	I will say to the **prisoners**, 'Go **free**!
	51.14	who are **prisoners** will soon be set **free**;
	61.1	release to **captives** And **freedom**
Jer	37.4	**prison** and was still moving about **freely**
Mt	27.15	**free** any one **prisoner** the crowd asked
Mk	15.6	**free** any one **prisoner** the people asked
Jn	18.39	set **free** a **prisoner** for you during
Phil	1.7	am in **prison** and also while I was **free**

Promise

Gen	24.8	you will be **free** from this **promise**.
Ps	119.154	me **free**; save me, as you have **promised**.
Rom	4.16	**promise**...be guaranteed as God's **free**
Gal	4.23	the **free** woman was born as a result of God's **promise**.
2 Pet	2.19	**promise** them **freedom** while they

Sin, Evil

Job	33.9	I am innocent and **free** from **sin**.
Ps	19.13	be perfect and **free** from the **evil** of **sin**.
Is	5.18	are unable to break **free** from your **sins**.
Ezek	37.23	I will **free** them from all the ways in which they **sin**
Dan	9.24	**freeing** your people and your holy city from **sin** and **evil**.
Acts	13.38	the **sins** from which the Law of Moses could not set you **free**.
Rom	5.15	God's **free** gift is not like Adam's **sin**.
	6.7	he is set **free** from the power of **sin**.
	6.18	You were set **free** from **sin**
	6.20	of **sin**, you were **free** from righteousness
	6.22	now you have been set **free** from **sin**
	8.2	has set me **free** from the law of **sin**
Gal	1.4	to set us **free** from this present **evil**
Eph	1.7	we are set **free**, that is, our **sins**
Col	1.14	whom we are set **free**, that is, our **sins**
	2.11	**freed** from the power of this sinful self.
1 Pet	2.16	use your **freedom** to cover up any **evil**,
Rev	1.5	death he has **freed** us from our **sins**

Slave

Gen	44.10	**slave**, and the rest of you can go **free**.
Ex	6.6	**free** from your **slavery** to the Egyptians.
	6.7	I set you **free** from **slavery** in Egypt.
	15.16	the people you set **free** from **slavery**.
	21.7	**slave**, she is not to be set **free**,
	21.26	he is to **free** the **slave** as payment
	21.27	he is to **free** the **slave** as payment
Deut	7.8	**free** from **slavery** to the king of Egypt.
	15.18	be resentful when you set a **slave free**;
Ezra	9.8	You have **freed** us from **slavery**
Job	3.19	and **slaves** at last are **free**.
Ps	129.4	has **freed** me from **slavery**.
Jer	34.10	**free** their **slaves** and never to **enslave**
	34.13	and set them **free** from **slavery**.
	34.14	**free** any Hebrew **slave** who had served
	34.16	the **slaves** whom you had set **free**

Ezek	34.27	**free** from those who made them **slaves**,
Rom	6.18	set **free** from sin and became the **slaves**
	6.20	**slaves** of sin, you were **free** from
	6.22	**free** from sin and are the **slaves** of God.
	8.21	be set **free** from its **slavery** to decay
1 Cor	9.19	I am a **free** man, nobody's **slave**
	12.13	Jews or Gentiles, whether **slaves** or **free**,
Gal	3.28	**slaves** and **free** men, between men and
	4.22	by a **slave-woman**, the other by a **free**
	4.31	of a **slave-woman** but of a **free** woman.
Eph	6.8	**slave** or **free**, for the good work
Col	3.11	savages, **slaves**, and **free** men,
Heb	2.15	this way set **free** those who were **slaves**
2 Pet	2.19	**freedom** while they themselves are **slaves**
Rev	6.15	**slave** and **free**,
	13.16	poor, **slave** and **free**, to have a mark
	19.18	**slave** and **free**, great and small!

Spirit of God

2 Cor	3.17	the **Spirit**...is present, there is **freedom**.
Phil	1.19	**Spirit** of Jesus Christ I shall be set **free**.

Will

Is	52.4	you did so of your own **free will**;
Jn	10.18	I give it up of my own **free will**.
2 Cor	8.3	Of their own **free will** they begged
	8.17	eager to help that of his own **free will**
Phil	2.7	his own **free will** he gave up all he had,
Phlm	.14	like you to do it of your own **free will**.

FRIEND

Prov	12.26	—	19.7	x14
2 Cor	4.9	—	7.1	x8
Lk	11.5	—	12.14	x7
Lk	14.10	—	16.9	x7
1 Jn	2.7	—	4.11	x6
Prov	27.6	—	29.5	x5
Jer	9.4 – 20			x5
Rom	16.2 – 12			x5
3 Jn	.2 – 15			x5
2 Sam	15.32	—	16.17	x4
Esth	5.10	—	6.13	x4
Job	16.20	—	17.12	x4
Jas	2.23	—	4.4	x4
2 Pet	3.1 – 17			x4
Job	6.14 – 27			x3
Job	19.14 – 21			x3
Job	42.7 – 11			x3
Is	5.1 – 3			x3
Jer	20.4 – 10			x3
Jn	15.13 – 15			x3
Rom	5.10 – 11			x3
Jude	.3 – 20			x3

Christ see Jesus

Enemy

Judg	5.31	your **enemies** die...but may your **friends**
2 Kgs	9.17	if they are **friends** or **enemies**.
Ps	7.3	**friend** or...done violence to my **enemy**
Prov	16.7	you can make your **enemies** into **friends**.
Mt	5.43	Love your **friends**, hate your **enemies**.
Lk	23.12	became **friends**...they had been **enemies**.
Rom	5.10	**enemies**, but he made us his **friends**
	11.15	from God's **enemies** into his **friends**.
2 Cor	4.9	many **enemies**, but we are never without a **friend**
	5.18	changed us from **enemies** into his **friends**
	5.20	you from **enemies** into his **friends**!
Jas	4.4	**friend** makes himself God's **enemy**.

Evil

Ps	28.3	**evil** — men whose words are **friendly**,
Prov	15.26	**evil** thoughts, but...pleased with **friendly**
	24.1	**evil** people...don't try to make **friends**
Tit	3.2	**evil** of anyone, but to be...**friendly**,

God

Job	29.4	**friendship** of **God** protected my home.
Rom	5.10	We were **God's** enemies, but he made us his **friends**
	5.11	who has now made us **God's friends**.
	11.15	from **God's** enemies into his **friends**.
	11.28	of **God's** choice, they are his **friends**
2 Cor	5.19	**God** was making all mankind his **friends**
	5.20	let **God** change you from enemies into his **friends**!
Col	1.22	**God** has made you his **friends**,
Jas	2.23	so Abraham was called **God's friend**.

Jesus, Christ

Rom	5.11	our Lord **Jesus Christ**, who has now made us God's **friends**.
2 Cor	5.18	**Christ** changed us...into his **friends**
	5.19	all mankind his **friends** through **Christ**.

Lord

Judg	5.31	O **Lord**, but may your **friends** shine
Ps	25.14	**Lord** is the **friend** of those who obey
Prov	16.7	please the **Lord**, you can make your enemies into **friends**.
Jn	11.3	**Lord**, your dear **friend** is ill.
Rom	16.8	**friend** in the fellowship of the **Lord**.

Love

Deut	13.6	the wife you **love** or your closest **friend**
Job	19.19	My closest **friends** look at me with disgust; those I **loved**
Prov	17.17	**Friends** always show their **love**
Mt	5.43	**Love** your **friends**,
Jn	15.13	**love** a person can have for his **friends**
1 Jn	4.7	Dear **friends**, let us **love** one another,
	4.11	**friends**, if this is how God **loved** us

Loyal

2 Sam	10.2	I must show **loyal friendship** to Hanun,
	16.17	happened to your **loyalty** to your **friend**
1 Chr	19.2	I must show **loyal friendship** to Hanun,
Job	6.14	trouble like this I need **loyal friends**
Prov	18.24	**friends** are more **loyal** than brothers.

Need

Job	6.14	trouble like this I **need loyal friends**
Acts	24.23	his **friends** to provide for his **needs**.
	27.3	his **friends**, to be given what he **needed**.

Peace

Mk	9.50	the salt of **friendship**...live in **peace**
Tit	3.2	but to be **peaceful** and **friendly**,
Jas	3.17	it is also **peaceful**, gentle, and **friendly**;

Words

Ps	28.3	men whose **words** are **friendly**,
Prov	15.26	but he is pleased with **friendly words**.
Jer	9.8	speaks **friendly words** to his neighbour,
	12.6	even though they speak **friendly words**.

GENEROUS

	2 Cor	8.2	— 9.13	x7
	Deut	15.8 – 14		x3

God

1 Tim	6.17	**God**, who **generously** gives us everything
Jas	1.5	**God** gives **generously** and graciously to

GENTILES

	Acts	13.16	— 15.23	x20
	Rom	1.13	— 3.30	x14
	Gal	1.16	— 3.28	x14
	Acts	17.17	— 22.21	x12
	Rom	9.24	— 11.30	x12
	Rom	15.9	— 16.4	x11
	Acts	9.15	— 11.20	x9
	Eph	2.11	— 3.8	x8

	Acts	26.17 – 23		x3
	1 Cor	9.21 — 10.32		x3

Believe see Faith

Blessings

Rom	11.12	brought rich **blessings** to the **Gentiles**.
	15.27	spiritual **blessings** with the **Gentiles**,
Eph	3.6	**Gentiles** have a part with the Jews in God's **blessings**;

Faith, Believe

Acts	11.1	**believers** throughout Judaea heard that the **Gentiles**
	14.1	and **Gentiles** became **believers**.
	14.2	not **believe** stirred up the **Gentiles**
	14.27	the way for the **Gentiles** to **believe**.
	15.7	to the **Gentiles**, so that they could hear and **believe**.
	21.25	the **Gentiles** who have become **believers**,
Rom	1.16	who **believe**, first the Jews and also the **Gentiles**.
	3.30	the **Gentiles** right through their **faith**.
Gal	3.8	**Gentiles** right with himself through **faith**.
1 Tim	2.7	of the **Gentiles**, to proclaim the message of **faith**

Good News, Gospel, Message, Preach

Mt	10.18	tell the **Good News** to them and to the **Gentiles**.
Acts	11.20	**Gentiles** also, telling them the **Good**
	15.7	**preach** the **Good News** to the **Gentiles**,
	26.20	**Gentiles**, I **preached** that they must
	28.28	**message**...has been sent to the **Gentiles**.
Rom	15.16	**Good News**...in order that the **Gentiles**
1 Cor	1.24	and **Gentiles**, this **message** is Christ,
Gal	1.16	**Good News** about him to the **Gentiles**,
	2.2	**gospel**...that I **preach** to the **Gentiles**.
	2.7	of **preaching** the **gospel** to the **Gentiles**,
Eph	2.17	**Good News** of peace...to you **Gentiles**
	3.6	by means of the **gospel** the **Gentiles**
	3.8	taking to the **Gentiles** the **Good News**
1 Thes	2.16	**preaching** to the **Gentiles** the **message**
1 Tim	2.7	the **Gentiles**, to proclaim the **message**
2 Tim	4.17	full **message** for all the **Gentiles** to hear;

Law

Acts	21.21	**Gentile** countries to abandon the **Law**
Rom	2.12	**Gentiles** do not have the **Law** of Moses
	2.14	The **Gentiles** do not have the **Law**;
	2.27	the **Gentiles** because you break the **Law**,
1 Cor	9.21	like a **Gentile**, outside the Jewish **Law**,
Col	2.13	were **Gentiles** without the **Law**.

Message see Good News

Preach see Good News

Salvation

Acts	26.23	of **salvation**...to the **Gentiles**.
	28.28	**salvation** has been sent to the **Gentiles**.
Rom	11.11	**salvation** has come to the **Gentiles**,
1 Thes	2.16	**Gentiles** the message that would bring them **salvation**.

Sin

Rom	2.12	**Gentiles** do not have the Law...they **sin**
	3.9	Jews and **Gentiles** alike are all under the power of **sin**.
	11.11	Because they **sinned**, salvation has come to the **Gentiles**,
Gal	2.15	and not "**Gentile sinners**,
	2.17	to be **sinners** as much as the **Gentiles**
Col	2.13	your **sins** and because you were **Gentiles**

Spirit of God

Acts	10.45	gift of the **Holy Spirit** on the **Gentiles**
	15.8	the **Gentiles** by giving the **Holy Spirit**
Eph	2.18	**Gentiles**, are able to come in the...**Spirit**

Worship

Acts	13.16	and all **Gentiles** here who **worship** God:
	13.26	and all **Gentiles** here who **worship** God:
	13.50	**Gentile** women...who **worshipped** God.
	17.17	with the **Gentiles** who **worshipped** God,
	18.7	**Gentile** named...Justus, who **worshipped**

GIFT

1 Cor	12.1	—	14.37	x18
Rom	3.24	—	6.23	x9
Num	6.20	—	8.21	x8
2 Chr	31.5	—	32.23	x8
Lev	7.29	—	10.14	x7
Eph	1.6	—	4.11	x6
1 Sam	6.3 – 17			x5
2 Cor	8.12	—	9.15	x5
Ex	29.24 – 28			x4
Num	18.6 – 32			x4
Deut	12.6 – 26			x4
Gen	43.15 – 26			x3
Lev	14.12 – 24			x3
Lev	23.17 – 38			x3
Judg	3.15 – 18			x3
1 Kgs	10.10 – 25			x3
2 Kgs	5.15 – 17			x3
1 Chr	26.20 – 28			x3
2 Chr	9.9 – 24			x3
Ezek	20.31 – 40			x3
Mt	5.23 – 24			x3
Mt	23.18 – 20			x3
Lk	21.1 – 5			x3
Rom	12.3 – 6			x3
1 Cor	7.7 – 17			x3
Gal	3.18 – 22			x3

Dedicate see Offer

Faith

Gal	3.22	**gift**...promised on the basis of **faith**

Free

Rom	3.24	**free gift** of God's grace all are put right
	4.16	**free gift** to all of Abraham's descendants
	5.15	God's **free gift** is not like Adam's sin.
	6.23	**free gift** is eternal life in union with
Eph	1.6	the **free gift** he gave us in his dear Son!

God

Gen	30.20	**God** has given me a fine **gift**.
1 Chr	26.20	storerooms for **gifts** dedicated to **God**.
	26.26	**gifts** dedicated to **God** by King David,
Ps	76.11	**God** what you promised him; bring **gifts**
Ecc	3.13	It is **God's gift**.
	5.19	It is a **gift** from **God**.
Mt	5.23	to offer your **gift** to **God** at the altar
	5.24	come back and offer your **gift** to **God**.
Lk	21.5	fine stones and the **gifts** offered to **God**.
Acts	2.38	will receive **God's gift**, the Holy Spirit.
	5.32	is **God's gift** to those who obey him.
	8.20	thinking that you can buy **God's gift**
	10.45	that **God** had poured out his **gift**
	11.17	**God** gave those Gentiles the same **gift**
Rom	3.24	But by the free **gift** of **God's** grace
	4.16	as **God's** free **gift** to all of Abraham's
	5.5	the Holy Spirit, who is **God's gift**
	5.15	**God's** free **gift** is not like Adam's sin.
	5.16	between **God's gift** and the sin
	6.23	but **God's** free **gift** is eternal life
	8.23	the Spirit as the first of **God's gifts**
	12.3	because of **God's** gracious **gift** to me
	12.6	different **gifts** in accordance with the grace that **God** has given
1 Cor	3.10	Using the **gift** that **God** gave me
	7.7	each one has a special **gift** from **God**,
2 Cor	8.12	**God** will accept your **gift** on the basis

2 Cor	9.11	that many will thank **God** for your **gifts**
	9.15	Let us thank **God** for his priceless **gift**!
Gal	3.18	For if **God's gift** depends on the Law
Eph	1.6	praise **God** for his glorious grace, for the free **gift**
	2.8	**God's gift**, so that no one can boast
	3.7	of the gospel by **God's** special **gift**
2 Tim	1.6	to keep alive the **gift** that **God** gave
Heb	6.4	in **God's** light; they tasted heaven's **gift**
	11.4	**God** himself approved of his **gifts**.
1 Pet	1.10	about this **gift** which **God** would give
	3.7	**God's gift** of life.
	4.10	a good manager of **God's** different **gifts**,

Lord

Ex	29.28	is the people's **gift** to me, the **Lord**.
Lev	7.29	as a special **gift** to the **Lord** Also: 7.30; 8.27; 8.29
	9.21	hind legs as the special **gift** to the **Lord**
	10.14	special **gift**...to the **Lord**
	14.12	them as a special **gift** to the **Lord**
	14.21	a special **gift** to the **Lord**
	14.24	as a special **gift** to the **Lord**
	23.17	them to the **Lord** as a special **gift**.
	23.20	two lambs as a special **gift** to the **Lord**
	27.9	then every **gift** made to the **Lord**
Num	6.20	as a special **gift** to the **Lord**;
	8.21	them as a special **gift** to the **Lord**.
	15.21	special **gift** is to be given to the **Lord**
Deut	12.6	the **gifts** that you promise to the **Lord**,
	12.11	**gifts** that you have promised to the **Lord**,
	12.17	the **gifts** that you promise to the **Lord**,
	12.26	**gifts** that you have promised the **Lord**.
1 Sam	6.17	five gold tumours to the **Lord** as a **gift**
1 Chr	28.12	and the **gifts** dedicated to the **Lord**.
2 Chr	31.6	**gifts**, which they dedicated to the **Lord**
	31.14	receiving the **gifts** offered to the **Lord**
Ps	76.11	Give the **Lord** your God what you promised him; bring **gifts**
	127.3	Children are a **gift** from the **Lord**;
Hos	3.5	the **Lord** and will receive his good **gifts**.
Acts	11.17	same **gift** that he gave us when we believed in the **Lord** Jesus
Rom	6.23	**gift** is eternal life in union with Christ Jesus our **Lord**.
1 Cor	7.17	go on living according to the **Lord's gift**

Message, Proclaim

Rom	12.6	If our **gift** is to speak God's **message**,
1 Cor	12.10	the **gift** of speaking God's **message**;
	13.9	our **gifts**...of inspired **messages**
	14.1	the **gift** of proclaiming God's **message**. Also: 14.5; 14.22; 14.32

Offer, Dedicate, Present

Gen	43.25	their **gifts** ready to **present** to Joseph
Ex	29.24	to **dedicate** it to me as a special **gift**.
	29.26	and **dedicate** it to me as a special **gift**.
	29.27	be **dedicated** to me as a special **gift**
Lev	7.29	**offering** must bring...it as a...**gift**
	7.30	**present** it as a special **gift** to the Lord
	8.27	**presented** it as a special **gift** to the
	8.29	**presented** it as a special **gift** to the
	10.14	**presented** as the special **gift** and the
	14.12	**present** them as a special **gift** to the
	14.24	**present** them as a special **gift** to the
	23.17	and **present** them to the Lord as a...**gift**.
	23.20	**gift** to the Lord...These **offerings**
	23.38	these **offerings** are in addition to your regular **gifts**,
	27.9	**offering** to the Lord, then every **gift**
Num	6.20	shall **present** them as a special **gift**

Num	7.10	they were ready to **present** their **gifts**
	7.11	to **present** his **gifts** for the **dedication**
	8.11	**dedicate** the Levites to me as a...**gift**
	8.13	**Dedicate** the Levites as a special **gift**
	8.21	Aaron **dedicated** them as a special **gift**
	18.6	as a **gift** to you. They are **dedicated**
	18.32	the **gifts** before the best part is **offered**;
Deut	12.6	**offerings**, the **gifts** that you promise
	12.11	your **offerings**, and those special **gifts**
	12.26	**offerings** and the **gifts** that you have
1 Kgs	10.10	She **presented** to King Solomon the **gifts**
1 Chr	26.20	storerooms for **gifts dedicated** to God.
	26.26	were in charge of all the **gifts dedicated**
	28.12	and the **gifts dedicated** to the Lord.
2 Chr	9.9	She **presented** to King Solomon the **gifts**
	31.6	**gifts**, which they **dedicated** to the Lord
	31.12	and put all the **gifts** and **tithes** in them
	31.14	receiving the **gifts offered** to the Lord
	32.23	**offerings** to the Lord and **gifts** to
Ps	72.10	and of the islands will **offer** him **gifts**;
Ezek	20.31	**offer** the same **gifts** and defile yourselves
	20.39	by **offering gifts** to your idols.
	20.40	your best **offerings**, and your holy **gifts**.
Dan	2.48	**presented** him with many splendid **gifts**,
	11.38	**offer** gold, silver...and other rich **gifts**
Mt	2.11	brought out their **gifts**...and **presented**
	5.23	to **offer** your **gift** to God at the altar
	5.24	come back and **offer** your **gift** to God.
Lk	21.4	**offered** their **gifts** from what they had
	21.5	fine stones and the **gifts offered** to God.
Phil	4.18	your **gifts**...like a sweet-smelling **offering**
Heb	8.4	there are priests who **offer** the **gifts**

Proclaim see Message

Promise

Deut	12.6	the **gifts** that you **promise** to the Lord,
	12.11	special **gifts** that you have **promised**
	12.17	the **gifts** that you **promise** to the Lord,
	12.26	**gifts** that you have **promised** the Lord.
Ps	76.11	you **promised** him; bring **gifts** to him,
Acts	1.4	the **gift** my Father **promised**.
Rom	4.16	**promise** should be guaranteed as God's free **gift**
2 Cor	9.5	the **gift** you **promised** to make.
Gal	3.18	**gift**...no longer depends on his **promise**.
	3.22	**gift** which is **promised** on the basis of
2 Pet	1.4	great and precious **gifts** he **promised**,

Sin

1 Sam	6.3	it a **gift** to him to pay for your **sin**.
	6.8	to him as a **gift** to pay for your **sins**.
	6.17	as a **gift** to pay for their **sins**,
Rom	5.15	God's free **gift** is not like Adam's **sin**.
	5.16	between God's **gift** and the **sin**

Spirit of God

Acts	2.38	will receive God's **gift**, the **Holy Spirit**.
	5.32	**Holy Spirit**, who is God's **gift**
	10.45	poured out his **gift** of the **Holy Spirit**
Rom	5.5	**Holy Spirit**, who is God's **gift** to us.
	8.23	the **Spirit** as the first of God's **gifts**.
1 Cor	2.14	the **gifts** that come from **God's Spirit**.
	12.1	about the **gifts** from the **Holy Spirit**.
	12.4	spiritual **gifts**, but the same **Spirit** gives
	12.10	**Spirit** gives one person...the **gift**
	14.12	are eager to have the **gifts** of the **Spirit**
Heb	2.4	distributing the **gifts** of the **Holy Spirit**
	6.4	**gift** and received...the **Holy Spirit**;

Spiritual

1 Cor	12.4	are different kinds of **spiritual gifts**
	14.1	Set your hearts on **spiritual gifts**,
	14.37	God's messenger or has a **spiritual gift**,
1 Tim	4.14	neglect the **spiritual gift** that is in you,

Tongues

1 Cor	13.8	are **gifts** of speaking in strange **tongues**,
	14.13	in strange **tongues**, then, must pray for the **gift**
	14.22	the **gift** of speaking in strange **tongues**

GLAD

Ps	97.1 – 12		x4
Jn	16.20 – 22		x4
2 Cor	11.4 —	13.9	x4
1 Chr	16.10 – 32		x3
Is	65.18 —	66.14	x3
Lk	1.14 – 47		x3
Phil	2.17 – 28		x3
Rev	18.20 —	19.7	x3

God, Lord

Ps	32.11	be **glad** and rejoice because of what the **Lord** has done.
	35.9	I will be **glad** because of the **Lord**;
	51.14	O **God**...I will **gladly** proclaim
	54.6	will **gladly** offer you a sacrifice, O **Lord**;
	68.4	is the **Lord** — be **glad** in his presence!
	69.32	will be **glad**; those who worship **God**
	86.4	Make your servant **glad**, O **Lord**,
	92.4	O **Lord**, make me **glad**;
	97.1	The **Lord** is king! Earth, be **glad**!
	97.12	**glad** because of what the **Lord** has
	122.1	**glad** when they said to me, "Let us go to the **Lord's** house.
Joel	2.21	**glad** because of all the **Lord** has done
	2.23	Be **glad**...at what the **Lord** your **God**
Hab	3.18	**glad**, because the **Lord God** is my
Zech	10.7	**glad** because of what the **Lord** has
Lk	1.47	my soul is **glad** because of **God**
Acts	13.48	**glad** and praised the **Lord's** message;
2 Cor	9.7	for **God** loves the one who gives **gladly**.
Jas	1.9	must be **glad** when **God** lifts him up
	1.10	be **glad** when **God** brings him down.

Joy, Happy, Rejoice

Deut	28.47	serve him with **glad** and **joyful** hearts.
2 Sam	1.20	**glad**; do not let...pagans **rejoice**
Ps	28.7	me **glad**; I praise him with **joyful** songs.
	31.7	I will be **glad** and **rejoice**
	32.11	be **glad** and **rejoice**
	35.9	I will be **glad**...I will be **happy**
	40.16	be **glad** and **joyful**.
	45.15	With **joy** and **gladness** they come
	51.8	me hear the sounds of **joy** and **gladness**;
	67.4	the nations be **glad** and sing for **joy**,
	68.3	But the righteous are **glad** and **rejoice**
	70.4	be **glad** and **joyful**.
	97.1	**glad**! **Rejoice**, you islands of the seas!
	97.8	are **glad**, and the cities of Judah **rejoice**
	106.5	**happiness** of your nation, in the **glad**
	149.2	**glad**...because of your Creator; **rejoice**,
Song	3.11	on the day of his **gladness** and **joy**.
Is	35.10	**gladness**, singing and shouting for **joy**.
	51.3	**Joy** and **gladness** will be there,
	51.11	**gladness**, singing and shouting for **joy**.
	61.3	**Joy** and **gladness** instead of grief,
	65.18	Be **glad** and **rejoice** for ever in what
	66.10	**Rejoice** with Jerusalem; be **glad** for her,
Jer	7.34	**joy** and **gladness** and to the happy
	16.9	silence the sounds of **joy** and **gladness**
	25.10	silence their shouts of **joy** and **gladness**
	31.13	into **joy**, their sorrow into **gladness**.
	33.11	the shouts of **gladness** and **joy**
	50.11	You are **happy** and **glad**,
Joel	2.21	but be **joyful** and **glad**
	2.23	Be **glad**, people of Zion, **rejoice** at what
Hab	3.18	I will still be **joyful** and **glad**,
Zech	8.19	of **joy** and **gladness** for the people

Mt	5.12	Be **happy** and **glad**, for a great reward
Lk	1.14	How **glad** and **happy** you will be,
	6.23	Be **glad**...and dance for **joy**,
Acts	2.26	**gladness**, and my words are full of **joy**.
2 Cor	2.3	make me **glad**. For...when I am **happy**,
Phil	2.17	am **glad** and share my **joy** with you all.
	2.18	must be **glad** and share your **joy**
Rev	19.7	Let us **rejoice** and be **glad**;

Lord see **God**

Rejoice see **Joy**

Righteous

Ps	32.11	that are **righteous**, be **glad** and rejoice
	51.14	will **gladly** proclaim your **righteousness**.
	58.10	**righteous** will be **glad** when they see
	68.3	But the **righteous** are **glad** and rejoice
	97.11	shines on the **righteous**, and **gladness**
	97.12	All you that are **righteous** be **glad**
	107.42	The **righteous** see this and are **glad**,

Sad, Sorrow

Jer	31.13	their **sorrow** into **gladness**.
Jn	16.20	but your **sadness** will turn into **gladness**.
2 Cor	2.3	made **sad** by the very people who should make me **glad**.
	6.10	although **saddened**, we are always **glad**
Phil	2.28	will be **glad** again...and my own **sorrow**
Heb	12.11	something to make us **sad**, not **glad**.
	13.17	do their work **gladly**; if not, they will do it with **sadness**,

GLORY

Jn	11.4	—	17.24	x23
2 Cor	3.7	—	4.17	x15
Rom	8.17	—	9.23	x7
1 Pet	4.11	—	5.10	x6
1 Pet	1.7 – 24			x5
2 Pet	1.3	—	3.18	x5
1 Chr	16.24 – 29			x4
Ps	29.1 – 9			x4
Ps	96.3 – 8			x4
Is	60.1 – 19			x4
Dan	4.30 – 37			x4
Lk	9.26 – 32			x4
Eph	1.6 – 17			x4
2 Thes	1.9	—	2.14	x4
Heb	1.3	—	2.10	x4
Rev	4.9	—	5.13	x4
1 Chr	29.11 – 25			x3
Ps	145.5 – 12			x3
Is	2.10 – 21			x3
Is	28.1 – 5			x3
Lk	2.9 – 32			x3
Jn	7.18 – 39			x3
Col	1.11 – 27			x3
Jude	.8 – 25			x3

Angels, Beings

Ps	29.1	you heavenly **beings**; praise his **glory**
Mt	16.27	the **glory** of his Father with his **angels**,
Mk	8.38	the **glory** of his Father with the...**angels**.
Lk	2.9	**angel**...appeared to them, and the **glory**
	9.26	**glory** of the Father and of the...**angels**.
Heb	2.7	the **angels**; you crowned him with **glory**
2 Pet	2.10	no respect for the **glorious beings** above;
Jude	.8	and insult the **glorious beings** above.

Christ see **Jesus**

God, Father

Deut	5.24	The Lord our **God** showed us his greatness and his **glory**
1 Sam	4.21	**God's glory** has left Israel
	4.22	**God's glory** has left Israel
1 Chr	29.13	**God**, we...praise your **glorious** name.

Job	37.22	and the **glory** of **God** fills us with awe.
Ps	19.1	How clearly the sky reveals **God's glory**!
	29.3	the **glorious God** thunders,
	29.9	**Glory** to **God**!
	57.5	**God**, and your **glory** over all the earth.
	57.11	**God**, and your **glory** over all the earth.
	76.4	How **glorious** you are, O **God**!
	106.20	they exchanged the **glory** of **God**
	108.5	**God**, and your **glory** over all the earth.
Is	4.5	**God's glory** will cover and protect
	42.8	**God**. No other god may share my **glory**;
Dan	4.34	**God** and gave honour and **glory**
Mt	16.27	to come in the **glory** of his **Father**
Mk	8.38	**glory** of his **Father** with the holy angels.
Lk	2.14	**Glory** to **God** in the highest heaven,
	9.26	**glory** of the **Father** and of the holy
	19.38	Peace in heaven and **glory** to **God**!
Jn	1.14	**glory** which he received as the **Father's**
	11.4	in order to bring **glory** to **God**,
	11.40	tell you that you would see **God's glory**
	12.28	**Father**, bring **glory** to your name!
	13.31	**God's glory** is revealed through him,
	13.32	if **God's glory** is revealed through him,
	14.13	**Father's glory** will be shown through
	15.8	**Father's glory** is shown by your bearing
	17.1	**Father**...Give **glory** to your Son,
	17.5	**Father**! Give me **glory** in your presence
	21.19	would die and bring **glory** to **God**.)
Acts	3.13	the **God** of our ancestors, has given divine **glory** to his Servant
	7.2	the **God** of **glory** appeared to him
	7.55	and saw **God's glory** and Jesus standing
Rom	2.10	But **God** will give **glory**
	3.7	what if my untruth serves **God's glory**
	5.2	hope we have of sharing **God's glory**!
	6.4	by the **glorious** power of the **Father**,
	11.36	To **God** be the **glory** for ever! Amen.
	15.7	for the **glory** of **God**,
	16.25	Let us give **glory** to **God**
	16.27	To the only **God**...be **glory**
1 Cor	6.20	So use your bodies for **God's glory**.
	10.31	do it all for **God's glory**.
	11.7	he reflects the image and **glory** of **God**.
2 Cor	1.20	"Amen" is said to the **glory** of **God**.
	3.7	**God's glory** appeared when it was given.
	4.6	bring us the knowledge of **God's glory**
	4.15	they will offer to the **glory** of **God**
	9.13	will give **glory** to **God** for your loyalty
Gal	1.5	To **God** be the **glory** for ever
Eph	1.6	Let us praise **God** for his **glorious** grace
	1.12	praise **God's glory**!
	1.17	the **God** of our Lord Jesus Christ, the **glorious Father**,
	3.16	I ask **God** from the wealth of his **glory**
	3.21	to **God** be the **glory** in the church
Phil	1.11	for the **glory** and praise of **God**.
	2.11	to the **glory** of **God** the **Father**.
	4.20	To our **God** and **Father** be the **glory**
Col	1.27	that you will share in the **glory** of **God**.
1 Tim	1.11	from the **glorious** and blessed **God**.
	1.17	only **God** — to him be honour and **glory**
Tit	2.13	the **glory** of our great **God** and Saviour
Heb	1.3	He reflects the brightness of **God's glory**
1 Pet	4.14	the **glorious** Spirit, the Spirit of **God**,
2 Pet	1.17	he was given honour and **glory** by **God**
Rev	4.11	**God**! You are worthy to receive **glory**,
	19.1	Praise **God**! Salvation, **glory**,
	21.11	and shining with the **glory** of **God**.
	21.23	because the **glory** of **God** shines on it,

God's People

Lev	10.3	I will reveal my **glory** to **my people**.
Is	28.5	**glorious** crown of flowers for **his people**
	43.7	**own people**...to bring me **glory**.

2 Thes 1.10 Day to receive **glory** from all **his people**

Heaven

Ps	29.1	you **heavenly** beings; praise his **glory**
	113.4	his **glory** is above the **heavens**.
	148.13	his **glory** is above earth and **heaven**.
Is	63.15	**heaven**, where you live in...**glory**.
Ezek	3.12	the **glory** of the Lord in **heaven** above!
Dan	4.37	and **glorify** the King of **Heaven**.
Mt	24.30	of **heaven** with power and great **glory**.
Lk	2.14	**Glory** to God in the highest **heaven**,
	9.31	in **heavenly glory** and talked with Jesus
	19.38	Peace in **heaven** and **glory** to God!
Acts	7.55	up to **heaven** and saw God's **glory**

Honour

Ps	8.5	crowned him with **glory** and **honour**.
	84.11	**glorious** king, blessing us with...**honour**.
Is	55.5	I will give you **honour** and **glory**.
Dan	4.34	**honour** and **glory** to the one who lives
	4.36	my **honour**, my majesty, and the **glory**
	4.37	**honour**, and **glorify** the King of Heaven.
Rom	2.7	and seek **glory**, **honour**,
	2.10	But God will give **glory**, **honour**,
2 Thes	1.10	**glory** from all his people and **honour**
1 Tim	1.17	be **honour** and **glory** for ever and ever!
Heb	2.7	crowned him with **glory** and **honour**.
	2.9	now crowned with **glory** and **honour**
1 Pet	1.7	will receive praise and **glory** and **honour**
2 Pet	1.17	when he was given **honour** and **glory**
Rev	4.9	songs of **glory** and **honour** and thanks
	4.11	to receive **glory**, **honour**, and power.
	5.12	**honour**, **glory**, and praise!
	5.13	be praise and **honour**, **glory** and might,
	7.12	**glory**, wisdom, thanksgiving, **honour**,

Jesus, Christ, Son of God, Son of Man

Mt	16.27	**Son of Man** is...to come in the **glory**
	19.28	**Son of Man** sits on his **glorious** throne
Lk	9.31	heavenly **glory** and talked with **Jesus**
	9.32	but they woke up and saw **Jesus'** **glory**
Jn	7.39	**Jesus** had not been raised to **glory**.
	11.4	the **Son of God** will receive **glory**.
	12.16	when **Jesus** had been raised to **glory**,
	12.23	the **Son of Man** to receive great **glory**.
	12.41	said this because he saw **Jesus'** **glory**
	13.31	the **Son of Man's** **glory** is revealed;
	13.32	will reveal the **glory** of the **Son of Man**
	14.13	**glory** will be shown through the **Son**.
	17.1	Give **glory** to your **Son**,
Acts	3.13	given divine **glory** to his Servant **Jesus**.
Rom	6.4	**Christ** was raised...by the **glorious** power
	8.17	share **Christ's** suffering, we will also share his **glory**.
	16.27	be **glory** through **Jesus Christ** for ever!
2 Cor	4.4	Good News about the **glory** of **Christ**,
	4.6	**glory** shining in the face of **Christ**.
	8.23	and bring **glory** to **Christ**.
Phil	2.11	**Jesus Christ** is Lord, to the **glory**
2 Thes	1.12	our Lord **Jesus** will receive **glory**
	2.14	share of the **glory** of our Lord **Jesus**
2 Tim	2.10	**Christ Jesus** and brings eternal **glory**.
Tit	2.13	the **glory** of our great God and Saviour **Jesus Christ**
Heb	13.20	And to **Christ** be the **glory**
Jas	2.1	Lord **Jesus Christ**, the Lord of **glory**,
1 Pet	1.11	that **Christ** would...endure and the **glory**
	4.11	**Jesus Christ**, to whom belong **glory**
	5.10	his eternal **glory** in union with **Christ**,
2 Pet	3.18	**Jesus Christ**. To him be the **glory**,
Jude	.25	through **Jesus Christ** our Lord, be **glory**,
Rev	1.6	To **Jesus Christ** be the **glory**

Light

Is	60.19	The **light** of my **glory** will shine on you.

Lord

Ex	15.1	the **Lord**, because he has won a **glorious**
	15.21	the **Lord**, because he has won a **glorious**
Deut	5.24	The **Lord** our God showed us his greatness and his **glory**
1 Chr	16.28	Praise the **Lord**...praise his **glory**
	16.29	Praise the **Lord's glorious** name;
	23.30	and to praise and **glorify** the **Lord**
Ps	26.8	**Lord**, the place where your **glory** dwells.
	29.1	Praise the **Lord**...praise his **glory**
	29.2	Praise the **Lord's glorious** name;
	84.11	**Lord** is our protector and **glorious** king,
	96.7	Praise the **Lord**...praise his **glory**
	96.8	Praise the **Lord's glorious** name;
	104.31	May the **glory** of the **Lord** last for ever!
	113.4	**Lord** rules over all nations; his **glory**
	115.1	O **Lord**, to you alone...must **glory** be
Is	6.3	**Lord** Almighty is holy! His **glory** fills
	28.5	the **Lord**...will be like a **glorious** crown
	30.27	The **Lord's** power and **glory** can be seen
	33.21	The **Lord** will show us his **glory**
	40.5	the **glory** of the **Lord** will be revealed,
	42.12	give praise and **glory** to the **Lord**!
	60.1	The **glory** of the **Lord** is shining
	60.19	the **Lord**, will be your eternal light; The light of my **glory**
Ezek	3.12	Praise the **glory** of the **Lord**
	3.23	and there I saw the **glory** of the **Lord**,
	39.21	The **Lord** said, "I will let the nations see my **glory**
	43.5	was filled with the **glory** of the **Lord**.
Hab	2.14	of the knowledge of the **Lord's glory**
Lk	2.9	the **glory** of the **Lord** shone over them.
Acts	2.20	the great and **glorious** Day of the **Lord**
1 Cor	2.8	not have crucified the **Lord** of **glory**.
2 Cor	3.18	reflect the **glory** of the **Lord**
	8.19	of love for the sake of the **Lord's glory**,
2 Thes	1.9	the **Lord** and from his **glorious** might,
Rev	4.11	Our **Lord** and God! You are worthy to receive **glory**,

Power, Might

1 Chr	16.24	**glory** to the nations, his **mighty** deeds
	16.27	**Glory** and majesty surround him, **power**
	16.28	praise his **glory** and **might**.
	29.11	You are great and **powerful**, **glorious**
Ps	29.1	praise his **glory** and **power**.
	45.3	**mighty** king; you are **glorious** and
	63.2	see how **mighty** and **glorious** you are.
	78.61	the symbol of his **power** and **glory**.
	90.16	our descendants see your **glorious** might
	96.3	**glory** to the nations, his **mighty** deeds
	96.6	**Glory** and majesty surround him; **power**
	96.7	praise his **glory** and **might**.
	145.11	speak of the **glory** of your royal **power**
	145.12	**mighty** deeds and the **glorious** majesty
Is	2.10	and to hide from his **power** and **glory**!
	2.19	and to hide from his **power** and **glory**,
	2.21	and to hide from his **power** and **glory**.
	30.27	Lord's **power** and **glory** can be seen
Jer	48.17	**powerful** rule has been broken; its **glory**
Ezek	39.21	see my **glory** and...how I use my **power**
Dan	4.30	display my **power** and **might**, my **glory**
Mt	24.30	of heaven with **power** and great **glory**.
Mk	13.26	the clouds with great **power** and **glory**.
Lk	21.27	in a cloud with great **power** and **glory**.
Rom	6.4	raised from death by the **glorious** power
Eph	3.16	wealth of his **glory** to give you **power**
Phil	3.21	own **glorious** body, using that **power**
Col	1.11	which comes from his **glorious** power,
2 Thes	1.9	the Lord and from his **glorious** might,
1 Pet	4.11	**glory** and **power** for ever and ever.
Jude	.25	be **glory**, majesty, **might**,
Rev	1.6	Christ be the **glory** and **power** for ever

Rev	4.11	to receive **glory**, honour, and **power**.
	5.13	and honour, **glory** and **might**,
	7.12	**glory**, wisdom, thanksgiving...**power**,
	15.8	from the **glory** and **power** of God,
	19.1	**glory**, and **power** belong to our God!

Son of God see **Jesus**

Son of Man see **Jesus**

World

Ps	72.19	May his **glory** fill the whole **world**.
Is	6.3	His **glory** fills the **world**.
Jn	17.5	**glory** I had with you before the **world**
1 Cor	2.7	**glory** even before the **world** was made.

GOD'S PEOPLE

Jer	4.12	—	16.5	x54
Is	40.1	—	52.10	x33
Is	55.3	—	63.18	x29
Ezek	33.31	—	39.28	x19
Ex	5.1	—	12.41	x17
Jer	23.1	—	25.38	x17
Jer	29.31	—	33.26	x17
Mic	1.9	—	6.5	x16
Zech	7.9	—	10.12	x15
Eph	1.1	—	6.18	x14
Deut	31.26	—	33.5	x13
Hos	4.6	—	9.17	x12
Rom	8.17	—	11.2	x12
Lev	17.3	—	21.8	x10
Ps	78.20	— 71		x10
Is	25.8	—	30.32	x10
Ezek	13.9	—	14.11	x10
Hos	1.2	—	2.23	x9
Ex	28.12	—	32.14	x8
1 Kgs	8.16	—	9.7	x8
Ps	106.9	— 43		x7
Ps	105.12	— 45		x6
Ex	3.7	— 21		x5
Ezek	21.10	— 15		x5
Col	1.2	— 27		x5
Lev	7.20	— 27		x4
Deut	23.1	— 8		x4
Lev	26.12	— 45		x3
Ps	81.8	— 13		x3
Ps	111.1	— 9		x3
Ps	136.14	— 21		x3
Ps	149.4	— 9		x3
Is	14.1	— 30		x3
Nah	1.7	— 12		x3
Mt	24.22	— 31		x3
Mk	13.20	— 27		x3
1 Cor	14.21	— 33		x3
Heb	8.6	— 10		x3

Abandon, Rebel, Reject, Turn, Unfaithful

Num	31.16	the **people** to be **unfaithful** to the Lord.
Deut	32.5	**unfaithful**, unworthy to be **his people**,
	32.15	**Lord's people** grew rich, but **rebellious**;
Ps	73.10	so that even **God's people turn** to them
	78.59	so he **rejected his people** completely.
	94.14	The Lord will not **abandon his people**;
	106.43	**his people**, but they chose to **rebel**
Jer	1.16	**people** because...they have **abandoned**
	2,13	**my people** have committed two sins: they have **turned** away
	5.7	of **my people**? They have **abandoned** me
	7.29	am angry, and have **rejected my people**.
	8.5	**my people**, do you **turn** away from me
	9.2	from **my people**. They are all **unfaithful**,
	9.5	Lord says that **his people reject** him.
	9.13	because **my people** have **abandoned**
	12.8	**chosen people** have **turned** against me;
	25.38	The Lord has **abandoned his people**

Jer	29.31	**people**, because he told them to **rebel**
Hos	1.2	**my people** have...become **unfaithful**.
	5.15	I will **abandon my people**
	9.17	The God I serve will **reject his people**
	11.2	**turned** away from me. **My people**
Mic	5.3	the Lord will **abandon his people**
Rom	11.1	**reject his own people**? Certainly not!
	11.2	God has not **rejected his people**

Afraid

Deut	28.10	his **own people**, and they will be **afraid**
Is	10.24	**his people**...in Zion, "Do not be **afraid**
	44.2	**afraid**...my servant, my **chosen people**
	44.8	Do not be **afraid, my people**!
Jer	23.4	**My people** will no longer be **afraid**
	30.10	**My people**, do not be **afraid**;
	46.27	**My people**, do not be **afraid**,

Believe see **Faith**

Bless

Ruth	1.6	the Lord had **blessed his people**
2 Sam	21.3	so that you will **bless** the **Lord's people**.
2 Chr	7.10	**blessings** that the Lord had given to **his people**
	31.10	the Lord has **blessed his people**.
Ps	3.8	may he **bless his people**.
	29.11	strength to **his people** and **blesses** them
	107.38	He **blessed his people**,
Is	19.25	I will **bless** you, Egypt, **my people**;
Jer	16.5	I will no longer **bless my people**
Acts	20.32	the **blessings** God has for all **his people**.
Rom	8.17	the **blessings** he keeps for **his people**,
Eph	1.18	**blessings** he promises **his people**,
1 Pet	1.4	**blessings** that God keeps for **his people**.

Blood

Rev	16.6	poured out the **blood** of **God's people**
	17.6	with the **blood** of **God's people**
	18.24	**blood** of prophets and of **God's people**

Chosen

Ex	19.5	but you will be my **chosen people**,
Deut	10.15	**chose** you instead of any other **people**,
	14.2	**chosen** you to be his **own people**
	28.10	has **chosen** you to be his **own people**,
1 Sam	10.1	**chosen** you to be the ruler of **his people**:
2 Sam	7.10	I have **chosen** a place for **my people**
1 Kgs	8.53	**chose** them...to be your **own people**,
1 Chr	17.9	I have **chosen** a place for **my people**
Ps	105.43	So he led his **chosen people** out,
	106.23	destroy **his people**, his **chosen** servant,
Is	14.1	**his people** Israel and **choose** them
	19.25	Israel, my **chosen people**.
	43.20	to give water to my **chosen people**.
	44.1	**chosen people**, the descendants of Jacob.
	44.2	my **chosen people** whom I love.
	65.9	My **chosen people**, who serve me
	65.15	My **chosen people** will use your name
Jer	10.16	has **chosen** Israel to be **his**...**people**.
	12.8	My **chosen people** have turned
	12.9	My **chosen people** are like a bird
	51.19	has **chosen** Israel to be **his**...**people**.
Ezek	37.28	**chosen** Israel to be my **own people**.
Mt	24.22	For the sake of his **chosen people**,
	24.24	to deceive...**God's chosen people**,
	24.31	will gather his **chosen people**
Mk	13.20	For the sake of his **chosen people**,
	13.22	to deceive...**God's chosen people**,
	13.27	to gather **God's chosen people**
Acts	26.18	their place among **God's chosen people**.
Rom	8.33	Who will accuse **God's chosen people**
	11.2	not rejected **his people**, whom he **chose**
Eph	1.11	God **chose** us to be his **own people**
	2.12	not belong to **God's chosen people**.
Col	3.12	the **people** of God; he...**chose** you

2 Tim	2.10	for the sake of **God's chosen people,**
Tit	1.1	to help the faith of **God's chosen people**
1 Pet	1.1	**God's chosen people**...refugees
	2.9	**God's own people, chosen** to proclaim

Comfort see **Protect**

Covenant see **Promise**

Deceive, Lie, Mislead

Deut	32.5	to be **his people,** a sinful and **deceitful**
Ps	105.25	**people** and treat his servants with **deceit.**
Is	3.12	**people,** your leaders are **misleading** you,
	63.8	are my **people;** they will not **deceive** me.
Jer	23.26	**mislead my people** with the **lies**
	23.32	lead my **people** astray with their **lies**
Ezek	13.10	The prophets **mislead my people**
	13.19	So you tell **lies** to **my people,**
Mic	3.5	**My people** are **deceived** by prophets
	3.6	Because you **mislead my people,**
Mt	24.24	to **deceive** even **God's chosen people,**
Mk	13.22	to **deceive** even **God's chosen people,**

Defend see **Protect**

Evil see **Sin**

Faith, Believe

Ps	73.10	**people** turn to them and eagerly **believe**
	106.12	Then **his people believed** his promises
Ezek	13.19	tell **lies** to **my people,** and they **believe**
2 Thes	1.10	**people** and honour from all who **believe.**
	2.13	**people** and by your **faith** in the truth.
Tit	1.1	to help the **faith** of **God's chosen people**
Phlm	.5	all **God's people** and the **faith** you have
Rev	13.10	and **faith** on the part of **God's people.**

Faithful

1 Kgs	8.61	**people,** always be **faithful** to the Lord
Is	61.8	I will **faithfully** reward **my people**
Eph	1.1	**people** in Ephesus, who are **faithful**
Col	1.2	**people** in Colossae, who are our **faithful**

Forget see **Remember**

Forgive see **Mercy**

Free see **Rescue**

Holy

Lev	21.8	I am **holy** and I make **my people holy.**
Ezra	9.2	**holy people** had become contaminated.
Ps	114.2	Judah became the **Lord's holy people,**
Is	5.16	his **holiness** by judging **his people.**
	12.6	**holy** God...lives among **his people.**
	52.10	his **holy** power; he will save **his people,**
	62.12	You will be called "**God's Holy People,**
	63.18	**your holy people,** were driven out
Ezek	39.7	**my people** Israel know **my holy** name,
	39.27	am **holy,** I will bring **my people** back
	44.23	teach **my people** the difference between what is **holy**
1 Pet	2.9	the **holy** nation, **God's own people,**

Joy

Ps	105.43	his **chosen people**...shouted for **joy.**
	149.5	Let **God's people**...sing **joyfully**
Is	12.3	brings **joy** to the thirsty, so **God's people** **rejoice**

Justice, Judge

Ps	50.4	to see him **judge his people.**
Is	3.13	he is ready to **judge his people.**
	3.14	and leaders of **his people** to **judgement.**
	5.16	his holiness by **judging his people.**
	56.1	says to **his people,** "Do what is **just**
Jer	4.12	is pronouncing **judgement** on **his people.**
Dan	7.22	**judgement** in favour of the **people**
Joel	3.2	I will **judge** them for all they have done to **my people.**

Zeph	3.5	he brings **justice** to **his people.**
Zech	7.9	**my people:** 'You must see that **justice**
Lk	18.7	not **judge** in favour of his **own people**
1 Cor	6.1	**judges** instead of letting **God's people**
	6.2	**God's people** will **judge** the world
Heb	10.30	The Lord will **judge his people.**
1 Pet	4.17	**own people** are the first to be **judged.**

Lie see **Deceive**

Mercy, Forgive

Ex	34.9	**people** are stubborn, but **forgive** our evil
Deut	32.43	and **forgives** the sins of **his people.**
Ps	78.38	But God was **merciful** to **his people.**
Is	14.1	will once again be **merciful** to **his people**
Jer	5.7	should I **forgive** the sins of **my people?**
	16.5	**people**...or show them love and **mercy.**
	30.18	**my people** to their land and have **mercy**
	33.26	I will be **merciful** to **my people**
Joel	2.18	he had **mercy** on **his people.**
1 Pet	2.10	**people**...you did not know God's **mercy,**

Message, Proclaim

Ps	147.19	He gives his **message** to **his people,**
Jer	23.22	**message** to **my people** and could have
Eph	1.13	**people** when you heard the true **message**
1 Pet	2.9	**God's own people, chosen** to **proclaim**

Mislead see **Deceive**

Mourn, Tears, Weep

Is	22.4	**weep** bitterly over all those of **my people**
Jer	7.29	**Mourn, people** of Jerusalem;
	8.21	**my people** are crushed; I **mourn;**
	13.17	**tears**...flow because the **Lord's people**
	25.34	of **my people,** cry out loud! **Mourn**
	31.9	**My people** will return **weeping,**
Lam	3.48	of **tears** at the destruction of **my people.**

Obey

2 Kgs	21.9	But the **people** of Judah did not **obey**
Ps	34.9	all **his people;** those who **obey** him
	105.45	so that **his people** would **obey** his laws
Jer	11.4	they **obeyed,** they would be **my people**
Ezek	11.20	**obey** all my commands. They will be **my** **people,**
	44.7	**people** who do not **obey** me,
Zech	10.12	**my people** strong; they will...**obey** me.
Mal	2.9	**people** of Israel despise you because you do not **obey**
Rev	14.12	**God's people,** those who **obey**

Peace

1 Kgs	8.56	Lord who has given **his people peace,**
1 Chr	23.25	of Israel has given **peace** to **his people,**
Ps	29.11	**his people** and blesses them with **peace.**
	85.8	promises **peace** to us, his **own people,**
Is	27.5	**my people** want my protection, let them make **peace**
Jer	16.5	no longer bless **my people** with **peace**
Hos	2.18	and will let **my people** live in **peace**
Mic	3.5	**My people** are **deceived** by prophets who promise **peace**
Hag	2.9	give **my people** prosperity and **peace.**

Poor

Ex	22.25	to any of **my people** who are **poor,**
Is	14.30	be a shepherd to the **poor** of **his people**
Rom	15.26	**poor** among **God's people** in Jerusalem.

Praise see **Worship**

Prayer

Is	65.1	ready to answer **my people's prayers,** but they did not **pray.**
Jer	31.9	**My people** will return weeping, **praying**
Hos	2.21	I will answer the **prayers** of **my people**
Eph	6.18	**pray** always for all **God's people.**
Rev	5.8	which are the **prayers** of **God's people.**

Rev   8.3   add to the **prayers** of all **God's people**
      8.4   with the **prayers** of **God's people**

Proclaim see Message

Promise, Covenant

Ex   19.5   **covenant**, you will be my **own people**.
Lev   26.42 renew my **promise** to give **my people**
Deut 26.18 as his **own people**, as he **promised** you;
      26.19 will be his **own people**, as he **promised**.
      28.9   his **own people**, as he has **promised**.
      29.13 **people** and be your God, as he **promised**
      29.25 the **Lord's people** broke the **covenant**
2 Sam 5.2   **promised**...you would lead **his people**
1 Kgs 8.56 given **his people** peace, as he **promised**
2 Kgs 11.17 **covenant** with the Lord that they would be the
            Lord's people;
1 Chr 11.2 **promised**...you would lead **his people**
2 Chr 23.16 a **covenant** that they would be the **Lord's
            people**.
Ps   85.8   **promises** peace to us, his **own people**,
      106.12 Then **his people** believed **his promises**
      116.14 all **his people** I will give him what I have
             promised.
Is   56.8   **his people** Israel home...has **promised**
Ezek 44.7   So **my people** have broken my **covenant**
Hos   8.1   **My people** have broken the **covenant**
Mic   3.5   **My people** are deceived by prophets who
             promise peace
Rom   9.6   the **promise** of God has failed; for not all the
             people
Eph   1.14   what God has **promised his people**,
      1.18   blessings he **promises his people**,
      2.12   based on God's **promises** to **his people**,
Heb   8.8   new **covenant** with the **people** of Israel
      8.10   the **covenant** that I will make with the **people**

Prosper, Rich

Deut 32.15 The **Lord's people** grew **rich**,
2 Sam 5.12   **prosperous** for the sake of **his people**.
1 Chr 14.2   **prosperous** for the sake of **his people**.
Jer   12.16 a part of **my people** and will **prosper**.
      33.26 **people** and make them **prosperous** again.
Hos   2.23   **my people**...and make them **prosper**.
      4.8   grow **rich** from the sins of **my people**,
      7.1   **people** Israel and make them **prosperous**
Hag   2.9   give **my people** prosperity and peace.

Protect, Comfort, Defend

Deut 33.3   loves **his people** and **protects** those
1 Sam 10.1   will rule **his people** and **protect** them
Ps   28.8   The Lord **protects his people**; he **defends**
      34.22 **people**...who go to him for **protection**
      97.10 he **protects** the lives of **his people**,
      135.14 The Lord will **defend his people**;
Is   22.4   **people** who have died. Don't try to **comfort**
      33.6   He always **protects his people**
      40.1   **Comfort my people**," says our God
      49.13 The Lord will **comfort his people**;
      51.16 You are **my people**...I **protect** you
      52.9   and **comfort his people**.
      59.20 **his people**, ¶I will come...to **defend** you
Ezek 34.30 I **protect** Israel...they are **my people**.
Joel 3.16   But he will **defend his people**.
Nah   1.7   **protects his people** in times of trouble;
Zech 9.15   Lord Almighty will **protect his people**,

Rebel see Abandon

Reject see Abandon

Religion

Jer   12.16 will accept the **religion** of **my people**.
Dan   11.28 to destroy the **religion** of **God's people**.
      11.30 the **religion** of **God's people**.

Remember, Forget

Ex   28.12 will always **remember my people**.
      28.29 will always **remember my people**.
2 Kgs 13.23 He has never **forgotten his people**.
Ps   69.33 does not **forget his people** in prison.
Is   56.5   **remembered**...among **my people**
Jer   18.15 Yet **my people** have **forgotten** me;
      23.27 will make **my people forget** me,
Mic   6.5   **My people, remember** what King Balak

Rescue, Free, Save, Slavery

Ex   18.10 who **saved his people** from **slavery**!
Deut 4.20   are the **people** he **rescued** from Egypt,
      9.26   **own people**, the **people** you **rescued**
      32.36 The Lord will **rescue his people**
1 Sam 9.16   **people** Israel, and he will **rescue** them
      17.47 swords or spears to **save his people**
2 Sam 3.18   servant David to **rescue my people** Israel
      7.23   **rescued**...to make them your **own people**.
1 Chr 17.21 You **rescued your people** from Egypt.
Neh   1.10   your **own people**. You **rescued** them
Ps   22.31 The Lord **saved his people**.
      28.8   protects **his people**; he defends and **saves**
      34.22 The Lord will **save his people**;
      97.10 the lives of **his people**; he **rescues** them
      106.43 Many times the Lord **rescued his people**,
      111.9 He set **his people free**
      130.8 He will **save his people** Israel
Is   12.3   **people** rejoice when he **saves** them.
      14.25 **free my people** from the Assyrian yoke
      32.18 **God's people** will be **free** from worries,
      44.23 by **saving his people** Israel.
      45.15 who **saves his people**,
      45.21 the God who **saves his people**?
      49.8   **people**, "When the time comes to **save**
      52.3   **his people**, "When you became **slaves**,
      52.9   **rescue** his city and comfort **his people**.
      52.10 he will **save his people**,
      61.2   When the Lord will **save his people**
      61.11 The Sovereign Lord will **save his people**,
      62.12 The **People** the Lord Has **Saved**.
      63.4   the time to **save my people** had come;
      63.11 who **saved** the leaders of **his people**
      65.8   I destroy all **my people** — I will **save**
Jer   31.7   has **saved his people**; he has **rescued** all
Ezek 13.23 **rescuing my people** from your power,
      34.27 **my people's** chains and set them **free**
Zech 8.7   I will **rescue my people** from the lands
      9.16   the Lord will **save his people**,
      10.8   I will call **my people**...I will **rescue** them
Mt   1.21   he will **save his people** from their sins.
Lk   1.68   of **his people** and has set them **free**.
      1.77   to tell his people that they will be **saved**
      4.19   when the Lord will **save his people**.
      7.16   God has come to **save his people**!
1 Cor 1.30   **God's** holy **people** and are set **free**.
2 Tim 1.9   He **saved** us...to be his **own people**.

Rich see Prosper

Safety

Is   14.30 **people** and will let them live in **safety**.
Hos   2.18   let **my people** live in peace and **safety**.
Mic   5.4   **His people** will live in **safety**

Save see Rescue

Serve

Neh   1.10   are your **servants**, your **own people**.
Ps   106.23 destroy **his people**, his chosen **servant**,
Is   44.1   my **servant**, my chosen **people**,
      44.2   you are my **servant**, my chosen **people**
      56.6   **his people**, who love him and **serve** him,
      65.9   **My** chosen **people**, who **serve** me,
Rom   15.25 Jerusalem in the **service** of **God's people**
1 Cor 16.15 to the **service** of **God's people**.

Eph	4.12	**people** for the work of Christian **service**,

Shepherd, Sheep

Ps	78.52	he led **his people** out like a **shepherd**
	78.71	the **shepherd** of the **people** of God.
Is	14.30	be a **shepherd** to the poor of **his people**
Jer	25.34	you **shepherds** of **my people**,
	50.6	**people** are like **sheep** whose **shepherds**
Ezek	34.31	my **sheep**...that I feed, are **my people**,
Mic	4.8	like a **shepherd**, watches over **his people**,
Zech	9.16	will save **his people**, as a **shepherd**
	13.7	the **sheep** will be scattered. I will attack **my people**

Sin, Evil

Ex	34.9	**evil**...and accept us as your **own people**
Deut	32.5	unworthy to be **his people**, a **sinful**
	32.43	and forgives the **sins** of **his people**.
1 Kgs	16.2	and have led **my people** into **sin**.
2 Kgs	21.15	**my people** because they have **sinned**
Ps	14.4	**evildoers**...live by robbing **my people**,
	53.4	**evildoers**...live by robbing **my people**,
	78.38	to **his people**. He forgave their **sin**
	97.10	**evil**; he protects the lives of **his people**;
	130.8	will save **his people**...from all their **sins**.
Is	58.1	Tell **my people**...about their **sins**!
Jer	1.16	**my people** because they have **sinned**;
	2.13	for **my people** have committed two **sins**:
	5.7	should I forgive the **sins** of **my people**?
	5.26	**Evil** men live among **my people**
	6.29	**my people**, because those who are **evil**
	7.12	to it because of the **sins** of **my people**
	9.3	**people** do one **evil** thing after another,
	9.7	**My people** have done **evil**
	14.7	**My people** cry out to me, 'Even though our **sins** accuse
	15.13	**my people**...to punish them for the **sins**
	23.22	**people** and...made them give up the **evil**
Dan	9.4	and confessed the **sins** of **my people**.
	9.20	my **sins** and the **sins** of **my people**
Hos	4.8	grow rich from the **sins** of **my people**,
Amos	9.10	The **sinners** among **my people**
Mic	3.2	what is **evil**. You skin **my people** alive
Mt	1.21	he will save **his people** from their **sins**.
Heb	11.25	**God's people** rather than to enjoy **sin**

Slavery see **Rescue**

Tears see **Mourn**

Turn see **Abandon**

Understand

Is	1.3	my **people** Israel...don't **understand**
Jer	23.20	days to come **his people** will **understand**
	30.23	days to come **his people** will **understand**
Rom	10.19	Did the **people** of Israel not **understand**?
Eph	3.18	all **God's people**, may have the power to **understand**

Unfaithful see **Abandon**

Weep see **Mourn**

Worship, Praise

Ex	7.16	**people** go, so that they can **worship** Also: 8.1; 8.20; 9.1; 9.13; 10.3
Deut	32.3	I will **praise**...the Lord, and **his people**
1 Kgs	8.56	**Praise** the Lord who has given **his people** peace,
Ps	26.12	of **his people** I **praise** the Lord.
	68.26	**Praise**...in the meeting of **his people**;
	106.12	**his people** believed...and sang **praises**
	106.28	**people** joined in the **worship** of Baal,
	106.36	**God's people worshipped** idols,
	148.14	so that all **his people praise** him
Is	56.3	will not let me **worship** with **his people**.

Is	61.11	**people**, And all the nations will **praise**
Jer	5.7	of **my people**? They have...**worshipped**
	13.11	be **my people** and would bring **praise**
	31.7	**praise**, 'The Lord has saved **his people**;
Hos	6.10	**my people** have defiled themselves by **worshipping** idols.
Zech	10.12	**my people** strong; they will **worship**

GODS (GODDESS)

Is	41.21	— 46.6	x27
Deut	28.14	— 33.26	x21
Dan	1.2	— 6.12	x21
2 Kgs	17.7	— 19.37	x18
Deut	3.24	— 8.19	x14
Deut	10.17	— 13.13	x13
1 Kgs	11.2	— 12.28	x11
Jer	1.16	— 3.24	x11
Josh	23.7	— 24.23	x10
Dan	11.8 – 39		x9
2 Chr	32.13	— 34.25	x8
Jer	43.12	— 44.23	x8
Jer	48.7	— 51.44	x8
Gen	31.19 – 35		x7
2 Kgs	1.2 – 16		x7
Is	57.5 – 11		x6
Jer	16.11 – 20		x6
Ex	32.1 – 31		x5
Ex	34.14 – 17		x5
Ezek	28.2 – 9		x5
Num	25.2 – 11		x3
Judg	16.23 – 24		x3
2 Kgs	5.15 – 18		x3
Jer	13.10 – 27		x3
Jer	46.15 – 25		x3

Disgusting

Deut	12.31	**gods** they do all the **disgusting** things
1 Kgs	11.5	Molech the **disgusting god** of Ammon.
	11.7	the **disgusting god** of Moab,
2 Kgs	23.13	of **disgusting** idols — Astarte the **goddess**
Jer	11.13	sacrifices to that **disgusting god** Baal
Ezek	20.8	**disgusting** idols or...the Egyptian **gods**.
Hos	9.10	as **disgusting** as the **gods** they loved.

Evil see **Sin**

False, Idol, Image, Real, Symbol

Ex	34.13	cut down the **symbols** of their **goddess**
Lev	19.4	**idols**; do not make **gods** of metal
Deut	7.5	the **symbols** of their **goddess** Asherah
	12.3	their **symbols** of the **goddess** Asherah
	16.21	a wooden **symbol** of the **goddess**
	32.17	sacrificed to **gods** that are **not real**,
	32.39	**no** other **god** is **real**.
Judg	6.25	the **symbol** of the **goddess** Asherah,
1 Sam	7.3	**gods** and the **images** of the **goddess**
	12.21	Don't go after **false gods**
2 Sam	12.30	head of the **idol** of the Ammonite **god**
1 Kgs	14.15	by making **idols** of the **goddess** Asherah.
	14.23	built places of worship for **false gods**
	15.13	**idol** of the fertility **goddess** Asherah.
	16.33	an **image** of the **goddess** Asherah.
2 Kgs	13.6	**image** of the **goddess** Asherah remained
	17.10	and **images** of the **goddess** Asherah,
	17.16	made an **image** of the **goddess** Asherah,
	17.30	made **idols** of the **god** Succoth Benoth;
	18.4	the **images** of the **goddess** Asherah.
	19.18	which were no **gods** at all, only **images**
	21.3	made an **image** of the **goddess** Asherah,
	21.7	the **symbol** of the **goddess** Asherah
	23.6	the **image** of the **goddess** Asherah.
	23.13	**idols** — Astarte the **goddess** of Sidon,
	23.14	the **symbols** of the **goddess** Asherah.
	23.24	and all the household **gods, idols,**
1 Chr	16.26	**gods** of all other nations are only **idols**,

GODS — False

2 Chr	14.3	the **symbols** of the **goddess** Asherah.
	15.16	**idol** of the fertility **goddess** Asherah.
	17.6	the **symbols** of the **goddess** Asherah
	19.3	removed all the **symbols** of the **goddess**
	24.18	**idols** and the **images** of the **goddess**
	31.1	the **symbols** of the **goddess** Asherah,
	32.19	**gods** of the other peoples, **idols** made
	33.3	made **images** of the **goddess** Asherah,
	33.15	**gods** and the **image** that he had placed
	33.19	the **goddess** Asherah...and the **idols**
	34.3	**goddess** Asherah, and all the other **idols**
Ps	31.6	You hate those who worship **false gods**,
	40.4	or join those who worship **false gods**.
	96.5	**gods** of all other nations are only **idols**,
	97.7	**idols** is put to shame; all the **gods** bow
Is	17.8	**symbols** of the **goddess** Asherah and
	27.9	or **symbols** of the **goddess** Asherah
	37.19	which were no **gods** at all, only **images**
	42.8	No other **god** may share my glory; I will not let **idols**
	42.17	in **idols**, who call **images** their **gods**,
	44.9	**idols** are worthless, and the **gods** they
	44.10	a metal **image** to worship as a **god**!
	44.20	**idol** he holds in his hand is not a **god**
	45.20	their **idols** of wood and pray to **gods**
Jer	1.16	to other **gods**, and have made **idols**
	2.11	**gods**, even though they were **not real**.
	5.7	have worshipped **gods** that are **not real**.
	10.14	because the **gods** they make are **false**
	13.25	and have trusted in **false gods**.
	16.18	and have filled it with their **false gods**.
	16.19	ancestors had nothing but **false gods**,
	17.2	the **symbols**...set up for the **goddess**
	44.8	**idols** and by sacrificing to other **gods**
	50.2	**god**...has been shattered! Babylon's **idols**
	51.17	because the **gods** they make are **false**
Ezek	20.7	unclean with the **false gods** of Egypt,
	20.8	**idols** or give up the Egyptian **gods**.
	30.13	will destroy the **idols** and the **false gods**
Dan	11.8	the **images** of their **gods** and the articles
Hos	8.6	the **idol**, and it is not a **god** at all!
Amos	2.4	been led astray by the same **false gods**
	5.26	**images** of Sakkuth, your king **god**,
	8.14	**idols** of Samaria, who say, 'By the **god**
Mic	5.14	down the **images** of the **goddess** Asherah
Nah	1.14	the **idols**...in the temples of their **gods**.
Acts	7.43	the **image** of Rephan, your star **god**;
Rom	11.4	have not worshipped the **false god** Baal.
1 Jn	5.21	keep yourselves safe from **false gods**!

Heaven

Deut	3.24	**god** in **heaven** or on earth who can do
1 Kgs	8.23	is no **god** like you in **heaven** above
2 Chr	6.14	in all **heaven** and earth there is no **god**
1 Cor	8.5	"**gods**," whether in **heaven** or on earth,

Holy see **Spirit**

Honour

Judg	9.9	which is used to **honour gods** and men.
1 Chr	16.25	to be **honoured** more than all the **gods**.
Ps	96.4	to be **honoured** more than all the **gods**.
Dan	11.38	**honour** the **god** who protects fortresses.

Idol see **False**

Image see **False**

Love

Jer	2.25	turn back. I have **loved** foreign **gods**
	3.13	have given your **love** to foreign **gods**
Dan	11.37	and also the **god** that women **love**.
Hos	9.1	to the **god** Baal and have **loved**
	9.10	as disgusting as the **gods** they **loved**.

Might see **Power**

Pagan

Ex	34.15	when they worship their **pagan gods**
	34.16	to me and to worship their **pagan gods**.
Deut	31.16	me and worship the **pagan gods**
2 Kgs	17.17	as burnt-offerings to **pagan gods**;
	23.24	**gods**, idols, and all other **pagan** objects
Jer	13.27	you go after **pagan gods** on the hills
Mt	6.7	**pagans** do, who think that their **gods**

Power, Might

Num	33.4	he was more **powerful** than the **gods**
Deut	3.24	no **god**...who can do the **mighty** things
	10.17	over all **gods** and over all **powers**.
	32.31	their own **gods** are weak, not **mighty**
	32.37	are those **mighty gods** you trusted?
1 Sam	4.8	can save us from those **powerful gods**?
Is	44.8	some **powerful god** I never heard of?
Jer	46.15	Why has your **mighty god** Apis fallen?
Hos	7.16	from me to a **god** that is **powerless**.
Hab	1.11	these men whose **power** is their **god**.

Pray

Ex	23.13	Do not **pray** to other **gods**;
1 Kgs	18.24	the prophets of Baal **pray** to their **god**,
	18.25	**Pray** to your **god**,
	18.27	**Pray** louder! He is a **god**!
Ps	44.20	and **prayed** to a foreign **god**,
Is	44.17	**prays** to it and says, "You are my **god**
	45.20	**pray** to **gods** that cannot save them
Jon	1.6	Get up and **pray** to your **god** for help.
Zeph	3.9	**pray** to me alone and not to other **gods**
Mt	6.7	**gods** will hear them because their **prayers**

Punish

Ex	12.12	and **punishing** all the **gods** of Egypt.
Josh	23.16	**gods**, then in his anger he will **punish**
	24.20	foreign **gods**, he will...**punish** you.
1 Sam	5.7	is **punishing** us and our **god** Dagon.
	6.5	he will stop **punishing** you, your **gods**,
Jer	51.44	I will **punish** Bel, the **god** of Babylonia,

Real see **False**

Rescue see **Save**

Rid

Gen	35.2	**rid** of the foreign **gods** that you have;
Josh	24.14	**rid** of the **gods** which your ancestors
	24.23	Then get **rid** of those foreign **gods**
Judg	10.16	So they got **rid** of their foreign **gods**
1 Sam	7.3	you must get **rid** of all the foreign **gods**

Save, Rescue

Judg	10.13	**gods**, so I am not going to **rescue** you
	10.14	**gods** you have chosen. Let them **rescue**
1 Sam	4.8	can **save** us from those powerful **gods**?
	12.21	**gods**; they cannot help you or **save** you,
2 Kgs	18.33	**gods** of any other nations **save** their
	18.35	the **gods** of all these countries ever **save**
	19.12	and none of their **gods** could **save** them.
2 Chr	25.15	foreign **gods** that could not even **save**
	32.13	**gods** of any other nation ever **save** their
	32.14	the **gods** of all those countries ever **save**
	32.15	**god** of any nation has...been able to **save**
	32.17	**gods** of the nations have not **saved** their
Is	36.18	**gods** of any other nations **save** their
	36.19	**gods** of Sepharvaim? Did anyone **save**
	36.20	the **gods** of all these countries ever **save**
	37.12	and none of their **gods** could **save** them.
	44.17	You are my **god** — **save** me!
	45.20	pray to **gods** that cannot **save** them
Jer	11.12	**gods** will not be able to **save** them
Dan	3.15	think there is any **god** who can **save**
	3.29	no other **god** who can **rescue** like this.

Serve

Deut	4.28	will **serve gods** made by human hands

Deut	8.19	other **gods** to worship and **serve** them.
	11.16	to worship and **serve** other **gods**.
	13.2	to lead you to worship and **serve gods**
	17.3	and **serving** other **gods** or the sun
	28.14	or worship and **serve** other **gods**.
	28.36	**serve gods** made of wood and stone.
	28.64	**serve gods** made of wood and stone,
	29.26	**served** other **gods** that they had never
Josh	23.16	if you **serve** and worship other **gods**,
	24.15	**serve**, the **gods** your ancestors
	24.16	leave the Lord to **serve** other **gods**!
	24.20	if you leave him to **serve** foreign **gods**,
Judg	2.19	would **serve** and worship other **gods**,
2 Kgs	10.18	Ahab **served** the **god** Baal a little,
	17.16	and **served** the **god** Baal.
	17.35	worship other **gods**; do not...**serve** them
Jer	5.19	**served** foreign **gods** in their own land,
	13.10	have worshipped and **served** other **gods**.
	16.11	and worshipped and **served** other **gods**,
	16.13	you will **serve** other **gods** day and night,
	22.9	have worshipped and **served** other **gods**.
	25.6	not to worship and **serve** other **gods**
	35.15	not to worship and **serve** other **gods**,
	44.3	sacrifices to other **gods** and **served gods**
Dan	11.37	will ignore the **god** his ancestors **served**,
Amos	2.4	false **gods** that their ancestors **served**.

Sin, Evil

Ex	32.31	a terrible **sin**. They have made a **god**
Deut	31.18	done **evil** and worshipped other **gods**.
Judg	2.19	**gods**, and refused to give up their...**evil**
Jer	44.5	**evil** practice of sacrificing to other **gods**.
	44.23	other **gods** and **sinned** against the Lord
2 Cor	4.4	the dark by the **evil god** of this world.

Spirit, Holy

Dan	4.8	The **spirit** of the **holy gods** is in him,
	4.9	the **spirit** of the **holy gods** is in you,
	4.18	the **spirit** of the **holy gods** is in me.
	5.11	has the **spirit** of the **holy gods** in him.
	5.14	the **spirit** of the **holy gods** is in you

Symbol see **False**

Temple

Judg	9.27	They went into the **temple** of their **god**,
1 Sam	5.2	into the **temple** of their **god** Dagon,
2 Kgs	5.18	**temple** of Rimmon, the **god** of Syria,
	19.37	worshipping in the **temple** of his **god**
1 Chr	10.10	head in the **temple** of their **god** Dagon.
2 Chr	32.21	when he was in the **temple** of his **god**.
Ezra	1.7	and had put in the **temple** of his **gods**.
Is	37.38	in the **temple** of his **god** Nisroch,
Jer	43.12	set fire to the **temples** of Egypt's **gods**,
	43.13	down the **temples** of the Egyptian **gods**.
Dan	1.2	back with him to the **temple** of his **gods**
Nah	1.14	that are in the **temples** of their **gods**.
Acts	14.13	of the **god** Zeus, whose **temple** stood

Trust

Deut	32.37	are those mighty **gods** you **trusted**?
Ps	31.6	who worship false **gods**, but I **trust**
Is	42.17	**trust** in idols...call images their **gods**,
Jer	13.25	and have **trusted** in false **gods**.
	48.13	Bethel, a **god** in whom they **trusted**.
Hab	2.18	to **trust** it — a **god** that can't even talk!

GOOD

	Prov	10.2	— 22.29	x52
	1 Pet	2.12	— 4.19	x16
	1 Tim	1.8	— 6.18	x14
	Rom	12.2	— 16.19	x12
	Ezek	33.12	— 34.22	x11
	Mt	12.33	— 13.49	x11
	Tit	1.8	— 3.14	x11
	Jas	1.17	— 5.16	x11

	Ps	37.3 — 37		x10
	Mt	5.16	— 7.19	x9
	Rom	7.12	— 9.11	x9
	Heb	9.11	— 13.20	x9
	Ps	119.17 — 121		x8
	Prov	1.2	— 5.16	x8
	Ezek	18.5 — 27		x8
	Lk	1.3	— 4.10	x8
	1 Cor	10.23	— 15.33	x8
	Gal	4.17	— 6.10	x8
	Gen	2.9	— 3.22	x7
	Prov	28.12	— 31.29	x7
	Lk	6.27 — 45		x6
	Ps	11.2 — 7		x4
	Ps	34.8 — 19		x4
	Ps	36.3 — 10		x4
	Ecc	9.2 — 18		x4
	Jn	10.11 — 33		x4
	Neh	9.13 — 25		x3
	Ps	25.7 — 21		x3
	Ps	30.5 — 9		x3
	Ps	112.2 — 6		x3
	Ps	116.5 — 12		x3
	Ps	118.1 — 29		x3
	Is	5.4 — 20		x3
	Ezek	3.20' — 21		x3
	Mt	19.16 — 17		x3
	Lk	14.14 — 35		x3
	Acts	24.2 — 25		x3
	3 Jn	.2 — 11		x3

God, Lord

Gen	33.5	**God** has been **good** enough to give
	50.20	but **God** turned it into **good**,
Ex	1.20	feared **God**, he was **good** to them
Deut	6.18	what the **Lord** says is right and **good**
	26.11	the **good** things that the **Lord** your **God**
	33.16	Blessed by the **goodness** of the **Lord**,
	33.23	blessed by the **Lord's good** favour;
Josh	23.13	**good** land which the **Lord** your **God**
	23.14	**God** has given you all the **good** things
Ruth	1.8	May the **Lord** be as **good** to you
1 Sam	25.30	the **Lord** has done all the **good** things
1 Chr	16.34	thanks to the **Lord**, because he is **good**;
2 Chr	5.11	Praise the **Lord**, because he is **good**,
	7.3	worshipping **God**...for his **goodness**
	30.19	O **Lord**...in your **goodness** forgive
Ezra	3.11	the refrain: "The **Lord** is **good**,
Job	2.10	When **God** sends us something **good**,
	13.9	If **God** looks at you closely, will he find
		anything **good**?
Ps	11.7	**Lord** is righteous and loves **good** deeds;
	13.6	O **Lord**, because you have been **good**
	16.2	You are my **Lord**; all the **good** things
	19.9	Reverence for the **Lord** is **good**;
	25.7	love and **goodness**, remember me, **Lord**!
	25.8	Because the **Lord** is righteous and **good**,
	27.13	the **Lord's goodness** in this present life.
	30.7	You were **good** to me, **Lord**;
	34.8	out for yourself how **good** the **Lord** is.
	34.10	who obey the **Lord** lack nothing **good**.
	37.3	Trust in the **Lord** and do **good**;
	54.6	O **Lord**; I will give you thanks because you
		are **good**.
	69.16	**Lord**, in the **goodness** of your constant
	71.16	**Lord**; I will proclaim your **goodness**,
	73.1	**God** is indeed **good** to Israel,
	86.17	Show me proof of your **goodness**, **Lord**;
	92.1	How **good** it is to give thanks to you, O
		Lord,
	100.5	The **Lord** is **good**;
	103.17	honour the **Lord**...his **goodness** endures
	106.1	to the **Lord**, because he is **good**;
	107.1	thanks to the **Lord**, because he is **good**;

Ps	116.5	The **Lord** is merciful and **good**;
	116.7	because the **Lord** has been **good** to me.
	116.12	I offer the **Lord** for all his **goodness**
	118.1	thanks to the **Lord**, because he is **good**,
	118.27	**Lord** is **God**; he has been **good** to us.
	118.29	thanks to the **Lord**, because he is **good**,
	119.65	**Lord**, and you are **good** to me,
	125.4	**Lord**, do **good** to those who are **good**,
	135.3	Praise the **Lord**, because he is **good**;
	136.1	thanks to the **Lord**, because he is **good**;
	143.10	You are my **God**...Be **good** to me,
	143.11	**Lord**...in your **goodness** save me
	147.1	It is **good** to sing praise to our **God**;
Prov	12.2	The **Lord** is pleased with **good** people
	15.8	**Lord** is pleased when **good** men pray
	15.29	**good** people pray, the **Lord** listens
	18.22	it shows that the **Lord** is **good** to you.
Is	26.7	**Lord**, you make the path smooth for **good** men;
Jer	33.11	the **Lord** Almighty, because he is **good**
Lam	3.25	**Lord** is **good** to everyone who trusts
Hos	3.5	the **Lord** and will receive his **good** gifts.
Mic	6.8	the **Lord** has told us what is **good**.
Nah	1.7	The **Lord** is **good**;
Mal	1.9	try asking **God** to be **good** to us.
Mk	10.18	No one is **good** except **God**
Lk	1.6	both lived **good** lives in **God's** sight
	1.58	wonderfully **good** the **Lord** had been
	18.19	No one is **good** except **God**
Acts	10.22	He is a **good** man who worships **God**
	27.24	And **God** in his **goodness** to you
Rom	1.10	I ask that **God** in his **good** will
	4.17	promise is **good** in the sight of **God**,
	8.28	that in all things **God** works for **good**
	12.2	know the will of **God** — what is **good**
	13.4	he is **God's** servant...for your own **good**.
1 Cor	14.17	prayer of thanks to **God** is quite **good**,
Phil	1.6	that **God**, who began this **good** work
1 Tim	2.3	This is **good** and it pleases **God**
	4.4	Everything that **God** has created is **good**
Heb	6.5	experience that **God's** word is **good**,
	12.10	but **God** does it for our own **good**.
	13.9	It is **good** to receive inner strength from **God's** grace,
	13.20	May the **God** of peace provide you with every **good** thing
1 Pet	2.12	your **good** deeds and so praise **God**
	3.17	**good**, if this should be **God's** will,
3 Jn	.11	Whoever does **good** belongs to **God**;

Shepherd

| Jn | 10.11 | I am the **good shepherd**, |
| | 10.14 | I am the **good shepherd**. |

GOOD NEWS (GOSPEL)

Gal	1.6	—	4.13	x14
Phil	1.5	—	2.22	x7
2 Sam	18.19 – 31			x6
Acts	13.32	—	16.10	x6
1 Thes	1.5	—	3.2	x6
Lk	1.19	—	4.43	x5
Rom	1.1	—	2.16	x5
1 Cor	9.14 – 23			x5
Acts	8.12 – 40			x4
Rom	15.16	—	16.25	x4
Col	1.6 – 23			x4
2 Tim	1.8	—	2.9	x4
Mt	9.35	—	11.5	x3
Mk	1.1 – 15			x3
Lk	7.22	—	9.6	x3
Rom	10.15	—	11.28	x3
2 Cor	10.14	—	11.7	x3
Eph	1.13	—	3.8	x3
Eph	6.19 – 20			x3

Announce see **Proclaim**

Christ see **Jesus**

God

Mk	1.14	preached the **Good News** from **God**.
Lk	4.43	**Good News** about the Kingdom of **God**
Acts	13.32	told **Good News** to you: what **God** promised
	15.7	**God** chose me...to preach the **Good**
	16.10	**God** had called us to preach the **Good**
	20.24	**Good News** about the grace of **God**.
Rom	1.1	by **God** to preach his **Good News**.
	1.2	The **Good News** was promised...by **God**
	1.9	**God** whom I serve...preaching the **Good**
	1.16	in the gospel; it is **God's** power
	1.17	gospel reveals how **God** puts people
	11.28	the **Good News**...are **God's** enemies
	15.16	in preaching the **Good News** from **God**,
2 Cor	9.13	to **God** for your loyalty to the gospel
	11.7	the **Good News** of **God** to you;
Gal	2.7	saw that **God** had given me the task of preaching the gospel
Eph	3.7	of the gospel by **God's** special gift
Phil	1.16	that **God** has given me the work of defending the gospel.
1 Thes	2.2	our **God** gave us courage to tell you the **Good News**
	2.8	not only the **Good News** from **God**
	2.9	to you the **Good News** from **God**.
	3.2	for **God** in preaching the **Good News**
2 Thes	1.8	who reject **God** and...the **Good News**
	2.14	**God** called you to this through the **Good News** we preached
1 Tim	1.11	the **Good News** from the glorious and blessed **God**.
2 Tim	1.8	**Good News**, as **God** gives you the
1 Pet	4.17	not believe the **Good News** from **God**?

Jesus, Christ

Mk	1.1	is the **Good News** about **Jesus Christ**,
	1.14	**Jesus** went to Galilee and preached the **Good News** from God.
Lk	8.1	**Jesus** travelled through towns and villages, preaching the **Good News**
Acts	5.42	**Good News** about **Jesus** the Messiah.
	8.35	told him the **Good News** about **Jesus**.
	10.36	the **Good News** of peace through **Jesus**
	11.20	the **Good News** about the Lord **Jesus**.
Rom	15.19	the **Good News** about **Christ**.
	15.20	**Good News** in places where **Christ**
	16.25	**Good News** I preach about **Jesus Christ**
1 Cor	9.12	way of the **Good News** about **Christ**.
2 Cor	2.12	to preach the **Good News** about **Christ**
	4.4	**Good News** about the glory of **Christ**,
	9.13	your loyalty to the gospel of **Christ**
	10.14	bringing the **Good News** about **Christ**.
Gal	1.7	trying to change the gospel of **Christ**
Eph	2.17	**Christ** came and preached the **Good**
	3.8	the **Good News** about...**Christ**,
Phil	1.27	as the gospel of **Christ** requires
1 Thes	3.2	preaching the **Good News** about **Christ**.
2 Thes	1.8	the **Good News** about our Lord **Jesus**.

Kingdom

Mt	4.23	the **Good News** about the **Kingdom**,
	9.35	the **Good News** about the **Kingdom**,
	24.14	**Good News** about the **Kingdom** will be
Lk	4.43	the **Good News** about the **Kingdom**
	8.1	**Good News** about the **Kingdom** of
	16.16	**Good News** about the **Kingdom** of God
Acts	8.12	about the **good news** of the **Kingdom**

Lord

| 2 Sam | 18.19 | **good news** that the **Lord** has saved him |
| Is | 21.10 | the **good news** that I have heard from the **Lord** Almighty, |

Is	60.6	**good news** of what the **Lord** has done!
Acts	11.20	the **Good News** about the **Lord** Jesus.
2 Thes	1.8	the **Good News** about our **Lord** Jesus.

Proclaim, Announce, Bring, Preach, Tell

1 Sam	31.9	to **tell** the **good news** to their idols
2 Sam	4.10	thought he was **bringing good news.**
	18.25	he is **bringing good news.**
	18.26	This one also is **bringing good news.**
	18.27	and he is **bringing good news.**
1 Kgs	1.42	you must be **bringing good news.**
1 Chr	10.9	to **tell** the **good news** to their idols
	16.23	**Proclaim** every day the **good news**
Ps	40.9	I **told** the **good news** that you save us.
	96.2	**Proclaim** every day the **good news**
Is	21.10	I have **announced** to you the **good news**
	40.9	and **proclaim** the **good news!**
	52.7	**bringing good news,** the news of peace!
	60.6	**tell** the **good news** of what the Lord
	61.1	To **bring good news** to the poor,
Nah	1.15	**good news!** He is...to **announce** the
Mt	4.23	**preaching** the **Good News** about the
	9.35	**preached** the **Good News** about the
	10.18	to **tell** the **Good News** to them
	11.5	the **Good News** is **preached** to the poor.
	24.14	this **Good News**...will be **preached**
	26.13	that wherever this **gospel** is **preached**
Mk	1.14	**preached** the **Good News** from God.
	13.9	to **tell** them the **Good News.**
	13.10	**gospel** must be **preached** to all peoples.
	14.9	you that wherever the **gospel** is **preached**
	16.15	and **preach** the **gospel** to all mankind.
Lk	1.19	and **tell** you this **good news.**
	3.18	**preached** the **Good News** to the people
	4.18	chosen me to **bring good news** to the
		poor....to **proclaim** liberty
	4.43	I must **preach** the **Good News**
	7.22	the **Good News** is **preached** to the poor.
	8.1	**preaching** the **Good News** about the
	9.6	**preaching** the **Good News** and healing
	20.1	people and **preaching** the **Good News,**
	21.13	your chance to **tell** the **Good News.**
Acts	5.42	and **preach** the **Good News** about Jesus
	8.25	**preached** the **Good News** in many
	8.35	he **told** him the **Good News** about Jesus.
	8.40	**preached** the **Good News** in every town.
	10.36	**proclaiming** the **Good News** of peace
	10.42	he commanded us to **preach** the **gospel**
	11.20	**telling** them the **Good News** about the Lord
	13.32	here to **bring** the **Good News** to you:
	14.7	There they **preached** the **Good News.**
	14.15	are here to **announce** the **Good News,**
	14.21	**preached** the **Good News** in Derbe
	15.7	among you to **preach** the **Good News**
	16.10	had called us to **preach** the **Good News**
Rom	1.1	by God to **preach** his **Good News.**
	1.9	by **preaching** the **Good News**
	1.15	to **preach** the **Good News** to you also
	2.16	according to the **Good News I preach,**
	10.15	messengers who **bring good news!**
	15.16	in **preaching** the **Good News** from God,
	15.19	I have **proclaimed** fully the **Good News**
	15.20	always been to **proclaim** the **Good News**
	16.25	**Good News I preach** about Jesus Christ
1 Cor	1.17	sent me to **tell** the **Good News.**
	4.15	by **bringing** the **Good News** to you.
	9.14	**preach** the **gospel** should get their living
	9.16	boast just because I **preach** the **gospel**
	9.18	privilege of **preaching** the **Good News**
	15.1	**Good News** which I **preached** to you,
	15.2	the **gospel,** the message that I **preached**
2 Cor	2.12	in Troas to **preach** the **Good News**

2 Cor	4.3	For if the **gospel** we **preach** is hidden
	8.18	for his work in **preaching** the **gospel.**
	10.14	**bringing** the **Good News** about Christ.
	10.16	**preach** the **Good News** in other
	11.4	we **preached;** and you accept...a **gospel**
	11.7	I **preached** the **Good News** of God
Gal	1.8	**preach** to you a **gospel** that is different
	1.9	if anyone **preaches** to you a **gospel**
	1.11	**gospel I preach** is not of human origin.
	1.16	**preach** the **Good News** about him
	2.2	the **gospel** message that I **preach**
	2.7	the task of **preaching** the **gospel**
	3.8	the scripture **announced** the **Good News**
	4.13	why I **preached** the **gospel** to you
Eph	2.17	and **preached** the **Good News** of peace
	6.15	readiness to **announce** the **Good News**
Phil	4.15	early days of **preaching** the **Good News,**
Col	1.23	**gospel** which has been **preached** to
1 Thes	1.5	For we **brought** the **Good News** to you,
	2.2	courage to **tell** you the **Good News**
	2.9	we **preached** to you the **Good News**
	3.2	**preaching** the **Good News** about Christ.
2 Thes	2.14	the **Good News** we **preached** to you;
1 Tim	1.11	to me to **announce,** the **Good News**
2 Tim	1.11	teacher to **proclaim** the **Good News,**
	2.8	is taught in the **Good News I preach.**
	2.9	I **preach** the **Good News,** I suffer
	4.5	work of a **preacher** of the **Good News,**
1 Pet	1.12	who **announced** the **Good News**
	1.25	is the **Good News** that was **proclaimed**
	4.6	is why the **Good News** was **preached**
Rev	14.6	message of **Good News** to **announce**

GRACE

Rom	5.2	—	6.15		x9
Eph	1.2	—	3.2		x7
Acts	13.43	—	15.40		x5
Rom	11.5	—	12.6		x5
Tit	1.4	—	3.15		x5
1 Cor	15.10	—	16.23		x4
Gal	1.3	—	2.21		x4
2 Thes	1.2	—	3.18		x4
2 Tim	1.2	—	2.1		x4
Ezra	7.28	—	9.8		x3
Jn	1.14 – 17				x3
2 Cor	8.1	—	9.14		x3
Col	1.2 – 7				x3
Heb	12.15	—	13.25		x3

Christ see Jesus

Father see God

Gift, Free

Rom	3.24	**free gift** of God's **grace** all are put right
	5.15	But God's **grace** is much greater, and so is his **free gift**
	5.17	**grace** and are **freely** put right with him
	12.3	**gracious gift** to me I say to every one
	12.6	**gifts** in accordance with the **grace**
Eph	1.6	glorious **grace,** for the **free gift** he gave

Glory

Jn	1.14	of **grace** and truth...We saw his **glory,**
Eph	1.6	praise God for his **glorious grace**
2 Thes	1.12	**glory** from you...by the **grace**
1 Pet	5.10	**grace,** who calls you to share his...**glory**

God, Father

Ezra	7.28	By God's **grace** I have won the favour
	8.18	Through God's **grace** they sent us
	9.8	our **God,** you have been **gracious** to us
Neh	9.17	a **God** who forgives; you are **gracious**
	9.31	You are a **gracious** and merciful **God!**
Lk	1.30	**God** has been **gracious** to you.

Jn	1.17	**God** gave the Law through Moses, but **grace** and truth
Acts	13.43	to keep on living in the **grace** of **God**.
	14.26	commended to the care of **God's grace**
	18.27	**God's grace** had become believers.
	20.24	Good News about the **grace** of **God**.
	20.32	to the care of **God** and...his **grace**,
Rom	1.7	our **Father**...give you **grace**
	3.24	by the free gift of **God's grace**
	5.2	into this experience of **God's grace**,
	5.15	But **God's grace** is much greater,
	5.17	All who receive **God's** abundant **grace**
	5.20	**God's grace** increased much more.
	5.21	**God's grace** rules by means of
	6.1	so that **God's grace** will increase?
	6.14	live under law but under **God's grace**.
	6.15	not under law but under **God's grace**?
	11.5	**God** has chosen because of his **grace**.
	11.6	if **God's** choice were based on what people do, then his **grace**
	12.3	because of **God's gracious** gift to me
	12.6	with the **grace** that **God** has given us.
1 Cor	1.3	our **Father**...give you **grace**
	1.4	to my **God** for you because of the **grace**
	15.10	But by **God's grace** I am what I am
2 Cor	1.2	our **Father**...give you **grace**
	1.12	by the power of **God's grace**,
	4.15	as **God's grace** reaches more and more
	6.1	you who have received **God's grace**
	8.1	what **God's grace** has accomplished
	9.14	the extraordinary **grace God** has shown
Gal	1.3	our **Father**...give you **grace**
	1.15	But **God** in his **grace** chose me
	2.21	I refuse to reject the **grace** of **God**
	5.4	You are outside **God's grace**.
Eph	1.2	our **Father**...give you **grace**
	1.6	Let us praise **God** for his glorious **grace**
	1.7	How great is the **grace** of **God**,
	2.5	**God's grace** that you have been saved.
	2.8	**God's grace** that you have been saved
	3.2	you have heard that **God's grace**
	6.24	May **God's grace** be with all those
Phil	1.2	our **Father**...give you **grace**
Col	1.2	May **God** our **Father** give you **grace**
	1.6	you first heard about the **grace** of **God**
	1.7	learnt of **God's grace** from Epaphras
	4.18	May **God's grace** be with you.
1 Thes	1.1	to **God** the **Father**...May **grace**
2 Thes	1.2	our **Father**...give you **grace**
	1.12	**grace** of our **God** and of the Lord Jesus
	2.16	and **God** our **Father**, who loved us and in his **grace** gave
1 Tim	1.2	**Father** and Christ Jesus...give you **grace**,
	6.21	**God's grace** be with you all.
2 Tim	1.2	**Father** and Christ Jesus...give you **grace**,
	4.22	**God's grace** be with you all.
Tit	2.11	For **God** has revealed his **grace**
	3.7	**grace** we might be put right with **God**
	3.15	**God's grace** be with you all.
Phlm	.3	our **Father**...give you **grace**
Heb	2.9	that through **God's grace** he should die
	4.16	**God's** throne, where there is **grace**.
	12.15	turning back from the **grace** of **God**.
	13.9	receive inner strength from **God's grace**,
	13.25	May **God's grace** be with you all.
Jas	1.5	**God** gives generously and **graciously**
	4.6	**grace** that **God** gives is even stronger.
1 Pet	5.10	the **God** of all **grace**,
	5.12	this is the true **grace** of **God**.
2 Jn	.3	**Father** and Jesus Christ...give us **grace**
Jude	1.4	the message about the **grace** of our **God**
Rev	1.4	**Grace** and peace be yours from **God**,

Jesus, Christ

Jn	1.17	**grace** and truth came through **Jesus**
Acts	15.11	saved by the **grace** of the Lord **Jesus**,
Rom	1.7	the Lord **Jesus Christ** give you **grace**
	5.15	through the **grace** of the one man, **Jesus**
	5.17	**receive grace**...through **Christ**.
	16.20	**grace** of our Lord **Jesus** be with you.
1 Cor	1.3	the Lord **Jesus Christ** give you **grace**
	1.4	because of the **grace** he has given you through **Christ Jesus**.
	16.23	**grace** of the Lord **Jesus** be with you.
2 Cor	1.2	the Lord **Jesus Christ** give you **grace**
	8.9	the **grace** of our Lord **Jesus Christ**;
	13.13	The **grace** of the Lord **Jesus Christ**
Gal	1.3	the Lord **Jesus Christ** give you **grace**
	1.6	who called you by the **grace** of **Christ**,
	6.18	May the **grace** of our Lord **Jesus Christ**
Eph	1.2	the Lord **Jesus Christ** give you **grace**
	2.7	his **grace** in the love he showed us in **Christ Jesus**.
Phil	1.2	the Lord **Jesus Christ** give you **grace**
	4.23	May the **grace** of the Lord **Jesus Christ**
1 Thes	5.28	The **grace** of our Lord **Jesus Christ**
2 Thes	1.2	the Lord **Jesus Christ** give you **grace**
	1.12	**grace** of our God and of the Lord **Jesus**
	3.18	May the **grace** of our Lord **Jesus Christ**
1 Tim	1.2	**Christ Jesus** our Lord give you **grace**,
2 Tim	1.2	**Christ Jesus** our Lord give you **grace**,
	1.9	us this **grace** by means of **Christ Jesus**
	2.1	through the **grace** that is ours in union with **Christ Jesus**.
Tit	1.4	**Christ Jesus** our Saviour give you **grace**
Phlm	.3	the Lord **Jesus Christ** give you **grace**
	.25	May the **grace** of the Lord **Jesus Christ**
2 Pet	3.18	grow in the **grace** and knowledge of our Lord and Saviour **Jesus**
2 Jn	.3	and **Jesus Christ**, the Father's Son, give us **grace**
Rev	22.21	May the **grace** of the Lord **Jesus**

Lord

Num	6.25	the **Lord** be kind and **gracious** to you;
Ezra	9.8	**Lord** our God, you have been **gracious**
Acts	15.40	believers to the care of the **Lord's grace**.
1 Tim	1.14	our **Lord** poured out his abundant **grace**

Peace, Mercy

Rom	1.7	Jesus Christ give you **grace** and **peace**.
1 Cor	1.3	Jesus Christ give you **grace** and **peace**.
2 Cor	1.2	Jesus Christ give you **grace** and **peace**.
Gal	1.3	Jesus Christ give you **grace** and **peace**.
Eph	1.2	Jesus Christ give you **grace** and **peace**.
Phil	1.2	Jesus Christ give you **grace** and **peace**.
Col	1.2	our Father give you **grace** and **peace**.
1 Thes	1.1	May **grace** and **peace** be yours.
2 Thes	1.2	Jesus Christ give you **grace** and **peace**.
1 Tim	1.2	give you **grace**, **mercy**, and **peace**.
2 Tim	1.2	give you **grace**, **mercy**, and **peace**.
Tit	1.4	give you **grace** and **peace**.
Phlm	.3	Jesus Christ give you **grace** and **peace**.
Heb	4.16	we will receive **mercy** and find **grace**
1 Pet	1.2	**grace** and **peace** be yours in full
2 Pet	1.2	**grace** and **peace** be yours in full
2 Jn	.3	give us **grace**, **mercy**, and **peace**;
Rev	1.4	**Grace** and **peace** be yours from God,

Saved

Eph	2.5	by...**grace** that you have been **saved**
	2.8	by...**grace** that you have been **saved**
Tit	2.11	his **grace** for the **salvation** of all

Sin

Rom	5.20	**sin** increased, God's **grace** increased
	5.21	**sin** ruled by means of death, so also God's **grace** rules

Rom 6.1 in **sin** so that God's **grace** will increase?
Eph 1.7 **sins** are forgiven. How great is the **grace**

Truth
Jn 1.14 full of **grace** and **truth**,
     1.17 **grace** and **truth** came through Jesus
Acts 14.3 message about his **grace** was **true**

GRAIN-OFFERING

Num	28.5	—	29.39	x14
Lev	5.11	—	7.37	x10
Ezek	44.29	—	46.11	x8
Num	15.4 – 24			x4
Lev	2.3 – 13			x3
Lev	9.4	—	10.12	x3
Lev	14.20 – 31			x3
Num	7.12	—	8.8	x3
2 Kgs	16.13 – 15			x3

Present
Lev 2.11 of the **grain-offerings** which you **present**
     6.14 priest shall **present** the **grain-offering**
     6.21 and **presented** as a **grain-offering**,
     9.17 He **presented** the **grain-offering**
     23.37 **presenting...grain-offerings**,
Num 15.6 are to be **presented** as a **grain-offering**,
Is 66.3 whether they **present** a **grain-offering**

Proper
Num 15.24 **proper grain-offering** and wine-offering.
     28.20 Offer the **proper grain-offering** of flour
         Also: 28.28; 29.3; 29.9; 29.14

GRATEFUL

Deut	24.13	—	27.7	x3

God, Lord
Lev 19.24 to show your **gratitude** to me, the **Lord**.
Deut 24.13 will be **grateful**, and the **Lord** your **God**
     26.11 Be **grateful** for the good things that the **Lord** your **God**
     27.7 be **grateful** in the presence of the **Lord** your **God**.
2 Chr 32.25 **gratitude** for what the **Lord** had done
Lk 6.35 **God**. For he is good to the **ungrateful**
2 Cor 9.12 an outpouring of **gratitude** to **God**.
Heb 12.28 Let us be **grateful** and worship **God**

GRAVE

Ezek	32.22 – 26	x6
1 Kgs	13.22 – 31	x3
Ps	49.9 – 17	x3
Jn	11.31 — 12.17	x3
Acts	2.27 – 31	x3
Acts	13.34 – 36	x3

Death
Num 19.18 bone or the **dead** body or the **grave**.
2 Sam 22.6 **death** was round me, and the **grave** set
Job 3.21 wait for **death**...they prefer a **grave**
Ps 18.5 **death** was round me, and the **grave** set
     30.9 from my **death**? What profit from my going to the **grave**?
     88.5 **dead**; I am like the slain...in their **graves**,
     116.3 **death** was all round me...the **grave**
Acts 2.31 **dead**; his body did not rot in the **grave**.

Keep From
Ps 30.3 you **kept** me **from** the **grave**.
     49.9 to **keep** him **from** the **grave**,
     71.20 you will **keep** me **from** the **grave**.
     89.48 can man **keep** himself **from** the **grave**?
     103.4 He **keeps** me **from** the **grave**

GRIEF

Ezra	9.3	—	10.6	x4
Job	1.20	—	3.20	x4
Is	15.2	—	16.11	x4
Lam	2.11	—	3.51	x4
Judg	11.37 – 40			x3
2 Sam	1.2 – 26			x3
Is	23.1 – 14			x3
Is	35.10	—	37.1	x3
Jer	15.5	—	16.6	x3
Rev	18.7 – 8			x3

Weep, Cry
Job 2.12 **weep**...tearing their clothes in **grief**
Ps 6.6 **grief**...my bed is damp from my **weeping**;
Is 15.5 **weeping** as they go...**grieving**
Lam 2.18 yourself out with **weeping** and **grief**!
Rev 21.4 no more **grief** or **crying** or pain

GUIDE

	Prov	11.3	— 12.26	x3

God
Prov 29.18 A nation without **God's guidance**

Lord
2 Chr 20.3 and prayed to the **Lord** for **guidance**
     20.4 to ask the **Lord** for **guidance**,
Ps 1.6 are **guided** and protected by the **Lord**,
     16.7 I praise the **Lord**, because he **guides** me,
     37.23 The **Lord guides** a man in the way
Jer 10.21 they do not ask the **Lord** for **guidance**.
1 Cor 12.3 Jesus is **Lord**," unless he is **guided**

GUILTY

Lev	4.3	—	6.4	x10
Num	35.16 – 30			x6
Job	9.20	—	10.7	x5
Ex	22.2	—	23.1	x4
Gen	18.23 – 25			x3
Num	5.8 – 31			x3
Deut	24.15	—	25.2	x3
Is	4.4	—	6.7	x3
Ezek	4.4 – 6			x3
Ezek	21.24	—	23.21	x3
Mt	12.5 – 37			x3
Jn	8.46	—	9.41	x3
Rom	4.5	—	5.16	x3
Heb	10.2 – 28			x3
Jas	2.4 – 10			x3

Innocent
Gen 18.23 to destroy the **innocent** with the **guilty**?
     18.25 won't kill the **innocent** with the **guilty**.
Deut 25.1 declared **innocent** and the other **guilty**.
Job 9.20 **innocent**...but my words sound **guilty**
     9.21 **innocent** or **guilty**, God will destroy us.
     33.9 I am not **guilty**...I am **innocent**
Prov 18.5 the **guilty** and prevent the **innocent**
     21.8 **Guilty** people walk a crooked path; the **innocent**
     24.24 he pronounces a **guilty** person **innocent**,
Is 5.23 let **guilty** men go free, and...the **innocent**
Jer 26.15 be **guilty** of killing an **innocent** man,
Lam 4.13 **guilty** of causing the death of **innocent**
Mt 12.37 to declare you either **innocent** or **guilty**.
Rom 4.5 who declares the **guilty** to be **innocent**,

Judge
Deut 25.2 If the **guilty** man is sentenced...the **judge**
1 Kgs 8.32 **judge** your servants. Punish the **guilty**
2 Chr 6.23 **judge** your servants. Punish the **guilty**
Prov 24.25 **Judges** who punish the **guilty**,
Mt 12.37 **judge** you ...either innocent or **guilty**.

Rom   5.16   came the **judgement** of "Guilty";
       14.22   **guilty** when he does something he **judges**
Heb   10.28   **judged guilty** on the evidence

Prove

Deut 19.15   necessary to **prove** that a man is **guilty**.
Job   16.8   people take that as **proof** of my **guilt**.
      19.5   regard my troubles as **proof** of my **guilt**.
Is   50.9   can **prove** me **guilty**?
Jn   8.46   one of you can **prove** that I am **guilty**

Punish

Gen   18.25   be **punished** along with the **guilty**.
Lev   22.16   **guilt** and **punishment** on such a person.
1 Kgs 8.32   **Punish** the **guilty** one as he deserves,
2 Chr 6.23   **Punish** the **guilty** one as he deserves
Ps   106.30   stood up and **punished** the **guilty**,
Prov 24.25   Judges who **punish** the **guilty**,
Lam   4.22   **punish** you; he will expose your **guilt**
Nah   1.3   and never lets the **guilty** go **unpunished**.

Suffer

Num   5.31   if **guilty**, must **suffer** the consequences.
      18.1   **suffer** the consequences of any **guilt**
Ezek   4.4   and **suffer** because of their **guilt**.
      4.6   **suffer** for the **guilt** of Judah for forty

HAPPY

Mt	5.3 – 12		x10
Prov	14.13	— 16.20	x9
Ps	119.1 – 174		x7
Prov	27.9	— 29.18	x7
Is	23.12	— 25.9	x5
Lk	6.20	— 7.23	x5
Lk	11.27	— 12.43	x5
Lk	14.15	— 15.32	x5
1 Chr	29.9 – 22		x4
Job	20.5	— 21.25	x4
Prov	7.18	— 8.34	x4
Prov	11.1	— 12.25	x4
Ecc	5.20	— 7.14	x4
Ecc	9.7	— 11.9	x4
Is	29.19	— 30.29	x4
Jer	48.33	— 51.39	x4
Lk	1.14 – 48		x4
Rom	4.6 – 9		x4
2 Cor	7.7 – 16		x4
Ps	84.4 – 12		x3
Prov	3.13 – 22		x3
Prov	23.15 – 25		x3

Believe see **Trust**

Celebrate, Feast

Esth   8.17   holiday with **feasting** and **happiness**.
Ps   118.24   let us be **happy**, let us **celebrate**!
Ecc   10.19   **Feasting** makes you **happy** and wine
Jer   7.34   the **happy** sounds of wedding **feasts**.
            Also: 16.9; 25.10; 33.11
     51.39   **feast** and make them drunk and **happy**.
Lk   14.15   How **happy** are those who will...**feast**
     15.6   I am so **happy** I found my lost sheep. Let us **celebrate**!
     15.9   I am so **happy** I found the coin I lost. Let us **celebrate**!,
    15.32   But we had to **celebrate** and be **happy**

Command see **Obey**

Faithful

Dan 12.12   **Happy** are those who remain **faithful**
Jas   1.12   **Happy** is the person who remains **faithful** under trials

Feast see **Celebrate**

Forgiven

Ps   32.1   **Happy** are those whose sins are **forgiven**,
Rom 4.8   **Happy** are those whose wrongs are **forgiven**

Glad

Ps   35.9   I will be **glad**...I will be **happy**
    106.5   **happiness** of your nation, in the **glad**
Jer   50.11   You are **happy** and **glad**,
Mt   5.12   Be **happy** and **glad**, for a great reward
Lk   1.14   How **glad** and **happy** you will be,
2 Cor 2.3   make me **glad**. For...when I am **happy**,

God

2 Chr 29.36   **happy**, because **God** had helped them
Neh 12.43   **God** had made them very **happy**.
Job   5.17   **Happy** is the person whom **God**
Ps   33.12   **Happy** is the nation whose **God** is the
     43.4   O **God**; you are the source of my **happiness**.
     45.7   **God**, has...poured out more **happiness**
     53.6   How **happy**...Israel will be when **God**
  144.15   **happy** are the people whose **God**
  146.5   **Happy** is the man who has the **God** of
Prov 29.18   **Happy** is the man who keeps **God's**
Ecc   2.26   **God** gives wisdom, knowledge, and **happiness**
     5.20   **God** has allowed him to be **happy**,
     7.14   **God** sends both **happiness** and trouble;
Is   29.19   **happiness** which the Lord, the holy **God**
    41.16   will be **happy** because I am your **God**;
Mt   5.4   **Happy** are those who mourn; **God** will
     5.7   **Happy** are those who are merciful...**God**
     5.8   **Happy** are the pure in heart; they will see **God**!
     5.9   **Happy** are those who work for peace; **God** will call them
Acts   5.41   were **happy**, because **God** had considered
Rom   4.6   **happiness** of the person whom **God**

Kingdom

Mt   5.3   **Happy** are those...spiritually poor; the **Kingdom** of heaven
     5.10   **Happy** are those who are persecuted ...the **Kingdom** of heaven
Lk   6.20   **Happy** are you poor; the **Kingdom** of God is yours!

Law see **Obey**

Lord

1 Kgs 8.66   **happy** because of all the blessings that the **Lord** had given
1 Chr 29.22   **happy** as they ate and drank in the presence of the **Lord**.
2 Chr 7.10   **happy** about all the blessings that the **Lord** had given
Ps   14.7   How **happy** the people of Israel will be when the **Lord**
     32.2   **Happy** is the man whom the **Lord** does
     33.12   **Happy** is the nation whose God is the **Lord**;
     35.9   because of the **Lord**; I will be **happy**
     37.4   Seek your **happiness** in the **Lord**,
     40.4   **Happy** are those who trust the **Lord**,
     84.12   **Lord** Almighty, how **happy** are those
     94.12   **Lord**, how **happy** is the person you
    100.2   the **Lord** with joy...with **happy** songs!
  104.31   May the **Lord** be **happy** with what he
  112.1   **Happy** is the person who honours the **Lord**,
  118.24   of the **Lord's** victory; let us be **happy**,
  119.174 O **Lord**! I find **happiness** in your law.
  128.1   **Happy** are those who obey the **Lord**,

D

Ps   144.15 **happy** are the people whose God is the **Lord**!
Prov 16.20   in the **Lord** and you will be **happy**.
      28.14   obey the **Lord** and you will be **happy**
Is   9.3   **Lord**; you have made them **happy**.
      25.9   He is the **Lord**...now we are **happy**.
      29.19   find the **happiness** which the **Lord**,
      30.18   **Happy** are those who put their trust in the **Lord**.
Lk   1.45   **happy** you are to believe that the **Lord's**
Rom   4.8   **Happy** is the person whose sins the **Lord**
Rev   14.13   **Happy** are those who from now on die in the service of the **Lord**!

Obey, Command, Law, Word

Ps   19.8   and those who **obey** them are **happy**.
      106.3   **Happy** are those who **obey** his
      119.2   **Happy** are those who follow his **commands**,
      119.56 **happiness** in **obeying** your **commands**.
      119.174 I find **happiness** in your **law**.
      128.1   **Happy** are those who **obey** the Lord,
Prov 28.14   **obey** the Lord and you will be **happy**
      29.18   **Happy** is the man who keeps God's **law**!
Jer   15.16   **words** filled my heart with...**happiness**.
Lk   11.28   **happy** are those who hear the **word**
Rev   1.3   **happy** are those who listen to the **words**
      22.7   **Happy** are those who **obey** the...**words**

Poor

Ps   41.1   **Happy** are those...concerned for the **poor**;
Prov 14.21   want to be **happy**, be kind to the **poor**
      15.15   **poor** is a constant struggle, but **happy**
      31.7   forget their **poverty** and **unhappiness**.
Mt   5.3   **Happy** are those...spiritually **poor**;
Lk   6.20   **Happy** are you **poor**;

Trust, Believe

Ps   40.4   **Happy** are those who **trust** the Lord,
      84.12   how **happy** are those who **trust** in you!
Prov 16.20   **trust** in the Lord...you will be **happy**.
Is   25.9   **trust** in him, and now we are **happy**
      30.18   **Happy** are those who put their **trust** in
Lk   1.45   How **happy** you are to believe
Jn   20.29   How **happy** are those who **believe**

Truth

Jn   13.17   know this **truth**, how **happy** you will be
1 Cor 13.6   but is **happy** with the **truth**.

Wise

Prov 3.13   **Happy** is the man who becomes **wise**
      3.18   Those who become **wise** are **happy**;
      15.20   A **wise** son makes his father **happy**
      15.21   are **happy** with...foolishness, but the **wise**
      16.14   A **wise** man will...keep the king **happy**
      23.15   you become **wise**, I will be very **happy**.
      23.24   **happy**. You can take pride in a **wise**
      27.11   Be **wise**, my son, and I will be **happy**

Word see Obey

HARVEST

Lev	25.5 —	26.10	x7
Ruth	1.6 —	2.23	x5
Ex	23.11 – 19		x4
Ex	34.21 – 26		x4
Lev	23.9 – 39		x4
Deut	16.9 – 16		x4
Is	16.9 —	18.4	x4
Mt	13.30 – 39		x4
Jn	4.35 – 38		x4
2 Kgs	4.18 – 42		x3
Ezek	44.30 —	45.13	x3
Hag	1.6 – 9		x3
Mt	9.37 – 38		x3
Lk	10.2		x3
Gal	6.8 – 9		x3
Rev	14.15 – 16		x3

Bless

Deut 16.15   the Lord has **blessed** your **harvest**
Ruth 1.6   had **blessed** his people by giving them a good **harvest**;
Ps   67.6   **harvest**; God, our God, has **blessed** us.

Bread

2 Kgs 4.42   **bread** made from the first barley **harvested**
2 Chr 8.13   Unleavened **Bread**, the **Harvest** Festival,
Is   62.9   **harvested** the corn Will eat the **bread**

Festival

Ex   23.16   Celebrate the **Harvest Festival**
      34.22   Keep the **Harvest Festival**
Lev   23.39   When you have **harvested** your fields, celebrate this **festival**
Num   28.26   On the first day of the **Harvest Festival**
Deut 16.10   and then celebrate the **Harvest Festival**
      16.16   **Harvest Festival**, and the **Festival** of
2 Chr 8.13   Unleavened Bread, the **Harvest Festival**,

Joy

Deut 16.15   Be **joyful**, because the Lord has blessed your **harvest**
Ps   126.5   gather the **harvest** with **joy**!
      126.6   for **joy**, as they bring in the **harvest**.

Offering

Gen   4.3   of his **harvest** and gave it as an **offering**
Lev   2.12   **offering**...the first corn that you **harvest**
      2.14   an **offering** of the first corn **harvested**,
      23.17   **offering** of the first corn to be **harvested**.
Num   28.26   **Harvest**...when you present the **offering**
Neh   10.35   an **offering** of the first corn we **harvest**
      10.37   corn **harvested**...and our other **offerings**
Ezek 44.30   **harvest** and of everything else...**offered** to

Plenty, Rich

Lev   26.5   **plentiful** that you will still be **harvesting**
      26.10   Your **harvests** will be so **plentiful**
Deut 28.38   **plenty** of seed, but...only a small **harvest**
Ps   65.11   a **rich harvest** your goodness provides!
      85.12   and our land will produce **rich harvests**.
Is   30.23   **harvest**...your livestock will have **plenty**
2 Cor 9.10   a **rich harvest** from your generosity.
Eph   5.9   **rich harvest** of every kind of goodness,

Reap

Deut 28.38   but **reap** only a small **harvest**,
Ps   107.37 and **reaped** an abundant **harvest**,
Hos   10.13   you planted evil and **reaped** its **harvest**
Mt   25.24   **reap harvests** where you did not sow,
      25.26   I **reap harvests** where I did not sow,
Jn   4.36   man who **reaps** the **harvest** is being paid
      4.38   sent you to **reap** a **harvest** in a field
Gal   6.9   come when we will **reap** the **harvest**.
Rev   14.15   Use your sickle and **reap** the **harvest**,
      14.16   and the earth's **harvest** was **reaped**.

Rich see Plenty

Ripe

Neh   10.35   **harvest** and of the first fruit that **ripens**
Job   5.26   Like wheat that **ripens** till **harvest** time,
Jn   4.35   are now **ripe** and ready to be **harvested**!
Rev   14.15   the earth is **ripe** for the **harvest**!

Seed

Gen   26.12   sowed **seed** in that land, and...**harvested**
Deut 28.38   of **seed**, but reap only a small **harvest**
Job   4.8   like **seed**; now they **harvest** wickedness
Ps   126.5   their **seed**, gather the **harvest** with joy!
Jer   50.16   not let **seeds** be sown...or let a **harvest**
Mt   6.26   they do not sow **seeds**, gather a **harvest**

Lk   12.24 don't sow **seeds** or gather a **harvest**;
Jas   3.18 **harvest** that is produced from the **seeds**

HATE

Prov	8.7	—	13.5	x12
Prov	24.9	—	26.28	x7
Prov	15.8	—	17.15	x6
Prov	28.9	—	30.23	x5
Ezek	16.27 – 57			x5
Jn	15.18 – 25			x5
1 Jn	2.9	—	4.20	x5
Ps	119.104 – 163			x4
Hos	7.4	—	9.15	x4
Amos	5.10	—	6.8	x4
Gen	37.4 – 8			x3
Deut	7.10 – 26			x3
Deut	16.22	—	18.12	x3
2 Sam	13.15 – 22			x3
Prov	20.10	—	21.27	x3
Jer	12.8	—	14.19	x3
Lam	2.16	—	3.60	x3
Mal	1.3	—	2.16	x3

Bad see **Sin**

Despise
Deut   7.26 You must **hate** and **despise** these idols,
Ps   139.21 **hate** those who **hate** you! How I **despise**
Is   49.7 who is deeply **despised**, who is **hated**
Amos   6.8 **hate** the pride of the people...I **despise**

Dishonest see **Justice**

Enemies
Num   10.35 **enemies** and put to flight those who **hate**
Deut   30.7 **enemies**, who **hated** you and oppressed
          32.41 **enemies** and punish those who **hate** me.
2 Sam 22.18 **enemies** and from all those who **hate** me
          22.41 **enemies** run from me...those who **hate**
Ps   18.17 **enemies** and from all those who **hate** me
          18.40 **enemies** run from me...those who **hate**
          21.8 **enemies**...capture everyone who **hates**
          25.19 **enemies** I have; see how much they **hate**
          44.7 **enemies** and defeated those who **hate** me.
          44.16 of my **enemies** and those who **hate** me.
          68.1 **enemies**. Those who **hate** him run away
          83.2 **enemies**...in revolt, and those who **hate**
          106.10 who **hated** them; he rescued them from their **enemies**.
Lam   2.16 your **enemies**...glare at you with **hate**.
          3.52 **enemies** who had no cause to **hate** me.
          3.60 You know how my **enemies hate** me
Ezek 25.15 age-long **enemies** and destroyed them in their **hate**.
Mt   5.43 **hate** your **enemies**.
Lk   1.71 **enemies**, from...all those who **hate** us.
          6.27 **enemies**, do good to those who **hate**

Evil see **Sin**

God, Lord
Lev   18.22 another man; **God hates** that.
Num   10.35 **Lord**...put to flight those who **hate** you!
Deut   1.27 The **Lord hates** us.
          7.25 because the **Lord hates** idolatry.
          12.31 disgusting things that the **Lord hates**.
          16.22 idol worship; the **Lord hates** them.
          17.1 any defects; the **Lord hates** this.
          18.12 **God hates** people who do these
          22.5 **God hates** people who do such things.
          23.18 The **Lord hates** temple prostitutes.
          25.16 The **Lord hates** people who cheat.
          27.15 the **Lord hates** idolatry.
2 Chr 19.2 the side of those who **hate** the **Lord**?
Ps   86.17 **Lord**; those who **hate** me will be
          97.10 The **Lord** loves those who **hate** evil;
          139.21 **Lord**, how I **hate** those who **hate** you!

Prov   3.32 the **Lord hates** people who do evil,
          6.16 are seven things that the **Lord hates**
          8.13 To honour the **Lord** is to **hate** evil;
          11.1 **Lord hates** people who use dishonest
          11.20 The **Lord hates** evil-minded people
          12.22 The **Lord hates** liars
          15.8 The **Lord...hates** the sacrifices that
          15.9 The **Lord hates** the ways of evil people
          15.26 The **Lord hates** evil thoughts
          16.5 **Lord hates** everyone who is arrogant
          17.15 both are **hateful** to the **Lord**.
          20.10 **Lord hates** people who use dishonest
          20.23 **Lord hates** people who use dishonest
          21.27 **Lord hates** it when wicked men offer
          28.9 **God** will find your prayers too **hateful**
Is   61.8 The **Lord** says, "I...**hate** oppression
Jer   14.19 **Lord**...Do you **hate** the people of Zion?
Ezek 13.20 **Lord** says: "I **hate** the wristbands
Amos   5.21 **Lord** says, "I **hate** your religious
          6.8 **Lord** Almighty has given this solemn warning: "I **hate** the pride
Mal   2.16 I **hate** divorce," says the **Lord God**
Rom   1.30 are **hateful** to **God**, insolent, proud,
1 Jn   4.20 he loves **God**, but **hates** his brother,

Idolatry, Worship
Deut   7.25 because the **Lord hates** idolatry.
          7.26 You must **hate** and despise these **idols**,
          16.22 for **idol** worship; the **Lord hates** them.
          27.15 the **Lord hates** idolatry.
Ps   31.6 You **hate** those who **worship** false gods,
Jer   4.1 to me and remove the **idols** I **hate**,
          7.30 have placed their **idols**, which I **hate**,
Hos   8.5 I **hate** the gold bull **worshipped**

Justice, Dishonest, Wrong
Job   34.17 Do you think that he **hates justice**?
Prov   11.1 **hates** people who use **dishonest** scales
          20.10 **hates** people who use **dishonest** weights
          20.23 **hates** people who use **dishonest** scales
          28.16 **hates dishonesty** will rule a long time.
Is   61.8 I love **justice** and I **hate** oppression
Mic   3.9 **hate justice** and turn right into **wrong**.
Heb   1.9 what is right and **hate** what is **wrong**.

Lies
Ps   10.7 **lies**...he is quick to speak **hateful**,
          119.163 I **hate** and detest all **lies**,
Prov   8.7 **lies** are **hateful** to me.
          10.18 A man who hides his **hatred** is a **liar**
          12.22 The **Lord hates** liars
          13.5 Honest people **hate lies**
          26.28 to **hate** someone...to hurt him with **lies**.
Zech   8.17 I **hate** lying, injustice, and violence.
1 Jn   4.20 but **hates** his brother, he is a **liar**.

Lord see **God**

Sin, Bad, Evil, Wicked
2 Chr 19.2 are **wicked** and...who **hate** the **Lord**?
Job   8.22 **hate** you, and the homes of the **wicked**
Ps   5.5 you **hate** all **wicked** people.
          10.7 he is quick to speak **hateful**, **evil** words.
          11.5 the **wicked** alike; the lawless he **hates**
          26.5 I **hate** the company of **evil** men and avoid the **wicked**.
          34.21 **Evil** will kill the **wicked**; those who **hate**
          45.7 love what is right and **hate** what is **evil**.
          97.10 The **Lord** loves those who **hate evil**;
          101.3 never tolerate **evil**. I **hate** the actions
          109.5 back **evil** for good and **hatred** for love.
          119.104 and so I **hate** all **bad** conduct.
Prov   3.32 the **Lord hates** people who do **evil**,
          8.13 To honour the **Lord** is to **hate evil**;
          11.20 The **Lord hates evil-minded** people
          13.5 **hate** lies, but the words of **wicked**

Prov	15.8	**hates** the sacrifices that **wicked** men
	15.9	The Lord **hates** the ways of **evil** people
	15.26	The Lord **hates evil** thoughts
	17.15	letting the **wicked** go — both are **hateful**
	21.27	Lord **hates** it when **wicked** men offer
	26.26	his **hatred**, but everyone will see the **evil**
	29.27	The righteous **hate** the **wicked**
Hos	9.7	**hate** me so much because your **sin** is so
Amos	5.15	**Hate** what is **evil**
Mic	3.2	**hate** what is good...love what is **evil**.
Jn	3.20	who does **evil** things **hates** the light
Rom	1.30	**evil** of one another; they are **hateful**
	12.9	**Hate** what is **evil**,
Heb	12.3	up with so much **hatred** from **sinners**!
Jude	.23	**hate** their very clothes, stained by their **sinful** lusts.

Worship see **Idolatry**

Wrong see **Justice**

HEAL

Lk	4.23	—	10.9	x17
Mt	8.3	—	10.8	x8
Mt	12.10	—	15.30	x7
Jn	4.47	—	6.2	x6
Acts	4.9	—	5.16	x5
Lev	13.16	—	14.3	x4
Mk	5.29	—	6.13	x4
Lk	13.14	—	14.4	x4
Is	57.18	—	58.8	x3
Jer	8.15 – 22			x3
Jer	14.19	—	15.18	x3
Jer	30.12 – 17			x3
Hos	5.13	—	7.1	x3
Acts	28.8 – 27			x3
1 Cor	12.9 – 30			x3

Demons see **Spirits**

God

Gen	20.17	Abimelech, and **God healed** him.
Num	12.13	cried out...O **God, heal** her!
1 Kgs	13.6	**Lord** your **God**, and ask him to **heal**
Ps	30.2	O **Lord** my **God**, and you **healed** me;
Mt	13.15	says **God**, and I would **heal** them.
Lk	17.15	was **healed**, he came back, praising **God**
Jn	12.40	turn to me, says **God**, for me to **heal**
Acts	28.27	says **God**, and I would **heal** them.

God's People

Is	30.26	and **heals** the wounds he has given his **people**.
	57.19	I will **heal my people**.
Jer	8.22	have **my people** not been **healed**?
Hos	7.1	I want to **heal my people** Israel

Heart

Ps	147.3	He **heals** the **broken-hearted**
Is	61.1	To **heal** the **broken-hearted**,
Jer	8.18	cannot be **healed**; I am sick at **heart**.
Mt	14.14	**heart** was filled with pity...and he **healed**

Hurt

Job	5.18	his hand **hurts** you, and his hand **heals**.
Jer	10.19	we are **hurt**! Our wounds will not **heal**.
	14.19	**hurt** us so...that we cannot be **healed**?
Ezek	34.16	those that are **hurt**, and **heal** those
Hos	6.1	**hurt** us, but he will be sure to **heal** us;
Zech	11.16	**heal** those that are **hurt**, or feed the

Jesus

Mt	4.24	paralytics — and **Jesus healed** them all.
	8.16	**Jesus**...**healed** all who were sick.
	12.22	**Jesus healed** the man,
	15.30	at **Jesus'** feet; and he **healed** them.
Mk	1.34	**Jesus healed** many who were sick
Lk	4.40	**Jesus**...**healed** them all.

Lk	5.17	was present for **Jesus** to **heal** the sick.
	9.42	**Jesus**...**healed** the boy,
	13.14	that **Jesus** had **healed** on the Sabbath,
	14.4	**Jesus** took the man, **healed** him,
Jn	5.13	**healed** did not know who **Jesus** was
	5.15	that it was **Jesus** who had **healed** him.
	5.16	**Jesus**, because he had done this **healing**

Lord

see also **God**

Ex	15.26	I am the **Lord**, the one who **heals** you.
2 Kgs	20.8	to prove that the **Lord** will **heal** me
Ps	41.4	**Lord**; be merciful to me and **heal** me.
Is	19.22	**Lord** will punish the Egyptians, but then he will **heal** them.
	30.26	**Lord** bandages and **heals** the wounds
	38.16	**Lord**, I will live for you...**Heal** me
	38.20	**Lord**, you have **healed** me.
Jer	3.22	away from the **Lord**; he will **heal** you
	17.14	**Lord, heal** me and I will be completely
Hos	6.1	the **Lord**...will be sure to **heal** us;
Lk	5.17	the **Lord** was present for Jesus to **heal**
Jas	5.15	the **Lord** will restore him to **health**,

Sabbath

Mt	12.10	our Law to **heal** on the **Sabbath**?
Mk	3.2	he would **heal** the man on the **Sabbath**.
Lk	6.7	to see if he would **heal** on the **Sabbath**,
	13.14	that Jesus had **healed** on the **Sabbath**,
	14.3	our Law allow **healing** on the **Sabbath**
Jn	5.10	had been **healed**, "This is a **Sabbath**,
	5.16	he had done this **healing** on a **Sabbath**.

Sin

Ps	103.3	He forgives all my **sins** and **heals**
Jas	5.15	will restore him to **health**, and the **sins**

Spirits, Demons

Mt	8.16	the evil **spirits** with a word and **healed**
	10.1	to drive out evil **spirits** and to **heal**
	12.22	he had a **demon**. Jesus **healed** the man,
Lk	6.18	evil **spirits** also came and were **healed**.
	8.2	been **healed** of evil **spirits** and diseases;
	9.42	to the evil **spirit**, **healed** the boy,
Acts	5.16	**spirits** in them; and they were all **healed**.

Suffer

Is	53.5	**healed** by the punishment he **suffered**,
Mt	10.8	**heal** those who **suffer** from dreaded

HEART

2 Cor	1.22	—	7.10	x14
Ps	119.2 – 167			x13
Rom	8.27	—	12.11	x6
Jer	3.17	—	4.19	x5
Lam	1.20	—	3.51	x5
Lk	6.45	—	8.15	x5
Rom	1.9	—	2.29	x5
Eph	3.17	—	6.6	x5
Col	3.1 – 23			x5
Heb	8.10	—	10.22	x5
Deut	30.2 – 10			x4
1 Chr	28.9	—	29.19	x4
Prov	6.21	—	7.25	x4
Mt	14.14	—	15.19	x4
Mk	6.34	—	7.21	x4
1 Kgs	8.23 – 39			x3
2 Chr	6.14 – 30			x3
Jer	17.1 – 10			x3
Ezek	11.19			x3
Ezek	36.26			x3
Acts	27.22 – 36			x3

Believe see **Faith**

Christ see **Jesus**

Command see Obey

Desire

1 Chr	29.19	a **wholehearted desire** to obey everything
Ps	21.2	You have given him his **heart's desire**;
	37.4	and he will give you your **heart's desire**.
Ecc	11.9	and follow your **heart's desire**.
Rom	1.24	the filthy things their **hearts desire**,
Heb	4.12	the **desires** and thoughts of man's **heart**.

Evil see Sin

Faith, Believe

Prov	26.25	but don't **believe** him, because his **heart**
Mk	11.23	does not doubt in his **heart**, but **believes**
Lk	8.12	**hearts** in order to keep them from **believing**
Jn	5.38	in your **hearts**, for you do not **believe**
Rom	10.8	**heart**" — that is, the message of **faith**
Eph	3.17	his home in your **hearts** through **faith**.
1 Tim	1.5	pure **heart**...and a genuine **faith**.
	6.10	the **faith** and have broken their **hearts**
Heb	10.22	with a sincere **heart** and a sure **faith**,
1 Jn	5.10	**believes** in the Son of God has this testimony in his own **heart**;

Faithful, True

Deut	26.16	obey them **faithfully** with all your **heart**.
1 Sam	12.24	serve him **faithfully** with all your **heart**.
1 Kgs	2.4	commands **faithfully** with all their **heart**
1 Chr	29.18	**hearts** and keep them always **faithful**
Acts	11.23	**true** to the Lord with all their **hearts**.

Glad see Joy

God

Deut	6.5	the **Lord** your **God** with all your **heart**
	11.13	**God** and serve him with all your **heart**.
Josh	23.14	**heart** and soul that the **Lord** your **God**
1 Sam	10.26	whose **hearts God** had touched,
2 Kgs	10.31	**heart** the law of the **Lord**, the **God** of
1 Chr	22.19	the **Lord** your **God** with all your **heart**
	28.9	**God**...with an undivided **heart**
2 Chr	15.12	the **God** of their ancestors, with all their **heart**
	20.33	not turn **wholeheartedly** to the worship of the **God**
Ezra	1.5	else whose **heart God** had moved
Ps	36.1	deep in his **heart**; he rejects **God**
	37.31	keeps the law of his **God** in his **heart**
	40.8	**God**! I keep your teaching in my **heart**.
	51.10	Create a pure **heart** in me, O **God**,
	86.12	with all my **heart**, O **Lord** my **God**;
Jer	15.16	**God** Almighty, and so your words filled my **heart** with joy
Lam	3.41	us open our **hearts** to **God** in heaven
Mt	5.8	the pure in **heart**; they will see **God**!
	15.8	says **God**, honour me with their words, but their **heart**
	22.37	the **Lord** your **God** with all your **heart**,
Mk	7.6	says **God**, honour me with their words, but their **heart**
	12.30	the **Lord** your **God** with all your **heart**,
	12.33	man must love **God** with all his **heart**
Lk	10.27	the **Lord** your **God** with all your **heart**,
	16.15	but **God** knows your **hearts**.
Jn	5.42	have no love for **God** in your **hearts**.
Acts	7.51	your **hearts**, how deaf you are to **God's**
	8.21	your **heart** is not right in **God's** sight.
Rom	1.9	**God** whom I serve with all my **heart**
	5.5	for **God** has poured out his love into our **hearts**
	8.27	And **God**, who sees into our **hearts**,
	11.8	**God** made their minds and **hearts** dull;
1 Cor	14.39	**heart** on proclaiming **God's** message,

2 Cor	1.23	I call **God** as my witness — he knows my **heart**
	4.6	the same **God** who made his light shine in our **hearts**,
	7.10	is used by **God** brings a change of **heart**
Gal	4.6	**God** sent the Spirit of his Son into our **hearts**,
Eph	6.6	with all your **heart** do what **God** wants,
Col	3.16	**God** with thanksgiving in your **hearts**.
Heb	9.9	**God** cannot make the worshipper's **heart**
	10.22	come near to **God** with a sincere **heart**
Rev	17.17	**God** has placed in their **hearts** the will

God's People

Jer	8.21	My **heart** has been crushed because **my people** are crushed;
Phlm	.7	cheered the **hearts** of all **God's people**.

Happy see Joy

Jesus, Christ

Eph	3.17	**Christ** will make his home in your **hearts** through faith
Phil	1.8	all comes from the **heart** of **Christ** Jesus
	4.7	your **hearts**...in union with **Christ** Jesus.
1 Pet	3.15	reverence for **Christ** in your **hearts**

Joy, Glad, Happy

Deut	28.47	serve him with **glad** and **joyful hearts**.
1 Sam	2.1	The Lord has filled my **heart** with **joy**;
Ps	119.111	they are the **joy** of my **heart**.
Jer	15.16	filled my **heart** with **joy** and **happiness**.
Mt	5.8	**Happy** are the pure in **heart**;
Jn	16.22	your **hearts** will be filled with **gladness**,
	17.13	they might have my **joy** in their **hearts**
Acts	2.46	eating with **glad** and humble **hearts**,
	14.17	and fills your **hearts** with **happiness**.

Law see Obey

Lord

see also **God**

Deut	13.3	you love the **Lord** with all your **heart**.
	30.2	the **Lord** and with all your **heart** obey
	30.6	The **Lord** your God will give you ...obedient **hearts**,
1 Sam	2.1	The **Lord** has filled my **heart** with joy;
	7.3	turn to the **Lord** with all your **hearts**.
	12.20	**Lord**, but serve him with all your **heart**.
	12.24	Obey the **Lord**...with all your **heart**.
2 Kgs	23.25	who served the **Lord** with all his **heart**,
Ps	35.10	all my **heart** I will say to the **Lord**,
	111.1	With all my **heart** I will thank the **Lord**
	116.7	**heart**, because the **Lord** has been good
	119.145	**heart** I call to you; answer me, **Lord**,
Prov	3.5	Trust in the **Lord** with all your **heart**
	17.3	a person's **heart** is tested by the **Lord**.
Jer	15.16	**Lord**...your words filled my **heart**
	17.10	the **Lord**...test the **hearts** of men.
	20.12	**Lord**, you test men justly; you know what is in their **hearts**
	23.9	**heart** is crushed...Because of the **Lord**,
	48.10	do the **Lord's** work with all his **heart**!
Lam	2.19	the **Lord**; Pour out your **heart** and beg
Lk	1.46	My **heart** praises the **Lord**;
	7.13	the **Lord** saw her, his **heart** was filled
Acts	11.23	**true** to the **Lord** with all their **hearts**.
Rom	12.11	the **Lord** with a **heart** full of devotion.
Eph	5.19	to the **Lord** with praise in your **hearts**.
Col	3.22	with a sincere **heart** because of your reverence for the **Lord**.
	3.23	with all your **heart**, as though you were working for the **Lord**
2 Tim	2.22	with a pure **heart** call out to the **Lord**
1 Pet	3.15	your **hearts**, and honour him as **Lord**.

Mind, New

2 Kgs	23.25	the Lord with all his **heart**, **mind**,
1 Chr	28.9	an undivided **heart** and a willing **mind**.
Ps	64.6	**heart** and **mind** of man are a mystery.
	73.7	**hearts** pour out evil, and their **minds**
Ecc	2.23	**heartache**. Even at night your **mind**
Is	1.5	and your **heart** and **mind** are sick.
Jer	17.10	the **minds** and test the **hearts** of men.
	20.12	know what is in their **hearts** and **minds**.
Ezek	11.19	give them a **new heart** and a **new mind**.
	18.31	get yourselves **new minds** and **hearts**.
	36.26	give you a **new heart** and a **new mind**.
Mk	12.30	all your **heart**...with all your **mind**,
	12.33	with all his **heart** and with all his **mind**
Acts	4.32	of believers was one in **mind** and **heart**
Rom	11.8	God made their **minds** and **hearts** dull;
Eph	4.23	**hearts** and **minds** must be made...**new**
Phil	4.7	will keep your **hearts** and **minds** safe
Heb	8.10	**minds** and write them on their **hearts**.
	10.16	**hearts** and write them on their **minds**.

Obey, Command, Law

Deut	10.12	**commands**...serve him with all your **heart**,
	26.16	**laws**; so **obey** them...with all your **heart**.
	30.2	with all your **heart obey** his **commands**
	30.6	and your descendants **obedient hearts**,
1 Kgs	2.4	**obey** his **commands**...with all their **heart**
	8.23	live in **whole-hearted obedience** to you.
2 Kgs	10.31	did not **obey** with all his **heart** the **law**
	23.3	**laws** and **commands** with all his **heart**
	23.25	with all·his **heart**...**obeying** all the **Law**
1 Chr	29.19	a **wholehearted** desire to **obey** everything
2 Chr	6.14	live in **wholehearted obedience** to you.
	34.31	**laws** and **commands** with all his **heart**
Ps	37.31	keeps the **law** of his God in his **heart**
	119.2	who **obey** him with all their **heart**.
	119.11	I keep your **law** in my **heart**,
	119.34	**obey** it; I will keep it with all my **heart**.
	119.69	all my **heart** I **obey** your instructions.
	119.129	I **obey** them with all my **heart**.
	119.160	The **heart** of your **law** is truth,
Jer	31.33	**law** within...and write it on their **hearts**.
Ezek	11.19	and will give them an **obedient heart**.
	36.26	and give you an **obedient heart**.
Lk	8.15	in a good and **obedient heart**,
Rom	2.15	**Law commands** is written in·their **hearts**.
	6.17	**obeyed** with all your **heart** the truths
Heb	8.10	**laws**...and write them on their **hearts**.
	10.16	I will put my **laws** in their **hearts**

Pity

Mt	9.36	his **heart** was filled with **pity** for them,
	14.14	his **heart** was filled with **pity** for them,
Mk	6.34	his **heart** was filled with **pity** for them,
Lk	7.13	his **heart** was filled with **pity** for her,
		Also: 10.33; 15.20

Praise see **Worship**

Pure

Ps	51.10	Create a **pure heart** in me, O God,
	73.1	to those who have **pure hearts**.
	119.7	I will praise you with a **pure heart**.
Prov	22.11	love **purity** of **heart** and graciousness
Mt	5.8	Happy are the **pure** in **heart**;
1 Tim	1.5	the love that comes from a **pure heart**
2 Tim	2.22	those who with a **pure heart** call out
Heb	10.22	with **hearts** that have been **purified**
Jas	4.8	**Purify** your **hearts**, you hypocrites!

Sin, Evil, Wicked

Job	15.35	do **evil**; their **hearts** are always full
Ps	36.1	**Sin** speaks to the **wicked** man deep in his **heart**;

Ps	55.15	**Evil** is in their homes and in their **hearts**.
	73.7	their **hearts** pour out evil,
	119.11	in my **heart**, so that I will not **sin**
Jer	3.17	their stubborn and **evil hearts** tell them.
	4.14	wash the **evil** from your **heart**,
	7.24	their stubborn and **evil hearts** told them
Lam	1.20	**heart** is broken in sorrow for my **sins**.
Mt	12.34	**evil**...the mouth speaks what the **heart**
	15.19	For from his **heart** come the **evil** ideas
Mk	7.21	a person's **heart**, come the **evil** ideas
Heb	3.12	has a **heart** so **evil** and unbelieving
Jas	4.8	you **sinners**! Purify your **hearts**,

Sincere

Eph	6.5	and do it with a **sincere heart**,
Col	3.22	but do it with a **sincere heart**
Heb	10.22	come near to God with a **sincere heart**

Soul

Deut	6.5	with all your **heart**, with all your **soul**,
Josh	22.5	serve him with all your **heart** and **soul**.
	23.14	one of you knows in his **heart** and **soul**
1 Kgs	2.4	with all their **heart** and **soul**.
2 Kgs	23.3	commands with all his **heart** and **soul**,
1 Chr	22.19	your God with all your **heart** and **soul**.
2 Chr	15.12	with all their **heart** and **soul**.
	34.31	commands with all his **heart** and **soul**,
Lam	1.20	anguish of my **soul**! My **heart** is broken
Mt	22.37	with all your **heart**, with all your **soul**,
Mk	12.30	with all your **heart**, with all your **soul**,
Lk	10.27	with all your **heart**, with all your **soul**,

Strength

2 Kgs	23.25	with all his **heart**, mind, and **strength**,
2 Chr	16.9	**strength** to those whose **hearts** are loyal
Ps	38.10	**heart** is pounding, my **strength** is gone,
Nah	2.10	**Hearts** melt with fear...**strength** is gone;
Lk	10.27	all your **heart**...with all your **strength**,

Stubborn

Jer	3.17	their **stubborn** and evil **hearts** tell them.
	7.24	whatever their **stubborn** and evil **hearts**
Ezek	11.19	take away their **stubborn heart** of stone
	36.26	take away your **stubborn heart** of stone
Rom	2.5	you have a hard and **stubborn heart**,

Test

1 Chr	29.17	I know that you **test** everyone's **heart**
Prov	17.3	a person's **heart** is **tested** by the Lord.
Jer	17.10	and **test** the **hearts** of men.
	20.12	**test** men justly; you know...their **hearts**

Thank see **Worship**

Trouble

Job	15.35	plan **trouble** and do evil; their **hearts**
Ps	13.2	**trouble**...will sorrow fill my **heart**
	38.8	my **heart** is **troubled**, and I groan
Jn	12.27	**heart** is **troubled** — and what shall I say
2 Cor	2.4	a greatly **troubled** and distressed **heart**

True see **Faithful**

Wicked see **Sin**

Worship, Praise, Thank

2 Chr	20.33	not turn **wholeheartedly** to the **worship**
	30.19	are **worshipping** you with all their **heart**,
Job	31.20	he would **praise** me with all his **heart**.
Ps	9.1	will **praise** you, Lord, with all my **heart**;
	86.12	I will **praise** you with all my **heart**
	111.1	**Praise** the Lord! With all my **heart** I will **thank** the Lord
	119.7	I will **praise** you with a **pure heart**.
	138.1	I **thank** you, Lord, with all my **heart**; I sing **praise** to you
Lk	1.46	My **heart praises** the Lord;
Eph	5.19	to the Lord with **praise** in your **hearts**.

Phil	4.6	asking him with a **thankful heart**.
Col	3.16	God with **thanksgiving** in your **hearts**.
Heb	9.9	make the **worshipper's heart** perfect,

HEAVEN

Rev	10.1	—	16.11	x23
Mt	5.12	—	7.21	x15
2 Chr	6.13	—	7.14	x14
Rev	18.1	—	21.10	x14
Dan	4.13	—	8.13	x11
1 Kgs	8.23 – 49			x10
Lk	9.16	—	12.33	x10
Jn	6.31 – 58			x10
Mt	18.10	—	19.21	x8
Acts	1.2	—	4.24	x8
Eph	1.3	—	4.10	x8
Heb	6.4	—	9.24	x8
Ezra	5.11	—	7.23	x7
Mt	22.30	—	24.36	x7
Mk	10.21	—	14.62	x7
Lk	15.7	—	19.38	x7
2 Pet	3.5 – 13			x7
Neh	9.6 – 28			x6
Lk	1.79	—	3.22	x6
1 Cor	15.40 – 49			x6
Deut	3.24	—	5.8	x5
2 Kgs	1.10	—	2.11	x5
Dan	2.18 – 44			x5
Mt	10.32	—	12.50	x5
Mt	14.19	—	16.19	x5
Acts	10.11	—	11.10	x5
Heb	11.16	—	12.26	x5
Rev	3.12	—	5.13	x5
Ps	89.5 – 11			x4
Ps	148.1 – 13			x4
Is	51.6 – 16			x4
Jer	44.17 – 24			x4
Jn	3.12 – 31			x4
Acts	7.42 – 56			x4
Ps	115.3 – 16			x3
2 Cor	5.1 – 4			x3
Col	1.5 – 20			x3

Above

Josh	2.11	Lord your God is God in **heaven above**
1 Kgs	8.23	is no god like you in **heaven above**
Ps	148.1	from **heaven**, you that live...**above**.
Ezek	3.12	the glory of the Lord in **heaven above**!
Jn	3.31	he who comes from **heaven** is **above** all.

Angel, Being

Gen	6.2	the **heavenly beings** saw that these girls
	6.4	human women and the **heavenly beings**.
	21.17	from **heaven** the **angel** of God spoke
	22.11	the **angel**...called to him from **heaven**,
	22.15	**angel**...called to Abraham from **heaven**
	28.12	to **heaven**, with **angels** going up
Judg	13.20	the Lord's **angel** go up towards **heaven**
1 Kgs	22.19	his throne in **heaven**, with all his **angels**
2 Chr	18.18	his throne in **heaven**, with all his **angels**
Job	1.6	came for the **heavenly beings** to appear
	2.1	came for the **heavenly beings** to appear
	38.7	and the **heavenly beings** shouted for joy.
Ps	29.1	you **heavenly beings**;
	89.6	none of the **heavenly beings**
	148.2	all his **angels**, all his **heavenly armies**.
Dan	4.13	saw coming down from **heaven** an **angel**,
	4.23	an **angel** came down from **heaven**
	4.35	**angels** in **heaven** and people on earth
Zech	3.4	**angel** said to his **heavenly** attendants
Mt	18.10	Their **angels** in **heaven**,
	22.30	they will be like the **angels** in **heaven**
	24.36	neither the **angels** in **heaven**
	28.2	an **angel**...came down from **heaven**,
Mk	12.25	they will be like the **angels** in **heaven**

Mk	13.32	neither the **angels** in **heaven**,
Lk	2.13	a great army of **heaven's angels**
	2.15	When the **angels** went...back into **heaven**
	22.43	An **angel** from **heaven** appeared to him
Jn	1.51	will see **heaven** open and God's **angels**
Rom	8.38	neither **angels** nor other **heavenly** rulers
Gal	1.8	But even if we or an **angel** from **heaven**
	4.14	me as you would an **angel** from **heaven**;
Eph	3.10	the **angelic** rulers...in the **heavenly** world
Phil	2.10	all **beings** in **heaven**, on earth,
2 Thes	1.7	from **heaven** with his mighty **angels**,
Heb	12.22	the **heavenly** Jerusalem, with its...**angels**.
1 Pet	1.12	**heaven**...things which even the **angels**
	3.22	over all **angels** and **heavenly** authorities
Rev	10.1	**angel** coming down out of **heaven**
	12.7	in **heaven**. Michael and his **angels**
	12.8	**angels**...not allowed to stay in **heaven**
	14.17	**angel** come out of the temple in **heaven**
	18.1	**angel** coming down out of **heaven**
	20.1	saw an **angel** coming down from **heaven**

Create

1 Chr	16.26	but the Lord **created** the **heavens**
2 Chr	2.12	**Creator** of **heaven** and earth!
Ps	33.6	The Lord **created** the **heavens**
	96.5	but the Lord **created** the **heavens**.
	146.6	the **Creator** of **heaven**, earth,
Is	42.5	God **created** the **heavens**
	45.18	The Lord **created** the **heavens**
Jer	10.12	he **created** the world and stretched out the **heavens**.
	51.15	he **created** the world and stretched out the **heavens**.
Acts	4.24	**Creator** of **heaven**, earth, and sea,
Eph	1.10	all **creation** together...in **heaven**
Col	1.16	God **created** everything in **heaven**
Jas	1.17	the **Creator** of the **heavenly** lights,
2 Pet	3.5	and the **heavens** and earth were **created**.
Rev	10.6	who **created** heaven, earth,

Father see God

Forgive see Mercy

Glad see Joy

God, Father

Gen	14.19	**God**, who made **heaven** and earth, bless
	14.22	High **God**, Maker of **heaven** and earth,
	24.3	the **God** of **heaven** and earth,
	24.7	The **Lord**, the **God** of **heaven**,
	27.28	May **God** give you dew from **heaven**
	28.17	**God**...the gate that opens into **heaven**.
Deut	4.39	**Lord** is **God** in **heaven** and on earth.
Josh	2.11	**Lord** your **God** is **God** in **heaven** above
1 Kgs	8.23	is no **god** like you in **heaven** above
	8.27	**God**...Not even all **heaven** is large
2 Chr	2.6	for **God**, because even...**heaven** cannot
	2.12	**Lord God** of Israel, Creator of **heaven**
	6.14	**God** of Israel, in all **heaven** and earth
	20.6	O **Lord God** of our ancestors, you rule in **heaven**
	30.27	in **heaven God** heard their prayers
	36.23	The **Lord**, the **God** of **Heaven**,
Ezra	1.2	The **Lord**, the **God** of **Heaven**,
	5.11	We are servants of the **God** of **heaven**
	5.12	made the **God** of **Heaven** angry,
	6.9	as offerings to the **God** of **Heaven**,
	6.10	**God** of **Heaven** and pray for his
	7.12	in the Law of the **God** of **Heaven**.
	7.21	in the Law of the **God** of **Heaven**,
	7.23	which the **God** of **Heaven** requires
Neh	1.5	**Lord God** of **Heaven**
	2.4	I prayed to the **God** of **Heaven**,
	2.20	The **God** of **Heaven** will give us success.
Job	4.18	**God** does not trust his **heavenly**

Job	9.8	one helped **God** spread out the **heavens**
	22.12	Doesn't **God** live in the highest **heavens**
Ps	50.6	**heavens** proclaim that **God** is righteous,
	53.2	**God** looks down from **heaven** at
	69.34	Praise **God**, O **heaven** and earth,
	73.9	They speak evil of **God** in **heaven**
	80.14	**God**! Look down from **heaven** at us;
	82.1	**God** presides in the **heavenly** council;
	85.11	and **God's** righteousness will look down from **heaven**.
	115.3	Our **God** is in **heaven**;
	136.26	Give thanks to the **God** of **heaven**;
	150.1	Praise **God**...his strength in **heaven**!
Ecc	5.2	rash promises to **God**. He is in **heaven**
Is	42.5	**God** created the **heavens**
Lam	3.41	us open our hearts to **God** in **heaven**
Dan	2.18	**God** of **heaven** for mercy and to ask
	2.19	and he praised the **God** of **heaven**:
	2.28	there is a **God** in **heaven**, who reveals
	2.37	**God** of **heaven** has made you emperor
	2.44	time of those rulers the **God** of **heaven**
Jon	1.9	the **Lord**, the **God** of **heaven**,
Mic	6.6	the **Lord**, the **God** of **heaven**,
Mt	5.16	and praise your **Father** in **heaven**.
	5.34	swear by **heaven**, for it is **God's** throne;
	5.45	the sons of your **Father** in **heaven**.
	5.48	just as your **Father** in **heaven** is perfect!
	6.1	any reward from your **Father** in **heaven**.
	6.9	Our **Father** in **heaven**:
	6.14	**Father** in **heaven** will also forgive you.
	6.26	**Father** in **heaven** takes care of them!
	6.32	**Father** in **heaven** knows that you need
	7.11	your **Father** in **heaven** give good things
	7.21	do what my **Father** in **heaven** wants
	10.32	for him before my **Father** in **heaven**.
	10.33	reject him before my **Father** in **heaven**.
	11.25	**Father**, **Lord** of **heaven** and earth!
	12.50	what my **Father** in **heaven** wants him to
	14.19	up to **heaven**, and gave thanks to **God**.
	15.13	my **Father** in **heaven** did not plant
	16.17	to you directly by my **Father** in **heaven**.
	18.10	in the presence of my **Father** in **heaven**.
	18.14	**Father** in **heaven** does not want any
	18.19	done for you by my **Father** in **heaven**.
	18.35	**Father** in **heaven** will treat every one
	23.9	have only the one **Father** in **heaven**.
	23.22	**heaven**, he is swearing by **God's** throne
Mk	6.41	up to **heaven**, and gave thanks to **God**.
	11.25	**Father** in **heaven** will forgive the wrongs
	16.19	**heaven** and sat at the right side of **God**.
Lk	2.14	Glory to **God** in the highest **heaven**,
	9.16	up to **heaven**, thanked **God** for them,
	10.21	**Father**, **Lord** of **heaven** and earth!
	11.13	**Father** in **heaven** give the Holy Spirit
	19.38	Peace in **heaven** and glory to **God**!
Jn	1.51	will see **heaven** open and **God's** angels
	6.32	my **Father** who gives you the real bread from **heaven**.
	6.33	bread that **God** gives is he who comes down from **heaven**
	17.1	looked up to **heaven** and said, "**Father**,
Acts	4.24	**God**: "Master and Creator of **heaven**,
	7.55	up to **heaven** and saw **God's** glory
	14.15	to the living **God**, who made **heaven**,
Rom	1.18	**God's** anger is revealed from **heaven**
2 Cor	5.1	**God** will have a house in **heaven** for us
Col	1.16	him **God** created everything in **heaven**
Heb	1.3	**heaven** at the right-hand side of **God**,
	6.4	in **God's** light; they tasted **heaven's** gift
	12.22	the living **God**, the **heavenly** Jerusalem,
	12.23	**God's** first-born sons, whose names are written in **heaven**.
Jas	1.17	from **heaven**; it comes down from **God**,

1 Pet	3.22	has gone to **heaven** and is at the right-hand side of **God**,
2 Pet	3.5	**God** gave a command, and the **heavens**
	3.13	what **God** has promised: new **heavens**
Rev	3.12	down out of **heaven** from my **God**.
	11.13	the greatness of the **God** of **heaven**.
	11.19	**God's** temple in **heaven** was opened
	15.5	**heaven** open, with the Tent of **God's**
	16.11	and they cursed the **God** of **heaven**
	21.2	coming down out of **heaven** from **God**,

Help see Save

Holy

Deut	26.15	your **holy** place in **heaven** and bless
Ps	11.4	is in his **holy** temple; he has his throne in **heaven**.
	20.6	he answers him from his **holy heaven**
	102.19	**holy** place...he looked down from **heaven**
Is	63.15	**heaven**, where you live in your **holiness**
Rev	21.10	**Holy** City, coming down out of **heaven**

Jesus, Son of God, Son of Man

Mt	3.17	**heaven**, "This is my own dear **Son**,
	24.30	**Son of Man**...on the clouds of **heaven**
	24.36	the angels in **heaven** nor the **Son**;
Mk	1.11	**heaven**, "You are my own dear **Son**.
	13.32	the angels in **heaven**, nor the **Son**;
	16.19	**Jesus**...was taken up to **heaven**
Lk	3.22	**heaven**, "You are my own dear **Son**.
	9.31	in **heavenly** glory and talked with **Jesus**
	9.51	**Jesus** would be taken up to **heaven**
Jn	3.13	up to **heaven** except the **Son of Man**,
Acts	1.11	This **Jesus**, who was taken from you into **heaven**,
	1.21	**Jesus** was taken up from us to **heaven**.
	7.55	**heaven** and saw **God's** glory and **Jesus**
	7.56	see **heaven** opened and the **Son of Man**
Eph	2.6	with Christ **Jesus**...in the **heavenly** world.
Phil	2.10	the name of **Jesus** all beings in **heaven**,
	3.20	**heaven**, and we eagerly wait for...**Jesus**
1 Thes	1.10	to come from **heaven** — his **Son Jesus**,
2 Thes	1.7	the **Lord Jesus** appears from **heaven**

Joy, Glad

Job	38.7	and the **heavenly** beings shouted for **joy**.
Is	44.23	Shout for **joy**, you **heavens**!
	49.13	Sing, **heavens**! Shout for **joy**,
Mt	5.12	**glad**, for a...reward is kept...in **heaven**.
Lk	10.20	be **glad** because your names are written in **heaven**.
	15.7	more **joy** in **heaven** over one sinner
Rev	12.12	**glad**, you **heavens**, and all you that live
	18.20	**glad**, **heaven**, because of her destruction

Last

Ps	119.89	will **last** for ever; it is eternal in **heaven**.
Mt	5.18	that as long as **heaven** and earth **last**,

Lord

see also **God**

Gen	22.11	the **Lord** called to him from **heaven**,
Ex	20.22	**Lord**, have spoken to you from **heaven**.
	31.17	the **Lord**, made **heaven** and earth
Deut	10.14	**Lord** belong even the highest **heavens**;
1 Sam	7.10	then the **Lord** thundered from **heaven**
1 Kgs	8.32	O **Lord**, listen in **heaven** and judge
	22.19	**Lord** sitting on his throne in **heaven**,
2 Kgs	2.1	the **Lord** to take Elijah up to **heaven**
1 Chr	16.26	but the **Lord** created the **heavens**.
	21.26	the **Lord** answered him by sending fire from **heaven**
2 Chr	6.23	O **Lord**, listen in **heaven** and judge
	6.27	O **Lord**, listen to them in **heaven**
	18.18	**Lord** sitting on his throne in **heaven**,
Neh	9.6	alone are **Lord**; you made the **heavens**

Job	1.6	for the **heavenly** beings to appear before the **Lord,**
	2.1	the **heavenly** beings to appear before the **Lord** again,
Ps	2.4	his throne in **heaven** the **Lord** laughs
	11.4	**Lord** is in his holy temple; he has his throne in **heaven.**
	14.2	The **Lord** looks down from **heaven**
	29.1	Praise the **Lord,** you **heavenly** beings;
	33.6	The **Lord** created the **heavens**
	33.13	The **Lord** looks down from **heaven**
	36.5	**Lord,** your constant love reaches the **heavens;**
	89.6	No one in **heaven** is like you, **Lord;**
	93.4	The **Lord** rules supreme in **heaven,**
	96.5	but the **Lord** created the **heavens.**
	103.19	The **Lord** placed his throne in **heaven;**
	103.21	the **Lord,** all you **heavenly** powers,
	113.4	The **Lord** rules over all nations; his glory is above the **heavens.**
	115.15	blessed by the **Lord,** who made **heaven**
	115.16	**Heaven** belongs to the **Lord** alone,
	121.2	come from the **Lord,** who made **heaven**
	123.1	**Lord,** I look up to you, up to **heaven,**
	124.8	comes from the **Lord,** who made **heaven**
	134.3	the **Lord,** who made **heaven** and earth,
	148.1	Praise the **Lord** from **heaven,**
Is	18.4	**Lord** said to me, "I will look down from **heaven**
	26.21	**Lord** is coming from his **heavenly**
	34.5	**Lord** has prepared his sword in **heaven**
	45.18	The **Lord** created the **heavens**
	51.13	the **Lord** who...stretched out the **heavens**
	63.15	**Lord,** look upon us from **heaven**
	65.17	The **Lord** says, "I am making a new earth and new **heavens.**
	66.1	The **Lord** says, "**Heaven** is my throne
Jer	25.30	The **Lord** will roar from **heaven**
Lam	3.50	Until the **Lord** looks down from **heaven**
Ezek	3.12	Praise the glory of the **Lord** in **heaven**
Dan	5.23	You acted against the **Lord** of **heaven**
Amos	9.6	**Lord** builds his home in the **heavens,**
Mic	6.6	bring to the **Lord,** the God of **heaven**
Mt	7.21	calls me '**Lord, Lord**' will enter the Kingdom of **heaven,**
	11.25	**Lord** of **heaven** and earth!
Lk	9.54	**Lord,** do you want us to call fire down from **heaven**
	10.21	**Lord** of **heaven** and earth!
Acts	7.49	**Heaven** is my throne, says the **Lord,**
	17.24	is **Lord** of **heaven** and earth
1 Thes	4.16	the **Lord** himself will come down from **heaven.**
2 Thes	1.7	the **Lord** Jesus appears from **heaven**

Mercy, Forgive

1 Kgs	8.30	home in **heaven** hear us and **forgive** us.
	8.34	to them in **heaven. Forgive** the sins
	8.36	to them in **heaven. Forgive** the sins
	8.39	in your home in **heaven, forgive** them,
	8.49	in **heaven** hear them and be **merciful**
2 Kgs	1.14	**heaven;** but please be **merciful** to me!
2 Chr	6.21	home in **heaven** hear us and **forgive** us.
	6.25	to them in **heaven. Forgive** the sins
	6.27	to them in **heaven** and **forgive** the sins
	6.30	your home in **heaven** and **forgive** them.
	6.39	in **heaven** hear them and be **merciful**
	7.14	hear them in **heaven, forgive** their sins,
Neh	9.27	them from **heaven.** In your great **mercy**
Dan	2.18	pray to the God of **heaven** for **mercy**
Mt	6.14	Father in **heaven** will also **forgive** you.
Mk	11.25	Father in **heaven** will **forgive** the wrongs

Peace

| Job | 25.1 | he keeps his **heavenly** kingdom in **peace.** |

| Lk | 2.14 | the highest **heaven,** and **peace** on earth |
| | 19.38 | **Peace** in **heaven** and glory to God! |

Power

Neh	9.6	**heavenly powers** bow down and worship
Ps	20.6	from his holy **heaven** and by his **power**
	29.1	you **heavenly** beings; praise his...**power.**
	103.21	all you **heavenly powers,**
Is	45.12	my **power** I stretched out the **heavens;**
	66.22	new **heavens** will endure by my **power,**
Dan	2.37	God of **heaven** has...given you **power,**
Mt	24.29	from **heaven,** and the **powers** in space
	24.30	of **heaven** with **power** and great glory.
Mk	13.25	from **heaven,** and the **powers** in space
Rom	8.38	nor other **heavenly** rulers or **powers,**
Eph	1.21	all **heavenly** rulers, authorities, **powers,**
	3.10	rulers and **powers** in the **heavenly** world
1 Pet	1.12	**power** of the...Spirit sent from **heaven.**
	3.22	and **heavenly** authorities and **powers.**

Praise see Worship

Promise

Jer	44.24	**promises** to the Queen of **Heaven.**
Mt	5.34	a **promise.** Do not swear by **heaven,**
Jas	5.12	a **promise.** Do not swear by **heaven**
2 Pet	3.13	what God has **promised:** new **heavens**

Rescue see Save

Right (hand)

Mk	16.19	up to **heaven** and sat at the **right** side
Eph	1.20	at his **right** side in the **heavenly** world.
Heb	1.3	**heaven** at the **right-hand** side of God,
1 Pet	3.22	gone to **heaven** and is at the **right-hand**
Rev	10.5	raised his **right hand** to **heaven**

Save, Help, Rescue

1 Kgs	8.39	in **heaven,** forgive them, and **help** them.
Neh	9.27	**help**...you answered them from **heaven.**
	9.28	to **save** them, in **heaven** you heard,
Esth	4.14	**help** will come from **heaven** to the Jews, and they will be **saved,**
Job	-9.8	**helped** God spread out the **heavens**
Ps	57.3	will answer from **heaven** and **save** me;
	80.14	down from **heaven** at us; come and **save**
Is	38.14	looking to **heaven.** Lord, **rescue** me
Lk	12.33	and **save** your riches in **heaven,**

Sin

Job	20.27	**Heaven** reveals this man's **sin,**
Lk	15.7	in **heaven** over one **sinner** who repents
Rom	1.18	revealed from **heaven** against all the **sin**
Heb	7.26	**sinners** and raised above the **heavens.**
Rev	18.5	her **sins** are piled up as high as **heaven,**

Son of God see Jesus

Son of Man see Jesus

Thank see Worship

Universe see World

Witness

Deut	4.26	**heaven** and earth as **witnesses** against
	30.19	**heaven** and earth to **witness** the choice
	31.28	**heaven** and earth to be my **witnesses**
Ps	50.4	He calls **heaven** and earth as **witnesses**

World, Universe

2 Chr	20.6	**heaven** over all the nations of the **world.**
Ps	76.8	from **heaven;** the **world** was afraid
Jer	10.12	the **world** and stretched out the **heavens.**
	51.15	the **world** and stretched out the **heavens.**
Ezek	32.8	lights of **heaven** and plunge your **world**
Jn	6.33	from **heaven** and gives life to the **world.**
Acts	17.24	who made the **world**...is Lord of **heaven**
Eph	1.3	spiritual blessing in the **heavenly** world
	1.20	at his right side in the **heavenly** world.

Eph	2.6	to rule with him in the **heavenly world**.
	3.10	rulers and powers in the **heavenly world**
	4.10	the **heavens**, to fill the whole **universe**
	6.12	spiritual forces in the **heavenly world**,
1 Tim	3.16	the **world**, and was taken up to **heaven**,
Jas	3.15	from **heaven**; it belongs to the **world**,

Worship, Praise, Thank

2 Chr	2.12	**Praise** the...Creator of **heaven** and earth!
Ps	8.1	Your **praise** reaches up to the **heavens**;
	29.1	**Praise** the Lord, you **heavenly** beings;
	69.34	**Praise** God, O **heaven** and earth,
	103.21	**Praise** the Lord, all you **heavenly**
	136.26	Give **thanks** to the God of **heaven**;
	148.1	**Praise** the Lord from **heaven**,
	148.2	**Praise** him...all his **heavenly** armies.
	148.4	**Praise** him, highest **heavens**,
	150.1	**Praise** his strength in **heaven**!
Ezek	3.12	**Praise**...the Lord in **heaven** above!
Dan	2.19	and he **praised** the God of **heaven**:
	4.37	**praise**...and glorify the King of **Heaven**.
Jon	1.9	I **worship** the Lord, the God of **heaven**,
Mic	6.6	**heaven**, when I come to **worship** him?
Hab	3.3	**heavens**...the earth is full of his **praise**.
Mt	5.16	and **praise** your Father in **heaven**.
	11.25	Lord of **heaven** and earth! I **thank** you
	14.19	up to **heaven**, and gave **thanks** to God.
Mk	6.41	up to **heaven**, and gave **thanks** to God.
Lk	9.16	up to **heaven**, **thanked** God for them,
	10.21	Lord of **heaven** and earth! I **thank** you
Rev	11.13	and **praised**...the God of **heaven**.
	14.7	**Worship** him who made **heaven**,
	19.1	people in **heaven**, saying, "**Praise** God!

HELP

2 Cor	6.2	—	9.3	x18
Ezra	1.4	—	7.8	x10
Ps	119.27	—	175	x10
2 Cor	1.3	—	16	x10
Is	30.2	—	31.3	x9
Job	34.28	—	37.18	x8
Acts	9.27	—	13.5	x8
Deut	31.18	—	33.11	x7
2 Chr	28.16	—	29.36	x7
Job	29.12	—	32.9	x7
Jer	14.2	—	16.19	x7
Lam	1.7	—	4.17	x7
Rom	14.19	—	16.2	x7
1 Cor	14.3	— 26		x7
Ex	21.18	—	24.13	x6
2 Sam	21.17	—	22.42	x6
Is	44.2	—	47.12	x6
Is	57.12	—	59.16	x6
Is	63.3	—	66.14	x6
Dan	9.22	—	11.45	x6
Acts	18.27	—	21.28	x6
Heb	1.14	—	4.16	x6
1 Sam	7.2 – 12			x4
Ps	18.6 – 41			x4
Ps	22.1 – 24			x4
Ps	142.1 – 6			x4
Ecc	4.1 – 10			x4
Phil	4.3 – 16			x4
Heb	13.6 – 17			x4
2 Sam	10.11 – 19			x3
Ps	28.2 – 7			x3
Ps	30.2 – 10			x3
Ps	37.5 – 40			x3
Ps	40.1 – 13			x3
Ps	41.1 – 6			x3
Ps	88.2 – 13			x3
Ps	115.9 – 11			x3
Is	19.3 – 20			x3
Is	36.5 – 10			x3

Jer	11.11 – 14	x3
Mk	1.13 – 40	x3
Mk	9.22 – 27	x3
Lk	1.25 – 68	x3
1 Cor	16.1 – 11	x3
1 Tim	5.5 – 23	x3
3 Jn	.6 – 8	x3

Beg see Plead

Believers see God's People

Church see God's People

Danger

2 Sam	22.20	He **helped** me out of **danger**;
Ps	18.19	He **helped** me out of **danger**;
	25.15	**help**...and he rescues me from **danger**.
Prov	13.14	**help** you...when your life is in **danger**.

Defend see Protect

Destroy

2 Kgs	13.23	let them be **destroyed**, but **helped** them,
	18.25	**destroyed** it without the Lord's **help**.
Prov	19.18	are **helping** them to **destroy** themselves.
Is	31.3	**helped** will fall. Both...will be **destroyed**.
	36.10	**destroyed** it without the Lord's **help**.
Jer	47.4	**destroy** Philistia, to cut off...the **help**
Hos	13.9	**destroy** you...Israel! Then who can **help**
Amos	9.4	to **destroy** them, not to **help** them.
Zech	11.16	**help** the sheep...threatened by **destruction**;
Mk	3.4	**help** or to harm? To save a man's life or to **destroy**
Lk	6.9	**help** or to harm? To save a man's life or **destroy**

Eager

1 Chr	28.21	every kind of skill are **eager** to **help**
Ps	130.5	I wait **eagerly** for the Lord's **help**,
2 Cor	8.7	your **eagerness** to **help** and in your love
	8.8	showing how **eager** others are to **help**,
	8.16	making Titus as **eager** as we are to **help**
	8.17	**eager** to **help** that of his own free will
	8.22	found him always very **eager** to **help**.
	9.2	**help** since last year." Your **eagerness** has

Faith, Trust

1 Chr	5.20	put their **trust** in God and prayed to him for **help**,
Ps	28.7	I **trust** in him. He gives me **help**
	37.5	**trust** in him, and he will **help** you;
	115.9	**Trust** in the Lord...He **helps** you
	115.10	**Trust** in the Lord...He **helps** you
	130.5	Lord's **help**, and in his word I **trust**.
Is	40.31	those who **trust** in the Lord for **help**
Zeph	3.2	**trust** in the Lord or asked for his **help**.
Mk	9.24	do have **faith**, but not enough. **Help** me
Rom	1.12	will be **helped**...you by my **faith**
	15.1	are strong in the **faith** ought to **help**
1 Thes	3.2	to strengthen you and **help** your **faith**,
Tit	1.1	to **help** the **faith** of God's chosen people

God

Gen	27.20	The **Lord** your **God helped** me
	35.3	the **God** who **helped** me in the time
	49.25	It is your father's **God** who **helps** you,
Ex	2.23	out for **help**. Their cry went up to **God**,
	18.4	The **God** of my father **helped** me
Num	10.9	the **Lord** your **God**, will **help** you
	10.10	will **help** you. I am the **Lord** your **God**.
1 Sam	2.1	joyful I am because **God** has **helped** me!
	14.45	he did today was done with **God's help**.
2 Sam	22.7	I called to my **God** for **help**.
1 Chr	5.20	in **God** and prayed to him for **help**,
	15.26	sure that **God** would **help** the Levites
2 Chr	14.11	**Lord** his **God**, "O **Lord**, you can **help**
	26.7	**God helped** him to defeat the

2 Chr	26.15	of the **help** he received from God.
	29.36	**God** had **helped** them to do all this
	32.8	we have the **Lord** our **God** to **help** us
	32.20	to **God** and cried out to him for **help**.
	33.12	**Lord** his **God**, and begged him for **help**.
Ezra	7.8	**God's help** they arrived in Jerusalem
Neh	2.18	**God** had been with me and **helped** me,
	6.16	work had been done with **God's help**.
Job	8.6	then **God** will come and **help** you
	9.8	one **helped God** spread out the heavens
	22.3	**God**, or does your being good **help**
	34.28	**God**, and he heard their calls for **help**.
	35.7	Do you **help God** by being so righteous?
	35.12	cry for **help**, but **God** doesn't answer,
	37.18	Can you **help God** stretch out the sky
Ps	3.2	**God** will not **help** him.
	5.2	Listen to my cry for **help**, my **God**
	18.6	I called to my **God** for **help**.
	30.2	cried to you for **help**, O **Lord** my **God**,
	51.18	O **God**, be kind to Zion and **help** her;
	54.4	But **God** is my **helper**.
	55.16	But I call to the **Lord God** for **help**,
	70.1	O **God! Lord, help** me now!
	79.9	**Help** us, O **God**, and save us;
	109.26	**Help** me, O **Lord** my **God**;
	115.10	you priests of **God**. He **helps** you
	140.6	are my **God**." Hear my cry for **help**,
	146.5	who has the **God** of Jacob to **help** him
Is	17.7	**help** to their Creator, the holy **God** of
	41.14	I will **help** you. I, the holy **God**
Lam	3.8	I cry aloud for **help**, but **God** refuses
Lk	1.68	**God**...has come to the **help** of his
Acts	26.22	very day I have been **helped** by **God**,
1 Cor	14.4	one who proclaims **God's** message **helps**
2 Cor	1.3	the **God** from whom all **help** comes!
	1.4	same **help** that we...received from **God**.
	1.5	we share in **God's** great **help**.
Eph	6.18	asking for **God's help**.
Heb	1.14	serve **God** and are sent by him to **help**

God's People, Believers, Church, One another

Deut	32.12	**people** without the **help** of a foreign
1 Sam	9.16	**people** and...heard their cries for **help**.
Ezra	1.4	his **people** in exile need **help** to return,
Jer	23.32	they are of no **help** at all to the **people**.
Dan	11.34	**God's people** will receive a little **help**,
Lk	1.68	He has come to the **help** of his **people**
	18.7	own **people** who cry to him...for **help**?
Acts	9.41	**helped** her get up. Then he called all the **believers**,
	11.29	to **help** their **fellow-believers**
	18.27	**helped** him by writing to the **believers**
Rom	14.19	and that **help** to strengthen **one another**.
	15.26	**help** the poor among **God's people**
	16.2	**people** should, and give her any **help**
1 Cor	14.4	**God's** message **helps** the whole **church**.
	14.5	that the whole **church** may be **helped**.
	14.12	which **help** to build up the **church**.
	14.26	must be of **help** to the **church**.
	16.1	raised to **help God's people** in Judaea.
2 Cor	8.4	part in **helping God's people** in Judaea.
	9.1	**help** being sent to **God's people**
Gal	6.2	**Help** to carry **one another's** burdens
Phil	4.15	you were the only **church** to **help** me;
1 Thes	5.11	**one another** and **help one another**,
Tit	1.1	to **help** the faith of **God's** chosen **people**
Heb	3.13	you must **help one another** every day,
	10.24	for **one another**, to **help one another**
	13.16	to do good and to **help one another**

Gods, Idols

Deut	32.12	without the **help** of a foreign **god**.
1 Sam	5.12	people cried out to their **gods** for **help**.
	12.21	after false **gods**; they cannot **help** you
Is	19.3	They will ask their **idols** to **help** them,

Is	57.12	your **idols** will not be able to **help** you.
	57.13	cry for **help**, let those **idols** of yours
Jer	11.12	out to them for **help**. But those **gods**
Jon	1.5	out for **help**, each one to his own **god**.
	1.6	Get up and pray to your **god** for **help**.

Happy, Joyful

1 Sam	2.1	**joyful** I am because God has **helped** me!
2 Chr	29.36	**happy**, because God had **helped** them
Ps	28.7	gives me **help**...I praise him with **joyful**
	119.174	saving **help**, O Lord! I find **happiness**

Heal

Ps	30.2	**help**, O Lord my God, and you **healed**
Is	57.18	**heal** them. I will lead them and **help**
Hos	5.13	for **help**, but he could not...**heal**
1 Cor	12.28	the power to **heal** or to **help** others

Idols see Gods

Jesus

Mt	4.11	left **Jesus**; and angels came and **helped**
	27.55	**Jesus** from Galilee and **helped** him.
Mk	1.40	came to **Jesus**, knelt down, and begged him for **help**.
	9.27	But **Jesus** took the boy by the hand and **helped** him
	15.41	followed **Jesus** while he was in Galilee and had **helped** him.
Lk	8.3	used their own resources to **help Jesus**
	19.35	and **helped Jesus** get on.
Phil	1.19	the **help** which comes from the Spirit of **Jesus** Christ

Joyful see Happy

Lord

see also **God**

Gen	4.1	the **Lord's help** I have acquired a son.
	10.9	the **Lord's help** he was a great hunter,
Ex	14.10	and cried out to the **Lord** for **help**.
	14.15	The **Lord** said to Moses, "Why are you crying out for **help**?
	22.23	the **Lord**, will answer them when they cry out to me for **help**,
Num	20.16	and we cried to the **Lord** for **help**.
	21.3	The **Lord** heard them and **helped** them
	32.3	which the **Lord** has **helped** the Israelites
Deut	1.45	So you cried out to the **Lord** for **help**,
	4.7	the **Lord** our God...answers us whenever we call for **help**.
	26.7	Then we cried out for **help** to the **Lord**
	33.7	**Lord**, listen to their cry for **help**;
	33.11	**Lord**, **help** their tribe to grow strong;
Judg	1.18	The **Lord helped** the people of Judah
	1.22	The **Lord helped** them.
	2.18	the **Lord** would **help** him
	4.3	cried out to the **Lord** for **help**.
	5.23	They did not come to **help** the **Lord**.
	6.7	Israel cried out to the **Lord** for **help**
	6.16	The **Lord** answered, "You can do it because I will **help** you
1 Sam	7.2	the Israelites cried to the **Lord** for **help**.
	7.9	he prayed to the **Lord** to **help** Israel,
	7.12	The **Lord** has **helped** us
	12.8	ancestors cried to the **Lord** for **help**,
	12.10	Then they cried to the **Lord** for **help**
	14.6	Maybe the **Lord** will **help** us;
2 Sam	22.36	O **Lord**, you protect me...your **help**
2 Kgs	6.27	If the **Lord** won't **help** you,
	18.25	destroyed it without the **Lord's help**?
1 Chr	16.11	Go to the **Lord** for **help**
2 Chr	13.14	They cried to the **Lord** for **help**,
	16.12	he did not turn to the **Lord** for **help**,
Ps	3.4	I call to the **Lord** for **help**,
	6.3	O **Lord**, will you wait to **help** me?

Ps	12.1	**Help** us, **Lord**!
	17.1	**Lord**...pay attention to my cry for **help**!
	22.8	**Lord** likes you, why doesn't he **help**
	25.15	I look to the **Lord** for **help**
	28.6	the **Lord**; he has heard my cry for **help**.
	28.7	The **Lord** protects...gives me **help**
	30.2	I cried to you for **help**, O **Lord**
	30.8	**Lord**; I begged for your **help**:
	30.10	be merciful! **Help** me, **Lord**!
	33.20	**Lord**; he is our protector and our **help**.
	37.5	to the **Lord**...and he will **help** you;
	37.24	because the **Lord** will **help** them up.
	38.22	**Help** me now, O **Lord** my saviour!
	40.1	I waited patiently for the **Lord's help**;
	40.13	**Lord**! **Help** me now!
	41.1	the **Lord** will **help** them when they are
	41.3	The **Lord** will **help** them
	51.15	**Help** me to speak, **Lord**,
	85.7	O **Lord**, and give us your saving **help**.
	86.6	**Lord**, to my prayer; hear my cries for **help**.
	88.13	**Lord**, I call to you for **help**;
	94.17	If the **Lord** had not **helped** me,
	102.1	O **Lord**, and hear my cry for **help**!
	105.4	Go to the **Lord** for **help**;
	106.4	**Lord**, when you **help** your people;
	109.21	But my Sovereign **Lord**, **help** me
	115.9	Trust in the **Lord**...He **helps** you
	115.11	Trust in the **Lord**...He **helps** you
	118.7	It is the **Lord** who **helps** me,
	118.13	but the **Lord helped** me.
	119.169	Let my cry for **help** reach you, **Lord**!
	119.174	I long for your saving **help**, O **Lord**!
	121.2	My **help** will come from the **Lord**,
	124.8	Our **help** comes from the **Lord**,
	130.2	O **Lord**; listen to my call for **help**!
	130.5	I wait eagerly for the **Lord's help**,
	141.1	**Lord**; **help** me now!
	142.1	I call to the **Lord** for **help**;
	142.5	**Lord**, I cry to you for **help**;
Prov	21.30	no **help** if the **Lord** is against you.
Is	12.4	to the **Lord**! Call for him to **help**
	19.20	and call out to the **Lord** for **help**,
	30.19	The **Lord** is compassionate, and when you cry to him for **help**,
	36.10	without the **Lord's help**?
	40.31	those who trust in the **Lord** for **help**
	44.2	I am the **Lord**...I have **helped** you.
	49.23	**Lord**; no one who waits for my **help**
	50.7	the Sovereign **Lord** gives me **help**.
	51.9	Wake up, **Lord**, and **help** us!
	66.14	the **Lord**, **help** those who obey me,
Jer	3.23	**Help**...comes only from the **Lord**
	14.7	**help** us, **Lord**, as you have promised.
	14.11	The **Lord** said...'Do not ask me to **help**
	15.15	**Lord**...Remember me and **help** me.
Joel	2.32	But all who ask the **Lord** for **help**
Hab	1.2	O **Lord**, how long must I call for **help**
Zeph	3.2	trust in the **Lord** or asked for his **help**.
Lk	1.25	Now at last the **Lord** has **helped** me,
Acts	2.21	whoever calls out to the **Lord** for **help**
Rom	10.13	who calls out to the **Lord** for **help**
2 Tim	2.22	heart call out to the **Lord** for **help**.
Heb	13.6	The **Lord** is my **helper**,

Offer

Ezra	2.68	**offerings** to **help** rebuild the Temple
Is	19.15	important or unknown, can **offer help**.
Rom	15.26	to give an **offering** to **help** the poor

One Another see God's People

Plead, Beg

Gen	42.21	he was in when he **begged** for **help**,
1 Sam	2.36	**beg** to be allowed to **help** the priests,

2 Chr	33.12	and **begged** him for **help**.
Job	19.16	even when I **beg** him to **help** me.
	30.28	I stand up in public and **plead** for **help**.
Ps	30.8	I **begged** for your **help**:
	142.1	I call to the Lord for **help**; I **plead**
Mt	8.5	officer met him and **begged** for **help**:
Mk	1.40	and **begged** him for **help**.
Lk	18.3	**pleading** for her rights, saying, 'Help me
Acts	16.9	**begging** him, "Come over to Macedonia and **help** us!

Pray

Num	11.2	Moses for **help**; he **prayed** to the Lord,
1 Sam	7.9	he **prayed** to the Lord to **help** Israel,
1 Kgs	8.52	hear their **prayer** whenever they call to you for **help**.
1 Chr	5.20	and **prayed** to him for **help**,
2 Chr	32.20	**prayed** to God...for **help**.
Job	36.13	they don't **pray** for **help**.
Ps	4.1	you **helped** me...hear my **prayer**.
	5.2	**help**, my God and king! I **pray** to you,
	6.9	cry for **help** and will answer my **prayer**.
	17.1	for **help**! Listen to my honest **prayer**.
	86.6	to my **prayer**; hear my cries for **help**.
	88.2	my **prayer**; listen to my cry for **help**!
	88.13	to you for **help**; every morning I **pray**
	102.1	my **prayer**...and hear my cry for **help**!
Is	64.7	in **prayer**; no one goes to you for **help**.
Hos	7.7	but no one **prays** to me for **help**.
Jon	1.6	Get up and **pray** to your god for **help**.
2 Cor	1.11	you **help** us by means of your **prayers**
Eph	6.18	all this in **prayer**, asking for God's **help**.
Phil	1.19	your **prayers** and the **help** which comes
1 Tim	5.5	to **pray** and ask him for his **help**

Protect, Defend

2 Sam	22.36	you **protect** me and save me; your **help**
Ps	4.1	my **defender**! When I was in trouble, you **helped** me.
	28.7	and **defends** me...He gives me **help**
	33.20	he is our **protector** and our **help**.
	54.4	is my **helper**. The Lord is my **defender**.
	115.9	He **helps** you and **protects** you.
	115.10	He **helps** you and **protects** you.
	115.11	He **helps** you and **protects** you.
	142.4	one to **help** me, no one to **protect** me.
	142.5	for **help**; you, Lord, are my **protector**;
Prov	2.7	**help** and **protection** for righteous,
	18.19	**Help** your brother and he will **protect**
Is	30.3	to **help** them, and Egypt's **protection**
	41.10	strong and **help** you; I will **protect** you
	49.8	for **help**. I will guard and **protect** you
Jer	16.19	the one who **protects** me...you **help** me
Dan	11.1	for **helping** and **defending** me.

Save, Rescue

Ex	18.4	of my father **helped** me and **saved** me
Num	10.9	your God, will **help** you and **save** you
Deut	32.38	and **help** you now...run to your **rescue**.
Josh	10.6	Come at once and **help** us! **Save** us!
Judg	2.18	**help** him and would **save** the people
1 Sam	12.21	they cannot **help** you or **save** you,
2 Sam	22.20	**helped** me out of danger; he **saved** me
	22.36	**save** me; your **help** has made me great;
	22.42	look for **help**, but no one **saves** them;
Ps	18.19	**helped** me out of danger; he **saved** me
	18.41	cry for **help**, but no one **saves** them;
	25.15	for **help** at all times, and he **rescues** me
	37.40	**helps** them and **rescues** them; he **saves**
	40.13	**Save** me, **Lord**! **Help** me now!
	55.16	God for **help**, and he will **save** me.
	70.1	**Save** me, O God! Lord, **help** me now!
	71.2	**help** me...Listen to me and **save** me!
	79.9	**Help** us, O God, and **save** us;
	85.7	and give us your **saving help**.

Ps 106.4 **help** your people...when you **save** them.
109.21 **help** me...and **rescue** me
119.123from watching for your **saving help**,
119.174I long for your **saving help**, O Lord!
142.6 **help**, for I am sunk in despair. **Save** me
Is 19.20 for **help**, he will send someone to **rescue**
41.10 **help** you; I will protect you and **save**
46.4 I will give you **help** and **rescue** you.
51.1 be **saved**, you that come to me for **help**.
51.9 **help** us! Use your power and **save** us;
57.13 **help**, let those idols of yours **save** you!
59.1 **save** you or...to hear your call for **help**!
Jer 11.12 for **help**. But those gods will not be able to **save** them
Joel 2.32 ask the Lord for **help** will be **saved**.
Hab 1.2 **help** before you listen, before you **save**
Mk 3.4 **help** or to harm? To **save** a man's life
Lk 6.9 **help** or to harm? To **save** a man's life
Acts 2.21 out to the Lord for **help** will be **saved**.
Rom 10.13 out to the Lord for **help** will be **saved**.
2 Cor 6.2 for me to **save** you I **helped** you.

Serve

Num 18.2 and **help** you while you...are **serving**
Ps 27.9 **servant** away. You have been my **help**;
119.122Promise that you will **help** your **servant**;
Is 44.2 I have **helped** you...you are my **servant**,
45.4 I appoint you to **help** my **servant** Israel,
Lk 1.54 and has come to the **help** of his **servant**
Jn 12.2 which Martha **helped** to **serve**;
2 Cor 8.6 **help** you complete this special **service**
Phil 2.25 **served** as your messenger in **helping** me.
Heb 1.14 **serve** God and are sent by him to **help**
3 Jn .7 the **service** of Christ without...any **help**

Spirit of God

Acts 9.31 Through the **help** of the **Holy Spirit**
Rom 8.26 the **Spirit** also comes to **help** us,
Phil 1.19 the **help** which comes from the **Spirit**

Strength

Deut 1.38 But **strengthen**...your **helper**
33.11 **help** their tribe to grow **strong**;
Job 36.19 all your **strength** can't **help** you now. .
Ps 46.1 and **strength**, always ready to **help**
Is 40.31 Lord for **help** will find their **strength**
41.10 I will make you **strong** and **help** you;
Jer 16.19 and gives me **strength**; you **help** me
Acts 9.31 **help** of the...**Spirit** it was **strengthened**
Rom 14.19 and that **help** to **strengthen** one another.
15.1 are **strong** in the faith ought to **help**
2 Cor 1.6 too are **helped** and given the **strength**
1 Thes 3.2 to **strengthen** you and **help** your faith,

Temple

Ezra 2.68 offerings to **help** rebuild the **Temple**
4.3 don't need your **help** to build a **temple**
5.2 **Temple**...and the two prophets **helped**
5.4 who were **helping** to build the **Temple**.
Neh 7.70 to **help** pay the cost of restoring the **Temple**:
10.32 to **help** pay the expenses of the **Temple**.
Ps 18.6 God for **help**. In his **temple** he heard
20.2 May he send you **help** from his **Temple**
Zech 6.15 come and **help** to rebuild the **Temple**

Trust see Faith

Weak

2 Chr 14.11 you can **help** a **weak** army
Job 26.1 **help** you are to me — poor, **weak** man
Is 31.3 and the **weak** nation it **helped** will fall.
Acts 20.35 in this way we must **help** the **weak**,
Rom 8.26 also comes to **help** us, **weak** as we are
15.1 to **help** the **weak** to carry their burdens.
1 Thes 5.14 encourage the timid, **help** the **weak**,

HIGH PRIEST

Heb	2.17	—		9.25	x21
Mt	26.3	—	69		x8
Jn	18.10	—	26		x8
Mk	14.47	—	66		x7
Neh	11.11	—		13.28	x5
Acts	4.6	—		5.27	x5
Acts	22.5	—		24.1	x5
Lev	4.3	—	16		x3
Num	35.25	—	32		x3
2 Kgs	22.4	—		23.24	x3
Hag	1.1	—		2.2	x3

Offer, Blood

Lev 4.5 **High Priest** shall take some of the bull's **blood**
4.16 The **High Priest** shall take some of the bull's **blood**
Heb 7.27 **high priests**; he does not need to **offer**
8.3 our **High Priest** must...have something to **offer**.
13.11 Jewish **High Priest** brings the **blood**

Slave

Mt 26.51 and struck at the **High Priest's slave**,
Mk 14.47 struck at the **High Priest's slave**,
Lk 22.50 of them struck the **High Priest's slave**
Jn 18.10 and struck the **High Priest's slave**,
18.26 One of the **High Priest's slaves**

HOLY

Lev	19.2	—		24.9	x24
Ezek	42.13	—		46.20	x22
Ex	28.30	—		30.37	x16
Lev	6.16	—		7.6	x10
Lev	10.1	—		12.4	x8
Neh	8.9	—		11.18	x7
Is	4.3	—		6.3	x6
Is	29.19	—		31.1	x6
Ezek	20.12	—	41		x6
Ezek	38.16	—		39.27	x6
Ezek	48.10	—	18		x6
1 Pet	1.2	—		2.9	x6
Ps	89.5	—	35		x5
Is	47.4	—		49.7	x5
Ezek	36.20	—	23		x5
Dan	4.8	—		5.14	x5
1 Thes	3.13	—		5.23	x5
1 Sam	9.6	—		11.15	x4
Is	40.25	—		41.20	x4
Is	62.12	—		63.18	x4
Ezek	28.14	—	25		x4
Hab	1.12	—		3.3	x4
Lk	1.35	—	75		x4
Acts	3.14	—		4.30	x4
Rev	21.2	—		22.19	x4
Lev	16.19	—	31		x3
Ps	99.3	—	9		x3
Is	43.3	—	15		x3
Is	52.1	—	11		x3
Ezek	22.8	—	26		x3
Dan	9.20	—	24		x3

Awe, Respect

Lev 10.3 who serve me must **respect** my **holiness**;
1 Sam 9.6 is a **holy** man who is highly **respected**
2 Kgs 19.22 been **disrespectful** to me, the **holy** God
Ps 89.7 **holy** ones; and all of them stand in **awe**
Is 8.14 Because of my **awesome holiness**
37.23 been **disrespectful** to me, the **holy** God
Ezek 22.8 You have no **respect** for the **holy** places,
22.26 and have no **respect** for what is **holy**.
2 Cor 7.1 us be completely **holy** by living in **awe**

Bow see Worship

Evil see **Sin**

Faithful

Ps	89.5	**holy** ones sing of your **faithfulness**,
Hos	11.12	the **faithful** and **holy** God.

God, Father, Lord, Name

Gen	4.26	began using the **Lord's holy** name
Ex	6.3	to them by my **holy** name, the **Lord**.
	30.10	**holy**, dedicated to me, the **Lord**.
	34.5	pronounced his **holy** name, the **Lord**.
Lev	11.44	I am...**God**...keep yourselves **holy**,
	11.45	could be your **God**. You must be **holy**,
	19.2	because I, the **Lord** your **God**, am **holy**.
	20.7	**holy**, because I am the **Lord** your **God**.
	20.8	I am the **Lord** and I make you **holy**.
	20.26	because I am the **Lord** and I am **holy**.
	21.8	I am the **Lord**; I am **holy**
	21.23	I am the **Lord** and I make them **holy**.
	22.9	I am the **Lord** and I make them **holy**.
	22.16	the **Lord** and I make the offerings **holy**.
	22.32	I am the **Lord** and I make you **holy**;
Num	20.13	**Lord**...showed them that he was **holy**.
Deut	5.12	keep it **holy**, as I, the **Lord** your **God**,
Josh	24.19	He is a **holy** God and will not forgive
1 Sam	2.2	No one is **holy** like the **Lord**;
	6.20	the **Lord**, this **holy** God?
2 Kgs	19.22	the **holy** God of Israel.
1 Chr	16.35	and praise your **holy** name.
	29.16	a temple to honour your **holy** name,
2 Chr	30.8	the **Lord** your **God** has made **holy**
	36.14	which the **Lord** himself had made **holy**.
Neh	8.9	This day is **holy** to the **Lord** your **God**,
	8.10	Today is **holy** to our **Lord**,
Job	6.10	I know that **God** is **holy**;
Ps	11.4	The **Lord** is in his **holy** temple;
	29.2	name; bow down before the **Holy** One
	33.21	we trust in his **holy** name.
	77.13	Everything you do, O **God**, is **holy**.
	78.41	and brought pain to the **Holy** God
	89.18	**Holy** God of Israel, gave us our king.
	89.35	I have promised by my **holy** name:
	97.12	Remember what the **holy** God has done,
	99.5	the **Lord** our **God**...**Holy** is he!
	99.9	The **Lord** our **God** is **holy**.
	103.1	praise his **holy** name!
	106.47	and praise your **holy** name.
	145.21	let all his creatures praise his **holy** name
Is	1.4	the **holy** God of Israel,
	5.19	Israel's **holy God** carry out his plans;
	5.24	Israel's **holy** God, has taught us.
	6.3	**Holy, holy, holy!** The **Lord** Almighty is **holy**!
	8.13	the **Lord** Almighty, am **holy**;
	10.17	Israel's **holy** God will become a flame,
	10.20	the **Lord**, Israel's **holy** God.
	12.6	Israel's **holy** God is great,
	17.7	the **holy** God of Israel.
	29.19	the **holy** God of Israel, gives.
	29.23	that I am the **holy** God of Israel.
	30.11	to hear about your **holy** God of Israel.
	30.12	this is what the **holy** God of Israel says
	30.15	the **holy** God of Israel,
	31.1	the **holy** God of Israel,
	37.23	the **holy** God of Israel.
	40.25	whom can the **holy** God be compared?
	41.14	the **holy** God of Israel,
	41.16	will praise me, the **holy** God of Israel.
	41.20	Israel's **holy** God has made it happen.
	43.3	the **holy** God of Israel, who saves you.
	43.14	Israel's **holy** God, the **Lord**
	43.15	I am the **Lord**, your **holy** God.
	45.11	the **holy** God of Israel,

Is	47.4	The **holy** God of Israel sets us free — his name is the **Lord**
	48.17	The **holy** God of Israel,
	49.7	Israel's **holy** God and saviour says
	52.10	The **Lord** will use his **holy** power;
	54.5	The **holy** God of Israel will save you
	55.5	**Lord** your **God**, the **holy** God of Israel,
	57.15	I am the high and **holy** God
	60.9	the name of the **Lord**, The **holy** God
	60.14	the City of Israel's **Holy** God.
	63.15	**Lord**, look upon us from heaven, where you live in your **holiness**
Jer	23.9	of the **Lord**, because of his **holy** words,
Ezek	20.12	I, the **Lord**, make them **holy**.
	20.39	and stop dishonouring my **holy** name
	28.22	the **Lord**, when I show how **holy** I am
	36.20	they brought disgrace on my **holy** name,
	36.21	made me concerned for my **holy** name,
	36.22	but for the sake of my **holy** name,
	39.7	my people Israel know my **holy** name,
	39.7	I, the **Lord**, am the **Holy** God of Israel.
	39.25	I will protect my **holy** name.
	43.7	**holy** name by worshipping other gods
	43.8	They disgraced my **holy** name
	48.14	It is **holy** and belongs to the **Lord**.
Hos	11.9	am **God** and not man. I, the **Holy** One,
	11.12	the faithful and **holy** God.
Amos	2.7	and so profane my **holy** name.
	4.2	As the Sovereign **Lord** is **holy**
Hab	1.12	You are my **God**, **holy** and eternal.
	3.3	the **holy** God is coming from the hills
Mt	6.9	**Father** in heaven: May your **holy** name
Mk	1.24	you are **God's holy** messenger!
	8.38	glory of his **Father** with the **holy** angels.
Lk	1.49	**God** has done...His name is **holy**;
	9.26	of the **Father** and of the **holy** angels.
	11.2	**Father**: May your **holy** name be
Jn	6.69	the **Holy** One who has come from **God**.
	17.11	**Holy Father!** Keep them safe
2 Cor	7.1	**holy** by living in awe of **God**.
1 Thes	3.13	and **holy** in the presence of our **God**
	4.3	**God** wants you to be **holy**
	5.23	**God** who gives us peace make you **holy**
1 Pet	1.2	**God** the Father and were made a **holy**
	1.15	just as **God** who called you is **holy**.
2 Pet	3.11	should be **holy** and dedicated to **God**,
Rev	4.8	**Holy, holy, holy**, is the **Lord** God
	6.10	Almighty **Lord**, **holy** and true!

Honour

1 Chr	29.16	a temple to **honour** your **holy** name,
2 Chr	2.4	other **holy** days **honouring** the **Lord**
Is	29.23	**holy** God of Israel. You will **honour** me
	58.13	if you value my **holy** day and **honour** it
	60.9	**honour** the name of the Lord, The **holy**
Mt	6.9	May your **holy** name be **honoured**;
Lk	11.2	May your **holy** name be **honoured**;
1 Thes	4.4	his wife in a **holy** and **honourable** way,

Jesus

Acts	4.27	against **Jesus**, your **holy** Servant,
	4.30	the name of your **holy** Servant **Jesus**.

Lord see **God**

Mighty, Strength

Ex	15.11	in **holiness**? Who can work...**mighty** acts
Ps	98.1	By his own power and **holy** strength
	111.9	**Holy** and **mighty** is he!
Lk	1.49	the **Mighty** God has done...His name is **holy**;
1 Thes	3.13	**strengthen** you, and you will be...**holy**

Name see **God**

Power

Lev	6.18	be harmed by the **power** of its **holiness**.

Num	20.12	**holy power** before the people of Israel,
	27.14	refused to acknowledge my **holy power**
Ps	98.1	By his own **power** and **holy** strength
Is	52.10	The Lord will use his **holy power**;
Lk	1.35	**Holy Spirit** will come...and God's **power**
Rom	1.4	**holiness**, he was shown with great **power**

Praise see Worship

Respect see Awe

Sin, Evil
Hab	1.13	Your eyes are too **holy** to look at **evil**,
Heb	7.26	He is **holy**; he has no fault or **sin**

Strength see Mighty

True
Eph	4.24	in the **true** life that is upright and **holy**.
Rev	3.7	from the one who is **holy** and **true**.
	6.10	Almighty Lord, **holy** and **true**!

Worship, Bow, Praise
Gen	4.26	using the Lord's **holy** name in **worship**.
1 Chr	16.29	**Bow** down before the **Holy One**
	16.35	and **praise** your **holy** name.
2 Chr	2.4	a **holy** place where...I will **worship**
	30.8	made **holy** for ever, and **worship** him
Ps	5.7	I can **worship** in your **holy** Temple
	22.3	**Holy One**, the one whom Israel **praises**.
	29.2	**bow** down before the **Holy One**
	96.9	**Bow** down before the **Holy One**
	99.3	**praise** his great and majestic name. **Holy**
	99.5	**worship** before his throne! **Holy** is he!
	103.1	All my being, **praise** his **holy** name!
	106.47	and **praise** your **holy** name.
	138.2	**holy** Temple, **bow** down, and **praise**
	145.21	let all his creatures **praise** his **holy** name
Is	41.16	will **praise** me, the **holy** God of Israel.
Lam	1.4	now to **worship** on the **holy** days.
Rev	15.4	**holy**. All the nations will...**worship** you,

AV HOLY OF HOLIES
see (Most) HOLY PLACE

HOLY PLACE
Lev	16.2 – 33			x11
1 Kgs	6.16	—	8.8	x10
Ezek	41.1 – 25			x9
2 Chr	3.8	—	5.9	x8
Heb	8.2	—	10.19	x8
Num	3.31	—	4.12	x5
Ex	28.29	—	29.30	x4
Ex	26.33 – 35			x3
Num	18.3 – 7			x3

Creatures
1 Kgs	8.6	**Holy Place**, beneath the winged **creatures**.
2 Chr	5.7	**Holy Place**, beneath the winged **creatures**.
Ezek	41.25	**creatures** carved on the doors of the **Holy Place**,

HONEST
Prov	10.2	—	16.11	x17
Prov	28.1	—	29.10	x7
Gen	42.11 – 34			x5
Prov	19.1	—	21.21	x5
Prov	24.15 – 26			x3

Dishonest see Justice

Happy
Prov	11.1	He is **happy** with **honest** weights.
	11.10	A city is **happy** when **honest** people
	28.20	**Honest** people will lead a full, **happy**
	29.6	while **honest** people are **happy** and free.

Help
Job	8.6	**honest** and pure, then God will...**help**
Prov	2.7	**help** and protection for righteous, **honest**
Eph	4.28	an **honest** living...and to be able to **help**

Justice, Dishonest
Lev	19.15	**honest** and **just** when you make
Prov	1.3	intelligently and how to be **honest**, **just**,
	10.2	**dishonesty** will do you no good, but **honesty** can save
	10.9	**Honest** people are safe...but the **dishonest**
	11.1	**dishonest** scales. He is happy with **honest** weights.
	20.28	long as his rule is **honest**, **just**, and fair.
	28.6	and **honest** than rich and **dishonest**.
	28.18	Be **honest**...If you are **dishonest**,
Is	29.21	to keep **honest** men from getting **justice**.
Mt	23.23	such as **justice** and mercy and **honesty**.

Life
Prov	10.2	but **honesty** can save your **life**.
	11.4	but **honesty** can save your **life**.
	11.5	**Honesty** makes a good man's **life** easier
	21.21	and **honest** and you will live a long **life**;
	28.20	**Honest** people will lead a full, happy **life**

Poor
Prov	19.1	It is better to be **poor** but **honest**
	28.6	Better to be **poor** and **honest**
Amos	2.6	**honest** men who cannot pay...**poor** men

Wicked
Prov	10.25	**wicked** are blown away, but **honest**
	12.5	**Honest** people will treat you fairly; the **wicked** only
	13.5	**Honest** people hate lies, but the words of **wicked** people
	24.15	**wicked** who scheme to rob an **honest**

HONOUR
Dan	4.34	—	5.29	x10
Ex	12.11	—	14.17	x6
Esth	6.3 – 11			x6
Deut	16.1	—	17.19	x5
Is	55.5	—	58.14	x5
Mal	1.6	—	2.2	x5
Heb	1.9	—	3.3	x5
Lev	23.5 – 44			x4
Deut	5.29	—	6.24	x4
2 Sam	6.5 – 21			x4
2 Chr	17.5	—	20.8	x4
Prov	3.9	—	4.8	x4
Is	42.21	—	43.23	x4
Is	49.5	—	50.10	x4
Jn	8.49 – 54			x4
Rom	13.7	—	14.6	x4
Rev	4.9	—	5.13	x4
1 Sam	2.8 – 30			x3
2 Chr	32.23 – 33			x3
Ps	34.7 – 11			x3
Ps	103.11 – 17			x3
Ps	111.3 – 10			x3
Dan	2.6 – 37			x3

Celebrate, Festival, Passover
Ex	5.1	a **festival** in the desert to **honour** me.
	10.9	hold a **festival** to **honour** the Lord.
	12.11	is the **Passover Festival** to **honour** me,
	12.27	of **Passover** to **honour** the Lord,
	12.48	**celebrate Passover** to **honour** the Lord.
	13.6	a **festival** to **honour** the Lord.
	23.14	**Celebrate** three festivals a year to **honour**
	32.5	will be a **festival** to **honour** the Lord.
Lev	23.5	The **Passover**, **celebrated** to **honour**
	23.37	**festivals** on which you **honour** the Lord
	23.40	a religious **festival** to **honour** the Lord

Lev	23.44	religious **festivals** to **honour** the Lord.
	26.2	religious **festivals** and **honour** the place
Num	28.16	**Passover Festival** in **honour** of the Lord
	29.12	**Celebrate** this **festival** in **honour** of the
Deut	16.1	**Honour**...God by **celebrating** Passover
	16.2	Passover meal to **honour** the Lord your
	16.10	**celebrate** the Harvest **Festival**, to **honour**
	16.15	**Honour** the Lord your God by **celebrating**
2 Kgs	23.21	**celebrate** the Passover in **honour**
2 Chr	2.4	**Festivals**, and other holy days **honouring**
	30.1	**celebrate** the Passover in **honour**
	35.1	**celebrated** the Passover...in **honour**
Hos	9.5	**festivals** in **honour** of the Lord,

Command

Deut	5.29	**honour** me and obey all my **commands**,
	6.24	God **commanded** us...to **honour** him.
	13.4	**honour** him...keep his **commands**;
2 Chr	2.4	**honouring** the Lord...He has **commanded**
Ezra	10.3	the others who **honour** God's **commands**
Ps	37.34	obey his **commands**; he will **honour** you

Covenant see **Promise**

Faithful

Deut	17.19	**honour** the Lord and to obey **faithfully**
Josh	24.14	**honour** the Lord and serve him sincerely and **faithfully**.
Dan	9.4	**honour** you. You are **faithful** to your

Father see **God**

Festival see **Celebrate**

God, Father

Gen	22.12	I know that you **honour** and obey **God**,
Lev	23.40	festival to **honour** the **Lord** your **God**
Deut	6.2	are to **honour** the **Lord** your **God**
	6.13	**Honour** the **Lord** your **God**,
	14.23	learn to **honour** the **Lord** your **God**
	16.1	**Honour** the **Lord** your **God**
	16.2	to **honour** the **Lord** your **God**
	16.10	to **honour** the **Lord** your **God**,
	16.15	**Honour** the **Lord** your **God**
	31.12	and learn to **honour** the **Lord** your **God**
Josh	4.24	and you will **honour** the **Lord** your **God**
1 Sam	6.5	must give **honour** to the **God** of Israel.
	12.14	you if you **honour** the **Lord** your **God**,
2 Kgs	23.21	in **honour** of the **Lord** their **God**,
1 Chr	13.8	with all their might to **honour** **God**.
	22.7	a temple to **honour** the **Lord** my **God**.
2 Chr	2.4	a temple to **honour** the **Lord** my **God**.
	30.1	**honour** of the **Lord**, the **God** of Israel.
Ezra	10.3	the others who **honour** **God's** commands
Neh	5.15	because I **honoured** **God**.
Ps	62.7	salvation and **honour** depend on **God**;
	66.16	all who **honour** **God**,
	76.1	**God** is known in Judah; his name is **honoured** in Israel.
	92.1	in your **honour**, O Most High **God**,
Prov	25.2	We **honour** **God** for what he conceals
Ecc	6.2	**God** will give someone wealth, **honour**,
Is	25.1	you are my **God**; I will **honour** you
	29.23	holy **God** of Israel. You will **honour** me
Jer	2.11	the **God** who has brought them **honour**,
	13.16	**Honour** the **Lord**, your **God**,
Dan	2.23	I praise you and **honour** you, **God**
	4.34	the Supreme **God** and gave **honour**
	5.23	But you did not **honour** the **God**
	9.4	**God**, you are great, and we **honour**
Mal	1.6	your **father** — why don't you **honour**
Mt	6.9	**Father**:May your...name be **honoured**;
	15.8	says **God**, **honour** me with their words,
Mk	7.6	says **God**, **honour** me with their words,
Lk	11.2	**Father**: May your...name be **honoured**;
Jn	5.23	same way as they **honour** the **Father**.

Jn	8.49	I **honour** my **Father**,
	8.54	The one who **honours** me is my **Father**
	12.26	**Father** will **honour** anyone who serves
Acts	12.23	because he did not give **honour** to **God**.
Rom	1.21	They know **God**, but they do not give him **honour**
	2.10	But **God** will give glory, **honour**
1 Tim	1.17	only **God** — to him be **honour** and glory
1 Pet	2.17	**honour** **God**,
2 Pet	1.17	he was given **honour** and glory by **God**
Rev	4.11	**God**! You are worthy to receive glory, **honour**, and power.
	7.12	**honour**, power, and might belong to our **God** for ever
	14.7	**Honour** **God** and praise his greatness!

Jesus

Acts	19.17	Lord **Jesus** was given greater **honour**.
Phil	2.10	in **honour** of the name of **Jesus**
Heb	3.3	**Jesus** is worthy of much greater **honour**
1 Pet	1.7	**honour** on the Day when **Jesus** Christ

Kind see **Love**

Law

Deut	6.2	**honour**...God and obey all his **laws**
	6.24	obey all these **laws** and to **honour** him.
Jer	44.10	not **honoured** me or lived according to all the **laws**

Lord

see also **God**

Ex	10.9	hold a festival to **honour** the **Lord**.
	12.11	Festival to **honour** me, the **Lord**.
	12.27	of Passover to **honour** the **Lord**,
	12.48	celebrate Passover to **honour** the **Lord**,
	13.6	a festival to **honour** the **Lord**.
	32.5	will be a festival to **honour** the **Lord**.
Lev	23.5	celebrated to **honour** the **Lord**,
	23.37	festivals on which you **honour** the **Lord**
	23.44	religious festivals to **honour** the **Lord**.
	25.2	you shall **honour** the **Lord**
Num	28.16	Passover Festival in **honour** of the **Lord**
	29.12	this festival in **honour** of the **Lord**
Deut	6.24	Then the **Lord** our God commanded us to ...**honour** him.
	13.4	Follow the **Lord** and **honour** him
	17.19	that he will learn to **honour** the **Lord**
	28.58	**honour** the wonderful and awesome name of the **Lord** your God,
Josh	24.14	**honour** the **Lord** and serve him
1 Sam	12.14	well with you if you **honour** the **Lord**
2 Sam	6.5	with all their might to **honour** the **Lord**.
	6.14	with all his might to **honour** the **Lord**.
	6.21	I was dancing to **honour** the **Lord**,
1 Chr	16.25	The **Lord** is great...he is to be **honoured**
	29.20	low and gave **honour** to the **Lord**
2 Chr	19.7	**Honour** the **Lord** and act carefully,
	35.1	at Jerusalem in **honour** of the **Lord**;
Ps	15.4	but **honours** those who obey the **Lord**.
	22.23	you servants of the **Lord**! **Honour** him,
	33.8	the **Lord**, all the earth! **Honour** him,
	34.7	guards those who **honour** the **Lord**
	34.9	**Honour** the **Lord**, all his people;
	34.11	I will teach you to **honour** the **Lord**.
	96.4	The **Lord** is...to be **honoured**
	103.13	**Lord** is kind to those who **honour** him.
	103.17	But for those who **honour** the **Lord**
	111.10	to become wise is to **honour** the **Lord**;
	112.1	is the person who **honours** the **Lord**,
	149.4	The **Lord**...**honours** the humble
Prov	3.9	**Honour** the **Lord** by making him an
	8.13	To **honour** the **Lord** is to hate evil;
	31.30	but a woman who **honours** the **Lord**
Is	49.5	The **Lord** gives me **honour**;

HONOUR — Lord

Is	50.10	All of you that **honour** the **Lord**
	56.4	The **Lord** says...'If you **honour** me
	60.9	To **honour** the name of the **Lord**,
Jer	26.19	Hezekiah **honoured** the **Lord**
Hos	9.5	festivals in **honour** of the **Lord**,
Acts	19.17	**Lord** Jesus was given greater **honour**.
Rom	14.6	day does so in **honour** of the **Lord**;
1 Pet	3.15	and **honour** him as **Lord**.

Love, Kind

2 Kgs	25.28	**kindly**, and gave him a position of greater **honour**
Ps	84.11	blessing us with **kindness** and **honour**.
	103.11	is his **love** for those who **honour** him.
	103.13	**Lord** is **kind** to those who **honour** him.
	103.17	who **honour** the **Lord**, his **love** lasts
	141.5	**kindness**, but I will never accept **honour**
Is	43.4	I **love** you and give you **honour**.
Jer	52.32	**kindly** and gave him a position of greater **honour**
1 Pet	2.17	**love** your fellow-believers, **honour** God,

Might see Power

Name

Deut	26.19	bring praise and **honour** to his **name**.
	28.58	not **honour** the wonderful...**name**
1 Chr	29.16	a temple to **honour** your holy **name**,
Ps	76.1	his **name** is **honoured** in Israel.
Is	25.1	will **honour** you and praise your **name**.
	60.9	To **honour** the **name** of the **Lord**,
	63.14	people and brought **honour** to his **name**.
Jer	13.11	bring praise and **honour** to my **name**;
Mt	6.9	May your holy **name** be **honoured**;
Lk	11.2	May your holy **name** be **honoured**;
Acts	19.17	the **name** of...Jesus was given...**honour**.
Phil	2.10	in **honour** of the **name** of Jesus

Obey

Gen	22.12	I know that you **honour** and **obey** God,
Deut	5.29	they would always **honour** me and **obey**
	6.2	**honour** the **Lord** your God and **obey** all
	6.24	**obey** all these laws and to **honour** him.
	13.4	the **Lord** and **honour** him; **obey** him
	17.19	**honour** the **Lord** and to **obey** faithfully
	31.12	**honour** the **Lord** your God and...**obey**
2 Chr	6.31	people may **honour** you and **obey** you
Ps	15.4	but **honours** those who **obey** the **Lord**.
	34.9	**Honour** the **Lord**...those who **obey**
	37.34	**obey** his commands; he will **honour** you
	50.23	**honours** me...I will...save all who **obey**
	112.1	who **honours** the **Lord**, who takes pleasure in **obeying**
Is	50.10	**honour** the **Lord** and **obey** the words
Jer	13.11	**honour** to my **name**; but they would not **obey** me.

Offer, Sacrifice

Ex	12.27	**sacrifice** of Passover to **honour** the
Ps	50.23	thanks is the **sacrifice** that **honours** me,
Prov	3.9	**Honour** the **Lord** by...an **offering**
	3.16	**offers** you long life, as well as...**honour**.
Is	43.23	**offerings** of sheep; you did not **honour**
Mal	1.11	**honour** me. Everywhere they...**offer**
Acts	7.41	**offered sacrifice**...had a feast in **honour**

Passover see Celebrate

Power, Might

Josh	4.24	**Lord**'s **power** is, and you will **honour**
2 Sam	6.5	with all their **might** to **honour** the **Lord**.
	6.14	with all his **might** to **honour** the **Lord**.
1 Chr	13.8	with all their **might** to **honour** God.
Is	53.12	**honour**, a place among...**powerful** men.
Dan	2.37	given you **power**, **might**, and **honour**.
	4.36	royal **power**, with even greater **honour**
	5.7	of **honour**...and be the third in **power**

Dan	5.16	of **honour**...and be the third in **power**
	7.14	**honour**, and royal **power**,
Rev	4.11	**honour**, and **power**.
	5.12	**power**, wealth, wisdom...**honour**,
	5.13	be praise and **honour**, glory and **might**,
	7.12	wisdom, thanksgiving, **honour**, **power**,

Praise see Worship

Promise, Covenant

2 Kgs	19.34	own **honour** and because of the **promise**
	20.6	own **honour** and because of the **promise**
Is	37.35	own **honour** and because of the **promise**
Ezek	16.60	I will **honour** the **covenant** I made

Protect

Josh	7.9	will you do to **protect** your **honour**?
2 Kgs	19.34	**protect** it, for the sake of my...**honour**
Ps	62.7	**honour** depend on God; he is my strong **protector**;
Is	37.35	**protect** it, for the sake of my...**honour**
Ezek	20.44	When I act to **protect** my **honour**,
Dan	11.38	**honour** the god who **protects** fortresses.

Rescue see Save

Reverence, Respect

Lev	19.32	and **honour** them. **Reverently** obey me;
Job	31.27	to **honour** them by kissing my hand in **reverence**
Prov	24.21	**reverence** for the **Lord**...and **honour** the
Is	49.23	**honour** you; they will...show...**respect**
Mal	1.6	**honour** me...why don't you **respect**
Rom	13.7	show **respect** and **honour** for them all.
1 Pet	2.17	**honour** God, and **respect** the Emperor.
	3.15	**reverence** for Christ...and **honour** him

Sacrifice see Offer

Save, Rescue

Ps	34.7	who **honour** the **Lord** and **rescues** them
	50.23	**honours** me, and I will surely **save** all
	85.9	is ready to **save** those who **honour** him,
	91.15	I will **rescue** them and **honour** them.
	145.19	**honour** him; he...**saves** them.
Is	46.13	I will **save** Jerusalem and bring **honour**

Serve

Gen	18.5	**honoured** me by coming to my home, so let me **serve** you.
Josh	24.14	**honour** the **Lord** and **serve** him sincerely
1 Sam	12.14	**honour** the **Lord** your God, **serve** him,
1 Chr	17.18	and yet you **honour** me, your **servant**.
Neh	1.11	other **servants** who want to **honour** you.
Ps	22.23	you **servants** of the **Lord**! **Honour** him,
Is	50.10	**honour** the **Lord** and obey the words of his **servant**,
	58.14	**serving** me. I will make you **honoured**
Mal	1.6	and a **servant honours** his master.
Jn	12.26	will **honour** anyone who **serves** me.

Thank see Worship

Wisdom

Ps	111.10	to become **wise** is to **honour** the **Lord**;
Prov	3.35	**Wise** men will gain an **honourable**
Ecc	10.12	a **wise** man says brings him **honour**,
Rev	5.12	**wisdom**, and strength, **honour**, glory,
	7.12	**wisdom**, thanksgiving, **honour**, power

World

Ps	33.8	**Honour** him, all peoples of the **world**!
Is	58.14	make you **honoured** all over the **world**,
Lam	1.1	Once **honoured** by the **world**,
Zeph	3.19	**honour**, and all the **world** will praise
Mal	1.11	of the **world** to the other **honour** me

Worship, Praise, Thank

Lev	19.30	and **honour** the place where I am **worshipped**.

Lev	23.37	**honour** the Lord by...**worship**
	26.2	and **honour** the place where I am **worshipped**.
Deut	6.13	**Honour** the Lord your God, **worship**
	13.4	**honour** him; obey him and...**worship** him
	26.19	bring **praise** and **honour** to his name.
1 Chr	16.25	be highly **praised**; he is to be **honoured**
Ps	22.23	**Honour** him...**Worship** him, you people
	33.8	**Worship** the Lord...**Honour** him,
	50.23	**thanks** is the sacrifice that **honours** me,
	92.1	give **thanks**...sing in your **honour**,
	96.4	be highly **praised**; he is to be **honoured**
Prov	31.30	**honours** the Lord should be **praised**.
Is	25.1	will **honour** you and **praise** your name.
	43.20	will **honour** me...ostriches will **praise** me
Jer	13.11	bring **praise** and **honour** to my name;
Dan	2.23	I **praise** you and **honour** you, God of
	4.34	**praised**...God and gave **honour** and glory
	4.37	I, Nebuchadnezzar, **praise**, **honour**, and
Zeph	3.19	**honour**, and all the world will **praise**
Rom	1.21	the **honour** that belongs to him, nor do they **thank** him.
	14.6	in **honour** of the Lord...he gives **thanks**
2 Cor	6.8	**honoured** and disgraced; we are...**praised**.
1 Pet	1.7	will receive **praise** and glory and **honour**
Rev	4.9	songs of glory and **honour** and **thanks**
	5.12	**honour**, glory, and **praise**!
	5.13	be **praise** and **honour**, glory and might,
	7.12	**Praise**, glory, wisdom, **thanksgiving**, **honour**,
	14.7	**Honour** God and **praise** his greatness!

HOPE

Job	3.9	—	8.13	x7
Ps	119.5	–	147	x6
Lam	2.13	—	3.29	x6
Acts	26.6	—	28.20	x6
Rom	8.20	–	25	x6
1 Pet	1.3	—	3.15	x6
Jer	28.6	—	31.17	x5
Rom	4.18	—	5.5	x5
Rom	15.4	–	24	x5
Job	13.15	—	15.22	x4
Job	17.11	–	16	x4
Jer	13.16	—	14.22	x4
2 Cor	1.7	–	13	x4
Phil	1.20	—	3.11	x4
1 Tim	3.14	—	6.17	x4
Heb	6.11	—	7.19	x4
Acts	23.6	—	24.26	x3
1 Cor	15.19	—	16.7	x3
Eph	1.12	—	2.12	x3
Col	1.5	–	23	x3
Tit	1.2	—	3.7	x3

Christ see **Jesus**

Darkness see **Trouble**

God, Lord

Job	8.13	**hope** is gone, once **God** is forgotten.
	11.18	full of **hope**; **God** will protect you
	27.8	What **hope** is there for **godless** men
	35.10	**God**, their Creator, who gives them **hope**
Ps	31.24	all you that **hope** in the **Lord**.
	33.20	We put our **hope** in the **Lord**;
	33.22	**Lord**, as we put our **hope** in you.
	37.34	Put your **hope** in the **Lord** and obey
	39.7	What...can I **hope** for, **Lord**?
	42.5	I will put my **hope** in **God**,
	42.11	I will put my **hope** in **God**,
	43.5	I will put my **hope** in **God**,
	62.5	on **God** alone; I put my **hope** in him.
	71.5	Sovereign **Lord**, I put my **hope** in you;
	143.7	**Lord**! I have lost all **hope**.

Is	33.2	**Lord**, have mercy on us. We have put our **hope** in you.
Jer	14.22	put our **hope** in you, O **Lord** our **God**,
	17.13	**Lord**, you are Israel's **hope**;
Lam	3.18	my **hope** in the **Lord** is gone.
	3.24	The **Lord** is all I have, and so I put my **hope** in him.
Acts	24.15	I have the same **hope** in **God**
	26.6	**hope** I have in the promise that **God**
Rom	5.2	**hope** we have of sharing **God's** glory!
	5.4	endurance brings **God's** approval, and his approval creates **hope**
	15.13	May **God**, the source of **hope**
Gal	5.5	our **hope** is that **God** will put us right
Eph	1.12	to **hope** in Christ, praise **God's** glory!
	2.12	without **hope** and without **God**.
	4.4	one **hope** to which **God** has called you.
1 Tim	4.10	have placed our **hope** in the living **God**,
	5.5	has placed her **hope** in **God**
Tit	2.13	blessed Day we **hope** for, when the glory of our great **God**
Phlm	.22	I **hope** that **God** will answer the prayers
Heb	10.23	firmly to the **hope** we profess, because we can trust **God**
1 Pet	1.21	your faith and **hope** are fixed on **God**.
	2.23	but placed his **hopes** in **God**,
	3.5	who placed their **hope** in **God**

Jesus, Christ, Lord

Lk	23.8	He was **hoping** to see **Jesus**
1 Cor	15.19	If our **hope** in **Christ** is good
Eph	1.12	who were the first to **hope** in **Christ**,
1 Thes	1.3	how your **hope** in our **Lord Jesus Christ**
1 Tim	1.1	and **Christ Jesus** our **hope**
1 Jn	3.3	Everyone who has this **hope** in **Christ**

Joy

Prov	10.28	The **hopes** of good men lead to **joy**
Rom	12.12	Let your **hope** keep you **joyful**
	15.13	the source of **hope**, fill you with all **joy**
1 Thes	2.19	who are our **hope**, our **joy**,

Lord see **God, Jesus**

Praise

Ps	42.5	**hope** in God, and...again I will **praise**
	42.11	**hope** in God, and...again I will **praise**
	43.5	**hope** in God, and...again I will **praise**
	71.14	put my **hope** in you; I will **praise** you
Eph	1.12	to **hope** in Christ, **praise** God's glory!

Trouble, Darkness

Job	15.22	has no **hope** of escaping from **darkness**,
	30.26	I **hoped** for happiness...but **trouble**
	35.10	gives them **hope** in their **darkest** hours.
Ps	42.5	so **troubled**? I will put my **hope** in God,
	42.11	so **troubled**? I will put my **hope** in God,
	43.5	so **troubled**? I will put my **hope** in God,
Hos	2.15	make **Trouble** Valley a door of **hope**.
Rom	12.12	your **hope** keep you joyful, be patient in your **troubles**,

HUMAN

Rom	7.5	—	9.5	x15
Dan	4.16	—	5.21	x10
1 Cor	1.17	—	2.13	x7
Gal	4.4	—	5.24	x6
Dan	7.4	—	8.25	x4
Col	2.8	—	3.22	x4
Gen	5.1	—	7.23	x3
Ezek	1.5	–	10	x3
Ezek	10.8	–	21	x3

Being

Gen	1.26	And now we will make **human beings**;
	1.27	So God created **human beings**
	3.20	she was the mother of all **human beings**.

Gen	5.1	(When God created **human beings**,
	6.4	**human** women and the heavenly **beings**.
	7.23	**beings** on the earth — **human beings**,
Lev	27.28	whether it is a **human being**, an animal,
	27.29	Not even a **human being** who has
Deut	5.26	Has any **human being** ever lived
Josh	10.14	when the Lord obeyed a **human being**.
Ps	56.4	can a mere **human being** do to me?
	56.11	can a mere **human being** do to me?
	146.3	no **human being** can save you.
Ecc	3.19	A **human being** is no better off
Is	44.11	who make idols are **human beings**
	66.3	or sacrifice a **human being**;
Ezek	29.11	No **human being** or animal
	38.20	**human being** on the face of the earth
	44.2	No **human being** is allowed to use it,
Dan	2.11	they do not live among **human beings**.
	7.13	I saw what looked like a **human being**.
Zeph	1.3	all **human beings** and animals
Mt	16.17	come to you from any **human being**,
Jn	1.14	The Word became a **human being**
Acts	14.15	are only **human beings** like you!
Rom	9.5	as a **human being**, belongs to their race.
1 Cor	15.39	**human beings** have one kind of flesh,
Eph	6.12	are not fighting against **human beings**
1 Jn	4.2	Jesus Christ came as a **human being**
2 Jn	.7	Jesus Christ came as a **human being**.
Rev	1.13	was what looked like a **human being**
	14.14	was what looked like a **human being**,

Death

Rom	5.12	**death** has spread to the whole **human**
	8.6	by **human** nature results in **death**;
2 Cor	7.10	that is merely **human** causes **death**.

Desire see Nature

Enemy

Rom	8.7	enemy of God when he is controlled by his **human** nature;
Gal	5.17	what our **human** nature wants. These two are enemies,

Gods, Idols

Deut	4.28	will serve **gods** made by **human** hands
2 Chr	32.19	**idols** made by **human** hands.
Ps	115.4	Their **gods** are...formed by **human** hands.
Is	31.3	are not **gods** — they are only **human**.
	44.11	who make **idols** are **human** beings
Dan	2.11	**gods**...do not live among **human** beings.
Hos	13.2	**idols** of silver, designed by **human**

Heart

1 Kgs	8.39	know the thoughts of the **human heart**.
2 Chr	6.30	know the thoughts of the **human heart**.
Jer	17.9	Who can understand the **human heart**?
2 Cor	3.3	on stone tablets but on **human hearts**.

Idols see Gods

Mind

Num	23.19	is not a **human** who changes his **mind**.
Dan	4.16	**human mind**, but the **mind** of an
	5.21	**human** society, and his **mind** became
	7.4	then a **human mind** was given to it.
Hos	13.2	**human minds**, made by **human** hands.
Rom	7.25	with my **mind**, while my **human** nature
	8.5	**minds** controlled by what **human** nature

Nature, Desire

Prov	27.20	**Human desires** are like the world of the
Rom	7.5	we lived according to our **human nature**
	7.18	in my **human** nature.
	7.25	my **human nature** serves the law of sin.
	8.3	**human nature** was weak, God did.
	8.3	He condemned sin in **human nature**.
	8.4	and not according to **human nature**.
	8.5	live as their **human nature** tells them

Rom	8.6	by **human nature** results in death;
	8.7	he is controlled by his **human nature**;
	8.8	their **human nature** cannot please God.
	8.9	not live as your **human nature** tells you
	8.12	live as our **human nature** wants us to.
	8.13	live according to your **human nature**,
Gal	5.16	satisfy the desires of the **human nature**.
	5.17	**human nature** wants is opposed to what
	5.19	What **human nature** does is quite plain
	5.24	their **human nature** with all its passions
Heb	2.14	them and shared their **human nature**.
1 Pet	4.2	God's will and not by **human desires**.

Obey

Josh	10.14	when the Lord **obeyed** a **human** being.
Rom	8.7	**human** nature; for he does not **obey**
	8.8	**obey** their **human** nature cannot please
Eph	6.5	**obey** your **human** masters with fear and
Col	3.22	**obey** your **human** masters in all things,

Power

2 Chr	32.8	He has **human power**
Is	31.8	but not by **human power**.
Dan	4.17	has **power** over **human** kingdoms
	4.32	God has **power** over **human** kingdoms
	8.25	without the use of any **human power**.
1 Cor	1.26	**human** point of view few of you were wise or **powerful**

Sin

Rom	5.12	**human** race because everyone has **sinned**.
	7.5	our **human** nature, the **sinful** desires
	7.25	my **human** nature serves the law of **sin**.
	8.3	He condemned **sin** in **human** nature

Spirit of God

Jn	3.6	**human** parents, but he is born **spiritually** of the **Spirit**.
Rom	8.4	**Spirit**, and not according to **human**
1 Cor	2.13	by **human** wisdom, but in words taught by the **Spirit**,
Gal	5.17	**human** nature is opposed to what the **Spirit** wants,
1 Tim	3.16	in **human** form, was shown to be right by the **Spirit**,
1 Jn	4.2	came as a **human** being has the **Spirit**

Wisdom

Job	11.6	**wisdom**...things too deep for **human**
	15.8	**human wisdom** belong to you alone?
Prov	21.30	**Human wisdom**, brilliance, insight
1 Cor	1.17	using the language of **human wisdom**,
	1.25	foolishness is wiser than **human wisdom**,
	2.4	with skilful words of **human wisdom**,
	2.5	on **human wisdom** but on God's power.
	2.13	in words taught by **human wisdom**,
2 Cor	1.12	and not by **human wisdom**.
Col	2.8	the worthless deceit of **human wisdom**,

HUMBLE

	2 Chr	32.26 —	34.27	x4
	Prov	14.19 —	16.19	x3
	Zeph	2.3 —	3.12	x3
	Zech	9.6 —	10.11	x3
	Col	2.18 —	3.12	x3
	Jas	3.13 —	4.10	x3
	1 Pet	5.5 – 6		x3

God, Lord

2 Chr	32.26	**humbled** themselves, and so the **Lord**
	33.12	**humble**, turned to the **Lord** his **God**,
	33.23	become **humble** and turn to the **Lord**;
	36.12	the **Lord** and did not listen **humbly**
Ezra	8.21	and **humble** ourselves before our **God**
Job	5.11	it is **God** who raises the **humble**
	22.23	you must **humbly** return to **God**
	22.29	**God**...saves the **humble**.

105

Ps	14.6	plans of the **humble** man, but the **Lord**
	51.17	My sacrifice is a **humble** spirit, O **God**;
	149.4	The **Lord**...honours the **humble**
Prov	22.4	Obey the **Lord**, be **humble**
Is	2.12	the **Lord** Almighty will **humble** everyone
	29.19	**humble** people will once again find the happiness which the **Lord**,
Jer	13.15	the **Lord** has spoken! Be **humble**
Mic	6.8	live in **humble** fellowship with our **God**.
Zeph	2.3	Turn to the **Lord**, all you **humble**
Zech	9.6	**Lord** says, "I will **humble** all these
Mt	5.5	**humble**; they will receive what **God** has
2 Cor	11.7	News of **God** to you; I **humbled** myself
Heb	5.7	Because he was **humble**...**God** heard him.
Jas	4.10	**Humble** yourselves before the **Lord**,
1 Pet	5.6	**Humble** yourselves...under **God's** mighty

Honour

Ps	149.4	he **honours** the **humble** with victory.
Prov	15.33	**humble** before you can...receive **honours**.
	22.4	**humble**, and you will get riches, **honour**,
Is	49.23	**honour** you; they will **humbly** show
Jer	44.10	not **humbled** yourselves. You have not **honoured** me

Lord see God

Proud

2 Sam	22.28	but you **humble** those who are **proud**.
Job	22.29	down the **proud** and saves the **humble**.
	40.11	**proud**; pour out your anger and **humble**
Ps	18.27	but you **humble** those who are **proud**.
	76.12	he **humbles** **proud** princes
Is	5.15	and all who are **proud** will be **humbled**.
	13.11	I will **humble** everyone who is **proud**
	26.5	He has **humbled** those who were **proud**;
Dan	4.37	can **humble** anyone who acts **proudly**.
Zech	9.6	I will **humble** all these **proud** Philistines.
	10.11	**Proud** Assyria will be **humbled**,
Rom	12.16	not be **proud**, but accept **humble** duties.
Jas	4.6	**proud**, but gives grace to the **humble**.
1 Pet	5.5	**proud**, but shows favour to the **humble**.

Repent, Turn

1 Kgs	8.33	**turn** to you...**humbly** praying
	8.35	**repent** and face this Temple, **humbly**
2 Kgs	22.19	**repented** and **humbled** yourself before
2 Chr	6.24	they **turn** to you...**humbly** praying
	6.26	**repent** and face this Temple, **humbly**
	33.12	he became **humble**, **turned** to the Lord
	33.23	become **humble** and **turn** to the Lord;
	34.27	**repented** and **humbled** yourself before
Ps	51.17	not reject a **humble** and **repentant** heart.
Is	57.15	people who are **humble** and **repentant**,
	66.2	those who are **humble** and **repentant**,
Zeph	2.3	**Turn** to the Lord, all you **humble**

HUNGER

Mt	25.35 – 44		x4
1 Sam	14.24 – 31		x3
Ps	107.5 – 36		x3
Prov	12.9	— 13.25	x3
Is	8.21	— 9.20	x3
Ezek	5.12 – 17		x3
Lk	6.3 – 25		x3

Jesus

Mt	4.2	**Jesus** was **hungry**.
	21.18	**Jesus** was **hungry**.
Mk	11.12	**Jesus** was **hungry**.

Lord

Prov	10.3	**Lord** will not let good people go **hungry**
Amos	8.11	will **hunger** and thirst for a message from the **Lord**.
Mt	25.37	**Lord**, did we ever see you **hungry**
	25.44	**Lord**, did we ever see you **hungry**

Need

Deut	8.9	will never go **hungry** or ever be in **need**
	28.48	**hungry**, thirsty, and naked — in **need** of
Is	58.10	food to the **hungry** and satisfy those who are in **need**,
Mk	2.25	**needed** something to eat? He and his men were **hungry**,

I AM

Jn	8.12	—	11.25	x10
Rev	21.6	—	22.20	x6
Jn	5.45	—	6.51	x5
Rev	1.8	—	3.11	x5
Jn	13.19	—	15.5	x4

Bread

Jn	6.35	**I am** the **bread** of life
	6.41	**I am** the **bread** that came down
	6.48	**I am** the **bread** of life
	6.51	**I am** the living **bread**

First

| Rev | 1.8 | **I am** the **first** and the last, |
| | 22.13 | **I am** the **first** and the last, |

Gate

| Jn | 10.7 | **I am** the **gate** for the sheep. |
| | 10.9 | **I am** the **gate**. |

God

Ex	3.14	**God** said, "**I am** who **I am**
Mt	22.32	**I am** the **God** of Abraham
Mk	12.26	**God** said to Moses, '**I am** the **God** of
Acts	7.32	**I am** the **God** of your ancestors
Rom	14.11	As surely as **I am** the living **God**,

Life

Jn	6.35	**I am** the bread of **life**," Jesus told them
	6.48	**I am** the bread of **life**.
	11.25	**I am** the resurrection and the **life**.
	14.6	**I am** the way, the truth, and the **life**;

Light

| Jn | 8.12 | **I am** the **light** of the world, |
| | 9.5 | **I am** the **light** for the world. |

Shepherd

| Jn | 10.11 | **I am** the good **shepherd**, |
| | 10.14 | **I am** the good **shepherd**. |

Vine

| Jn | 15.1 | **I am** the real **vine**, |
| | 15.5 | **I am** the **vine**, |

IDOLS

Ezek	20.7	—	23.49	x20
2 Kgs	16.3	—	17.41	x10
Is	44.9	—	46.2	x10
Judg	17.3	—	18.31	x9
Ezek	6.3	—	8.5	x9
Hos	10.5	—	14.8	x9
Jer	7.30	—	10.14	x8
Ezek	16.19 – 39			x8
1 Kgs	14.9	—	16.26	x7
2 Chr	32.19	—	34.33	x7
Ezek	14.3 – 7			x7
1 Cor	8.1 – 10			x7
Deut	7.5 – 26			x5
Is	40.19	—	42.17	x5
Jer	50.2	—	51.52	x5
Hos	3.1	—	6.10	x5
2 Chr	15.8 – 16			x4
Is	57.8 – 13			x4
1 Cor	10.7 – 28			x4
2 Kgs	21.11 – 21			x3
Ps	106.19 – 37			x3
Is	2.8 – 20			x3

Is	10.10 – 11	x3
Ezek	18.6 – 15	x3
Hos	8.4 – 6	x3
Zech	13.1 – 2	x3

Bow see **Worship**

Disgusting

Deut	29.17 **disgusting idols** made of wood, stone,
2 Kgs	16.3 to **idols**, imitating the **disgusting** practice
	23.13 the worship of **disgusting idols** — Astarte
2 Chr	28.3 to **idols**, imitating the **disgusting** practice
	34.33 **disgusting idols** that were in the
Jer	32.34 their **disgusting idols** in the Temple
	50.2 **idols** are put to shame, her **disgusting**
Ezek	7.20 they used them to make **disgusting idols**.
	11.18 **disgusting idols** they find.
	11.21 filthy, **disgusting idols**.
	14.6 back and leave your **disgusting idols**
	16.36 lovers and to all your **disgusting idols**,
	18.12 worships **disgusting idols**,
	20.7 them to throw away the **disgusting idols**
	20.8 not throw away their **disgusting idols**
	37 23 defile themselves with **disgusting idols**
1 Pet	4.3 and the **disgusting** worship of **idols**.

Evil see **Sin**

God, Lord

Ex	20.5 any **idol** or worship it, because I am the **Lord**
Lev	26.1 The **Lord** said, "Do not make **idols**
Deut	4.25 an **idol** in any form at all. This is evil in the **Lord's** sight,
	5.9 **idol** or worship it, for I am the **Lord**
	7.25 because the **Lord** hates **idolatry**.
	7.26 **idols**...are under the **Lord's** curse.
	16.22 for **idol** worship; the **Lord** hates them.
	27.15 **God's** curse on anyone who makes an **idol**
	27.15 the **Lord** hates **idolatry**.
	32.16 Their **idolatry** made the **Lord** jealous;
Judg	8.27 abandoned **God**...to worship the **idol**.
1 Sam	12.10 you, **Lord**, and worshipped the **idols**
1 Kgs	18.18 the **Lord's** commands and worshipping the **idols**
2 Kgs	17.12 **Lord's** command not to worship **idols**.
	17.41 worshipped the **Lord**, but they also worshipped their **idols**;
	21.16 into **idolatry**, causing them to sin against the **Lord**.
1 Chr	16.26 are only **idols**, but the **Lord** created
2 Chr	33.22 the **Lord**, and he worshipped the **idols**
Ps	40.4 the **Lord**, who do not turn to **idols**
	96.5 are only **idols**, but the **Lord** created
Is	2.17 **Idols** will completely disappear, and the **Lord** alone
Jer	25.6 the **Lord** angry by worshipping the **idols**
Ezek	8.3 an **idol** that was an outrage to **God**.
	8.5 the **idol** that was an outrage to **God**.
	14.6 **Lord**, am saying: Turn back and leave your disgusting **idols**.
	30.13 **Lord** says, "I will destroy the **idols**
Hos	14.3 say to our **idols** that they are our **God**.
2 Cor	6.16 can **God's** temple come to terms with pagan **idols**?
1 Thes	1.9 you turned away from **idols** to **God**,

Immoral

Ezek	23.49 your **immorality** and...worshipping **idols**.
1 Cor	5.11 is **immoral** or greedy or worships **idols**
	6.9 who are **immoral** or who worship **idols**
Rev	2.14 food...offered to **idols** and to practise sexual **immorality**.

Lord see **God**

Pagan

2 Kgs	23.24 **idols**, and all other **pagan** objects of
Ezek	18.12 **pagan** shrines, worships disgusting **idols**,
2 Cor	6.16 temple come to terms with **pagan idols**?

Save

Is	45.20 **idols** of wood and pray to gods that cannot **save** them —
	46.2 The **idols** cannot **save** themselves;
	57.13 let those **idols** of yours **save** you!

Serve

Ezek	20.24 same **idols** their ancestors had **served**.
	20.39 Go on and **serve** your **idols**!
Hos	10.5 who **serve** the **idol** will weep over it.
1 Thes	1.9 from **idols** to God, to **serve** the true

Shame

1 Kgs	21.26 most **shameful** sins by worshipping **idols**,
Ps	97.7 who worships **idols** is put to **shame**;
Jer	50.2 Babylon's **idols** are put to **shame**,
	51.47 **idols**. The whole country will be put to **shame**,

Sin, Evil

Deut	4.16 not **sin** by making for yourselves an **idol**
	4.25 not **sin** by making for yourselves an **idol** in any form at all. This is **evil**
	32.16 **idolatry** made the Lord jealous; the **evil**
Judg	3.7 they **sinned** against him and worshipped the **idols**
1 Sam	15.23 and arrogance is as **sinful** as **idolatry**.
1 Kgs	16.13 their **idolatry** and because they led Israel into **sin**,
	16.26 leading the people into **sin** and **idolatry**.
	21.26 most shameful **sins** by worshipping **idols**,
2 Kgs	21.11 with his **idols** he has led the people of Judah into **sin**.
	21.16 Judah into **idolatry**, causing them to **sin**
Is	31.7 throw away the **sinful idols** you made
Jer	7.30 **evil** thing. They have placed their **idols**,
Ezek	14.3 and are letting **idols** lead them into **sin**.
	14.4 to **idols** and lets them lead him into **sin**
	23.49 and your **sin** of worshipping **idols**.
	37.23 **idols**...or corrupt themselves with **sin**.
Hos	13.2 **sinning** by making...**idols** of silver,
Zech	13.1 of Jerusalem from their **sin** and **idolatry**.

Trust

Ps	115.8 who **trust** in them become like the **idols**
	135.18 who **trust** in them become like the **idols**
Is	42.17 All who **trust** in **idols**,

Useless

Is	41.29 All these gods are **useless**...these **idols**
Jer	2.8 and worshipped **useless idols**.
	8.19 **idols**...your **useless** foreign gods?
	16.19 nothing but **useless idols**.

Worship, Bow

Ex	20.5 **bow** down to any **idol** or **worship** it,
Lev	19.4 Do not abandon me and **worship idols**
Deut	5.9 **bow** down to any **idol** or **worship** it,
	12.3 **idols**, so that they will never again be **worshipped**
	16.22 set up any stone pillar for **idol worship**
	27.15 **idol** of stone...and secretly **worships** it;
Judg	3.7 against him and **worshipped** the **idols**
	8.27 and went there to **worship** the **idol**.
	18.30 Dan set up the **idol** to be **worshipped**,
1 Sam	12.10 **worshipped** the **idols** of Baal and
1 Kgs	14.9 **idols** and metal images to **worship**.
	18.18 and **worshipping** the **idols** of Baal.
	19.18 not **bowed** to Baal or kissed his **idol**.
	21.26 most shameful sins by **worshipping idols**,
2 Kgs	17.12 Lord's command not to **worship idols**.
	17.15 **worshipped** worthless **idols** and became

2 Kgs	17.41	but they also **worshipped** their **idols**;
	21.21	**worshipped** the **idols** that his father
	23.13	the **worship** of disgusting **idols** — Astarte
	23.24	**idols**, and all...pagan objects of **worship**.
2 Chr	11.15	**worship** demons and the **idols** he made
	24.18	began to **worship idols** and the images
	25.14	**idols** back with him...**worshipped** them,
	25.20	he had **worshipped** the Edomite **idols**.
	33.19	and the **idols** that he **worshipped**
	33.22	**worshipped** the **idols** that his father
	36.14	round them in **worshipping idols**,
Ps	24.4	who do not **worship idols**
	40.4	turn to **idols** or join those who **worship**
	97.7	who **worships idols** is put to shame; all the gods **bow**
	106.19	and **worshipped** that **idol**;
	106.36	God's people **worshipped idols**,
Is	2.8	land is full of **idols**, and they **worship**
	10.10	those kingdoms that **worship idols**,
	21.9	the **idols** they **worshipped** lie shattered
	44.17	into an **idol**, and then he...**worships** it.
	44.19	into an **idol**. Here I am **bowing** down
Jer	1.16	have made **idols** and **worshipped** them.
	2.5	They **worshipped** worthless **idols**
	2.8	and **worshipped** useless **idols**.
	8.19	me angry by **worshipping** your **idols** and by **bowing** down
	9.14	and have **worshipped** the **idols** of Baal
	25.6	the Lord angry by **worshipping** the **idols**
	44.8	make me angry by **worshipping idols**
Ezek	6.3	the places where people **worship idols**.
	11.21	love to **worship** filthy, disgusting **idols**.
	14.7	turns away from me and **worships idols**,
	16.24	you built places to **worship idols**
	16.31	street you built places to **worship idols**
	16.39	engage in prostitution and **worship idols**.
	18.6	**worship** the **idols** of the Israelites
	18.12	**worships** disgusting **idols**,
	18.15	**worship** the **idols** of the Israelites
	20.16	they preferred to **worship** their **idols**.
	20.24	**worshipped** the same **idols** their
	22.3	defiled yourself by **worshipping idols**,
	23.7	herself by **worshipping** Assyrian **idols**.
	23.49	and your sin of **worshipping idols**.
	33.25	You **worship idols**.
	44.10	deserted me and **worshipped idols**.
	44.12	they conducted the **worship** of **idols**
Hos	6.10	defiled themselves by **worshipping idols**.
	10.8	where the people of Israel **worship idols**,
	12.11	Yet **idols** are **worshipped** in Gilead,
	13.2	images to **worship** — **idols** of silver,
Jon	2.8	Those who **worship** worthless **idols**
Zech	13.2	take away the desire to **worship idols**.
Acts	7.43	**idols** that you had made to **worship**.
1 Cor	5.10	or are thieves or who **worship idols**.
	5.11	is immoral or greedy or **worships idols**
	6.9	who are immoral or who **worship idols**
	10.7	to **worship idols**, as some of them did
	10.14	keep away from the **worship** of **idols**.
	12.2	to the **worship** of lifeless **idols**.
Gal	5.20	in **worship** of **idols** and witchcraft
1 Pet	4.3	and the disgusting **worship** of **idols**.
Rev	9.20	stop **worshipping** demons, nor the **idols**
	21.8	practise magic, those who **worship idols**,
	22.15	**worship idols** and those who are liars

IMAGE

	Rev	13.14 —	16.2	x7
	2 Kgs	17.10 —	19.18	x4
	2 Chr	33.3 —	34.4	x4

God
Ps	106.20	the glory of **God** for the **image**
Rom	1.23	immortal **God**, they worship **images**

1 Cor	11.7	he reflects the **image** and glory of **God**.

Gods, Goddess, Idols
1 Sam	7.3	**gods** and the **images** of the **goddess**
1 Kgs	14.9	anger by making **idols** and metal **images**
	16.33	an **image** of the **goddess** Asherah.
2 Kgs	13.6	**image** of the **goddess** Asherah remained
	17.10	and **images** of the **goddess** Asherah,
	18.4	the **images** of the **goddess** Asherah.
	19.18	which were no **gods** at all, only **images**
	21.3	made an **image** of the **goddess** Asherah,
2 Chr	24.18	**idols** and the **images** of the **goddess**
	33.3	made **images** of the **goddess** Asherah,
	33.15	**gods** and the **image** that he had placed
	34.4	**images** of Asherah and...the other **idols**
Is	37.19	which were no **gods** at all, only **images**
	42.17	who call **images** their **gods**,
	44.10	a metal **image** to worship as a **god**!
	48.5	**idols** and **images** made them happen.
Jer	50.2	**idols** are put to shame, her...**images**
Dan	11.8	the **images** of their **gods** and the articles
Hos	3.4	**idols** or **images** to use for divination.
	13.2	**images** to worship — **idols** of silver,
Amos	5.26	**images** of Sakkuth, your king **god**,
Mic	5.14	down the **images** of the **goddess** Asherah
Acts	7.43	the **image** of Rephan, your star **god**;

Sin
Hos	13.2	keep on **sinning** by making metal **images**

IMMORALITY

1 Cor	5.1 —	7.2	x9
Ezek	23.13 —	24.13	x7
Rev	17.2 —	19.2	x7
2 Pet	2.2 – 18		x4
Judg	19.23 —	20.10	x3
Rev	2.14 – 21		x3

Evil see Sin

Greed, Lust
1 Cor	5.10	mean pagans who are **immoral** or **greedy**
	5.11	is **immoral** or **greedy** or worships idols
2 Cor	12.21	the **immoral** things they have done...**lust**
Eph	5.3	sexual **immorality** or indecency or **greed**
	5.5	**immoral**, indecent, or **greedy**
Col	3.5	as sexual **immorality**, indecency, **lust**,
2 Pet	2.18	use **immoral** bodily **lusts** to trap those
Rev	14.8	the strong wine of her **immoral lust**!
	18.3	the strong wine of her **immoral lust**.
	18.9	**immorality** and **lust** will cry and weep

Perversion
1 Tim	1.10	for the **immoral**, for sexual **perverts**
Jude	.7	in sexual **immorality** and **perversion**:
Rev	21.8	**perverts**, murderers, the **immoral**,
	22.15	the **perverts** and...the **immoral**

Sin, Evil
Gen	39.9	I do such an **immoral** thing and **sin**
Judg	19.23	Don't do such an **evil**, **immoral** thing!
	20.6	have committed an **evil** and **immoral** act
Ezek	23.49	you for your **immorality** and your **sin**
Mk	7.21	**evil** ideas which lead him to do **immoral**
1 Cor	6.18	**immorality**. Any other **sin** a man
Col	3.5	sexual **immorality**, indecency, lust, **evil**
2 Pet	2.14	**immoral** women; their appetite for **sin**

IMPOSSIBLE

	Gen	18.25 — 20.17	x3

God
Mt	19.26	This is **impossible** for man, but for **God**
Mk	10.27	**impossible** for man, but not for **God**;
Lk	18.27	**impossible** for man is possible for **God**,
Acts	26.8	it **impossible** to believe that **God** raises
1 Cor	1.21	**God** in his wisdom made it **impossible**

INCENSE

	2 Chr	25.14 —	30.14	x12
	Ex	30.1 —	31.11	x10
	Num	16.6 – 47		x7
	2 Kgs	14.4 —	18.4	x6
	Ex	35.8 – 28		x4
	Lev	2.1 – 16		x4
	Lev	4.7 —	6.15	x4
	Song·	3.6 —	4.14	x4
	Rev	8.3 – 5		x4
	Ex	39.38 —	40.27	x3
	Lev	16.12 – 13		x3
	Num	4.7 —	5.15	x3
	Is	65.3 —	66.3	x3
	Jer	17.26 —	19.13	x3
	Lk	1.9 – 11		x3

Altar

Ex 30.1 Make an **altar**...for burning **incense**.
     30.9 offer on this **altar** any forbidden **incense**,
     30.27 the **altar** for burning **incense**,
     31.8 the **altar** for burning **incense**,
     35.15 the **altar** for burning **incense**
     37.25 He made an **altar**...for burning **incense**.
     40.5 Put the gold **altar** for burning **incense**
Lev 2.2 the **incense** and burn it on the **altar**
     4.7 corners of the **incense-altar** in the Tent.
     4.18 the **incense-altar** inside the Tent
     6.15 **incense** on it, and burn it on the **altar**
     16.12 **altar** and two handfuls of fine **incense**
     26.30 tear down your **incense-altars**,
Num 16.6 and **incense**...and take them to the **altar**.
     16.17 **incense** on it...present it at the **altar**.
     16.40 come to the **altar** to burn **incense**
1 Sam 2.28 serve at the **altar**, to burn the **incense**,
2 Kgs 17.11 burnt **incense** on all the pagan **altars**
1 Chr 28.18 the **altar** on which **incense** was burnt
2 Chr 14.5 **incense-altars** from all the cities
     26.16 to burn **incense** on the **altar** of incense.
     26.19 in the Temple beside the **incense altar**
     32.12 worship and burn **incense** at one **altar**
     34.4 and tore down the **incense-altars**
     34.7 broke in pieces all the **incense-altars**.
Is 17.8 and **altars** for burning **incense**.
     27.9 no more **incense-altars** or symbols
     65.3 and burn **incense** on pagan **altars**.
Ezek 6.4 and the **incense-altars** broken.
     6.6 **incense-altars** will be shattered,
Lk 1.9 by lot to burn **incense** on the **altar**.
     1.11 the **altar** where the **incense** was burnt.
Heb 9.4 gold **altar** for the burning of **incense**
Rev 8.3 gold **incense-burner**...stood at the **altar**.

God's People

Jer 18.15 Yet **my people**...burn **incense** to idols.
Hos 11.2 **My people**...burnt **incense** to idols.
Rev 5.8 **incense**...the prayers of **God's people**.
     8.3 **incense** to add to the prayers of all **God's people**
     8.4 **incense** went up with the prayers of **God's people**

Idols

2 Chr 34.7 **idols** to dust, and broke in pieces all the **incense-altars**.
Is 66.3 they offer **incense** or pray to an **idol**.
Jer 18.15 they burn **incense** to **idols**.
Ezek 6.6 **idols** will be smashed...their **incense-altars**
Hos 11.2 they burnt **incense** to **idols**.

Offer, Present, Sacrifice

Ex 30.8 This **offering** of **incense** is to continue
     30.9 **offer** on this altar any forbidden **incense**,
Lev 10.1 **incense**, and **presented** it to the Lord.
Num 16.17 put **incense** on it, and then **present** it

Num 16.35 250 men who had **presented** the **incense**.
1 Kgs 11.8 could burn **incense** and **offer sacrifices**
     22.43 **offer sacrifices** and burn **incense** there.
2 Kgs 12.3 **offer sacrifices** and burn **incense** there.
            Also: 14.4; 15.4; 15.35
     16.4 **offered sacrifices** and burnt **incense**.
1 Chr 6.49 **presented** the **offerings** of incense
2 Chr 2.4 **incense** of...spices, where we will **present**
     13.11 **offer** him **incense** and animal **sacrifices**
     28.3 burnt **incense**...and even **sacrificed**
     28.4 **offered sacrifices** and burnt **incense**.
     29.7 to burn **incense** or **offer burnt-offerings**
     30.14 **offering sacrifices** and burning **incense**
Neh 13.5 for storing **offerings** of corn and **incense**,
Ps 141.2 as **incense**...as an evening **sacrifice**.
Is 43.23 **offerings** or...asking for **incense**.
     65.3 **offer** pagan **sacrifices**...and burn **incense**
     66.3 they **offer incense** or pray to an idol.
Jer 17.26 **sacrifices**, grain-offerings and **incense**,
     41.5 corn and **incense** to **offer** in the Temple.
     52.19 **incense**, and...for pouring out **offerings**
Ezek 16.18 you **offered** to the images the...**incense**
Hos 4.13 **offer sacrifices**, and...burn **incense**
     11.2 **sacrificed** to Baal; they burnt **incense**
Mal 1.11 they burn **incense** to me and **offer**
2 Cor 2.15 sweet-smelling **incense** offered by Christ

Temple

2 Chr 26.16 into the **Temple** to burn **incense**
     26.19 in the **Temple** beside the **incense** altar
     27.2 sin by burning **incense** in the **Temple**.
Jer 41.5 corn and **incense** to offer in the **Temple**.
Lk 1.9 **incense**...So he went into the **Temple**

Worship

1 Chr 23.13 **incense** in the **worship** of the Lord,
2 Chr 2.4 I will **worship** him by burning **incense**
     29.11 burn **incense** to him and to lead the people in **worshipping**
     32.12 **worship** and burn **incense** at one altar

INNOCENT

	Gen	18.23 – 28		x7
	Job	9.15 – 23		x5
	Job	31.6 —	35.1	x5
	1 Kgs	2.5 – 32		x3
	Job	22.19 —	23.7	x3
	Prov	17.15 —	18.5	x3
	Mt	27.4 —	28.14	x3

Evil see Sin

God, Lord

Gen 18.26 **Lord** answered, "If I find fifty **innocent**
     20.4 **Lord**, I am **innocent**!
Job 9.21 **innocent** or guilty, **God** will destroy us.
     9.23 **innocent** man suddenly dies, **God** laughs.
     23.7 with **God**; he would declare me **innocent**
     34.5 that he is **innocent**, that **God** refuses
     35.1 that you are **innocent** in **God's** sight,
Ps 7.8 O **Lord**; you know that I am **innocent**
     24.5 **God** will declare them **innocent**.
     26.1 Declare me **innocent**, O **Lord**,
     26.6 **Lord**, I wash my hands to show that I am **innocent**
     35.24 O **Lord**, so declare me **innocent**;
     43.1 O **God**, declare me **innocent**,
Is 50.8 for **God**...will prove me **innocent**.
Rom 4.5 in the **God** who declares the guilty to be **innocent**,
Phil 2.15 be **innocent** and pure as **God's** perfect

Right

Ex 23.8 **right** and ruins the cause of those who are **innocent**.

INNOCENT — Right

2 Sam	22.21	I do what is **right**...I am **innocent**.
	22.25	**right**, because he knows...I am **innocent**.
Job	22.30	are **innocent**, if what you do is **right**.
	27.5	are **right**; I will insist on my **innocence**
	35.1	not **right**...to say that you are **innocent**
Ps	18.20	what is **right**...I am **innocent**.
	18.24	**right**, because he knows...I am **innocent**.
	26.1	me **innocent**...because I do what is **right**
Prov	17.26	not **right** to make an **innocent** person
	18.5	not **right** to...prevent the **innocent**
	21.8	the **innocent** do what is **right**.

Sin, Evil

2 Sam	4.11	**evil** men who murder an **innocent** man
Job	33.9	I am **innocent** and free from **sin**.
Prov	13.6	protects the **innocent**; wickedness is the downfall of **sinners**.
Mt	27.4	**sinned** by betraying an **innocent** man
Rom	16.19	but **innocent** in what is **evil**.

JEALOUS

| Deut | 32.16 — 21 | x3 |
| Rom | 10.19 — 11.14 | x3 |

Anger

Deut	32.16	Lord **jealous**; the evil...made him **angry**.
	32.21	idols they have made me **angry**, **jealous**
Prov	6.34	is never **angrier** than when he is **jealous**;
Ezek	35.11	you back for your **anger**, your **jealousy**,
	36.6	in **jealous anger** because of the way
Gal	5.20	they become **jealous**, **angry**,

Evil

Deut	32.16	made the Lord **jealous**; the **evil** they did
Mk	7.22	**evil** things; deceit, indecency, **jealousy**,
Rom	1.29	**evil**...and vice; they are full of **jealousy**,
1 Tim	6.4	**jealousy**, disputes, insults, **evil** suspicions;
1 Pet	2.1	of all **evil**; no more lying...or **jealousy**

Insult

2 Cor	12.20	**jealousy**, hot tempers and...**insults**
1 Tim	6.4	this brings on **jealousy**, disputes, **insults**,
1 Pet	2.1	or **jealousy** or **insulting** language.

Proud

Ps	73.3	because I was **jealous** of the **proud**
Mk	7.22	**jealousy**, slander, **pride**,
1 Cor	13.4	it is not **jealous** or conceited or **proud**;
Gal	5.26	We must not be **proud**...or be **jealous**

JESUS

see also **CHRIST**

Lk	1.31 — 24.28	x248
Mk	1.1 — 16.19	x240
Mt	7.28 — 24.3	x144
Jn	1.17 — 13.29	x134
Jn	16.19 — 21.25	x68
Mt	26.1 — 28.18	x53
Acts	1.1 — 11.20	x49
Rom	1.1 — 8.39	x24
Acts	15.11 — 22.8	x22
Mt	1.1 — 5.1	x21
Phil	1.1 — 4.23	x21
Eph	1.1 — 6.24	x20
1 Cor	1.1 — 6.11	x17
Gal	1.1 — 6.18	x17
1 Thes	1.1 — 5.28	x16
Heb	2.9 — 8.6	x15
1 Tim	1.1 — 6.14	x14
2 Thes	1.1 — 3.18	x13
2 Tim	1.1 — 4.1	x13
1 Jn	1.3 — 5.20	x13
Rom	13.14 — 16.27	x11
1 Pet	1.1 — 4.11	x9
2 Pet	1.1 — 3.18	x9

Heb	12.2 — 13.20	x7
2 Cor	1.1 — 20	x6
2 Cor	4.5 — 14	x6
Col	1.1 — 4.12	x6
Phlm	.3 — 25	x6
Jude	.1 — 25	x6
Rev	1.1 — 9	x6
Acts	13.23 — 38	x5
Acts	24.24 — 26.15	x4
1 Cor	15.31 — 16.24	x4
Tit	1.1 — 3.6	x4
1 Cor	11.23 — 12.3	x3
Rev	19.10 — 20.4	x3
Rev	22.16 — 21	x3

Children

Mt	18.2	So **Jesus** called a **child**, made him stand
	19.13	people brought **children** to **Jesus** for him
	19.14	**Jesus** said, "Let the **children** come
Mk	10.13	people brought **children** to **Jesus** for him
Lk	2.27	the parents brought the **child Jesus** into
	18.16	but **Jesus** called the **children** to him

God

Mk	5.7	**Jesus**, Son of the Most High **God**!
Lk	18.43	followed **Jesus**, giving thanks to **God**.
	22.17	**Jesus** took a cup, gave thanks to **God**
Jn	6.11	**Jesus** took the bread, gave thanks to **God**
	17.3	true **God**, and knowing **Jesus** Christ,
Acts	2.23	plan **God** had already decided that **Jesus**
	2.32	**God** has raised this very **Jesus** from
	2.36	this **Jesus**, whom you crucified, is the one that **God**
	4.33	**Jesus**, and **God** poured rich blessings
	5.30	The **God** of our ancestors raised **Jesus**
	7.55	heaven and saw **God's** glory and **Jesus**
	10.38	**Jesus** of Nazareth and how **God** poured
	13.23	**Jesus**...whom **God** made the Saviour
	20.21	to **God** and believe in our Lord **Jesus**.
Rom	1.6	**God** has called to belong to **Jesus**
	1.7	**God** our Father and the Lord **Jesus**
	1.8	I thank my **God** through **Jesus** Christ
	2.16	**God** through **Jesus** Christ will judge
	3.22	**God** puts people right through their faith in **Jesus** Christ.
	5.1	**God** through our Lord **Jesus** Christ.
	5.11	**God** has done through our Lord **Jesus**
	6.11	with **God** through Christ **Jesus**.
	7.25	Thanks be to **God**, who does this through our Lord **Jesus** Christ!
	8.11	If the Spirit of **God**, who raised **Jesus**
	8.39	**God** which is ours through Christ **Jesus**
	10.9	**Jesus** is Lord and believe that **God**
	15.6	**God** and Father of our Lord **Jesus**
1 Cor	1.3	**God** our Father and the Lord **Jesus**
	1.30	**God** has brought you into union with Christ **Jesus**,
	3.11	For **God** has already placed **Jesus** Christ
	6.11	right with **God** by the Lord **Jesus** Christ
2 Cor	1.1	apostle of Christ **Jesus** by **God's** will,
	1.2	**God** our Father and the Lord **Jesus**
	1.3	**God** and Father of our Lord **Jesus**
	1.19	For **Jesus** Christ, the Son of **God**
	1.20	through **Jesus** Christ our "Amen" is said to the glory of **God**.
	4.14	that **God**, who raised the Lord **Jesus**
	11.31	The **God** and Father of the Lord **Jesus**
	13.13	the Lord **Jesus** Christ, the love of **God**
Gal	1.1	from **Jesus** Christ and **God** the Father,
	1.3	**God** our Father and the Lord **Jesus**
	2.16	**God** only through faith in **Jesus** Christ,
	3.26	**God's** sons in union with Christ **Jesus**.
Eph	1.1	**God's** will is an apostle of Christ **Jesus**
	1.2	**God** our Father and the Lord **Jesus**

Eph	1.3	**God** and Father of our **Lord Jesus**
	1.5	**God** had already decided that through **Jesus** Christ
	1.17	ask the **God** of our **Lord Jesus** Christ,
	3.6	that **God** made through Christ **Jesus**.
	6.23	**God** the Father and the **Lord Jesus**
Phil	1.2	**God** our Father and the **Lord Jesus**
	2.11	that **Jesus** Christ is Lord, to the glory of **God**
	3.14	which is **God's** call through Christ **Jesus**
	4.19	Christ **Jesus**, my **God** will supply all
Col	1.1	**God's** will is an apostle of Christ **Jesus**,
	1.3	**God**, the Father of our **Lord Jesus**.
	3.17	Lord **Jesus**, as you give thanks...to **God**
1 Thes	1.1	to **God** the Father and the **Lord Jesus**
	3.11	May our **God** and Father himself and our Lord **Jesus** prepare
	3.13	**God** and Father when our Lord **Jesus**
	4.14	**God** will take back with **Jesus** those
2 Thes	1.1	to **God** our Father and the **Lord Jesus**
	1.2	**God** our Father and the **Lord Jesus**
	1.12	grace of our **God** and of the Lord **Jesus**
	2.16	our Lord **Jesus** Christ himself and **God**
1 Tim	1.1	of **God** our Saviour and Christ **Jesus**
	1.2	**God** the Father and Christ **Jesus** our
	1.16	**God** was merciful to me in order that Christ **Jesus** might show
	5.21	**God** and of Christ **Jesus** and of the
2 Tim	1.1	apostle of Christ **Jesus** by **God's** will,
	1.2	**God** the Father and Christ **Jesus** our
	4.1	the presence of **God** and of Christ **Jesus**
Tit	1.1	servant of **God** and an apostle of **Jesus**
	1.4	May **God** the Father and Christ **Jesus**
	2.13	of our great **God** and Saviour **Jesus**
Phlm	.3	**God** our Father and the **Lord Jesus**
Heb	3.1	Think of **Jesus**, whom **God** sent
	4.14	into the very presence of **God** — **Jesus**,
	10.10	**Jesus** Christ did what **God** wanted
	13.15	to **God** as our sacrifice through **Jesus**,
	13.20	**God** has raised from death our Lord **Jesus**
Jas	1.1	of **God** and of the Lord **Jesus** Christ:
1 Pet	1.3	**God** and Father of our **Lord Jesus**
	2.5	sacrifices to **God** through **Jesus** Christ.
	4.11	may be given to **God** through **Jesus**
2 Pet	1.1	of our **God** and Saviour **Jesus**
	1.2	your knowledge of **God** and of **Jesus**
1 Jn	2.6	with **God** should live just as **Jesus**
	5.20	true **God** — in union with his Son **Jesus**
2 Jn	1.3	May **God** the Father and **Jesus** Christ
Jude	.21	**God**, as you wait for our Lord **Jesus**
	.25	only **God** our Saviour, through **Jesus**
Rev	1.2	**God** and the truth revealed by **Jesus**
	1.9	**God's** word and the truth that **Jesus**
	14.12	who obey **God's** commandments and are faithful to **Jesus**.

Lord

Mk	16.19	the **Lord Jesus** had talked with them
Lk	24.3	not find the body of the **Lord Jesus**.
Acts	1.21	to the resurrection of the **Lord Jesus**.
	2.36	**Jesus**, whom you crucified, is the one that God has made **Lord**
	4.33	to the resurrection of the **Lord Jesus**,
	7.59	**Lord Jesus**, receive my spirit!
	8.16	baptized in the name of the **Lord Jesus**.
	9.17	the **Lord** has sent me — **Jesus** himself,
	10.36	peace through **Jesus** Christ, who is **Lord**
	11.17	we believed in the **Lord Jesus** Christ;
	11.20	the Good News about the **Lord Jesus**.
	15.11	saved by the grace of the **Lord Jesus**,
	15.26	in the service of our **Lord Jesus** Christ.
	16.31	Believe in the **Lord Jesus**,
	19.5	baptized in the name of the **Lord Jesus**

Acts	19.13	tried to use the name of the **Lord Jesus**
	19.17	**Lord Jesus** was given greater honour.
	20.21	and believe in our **Lord Jesus**.
	20.24	the work that the **Lord Jesus** gave me
	20.35	words that the **Lord Jesus** himself said,
	21.13	die there for the sake of the **Lord Jesus**.
	26.15	And the **Lord** answered, 'I am **Jesus**,
	28.31	and taught about the **Lord Jesus** Christ,
Rom	1.3	**Lord Jesus** Christ: as to his humanity,
	1.7	the **Lord Jesus** Christ give you grace
	4.24	in him who raised **Jesus** our **Lord**
	5.1	peace with God through our **Lord Jesus**
	5.11	God has done through our **Lord Jesus**
	5.21	life through **Jesus** Christ our **Lord**.
	6.23	in union with Christ **Jesus** our **Lord**.
	7.25	does this through our **Lord Jesus** Christ!
	8.39	is ours through Christ **Jesus** our **Lord**.
	10.9	confess that **Jesus** is **Lord** and believe
	13.14	take up the weapons of the **Lord Jesus**
	14.14	with the **Lord Jesus** makes me certain
	15.6	and Father of our **Lord Jesus**
	15.30	our **Lord Jesus** Christ and by the love
	16.20	grace of our **Lord Jesus** be with you.
1 Cor	1.2	who worship our **Lord Jesus** Christ,
	1.3	the **Lord Jesus** Christ give you grace
	1.7	as you wait for our **Lord Jesus** Christ
	1.8	on the Day of our **Lord Jesus** Christ.
	1.9	with his Son **Jesus** Christ, our **Lord**.
	1.10	the authority of our **Lord Jesus** Christ
	5.3	our **Lord Jesus** already passed judgement
	6.11	right with God by the **Lord Jesus** Christ
	8.6	there is only one **Lord**, **Jesus** Christ,
	9.1	Haven't I seen **Jesus** our **Lord**?
	11.23	passed on to you: that the **Lord Jesus**,
	12.3	can confess "**Jesus** is **Lord**," unless
	15.31	in union with Christ **Jesus** our **Lord**,
	15.57	us the victory through our **Lord Jesus**
	16.23	grace of the **Lord Jesus** be with you.
2 Cor	1.2	the **Lord Jesus** Christ give you grace
	1.3	the God and Father of our **Lord Jesus**
	1.13	of our **Lord Jesus** you can be as proud
	4.5	we preach **Jesus** Christ as **Lord**,
	4.14	who raised the **Lord Jesus** to life,
	8.9	the grace of our **Lord Jesus** Christ;
	11.31	of the **Lord Jesus** — blessed be his name
	13.13	The grace of the **Lord Jesus** Christ
Gal	1.3	the **Lord Jesus** Christ give you grace
	6.14	only about the cross of our **Lord Jesus**
	6.18	May the grace of our **Lord Jesus** Christ
Eph	1.2	the **Lord Jesus** Christ give you grace
	1.3	the God and Father of our **Lord Jesus**
	1.15	I heard of your faith in the **Lord Jesus**
	1.17	ask the God of our **Lord Jesus** Christ,
	3.11	achieved through Christ **Jesus** our **Lord**.
	5.20	In the name of our **Lord Jesus** Christ
	6.23	the Father and the **Lord Jesus** Christ
	6.24	those who love our **Lord Jesus** Christ
Phil	1.2	the **Lord Jesus** Christ give you grace
	2.11	proclaim that **Jesus** Christ is **Lord**,
	3.8	the knowledge of Christ **Jesus** my **Lord**.
	3.20	the **Lord Jesus** Christ,
	4.23	May the grace of the **Lord Jesus** Christ
Col	1.3	the Father of our **Lord Jesus** Christ,
	2.6	you have accepted Christ **Jesus** as our **Lord**
	3.17	be done in the name of the **Lord Jesus**,
1 Thes	1.1	to God the Father and the **Lord Jesus**
	1.3	how your hope in our **Lord Jesus** Christ
	2.15	killed the **Lord Jesus** and the prophets,
	2.19	in the presence of our **Lord Jesus**
	3.11	and Father himself and our **Lord Jesus**
	3.13	and Father when our **Lord Jesus** comes
	4.1	urge you in the name of the **Lord Jesus**
	4.2	by the authority of the **Lord Jesus**.
	5.9	possess salvation through our **Lord Jesus**

1 Thes	5.23	at the coming of our **Lord Jesus** Christ.
	5.28	The grace of our **Lord Jesus** Christ
2 Thes	1.1	to God our Father and the **Lord Jesus**
	1.2	the **Lord Jesus** Christ give you grace
	1.7	do this when the **Lord Jesus** appears
	1.8	the Good News about our **Lord Jesus**.
	1.12	of our **Lord Jesus** will receive glory
	2.1	the coming of our **Lord Jesus** Christ
	2.8	but when the **Lord Jesus** comes,
	2.14	of the glory of our **Lord Jesus** Christ.
	2.16	our **Lord Jesus** Christ himself and God
	3.6	**Lord Jesus** Christ to keep away from all
	3.12	**Lord Jesus** Christ we command these
	3.18	May the grace of our **Lord Jesus** Christ
1 Tim	1.2	Christ **Jesus** our **Lord** give you grace,
	1.12	I give thanks to Christ **Jesus** our **Lord**
	6.3	**Lord Jesus** Christ and with the teaching
	6.14	when our **Lord Jesus** Christ will appear.
2 Tim	1.2	Christ **Jesus** our **Lord** give you grace,
Phlm	.3	the **Lord Jesus** Christ give you grace
	.5	the faith you have in the **Lord Jesus**.
	.25	of the **Lord Jesus** Christ be with you
Heb	13.20	has raised from death our **Lord Jesus**
Jas	1.1	of God and of the **Lord Jesus** Christ:
	2.1	as believers in our **Lord Jesus** Christ,
1 Pet	1.3	the God and Father of our **Lord Jesus**
2 Pet	1.2	of God and of **Jesus** our **Lord**.
	1.8	knowledge of our **Lord Jesus** Christ.
	1.11	Kingdom of our **Lord** and Saviour **Jesus**
	1.14	our **Lord Jesus** Christ plainly told me.
	1.16	mighty coming of our **Lord Jesus** Christ.
	2.20	our **Lord** and Saviour **Jesus** Christ,
	3.18	of our **Lord** and Saviour **Jesus** Christ.
Jude	.4	**Jesus** Christ, our only Master and **Lord**.
	.17	the apostles of our **Lord Jesus** Christ.
	.21	for our **Lord Jesus** Christ in his mercy
	.25	through **Jesus** Christ our **Lord**,
Rev	22.20	So be it. Come, **Lord Jesus**!
	22.21	May the grace of the **Lord Jesus**

Mercy

1 Tim	1.2	**Jesus** our **Lord** give you grace, **mercy**,
2 Tim	1.2	**Jesus** our **Lord** give you grace, **mercy**,
2 Jn	.3	**Jesus** Christ, the Father's Son, give us grace, **mercy**,
Jude	.21	our **Lord Jesus** Christ in his **mercy**

Messiah

Mt	1.12	of **Jesus**, who was called the **Messiah**.
	27.17	**Jesus** Barabbas or **Jesus** called the **Messiah**?
	27.22	shall I do with **Jesus** called the **Messiah**?
Jn	9.22	he believed that **Jesus** was the **Messiah**
	20.31	may believe that **Jesus** is the **Messiah**,
Acts	3.20	he will send **Jesus**, who is the **Messiah**
	4.27	**Jesus**, your holy Servant, whom you made **Messiah**.
	5.42	about **Jesus** the **Messiah**.
	9.22	his proofs that **Jesus** was the **Messiah**
	17.3	This **Jesus**...is the **Messiah**.
	18.5	that **Jesus** is the **Messiah**.
	18.28	that **Jesus** is the **Messiah**.
1 Jn	2.22	who says that **Jesus** is not the **Messiah**.
	5.1	believes that **Jesus** is the **Messiah**

JEWS

Acts	16.1	—	26.23	x59
Esth	8.1	—	10.3	x43
Acts	9.22	—	14.19	x19
Esth	2.5	—	6.13	x17
Rom	1.16	—	3.30	x17
Jn	18.12	—	20.19	x15
Jn	1.19	—	5.18	x13
Rom	9.24	—	11.31	x13
Neh	4.1	—	7.65	x12

Gal	1.13	—	3.28	x12
Jn	7.1	—	9.22	x8
Ezra	4.4	—	6.14	x7
Acts	4.5	—	6.9	x6
Rom	15.8	—	16.21	x6
Mt	27.11	—	28.15	x5
Mk	15.2 – 26			x5
Jn	11.51	—	13.33	x5
Eph	2.11	—	3.6	x5
Lk	23.3 – 38			x4
Dan	2.25	—	3.12	x3
Acts	2.5 – 14			x3
1 Cor	1.22 – 24			x3
1 Cor	9.20	—	10.32	x3

Authorities

Mt	27.18	very well that the **Jewish authorities**
Jn	1.19	The **Jewish authorities** in Jerusalem
	2.18	The **Jewish authorities** replied
	5.10	**Jewish authorities** told the man
	5.15	man left and told the **Jewish authorities**
	5.18	This saying made the **Jewish authorities**
	7.1	because the **Jewish authorities** there
	7.11	**Jewish authorities** were looking for him
	7.13	were afraid of the **Jewish authorities**.
	7.15	**Jewish authorities** were greatly surprised
	7.35	The **Jewish authorities** said
	8.22	So the **Jewish authorities** said
	9.18	The **Jewish authorities**
	9.22	were afraid of the **Jewish authorities**,
	11.53	on the **Jewish authorities** made plans
	12.42	many of the **Jewish authorities** believed
	13.33	what I told the **Jewish authorities**,
	18.14	who had advised the **Jewish authorities**
	18.28	The **Jewish authorities** did not go inside
	18.36	handed over to the **Jewish authorities**
	19.31	Then the **Jewish authorities** asked Pilate
	19.38	he was afraid of the **Jewish authorities**,
	20.19	were afraid of the **Jewish authorities**.
Acts	23.20	The **Jewish authorities** have agreed

Believe

Jn	12.11	**Jews** were rejecting them and **believing**
	12.42	**Jewish authorities believed** in Jesus;
Acts	10.45	**Jewish believers** who had come from
	14.1	of **Jews** and Gentiles became **believers**.
	14.2	the **Jews** who would not **believe**
	21.20	of **Jews** have become **believers**,
Rom	1.16	to save all who **believe**, first the **Jews**
Col	4.11	only **Jewish believers** who work with me

Custom

Jn	19.40	the **Jewish custom** of preparing a body
Acts	21.21	or follow the **Jewish customs**.
	26.3	know so well all the **Jewish customs**

Gentiles

Acts	2.11	**Jews** and **Gentiles** converted to Judaism
	13.43	by many **Jews** and by many **Gentiles**
	14.1	of **Jews** and **Gentiles** became believers.
	14.2	the **Jews**...stirred up the **Gentiles**
	14.5	Then some **Gentiles** and **Jews**
	17.17	with the **Jews** and with the **Gentiles**
	19.10	both **Jews** and **Gentiles**,
	19.17	**Jews** and **Gentiles** who lived in Ephesus
	20.21	**Jews** and **Gentiles** alike I gave solemn
	21.21	the **Jews** who live in **Gentile** countries
	26.23	to the **Jews** and to the **Gentiles**.
Rom	1.16	first the **Jews** and also the **Gentiles**.
	2.9	the **Jews** first and also for the **Gentiles**.
	2.10	the **Jews** first and also to the **Gentiles**.
	2.24	of you **Jews**, the **Gentiles** speak evil
	2.27	**Jews** will be condemned by the **Gentiles**
	3.1	**Jews**...any advantage over the **Gentiles**
	3.9	that **Jews** and **Gentiles** alike are all

Rom	3.29	of the **Jews** only? Is he not the God of the **Gentiles**
	9.24	**Jews** but also from among the **Gentiles**.
	10.12	no difference between **Jews** and **Gentiles**;
	11.11	to the **Gentiles**, to make the **Jews**
	11.28	**Jews** are God's enemies for the sake of you **Gentiles**.
1 Cor	1.23	the **Jews** and nonsense to the **Gentiles**;
	1.24	both **Jews** and **Gentiles**,
	10.32	no trouble either to **Jews** or **Gentiles**
	12.13	whether **Jews** or **Gentiles**,
2 Cor	11.26	from **fellow-Jews** and from **Gentiles**;
Gal	2.9	the **Gentiles** and they among the **Jews**.
	2.14	like a **Gentile**, not like a **Jew**.
	2.15	**Jews** by birth and not "**Gentile** sinners,
	3.28	no difference between **Jews** and **Gentiles**,
Eph	2.14	making **Jews** and **Gentiles** one people.
	2.18	all of us, **Jews** and **Gentiles**,
	3.6	the **Gentiles** have a part with the **Jews**
Col	3.11	distinction between **Gentiles** and **Jews**,

High Priest see Priest

Law

Acts	25.8	wrong against the **Law** of the **Jews**
Rom	2.12	from the **Law**. The **Jews** have the **Law**;
	2.17	yourself a **Jew**; you depend on the **Law**

Message, Preach

Acts	11.19	telling the **message** to **Jews** only.
	17.13	the **Jews**...heard that Paul had **preached**
	18.5	the **message**, testifying to the **Jews**
Rom	3.2	God trusted his **message** to the **Jews**.
1 Cor	1.23	a **message** that is offensive to the **Jews**
	1.24	both **Jews** and Gentiles, this **message**
Gal	2.7	of **preaching** the gospel to the **Jews**.

Peace

Esth	9.30	It wished the **Jews** **peace** and security
Rom	2.10	**peace** to all who do...good, to the **Jews**
Eph	2.14	has brought us **peace** by making **Jews**

Plan

Esth	3.6	He made **plans** to kill every **Jew**
	9.24	**Jews**; he had **planned** to wipe them out.
	9.25	the fate he had **planned** for the **Jews**
Jn	11.53	**Jewish** authorities made **plans** to kill
Acts	9.23	**Jews** met together and made **plans** to
	23.12	**Jews** met together and made a **plan**

Preach see Message

Priest, High Priest

Neh	2.16	to any of my **fellow-Jews** — the **priests**,
Jn	1.19	The **Jewish** authorities...sent some **priests**
Acts	19.14	were the sons of a **Jewish High Priest**
Heb	9.25	**Jewish High Priest** goes into the Most
	10.11	Every **Jewish priest** performs his services
	13.10	**priests** who serve in the **Jewish** place
	13.11	The **Jewish High Priest** brings the blood

Religion

Acts	2.5	**Jews** living in Jerusalem, **religious** men
	10.28	a **Jew** is not allowed by his **religion**
Gal	1.13	I was devoted to the **Jewish religion**,
	1.14	in my practice of the **Jewish religion**,

Synagogue

Acts	17.17	in the **synagogue** with the **Jews**
	18.19	**synagogue**...discussions with the **Jews**.

Temple

Ezra	6.7	the **Jewish** leaders rebuild the **Temple**
Lk	2.46	**Temple**, sitting with the **Jewish** teachers,
Acts	25.8	Law of the **Jews** or against the **Temple**
	26.21	the **Jews** seized me...in the **Temple**,

Worship

Jn	4.20	**Jews** say that Jerusalem is...where we should **worship**
Jn	4.22	but we **Jews** know whom we **worship**,
Heb	13.10	serve in the **Jewish** place of **worship**

JOY

Is	51.3	—	56.7	x9
Phil	1.4	—	4.10	x8
Esth	8.15	—	9.22	x6
Prov	10.28	—	15.23	x6
1 Chr	15.16	—	16.33	x5
Is	23.7	—	26.19	x5
Jer	30.19	—	31.13	x5
2 Chr	29.30	—	30.26	x4
Ps	98.4 — 8			x4
Is	60.5	—	61.7	x4
Is	64.5	—	65.19	x4
1 Thes	1.6	—	3.9	x4
Ezra	6.16 — 22			x3
Ps	30.5 — 11			x3
Ps	65.8 — 13			x3
Ps	119.92 — 143			x3
Ps	126.2 — 6			x3
Is	35.2 — 10			x3
Lam	2.4 — 17			x3
Joel	1.12	—	2.21	x3
Zeph	3.14 — 18			x3
Acts	15.3	—	16.34	x3
Rom	14.17	—	15.32	x3

Celebrate, Feast, Festival

2 Chr	30.21	**Festival** of Unleavened Bread with...**joy**,
	30.23	So they **celebrated** with **joy**.
Ezra	6.22	seven days they **joyfully celebrated**
Esth	8.17	**Jews** held a **joyful** holiday with **feasting**
	9.17	they made it a **joyful** day of **feasting**.
	9.19	as a **joyous** holiday, a time for **feasting**
Ps	20.5	**joy** over your victory and **celebrate**
Zeph	3.18	as **joyful** as people at a **festival**.
Zech	8.19	become **festivals** of **joy** and gladness

Glad see Happy

God

Gen	21.6	**God** has brought me **joy** and laughter.
1 Sam	2.1	**joyful** I am because **God** has helped
2 Chr	29.30	**joy** as they knelt and worshipped **God**.
Neh	12.43	the people were full of **joy** because **God**
Job	5.11	it is **God** who raises the humble and gives **joy**
	22.26	in **God**...he is the source of your **joy**.
	33.26	he will worship **God** with **joy**;
Ps	47.1	Clap your hands for **joy**...Praise **God**
	66.1	Praise **God** with shouts of **joy**,
	81.1	Shout for **joy** to **God** our defender;
	84.2	I sing for **joy** to the living **God**.
	95.1	Let us sing for **joy** to **God**,
Joel	1.16	is no **joy** in the Temple of our **God**.
Hab	3.18	**joyful** and glad, because the Lord **God**
Acts	16.34	**joy**, because they now believed in **God**.
Rom	15.13	May **God**...fill you with all **joy**
	15.32	to you full of **joy**, if it is **God's** will,
Heb	1.9	**God**, has...given you the **joy** of an
	12.23	the **joyful** gathering of **God's** first-born

Happy, Glad, Rejoice

Deut	28.47	serve him with **glad** and **joyful** hearts.
1 Sam	2.1	my heart with **joy**; how **happy** I am
Neh	12.43	**joy** because God had made them...**happy**.
Esth	8.16	**Jews** there was **joy** and relief, **happiness**
	8.17	held a **joyful** holiday with feasting and **happiness**.
	9.22	into a time of **joy** and **happiness**.
Ps	5.11	**rejoice**; they can always sing for **joy**.
	28.7	me **glad**; I praise him with **joyful** songs.
	40.16	be **glad** and **joyful**.
	45.15	With **joy** and **gladness** they come
	51.8	me hear the sounds of **joy** and **gladness**;

113

Ps	67.4	the nations be **glad** and sing for **joy**,
	68.3	they are **happy** and shout for **joy**.
	70.4	be **glad** and **joyful**.
	100.2	**joy**; come before him with **happy** songs!
	149.5	**rejoice** in their triumph and sing **joyfully**
Prov	5.18	**happy** with your wife and find your **joy**
Song	3.11	on the day of his **gladness** and **joy**.
Is	9.3	**joy**, Lord; you have made them **happy**.
	12.3	**joy** to the thirsty...God's people **rejoice**
	25.9	**happy** and **joyful** because he has saved
	35.10	shouting for **joy**. They will be **happy**
	51.3	**Joy** and **gladness** will be there,
	51.11	shouting for **joy**. They will be **happy**
	61.3	**Joy** and **gladness** instead of grief,
	65.18	of **joy**, and her people will be **happy**.
Jer	7.34	**joy** and **gladness** and to the **happy**
	15.16	filled my heart with **joy** and **happiness**.
	16.9	**joy** and **gladness** and the **happy** sounds
	25.10	**joy** and **gladness** and the **happy** sounds
	31.13	into **joy**, their sorrow into **gladness**.
	33.11	**gladness** and **joy** and the **happy** sounds
	48.33	**Happiness** and **joy** have been taken
Joel	2.21	but be **joyful** and **glad**
Hab	3.18	I will still be **joyful** and **glad**,
Zeph	3.14	shout for **joy**, people of Israel! **Rejoice**
Zech	8.19	of **joy** and **gladness** for the people
	9.9	**rejoice**, people of Zion! Shout for **joy**,
Mt	2.9	**happy** they were, what **joy** was theirs!
Lk	6.23	Be **glad**...and dance for **joy**,
Acts	2.26	**gladness**, and my words are full of **joy**.
Phil	2.17	am **glad** and share my **joy** with you all.
	2.18	must be **glad** and share your **joy**
1 Pet	1.8	**rejoice** with a great and glorious **joy**

Honour

| Jer | 33.9 | will be a source of **joy**, **honour** |
| Heb | 1.9 | the **joy** of an **honour** far greater |

Jesus

| Lk | 10.21 | **Jesus** was filled with **joy** by the Holy |

Lord

Deut	16.11	Be **joyful** in the **Lord's** presence,
1 Sam	2.1	The **Lord** has filled my heart with **joy**;
1 Chr	16.33	for **joy** when the **Lord** comes to rule
Ezra	6.22	They were full of **joy** because the **Lord**
Neh	8.10	The **joy** that the **Lord** gives you
Ps	1.2	**joy** in obeying the Law of the **Lord**,
	32.11	the **Lord** has done. You that obey him, shout for **joy**!
	33.1	for **joy** for what the **Lord** has done;
	47.5	shouts of **joy**...as the **Lord** goes up.
	95.1	us praise the **Lord**! Let us sing for **joy**
	98.4	Sing for **joy** to the **Lord**, all the earth;
	98.6	and shout for **joy** to the **Lord**,
	98.8	sing together with **joy** before the **Lord**,
	100.2	Worship the **Lord** with **joy**;
Is	9.3	You have given them great **joy**, **Lord**;
Jer	31.7	The **Lord** says, "Sing with **joy**
Joel	2.21	**joyful** and glad because of all the **Lord**
Hab	3.18	be **joyful** and glad, because the **Lord**
Zech	2.10	The **Lord** said, "Sing for **joy**
Jn	20.20	were filled with **joy** at seeing the **Lord**.
Phil	2.29	with **joy**, as a brother in the **Lord**.
	3.1	be **joyful** in your union with the **Lord**.
	4.4	be **joyful** in your union with the **Lord**

Mourn

Job	5.11	and gives **joy** to all who **mourn**.
	30.31	**joyful** music, now I hear only **mourning**
Is	61.3	give to those who **mourn** in Zion **Joy**

Power

| 1 Chr | 16.27 | **power** and **joy** fill his Temple. |

Rejoice see Happy

Spirit of God

Lk	10.21	was filled with **joy** by the **Holy Spirit**
Acts	13.52	were full of **joy** and the **Holy Spirit**
Rom	14.17	and **joy** which the **Holy Spirit** gives.
Gal	5.22	But the **Spirit** produces love, **joy**
1 Thes	1.6	the **joy** that comes from the **Holy Spirit**

World

Ps	48.2	brings **joy** to all the **world**.
Is	14.7	**world enjoys** rest and peace, and everyone sings for **joy**.
Jn	17.13	**world** so that they might have my **joy**

JUDGE

Jas	2.4	—	5.12	x15
Ps	119.7	—	164	x11
1 Cor	4.3	—	6.6	x11
Rom	2.1	—	3.19	x9
Deut	16.18	—	17.12	x6
Is	3.2	—	5.16	x6
Jn	5.22	—	30	x6
Jn	7.24	—	9.39	x6
Rom	12.3	—	14.22	x6
1 Cor	10.15	—	11.34	x6
Rev	18.8	—	20.13	x6
Ps	9.4	—	19	x5
Joel	3.2	—	14	x5
Lk	18.2	—	8	x5
Jn	12.31	—	48	x5
1 Pet	4.5	—	17	x5
Ps	7.8	—	11	x4
Ps	75.2	—	7	x4
Ezek	21.30	—	23.36	x4
Ezek	33.20	—	34.22	x4
Jn	3.17	—	19	x4
Acts	23.3	—	25.10	x4
Heb	9.27	—	10.30	x4
Gen	30.6	—	31.53	x3
Deut	19.17	—	18	x3
1 Sam	7.17	—	8.2	x3
1 Kgs	7.7	—	8.32	x3
2 Chr	19.5	—	8	x3
Job	9.15	—	33	x3
Prov	24.12	—	25	x3
Jer	48.21	—	49.7	x3
Ezek	7.3	—	27	x3
Hos	5.1	—	6.5	x3
Mt	7.1	—	2	x3
Lk	12.14	—	58	x3
Jn	16.8	—	11	x3
1 Cor	2.14	—	15	x3
2 Cor	5.10	—	16	x3

Case, Court, Dispute

Num	35.24	such **cases** the community shall **judge**
Deut	1.16	**Judge** every **dispute** fairly,
	17.8	that some **cases** will be too difficult for the local **judges**
	17.9	present your **case**...to the **judge**
	19.18	The **judges** will investigate the **case**
2 Sam	15.4	**judge**! Then anyone who had a **dispute**
1 Kgs	7.7	**Judgement**, where Solomon decided **cases**,
2 Chr	19.8	as **judges** in **cases** involving a violation
Job	13.8	you going to argue his **case** in **court**?
Is	1.23	**court**...when widows present their **case**.
	3.13	to state his **case**; he is ready to **judge**
	41.1	Get ready to present your **case** in **court**;
	43.26	go to **court**...Present your **case**
	45.21	Come and present your **case** in **court**;
Dan	7.26	the heavenly **court** will sit in **judgement**,
Acts	25.6	sat down in the **court** of **judgement**
	25.10	the Emperor's own **court** of **judgement**,
1 Cor	6.6	and lets unbelievers **judge** the **case**!

Christ see Jesus

Condemn

Ps	7.11	judge and...condemns the wicked.
	51.4	right in judging me...condemning me.
	75.7	God who is the judge, condemning some
Lk	6.37	will not judge you; do not condemn
Jude	.15	judgement on all, to condemn them
Rev	19.2	are his judgements! He has condemned

Corrupt

Ps	94.20	nothing to do with corrupt judges,
	109.6	some corrupt judge to try my enemy,
Prov	17.23	Corrupt judges accept secret bribes
Lk	18.6	Listen to what that corrupt judge said.

Court see Case

Dead

Acts	10.42	judge of the living and the dead.
2 Tim	4.1	who will judge the living and the dead,
Heb	6.2	of the dead and the eternal judgement.
Pet	4.5	ready to judge the living and the dead.
	4.6	the dead, to those who had been judged
Rev	11.18	the time for the dead to be judged.
	20.12	dead were judged according to what
	20.13	the dead they held. And all were judged

Destroy

er	23.1	judgement on those rulers who destroy
Dan	7.26	sit in judgement...and destroy
Hos	6.5	message of judgement and destruction.
Heb	10.27	Judgement and...fire which will destroy
as	4.12	judge. He alone can save and destroy.
Pet	3.7	people will be judged and destroyed.

Dispute see Case

Evil see Sin

Favour

Gen	30.6	God has judged in my favour.
Num	35.24	shall judge in favour of the man
s	7.8	Judge in my favour, O Lord;
	9.4	and you have judged in my favour.
	10.18	you will judge in their favour,
	17.2	You will judge in my favour,
	103.6	Lord judges in favour of the oppressed
	146.7	he judges in favour of the oppressed
am	3.59	Judge in my favour
an	7.22	judgement in favour of the people of
k	18.7	judge in favour of his own people who
	18.8	he will judge in their favour and do it
n	8.50	and who judges in my favour.

God, Lord

en	16.5	the Lord judge which of us is right,
	30.6	God has judged in my favour.
	31.53	God of Nahor will judge between us.
eut	28.46	will be the evidence of God's judgement
dg	11.27	The Lord is the judge.
Sam	2.3	is a God who knows, and he judges all
	2.10	The Lord will judge the whole world;
	24.12	Lord judge which one of us is wrong
	24.15	The Lord will judge, and he will decide
Kgs	8.32	O Lord, listen in heaven and judge
Chr	16.12	that God performed and the judgements
Chr	6.23	O Lord, listen in heaven and judge
ob	9.15	is beg for mercy from God my judge.
	9.33	no one to judge both God and me.
	21.22	Can a man teach God, who judges
	22.13	What does God know...can he judge
	24.1	doesn't God set a time for judging,
	31.14	I say when God came to judge me?
s	7.8	Judge in my favour, O Lord;
	7.9	a righteous God and judge our thoughts
	7.11	God is a righteous judge
	9.7	the Lord...has set up his throne for judgement.

Ps	9.16	The Lord has revealed himself by his righteous judgements,
	10.5	He cannot understand God's judgements;
	19.9	The judgements of the Lord are just;
	26.2	Lord; judge my desires and thoughts.
	50.6	that God is righteous, that he...is judge.
	58.11	is indeed a God who judges the world.
	75.2	set a time for judgement," says God,
	75.7	it is God who is the judge,
	97.8	because of your judgements, O Lord.
	103.6	Lord judges in favour of the oppressed
	105.5	that God performed and the judgements
	111.10	the Lord; he gives sound judgement
	119.52	judgements...bring me comfort, O Lord.
	119.75	your judgements are righteous, Lord,
Prov	16.2	but the Lord judges your motives.
	21.2	that the Lord judges your motives.
	24.12	God knows and judges your motives.
Ecc	3.17	God is going to judge the righteous
	11.9	that God is going to judge you
	12.14	God is going to judge everything we do,
Is	3.13	The Lord is ready...to judge his people.
	3.14	The Lord is bringing...his people to judgement.
	4.4	Lord will judge and purify the nation
	9.8	The Lord has pronounced judgement
	33.14	God's judgement is like a fire that
Jer	4.12	the Lord himself who is pronouncing judgement
	11.20	Almighty Lord, you are a just judge;
	23.1	terrible will be the Lord's judgement
Ezek	5.8	the Sovereign Lord...will pass judgement
	18.30	the Sovereign Lord...will judge each
	34.17	the Sovereign Lord...will judge each
	34.20	Lord, tell you that I will judge
Joel	3.12	There I, the Lord, will sit to judge
Obad	.15	the Lord, will judge all nations.
Zeph	1.7	when the Lord will sit in judgement;
Zech	14.1	day when the Lord will sit in judgement
Mal	3.5	The Lord Almighty says, "I will appear among you to judge,
Mt	7.1	judge others, so that God will not judge
	7.2	God will judge you in the same way as you judge others,
Mk	4.24	rules you use to judge others will be used by God to judge
Lk	6.37	judge others, and God will not judge
	18.7	God not judge in favour of his own
Jn	5.30	I judge only as God tells me,
	16.8	is right and about God's judgement.
Acts	10.42	the one whom God has appointed judge
Rom	2.2	know that God is right when he judges
	2.3	think you will escape God's judgement?
	2.5	God's anger and righteous judgements
	2.11	God judges everyone by the same
	2.16	God through Jesus Christ will judge
	3.6	If God is not just, how can he judge
	3.19	the whole world under God's judgement.
	14.10	will stand before God to be judged
1 Cor	5.12	God will judge them.
	11.31	would not come under God's judgement.
	11.34	will not come under God's judgement
Gal	2.6	God does not judge by outward
Col	3.25	God judges everyone by the same
1 Thes	2.4	God wants us to, because he has judged
2 Thes	1.5	this proves that God's judgement is just
Heb	9.27	and after that be judged by God.
	10.30	The Lord will judge his people.
	12.23	have come to God, who is the judge
	13.4	God will judge those who are immoral
Jas	2.13	For God will not show mercy when he judges
	4.12	God is the only lawgiver and judge
	5.9	so that God will not judge you.

Jas	5.12	will not come under **God's judgement**.
1 Pet	1.17	you pray to **God**, who **judges** all people
	2.23	his hopes in **God**, the righteous **Judge**.
	4.5	to **God**, who is ready to **judge**
Rev	6.10	**Lord**...How long will it be until you **judge** the people
	16.7	**Lord God** Almighty! True and just indeed are your **judgements**!
	18.8	because the **Lord God**, who **judges** her,

Heaven

1 Kgs	8.32	listen in **heaven** and **judge** your servants.
2 Chr	6.23	listen in **heaven** and **judge** your servants.
Ps	50.4	**heaven** and earth...to see him **judge**
	76.8	your **judgement** known from **heaven**;
Dan	7.26	the **heavenly** court will sit in **judgement**,
Eph	6.9	Master in **heaven**, who **judges** everyone

Human

2 Chr	19.6	**judgement**; you are not acting on **human**
Jn	8.15	**judgements** in a purely **human** way;
1 Cor	4.3	**judged** by you or by any **human**
2 Cor	5.16	we **judge** anyone by **human** standards.

Jesus, Christ, Lord, Son of God

Jn	5.22	given his **Son** the full right to **judge**
	5.27	given the **Son** the right to **judge**
	19.13	he took **Jesus** outside and sat down on the **judge's** seat
Rom	2.16	God through **Jesus Christ** will **judge**
1 Cor	4.5	**judgement** must wait until the **Lord**
	11.32	are **judged** and punished by the **Lord**
2 Cor	5.10	before **Christ** to be **judged** by him
	5.16	at one time we **judged Christ**
2 Tim	4.1	God and of **Christ Jesus**, who will **judge**
	4.8	which the **Lord**, the righteous **Judge**,

Justice, Oppress, Poor, Right(eous), True

Gen	16.5	the Lord **judge** which of us is **right**,
	18.25	**judge** of all the earth has to act **justly**.
Job	24.1	set a time for **judging**, a day of **justice**
Ps	7.9	a **righteous** God and **judge** our thoughts
	7.11	God is a **righteous judge**
	9.8	he **judges** the nations with **justice**.
	9.16	himself by his **righteous judgements**,
	10.18	cries of the **oppressed**...you will **judge**
	19.9	The **judgements** of the Lord are **just**;
	48.11	You give **right judgements**;
	50.6	is **righteous**, that he himself is **judge**.
	51.4	So you are **right** in **judging** me;
	58.1	**just** decision? Do you **judge** all men
	67.4	you **judge** the peoples with **justice**
	72.1	king to **judge** with your **righteousness**
	72.4	May the king **judge** the **poor** fairly;
	76.9	**judgement**, to save all the **oppressed** on
	96.10	he will **judge** the peoples with **justice**.
	103.6	Lord **judges** in favour of the **oppressed**
	119.7	As I learn your **righteous judgements**,
	119.62	you for your **righteous judgements**.
	119.75	know that your **judgements** are **righteous**
	119.160	your **righteous judgements** are eternal.
	119.164	for your **righteous judgements**.
	146.7	he **judges** in favour of the **oppressed**
Prov	16.2	you do is **right**, but the Lord **judges**
	17.23	**judges** accept secret bribes, and...**justice**
	21.2	do is **right**, but...the Lord **judges**
	31.9	for them and be a **righteous judge**.
Ecc	3.17	to **judge** the **righteous** and the evil
Is	5.16	**right**...he reveals his holiness by **judging**
	11.4	**judge** the **poor** fairly...defend the **rights**
	28.6	of **justice** to those who serve as **judges**,
Jer	11.20	a **just judge**; you test people's thoughts
Hos	5.1	**judge** with **justice** — so **judgement** will
Lk	12.14	**right** to **judge** or to divide the property
	12.57	not **judge** for yourselves the **right** thing
Jn	5.22	given his Son the full **right** to **judge**,

Jn	5.27	he has given the Son the **right** to **judge**,
	5.30	so my **judgement** is **right**,
	7.24	and **judge** by **true** standards.
	8.16	**judgement** would be **true**, because I am
	16.8	is **right** and about God's **judgement**.
Acts	4.19	**judge** which is **right** in God's sight
	17.31	will **judge** the whole world with **justice**
Rom	2.2	God is **right** when he **judges** the people
	2.5	**righteous judgements** will be revealed.
	3.6	is not **just**, how can he **judge** the world?
	14.22	he does something he **judges** is **right**!
1 Cor	4.5	**judgement** on anyone before the **right**
Phil	1.9	**true** knowledge and perfect **judgement**,
2 Thes	1.5	this proves that God's **judgement** is **just**
2 Tim	4.8	which the Lord, the **righteous Judge**,
Jas	2.6	who **oppress** you and drag you before the **judges**?
1 Pet	2.23	hopes in God, the **righteous Judge**.
Rev	16.5	The **judgements** you have made are **just**,
	16.7	and **just** indeed are your **judgements**!
	19.2	**True** and **just** are his **judgements**
	19.11	it is with **justice** that he **judges**

Lord see **God, Jesus**

Motives

Prov	16.2	but the Lord **judges** your **motives**.
	21.2	that the Lord **judges** your **motives**.
	24.12	God knows and **judges** your **motives**.
Jas	2.4	**judgements** based on evil **motives**.

Oppress see **Justice**

Pass

Jn	8.15	I **pass judgement** on no one.
Rom	2.1	**pass judgement** on others?
	2.3	things for which you **pass judgement**
	14.10	vegetables — why do you **pass judgement**
1 Cor	4.3	I don't even **pass judgement** on myself.
	4.5	should not **pass judgement** on anyone

Poor see **Justice**

Punish

1 Sam	24.12	Lord **judge** which one of us is wrong! May he **punish**
1 Kgs	8.32	**judge** your servants. **Punish** the guilty
2 Chr	6.23	**judge** your servants. **Punish** the guilty
Prov	24.25	**Judges** who **punish** the guilty,
Ezek	7.27	I will **punish** you...and will **judge** you
1 Cor	11.32	are **judged** and **punished** by the Lord
Rev	6.10	**judge** the people on earth and **punish**

Right(eous) see **Justice**

Save

Ps	76.9	to pronounce **judgement**, to **save**
Jn	12.47	not to **judge** the world, but to **save** it.
Jas	4.12	**judge**. He alone can **save** and destroy.

Serve

Ex	18.22	Let them **serve** as **judges** for the people
	18.26	They **served** as **judges** for the people
Judg	4.4	was **serving** as a **judge** for the Israelites
1 Sam	7.17	where also he would **serve** as **judge**.
Job	24.1	for **judging**...for those who **serve** him?
Is	28.6	of **justice** to those who **serve** as **judges**,

Sin, Evil, Wicked

Ps	7.9	**judge** our thoughts...Stop the **wickedness**
	7.11	**judge** and always condemns the **wicked**.
	9.16	**judgements**, and the **wicked** are trapped
	51.4	**evil**. So you are **right** in **judging** me;
Prov	20.8	king sits in **judgement** and knows **evil**
Ecc	3.17	to **judge** the **righteous** and the **evil**
Is	57.3	Come here to be **judged**, you **sinners**
Mic	7.3	**evil**. Officials and **judges** ask for bribes.
Jn	16.8	wrong about **sin** and...God's **judgement**.
Rom	2.12	they **sin** and are **judged** by the Law.

Rom	5.16	After the one **sin**, cáme the **judgement**
1 Cor	14.24	convinced of his **sin**...He will be **judged**
1 Tim	5.24	**sins** go ahead of them to **judgement**;
Jas	2.4	**judgements** based on **evil** motives.

Son of God see Jesus

True see Justice

Wicked see Sin

JUSTICE

Prov	16.12	—	21.15	x7
Is	58.2	—	61.8	x7
Jer	20.12	—	23.5	x5
Amos	5.7	—	6.12	x5
Ps	119.106	—	172	x4
Is	42.1	—	6	x4
Job	36.3	—	37.23	x3
Prov	28.5	—	29.26	x3
Is	9.7	—	11.5	x3
Is	28.6	—	29.21	x3
Is	32.1	—	33.5	x3
Mic	3.1	–9		x3
Zech	7.9	—	8.16	x3
Rev	15.4	—	16.7	x3

Court

Ex	23.6	**justice** to a poor man...in **court**.
Ps	94.15	**Justice** will again be found in the **courts**,
Is	59.4	go to **court**, but you haven't got **justice**
Lam	3.36	When **justice** is perverted in **court**,
Amos	5.12	poor from getting **justice** in the **courts**.
	5.15	see that **justice** prevails in the **courts**.
Zech	8.16	In the **courts**, give real **justice**

Prevent

Prov	18.5	**prevent** the innocent...receiving **justice**.
Is	5.23	**prevent** the innocent from getting **justice**.
Amos	5.12	**prevent** the poor from getting **justice**

KIND

Prov	14.21	—	16.24	x4
Rom	11.22	—	12.8	x4
2 Sam	9.1	–7		x3
Ps	103.2	–13		x3
Prov	10.32	—	12.25	x3
Rom	1.31	—	2.4	x3
1 Pet	2.3	—	3.8	x3

Faithful

Gen	32.10	worth all the **kindness** and **faithfulness**
2 Sam	2.6	the Lord be **kind** and **faithful** to you
	15.20	the Lord be **kind** and **faithful** to you.
Ps	86.15	loving God...always **kind** and **faithful**.
Gal	5.22	patience, **kindness**, goodness, **faithfulness**,

God

Gen	33.11	**God** has been **kind** to me
Ps	51.18	**God** is **kind** and merciful.
	51.18	**God**, be **kind** to Zion and help her;
	86.15	loving **God**, always patient, always **kind**
Joel	2.13	**God**. He is **kind** and full of mercy;
Jon	4.2	**God**, always patient, always **kind**.
Rom	2.4	Surely you know that **God** is **kind**,
	11.22	see how **kind** and how severe **God** is
Tit	3.4	**kindness** ánd love of **God** our Saviour

Lord

Num	6.25	**Lord** be **kind** and gracious
Sam	2.6	**Lord** be **kind** and faithful to you
	15.20	**Lord** be **kind** and faithful to you.
Kgs	13.23	**Lord** was **kind** and merciful to them
Chr	30.9	The **Lord** your God is **kind**
Ps	4.6	**Lord**. Look on us with **kindness**!
	25.6	**Lord**, your **kindness** and constant love
	84.11	**Lord** is...blessing us with **kindness**
	103.2	**Lord**...do not forget how **kind** he is.

Ps	103.13	**kind** to his children, so the **Lord** is **kind**
	111.4	The **Lord**...is **kind**
Joel	2.13	the **Lord**...is **kind** and full of mercy;
Mk	5.19	**Lord** has done for you and how **kind**
1 Pet	2.3	have found out...how **kind** the **Lord** is.

Love

Ps	25.6	your **kindness** and constant **love**
	31.16	**kindness**; save me in your constant **love**.
	86.15	**loving** God, always patient, always **kind**
1 Cor	13.4	**Love** is patient and **kind**
Gal	5.22	**love**, joy, peace, patience, **kindness**
Tit	3.4	**kindness** and **love** of God our Saviour
1 Pet	3.8	**love** one another...and be **kind** and

Need

Gen	33.11	**kind**...and given me everything I **need**.
Ps	112.9	to the **needy**, and his **kindness**
2 Cor	9.9	generously to the **needy**; his **kindness**

KING

God, Lord

Ex	15.18	**Lord**, will be **king** for ever
Deut	33.5	The **Lord** became **king** of his people
1 Chr	16.31	Tell the nations that the **Lord** is **king**.
Job	34.18	**God** condemns **kings** and rulers
Ps	5.2	my **God** and **king**!
	9.7	the **Lord** is **king** for ever;
	10.16	**Lord** is **king** for ever and ever.
	18.50	**God** gives great victories to his **king**;
	20.6	**Lord** gives victory to his chosen **king**;
	20.9	victory to the **king**, O **Lord**;
	21.1	The **king** is glad, O **Lord**
	21.7	The **king** trusts in the **Lord**
	22.28	The **Lord** is **king**,
	24.8	Who is this great **king**? He is the **Lord**,
	24.10	is this great **king**? The triumphant **Lord**
	28.8	**Lord**...defends and saves his chosen **king**.
	29.10	The **Lord** rules...as **king**
	44.4	You are my **king** and my **God**;
	47.2	The **Lord**...is a great **king**,
	47.6	praise to **God**; sing praise to our **king**!
	47.7	**God** is **king** over all the world;
	68.14	**God** scattered the **kings** on Mount
	68.24	the procession of **God**, my **king**,
	72.1	the **king** to judge with your righteousness, O **God**;
	74.12	our **king** from the beginning, O **God**;
	84.3	my **king** and my **God**.
	84.9	Bless our **king**, O **God**,
	84.11	**Lord** is our protector and glorious **king**,
	89.18	Holy **God** of Israel, gave us our **king**.
	93.1	The **Lord** is **king**.
	95.3	mighty **God**, a mighty **king**
	96.10	The **Lord** is **king**!
	97.1	The **Lord** is **king**! Earth, be glad!
	98.6	shout for joy to the **Lord**, our **king**.
	99.1	The **Lord** is **king**;
	102.12	O **Lord**, are **king** for ever;
	103.19	The **Lord**...is **king**
	110.1	**Lord** said to my lord, the **king**,
	145.1	my **God** and **king**;
	146.10	**Lord** is **king** for ever.
Is	6.5	seen the **King**, the **Lord** Almighty!
	8.21	they will curse their **king** and their **God**.
	24.23	the **Lord** Almighty will be **king**.
	33.22	The **Lord** himself will be our **king**;
	41.21	The **Lord**, the **king** of Israel
	43.15	**God**. I created you...I am your **king**.
	52.7	Your **God** is **king**!
Jer	8.19	**Lord** no longer in Zion? Is Zion's **king**
	10.10	living **God** and the eternal **king**.
	46.18	am **king**. I am the living **God**.
	48.15	I am the **king**, the **Lord**

Jer	51.57	the **king**, have spoken, I am the **Lord**
Lam	5.19	O **Lord**, are **king** for ever,
Dan	2.47	Your **God** is...the **Lord** over **kings**,
	4.3	**God** is **king** for ever; he will rule
Obad	.21	the **Lord** himself will be **King**.
Mic	2.13	Their **king**, the **Lord** himself,
Zeph	3.15	**Lord**, the **king** of Israel, is with you;
Zech	14.9	**Lord** will be **king** over all the earth
	14.16	worship the **Lord** Almighty as **king**,
	14.17	**Lord** Almighty as **king**, then rain will
Lk	1.32	**God** will make him a **king**,
	19.38	**God** bless the **king** who comes
Jn	12.13	**God** bless him who comes...the **King**
Acts	13.22	**God** made David their **king**.
1 Tim	1.17	**King**, immortal and invisible...be honour
	6.15	**God**...**King** of kings and the **Lord**
Rev	12.10	**God** has shown his power as **King**!
	15.3	**Lord**...how great...are your deeds! **King**
	19.6	the **Lord**, our Almighty **God**, is **King**!

Jesus, Lord

Mt	27.37	**Jesus**, the **King** of the Jews.
Lk	23.42	me, **Jesus**, when you come as **King**!
Jn	19.19	**Jesus** of Nazareth, the **King** of the
Acts	17.7	another **king**, whose name is **Jesus**.
Rev	17.14	**Lord** of lords and **King** of kings.
	19.16	**King** of kings and **Lord** of lords.

KINGDOM

Mt	3.2	— 13.52	x31
Lk	6.20	— 14.15	x20
Mt	18.1	— 26.29	x18
Mk	9.1	— 12.34	x10
Lk	16.16	— 19.11	x10
Lk	21.31	— 23.50	x5
Mk	4.11 – 30		x3
Jn	18.36		x3

Christ, Son of God

Eph	5.5	the **Kingdom** of **Christ** and of God
Col	1.13	the **Kingdom** of his dear **Son**
2 Pet	1.11	eternal **Kingdom** of Jesus **Christ**

Father

Mt	13.43	like the sun in their **Father's Kingdom**.
	26.29	wine with you in my **Father's Kingdom**.
Lk	12.32	your **Father** is pleased to give you the **Kingdom**.
1 Cor	15.24	over the **Kingdom** to God the **Father**.
Rev	1.6	**kingdom** of priests to serve his...**Father**.

Glory

Ps	145.12	the **glorious** majesty of your **kingdom**.
Mk	10.37	your throne in your **glorious Kingdom**,
1 Thes	2.12	to share in his own **Kingdom** and **glory**.

God, Lord

1 Chr	28.5	to rule over Israel, the **Lord's kingdom**.
Ps	45.6	The **kingdom** that **God** has given you
Mt	6.33	else with the **Kingdom of God**
	12.28	the **Kingdom of God** has already come
	19.24	enter the **Kingdom of God** than for a
	21.31	going into the **Kingdom of God** ahead
	21.43	the **Kingdom of God** will be taken
Mk	1.15	and the **Kingdom of God** is near!
	4.11	the secret of the **Kingdom of God**,
	4.26	The **Kingdom of God** is like this.
	4.30	say the **Kingdom of God** is like?
	9.1	**Kingdom of God** come with power.
	9.47	enter the **Kingdom of God** with only
	10.14	**Kingdom of God** belongs to such as
	10.15	not receive the **Kingdom of God** like a child
	10.23	to enter the **Kingdom of God**!
	10.24	it is to enter the **Kingdom of God**!
	10.25	enter the **Kingdom of God** than for a

Mk	11.10	**God** bless the coming **kingdom**
	12.34	not far from the **Kingdom of God**.
	14.25	the new wine in the **Kingdom of God**.
	15.42	the coming of the **Kingdom of God**.
Lk	4.43	about the **Kingdom of God**
	6.20	the **Kingdom of God** is yours!
	7.28	who is least in the **Kingdom of God**
	8.1	about the **Kingdom of God**.
	8.10	the secrets of the **Kingdom of God**
	9.2	to preach the **Kingdom of God**
	9.11	about the **Kingdom of God**, and healed
	9.27	they have seen the **Kingdom of God**.
	9.60	proclaim the **Kingdom of God**.
	9.62	no use to the **Kingdom of God**.
	10.9	The **Kingdom of God** has come near
	10.11	the **Kingdom of God** has come near
	11.20	the **Kingdom of God** has already come
	13.18	What is the **Kingdom of God** like?
	13.20	compare the **Kingdom of God** with?
	13.28	prophets in the **Kingdom of God**,
	13.29	at the feast in the **Kingdom of God**.
	14.15	at the feast in the **Kingdom of God**!
	16.16	about the **Kingdom of God**
	17.20	when the **Kingdom of God** would
	17.20	The **Kingdom of God** does not come in
	17.21	because the **Kingdom of God** is within
	18.16	**Kingdom of God** belongs to such as
	18.17	not receive the **Kingdom of God** like a
	18.24	to enter the **Kingdom of God**!
	18.25	enter the **Kingdom of God** than for a
	18.29	for the sake of the **Kingdom of God**
	19.11	**Kingdom of God** was just about to
	21.31	the **Kingdom of God** is about to come.
	22.16	meaning in the **Kingdom of God**.
	22.18	this wine until the **Kingdom of God**
	23.50	coming of the **Kingdom of God**.
Jn	3.3	no one can see the **Kingdom of God**
	3.5	no one can enter the **Kingdom of God**
Acts	1.3	with them about the **Kingdom of God**.
	8.12	good news of the **Kingdom of God**
	14.22	troubles to enter the **Kingdom of God**,
	20.25	preaching the **Kingdom of God**.
	28.23	about the **Kingdom of God**,
	28.31	about the **Kingdom of God**.
Rom	14.17	For **God's Kingdom** is not a matter of
1 Cor	4.20	**Kingdom of God** is not a matter of
	6.9	will not possess **God's Kingdom**.
	6.10	of these will possess **God's Kingdom**.
	15.24	hand over the **Kingdom** to **God**
	15.50	blood cannot share in **God's Kingdom**,
Gal	5.21	will not possess the **Kingdom of God**.
Col	4.11	with me for the **Kingdom of God**,
Heb	1.8	Your **kingdom**, O **God**, will last

Heaven

Job	25.1	he keeps his **heavenly kingdom**
Dan	2.44	**God of heaven** will establish a **kingdom**
Mt	3.2	the **Kingdom of heaven** is near!
	4.17	the **Kingdom of heaven** is near!
	5.3	the **Kingdom of heaven** belongs to
	5.10	the **Kingdom of heaven** belongs to
	5.19	be least in the **Kingdom of heaven**.
	5.19	be great in the **Kingdom of heaven**.
	5.20	able to enter the **Kingdom of heaven**
	7.21	will enter the **Kingdom of heaven**,
	8.11	at the feast in the **Kingdom of heaven**
	10.7	The **Kingdom of heaven** is near!
	11.11	who is least in the **Kingdom of heaven**
	11.12	the **Kingdom of heaven** has suffered
	13.11	the secrets of the **Kingdom of heaven**
	13.24	The **Kingdom of heaven** is like this.
		Also: 13.31, 33, 44, 45, 47
	13.52	a disciple in the **Kingdom of heaven**

118

Mt	16.19	the keys of the **Kingdom of heaven**;
	18.1	the greatest in the **Kingdom of heaven**?
	18.3	never enter the **Kingdom of heaven**.
	18.4	The greatest in the **Kingdom of heaven**
	18.23	because the **Kingdom of heaven** is like
	19.12	for the sake of the **Kingdom of heaven**.
	19.14	because the **Kingdom of heaven** belongs
	19.23	to enter the **Kingdom of heaven**.
	20.1	The **Kingdom of heaven** is like this.
	22.2	The **Kingdom of heaven** is like this.
	23.13	the door to the **Kingdom of heaven**
	25.1	the **Kingdom of heaven** will be like
	25.14	the **Kingdom of heaven** will be like
2 Tim	4.18	safely into his **heavenly Kingdom**.

Justice
Ps	89.14	Your **kingdom** is founded on...**justice**;

Last
Ps	45.6	**kingdom**...God has given you will **last**
Dan	4.34	and his **kingdom** will **last** for all time.
	7.14	would **last** for ever, and his **kingdom**
Heb	1.8	**kingdom**, O God, will **last** for ever

Lord see God

Possess
Mt	25.34	Come and **possess** the **kingdom**
1 Cor	6.9	wicked will not **possess** God's **Kingdom**
	6.10	of these will **possess** God's **Kingdom**.
	15.50	**Kingdom**, and...mortal cannot **possess**
Gal	5.21	will not **possess** the **Kingdom** of God.
Jas	2.5	**possess** the **kingdom** which he promised

Power
Is	9.7	His royal **power** will...grow; his **kingdom**
Dan	6.26	His **kingdom** will never be destroyed, and his **power**
Mk	9.1	the **Kingdom** of God come with **power**.
1 Cor	15.24	**powers**, and will hand over the **Kingdom**

Son of God see Christ

World
Mt	24.14	**Kingdom** will be preached through all the **world**
Jn	18.36	**kingdom** does not belong to this **world**;

KNOWLEDGE

Prov	1.5	—	3.19	x9
2 Pet	1.2	—	3.18	x7
1 Cor	12.8	—	14.6	x6
Prov	8.10	—	10.14	x5
Prov	14.18	—	16.16	x4
Ecc	1.16	—	2.26	x4
1 Cor	8.1 – 11			x4
Col	1.9	—	3.10	x4
Gen	2.9	—	3.22	x3
2 Chr	1.10 – 12			x3

Life
Gen	2.9	**life** and the tree that gives **knowledge**
2 Pet	1.3	**life** through our **knowledge** of the one

Understand
Prov	2.6	him come **knowledge** and **understanding**.
1 Cor	13.2	all **knowledge** and **understand** all secrets;

Wisdom
1 Kgs	4.29	**wisdom** and insight, and **knowledge**
2 Chr	1.10	**wisdom** and **knowledge** I need to rule
	1.11	have asked for **wisdom** and **knowledge**
	1.12	I will give you **wisdom** and **knowledge**
Ps	119.66	Give me **wisdom** and **knowledge**,
Prov	1.5	even add to the **knowledge** of **wise** men
	2.6	gives **wisdom**; from him come **knowledge**
	2.10	**wise**, and your **knowledge** will give you
	3.19	by his **wisdom**; by his **knowledge** he set
	8.12	I am **Wisdom**, and...I have **knowledge**

Prov	10.14	The **wise** get all the **knowledge** they can
	15.2	**wise** people speak, they make **knowledge**
	15.7	**Knowledge**...by people who are **wise**
	16.16	have **wisdom** and **knowledge** than gold
	24.5	Being **wise** is better...**knowledge** is more
Ecc	1.16	what **wisdom** and **knowledge** really are.
	1.17	**knowledge** and foolishness, **wisdom** and
	2.21	with all your **wisdom**, **knowledge**,
	2.26	God gives **wisdom**, **knowledge**
	9.10	no **knowledge**, no **wisdom** in the world
Is	11.2	give him **wisdom**, and the **knowledge**
	33.6	and gives them **wisdom** and **knowledge**.
	47.10	**wisdom** and **knowledge** led you astray,
Dan	5.11	**knowledge**, and **wisdom** like the **wisdom**
	5.14	skilful and have **knowledge** and **wisdom**.
Rom	11.33	deep are his **wisdom** and **knowledge**!
Col	1.9	**knowledge** of his will, with...the **wisdom**
	2.3	of God's **wisdom** and **knowledge**.

LAMB

Num	28.3	—	29.36	x25
Rev	5.6	—	8.1	x18
Lev	14.10 – 25			x8
Rev	12.11	—	15.3	x8
Num	6.12	—	7.84	x7
Ezek	46.4 – 15			x7
Rev	21.9	—	22.3	x7
Lev	22.26	—	23.20	x6
2 Chr	29.21	—	30.17	x6
2 Chr	35.6 – 11			x5
Ex	29.38 – 41			x4
Ezra	6.9	—	8.35	x4
Gen	21.28	—	22.7	x3
Ex	12.3	—	13.13	x3
2 Sam	12.3 – 4			x3

Christ
1 Cor	5.7	now that **Christ**, our Passover **lamb**,
1 Pet	1.19	**Christ**, who was like a **lamb**

Dedicate see Present

God
Jn	1.29	There is the **Lamb** of God,
	1.36	There is the **Lamb** of God!
Rev	7.10	from our God...and from the **Lamb**!
	14.4	to be offered to God and to the **Lamb**.
	21.22	the Lord God Almighty and the **Lamb**.
	21.23	the glory of God...and the **Lamb**
	22.1	the throne of God and of the **Lamb**
	22.3	The throne of God and of the **Lamb**

Offering see Sacrifice

Passover
2 Chr	30.17	they could not kill the **Passover lambs**,
	35.6	to kill the **Passover lambs** and goats.
Mk	14.12	**lambs** for the **Passover** meal were killed,
Lk	22.7	**lambs** for the **Passover** meal were to be
1 Cor	5.7	our **Passover lamb**, has been sacrificed.

Present, Dedicate
Lev	14.24	**lamb** and the olive-oil and **present** them
	23.18	to **present** seven one-year-old **lambs**
	23.20	**present** the bread with the two **lambs**
2 Chr	30.17	and **dedicated** the **lambs** to the Lord.

Sacrifice, Offering
Gen	22.7	but where is the **lamb** for the **sacrifice**?
Ex	29.38	**sacrifice**...two one-year-old **lambs**.
	29.39	**Sacrifice** one of the **lambs** in the
	29.41	**Sacrifice** the second **lamb** in the evening
Lev	9.3	**lamb** without any defects for a **burnt-offering**
	12.6	one-year-old **lamb** for a **burnt-offering**
	14.13	**lamb** in the place...for the **sin-offerings**
	23.12	**burnt-offering** a one-year-old male **lamb**

E

Num	6.14	a...male **lamb** for a **burnt-offering**, a...ewe **lamb** for a **sin-offering**,
	7.12	**lamb**, for the **burnt-offering**;
	28.3	**burnt-offering**, two one-year-old male **lambs**
	28.13	**lamb**, one kilogramme. These **burnt-offerings**
	28.14	**lamb**. This is the regulation for the **burnt-offering**
1 Sam	7.9	**lamb** and burnt it whole as a **sacrifice**
2 Chr	29.22	the **lambs**, and sprinkled the blood of each **sacrifice**
	29.32	two hundred **lambs** as **burnt-offerings**
	30.15	the **lambs** for the Passover **sacrifice**.
Ezra	6.17	and four hundred **lambs** as **sacrifices**,
Is	34.6	of **lambs** and goats that are **sacrificed**.
	66.3	whether they **sacrifice** a **lamb**
Ezek	46.4	**sacrifices** to be burnt whole, six **lambs**
1 Cor	5.7	our Passover **lamb**, has been **sacrificed**.
1 Pet	1.19	**sacrifice** of Christ, who was like a **lamb**

Seal

Rev	6.1	I saw the **Lamb** break open the first of the seven **seals**
	6.3	the **Lamb** broke open the second **seal**
	6.5	the **Lamb** broke open the third **seal**
	6.7	the **Lamb** broke open the fourth **seal**
	6.9	the **Lamb** broke open the fifth **seal**
	6.12	saw the **Lamb** break open the sixth **seal**
	8.1	the **Lamb** broke open the seventh **seal**

Throne

Rev	5.6	saw a **Lamb**...in the centre of the **throne**
	5.13	sits on the **throne** and to the **Lamb**,
	6.16	**throne** and from the anger of the **Lamb**!
	7.9	in front of the **throne** and of the **Lamb**,
	7.10	sits on the **throne**, and from the **Lamb**!
	7.17	the **Lamb**...in the centre of the **throne**
	22.1	the **throne** of God and of the **Lamb**
	22.3	The **throne** of God and of the **Lamb**

LAW

	Rom	1.32 —	10.5	x75
	Ps	119.1 —	176	x52
	Gal	2.16 —	6.13	x36
	Neh	8.1 —	10.36	x25
	Deut	4.1 —	8.11	x21
	Deut	26.16 —	31.26	x17
	Heb	7.5 —	10.28	x17
	Acts	21.20 —	25.11	x12
	Ezra	7.6 — 26		x10
	Jn	7.19 —	10.34	x10
	1 Kgs	8.58 —	11.38	x8
	2 Kgs	17.13 —	18.12	x8
	Ezek	20.11 — 25		x8
	Lev	17.3 —	20.22	x7
	2 Chr	33.8 —	35.26	x7
	Mt	11.13 —	12.12	x7
	Acts	15.1 —	18.15	x7
	Lev	24.22 —	26.46	x6
	Deut	10.13 —	12.1	x6
	2 Kgs	21.8 —	23.25	x6
	2 Chr	29.15 —	31.21	x6
	Lk	1.6 —	2.39	x6
	1 Cor	9.8 — 21		x6
	2 Cor	3.6 — 15		x5
	Josh	8.31 — 34		x4
	Ezek	18.9 — 21		x4
	Dan	9.10 — 13		x4
	Deut	33.4 — 21		x3
	Esth	1.13 — 19		x3
	Ps	78.5 — 10		x3
	Jer	8.7 — 8		x3
	Ezek	11.12 — 20		x3
	Mt	5.17 — 19		x3

	Mk	10.2 — 5	x3
	Lk	6.2 — 9	x3
	Phil	3.5 — 9	x3
	Jas	4.11	x3

Anger, Curse

Josh	8.34	whole **Law**...blessings and the **curses**,
Ps	119.53	your **law**, I am filled with **anger**.
Dan	9.11	the **curses** that are written in the **Law**
Jn	7.23	**Law** is not broken, why are you **angry**
	7.49	know the **Law**...are under God's **curse**!
Rom	4.15	The **Law** brings down God's **anger**;
Gal	3.10	depend on...the **Law** live under a **curse**
	3.13	us from the **curse** that the **Law** brings;

Believe see **Faith**

Case see **Judge**

Change

Jer	8.8	Look, the **laws** have been **changed**
Dan	7.25	will try to **change** their religious **laws**
Heb	7.12	has to be a **change** in the **law**.

Christ, Jesus

Rom	8.2	**Jesus**, has set me free from the **law** of
	10.4	**Christ** has brought the **Law** to an end,
1 Cor	9.21	I am really under **Christ's law**.
Gal	2.16	faith in **Jesus**...never by...the **law**
	2.21	the **Law**, it means that **Christ** died
	3.24	**Law** was in charge of us until **Christ**
	5.4	**Law** have cut yourselves off from **Christ**.
	6.2	you will obey the **law** of **Christ**.

Command, Requirement

Gen	26.5	and kept all my **laws** and **commands**.
Ex	18.16	I tell them God's **commands** and **laws**.
Lev	18.4	Obey my **laws** and do what I **command**.
	18.26	keep the Lord's **laws** and **commands**,
	19.37	Obey all my **laws** and **commands**
	20.22	Keep all my **laws** and **commands**,
	25.18	Obey all the Lord's **laws** and **commands**
	26.3	to my **laws** and obey my **commands**,
	26.15	refuse to obey my **laws** and **commands**
	26.43	rejected my **laws** and my **commands**.
	26.46	All these are the **laws** and **commands**
Deut	5.31	give you all my **laws** and **commands**.
	5.32	God has **commanded** you. Do not disobey any of his **laws**.
	6.1	the **laws** that the Lord your God **commanded**
	6.20	**command** us to obey all these **laws**?
	6.24	**commanded** us to obey all these **laws**
	8.6	Lord has **commanded** you: live according to his **laws**
	26.16	**commands** you to obey all his **laws**;
	26.17	**laws**, and to do all that he **commands**.
	26.18	he **commands** you to obey all his **laws**.
	28.15	**commands** and **laws** that I am giving
	33.21	obeyed the Lord's **commands** and **laws**
Josh	22.5	obey the **law** that Moses **commanded**
	24.26	these **commands** in the book of the **Law**
2 Sam	22.23	observed all his **laws**...his **commands**.
1 Kgs	2.3	Obey all his **laws** and **commands**,
	3.14	me and keep my **laws** and **commands**,
	6.12	If you obey all my **laws** and **commands**,
	8.58	and keep all the **laws** and **commands**
	8.61	obeying all his **laws** and **commands**
	9.4	**laws** and do everything I have **commanded**
	9.6	if you disobey the **laws** and **commands**
	11.33	has not kept my **laws** and **commands**.
	11.34	who obeyed my **laws** and **commands**.
	11.38	my **laws**...by doing what I **command**,
2 Kgs	14.6	the Lord had **commanded** in the **Law**
	17.13	my **commands**, which are...in the **Law**
	17.34	do they obey the **laws** and **commands**

2 Kgs	17.37	always obey the **laws** and **commands**
	21.8	all my **commands** and...the whole **Law**
	23.3	to keep his **laws** and **commands**
1 Chr	28.7	carefully all my **laws** and **commands**
2 Chr	7.17	**laws** and...everything I have **commanded**
	7.19	**laws** and **commands** I have given you,
	8.13	the **requirements** of the **Law** of Moses
	19.10	violation of a **law** or **commandment**,
	25.4	the Lord had **commanded** in the **Law**
	31.3	are **required** by the **Law** of the Lord.
	31.4	time to the **requirements** of the **Law**
	33.8	all my **commands** and...the whole **Law**
	34.31	to keep his **laws** and **commands**
Ezra	7.11	knowledge of the **laws** and **commands**
Neh	8.9	the people heard what the **Law required**
	8.18	ceremony, as **required** in the **Law**.
	9.34	not kept your **Law**...your **commands**
	10.29	will keep all his **laws** and **requirements**.
	10.34	to the **requirements** of the **Law**.
	10.36	**required** by the **Law**, dedicate him to
	12.44	and the Levites which the **Law required**.
Ps	18.22	observed all his **laws**...his **commands**.
	78.5	gave **laws** to...Israel and **commandments**
	89.30	disobey my **law** and...my **commands**,
	99.7	**laws** and **commands** that he gave them.
	105.45	obey his **laws** and...all his **commands**.
	119.16	pleasure in your **laws**; your **commands**
	119.172	about your **law**, because your **commands**
Ezek	5.6	rejected my **commands** and...my **laws**.
	5.7	By not obeying my **laws** or...**commands**,
	11.20	my **laws** and...obey all my **commands**.
	18.9	obeys my **commands** and...my **laws**.
	18.17	He keeps my **laws** and...**commands**.
	20.11	gave them my **commands** and...my **laws**
	20.13	broke my **laws** and...my **commands**,
	20.16	had rejected my **commands**...my **laws**,
	20.19	Obey my **laws** and my **commands**.
	20.21	**laws** and did not keep my **commands**,
	20.24	had rejected my **commands**...my **laws**,
	20.25	**laws** that are not good and **commands**
	36.27	my **laws** and keep all the **commands**
Mal	4.4	**laws** and **commands** which I gave him
Mt	22.36	the greatest **commandment** in the **Law**?
Lk	1.6	all the Lord's **laws** and **commands**.
	2.22	as the **Law** of Moses **commanded**.
	2.24	as **required** by the **law** of the Lord.
	2.27	to do for him what the **Law required**,
	2.39	was **required** by the **law** of the Lord,
	23.56	as the **Law commanded**.
Jn	8.5	In our **Law** Moses **commanded**
Acts	15.1	as the **Law** of Moses **requires**.
Rom	2.13	but by doing what the **Law commands**.
	2.14	do by instinct what the **Law commands**,
	2.15	shows that what the **Law commands**
	2.26	obeys the **commands** of the **Law**,
	3.20	by doing what the **Law requires**;
	3.28	not by doing what the **Law requires**.
	7.12	the **Law**...is holy, and the **commandment**
	10.5	obeys the **commands** of the **Law**
Gal	2.16	never by doing what the **Law requires**.
	3.2	Spirit by doing what the **Law requires**
	3.5	the **Law requires** or because you hear
	3.12	does everything the **Law requires**
	5.14	whole **Law** is summed up in one **commandment**:
Eph	2.15	the Jewish **Law** with its **commandments**
Phil	3.6	by obeying the **commands** of the **Law**,
Heb	7.5	are priests are **commanded** by the **Law**
	8.4	the gifts **required** by the Jewish **Law**.
	9.19	**commandments** as set forth in the **Law**.

Curse see **Anger**

Death

Rom	7.8	Apart from **law**, sin is a **dead** thing.

Rom	8.2	me free from the **law** of sin and **death**.
2 Cor	3.6	The written **law** brings **death**,
	3.7	If the **Law**, which brings **death**
Gal	2.19	I am **dead** — killed by the **Law**
Heb	10.28	the **Law** of Moses is put to **death**

Disobey, Refuse

Lev	26.15	**refuse to obey** my **laws** and commands
Deut	5.32	Do not **disobey** any of his **laws**.
2 Sam	22.23	all his **laws**; I have not **disobeyed**
1 Kgs	9.6	**disobey** the **laws** and commands I have
2 Kgs	18.12	**disobeyed** all the **laws** given by Moses,
2 Chr	7.19	and your people ever **disobey** the **laws**,
Ezra	7.26	**disobeys** the **laws** of your God
Ps	18.22	all his **laws**; I have not **disobeyed**
	78.10	they **refused to obey** his **law**.
	89.30	But if his descendants **disobey** my **law**
	119.118	reject everyone who **disobeys** your **laws**;
	119.126	because people are **disobeying** your **law**.
Ezek	5.6	commands and **refused to keep** my **laws**.
Dan	9.11	broke your **laws** and **refused** to listen
Rom	2.25	is of value; but if you **disobey** the **Law**,
	4.15	**law**, there is no **disobeying** of the **law**.
Heb	10.28	who **disobeys** the **Law** of Moses is put

Faith, Believe

Acts	24.14	**believe** in everything written in the **Law**
Rom	3.27	obey the **Law**? No, but that we **believe**.
	3.28	**faith**, and not by doing what the **Law**
	3.31	by this **faith** we do away with the **Law**
	4.13	obeyed the **Law**, but because he **believed**
	4.14	**Law**, then man's **faith** means nothing
	4.16	the **Law**, but also to those who **believe**
	10.4	**Law** to an end, so that everyone who **believes**
Gal	2.16	**faith**...never by doing what the **Law**
	3.2	**Law** requires or by hearing the gospel and **believing**
	3.12	the **Law** has nothing to do with **faith**
	3.23	**faith** came, the **Law** kept us all locked
	3.25	for **faith** is here, the **Law** is no longer

Faithful see **Obey**

Free see **Save**

God see **Lord**

God's People

Neh	13.1	the **Law**...was being read...to the **people**,
Ps	105.45	so that **his people** would obey his **laws**
	147.19	to **his people**, his instructions and **laws**
Is	10.1	unjust **laws** that oppress **my people**.
	42.21	his **laws**...and he wanted **his people**
Jer	8.7	**my people**, you do not know the **laws**
Dan	7.25	**people**. He will try to change their...**laws**
Rom	9.31	**God's people**, who were seeking a **law**

Grace

Jn	1.17	gave the **Law** through Moses, but **grace**
Rom	6.14	live under **law** but under God's **grace**.
	6.15	not under **law** but under God's **grace**?

Help

Ps	119.27	**Help** me to understand your **laws**,
Mt	12.12	our **Law** does allow us to **help** someone
Mk	3.4	does our **Law** allow us to do...To **help**
Lk	6.9	does our **Law** allow us to do...To **help**

Holy

Rom	7.12	the **Law** itself is **holy**,

Human

Rom	3.19	**Law**, in order to stop all **human** excuses
	7.25	my **human** nature serves the **law** of sin.
	8.3	**Law** could not do, because **human**
	8.7	by his **human** nature; for he does not obey God's **law**,
Gal	4.4	a **human** mother...under the Jewish **Law**,

Jesus see **Christ**

Judge, Case
Num	5.29	the **law** in **cases** where a man is jealous
2 Chr	19.8	**cases** involving a violation of the **Law**
Ps	119.160	**law** is truth, and all your...**judgements**
Ezek	23.24	they will **judge** you by their own **laws**.
	44.24	to decide the **case** according to my **laws**.
Acts	23.3	there to **judge** me according to the **Law**,
Rom	2.12	they sin and are **judged** by the **Law**.
Jas	2.12	be **judged** by the **law** that sets us free.
	4.11	**judges** him, criticizes the **Law** and **judges**

Justice, Righteousness
Deut	4.8	**laws** so **just** as those that I have taught
1 Kgs	10.9	that you can maintain **law** and **justice**.
2 Chr	9.8	that you can maintain **law** and **justice**.
Ps	119.137	and your **laws** are **just**.
	119.142	**righteousness** will last...and your **law**
	119.160	your **law** is truth, and all your **righteous**
	119.172	**law**, because your commands are **just**.
Is	58.2	they want me to give them **just laws**
Ezek	18.9	carefully keeps my **laws**. He is **righteous**,
Hab	1.4	The **law** is weak and useless, and **justice**
Rom	8.4	that the **righteous** demands of the **Law**
Phil	3.6	be **righteous** by obeying...the **Law**,

Keep see **Obey**

Kingdom
Mt	11.13	and the **Law** of Moses spoke about the **Kingdom**;
Jas	2.8	if you obey the **law** of the **Kingdom**

Lord, God
Ex	13.9	recite and study the **Law** of the **Lord**,
	15.25	the **Lord** gave them **laws** to live by,
	18.16	I tell them **God's** commands and **laws**.
	34.32	the **laws** that the **Lord** had given
Lev	18.4	my **laws**...I am the **Lord** your **God**.
	25.18	Obey all the **Lord's laws** and commands
	26.46	**laws** and commands that the **Lord** gave
Deut	1.5	Moses began to explain **God's laws**
	4.44	**God's laws** and teachings to the people
	6.1	are all the **laws** that the **Lord** your **God**
	6.2	**Lord** your **God** and obey all his **laws**
	6.20	**God** command us to obey all these **laws**?
	6.24	**Lord** our **God** commanded us to obey all these **laws**
	8.6	**Lord** has commanded you: live according to his **laws**
	11.1	your **God** and always obey all his **laws**
	17.18	have a copy of the book of **God's laws**
	26.16	**God** commands you to obey all his **laws**;
	27.8	write clearly every word of **God's laws**.
	27.26	**God's** curse on anyone who does not obey all of **God's laws**
	28.61	this book of **God's laws** and teachings,
	29.29	our **God** has kept secret; but he has revealed his **Law**,
	31.9	Moses wrote down **God's Law**
	31.13	heard the **Law** of the **Lord** your **God**
	31.24	Moses wrote **God's Law** in a book
	31.26	Take this book of **God's Law**
	33.21	obeyed the **Lord's** commands and **laws**
Josh	24.26	in the book of the **Law** of **God**.
2 Sam	22.22	I have obeyed the **law** of the **Lord**;
1 Kgs	2.3	**God** orders you to do. Obey all his **laws**
	8.61	**Lord** our **God**, obeying all his **laws**
2 Kgs	10.31	with all his heart the **law** of the **Lord**,
	14.6	**Lord** had commanded in the **Law** of
	17.16	all the **laws** of the **Lord** their **God**
	17.19	obey the **laws** of the **Lord** their **God**;
	22.2	strictly obeying all the **laws** of **God**.
1 Chr	16.40	the **Law** which the **Lord** gave to Israel.
	22.13	obey all the **laws** which the **Lord** gave

2 Chr	12.1	people abandoned the **Law** of the **Lord**.
	17.9	took the book of the **Law** of the **Lord**
	19.8	the **Law** of the **Lord** or legal disputes
	25.4	the **Lord** had commanded in the **Law**
	29.15	according to the **Law** of the **Lord**.
	31.3	are required by the **Law** of the **Lord**.
	31.4	requirements of the **Law** of the **Lord**.
	34.2	strictly obeying all the **laws** of **God**.
	34.14	the **Law** that **God** had given
Ezra	7.6	knowledge of the **Law** which the **Lord**,
	7.10	life to studying the **Law** of the **Lord**,
	7.11	**laws** and commands which the **Lord** had
	7.12	in the **Law** of the **God** of Heaven.
	7.14	the **Law** of your **God**,
	7.21	the **Law** of the **God** of Heaven,
	7.25	who live by the **Law** of your **God**.
	7.26	**laws** of your **God** or the **laws** of the
	10.3	We will do what **God's Law** demands
Neh	8.1	and scholar of the **Law** which the **Lord**
	8.8	gave an oral translation of **God's Law**
	8.14	that the **Law**, which the **Lord** gave
	8.18	read a part of **God's Law** every day.
	9.3	hours the **Law** of the **Lord** their **God**
	10.28	others who in obedience to **God's Law**
	10.29	we will live according to **God's Law**,
Ps	1.2	joy in obeying the **Law** of the **Lord**,
	18.21	I have obeyed the **law** of the **Lord**;
	19.7	The **law** of the **Lord** is perfect;
	19.8	The **laws** of the **Lord** are right,
	37.31	keeps the **law** of his **God** in his heart
	93.5	Your **laws** are eternal, **Lord**,
	119.1	live according to the **law** of the **Lord**.
	119.4	**Lord**, you have given us your **laws**
	119.33	**Lord**, the meaning of your **laws**,
	119.55	**Lord**, and I think about your **law**.
	119.57	O **Lord**; I promise to obey your **laws**.
	119.137	**Lord**, and your **laws** are just.
	119.174	O **Lord**! I find happiness in your **law**
Prov	19.16	**God's laws** and you will live longer
	29.18	is the man who keeps **God's law**!
Is	24.5	by breaking **God's laws**
	42.21	**God** who is eager to save, so he exalted his **laws**
Ezek	20.19	I am the **Lord** your **God**. Obey my **laws**
Zeph	3.4	and twist the **law** of **God**
Mk	7.7	as though they were **God's laws**!
	7.9	a clever way of rejecting **God's law**
Lk	1.6	and obeyed fully all the **Lord's laws**
	2.23	as it is written in the **law** of the **Lord**:
	2.24	as required by the **law** of the **Lord**.
	2.39	was required by the **law** of the **Lord**,
Jn	1.17	**God** gave the **Law** through Moses
	10.34	written in your own **Law** that **God** said,
Acts	7.53	are the ones who received **God's law**,
Rom	1.32	**God's law** says that people who live
	2.13	**Law** that people are put right with **God**
	2.17	on the **Law** and boast about **God**;
	2.23	You boast about having **God's law**
	4.15	The **Law** brings down **God's** anger;
	6.14	not...under **law** but...**God's** grace
	6.15	not under **law** but under **God's** grace?
	7.22	inner being delights in the **law** of **God**.
	7.25	serve **God's law** only with my mind,
	8.3	What the **Law** could not do...**God** did
	8.7	for he does not obey **God's law**,
	9.31	were seeking a **law** that would put them right with **God**,
	10.5	put right with **God** by obeying the **Law**
1 Cor	9.21	not mean that I don't obey **God's law**;
Gal	3.11	right with **God** by means of the **Law**
	3.18	For if **God's** gift depends on the **Law**
	3.21	that the **Law** is against **God's** promises
1 Tim	2.14	who was deceived and broke **God's law**.
Heb	8.10	says the **Lord**: I will put my **laws**

Heb	10.16	says the Lord: I will put my **laws**
1 Jn	3.4	sins is guilty of breaking **God's law**

Love

Ex	20.6	those who **love** me and obey my **laws**.
Deut	5.10	those who **love** me and obey my **laws**.
	11.22	**laws** that I have given you: **Love** the
	30.16	if you **love** him...keep all his **laws**,
Josh	22.5	**law** that Moses commanded you: **love**
Ps	119.88	**love** be good to me, so that I may obey your **laws**.
	119.97	How I **love** your **law**!
	119.113	but I **love** your **law**.
	119.163	but I **love** your **law**.
	119.165	who **love** your **law** have perfect security,
Rom	13.10	**love**, then, is to obey the whole **Law**.
Gal	5.14	whole **Law** is summed up in one commandment: "**Love**

Mind

2 Kgs	23.25	**mind**, and strength, obeying all the **Law**
Rom	7.23	the **law** which my **mind** approves of.
	7.25	serve God's **law** only with my **mind**,
2 Cor	3.15	**Law**...the veil still covers their **minds**.
Heb	8.10	I will put my **laws** in their **minds**

Obey, Faithful, Follow, Keep, Observe

Gen	26.5	**obeyed** me and **kept** all my **laws**
Ex	20.6	those who love me and **obey** my **laws**.
	34.11	**Obey** the **laws** that I am giving you
Lev	10.9	a **law** to be **kept** by all your
	18.4	**Obey** my **laws** and do what I **command**.
	18.26	**keep** the Lord's **laws** and **commands**
	19.37	**Obey** all my **laws** and **commands**
	20.8	**Obey** my **laws**
	20.22	**Keep** all my **laws** and **commands**,
	25.18	**Obey** all the Lord's **laws** and **commands**
	26.3	you live according to my **laws** and **obey**
	26.15	refuse to **obey** my **laws** and **commands**
Deut	4.1	**Obey** all the **laws** that I am teaching
	4.14	**laws** that you are to **obey** in the land
	4.40	**Obey** all his **laws** that I have given you
	5.10	those who love me and **obey** my **laws**.
	6.2	Lord your God and **obey** all his **laws**
	6.17	**obey** all the **laws** that he has given you
	6.20	**command** us to **obey** all these **laws**?
	6.24	**commanded** us to **obey** all these **laws**
	7.11	**obey** all the **laws** that I have given
	8.1	**Obey** faithfully all the **laws** that I have
	8.6	live according to his **laws** and **obey** him.
	8.11	do not fail to **obey** any of his **laws**
	10.13	and **obey** all his **laws**
	11.1	and always **obey** all his **laws**
	11.8	**Obey** all the **laws** that I have given you
	11.22	**Obey** faithfully all the **laws** that I have
	11.32	**obey** all the **laws** that I am giving you
	12.1	Here are the **laws** that you are to **obey**
	26.16	**commands** you to **obey** his **laws**;
	26.17	to **obey** him, to **keep** all his **laws**,
	26.18	he **commands** you to **obey** all his **laws**.
	27.10	so **obey** him and **keep** all his **laws**
	27.26	**obey** all of God's **laws** and teachings.
	28.15	faithfully **keep** all his...**laws**
	28.45	**obey** the **Lord**...and **keep** all the **laws**
	29.29	his **Law**, and we...are to **obey** it
	30.10	have to **obey** him and **keep** all his **laws**
	30.16	him, **obey** him, and **keep** all his **laws**,
	33.4	We **obey** the **Law** that Moses gave us,
	33.10	teach your people to **obey** your **Law**;
	33.21	**obeyed** the Lord's **commands** and **laws**
Josh	1.7	make sure that you **obey** the whole **Law**
	1.8	**sure** that the book of the **Law** is always
	22.5	**obey** the **law** that Moses **commanded**
2 Sam	22.22	I have **obeyed** the **law** of the Lord;
	22.23	I have **observed** all his **laws**;

1 Kgs	2.3	**Obey** all his **laws** and **commands**,
	3.14	And if you **obey** me and **keep** my **laws**
	6.12	If you **obey** all my **laws** and **commands**,
	8.58	**keep** all the **laws** and **commands** he
	8.61	**obeying** all his **laws** and **commands**,
	9.4	if you **obey** my **laws** and do everything
	11.33	not **kept** my **laws** and **commands**
	11.34	who **obeyed** my **laws** and **commands**.
	11.38	**obey** me completely, live by my **laws**,
2 Kgs	10.31	did not **obey** with all his heart the **law**
	17.19	did not **obey** the **laws** of the Lord
	17.34	do they **obey** the **laws** and **commands**
	17.37	always **obey** the **laws** and **commands**
	21.8	obey...my **commands** and **keep** the...**Law**
	22.2	strictly **obeying** all the **laws** of God.
	23.3	the Lord to **obey** him, to **keep** his **laws**
	23.25	strength, **obeying** all the **Law** of Moses;
1 Chr	22.13	**obey** all the **laws** which the Lord gave
	28.7	**obey** carefully all my **laws** and
2 Chr	6.16	that they carefully **obeyed** your **Law**
	7.17	**obeying** my **laws** and doing everything I
	31.21	or in **observance** of the **Law**,
	33.8	obey...my **commands** and **keep** the...**Law**
	34.2	strictly **obeying** all the **laws** of God.
	34.31	the Lord to **obey** him, to **keep** his **laws**
	35.26	his **obedience** to the **Law**,
Neh	1.7	We have not **kept** the **laws** which you
	9.29	although **keeping** your **Law** is the way
	9.34	priests have not **kept** your **Law**.
	10.28	others who in **obedience** to God's **Law**
	10.29	we will **keep** all his **laws**
Esth	3.8	do not **obey** the **laws** of the empire,
Ps	1.2	joy in **obeying** the **Law** of the Lord,
	18.21	I have **obeyed** the **law** of the Lord;
	18.22	I have **observed** all his **laws**;
	19.8	The **laws**...are right, and those who **obey**
	37.31	He **keeps** the **law** of his God in his
	78.10	they refused to **obey** his **law**.
	99.7	**obeyed** the **laws** and **commands** that he
	105.45	so that his people would **obey** his **laws**
	119.4	given us your **laws** and told us to **obey**
	119.8	I will **obey** your **laws**;
	119.33	of your **laws**, and I will **obey** them
	119.34	your **law** to me, and I will **obey** it;
	119.36	Give me the desire to **obey** your **laws**
	119.44	I will always **obey** your **law**,
	119.57	I promise to **obey** your **laws**.
	119.63	of all who **obey** your **laws**.
	119.85	who do not **obey** your **law**,
	119.88	so that I may **obey** your **laws**.
	119.112	I have decided to **obey** your **laws**
	119.136	because people do not **obey** your **law**.
	119.146	save me, and I will **keep** your **laws**.
	119.150	people who never **keep** your **law**.
	119.155	for they do not **obey** your **laws**.
	119.157	but I do not fail to **obey** your **laws**.
Prov	19.16	**Keep** God's **laws** and you will live
	28.7	man who **obeys** the **law** is intelligent
	28.9	If you do not **obey** the **law**
	29.18	the man who **keeps** God's **law**!
Is	58.2	to know my ways and **obey** my **laws**.
Ezek	5.6	and refused to **keep** my **laws**.
	5.7	By not **obeying** my **laws** or **keeping**
	11.12	**keeping** the **laws** of the neighbouring
	11.20	will **keep** my **laws** and faithfully **obey**
	18.9	a man **obeys** my **commands** and...**keeps** my **laws**.
	18.17	**keeps** my **laws** and **obeys** my **commands**.
	18.19	**kept** my **laws** and **followed** them
	18.21	man stops sinning and **keeps** my **laws**,
	20.11	**laws**...bring life to anyone who **obeys**
	20.18	Do not **keep** the **laws** your ancestors
	20.19	**Obey** my **laws** and my **commands**.
	20.21	my **laws** and did not **keep** my

Ezek	33.15	sinning and **follows** the **laws** that give
	36.27	**follow** my **laws** and **keep** all the
	37.24	under one ruler and will **obey** my **laws**
Zech	3.7	**obey** my **laws** and perform the duties
Mt	5.19	**obeys** the **Law** and teaches others to do
Lk	1.6	**obeyed** fully all the Lord's **laws** and
Jn	7.19	But not one of you **obeys** the **Law**.
	9.16	for he does not **obey** the Sabbath **law**.
Acts	15.5	circumcised and told to **obey** the **Law**
	22.12	a religious man who **obeyed** our **Law**
Rom	2.25	If you **obey** the **Law**, your circumcision
	2.26	**obeys** the **commands** of the **Law**,
	2.27	**obey** the **Law**, even though they are not
	3.27	**obey** the **Law**? No, but that we believe.
	4.13	not because Abraham **obeyed** the **Law**,
	4.14	to be given to those who **obey** the **Law**,
	4.16	not just to those who **obey** the **Law**,
	8.7	for he does not **obey** God's **law**,
	10.5	**obeys** the **commands** of the **Law**.
	13.8	Whoever does this has **obeyed** the **Law**.
	13.10	is to **obey** the whole **Law**.
1 Cor	9.21	not mean that I don't **obey** God's **law**;
Gal	3.10	on **obeying** the **Law** live under a curse
	5.3	he is obliged to **obey** the whole **Law**.
	5.4	**obeying** the **Law** have cut yourselves off
	6.2	you will **obey** the **law** of Christ.
	6.13	circumcision do not **obey** the **Law**;
Phil	3.5	as **keeping** the Jewish **Law** is concerned,
	3.6	by **obeying** the **commands** of the **Law**,
	3.9	kind that is gained by **obeying** the **Law**.
Jas	2.8	if you **obey** the **law** of the Kingdom
	4.11	are no longer one who **obeys** the **Law**,

Perfect

Ps	19.7	The **law** of the Lord is **perfect**;
	119.165	who love your **law** have **perfect** security,
Heb	7.19	**Law**...could not make anything **perfect**.
Jas	1.25	the **perfect law** that sets people free,

Prophets

Neh	9.26	on your **Law**. They killed the **prophets**
Lam	2.9	**Law** is no longer taught...the **prophets**
Mt	5.17	the **Law** of Moses and the teachings of the **prophets**.
	7.12	**Law**...and...the teachings of the **prophets**.
	11.13	**prophets** and the **Law** of Moses spoke
	22.40	**Law**...and the teachings of the **prophets**
Lk	16.16	**Law**...and the writings of the **prophets**
	24.44	the **Law**...the writings of the **prophets**,
Jn	1.45	of the **Law** and whom the **prophets**
Acts	13.15	**Law**...and...the writings of the **prophets**,
	24.14	**Law**...and the books of the **prophets**.
	28.23	**Law**...and the writings of the **prophets**.
Rom	3.21	the **Law** of Moses and the **prophets**

Refuse see **Disobey**

Requirement see **Command**

Right With God see **Save**

Righteousness see **Justice**

Save, Free, Right With God

Lev	18.5	the **laws** that I give you; you will **save**
Ps	119.146	**save** me, and I will keep your **laws**.
	119.153	**save** me...I have not neglected your **law**.
	119.155	**saved**, for they do not obey your **laws**.
Is	42.21	is eager to **save**, so he exalted his **laws**
Acts	13.38	**Law** of Moses could not set you **free**.
	15.1	be **saved** unless...circumcised as the **Law**
Rom	2.13	the **Law** that people are put **right**
	3.20	**right**...by doing what the **Law** requires;
	7.2	if he dies, then she is **free** from the **Law**
	7.6	**free** from the **Law**, because we died to
	8.2	has set me **free** from the **law** of sin
	9.31	seeking a **law** that would put them **right**

Rom	10.5	put **right with God** by obeying the **Law**:
Gal	2.21	is put **right with God** through the **Law**,
	3.11	**right with God** by means of the **Law**,
	5.4	put **right with God** by obeying the **Law**
Jas	1.25	the perfect **law** that sets people **free**,
	2.12	be judged by the **law** that sets us **free**.

Scholar

Ezra	7.6	a **scholar** with a thorough knowledge of the **Law**
	7.12	**scholar** in the **Law** of the God of
	7.21	and **scholar** in the **Law** of the God
Neh	8.1	and **scholar** of the **Law** which the Lord
	8.9	Ezra, the priest and **scholar** of the **Law**,
	12.26	priest who was a **scholar** of the **Law**.
	13.13	a **scholar** of the **Law**;

Servant

Josh	1.7	**Law** that my **servant** Moses gave you.
2 Kgs	18.12	the **laws** given by Moses, the **servant**
	21.8	**Law** that my **servant** Moses gave them,
2 Chr	33.8	**Law** that my **servant** Moses gave them,
Neh	1.7	**laws**...through Moses, your **servant**.
	9.14	**servant** Moses you gave them your **laws**.
	10.29	God's **Law**, which God gave through his **servant** Moses;
Ps	119.176	**servant**...I have not neglected your **laws**.
Dan	9.10	the **laws** which you gave us through your **servants**
	9.11	in the **Law** of Moses, your **servant**.
Mal	4.4	teachings of my **servant** Moses, the **laws**

Serve

Ps	119.63	**serve** you, of all who obey your **laws**.
Rom	7.6	**serve** in the old way of a written **law**,
	7.25	**serve** God's **law** only with my mind,

Sin

Ezek	18.21	stops **sinning** and keeps my **laws**,
	33.15	stops **sinning** and follows the **laws**
Acts	13.38	**sins** from which the **Law** of Moses
Rom	2.12	they **sin** and are lost apart from the **Law**.
	2.12	they **sin** and are judged by the **Law**.
	5.13	was **sin** in the world before the **Law**
	5.13	no **law**, no account is kept of **sins**.
	6.15	we **sin**, because we are not under **law**
	7.7	say, then, that the **Law** itself is **sinful**?
	7.7	**Law** that made me know what **sin** is.
	7.8	Apart from **law**, **sin** is a dead thing.
	7.23	a prisoner to the **law** of **sin**
	7.25	human nature serves the **law** of **sin**.
	8.2	free from the **law** of **sin** and death.
1 Cor	15.56	**sin** gets its power from the **Law**.
1 Jn	3.4	because **sin** is a breaking of the **law**.

Spirit of God

Rom	2.29	**God's Spirit**, not of the written **Law**.
	7.6	**law**, but in the new way of the **Spirit**.
	8.2	For the **law** of the **Spirit**
2 Cor	3.6	not of a written **law** but of the **Spirit**.
	3.6	written **law** brings death, but the **Spirit**
Gal	3.2	**Spirit** by doing what the **Law** requires

Study

Ex	13.9	recite and **study** the **Law** of the Lord,
Josh	1.8	**Law** is...read in your worship. **Study** it
Ezra	7.10	had devoted his life to **studying** the **Law**.
Neh	8.13	Ezra to **study** the teachings of the **Law**.
Ps	1.2	the **Law** of the Lord, and they **study** it

True

Ps	119.18	the wonderful **truths** in your **law**.
	119.142	and your **law** is always **true**.
	119.160	The heart of your **law** is **truth**,
Jn	1.17	**Law** through Moses, but grace and **truth**
	15.25	is written in their **Law** may come **true**:

Wisdom

Deut 4.6 these **laws**, they will say, 'What **wisdom**
Ps 119.104 I gain **wisdom** from your **laws**,

LEARN

Prov	13.18	—	19.27	x15
Prov	21.11	—	25.10	x7
Ps	119.7	—	152	x5
Prov	1.7	—	2.5	x4
Eph	3.4	—	5.10	x4
Esth	2.22	—	4.1	x3
Prov	4.13	—	6.6	x3
Ecc	7.25	—	8.16	x3
Jer	5.3	—	7.28	x3
Mt	11.25 – 29			x3
Phil	4.9 – 12			x3
1 Tim	5.4 – 13			x3

Fool, Stupid

Ps	94.8 **stupid fools**? When will you ever **learn**?
Prov	8.5 Are you **foolish**? **Learn** to have sense.
	15.14 people want to **learn**, but **stupid** people
	17.10 **learns** more...than a **fool learns**
Ecc	1.17 **learn** the difference between knowledge and **foolishness**,
	5.1 **learn** than to offer sacrifices as **foolish**
	7.25 **learn** how wicked and **foolish stupidity**
Is	29.24 **Foolish** people will **learn** to understand,
Jer	10.8 **stupid** and **foolish**. What can they **learn**

Intelligent see Wisdom

Knowledge see Wisdom

Lesson

Ps 2.10 **learn** this **lesson**, you rulers of the
Prov 6.6 should **learn** a **lesson** from the way ants
24.32 know any better can **learn** a **lesson**.
21.11 an unthinking person **learns** a **lesson**.
24.32 and **learned** a **lesson** from it:

Obey

Deut	4.10 **learn** to **obey** me as long as they live
	5.1 **Learn** them and be sure that you **obey**
	17.19 **learn** to honour the Lord and to **obey**
	31.12 **learn** to honour...God and to **obey**
	31.13 **learn** to **obey** him as long as they live
Jer	7.28 **obey** me, the Lord their God, or **learn**
	17.23 would not **obey** me or **learn** from me.
Heb	5.8 **learnt** through...sufferings to be **obedient**.

Right

Is 1.17 and **learn** to do **right**.
26.10 they never **learn** to do what is **right**.
Jer 13.23 could **learn** to do what is **right**.
Rom 2.18 have **learnt**...to choose what is **right**;

Secret

Job 15.18 **learnt** from their fathers, and they kept no **secrets**
Prov 25.10 will **learn** that you can't keep a **secret**,
Eph 3.4 **learn** about...the **secret** of Christ.
Phil 4.12 I have **learnt** this **secret**,
Rev 2.24 **learnt** what...others call 'the deep **secrets**

Stupid see Fool

Teach

Job 15.18 have **taught** me truths which they **learnt**
Prov 2.1 **Learn** what I **teach** you
21.11 wise will **learn** from what he is **taught**.
Jer 32.33 **teaching** them, they would not...**learn**.
Rev 2.24 this evil **teaching**; you have not **learnt**

Truth

Job 8.8 consider the **truths** our fathers **learnt**.
15.18 have **taught** me **truths** which they **learnt**
Prov 23.23 **Truth**, wisdom, **learning**

1 Cor 2.1 **truth**, I did not use...great **learning**.
2 Tim 3.7 trying to **learn** but who can never come to know the **truth**.

Understand

Job	28.12 Where can we **learn** to **understand**?
	28.20 Where can we **learn** to **understand**?
Ps	119.73 me **understanding**, so that I may **learn**
Is	29.24 Foolish people will **learn** to **understand**,
	40.14 to know and **understand** and to **learn**
Dan	2.30 may **learn** the meaning of your dream and **understand**
Eph	3.4 **learn** about my **understanding** of the

Wisdom, Intelligent, Knowledge

Job	8.8 **wisdom**...the truths our fathers **learnt**.
	15.10 **learnt** our **wisdom** from grey-haired men
	15.18 **Wise** men have taught me truths...**learnt**
	28.12 **wisdom** be found? Where can we **learn**
	28.20 source of **wisdom**? Where can we **learn**
Prov	1.7 respect for **wisdom** and refuse to **learn**.
	1.22 on **knowledge**? Will you never **learn**?
	14.6 **wise**, but **intelligent** people **learn** easily.
	15.14 **Intelligent** people want to **learn**
	17.10 An **intelligent** person **learns** more
	19.20 to **learn**, one day you will be **wise**.
	19.25 If you are **wise**, you will **learn**
	21.11 One who is **wise** will **learn**
	23.23 **wisdom**, **learning**,
	30.3 I have never **learned** any **wisdom**,
Ecc	1.17 **learn** the difference between **knowledge**
	8.16 to become **wise** and **learn** what goes on
Dan	1.4 **intelligent**, well-trained, quick to **learn**,
Mt	11.25 have hidden from the **wise** and **learned**.
Lk	10.21 have hidden from the **wise** and **learned**.
Eph	3.10 **learn** of his **wisdom** in all its different

LEVITES

Neh	7.1	—	13.30	x43
2 Chr	29.4	—	31.19	x27
Num	1.47	—	4.34	x21
Num	7.5	—	8.26	x20
1 Chr	15.2	—	16.37	x18
1 Chr	23.2	—	26.20	x18
Ezra	6.16	—	10.23	x17
2 Chr	34.9	—	35.18	x16
Judg	17.7	—	20.4	x13
2 Chr	23.2	—	24.11	x11
Ezra	1.5	—	3.12	x9
Josh	21.1 – 41			x8
1 Chr	9.2 – 34			x8
Num	18.1 – 26			x6
Deut	16.11	—	18.7	x6
Deut	26.11	—	27.14	x5
Lev	25.32 – 34			x4
Num	16.1 – 10			x4
Num	35.2 – 8			x4
Deut	12.12 – 19			x4
2 Chr	5.4 – 11			x4
2 Chr	19.8	—	20.19	x4
Ex	32.26 – 29			x3
1 Chr	6.48 – 64			x3
1 Chr	28.13	—	29.8	x3
2 Chr	7.6	—	8.15	x3
2 Chr	11.13 – 16			x3
Ezek	48.12 – 21			x3

Consecrate see Dedicate

Contribute see Offer

Dedicate, Consecrate, Purify

Ex 32.29 **Levites**, "Today you have **consecrated**
Num 3.45 Now **dedicate** the **Levites**
8.11 then Aaron shall **dedicate** the **Levites**
8.12 the ritual of **purification** for the **Levites**.

Num 8.13 **Dedicate** the **Levites** as a special gift
      8.15 have **purified** and **dedicated** the **Levites**,
      8.20 people of Israel **dedicated** the **Levites**,
      8.21 **Levites purified** themselves and washed
1 Chr 15.12 **Purify** yourselves and your **fellow-Levites**,
      15.14 and the **Levites purified** themselves
2 Chr 29.5 You **Levites** are to **consecrate** yourselves
      30.17 **Levites** did it for them, and **dedicated**
      35.3   the **Levites**...who were **dedicated**
Ezra 6.20 and the **Levites** had **purified** themselves
Neh   12.30 the **Levites** performed ritual **purification**
      13.22 ordered the **Levites** to **purify** themselves

Duty
Num 8.24 **Levite** shall perform his **duties** in the
      8.26 **fellow-Levites** in performing their **duties**
1 Chr 6.48 **Levites** were assigned all the other **duties**
      23.31 The **Levites** were assigned the **duty**
      26.12 **duties**...just as the other **Levites** were.
      28.13 and **Levites** to perform their **duties**,
      28.21 **Levites** have been assigned **duties** to
2 Chr 13.10 perform their **duties**, and **Levites** assist
      23.4   the priests and **Levites** come on **duty**
      23.6   priests and the **Levites** who are on **duty**.
      31.2   **Levites**, under which they each had specific
             duties.
      31.15 **fellow-Levites** according to what their **duties**
             were,
      31.17 **duties** by clans, and the **Levites** twenty
Neh   13.30 the **Levites** so that each one would know his
             duty;

Gift see **Offer**
Help
Num 8.26 **help** his **fellow-Levites** in performing
1 Chr 15.26 **help** the **Levites** who were carrying
2 Chr 29.34 the **Levites helped** them until the work
Ezra 3.9   They were **helped** by the **Levites**

Law
Deut 31.9 **Law** and gave it to the **levitical** priests,
Neh   8.7 **Levites** explained the **Law** to them:
      8.9 **Levites** who were explaining the **Law**
      12.44 and the **Levites** which the **Law** required.
Heb   7.11 of the **levitical** priesthood that the **Law**

Offer, Contribute, Gift, Sacrifice, Tithe
Num 8.11 the **Levites** to me as a special **gift**
      8.13 the **Levites** as a special **gift** to me,
      8.19 **Levites** to Aaron and his sons, as a **gift**
      18.6 the **Levites**...as a **gift** to you.
      18.21 I have given to the **Levites** every **tithe**
Deut 26.12 give the **tithe** ...to the **Levites**,
2 Chr 11.16 **Levites** to Jerusalem, so...they could **offer**
      24.8   **Levites** to make a box for **contributions**
      30.16 **Levites** gave the blood of the **sacrifices**
      31.4   **offerings** to which...the **Levites**
      31.9   priests and the **Levites** about these **gifts**,
      35.9   for the **Levites** to **offer** as **sacrifices**.
      35.13 **Levites** roasted the Passover **sacrifices**
Ezra 6.20 The **Levites** killed the animals for the Passover
             sacrifices
Neh   10.37 take to the **Levites**, who collect **tithes**
      10.38 the **Levites** when **tithes** are collected,
      10.39 **Levites** are to take the **contributions**
      12.44 the **contributions** for...the **Levites**
      12.47 gave a sacred **offering** to the **Levites**,

Passover
2 Chr 30.17 the **Passover** lambs, so the **Levites** did it
      35.10 **Passover**, the priests and the **Levites**
      35.13 **Levites** roasted the **Passover** sacrifices
      35.15 **Levites** prepared the **Passover** for them.
Ezra 6.20 **Levites** killed the animals for...**Passover**

Praise
1 Chr 16.7 **Levites**...responsibility for singing **praises**
2 Chr 7.6 the **Levites**, **praising** the Lord
      29.30 the **Levites** to sing...the songs of **praise**
      30.21 **Levites** and the priests **praised** the Lord
      30.22 **praised** the **Levites** for their skill
Ps   135.20 **Praise** the Lord, you **Levites**;

Purify see **Dedicate**

Sacrifice see **Offer**
Separate
Num 8.6   **Separate** the **Levites** from the rest of the
      8.14 **Separate** the **Levites** in this way from
Ezra 9.1 **Levites** had not kept themselves **separate**

Serve
Num 3.9   the **Levites** have is to **serve** Aaron
Deut 12.12 your **servants**, and the **Levites** who live
      12.18 with your **servants** and the **Levites**
      16.11 **servants**, and the **Levites**, foreigners,
      16.14 your **servants**, and the **Levites**,
      33.8   your faithful **servants**, the **Levites**;
1 Chr 23.27 all **Levites** were registered for **service**
      25.1   **Levite** clans to lead the **services**
      26.1   **Levites** who **served** as temple guards.
Ezra 6.18 and the **Levites** for the temple **services**

Tent
Num 1.50 put the **Levites** in charge of the **Tent**
      1.51 the **Levites** shall take the **Tent** down
      1.53 the **Levites** shall camp round the **Tent**
      2.17 **Levites** are to march carrying the **Tent**.
      7.5   for the **Tent**; give them to the **Levites**
      8.9   the **Levites** stand in front of the **Tent**
      8.22 **Levites**...qualified to work in the **Tent**
      8.24 **Levite**...perform his duties in the **Tent**
      8.26 **Levites** in...their duties in the **Tent**,
      18.23 the **Levites** will take care of the **Tent**
      31.30 **Levites** who are in charge of the...**Tent**.
      31.47 **Levites** who were in charge of the...**Tent**.
1 Kgs 8.4 The **Levites**...also moved the **Tent**
1 Chr 23.26 need for the **Levites** to carry the **Tent**
2 Chr 5.5 and the **Levites** also moved the **Tent**

Tithe see **Offer**

LIE

Jer	27.15 —	29.31	x8
Prov	12.17 —	14.25	x6
Jer	23.14 — 32		x5
Ezek	13.6 — 22		x5
1 Jn	1.6 —	2.22	x5
Prov	19.1 — 22		x4
Is	28.15 —	30.9	x4
2 Cor	11.3 —	12.16	x4
Job	13.4 — 7		x3
Ps	119.69 — 163		x3
Prov	6.12 — 16		x3
Prov	29.12 —	30.8	x3
Is	59.3 — 13		x3
Jer	9.3 — 8		x3
Mt	26.60 —	27.64	x3
Acts	5.3 —	6.13	x3
1 Pet	2.1 —	3.10	x3
Rev	21.8 —	22.15	x3

False, Claim, Deceive
Ps   5.6   all **liars** and despise violent, **deceitful**
      12.2 of them **lie** to one another; they **deceive**
      120.2 from **liars** and **deceivers**.
Prov 29.12 **false** information...officials will be **liars**.
Is   28.15 you depend on **lies** and **deceit**
      59.13 thoughts are **false**; our words are **lies**.
Jer 23.25 who speak **lies** in my name and **claim**
Lam 2.14 but **lies**; Their preaching **deceived** you

Ezek	13.6	are **false**, and their predictions are **lies**.
	13.7	are **false**, and the predictions...are **lies**.
	13.8	are **false**, and your visions are **lies**.
	21.29	are **false**, and the predictions...are **lies**.
Hos	11.12	have surrounded me with **lies** and **deceit**,
Mic	2.11	who goes about full of **lies** and **deceit**
Zeph	3.13	tell no **lies**, nor try to **deceive**.
Zech	8.17	**false** testimony under oath. I hate **lying**,
Rom	3.13	full of deadly **deceit**; wicked **lies** roll
2 Cor	11.3	was **deceived** by the snake's clever **lies**.
	11.13	**false** apostles, who **lie** about their work
1 Tim	1.10	those who **lie** and give **false** testimony
	4.2	teachings are spread by **deceitful liars**
Rev	3.9	those **liars** who **claim** that they are Jews

Oath, Promise

Ps	89.35	**promised** by my...name: I will never **lie**
	144.8	and **lie** even under **oath**.
	144.11	and **lie** even under **oath**.
Jer	7.9	commit adultery, tell **lies** under **oath**,
Hos	4.2	make **promises** and break them; they **lie**
Zech	5.3	that everyone who tells **lies** under **oath**
	5.4	of everyone who tells **lies** under **oath**.
	8.17	**false** testimony under **oath**. I hate **lying**,
Tit	1.2	who does not **lie**, **promised** us this life

Prophet

1 Kgs	13.18	But the old **prophet** was **lying**.
	22.22	and make all Ahab's **prophets** tell **lies**.
	22.23	has made these **prophets** of yours **lie**
2 Chr	18.21	and make all Ahab's **prophets** tell **lies**.
	18.22	has made these **prophets** of yours **lie**
Is	9.15	is the **prophets** whose teachings are **lies**!
Jer	5.31	**prophets** speak nothing but **lies**
	14.14	**prophets** are telling **lies** in my name;
	23.25	those **prophets** have said who speak **lies**
	23.26	**prophets** mislead my people with the **lies**
	27.15	**prophets** who are telling you these **lies**.
	29.31	a **prophet**, and he made you believe **lies**.
	50.36	Death to its **lying prophets**
Lam	2.14	Your **prophets** had nothing to tell you but **lies**;
Mic	2.11	of **prophet** who goes about full of **lies**

Punish

Ps	120.3	**liars**, what will God do to you? How will he **punish**
Prov	19.5	tell **lies** in court, you will be **punished**
	19.9	tells **lies** in court can escape **punishment**
Is	29.21	**punishment** of criminals, and...tell **lies**

Steal

Lev	19.11	Do not **steal** or cheat or **lie**
Josh	7.11	They **stole** them, **lied** about it,
Jer	7.9	**steal**, murder, commit adultery, tell **lies**
Hos	4.2	**lie**, murder, **steal**, and commit adultery.

Testimony see Word

Truth

Ps	144.8	tell the **truth** and **lie** even under oath.
	144.11	tell the **truth** and **lie** even under oath.
Prov	4.24	isn't **true**. Have nothing to do with **lies**
	8.7	say is the **truth**; **lies** are hateful to me.
	12.17	tell the **truth**, justice is done, but **lies**
	12.19	**lie** has a short life, but **truth** lives on
	14.25	the **truth**; when he tells **lies**, he betrays
Jer	9.3	to tell **lies**; dishonesty instead of **truth**
	9.5	**truth**; they...taught their tongues to **lie**
Jn	8.44	is no **truth** in him. When he tells a **lie**,
Acts	13.10	to turn the Lord's **truths** into **lies**!
Rom	1.25	exchange the **truth** about God for a **lie**;
	3.4	**true**, even though every man is a **liar**.
	9.1	I am speaking the **truth**...I do not **lie**
2 Cor	6.8	treated as **liars**, yet we speak the **truth**;
	11.13	not **true** apostles — they are false apostles, who **lie**

Gal	1.20	is **true**. God knows that I am not **lying**!
Eph	4.25	**lying**, then! Everyone must tell the **truth**
1 Tim	2.7	I am not **lying**; I am telling the **truth**!
Tit	1.12	spoke the **truth** when he said, "Cretans are always **liars**,
1 Jn	2.4	is a **liar** and there is no **truth** in him.
	2.21	that no **lie** ever comes from the **truth**.

Word, Testimony, Witness

Ps	52.4	hurt people with your **words**, you **liar**!
	78.36	But their **words** were all **lies**;
Prov	4.24	to do with **lies** and misleading **words**.
	6.16	**witness** who tells one **lie** after another,
	13.5	hate **lies**, but the **words** of wicked
	21.28	a **liar** is not believed, but the **word**
	22.12	safe by disproving the **words** of **liars**.
Is	59.13	our **words** are **lies**.
Ezek	13.8	Your **words** are false, and your visions are **lies**.
Zech	8.17	false **testimony** under oath. I hate **lying**,
	13.3	to speak the Lord's **word**, but spoke **lies**
Mk	14.56	Many **witnesses** told **lies** against Jesus
Rom	3.13	**words** are full of...deceit; wicked **lies**
1 Tim	1.10	those who **lie** and give false **testimony**
1 Jn	1.6	we are **lying** both in our **words**
	1.10	to be a **liar**, and his **word** is not in us.
Rev	22.15	who are **liars** both in **words** and deeds.

LIFE

Jn	3.15	—	8.12	x32
Prov	7.23	—	16.31	x25
Ecc	1.2	—	9.9	x21
Job	7.1	—	14.19	x18
Rom	4.12	—	8.38	x17
1 Jn	1.1	—	5.20	x17
Prov	1.19	—	5.6	x14
Phil	1.11	—	4.10	x14
Prov	18.21	—	23.26	x12
Lk	6.9	—	10.25	x12
2 Cor	1.12	—	5.10	x11
Gen	1.24	—	6.12	x10
Gen	42.18	—	47.25	x9
Ezek	13.18	—	14.20	x9
Ezek	32.10	—	33.19	x9
Mk	8.35	—	10.45	x9
Jn	10.10	—	12.50	x9
Ps	119.1	—	175	x8
Jer	48.6	—	52.33	x8
Tit	1.2	—	3.14	x8
Jer	20.18	—	23.22	x7
Col	1.10	—	3.7	x7
Is	38.10	—	17	x6
1 Tim	6.12	—	19	x5
Ps	90.9	—	14	x4
Ps	102.3	—	27	x4
Ezek	20.11	—	25	x4
Mt	16.25	—	26	x4
Lk	12.15	—	23	x4
1 Cor	15.19	—	45	x4
Gal	2.20	—	3.27	x4
Heb	11.35	—	13.5	x4
1 Pet	1.3	—	18	x4

Accept see Faith

Believe see Faith

Change

Is	55.7	leave their way of **life** and **change**
Jer	18.11	to stop living sinful **lives** — to **change**
Ezek	3.18	**change** his ways so that he can save his **life**,
	33.8	**change** his ways so that he can save his **life**,

Christ, I Am, Jesus, Son of God

Jn	3.36 believes in the **Son** has eternal **life**
	5.21 **life**, in the same way the **Son** gives **life**
	5.26 made his **Son** to be the source of **life**.
	6.35 **I am** the bread of **life**," **Jesus** told them
	6.40 see the **Son**...should have eternal **life**.
	6.48 **I am** the bread of **life**.
	11.23 brother will rise to **life**," **Jesus** told
	11.25 **Jesus** said to her, "**I am** the resurrection and the **life**.
	14.6 **I am** the way, the truth, and the **life**;
Acts	13.32 by raising **Jesus** to **life**.
Rom	5.10 more will we be saved by **Christ's life**!
	5.17 will rule in **life** through **Christ**.
	5.21 leading us to eternal **life** through **Jesus**
	8.2 brings us **life** in union with...**Jesus**,
	8.11 who raised **Christ**...will...give **life**
	14.9 For **Christ** died and rose to **life**
	15.8· I tell you that **Christ's life** of service
1 Cor	4.15 your **life** in union with **Christ Jesus**
	4.17 new **life** in union with **Christ Jesus**
	15.15 to **life**, then he did not raise **Christ**.
	15.19· our hope in **Christ** is good for this **life**
	15.22 will be raised to **life**...with **Christ**.
	15.31 our **life** in union with **Christ Jesus**
2 Cor	1.21 sure of our **life** in union with **Christ**;
	4.14 who raised the Lord **Jesus** to **life**,
Gal	2.20 it is **Christ** who lives in me. This **life**
	3.27 clothed...with the **life** of **Christ**
Eph	1.1 their **life** in union with **Christ Jesus**:
	2.5 he brought us to **life** with **Christ**.
	5.2 as **Christ** loved us and gave his **life**
	5.25 **Christ** loved the church and gave his **life**
Phil	1.21 For what is **life**? To me, it is **Christ**
	1.23 to leave this **life** and be with **Christ**,
	1.26 your **life** in union with **Christ Jesus**.
	1.27 of **life** should be as the gospel of **Christ**
	2.1 Your **life** in **Christ** makes you strong,
	3.3 our **life** in union with **Christ Jesus**.
	3.14 through **Christ Jesus** to the **life** above.
	3.18 **lives** make them enemies of **Christ's**
Col	2.13 now brought you to **life** with **Christ**.
	3.1 You have been raised to **life** with **Christ**
	3.3 your **life** is hidden with **Christ**
	3.4 Your real **life** is **Christ**
1 Thes	4.16 believing in **Christ** will rise to **life**
	5.18 your **life** in union with **Christ Jesus**.
2 Tim	3.12 a godly **life** in union with...**Jesus**
Phlm	.6 our **life** in union with **Christ**.
Heb	5.7 In his **life** on earth **Jesus** made
1 Pet	1.3 gave us new **life** by raising **Jesus**
1 Jn	2.25 what **Christ** himself promised...**life**.
	3.16 **Christ** gave his **life** for us.
	4.9 only **Son** into the world, so that we might have **life**
	4.17 our **life**...is the same as **Christ's**.
	5.11 and this **life** has its source in his **Son**.
	5.12 Whoever has the **Son** has this **life**
	5.13 **life** — you that believe in the **Son** of
Jude	.21 Lord **Jesus**...to give you eternal **life**.
Rev	20.4 They came to **life**...with **Christ**

Church see God's People

Command see Law

Danger see Trouble

Death

Deut	30.15 between **life** and **death**.
	30.19 you the choice between **life** and **death**,
Judg	16.30 **death** than he had killed during his **life**.
2 Sam	1.23 together in **life**, together in **death**;
	14.14 does not bring the **dead** back to **life**,
1 Kgs	3.11 **life** for yourself or riches or the **death**

1 Kgs	19.4 away my **life**; I might as well be **dead**!
2 Kgs	5.7 with the power of **life** and **death**?
	8.5 had brought a **dead** person back to **life**,
2 Chr	1.11 **death** of your enemies or...for long **life**
Prov	11.4 **death**, but honesty can save your **life**.
	12.28 to **life**; wickedness is the road to **death**.
	15.24 **life**, not the road that leads...to **death**.
Is	57.2 good **lives** find peace and rest in **death**.
Jer	21.8 to **life** and the way that leads to **death**.
Ezek	13.18 to possess the power of **life** and **death**
	13.20 your attempt to control **life** and **death**.
	32.24 In **life** they spread terror, but now they lie **dead**
	32.25 In **life** they spread terror, but now they lie **dead**
	37.9 **dead** bodies...bring them back to **life**.
Jon	1.14 with **death** for taking this man's **life**!
Mt	10.8 bring the **dead** back to **life**,
	11.5 the **dead** are brought back to **life**,
	22.28 on the day when the **dead** rise to **life**,
	22.30 For when the **dead** rise to **life**
	22.31 as for the **dead** rising to **life**:
Mk	12.23 all the **dead** rise to **life**
	12.25 For when the **dead** rise to **life**,
Lk	7.22 the **dead** are raised to **life**,
	20.33 on the day when the **dead** rise to **life**,
	20.37 proves that the **dead** are raised to **life**.
Jn	5.21 raises the **dead** and gives them **life**,
	5.24 has already passed from **death** to **life**.
Acts	3.15 to **life**, but God raised him from **death**
	4.2 proved that the **dead** will rise to **life**.
	23.6 I have that the **dead** will rise to **life**!
	24.21 that the **dead** will rise to **life**.
Rom	4.17 The God who brings the **dead** to **life**
	6.13 have been brought from **death** to **life**,
	6.23 **death**; but God's free gift is eternal **life**
	7.10 to bring **life**, in my case brought **death**.
	8.11 **Christ** from **death** will also give **life**
	8.38 neither **death** nor **life**,
	11.15 It will be **life** for the **dead**!
1 Cor	3.22 **life** and **death**,
	15.12 that the **dead** will not be raised to **life**?
	15.15 true that the **dead** are not raised to **life**,
	15.29 that the **dead** are not raised to **life**,
	15.32 But if the **dead** are not raised to **life**,
	15.35 How can the **dead** be raised to **life**?
	15.42 will be when the **dead** are raised to **life**
2 Cor	3.6 brings **death**, but the Spirit gives **life**.
	4.10 the **death** of Jesus, so that his **life** also
	4.11 of **death** for Jesus' sake...that his **life**
	4.12 that **death** is at work in us, but **life**
Eph	2.5 spiritually **dead**...he brought us to **life**
Phil	3.11 myself will be raised from **death** to **life**.
Heb	11.35 their **dead** relatives raised back to **life**.
1 Pet	1.3 **life** by raising Jesus Christ from **death**.
1 Jn	3.14 have left **death** and come over into **life**
Rev	2.10 it means **death**, and I will give you **life**
	20.5 rest of the **dead** did not come to **life**

Destroy

Gen	19.15 your **lives** when the city is **destroyed**.
1 Kgs	20.42 **life**, and your army will be **destroyed**
Job	14.19 so you **destroy** man's hope for **life**.
Prov	18.21 you say can preserve **life** or **destroy** it;
Mk	3.4 To save a man's **life** or to **destroy** it?
Lk	6.9 To save a man's **life** or **destroy** it?

Disaster see Trouble

Disgrace

Job	36.14 worn out by a **life** of **disgrace**.
Jer	20.18 to end my **life** in **disgrace**?
Dan	12.2 eternal **life**, and some will suffer eternal **disgrace**.

128

Enjoy see **Joy**

Eternal, Last

Ps	21.4	and you gave it, a long and **lasting life**.
Dan	12.2	some will enjoy **eternal life**,
Mt	19.16	must I do to receive **eternal life**?
	19.29	and will be given **eternal life**.
	25.46	but the righteous will go to **eternal life**.
Mk	10.17	what must I do to receive **eternal life**?
	10.30	age to come he will receive **eternal life**.
Lk	10.25	what must I do to receive **eternal life**?
	18.18	what must I do to receive **eternal life**?
	18.30	and **eternal life** in the age to come.
Jn	3.15	believes in him may have **eternal life**.
	3.16	may not die but have **eternal life**.
	3.36	believes in the Son has **eternal life**
	4.14	and give him **eternal life**;
	4.36	and gathers the crops for **eternal life**;
	5.24	in him who sent me has **eternal life**.
	5.39	that in them you will find **eternal life**.
	6.27	for the food that **lasts** for **eternal life**.
	6.40	believe in him should have **eternal life**.
	6.47	he who believes has **eternal life**.
	6.54	and drinks my blood has **eternal life**,
	6.68	have the words that give **eternal life**.
	10.28	I give them **eternal life**,
	12.25	will keep it for **life eternal**.
	12.50	that his command brings **eternal life**.
	17.2	so that he might give **eternal life** to all
	17.3	And **eternal life** means knowing you,
Acts	13.46	yourselves worthy of **eternal life**,
	13.48	who had been chosen for **eternal life**
Rom	2.7	to them God will give **eternal life**.
	5.21	to **eternal life** through Jesus Christ
	6.22	and the result is **eternal life**.
	6.23	God's free gift is **eternal life**
Gal	6.8	he will gather the harvest of **eternal life**.
1 Tim	1.16	believe in him and receive **eternal life**.
	6.12	and win **eternal life** for yourself;
Tit	1.2	is based on the hope for **eternal life**.
	3.7	of the **eternal life** we hope for.
1 Jn	1.2	and tell you about the **eternal life**
	2.25	promised to give us — **eternal life**.
	3.15	murderer has not got **eternal life** in him.
	5.11	God has given us **eternal life**,
	5.13	you have **eternal life** — you that believe
	5.20	and this is **eternal life**.
Jude	.21	in his mercy to give you **eternal life**.

Evil, Wicked

Gen	6.12	for the people were all living **evil lives**.
Deut	30.15	good and evil, between **life** and death.
1 Sam	2.9	the **lives** of his...people, but the **wicked**
Ps	58.3	**Evil** men go wrong all their **lives**;
	97.10	**evil**; he protects the **lives** of his people;
Prov	10.11	of **life**, but a **wicked** man's words
	11.5	man's **life** easier, but a **wicked** man
	12.28	is the road to **life**; **wickedness**
Ecc	8.13	go well for the **wicked**. Their **life** is like
Is	53.12	his **life** and shared the fate of **evil** men.
	55.7	Let the **wicked** leave their way of **life**
Jer	23.10	**live wicked lives** and misuse their power.
	23.22	**evil lives** they **live** and the wicked things
	25.5	way of **life** and from the **evil** things
Ezek	13.22	giving up **evil** and saving their **lives**.
Zech	1.4	telling them not to **live evil**, sinful

Faith, Accept, Believe, Hope

Job	14.19	so you destroy man's **hope** for **life**.
Jn	3.15	**believes** in him may have **eternal life**
	3.36	**believes** in the Son has **eternal life**
	5.24	and **believes** in him who sent me has **eternal life**.
	6.40	believe in him should have **eternal life**.
	6.47	he who **believes** has **eternal life**.

Jn	7.38	**believes** in me, streams of **life-giving**
	11.25	and the **life**. Whoever **believes** in me
	20.31	your **faith** in him you may have **life**.
Acts	24.21	**believing** that the dead will rise to **life**.
Rom	4.12	**life** of **faith** that our father Abraham
	4.17	**believed** — the God who brings the dead to **life**
	11.15	when they are **accepted**? It will be **life**
1 Cor	15.19	**hope** in Christ is good for this **life** only
2 Cor	5.7	For our **life** is a matter of **faith**,
Gal	2.20	This **life** that I live now, I live by **faith**
Col	2.7	**lives** on him, and become stronger in your **faith**,
1 Thes	4.16	**believing** in Christ will rise to **life** first;
1 Tim	1.16	**believe** in him and receive eternal life.
	6.12	**faith**, and win eternal **life** for yourself;
2 Tim	3.10	in **life**; you have observed my **faith**,
Tit	1.2	is based on the **hope** for eternal **life**.
	3.7	of the eternal **life** we **hope** for.
Heb	6.19	this **hope** as an anchor for our **lives**.
1 Jn	5.13	have eternal **life** — you that believe
Rev	22.17	**accept** the water of **life** as a gift,

Give Up

Lk	12.20	night you will have to **give up** your **life**;
Jn	10.17	because I am willing to **give up** my **life**
	10.18	my **life** away from me. I **give it up**
Rev	12.11	they were willing to **give up** their **lives**

Glad see **Joy**

God's People, Church

Ps	97.10	he protects the **lives** of **his people**;
Is	57.16	I gave **my people life**,
Ezek	13.18	power of **life** and death over **my people**
Eph	5.25	Christ loved the **church** and gave his **life**
Col	1.18	**church**...the source of the body's **life**.

Happy see **Joy**

Holy

Eph	4.24	in the true **life** that is upright and **holy**.
Tit	2.3	as women should who live a **holy life**.
Heb	12.14	and try to live a **holy life**,
2 Pet	3.11	Your **lives** should be **holy** and dedicated

Hope see **Faith**

I Am see **Christ**

Jesus see **Christ**

Joy, Enjoy, Glad, Happy

Job	7.7	my **life** is only a breath; my **happiness**
	10.20	**life** almost over...Let me **enjoy**
	14.6	let him **enjoy** his hard **life** — if he can.
	33.30	a person's **life**, and gives him the **joy**
Ps	16.11	to **life**; your presence fills me with **joy**
	34.12	Would you like to **enjoy life**?
	34.12	Do you want long **life** and **happiness**?
	41.2	their **lives**; he will make them **happy**
	90.14	we may sing and be **glad** all our **life**.
	119.1	**Happy** are those whose **lives** are
Prov	3.18	are **happy**; wisdom will give them **life**.
	3.22	with **life** — a pleasant and **happy life**.
	15.15	but **happy** people always **enjoy life**.
	28.20	lead a full, **happy life**.
Ecc	6.6	so than the man who never **enjoys life**,
	8.15	**life** is eating and drinking and **enjoying**
	9.9	**Enjoy life** with the woman you love,
	12.1	I don't **enjoy life**.
Is	53.11	**life** of suffering, he will again have **joy**;
Jer	22.15	Your father **enjoyed** a full **life**.
Lam	5.15	**Happiness** has gone out of our **lives**.
Dan	12.2	some will **enjoy** eternal **life**,
Zeph	3.17	new **life**. He will sing and be **joyful**
Lk	12.19	**life** easy, eat, drink, and **enjoy** yourself!
Acts	2.28	**life**...your presence will fill me with **joy**.

129

Phil   4.10   In my **life**...it is a great **joy** to me
1 Pet   3.10   Whoever wants to **enjoy life**

Last see **Eternal**

Law, Command, Obey

Lev   18.5   **laws**...I give you; you will save your **life**
Deut   13.5   **life** that the Lord has **commanded** you
         32.47 they are your very **life**. **Obey** them
Ezra   7.10   had devoted his **life** to studying the **Law**
Neh   9.29   keeping your **Law** is the way to **life**.
Job   36.11 **obey** God...they **live** out their **lives**
Ps   119.1   who **live** according to the **law**
         119.9   man keep his **life** pure? By **obeying** your
                    commands.
         119.40 **obey** your **commands**; give me new **life**,
         119.54 **life** I compose songs about your **commands**.
         119.109 my **life**; I have not forgotten your **law**.
Prov   19.23 **Obey** the Lord...live a long **life**
Jer   22.21 **life**; you never would **obey** the Lord.
Ezek 20.11 **laws**, which bring **life** to anyone who **obeys**
                    them.
         20.13 broke my **laws** and...my **commands**, which
                    bring **life** to anyone who **obeys** them.
         20.21 not keep my **commands**, which bring **life**
         20.25 and **commands** that do not bring **life**.
         33.15 and follows the **laws** that give **life**,
Lk   1.6   They both **lived** good **lives**...and **obeyed**
Jn   12.50 that his **command** brings eternal **life**.
Rom   8.2   **law** of the Spirit, which brings us **life**
2 Cor   3.6   The written **law** brings death, but the Spirit
                    gives **life**.
Gal   3.21   had received a **law** that could bring **life**,
1 Pet   1.14   **obedient**...and do not allow your **lives**

Mercy see **Spare**

Obey see **Law**

Offer

Num   31.50 **offer** them...as a payment for our **lives**,
Prov   3.16   Wisdom **offers** you long **life**
Eph   5.2   **life** for us as a sweet-smelling **offering**
Phil   2.16   as you **offer** them the message of **life**
         2.17   **life's** blood...poured out like an **offering**

Peace

Job   21.13 They **live** out their **lives** in **peace**
         36.11 they **live** out their **lives** in **peace**
Is   57.2   who **live** good **lives** find **peace** and rest
Rom   8.6   by the Spirit results in **life** and **peace**.
Gal   6.16   their **lives**, may **peace** and mercy
1 Tim 2.2   we may live a quiet and **peaceful life**
Heb   12.11 the **peaceful** reward of a righteous **life**.
         12.14 at **peace** with everyone...live a holy **life**

Please

2 Kgs 12.2   his **life** he did what **pleased** the Lord,
Prov   8.35   finds **life**, and the Lord will be **pleased**
Col   1.10   always do what **pleases** him. Your **lives**
1 Thes 2.12 live the kind of **life** that **pleases** God,

Pleasure

Ecc   8.15   **pleasure** he has in this **life** is eating
Lk   8.14   **pleasures** of this **life** crowd in and choke
Tit   3.3   **pleasures** of all kinds. We spent our **lives**

Pray

1 Kgs 19.4   Lord," he **prayed**. "Take away my **life**;
Ps   42.8   a **prayer** to the God of my **life**.
         64.1   listen to my **prayer**...save my **life**!
Jon   2.7   felt my **life** slipping away...I **prayed**
Heb   5.7   his **life** on earth Jesus made his **prayers**
1 Jn   5.16   **pray** to God, who will give him **life**.

Promise

Ps   119.50 because your **promise** gave me **life**.
         133.3   **promised** his blessing — **life** that never

Ezek 33.13 I may **promise life** to a good man,
Mal   2.5   In my covenant I **promised** them **life**
1 Tim 4.8   it **promises life** both for the present
2 Tim 1.1   the **promised life** which we have
Tit   1.2   who does not lie, **promised** us this **life**
Jas   1.12   **life** which God has **promised** to those
1 Jn   2.25   **promised** to give us — eternal **life**.

Protect see **Safe**

Purpose see **Will**

Rescue see **Save**

Reward

Ps   91.16 I will **reward** them with long **life**;
Prov   10.16 The **reward** for doing good is **life**
         16.31 Long **life** is the **reward** of the righteous
Heb   12.11 the peaceful **reward** of a righteous **life**.
Jas   1.12   receive as his **reward** the **life** which God

Riches

1 Kgs 3.11   instead of long **life** for yourself or **riches**
Prov   13.8   A **rich** man has to use his money to save his
                    life
         22.4   will get **riches**, honour, and a long **life**.
Jer   17.11 the prime of **life** he will lose his **riches**,
Mt   13.22 about this **life** and the love for **riches**
Mk   4.19   about this **life**, the love for **riches**,
Lk   6.24   **rich** now; you have had your easy **life**!
         8.14   **riches** and pleasures of this **life** crowd in
1 Tim 6.17   who are **rich** in the things of this **life**

Righteous

Ps   119.40 give me new **life**, for you are **righteous**.
Prov   2.13   who have abandoned a **righteous life**
         2.20   of good men and live a **righteous life**.
         11.30 **Righteousness** gives **life**
         12.28 **Righteousness** is the road to **life**
         16.31 Long **life** is the reward of the **righteous**
         29.10 but **righteous** people will protect the **life**
Mt   25.46 but the **righteous** will go to eternal **life**.
Lk   1.75   **righteous** before him all...our **life**.
Rom   5.21   **righteousness**, leading us to eternal **life**
Heb   12.11 the peaceful reward of a **righteous life**.

Safe, Protect

Ex   30.16 **lives**, and I will remember to **protect**
Num   31.50 for our **lives**, so that he will **protect** us.
1 Sam 2.9   **protects** the **lives** of his faithful people,
Ps   41.2   **protect** them and preserve their **lives**;
         61.4   sanctuary all my **life**; let me find **safety**
         71.6   you all my **life**; you have **protected** me
         97.10 he **protects** the **lives** of his people;
       142.5   **protector**; you are all I want in this **life**.
Prov   3.17   your **life** pleasant and lead you **safely**
         13.3   what you say and **protect** your **life**
         19.23 will live a long **life**, content and **safe**
         29.10 righteous people will **protect** the **life**
Amos   6.1   **life** in Zion and for you that feel **safe**
Heb   6.19   anchor for our **lives**. It is **safe** and sure,

Sake

Mt   10.39 whoever loses his **life** for my **sake**
         16.25 whoever loses his **life** for my **sake**
Lk   9.24   whoever loses his **life** for my **sake**
2 Cor   4.11   **sake**, in order that his **life** may be seen
Phil   2.30   his **life** and nearly died for the **sake**

Save, Rescue

Gen   19.19 me a great favour and **saved** my **life**.
         45.5   ahead of you to **save** people's **lives**.
         47.25 You have **saved** our **lives**;
Ex   21.30 is allowed to pay a fine to **save** his **life**,
Lev   18.5   you will **save** your **life** by doing so.
Judg   9.17   his **life** to **save** you from the Midianites.
2 Sam 19.5   **saved** your **life** and the lives of your
1 Kgs 1.12   **save** your **life** and the **life** of your son

Neh	6.11	to **save** my **life** by hiding in the Temple?
Esth	7.9	who **saved** Your Majesty's **life**.
Job	33.30	he **saves** a person's **life**,
Ps	17.14	**save** me from those who in this **life**
	22.20	**Save** me from the sword; **save** my **life**
	35.17	**save** my **life** from these lions!
	51.14	Spare my **life**, O God, and **save** me,
	64.1	am afraid of my enemies — **save** my **life**!
	72.13	he **saves** the **lives** of those in need.
	91.16	with long **life**; I will **save** them
	97.10	the **lives** of his people; he **rescues** them
Prov	10.2	but honesty can **save** your **life**.
	11.4	but honesty can **save** your **life**.
	13.8	has to use his money to **save** his **life**
	14.25	**saves** lives when he tells the truth
	16.17	you are going — it may **save** your **life**.
	23.14	it may **save** his **life**.
Is	38.17	You **save** my **life** from all danger;
	43.4	whole nations to **save** your **life**,
Lam	3.58	and **saved** my **life**.
Ezek	3.18	his ways so that he can **save** his **life**,
	13.22	giving up evil and **saving** their **lives**.
	14.14	would **save** only their own **lives**.
	14.16	They would **save** only their own **lives**.
	14.18	**save**...children, but only their own **lives**.
	14.20	would **save** only their own **lives**.
	18.27	he **saves** his **life**.
	33.8	his ways so that he can **save** his **life**,
	33.19	he has **saved** his **life**.
Amos	2.14	will not be able to **save** their own **lives**.
Mt	16.25	wants to **save** his own **life** will lose it;
Mk	3.4	To **save** a man's **life** or to destroy it?
	8.35	wants to **save** his own **life** will lose it;
Lk	6.9	To **save** a man's **life** or destroy it?
	9.24	wants to **save** his own **life** will lose it,
	17.33	tries to **save** his own **life** will lose it;
Rom	5.10	more will we be **saved** by Christ's **life**!
2 Cor	2.16	**saved**, it is a fragrance that brings **life**.

Son of God see **Christ**

Spare, Mercy

Gen	42.18	I will **spare** your **lives** on one condition.
Ex	4.25	And so the Lord **spared** Moses' **life**.
Deut	19.21	no **mercy**; the punishment is to be a **life**
Josh	6.25	**spared** the **lives** of the prostitute Rahab
1 Sam	15.9	Saul and his men **spared** Agag's **life**
	26.21	because you have **spared** my **life** tonight.
	26.24	Just as I have **spared** your **life** today,
1 Kgs	20.31	and maybe he will **spare** your **life**.
2 Kgs	1.13	be **merciful** to me...Spare our **lives**!
	7.4	but maybe they will **spare** our **lives**.
Esth	4.11	then that person's **life** is **spared**.
Ps	51.14	**Spare** my **life**, O God, and save me,
	78.50	or **spare** their **lives**,
	119.149	show your **mercy**, and preserve my **life**!
Jer	38.17	your **life** will be **spared**, and this city
	38.20	and your **life** will be **spared**.
	50.20	those people whose **lives** I have **spared**.
Ezek	3.19	but your **life** will be **spared**.
	3.21	and your **life** will also be **spared**.
	33.9	but your **life** will be **spared**.
	33.12	his **life** will not be **spared**.
Jon	1.6	feel sorry for us and **spare** our **lives**.
Acts	27.24	his goodness to you has **spared** the **lives**
Gal	6.16	their **lives**, may peace and **mercy**
1 Pet	1.3	of his great **mercy** he gave us new **life**
Jude	.21	in his **mercy** to give you eternal **life**.

Strong

Rom	11.17	the **strong** spiritual **life** of the Jews.
Phil	2.1	Your **life** in Christ makes you **strong**,
Col	2.7	your **lives** on him, and become **stronger**

Tree

Gen	2.9	stood the **tree** that gives **life**

Gen	3.22	fruit from the **tree** that gives **life**,
	3.24	near the **tree** that gives **life**.
Rev	22.2	was the **tree** of **life**, which bears fruit
	22.14	eat the fruit from the **tree** of **life**
	22.19	share of the fruit of the **tree** of **life**

Trouble, Danger, Disaster

Ex	30.12	**life**, so that no **disaster** will come on
Deut	28.66	Your **life** will always be in **danger**
2 Sam	19.7	worst **disaster** you have suffered in all your **life**.
Job	14.1	the same short, **troubled life**.
Ps	78.33	and their **lives** with sudden **disaster**.
	90.10	is **trouble** and sorrow; **life** is soon over,
Prov	7.23	not know that his **life** was in **danger**.
	13.14	you escape when your **life** is in **danger**.
Is	38.17	You save my **life** from all **danger**;
Jer	20.18	have **trouble** and sorrow, to end my **life**
	38.24	and your **life** will not be in **danger**.

Union

Rom	6.23	gift is eternal **life** in **union** with Christ
	8.2	brings us **life** in **union** with Christ Jesus,
1 Cor	4.15	in your **life** in **union** with Christ Jesus
	4.17	the new **life** in **union** with Christ Jesus
	9.2	of your **life** in **union** with the Lord
	15.31	in our **life** in **union** with Christ Jesus
2 Cor	1.21	sure of our **life** in **union** with Christ;
Gal	5.10	**life** in **union** with the Lord makes me
Eph	1.1	faithful in their **life** in **union** with Christ
Phil	1.26	in your **life** in **union** with Christ Jesus.
	3.3	rejoice in our **life** in **union** with Christ
	4.10	**life** in **union** with the Lord it is a great
Col	2.10	been given full **life** in **union** with him
1 Thes	3.8	in your **life** in **union** with the Lord.
	5.18	in your **life** in **union** with Christ Jesus
2 Tim	1.1	**life** which we have in **union** with Christ
	3.12	to live a godly **life** in **union** with Christ
Phlm	.6	have in our **life** in **union** with Christ.

Useless

Ecc	1.2	**Life** is **useless**, all **useless**.
	4.7	something else in **life** that is **useless**.
	6.12	in this short, **useless life** of his
	7.15	My **life** has been **useless**
	9.9	as long as you live the **useless life**
Tit	3.14	they should not **live useless lives**.

Wicked see **Evil**

Will, Purpose

Job	21.14	want to know his **will** for their **lives**.
Is	53.10	long **life**, and through him my **purpose**
Jer	32.39	I will give them a single **purpose** in **life**
2 Tim	1.1	**will**, sent to proclaim the promised **life**
	3.10	and my **purpose** in **life**;
1 Pet	4.2	earthly **lives** controlled by God's **will**

World

Ecc	8.15	during the **life**...in this **world**.
	9.9	the useless **life**...in this **world**.
Mt	16.26	wins the whole **world** but loses his **life**?
Mk	8.36	wins the whole **world** but loses his **life**?
Jn	6.33	from heaven and gives **life** to the **world**
	12.25	whoever hates his own **life** in this **world**
1 Cor	3.22	this **world**, **life** and death,
2 Cor	1.12	assures us that our **lives** in this **world**,
Tit	2.12	and godly **lives** in this **world**,
1 Jn	4.9	**world**, so that we might have **life**
	4.17	have it because our **life** in this **world**

Worry

Ecc	2.22	work and **worry** your way through **life**
	5.17	to **live** our **lives** in darkness...**worried**,
	5.20	**worry** too much about how short **life** is.
Is	32.9	who **live** an easy **life**, free from **worries**
	32.11	living an easy **life**, free from **worries**;

Mt	13.22	the **worries** about this **life** and the love
Mk	4.19	but the **worries** about this **life**
Lk	8.14	the **worries**...and pleasures of this **life**
	21.34	and with the **worries** of this **life**,

LIGHT

Gen	1.3 – 18			x8
Is	59.9	—	60.20	x8
Ezek	8.4	—	11.23	x8
Mt	4.16	—	6.23	x7
Jn	11.9	—	12.46	x7
Jn	1.4 – 9			x6
Jn	3.19 – 21			x6
Eph	5.8 – 14			x6
1 Jn	1.5	—	2.10	x6
Job	24.13	—	26.10	x5
2 Cor	4.2 – 6			x5
Ezek	43.2	—	44.4	x4
Lk	11.33 – 36			x4
Lev	13.21 – 28			x3
2 Chr	7.1 – 3			x3
Job	17.12	—	18.18	x3
Job	28.11	—	30.26	x3
Job	37.21	—	38.19	x3
Is	9.2	—	10.17	x3
Jn	8.12	—	9.5	x3
Acts	12.7	—	13.47	x3
Acts	22.6 – 11			x3
Acts	26.13 – 23			x3

Darkness

Gen	1.4	he separated the **light** from the **darkness**,
	1.5	**light** "Day" and the **darkness** "Night".
	1.18	and to separate **light** from **darkness**.
Ex	14.20	**dark** for the Egyptians, but gave **light**
2 Sam	22.29	are my **light**; you dispel my **darkness**
Job	10.22	where the **light** itself is **darkness**.
	12.22	He sends **light** to places **dark** as death.
	17.12	**light** is near, but...I remain in **darkness**.
	18.18	driven from **light** into **darkness**.
	24.17	They fear the **light** of day, but **darkness**
	26.10	He divided **light** from **darkness**
	29.3	**light** as I walked through the **darkness**.
	30.26	and **light**, but trouble and **darkness**
	38.19	the **light** comes from or what the source of **darkness** is?
Ps	18.28	give me **light**; you dispel my **darkness**.
	112.4	**Light** shines in the **darkness** for good
	139.11	**darkness** to hide me or the **light** round
	139.12	**Darkness** and **light** are the same to you.
Ecc	2.13	just as **light** is better than **darkness**.
Is	5.20	**darkness** into **light** and **light** into
	5.30	The **light** is swallowed by **darkness**.
	9.2	in **darkness** have seen a great **light**.
	42.16	I will turn their **darkness** into **light**
	45.7	I create both **light** and **darkness**;
	49.9	are in **darkness**, 'Come out to the **light**!
	59.9	for **light**...but there is only **darkness**,
	60.2	by **darkness**, But on you the **light**
Jer	13.16	deep **darkness** the **light** you hoped for.
Ezek	32.8	**lights** of heaven and plunge your world into **darkness**.
Dan	2.22	**darkness**, and he...is surrounded by **light**.
Amos	5.18	be a day of **darkness** and not of **light**.
	5.20	Lord will bring **darkness** and not **light**;
Mic	7.8	in **darkness** now, but the Lord will give us **light**.
Mt	4.16	live in **darkness** will see a great **light**.
	6.23	So if the **light** in you is **darkness**,
Lk	11.35	that the **light** in you is not **darkness**.
	11.36	of **light**, with no part of it in **darkness**,
Jn	1.5	The **light** shines in the **darkness**
	3.19	love the **darkness** rather than the **light**,
	8.12	**light**...and will never walk in **darkness**.

Jn	12.35	the **light**, so that the **darkness** will not
Acts	26.18	them from the **darkness** to the **light**
Rom	2.19	a **light** for those who are in **darkness**,
1 Cor	4.5	he will bring to **light** the **dark** secrets
2 Cor	4.6	Out of **darkness** the **light** shall shine!
	6.14	can **light** and **darkness** live together?
Eph	5.11	**darkness**...bring them out to **light**
Jas	1.17	**lights**, who does not...cause **darkness**
1 Pet	2.9	**darkness** into his own marvellous **light**.
2 Pet	1.19	in a **dark** place until...the **light**
1 Jn	1.5	God is **light**, and there is no **darkness**
	2.8	**darkness** is passing away, and the...**light**
	2.9	in the **light**, yet hates his brother, is in the **darkness**

Dazzling, Presence

Ex	16.7	morning you will see the **dazzling light**
	16.10	the **dazzling light** of the Lord appeared
	24.16	**dazzling light** of the Lord's **presence**
	29.43	and the **dazzling light** of my **presence**
	33.18	see the **dazzling light** of your **presence**.
	33.22	When the **dazzling light** of my **presence**
	40.34	**dazzling light** of the Lord's **presence**
Lev	9.6	the **dazzling light** of his **presence**
	9.23	the **dazzling light** of the Lord's **presence**
Num	14.10	the people saw the **dazzling light**
	14.22	They have seen the **dazzling light**
	16.19	the **dazzling light** of the Lord's **presence**
		Also: 16.42; 20.6
1 Kgs	8.11	**dazzling light** of the Lord's **presence**,
2 Chr	5.11	a cloud shining with the **dazzling light**
	7.1	the **dazzling light** of the Lord's **presence**
	7.2	Temple was full of the **dazzling light**,
Job	37.21	now the **light** in the sky is **dazzling**,
Ps	56.13	in the **presence** of God, in the **light**
Ezek	1.28	**dazzling light** that shows the **presence**
	8.4	**dazzling light** that shows the **presence**
	9.3	**dazzling light** of the **presence** of the
	10.4	**dazzling light** of the Lord's **presence**
	10.18	the **dazzling light** of the Lord's **presence**
	10.19	and the **dazzling light** was over them.
	11.22	**dazzling light** of the **presence** of the
	11.23	the **dazzling light** left the city
	43.2	coming from the east the **dazzling light**
	43.4	The **dazzling light** passed through
	44.4	with the **dazzling light** of his **presence**.

God, Eternal, Lord

Gen	1.3	**God** commanded, "Let there be **light**
	1.14	**God** commanded, "Let **lights** appear
	1.16	So **God** made the two larger **lights**,
2 Sam	22.29	You, **Lord**, are my **light**;
Job	25.3	place where **God's light** does not shine?
	29.3	**God**...gave me **light** as I walked
Ps	18.28	O **Lord**, you give me **light**;
	27.1	The **Lord** is my **light** and my salvation;
	56.13	in the presence of God, in the **light**
Is	2.5	walk in the **light** which the **Lord** gives
	10.17	**God**, the **light** of Israel, will become
	60.2	on you the **light** of the **Lord** will shine;
	60.19	the **Lord**, will be your eternal **light**;
	60.20	the **Lord**, will be your eternal **light**,
Jer	31.35	The **Lord** provides the sun for **light**
Ezek	8.4	**light** that shows the presence of Israel's **God**,
	9.3	**light** of the presence of the **God**
	11.22	**light** of the presence of the **God**
	43.2	**light** of the presence of the **God**
Mic	7.8	but the **Lord** will give us **light**.
1 Cor	4.5	the **Lord** comes; he will bring to **light**
2 Cor	4.6	The **God** who said, "Out of darkness the **light** shall shine
Col	1.11	what **God** has reserved...in the kingdom of **light**.

Heb	6.4	They were once in **God's light**;	
	10.32	after **God's light** had shone on you,	
Jas	1.17	**God**, the Creator of the heavenly **lights**,	
1 Jn	1.5	**God** is **light**, and there is no darkness	
Rev	22.5	the **Lord God** will be their **light**,	

Presence see **Dazzling**

Truth
Num	5.15	made to bring the **truth** to **light**.
Ps	43.3	Send your **light** and your **truth**;
2 Cor	4.2	In the full **light** of **truth** we live

World
Ps	77.18	flashes of lightning **lit** up the **world**;
	97.4	His lightning **lights** up the **world**;
Is	49.6	**light** to the nations — so...all the **world**
Ezek	32.8	**lights** of heaven and plunge your **world**
Mt	5.14	You are like **light** for the whole **world**
Jn	1.9	the **light** that comes into the **world**,
	3.19	the **light** has come into the **world**,
	8.12	I am the **light** of the **world**,
	9.5	the **world**, I am the **light** for the **world**.
	11.9	for he sees the **light** of this **world**.
	12.46	I have come into the **world** as **light**
Acts	13.47	**light** for the Gentiles, so...all the **world**
2 Cor	4.4	**world**...keeps them from seeing the **light**
Rev	21.24	of the **world** will walk by its **light**

LOT
	1 Chr	24.5 — 26.13	x5
	Josh	18.6 — 19.51	x4

Choose
Lev	16.9	sacrifice the goat **chosen** by **lot**
Judg	20.9	we will draw **lots** and **choose** some men
Neh	11.1	drew **lots** to **choose** one family
Lk	1.9	he was **chosen** by **lot** to burn incense
Acts	1.26	drew **lots** to **choose** between the two

Determine
Josh	14.2	were **determined** by drawing **lots**.
Neh	10.34	**lots** each year to **determine** which clans
Esth	9.24	cast **lots**...to **determine** the day
Prov	16.33	**lots** to learn God's will, but God himself **determines**

LOVE
	1 Jn	2.5 — 5.3	x42
	Song	1.2 — 8.13	x34
	Jn	10.17 — 17.26	x33
	Ps	119.41 – 167	x19
	Eph	1.4 — 6.24	x17
	1 Cor	13.1 — 14.1	x12
	Jn	19.26 — 21.20	x11
	Deut	4.37 — 7.13	x10
	2 Cor	5.14 — 9.7	x10
	1 Thes	1.3 — 5.13	x10
	Hos	1.6 — 4.1	x8
	Lk	6.27 — 7.47	x8
	Rom	8.28 — 9.25	x8
	Rom	12.9 — 15.30	x8
	Deut	10.12 — 11.22	x7
	2 Sam	11.4 — 13.15	x7
	Ps	89.1 – 49	x7
	Is	61.8 — 64.11	x7
	Col	1.4 — 3.19	x7
	2 Tim	1.7 — 4.10	x7
	1 Pet	1.8 — 5.14	x7
	Gen	29.18 – 33	x6
	Ps	107.1 – 43	x6
	2 Jn	.1 – 6	x6
	Ps	103.4 – 17	x5
	Ps	109.4 – 26	x5
	Ps	118.1 – 29	x5
	1 Sam	18.1 – 28	x4
	1 Kgs	3.3 – 26	x4
	Ps	31.7 – 23	x4
	Ps	33.5 – 22	x4
	Is	54.7 – 10	x4
	Ezek	16.5 – 32	x4
	Mk	12.30 – 33	x4
	Gal	5.6 – 22	x4

Anger
Ex	34.6	easily **angered** and who shows great **love**
Num	14.18	easily **angered**, and I show great **love**
Neh	9.17	gracious and **loving**, slow to be **angry**.
Ps	103.8	become **angry** and full of constant **love**.
	145.8	become **angry** and full of constant **love**.
Hos	14.4	I will **love** them...no longer am I **angry**
Zech	8.2	a **love** which has made me **angry**

Believe see **Faith**

Believer see **God's People**

Body see **God's People**

Brother see **God's People**

Child of God see **God's People**

Children
Hos	11.1	When Israel was a **child**, I **loved** him
Mic	1.16	in mourning for the **children** you **love**.
Tit	2.4	to **love** their husbands and **children**,
1 Jn	5.1	whoever **loves** a father **loves** his **child**

Christ, Jesus, Son of God
Mt	22.37	**Jesus** answered, "**Love** the Lord
Mk	10.21	**Jesus** looked straight at him with **love**
Jn	3.35	**loves** his **Son** and has put everything
	5.20	Father **loves** the **Son** and shows him all
	11.5	**Jesus loved** Martha and her sister
	13.23	the one whom **Jesus loved**,
	14.23	**Jesus** answered...Whoever **loves** me
	19.26	**Jesus** saw...the disciple he **loved**
	20.2	other disciple, whom **Jesus loved**,
	21.7	The disciple whom **Jesus loved**
	21.17	**Jesus** said, "Simon son of John, do you **love** me?
	21.20	other disciple, whom **Jesus loved**
Rom	8.35	can separate us from the **love** of **Christ**?
	8.39	the **love** of God which is ours through **Christ Jesus**
	15.30	**Jesus Christ** and by the **love** that
1 Cor	16.24	My **love** be with you all in **Christ Jesus**.
2 Cor	5.14	We are ruled by the **love** of **Christ**,
Gal	2.20	faith in the **Son** of God, who **loved** me
Eph	2.7	the **love** he showed us in **Christ Jesus**.
	3.18	high and deep, is **Christ's love**.
	4.15	of **love**, we must grow up...to **Christ**,
	5.2	by **love**, just as **Christ loved** us
	5.25	just as **Christ loved** the church
	6.24	those who **love** our Lord **Jesus Christ**
Phil	2.1	Your life in **Christ**...and his **love**
1 Tim	1.14	and **love** which are ours in union with **Christ Jesus**.
2 Tim	1.13	and **love** that are ours in union with **Christ Jesus**.
1 Jn	3.16	what **love** is: **Christ** gave his life
	3.23	**love** one another, just as **Christ**
	4.9	his **love** for us by sending his only **Son**
	4.10	but that he **loved** us and sent his **Son**
	4.21	command...**Christ** has given...**love**

Christian see **God's People**

Comfort see **Help**

Command
Deut	7.9	who **love** him and obey his **commands**,
	10.12	do all that he **commands**. **Love** him,
	11.13	obey the **commands**...**love** the Lord

133

Deut 11.22 **Love**...God, do everything he **commands**,
      19.9   I **command** you...if you **love** the Lord
Josh 22.5   Moses **commanded** you: **love** the Lord
Neh   1.5   **love** you and do what you **command**.
Ps   119.47 your **commands**, because I **love** them.
      119.48 I respect and **love** your **commandments**;
      119.64 **love**; teach me your **commandments**.
      119.124**love**, and teach me your **commands**.
      119.127I **love** your **commands** more than gold,
Dan   9.4   **love** you and do what you **command**.
Mt   22.39 **commandment** is...**Love** your neighbour
Mk   12.31 **commandment** is this: '**Love** your
Jn   13.34 a new **commandment**: **love** one another
      14.15 you **love** me...obey my **commandments**
      14.21 **commandments**...is the one who **loves**
      15.10 obey my **commands**...remain in my **love**
      15.12 **commandment** is this: **love** one another
      15.17 what I **command** you: **love** one another.
Rom   13.9   one **command**. "**Love** your neighbour
Gal   5.14   **commandment**: "**Love** your neighbour
1 Jn 3.23   **love** one another...as Christ **commanded**
      5.3   **love**...means that we obey his **commands**
2 Jn .5   let us all **love** one another. This is no new
             command

Compassion see **Mercy**

Constant, Enduring, Eternal

Deut 7.9   **constant love** to a thousand generations
      7.12   and will show you his **constant love**,
2 Sam 22.51 he shows **constant love**
1 Kgs 3.6   your great and **constant love**
      10.9   Because his **love** for Israel is **eternal**,
1 Chr 16.34 his **love** is **eternal**.
      16.41 praises to the Lord for his **eternal love**.
2 Chr 5.11   And his **love** is **eternal**.
      7.3   for his goodness and his **eternal love**.
      7.6   His **Love Is Eternal**!
      20.21 His **love** is **eternal**!
Ezra 3.11   and his **love** for Israel is **eternal**.
Job   10.12 have given me life and **constant love**,
Ps   13.5   I rely on your **constant love**;
      18.50 he shows **constant love**
      21.7   and because of the Lord's **constant love**
      25.6   your kindness and **constant love**
      25.7   In your **constant love** and goodness,
      26.3   Your **constant love** is my guide;
      31.7   because of your **constant love**.
      31.16 save me in your **constant love**.
      32.10 are protected by his **constant love**.
      33.5   his **constant love** fills the earth.
      33.18 those who trust in his **constant love**.
      33.22 May your **constant love** be with us,
      36.5   your **constant love** reaches the heavens;
      36.7   precious...is your **constant love**!
      40.10 your loyalty and **constant love**.
      42.8   May the Lord show his **constant love**
      44.26 Because of your **constant love** save us!
      48.9   we think of your **constant love**.
      51.1   because of your **constant love**.
      52.8   I trust in his **constant love**
      57.3   God will show me his **constant love**
      57.10 Your **constant love** reaches the heavens;
      59.16 sing aloud of your **constant love**,
      61.7   protect him with your **constant love**
      62.12 and that his **love** is **constant**.
      63.3   Your **constant love** is better than life
      66.20 or keep back his **constant love**
      69.16 in the goodness of your **constant love**;
      85.7   Show us your **constant love**,
      86.5   full of **constant love** for all
      86.13 How great is your **constant love**
      88.11 **constant love** spoken of in the grave
      89.1   I will always sing of your **constant love**;
      90.14 Fill us...with your **constant love**,

Ps   92.2   to proclaim your **constant love**
      94.18 but your **constant love**...held me up.
      98.3   with loyalty and **constant love**
      100.5 his **love** is **eternal**
      103.8 and full of **constant love**.
      103.17 his **love** lasts...and his goodness **endures**
      106.1 his **love** is **eternal**.
      107.1 his **love** is **eternal**!
      107.8 thank the Lord for his **constant love**,
             Also: 107.15, 21, 31
      107.43 consider the Lord's **constant love**.
      108.4 **constant love** reaches above the heavens;
      109.26 because of your **constant love**, save me!
      115.1 because of your **constant love**
      118.1 and his **love** is **eternal**.
             Also: 118.2, 3, 4, 29
      119.64 the earth is full of your **constant love**;
      119.76 Let your **constant love** comfort me,
      119.88 of your **constant love** be good to me,
      119.124me according to your **constant love**,
      119.149Because your **love** is **constant**
      130.7 because his **love** is **constant**
      136.1 his **love** is **eternal**.
             Also: 136.2 – 26
      138.2 because of your **constant love**
      138.8 your **love** is **eternal**.
      143.8 Remind me...of your **constant love**,
      145.8 and full of **constant love**.
      147.11 who trust in his **constant love**.
Is   63.7   his mercy and **constant love**.
Jer   9.24   because my **love** is **constant**,
      31.3   to show you my **constant love**.
      32.18 have shown **constant love** to thousands,
      33.11 and his **love** is **eternal**.
Dan   9.4   **constant love** to those who **love** you
Hos   2.19   will show you **constant love** and mercy
      6.6   I want your **constant love**,
Mic   6.8   to show **constant love**,
      7.18   in showing us your **constant love**.
      7.20   show your faithfulness and **constant love**
1 Cor 13.8   **Love** is **eternal**
2 Thes 3.5   of God's **love** and the **endurance**
1 Tim 6.11   **love**, **endurance**, and gentleness.
2 Tim 3.10   my patience, my **love**, my **endurance**,
Tit   2.2   **love**, and **endurance**.

Covenant see **Promise**

Dear

Ps   78.68 and Mount Zion, which he **dearly loves**.
Jer   31.20 you are my **dearest** son, the child I **love**
Phlm .7   Your **love**, **dear** brother
1 Jn 4.7   **Dear** friends, let us **love** one another,

Death

Prov 8.36   anyone who hates me **loves death**.
Song 8.6   **Love** is as powerful as **death**;
Rom   8.38   separate us from his **love**: neither **death**
1 Jn 3.14   **love** is still under the power of **death**.
Rev   1.5   **loves** us, and by his **death** he has freed

Destroy

Ps   39.11 like a moth you **destroy** what he **loves**.
      102.14 **love** her, even though she is **destroyed**;
      143.12 **love** for me, kill my enemies and **destroy**
      145.20 who **loves** him, but he will **destroy**
Is   64.11 **destroyed** by fire...the places we **loved**

Enduring see **Constant**

Enemies

Ps   143.12 of your **love** for me, kill my **enemies**
Jer   12.7   I **love** into the power of their **enemies**.

Zech	8.2	**love** which has made me angry with her **enemies.**
Mt	5.44	**love** your **enemies** and pray for those
Lk	6.27	**Love** your **enemies,**
	6.35	**Love** your **enemies** and do good to

Eternal see **Constant**

Evil, Wicked

Ps	45.7	**love** what is right and hate what is **evil.**
	52.3	You **love evil** more than good
	97.10	The Lord **loves** those who hate **evil;**
	109.5	back **evil** for good and hatred for **love.**
	119.119	the **wicked** like rubbish, and so I **love**
	145.20	who **loves** him, but he will destroy the **wicked.**
Prov	11.20	**evil-minded** people, but **loves** those
	15.9	the ways of **evil** people, but **loves** those
	19.28	**Wicked** people **love** the taste of **evil.**
Jer	11.15	The people I **love** are doing **evil** things.
Amos	5.15	Hate what is **evil, love** what is right
Mic	3.2	what is good and you **love** what is **evil.**
Mt	24.12	**evil** that many people's **love** will grow
1 Cor	13.6	**love** is not happy with **evil**
1 Tim	6.10	the **love** of money is a source of...**evil.**

Faith, Believe, Hope, Trust

Ps	33.18	those who **trust** in his constant **love.**
	33.22	**love** be with us...as we put our **hope** in
	52.8	I **trust** in his constant **love** for ever
	130.7	**trust** in the Lord, because his **love**
	143.8	**love,** for I put my **trust** in you.
	147.11	in those who **trust** in his constant **love.**
Jn	16.27	because you **love** me and have **believed**
1 Cor	13.7	**Love** never gives up; and its **faith**
	13.13	**faith,** hope, and **love;**
Gal	2.20	**faith** in the Son of God, who **loved** me
	5.6	matters is **faith** that works through **love.**
Eph	1.15	**faith** in the Lord Jesus and your **love**
	6.23	brothers peace and **love** with **faith.**
Col	1.4	**faith** in Christ Jesus and of your **love**
	1.5	your **faith** and **love** are based on what
1 Thes	1.3	**faith** into practice, how your **love** made
	3.6	news about your **faith** and **love.**
	5.8	wear **faith** and **love** as a breastplate,
2 Thes	1.3	**faith** is growing so much and the **love**
1 Tim	1.14	me the **faith** and **love** which are ours
	2.15	in **faith** and **love** and holiness,
	4.12	your **love, faith,** and purity.
	6.11	**faith, love,** endurance, and gentleness.
2 Tim	1.13	in the **faith** and **love** that are ours
	2.22	**faith, love,**
	3.10	my **faith,** my patience, my **love,**
Tit	2.2	in their **faith, love,** and endurance.
Phlm	.5	**love** for all God's people and the **faith**
1 Jn	3.23	**believe** in his Son Jesus Christ and **love**
	4.16	we ourselves know and **believe** the **love**

Faithfulness, Loyalty

Ex	34.6	who shows great **love** and **faithfulness.**
Num	14.18	**love** and **faithfulness** and forgive sin
Deut	30.20	**Love** the Lord your God...be **faithful**
Ps	25.10	With **faithfulness** and **love** he leads
	26.3	**love** is my guide; your **faithfulness**
	31.23	**Love** the Lord, all his **faithful** people.
	36.5	your constant **love** reaches the heavens; your **faithfulness**
	40.10	about your **loyalty** and constant **love.**
	40.11	**love** and **loyalty** will always keep me
	57.3	me his constant **love** and **faithfulness.**
	57.10	Your constant **love** reaches the heavens; your **faithfulness**
	61.7	with your constant **love** and **faithfulness.**
	85.10	**Love** and **faithfulness** will meet;
	86.15	**loving** God...always kind and **faithful.**

Ps	88.11	constant **love** spoken of in the grave or your **faithfulness**
	89.1	**love;** I will proclaim your **faithfulness**
	89.2	your **love** will last...your **faithfulness**
	89.14	**love** and **faithfulness** are shown in all
	89.24	I will **love** him and be **loyal** to him;
	92.2	**love** every morning and your **faithfulness**
	98.3	with **loyalty** and constant **love** for them.
	100.5	**love** is eternal and his **faithfulness** lasts
	108.4	Your constant **love** reaches above the heavens; your **faithfulness**
	115.1	of your constant **love** and **faithfulness.**
	117.2	**love** for us is strong and his **faithfulness**
	138.2	of your constant **love** and **faithfulness,**
Prov	5.15	**faithful** to your...wife and give your **love**
Is	16.5	the people with **faithfulness** and **love.**
Dan	9.4	**faithful** to your covenant and show constant **love**
Hos	2.19	**faithful;** I will show you constant **love**
	4.1	is no **faithfulness** or **love** in the land,
Mic	7.20	show your **faithfulness** and constant **love**
Mt	6.24	**love** the other; he will be **loyal** to one
Lk	16.13	**love** the other; he will be **loyal** to one
Rev	2.19	**love,** your **faithfulness,** your service,

Forgive see **Mercy**

Gentleness

1 Cor	4.21	or in a spirit of **love** and **gentleness?**
Eph	4.2	**gentle,** and patient. Show your **love**
1 Tim	6.11	**love,** endurance, and **gentleness.**

Glad see **Joy**

God

Deut	6.5	**Love** the **Lord** your **God** with all your
	11.1	**Love** the **Lord** your **God** and always
	11.13	**love** the **Lord** your **God** and serve him
	11.22	**Love** the **Lord** your **God,**
	13.3	**God** is using him to test you, to see if you **love**
	19.9	and if you **love** the **Lord** your **God**
	30.20	**Love** the **Lord** your **God,**
Josh	22.5	**love** the **Lord** your **God,**
	23.11	to **love** the **Lord** your **God.**
2 Sam	22.51	**God**...shows constant **love**
2 Chr	7.3	worshipping **God**...for his...eternal **love.**
Neh	9.17	**God** who forgives...gracious and **loving,**
	13.26	**God** loved him and made him king
Ps	18.50	**God**...shows constant **love**
	36.7	precious, O **God,** is your constant **love!**
	48.9	O **God,** we think of your constant **love.**
	51.1	O **God,** because of your constant **love.**
	57.3	**God** will show me his constant **love**
	59.10	My **God loves** me and will come to me;
	59.17	refuge is **God,** the **God** who **loves** me.
	61.7	O **God;** protect him with your constant **love**
	86.15	are a merciful and **loving God,**
	91.14	**God** says, "I will save those who **love**
	109.26	**God;** because of your constant **love,**
	118.3	Let the priests of **God** say, "His **love**
Is	62.12	The City That **God Loves,**
Dan	10.11	**God loves** you.
	10.19	**God loves** you, so don't...worry
Hos	1.7	will show **love.** I, the **Lord** their **God,**
Jon	4.2	that you are a **loving** and merciful **God,**
Mt	22.37	**Love** the **Lord** your **God** with all your
Mk	12.30	**Love** the **Lord** your **God** with all your
	12.33	man must **love God** with all his heart
Lk	10.27	**Love** the **Lord** your **God** with all your
	11.42	you neglect justice and **love** for **God.**
Jn	3.16	For **God** loved the world so much
	5.42	I know that you have no **love** for **God**
	8.42	**love** me, because I came from **God**

Jn	12.43	**loved** the approval of men rather than the approval of **God.**
Rom	1.7	all of you in Rome whom **God loves**
	5.5	**God** has poured out his **love** into our
	5.8	**God** has shown us how much he **loves**
	8.28	**God** works for good with those who **love** him,
	8.39	the **love** of **God** which is ours
1 Cor	2.9	**God** prepared for those who **love** him.
	8.3	who **loves God** is known by him.
2 Cor	6.6	to be **God's** servants...by our true **love**,
	9.7	for **God loves** the one who gives gladly.
	13.11	**God** of **love** and peace will be with
	13.13	the **love** of **God**,
Eph	2.4	**God's**...**love** for us is so great
Col	3.12	are the people of **God**; he **loved** you
1 Thes	1.4	**God loves** you and has chosen you
	4.9	taught by **God** how you should **love**
2 Thes	2.16	and **God** our Father, who **loved** us
	3.5	a greater understanding of **God's love**
1 Tim	6.11	righteousness, **godliness**, faith, **love**,
2 Tim	3.4	they will **love** pleasure rather than **God**;
Tit	3.4	kindness and **love** of **God** our Saviour
Jas	1.12	**God** has promised to those who **love**
1 Jn	2.5	**love** for **God** has really been made
	3.17	how can he claim that he **loves God**?
	4.7	**love** one another, because **love** comes from **God**.
	4.8	does not **love** does not know **God**, for **God** is **love**.
	4.9	And **God** showed his **love** for us
	4.10	is what **love** is: it is not that we have **loved God**
	4.10	but that **he loved** us
	4.11	if this is how **God loved** us,
	4.16	believe the **love** which **God** has for us.
	4.19	We **love** because **God** first **loved** us
	4.20	he **loves God**, but hates his brother,
	4.21	**loves God** must **love** his brother also.
	5.2	it is by **loving God** and obeying
	5.3	our **love** for **God** means that we obey
2 Jn	.6	**love**...means...obedience to **God's**
Jude	.1	who live in the **love** of **God**
	.21	and keep yourselves in the **love** of **God**,

God's People, Believer, Body, Brother, Child of God, Christian, One Another

Deut	33.3	The Lord **loves his people**
2 Chr	2.11	Because the Lord **loves his people**,
	9.8	Because he **loves his people** Israel
Ps	47.4	possession of **his people**, whom he **loves**.
Prov	17.17	show their **love**. What are **brothers** for
Is	44.2	**my chosen people** whom I **love**.
	56.6	part of **his people**, who **love** him
Jer	16.5	**people** with peace or show them **love**
Hos	14.4	**my people** back to me. I will **love** them
Mic	2.9	**my people** out of the homes they **love**,
Mal	1.2	to **his people**, "I have always **loved** you.
Jn	13.34	**love one another.**
	13.35	If you have **love** for **one another**,
	15.12	**love one another**,
	15.17	**love one another.**
Rom	1.7	**loves** and...called to be **his own people**:
	12.10	**Love one another** warmly as **Christian brothers**
	13.8	you have is to **love one another.**
Gal	5.13	let **love** make you serve **one another.**
Eph	1.15	and your **love** for all **God's people**,
	4.2	**love** by being tolerant with **one another**,
	4.16	whole **body** grows...through **love**
	6.23	to all **Christian brothers** peace and **love**
Col	1.4	and of your **love** for all **God's people.**
	3.12	are the **people** of **God**; he **loved** you
1 Thes	1.4	**brothers**, we know that **God loves** you

1 Thes	3.12	**love** for **one another** and for all people
	4.9	you about **love** for your **fellow-believers**
	4.9	how you should **love one another.**
2 Thes	2.13	**brothers**, you whom the Lord **loves.**
1 Tim	6.2	their work are **believers** whom they **love.**
Phlm	.5	I hear of your **love** for all **God's people**
	.7	Your **love**, dear **brother**
Heb	10.24	to help **one another** to show **love**
	12.6	everyone he **loves**...as a **son.**
	13.1	**loving one another** as **Christian brothers**
1 Pet	1.22	a sincere **love** for your **fellow-believers**,
	1.22	**love one another** earnestly
	2.17	**love** your **fellow-believers**,
	3.8	**love one another** as **brothers**,
	4.8	**love one another** earnestly,
	5.14	with the kiss of **Christian love.**
2 Pet	1.7	to your **brotherly affection** add **love.**
1 Jn	2.10	**loves** his **brother** lives in the light,
	3.1	His **love** is so great that we are called **God's children**
	3.10	or does not **love** his **brother** is not **God's child.**
	3.11	we must **love one another.**
	3.14	know it because we **love** our **brothers.**
	3.17	**brother**, how can he claim that he **loves**
	3.23	Son Jesus Christ and **love one another**,
	4.7	**love** one another, because **love** comes
	4.7	Whoever **loves** is a **child of God**
	4.11	**God loved** us, then we should **love one another.**
	4.12	seen God, but if we **love one another**
	4.20	he **loves** God, but hates his **brother**,
	4.21	**loves** God must **love** his **brother**
	5.1	whoever **loves** a father **loves** his **child**
	5.2	we know that we **love God's children**:
2 Jn	.5	let us all **love one another.**
Rev	20.9	**God's people** and the city that he **loves.**

Grace see **Mercy**

Happy see **Joy**

Hate

Gen	37.4	he **loved** them, they **hated** their brother
Lev	19.18	to **hate** him, but **love** your neighbour
Judg	14.16	You don't **love** me! You just **hate** me!
2 Sam	13.15	**hated** her now...more than he had **loved**
	19.6	**love** you and support those who **hate**
Ps	45.7	**love** what is right and **hate** what is evil.
	97.10	The Lord **loves** those who **hate** evil;
	109.5	and **hatred** for **love.**
	109.17	**loved** to curse...He **hated** to give
	119.163	I **hate** and detest all lies, but I **love**
Prov	8.36	anyone who **hates** me **loves** death.
	10.12	**Hate** stirs up trouble, but **love** overlooks
	11.20	Lord **hates** evil-minded people, but **love**
	15.9	**hates** the ways of evil people, but **loves**
Ecc	3.8	the time for **love** and the time for **hate**,
	9.1	even their **love** and their **hate.**
	9.6	Their **loves**, their **hates**
Is	61.8	I **love** justice and I **hate** oppression
Amos	5.15	**Hate** what is evil, **love** what is right
Mic	3.2	you **hate** what is good and you **love**
Mt	5.43	**Love** your friends, **hate** your enemies.
	6.24	he will **hate** one and **love** the other;
Lk	6.27	**Love** your enemies...those who **hate**
	16.13	he will **hate** one and **love** the other;
Jn	12.25	**loves** his...life will lose it; whoever **hates**
Rom	9.13	I **loved** Jacob, but I **hated** Esau.
Heb	1.9	You **love** what is right and **hate**
1 Jn	4.20	he **loves** God, but **hates** his brother,

Heart, Mind

Deut	6.5	**Love** the Lord...with all your **heart**
	10.12	**Love** him, serve him with all your **heart**,
	13.3	you **love** the Lord with all your **heart.**

Deut	30.6	you will **love** him with all your **heart**,
1 Kgs	3.26	her **heart** full of **love** for her son,
	8.23	**love** when they live in **whole-hearted**
2 Chr	6.14	**love** when they live in **wholehearted**
Ps	119.167	I **love** them with all my **heart**.
Prov	22.11	**love** purity of **heart** and graciousness
Song	8.6	your **heart** to every **love** but mine;
Jer	31.20	of you with **love**. My **heart** goes out
Hos	11.8	**heart** will not let me do it! My **love** for
	14.4	I will **love** them with all my **heart**;
Mt	22.37	**Love** the Lord...with all your **heart**,
Mk	12.30	**Love** the Lord...with all your **heart**,
	12.33	man must **love** God with all his **heart** ...all his **mind**
Lk	10.27	**Love** the Lord...with all your **heart**,
Jn	5.42	have no **love** for God in your **hearts**.
Rom	5.5	has poured out his **love** into our **hearts**
Phil	2.2	**love**, and being one in soul and **mind**.
1 Tim	1.5	the **love** that comes from a pure **heart**,
1 Pet	1.22	**love** one another...with all your **heart**.

Heaven

Ps	36.5	your constant **love** reaches the **heavens**;
	57.10	Your constant **love** reaches the **heavens**;
	108.4	constant **love** reaches above the **heavens**;

Help, Comfort, Protect

Gen	24.67	**loved** Rebecca, and so he was **comforted**
Deut	33.3	The Lord **loves** his people and **protects**
	33.12	tribe the Lord **loves** and **protects**;
Ps	5.11	**Protect** those who **love** you;
	5.12	your **love protects** them like a shield.
	32.10	are **protected** by his constant **love**.
	36.7	your constant **love**! We find **protection**
	61.7	**protect** him with your constant **love**
	85.7	**love**, O Lord, and give us your...**help**.
	91.14	save those who **love** me and will **protect**
	97.10	**loves** those who hate evil; he **protects**
	119.76	Let your constant **love comfort** me,
	145.20	He **protects** everyone who **loves** him,
Prov	4.6	will **protect** you; **love** her, and she will
Jer	16.7	to **comfort** him when a **loved** one dies.
Lam	2.13	**beloved** Jerusalem...How can I **comfort**
Zech	8.2	**help** Jerusalem because of my deep **love**
2 Cor	8.6	**help** you complete this...service of **love**.
	8.7	your eagerness to **help** and in your **love**
Phil	2.1	and his **love comforts** you.
Heb	6.10	**love** you showed for him in the **help**
	10.24	to **help** one another to show **love** and
Jude	.1	the **love** of God...and the **protection**

Honour see Respect

Hope see Faith

Husband

Gen	29.32	and now my **husband** will **love** me
Deut	28.56	share them with the **husband** she **loves**
Eph	5.25	**Husbands**, **love** your wives just as Christ
	5.33	every **husband** must **love** his wife
Col	3.19	**Husbands**, **love** your wives and do not
Tit	2.4	younger women to **love** their **husbands**

Jesus see Christ

Joy, Glad, Happy

Ps	5.11	who **love** you; because of you they are ...**happy**.
	13.5	on your constant **love**; I will be **glad**,
	31.7	be **glad**...because of your constant **love**.
	90.14	**love**, so that we may sing and be **glad**
Prov	5.19	you **happy**...surround you with her **love**.
	7.18	**love** all night long. We'll be **happy**
Is	66.10	**glad** for her, all you that **love** this city!
Jn	14.28	**loved** me, you would be **glad** that I am
1 Cor	13.6	**love** is not **happy** with evil
2 Cor	9.7	for God **loves** the one who gives **gladly**.

Gal	5.22	But the Spirit produces **love**, **joy**
Phlm	.7	Your **love**...has brought me great **joy**

Justice, Right(eous)

Ps	11.7	Lord is **righteous** and **loves** good deeds;
	33.5	Lord **loves** what is righteous and **just**;
	37.28	for the Lord **loves** what is **right**
	45.7	**love** what is **right** and hate what is evil.
	85.10	**Love** and faithfulness...meet; **righteousness**
	89.14	**righteousness** and **justice**; your **love**
	99.4	you **love** what is right; you have established **justice**
	146.8	he **loves** his **righteous** people.
Prov	11.20	but **loves** those who do **right**.
	15.9	but **loves** those who do what is **right**.
Ecc	9.1	**righteous** men, even their **love** and their
Is	16.5	and **love**. He will...do what is **right**,
	61.8	I **love justice** and I hate oppression
Jer	9.24	**love** is constant, and I do what is **just**
Amos	5.15	**love** what is right, and see that **justice**
Mic	6.8	do what is **just**, to show constant **love**,
Lk	11.42	you neglect **justice** and **love** for God.
1 Tim	6.11	for **righteousness**, godliness, faith, **love**,
2 Tim	2.22	and strive for **righteousness**, faith, **love**,
Heb	1.9	**love** what is **right** and hate what is
1 Jn	3.10	is **right** or does not **love** his brother

Life

Gen	25.27	a man who **loved** the outdoor **life**,
Job	10.12	have given me **life** and constant **love**,
Ps	23.6	and **love** will be with me all my **life**;
	63.3	constant **love** is better than **life** itself,
	97.10	**loves** those who hate evil; he protects the **lives**
Prov	22.5	If you **love** your **life**
Ecc	9.9	Enjoy **life** with the woman you **love**,
Jer	17.21	Tell them that if they **love** their **lives**,
Zeph	3.17	in his **love** he will give you new **life**.
Mt	13.22	about this **life** and the **love** for riches
Mk	4.19	about this **life**, the **love** for riches,
Jn	10.17	**loves** me because I...give up my **life**
	12.25	Whoever **loves** his own **life** will lose it;
Rom	8.38	us from his **love**: neither death nor **life**,
Gal	2.20	of God, who **loved** me and gave his **life**
Eph	5.2	Your **life** must be controlled by **love**,
	5.25	Christ **loved** the church and gave his **life**
Phil	2.1	Your **life** in Christ makes you strong, and his
Heb	13.5	your **lives** free from the **love** of money
Jas	1.12	**life**...promised to those who **love** him.
1 Jn	3.14	into **life**; we know it because we **love**
	3.16	what **love** is: Christ gave his **life** for us.

Lord

see also **God**

Num	14.18	I, the **Lord**...show great **love**
	14.19	**Lord**, according to...your unchanging **love**,
Deut	7.7	**Lord** did not **love** you and choose you
	7.8	the **Lord loved** you and wanted to keep
	10.12	Worship the **Lord**...**Love** him,
	10.15	But the **Lord's love** for your ancestors
	13.3	to see if you **love** the **Lord**
	33.3	The **Lord loves** his people
	33.12	This is the tribe the **Lord loves**
2 Sam	12.24	The **Lord loved** the boy
	12.25	because the **Lord loved** him.
1 Kgs	3.3	Solomon **loved** the **Lord**
1 Chr	16.34	the **Lord**...his **love** is eternal.
	16.41	praises to the **Lord** for his eternal **love**.
2 Chr	2.11	Because the **Lord loves** his people,
	5.11	Praise the **Lord**...his **love** is eternal.
	20.21	Praise the **Lord**! His **love** is eternal!
Ezra	3.11	The **Lord** is good, and his **love**

Ps	5.12	**Lord**; your **love** protects them
	18.1	How I **love** you, **Lord**!
	21.7	because of the **Lord's** constant **love**
	25.6	**Lord**, your kindness and constant **love**
	25.7	your constant **love** and goodness...**Lord**!
	31.21	Praise the **Lord**! How wonderfully he showed his **love**
	31.23	**Love the Lord**, all his faithful people.
	33.5	**Lord loves** what is righteous and just;
	33.22	your constant **love** be with us, **Lord**,
	36.5	**Lord**, your constant **love** reaches the
	37.28	for the **Lord loves** what is right
	42.8	May the **Lord** show his constant **love**
	69.16	**Lord**, in the goodness of your constant **love**;
	85.7	Show us your constant **love**, O **Lord**,
	89.1	**Lord**, I will always sing of your constant **love**;
	89.49	**Lord**, where are the former proofs of your **love**?
	94.18	constant **love**, O **Lord**, held me up.
	97.10	The **Lord loves** those who hate evil;
	100.5	The **Lord** is good; his **love** is eternal
	103.17	who honour the **Lord**, his **love** lasts
	106.1	Give thanks to the **Lord**...his **love**
	107.1	Give thanks to the **Lord**...his **love**
	107.8	thank the **Lord** for his constant **love**, Also: 107.15, 21, 31
	107.43	the **Lord's** constant **love**.
	116.1	I **love** the **Lord**, because he hears me;
	118.1	Give thanks to the **Lord**...his **love**
	118.29	Give thanks to the **Lord**...his **love**
	119.41	Show me how much you **love** me, **Lord**,
	119.64	**Lord**, the earth is full of your constant **love**;
	119.149	your **love** is constant, hear me, O **Lord**;
	119.159	See how I **love** your instructions, **Lord**.
	127.2	the **Lord** provides for those he **loves**,
	130.7	trust in the **Lord**...his **love** is constant
	138.8	**Lord**, your **love** is eternal.
Prov	3.12	The **Lord** corrects those he **loves**,
	11.20	The **Lord...loves** those who do right.
	15.9	**Lord...loves** those who do what is right.
Is	54.10	So says the **Lord** who **loves** you.
	63.7	I will tell of the **Lord's** unfailing **love**;
Jer	11.15	**Lord** says, "The people I **love** are doing
	12.3	**Lord**, you know...how I **love** you.
Lam	3.22	The **Lord's** unfailing **love** and mercy
Hos	11.1	The **Lord** says, "When Israel was a child, I **loved** him
	14.4	The **Lord** says...I will **love** them
Zech	3.2	May the **Lord**, who **loves** Jerusalem,
Mal	1.2	**Lord** says...I have always **loved** you.
	2.11	Temple which the **Lord loves**
1 Cor	16.22	not **love** the **Lord** — a curse on him!
2 Cor	8.19	of **love** for the sake of the **Lord's** glory,
2 Thes	2.13	you whom the **Lord loves**.
Heb	12.6	the **Lord** corrects everyone he **loves**,

Loyalty see **Faithfulness**

Mercy, Compassion, Forgive, Grace

Num	14.18	**love** and faithfulness and **forgive** sin
	14.19	of your unchanging **love**, **forgive**,
Neh	9.17	**gracious** and **loving**, slow to be angry. Your **mercy** is great;
Ps	40.11	**merciful** to me. Your **love** and loyalty
	51.1	**love**. Because of your great **mercy**
	69.16	your constant **love**...great **compassion**
	86.5	**forgiving**, full of constant **love** for all
	86.15	are a **merciful** and **loving** God,
	103.4	and blesses me with **love** and **mercy**.
	119.132	**mercy** on me as you do on all those who **love** you.

Prov	22.11	**love** purity of heart and **graciousness**
Is	63.7	because of his **mercy** and constant **love**.
	63.9	**love** and **compassion** he rescued them.
	63.15	Where are your **love** and **compassion**?
Jer	16.5	peace or show them **love** and **mercy**.
	31.20	of you with **love**...I will be **merciful**.
Lam	3.22	unfailing **love** and **mercy** still continue,
Hos	1.6	**love** to the people of Israel or **forgive**
	2.19	will show you constant **love** and **mercy**
Jon	4.2	that you are a **loving** and **merciful** God,
Lk	7.47	**forgiven** little shows only a little **love**
2 Cor	13.13	**grace** of the Lord Jesus Christ, the **love**
Eph	2.4	**mercy** is so abundant, and his **love**
	2.7	his **grace** in the **love** he showed us
	6.24	God's **grace** be with all those who **love**
2 Thes	2.16	**loved** us and in his **grace** gave us
1 Tim	1.14	**grace** on me and gave me the...**love**
Jude	.2	**mercy**, peace, and **love** be yours in full

Mind see **Heart**

Money, Greedy

Ecc	5.10	if you **love money** you will never
Lk	16.14	because they **loved money**.
1 Tim	3.3	he must not **love money**;
	3.8	not...be **greedy** for **money**
	6.10	the **love** of **money** is a source of
Tit	1.7	violent or **greedy** for **money**
Heb	13.5	free from the **love** of **money**
2 Pet	2.15	Beor, who **loved** the **money** he would get

Neighbour

Lev	19.18	**love** your **neighbour** as you **love**
Mt	19.19	**love** your **neighbour** as you **love**
	22.39	**Love** your **neighbour** as you **love**
Mk	12.31	**Love** your **neighbour** as you **love**
	12.33	**love** his **neighbour** as he **loves** himself.
.k	10.27	**Love** your **neighbour** as you **love**
Rom	13.9	**Love** your **neighbour** as you **love**
Gal	5.14	**Love** your **neighbour** as you **love**
Jas	2.8	**Love** your **neighbour** as you **love**

One Another see **God's People**

Peace

Ps	122.6	**peace** of Jerusalem: "May those who **love** you prosper.
Is	54.10	my **love** for you...my promise of **peace**.
Jer	16.5	people with **peace** or show them **love**
Zech	8.19	You must **love** truth and **peace**.
2 Cor	13.11	And the God of **love** and **peace**
Gal	5.22	But the Spirit produces **love**, joy, **peace**
Eph	6.23	to all Christian brothers **peace** and **love**
2 Tim	2.22	**love**, and **peace**,
2 Jn	.3	and **peace**; may they be ours in...**love**.
Jude	.2	**peace**, and **love** be yours in full

Perfect

Col	3.14	**love**, which binds all things...in **perfect**
1 Jn	2.5	**love** for God has...been made **perfect**.
	4.12	his **love** is made **perfect** in us.
	4.17	**Love** is made **perfect** in us in order that
	4.18	**perfect love** drives out all fear.

Praise, Thank

1 Chr	16.34	Give **thanks** to the Lord...his **love**
	16.41	**praises** to the Lord for his eternal **love**
2 Chr	20.21	**Praise** the Lord! His **love** is eternal!
Ps	106.1	Give **thanks** to the Lord...his **love**
	107.1	Give **thanks** to the Lord...his **love**
	107.8	thank the Lord for his constant **love**, Also: 107.15, 21, 31
	138.2	**praise** your name because of your...**love**
Is	63.7	unfailing **love**; I **praise** him for all

Promise, Covenant

Deut	7.8	**loved** you...wanted to keep the **promise**

Deut	7.12	**love**, as he **promised** your ancestors.
1 Sam	20.17	made David **promise** to **love** him
Neh	1.5	your **covenant** with those who **love** you
Ps	69.13	**love**, because you keep your **promise**
	77.8	he stopped **loving** us? Does his **promise**
	89.33	**loving** David or fail to keep my **promise**
	119.76	**love** comfort me, as you have **promised**
	119.140	certain your **promise** is! How I **love** it!
	138.8	**promised**; Lord, your **love** is eternal.
Is	54.10	**love** for you will never end...my **promise**
Ezek	16.8	with my coat and **promised** to **love** you.
Dan	9.4	your **covenant** and show constant **love**
Jas	1.12	has **promised** to those who **love** him.
	2.5	he **promised** to those who **love** him.

Protect see **Help**

Purity

Prov	22.11	**love purity** of heart and graciousness
1 Tim	1.5	the **love** that comes from a **pure** heart,
	4.12	your **love**, faith, and **purity**.

Rescue see **Save**

Respect, Honour

Ps	103.11	is his **love** for those who **honour** him.
	103.17	who **honour** the Lord, his **love** lasts
	119.48	I **respect** and **love** your commandments;
Is	43.4	I **love** you and give you **honour**.
Mt	19.19	**respect** your father and...mother...**love**
	23.7	they **love** to be greeted with **respect**
Lk	20.46	and **love** to be greeted with **respect**
1 Thes	5.13	them with the greatest **respect** and **love**
1 Pet	2.17	**Respect** everyone, **love** your

Right(eous) see **Justice**

Save, Rescue

Ps	13.5	your constant **love**...you will **rescue** me.
	17.7	your wonderful **love** and **save** me;
	31.16	**save** me in your constant **love**.
	44.26	Because of your constant **love save** us!
	60.5	the people you **love** may be **rescued**.
	69.13	**love**...you keep your promise to **save**.
	85.7	**love**, O Lord, and give us your **saving**
	86.13	**love** for me! You have **saved** me
	91.14	I will **save** those who **love** me
	108.6	the people you **love** may be **rescued**.
	109.21	**rescue** me because of...your **love**.
	109.26	because of your constant **love**, **save** me!
	119.41	much you **love** me, Lord, and **save** me
	119.159	Your **love** never changes, so **save** me!
Is	54.8	my **love** for ever." So says the Lord who **saves** you.
	63.9	himself who **saved** them. In his **love**
Hos	1.7	**love**. I, the Lord their God, will **save**
2 Thes	2.10	and **love** the truth so as to be **saved**.

Servant, Slave

Ex	21.5	**slave** declares that he **loves** his master
Deut	15.16	your **slave** may not want to leave; he may **love** you
1 Kgs	3.6	**love** for my father David, your **servant**,
2 Chr	6.42	the **love** you had for your **servant**
Ps	102.14	Your **servants love** her,
Is	44.2	**servant**, my chosen people whom I **love**.
Mt	6.24	**slave** of two masters; he will hate one and **love** the other;
	12.18	my **servant**...the one I **love**,
Lk	16.13	**slave** of two masters; he will hate one and **love** the other;
2 Cor	6.6	God's **servants**...by our true **love**,

Serve

Deut	10.12	**Love** him, **serve** him with all your
	11.13	**love** the Lord your God and **serve** him
Is	56.6	who **love** him and **serve** him,
Jer	8.2	these people have **loved** and **served**,

Dan	11.37	**served**...the god that women **love**.
2 Cor	8.6	you complete this special **service** of **love**.
	8.7	be generous also in this **service** of **love**.
	8.19	as we carry out this **service** of **love**
Gal	5.13	let **love** make you **serve** one another.
Rev	2.19	**love**, your faithfulness, your **service**,

Sin

Lk	6.32	Even **sinners love** those who **love**
	7.47	the great **love** she has shown proves that her many **sins**
1 Pet	4.8	because **love** covers over many **sins**.

Slave see **Servant**

Son of God see **Christ**

Strong

Deut	10.15	**love** for your ancestors was so **strong**
Ps	117.2	His **love** for us is **strong**
Song	8.6	**Love** is as powerful as death; passion is as **strong**
Lam	3.32	but his **love** for us is sure and **strong**.
Hos	11.8	My **love** for you is too **strong**.
2 Cor	7.15	so his **love** for you grows **stronger**
Phil	2.1	makes you **strong**, and his **love** comforts

Teach

Ps	40.8	**love** to do your will, my God! I keep your **teaching**
	119.64	is full of your constant **love**; **teach** me
	119.124	**love**, and **teach** me your commands.
	119.167	I obey your **teachings**; I **love** them
Song	8.2	where you could **teach** me **love**.
Jn	14.23	**loves** me will obey my **teaching**.
	14.24	not **love** me does not obey my **teaching**
1 Thes	4.9	**taught** by God how you should **love**

Temple

Ps	48.9	**Temple**, O God, we think of your...**love**.
	84.1	I **love** your **Temple**, Lord Almighty!
Mal	2.11	the **Temple** which the Lord **loves**.

Thank see **Praise**

Trust see **Faith**

Truth

Zech	8.19	You must **love truth** and peace.
Eph	4.15	speaking the **truth** in a spirit of **love**,
2 Thes	2.10	and **love** the **truth** so as to be saved.
2 Jn	.1	all who know the **truth love** you,
	.3	may they be ours in **truth** and **love**.

Union

1 Tim	1.14	**love** which are ours in **union** with
2 Tim	1.13	**love** that are ours in **union** with Christ
1 Jn	4.12	lives in **union** with us, and his **love**
	4.16	whoever lives in **love** lives in **union**

Wicked see **Evil**

Wife

Prov	5.15	to your own **wife** and give your **love**
Eph	5.25	Husbands, **love** your **wives** just as Christ
	5.28	Men ought to **love** their **wives**
	5.28	A man who **loves** his **wife loves** himself.
	5.33	every husband must **love** his **wife**
Col	3.19	Husbands, **love** your **wives**

World

Jn	3.16	**loved** the **world** so much that he gave
	3.19	come into the **world**, but people **love**
	13.1	He had always **loved** those in the **world**
	14.31	**world** must know that I **love** the
	15.19	the **world** would **love** you as its own.
	17.24	**loved** me before the **world** was made.
2 Tim	4.10	fell in **love** with this present **world**
1 Jn	2.15	Do not **love** the **world** or anything

LOYAL

2 Sam	2.5	—	3.8	x4
1 Kgs	11.2	—	12.20	x4
Gen	20.13	—	21.23	x3
2 Sam	15.6	—	16.17	x3
2 Sam	19.14	—	20.19	x3
2 Kgs	2.2 – 6			x3

Promise, Swear

Gen	21.23	so **promise** that you will also be **loyal**
Num	32.11	I **swear** that...they did not remain **loyal**
1 Sam	20.14	your sacred **promise** and be **loyal** to me;
2 Sam	9.3	**loyalty** and kindness, as I **promised** God
2 Kgs	2.2	**swear** by my **loyalty** to the living Lord
		Also: 2.4, 6; 4.30
1 Chr	29.24	sons **promised** to be **loyal** to Solomon
2 Chr	36.13	to **swear**...that he would be **loyal**.
Ps	98.3	kept his **promise** to...Israel with **loyalty**
Ezek	17.13	and made him **swear** to be **loyal**.
Zeph	1.5	worship me and **swear loyalty** to me,

Serve

Judg	9.28	but why should we **serve** him? Be **loyal**
1 Sam	18.17	**serve** me as a brave and **loyal** soldier,
1 Kgs	3.6	your **servant**, and he was good, **loyal**,
	12.7	they will always **serve** you **loyally**.
	14.8	**servant**·David, who was completely **loyal**
2 Kgs	20.3	I have **served** you faithfully and **loyally**,
2 Chr	10.7	they will always **serve** you **loyally**.
Ps	86.2	I am **loyal** to you...I am your **servant**
Is	38.3	I have **served** you faithfully and **loyally**,
Dan	6.16	whom you **serve** so **loyally**, rescue you.
	6.20	you **serve** so **loyally** able to save you

Swear see Promise

MAGIC

Ex	7.11	—	9.11	x8
Dan	1.20	—	2.27	x4
Dan	4.7	—	5.15	x4
Is	2.6	—	3.20	x3
Is	47.9 – 12			x3
Acts	13.6 – 9			x3

Practice

Ex	22.18	death any woman who **practises magic**.
Lev	19.26	Do not **practise** any kind of **magic**.
2 Kgs	21.6	He **practised** divination and **magic**
2 Chr	33.6	He **practised** divination and **magic**
Is	2.6	The land is full of **magic practices**
Mal	3.5	against those who **practise magic**,
Acts	19.19	Many of those who had **practised magic**
Rev	21.8	the immoral, those who **practise magic**,
	22.15	perverts and those who **practise magic**,

MAJESTY

Dan	2.4	—	6.22	x38
2 Sam	13.24	—	16.9	x16
2 Sam	18.28	—	19.41	x13
1 Kgs	1.2	—	3.26	x12
Ezra	4.12	—	5.17	x6
2 Sam	24.3 – 22			x4
Esth	7.3	—	9.13	x4
1 Sam	17.32 – 55			x3
1 Sam	22.15	—	24.8	x3
1 Sam	26.17 – 22			x3

Glory

1 Chr	16.27	**Glory** and **majesty** surround him,
	29.11	**glorious**, splendid, and **majestic**.
Job	40.10	clothe yourself with **majesty** and **glory**.
Ps	45.3	you are **glorious** and **majestic**.
	76.4	**glorious** you are, O God! How **majestic**,
	96.6	**Glory** and **majesty** surround him;

Ps	104.1	You are clothed with **majesty** and **glory**;
	145.5	will speak of your **glory** and **majesty**,
	145.12	the **glorious majesty** of your kingdom.
Dan	4.30	my **glory** and **majesty**.
	4.36	**majesty**, and the **glory** of my kingdom
Jude	.25	be **glory**, **majesty**,

God, Lord

1 Sam	15.29	Israel's **majestic** God does not lie
Ps	29.4	voice of the **Lord** is heard in...**majesty**.
	68.34	Proclaim **God's** power; his **majesty**
	76.4	O **God**! How **majestic**, as you return
	93.1	The **Lord** is...clothed with **majesty**
	104.1	**God**...clothed with **majesty** and **glory**;
Is	30.30	**Lord** will let everyone hear his **majestic**
Mic	5.4	and with the **majesty** of the **Lord God**
Jude	.25	**God** our Saviour...be **glory**, **majesty**,

Power, Might

1 Chr	16.27	**Glory** and **majesty** surround him, **power**
	29.11	**powerful**, glorious, splendid, and **majestic**.
Ps	29.4	in all its **might** and **majesty**.
	45.3	**mighty** king; you are glorious and **majestic**.
	68.34	**God's** power; his **majesty** is over Israel,
	96.6	**Glory** and **majesty** surround him; **power**
	145.12	**mighty** deeds and the glorious **majesty**
Dan	4.30	**power** and might, my **glory** and **majesty**.
Jude	.25	**majesty**, **might**,

MANKIND

Eph	3.5	—	4.11	x4
Gen	5.2	—	6.13	x3
Rom	5.14 – 18			x3
Rev	9.15 – 20			x3
Rev	14.3 – 7			x3

God, Lord

Gen	6.13	**God**...decided to put an end to all **mankind**.
Ps	7.8	the judge of all **mankind**...O **Lord**;
	14.2	The **Lord** looks down from heaven at **mankind**
	33.13	The **Lord** looks down from heaven and sees all **mankind**.
	53.2	**God** looks down from heaven at **mankind**
Is	40.5	**Lord** will be revealed, and all **mankind**
	49.26	**mankind** will know that I am the **Lord**,
Jer	32.27	I am the **Lord**, the **God** of all **mankind**.
Lk	3.6	All **mankind** will see **God's** salvation!
Rom	11.15	**mankind** was changed from **God's**
1 Cor	2.7	**God's** secret wisdom...hidden from **mankind**,
2 Cor	5.19	**God** was making all **mankind** his friends
Gal	3.8	you **God** will bless all **mankind**.
Eph	4.6	is one **God** and Father of all **mankind**,
1 Tim	2.5	who brings **God** and **mankind** together,
Tit	2.11	**God** has revealed his grace for the salvation of all **mankind**
Heb	12.23	**God**, who is the judge of all **mankind**,
Rev	21.3	Now **God's** home is with **mankind**!

Life

Jn	1.4	and this **life** brought light to **mankind**.
	17.2	**mankind**, so...he might give eternal **life**
Rom	5.18	all **mankind** free and gives them **life**.
Gal	3.21	if **mankind** had received a law that could bring **life**,

Lord see God

Sin

Rom	5.14	over all **mankind**, even over those who did not **sin**
	5.18	one **sin** condemned all **mankind**,

| Heb | 1.3 | forgiveness for the **sins** of **mankind**, |

World

Gen	6.1	**mankind** had spread all over the **world**
Jer	27.5	I created the **world**, **mankind**,
Mt	24.14	the **world** for a witness to all **mankind**;
Mk	16.15	**world** and preach the gospel to all **mankind**.
Jn	1.9	the **world** and shines on all **mankind**.
1 Cor	4.9	whole **world** of angels and of **mankind**.

MANNA

| | Ex | 16.31 – 35 | | x4 |

Eat, Food

Ex	16.31	of Israel called the **food** manna.
	16.35	The Israelites **ate** manna
Num	11.6	to **eat** — nothing but this **manna**
Deut	8.3	then he gave you **manna** to **eat**,
	8.16	he gave you **manna** to **eat**, **food**
Esth	9.20	you **fed** them with **manna**
Ps	78.24	sending down **manna**...to **eat**
Jn	6.31	ancestors **ate manna** in the desert,
	6.49	ancestors **ate manna** in the desert,

MARK

| | Rev | 13.16 — 14.11 | | x4 |

Forehead

Ezek	9.4	**mark** on the **forehead** of everyone who
	9.6	who has the **mark** on his **forehead**.
Rev	7.4	who were **marked** with God's seal on their **foreheads**
	9.4	**mark** of God's seal on their **foreheads**.
	14.9	**mark** on his **forehead** or on his hand
	20.4	the **mark** of the beast on their **foreheads**

Image

Rev	14.9	**image** and receives the **mark** on his
	14.11	its **image**, for anyone who has the **mark**
	20.4	**image**, nor had they received the **mark**

MASTER

	Gen	24.9 – 65		x23
	Lk	12.36 — 14.23		x14
	Mt	24.45 — 25.26		x11
	Lk	16.1 — 17.13		x7
	Ex	21.4 – 21		x6
	1 Sam	24.6 — 26.16		x6
	Gen	39.2 – 19		x5
	1 Sam	29.4 — 30.15		x5
	Lk	8.24 — 9.49		x4
	Col	3.22 — 4.1		x4
	Gen	32.4 – 18		x3
	2 Kgs	2.3 – 16		x3
	2 Kgs	5.3 – 22		x3
	Eph	6.5 – 9		x3

Obey

Gen	24.37	My **master** made me promise with a vow to **obey**
	32.4	**obedient** servant, report to my **master**
Ps	45.11	is your **master**, so you must **obey** him.
Rom	6.16	of the **master** you **obey** — either of sin,
Eph	6.5	**obey** your human **masters** with fear and
Col	3.22	**obey** your human **masters** in all things,
1 Pet	3.6	**obeyed** Abraham and called him **master**.

Servant, Slave

Ex	21.5	**slave** declares that he loves his **master**
	21.21	**slave** does not die for a day or two, the **master**
2 Sam	16.19	should I **serve**, if not my **master's** son?
Ps	123.2	As a **servant** depends on his **master**,
Prov	17.2	**servant** will gain authority over a **master's**
Prov	27.18	A **servant** who takes care of his **master**
	30.10	Never criticize a **servant** to his **master**
Is	24.2	**slaves** and **masters**,
Dan	10.17	like a **slave** standing before his **master**
Mal	1.6	and a **servant** honours his **master**.
Mt	6.24	No one can be a **slave** of two **masters**
	10.24	no **slave** is greater than his **master**.
	10.25	and a **slave** like his **master**.
	24.45	**master** has placed in charge of the other **servants**
	24.46	How happy that **servant** is if his **master**
	24.47	**master** will put that **servant** in charge
	24.48	bad **servant**, he will tell himself that his **master**
	24.50	that **servant's master** will come back
	25.19	the **master** of those **servants** came back
	25.21	and faithful **servant**!' said his **master**.
	25.23	and faithful **servant**!' said his **master**.
	25.26	bad and lazy **servant**!' his **master** said
Lk	12.36	**servants** who are waiting for their **master**
	12.37	happy are those **servants** whose **master**
	12.42	**servant**? He is the one that his **master**
	12.43	How happy that **servant** is if his **master**
	12.44	**master** will put that **servant** in charge
	12.45	**servant** says to himself that his **master**
	12.46	**master** will come back one day when the **servant**
	12.47	**servant** who knows what his **master**
	12.48	**servant** who does not know what his **master**
	14.21	**servant** went back and told all this to his **master**
	14.23	So the **master** said to the **servant**,
	16.3	**servant** said to himself, 'My **master** is
	16.13	**servant** can be the slave of two **masters**
Jn	13.16	no **slave** is greater than his **master**,
	15.15	**servant** does not know what his **master**
	15.20	No **slave** is greater than his **master**.
Rom	6.16	**slaves** of the **master** you obey — either
	14.4	**servant** of someone else? It is his own **Master**
1 Cor	4.2	**servant** is that he be faithful to his **master**.
Eph	6.5	**Slaves**, obey your human **masters** with
	6.9	**Masters**, behave in the same way towards your **slaves**
Col	3.22	**Slaves**, obey your human **masters** in all
	3.24	For Christ is the real **Master** you **serve**.
	4.1	**Masters**, be fair and just in the way you treat your **slaves**
1 Tim	6.1	**slaves** must consider their **masters**
	6.2	**Slaves** belonging to Christian **masters**
Tit	2.9	**Slaves** are to submit to their **masters**
1 Pet	2.18	**servants** must submit to your **masters**

MERCY

	Lam	1.9 — 3.43		x9
	Neh	9.17 – 31		x6
	Ps	119.58 – 156		x5
	Rom	11.30 — 12.1		x5
	Ezek	7.4 — 9.5		x4
	Lk	1.50 – 78		x4
	Rom	9.15 – 23		x4
	Jude	.2 – 23		x4
	Deut	13.8 – 17		x3
	Ps	80.3 – 19		x3
	Ps	86.3 – 16		x3
	Ps	145.8 – 17		x3
	Jer	15.1 — 16.13		x3
	Jer	30.18 — 31.20		x3
	Mt	10.15 — 11.24		x3
	Mt	17.15 — 18.33		x3
	1 Tim	1.2 – 16		x3
	2 Tim	1.2 – 18		x3

	Jas	2.13	x3

Beg

Deut	33.29	enemies will come **begging** for **mercy**,
Esth	4.8	**beg** him to have **mercy** on her people.
	7.8	on Esther's couch to **beg** for **mercy**,
Job	9.15	is **beg** for **mercy** from God my judge.
Lam	2.19	out your heart and **beg** him for **mercy**

Compassion, Kind, Pity

Deut	13.8	Show him no **mercy** or **pity**,
2 Kgs	13.23	the Lord was **kind** and **merciful** to them
2 Chr	30.9	Lord your God is **kind** and **merciful**,
Ps	67.1	be **merciful** to us...look on us with **kindness**,
	77.9	**merciful**? Has anger taken the place of his **compassion**?
	102.13	**pity** on Zion; the time has come to have **mercy**
	111.4	he is **kind** and **merciful**.
	112.4	those who are **merciful**, **kind**, and just.
	116.5	Lord is **merciful** and...**compassionate**.
	119.156	**compassion**, Lord...show your **mercy**
Is	13.18	no **mercy** to babies and take no **pity**
	27.11	not **pity** them or show them any **mercy**.
	30.18	**merciful** to you. He is ready to take **pity**
Jer	13.14	**compassion**, or **mercy** will stop me
	21.7	or show **mercy** or **pity**
Ezek	24.14	or show **pity** or be **merciful**.
Joel	2.13	He is **kind** and full of **mercy**;
Jon	4.2	loving and **merciful** God...always **kind**,
Zech	7.9	**kindness** and **mercy** to one another.
Rom	9.15	**mercy** on anyone I wish; I will take **pity**
Jas	5.11	Lord is full of **mercy** and **compassion**.

Destroy, Death

Deut	4.31	**merciful** God. He will not...**destroy** you,
Josh	11.20	to total **destruction** and all be killed without **mercy**.
2 Kgs	13.23	**merciful** to them. He would not let them be **destroyed**,
Neh	9.31	**mercy** is great, you did not...**destroy**
Jer	20.16	that the Lord **destroyed** without **mercy**.
	21.7	you to **death**. He will not...show **mercy**
Lam	2.2	The Lord **destroyed** without **mercy**,
	2.17	He has **destroyed** us without **mercy**,
Hab	1.17	on **destroying** nations without **mercy**?
Heb	10.28	is put to **death** without any **mercy**

Father see God

Forgive, Spare

2 Kgs	1.13	**merciful** to me and my men. **Spare** our
2 Chr	6.39	**merciful** to them and **forgive** all the sins
Ps	78.38	**merciful** to his people. He **forgave** their
Is	55.7	he is **merciful** and quick to **forgive**.
Jer	21.7	not **spare** any of you or show **mercy**
Ezek	7.4	not **spare** you or show you any **mercy**.
	7.9	not **spare** you or show you any **mercy**.
	8.18	**spare** them or show them any **mercy**.
	9.5	**Spare** no one; have **mercy** on no one.
Dan	9.9	You are **merciful** and **forgiving**,

God, Father

Deut	4.31	He is a **merciful God**
	30.3	the Lord your **God** will have **mercy**
2 Chr	30.9	Lord your **God** is kind and **merciful**.
Job	9.15	is beg for **mercy** from **God** my judge.
Ps	51.1	**God**, because of your...great **mercy**
	56.1	Be **merciful** to me, O **God**,
	57.1	Be **merciful** to me, O **God**, be **merciful**,
	67.1	**God**, be **merciful** to us and bless us;
	77.9	Has **God** forgotten to be **merciful**?
	78.38	But **God** was **merciful** to his people.
	80.3	O **God**! Show us your **mercy**,
	80.7	Almighty **God**! Show us your **mercy**,
	80.19	**God** Almighty. Show us your **mercy**,

Ps	86.3	You are my **God**, so be **merciful** to me;
	86.15	are a **merciful** and loving **God**,
Prov	28.13	then **God** will show **mercy** to you.
Is	55.7	our **God**; he is **merciful**
Joel	2.13	your **God**...is kind and full of **mercy**;
Jon	4.2	that you are a loving and **merciful God**,
Mt	5.7	**God** will be **merciful** to them!
	10.15	**God** will show more **mercy** to the
	11.22	**God** will show more **mercy** to the
	11.24	**God** will show more **mercy** to Sodom
Lk	1.78	Our **God** is **merciful** and tender.
	6.36	**merciful** just as your **Father** is **merciful**.
	10.12	**God** will show more **mercy** to Sodom
	10.14	**God** will show more **mercy**...to Tyre
Rom	9.16	but only on **God's mercy**.
	9.18	**God** has **mercy** on anyone he wishes,
	11.30	but now you have received **God's mercy**
	12.1	because of **God's** great **mercy** to us
	15.9	Gentiles to praise **God** for his **mercy**.
2 Cor	1.3	the **merciful Father**, the **God**
	4.1	**God** in his **mercy** has given us this
Eph	2.4	But **God's mercy** is so abundant
1 Tim	1.2	**God** the **Father**...give you grace, **mercy**,
	1.13	But **God** was **merciful** to me
	1.16	but **God** was **merciful** to me
2 Tim	1.2	**God** the **Father**...give you grace, **mercy**,
Jas	2.13	**God** will not show **mercy** when he
1 Pet	2.10	you did not know **God's mercy**,
2 Jn	.3	God the **Father**...give us...**mercy**,

Help, Protect

Ex	22.27	cries out to me for **help**...I am **merciful**.
Deut	13.8	**mercy** or pity, and do not **protect** him.
Ps	30.10	and be **merciful**! **Help** me, Lord!
Is	33.2	have **mercy** on us...**Protect** us
2 Cor	1.3	**merciful** Father...from whom all **help**
Heb	4.16	receive **mercy** and find grace to **help**

Kind see Compassion

Lord

see also **God**

Deut	13.17	**Lord** will turn...and show you **mercy**.
Judg	2.18	The **Lord** would have **mercy** on them
2 Sam	12.22	that the **Lord** might be **merciful** to me
	24.14	**Lord** himself be the one to punish us, for he is **merciful**.
2 Kgs	13.23	but the **Lord** was kind and **merciful**
1 Chr	21.13	**Lord** himself be the one to punish me, because he is **merciful**.
Ps	6.4	**Lord**; in your **mercy** rescue me from
	9.13	Be **merciful** to me, O **Lord**!
	25.16	**Lord**, and be **merciful** to me,
	27.7	**Lord**, when I call to you! Be **merciful**
	30.10	**Lord**, and be **merciful**!
	31.9	Be **merciful** to me, **Lord**,
	40.11	**Lord**...you will never stop being **merciful**
	41.4	**Lord**; be **merciful** to me and heal me.
	41.10	Be **merciful** to me, **Lord**
	85.1	**Lord**, you have been **merciful** to your
	103.8	The **Lord** is **merciful** and loving,
	116.5	The **Lord** is **merciful** and good;
	119.149	O **Lord**; show your **mercy**,
	119.156	**Lord**, is great; show your **mercy**
	123.3	Be **merciful** to us, **Lord**, be **merciful**;
	145.8	The **Lord** is loving and **merciful**,
	145.13	The **Lord** is...**merciful**
	145.17	The **Lord** is...**merciful**
Is	14.1	The **Lord** will once again be **merciful**
	30.18	yet the **Lord** is waiting to be **merciful**
	33.2	**Lord**, have **mercy** on us
Lam	1.9	and she cries to the **Lord** for **mercy**.
	3.22	The **Lord's** unfailing love and **mercy**
	3.31	The **Lord** is **merciful**

Hos	14.3	O **Lord**, you show **mercy** to those
Amos	5.15	Perhaps the **Lord** will be **merciful**
1 Cor	7.25	who by the **Lord's mercy** is worthy
2 Tim	1.16	May the **Lord** show **mercy** to the family
	1.18	May the **Lord** grant him his **mercy**
Jas	5.11	For the **Lord** is full of **mercy**

Patient
Ps	86.15	**merciful** and loving God, always **patient**,
Joel	2.13	is kind and full of **mercy**; he is **patient**
Jon	4.2	loving and **merciful** God, always **patient**,

Peace
Jer	16.5	**peace** or show them love and **mercy**.
Gal	6.16	may **peace** and **mercy** be with them
1 Tim	1.2	**mercy**, and **peace**.
2 Tim	1.2	**mercy**, and **peace**.
2 Jn	.3	**mercy**, and **peace**; may they be ours in
Jude	.2	May **mercy**, **peace**, and love be yours

Pity see **Compassion**

Protect see **Help**

Save, Rescue
Neh	9.27	**mercy** you sent them leaders who **rescued**
	9.28	you **rescued** them in your great **mercy**.
Ps	6.4	and **save** me, Lord; in your **mercy**
	26.11	be **merciful** to me and **save** me!
	80.3	us your **mercy**, and we will be **saved!**
	80.7	us your **mercy**, and we will be **saved!**
	80.19	us your **mercy**, and we will be **saved**.
	86.16	**mercy** on me; strengthen me and **save**
	119.156	show your **mercy** and **save** me!
Tit	3.5	of his own **mercy** that he **saved** us,

Sin
Ps	51.1	great **mercy** wipe away my **sins**!
Ezek	24.14	not ignore your **sins**...or be **merciful**.
Dan	4.27	Stop **sinning**, do what is right, and be **merciful**

Spare see **Forgive**

MESSAGE
1 Cor	11.4 — 15.12	x24
Acts	13.15 — 21.9	x18
Acts	7.14 — 11.20	x12
Mk	2.2 — 4.33	x10
Jer	23.18 – 36	x9
Rom	10.8 – 18	x9
Rev	1.2 — 3.14	x9
Jer	17.19 — 21.11	x8
Acts	1.21 — 4.31	x8
Num	22.5 — 24.15	x7
Zech	6.9 — 9.1	x7
1 Cor	1.6 — 2.6	x7
Is	6.9 — 8.19	x6
Mt	13.19 – 23	x6
Lk	1.2 – 67	x6
1 Kgs	19.2 — 21.15	x5
2 Kgs	18.14 — 20.19	x5
2 Chr	32.9 — 35.21	x5
Is	21.1 — 23.1	x5
Jn	3.11 — 5.38	x5
Jn	10.35 — 12.48	x5
1 Thes	1.6 — 2.16	x5
1 Jn	1.5 — 3.11	x5
1 Kgs	5.2 – 8	x4
Gen	50.4 – 17	x3
Deut	18.20 – 22	x3
1 Chr	25.1 – 3	x3
Neh	6.2 – 5	x3
Is	37.3 – 21	x3
Jer	29.19 – 31	x3
Lk	8.12 – 15	x3
Jn	17.8 – 20	x3

2 Thes	3.1 – 14	x3
2 Tim	4.2 – 17	x3
2 Pet	1.19 – 21	x3

Accept see **Faith**

Baptize
Acts	1.21	John preached his **message** of **baptism**
	2.41	believed his **message** and were **baptized**
	10.37	John preached his **message** of **baptism**.
	18.8	**message**, believed, and were **baptized**.

Believe see **Faith**

Bold see **Proclaim**

Christ, Jesus
Mk	2.2	**Jesus** was preaching the **message**
	4.33	**Jesus** preached his **message**
Jn	11.3	The sisters sent **Jesus** a **message**:
Acts	13.38	it is through **Jesus** that the **message**
Rom	10.17	**message** comes through preaching **Christ**.
1 Cor	1.6	The **message** about **Christ** has become
	1.18	For the **message** about **Christ's** death
	1.23	**Christ**, a **message** that is offensive
	1.24	this **message** is **Christ**,
	15.12	**message** is that **Christ** has been raised
Col	3.16	**Christ's message** in all its richness
	4.3	his **message** about the secret of **Christ**.

Dream see **Vision**

Encourage see **Help**

Faith, Accept, Believe
Jon	3.5	of Nineveh **believed** God's **message**
Mt	11.14	you are willing to **believe** their **message**
Mk	4.20	They hear the **message**, **accept** it,
Lk	1.20	But you have not **believed** my **message**,
	1.45	to **believe** that the Lord's **message**
Jn	1.7	all should hear the **message** and **believe**.
	3.11	of you is willing to **accept** our **message**.
	3.32	yet no one **accepts** his **message**.
	3.33	But whoever **accepts** his **message**
	4.41	more **believed** because of his **message**
	5.38	**message** in your hearts, for you do not **believe**
	12.38	who **believed** the **message** we told?
	12.48	me and does not **accept** my **message**
	17.20	**believe** in me because of their **message**.
Acts	2.41	Many of them **believed** his **message**
	4.4	many who heard the **message believed**
	8.12	But when they **believed** Philip's **message**
	18.8	in Corinth heard the **message**, **believed**,
Rom	10.8	heart" — that is, the **message** of **faith**
	10.14	**believe** if they have not heard the **message**?
	10.16	who **believed** our **message**?
	10.17	**faith** comes from hearing the **message**,
	12.6	God's **message**...according to the **faith**
1 Cor	14.22	God's **message** is proof for **believers**,
1 Thes	2.13	**message**, you heard it and **accepted** it,
2 Thes	1.10	because you have **believed** the **message**
	3.2	for not everyone **believes** the **message**.
1 Tim	2.7	proclaim the **message** of **faith** and truth.

God
Judg	3.20	I have a **message** from **God** for you.
1 Chr	25.1	They were to proclaim **God's messages**,
	25.2	who proclaimed **God's messages**
	25.3	they proclaimed **God's message**,
Is	2.1	the **message** which **God** gave to Isaiah
	8.16	the **messages** that **God** has given me.
	28.19	Each new **message** from **God** will bring
	30.6	This is **God's message** about the animals
Jer	18.18	prophets to proclaim **God's message**.
	29.24	**God** of Israel, gave me a **message** for
Jon	3.5	of Nineveh **believed God's message**

Mt	7.22	In your name we spoke **God's message,**
Mk	4.14	The sower sows **God's message.**
Lk	1.67	and he spoke **God's message:**
Acts	4.31	and began to proclaim **God's message**
	7.38	and he received **God's living messages**
	7.51	how deaf you are to **God's message!**
	19.6	and also proclaimed **God's message.**
	20.32	to the care of **God** and to the **message**
	21.9	who proclaimed **God's message.**
	28.28	**God's message** of salvation has been
Rom	3.2	**God** trusted his **message** to the Jews.
	10.8	**God's message** is near you,
	12.6	If our gift is to speak **God's message,**
1 Cor	11.4	or proclaims **God's message** in public
	11.5	who prays or proclaims **God's message**
	12.10	the gift of speaking **God's message;**
	14.1	the gift of proclaiming **God's message.**
	14.3	who proclaims **God's message** speaks
	14.4	one who proclaims **God's message** helps
	14.5	the gift of proclaiming **God's message.**
	14.22	of proclaiming **God's message** is proof
	14.24	if everyone is proclaiming **God's message**
	14.29	or three who are given **God's message**
	14.30	meeting receives a **message** from **God,**
	14.31	All of you may proclaim **God's message**
	14.32	The gift of proclaiming **God's message**
	14.39	heart on proclaiming **God's message,**
2 Cor	2.17	**God's message** as if it were cheap
	5.19	message is that **God** was making all
Eph	6.19	**God** will give me a **message** when I am
Col	4.3	**God** will give us a good opportunity to preach his **message**
1 Thes	2.13	When we brought you **God's message,**
2 Tim	2.15	teaches the **message** of **God's** truth.
Tit	2.5	of the **message** that comes from **God.**
Heb	5.12	you the first lessons of **God's message.**
	13.7	who spoke **God's message** to you.
1 Pet	4.11	preaches must preach **God's messages**
2 Pet	1.21	spoke the **message** that came from **God.**
Jude	.4	the **message** about the grace of our **God**
Rev	1.2	report concerning the **message** from **God**
	10.11	again you must proclaim **God's message**
	11.3	and they will proclaim **God's message**
	11.6	the time they proclaim **God's message.**

Good News, Salvation, Save

Acts	8.12	Philip's **message** about the **good news**
	11.20	**message** to Gentiles also...the **Good**
	13.26	this **message** of **salvation** has been sent!
	28.28	**message** of **salvation** has been sent
1 Cor	1.21	**message** we preach, God decided to **save**
	15.2	the **message** that I preached to you. You are **saved**
Eph	1.13	the true **message,** the **Good News**
Col	1.5	**message,** the **Good News,** first came
1 Thes	2.16	**message** that would bring them **salvation.**
Heb	4.2	**Good News**...They heard the **message,**
Rev	14.6	**message** of **Good News** to announce

Heart

Lk	8.12	the **message** away from their **hearts**
Jn	5.38	do not keep his **message** in your **hearts,**
Acts	7.51	**hearts,** how deaf...to **God's message!**
Rom	10.8	**message** is near you...in your **heart**
1 Cor	14.39	**heart** on proclaiming **God's message,**
1 Jn	2.24	in your **hearts** the **message** you heard

Help, Encourage

Acts	13.15	a **message** of **encouragement** for them.
	15.31	joy by the **message** of **encouragement.**
	20.2	**encouraged** the people with...**messages.**
1 Cor	14.3	**God's message** speaks to people and gives them **help,**
	14.4	**God's message helps** the whole church.
Heb	13.22	to this **message** of **encouragement;**

Jesus see Christ

Lord

Deut	18.21	**message** does not come from the **Lord.**
	18.22	then it is not the **Lord's message.**
Judg	6.8	them this **message** from the **Lord,**
1 Sam	2.27	with this **message** from the **Lord**
	3.1	were very few **messages** from the **Lord,**
2 Sam	23.2	**Lord** speaks through me; his **message** is
1 Kgs	16.7	**message** from the **Lord** against Baasha
2 Kgs	20.19	The **message** you have given me from the **Lord** is good.
	22.16	the following **message** from the **Lord**
2 Chr	12.5	This is the **Lord's message** to you:
	34.24	the following **message** from the **Lord**
Is	7.10	The **Lord** sent another **message** to Ahaz
	16.13	is the **message** the **Lord** gave earlier
	39.8	The **message** you have given me from the **Lord**
Jer	2.4	Listen to the **Lord's message**
	5.13	they have no **message** from the **Lord.**
	10.1	listen to the **message** that the **Lord** has
	11.21	kept on proclaiming the **Lord's message.**
	17.19	**Lord** said to me, "Jeremiah, go and announce my **message**
	19.14	the **Lord** had sent me to proclaim his **message.**
	21.11	The **Lord** told me to give this **message**
	23.33	asks you, 'What is the **Lord's message?**
	25.1	I received a **message** from the **Lord**
	27.18	**message,** let them ask me, the **Lord**
	29.24	**Lord** Almighty, the God of Israel, gave me a **message**
	33.1	the **Lord's message** came to me again.
	37.2	**message** which the **Lord** had given me.
	37.17	Is there any **message** from the **Lord?**
	38.20	I beg you to obey the **Lord's message;**
	49.14	have received a **message** from the **Lord.**
	50.1	is the **message** that the **Lord** gave me
Ezek	11.5	the **Lord** told me to give the people this **message:**
	12.19	**message** of the Sovereign **Lord** to the
	36.22	the **message** that I, the Sovereign **Lord,**
Hos	1.1	the **message** which the **Lord** gave Hosea
Joel	1.1	This is the **Lord's message** to Joel
Amos	3.1	this **message** which the **Lord** has spoken
	3.8	**Lord** speaks, who can avoid proclaiming his **message?**
	8.11	and thirst for a **message** from the **Lord.**
	8.12	for a **message** from the **Lord,**
Mic	1.1	the **Lord** gave this **message** to Micah,
Hab	1.1	**message** that the **Lord** revealed
Zeph	1.1	**message** that the **Lord** gave to
Hag	1.3	**Lord** then gave this **message** to the
	1.13	Haggai gave the **Lord's message**
	2.20	the **Lord** gave Haggai a second **message**
Zech	1.1	**Lord** gave this **message** to the prophet
	1.7	the **Lord** gave me a **message** in a vision
	2.8	So the **Lord** Almighty sent me with this **message**
	4.6	Zerubbabel this **message** from the **Lord:**
	4.8	**message** came to me from the **Lord**
	6.9	The **Lord** gave me this **message**
	7.1	the **Lord** gave me a **message.**
	7.4	This is the **message** of the **Lord**
	7.8	**Lord** gave this **message** to Zechariah
	8.1	The **Lord** Almighty gave this **message**
	8.18	The **Lord** Almighty gave this **message**
	9.1	This is the **Lord's message:**
	12.1	is a **message** about Israel from the **Lord**
Mal	1.1	the **message** that the **Lord** gave Malachi
Mt	7.22	**Lord, Lord!** In your name we spoke **God's message,**
Lk	1.45	**Lord's message** to you will come true!

Jn	12.38	**Lord**, who believed the **message** we told?
Acts	8.25	and proclaimed the **Lord's message**,
	13.48	glad and praised the **Lord's message**;
Rom	10.16	**Lord**, who believed our **message**?
1 Thes	1.8	did the **message** about the **Lord** go out
2 Thes	3.1	**Lord's message** may continue to spread

Name

Deut	18.20	**message** in my **name** when I did not
Jer	20.9	**name**," then your **message** is like a fire
	23.21	**message**, but still they spoke in my **name**.
	23.25	my **name** and claim that I have given them my **messages**
Mt	7.22	In your **name** we spoke God's **message**,
Lk	24.47	his **name** the **message** about repentance

Obey

Jer	29.19	**obey** the **message** that I kept on sending
	37.2	**obeyed** the **message** which the Lord had
	38.20	I beg you to **obey** the **Lord's message**;
Lk	8.15	**message** and retain it in a good and **obedient**
Jn	12.47	hears my **message** and does not **obey**
2 Thes	3.14	will not **obey** the **message** we send you
Rev	1.3	**message** and **obey** what is written

Proclaim, Bold, Preach

1 Chr	25.1	They were to **proclaim** God's **messages**,
	25.2	**proclaimed** God's **messages** whenever the
	25.3	they **proclaimed** God's **message**,
Is	14.28	This is a **message** that was **proclaimed**
	40.6	**Proclaim** a **message**!
Jer	2.2	**proclaim** this **message** to everyone
	11.6	**Proclaim** my **message** there and tell
	11.21	kept on **proclaiming** the **Lord's message**.
	15.19	you **proclaim** a worthwhile **message**,
	18.18	prophets to **proclaim** God's **message**.
	19.2	I was to **proclaim** the **message**
	19.14	had sent me to **proclaim** his **message**.
	20.8	because I **proclaim** your **message**.
	23.22	**proclaimed** my **message** to my people
	23.28	should **proclaim** that **message** faithfully.
	23.30	and **proclaim** them as my **message**.
Joel	2.28	and daughters will **proclaim** my **message**;
Amos	3.8	who can avoid **proclaiming** his **message**?
Jon	3.2	and **proclaim** to the people the **message**
Mt	4.17	Jesus began to **preach** his **message**
	11.12	**preached** his **message** until this very
Mk	2.2	was **preaching** the **message** to them
	4.33	Jesus **preached** his **message** to the people
Lk	1.2	who **proclaimed** the **message**.
Acts	1.21	John **preached** his **message** of baptism
	2.17	and daughters will **proclaim** my **message**;
	2.18	and they will **proclaim** my **message**.
	4.29	to speak your **message** with all **boldness**.
	4.31	**proclaim** God's **message** with **boldness**.
	8.4	**preaching** the **message**.
	8.25	and **proclaimed** the **Lord's message**,
	10.36	**message** he sent to the people of Israel, **proclaiming**
	10.37	after John **preached** his **message**
	11.20	**proclaimed** the **message** to Gentiles also,
	13.38	**message** about forgiveness of sins is **preached**
	14.25	they **preached** the **message** in Perga
	16.6	**preach** the **message** in the province of
	18.5	whole time to **preaching** the **message**,
	19.6	and also **proclaimed** God's **message**.
	21.9	who **proclaimed** God's **message**.
Rom	10.8	the **message** of faith that we **preach**.
	10.14	hear if the **message** is not **proclaimed**?
	10.15	**message** be **proclaimed** if the messengers
	10.17	**message** comes through **preaching** Christ.
1 Cor	1.21	so-called "foolish" **message** we **preach**,

1 Cor	1.23	**proclaim** the crucified Christ, a **message**
	2.6	Yet I do **proclaim** a **message** of wisdom
	11.4	or **proclaims** God's **message** in public
	11.5	who prays or **proclaims** God's **message**
	14.1	the gift of **proclaiming** God's **message**.
	14.3	who **proclaims** God's **message** speaks
	14.4	one who **proclaims** God's **message** helps
	14.5	the gift of **proclaiming** God's **message**.
	14.22	the gift of **proclaiming** God's **message**
	14.24	if everyone is **proclaiming** God's **message**
	14.31	All of you may **proclaim** God's **message**
	14.32	The gift of **proclaiming** God's **message**
	14.39	heart on **proclaiming** God's **message**,
	15.2	the **message** that I **preached** to you.
Gal	2.2	the gospel **message** that I **preach**
Phil	1.14	**bolder** all the time to **preach** the **message** fearlessly.
Col	1.25	task of fully **proclaiming** his **message**,
	4.3	to **preach** his **message** about the secret
1 Thes	2.16	**preaching** to the Gentiles the **message**
1 Tim	2.7	**proclaim** the **message** of faith and truth.
2 Tim	4.2	**message**, to insist upon **proclaiming** it
	4.17	I was able to **proclaim** the full **message**
Tit	1.3	**message**. This was entrusted to me, and I **proclaim** it
1 Pet	4.11	**preaches** must **preach** God's **message**
2 Pet	1.19	the **message proclaimed** by the prophets.
Rev	10.11	again you must **proclaim** God's **message**
	11.3	they will **proclaim** God's **message**
	11.6	the time they **proclaim** God's **message**
	11.7	they finish **proclaiming** their **message**

Revealed

Dan	10.1	a **message** was **revealed** to Daniel,
Hab	1.1	is the **message** that the Lord **revealed**
1 Cor	14.26	**revelation** from God, another a **message**
Tit	1.3	he **revealed** it in his **message**.
Rev	1.2	**message** from God and the truth **revealed**

Salvation see Good News

Save see Good News

Tongues

Acts	19.6	strange **tongues** and also proclaimed God's **message**.
1 Cor	14.9	**message** given in strange **tongues** is not
	14.26	another a **message** in strange **tongues**,
	14.39	**message**, but do not forbid the speaking in strange **tongues**.

True

Deut	18.22	**true**, then it is not the **Lord's message**.
Dan	10.1	**message** was **true** but extremely hard
Lk	1.20	**message**, which will come **true** at the
	1.45	**Lord's message** to you will come **true**!
Jn	3.33	his **message** confirms by this that God is **truthful**.
Acts	14.3	their **message** about his grace was **true**
Rom	10.18	**true** that they did not hear the **message**?
2 Cor	6.7	our **message** of **truth**, and by the power
Eph	1.13	people when you heard the **true message**
Col	1.5	When the **true message**
1 Tim	2.7	proclaim the **message** of faith and **truth**.
2 Tim	2.15	teaches the **message** of God's **truth**.
Rev	1.2	**message** from God and the
	3.7	**message** from the one who is holy and **true**.
	3.14	**message** from the Amen, the faithful and **true**

Vision, Dream

1 Sam	3.1	few **messages** from the Lord, and **visions**
Is	22.1	a **message** about the **Valley of Vision**.
Jer	23.25	given them my **messages** in their **dreams**.

Jer	23.28	only a **dream**, but the prophet who has heard my **message**
Dan	4.19	let the **dream** and its **message** alarm
Joel	2.28	**message**; your old men will have **dreams**,
Nah	1.1	**message** about Nineveh, the account of a **vision**
Zech	1.7	the Lord gave me a **message** in a **vision**
Acts	2.17	**message**; your young men will see **visions**,

Wisdom

1 Cor	2.6	Yet I do proclaim a **message** of **wisdom**
	12.8	one person a **message** full of **wisdom**

World

Ps	19.4	their **message** goes out to all the **world**
Jn	17.14	gave them your **message**, and the **world**

Worship

Acts	13.26	**worship** God: it is to us that this **message**
1 Cor	11.4	God's **message** in public **worship**
	11.5	God's **message** in public **worship**

MESSIAH

Acts	2.31	—	5.42	x7
Mt	22.42	—	24.24	x6
Mk	12.35	—	15.32	x6
Lk	22.67	—	24.46	x6
Jn	7.26 – 42			x6
Mt	26.63	—	27.22	x4
Jn	9.22	—	12.34	x4
Acts	17.3	—	18.28	x4
Mt	1.12	—	2.4	x3
Lk	2.26	—	4.41	x3
Jn	1.20 – 41			x3
Jn	3.28	—	4.29	x3

Believe

Mt	24.23	the **Messiah**!' or 'There he is!' — do not **believe** him.
Mk	13.21	**Messiah**!' or, 'Look, there he is!' — do not **believe**
Jn	7.31	**believed** in him and said, "When the **Messiah** comes,
	9.22	he **believed** that Jesus was the **Messiah**
	11.27	I do **believe** that you are the **Messiah**,
	20.31	may **believe** that Jesus is the **Messiah**,
1 Jn	5.1	**believes** that Jesus is the **Messiah**

MIGHT

Deut	32.4 – 37			x6
Ps	68.15 – 34			x5
Lk	1.17 – 69			x5
Ps	145.4 – 12			x4
Jer	31.11	—	32.21	x4
Deut	2.10	—	3.24	x3
Deut	5.22	—	7.8	x3
Deut	9.29	—	11.2	x3
Jer	48.1 – 25			x3
Jer	50.41	—	51.58	x3
Rev	18.8 – 21			x3

Acts, Miracles

Ex	15.11	Who can work **miracles** and **mighty acts**
Ps	77.12	I will meditate on all your **mighty acts**.
	77.14	works **miracles**; you showed your **might**
	78.43	performed his **mighty acts** and **miracles**
	105.27	They did God's **mighty acts**
	106.21	by his **mighty acts** in Egypt.
	145.4	they will proclaim your **mighty acts**.

God

Gen	49.24	the power of the **Mighty God** of Jacob,
Deut	10.17	**God** is supreme...great and **mighty**,
	32.18	forgot their **God**, their **mighty saviour**,
	32.30	their **mighty God** had given them up.
Deut	32.31	are weak, not **mighty** like Israel's **God**.
Josh	22.22	The **Mighty One** is **God**
Ps	54.1	O **God**; set me free by your **might**!
	68.34	**God's** power; his majesty...his **might**
	71.18	**God**...I proclaim your power and **might**
	77.14	**God** who works miracles; you showed your **might**
	86.10	You are **mighty**...you alone are **God**.
	89.8	**God** Almighty, none is as **mighty** as
	95.3	For the **Lord** is a **mighty God**,
	105.27	They did **God's mighty** acts
	106.21	**God** who had saved them by his **mighty**
	132.2	the **Mighty God** of Jacob:
	132.5	a home for the **Mighty God** of Jacob.
Is	9.6	**Mighty God**," "Eternal Father,
	10.21	will come back to their **mighty God**.
	60.16	the **mighty God** of Israel sets you free.
Lk	1.49	great things the **Mighty God** has done
1 Pet	5.6	under **God's mighty hand**,
Rev	7.12	and **might** belong to our **God** for ever
	18.8	**God**, who judges her, is **mighty**.

Lord

see also **God**

Deut	11.2	**Lord's** greatness, his power, his **might**,
	32.4	The **Lord** is your **mighty** defender,
1 Sam	12.7	of all the **mighty** actions the **Lord** did
1 Chr	16.28	the **Lord**...praise his glory and **might**.
Ps	24.8	He is the **Lord**, strong and **mighty**,
	29.4	of the **Lord** is heard in all its **might**
	92.4	**mighty** deeds, O **Lord**, make me glad;
	96.7	the **Lord**...praise his glory and **might**.
	99.2	The **Lord** is **mighty** in Zion;
	118.15	The **Lord's mighty** power has done it!
	147.5	Great and **mighty** is our **Lord**;
Jer	10.6	**Lord**, there is no one like you; you are **mighty**,
	20.11	**Lord**, are on my side, strong and **mighty**,
Mal	1.5	The **Lord** is **mighty** even outside...Israel!
Eph	6.10	**Lord** and by means of his **mighty**
2 Thes	1.9	the **Lord** and from his glorious **might**,
2 Pet	1.16	**mighty** coming of our **Lord** Jesus Christ.
Jude	.25	our **Lord**, be glory, majesty, **might**,

Miracles see **Acts**

Power

Gen	49.24	the **power** of the **Mighty God** of Jacob,
Ex	32.11	from Egypt with great **might** and **power**?
Deut	9.29	by your great **power** and **might**.
	10.17	over all **powers**. He is great and **mighty**,
	11.2	his **power**, his **might**,
2 Chr	20.6	are **powerful** and **mighty**, and no one
Ps	54.1	**power**, O **God**; set me free by your **might**!
	65.6	showing your **mighty power**.
	68.34	**power**; his majesty is over Israel, his **might**
	71.18	while I proclaim your **power** and **might**
	118.15	The **Lord's mighty power** has done it!
	118.16	his **mighty power** in battle!
	145.11	royal **power** and tell of your **might**,
Jer	10.6	you are **mighty**...great and **powerful**.
	16.21	nations know my **power** and my **might**;
	32.17	by your great **power** and **might**;
	32.21	**power** and **might** to bring your people
	48.25	**might** has been crushed; its **power**
Dan	2.37	emperor and given you **power**, **might**,
	4.30	city to display my **power** and **might**,
Zech	10.11	and **mighty** Egypt will lose her **power**.
Lk	9.43	amazed at the **mighty power** of God.
Eph	1.19	**power** working in us is the same as the **mighty strength**

| Eph | 6.10 | and by means of his **mighty power**. |
| Rev | 7.12 | **power**, and **might** belong to our God |

MIND

2 Cor	2.1	—	4.4	x5
Jer	25.16	—	26.19	x4
Amos	7.3	—	8.1	x4
Rom	7.23	—	8.5	x4
Rom	11.8	—	12.2	x4
Jer	19.5	—	21.10	x3
Jer	34.11 — 16			x3
Dan	1.8	—	2.8	x3
Jon	3.9	—	4.2	x3
Mt	21.29	—	22.37	x3
Lk	8.35	—	10.27	x3
Acts	28.6 — 27			x3
Rom	1.21 — 28			x3
1 Cor	2.2 — 16			x3
1 Cor	14.14 — 15			x3

Change

Ex	13.17	want the people to **change** their **minds**
	14.5	he and his officials **changed** their **minds**
	32.12	**change** your **mind** and do not bring this
	32.14	So the Lord **changed** his **mind**
Num	23.19	is not a human who **changes** his **mind**.
1 Sam	15.29	God does not...**change** his **mind**.
	26.19	to him will make him **change** his **mind**;
2 Sam	24.16	the Lord **changed** his **mind**
1 Chr	21.15	but he **changed** his **mind** and said
Jer	4.28	and will not **change** his **mind**.
	26.3	then I will **change** my **mind**
	26.13	If you do, he will **change** his **mind**
	26.19	And the Lord **changed** his **mind**
	34.11	but later they **changed** their **minds**,
	34.15	a few days ago you **changed** your **minds**
	34.16	But then you **changed** your **minds** again
Joel	2.14	Lord your God will **change** his **mind**
Amos	7.3	The Lord **changed** his **mind** and said
	7.6	The Lord **changed** his **mind** again
	7.8	I will not **change** my **mind** again
	8.1	I will not **change** my **mind** again
Jon	3.9	Perhaps God will **change** his **mind**
	3.10	So he **changed** his **mind**
	4.2	and always ready to **change** your **mind**
Zech	8.14	and did not **change** my **mind**,
Mt	3.14	tried to make him **change** his **mind**.
	21.29	but later he **changed** his **mind** and went.
	21.32	you did not later **change** your **minds**
Acts	28.6	they **changed** their **minds** and said,
Rom	11.29	For God does not **change** his **mind**
	12.2	by a complete **change** of your **mind**.

Dark

Rom	1.21	empty **minds** are filled with **darkness**.
2 Cor	4.4	their **minds** have been kept in the **dark**
Eph	4.18	and whose **minds** are in the **dark**.

Peace

Prov	14.30	**Peace** of **mind** makes the body healthy
	17.1	a dry crust of bread with **peace** of **mind**
	27.9	but trouble shatters your **peace** of **mind**.
Ecc	4.6	with **peace** of **mind**,

Right

| Mk | 5.15 | his **right mind**; and they were all afraid. |
| Lk | 8.35 | clothed and in his **right mind**; |

Understand

Ps	19.8	and give **understanding** to the **mind**.
Mt	13.15	their **minds** would **understand**,
Mk	8.17	**understand** yet? Are your **minds** so dull?
Lk	24.45	their **minds** to **understand** the Scriptures
Jn	12.40	and their **minds** would not **understand**,
Acts	28.27	their **minds** would **understand**,

| Phil | 4.7 | **understanding**, will keep your hearts and minds |

MIRACLE

Mt	11.20	—	14.2	x10
Acts	4.16	—	8.13	x8
Ex	4.8 — 30			x6
Jn	2.11	—	4.54	x6
Jn	6.2	—	7.31	x6
Jn	9.16	—	12.37	x5
Ex	10.1	—	11.10	x4
Ps	78.11 — 43			x4
Lk	10.13	—	11.29	x4
Mt	16.1 — 4			x3
Mk	6.2 — 14			x3
Mk	8.11	—	9.39	x3
Acts	2.19 — 43			x3
1 Cor	12.10 — 29			x3

God, Lord

Ex	4.28	**miracles** which the **Lord** had ordered
Deut	11.3	**Lord's** greatness...and his **miracles**.
Josh	3.5	the **Lord** will perform **miracles**
1 Chr	16.12	the **miracles** that **God** performed
Ps	77.14	You are the **God** who works **miracles**;
	78.12	**God** performed **miracles** in the plain
	105.5	the **miracles** that **God** performed
Jer	21.2	the **Lord** will perform...**miracles**
Dan	4.2	and **miracles** which the Supreme **God**
Mic	7.15	Work **miracles** for us, **Lord**,
Mt	16.1	perform a **miracle**...to show that **God**
Mk	8.11	a **miracle** to show that **God** approved
Lk	11.16	a **miracle** to show that **God** approved
Jn	3.2	the **miracles** you are doing unless **God**
Acts	2.22	the **miracles**...which **God** performed
	15.12	the **miracles**...that **God** had performed
	19.11	**God** was performing unusual **miracles**

Healing

Jn	6.2	they had seen his **miracles** of **healing**
Acts	4.22	**miracle** of **healing** had been performed
	4.30	to **heal**, and grant that...**miracles**

Jesus

Mt	11.20	**Jesus** had performed...his **miracles**
Lk	23.8	to see **Jesus** perform some **miracle**.
Jn	2.11	**Jesus** performed this first **miracle**
	4.54	second **miracle** that **Jesus** performed
	6.14	this **miracle** that **Jesus** had performed,
	20.30	**Jesus** performed many other **miracles**

Lord see God

Might see Wonder

Prophet

Deut	34.11	No other **prophet** has ever done **miracles**
Mt	12.39	is the **miracle** of the **prophet** Jonah.
Mk	13.22	**prophets** will appear. They will perform miracles
Rev	19.20	**prophet** who had performed **miracles**

Prove

Ex	7.9	**prove** yourselves by performing a **miracle**,
Mk	8.12	**miracle**? No, I tell you! No such **proof**
	16.20	**proved** that their preaching was true by the miracles
Acts	2.22	clearly **proven** to you by all the **miracles**
1 Cor	1.22	Jews want **miracles** for **proof**,
2 Cor	12.12	many **miracles** and wonders that **prove**

Wonder, Might

Ex	15.11	**wonderful** in holiness? Who can work **miracles** and **mighty** acts
Deut	4.34	worked **miracles** and **wonders**,
	7.19	the **miracles** and **wonders**,
	13.1	may promise a **miracle** or a **wonder**,

147

Deut	26.8	He worked **miracles** and **wonders**,
	29.3	the **miracles**, and the great **wonders**
	34.11	has ever done **miracles** and **wonders**
Ps	77.14	works **miracles**; you showed your **might**
	78.43	performed his **mighty** acts and **miracles**
	105.27	**mighty** acts and performed **miracles**
	135.9	he performed **miracles** and **wonders**
Jer	32.20	**miracles** and **wonders** in Egypt,
	32.21	By means of **miracles** and **wonders**
Dan	4.2	my account of the **wonders** and **miracles**
	4.3	**wonders** God shows us! How powerful are the **miracles**
	6.27	he performs **wonders** and **miracles**
Mt	24.24	perform great **miracles** and **wonders**
Mk	13.22	They will perform **miracles** and **wonders**
Jn	4.48	unless you see **miracles** and **wonders**.
Acts	2.19	**miracles** in the sky above and wonders
	2.22	**miracles** and **wonders** which God
	2.43	**miracles** and **wonders** were being done
	4.30	**wonders** and **miracles** may be performed
	5.12	**miracles** and **wonders** were being
	6.8	performed great **miracles** and **wonders**
	7.36	**miracles** and **wonders** in Egypt
	8.13	the great **wonders** and **miracles**
	14.3	power to perform **miracles** and **wonders**.
	15.12	**miracles** and **wonders** that God had
Rom	15.19	by the power of **miracles** and **wonders**,
2 Cor	12.12	many **miracles** and **wonders** that prove
2 Thes	2.9	all kinds of false **miracles** and **wonders**,
Heb	2.4	all kinds of **miracles** and **wonders**

MORTAL

Ezek	20.3	—	40.4	x50
Ezek	2.1	—	8.17	x21
Ezek	11.2	—	17.2	x16
Ezek	43.7	—	44.5	x4
1 Cor	15.42 – 54			x4
Rom	6.12	—	8.11	x3
2 Cor	4.10	—	5.4	x3

Body

Rom	6.12	no longer rule in your **mortal bodies**
	8.11	give life to your **mortal bodies**
1 Cor	15.42	When the **body** is buried, it is **mortal**;
2 Cor	4.10	we carry in our **mortal bodies** the death
	4.11	his life may be seen in this **mortal body**
2 Pet	1.14	I shall soon put off this **mortal body**,

Immortal

1 Cor	15.42	**mortal**; when raised, it will be **immortal**.
	15.50	is **mortal** cannot possess **immortality**.
	15.53	**mortal** must be changed into...**immortal**
	15.54	**mortal** has been changed into...**immortal**,
1 Pet	1.23	a parent who is **immortal**, not **mortal**.

Life

Rom	8.11	will also give **life** to your **mortal** bodies
2 Cor	4.11	his **life** may be seen in this **mortal** body
	5.4	is **mortal** will be transformed by **life**.

MOURN

Zech	12.10 – 12			x7
Gen	50.3 – 11			x6
Jer	6.26*	—	9.20	x6
Jer	47.5	—	49.3	x6
Joel	1.8	—	2.12	x5
Gen	37.34	—	38.12	x4
2 Sam	13.37	—	14.2	x4
1 Kgs	13.29	—	14.18	x4
Ezek	24.17 – 23			x4
Judg	20.22	—	21.2	x3
Ps	35.13 – 14			x3
Jer	16.4 – 6			x3
Jer	22.10	—	23.10	x3
Ezek	31.15	—	32.18	x3

Amos	8.3	—	9.5	x3
Mic	1.8 – 16			x3
Rev	18.11 – 19			x3

Bitterly

Num	14.39	they **mourned bitterly**.
Judg	21.2	Loudly and **bitterly** they **mourned**:
Jer	6.26	**Mourn** with **bitter** tears
	22.10	not **mourn** his death. But weep **bitterly**
Ezek	27.30	They all **mourn bitterly** for you,
Zech	12.10	They will **mourn bitterly**,

Comfort, Joy

Job	5.11	and gives **joy** to all who **mourn**.
	30.31	**joyful** music, now I hear only **mourning**
Ecc	3.4	the time for **joy**, the time for **mourning**
Is	57.18	and I will **comfort** those who **mourn**.
	61.2	has sent me to **comfort** all who **mourn**,
	61.3	give to those who **mourn** in Zion **Joy**
Jer	31.13	**comfort** them and turn their **mourning** into **joy**,
Mt	5.4	are those who **mourn**; God will **comfort**

Dead

Gen	23.2	and Abraham **mourned** her **death**.
	27.41	to **mourn** my father's **death** is near;
Lev	10.6	are allowed to **mourn** this **death**
	19.28	in your body to **mourn** for the **dead**.
Deut	14.1	So when you **mourn** for the **dead**,
2 Chr	16.14	built a huge bonfire to **mourn** his **death**.
	35.24	Judah and Jerusalem **mourned** his **death**.
Job	27.15	their widows will not **mourn** their **death**.
Is	50.3	as if it were in **mourning** for the **dead**.
Jer	22.10	do not **mourn** his **death**.
	22.18	No one will **mourn** his **death** or say,
	34.5	**mourn**...and say, 'Our king is **dead**!
Joel	1.8	like a girl who **mourns** the **death**
Amos	5.16	will be called to **mourn** the **dead**
	8.3	of **mourning**. There will be **dead** bodies

Grief see Sorrow

Joy see Comfort

Sackcloth

Gen	37.34	on **sackcloth**. He **mourned** for his son
2 Sam	3.31	wear **sackcloth**, and **mourn** for Abner.
Job	16.15	I **mourn** and wear clothes made of **sackcloth**,
Is	22.12	and **mourn**, to shave your heads and wear **sackcloth**.
Jer	6.26	on **sackcloth** and roll in ashes. **Mourn**
	49.3	**mourning**! Put on **sackcloth** and **mourn**.
Amos	8.10	**sackcloth**, and you will be like parents **mourning**

Sorrow, Grief

Gen	37.34	in **sorrow** and put on sackcloth. He **mourned**
2 Sam	1.12	They **grieved** and **mourned** and fasted
Ecc	3.4	**sorrow** and the time for joy, the time for **mourning**
Is	61.3	**mourn** in Zion...gladness instead of **grief**,
Jer	16.5	is **mourning**. Do not **grieve** for anyone.
	31.13	their **mourning** into joy, their **sorrow**
Mic	1.8	**mourn** and lament. To show my **sorrow**,

NAKED

Ezek	16.7 – 39			x5
Gen	2.25	—	3.11	x4
Is	20.2 – 4			x4
Mt	25.36 – 44			x4
Gen	9.21 – 23			x3

Strip

Is	3.26	a woman...**stripped naked**.
Ezek	16.37	**strip** off your clothes and let them see you **naked**.

Ezek	23.10	They **stripped** her **naked**
	23.29	**stripped naked**, exposed like a prostitute.
Hos	2.3	I will **strip** her as **naked** as she was
	2.10	I will **strip** her **naked** in front of her
Nah	3.5	I will **strip** you **naked**

NAME

	Acts	2.38	—	5.40	x10
	Jn	14.13	—	17.12	x9
	Lev	18.21	—	22.32	x7
	Acts	8.16	—	10.48	x6
	1 Kgs	1.17	—	2.42	x5
	Is	47.4	—	48.11	x5
	Jer	26.9	—	27.15	x4
	Ezek	20.9 – 39			x4
	Ezek	36.20 – 23			x4
	Amos	4.13	—	6.10	x4
	Lk	9.48	—	11.2	x4
	Acts	19.5 – 17			x4
	Deut	5.11	—	6.13	x3
	Deut	18.19 – 22			x3
	1 Chr	16.2 – 35			x3
	1 Chr	29.13 – 22			x3
	Ps	113.1 – 3			x3
	Ps	148.5 – 13			x3
	Jer	13.11	—	14.15	x3
	Jer	29.9 – 23			x3
	Jer	44.16 – 26			x3
	Ezek	39.7 – 25			x3
	Mt	6.9	—	7.22	x3
	Mk	9.37 – 39			x3
	Lk	1.31	—	2.21	x3

Command see **Power**

Demons see **Power**

Dishonour, Disgrace, Lie

Ps	89.35	by my holy **name**: I will never **lie**
Is	48.11	I will not let my **name** be **dishonoured**
Jer	14.14	prophets are telling **lies** in my **name**;
	23.25	have said who speak **lies** in my **name**
	29.9	They are telling you **lies** in my **name**.
	29.21	who are telling you **lies** in his **name**.
	29.23	and have told **lies** in the Lord's **name**.
Ezek	20.9	have brought **dishonour** to my **name**,
	20.14	brought **dishonour** to my **name**
	20.22	have brought **dishonour** to my **name**
	20.39	**dishonouring** my holy **name** by offering
	36.20	they brought **disgrace** on my holy **name**,
	36.21	my holy **name**, since the Israelites brought **disgrace** on it
	36.22	holy **name**, which you have **disgraced**
	36.23	great **name** — the **name** you **disgraced**
	39.7	and I will not let my **name** be **disgraced**
	43.7	**disgrace** my holy **name** by worshipping
	43.8	They **disgraced** my holy **name** by all

Father

Mt	6.9	**Father** in heaven: May your holy **name**
	28.19	baptize them in the **name** of the **Father**,
Lk	11.2	**Father**: May your holy **name**
Jn	12.28	**Father**, bring glory to your **name**!
	14.13	my **name**, so that the **Father's** glory
	14.26	whom the **Father** will send in my **name**,
	17.11	Holy **Father**! Keep them safe by the power of your **name**,
2 Cor	11.31	**Father** of...Jesus — blessed be his **name**
Rev	14.1	have his **name** and his **Father's name**

Glory

1 Chr	16.29	Praise the Lord's **glorious name**;
	29.13	and we praise your **glorious name**.
Neh	9.5	Let everyone praise his **glorious name**,
Ps	29.2	Praise the Lord's **glorious name**;
	66.2	Sing to the **glory** of his **name**;

Ps	72.19	glorious **name** for ever! May his **glory**
	96.8	Praise the Lord's **glorious name**;
	148.13	**name** is greater than all others; his **glory**
Jn	12.28	bring **glory** to your **name**!
	14.13	my **name**, so that the **Father's glory**
2 Thes	1.12	the **name** of...Jesus will receive **glory**

Lie see **Dishonour**

Oath see **Promise**

Power, Command, Demons

Ps	138.2	your **name** and your **commands**
	148.5	the **name** of the Lord! He **commanded**,
Jer	10.6	and your **name** is great and **powerful**.
Mt	7.22	your **name** we drove out many **demons**
Mk	9.38	was driving out **demons** in your **name**,
	16.17	they will drive out **demons** in my **name**;
Lk	9.49	man driving out **demons** in your **name**,
	10.17	gave them a **command** in your **name**!
Jn	17.11	them safe by the **power** of your **name**,
	17.12	them safe by the **power** of your **name**,
Acts	3.16	It was the **power** of his **name**
	4.10	the **power** of the **name** of Jesus Christ
	10.43	forgiven through the **power** of his **name**.
	19.13	I **command** you in the **name** of Jesus,
2 Thes	3.6	we **command** you in the **name** of...Jesus
	3.12	**name** of...Christ we **command** these

Promise, Oath, Swear

2 Sam	15.21	I **swear** to you in the Lord's **name**
	19.7	I **swear** by the Lord's **name**
1 Kgs	1.17	solemn **promise** in the **name** of the Lord
	1.30	the **promise** I made to you in the **name**
	2.8	solemn **promise** in the **name** of the Lord
	2.23	a solemn **promise** in the Lord's **name**,
	2.42	I made you **promise** in the Lord's **name**
2 Chr	15.14	they took an **oath** in the Lord's **name**
	36.13	had forced him to **swear** in God's **name**
Neh	13.25	made them take an **oath** in God's **name**
Ps	63.11	who make **promises** in God's **name**
	89.35	I have **promised** by my holy **name**:
Is	19.18	will take their **oaths** in the **name**
	48.1	You **swear** by the **name** of the Lord
	65.16	takes an **oath** will **swear** by the **name**
Jer	4.2	be right for you to **swear** by my **name**.
	44.26	**name** to make a vow by saying, 'I **swear**
Ezek	17.19	which he **swore** in my **name** to keep.
Dan	12.7	**promise** in the **name** of the Eternal
Hos	4.15	or make **promises** there in the **name**
Mt	26.63	**name** of the living God I now put you on **oath**:

NEED

	Prov	30.8	—	31.27	x8
	Lk	9.11	—	12.30	x8
	2 Cor	8.13	—	9.12	x8
	Mt	6.2 – 34			x7
	1 Cor	11.7	—	13.2	x7
	1 Kgs	3.9	—	4.28	x5
	Phil	4.6 – 19			x5
	Deut	14.29	—	15.11	x4
	Lk	18.22	—	19.42	x4
	1 Thes	3.10	—	5.1	x4
	Heb	7.11	—	8.7	x4
	Ex	16.16 – 21			x3
	Ex	22.11 – 15			x3
	Ex	35.21	—	36.5	x3
	Deut	23.12	—	24.15	x3
	2 Kgs	4.13 – 22			x3
	Job	34.23	—	35.7	x3
	Ps	72.4 – 13			x3
	Ps	145.15 – 19			x3
	Acts	27.3	—	28.10	x3
	2 Cor	11.9	—	12.9	x3
	1 Jn	2.27	—	3.17	x3

Enough

Ps	145.16	give them **enough** and satisfy the **needs**
Mt	6.34	**enough** worries...There is no **need**
2 Cor	9.8	all you **need**...and more than **enough**
Phil	4.12	in **need** and what it is to have...**enough**.
	4.18	than **enough!** I have all I **need** now that
Jas	2.15	**need** clothes and don't have **enough** to

Generous see **Help**

God, Lord

Gen	33.11	**God** has...given me everything I **need**.
Num	18.20	I, the **Lord**, am all you **need**.
Deut	4.7	near when they **need** him as...**God** is
	29.6	the **Lord** provided for your **needs**
1 Sam	17.47	the **Lord** does not **need** swords
Job	21.15	think there is no **need** to serve **God**
	34.23	**God** does not **need** to set a time
	35.7	There is nothing **God needs** from you.
Ps	16.5	**Lord**...you give me all I **need**;
	57.2	to **God**, who supplies my every **need**.
	69.33	The **Lord** listens to those in **need**
	73.26	**God**...is all I ever **need**.
Mt	4.4	but **needs** every word that **God** speaks.
Phil	4.6	ask **God** for what you **need**,
	4.19	my **God** will supply all your **needs**.
2 Pet	1.3	**God's** divine power...everything we **need**

God's People

Ezra	1.4	**his people** in exile **need** help to return,
Ps	34.9	**his people**...have all they **need**.
	69.33	in **need** and does not forget **his people**
Is	41.17	**my people** in their **need** look for water,
Jer	31.14	and satisfy all the **needs** of **my people**.
Zeph	3.11	**people**, will no longer **need** to be
2 Cor	9.12	only meets the **needs** of **God's people**,

Help, Generous

Deut	15.7	in **need**, then do not...refuse to **help**
	15.8	**generous** and lend...as much as he **needs**.
	15.11	**need**...so I command you to be **generous**
Ezra	1.4	If any of his people in exile **need help**
	4.3	don't **need** your **help** to build a temple
Ps	10.14	you have always **helped** the needy.
	72.4	may he **help** the needy
	112.9	He gives **generously** to the needy,
Prov	31.20	She is **generous** to the poor and **needy**.
Mt	6.3	But when you **help** a **needy** person
Rom	16.2	her any **help** she may **need** from you;
2 Cor	8.13	you should **help** those who are in **need**.
	9.1	no **need** for me to write...about the **help**
	9.9	He gives **generously** to the **needy**;
	11.9	you for **help** when I **needed** money;
Phil	4.16	**needed help** in Thessalonica, you sent it
Heb	4.16	grace to **help** us just when we **need** it.

Lord see **God**

Provide

Deut	29.6	the Lord **provided** for your **needs**
2 Sam	20.3	He **provided** for their **needs**,
2 Kgs	4.13	in **providing** for our **needs**.
Neh	9.21	you **provided** all that they **needed**;
Ps	128.2	Your work will **provide** for your **needs**;
	132.15	richly **provide** Zion with all she **needs**;
Acts	24.23	his friends to **provide** for his needs.
Eph	4.29	build up and **provide** what is **needed**,
Tit	3.14	in order to **provide** for real **needs**;
Heb	13.20	**provide** you with every good thing you **need**

Teach

Deut	29.6	for your **needs** in order to **teach** you
Is	28.9	he's **teaching**? Who **needs** his message?
Heb	5.12	you still **need** someone to **teach** you
1 Jn	2.27	you do not **need** anyone to **teach** you.

Trouble

2 Kgs	4.13	the **trouble** she has had in providing for our **needs**.
Job	6.14	**trouble** like this I **need** loyal friends
	30.25	**trouble** and feel sorry for those in **need**?
Ps	32.6	of **need**; when a great flood of **trouble**
Mt	6.34	There is no **need** to add to the **troubles**

NEIGHBOUR

Jer	25.9 – 11	x3
Lk	10.27 – 36	x3
Lk	14.12 – 15.9	x3

Friend

Ex	32.27	his **friends**, and his **neighbours**.
Ps	15.3	his **friends** nor spreads rumours about his **neighbours**.
	38.11	**friends** and **neighbours** will not come
Jer	6.21	and so will **friends** and **neighbours**.
	9.8	speaks **friendly** words to his **neighbour**,
Mic	7.5	your **neighbour** or trust your **friend**.
Lk	15.6	calls his **friends** and **neighbours** together
	15.9	calls her **friends** and **neighbours** together,

NEW

Lk	5.36 – 39	x7
Judg	15.13 – 16.12	x5
Mk	1.27 – 2.22	x5
Heb	8.8 – 10.20	x5
Is	41.15 – 43.19	x4
Is	65.15 – 66.22	x4
Mt	9.16 – 17	x4
Is	11.1 – 10	x3
Jer	31.22 – 33	x3
Rev	2.17 – 3.12	x3
Rev	21.1 – 5	x3

Covenant

Jer	31.31	I will make a **new covenant**
	31.33	The **new covenant** that I will make
Lk	22.20	**new covenant** sealed with my blood,
1 Cor	11.25	This cup is God's **new covenant**,
2 Cor	3.6	capable of serving the **new covenant**,
Heb	8.8	a **new covenant** with the people
	8.13	By speaking of a **new covenant**,
	9.15	the one who arranges a **new covenant**
	12.24	who arranged the **new covenant**,

Heaven

Is	65.17	making a **new earth** and **new heavens**.
	66.22	**new heavens** will endure by my power,
2 Pet	3.13	**new heavens** and a **new earth**,
Rev	21.1	I saw a **new heaven** and a **new earth**
	21.2	**new Jerusalem**, coming...out of **heaven**

Jerusalem

Is	65.18	The **new Jerusalem** I make
Gal	4.26	But the heavenly **Jerusalem** is free,
Heb	12.22	the heavenly **Jerusalem**,
Rev	3.12	city of my God, the **new Jerusalem**,
	21.2	the Holy City, the **new Jerusalem**,

Life

Ruth	4.15	who will bring **new life** to you
Ezra	9.8	us from slavery and given us **new life**.
Ps	104.30	you give **new life** to the earth.
	119.40	give me **new life**, for you are righteous.
Ecc	11.5	how **new life** begins in the womb
Zeph	3.17	in his love he will give you **new life**.
Acts	5.20	tell the people all about this **new life**.
Rom	6.4	so also we might live a **new life**.
1 Cor	4.17	principles which I follow in the **new life**
Tit	3.5	**new birth** and **new life** by washing us.
1 Pet	1.3	of his great mercy he gave us **new life**

OBEY

Deut	4.1	—	13.18	x47
Deut	26.14	—	34.9	x39
Ps	119.2	—	168	x39
Rom	1.5	—	6.17	x14
2 Kgs	17.13	—	18.12	x11
Lev	25.17	—	26.27	x10
Jer	11.3	—	13.11	x9
Jer	35.8	—	18	x8
Lev	18.4	—	20.8	x7
Josh	22.2	—	24.24	x7
1 Kgs	8.23	—	9.4	x7
Jn	14.15	—	15.20	x7
Neh	9.16	—	10.29	x6
Ezek	20.11	—	39	x6
Phil	2.8	—	3.9	x6
1 Jn	2.3	—	3.24	x6
1 Sam	15.13	—	22	x5
1 Kgs	2.3	—	3.14	x5
2 Chr	6.14	—	7.17	x5
Is	65.13	—	66.14	x5
Gal	5.3	—	6.13	x5
Prov	28.4	—	14	x4
Rom	13.1	—	10	x4
Heb	13.9	—	17	x4
Josh	1.7	—	17	x3
Ps	78.7	—	56	x3
Ecc	8.5	—	13	x3
Gal	3.10	—	21	x3
1 Pet	1.2	—	22	x3

Abandon, Forget

Deut	8.11	not **forget** the Lord...do not fail to **obey**
	16.12	you **obey** these commands; do not **forget**
2 Kgs	17.13	**Abandon** your evil ways and obey
Neh	9.17	refused to **obey**; they **forgot** all you did;
Ps	78.7	not **forget** what he has done, but...**obey**
	119.8	will **obey** your laws; never **abandon** me!
Jer	16.11	They **abandoned** me and did not **obey**
1 Tim	4.1	will **abandon** the faith...they will **obey**

Afraid see Fear

Anger, Curse, Destroy

Deut	8.20	If you do not **obey** the Lord, then you will be **destroyed**
	27.26	**curse** on anyone who does not **obey** .
	28.45	**destroyed**, because you did not **obey**
Is	66.14	who **obey** me, and I show my **anger**
Jer	11.3	a **curse** on everyone who does not **obey**
	12.17	**obey**, then I will...uproot it and **destroy**
Gal	3.10	depend on **obeying**...live under a **curse**
Eph	5.6	**anger**...upon those who do not **obey**
Col	3.6	**anger**...upon those who do not **obey**

Bow see Worship

Christ

1 Cor	9.21	I don't **obey** God's law; I am really under **Christ's** law.
2 Cor	10.5	every thought...and make it **obey Christ**
Gal	1.4	**Christ** gave himself...in **obedience**
	6.2	you will **obey** the law of **Christ**.

Command, Commandment, Follow, Keep
see also **LAW — Obey**

Gen	18.19	may **command** his sons...to **obey** me
	22.18	because you **obeyed** my **command**
	24.37	with a vow to **obey** his **command**.
Ex	12.50	**obeyed**...what the Lord had **commanded**
	16.28	people refuse to **obey** my **commands**?
	23.22	**obey** him and do everything I **command**,
	24.7	**obey**...everything that he has **commanded**.
	27.21	This **command** is to be **kept** for ever
Lev	18.30	**Obey** the **commands** I give

Lev	19.3	**keep** the Sabbath, as I have **commanded**.
	19.19	**Obey** my **commands**
	22.31	**Obey** my **commands**;
	26.14	If you will not **obey** my **commands**,
Num	9.23	in **obedience** to the **commands**
	15.39	all my **commands** and obey them;
	15.40	remind you to **keep** all my **commands**,
Deut	4.2	**Obey** the **commands** of the Lord
	4.13	you must **obey** the Ten **Commandments**,
	4.23	**Obey** his **command**
	5.29	honour me and **obey** all my **commands**,
	6.25	**obey** everything that God has **commanded** us,
	7.9	who love him and **obey** his **commands**,
	7.12	you listen to these **commands** and **obey**
	8.2	whether you would **obey** his **commands**.
	11.13	**obey** the **commands** that I have given
	11.27	if you **obey** the **commands**
	12.25	If you **obey** this **command**
	12.28	**Obey**...everything that I have **commanded**
	13.4	**obey** him and keep his **commands**;
	13.18	if you **obey** all his **commands**
	16.12	Be sure that you **obey** these **commands**;
	17.19	**obey**...everything that is **commanded**
	28.1	faithfully **keep** all his **commands**
	28.9	**obey**...everything he **commands**,
	28.13	**obey** faithfully all his **commands**
	28.15	not faithfully **keep** all his **commands**
	30.8	**obey** him and keep all his **commands**
	30.2	**obey** his **commands** that I am giving
	30.8	**obey** him and **keep** all his **commands**
	30.16	If you **obey** the **commands**
	32.46	Make sure you **obey** all these **commands**
	33.3	and **obey** his **commands**.
	33.9	They **obeyed** your **commands**
	34.9	**obeyed** Joshua and **kept** the **commands**
Josh	22.2	and you have **obeyed** all my **commands**.
	22.3	have been careful to **obey** the **commands**
	22.20	Achan...refused to **obey** the **command**
	23.16	the Lord your God **commanded** you to **keep**
	24.24	We will **obey** his **commands**.
Judg	2.17	had **obeyed** the Lord's **commands**,
	3.4	the Israelites would **obey** the **commands**
1 Sam	12.14	and **obey** his **commands**,
	13.13	You have not **obeyed** the **command**
	15.13	I have **obeyed** the Lord's **command**.
2 Sam	24.19	David **obeyed** the Lord's **command**
1 Kgs	2.4	they were careful to **obey** his **commands**
	3.14	you **obey** me and keep my...**commands**,
	12.24	They all **obeyed** the Lord's **command**
	14.8	**obeyed** my **commands**,
	17.5	Elijah **obeyed** the Lord's **command**
2 Kgs	17.13	and **obey** my **commands**,
	18.6	**kept** all the **commands** that the Lord
	23.3	to **obey** him, to **keep** his...**commands**
1 Chr	21.19	David **obeyed** the Lord's **command**
	24.19	**obedience** to the **commands** of the Lord
	29.19	to **obey** everything that you **command**
2 Chr	7.17	**obeying**...everything I have **commanded**
	11.4	They **obeyed** the Lord's **command**
	14.4	to **obey** his teachings and **commands**.
	17.4	**obeyed** God's **commands**, and did not
	30.12	**obey** his will by following the **commands**
Neh	9.16	and refused to **obey** your **commands**.
	10.29	**obey** all that the Lord...**commands**
Esth	1.15	a **command**, and she refused to **obey**
Ps	17.4	I have **obeyed** your **command**
	25.10	his covenant and **obey** his **commands**.
	37.34	and **obey** his **commands**;
	78.7	but always **obey** his **commandments**.
	78.56	They did not **obey** his **commandments**,
	89.31	and do not **keep** my **commandments**,

151

Ps	95.10	They refuse to **obey** my **commands**.
	103.18	and who faithfully **obey** his **commands**.
	103.20	who **obey** his **commands**,
	105.28	Egyptians did not **obey** his **command**.
	105.45	**obey** his laws and **keep** all his **commands**,
	106.3	are those who **obey** his **commands**,
	111.10	who **obey** his **commands**.
	112.1	takes pleasure in **obeying** his **commands**.
	119.2	who **follow** his **commands**, who **obey**
	119.9	By **obeying** your **commands**.
	119.14	I delight in **following** your **commands**
	119.32	I will eagerly **obey** your **commands**.
	119.35	me **obedient** to your **commandments**,
	119.40	I want to **obey** your **commands**;
	119.47	find pleasure in **obeying** your **commands**,
	119.56	in **obeying** your **commands**.
	119.60	to **obey** your **commands**.
	119.80	I perfectly **obey** your **commandments**
	119.94	I have tried to **obey** your **commands**.
	119.100	because I **obey** your **commands**.
	119.115	I will **obey** the **commands** of my God.
	119.134	so that I may **obey** your **commands**.
	119.145	and I will **obey** your **commands**!
	119.158	because they do not **keep** your **commands**.
	119.168	I **obey** your **commands**
	119.173	because I **follow** your **commands**.
	125.4	to those who **obey** your **commands**.
	128.1	who **obey** the Lord...his **commands**.
	148.8	strong winds that **obey** his **command**.
Ecc	8.5	As long as you **obey** his **commands**,
	12.13	and **obey** his **commands**,
Jer	3.13	you have not **obeyed** my **commands**.
	3.25	we have never **obeyed** his **commands**.
	7.23	But I did **command** them to **obey** me
	11.4	**obey**...everything that I had **commanded**.
	17.24	that they must **obey** all my **commands**.
	22.5	But if you do not **obey** my **commands**,
	32.23	they did not **obey** your **commands**.
	35.9	**obeyed** everything that...Jonadab **commanded**
	35.14	descendants have **obeyed** his **command**
	35.16	descendants have **obeyed** the **command**
	35.18	You have **obeyed** the **command**
	42.5	**obey** all the **commands** that the Lord
	43.4	would **obey** the Lord's **command**
	44.23	by not **obeying** all his **commands**.
Ezek	20.13	**commands**...bring life to anyone who **obeys**
	20.21	**commands**...bring life to anyone who **obeys**
	36.27	**keep** all the **commands** I have given
Joel	2.11	**commands**...The troops that **obey**
Amos	2.4	and have not **kept** my **commands**.
Zeph	2.3	who **obey** his **commands**.
Zech	6.15	if you fully **obey** the **commands**
Mt	19.17	**Keep** the **commandments** if you want
	19.20	I have **obeyed** all these **commandments**,
	28.20	to **obey** everything I have **commanded**
Mk	7.8	put aside God's **command** and **obey**
	10.20	I have **obeyed** all these **commandments**.
	12.33	to **obey** these two **commandments**
Lk	10.17	demons **obeyed** us when we gave them a **command**
	18.21	I have **obeyed** all these **commandments**.
Jn	14.15	you will **obey** my **commandments**.
	14.21	accepts my **commandments** and **obeys**
	15.10	If you **obey** my **commands**
1 Cor	7.19	is to **obey** God's **commandments**.
Heb	3.10	and refuse to **obey** my **commands**.
	9.20	that God has **commanded** you to **obey**.
1 Jn	2.3	If we **obey** God's **commands**,
	2.4	but does not **obey** his **commands**,

1 Jn	3.22	because we **obey** his **commands**
	3.24	Whoever **obeys** God's **commands**
	5.2	loving God and **obeying** his **commands**.
	5.3	means that we **obey** his **commands**
2 Jn	.6	live in **obedience** to God's **commands**.
Rev	12.17	those who **obey** God's **commandments**
	14.12	those who **obey** God's **commandments**

Covenant see **Promise**

Curse see **Anger**

Desire

1 Chr	29.19	wholehearted **desire** to **obey** everything
Ps	119.36	Give me the **desire** to **obey** your laws
Rom	6.12	**obey** the **desires** of your natural self.

Destroy see **Anger**

Father

Jn	15.10	as I have **obeyed** my **Father's** commands
Gal	1.4	in **obedience** to the will of our...**Father**.

Fear, Afraid

Ex	1.17	**feared** God and so did not **obey**
Josh	14.8	people **afraid**. But I faithfully **obeyed**
Is	66.2	who **fear** me and **obey** me.
	66.5	you that **fear** him and **obey** him:
Hag	1.12	**afraid** and **obeyed** the prophet Haggai,
Eph	6.5	**obey** your human masters with **fear** and

Forget see **Abandon**

Gods

Deut	32.17	**gods** that Israel had never **obeyed**,
1 Kgs	11.9	foreign **gods**, Solomon did not **obey**
2 Kgs	17.37	You shall not **obey** other **gods**,
Jer	3.13	**gods** and that you have not **obeyed**
	16.11	other **gods**. They...did not **obey**
	44.23	other **gods** and sinned...by not **obeying**
Mic	4.5	nation worships and **obeys** its own **god**
Zeph	3.9	to other **gods**. They will all **obey** me.

Justice, Judge

Gen	18.19	to **obey** me and to do what is...**just**.
2 Sam	23.3	**justice**, who rules in **obedience** to God,
Ps	111.10	sound **judgement** to all who **obey**
	119.30	to be **obedient**...to your **judgements**.
	119.106	to **obey** your **just** instructions.
Is	11.3	in **obeying** him. He will not **judge**
Jn	12.47	does not **obey** it, I will not **judge** him.
Acts	4.19	**judge** which is right...to **obey** you
Jas	4.11	If you **judge** the Law, then you are no longer one who **obeys**

Life, Save

Deut	32.47	they are your very **life**. **Obey** them
Job	36.11	**obey** God...they **live** out their **lives**
Ps	7.10	he **saves** those who **obey** him.
	50.23	I will surely **save** all who **obey** me.
	119.9	man keep his **life** pure? By **obeying**
	119.40	**obey** your commands; give me new **life**,
	119.94	yours — **save** me! I have tried to **obey**
	119.155	will not be **saved**, for they do not **obey**
Prov	19.23	**Obey** the Lord...**live** a long **life**
Jer	22.21	**life**; you never would **obey** the Lord.
Ezek	20.11	bring **life** to anyone who **obeys** them.
	20.13	bring **life** to anyone who **obeys** them.
	20.21	bring **life** to anyone who **obeys** them.
Mal	4.2	for you who **obey** me, my **saving** power
Lk	1.6	They both **lived** good **lives**...and **obeyed**
1 Pet	1.14	**obedient**...and do not allow your **lives**

Love

Ex	20.6	those who **love** me and **obey** my laws.
Deut	5.10	those who **love** me and **obey** my laws.
	7.9	who **love** him and **obey** his commands,
	11.1	**Love** the Lord...and always **obey** all his
	30.6	**obedient** hearts, so that you will **love**

Deut	30.16	if you **love** him, **obey** him,
	30.20	**Love** the Lord your God, **obey** him and
Josh	22.5	**obey** the law...**love** the Lord
1 Kgs	8.23	your **love** when they live in...**obedience**
2 Chr	6.14	your **love** when they live in...**obedience**
Ps	5.12	those who **obey** you, Lord; your **love**
	25.10	**love** he leads all who...**obey** his
	119.47	**obeying** your commands, because I **love**
	119.88	**love** be good to me, so that I may **obey**
	119.167	I **obey** your teachings; I **love** them
Jn	14.15	If you **love** me, you will **obey**
	14.21	**obeys** them is the one who **loves** me.
	14.23	**loves** me will **obey** my teaching.
	14.24	does not **love** me does not **obey** my
	15.10	If you **obey**...you will remain in my **love**
Rom	13.8	**love** one another. Whoever does this has **obeyed** the Law.
	13.10	**love**, then, is to **obey** the whole Law.
1 Jn	2.5	**obeys** his word is the one whose **love**
	5.3	our **love** for God means that we **obey**
2 Jn	.6	**love**...means...we must live in **obedience**

Power

2 Chr	27.6	**powerful** because he faithfully **obeyed**
Mal	4.2	for you who **obey** me, my saving **power**
Eph	2.2	**obeyed** the ruler of the spiritual **powers**

Praise see Worship

Promise, Covenant

Gen	24.37	made me **promise** with a vow to **obey**
Ex	19.5	will **obey** me and keep my **covenant**,
Lev	26.15	refuse to **obey**...and break the **covenant**
Deut	26.17	you have **promised** to **obey** him,
	26.18	he **promised** you; and he commands you to **obey**
	29.9	**Obey**...all the terms of this **covenant**,
1 Kgs	2.4	**obey** him, the Lord will keep the **promise**
2 Kgs	18.12	**obey** the Lord...but broke the **covenant**
	23.3	a **covenant** with the Lord to **obey** him,
2 Chr	34.31	a **covenant** with the Lord to **obey** him,
	34.32	**obeyed** the requirements of the **covenant**
Ps	25.10	all who keep his **covenant** and **obey**
	25.14	**obey** him and he affirms his **covenant**
	78.10	**covenant** with God; they refused to **obey**
	103.18	**covenant** and who faithfully **obey**
	119.38	**promise** you make to those who **obey**
	119.57	I **promise** to **obey** your laws.
	119.106	I will keep my solemn **promise** to **obey**
Jer	11.3	not **obey** the terms of this **covenant**.
	11.6	of the **covenant** and to **obey** them.
Ezek	20.37	and make you **obey** my **covenant**.
Rom	4.14	**promises** is to be given to those who **obey**
Heb	9.20	the **covenant** that God has commanded you to **obey**.

Prophet

Hag	1.12	afraid and **obeyed** the **prophet** Haggai,
Acts	3.23	Anyone who does not **obey** that **prophet**
Rev	1.3	of this **prophetic** message and **obey**
	22.7	are those who **obey** the **prophetic** words
	22.9	**prophets** and of all those who **obey** the

Proud see Stubborn

Rebellious see Stubborn

Refuse, Reject

Ex	16.28	people **refuse** to **obey** my commands?
Lev	26.15	If you **refuse** to **obey** my laws
	26.21	to resist me and **refuse** to **obey** me,
	26.27	to defy me and **refuse** to **obey** me,
Num	14.22	and have **refused** to **obey** me.
Deut	18.19	will punish anyone who **refuses** to **obey**

Deut	21.20	rebellious and **refuses** to **obey** us;
Josh	22.20	Achan son of Zerah **refused** to **obey**
2 Kgs	17.15	They **refused** to **obey** his instructions
Neh	9.16	and **refused** to **obey** your commands.
	9.17	They **refused** to **obey**
	9.29	stubborn, they **refused** to **obey**.
Esth	1.15	and she **refused** to **obey** it!
Ps	15.4	**rejects**, but honours those who **obey**
	78.10	they **refused** to **obey** his law.
	95.10	They **refuse** to **obey** my commands.
Prov	1.29	always **refused** to **obey** the Lord.
	3.7	**obey** the Lord and **refuse** to do wrong.
Jer	2.20	**refused** to **obey** me and worship me.
	5.5	and **refuse** to **obey** him.
	6.19	**rejected** my teaching and have not **obeyed**
	13.10	evil people have **refused** to **obey** me.
	35.12	you **refuse** to listen to me and to **obey**
Acts	7.39	But our ancestors **refused** to **obey** him
2 Thes	1.8	who **reject** God and who do not **obey**
Heb	3.10	and **refuse** to **obey** my commands.

Right

Gen	17.1	**Obey** me and always do what is **right**.
	18.19	**obey** me and to do what is **right**
Ex	15.26	**obey** me completely by doing what I consider **right**
Neh	5.9	ought to **obey** God and do what's **right**.
Ps	19.8	are **right**, and those who **obey** them
	106.3	who **obey** his commands, who always do what is **right**.
Zeph	2.3	**obey** his commands. Do what is **right**,
Acts	4.19	**right** in God's sight — to **obey** you or to **obey**
Eph	6.1	**obey** your parents, for this is the **right**
Jas	2.8	be doing the **right** thing if you **obey**

Right With God, Righteous

Lk	7.29	had **obeyed** God's **righteous** demands
Rom	5.19	**right with God** as the result of the **obedience**
	10.5	**right with God** by **obeying** the Law:
Gal	3.21	be put **right with God** by **obeying** it.
	5.4	**right with God** by **obeying** the Law
Phil	3.6	a person can be **righteous** by **obeying**
	3.9	**righteousness**...that is gained by **obeying**

Save see Life

Spirit of God

Acts	5.32	**Spirit**, who is God's gift to those who **obey**
	20.22	in **obedience** to the Holy **Spirit**
1 Pet	1.2	his **Spirit**, to **obey** Jesus Christ
1 Jn	2.27	**Obey** the **Spirit's** teaching,

Spirits

Mk	1.27	the evil **spirits**, and they **obey** him!
Lk	10.20	be glad because the evil **spirits obey**
Eph	2.2	**obeyed** the ruler of the spiritual **powers**
1 Tim	4.1	they will **obey** lying **spirits**
1 Pet	3.20	**spirits** of those who had not **obeyed**

Stubborn, Proud, Rebellious

Ex	23.21	**obey** him. Do not **rebel** against him,
Deut	10.16	**obedient** to the Lord and stop being **stubborn**.
	21.18	**stubborn** and **rebellious**, a son who will not **obey**
	21.20	**stubborn** and **rebellious** and refuses to **obey**
2 Kgs	17.14	would not **obey**; they were **stubborn**
2 Chr	30.8	not be **stubborn** as they were, but **obey**
Neh	9.16	**stubborn** and refused to **obey** your
	9.29	**stubborn**, they refused to **obey**.
Ps	119.85	**Proud** men, who do not **obey** your law,

Jer	11.8	**obey**. Instead, everyone continued to be as **stubborn**
	13.10	to **obey** me. They have been as **stubborn**
	16.12	**stubborn** and evil, and you do not **obey**
	17.23	**stubborn**; they would not **obey** me
Ezek	11.19	**stubborn** heart of stone and will give them an **obedient**
	36.26	**stubborn** heart of stone and give you an **obedient**

True

Ps	103.18	**true** to his covenant and who faithfully **obey**
Rom	6.17	**obeyed** with all your heart the **truths**
Gal	5.7	Who made you stop **obeying** the **truth**?
Heb	2.2	**true**, and anyone who did not follow it or **obey**
1 Pet	1.22	by your **obedience** to the **truth**
1 Jn	2.27	what he teaches is **true**, not false. **Obey**

Turn

Num	15.39	**obey** them; then you will not **turn** away
Deut	4.30	will finally **turn** to the Lord and **obey**
2 Sam	22.22	**obeyed** the law of the Lord; I have not **turned**
1 Kgs	11.9	did not **obey** the Lord, but **turned** away
Ps	18.21	**obeyed** the law of the Lord; I have not **turned**
Rev	3.3	**obey** it and **turn** from your sins.

Word, Will

Deut	32.47	**words**; they are your very life. **Obey**
2 Chr	30.12	**obey** his **will** by following the
	34.21	not **obeyed** the **word** of the Lord
Ps	119.67	but now I **obey** your **word**.
	119.101	because I want to **obey** your **word**.
Is	50.10	and **obey** the **words** of his servant,
Jer	6.19	and have not **obeyed** my **words**.
Ezek	33.32	listen to all your **words** and don't **obey**
Mal	2.9	because you do not **obey** my **will**,
Mt	7.24	these **words** of mine and obeys them
	7.26	**words** of mine and does not **obey** them
Lk	6.47	and listens to my **words** and **obeys**
	6.49	who hears my **words** and does not **obey**
	8.21	who hear the **word** of God and **obey**
	11.28	who hear the **word** of God and **obey** it!
Jn	4.34	**obey** the **will** of the one who sent me
	8.55	and I **obey** his **word**.
	17.6	They have **obeyed** your **word**,
Gal	1.4	in **obedience** to the **will** of our God
Col	4.12	in complete **obedience** to God's **will**.
2 Tim	2.26	them and made them **obey** his **will**.
1 Jn	2.5	whoever **obeys** his **word** is the one
Rev	1.3	**words** of this prophetic message and **obey**
	22.7	are those who **obey** the prophetic **words**
	22.9	those who **obey** the **words** in this book.

Worship, Bow, Praise

Gen	49.10	And **bow** in **obedience** before him.
Deut	10.20	**Obey** the Lord your God and **worship**
	13.4	**obey** him and keep his commands; **worship** him
	33.3	So we **bow** at his feet and **obey**
2 Sam	22.45	**bow** before me; when they hear me, they **obey**.
2 Kgs	17.34	not **worship** the Lord nor do they **obey**
Ps	18.44	**bow** before me; when they hear me, they **obey**.
	33.1	**praise** him, all you that **obey** him.
Is	65.13	those who **worship** and **obey** me
Jer	2.20	refused to **obey** me and **worship** me.
Mic	4.5	nation **worships** and **obeys** its own god
Zech	10.12	they will **worship** and **obey** me.

OFFER
see also **SACRIFICE**

Lev	1.2	—	10.14	x86
Num	28.4	—	29.39	x48
Ezek	42.13	—	46.24	x41
Lev	21.6	—	24.9	x38
Num	3.4	—	9.13	x27
2 Chr	28.4	—	35.16	x24
Heb	7.27	—	11.17	x24
Ex	28.38	—	30.28	x20
Lev	14.11	—	17.9	x15
Deut	12.6	—	13.16	x14
Ezra	6.3	—	10.19	x14
Ex	34.15	—	36.3	x13
1 Kgs	7.48	—	13.18	x13
Num	15.3	—	16.15	x11
1 Sam	1.3	—	3.14	x11
1 Chr	21.23	—	23.31	x11
Ezra	1.4	—	4.2	x11
2 Chr	6.40	—	9.4	x10
Mal	1.7	—	3.8	x10
1 Cor	8.1	—	10.28	x8
Num	18.9 – 32			x7
Jer	44.3 – 24			x7
1 Sam	15.15	—	16.11	x6
2 Sam	23.16	—	24.25	x6
Neh	10.33 – 37			x6
Neh	12.43	—	13.31	x6
Ezek	20.26 – 40			x6
1 Kgs	3.2 – 15			x5
2 Kgs	12.3 – 18			x5
Gen	4.3 – 5			x4
Ex	25.2 – 30			x4
Num	23.2 – 30			x4
Josh	22.26 – 29			x4
Ezek	16.18 – 25			x4
Ex	5.3 – 17			x3
Ex	8.8 – 27			x3
Lev	19.5 – 24			x3
Lev	27.9 – 26			x3
Judg	13.15 – 23			x3
2 Sam	6.13 – 18			x3
1 Kgs	1.9 – 25			x3
2 Kgs	10.19 – 25			x3
1 Chr	16.1 – 29			x3
Ps	66.2 – 15			x3
Jer	11.12 – 17			x3
Ezek	18.6 – 15			x3
Ezek	40.39 – 43			x3
Phil	2.16 – 17			x3
Heb	13.11 – 15			x3

Best, Perfect

Gen	4.4	gave the **best** parts of it as an **offering**.
Lev	22.23	may **offer** an animal that is stunted or not **perfectly**
Num	18.32	before the **best** part is **offered**;
1 Sam	15.15	kept the **best** sheep and cattle to **offer**
Prov	3.9	making him an **offering** from the **best**
Ezek	16.19	**best** flour, olive-oil, and honey — but you **offered**
	20.40	your **best offerings**,
Mic	6.6	the **best** calves to burn as **offerings**
Mt	21.16	babies to **offer perfect** praise.
Heb	9.14	**offered** himself as a **perfect** sacrifice

Bow see Worship

Defile, Unclean

Lev	22.3	**unclean**, comes near the sacred **offerings**
Jer	19.4	**defiled** this place by **offering** sacrifices
Ezek	20.26	**defile** themselves with their...**offerings**,
	20.31	**offer** the same gifts and **defile** yourselves

Hag	2.14	they **offer** on the altar is **defiled**.
Acts	15.20	**unclean** because it has been **offered** to

Faith

Phil	2.17	the sacrifice that your **faith offers**
Heb	11.4	was **faith** that made Abel **offer** to God
	11.17	**faith** that made Abraham **offer** his son

First-born

Ex	13.12	**offer** every **first-born** male to the Lord.
	13.13	every **first-born** male donkey by **offering**
	34.20	**first-born** donkey by **offering** a lamb in
Deut	12.6	freewill **offerings**, and the **first-born**
Ezek	20.26	**offerings**, and I let them sacrifice their
		first-born
Mic	6.7	**offer** him my **first-born** child to pay for

Forgive, Take Away (sin)

Ex	29.14	is an **offering** to **take away the sins**
Lev	4.24	This is an **offering** to **take away sin**.
	5.9	This is an **offering** to **take away sin**.
	9.7	**burnt-offering** to **take away your sins**
	16.6	**offer** a bull as a sacrifice to **take away**
2 Chr	29.21	an **offering** to **take away the sins**
Neh	10.33	**offerings** to **take away the sins**
Ezek	45.13	-**offerings**, so...your sins will be **forgiven**.
	45.17	the **fellowship-offerings**, to **take away**
Hos	14.2	**offering** to him: "**Forgive** all our sins
Heb	9.28	**offered** in sacrifice once to **take away**
	10.18	these have been **forgiven**, an **offering**

Freewill

Lev	7.16	a vow or as his own **freewill offering**,
	22.18	of a vow or as a **freewill offering**,
	22.21	of a vow or as a **freewill offering**,
	22.23	As a **freewill offering** you may **offer**
	27.26	to him as a **freewill offering**.
Num	15.3	as a **freewill offering** or as an **offering**
	29.39	of a vow or as a **freewill offerings**.
Deut	12.17	to the Lord, your **freewill offerings**,
	16.10	him a **freewill offering** in proportion
Ezra	2.68	gave **freewill offerings** to help rebuild
	8.28	brought to him as **freewill offerings**.

Gods, Idols

Ex	22.20	who **offers** sacrifices to any **god** except
	34.15	to eat the food they **offer** to their **gods**.
Judg	16.23	**offer** a great sacrifice to their **god**
1 Kgs	11.8	and **offer** sacrifices to their own **gods**.
2 Kgs	5.17	not **offer** sacrifices...to any **god**
	22.17	have **offered** sacrifices to other **gods**,
2 Chr	34.25	have **offered** sacrifices to other **gods**,
Ps	106.28	ate sacrifices **offered** to lifeless **gods**.
Is	57.6	as **gods**. You pour out wine as **offerings**
	66.3	they **offer** incense or pray to an **idol**.
Jer	7.9	**offer** sacrifices to Baal, and worship **gods**
	11.12	the **gods** to whom they **offer** sacrifices
	19.4	by **offering** sacrifices here to other **gods**
	19.13	an **offering** to other **gods** — they will all
	44.3	**offered** sacrifices to other **gods**
	44.15	wives **offered** sacrifices to other **gods**,
	44.23	**offered** sacrifices to other **gods**
	48.35	from **offering** sacrifices to their **gods**.
Ezek	16.20	and **offered** them as sacrifices to **idols**.
	20.39	by **offering** gifts to your **idols**.
	22.9	of them eat sacrifices **offered** to **idols**.
Hos	3.1	to other **gods** and like to take **offerings**
Acts	7.41	**idol** in the shape of a bull, **offered**
	15.20	because it has been **offered** to **idols**;
	15.29	no food that has been **offered** to **idols**;
	21.25	any food that has been **offered** to **idols**,
1 Cor	8.1	you wrote about food **offered** to **idols**.
	8.4	about eating the food **offered** to **idols**:
	8.10	him to eat food **offered** to **idols**?
	10.19	**idol** or the food **offered** to it
	10.28	This food was **offered** to **idols**,

Rev	2.14	eat food that had been **offered** to **idols**
	2.20	food that has been **offered** to **idols**.

Holy, Sacred

Ex	25.30	the **sacred** bread **offered** to me.
Lev	2.10	the **offering** belongs to the priests; it
		is...**holy**,
	6.25	This is a very **holy offering**.
	6.29	may eat this **offering**; it is very **holy**.
	10.12	because this **offering** is very **holy**.
	21.6	He **offers food-offerings** to me, and he must
		be **holy**.
	21.22	the food **offered** to me, both the **holy**
	22.2	treat with respect the **sacred offerings**
	22.3	comes near the **sacred offerings**
	22.4	may eat any of the **sacred offerings**
	22.6	may not eat any of the **sacred offerings**
	22.7	then he may eat the **sacred offerings**,
	22.10	may eat any of the **sacred offerings**;
	22.12	may not eat any of the **sacred offerings**.
	22.14	eats any of the **sacred offerings**
	22.15	shall not profane the **sacred offerings**
	22.16	the Lord and I make the **offerings holy**.
	23.20	These **offerings** are **holy**.
	24.9	is a very **holy** part of the food **offered**
Num	6.20	a **sacred offering** for the priest,
	18.9	the most **sacred offerings** not burnt
2 Chr	2.4	we will present **offerings** of **sacred** bread
	35.13	boiled the **sacred offerings** in pots,
Neh	12.47	The people gave a **sacred offering**
Heb	13.11	**Holy** Place to **offer** it as a sacrifice

Idols see **Gods**

Perfect see **Best**

Praise see **Worship**

Prayer

1 Chr	21.28	had answered his **prayer**, so he **offered**
2 Chr	6.40	on us and listen to the **prayers offered**
	7.15	to hear all the **prayers** that are **offered**
	30.18	Hezekiah **offered** this **prayer** for them:
Ps	5.3	at sunrise I **offer** my **prayer**
	25.1	I **offer** my **prayer**;
	116.17	and **offer** my **prayer** to you.
Is	66.3	whether they **offer** incense or **pray**
Hos	14.2	let this **prayer** be your **offering** to him:
Lk	5.33	John fast frequently and **offer prayers**,
2 Cor	4.15	**offer** to the glory of God more **prayers**
1 Tim	2.1	**prayers**, requests, and thanksgivings be
		offered
Rev	8.3	**prayers** of all God's people and to **offer**

Present

Lev	2.1	anyone **presents** an **offering** of grain
	2.6	when you **present** it as an **offering**.
	2.8	an **offering** to the Lord and **present** it
	2.11	the **grain-offerings** which you **present**
	6.20	**present** as an **offering** to the Lord
	7.12	**thank-offering** to God, he shall **present**,
	9.7	**Present** this **offering** to take away
	9.15	he **presented** the people's **offerings**.
	12.7	The priest shall **present** her **offering**
	14.12	a **repayment-offering**. He shall **present**
	22.18	in Israel **presents** a **burnt-offering**,
	22.21	anyone **presents** a **fellowship-offering**
	23.11	He shall **present** it as a special **offering**
	23.12	On the day you **present** the **offering**
	23.13	**present** with it an **offering** of one litre
	23.16	**present** to the Lord another new **offering**
	23.17	be **presented** to the Lord as an **offering**
Num	5.10	priest shall keep the **offerings presented**
	6.16	**present** all these to the Lord and **offer**
	6.17	he shall also **present** the **offerings**
	7.12	They **presented** their **offerings**
	9.7	from **presenting** the Lord's **offering**

Num	9.13	he did not **present** the **offering** to me
	15.3	**presented** to the Lord as a **burnt-offering**
	15.6	are to be **presented** as a **grain-offering**,
	18.9	**presented** to me as a sacred **offering**
	28.26	you **present** the **offering** of new corn
Josh	8.31	also **presented** their **fellowship-offerings**.
2 Kgs	10.25	soon as Jehu had **presented** the **offerings**
1 Chr	6.49	**presented** the **offerings** of incense
2 Chr	2.4	we will **present offerings** of sacred bread
	13.11	They **present** the **offerings** of bread
	29.27	for the **burnt-offering** to be **presented**;
	29.35	**presented** with the **burnt-offerings**.
Ezra	1.4	**offerings** to **present** in the Temple of
Is	66.3	they **present** a **grain-offering** or **offer**
Heb	8.3	is appointed to **present offerings**
	9.9	**offerings** and animal sacrifices **presented**
	13.15	the **offering presented** by lips

Proper see **Right**

Regulation

Lev	5.10	a **burnt-offering**, according to the **regulations**.
	6.25	following **regulations** for **sin-offerings**.
	7.7	**regulation** that applies to both the **sin-offering**
	7.36	the **offering**. It is a **regulation**
	9.16	**offered** it according to the **regulations**.
	19.5	**fellowship-offering**, keep the **regulations**
	23.14	this **offering** to God. This **regulation** is
Num	29.39	**regulations** concerning the **burnt-offerings**
2 Chr	35.13	**regulations**, and boiled the sacred **offerings**

Required

Lev	14.32	**offerings required** for his purification.
Num	5.15	He shall also take the **required offering**
	6.15	the **required offerings** of corn and wine.
	6.21	**offering** beyond what his vow **requires**
	29.18	all the other **offerings required**
		Also: 29.21, 24, 27, 30, 33, 37
1 Sam	2.29	sacrifices and **offerings** which I **require**
2 Chr	8.13	**offered** burnt-offerings according to the **requirements**
Ezra	3.4	they **offered** the sacrifices **required**
Heb	8.4	priests who **offer** the gifts **required**

Right, Proper, True

Num	28.20	**Offer** the **proper** grain-offering
		Also: 28.28; 29.3, 9, 14
Deut	33.19	And **offer** the **right** sacrifices there.
Neh	13.31	**offerings** to be brought at the **proper**
Ps	4.5	**Offer** the **right** sacrifices to the Lord,
Dan	8.12	**offering** the **proper** daily sacrifices,
Mal	3.3	the **right** kind of **offerings**.
Jn	4.23	**offering** him the **true** worship that he
Rom	12.1	the **true** worship that you should **offer**.

Sacred see **Holy**

Sacrifice, Sin-offering

Gen	22.2	**offer** him as a **sacrifice** to me.
	31.54	which he **offered** as a **sacrifice**
	46.1	he **offered sacrifices** to the God
Ex	3.18	into the desert to **offer sacrifices**
	5.3	into the desert to **offer sacrifices**
	5.8	go and **offer sacrifices** to their God!
	5.17	you go and **offer sacrifices** to the Lord.
	8.8	they can **offer sacrifices** to the Lord.
	8.25	Go and **offer sacrifices** to your God
	8.27	into the desert to **offer sacrifices**
	10.25	**sacrifices** and **burnt-offerings** to **offer**
	18.12	and other **sacrifices** to be **offered**

Ex	20.24	**sacrifice** your sheep and your cattle as **offerings**
	22.20	to death anyone who **offers sacrifices**
	23.18	**offer** bread made with yeast when you **sacrifice**
	24.5	**sacrificed**...cattle as **fellowship-offerings**.
	29.3	**offer** them to me when you **sacrifice**
	29.36	you must **offer** a bull as a **sacrifice**
	32.6	burn as **sacrifices** and others to eat as **fellowship-offerings**.
	32.8	it and **offered sacrifices** to it.
	34.25	not **offer** bread made with yeast when you **sacrifice**
	40.29	he **sacrificed** the **burnt-offering**
Lev	1.2	observe when they **offer** their **sacrifices**.
	1.9	**sacrifice**...The smell of this **food-offering**
	4.26	the priest shall **offer** the **sacrifice**
		Also: 4.31, 35; 5.6
	5.8	first **offer** the bird for the **sin-offering**.
	5.10	the priest shall **offer** the **sacrifice**
	5.13	the priest shall **offer** the **sacrifice**
	5.16	shall **offer** the animal as a **sacrifice**
	5.18	The priest shall **offer** the **sacrifice**
	6.7	The priest shall **offer** the **sacrifice**
	7.7	the priest who **offers** the **sacrifice**.
	7.8	the priest who **offers** the **sacrifice**.
	7.12	the animal to be **sacrificed**, an **offering**
	9.2	**offer** them to the Lord, the bull for a **sin-offering**
	9.4	**sacrifice** them...with the **grain-offering**
	9.7	and **offer** the **sin-offering**
	14.19	the priest shall **offer** the **sin-offering**
	15.15	**offer** one of them as a **sin-offering**
	15.30	**offer** one of them as a **sin-offering**
	16.6	He shall **offer** a bull as a **sacrifice**
	16.9	and **offer** it as a **sin-offering**.
	16.11	**sacrifices** the bull as the **sin-offering**
	17.8	a **burnt-offering** or any other **sacrifice**
	22.29	you **offer** a **sacrifice** of thanksgiving
	23.12	also **sacrifice** as a **burnt-offering**
	23.19	**offer** one male goat as a **sin-offering**
	23.37	**grain-offerings**, **sacrifices**, and **wine-offerings**,
Num	6.11	shall **offer** one as a **sin-offering**
	6.16	and **offer** the **sin-offering**
	6.17	**sacrifice** the ram to the Lord as a **fellowship-offering**,
	8.12	is to be **offered** as a **sin-offering**
	15.8	**sacrifice** in fulfilment of a vow or as a **fellowship-offering**,
	15.24	to **offer** a male goat as a **sin-offering**.
	15.27	**offer** a one-year-old female goat as a **sin-offering**.
	28.15	**offer** one male goat as a **sin-offering**.
		Also: 28.22, 30; 29.5, 11, 16
Deut	12.6	you are to **offer** your **sacrifices**
	12.11	**sacrifices**, your tithes and your **offerings**,
	12.13	not to **offer** your **sacrifices** wherever you
	12.14	there are you to **offer** your **sacrifices**
	12.27	**Offer** there the **sacrifices**
	18.1	live on the **offerings** and other **sacrifices**
	27.6	There you are to **offer** the **sacrifices**
	27.7	**sacrifice** and eat your **fellowship-offerings**
	33.10	They will **offer sacrifices** on your altar.
	33.19	**offer** the right **sacrifices** there.
Josh	8.31	**offered** burnt **sacrifices** to the Lord,
	22.23	**sacrifices** on or to use for **grain-offerings**
	22.26	not to burn **sacrifices** or make **offerings**,
	22.27	**offerings** to be burnt and with **sacrifices**
	22.28	not for burning **offerings** or for **sacrifice**,
	22.29	for **grain-offerings** or **sacrifices**.
Judg	2.5	they **offered sacrifices** to the Lord.

Judg	11.31	**offer** that person to you as a **sacrifice**.
	16.23	**offer** a great **sacrifice** to their god
	20.26	They **offered** fellowship **sacrifices**
	21.4	**offered** fellowship **sacrifices** and burnt
1 Sam	1.3	worship and **offer sacrifices** to the Lord
	1.4	Each time Elkanah **offered** his **sacrifice**,
	1.21	**offer** to the Lord the yearly **sacrifice**
	2.13	when a man was **offering** his **sacrifice**,
	2.14	came to Shiloh to **offer sacrifices**
	2.15	say to the man **offering** the **sacrifice**,
	2.19	her husband to **offer** the yearly **sacrifice**.
	2.29	**sacrifices** and **offerings** which I require
	3.14	no **sacrifice** or **offering** will ever be able
	6.15	**offered burnt-sacrifices** and other **sacrifices**
	7.10	Samuel was **offering** the **sacrifice**,
	9.12	to **offer** a **sacrifice** on the altar
	10.3	to **offer** a **sacrifice** to God at Bethel.
	10.8	and **offer**...**fellowship-sacrifices**.
	11.15	They **offered fellowship-sacrifices**,
	13.12	I felt I had to **offer** a **sacrifice**.
	15.15	cattle to **offer** as a **sacrifice**
	15.21	to Gilgal to **offer** as a **sacrifice**
	15.22	obedience or **offerings** and **sacrifices**?
	16.2	that you are there to **offer** a **sacrifice**
	16.5	I have come to **offer** a **sacrifice**
	16.11	won't **offer** the **sacrifice** until he comes.
2 Sam	6.13	**offered** the Lord a **sacrifice** of a bull
	6.17	**offered sacrifices** and **fellowship-offerings**
	6.18	he had finished **offering** the **sacrifices**
	15.12	while he was **offering sacrifices**,
	24.24	not **offer** to the Lord my God **sacrifices**
1 Kgs	1.9	Adonijah **offered** a **sacrifice** of sheep
	1.19	He has **offered** a **sacrifice** of many bulls,
	1.25	he has gone and **offered** a **sacrifice**
	3.2	the people were still **offering sacrifices**
	3.3	**offered** them as **sacrifices** on various
	3.4	went to Gibeon to **offer sacrifices**
	8.62	all the people there **offered sacrifices**
	8.64	**offered** there the **sacrifices** burnt whole,
	10.5	the **sacrifices** he **offered** in the Temple.
	11.8	and **offer sacrifices** to their own gods.
	12.26	go to Jerusalem and **offer sacrifices**
	12.32	**offered sacrifices** to the gold bull-calves
	12.33	**offered** a **sacrifice** on the altar
	13.1	to **offer** the **sacrifice**.
	13.2	at the pagan altars who **offer sacrifices**
	22.43	the people continued to **offer sacrifices**
2 Kgs	3.27	**offered** him on the city wall as a **sacrifice**
	5.17	not **offer sacrifices** or **burnt-offerings**
	10.19	to **offer** a great **sacrifice** to Baal,
	10.24	to **offer sacrifices** and **burnt-offerings**
	12.3	the people continued to **offer sacrifices**
		Also: 14.4; 15.4; 15.35
	16.4	**offered sacrifices** and burnt incense.
	16.13	animal **sacrifices** and **grain-offerings**
	17.32	to **offer sacrifices** for them
	17.35	serve them or **offer sacrifices** to them.
	17.36	to bow down to me and **offer sacrifices**
	22.17	rejected me and have **offered sacrifices**
	23.5	**offer sacrifices** on the pagan altars
	23.8	altars where they had **offered sacrifices**.
1 Chr	6.49	**offered** the **sacrifices** that were burnt
	16.1	**offered sacrifices** and **fellowship-offerings**
	16.2	had finished **offering** the **sacrifices**,
	21.28	he **offered sacrifices** on the altar
2 Chr	1.6	**offering sacrifices** on the bronze altar;
	7.1	the **sacrifices** that had been **offered**,
	7.4	and all the people **offered sacrifices**
	7.7	**offered** there the **sacrifices** burnt whole,
	7.12	place where **sacrifices** are to be **offered**
	8.12	Solomon **offered sacrifices** to the Lord

2 Chr	9.4	the **sacrifices** he **offered** in the Temple.
	11.16	so that they could **offer sacrifices**
	13.11	**offer** him incense and animal **sacrifices**
	15.11	On that day they **offered sacrifices**
	23.18	to burn the **sacrifices offered**
	24.14	**sacrifices** were **offered** regularly
	28.4	**offered sacrifices** and burnt incense.
	28.23	He **offered sacrifices** to the gods
	29.21	to **offer** the animals as **sacrifices**
	29.31	**sacrifices** as **offerings** of thanksgiving
	29.35	In addition to **offering** the **sacrifices**
	30.14	used in Jerusalem for **offering sacrifices**
	30.22	**offered sacrifices** in praise of the Lord,
	33.16	and he **sacrificed fellowship-offerings**
	33.17	the people continued to **offer sacrifices**
	34.25	**offered sacrifices** to other gods,
	35.9	to **offer** as **sacrifices**.
Ezra	3.4	they **offered** the **sacrifices** required
	3.5	**offered** the regular **sacrifices**
	4.2	we have been **offering sacrifices** to him
	6.3	**sacrifices** are made and **offerings** are
	6.10	**offer sacrifices** that are acceptable
	8.35	**offerings** to be burnt as **sacrifices**
	9.4	for the evening **sacrifice** to be **offered**,
	10.19	they **offered** a ram as a **sacrifice**
Neh	4.2	Do they think that by **offering sacrifices**
	10.34	**sacrifices offered** to the Lord our God,
	12.43	That day many **sacrifices** were **offered**
Job	1.5	would get up early and **offer sacrifices**
	42.8	**offer** them as a **sacrifice** for yourselves.
Ps	4.5	**Offer** the right **sacrifices** to the Lord,
	20.3	**offerings** and be pleased with all your **sacrifices**.
	22.25	I will **offer** the **sacrifices** I promised.
	27.6	will **offer sacrifices** in his Temple;
	40.6	do not want **sacrifices** and **offerings**;
	50.5	by **offering** a **sacrifice**.
	51.16	do not want **sacrifices**, or I would **offer**
	54.6	I will gladly **offer** you a **sacrifice**,
	69.31	**offering** him cattle, more than **sacrificing**
	106.28	ate **sacrifices offered** to lifeless gods.
	106.37	**offered** their own sons and daughters as **sacrifices**
	116.17	a **sacrifice** of thanksgiving and **offer**
Prov	7.14	**offerings** today and have the meat from the **sacrifices**.
	21.27	when wicked men **offer** him **sacrifices**,
Ecc	5.1	to **offer sacrifices** as foolish people do,
Is	9.2	those who **offer sacrifices** and those
	1.11	all these **sacrifices** you keep **offering**
	19.21	bring him **sacrifices** and **offerings**.
	34.6	The Lord will **offer** this **sacrifice**
	56.7	accept the **sacrifices** you **offer**
	57.5	You **offer** your children as **sacrifices**
	57.7	to the high mountains to **offer sacrifices**
	60.7	brought to you as **sacrifices** And **offered**
	65.3	**offer** pagan **sacrifices** in sacred gardens
	65.4	from meat **offered** in pagan **sacrifices**.
Jer	1.16	have **offered sacrifices** to other gods,
	6.20	**offerings** or be pleased with their **sacrifices**.
	7.9	**offer sacrifices** to Baal,
	11.12	gods to whom they **offer sacrifices**
	11.15	and by **offering** animal **sacrifices**?
	11.17	me angry by **offering sacrifices** to Baal.
	17.26	**sacrifices**, **grain-offerings** and incense,
	19.4	**offering sacrifices** here to other gods
	33.18	**grain-offerings**, and **sacrifices**.
	44.3	They **offered sacrifices** to other gods
	44.15	wives **offered sacrifices** to other gods,
	44.17	We will **offer sacrifices** to our goddess,
	44.19	**offered sacrifices** to her,
	44.23	you **offered sacrifices** to other gods
	44.24	you would **offer sacrifices** to her

Jer	48.35	**offering sacrifices** to their gods.
Ezek	16.19	you **offered** it as a **sacrifice** to win
	16.20	**offered** them as **sacrifices** to idols.
	18.6	**sacrifices offered** at forbidden shrines.
	18.11	**sacrifices offered** at forbidden shrines
	18.15	**sacrifices offered** at forbidden shrines.
	20.26	own **offerings**, and I let them **sacrifice**
	20.28	**offered sacrifices** at all of them.
	20.40	your **sacrifices**, your best **offerings**,
	22.9	of them eat **sacrifices offered** to idols.
	36.38	**offered** as **sacrifices** at a festival.
	40.39	the animals to be **offered** as **sacrifices**,
	40.43	All the meat to be **offered** in **sacrifice**
	42.13	the **sacrifices offered** for sin
	43.19	bull to **offer** as a **sacrifice** for sin.
	43.21	is **offered** as a **sacrifice** for sin
	43.22	and **offer** it as a **sacrifice** for sin.
	43.25	**offer** a goat, a bull, and a ram as **sacrifices**
	44.7	blood of the **sacrifices** are being **offered**
	44.11	for **burnt-offerings** and for **sacrifices**,
	44.15	to **offer** me the fat and the blood of the **sacrifices**.
	44.27	**offer** a **sacrifice** for his purification,
	45.22	**offer** a bull as a **sacrifice** for his sins
	45.23	**sacrifice** a male goat...as a **sin-offering**.
	45.24	is **sacrificed**, there is to be an **offering**
	45.25	**offer** on each of the seven days the same **sacrifice**
	46.2	**sacrifices** whole and **offer** his **fellowship-offerings**.
	46.20	meat **offered** as **sacrifices** for sin
Dan	2.46	**sacrifices** and **offerings** to be made
	8.11	the daily **sacrifices offered** to him,
	8.12	**offering** the proper daily **sacrifices**,
	8.14	morning **sacrifices** will not be **offered**.
	9.21	for the evening **sacrifice** to be **offered**.
	9.27	put an end to **sacrifices** and **offerings**.
Hos	4.13	the mountain-tops they **offer sacrifices**
	4.14	you **offer** pagan **sacrifices**.
	5.6	sheep and cattle to **offer** as **sacrifices**
	8.13	**offer sacrifices** to me and eat the meat
	13.2	**Offer sacrifices** to them!
Amos	5.25	I did not demand **sacrifices** and **offerings**
Jon	1.16	**offered** a **sacrifice** and promised to serve
	2.9	I will **offer** you a **sacrifice**
Hab	1.16	**worship** their nets and **offer sacrifices**
Zech	14.21	people who **offer sacrifices** will use them
Mal	1.11	and **offer** acceptable **sacrifices**.
Mt	8.4	**offer** the **sacrifice** that Moses ordered.
Mk	1.44	**offer** the **sacrifice** that Moses ordered.
	12.33	to **offer** animals and other **sacrifices**
Lk	2.24	to **offer** a **sacrifice** of a pair of doves
	5.14	**offer** the **sacrifice** as Moses ordered.
	13.1	killed while they were **offering sacrifices**
Acts	7.41	**offered sacrifice** to it,
	14.13	wanted to **offer sacrifice** to the apostles.
	14.18	keep the crowd from **offering** a **sacrifice**
	21.26	**sacrifice** would be **offered** for each one
	24.17	my own people and to **offer sacrifices**.
Rom	3.25	**offered** him, so that by his **sacrificial**
	12.1	**Offer** yourselves as a living **sacrifice**
1 Cor	9.13	**offer** the **sacrifices** on the altar
	10.18	who eat what is **offered** in **sacrifice**
	10.20	**sacrificed** on pagan altars is **offered**
Eph	5.2	sweet-smelling **offering** and **sacrifice**
Phil	2.17	**offering** on the **sacrifice** that your faith **offers**
	4.18	**offering** to God, a **sacrifice**
Heb	5.1	to **offer sacrifices** and **offerings** for sins.
	5.3	**offer sacrifices** not only for the sins
	7.27	not need to **offer sacrifices** every day
	8.3	to present **offerings** and animal **sacrifices**
	9.9	that the **offerings** and animal **sacrifices**

Heb	9.12	goats and bulls to **offer** as a **sacrifice**;
	9.14	he **offered** himself as a perfect **sacrifice**
	9.28	Christ also was **offered** in **sacrifice** once
	10.1	The same **sacrifices** are **offered** for ever,
	10.5	do not want **sacrifices** and **offerings**,
	10.8	with **sacrifices** and **offerings**
	10.11	**offers** the same **sacrifices** many times;
	10.12	**offered** one **sacrifice** for sins,
	11.4	Abel **offer** to God a better **sacrifice**
	11.17	**offer** his son Isaac as a **sacrifice**
	13.11	Holy Place to **offer** it as a **sacrifice**
	13.15	**offer** praise to God as our **sacrifice**
1 Pet	2.5	**offer** spiritual and acceptable **sacrifices**

Take Away (sin) see Forgive

Tithes

Neh	13.5	**offerings** for the priests, and the **tithes**
Mal	3.8	In the matter of **tithes** and **offerings**.

True see Right

Unclean see Defile

Vow

Lev	7.16	**offering** in fulfilment of a **vow**
	22.18	**offering**, whether in fulfilment of a **vow** or as a freewill **offering**,
	22.21	**offering**...in fulfilment of a **vow**
	23.38	your **offerings** in fulfilment of **vows**,
Num	29.39	**offerings** you give in fulfilment of a **vow**

Worship, Bow, Praise

Ex	23.15	**worship** me without bringing an **offering**.
	32.8	have **worshipped** it and **offered** sacrifices
1 Sam	1.3	Ramah to **worship** and **offer** sacrifices
2 Kgs	17.36	you are to **bow** down to me and **offer**
1 Chr	16.29	**offering** and come into his Temple. **Bow**
2 Chr	1.6	king **worshipped** the Lord by **offering**
	29.27	**offering** began, the people sang **praise**
	30.22	**offered** sacrifices in **praise** of the Lord,
Ezra	4.2	you **worship**, and we have been **offering**
Ps	22.25	**worship** you I will **offer** the sacrifices
	61.8	always sing **praises** to you, as I **offer**
	66.2	**offer** him glorious **praise**!
	68.30	until they all **bow** down and **offer** you
	96.8	**Praise** the Lord's glorious name; bring an **offering**
Is	19.21	**worship** him, and bring him sacrifices and **offerings**.
Jon	2.9	I will sing **praises** to you; I will **offer**
Hab	1.16	**worship** their nets and **offer** sacrifices
Mt	21.16	babies to **offer** perfect **praise**.
Jn	4.23	**offering** him the true **worship**
Rom	12.1	the true **worship** that you should **offer**.
Heb	13.15	**offer** praise to God as our **sacrifice**

OPPRESS

Is	58.3	— 61.8	x11
Deut	28.29	— 48	x3
1 Sam	12.3	— 8	x3
Ps	72.2	— 14	x3
Ps	119.122	— 157	x3
Ecc	4.1	— 5.8	x3
Is	9.4	— 10.24	x3
Is	14.2	— 6	x3
Ezek	45.8	— 46.18	x3
Amos	4.1	— 6.14	x3

God's People

Ex	3.9	**my people**, and I see how the Egyptians are **oppressing**
Is	3.12	Money-lenders **oppress my people**
	10.1	unjust laws that **oppress my people**.
Ezek	46.18	he will not **oppress** any of **my people**
Dan	7.25	and **oppress God's people**.
Zech	9.8	not allow tyrants to **oppress my people**

Help, Protect

1 Chr	16.21	no one **oppress** them; to **protect** them,
Ps	72.4	**help** the needy...defeat their **oppressors**.
	105.14	no one **oppress** them; to **protect** them,
	119.122	**help** your servant; don't let...men **oppress**
Ecc	4.1	The **oppressed** were weeping, and no one would **help**
Is	1.17	**help** those who are **oppressed**,
	19.20	are **oppressed** and call out...for **help**,
	59.16	there is no one to **help** the **oppressed**.

Justice, Judge

Ps	10.18	cries of the **oppressed**...you will **judge**
	72.2	with **justice** and govern the **oppressed**
	76.9	**judgement**, to save all the **oppressed** on
	103.6	Lord **judges** in favour of the **oppressed**
	146.7	he **judges** in favour of the **oppressed**
Ecc	5.8	**oppresses** the poor...denies them **justice**
Is	1.17	that **justice** is done — help those who are **oppressed**,
	60.17	no longer **oppress** you; I will make them rule with **justice**
	61.8	**justice** and I hate **oppression** and crime.
Jer	5.28	rights or show **justice** to the **oppressed**
Ezek	45.9	**oppression**. Do what is right and **just**.
Jas	2.6	who **oppress** you and drag you before the **judges**?

Protect see Help

Rescue see Save

Rights

Ps	103.6	**oppressed** and gives them their **rights**.
Jer	5.28	**rights** or show justice to the **oppressed**.
Hos	5.11	**oppression**; she has lost land that was **rightfully**

Save, Rescue

Job	5.15	he **saves** the needy from **oppression**.
Ps	57.3	**save** me; he will defeat my **oppressors**.
	72.14	He **rescues** them from **oppression**
	76.9	to **save** all the **oppressed** on earth.
	119.134	**Save** me from those who **oppress** me,
Is	59.9	not **save** us from those who **oppress**
	59.11	for God to **save** us from **oppression**
	59.16	**oppressed**. So he will use his own power to **rescue**
Jer	20.13	He **rescues** the **oppressed**
Zeph	3.19	punish your **oppressors**; I will **rescue**

ORDAIN

Lev	6.20	—	9.1	x11
Ex	28.41	—	30.30	x9

Offer

Lev	6.20	**ordained**, he shall present as an **offering**
	7.37	regulations for...**ordination-offerings**,
	8.28	as an **ordination offering**.
	8.31	in the basket of **ordination offerings**,
1 Kgs	23.5	had **ordained** to **offer** sacrifices

ORPHAN

Deut	24.17 – 21			x4
Deut	26.12	—	27.19	x3

Oppress

Ps	10.18	cries of the **oppressed** and the **orphans**;
Is	1.17	those who are **oppressed**, give **orphans**
Jer	5.28	**orphans** their rights or show justice to the **oppressed**.
	22.3	ill-treat or **oppress** foreigners, **orphans**,
Zech	7.10	Do not **oppress** widows, **orphans**,

Widow

Ex	22.22	Do not ill-treat any **widow** or **orphan**.
Deut	10.18	**orphans** and **widows** are treated fairly;

Deut	14.29	**orphans**, and **widows** who live in your
	16.11	**orphans**, and **widows** who live in your
	16.14	**orphans**, and **widows** who live in your
	24.17	**orphans** of their rights; and do not take a **widow's**
	24.19	**orphans**, and **widows**,
	24.20	**orphans**, and **widows**.
	24.21	**orphans**, and **widows**.
	26.12	the **orphans**, and the **widows**,
	26.13	the **orphans**, and the **widows**,
	27.19	**orphans**, and **widows** of their rights.
Job	22.9	**widows**, but you also robbed and ill-treated **orphans**.
	24.3	to **orphans**, and keep a **widow's** ox
Ps	68.5	cares for **orphans** and protects **widows**.
	94.6	They kill **widows** and **orphans**,
	109.9	become **orphans**, and his wife a **widow**!
	146.9	he helps **widows** and **orphans**,
Is	1.17	**orphans** their rights, and defend **widows**.
	1.23	**orphans** in court or listen when **widows**
	9.17	pity to any of the **widows** and **orphans**,
	10.2	that belongs to **widows** and **orphans**.
Jer	7.6	**orphans**, and **widows**.
	22.3	**orphans**, or **widows**;
Ezek	22.7	take advantage of **widows** and **orphans**.
Zech	7.10	Do not oppress **widows**, **orphans**,
Mal	3.5	who take advantage of **widows**, **orphans**,
Jas	1.27	to take care of **orphans** and **widows**

PAGAN

	2 Kgs	14.4	— 18.4	x9
	2 Chr	33.3	— 34.8	x7
	2 Kgs	23.5 – 24		x5
	Is	65.3	— 66.17	x5
	1 Kgs	13.2	— 15.14	x4
	Lev	18.24 – 28		x3
	2 Chr	14.3	— 15.17	x3
	Mt	5.47	— 6.32	x3

Altars

1 Kgs	13.2	priests serving at the **pagan altars**
	22.46	prostitutes serving at the **pagan altars**
2 Kgs	17.11	burnt incense on all the **pagan altars**
	21.4	He built **pagan altars** in the Temple,
	23.5	the **pagan altars** in the cities of Judah
	23.20	killed all the **pagan** priests on the **altars**
2 Chr	14.3	the foreign **altars** and the **pagan** places
	14.5	the **pagan** places...and the **incense-altars**
	31.1	**altars** and the **pagan** places of worship.
	33.4	He built **pagan altars** in the Temple,
	33.15	the **pagan altars** that were on the hill
	34.5	bones of the **pagan** priests on the **altars**
Is	27.9	stones of **pagan altars** are ground up
	65.3	and burn incense on **pagan altars**.
1 Cor	10.20	what is sacrificed on **pagan altars**

Offer, Sacrifice

1 Kgs	13.2	at the **pagan** altars who **offer sacrifices**
2 Kgs	17.32	**pagan** places of worship and to **offer**
	23.5	to **offer** sacrifices on the **pagan** altars
Is	65.3	They **offer pagan sacrifices**
	65.4	from meat **offered** in **pagan sacrifices**.
Hos	4.14	with them you **offer pagan sacrifices**.
1 Cor	10.20	on **pagan** altars is **offered** to demons,

Places of Worship

1 Kgs	14.24	at those **pagan places of worship**.
	15.12	serving at the **pagan places of worship**,
	15.14	did not destroy all the **pagan places**
	22.43	**pagan places of worship** were not
2 Kgs	12.3	**pagan places of worship** were not
	14.4	did not tear down the **pagan places of**
	15.4	**pagan places of worship** were not
	15.35	**pagan places of worship** were not
	16.4	At the **pagan places of worship**

2 Kgs	17.9	They built **pagan places of worship**	
	17.32	**pagan places of worship** and to offer	
	18.4	destroyed the **pagan places of worship**	
	21.3	rebuilt the **pagan places of worship**	
	23.10	**pagan place of worship** in the Valley	
	23.19	down all the **pagan places of worship**	
2 Chr	11.15	**pagan places of worship** and to worship	
	14.3	the foreign altars and the **pagan places**	
	14.5	abolished the **pagan places of worship**	
	15.17	destroy all the **pagan places of worship**	
	17.6	**pagan places of worship** and the	
	20.33	**pagan places of worship** were not	
	21.11	He even built **pagan places of worship**	
	28.4	At the **pagan places of worship**,	
	28.25	he built **pagan places of worship**,	
	31.1	the **pagan places of worship**.	
	33.3	rebuilt the **pagan places of worship**	
	33.19	**pagan places of worship** and the	
	34.3	to destroy the **pagan places of worship**,	

Priests

1 Kgs	13.2	**priests** serving at the **pagan** altars
2 Kgs	17.32	**priests** at the **pagan** places of worship
	23.20	He killed all the **pagan priests**
2 Chr	11.15	**priests** of his own to serve at the **pagan**
	34.5	He burnt the bones of the **pagan priests**
Zeph	1.4	will even remember the **pagan priests**

Sacrifice see **Offer**

Worship

Ex	34.15	when they **worship** their **pagan** gods
	34.16	and to **worship** their **pagan** gods.
Deut	31.16	abandon me and **worship** the **pagan**
2 Kgs	23.24	all other **pagan** objects of **worship**.
2 Chr	11.15	**pagan** places of **worship** and to **worship**
	34.5	**pagan** priests on the altars where they had **worshipped**.
	34.8	by ending **pagan worship**,
Is	66.17	purify themselves for **pagan worship**,
Jer	3.23	not helped at all by our **pagan worship**
Ezek	18.12	He goes to **pagan** shrines, **worships**
Zeph	1.9	who **worship** like **pagans** and who steal

PAIN

Lam	1.12 – 18		x4
Lk	16.23 – 28		x4
Ps	38.3 – 17		x3
Is	13.6	– 14.3	x3
Rev	16.2 – 11		x3

Birth

Gen	3.16	and your **pain** in giving **birth**.
1 Chr	4.9	because his **birth** had been very **painful**.
Is	26.18	in **pain** and agony, but we gave **birth** to
Jer	13.21	be in **pain** like a woman giving **birth**.
Rev	12.2	was soon to give **birth**, and the **pains**

Suffer

2 Chr	21.15	yourself will **suffer** a **painful** disease
Job	9.27	my **pain**, all my **suffering** comes back
	30.27	and **pain**...day after day of **suffering**.
Ps	73.4	They do not **suffer pain**;
Is	14.3	relief from their **pain** and **suffering**,
	53.3	he endured **suffering** and **pain**.
	53.4	But he endured the **suffering**...the **pain**
Zech	9.5	Gaza will see it and **suffer** great **pain**.
Rom	2.9	There will be **suffering** and **pain**
1 Pet	2.19	endure the **pain** of undeserved **suffering**
	4.12	the **painful** test you are **suffering**,
Rev	12.2	the **pains** and **suffering** of childbirth

PASSOVER

	2 Chr	35.1 – 18	x10
	Ex	12.11 – 48	x8
	Num	9.2 – 14	x7

	2 Chr	30.1 – 18	x6
	Mk	14.1 – 15.6	x6
	Lk	22.1 – 15	x6
	Mt	26.2 – 27.15	x5
	Deut	16.1 – 16	x4
	Jn	11.55 – 13.1	x4
	2 Kgs	23.21 – 23	x3
	Jn	18.28 – 19.14	x3
	1 Cor	5.7 – 8	x3

Observe

Num	9.2	Israel are to **observe** the **Passover**
	9.4	told the people to **observe** the **Passover**,
	9.12	**Observe** the **Passover** according to all
	9.13	and who does not **observe** the **Passover**,
	9.14	keep the **Passover**, he must **observe** it
Josh	5.10	they **observed Passover** on the evening
2 Chr	30.18	they were **observing Passover** improperly.

Regulations

Ex	12.43	These are the **Passover regulations**:
Num	9.2	**Passover** according to all the...**regulations**
	9.12	**Passover** according to all the **regulations**.

Sacrifice

Ex	12.27	**sacrifice** of **Passover** to honour the
2 Chr	30.15	the lambs for the **Passover sacrifice**
	35.13	Levites roasted the **Passover sacrifices**
Ezra	6.20	**Passover sacrifices** for all the people
1 Cor	5.7	our **Passover** lamb, has been **sacrificed**.

Unleavened Bread

2 Chr	35.17	**Passover** and the Festival of **Unleavened**
Mk	14.1	of **Passover** and **Unleavened Bread**.
	14.12	**Unleavened Bread**, the day the lambs for the **Passover**
Lk	22.1	**Unleavened Bread**...called the **Passover**.
	22.7	**Unleavened Bread** when the lambs for the **Passover**

PATIENT

	Jas	5.7 – 11	x6
	Rev	1.9 – 2.19	x4
	Lam	3.26 – 28	x3
	2 Tim	2.24 – 4.2	x3

Encourage

Rom	15.4	through the **patience** and **encouragement**
	15.5	source of **patience** and **encouragement**,
1 Thes	5.14	**encourage** the timid...be **patient**
2 Tim	4.2	and **encourage**, as you teach with all **patience**.
Heb	13.22	listen **patiently** to this message of **encouragement**;

Endure

Rom	9.22	he was very **patient** in **enduring** those
2 Cor	1.6	**endure** with **patience** the same sufferings
	6.4	are God's servants by **patiently enduring**
Col	1.11	able to **endure** everything with **patience**.
2 Tim	3.10	my **patience**, my love, my **endurance**,
Jas	5.10	them as examples of **patient endurance**,
Rev	1.9	**patiently enduring** the suffering that

God, Lord

Ps	37.7	Be **patient** and wait for the **Lord**
	40.1	I waited **patiently** for the **Lord's** help;
	62.1	I wait **patiently** for **God** to save me;
	86.15	loving **God**, always **patient**,
Is	7.13	must you wear out **God's patience** too?
Hos	12.6	wait **patiently** for your **God** to act.
Joel	2.13	**God**...is **patient** and keeps his promise.
Jon	4.2	merciful **God**, always **patient**,
Mic	2.7	Has the **Lord** lost his **patience**?
Mal	3.15	but they test **God's patience**
Rom	15.5	may **God**, the source of **patience**
1 Pet	3.20	obeyed **God** when he waited **patiently**

2 Pet 3.15 Look on our **Lord's patience** as

Hope
Rom 12.12 your **hope** keep you joyful, be **patient**
15.4 might have **hope** through the **patience**
1 Cor 13.7 **hope**, and **patience** never fail.
Jas 5.8 must be **patient**. Keep your **hopes** high,

Lord see God

Love, Kind
Ps 86.15 merciful and **loving** God, always **patient**, always **kind** and faithful.
Joel 2.13 is **kind** and full of mercy; he is **patient**
Jon 4.2 **loving** and merciful God, always **patient**, always **kind**,
Rom 2.4 great **kindness**, tolerance, and **patience**.
1 Cor 13.4 **Love** is **patient** and **kind**
2 Cor 6.6 **patience**, and **kindness** we have shown
Gal 5.22 Spirit produces **love**, joy, peace, **patience kindness**,
Col 3.12 **kindness**, humility...and **patience**.
2 Tim 2.24 **kind** towards all, a good and **patient**
3.10 my **patience**, my **love**,

Promise
Joel 2.13 he is **patient** and keeps his **promise**;
Heb 6.12 **patient**...receive what God has **promised**.
6.15 **patient**, and so he received what God had **promised**,
2 Pet 3.9 do what he has **promised**...he is **patient**

PEACE

Judg	3.11 —	6.24		x6
1 Chr	22.9 —	23.25		x5
Rom	14.17 —	16.20		x5
2 Chr	14.1 —	15.15		x4
Zech	8.12 —	9.10		x4
Mt	10.12 – 34			x4
Lk	1.28 —	2.29		x4
Lk	10.5 – 6			x4
Eph	1.2 —	2.17		x4
Josh	10.1 —	11.19		x3
1 Kgs	4.24 —	5.12		x3
1 Kgs	22.1 – 44			x3
Ps	122.6 – 8			x3
Prov	13.17 —	15.18		x3
Is	26.3 —	27.5		x3
Is	32.17 —	33.7		x3
Is	54.10 —	55.12		x3
Mic	3.5 —	5.5		x3
Jn	20.19 – 26			x3
Rom	1.7 —	3.17		x3
1 Tim	1.2 —	3.3		x3
Heb	12.11 —	13.20		x3
2 Jn	.3 – 11			x3

Christ, Jesus
Mt 28.9 **Jesus**...said, "**Peace** be with you.
Jn 20.21 **Jesus** said..."**Peace** be with you.
20.26 **Jesus**...said, "**Peace** be with you.
Acts 10.36 Good News of **peace** through **Jesus**
Rom 1.7 **Jesus Christ** give you grace and **peace**.
5.1 **peace** with God through our Lord **Jesus**
1 Cor 1.3 **Jesus Christ** give you grace and **peace**.
2 Cor 1.2 **Jesus Christ** give you grace and **peace**.
Gal 1.3 **Jesus Christ** give you grace and **peace**.
Eph 1.2 **Jesus Christ** give you grace and **peace**.
2.14 For **Christ** himself has brought us **peace**
2.17 So **Christ**...preached the Good News of **peace**
Phil 1.2 **Jesus Christ** give you grace and **peace**.
Col 3.15 The **peace** that **Christ** gives
1 Thes 1.2 **Jesus Christ** give you grace and **peace**.
1 Tim 1.2 **Jesus** our Lord give you...**peace**.
2 Tim 1.2 **Jesus** our Lord give you...**peace**.

Tit 1.4 **Jesus** our Saviour give you...**peace**.
Phlm .3 **Jesus Christ** give you grace and **peace**.
2 Jn .3 **Jesus Christ**...give us...**peace**;

Enjoy see Joy

God, Lord
Num 6.26 May the **Lord**...give you **peace**.
Josh 21.44 The **Lord** gave them **peace** throughout
22.4 the **Lord** your **God** has given...**peace**.
Judg 6.23 But the **Lord** said to him, "**Peace**.
6.24 and named it "The **Lord** is **Peace**.
1 Kgs 5.4 the **Lord** my **God** has given me **peace**
8.56 **Lord** who has given his people **peace**,
1 Chr 22.18 **God** has...given you **peace**
23.25 **God** of Israel has given **peace**
2 Chr 14.6 because the **Lord** gave him **peace**.
Job 16.12 I was living in **peace**, but **God** took me
22.21 Now, Job, make **peace** with **God**
Ps 29.11 The **Lord**...blesses them with **peace**.
85.8 The **Lord God**...promises **peace**
Is 26.3 You, **Lord**, give perfect **peace**
Lk 19.38 **Peace** in heaven and glory to **God**!
Rom 5.1 we have **peace** with **God**
15.33 May **God**, our source of **peace**,
16.20 And **God**, our source of **peace**,
1 Cor 7.15 **God** has called you to live in **peace**.
2 Cor 13.11 **God** of love and **peace** will be
Col 1.20 **God** made **peace** through his Son's
3.15 to this **peace** that **God** has called you
1 Thes 5.23 May the **God** who gives us **peace**
2 Thes 3.16 **Lord**...who is our source of **peace**,
Heb 13.20 May the **God** of **peace** provide you
Rev 1.4 Grace and **peace** be yours from **God**,

Heal
Is 57.19 **peace** to all...I will **heal** my people.
Jer 8.15 hoped for **peace** and a time of **healing**,
Mk 5.34 in **peace**, and be **healed** of your trouble.

Heart
Ps 34.14 strive for **peace** with all your **heart**.
2 Tim 2.22 **peace**...with those who with a pure **heart**
1 Pet 3.11 must strive for **peace** with all his **heart**.

Jesus see Christ

Joy, Enjoy
2 Chr 14.1 the land **enjoyed peace** for ten years.
Job 3.18 Even prisoners **enjoy peace**,
Ps 37.11 and **enjoy** prosperity and **peace**.
Is 14.7 and **peace**, and everyone sings for **joy**.
55.12 leave Babylon with **joy**...in **peace**.
Zech 1.15 the nations that **enjoy** quiet and **peace**.
3.10 to come and **enjoy peace** and security,
Rom 14.17 **peace**, and **joy** which the Holy Spirit
15.13 **joy** and **peace** by means of your faith
Gal 5.22 love, **joy**, **peace**,

Lord see God

Righteous
Num 23.10 Let me die in **peace** like the **righteous**.
Ps 37.37 the **righteous** man; a **peaceful** man
85.10 **righteousness** and **peace** will embrace.
Rom 14.17 of the **righteousness**, **peace**, and joy
2 Tim 2.22 for **righteousness**, faith, love, and **peace**,
Heb 12.11 the **peaceful** reward of a **righteous** life.

Security, Safety
Deut 33.28 Jacob's descendants live in **peace**, **secure**
2 Kgs 20.19 **peace** and **security** during his lifetime,
1 Chr 22.9 I will give Israel **peace** and **security**.
2 Chr 20.30 in **peace**, and God gave him **security**
Esth 9.30 It wished the Jews **peace** and **security**
Ps 4.8 in **peace**; you...O Lord, keep me...**safe**.
122.7 **peace** inside your walls and **safety**

Is	32.17	will be **peace** and **security** for ever.
	32.18	and their homes **peaceful** and **safe**.
	39.8	**peace** and **security** during his lifetime,
Jer	23.6	**safe**, and the people...will live in **peace**.
	30.10	live in **peace**; you will be **secure**,
	33.6	show them abundant **peace** and **security**.
	46.27	live in **peace**; you will be **secure**,
Ezek	38.11	**peace** and **security** in unwalled towns
Hos	2.18	let my people live in **peace** and **safety**.
Zech	3.10	to come and enjoy **peace** and **security**,

Trouble

Job	3.26	have no **peace**, no rest, and my **troubles**
Prov	13.17	**trouble**, but those who can be trusted bring **peace**.
	27.9	**trouble** shatters your **peace** of mind.
Jer	50.34	bring **peace** to the earth, but **trouble**
Mk	5.34	in **peace**, and be healed of your **trouble**.

World

Is	14.7	the whole **world** enjoys rest and **peace**,
Mt	10.34	have come to bring **peace** to the **world**
Lk	12.51	**peace** to the **world**? No, not **peace**,

PERSECUTION

1 Thes	2.14 —	3.4	x5
Mt	5.10 — 44		x4
Acts	7.52 —	9.5	x4
Ps	119.84 — 150		x3
Acts	11.19 —	13.50	x3
Acts	22.4 — 8		x3
Acts	26.11 — 15		x3
Gal	4.29 —	6.12	x3
2 Tim	3.11 — 12		x3

Church

Acts	8.1	**church**...suffer cruel **persecution**.
	12.1	**persecute** some members of the **church**.
1 Cor	15.9	because I **persecuted** God's **church**.
Gal	1.13	I **persecuted**...the **church** of God
Phil	3.6	that I **persecuted** the **church**

Jesus

Jn	5.16	they began to **persecute Jesus**,
Acts	9.5	I am **Jesus**, whom you **persecute**,
	22.8	I am **Jesus**...whom you **persecute**,
	26.15	I am **Jesus**, whom you **persecute**.

Suffer

Acts	8.1	began to **suffer** cruel **persecution**.
1 Thes	2.14	You **suffered** the same **persecutions**
2 Thes	1.4	all the **persecutions** and **sufferings**
2 Tim	3.11	my **persecutions**, and my **sufferings**

PHARISEES

	Lk	11.37 —	19.39	x17
	Jn	7.32 —	9.40	x13
	Mt	21.45 —	23.29	x12
	Lk	5.17 —	7.39	x10
	Mt	15.1 —	16.12	x6
	Mk	7.1 —	8.15	x6
	Mk	2.16 —	3.6	x5
	Jn	11.46 —	12.42	x5
	Acts	23.6 — 9		x5
	Mt	12.2 — 38		x4
	Mt	9.11 — 34		x3

Disciples

Mt	9.11	**Pharisees** saw this and asked his **disciples**
	9.14	**Pharisees** fast often, but your **disciples**
Mk	2.18	**disciples** of the **Pharisees** fast, but yours
Lk	5.33	**disciples** of the **Pharisees** do the same;

Hypocrites

Mt	23.13	the Law and **Pharisees**! You **hypocrites**!
		Also: 23.15, 23, 25, 27, 29

Lk	12.1	the **Pharisees** — I mean their **hypocrisy**.

Jesus

Mt	12.14	**Pharisees**...plans to kill **Jesus**.
	16.1	**Pharisees**...who came to **Jesus**
	21.45	the **Pharisees** heard **Jesus'** parables
	22.15	The **Pharisees**...made a plan to trap **Jesus**
	22.34	the **Pharisees** heard that **Jesus** had
	22.41	some **Pharisees** gathered together, **Jesus**
Mk	2.16	**Pharisees**, saw that **Jesus** was eating
	2.24	So the **Pharisees** said to **Jesus**,
	8.11	Some **Pharisees** came to **Jesus** and
	12.13	**Pharisees**...were sent to **Jesus**
Lk	5.17	when **Jesus** was teaching, some **Pharisees**
	7.36	A **Pharisee** invited **Jesus** to have dinner
	7.37	**Jesus** was eating in the **Pharisee's** house,
	11.37	**Jesus** finished speaking, a **Pharisee**
	11.38	**Pharisee** was surprised when...**Jesus**
	13.31	some **Pharisees** came to **Jesus** and said
	16.14	**Pharisees** heard all this, they sneered at **Jesus**,
	17.20	**Pharisees** asked **Jesus** when the Kingdom
	19.39	the **Pharisees** in the crowd spoke to **Jesus**.
Jn	4.1	**Pharisees** heard that **Jesus** was winning
	8.12	**Jesus** spoke to the **Pharisees** again.
	11.46	to the **Pharisees** and told them what **Jesus**

Law

Mt	23.2	**Pharisees** are the authorized interpreters of Moses' **Law**.
Phil	3.5	**Law** is concerned, I was a **Pharisee**,

Sadducees

Mt	3.7	John saw many **Pharisees** and **Sadducees**
	16.1	**Pharisees** and **Sadducees** who came to
	16.6	yeast of the **Pharisees** and **Sadducees**.
	16.11	yeast of the **Pharisees** and **Sadducees**!
	16.12	teaching of the **Pharisees** and **Sadducees**.
	22.34	**Pharisees** heard that Jesus had silenced the **Sadducees**
Acts	23.6	**Sadducees** and the others were **Pharisees**,
	23.7	**Pharisees** and **Sadducees** started to

Teachers of the Law

Mt	5.20	**teachers of the Law** and the **Pharisees**
	12.38	**teachers of the Law** and some **Pharisees**
	15.1	**Pharisees** and **teachers of the Law** came
	23.2	**teachers of the Law** and the **Pharisees**
	23.13	**teachers of the Law** and **Pharisees**!
		Also: 23.15, 23, 25, 27, 29
Mk	2.16	**teachers of the Law**, who were **Pharisees**,
	7.1	**Pharisees** and **teachers of the Law**
	7.5	**Pharisees** and the **teachers of the Law**
Lk	5.17	some **Pharisees** and **teachers of the Law**
	5.21	**teachers of the Law** and the **Pharisees**
	5.30	**Pharisees** and some **teachers of the Law**
	6.7	**Pharisees** and some **teachers of the Law**
	7.30	**Pharisees** and the **teachers of the Law**
	11.53	**teachers of the Law** and the **Pharisees**
	14.3	**teachers of the Law** and the **Pharisees**,
	15.2	**Pharisees** and the **teachers of the Law**
Jn	8.3	**teachers of the Law** and the **Pharisees**
Acts	5.34	**Pharisee** named Gamaliel, who was a **teacher** of the **Law**

Terrible

Mt	23.13	How **terrible** for you...**Pharisees**
		Also: 23.15, 23, 25, 27, 29
Lk	11.42	How **terrible** for you **Pharisees**
	11.43	How **terrible** for you **Pharisees**

Trap

Mt	19.3	**Pharisees** came to him and tried to **trap**
	22.15	**Pharisees** went...and made a plan to **trap**
Mk	10.2	**Pharisees** came to him and tried to **trap**

AV PIT see WORLD OF THE DEAD

PITY

Lk	15.20	—	18.39		x6
Mt	20.30 – 34				x3
Mk	9.22	—	10.48		x3

Lord, God

Gen	19.16	The **Lord**, however, had **pity** on him;
Ex	33.19	I am the **Lord**, and I show...**pity**
	34.6	a **God** who is full of...**pity**,
Ps	90.13	Have **pity**, O **Lord**, on your servants!
Is	27.11	**God** their Creator will not **pity** them
Joel	2.17	Have **pity** on your people, **Lord**.
Zech	11.6	The **Lord** said, "I will no longer **pity**
Lk	18.13	**God**, have **pity** on me, a sinner!
Phil	2.27	But **God** had **pity** on him,

PLACE OF WORSHIP

Deut	14.24	—	19.17		x12
1 Kgs	11.8	—	15.14		x8
2 Kgs	14.4	—	18.4		x7
Ex	21.6	—	22.11		x4
2 Chr	33.3	—	34.3		x4
Deut	12.18 – 26				x3
1 Sam	9.14 – 25				x3
2 Kgs	23.10 – 19				x3
2 Chr	14.3	—	15.17		x3

Altar

1 Kgs	13.32	**altar** in Bethel and against all the **places**
2 Chr	14.3	**altars** and the pagan **places of worship**,
	14.5	**places of worship** and the **incense-altars**
	31.1	**altars** and the pagan **places of worship**.
Acts	17.23	the **places** where you worship...an **altar**

Idols, Gods

Num	33.52	**idols** and all their **places of worship**.
Judg	17.5	**place of worship**. He made some **idols**
1 Kgs	14.23	built **places of worship** for false **gods**
	15.12	**places of worship**, and...all the **idols**
Ps	78.58	**places of worship**, and with their **idols**

Offer, Sacrifice

Deut	12.26	the one **place of worship** your **offerings**
2 Kgs	17.32	pagan **places of worship** and to **offer sacrifices**
1 Chr	21.29	**sacrifices** were burnt were...at the **place**
2 Chr	33.17	**offer sacrifices** at other **places of worship**
Jer	48.35	**places of worship** and...**offering sacrifices**

Serve

1 Kgs	12.32	**serving** at the **places of worship**
	14.24	**served** as prostitutes at...pagan **places**
	15.12	**serving** at the pagan **places of worship**,
2 Kgs	17.32	**serve** as priests at the pagan **places of**
2 Chr	11.15	to **serve** at the pagan **places of worship**
Heb	13.10	**serve** in the Jewish **place of worship**

Worship

Deut	16.16	**worship** the Lord...at the one **place**
	31.11	**worship** the Lord...at the one **place**
1 Chr	16.39	**worship** of the Lord at the **place**

PLAGUE

Ex	7.14	—	10.29		
Rev	15.1	—	16.21		x6
Num	16.47 – 50				x3

Terrible

Deut	7.19	the **terrible plagues** that you saw
	29.3	You saw the **terrible plagues**,

Lk	21.11	**terrible** earthquakes, famines, and **plagues**
Rev	16.21	because it was such a **terrible plague**.

PLAN (PLOT)

Is	28.29	—	30.28		x5
Zech	7.10	—	8.17		x5
2 Cor	1.15	—	2.11		x5
Ex	25.9	—	27.8		x4
1 Chr	28.11 – 19				x4
Prov	6.14	—	8.14		x4
Is	22.11	—	23.9		x4
Dan	11.17 – 36				x4
Ex	31.4	—	33.13		x3
1 Sam	18.25	—	20.3		x3
1 Sam	23.9 – 13				x3
2 Chr	6.7	—	8.6		x3
Ps	64.5 – 6				x3
Prov	16.1 – 9				x3
Prov	19.21	—	21.5		x3
Jer	29.11				x3
Jer	49.20	—	51.29		x3
Mic	2.1 – 3				x3
Mt	26.4	—	28.12		x3
Jn	11.8	—	12.10		x3
Acts	8.22	—	9.24		x3
Eph	1.9 – 11				x3

Evil, Hurt, Trouble

Gen	50.20	You **plotted evil** against me,
1 Sam	20.3	**plans** to do, because you would be...**hurt**.
Esth	8.3	to do something to stop the **evil plot**
Job	15.35	the men who **plan trouble** and do **evil**;
Ps	7.14	people think up **evil**; they **plan trouble**
	14.6	**Evildoers** frustrate the **plans** of the
	36.4	He makes **evil plans** as he lies in bed;
	37.7	or those who succeed in their **evil plans**.
	56.5	are always **planning** how to **hurt** me!
	64.2	**plots** of the wicked, from mobs of **evil**
	64.5	their **evil plots**; they **plan** where to place
	64.6	They make **evil plans** and say,
	73.8	speak of **evil things**; they...make **plans**
	140.2	They are always **plotting evil**,
Prov	3.29	**plan** anything that will **hurt** your
	6.14	**planning evil** in their perverted minds,
	6.16	**plans**, feet that hurry off to do **evil**,
	12.2	but condemns those who **plan evil**.
	12.20	who **plan evil** are in for a rude surprise
	24.8	If you are always **planning evil**
	30.32	arrogant and **plan evil**, stop and think!
Is	30.28	and puts an end to their **evil plans**.
	32.7	**evil things**; he **plots** to ruin the poor
	33.15	**plan** to...murder or to do other **evil**
	59.4	carry out your **plans** to **hurt** others.
	59.5	The **evil plots** you make are as deadly
	59.7	You are always **planning** something **evil**,
Jer	11.19	me that they were **planning evil** things.
	18.23	their **plots** to kill me. Do not forgive their **evil**
Ezek	11.2	make **evil plans** and give bad advice
	38.10	you will start thinking up an **evil plan**.
Hos	7.3	king and his officers by their **evil plots**.
Mic	2.1	for those who lie awake and **plan evil**!
Mt	22.18	was aware of their **evil plan**,
Acts	8.22	of this **evil plan** of yours,

Purpose

Ps	33.11	**plans** endure for ever; his **purposes** last
Eph	1.9	**purposed**, and made known...the...**plan**
Heb	11.40	better **plan** for us. His **purpose** was that

Secret

Job	10.13	you were **secretly planning** to harm me.
Ps	83.3	making **secret plans** against your people;
Mt	26.4	made **plans** to arrest Jesus **secretly**
Eph	1.9	made known to us the **secret plan**

Eph	3.3	God revealed his **secret plan**
	3.9	**secret plan** is to be put into effect.
Col	1.27	God's **plan** is to make known his **secret**
Rev	10.7	God will accomplish his **secret plan,**

Succeed

2 Chr	7.11	**successfully** completing all his **plans**
Ps	20.4	and make all your **plans succeed**
	37.7	those who **succeed** in their evil **plans**.
Prov	16.3	your **plans**, and you will be **successful**
Is	8.10	your **plans**! But they will never **succeed**.
	28.29	The **plans** God makes...always **succeed**!
Dan	11.17	but his **plan** will not **succeed**.

Trouble see Evil

PLEASE

Num	28.2	—	29.36	x11
2 Chr	24.2	—	31.20	x9
Lev	1.9	—	4.31	x8
Heb	10.6	—	13.20	x8
Gen	1.4–31			x7
Num	14.8	—	15.24	x7
Ex	33.12	—	34.9	x5
2 Kgs	14.3	—	16.18	x5
Acts	6.5	—	10.4	x5
2 Sam	14.22	—	16.4	x4
Prov	14.35	—	16.7	x4
Is	56.4	—	58.5	x4
Rom	14.18	—	15.3	x4
Ex	29.18–41			x3
Deut	12.8–28			x3
1 Sam	18.5–22			x3
1 Kgs	14.13	—	15.11	x3
Esth	7.3	—	9.13	x3
Dan	11.16–36			x3
1 Cor	7.32–34			x3

Accept

Gen	15.6	Lord was **pleased** with him and **accepted**
Ps	20.3	**accept** all your offerings and be **pleased**
Jer	6.20	not **accept** their offerings or be **pleased**
Mal	1.10	not **pleased** with you; I will not **accept**
Lk	14.18	**please accept** my apologies.
	14.19	**please accept** my apologies.
Phil	4.18	sacrifice which is **acceptable** and **pleasing**

Dear see Son of God

Love see Son of God

Offer, Sacrifice

Gen	4.4	was **pleased** with Abel and his **offering**,
	8.21	odour of the **sacrifice pleased** the Lord
Ex	29.18	The odour of this **offering pleases** me.
	29.25	The odour of this **offering pleases** me.
	29.41	food **offering** to me, the Lord, and its odour **pleases** me.
Lev	2.2	smell of this **food-offering** is **pleasing**
	2.9	smell of this **food-offering** is **pleasing**
	6.15	The smell of this **offering** is **pleasing**
	8.28	**food-offering**, and the smell was **pleasing**
	23.13	The smell of this **offering** is **pleasing**
	23.18	The smell of this **offering** is **pleasing**
Num	15.3	smell of these **food-offerings** is **pleasing**
	15.7	The smell of these **sacrifices** is **pleasing**
	15.10	The smell of this **sacrifice** is **pleasing**
	15.24	a **burnt-offering**, a smell that **pleases**
	28.6	as a **food-offering**, a smell **pleasing**
	28.8	also is a **food-offering**, a smell **pleasing**
	28.24	a **food-offering**, a smell **pleasing**
	28.27	**Offer** a **burnt-offering** as a smell **pleasing**
	29.6	These **food-offerings** are a smell **pleasing**
	29.8	**Offer** a **burnt-offering** to the Lord, a smell **pleasing**
	29.13	**offer** a **food-offering** to the Lord, a smell **pleasing**

Num	29.36	**food-offering** to the Lord, a smell **pleasing**
Ps	20.3	accept all your **offerings** and be **pleased** with all your **sacrifices**.
	51.16	you are not **pleased** with **burnt-offerings**.
	51.19	will be **pleased** with proper **sacrifices**
	69.31	will **please** the Lord more than **offering**
Prov	15.8	**pleased** when good men pray, but hates the **sacrifices**
	21.3	**pleases** the Lord more than bringing him **sacrifices**.
Is	57.6	**grain-offerings**. Do you think I am **pleased**
	60.7	**sacrifices...offered** on the altar to **please**
	66.3	**offer** incense or pray to an idol. They take **pleasure**
Jer	6.20	not accept their **offerings** or be **pleased** with their **sacrifices**.
	14.12	**grain-offerings**, I will not be **pleased**
Ezek	43.27	**-offerings** of the people. Then I will be **pleased**
Hos	8.13	**sacrifices**. But I...am not **pleased**
Mal	1.10	not **pleased** with you; I will not accept the **offerings**
Lk	22.5	were **pleased** and **offered** to pay him
Eph	5.2	**offering** and **sacrifice** that **pleases** God.
Phil	4.18	**sacrifice** which is acceptable and **pleasing**
Heb	10.8	**pleased** with **sacrifices** and **offerings**
	13.16	the **sacrifices** that **please** God.

Son of God, Dear, Love

Mt	3.17	**dear Son**, with whom I am **pleased**.
	12.18	I **love**, and with whom I am **pleased**.
	17.5	**dear Son** with whom I am **pleased**
Mk	1.11	own **dear Son**. I am **pleased** with you.
Lk	3.22	own **dear Son**. I am **pleased** with you.
2 Pet	1.17	**dear Son**, with whom I am **pleased!**

POOR

Prov	13.7	—	24.34	x28
Prov	28.3	—	31.20	x19
Job	24.4–14			x5
Job	29.12	—	31.19	x5
Jas	1.9	—	2.6	x5
Ex	22.25	—	23.11	x4
Lev	25.25–47			x4
2 Kgs	23.2	—	25.26	x4
Ecc	4.13	—	6.8	x4
Jn	12.5	—	13.29	x4
2 Sam	12.1–4			x3
Ps	72.4–13			x3
Ps	109.16–31			x3
Prov	10.4	—	11.24	x3
Is	23.16	—	25.4	x3
Amos	2.6–8			x3
Amos	4.1	—	5.12	x3
Mk	12.42–44			x3
Lk	6.20	—	7.22	x3
Lk	21.2–4			x3
2 Cor	8.2–9			x3

Advantage see Needy

Defend see Help

God, Lord

Job	5.15	But **God** saves the **poor** from death;
	34.28	forced the **poor** to cry out to **God**,
Ps	40.17	I am weak and **poor**, O **Lord**,
	140.12	**Lord**...you defend the cause of the **poor**
Prov	14.31	oppress **poor** people, you insult the **God**
	15.16	Better to be **poor** and fear the **Lord**
	17.5	at **poor** people, you insult the **God**
Jas	2.5	**God** chose the **poor** people

Help, Defend, Protect

Job	26.1	**help** you are to me — **poor**, weak man
	29.12	the **poor** cried out, I **helped** them;
	31.16	I have never refused to **help** the **poor**;
Ps	35.10	You **protect** the weak...the **poor**
	41.1	for the **poor**; the Lord will **help** them
	72.4	king judge the **poor** fairly; may he **help**
	82.3	**Defend** the rights of the **poor**
	109.31	because he **defends** the **poor** man
	140.12	that you **defend** the cause of the **poor**
Prov	10.15	Wealth **protects** the rich; poverty destroys the **poor**.
	21.13	cry of the **poor**, your own cry for **help**
	29.14	If a king **defends** the rights of the **poor**
	31.9	**Protect** the rights of the **poor** and
Is	11.4	he will judge the **poor** fairly and **defend**
	19.15	rich or **poor**...can offer **help**.
Acts	9.36	doing good and **helping** the **poor**.
	10.2	much to **help** the Jewish **poor** people
Rom	15.26	to **help** the **poor** among God's people
Eph	4.28	and to be able to **help** the **poor**.

Helpless, Weak

Job	26.1	**poor**, **weak** man that I am!
Ps	35.10	the **weak** from the strong, the **poor**
	40.17	I am **weak** and **poor**, O Lord,
	70.5	I am **weak** and **poor**;
	72.13	He has pity on the **weak** and **poor**;
	109.16	the **poor**, the needy, and the **helpless**.
Prov	28.15	**Poor** people are **helpless** against a
Is	11.4	the **poor** fairly and defend...the **helpless**.
	25.4	**poor** and the **helpless** have fled to you
Amos	2.7	**weak** and **helpless** and push the **poor**
	4.1	ill-treat the **weak**, oppress the **poor**,

Justice, Judge, Rights

Ex	23.6	Do not deny **justice** to a **poor** man
Job	24.4	the **poor** from getting their **rights**
	36.6	he always treats the **poor** with **justice**.
Ps	72.4	May the king **judge** the **poor** fairly;
	82.3	Defend the **rights** of the **poor**
	140.12	of the **poor** and the **rights** of the needy.
Prov	29.7	person knows the **rights** of the **poor**
	29.14	If a king defends the **rights** of the **poor**
	31.9	**judge**. Protect the **rights** of the **poor**
Ecc	5.8	the **poor** and denies them **justice**
Is	10.2	the **poor** from having their **rights**
	11.4	he will **judge** the **poor** fairly and defend the **rights**
Amos	5.12	prevent the **poor** from getting **justice**

Lord see God

Needy, Advantage, Oppress, Persecute

Deut	15.11	Israelites who are **poor** and in **need**,
	24.14	cheat a **poor** and **needy** hired servant
1 Sam	2.8	**poor** from the dust and raises the **needy**
Job	5.15	**poor** from death; he saves the **needy** from **oppression**.
	20.19	he **oppressed** and neglected the **poor**
	31.19	someone in **need**, too **poor** to buy
Ps	10.2	are proud and **persecute** the **poor**;
	12.5	because the **needy** are **oppressed**
	35.10	the **poor** from the **oppressor**
	37.14	to kill the **poor** and **needy**,
	72.4	the **poor** fairly; may he help the **needy** and defeat their **oppressors**.
	72.12	**poor** who call to him, and those who are **needy**
	72.13	**poor**; he saves the lives of those in **need**.
	74.21	**oppressed** not to shame; let those **poor** and **needy** people praise him.
	82.3	**poor** and the orphans; be fair to the **needy**

Ps	109.16	he **persecuted** and killed the **poor**, the **needy**, and the helpless.
	109.22	I am **poor** and **needy**;
	113.7	**poor** from the dust; he lifts the **needy**
	132.15	all she **needs**; I will satisfy her **poor**
	140.12	of the **poor** and the rights of the **needy**.
Prov	14.31	If you **oppress poor** people
	22.16	**oppress** the **poor** to get rich, you will become **poor**
	22.22	Don't take **advantage** of the **poor**
	28.3	in authority who **oppresses poor** people
	28.27	the **poor** and you will never be in **need**
	29.13	A **poor** man and his **oppressor**
	30.14	who take cruel **advantage** of the **poor** and **needy**;
	31.9	the rights of the **poor** and **needy**.
	31.20	She is generous to the **poor** and **needy**.
Ecc	5.8	The government **oppresses** the **poor**
Is	3.15	people and take **advantage** of the **poor**.
Ezek	22.29	ill-treat the **poor** and take **advantage**
Amos	4.1	**oppress** the **poor**,
	5.11	You have **oppressed** the **poor**
	8.4	the **needy** and try to destroy the **poor**
Hab	3.14	secretly **oppress** the **poor**.
Rom	8.35	or **persecution** or hunger or **poverty**
Heb	11.37	**poor**, **persecuted**, and ill-treated.

Protect see Help

Rights see Justice

Weak see Helpless

POWER

Dan	2.10	—	9.26	x34
Deut	2.24	—	11.23	x23
Acts	8.10	—	14.3	x11
Is	40.10	—	45.12	x10
Ezek	30.12	—	33.28	x10
Jer	26.14	—	30.20	x9
Acts	1.2	—	4.33	x9
1 Cor	1.17	—	2.6	x9
Eph	1.19	—	3.20	x9
Job	11.7	—	13.11	x8
Lk	8.46	—	11.20	x8
Job	25.1	—	30.21	x7
Dan	11.2 – 40			x7
Rev	3.8	—	7.12	x7
Ex	13.3	—	15.6	x6
2 Chr	25.3	—	27.6	x6
Ps	118.10 – 16			x6
Is	1.24	—	2.21	x6
Is	8.11	—	12.2	x6
Is	62.8	—	64.2	x6
Col	1.11	—	2.15	x6
Rev	17.13	—	20.6	x6
2 Chr	32.7 – 22			x5
Ps	78.4 – 61			x4
Ezek	13.18 – 23			x4
Mt	12.24 – 28			x4
Rom	6.4 – 10			x4
1 Cor	12.9 – 29			x4

Afraid see Fear

Authority, Means

Ps	105.22	**power** over the...officials and **authority**
Dan	7.14	**authority**, honour, and royal **power**,
Lk	4.36	**authority** and **power** this man gives
	9.1	**power** and **authority** to drive out all
	11.20	**means** of God's **power** that I drive out
	20.20	**authority** and **power** of the Roman
Acts	3.12	that it was by **means** of our own **power**
1 Cor	15.24	**authorities**, and **powers**,
Eph	1.21	**authorities**, **powers**, and lords;

165

Eph	3.10	**means** of the church, the angelic rulers and **powers**
	3.20	by **means** of his **power** working in us
	6.10	and by **means** of his mighty **power**.
	6.12	**authorities**, and cosmic **powers**
Col	1.16	**powers**, lords, rulers, and **authorities**.
	2.15	the **power** of the spiritual...**authorities**;
1 Pet	3.22	and heavenly **authorities** and **powers**.
Rev	13.2	his own **power**...and his vast **authority**.
	17.13	their **power** and **authority** to the beast.

Believe see Faith

Christ, Jesus, Name, Son of Man

Mt	24.30	the **Son of Man** coming on the clouds of heaven with **power**
	26.45	for the **Son of Man** to be handed over to the **power**
Mk	5.30	**Jesus** knew that **power** had gone out
	13.26	the **Son of Man** will appear, coming in the clouds with great **power**
	14.41	**Son of Man** is now being handed over to the **power**
Lk	5.17	**power** of the Lord was present for **Jesus**
	21.27	the **Son of Man** will appear, coming in a cloud with great **power**
Jn	13.3	**Jesus** knew that the Father had given him complete **power**;
	17.11	them safe by the **power** of your **name**,
	17.12	them safe by the **power** of your **name**,
Acts	3.16	It was the **power** of his **name**
	4.10	the **power** of the **name** of **Jesus Christ**
	10.43	forgiven through the **power** of his **name**.
1 Cor	1.24	**Christ**, who is the **power** of God
	5.3	by the **power** of our Lord **Jesus**
2 Cor	12.9	to feel the protection of **Christ's power**
Phil	3.10	to know **Christ** and...the **power**
	4.13	by the **power** that **Christ** gives
Col	2.15	**Christ** freed himself from the **power**
1 Pet	4.11	**Jesus Christ**, to whom belong...**power**
Rev	1.6	To **Jesus Christ** be the glory and **power**

Cross see Death

Cruel see Evil

Death, Cross

2 Kgs	5.7	with the **power** of life and **death**?
Ps	16.10	protect me from the **power** of **death**.
	49.15	will save me from the **power** of **death**.
Song	8.6	Love is as **powerful** as **death**;
Ezek	13.18	to possess the **power** of life and **death**
Hos	13.14	rescue them from the **power** of **death**
Acts	2.24	**death**, setting him free from its **power**,
Rom	6.4	raised from **death** by the glorious **power**
	6.6	on his **cross**, in order that the **power**
1 Cor	1.17	**death**...is not robbed of its **power**.
	6.14	from **death**, and he will...raise us by his **power**.
	15.55	Where, **Death**, is your **power** to hurt?
	15.56	**Death** gets its **power** to hurt from sin
2 Cor	13.4	on the **cross**, it is by God's **power**
Col	2.12	the active **power** of God, who raised him from **death**.
	2.15	**cross Christ** freed himself from the **power**
2 Tim	1.10	He has ended the **power** of **death**
Heb	2.14	Devil, who has the **power** over **death**,
1 Jn	3.14	is still under the **power** of **death**.
Rev	20.6	second **death** has no **power** over them;

Destroy

Deut	7.23	in your **power**...until they are **destroyed**.
Job	27.23	frightening them with **destructive power**.
	29.17	I **destroyed** the **power** of cruel men
Ps	118.10	but I **destroyed** them by the **power**
	118.11	but I **destroyed** them by the **power**

Ps	118.12	**power** of the Lord I **destroyed** them.
	135.10	**destroyed**...nations and killed **powerful**
Is	1.31	**powerful** men will be **destroyed**
	31.8	be **destroyed**...but not by human **power**.
Jer	48.25	its **power** has been **destroyed**.
Dan	6.26	will never be **destroyed**, and his **power**
	7.26	take away his **power**, and **destroy** him
	8.24	will bring **destruction** on **powerful** men
	8.25	will be **destroyed** without...human **power**.
	9.26	**destroyed** by the...army of a **powerful**
Hos	1.5	**destroy** Israel's military **power**.
Zeph	2.13	will use his **power** to **destroy** Assyria
Zech	11.17	War will totally **destroy** his **power**.
Rom	6.6	**power** of the...self might be **destroyed**,
2 Cor	10.4	God's **powerful** weapons, which...**destroy**
Heb	2.14	**destroy** the Devil, who has the **power**

Evil, Cruel, Wicked

Job	29.17	I destroyed the **power** of **cruel** men
	30.21	me **cruelly**...with all your **power**.
Ps	10.15	the **power** of **wicked** and **evil** men;
	71.4	from the **power** of **cruel** and **evil** men.
	75.10	He will break the **power** of the **wicked**,
	82.4	them from the **power** of **evil** men.
	97.10	them from the **power** of the **wicked**.
	140.4	from the **power** of the **wicked**;
	144.11	from my **cruel** enemies...the **power**
Prov	29.16	**evil** men are in **power**, crime increases
Is	1.31	so **powerful** men will be destroyed by their own **evil**
	14.5	has ended the **power** of the **evil** rulers
Jer	15.21	rescue you from the **power** of **wicked**
	20.13	the oppressed from the **power** of **evil**
	23.10	live **wicked** lives and misuse their **power**.
Ezek	30.12	put Egypt under the **power** of **evil** men.
Rom	13.4	do **evil**, then be afraid of him, because his **power**
2 Thes	2.9	**Wicked** One will come with the **power**

Faith, Believe

Num	20.12	**faith** to acknowledge my holy **power**
Rom	1.16	God's **power** to save all who **believe**,
	4.20	his **faith** filled him with **power**,
Gal	5.5	the **power** of God's Spirit working through our **faith**.
Eph	1.19	is his **power** at work in us who **believe**.
Col	2.12	your **faith** in the active **power** of God,
2 Thes	2.11	**power** of error to work in them so that they **believe**
1 Pet	1.5	**faith** are kept safe by God's **power**

Fear, Afraid

Ps	102.15	kings of the earth will **fear** his **power**.
Is	59.19	will **fear** him and his great **power**.
Rom	13.4	be **afraid** of him, because his **power**

God

Gen	1.2	the **power** of **God** was moving
	49.24	the **power** of the mighty **God** of Jacob,
Ex	35.31	**God** has filled him with his **power**
Deut	2.33	**God** put him in our **power**,
	5.15	**God**, rescued you by my great **power**
	8.18	your **God** who gives you the **power**
Judg	8.3	through the **power** of **God** you killed
2 Kgs	5.7	**God**, with the **power** of life and death?
2 Chr	25.8	**God** who has the **power** to give victory
Job	11.7	of the greatness and **power** of **God**?
	12.12	but **God** has wisdom and **power**
	12.12	**God** has insight and **power** to act.
	25.1	**God** is **powerful**;
	27.11	teach you how great is **God's power**,
	28.25	**God** gave the wind its **power**
	34.13	Did **God** get his **power** from
	36.22	Remember how great is **God's power**;
	37.23	**God's power** is so great that
Ps	20.7	we trust in the **power** of...**God**.

Ps	54.1	Save me by your **power**, O **God**;
	62.11	**God** say that **power** belongs to him
	68.28	**power**, O **God**; the **power** you have used
	68.34	Proclaim **God's power**;
	77.10	that **God** is no longer **powerful**.
Is	1.24	**Lord** Almighty, Israel's **powerful God**,
	49.26	know that I am Israel's **powerful God**.
Jer	32.18	You are a great and **powerful God**;
Dan	2.20	**God** is wise and **powerful**!
	4.17	**God** has **power** over human kingdoms
	4.32	**God** has **power** over human kingdoms
	7.18	Supreme **God** will receive royal **power**
	9.15	**God**, you showed your **power**
Mt	22.29	you don't know...**God's power**.
Mk	12.24	you don't know...**God's power**.
Lk	1.35	and **God's power** will rest upon you.
	11.20	rather by means of **God's power**
Jn	9.3	**God's power** might be seen at work
Rom	1.16	**God's power** to save all who believe,
1 Cor	1.18	but for us...it is **God's power**.
	1.24	Christ, who is the **power** of **God**
	2.4	proof of the **power** of **God's** Spirit.
	2.5	rest...on **God's power**.
2 Cor	1.12	by the **power** of **God's** grace,
	4.7	the supreme **power** belongs to **God**,
	10.4	but **God's powerful** weapons,
	13.4	it is by **God's power** that he lives.
Gal	2.8	by **God's power** I was made an apostle
	5.5	for by the **power** of **God's** Spirit
Heb	1.3	of **God**, the Supreme **Power**.
1 Pet	1.5	are kept safe by **God's power**
2 Pet	1.3	**God's** divine **power** has given us
Rev	7.2	to whom **God** had given the **power**
	7.12	**power**, and might belong to our **God**
	12.10	**God** has shown his **power** as King!
	19.1	glory, and **power** belong to our **God**!

God's People

Lev	26.45	my **power** by bringing **my people** out
Ps	68.35	gives strength and **power** to **his people**.
	111.6	He has shown his **power** to **his people**
Is	11.11	**power** and bring back home...**his people**
	52.10	his holy **power**; he will save **his people**,
Ezek	13.21	**people** escape from your **power** once
	13.23	rescuing **my people** from your **power**,
Dan	7.22	for **God's people** to receive royal **power**.
	7.25	**God's people** will be under his **power**
Eph	3.18	all **God's people**, may have the **power**
2 Thes	2.13	**power** to make you **his holy people**

Harm see Hurt

Heal

Lk	5.17	**power** of the Lord...for Jesus to **heal**
	6.19	**power** was going...from him and **healing**
Acts	10.38	**healing** all who were under the **power**
1 Cor	12.9	person he gives the **power** to **heal**.
	12.28	those who are given the **power** to **heal**

Hurt, Harm

Gen	31.29	I have the **power** to do you **harm**
Ex	29.37	be **harmed** by the **power** of its holiness.
	30.29	be **harmed** by the **power** of its holiness.
Lev	6.18	be **harmed** by the **power** of its holiness.
	6.27	be **harmed** by the **power** of its holiness.
1 Sam	26.23	in my **power**, but I did not **harm** you,
Job	1.12	your **power**, but you must not **hurt** Job
Ps	3.7	and leave them **powerless** to **harm** me.
Lk	10.19	the **power** of the Enemy, and nothing will **hurt** you.
1 Cor	15.55	is your **power** to **hurt**?
	15.56	Death gets its **power** to **hurt** from sin
Rev	9.10	**power** to **hurt** people for five months.

Jesus see Christ

Justice, Judge, Right

Josh	9.25	**power**; do...what you think is **right**.
1 Sam	2.10	will **judge** the...world; he will give **power**
Prov	20.28	**power** as long as his rule is honest, **just**,
Is	4.4	**power** the Lord will **judge** and purify
	9.7	basing his **power** on right and **justice**,
	42.6	you **power** to see that **justice** is done
	59.17	**justice** like...armour and saving **power**
Ezek	39.21	**power** to carry out my **just** decisions.
Dan	7.26	sit in **judgement**, take away his **power**,
Mic	3.8	**power**, and gives me a sense of **justice**
Rev	20.4	on them were given the **power** to **judge**.

Life, Raise

2 Kgs	5.7	with the **power** of **life** and death?
Job	12.10	every man's **life** is in his **power**.
Jer	23.10	**live** wicked **lives** and misuse their **power**.
Ezek	13.18	to possess the **power** of **life** and death
	21.26	**Raise** the poor to **power**!
Jn	6.63	gives **life** is God's Spirit; man's **power**
Rom	1.4	**power** to be the Son...by being **raised**
	6.4	**raised** from death by the glorious **power**
1 Cor	6.14	he will also **raise** us by his **power**.
2 Cor	13.4	we shall share God's **power** in his **life**.
Col	2.12	**power** of God, who **raised** him
Heb	7.16	the **power** of a **life** which has no end.

Lord

see also **God**

Ex	13.3	**Lord** brought you out by his great **power**.
	13.9	**Lord** brought you out...by his great **power**.
	13.14	using great **power** the **Lord** brought us
	13.16	**Lord** brought us out...by his great **power**.
	14.31	the great **power** with which the **Lord**
	15.6	hand, **Lord**, is awesome in **power**;
Num	22.28	the **Lord** gave...the **power** of speech,
	33.4	**Lord** showed that he was more **powerful**
Deut	11.2	the **Lord's** greatness, his **power**,
Josh	4.24	know how great the **Lord's power** is,
Judg	13.25	**Lord's power** began to strengthen him
	14.6	**power** of the **Lord** made Samson strong,
	14.19	the **power** of the **Lord** made him strong,
	15.14	the **power** of the **Lord** made him strong,
1 Kgs	18.46	The **power** of the **Lord** came on Elijah;
2 Kgs	3.15	the **power** of the **Lord** came on Elisha.
Job	42.2	I know, **Lord**, that you are **all-powerful**;
Ps	71.16	I will praise your **power**...**Lord**;
	78.4	about the **Lord's power** and his great
	110.2	the **Lord** will extend your royal **power**.
	118.10	destroyed...by the **power** of the **Lord**!
	118.11	destroyed...by the **power** of the **Lord**!
	118.12	by the **power** of the **Lord**
	118.14	The **Lord** makes me **powerful**
	118.15	The **Lord's** mighty **power** has done it!
Prov	23.11	The **Lord** is their **powerful** defender,
Is	4.4	By his **power** the **Lord** will judge
	8.11	With his great **power** the **Lord** warned
	12.2	The **Lord** gives me **power** and strength;
	14.5	The **Lord** has ended the **power** of
	24.21	the **Lord** will punish the **powers** above
	27.1	the **Lord** will use his **powerful**...sword
	28.2	The **Lord** has someone...**powerful**
	30.27	**Lord's power** and glory can be seen
	35.2	see the **Lord's** splendour...and **power**.
	48.16	Sovereign **Lord** has given me his **power**
	52.10	The **Lord** will use his holy **power**;
	63.1	It is the **Lord**, **powerful** to save,

Is	63.12	the **Lord**, who by his **power**
Jer	10.12	The **Lord** made the earth by his **power**;
	51.15	The **Lord** made the earth by his **power**;
Ezek	1.3	I heard the **Lord**...I felt his **power**.
	3.14	The **power** of the **Lord** came on me
	3.22	the **powerful** presence of the **Lord**
	8.1	the **power** of the Sovereign **Lord**
	33.22	the **powerful** presence of the **Lord**.
	37.1	the **powerful** presence of the **Lord**,
	40.1	the **powerful** presence of the **Lord**,
Zeph	2.13	The **Lord** will use his **power**
Lk	1.66	the **Lord's power** was upon him.
	5.17	The **power** of the **Lord** was present
Jn	12.38	did the **Lord** reveal his **power**?
Acts	11.21	The **Lord's power** was with them,
	19.20	**powerful** way the word of the **Lord**
1 Cor	5.3	by the **power** of our **Lord** Jesus
Eph	6.10	the **Lord** and...his mighty **power**.

Love

Song	8.6	**Love** is as **powerful** as death;
Is	63.15	is your **power**? Where are your **love** and
Jer	12.7	I **love** into the **power** of their enemies.
Jn	3.35	**loves** his Son and has put everything in his **power**.
2 Tim	1.7	his Spirit fills us with **power**, **love**,
1 Jn	3.14	**love** is still under the **power** of death.

Majesty

1 Chr	16.27	Glory and **majesty** surround him, **power**
Ps	68.34	God's **power**; his **majesty** is over Israel,
	96.6	Glory and **majesty** surround him; **power**

Means see **Authority**

Might see **Strength**

Miracles, Wonders

Ex	4.21	**miracles** which I have given you the **power**
Deut	7.19	**miracles** and **wonders**, and the great **power**
Ps	66.3	How **wonderful** are the things you do! Your **power**
	78.4	**Lord's power**...and the **wonderful** things
	98.1	**wonderful** things! By his own **power**
Dan	4.3	**wonders** God shows us! How **powerful** are the **miracles** he performs!
Mt	14.2	he has this **power** to perform **miracles**.
Mk	6.14	he has this **power** to perform **miracles**.
	16.17	be given the **power** to perform **miracles**:
Acts	6.8	**power**, performed...**miracles** and **wonders**
	14.3	**power** to perform **miracles** and **wonders**.
Rom	15.19	by the **power** of **miracles** and **wonders**,
1 Cor	12.10	one person the **power** to work **miracles**;
	12.29	has the **power** to work **miracles**

Name see **Christ**

Praise, Worship

Neh	9.6	**powers** bow down and **worship** you.
Ps	21.13	We will sing and **praise** your **power**.
	29.1	**praise** his glory and **power**.
	71.16	will **praise** your **power**, Sovereign Lord;
	103.21	**Praise** the Lord...you heavenly **powers**,
Is	25.3	**powerful** nations will **praise** you;
Dan	2.20	God is wise and **powerful**! **praise** him
Zech	8.22	**powerful** nations will come...to **worship**
Jn	4.23	by the **power** of God's Spirit people will **worship** the Father
	4.24	**power** of his Spirit can people **worship**
Rom	4.20	him with **power**, and he gave **praise**
Rev	19.1	**Praise** God! Salvation...and **power**

Protect see **Safe**

Raise see **Life**

Rescue

Ex	32.11	**rescued** from Egypt with great...**power**?
Deut	5.15	**rescued** you by my great **power** and
	6.21	the Lord **rescued** us by his great **power**.
	26.8	great **power** and strength he **rescued** us
1 Sam	7.3	he will **rescue** you from the **power**
2 Sam	22.18	**rescued** me from my **powerful** enemies
Neh	1.10	You **rescued** them by your great **power**
Job	29.17	the **power** of cruel men and **rescued**
Ps	18.17	**rescued** me from my **powerful** enemies
	71.4	**rescue** me from wicked men, from the **power**
	82.4	**Rescue** them from the **power** of evil
	97.10	**rescues** the oppressed from the **power**
	144.11	**rescue** me from the **power** of foreigners,
Is	40.10	**power**, bringing with him the people he has **rescued**.
	59.16	will use his own **power** to **rescue** them
Jer	15.21	**rescue** you from the **power** of wicked
	20.13	**rescues** the oppressed from the **power**
	42.11	I will **rescue** you from his **power**.
Ezek	13.23	**rescuing** my people from your **power**,
Hos	13.14	**rescue** them from the **power** of death.
Acts	12.11	to **rescue** me from Herod's **power**
Col	1.13	**rescued** us from the **power** of darkness

Right see **Justice**

Safe, Protect

Ps	16.10	**protect** me from the **power** of death.
	18.35	your **power** has kept me **safe**.
	139.5	you **protect** me with your **power**.
	140.4	the **power** of the wicked; keep me **safe**
Is	30.3	**powerless** to help...Egypt's **protection**
Zeph	2.15	of its own **power** and thinks it is **safe**.
Jn	17.11	them **safe** by the **power** of your name,
	17.12	them **safe** by the **power** of your name,
2 Cor	12.9	to feel the **protection** of Christ's **power**
Col	1.13	**power** of darkness and brought us **safe**
1 Pet	1.5	faith are kept **safe** by God's **power**

Sin

Mt	26.45	to the **power** of **sinful** men.
Mk	14.41	to the **power** of **sinful** men.
Acts	10.43	his **sins** forgiven through the **power**
Rom	3.9	alike are all under the **power** of **sin**.
	6.6	the **power** of the **sinful** self might be
	6.7	he is set free from the **power** of **sin**.
	6.10	he died, **sin** has no **power** over him;
1 Cor	15.56	Death gets its **power** to hurt from **sin**,
	15.56	and **sin** gets its **power** from the Law.
Gal	3.22	whole world is under the **power** of **sin**;
Col	2.11	from the **power** of this **sinful** self.

Son of Man see **Christ**

Spirit of God

Ezek	37.1	the **powerful** presence of the Lord, and his **spirit**
Mic	3.8	fills me with his **spirit** and **power**,
Mt	12.28	**Spirit**, who gives me the **power** to drive
Lk	1.35	The **Holy Spirit** will come on you, and God's **power**
	4.14	**power** of the **Holy Spirit** was with him.
Jn	4.23	by the **power** of **God's Spirit** people
	4.24	and only by the **power** of his **Spirit**
	6.63	**God's Spirit**; man's **power** is of no use
Acts	1.2	by the **power** of the **Holy Spirit**
	10.38	on him the **Holy Spirit** and **power**.
	11.28	by the **power** of the **Spirit** predicted
	21.4	the **power** of the **Spirit** they told Paul
Rom	8.15	by the **Spirit's power** we cry out
	15.13	grow by the **power** of the **Holy Spirit**.
	15.19	the **power** of the **Spirit** of **God**.
1 Cor	2.4	proof of the **power** of **God's Spirit**.
	12.10	The **Spirit** gives one person the **power**

1 Cor	14.2	secret truths by the **power** of the **Spirit**.
Gal	5.5	**power** of **God's Spirit** working through
Eph	3.16	**power** through his **Spirit** to be strong
1 Thes	1.5	with **power** and the **Holy Spirit**,
2 Thes	2.13	the **Spirit's power** to make you his holy
2 Tim	1.7	his **Spirit** fills us with **power**,
	1.14	Through the **power** of the **Holy Spirit**,
1 Pet	1.12	**power** of the **Holy Spirit** sent from
1 Jn	4.4	**Spirit** who is in you is more **powerful**
Jude	.20	Pray in the **power** of the **Holy Spirit**,

Strength, Might

Gen	49.24	his arms are made **strong** By the **power**
Ex	32.11	from Egypt with great **might** and **power**?
Deut	4.34	he used his great **power** and **strength**;
	5.15	you by my great **power** and **strength**.
	7.19	**power** and **strength** by which the Lord
	8.17	by your own **power** and **strength**.
	9.26	by your great **strength** and **power**.
	9.29	by your great **power** and **might**.
	10.17	over all **powers**. He is great and **mighty**,
	11.2	his **power**, his **might**,
	26.8	great **power** and **strength** he rescued us
Judg	13.25	Lord's **power** began to **strengthen** him
	14.6	**power** of the Lord made Samson **strong**
	14.19	**power** of the Lord made him **strong**
	15.14	**power** of the Lord made him **strong**,
2 Sam	22.30	**strength** to attack my enemies and **power**
2 Kgs	15.19	in **strengthening** Menaham's **power**
	17.36	with great **power** and **strength**;
1 Chr	29.12	everything by your **strength** and **power**;
2 Chr	20.6	are **powerful** and **mighty**, and no one
Neh	1.10	them by your great **power** and **strength**.
Job	12.21	**power** and puts an end to the **strength**
	40.16	what **strength** there is...and what **power**
Ps	18.29	**strength** to attack my enemies and **power**
	21.13	**strength**! We will...praise your **power**.
	44.3	it was by your **power** and your **strength**,
	54.1	**power**, O God; set me free by your **might**!
	65.6	**strength**, showing your **mighty power**.
	68.34	**power**; his majesty is over Israel, his **might**
	68.35	gives **strength** and **power** to his people.
	71.18	while I proclaim your **power** and **might**
	89.13	How **powerful** you are! How great is your **strength**!
	89.21	my **power** will make him **strong**.
	98.1	By his own **power** and holy **strength**
	118.14	Lord makes me **powerful** and **strong**;
	118.15	The Lord's **mighty power** has done it!
	118.16	his **mighty power** in battle!
	136.12	his **strong** hand, his **powerful** arm;
	145.11	royal **power** and tell of your **might**,
Song	8.6	**powerful** as death; passion is as **strong**
Is	12.2	The Lord gives me **power** and **strength**;
	18.2	to your **strong** and **powerful** nation,
	18.7	this **strong** and **powerful** nation,
	28.2	Lord has someone **strong** and **powerful**
	63.1	marching along in **power** and **strength**?
Jer	10.6	you are **mighty**...great and **powerful**.
	16.21	nations know my **power** and my **might**;
	27.5	my great **power** and **strength** I created
	32.17	by your great **power** and **might**;
	32.21	**power** and **might** to bring your people
	48.25	**might** has been crushed; its **power**
Ezek	20.33	with a **strong** hand, with all my **power**.
	30.18	**power**...and put an end to the **strength**
Dan	2.37	emperor and given you **power**, **might**,
	4.30	city to display my **power** and **might**,
	8.24	**strong** — but not by his own **power**.
Zech	10.11	and **mighty** Egypt will lose her **power**.
Lk	9.43	amazed at the **mighty power** of God.
Acts	3.16	**power** of his name that gave **strength**

Eph	1.19	**power** working in us is the same as the **mighty strength**
	3.16	**power** through his Spirit to be **strong**
	6.10	and by means of his **mighty power**.
Phil	4.13	I have the **strength** to face all conditions by the **power**
Col	1.11	**strength** which comes from his...**power**,
Rev	5.12	**power**, wealth, wisdom, and **strength**,
	7.12	**power**, and **might** belong to our God

Victory, Win

2 Chr	25.8	who has the **power** to give **victory**
Ps	20.6	his **power** gives him great **victories**.
	33.16	not **win** because of his **powerful** army;
	44.3	they did not **win** it by their own **power**;
	98.1	his own **power**...he has won the **victory**.
	98.2	**victory**; he made his saving **power**
	118.16	His **power** has brought us **victory**
Is	59.16	his own **power**...to win the **victory**.
	63.1	**powerful**...coming to announce his **victory**.
Zeph	3.17	his **power** gives you **victory**.
1 Cor	15.55	**victory**? Where, Death, is your **power**

Wicked see Evil

Win see Victory

Wisdom

Job	9.4	God is so **wise** and **powerful**;
	12.12	but God has **wisdom** and **power**.
Jer	10.12	the earth by his **power**; by his **wisdom**
	51.15	the earth by his **power**; by his **wisdom**
Dan	2.20	God is **wise** and **powerful**!
1 Cor	1.24	**power** of God and the **wisdom** of God.
	1.26	few of you were **wise** or **powerful**
	2.4	**wisdom**, but with...proof of the **power**
	2.5	on human **wisdom** but on God's **power**.
2 Cor	1.12	by the **power** of God's grace, and not by human **wisdom**.
Rev	5.12	to receive **power**, wealth, **wisdom**,
	7.12	**wisdom**, thanksgiving, honour, **power**,

Wonders see Miracles

World

1 Sam	2.10	the whole **world**; he will give **power**
Ecc	8.9	a **world** where some men have **power**
Jer	10.12	by his **power**...he created the **world**
	27.5	**power** and strength I created the **world**,
	51.15	by his **power**...he created the **world**
Dan	4.22	**power** extends over the whole **world**.
Zech	1.19	They stand for the **world powers**
Jn	14.30	this **world** is coming. He has no **power**
Rom	9.17	my **power** and to spread my fame over the whole **world**.
1 Cor	1.27	what the **world** considers weak in order to shame the **powerful**.
	2.6	the **powers** that rule this **world**
2 Cor	10.4	**world's** weapons but God's **powerful**
Gal	3.22	whole **world** is under the **power** of sin;
Eph	3.10	rulers and **powers** in the heavenly **world**
	6.12	**world**, the rulers...and cosmic **powers**
Rev	11.15	The **power** to rule over the **world**
	18.23	the most **powerful** in all the **world**,

Worship see Praise

PRAISE

Ps	148.1 – 14		x13
Ps	150.1 – 6		x13
1 Chr	16.4 – 42		x12
Ps	135.1 – 21		x10
Is	41.16	– 43.21	x10
Is	60.18	– 64.11	x8
Dan	2.19	– 5.23	x8
2 Chr	29.27	– 31.8	x7

Ps	66.1 – 20	x7
Ps	103.1 – 22	x7
Ps	106.1 – 48	x7
Ps	147.1 – 20	x7
Ps	68.4 – 35	x6
Ps	71.6 – 22	x6
Ps	145.2 – 21	x6
Ps	149.1 – 9	x6
Rom	15.6 – 11	x6
Rev	19.1 – 7	x6
1 Chr	29.10 – 20	x5
Ps	22.3 – 26	x5
Ps	96.2 – 8	x5
Ps	113.1 – 9	x5
Ps	119.7 – 175	x5
2 Sam	22.4 – 50	x4
Ps	9.1 – 14	x4
Ps	18.3 – 49	x4
Ps	30.1 – 12	x4
Ps	47.1 – 7	x4
Ps	67.3 – 5	x4
Ps	104.1 – 35	x4
Ps	146.1 – 10	x4
Is	38.9 – 20	x4
Mt	21.9 – 16	x4

Bow see Worship

Defender, Protector
2 Sam 22.47 **Praise** my **defender!**
Ps   18.46 **Praise** my **defender!**
     59.17 I will **praise** you, my **defender.**
     81.1 to God our **defender;** sing **praise**
   144.1 **Praise** the Lord, my **protector!**
Is   60.18 **defend** you like a wall; You will **praise**

Glad see Happy

Glory see Name

God's People, Servants
Deut 32.43 you must **praise** the **Lord's people**
1 Kgs 8.56 **Praise** the Lord who has given **his people**
              peace,
2 Chr 31.8 and **praised his people** Israel.
Ps   22.23 **Praise** him, you **servants** of God!
    26.12 of **his people** I **praise** the Lord.
    68.26 **Praise**...in the meeting of **his people;**
  106.12 **his people** believed...and sang **praises**
  113.1 **servants** of the Lord, **praise his** name!
  134.1 **praise** the Lord, all **his servants,**
  135.1 **Praise** his name, you **servants**
  148.14 so that all **his people praise** him
Is   49.3 you are my **servant;** because of you, people
          will **praise** me.
Jer   13.11 be my **people** and would bring **praise**
    31.7 **praise,** 'The Lord has saved **his people;**
Rev   19.5 **Praise** our God, all **his servants**

Happy, Glad, Joy, Rejoice
1 Kgs 8.66 all **praised** him and went home **happy**
Ps   9.2 **joy** because of you. I will sing **praise**
    9.14 I **praise** you. I will **rejoice**
    28.7 help and makes me **glad;** I **praise** him with
         joyful songs.
    33.1 **joy** for what the Lord has done; **praise**
    42.4 **happy** crowd, singing and shouting **praise**
    43.4 of my **happiness.** I will...sing **praise**
    47.1 hands for **joy,** all peoples! **Praise** God
    63.5 I will sing **glad** songs of **praise** to you.
    66.1 **Praise** God with shouts of **joy,** all
    81.1 for **joy** to God our defender; sing **praise**
    89.16 **rejoice** all day long, and they **praise** you
    95.1 us **praise** the Lord! Let us sing for **joy**
    95.2 and sing **joyful** songs of **praise.**
    98.4 **praise** him with songs and shouts of **joy!**
Is   41.16 **happy** because I am your God...**praise**

Is   51.3 **Joy** and **gladness**...and songs of **praise**
    61.3 **Joy** and **gladness**...A song of **praise**
Jer   30.19 will sing **praise;** they will shout for **joy.**
Acts 13.48 **glad** and **praised** the Lord's message;
1 Cor 12.26 **praised**...other parts share its **happiness.**
Jas   5.13 anyone **happy?** He should sing **praises.**
Rev   19.7 Let us **rejoice** and be **glad;** let us **praise**

Holy see Name

Honour see Name

Joy see Happy

Justice
Ps   7.17 the Lord for his **justice,** I sing **praises**
  119.7 righteous **judgements,** I will **praise** you
  119.62 **praise** you for your righteous **judgements.**

Might see Strength

Name, Glory, Holy, Honour, Sacred
Deut 26.19 bring **praise** and **honour** to his **name.**
1 Chr 16.25 be highly **praised;** he is to be **honoured**
   16.28 **praise** his **glory** and might.
   16.29 **Praise** the Lord's **glorious name;**
   16.35 and **praise** your **holy name.**
   23.30 **praise** and **glorify** the Lord every
   29.13 and we **praise** your **glorious name.**
Neh   9.5 Let everyone **praise-**his **glorious name,**
Job   1.21 May his **name** be **praised!**
Ps   22.3 **Holy** One, the one whom Israel **praises.**
   22.23 **Honour** him...**Honour** him,
   29.1 **praise** his **glory** and power.
   29.2 **Praise** the Lord's **glorious name;**
   34.3 let us **praise** his **name** together!
   48.1 highly **praised**...on his **sacred** hill.
   63.11 promises in God's **name** will **praise** him,
   66.2 his **name;** offer him **glorious praise!**
   66.4 they sing **praises** to your **name.**
   68.4 sing **praises** to his **name;**
   71.8 I **praise** you and proclaim your **glory.**
   72.19 **Praise** his **glorious name** for ever!
   96.4 be highly **praised;** he is to be **honoured**
   96.7 **praise** his **glory** and might.
   96.8 **Praise** the Lord's **glorious name;**
   99.3 **praise** his great and majestic **name.**
   99.9 **Praise** the Lord...at his **sacred**
  103.1 All my being, **praise** his **holy name!**
  106.47 and **praise** your **holy name.**
  113.1 servants of the Lord, **praise** his **name!**
  113.2 May his **name** be **praised;**
  113.3 **praise** the **name** of the Lord!
  135.1 **Praise** the Lord! **Praise** his **name,**
  135.3 sing **praises** to his **name,**
  138.2 and **praise** your **name**
  145.21 let all his creatures **praise** his **holy name**
  148.5 them all **praise** the **name** of the Lord!
  148.13 them all **praise** the **name** of the Lord!
  149.3 **Praise** his **name** with dancing;
Prov 31.30 **honours** the Lord should be **praised.**
Is   25.1 will **honour** you and **praise** your **name.**
   41.16 will **praise** me, the **holy** God of Israel.
   42.12 give **praise** and **glory** to the Lord!
   43.20 will **honour** me...ostriches will **praise** me
   48.9 order that people will **praise** my **name,**
Jer   13.11 bring **praise** and **honour** to my **name.**
Ezek   3.12 **Praise** the **glory** of the Lord in heaven
Dan   2.23 I **praise** you and **honour** you,
   4.34 I **praised**...God and gave...**glory**
   4.37 **praise, honour,** and **glorify** the King
Zeph   3.19 **honour,** and all the world will **praise**
Mt   21.9 in the **name** of the Lord! **Praise** God!
Mk   11.9 **Praise** God! God bless him who comes in the
        name
Jn   12.13 **Praise** God! God bless him who comes in the
        name

Eph	1.6	**praise** God for his **glorious** grace·
	1.12	to hope in Christ, **praise** God's **glory**!
	1.14	Let us **praise** his **glory**!
Phil	1.11	for the **glory** and **praise** of God.
1 Pet	1.7	Then you will receive **praise** and **glory**
Rev	5.12	**glory**, and **praise**!
	5.13	be **praise** and **honour**, **glory** and might,
	7.12	**Praise**, **glory**,
	14.7	**Honour** God and **praise** his greatness!
	19.1	**Praise** God! Salvation, **glory**,

Protector see **Defender**

Rejoice see **Happy**

Rescue see **Save**

Sacred see **Name**

Save, Rescue

Ex	15.2	who has **saved** me...I will **praise** him,
	18.10	**Praise** the Lord, who **saved** you from
2 Sam	22.4	he **saves** me from my enemies. **Praise**
Ps	9.14	I **praise** you...because you **saved** me.
	18.3	he **saves** me from my enemies. **Praise**
	30.1	**praise** you...because you have **saved** me
	50.15	I will **save** you, and you will **praise** me.
	107.2	in **praise** to the Lord, all you whom he has **saved**.
Is	60.18	will **praise** me because I have **saved** you.
	61.11	**save** his people, And all...will **praise**
Jer	20.13	**Praise** the Lord! He **rescues** the
	31.7	song of **praise**, 'The Lord has **saved**

Servants see **God's People**

Soul

Ps	103.1	**Praise** the Lord, my **soul**!
		Also: 103.2, 22; 104.1, 35
	108.1	sing and **praise** you! Wake up, my **soul**!
	146.1	**Praise** the Lord, my **soul**!

Strength, Might

1 Chr	16.28	**praise** his glory and **might**.
2 Chr	30.21	**praised** the Lord with all their **strength**.
Ezra	3.11	with all his **might**, **praising** the Lord
Job	29.20	always **praising** me, and my **strength**
Ps	21.13	We **praise** you...for your great **strength**!
	85.6	**strong** again, and we...will **praise** you.
	96.7	**praise** his glory and **might**.
	103.20	**Praise** the Lord, you **strong** and **mighty**
	148.14	**strong**, so that all his people **praise** him
	150.1	**Praise** his **strength** in heaven!
	150.2	**Praise** him for the **mighty** things he has
Rev	5.12	**strength**, honour, glory, and **praise**!
	5.13	be **praise** and honour, glory and **might**,

Wonderful

1 Chr	16.9	**praise** to the Lord; tell the **wonderful**
Ps	31.21	**Praise** the Lord! How **wonderfully** he
	105.2	**praise** to the Lord; tell of the **wonderful**
Joel	2.26	**praise** the Lord your God, who has done **wonderful**

World

Ps	8.1	in all the **world**! Your **praise** reaches up
	47.7	is king over all the **world**; **praise** him
	68.32	kingdoms of the **world**, sing **praise**
	138.4	the kings in the **world** will **praise** you,
Is	24.16	the **world** we will hear songs in **praise**
	42.10	sing his **praise**, all the **world**!
	62.7	makes it a city the whole **world praises**.
Jer	51.41	The city that the whole **world praised**
Zeph	3.19	and all the **world** will **praise** them.

Worship, Bow

Gen	24.48	and **worshipped** the Lord. I **praised**
2 Chr	7.3	**worshipping** God and **praising** him for
2 Chr	31.2	**worship**, and giving **praise** and thanks
Ps	29.2	**Praise** the Lord's glorious name; **bow**
	66.4	**worships** you; they sing **praises** to you,
	86.9	and **bow** down to you; they will **praise**
	99.5	**Praise** the Lord our God; **worship**
	99.9	**Praise** the Lord our God, and **worship**
	135.20	**praise** him, all you that **worship** him!
	138.2	**bow** down, and **praise** your name

PRAY

1 Kgs	8.12	–	54	x12
Acts	8.15	—	13.3	x12
Ex	8.8	—	10.18	x11
2 Chr	6.1	—	7.14	x11
1 Kgs	17.20	—	19.4	x10
1 Sam	1.9	—	2.1	x7
Mt	5.44	—	6.9	x7
Lk	9.18	—	11.2	x7
Jer	42.2	–	20	x6
Jon	1.6	—	4.2	x6
Mk	13.18	—	14.39	x6
Lk	21.36	—	22.46	x6
2 Kgs	4.33	—	6.20	x5
Neh	4.4	—	6.14	x5
Dan	9.3	–	21	x5
Mt	26.36	–	44	x5
Jas	5.13	–	18	x5
1 Sam	12.17	–	23	x4
Jn	17.9	–	21	x4
1 Cor	14.13	–	15	x4
Eph	6.18	–	20	x4
Col	4.2	–	12	x4
2 Chr	20.3	–	9	x3
Dan	6.10	–	13	x3
Hos	7.7	–	14	x3
Lk	18.1	–	11	x3
1 Cor	11.4	–	13	x3
Eph	3.1	–	17	x3

Alone

Zeph	3.9	and they will **pray** to me **alone**
Mt	14.23	himself to **pray**...Jesus was there **alone**;
Lk	9.18	when Jesus was **praying alone**,

Believe

Mt	21.22	**believe**, you will receive whatever you ask for in **prayer**.
Mk	11.24	you **pray** and ask for something, **believe**
Jas	1.6	But when you **pray**, you must **believe**

Confess see **Repent**

Earnestly

Ex	15.25	Moses **prayed earnestly** to the Lord
	17.4	**prayed earnestly** to the Lord and said
Deut	3.23	At that time I **earnestly prayed**
Ps	78.34	would repent and **pray earnestly** to him.
Dan	9.3	And I **prayed earnestly** to the Lord God
Jon	3.8	Everyone must **pray earnestly** to God
Acts	12.5	of the church were **praying earnestly**
Rom	12.12	and **pray** at all times.
Col	4.2	Be persistent in **prayer**,
1 Thes	5.17	**pray** at all times,
Heb	13.19	I beg you even more **earnestly** to **pray**
Jas	5.17	**prayed earnestly** that there would be no

Father

Mt	6.6	the door, and **pray** to your **Father**,
	6.9	is how you should **pray**: 'Our **Father**
	18.19	**pray** for, it will be done...by my **Father**
	26.39	and **prayed**, "My **Father**
	26.42	went away and **prayed**, "My **Father**
Mk	14.36	**Father**," he **prayed**, "my **Father**
Lk	11.2	When you **pray**, say this: 'Father:
Jn	17.21	I **pray** that they may all be one. **Father**
Col	1.3	**Father** of our Lord Jesus...when we **pray**

171

1 Pet 1.17 call him **Father**, when you **pray** to God

Heaven

1 Kgs	8.39	**prayer**. Listen to them...in **heaven**,
	8.43	listen to his **prayer**. In **heaven**,
	8.45	to their **prayers**. Hear them in **heaven**
	8.49	their **prayers**. In your home in **heaven**
2 Chr	6.30	their **prayer**. Listen to them...in **heaven**
	6.33	listen to his **prayer**. In **heaven**
	6.35	to their **prayers**. Hear them in **heaven**
	6.39	their **prayers**. In your home in **heaven**
	7.1	his **prayer**, fire came down from **heaven**
	30.27	home in **heaven** God heard their **prayers**
Ezra	6.10	**Heaven** and **pray** for his blessing on me
Neh	2.4	I **prayed** to the God of **Heaven**,
Lam	3.41	our hearts to God in **heaven** and **pray**,
Dan	2.18	to **pray** to the God of **heaven** for mercy
Mt	6.9	you should **pray**: 'Our Father in **heaven**:
Lk	3.21	he was **praying**, **heaven** was opened,

Jesus

Mt	26.26	**Jesus**...gave a **prayer** of thanks,
	26.42	**Jesus** went away and **prayed**,
	26.44	**Jesus**...**prayed** the third time,
Mk	14.22	**Jesus**...gave a **prayer** of thanks,
Lk	6.12	**Jesus** went up a hill to **pray**
	9.18	when **Jesus** was **praying** alone,
	11.1	One day **Jesus** was **praying**
Jn	18.1	After **Jesus** had said this **prayer**,
Heb	5.7	**Jesus** made his **prayers** and requests

Love

Ps	60.5	our **prayer**, so that the people you **love**
	66.20	**prayer** or keep back his constant **love**
	86.5	constant **love** for all who **pray** to you.
	108.6	my **prayer**, so that the people you **love**
	109.4	I **love** them and have **prayed** for them.
Mt	5.44	**love** your enemies and **pray** for those
	6.5	They **love** to stand up and **pray**
Phil	1.9	**pray** that your **love** will keep on

Power

Num	14.17	I **pray**, show us your **power**
Jas	5.16	**prayer** of a good person has a **powerful**
Jude	.20	**Pray** in the **power** of the Holy Spirit,

Repent, Confess, Turn

1 Kgs	8.33	when they **turn** to you...humbly **praying**
	8.35	**repent** and face this Temple...**praying**
	8.47	**repent** and **pray** to you, **confessing**
	8.48	sincerely **repent**, and **pray** to you
2 Kgs	20.2	**turned** his face to the wall and **prayed**
2 Chr	6.24	when they **turn** to you...humbly **praying**
	6.26	**repent** and face this Temple...**praying**
	6.37	**repent** and **pray** to you, **confessing**
	6.38	sincerely **repent** and **pray** to you
	7.14	**pray** to me and **repent** and **turn** away
Ezra	10.1	in **prayer**...weeping and **confessing**
Ps	55.1	my **prayer**, O God; don't **turn** away
	78.34	**turn** to him; they would **repent** and **pray**
Is	19.22	**turn** to him...he will hear their **prayers**
	38.2	**turned** his face to the wall and **prayed**
	55.6	**Turn** to the Lord and **pray** to him,
	64.7	No one **turns** to you in **prayer**
Jer	36.7	they will **pray** to the Lord and **turn**
Dan	9.4	I **prayed** to...God and **confessed** the sins
	9.20	I went on **praying**, **confessing** my sins
Jas	5.16	**confess** your sins to one another and **pray**

Spirit

1 Cor	14.14	my **spirit prays** indeed, but my mind
	14.15	**pray** with my **spirit**, but I will **pray** also

Spirit of God

Rom	8.26	we ought to **pray**; the **Spirit** himself
	15.30	**Spirit** gives: join me in **praying** fervently

Eph	6.18	**Pray** on every occasion, as the **Spirit**
Jude	.20	**Pray** in the power of the **Holy Spirit**,

Trouble

1 Sam	1.15	been **praying**, pouring out my **troubles**
2 Chr	20.9	They could **pray** to you in their **trouble**,
Ps	77.2	In times of **trouble** I **pray** to the Lord;
Rom	12.12	be patient in your **troubles**, and **pray**
Jas	5.13	among you in **trouble**? He should **pray**

Turn see Repent

Watch

Mt	26.41	**watch** and **pray** that you will not fall
Mk	14.38	**watch**, and **pray** that you will not fall

PREACH

see also PROCLAIM

Acts	13.5	—	20.25	x19
Acts	8.4	—	10.42	x10
Gal	1.8	—	2.7	x9
Mk	1.4	—	4.33	x7
Mt	9.35	—	12.41	x6
Rom	1.1	—	2.21	x5
Lk	3.3	—	4.44	x4
Lk	7.22	—	9.6	x4
1 Cor	9.14–18			x4
1 Cor	15.1–14			x4
2 Cor	10.16	—	11.7	x4
1 Tim	3.16	—	6.2	x4
1 Pet	3.19	—	4.11	x4
Mt	3.1	—	4.23	x3
Mk	16.15–20			x3
Acts	5.42	—	6.4	x3
2 Cor	4.3–5			x3
Gal	4.13	—	5.11	x3
Phil	1.14–18			x3
1 Thes	2.9	—	3.2	x3
2 Thes	2.2–15			x3

Good News see Message

Kingdom

Mt	4.23	**preaching**...about the **Kingdom**,
	9.35	**preached**...about the **Kingdom**,
	10.7	and **preach**, 'The **Kingdom** of heaven
	24.14	about the **Kingdom** will be **preached**
Lk	4.43	I must **preach**...about the **Kingdom**
	8.1	**preaching**...about the **Kingdom**
	9.2	sent them out to **preach** the **Kingdom**
Acts	20.25	**preaching** the **Kingdom** of God.
	28.31	**preached** about the **Kingdom** of God

Message, Good News, Turn, Word

Mt	4.17	Jesus began to **preach** his **message**
	4.23	**preaching** the **Good News** about the
	9.35	**preached** the **Good News** about the
	11.5	the **Good News** is **preached** to the poor.
	11.12	**preached** his **message** until this very
	24.14	this **Good News**...will be **preached**
Mk	1.4	**preaching**. "**Turn** away from your sins
	1.14	**preached** the **Good News** from God.
	2.2	was **preaching** the **message** to them
	4.33	Jesus **preached** his **message** to the people
	6.12	**preached** that people should **turn** away
Lk	3.3	**preaching**, "**Turn** away from your sins
	3.18	**preached** the **Good News** to the people
	4.43	I must **preach** the **Good News**
	7.22	the **Good News** is **preached** to the poor.
	8.1	**preaching** the **Good News** about the
	9.6	**preaching** the **Good News** and healing
	20.1	people and **preaching** the **Good News**,
Acts	1.21	John **preached** his **message** of baptism
	5.42	and **preach** the **Good News** about Jesus
	6.2	to neglect the **preaching** of God's **word**

Acts	8.4	**preaching** the **message**.
	8.25	**preached** the **Good News** in many
	8.40	**preached** the **Good News** in every town.
	10.37	after John **preached** his **message**
	13.5	they **preached** the **word** of God
	13.38	**message** about forgiveness of sins is **preached**
	14.7	There they **preached** the **Good News**.
	14.21	**preached** the **Good News** in Derbe
	14.25	they **preached** the **message** in Perga
	15.7	among you to **preach** the **Good News**
	15.21	his **words** are **preached** in every town.
	15.35	and **preached** the **word** of the Lord.
	15.36	we **preached** the **word** of the Lord,
	16.6	**preach** the **message** in the province of
	16.10	had called us to **preach** the **Good News**
	16.32	they **preached** the **word** of the Lord
	17.13	had **preached** the **word** of God in Berea
	18.5	whole time to **preaching** the **message**,
Rom	1.1	by God to **preach** his **Good News**.
	1.9	**preaching** the **Good News** about his
	1.15	to **preach** the **Good News** to you also
	2.16	according to the **Good News** I **preach**,
	10.8	the **message** of faith that we **preach**.
	10.17	**message** comes through **preaching** Christ.
	15.16	in **preaching** the **Good News** from God,
	16.25	**Good News** I **preach** about Jesus Christ
1 Cor	1.21	so-called "foolish" **message** we **preach**,
	9.18	privilege of **preaching** the **Good News**
	15.1	**Good News** which I **preached** to you,
	15.2	the **message** that I **preached** to you.
2 Cor	2.12	in Troas to **preach** the **Good News**
	10.16	**preach** the **Good News** in other
	11.7	I **preached** the **Good News** of God
Gal	1.16	**preach** the **Good News** about him
	2.2	the gospel **message** that I **preach**
Eph	2.17	and **preached** the **Good News** of peace
Phil	1.14	to **preach** the **message** fearlessly.
	4.15	early days of **preaching** the **Good News**,
Col	4.3	to **preach** his **message** about the secret
1 Thes	2.9	**preached** to you the **Good News** from
	2.16	**preaching** to the Gentiles the **message**
	3.2	**preaching** the **Good News** about Christ.
2 Thes	2.14	the **Good News** we **preached** to you;
2 Tim	2.8	is taught in the **Good News** I **preach**.
	2.9	I **preach** the **Good News**, I suffer
	4.2	to **preach** the **message**
	4.5	work of a **preacher** of the **Good News**,
1 Pet	4.6	is why the **Good News** was **preached**
	4.11	**preaches** must **preach** God's **messages**

Teach

Mt	4.23	**teaching** in the synagogues, **preaching**
	9.35	**taught** in the synagogues, **preached**
	11.1	and went off to **teach** and **preach**
Lk	20.1	**teaching** the people and **preaching**
Acts	5.42	to **teach** and **preach** the **Good News**
	15.35	they **taught** and **preached** the **word**
	20.20	I **preached** and **taught** in public
	28.31	He **preached** about the Kingdom of God and **taught**
2 Thes	2.15	**taught** you, both in our **preaching** and
1 Tim	4.13	and to **preaching** and **teaching**.
	5.17	work hard at **preaching** and **teaching**.
	6.2	You must **teach** and **preach** these things.
2 Tim	2.8	is **taught** in the **Good News** I **preach**.

Turn see **Message**

Word see **Message**

PRESENCE

	Ezek	40.1	— 44.15	x9
	Ex	27.21	— 29.43	x6
	Judg	20.1	— 21.5	x6

	Ex	33.16	— 34.10	x5
	Ezek	8.4	— 11.22	x5
	Gen	43.3	— 44.26	x4
	Lev	24.3 – 8		x4
	Deut	12.5 – 18		x4
	Deut	14.23	— 16.11	x4
	Deut	25.9	— 27.7	x4
	Ex	16.7	— 17.6	x3
	Ex	40.25 – 38		x3
	Lev	9.6	— 10.2	x3
	Num	14.10 – 22		x3
	Num	19.3	— 20.6	x3
	Deut	31.7	— 32.51	x3
	2 Chr	5.11	— 7.1	x3
	Ps	68.2 – 4		x3
	Jer	28.1 – 11		x3
	Lk	23.14	— 24.43	x3
	Eph	2.18	— 4.10	x3
	1 Thes	2.19	— 3.13	x3

Christ, Jesus

2 Cor	2.10	I do it in **Christ's presence**
	2.17	in his **presence**, as servants of **Christ**.
	12.19	as **Christ** would wish...in the **presence**
1 Thes	2.19	in the **presence** of our Lord **Jesus**
1 Tim	5.21	In the **presence** of...**Christ Jesus**
2 Tim	4.1	In the **presence** of...**Christ Jesus**,

Dazzling see Light

Father

Mt	18.10	are always in the **presence** of my **Father**
Jn	17.5	**Father**! Give me glory in your **presence**
Eph	2.18	into the **presence** of the **Father**.
1 Thes	3.13	in the **presence** of our God and **Father**
Rev	3.5	**presence** of my **Father** and of his angels

Holy

Ex	28.30	when he comes into my **holy presence**.
	29.11	Kill the bull there in my **holy presence**
	29.43	my **presence** will make the place **holy**.
Col	1.22	**holy**...and faultless, into his **presence**.
1 Thes	3.13	and **holy** in the **presence** of our God

Jesus see Christ

Joy

Deut	12.12	Be **joyful** there in his **presence**,
	16.11	Be **joyful** in the Lord's **presence**,
Ps	16.11	your **presence** fills me with **joy**
	17.15	your **presence** will fill me with **joy**.
	21.6	and your **presence** fills him with **joy**.
	68.3	in his **presence**; they...shout for **joy**.
Prov	8.30	of **joy**, always happy in his **presence**
Acts	2.28	and your **presence** will fill me with **joy**.
1 Thes	3.9	him for the **joy** we have in his **presence**
Jude	.24	and **joyful** before his glorious **presence**

Light, Dazzling

Ex	16.7	**dazzling light** of the Lord's **presence**.
	24.16	**dazzling light** of the Lord's **presence**
	29.43	and the **dazzling light** of my **presence**
	33.18	see the **dazzling light** of your **presence**.
	33.22	When the **dazzling light** of my **presence**
	40.34	**dazzling light** of the Lord's **presence**
Lev	9.6	that the **dazzling light** of his **presence**
Num	14.10	the **dazzling light** of the Lord's **presence**
	14.22	seen the **dazzling light** of my **presence**
	16.19	the **dazzling light** of the Lord's **presence**
	16.42	the **dazzling light** of the Lord's **presence**
	20.6	the **dazzling light** of the Lord's **presence**
1 Kgs	8.11	**dazzling light** of the Lord's **presence**,
2 Chr	5.11	**dazzling light** of the Lord's **presence**,
	7.1	the **dazzling light** of the Lord's **presence**
Ps	56.13	in the **presence** of God, in the **light**
Ezek	1.28	**dazzling light** that shows the **presence**

173

Ezek	8.4	**dazzling light** that shows the **presence**
	9.3	Then the **dazzling light** of the **presence**
	10.4	**dazzling light** of the Lord's **presence**
	10.18	the **dazzling light** of the Lord's **presence**
	11.22	**dazzling light** of the **presence** of the
	43.2	**dazzling light** of the **presence** of the
	44.4	with the **dazzling light** of his **presence**.
2 Thes	2.8	destroy him with his **dazzling presence**.

Powerful

Ezek	3.22	I felt the **powerful presence** of the Lord
	33.22	felt the **powerful presence** of the Lord.
	37.1	I felt the **powerful presence** of the Lord
	40.1	I felt the **powerful presence** of the Lord,

Spirit of God

Ps	51.11	**presence**; do not take your **holy spirit**
Ezek	37.1	**presence** of the Lord, and his **spirit**
Rom	8.11	by the **presence** of his **Spirit** in you.
1 Cor	12.7	**Spirit's presence** is shown in some way
Eph	2.18	come in the one **Spirit** into the **presence**

Temple

2 Kgs	19.14	to the **Temple**, placed the letter there in the **presence**
2 Chr	7.1	Lord's **presence** filled the **Temple**.
Is	37.14	to the **Temple**, placed the letter there in the **presence**
Jer	7.10	in my **presence**, in my own **Temple**,
	34.15	covenant in my **presence**, in the **Temple**
Ezek	10.18	**presence** left the entrance of the **Temple**
Jon	2.4	from your **presence** and would never see your holy **Temple**

PRIDE

Is	2.11	—	5.15	x7
Jer	48.29	—	50.32	x6
Ps	119.21	−	85	x5
Ezek	30.6	−	33.28	x5
1 Cor	4.6	−	5.6	x5
Is	13.2	−	19	x4
Rom	11.13	−	12.16	x4
2 Cor	12.7	−	20	x4
Phil	1.26	−	4.1	x4
Neh	9.16	−	29	x3
Job	40.10	−	41.34	x3
Ps	10.2	−	4	x3
Ps	73.3	−	8	x3
Prov	10.1	−	12.4	x3
Prov	16.18	−	17.6	x3
Prov	23.16	−	25	x3
Is	9.9	−	10.33	x3
Is	28.1	−	4	x3
Jer	13.9	−	20	x3
Ezek	16.49	−	56	x3
Ezek	28.2	−	17	x3
Dan	7.8	−	8.25	x3
Zeph	2.10	−	3.11	x3

Arrogant, Boast, Conceited

1 Sam	2.3	your loud **boasting**; silence your **proud**
Ps	31.18	all the **proud** and **arrogant**
	94.4	longer will criminals be **proud** and **boast**
	101.5	who is **proud** and **arrogant**.
	131.1	given up my **pride** and...my **arrogance**.
Prov	8.13	I hate **pride** and **arrogance**,
	16.18	**Pride** leads to destruction, and **arrogance**
	21.24	you someone who is **arrogant**, **proud**,
Is	2.11	**pride** will be ended...**arrogance** destroyed.
	2.12	everyone who is **proud** and **conceited**.
	2.17	Human **pride** will be ended...**arrogance**
	9.9	Now they are **proud** and **arrogant**.
	10.12	for all his **boasting** and all his **pride**.
	13.11	**proud** and punish everyone...**arrogant**
Jer	48.29	I have heard how **proud**, **arrogant**,
Dan	7.8	a mouth that was **boasting proudly**.

Dan	7.20	a mouth and was **boasting proudly**.
Zeph	2.10	punished for their **pride** and **arrogance**
	3.11	everyone who is **proud** and **arrogant**,
Rom	1.30	insolent, **proud**, and **boastful**;
1 Cor	13.4	it is not jealous or **conceited** or **proud**;
Jas	4.16	now you are **proud**, and you **boast**;

Cruel see Evil

Deceive

Jer	49.16	Your **pride** has **deceived** you.
Dan	8.25	in his **deceitful** ways. He will be **proud**
Obad	.3	Your **pride** has **deceived** you.
Hab	2.5	is **deceitful**. Greedy men are **proud**
Mk	7.22	**deceit**, indecency, jealousy, slander, **pride**,

Evil, Cruel, Wicked

Job	35.12	for they are **proud** and **evil** men.
Ps	5.5	**proud** men; you hate all **wicked** people.
	10.2	The **wicked** are **proud** and persecute
	10.3	**wicked** man is **proud** of his **evil** desires;
	36.11	let **proud** men attack me or **wicked** men
	54.3	**Proud** men are coming...**cruel** men
	73.8	**evil** things; they are **proud** and make
Prov	8.13	I hate **pride** and **arrogance**, **evil** ways
Dan	5.20	he became **proud**, stubborn, and **cruel**,
Mal	3.15	**proud** people...are happy. **Evil** men
	4.1	all **proud** and **evil** people will burn

Happy see Joy

Hate

Ps	5.5	**proud** men; you **hate** all wicked people.
Prov	6.16	**hates** and cannot tolerate: A **proud**
	8.13	I **hate** **pride** and arrogance,
Amos	6.8	I **hate** the **pride** of the people of Israel;
Rom	1.30	are **hateful** to God, insolent, **proud**,

Joy, Happy

Ps	106.5	in the **happiness**...in the glad **pride**
Prov	12.4	wife is her husband's **pride** and **joy**
	23.24	**happy**. You can take **pride** in a wise
	23.25	**proud**...give your mother that **happiness**.
Jer	33.9	source of **joy**, honour, and **pride** to me;
Ezek	24.25	Temple that was their **pride** and **joy**,
Mal	3.15	**proud** people...are **happy**.
2 Cor	12.9	most **happy**, then, to be **proud**
Phil	4.1	**happy** you make me, and how **proud**
1 Thes	2.20	you are our **pride** and our **joy**!

Plan

Ps	73.8	are **proud** and make **plans** to oppress
Is	23.9	**planned** it...to put an end to their **pride**
Lk	1.51	scattered the **proud** with all their **plans**.

Wicked see Evil

PRIESTS

Lev	12.6	—	17.6	x78
Lev	1.5	—	10.14	x64
Neh	7.39	—	13.30	x43
Heb	5.6	—	10.21	x31
Ezek	40.45	—	46.20	x30
Num	3.3	—	6.20	x29
Lev	21.1	—	24.9	x26
Ezra	6.9	—	10.18	x26
Ex	28.1	—	32.29	x24
2 Chr	29.4	—	31.19	x24
Judg	17.5	—	18.30	x15
1 Sam	1.3	—	2.36	x15
2 Kgs	10.11	—	12.16	x14
2 Chr	4.6	—	8.15	x14
Josh	3.3	—	4.18	x13
Deut	17.9	—	21.5	x12
2 Chr	22.11	—	24.25	x12
Ezra	1.5	—	3.12	x12
1 Sam	21.1	—	23.9	x11
1 Kgs	1.7	—	2.35	x11

174

2 Chr	34.5 — 36.14	x11
Josh	6.4 – 20	x10
2 Kgs	22.4 — 23.20	x10
Ex	38.21 — 40.15	x9
Jer	26.7 — 29.26	x9
Lev	27.8 – 23	x8
Num	18.1 — 20.28	x8
1 Chr	23.2 — 24.31	x8
Josh	21.1 — 22.31	x7
Mal	1.6 — 3.3	x7
2 Chr	13.9 – 14	x6
1 Sam	14.3 – 36	x5
2 Chr	26.17 – 20	x5
Lk	1.5, – 9	x5
Num	27.2 – 22	x4
1 Kgs	8.3 – 10	x4
1 Chr	9.2 – 30	x4
Ezek	48.10 – 21	x4
Ex	35.19 – 21	x3
Num	31.6 – 29	x3
Deut	10.6 – 9	x3
2 Sam	15.24 – 35	x3
1 Kgs	4.2 – 5	x3
2 Chr	11.13 – 15	x3
Jer	23.11 – 34	x3
Hag	2.11 – 13	x3

Altar

Ex	28.43	the **altar** to serve as **priests** in the Holy
Lev	1.7	**priests**...arrange firewood on the **altar**.
	1.9	**priest** will burn...sacrifice on the **altar**.
	1.11	**priests**...throw its blood on...the **altar**.
	1.15	The **priest** shall present it at the **altar**,
	2.8	the **priest**, who will take it to the **altar**.
	3.5	**priests** shall burn all this on the **altar**
	3.11	**priest** shall burn all this on the **altar**
	3.16	**priest** shall burn all this on the **altar**
	7.5	**priest** shall burn all the fat on the **altar**
	7.31	**priest** shall burn the fat on the **altar**,
	16.33	the **altar**, the **priests**,
Num	3.31	the **altars**, the utensils the **priests** use
	15.28	At the **altar** the **priest** shall perform
	18.7	**priesthood** that concern the **altar**
1 Sam	2.28	to be my **priests**, to serve at the **altar**,
1 Kgs	13.2	the **priests** serving at the pagan **altars**
	13.33	to choose **priests**...to serve at the **altars**
2 Kgs	23.20	the pagan **priests** on the **altars**
2 Chr	30.16	**priests**, who sprinkled it on the **altar**.
	34.5	bones of the pagan **priests** on the **altars**
	35.11	**priests** sprinkled the blood on the **altar**.
Ezek	40.46	for the **priests** who served at the **altar**.
	43.26	**priests** are to consecrate the **altar**
	43.27	**priests** are to begin offering on the **altar**
Joel	1.13	you **priests** who serve at the **altar**!
	2.17	The **priests**, serving...between the **altar**

Anoint see **Consecrate**

Bless

Deut	10.8	as **priests**, and to pronounce **blessings**
2 Chr	6.41	**Bless** your **priests** in all they do,
	30.27	**priests** and the Levites asked the Lord's **blessing**
Ps	115.12	**bless** the people of Israel and all the **priests**
	132.16	I will **bless** her **priests** in all they do,

Blood see **Offer**

Clean see **Pure**

Consecrate, Anoint, Dedicate, Holy, Ordain, Sacred

Ex	28.3	so that he may be **dedicated** as a **priest**
	29.1	and his sons to **dedicate** them as **priests**
	29.27	When a **priest** is **ordained**
	30.30	**ordain** them as **priests** in my service.
	32.29	have **consecrated** yourselves as **priests**

Ex	35.19	**sacred** clothes for Aaron the **priest**
	39.41	**sacred** clothes for Aaron the **priest**
	40.13	**priestly** garments...and...**consecrate** him,
	40.15	**anoint** them...can serve me as **priests**.
Lev	2.3	belongs to the **priests**; it is very **holy**,
	2.10	belongs to the **priests**; it is very **holy**,
	6.20	the **ordination** of an Aaronite **priest**.
	7.35	were **ordained** as **priests**.
	8.2	the **priestly** garments, the **anointing** oil,
	8.22	for the **ordination** of **priests**,
	14.13	belongs to the **priest** and is very **holy**.
	16.32	**Priest**, properly **ordained** and **consecrated**
	21.8	The people must consider the **priest** holy
	21.10	**consecrated** to wear the **priestly**
	22.10	**priestly** family may eat any of the **sacred**
	22.12	a **priest** may not eat any of the **sacred**
	22.14	**priestly** family eats any of the **sacred**
	22.15	The **priests** shall not profane the **sacred**
Num	3.3	were **anointed** and **ordained** as **priests**,
	4.20	**priests** preparing the **sacred** objects
	6.20	a **sacred** offering for the **priest**,
	31.6	**priest**, who took charge of the **sacred**
Judg	18.20	**priest** very happy, so he took the **sacred**
1 Sam	21.6	the **priest** gave David the **sacred** bread
1 Kgs	13.33	He **ordained** as **priest** anyone
2 Kgs	10.22	the **priest** in charge of the **sacred**
	23.5	**priests** that the kings of Judah had **ordained**
1 Chr	29.22	they **anointed**...Zadok as **priest**.
2 Chr	13.9	can get himself **consecrated** as a **priest**
	23.11	the **priest** and his sons **anointed** Joash,
Ezek	43.26	the **priests** are to **consecrate** the altar
	45.4	**holy**...country, set aside for the **priests**
	46.19	These are **holy** rooms for the **priests**.
	48.10	**priests** are to have a portion of this **holy**
	48.11	This **holy** area is to be for the **priests**
Zeph	3.4	the **priests** defile what is **sacred**,
1 Pet	2.5	where you will serve as **holy priests**
	2.9	the King's **priests**, the **holy** nation,

Contribution see **Gift**

Dedicate see **Consecrate**

Defile see **Unclean**

Dove see **Offer**

Duty

Num	3.7	and perform **duties** for the **priests**
	3.10	carry out the **duties** of the **priesthood**;
Deut	17.12	**priest** on **duty** is to be put to death;
2 Kgs	12.9	**priests** on **duty** at the entrance put in
	22.4	of money that the **priests** on **duty**
	23.4	assistant **priests**, and the guards on **duty**
1 Chr	23.28	the following **duties**: to help the **priests**
	28.13	the **priests**...to perform their **duties**,
	28.21	**priests**...have been assigned **duties**
2 Chr	13.10	**Priests**...perform their **duties**,
	23.4	the **priests** and Levites come on **duty**
	23.6	**priests** and the Levites who are on **duty**.
	31.17	The **priests** were assigned their **duties**
	35.2	**priests** the **duties** they were to perform
Neh	10.39	and where the **priests** who are on **duty**,
Mal	2.7	**duty** of **priests** to teach the true

Gift, Contribution, Special, Tithe

Ex	29.27	**special gift** and set aside for the **priests**.
Lev	7.14	**contribution**...belongs to the **priest**
	9.21	**special gift** to the Lord for the **priests**,
	10.14	**special contribution**...for the **priests**.
	14.12	a **special gift** to the Lord for the **priest**.
	14.21	a **special gift** to the Lord for the **priest**.
	14.24	a **special gift** to the Lord for the **priest**.
	23.20	**special gift** to the Lord for the **priests**.
Num	6.20	**priest** shall present them as a **special gift**
	18.7	given you the **gift** of the **priesthood**.

Num 18.28 **special contribution**...to Aaron the **priest**.
    31.29 to...the **priest** as a **special contribution**,
2 Chr 31.9 **priests** and the Levites about these **gifts**,
    35.8 **contributions** for the people, the **priests**,
Neh 12.44 the **contributions** for the **priests**
    13.5 offerings for the **priests**, and the **tithes**
Heb 8.4 are **priests** who offer the **gifts** required

God's People
Jer 23.33 **my people** or a prophet or a **priest** asks
    23.34 of **my people** or a prophet or a **priest**
Ezek 44.23 The **priests** are to teach **my people**
1 Pet 2.9 King's **priests...God's own people**,

Gods, Idols
Judg 18.24 my **priest** and the **gods** that I made,
2 Kgs 11.18 the **idols**, and killed Mattan, the **priest**
2 Chr 13.9 as a **priest** of those so-called **gods**
    23.17 **idols** there and killed Mattan, the **priest**
Hos 10.5 the **priests** who serve the **idol** will weep
Acts 14.13 The **priest** of the **god** Zeus

Holy see **Consecrate**

Holy Place
Ex 28.43 as **priests** in the **Holy Place**,
    35.19 **priests** are to wear when they serve in the **Holy Place**
    39.1 **priests** were to wear when they served in the **Holy Place**.
    39.41 **priests** were to wear in the **Holy Place**
Num 3.31 the **priests** use in the **Holy Place**,

Idols see **Gods**

Incense see **Worship**

Lamb see **Offer**

Law, Regulation, Scholar
Lev 5.10 the **regulations**. In this way the **priest**
    22.9 All **priests** shall observe the **regulations**
Num 6.20 ram which by **law** belong to the **priest**.
Deut 31.9 **Law** and gave it to the levitical **priests**,
1 Sam 2.13 **regulations** concerning what the **priests**
2 Chr 15.3 without **priests** to teach them, and without a **law**.
Ezra 7.11 the **priest** and **scholar**,
    7.12 to Ezra the **priest**, **scholar** in the **Law**
    7.21 **priest** and **scholar** in the **Law** of the
Neh 8.1 **priest** and **scholar** of the **Law** which the
    8.9 Ezra, the **priest** and **scholar** of the **Law**,
    9.34 and **priests** have not kept your **Law**.
    12.26 **priest** who was a **scholar** of the **Law**.
    12.44 **priests** and the Levites which the **Law**
    13.13 a **priest**; Zadok, a **scholar** of the **Law**;
    13.30 I prepared **regulations** for the **priests**
Ezek 22.26 **priests** break my **law** and have no
Mic 3.11 the **priests** interpret the **Law** for pay,
Mt 12.5 **priests**...break the Sabbath **law**,
Mk 2.26 According to our **Law** only the **priests**
Lk 6.4 our **Law** for anyone except the **priests**
Heb 7.5 **priests** are commanded by the **Law**
    7.11 of the levitical **priesthood** that the **Law**
    7.16 a **priest**, not by human...**regulations**,

Levites
Deut 17.9 present your case to the **levitical priests**
    17.18 copy kept by the **levitical priests**.
    18.7 a **priest** of...God, like the other **Levites**
    21.5 The **levitical priests** are to go there also,
    24.8 exactly what the **levitical priests** tell you;
    27.9 together with the **levitical priests**,
    31.9 and gave it to the **levitical priests**,
    31.25 he said to the **levitical priests**,
Josh 8.33 facing the **levitical priests** who carried it.
    21.1 leaders of the **Levite** families went to Eleazar the **priest**,

Judg 17.13 I have a **Levite** as my **priest**,
2 Sam 15.24 the **priest** was there, and with him were the **Levites**
1 Kgs 8.4 The **Levites** and the **priests** also moved
1 Chr 9.2 **priests**, **Levites**, and temple workmen.
    13.2 the **priests** and **Levites** in their towns,
    15.11 the **priests**...and the six **Levites**,
    15.14 **priests** and the **Levites** purified
    23.2 leaders and all the **priests** and **Levites**.
    24.6 **priestly** families and of the **Levite**
    24.31 families of the **priests** and of the **Levites**
    28.13 **priests** and **Levites** to perform their
    28.21 **priests** and the **Levites** have been
2 Chr 5.5 The **priests** and the **Levites** also moved
    8.14 the **Levites** who assisted the **priests**
    8.15 given the **priests** and the **Levites**
    11.13 **priests** and **Levites** came south to Judah.
    13.9 **priests**...and you drove out the **Levites**.
    17.8 by nine **Levites** and two **priests**.
    19.8 Jehoshaphat appointed **Levites**, **priests**
    23.4 the **priests** and **Levites** come on duty
    23.6 **priests** and the **Levites** who are on duty.
    23.18 put the **priests** and **Levites** in charge
    24.5 **priests** and the **Levites** to go to the
    29.4 assembled a group of **priests** and **Levites**
    29.34 **priests** to kill...these animals, the **Levites**
    30.15 **priests** and **Levites** who were not ritually
    30.21 the **Levites** and the **priests** praised
    30.25 the **priests**, the **Levites**,
    30.27 **priests** and the **Levites** asked the Lord's
    31.2 organization of the **priests** and **Levites**,
    31.4 the **priests** and the **Levites** were entitled,
    31.9 spoke to the **priests** and the **Levites**
    34.30 by the **priests** and the **Levites**
    35.8 the **priests**, and the **Levites** to use.
    35.10 **priests** and the **Levites** took their places,
    35.11 **Levites** skinned them, and the **priests**
    35.18 the **priests**, the **Levites**,
Ezra 1.5 the **priests** and **Levites**,
    2.70 The **priests**, the **Levites**
    3.8 the **priests**, and the **Levites**,
    3.12 Many of the older **priests**, **Levites**,
    6.16 of Israel — the **priests**, the **Levites**,
    6.18 organized the **priests** and the **Levites**
    6.20 **priests** and the **Levites** had purified
    7.6 Israelites which included **priests**, **Levites**,
    7.13 **priests**, and **Levites** that so desire
    7.24 any taxes from the **priests**, **Levites**,
    8.15 **priests** in the group, but no **Levites**.
    8.29 leaders of the **priests** and of the **Levites**
    8.30 the **priests** and the **Levites** took charge
    9.1 **priests**, and the **Levites** had not kept
    10.5 the leaders of the **priests**, of the **Levites**,
Neh 7.73 The **priests**, the **Levites**
    8.9 Ezra, the **priest**...and the **Levites**
    8.13 with the **priests** and the **Levites**,
    9.38 **Levites**, and our **priests** put their seals
    10.28 the **priests**, the **Levites**,
    10.34 **priests**, and **Levites**,
    11.3 the **priests**, the **Levites**,
    11.20 **priests** and **Levites** lived on their own
    12.1 **priests** and **Levites** who returned from
    12.22 **Levite** families and of the **priestly**
    12.30 **priests** and the **Levites** performed ritual
    12.44 for the **priests** and the **Levites**
    12.47 **Levites** gave the...portion to the **priests**.
    13.29 made with the **priests** and the **Levites**.
    13.30 for the **priests** and the **Levites**
Is 66.21 make some of them **priests** and **Levites**.
Ezek 48.21 the **priests'** land, the **Levites'** land,
Jn 1.19 **priests** and **Levites** to John, to ask him,
Heb 7.11 on the basis of the **levitical priesthood**

Offer, Blood, Dove, Lamb, Present, Sacrifice, Sheep

Ex	29.14	offering to take away the sins of the priests.
Lev	1.5	Aaronite priests shall present the blood
	1.9	priest will burn the whole sacrifice
	1.11	and the priests shall throw its blood
	1.13	the priest will present the sacrifice
	1.15	The priest shall present it at the altar,
	2.3	the grain-offering belongs to the priests;
	2.8	offering to the Lord and present it to the priest,
	2.10	of the offering belongs to the priests;
	3.2	Aaronite priests shall throw the blood
	3.8	The priests shall throw its blood
	3.13	The priests shall throw its blood
	4.25	priest shall dip his finger in the blood
	4.26	the priest shall offer the sacrifice
	4.30	priest shall dip his finger in the blood
	4.31	the priest shall offer the sacrifice
	4.34	priest shall dip his finger in the blood
	4.35	the priest shall offer the sacrifice
	5.6	sheep or goat as an offering. The priest shall offer the sacrifice
	5.8	priest, who will first offer the bird
	5.10	the priest shall offer the sacrifice
	5.13	the priest shall offer the sacrifice
	5.16	the priest shall offer the animal
	5.18	to the priest as a repayment-offering
	6.6	to the priest as his repayment-offering
	6.7	The priest shall offer the sacrifice
	6.14	priest shall present the grain-offering
	6.16	to the priests as their part of the food-offerings.
	6.20	Aaronite priest...shall present
	6.23	No part of a grain-offering that a priest
	6.26	The priest who sacrifices the animal
	6.29	priestly families may eat this offering;
	7.7	the priest who offers the sacrifice.
	7.8	the priest who offers the sacrifice.
	7.9	the priest who has offered it to God.
	7.14	to the priest who takes the blood
	7.33	to the priest who offers the blood
	12.7	The priest shall present her offering
	12.8	sin-offering, and the priest shall perform
	14.11	priest shall take the man and these offerings
	14.12	priest shall take one of the male lambs
	14.13	sin-offering, belongs to the priest
	14.14	priest shall take...the blood of the lamb
	14.19	the priest shall offer the sin-offering
	14.24	The priest shall take the lamb
	15.15	priest shall offer one of them
	15.29	two doves or two pigeons to the priest
	15.30	the priest shall offer one of them
	17.6	The priest shall throw the blood
	21.8	priest holy, because he presents the food-offerings
	21.21	priest who has any...defect may present
	22.10	priestly family may eat any of the sacred offerings;
	22.14	priestly family eats any of the sacred offerings
	22.15	priests shall not profane the sacred offerings
	23.11	The priest shall present it the day after
	23.20	The priest shall present the bread ...the two lambs
	24.9	food offered to the Lord for the priests.
Num	5.9	offer to the Lord belongs to the priest
	5.10	Each priest shall keep the offerings
	5.25	the priest shall take the offering of flour
	6.10	two doves or two pigeons to the priest

Num	6.11	priest shall offer one as a sin-offering
	6.16	The priest shall present all these
	6.20	they are a sacred offering for the priest,
Deut	17.9	present your case to the levitical priests
	18.3	sheep are sacrificed, the priests are to be
1 Sam	2.13	offering his sacrifice, the priest's servant
1 Kgs	13.2	priests serving at the pagan altars who offer
2 Kgs	23.5	priests who offered sacrifices to Baal,
2 Chr	29.22	priests killed the bulls...then the sheep
	29.24	priests killed the goats and poured their blood
	29.35	sacrifices...burnt whole, the priests
	30.16	the blood of the sacrifices to the priests,
	31.4	the offerings to which the priests
	35.8	priests two thousand six hundred lambs
	35.11	and the priests sprinkled the blood
Ezra	2.63	offered to God until there was a priest
Neh	7.65	offered to God until there was a priest
	13.5	the offerings for the priests,
Ezek	42.13	the priests will place the holiest offerings
	43.27	priests are to begin offering on the altar
	44.29	repayment-offerings will be the priests'
	44.30	the priests the first loaf as an offering
	45.19	priest will take some of the blood of this sin-offering
	46.2	priests burn his sacrifices whole and offer
	46.20	priests are to boil the meat offered
Joel	1.9	priests mourn because they have no offerings
Heb	7.27	high priests; he does not need to offer
	8.3	our High Priest must...have something to offer.
	8.4	there are priests who offer the gifts
	10.11	priest performs his services every day and offers
1 Pet	2.5	you will serve as holy priests to offer

Ordain see Consecrate

Praise see Worship

Present see Offer

Pure, Clean, Take Away (sin)

Ex	19.22	priests who come near me must purify
	29.14	to take away the sins of the priests.
Lev	12.8	priest shall perform the ritual to take
	13.7	priest has...pronounced him clean,
	13.17	the priest shall pronounce him clean.
	13.23	the priest shall pronounce him...clean.
	13.28	The priest shall pronounce him...clean,
	13.37	the priest shall pronounce him...clean.
	14.2	pronounced clean...brought to the priest,
	14.4	the priest shall order two...clean birds
	14.20	priest...perform the ritual of purification,
	14.23	of his purification he shall bring them to the priest
	14.31	priest...perform the ritual of purification.
	16.32	Priest...perform the ritual of purification.
	19.22	priest...perform the ritual of purification
Num	15.25	priest...perform the ritual of purification
	15.28	priest...perform the ritual of purification
1 Chr	15.14	priests and the Levites purified
2 Chr	29.16	priests went inside the Temple to purify
	29.34	more priests had made themselves...clean.
	30.1	because not enough priests were...clean
	30.15	The priests...who were not ritually clean
	30.24	number of priests went through the ritual of purification.
Ezra	6.20	priests and the Levites had purified
Neh	12.30	priests...performed ritual purification
Mal	3.3	Lord's messenger will purify the priests,

Regulation see Law

Ritual

Lev	12.8	the **priest** shall perform the **ritual**
	14.20	the **priest** shall perform the **ritual**
	14.31	the **priest** shall perform the **ritual**
	16.32	**High Priest**...is to perform the **ritual**
	19.22	the **priest** shall perform the **ritual**
Num	5.29	the **priest** shall perform this **ritual**.
	15.25	The **priest** shall perform the **ritual**
	15.28	the **priest** shall perform the **ritual**
2 Chr	30.24	of **priests** went through the **ritual**
Neh	12.30	**priests** and the Levites performed **ritual**

Sacred see **Consecrate**

Sacrifice see **Offer**

Scholar see **Law**

Serve

Ex	19.6	and you will **serve** me as **priests**.
	28.1	so that they may **serve** me as **priests**.
	28.3	dedicated as a **priest** in my **service**.
	28.4	so that they can **serve** me as **priests**.
	28.35	wear this robe when he **serves** as **priest**.
	28.41	so that they may **serve** me as **priests**.
	28.43	to **serve** as **priests** in the Holy Place,
	29.1	dedicate them as **priests** in my **service**.
	29.9	descendants are to **serve** me as **priests**
	29.44	his sons apart to **serve** me as **priests**.
	30.30	ordain them as **priests** in my **service**.
	31.10	to use when they **serve** as **priests**,
	32.29	as **priests** in the **service** of the Lord
	35.19	**priests** are to wear when they **serve**
	39.1	**priests** were to wear when they **served**
	40.13	so that he can **serve** me as **priest**.
	40.15	so that they can **serve** me as **priest**.
Num	3.4	Eleazar and Ithamar **served** as **priests**
	3.6	them as **servants** of Aaron the **priest**.
	18.1	of **service** in the **priesthood**.
Deut	10.8	**serve** him as **priests**, and to pronounce
	18.5	tribe of Levi to **serve** him as **priests**
	18.7	may **serve** there as a **priest** of the Lord
Josh	18.7	share is to **serve** as the Lord's **priests**.
Judg	18.4	who pays me to **serve** as his **priest**.
	18.30	**served** as a **priest** for the tribe of Dan,
1 Sam	2.11	**served** the Lord under the **priest** Eli.
	2.13	the **priest's servant** would come
	2.15	the **priest's servant** would come and say
	2.16	the **priest's servant** would say,
	2.28	his family to be my **priests**, to **serve**
	2.30	your clan would **serve** me as **priests**
	2.33	and he will **serve** me as **priest**.
1 Kgs	2.27	Abiathar from **serving** as a **priest**
	12.32	**priests serving** at the places of worship
	13.2	will slaughter on you the **priests serving**
	13.33	**priests** from ordinary families to **serve**
2 Kgs	17.32	to **serve** as **priests** at the pagan places
	23.9	Those **priests** were not allowed to **serve**
	23.20	**priests** on the altars where they **served**,
2 Chr	11.14	let them **serve** as **priests** of the Lord.
	11.15	appointed **priests** of his own to **serve**
Ezra	6.18	the **priests**...for the temple **services**
Is	61.6	the **priests** of the Lord, The **servants**
Jer	33.18	**priests** from the tribe of Levi to **serve**
Ezek	40.45	the **priests** who **served** in the Temple,
	40.46	for the **priests** who **served** at the altar.
	44.13	They are not to **serve** me as **priests**
	45.4	aside for the **priests** who **serve** the Lord
	48.11	**priests** who are descendants of Zadok. They **served**
Hos	10.5	the **priests** who **serve** the idol will weep
Joel	1.13	you **priests** who **serve** at the altar!
	2.17	The **priests**, **serving** the Lord
Zeph	1.4	the pagan **priests** who **serve** him.
Rom	15.16	I **serve** like a **priest** in preaching

Heb	7.13	of his tribe ever **served** as a **priest**.
	10.11	**priest** performs his **services** every day
	13.10	**priests** who **serve** in the Jewish place
1 Pet	2.5	where you will **serve** as holy **priests**
Rev	1.6	a kingdom of **priests** to **serve** his God
	5.10	a kingdom of **priests** to **serve** our God,

Sheep see **Offer**

Special see **Gift**

Take Away (sin) see **Pure**

Teach

2 Chr	15.3	without **priests** to **teach** them,
Ezek	7.26	The **priests** will have nothing to **teach**
	44.23	The **priests** are to **teach** my people
Mal	2.7	of **priests** to **teach** the true knowledge

Tithe see **Gift**

Unclean, Defile

Lev	13.3	**priest** shall pronounce the person **unclean**
	13.11	The **priest** shall pronounce him **unclean**; Also: 13.22, 25, 27, 44
	21.1	**priest** is to make himself ritually **unclean**
	22.4	Any **priest** is **unclean** if he touches
	22.6	Any **priest** who becomes **unclean** remains
Neh	13.29	**defiled** both the office of **priest**
Ezek	44.25	**priest** is not to become ritually **unclean**
Zeph	3.4	the **priests defile** what is sacred,

Worship, Incense, Praise

Ex	35.21	**worship** and for making the **priestly**
1 Sam	2.28	my **priests**...to burn the **incense**,
1 Chr	16.39	**fellow-priests**, however, were in charge of the **worship**
	23.32	the **priests**...in the temple **worship**.
2 Chr	26.18	**incense** to the Lord. Only the **priests**
	.30.21	and the **priests praised** the Lord
Ps	135.19	**praise** him, you **priests** of God!
Lk	1.9	**priests**, he was chosen...to burn **incense**

PRISON

Gen	39.20	—	42.19	x13
Jer	37.4	—	41.16	x13
Acts	22.4	—	28.17	x12
2 Chr	28.5	—	30.9	x11
Jer	28.6	—	30.16	x10
2 Kgs	23.33	—	25.29	x8
Acts	16.25	—	40	x8
2 Kgs	14.13	—	18.11	x7
Jer	52.11	—	33	x6
Num	31.11	—	47	x5
Lk	21.12	—	23.25	x5
Phlm	.1	—	23	x5
Mt	25.36	—	44	x4
Acts	5.19	—	25	x4
Phil	1.7	—	17	x4
Judg	15.10	—	16.24	x3
Is	49.9	—	25	x3
Lam	3.5	—	34	x3
Acts	12.6	—	17	x3
Heb	13.3	—	23	x3

Christ

Mt	11.2	in **prison** about the things that **Christ**
2 Cor	2.14	led by God as **prisoners** in **Christ's**
Eph	3.1	Paul, the **prisoner** of **Christ** Jesus
Phil	1.13	**prison** because I am a servant of **Christ**.
Col	4.3	**Christ**. For that is why I am now in **prison**.
2 Tim	1.8	a **prisoner** for **Christ's** sake.
Phlm	.1	**prisoner** for the sake of **Christ** Jesus,
	.10	own son in **Christ**; for while in **prison**
	.23	in **prison** with me for the sake of **Christ**

God's People

Ps	69.33	does not forget **his** people in **prison**.
Acts	26.10	put many of **God's people** in **prison**;

Help

Gen	40.14	and **help** me to get out of this **prison**.
Mt	25.44	in **prison**, and would not **help** you?

Law

Rom	7.23	makes me a **prisoner** to the **law** of sin
Gal	3.23	**Law** kept us all locked up as **prisoners**

Sake

Eph	3.1	**prisoner** of Christ Jesus for the **sake** of
2 Tim	1.8	a **prisoner** for Christ's **sake**.
Phlm	.1	a **prisoner** for the **sake** of Christ Jesus,
	.9	at present also a **prisoner** for his **sake**.
	.13	I am in **prison** for the gospel's **sake**,
	.23	in **prison** with me for the **sake** of Christ

Suffer

Ps	107.10	**prisoners suffering** in chains,
Heb	10.34	You shared the **sufferings** of **prisoners**

PROCLAIM

see also **PREACH**

Esth	1.19	—	4.8	x11
1 Cor	14.1 − 39			x10
2 Kgs	9.3	—	11.12	x6
Esth	8.5	—	9.14	x6
Jer	18.18	—	20.8	x5
Rev	10.11	—	12.11	x5
Is	40.6 − 9			x4
1 Chr	16.8 − 24			x3
1 Chr	25.1 − 3			x3
Ps	71.8 − 18			x3
Ps	145.1 − 6			x3
Jer	23.22 − 30			x3
Jer	25.30	—	26.12	x3
Jon	3.2 − 7			x3
Acts	17.23	—	19.6	x3
1 Cor	1.23	—	2.7	x3
1 Cor	11.4 − 26			x3
2 Tim	1.1	—	2.2	x3

Glory, Might, Power, Wonderful

Chr	16.24	**Proclaim** his **glory** to the nations, his **mighty** deeds
Ps	68.34	**Proclaim** God's **power**;
	71.8	and **proclaim** your **glory**.
	71.16	**power**, Sovereign Lord; I will **proclaim**
	71.18	while I **proclaim** your **power** and **might**
	75.1	**proclaim** how great you are and tell of the **wonderful**
	96.3	**Proclaim** his **glory** to the nations, his **mighty** deeds
	145.4	they will **proclaim** your **mighty** acts.
	145.6	your **mighty** deeds, and I will **proclaim**
Phil	2.11	**proclaim** that Jesus...is Lord, to the **glory**
Pet	2.9	to **proclaim** the **wonderful** acts of God,

Praise see **Worship**

Spirit of God

Acts	2.18	my **Spirit**...and they will **proclaim**
	4.31	the Holy **Spirit** and began to **proclaim**
	19.6	**Spirit** came on them; they spoke in strange tongues and also **proclaimed**

Thank see **Worship**

Wonderful see **Glory**

Worship, Praise, Thank

Sam	22.47	**Praise** my defender! **Proclaim**
Chr	16.8	**thanks** to the Lord, **proclaim**

Ps	18.46	**Praise** my defender! **Proclaim**
	30.9	able to **praise** you? Can they **proclaim**
	35.28	**proclaim** your righteousness, and...**praise**
	69.30	**praise** God with a song; I will **proclaim** his greatness by giving...**thanks**.
	71.8	I **praise** you and **proclaim** your **glory**.
	71.16	will **praise** your **power**...I will **proclaim**
	75.1	**thanks** to you! We **proclaim** how great!
	96.2	**praise** him! **Proclaim** every day the good
	102.21	**proclaimed** in Zion...he will be **praised**
	105.1	Give **thanks** to the Lord, **proclaim**
	118.28	**thanks**; I will **proclaim** your greatness.
1 Cor	11.4	**proclaims** God's message in...**worship**
	11.5	**proclaims** God's message in...**worship**

PROMISE

Ps	119.25 − 170			x28
Deut	6.3	—	13.17	x27
Heb	6.12	—	12.26	x26
Deut	26.3	—	31.23	x14
Gal	3.14	—	4.28	x13
Num	30.2 − 14			x10
1 Kgs	1.13	—	2.43	x10
Josh	21.43	—	23.15	x9
Mal	1.14	—	2.16	x9
1 Kgs	8.15	—	9.5	x8
Lk	1.20	—	2.29	x8
Rom	4.13 − 21			x8
Heb	3.11	—	4.10	x8
2 Chr	6.4	—	7.18	x7
Ezek	20.5 − 42			x7
Gen	24.7 − 37			x6
1 Sam	20.8 − 42			x6
2 Sam	7.10 − 29			x6
Ps	89.3 − 49			x6
Num	14.16 − 30			x5
Neh	9.8 − 32			x5
Ecc	5.2 − 5			x5
Jer	44.24 − 29			x5
Rom	9.4 − 9			x5
Gen	26.3 − 31			x4
Gen	50.5 − 25			x4
Num	32.10 − 24			x4
Josh	9.15 − 20			x4
Judg	11.30 − 39			x4

Believe see **Trust**

Christ

2 Cor	11.2	I have **promised** in marriage to...**Christ**
	11.10	By **Christ's** truth in me, I **promise**
1 Jn	2.25	this is what **Christ** himself **promised**

Command see **Law**

Fail

Josh	23.14	Every **promise** he made has been kept; not one has **failed**.
Ps	89.33	or **fail** to keep my **promise** to him.
Is	42.16	**promises**, and...keep them without **fail**.
Rom	9.6	that the **promise** of God has **failed**
Heb	4.1	have **failed** to receive that **promised** rest.

Faith, Hope

Ps	119.114	I put my **hope** in your **promise**.
	119.147	I place my **hope** in your **promise**.
Acts	26.6	**hope** I have in the **promise** that God
Rom	4.14	**faith** means nothing and God's **promise**
	4.16	so the **promise** was based on **faith**,
	4.20	did not doubt God's **promise**; his **faith**
Gal	3.14	through **faith** we might receive the Spirit **promised**
	3.22	**promised** on the basis of **faith** in Jesus
Heb	11.20	**faith** that made Isaac **promise** blessings
Jas	2.5	**faith** and to possess the kingdom which he **promised**

Faithful, Honour, Loyal, True

Gen	21.23	so **promise** that you will also be **loyal**
	24.27	**faithfully** kept his **promise** to my
Ex	15.13	**Faithful** to your **promise**
Deut	10.20	**faithful** to him and make your **promises**
	13.2	Even if what he **promises** comes **true**,
1 Sam	1.23	the Lord make your **promise** come **true**.
	20.14	your sacred **promise** and be **loyal** to me;
2 Sam	9.3	**loyalty** and kindness, as I **promised** God
1 Kgs	8.26	everything come **true** that you **promised**
2 Kgs	10.10	come **true**. The Lord has done what he **promised**
	19.34	own **honour** and because of the **promise**
	20.6	own **honour** and because of the **promise**
1 Chr	29.24	sons **promised** to be **loyal** to Solomon
2 Chr	6.17	everything come **true** that you **promised**
Neh	9.8	your **promise**, because you are **faithful**
	9.32	**faithfully** keep your covenant **promises**.
Ps	98.3	kept his **promise** to...Israel with **loyalty**
	145.13	The Lord is **faithful** to his **promises**,
Is	37.35	own **honour** and because of the **promise**
	45.23	My **promise** is **true**,
Mal	2.14	**promised**...that you would be **faithful**
	2.16	**promise** to be **faithful** to your wife.
Lk	1.20	the day my **promise** to you comes **true**.
Rom	9.8	God's **promise** are regarded as the **true**
	15.8	God is **faithful**, to make his **promises**

Father

Lk	24.49	upon you what my **Father** has **promised**
Acts	1.4	the gift my **Father promised**.

Fulfil

Num	6.21	must **fulfil** exactly the **promise** he made.
2 Sam	7.25	**fulfil** for all time the **promise** you made
2 Kgs	9.26	so as to **fulfil** the Lord's **promise**.
	15.12	**promise** was **fulfilled** which the Lord
1 Chr	17.23	**fulfil** for all time the **promise** you made
2 Chr	1.9	**fulfil** the **promise** you made to my
Jer	33.14	**fulfil** the **promise** that I made to the

Help, Protect, Strengthen

2 Sam	21.2	Israelites had **promised** to **protect**,
1 Chr	11.10	**helped** him...as the Lord had **promised**,
Ps	109.21	**help** me as you have **promised**,
	119.28	**strengthen** me, as you have **promised**.
	119.114	**protector**; I...hope in your **promise**.
	119.116	Give me **strength**, as you **promised**
	119.122	**Promise** that you will **help** your servant;
	119.123	**help**, for the deliverance you **promised**;
	119.147	**help**; I place my hope in your **promise**.
Jer	14.7	**help** us, Lord, as you have **promised**.

Holy, Sacred

1 Sam	20.8	the **sacred promise** you made to me.
	20.14	please keep your **sacred promise**
	20.42	keep the **sacred promise** we have made
	23.18	made a **sacred promise** of friendship
	28.10	**sacred** vow. "By the...Lord I **promise**
2 Sam	21.7	But because of the **sacred promise**
Ps	89.35	I have **promised** by my **holy** name:
	105.42	He remembered his **sacred promise**
Is	49.7	**holy** God of Israel keeps his **promises**.
Amos	4.2	Lord is **holy**, he has **promised**,
Lk	1.70	**promised** through his **holy** prophets long
Acts	13.34	**sacred** and sure blessings that I **promised**

Honour see **Faithful**

Hope see **Faith**

Land

Gen	15.18	I **promise** to give your descendants all this **land**
	50.24	the **land** he solemnly **promised** to
Ex	6.4	**promising** to give them the **land**
	6.8	the **land** that I solemnly **promised** to

Ex	12.25	**land** that the Lord has **promised** to give
	32.13	all that **land** you **promised** would be
	33.1	the **land** that I **promised** to give to
Lev	20.24	**promised** you this rich and fertile **land**
	26.42	my **promise** to give my people the **land**.
Num	11.12	the **land** you **promised** to their
	14.16	into the **land** you **promised** to give
	14.23	the **land** which I **promised** to their
	20.12	into the **land** that I **promised** to give
	20.24	the **land** which I **promised** to give to
	32.11	the **land** that I **promised** to Abraham,
Deut	1.8	**land** which I, the Lord, **promised** to
	1.35	the fertile **land** that I **promised** to give
	6.18	the fertile **land** that the Lord **promised**
	6.23	give us this **land**, as he had **promised**
	7.13	the **land** that he **promised** your
	8.1	the **land** which the Lord **promised**
	9.28	into the **land** that you had **promised**
	10.11	the **land** that he had **promised**
	11.9	fertile **land** that the Lord **promised**
	19.8	gives you all the **land** he has **promised**,
	26.3	the **land** that he **promised**
	28.11	in the **land** that he **promised** your
	30.20	long in the **land** that he **promised** to
	31.7	occupy the **land** that the Lord **promised**
	31.20	this rich and fertile **land**, as I **promised**
	31.21	take them into the **land** that I **promised**
	31.23	of Israel into the **land** that I **promised**
	34.4	This is the **land** that I **promised**
Josh	1.6	this **land** which I **promised** their
	5.4	fertile **land** that he had **promised**
	21.44	the **land**, just as he had **promised**
Judg	2.1	the **land** that I **promised** to your
Neh	9.8	You **promised** to give him the **land**
	9.15	the **land** which you had **promised**
	9.23	**land** that you had **promised** their
Ezek	20.28	to the **land** I had **promised** to give
	20.42	Israel, the **land** that I **promised** I would
Dan	8.9	and towards the **Promised Land**.
	11.16	He will stand in the **Promised Land**
	11.41	He will even invade the **Promised Land**

Law, Command

Gen	24.37	**promise** with a vow to obey his **command**.
Deut	26.17	**promised** to obey...to keep all his **laws**,
1 Kgs	2.43	**promise** and disobeyed my **command**?
	6.12	**laws** and **commands**, I will do for you what I **promised**
	11.11	**commands**, I **promise** that I will take
Ps	119.57	I **promise** to obey your **laws**.
Ezek	20.16	**promise** because they had rejected my **commands**,
Gal	3.18	on the **Law**, then it no longer depends on his **promise**.
	3.21	that the **Law** is against God's **promises**

Loyal see **Faithful**

Offer, Sacrifice

Num	6.21	if a Nazirite **promises** an **offering**
Deut	12.6	**offerings**, the gifts that you **promise**
	12.17	you **promise** to the Lord, your freewill **offerings**,
	12.26	**offerings** and the gifts that you have **promised**
1 Sam	1.21	the special **sacrifice** he had **promised**.
Ps	22.25	I will **offer** the **sacrifices** I **promised**.
	56.12	I will **offer** you what I have **promised**;
	61.8	I **offer** you daily what I have **promised**.
	66.13	I will **offer** you what I **promised**.
Prov	20.25	before you **promise** an **offering** to God.
Is	19.21	**offerings**. They will make solemn **promises**
Jer	11.15	making **promises** and by **offering** animal

Jer	44.24	**promised** that you would **offer sacrifices**
Jon	1.16	**offered** a **sacrifice** and do what I have
	2.9	**offer** you a **sacrifice** and do what I have **promised.**
Heb	4.1	God has **offered** us the **promise**
	11.17	the **promise**, yet he was ready to **offer**

Peace, Rest

Josh	21.44	gave them **peace**...as he had **promised**
1 Kgs	8.56	given his people **peace**, as he **promised**
Ps	85.8	**promises peace** to us, his own people,
Is	54.10	will keep for ever my **promise** of **peace.**
Jer	14.13	**promised**...that there will be only **peace**
Mic	3.5	who **promise peace** to those who pay
Lk	2.29	**promise**...let your servant go in **peace.**
Heb	4.1	**promise** that we may receive that **rest**
	4.3	receive that **rest** which God **promised.**
	4.8	people the **rest** that God had **promised**
	4.10	receives that **rest** which God **promised**

Possess

Ex	32.13	you **promised** would be their **possession**
Deut	10.11	**possession** of the land...he had **promised**
Jas	2.5	**possess** the kingdom which he **promised**

Praise see Worship

Protect see Help

Rescue see Save

Rest see Peace

Sacred see Holy

Sacrifice see Offer

Save, Rescue

Ex	15.13	your **promise**, you led the people you had **rescued;**
Josh	2.13	**Promise** me that you will **save** my father
1 Kgs	1.29	I **promise** you by the living Lord, who has **rescued**
Ps	35.3	**Promise** that you will **save** me.
	69.13	because you keep your **promise** to **save.**
	106.8	But he **saved** them, as he had **promised,**
	109.21	as you have **promised**, and **rescue** me
	119.41	**save** me according to your **promise.**
	119.123	for your **saving** help, for the deliverance you **promised.**
	119.154	**save** me, as you have **promised.**
	119.170	**save** me according to your **promise!**
	143.11	**promised**; in your goodness **save** me
Lk	1.73	**promised** to **rescue** us from our enemies

Solemn

Gen	24.7	**solemnly promised** me that he would
	26.28	**solemn** agreement between us. We want you to **promise**
	31.53	**solemnly** vowed to keep this **promise.**
	50.24	**solemnly promised** to Abraham, Isaac,
Ex	6.8	**solemnly promised** to give to Abraham,
	13.5	Lord **solemnly promised** your ancestors
	13.11	which he **solemnly promised** to you
	13.19	made the Israelites **solemnly promise**
	32.13	the **solemn promise** you made to them
Josh	9.15	**solemn promise** to keep the treaty.
	9.18	their leaders had made a **solemn promise**
	9.19	have made our **solemn promise** to them
	21.43	the land that he had **solemnly promised**
Judg	11.35	made a **solemn promise** to the Lord,
	21.1	made a **solemn promise** to the Lord:
	21.7	made a **solemn promise** to the Lord
1 Sam	1.11	Hannah made a **solemn promise:**
	12.22	The Lord has made a **solemn promise,**
1 Sam	3.35	but he made a **solemn promise,**
1 Kgs	1.13	you **solemnly promise** me that my son
	1.17	**solemn promise** in the name of the Lord
	2.8	I gave him my **solemn promise**

1 Kgs	2.23	Solomon made a **solemn promise**
Ezra	10.3	make a **solemn promise** to our God
Job	31.1	I have made a **solemn promise**
Ps	95.11	was angry and made a **solemn promise:**
	110.4	The Lord made a **solemn promise**
	119.106	I will keep my **solemn promise**
	132.11	You made a **solemn promise** to David
Is	19.21	They will make **solemn promises** to him
	45.23	I **solemnly promise** by all that I am:
	62.8	The Lord has made a **solemn promise,**
Jer	44.24	**solemn promises** to the Queen of
Ezek	36.7	**solemnly promise** that the surrounding
	47.14	I **solemnly promised** your ancestors
Dan	12.7	**solemn promise** in the name of the
Nah	1.15	give God what you **solemnly promised**
Lk	1.73	a **solemn** oath to...Abraham he **promised**
Heb	3.11	was angry and made a **solemn promise:**
	3.18	When God made his **solemn promise**
	4.3	was angry and made a **solemn promise:**
	7.21	The Lord has made a **solemn promise**

Strengthen see Help

Swear

Neh	5.12	the leaders **swear**...to keep the **promise**
Song	2.7	**Promise** me, women of Jerusalem; **swear**
	3.5	**Promise** me, women of Jerusalem; **swear**
Jer	38.16	**promised** me in secret, "I **swear**
Mt	14.7	that he **promised** her, "I **swear**
Jas	5.12	a **promise**. Do not **swear** by heaven

True see Faithful

Trust, Believe

Ps	12.6	**promises** of the Lord can be **trusted;**
	106.12	Then his people **believed** his **promises**
	106.24	they did not **believe** God's **promise.**
	119.74	because I **trust** in your **promise.**
Heb	10.23	we can **trust** God to keep his **promise.**
	11.11	He **trusted** God to keep his **promise.**

Worship, Praise

Deut	6.13	**worship**...him, and make your **promises**
2 Chr	6.20	**promised** that this is where you will be **worshipped,**
Ps	22.25	**worship** you I will offer the sacrifices I **promised.**
	56.4	I **praise** him for what he has **promised.**
	56.10	whose **promises** I **praise.**
	63.11	**promises** in God's name will **praise**
	65.1	to **praise** you...and keep our **promises**
	106.12	believed his **promises** and sang **praises**
Hos	14.2	we will **praise** you as we have **promised.**
Rom	9.4	**worship**; they...received God's **promises;**

PROPHETS

1 Kgs	11.29	—	22.24	x77
Jer	25.4	—	29.31	x23
2 Kgs	1.3	—	6.12	x21
Jer	23.11 – 37			x17
2 Chr	32.20	—	36.22	x13
Mt	21.4	—	24.24	x13
Ezek	13.2	—	14.10	x12
2 Kgs	19.2	—	24.2	x11
2 Chr	18.5	—	21.12	x11
Mt	1.22	—	5.17	x9
Mt	11.9	—	14.5	x9
Lk	9.8	—	11.50	x9
2 Kgs	8.8	—	10.19	x8
2 Chr	9.29	—	13.22	x8
2 Chr	24.19	—	26.22	x8
Jer	4.9	—	8.10	x8
Lk	1.17	—	4.27	x8
Acts	2.16	—	3.25	x8
Deut	18.15 – 22			x7
Jn	6.14	—	9.17	x7

181

Acts	7.37 —	8.34	x7
Acts	13.1 – 40		x7
1 Sam	9.9 —	10.12	x6
Jer	13.13 —	15.19	x6
Mic	2.11 —	3.11	x6
Lk	6.23 —	7.39	x6
Rev	18.20 —	20.10	x6
Rev	22.6 – 19		x6
Zech	13.2 – 5		x5
Zech	1.1 – 6		x4
Lk	24.19 – 44		x4
Jn	1.21 – 45		x4

Announce see Proclaim

Believe, Convince

2 Chr	20.20	**Believe** what his **prophets** tell you,
Jer	29.31	a **prophet**, and he made you **believe** lies.
Mt	21.26	all **convinced** that John was a **prophet**.
Mk	11.32	**convinced** that John had been a **prophet**.
Lk	16.31	the **prophets**, they will not be **convinced**
	20.6	are **convinced** that John was a **prophet**.
	24.25	to **believe** everything the **prophets** said!
Acts	26.27	do you **believe** the **prophets**?

Deceive, False, Lie

1 Kgs	13.18	But the old **prophet** was **lying**.
	22.22	**prophets** tell **lies**.' The Lord said, 'Go and **deceive**
	22.23	has made these **prophets** of yours **lie**
2 Chr	18.21	**prophets** tell **lies**.' The Lord said, 'Go and **deceive**
	18.22	has made these **prophets** of yours **lie**
Is	9.15	is the **prophets** whose teachings are **lies**!
Jer	5.31	**prophets** speak nothing but **lies**
	14.14	**prophets** are telling **lies** in my name;
	23.16	**prophets** say; they are filling you with **false** hopes.
	23.25	those **prophets** have said who speak **lies**
	23.26	**prophets** mislead my people with the **lies**
	27.15	**prophets** who are telling you these **lies**.
	29.8	yourselves **deceived** by the **prophets**
	29.31	a **prophet**, and he made you **believe** lies.
	50.36	Death to its **lying prophets**
Lam	2.14	Your **prophets** had nothing to tell you but **lies**;
Ezek	13.9	you **prophets** who have **false** visions
	14.9	If a **prophet** is **deceived** into giving
Mic	2.11	**prophet** who goes about full of...**deceit**
	3.5	My people are **deceived** by **prophets**
Zech	13.4	a **prophet's**...garment in order to **deceive**
Mt	7.15	Be on your guard against **false prophets**
	7.20	the **false prophets** by what they do.
	24.11	**false prophets** will appear and **deceive**
	24.24	**false** Messiahs and **false prophets** will
Mk	13.22	**false** Messiahs and **false prophets** will
Lk	6.26	same things about the **false prophets**.
2 Pet	2.1	**False prophets** appeared in the past
1 Jn	4.1	For many **false prophets** have gone out
	4.4	and have defeated the **false prophets**,
	4.5	**false prophets** speak about matters
Rev	16.13	and the mouth of the **false prophet**.
	19.20	**false prophet** who had performed
	20.10	beast and the **false prophet** had already

Dream see Vision

False see Deceive

Holy

Lk	1.70	through his **holy prophets** long ago
Acts	3.21	announced through his **holy prophets**
Eph	3.5	to his **holy** apostles and **prophets**.
2 Pet	3.2	spoken long ago by the **holy prophets**,

Lie see Deceive

Message, Word

Deut	18.20	if any **prophet** dares to speak a **message**
	18.21	a **prophet's message** does not come
Judg	6.8	**prophet** who brought them this **message**
1 Sam	2.27	**prophet** came to Eli with this **message**
1 Kgs	13.20	**word** of the Lord came to the...**prophet**,
2 Chr	33.18	the **messages** of the **prophets** who spoke
	36.12	**prophet** Jeremiah, who spoke the **word**
	36.16	his **words** and laughing at his **prophets**,
Jer	15.19	**message**, you will be my **prophet**
	18.18	**prophets** to proclaim God's **message**.
	23.28	the **prophet** who has heard my **message**
	23.30	**prophets** who take each other's **words**
	23.31	**prophets** who speak their own **words**
	23.34	**prophet** or a priest even uses the **words**
	26.5	the **words** of my servants, the **prophets**,
	27.18	**prophets** and if they have my **message**,
Hos	6.5	my **prophets** to you with my **message**
Amos	2.12	the **prophets** not to speak my **message**.
Hab	1.1	**message** that the Lord revealed to the **prophet**
Hag	1.1	the **prophet** Haggai. The **message**
	1.3	**message** to the people through the **prophet**
Zech	1.1	Lord gave this **message** to the **prophet**
	1.4	ago the **prophets** gave them my **message**,
	8.9	the same **words** the **prophets** spoke
Acts	3.24	all the **prophets** who had a **message**
	13.27	the **words** of the **prophets** that are read
	13.27	made the **prophets'** **words** come true
	15.15	**words** of the **prophets** agree completely
2 Pet	1.19	the **message** proclaimed by the **prophets**.
	1.21	For no **prophetic message** ever came
	3.2	**words**...spoken...by the holy **prophets**,
Rev	1.3	to the **words** of this **prophetic message**
	22.7	are those who obey the **prophetic words**
	22.9	**prophets** and of all...who obey the **words**
	22.10	**prophetic words** of this book a secret,
	22.18	the **prophetic words** of this book:
	22.19	from the **prophetic words** of this book,

Predict see Prophesy

Proclaim, Announce

Neh	6.7	some **prophets** to **proclaim** in Jerusalem
Jer	18.18	**prophets** to **proclaim** God's message.
	23.28	the **prophet** who has heard my message should **proclaim**
	23.30	am against those **prophets** who...**proclaim**
Ezek	38.17	when I **announced** through...the **prophets**
Acts	3.18	**announced**...through all the **prophets**
	3.21	**announced** through all his holy **prophets**
2 Pet	1.19	the message **proclaimed** by the **prophets**.
Rev	10.7	as he **announced** to...the **prophets**.

Prophesy, Predict

1 Kgs	13.5	as the **prophet** had **predicted**
	22.10	and all the **prophets** were **prophesying**
	22.13	other **prophets** have **prophesied** success
2 Kgs	23.16	the **prophet** had **predicted** long before
	23.17	the **prophet** who came...and **predicted**
2 Chr	18.9	all the **prophets** were **prophesying**
	18.12	other **prophets** have **prophesied** success
Jer	27.9	**prophets** or to anyone who claims he can **predict**
	28.9	that **prophet's predictions** come true.
Ezek	13.2	the **prophets**...who make up...**prophecies**.
Amos	7.14	kind of **prophet** who **prophesies** for pay.

Teachers

Mt	23.34	**prophets** and wise men and **teachers**;
Acts	13.1	there were some **prophets** and **teachers**
1 Cor	12.28	**prophets**, and in the third place **teachers**;
	12.29	not all apostles or **prophets** or **teachers**

Vision, Dream

Num 24.21 **vision** he saw the Kenites, and uttered this
prophecy:
Deut 13.1 **prophet** or an interpreter of **dreams** may
13.5 any interpreter of **dreams** or **prophet**
1 Sam 28.15 either by **prophets** or by **dreams**.
2 Chr 9.29 The **Visions** of Iddo the **Prophet**,
32.32 The **Vision** of the **Prophet** Isaiah
Is 28.7 The **prophets** are too drunk to understand the
visions
29.11 every **prophetic vision** will be hidden
Jer 23.28 The **prophet** who has had a **dream**
23.32 the **prophets** who tell their **dreams**
Lam 2.9 the **prophets** have no **visions**
Ezek 12.24 false **visions** or misleading **prophecies**.
12.27 think that your **visions** and **prophecies**
13.9 you **prophets** who have false **visions**
Dan 9.24 **vision** and the **prophecy** will come true,
Hos 12.10 **prophets** and gave them many **visions**
Mic 3.6 will have no more **prophetic visions**,
Zech 13.4 no **prophet** will be proud of his **visions**,

Warn

2 Kgs 17.13 messengers and **prophets** to **warn** Israel
17.23 **warned** through his servants the **prophets**
2 Chr 24.19 sent **prophets** to **warn** them to return
36.15 to send **prophets** to **warn** his people,
Neh 9.26 killed the **prophets** who **warned** them,
9.30 **warned** them. You inspired...**prophets**
Hos 9.8 me as a **prophet** to **warn** his people
12.10 the **prophets** I gave my people **warnings**.
Mic 7.4 he **warned** them through...the **prophets**.
Zech 1.6 Through...the **prophets** I gave...**warnings**,
Lk 16.29 Moses and the **prophets** to **warn** them;
Rev 22.18 **warn** everyone who hears the **prophetic**

Word see Message

AV PROPITIATION see FORGIVE

PROSPERITY

Deut	30.3 – 16			x6
Jer	33.7 – 26			x4
Deut	28.13 – 63			x3
1 Kgs	1.37	—	2.3	x3
Job	20.21	—	22.18	x3
Jer	48.47	—	49.39	x3
Ezek	16.53 – 55			x3
Zeph	2.7	—	3.20	x3

Enjoy see Happy

Evil, Wicked

Job 21.7 let **evil** men live...grow old and **prosper**?
24.24 For a while the **wicked** man **prospers**,
Ps 37.7 **prosper** or...succeed in their **evil** plans.
Jer 12.1 Why are **wicked** men so **prosperous**?
Hos 7.1 **prosperous** again, all I can see is their
wickedness
Mal 3.15 **Evil** men not only **prosper**,

Fail see Succeed

Happy, Enjoy

Ezra 9.12 **prosper** or succeed if we wanted to **enjoy**
Ps 37.11 and **enjoy prosperity** and peace.
72.3 May the land **enjoy prosperity**;
106.5 **prosperity**...and share in the **happiness**
128.2 you will be **happy** and **prosperous**.
Prov 24.25 **prosperous** and **enjoy** a good reputation.
Is 66.11 You will **enjoy** her **prosperity**,
Dan 4.4 **enjoying** great **prosperity**.

Life

Deut 22.7 you will live a long and **prosperous life**.
Job 36.11 live out their **lives** in...**prosperity**.
Ps 128.5 **prosper** all the days of your **life**!

Prov 3.2 will give you a long and **prosperous life**.

Mercy

Ps 85.1 **merciful** to your land; you have made Israel
prosperous
Jer 33.26 **merciful** to my people and make them
prosperous

Peace

Job 36.11 out their lives in **peace** and **prosperity**.
Ps 37.11 and enjoy **prosperity** and **peace**.
Is 54.13 and give them **prosperity** and **peace**.
Hag 2.9 give my people **prosperity** and **peace**.

Succeed, Fail

Deut 28.13 **prosper** and never **fail** if you obey
Josh 1.8 you will be **prosperous** and **successful**.
Ezra 9.12 **prosper** or **succeed** if we wanted to
Ps 37.7 those who **prosper** or those who **succeed**
Prov 8.18 **prosperity** and **success**.
Jer 12.1 wicked men so **prosperous**? Why do dishonest
men **succeed**?

Wicked see Evil

PROTECT

2 Sam	21.2	—	23.3	x11
Ps	18.2 – 48			x7
Ps	91.1 – 14			x6
Is	30.2	—	31.5	x6
Deut	32.10	—	33.25	x5
Ps	37.17 – 40			x5
Ps	121.3 – 8			x5
Prov	13.3	—	15.25	x5
1 Sam	25.16	—	26.16	x4
Ps	31.1 – 23			x4
Prov	29.10	—	31.9	x4
Ezra	8.21 – 31			x3
Ps	62.2 – 7			x3
Ps	71.1 – 6			x3
Ps	115.9 – 11			x3
Prov	2.7 – 11			x3
Prov	10.15	—	11.8	x3
Is	16.3	—	17.10	x3
Is	25.10	—	27.5	x3
Is	33.2 – 22			x3
Ezek	11.3 – 11			x3

Afraid see Trust

Care see Love

Defend, Shelter

2 Sam 22.3 **protects** me like a shield; he **defends** me
2 Kgs 19.34 I will **defend** this city and **protect** it,
Ps 18.2 **protects** me like a shield; he **defends** me
28.7 The Lord **protects** and **defends** me;
28.8 The Lord **protects** his people; he **defends**
31.2 Be my refuge to **protect** me; my **defence**
61.3 you are my **protector**, my strong **defence**
62.2 **protects** and saves me; he is my **defender**,
62.6 **protects** and saves me; he is my **defender**,
62.7 my strong **protector**; he is my **shelter**.
71.3 **protect** me; you are my...**defence**.
91.2 You are my **defender** and **protector**.
91.4 faithfulness will **protect** and **defend** you.
91.9 **defender**, the Most High your **protector**,
94.22 Lord **defends** me; my God **protects** me.
119.114 You are my **defender** and **protector**;
140.7 strong **defender**, you have **protected** me
144.2 He is my **protector** and **defender**,
Is 31.5 will **protect** Jerusalem and **defend** it.
37.35 I will **defend** this city and **protect** it,
60.18 will **protect** and **defend** you like a wall;
Nah 3.8 **protect** her...the Nile was her **defence**.

G

Evil, Violent, Wicked

2 Sam	22.3	**protects** me and saves me from **violence**.
	22.49	and **protect** me from **violent** men.
Ps	1.6	and **protected** by the Lord, but the **evil**
	18.48	and **protect** me from **violent** men.
	37.17	**wicked**, but **protect** those who are good.
	37.40	from the **wicked**, because they go to him for **protection**.
	64.2	**Protect** me from the plots of the **wicked**,
	97.10	loves those who hate **evil**; he **protects**
	140.4	**Protect** me, Lord, from...the **wicked**;
Prov	11.8	righteous are **protected** from trouble; it comes to the **wicked**
	13.6	**protects** the innocent; **wickedness**
	14.32	**evil** deeds, but good people are **protected**
Is	31.2	**evil** men and those who **protect** them.

Faithful

1 Sam	2.9	**protects** the lives of his **faithful** people,
Ps	31.23	The Lord **protects** the **faithful**,
	37.28	his **faithful** people. He **protects** them
	61.7	**protect** him with your...**faithfulness**.
	91.4	**faithfulness** will **protect** and defend you.

God, Lord

Gen	49.24	Mighty **God**...the **Protector** of Israel.
Num	31.54	**Lord** would **protect** the people of Israel.
	33.3	Under the **Lord's protection** they left
Deut	7.15	**Lord** will **protect** you from all sickness,
	33.3	The **Lord** loves his people and **protects**
	33.12	the tribe the **Lord** loves and **protects**;
1 Sam	2.2	no **protector** like our **God**.
	23.16	with assurances of **God's protection**,
2 Sam	22.2	The **Lord** is my **protector**;
	22.3	My **God** is my **protection**,
	22.19	but the **Lord protected** me.
	22.36	O **Lord**, you **protect** me and save me;
Job	29.4	friendship of **God protected** my home.
Ps	1.6	righteous are...**protected** by the **Lord**,
	3.5	all night long the **Lord protects** me.
	7.1	O **Lord**...I come to you for **protection**;
	7.10	**God** is my **protector**;
	14.6	but the **Lord** is his **protection**.
	16.1	**Protect** me, O **God**;
	18.2	The **Lord** is my **protector**;
	18.2	My **God** is my **protection**,
	18.18	but the **Lord protected** me.
	18.35	O **Lord**, you **protect** me and save me;
	20.1	May the **God** of Jacob **protect** you!
	27.1	The **Lord protects** me from all danger;
	28.7	The **Lord protects** and defends me;
	28.8	The **Lord protects** his people;
	31.1	I come to you, **Lord**, for **protection**;
	31.23	The **Lord protects** the faithful,
	37.39	The **Lord** saves...and **protects** them.
	41.2	The **Lord** will **protect** them
	59.11	defeat them, O **Lord**, our **protector**.
	71.1	**Lord**, I have come to you for **protection**;
	78.35	that **God** was their **protector**,
	84.11	The **Lord** is our **protector**
	89.18	You, O **Lord**, chose our **protector**;
	94.22	my **God protects** me.
	95.1	sing for joy to **God**, who **protects** us!
	116.6	The **Lord protects** the helpless;
	121.7	**Lord** will **protect** you from all danger;
	127.1	if the **Lord** does not **protect** the city,
	140.4	**Protect** me, **Lord**, from the power
	140.7	Sovereign **Lord**...you have **protected** me
	142.5	you, **Lord**, are my **protector**;
	143.9	I go to you for **protection**, **Lord**;
	144.1	Praise the **Lord**, my **protector**!
Prov	10.29	The **Lord protects** honest people,
Is	4.5	**God's** glory will cover and **protect**

Is	17.10	**God** who rescues you and who **protects**
	25.10	The **Lord** will **protect** Mount Zion,
	31.5	I, the **Lord**...will **protect** Jerusalem
	44.6	The **Lord**, who rules and **protects** Israel,
	52.12	**God** will lead you and **protect** you
Jer	16.19	**Lord**, you are the one who **protects** me
	39.17	But I, the **Lord**, will **protect** you,
Hab	1.12	**Lord**, my **God** and **protector**,
Zech	9.15	**Lord** Almighty will **protect** his people,
	12.8	the **Lord** will **protect** those who

Love, Care

Deut	32.10	He **protected**...and **cared** for them,
	33.3	The Lord **loves** his people and **protects**
	33.12	tribe the Lord **loves** and **protects**;
Ps	5.11	**Protect** those who **love** you;
	5.12	your **love protects** them like a shield.
	18.35	you **protect** me and save me; your **care**
	32.10	are **protected** by his constant **love**.
	36.7	your constant **love**! We find **protection**
	61.7	**protect** him with your constant **love**
	68.5	**cares** for orphans and **protects** widows.
	91.4	his **care**...will **protect** and defend
	91.14	save those who **love** me and will **protect**
	97.10	**loves** those who hate evil; he **protects**
	142.4	no one to **protect** me. No one **cares**
	145.20	He **protects** everyone who **loves** him,
Prov	4.6	will **protect** you; **love** her, and she will
Jude	.1	the **love** of God...and the **protection**

Righteous

Job	36.7	He **protects** those who are **righteous**;
Ps	1.6	The **righteous** are guided and **protected**
	37.39	saves **righteous** men and **protects** them
Prov	2.7	help and **protection** for **righteous**,
	11.8	The **righteous** are **protected** from trouble
	13.6	**Righteousness protects** the innocent
	29.10	**righteous** people will **protect** the life

Secure

2 Chr	14.7	has **protected** us and given us **security**
Job	11.18	**secure** and full of hope; God will **protect**
Ps	31.19	**securely** you **protect** those who trust
	71.3	**secure** shelter and a...fortress to **protect**

Shelter see Defend

Trust, Afraid

Num	14.9	who **protected** them; so don't be **afraid**.
Ps	16.1	**Protect** me, O God; I **trust** in you
	28.7	**protects** and defends me; I **trust** in him.
	31.19	you **protect** those who **trust** you.
	32.10	who **trust** in the Lord are **protected**
	91.2	and **protector**...my God; in you I **trust**.
Is	26.4	**Trust** in the Lord...he will...**protect** us.
	30.2	to **protect** them, so they put their **trust**
Jer	1.8	**afraid**...I will be with you to **protect**
Lam	4.20	the one we had **trusted** to **protect** us

Violent see Evil

Wicked see Evil

PROVE

1 Cor	1.22	—	4.4	x4
Deut	22.15 − 20			x3
Ezra	2.59 − 61			x3
Neh	7.61 − 63			x3
Acts	17.3	—	18.28	x3

True

Gen	42.20	**prove**...you have been telling the **truth**,
Deut	22.20	the charge is **true** and there is no **proof**
	33.8	**proved** them **true** at the waters of
Job	24.25	**prove** that my words are not **true**?
Ps	105.19	**true**. The word of the Lord **proved** him
Prov	22.12	that **truth** is kept safe by **disproving**
Mk	16.20	**proved** that their preaching was **true**

Acts 22.5 can **prove** that I am telling the **truth**.
2 Cor 7.14 made to Titus has **proved true**.
Heb 2.3 heard him **proved** to us that it is **true**.

AV PUBLICAN see TAX COLLECTOR

PUNISHMENT

Hos	4.9	—	13.16	x18
Is	9.12	—	11.4	x15
Jer	5.9	—	11.22	x13
Amos	1.3	—	5.17	x13
Ex	5.21	—	12.13	x12
Jer	49.8	—	51.56	x12
Ezek	13.9	—	17.20	x12
Ezek	20.26	—	25.17	x12
Ezek	4.4	—	7.27	x11
Ex	19.22	—	21.28	x10
Lev	26.14 − 28			x8
1 Sam	5.6	—	6.5	x8
Is	26.11	—	27.8	x8
Jer	29.31	—	32.18	x8
Zeph	1.4	—	3.19	x8
Heb	12.6 − 11			x8
Job	20.23	—	22.19	x7
Is	65.6	—	66.19	x7
Josh	22.17	—	24.20	x6
Prov	13.24	—	17.26	x6
Is	53.4	—	54.9	x6
Jer	25.6 − 29			x6
Deut	32.34 − 43			x4
2 Sam	24.14 − 17			x4
1 Kgs	2.9 − 44			x4
1 Chr	21.7 − 17			x4
Ps	119.67 − 84			x4
Jer	23.2 − 34			x4
Jer	46.10 − 28			x4
2 Chr	34.24 − 28			x3
Ps	10.12 − 15			x3
Ps	28.4 − 5			x3
Ps	94.1 − 23			x3
Jer	44.13 − 29			x3
Ezek	11.11 − 21			x3
Ezek	44.10 − 13			x3
Obad	.8 − 16			x3
Mic	4.6 − 13			x3
Rom	13.4 − 5			x3

Afraid see Fear

Anger, Fury
Josh 23.16 then in his **anger** he will **punish** you,
2 Sam 6.8 had **punished** Uzzah in **anger**.
1 Chr 13.11 had **punished** Uzzah in **anger**.
2 Chr 28.11 the Lord will **punish** you in his **anger**.
28.13 made him **angry** enough to **punish** us.
Job 20.23 God will **punish** him in **fury** and **anger**.
21.17 God ever **punish** the wicked in **anger**
21.30 On the day God is **angry** and **punishes**,
36.13 being **angry**, and even when **punished**,
Ps 6.1 Don't **punish** me in your **anger**!
38.1 don't **punish** me in your **anger**!
94.1 God who **punishes**; reveal your **anger**!
Is 9.19 Almighty is **angry**, his **punishment** burns
10.5 to **punish** those with whom I am **angry**.
13.3 war and **punish** those he is **angry** with.
51.17 **punishment** that the Lord in his **anger**
60.10 In my **anger** I **punished** you,
66.15 storm to **punish** those he is **angry** with.
Jer 2.35 **angry**...But I, the Lord, will **punish**
10.24 or **punish** us when you are **angry**;
25.7 **angry**...and have brought his **punishment**
Ezek 5.15 **angry** and **furious** with you and **punish**
16.38 in my **anger** and **fury** I will **punish** you
22.24 and so I am **punishing** it in my **anger**.
Hos 11.9 I will not **punish** you in my **anger**;

Nah 1.2 he **punishes**...In his **anger** he pays them

Correct
Deut 8.5 God **corrects** and **punishes** you
Heb 12.6 **corrects** everyone he loves, and **punishes**

Death see Destroy

Deserve
2 Sam 3.39 **punish** these criminals as they **deserve**!
1 Kgs 8.32 **Punish** the guilty one as he **deserves**,
2 Chr 6.23 **Punish** the guilty one as he **deserves**
Ezra 9.13 have **punished** us less than we **deserve**
Job 8.4 so he **punished** them as they **deserved**.
11.6 is **punishing** you less than you **deserve**.
36.17 you are being **punished** as you **deserve**.
Ps 31.23 but **punishes** the proud as they **deserve**.
103.10 He does not **punish** us as we **deserve**
Is 53.6 the **punishment** all of us **deserved**.
65.7 **punish** them as their past deeds **deserve**.
Jer 49.12 not **deserve** to be **punished** had to drink
51.6 revenge and **punishing** it as it **deserves**.
Zech 1.6 had **punished** them as they **deserved**
Lk 12.48 he **deserves** a whipping, will be **punished**
Rom 1.27 themselves the **punishment** they **deserve**
Heb 2.2 it received the **punishment** he **deserved**.
10.29 worse is the **punishment** he will **deserve**!

Destroy, Death
Gen 9.5 I will **punish** with **death** any animal
Lev 19.20 will be **punished** but not put to **death**,
Num 16.29 natural **death** without some **punishment**
Josh 24.20 and **punish** you. He will **destroy** you,
Ezra 7.26 he is to be **punished** promptly: by **death**
Neh 13.18 God **punished** your ancestors when he brought **destruction**
Job 31.11 wickedness should be **punished** by **death**.
31.28 Such a sin should be **punished** by **death**;
Ps 28.5 he will **punish** them and **destroy** them
54.5 **punish** my enemies. He will **destroy**
94.23 He will **punish** them...and **destroy** them
Is 10.25 **punishing** you, and then I will **destroy**
26.14 have **punished** them and **destroyed** them.
Ezek 16.38 and fury I will **punish** you with **death**.
Hos 11.9 will not **punish** you...I will not **destroy**
12.14 **death**...The Lord will **punish** them
Obad .8 the day I **punish** Edom, I will **destroy**
Jon 1.14 don't **punish** us with **death**
Mt 24.9 to be **punished** and be put to **death**.
2 Thes 1.9 the **punishment** of eternal **destruction**,

Disgrace, Shame
2 Kgs 19.3 are being **punished** and are in **disgrace**.
Is 26.11 **punish** them. Lord, put them to **shame**.
37.3 are being **punished** and are in **disgrace**.
Ezek 6.9 have **punished** them and **disgraced** them
Hos 12.14 **punish** them for the **disgrace** they have

Disgusting see Evil

Enemies, Hate
Ex 20.5 bring **punishment** on those who **hate** me
Deut 5.9 bring **punishment** on those who **hate** me
7.10 hesitate to **punish** those who **hate** him.
32.41 take revenge on my **enemies** and **punish** those who **hate** me.
Ps 3.7 You **punish** all my **enemies**
34.21 who **hate** the righteous will be **punished**.
54.5 their own evil to **punish** my **enemies**.
81.15 **hate** me would bow in fear before me; their **punishment**
109.20 **punish** my **enemies** in that way
Prov 29.24 own worst **enemy**. He will be **punished**
Is 26.11 Your **enemies** do not know that you will **punish** them.
27.7 **punished**...as severely as its **enemies**,
35.4 coming to **punish** your **enemies**.

Is　59.18　He will **punish** his **enemies**.
　　63.4　it was time to **punish** their **enemies**.
　　66.6　the Lord **punishing** his **enemies**!
Jer　30.14　you like an **enemy**; your **punishment**
　　46.10　today he will **punish** his **enemies**.
Ezek　5.9　hate, I will **punish** Jerusalem as I have
Mic　4.13　go and **punish** your **enemies**!
Zeph　3.15　your **punishment**; he has removed all your
　　　　　enemies.

Evil, Disgusting, Immoral, Wicked

Gen　15.16　so **wicked** that they must be **punished**.
Ex　34.7　forgive **evil** and sin; but I will...**punish**
Judg　20.10　and **punish** Gibeah for this **immoral** act
1 Sam　25.39　Lord has **punished** Nabal for his **evil**.
Job　21.17　Did God ever **punish** the **wicked**
　　21.30　and **punishes**, it is the **wicked** man
　　22.19　when they see the **wicked punished**.
　　27.7　**punished** like **wicked**, unrighteous men.
　　27.13　**punishes wicked**, violent men.
　　31.11　**wickedness** should be **punished** by death.
Ps　7.16　So they are **punished** by their own **evil**
　　10.12　**punish** those **wicked** men!
　　10.15　of **wicked** and **evil** men; **punish** them
　　11.6　on the **wicked**; he **punishes** them
　　28.4　**Punish** them...for the **evil** they have
　　54.5　their own **evil** to **punish** my enemies.
　　56.7　**Punish** them, O God, for their **evil**;
　　59.5　**punish** the heathen; show no mercy to **evil**
　　　　　traitors!
　　91.8　how the **wicked** are **punished**.
　　94.23　will **punish** them for their **wickedness**
　　125.5　But when you **punish** the **wicked**,
Prov　11.21　be sure that **evil** men will be **punished**.
　　11.31　**wicked** and sinful people will be **punished**.
Ecc　8.14　get the **punishment** of the **wicked**,
Is　11.4　be **punished**, and **evil** persons will die.
　　13.11　**punish** all **wicked** people for their sins.
　　31.2　his threats to **punish evil** men
　　53.5　because of the **evil** we did. We are healed by
　　　　　the **punishment**
　　65.7　**evil** of me. So I will **punish** them
Jer　2.19　Your own **evil** will **punish** you,
　　23.2　**punish** you for the **evil** you have done.
　　51.56　I am a God who **punishes evil**,
Lam　1.22　**wickedness**; **Punish** them as you **punished**
Ezek　7.4　to **punish** you for the **disgusting** things
　　7.9　to **punish** you for the **disgusting** things
　　11.21　**punish** the people who love...**disgusting**
　　14.22　See how **evil** they are...the **punishment**
　　23.49　I will **punish** you for your **immorality**
　　33.12　stops doing **evil**, he won't be **punished**,
　　44.13　the **punishment** for the **disgusting** things
Dan　8.23　so **wicked** that they must be **punished**,
Hos　4.9　I will **punish** you...for the **evil** you do.
　　7.12　**punish** them for the **evil** they have
Acts　2.40　**punishment** coming on this **wicked**
Rom　13.4　God's **punishment** on those who do **evil**
1 Pet　2.14　by him to **punish** the **evildoers**
2 Pet　2.9　to keep the **wicked** under **punishment**
Jude　7　**immorality**...they suffer the **punishment**
Rev　19.2　her **immorality**. God has **punished** her

Fear, Afraid

Job　31.23　Because I **fear** God's **punishment**,
Ps　81.15　**fear** before me; their **punishment** would
Jer　23.4　**afraid** or terrified, and I will not **punish**
Ezek　7.27　will shake with **fear**. I will **punish**
Rom　13.4　be **afraid**...his power to **punish** is real.
1 Jn　4.18　because **fear** has to do with **punishment**.

Forgive see **Mercy**

Fury see **Anger**

God

Ex　10.17　God to take away this fatal **punishment**
　　20.7　**Lord** your **God**, will **punish** anyone
Num　16.29　without some **punishment** from **God**,
Deut　5.11　**Lord** your **God**, will **punish** anyone
　　8.5　**God** corrects and **punishes** you
Josh　9.20　if we don't, **God** will **punish** us.
1 Sam　3.17　**God** will **punish** you severely
　　5.7　The **God** of Israel is **punishing** us
　　5.11　**God** was **punishing** them so severely.
2 Kgs　19.4　**God** hear these insults and **punish**
1 Chr　12.17　**God**...will know it and **punish** you.
　　15.13　the **Lord** our **God** punished us
　　21.7　**God**...**punished** Israel.
　　21.17　my **God**, **punish** me and my family,
　　27.24　**God punished** Israel because of this
Ezra　9.13　that you, our **God**, have **punished** us
Neh　13.18　why **God punished** your ancestors
Job　8.4　against **God**, and so he **punished** them
　　9.34　Stop **punishing** me, **God**!
　　11.6　**God** is **punishing** you less than
　　20.23　**God** will **punish** him in fury and anger.
　　21.17　**God** ever **punish** the wicked in anger
　　21.19　You claim **God punishes** a child
　　21.19　Let **God punish** the sinners themselves;
　　21.30　On the day **God** is angry and **punishes**,
　　27.13　**God punishes** wicked, violent men.
　　31.23　Because I fear **God's punishment**,
　　32.22　**God** would quickly **punish** me if I did.
　　35.15　You think that **God** does not **punish**,
Ps　5.10　Condemn and **punish** them, O **God**;
　　54.5　May **God** use their own evil to **punish**
　　56.7　**Punish** them, O **God**, for their evil;
　　94.1　**Lord**, you are a **God** who **punishes**;
　　99.8　**God**...even though you **punished**
Is　10.3　What will you do when **God punishes**
　　35.4　**God** is coming...to **punish**
　　37.4　**God** hear these insults and **punish**
　　53.4　was **punishment** sent by **God**.
Jer　50.18　**God**...will **punish** King Nebuchadnezzar
　　51.9　**God** has **punished** Babylonia
　　51.56　I am a **God** who **punishes** evil,
Lam　3.1　knows what it is to be **punished** by **God**.
Ezek　7.12　**God's punishment** will fall on everyone
Dan　9.14　our **God**, were prepared to **punish** us,
　　11.36　until the time when **God punishes** him.
Hos　9.9　**God** will...**punish** them for it.
Mic　7.4　**God** will **punish** the people,
Hab　3.16　**God** will **punish** those who attack us.
Mt　3.7　the **punishment God** is about to send?
　　26.74　May **God punish** me if I am not!
Mk　5.7　For **God's** sake...don't **punish** me!
　　14.71　May **God punish** me if I am not!
Lk　3.7　the **punishment God** is about to send?
　　21.23　**God's punishment** will fall on this people.
Jn　3.36　will remain under **God's punishment**.
Rom　1.19　**God punishes** them, because
　　3.5　**God** does wrong when he **punishes** us?
　　13.4　and carries out **God's punishment**
　　13.5　not just because of **God's punishment**,
Gal　5.10　whoever he is, will be **punished** by **God**.
2 Thes　1.8　to **punish** those who reject **God**
Rev　19.2　**God** has **punished** her because
　　22.18　**God** will add to his **punishment**

God's People

Josh　22.17　the Lord **punished** his own **people**
Is　5.25　angry with his **people**...to **punish** them.
　　27.8　**punished** his **people** by sending them
Jer　1.16　**punish** my **people** because they have
　　15.13　my **people**, in order to **punish** them
Lam　4.6　**people** have been **punished** even more

Ezek	21.10	**my people** have disregarded,..**punishment**.
Amos	7.4	saw him preparing to **punish his people**
Obad	.16	**people** have drunk a...cup of **punishment**

Hate see **Enemies**

Immoral see **Evil**

Life

Gen	9.5	takes human **life**, he will be **punished**.
Ex	21.23	the **punishment** shall be **life** for **life**,
Deut	19.21	the **punishment** is to be a **life** for a **life**,
Jer	18.11	to **punish** them. Tell them to stop living sinful **lives**
Jon	1.14	**punish** us...for taking this man's **life**!
Jn	3.36	**life**, but will remain under...**punishment**.

Lord

see also **God**

Lev	18.25	and so the **Lord** is **punishing** the land
Deut	32.35	the **Lord** will...**punish** them;
Josh	22.17	the **Lord punished** his own people
	22.23	let the **Lord** himself **punish** us.
	22.31	of Israel from the **Lord's punishment**.
Ruth	1.17	May the **Lord's** worst **punishment**
1 Sam	5.6	the **Lord punished** the people of Ashdod
	5.9	the **Lord punished** that city too
	20.16	the **Lord** will **punish** you.
	25.39	The **Lord** has **punished** Nabal
	26.9	The **Lord** will certainly **punish**
2 Sam	3.39	the **Lord punish** these criminals
	6.8	the **Lord** had **punished** Uzzah in anger.
	16.8	**Lord** is **punishing** you for murdering
	24.14	**Lord** himself be the one to **punish** us,
1 Kgs	2.32	The **Lord** will **punish** Joab
	2.44	The **Lord** will **punish** you for it.
	14.15	The **Lord** will **punish** Israel,
1 Chr	13.11	the **Lord** had **punished** Uzzah in anger.
	21.13	**Lord** himself be the one to **punish** me,
2 Chr	12.2	disloyalty to the **Lord** was **punished**.
	21.14	**Lord** will severely **punish** your people,
	24.22	May the **Lord**...**punish** you!
	26.20	because the **Lord** had **punished** him.
	28.11	or the **Lord** will **punish** you
	32.26	so the **Lord** did not **punish** the people
Ps	10.12	O **Lord**, **punish** those wicked men!
	31.23	The **Lord**...**punishes** the proud
	32.4	Day and night you **punished** me, **Lord**;
	38.1	O **Lord**, don't **punish** me in your anger!
	109.20	**Lord**, **punish** my enemies in that way
Is	9.13	the **Lord** Almighty has **punished** them,
	9.14	the **Lord** will **punish** Israel's leaders
	19.22	The **Lord** will **punish** the Egyptians,
	24.21	the **Lord** will **punish** the powers above
	26.16	You **punished** your people, **Lord**,
	27.8	The **Lord punished** his people
	53.6	**Lord** made the **punishment** fall on him.
	66.6	of the **Lord punishing** his enemies!
Jer	2.35	But I, the **Lord**, will **punish** you
	5.29	But I, the **Lord**, will **punish** them
	11.22	**Lord** Almighty said, "I will **punish**
	29.31	I, the **Lord**, will **punish** Shemaiah
Lam	3.64	**Punish** them...O **Lord**;
	4.22	But Edom, the **Lord** will **punish** you;
Hos	12.14	The **Lord** will **punish** them
Jon	1.14	O **Lord**, we pray, don't **punish** us
Zeph	1.8	says the **Lord**, "I will **punish**
	3.15	The **Lord** has ended your **punishment**;
Zech	1.6	I, the **Lord**...had **punished** them
1 Cor	11.32	are judged and **punished** by the **Lord**,
1 Thes	4.6	the **Lord** will **punish** those who do that.

Love

Prov	13.24	**punish** your son, you don't **love** him.
Jer	32.18	**love** to thousands, but you also **punish**

Ezek	11.21	**punish** the people who **love** to worship
Heb	12.6	corrects everyone he **loves**, and **punishes**
Rev	3.19	I rebuke and **punish** all whom I **love**.

Mercy, Forgive, Mind, Spare

Deut	19.21	show no **mercy**; the **punishment** is to be
2 Sam	24.14	the one to **punish** us, for he is **merciful**
	24.16	**Lord changed his mind** about **punishing**
1 Chr	21.13	to **punish** me, because he is **merciful**.
	21.17	**punish** me and my family, and **spare**
Ps	59.5	**punish** the heathen; show no **mercy**
	99.8	**forgives**, even though you **punished** them
Is	40.2	are now **forgiven**. I have **punished** them
	53.11	**punishment** of many and...I will **forgive**
	66.19	**punishes** them. "But I will **spare** some
Ezek	7.4	any **mercy**. I am going to **punish** you
	7.9	any **mercy**. I am going to **punish** you
	24.14	or be **merciful**. You will be **punished**
Joel	2.13	always ready to **forgive** and not **punish**.
Amos	7.8	**change my mind** again about **punishing**
	8.1	**change my mind** again about **punishing**
Jon	3.10	**his mind** and did not **punish** them
	4.2	to **change your mind** and not **punish**.
2 Cor	2.6	been **punished**...now...**forgive** him

Power

Ex	3.20	use my **power** and will **punish** Egypt
Ps	3.7	You **punish** all my enemies and leave them **powerless**
	10.15	**power** of wicked and evil men; **punish**
Is	24.21	the Lord will **punish** the **powers** above
	27.1	**powerful** and deadly sword to **punish**
Jer	30.20	restore the nation's...**power**...I will **punish**
Nah	1.3	**powerful** and never lets the guilty go **unpunished**.
Rom	13.4	his **power** to **punish** is real.
1 Tim	1.20	**punished** by handing them over to the **power** of Satan;

Proud

Ps	31.23	**punishes** the **proud** as they deserve
Is	13.11	everyone who is **proud** and **punish**
Zeph	2.10	Ammon will be **punished** for their **pride**

Rescue see **Save**

Righteous

Job	27.7	**punished** like wicked, **unrighteous** men.
Ps	34.21	who hate the **righteous** will be **punished**.
	119.75	**righteous**, Lord, and that you **punished**
Prov	11.21	**punished**, but **righteous** men will escape.
Ecc	8.14	**righteous** men get the **punishment**
Mt	25.46	eternal **punishment**, but the **righteous**
Heb	12.11	**punishment** reap the peaceful reward of a **righteous** life.

Save, Rescue

Ex	6.6	**punishment** upon them, and I will **save**
Josh	22.31	**saved** the people...from...**punishment**.
Ps	3.7	**Save** me, my God! You **punish** all my
Is	35.4	to your **rescue**, coming to **punish**
	63.4	time to **save** my people...time to **punish**
Zeph	3.19	**punish** your oppressors; I will **rescue**
Acts	2.40	**Save** yourselves from the **punishment**

Shame see **Disgrace**

Sin

Ex	32.34	**punish** these people for their **sin**"
Num	12.11	this **punishment** for our foolish **sin**.
	32.23	you will be **punished** for your **sin**.
1 Chr	9.1	Babylon as **punishment** for their **sins**.
Ezra	9.13	in **punishment** for our **sins**
Job	21.19	God **punishes** a child for the **sins**
	21.19	Let God **punish** the **sinners** themselves;
	21.20	Let **sinners** bear their own **punishment**;
	31.28	Such a **sin** should be **punished** by
	34.26	He **punishes sinners** where all can see

Ps	39.11	You **punish** a man's **sins** by your
	58.10	when they see **sinners punished**;
	79.8	Do not **punish** us for the **sins**;
	89.32	then I will **punish** them for their **sins**;
	99.8	you **punished** them for their **sins**.
Prov	11.31	and **sinful** people will be **punished**.
Is	13.11	**punish** all wicked people for their **sins**.
	57.17	**sin** and greed, and so I **punished** them
Jer	1.16	I will **punish** my people because they have **sinned**;
	14.10	and **punish** them because of their **sins**."
	15.13	in order to **punish** them for the **sins**
	25.12	will **punish** Babylonia...for their **sin**
	30.14	your **punishment**...because your **sins**
	30.15	I **punished** you...because your **sins**
Lam	1.22	as you **punished** me for my **sins**.
	3.39	when we are **punished** for our **sin**?
Ezek	33.29	**punish** the people for their **sins**
	35.5	time of final **punishment** for her **sins**.
Hos	8.13	remember their **sin** and **punish** them
	9.9	remember their **sin** and **punish** them
	10.10	attack this **sinful** people and **punish**
	10.10	will be **punished** for their many **sins**.

Spare see **Mercy**

Wicked see **Evil**

PURE

Lev	14.2	— 16.34	x24
Ex	28.14	— 31.8	x10
Ex	37.2 – 29		x10
Heb	9.10	— 10.29	x10
Num	19.12 – 21		x9
Ex	25.11 – 39		x8
Num	8.6 – 21		x6
2 Chr	29.5	— 30.24	x6
Num	15.25	— 16.47	x5
Num	31.19 – 22		x5
Neh	12.30	— 13.30	x5
Ex	39.15 – 37		x4
Lev	24.2 – 7		x4
Num	28.22	— 29.11	x4
Ezek	43.20	— 45.18	x4
Tit	1.15	— 2.14	x4
1 Pet	1.2	— 3.2	x4
1 Chr	28.17	— 29.4	x3
Ezek	24.11 – 13		x3
Zech	13.1 – 9		x3
Acts	21.24 – 26		x3
1 Cor	5.7	— 6.11	x3
Phil	2.15	— 4.8	x3
1 Tim	4.12	— 5.22	x3

Blood

Lev	14.7	**blood** seven times on the person who is to be **purified**
	14.52	**purify** the house with the bird's **blood**,
	16.18	**purify** it. He must take some of the bull's **blood**
Ezek	43.22	**Purify** the altar with its **blood**
Heb	9.14	His **blood** will **purify** our consciences
	9.22	almost everything is **purified** by **blood**,
	10.29	**blood** of God's covenant which **purified**
	13.12	to **purify** the people from sin with his own **blood**.
1 Pet	1.2	and be **purified** by his **blood**.
1 Jn	1.7	the **blood** of Jesus, his Son, **purifies** us

Ceremony, Sprinkle

Num	8.7	**sprinkle**...with the water of **purification**
	19.21	who **sprinkles** the water for **purification**
Neh	12.45	performed the **ceremonies** of **purification**
Lk	2.22	to perform the **ceremony** of **purification**,
Acts	21.24	in the **ceremony** of **purification**

Acts	21.26	performed the **ceremony** of **purification**
	24.18	completed the **ceremony** of **purification**.
Heb	9.10	and various **purification ceremonies**.

Clean see **Holy**

Defile, Unclean

Lev	16.16	**purify** the Most Holy Place from the **uncleanness**
Num	19.13	does not **purify** himself remains **unclean**,
	19.19	water on the **unclean** person...to **purify**
	19.20	does not **purify** himself remains **unclean**,
Lam	4.7	were **undefiled** and **pure** as snow,
Ezek	24.13	to **purify** you, you remained **defiled**.
Tit	1.15	nothing is **pure** to those who are **defiled**
Heb	9.13	**unclean**, and this **purifies** them

Faultless see **Holy**

Forgive

Num	15.28	**purify** the man...and he will be **forgiven**.
Heb	9.22	**purified** by blood, and sins are **forgiven**
1 Jn	1.9	he will **forgive** us our sins and **purify** us

Holy, Clean, Faultless

Gen	35.2	**purify** yourselves and put on **clean**
Ex	30.35	Add salt to keep it **pure** and **holy**.
Lev	14.20	**purification**, and the man will be...**clean**.
Ezra	6.20	had **purified** themselves and were...**clean**.
Eph	5.27	in all its beauty — **pure** and **faultless**,
Col	1.22	**holy**, **pure**, and **faultless**,
1 Thes	2.10	was **pure**, right, and **without fault**.
2 Pet	3.14	to be **pure** and **faultless** in God's sight

Holy Place

Lev	16.16	to **purify** the Most Holy Place
	16.17	**Holy Place** to perform...**purification**
	16.20	ritual to **purify** the Most Holy Place,
	16.33	ritual to **purify** the Most Holy Place,

Sight

Job	11.4	claim you are **pure** in the **sight** of God.
	15.15	even they are not **pure** in his **sight**.
	25.4	be righteous or **pure** in God's **sight**?
2 Pet	3.14	to be **pure** and faultless in God's **sight**

Sin

Lev	16.19	to **purify** it from the **sins**
	16.30	to **purify** them from all their **sins**,
	19.22	**purification** to remove the man's **sin**,
Num	15.28	to **purify** the man from his **sin**,
Ezra	8.35	goats to **purify** themselves from **sin**.
Ps	73.13	**pure** and have not committed **sin**?
Jer	33.8	I will **purify** them from the **sins** that
1 Cor	6.11	But you have been **purified** from **sin**;
Heb	2.11	He **purifies** people from their **sins**,
	9.22	**purified** by blood, and **sins** are forgiven
	10.2	really been **purified** from their **sins**,
	10.10	all **purified** from **sin** by the offering
	10.14	those who are **purified** from **sin**.
	10.29	covenant which **purified** him from **sin**?
	13.12	in order to **purify** the people from **sin**
2 Pet	1.9	has been **purified** from his past **sins**.
1 Jn	1.7	his Son, **purifies** us from every **sin**.
	1.9	forgives us our **sins** and **purify** us

Sprinkle see **Ceremony**

Unclean see **Defile**

PURPOSE

Rom	6.13 – 19		x4
Rom	8.20	— 9.11	x3
1 Cor	1.10	— 2.10	x3
Eph	1.5 – 11		x3
2 Tim	1.9	— 3.10	x3
1 Pet	1.2 – 9		x3

God, Lord

2 Kgs	14.27	was not the **Lord's purpose** to destroy
Ps	33.10	The **Lord** frustrates the **purposes**
Lk	7.30	rejected **God's purpose** for themselves
	9.31	he would soon fulfil **God's purpose**
Acts	13.36	David served **God's purposes**
	20.27	the whole **purpose** of God.
Rom	9.11	the result of **God's** own **purpose**,
1 Cor	1.27	**God purposely** chose what the world
	2.10	the hidden depths of **God's purposes.**
Eph	1.9	**God** did what he had **purposed**,
	3.11	**God**...according to his eternal **purpose**
Jas	1.20	not achieve **God's** righteous **purpose.**
1 Pet	1.2	according to the **purpose** of God

AV QUICK see ALIVE

RAGE

2 Kgs	19.27 – 28	x2
Is	37.28 – 29	x2

Anger, Fury

Job	19.11	God is **angry** and **rages** against me;
Ps	50.3	**raging** fire is in front of him, a **furious**
	78.49	pouring out his **anger** and fierce **rage**,
	85.3	**angry**...and held back your **furious rage.**
Jer	23.19	His **anger** is a storm...that will **rage**
	30.23	Lord's **anger** is a storm...that will **rage**
Ezek	5.13	feel all the force of my **anger** and **rage**
	22.20	My **anger** and **rage** will melt them
Rev	11.18	**rage**, because the time for your **anger**

RAISE (RISE)

1 Cor	15.4	—	16.1	x23
Acts	2.24	—	5.31	x7
Rom	6.4	—	8.34	x7
Mt	26.32	—	28.7	x6
Mk	8.31	—	10.34	x6
Jn	5.21	—	7.39	x6
Lk	22.45	—	24.46	x5
Mt	22.23 – 31			x4
Lk	20.27 – 36			x4
Jn	12.1 – 17			x4
Acts	13.30 – 37			x4
Acts	23.6	—	24.21	x4
Col	1.18	—	3.1	x4
Dan	10.10	—	12.7	x3
Mt	16.21	—	17.23	x3
Mk	12.18 – 25			x3
2 Cor	4.14	—	5.15	x3
Heb	11.19 – 35			x3

Christ, Jesus, Son of God

Mt	27.53	and after **Jesus rose** from death,
Jn	7.39	because **Jesus** had not been **raised**
	12.9	Lazarus, whom **Jesus** had **raised**
	12.16	but when **Jesus** had been **raised**
	21.14	**Jesus** appeared...after he was **raised**
Acts	2.32	God has **raised** this very **Jesus**
	4.2	that **Jesus** had **risen** from death,
	5.30	The God of our ancestors **raised Jesus**
	13.32	by **raising Jesus** to life.
Rom	1.4	to be the **Son** of God by being **raised**
	4.24	who **raised Jesus** our Lord from death.
	6.4	just as **Christ** was **raised** from death
	6.9	we know that **Christ** has been **raised**
	7.4	of **Christ**; and now you belong to him who was **raised**
	8.11	Spirit of God, who **raised Jesus**
	8.11	he who **raised Christ** from death
	14.9	**Christ** died and **rose** to life
1 Cor	15.12	message is that **Christ** has been **raised**
	15.13	it means that **Christ** was not **raised**;
	15.14	and if **Christ** has not been **raised**
	15.15	that he **raised Christ** from death

1 Cor	15.16	neither has **Christ** been **raised**
	15.17	And if **Christ** has not been **raised**,
	15.20	the truth is that **Christ** has been **raised**
	15.22	be **raised** to life because of...**Christ.**
	15.23	each one will be **raised**...**Christ**, first
2 Cor	4.14	God, who **raised** the Lord **Jesus** to life,
	4.14	will also **raise** us up with **Jesus**
Eph	1.20	when he **raised Christ** from death
	2.6	union with **Christ Jesus** he **raised** us up
Col	1.18	the first-born **Son**, who was **raised**
	2.12	you were also **raised** with **Christ**
	3.1	You have been **raised** to life with **Christ**
1 Thes	1.10	his **Son Jesus**, whom he **raised**
	4.14	that **Jesus** died and **rose** again,
2 Tim	2.8	**Jesus Christ**, who was **raised**
Heb	13.20	God has **raised** from death our Lord **Jesus**.
1 Pet	1.3	he gave us new life by **raising Jesus**

Dead

Job	14.12	people **die**, never to **rise**.
Ps	88.10	miracles for the **dead**? Do they **rise**
Mt	17.9	Son of Man has been **raised** from **death**.
	22.23	that people will not **rise** from **death**.
	22.28	on the day when the **dead rise** to life,
	22.30	For when the **dead rise** to life
	22.31	as for the **dead rising** to life:
	27.53	and after **Jesus rose** from **death**,
	27.64	people that he was **raised** from **death**.
	28.7	He has been **raised** from **death**,
Mk	8.31	put to **death**, but...he will **rise**
	9.9	Son of Man has **risen** from **death**.
	9.10	about this 'rising from death'
	12.18	that people will not **rise** from **death**,
	12.23	when all the **dead rise** to life
	12.25	For when the **dead rise** to life,
	12.26	as for the **dead** being **raised**:
	16.9	After Jesus **rose** from **death**
Lk	7.22	the **dead** are **raised** to life,
	14.14	the good people **rise** from **death**.
	16.30	if someone were to **rise** from **death**.
	16.31	if someone were to **rise** from **death**.
	20.27	that people will not **rise** from **death**,
	20.33	on the day when the **dead rise** to life,
	20.35	who are worthy to **rise** from **death**
	20.36	because they have **risen** from **death**
	20.37	clearly proves that the **dead** are **raised**
	24.46	and must **rise** from **death**...later.
Jn	2.22	So when he was **raised** from **death**,
	5.21	Just as the Father **raises** the **dead**
	12.1	the man he had **raised** from **death**.
	12.9	whom Jesus had **raised** from **death**
	12.17	of the grave and **raised** him from **death**
	20.9	said that he must **rise** from **death**.
	21.14	disciples after he was **raised** from **death**.
Acts	2.24	But God **raised** him from **death**,
	2.32	has **raised** this very Jesus from **death**
	3.15	but God **raised** him from **death** – and
	4.2	that Jesus had **risen** from **death**
	4.2	which proved that the **dead** will **rise**
	4.10	and whom God **raised** from **death**.
	5.30	of our ancestors **raised** Jesus from **death**
	10.40	But God **raised** him from **death**
	10.41	after he **rose** from **death**.
	13.30	But God **raised** him from **death**
	13.34	God said about **raising** him from **death**
	13.37	the one whom God **raised** from **death**.
	17.3	had to suffer and **rise** from **death**.
	17.31	by **raising** that man from **death**!
	17.32	Paul speak about a **raising** from **death**
	23.6	I have that the **dead** will **rise** to life!
	23.8	that people will not **rise** from **death**
	24.15	good and the bad, will **rise** from **death**.
	24.21	for believing that the **dead** will **rise**

Acts	26.8	to believe that God **raises** the **dead**?
	26.23	the first one to **rise** from **death**,
Rom	1.4	Son of God by being **raised** from **death**.
	4.24	who **raised** Jesus our Lord from **death**.
	6.4	just as Christ was **raised** from **death**
	6.9	Christ has been **raised** from **death**
	7.4	was **raised** from **death** in order that we
	8.11	who **raised** Jesus from **death**,
	10.9	believe that God **raised** him from **death**,
1 Cor	6.14	God **raised** the Lord from **death**
	15.12	you say that the **dead** will not be **raised**
	15.14	Christ has not been **raised** from **death**,
	15.15	if it is true that the **dead** are not **raised**
	15.16	For if the **dead** are not **raised**,
	15.20	Christ has been **raised** from **death**
	15.21	the **rising** from **death** comes
	15.29	some claim, that the **dead** are not **raised**
	15.32	But if the **dead** are not **raised** to life,
	15.35	How can the **dead** be **raised** to life?
	15.42	how it will be when the **dead** are **raised**
	15.51	the **dead** will be **raised**,
2 Cor	1.9	God, who **raises** the **dead**.
Gal	1.1	who **raised** him from **death**.
Eph	1.20	when he **raised** Christ from **death**
	5.14	Wake up...and **rise** from **death**,
Phil	3.11	myself to be **raised** from **death** to life.
Col	1.18	who was **raised** from **death**,
	2.12	of God, who **raised** him from **death**.
1 Thes	1.10	**raised** from **death** and who rescues us
	4.14	Jesus **died** and **rose** again
2 Tim	2.8	who was **raised** from **death**,
Heb	11.19	God was able to **raise** Isaac from **death**
	11.35	received their **dead** relatives **raised**
	13.20	has **raised** from **death** our Lord Jesus
1 Pet	1.3	life by **raising** Jesus Christ from **death**.
	1.21	**raised** him from **death** and gave him
Rev	1.5	the first to be **raised** from **death**
	20.5	This is the first **raising** of the **dead**.
	20.6	included in this first **raising** of the **dead**.

Glory

Jn	7.39	Jesus had not been **raised** to **glory**.
	12.16	when Jesus had been **raised** to **glory**,
Rom	6.4	**raised** from **death** by the **glorious** power
1 Pet	1.21	who **raised** him...and gave him **glory**;

God

Acts	2.24	But **God raised** him from death,
	2.32	**God** has **raised** this very Jesus
	2.33	**raised** to the right-hand side of **God**,
	3.15	but **God raised** him from death
	4.10	and whom **God raised** from death.
	5.30	The **God** of our ancestors **raised** Jesus
	5.31	**God raised** him to his right-hand side
	10.40	**God raised** him from death three days
	13.30	**God raised** him from death,
	13.34	**God** said about **raising** him from death,
	13.37	to the one whom **God raised**
	26.8	to believe that **God raises** the dead?
Rom	8.11	Spirit of **God**, who **raised** Jesus
	10.9	believe that **God raised** him from death,
1 Cor	6.14	**God raised** the Lord from death,
2 Cor	1.9	only on **God**, who **raises** the dead.
	4.14	**God**, who **raised** the Lord Jesus to life,
Gal	1.1	**God** the Father, who **raised** him
Phil	2.9	**God raised** him to the highest place
Col	2.12	power of **God**, who **raised** him
Heb	11.19	**God** was able to **raise** Isaac from death
	13.20	has **raised** from death our Lord
1 Pet	1.21	you believe in **God**, who **raised** him

Jesus see Christ

Last

Jn	6.39	**raise** them all to life on the **last** day.
	6.40	I will **raise** them to life on the **last** day.

Jn	6.44	I will **raise** him to life on the **last** day.
	6.54	I will **raise** him to life on the **last** day.

Life

Mt	16.21	three days later I will be **raised** to **life**.
	17.23	three days later he will be **raised** to **life**.
	20.19	three days later he will be **raised** to **life**.
	22.28	the day when the dead **rise** to **life**,
	22.30	For when the dead **rise** to **life**
	22.31	as for the dead **rising** to **life**:
	26.32	I am **raised** to **life**, I will go to Galilee
	27.52	people who had died were **raised** to **life**.
	27.63	I will be **raised** to **life** three days later.
Mk	8.31	three days later he will **rise** to **life**.
	9.31	Three days later...he will **rise** to **life**.
	10.34	three days later he will **rise** to **life**.
	12.23	when all the dead **rise** to **life**
	12.25	For when the dead **rise** to **life**,
	14.28	But after I am **raised** to **life**
Lk	7.22	the dead are **raised** to **life**,
	9.22	three days later he will **rise** to **life**.
	18.33	three days later he will **rise** to **life**.
	20.33	the day when the dead **rise** to **life**,
	20.37	proves that the dead are **raised** to **life**.
	24.7	and three days later **rise** to **life**.
Jn	5.21	**raises** the dead and gives them **life**,
	5.29	who have done good will **rise** and **live**,
	6.39	**raise** them all to **life** on the last day.
	6.40	I will **raise** them to **life** on the last day.
	6.44	I will **raise** him to **life** on the last day.
	6.54	I will **raise** him to **life** on the last day.
	11.23	Your brother will **rise** to **life**,
	11.24	he will **rise** to **life** on the last day.
Acts	3.15	who leads to **life**, but God **raised** him
	4.2	proved that the dead will **rise** to **life**.
	13.32	by **raising** Jesus to **life**.
	23.6	that the dead will **rise** to **life**!
	24.21	that the dead will **rise** to **life**.
Rom	4.25	**raised** to **life** in order to put us right
	6.5	by being **raised** to **life** as he was.
	8.11	he who **raised** Christ...will also give **life**
	8.34	**raised** to **life** and is at the right-hand
	14.9	For Christ died and **rose** to **life**
1 Cor	15.4	buried and that he was **raised** to **life**
	15.12	that the dead will not be **raised** to **life**?
	15.15	true that the dead are not **raised** to **life**,
	15.22	the same way all will be **raised** to **life**
	15.29	that the dead are not **raised** to **life**,
	15.32	But if the dead are not **raised** to **life**,
	15.35	How can the dead be **raised** to **life**?
	15.42	when the dead are **raised** to **life**
2 Cor	4.14	who **raised** the Lord Jesus to **life**,
	5.15	for him who died and was **raised** to **life**
Phil	3.11	myself will be **raised** from death to **life**.
Col	3.1	You have been **raised** to **life** with Christ
1 Thes	4.16	will **rise** to **life** first;
Heb	11.35	their dead relatives **raised** back to **life**.
1 Pet	1.3	**life** by **raising** Jesus Christ from death.

Prayer

2 Chr	6.12	and **raised** his arms in **prayer**.
Ps	63.4	I will **raise** my hands to you in **prayer**.
	68.31	Sudanese will **raise** their hands in **prayer**
	134.2	**Raise** your hands in **prayer** in the

Right (hand)

Acts	2.33	been **raised** to the **right-hand** side
	5.31	God **raised** him to his **right-hand** side
Rom	8.34	**raised** to life and is at the **right-hand**
Rev	10.5	**raised** his **right hand** to heaven

Son of God see Christ

REBEL

	Ezek	2.3	—	3.27	x9
	Josh	22.16 – 31			x7

Jer	2.8	—	7.26	x7
Ps	78.8 – 57			x5
Ezek	12.2 – 25			x5
Num	16.1	—	17.10	x4
Deut	31.27	—	32.15	x4
Is	1.2 – 28			x4
Hos	7.13	—	9.15	x4
Heb	3.8 – 18			x4
Num	26.9	—	27.14	x3
Deut	1.26	—	2.30	x3
Deut	9.7 – 24			x3
2 Sam	18.28 – 32			x3
Ezra	4.12 – 19			x3
Zeph	3.1 – 11			x3

Lord, God

Num	14.9	Do not **rebel** against the **Lord**
	26.9	when they **rebelled** against the **Lord**.
	27.3	Korah, who **rebelled** against the **Lord**;
Deut	1.26	you **rebelled** against...the **Lord**
	9.24	you have **rebelled** against the **Lord**.
	13.5	tells you to **rebel** against the **Lord**,
	31.27	They have **rebelled** against the **Lord**
Josh	22.16	You have **rebelled** against the **Lord**
	22.18	If you **rebel** against the **Lord** today,
	22.19	but don't **rebel** against the **Lord**
	22.29	certainly not **rebel** against the **Lord**
	24.47	from **rebelling** against your **God**.
2 Chr	25.27	when he **rebelled** against the **Lord**,
Job	23.1	I still **rebel** and complain against **God**;
Ps	78.56	they **rebelled** against Almighty **God**
	107.11	they had **rebelled** against...**God**
Is	30.9	They are always **rebelling** against **God**,
Jer	3.13	you have **rebelled** against the **Lord**,
	4.17	people have **rebelled** against the **Lord**.
	28.16	told the people to **rebel** against the **Lord**.
Mic	1.5	Israel have...**rebelled** against **God**.
Heb	3.8	when they **rebelled** against **God**,
	3.15	when they **rebelled** against **God**.
	3.16	who heard **God's** voice and **rebelled**

Punish

Num	14.18	**rebellion**. Yet I will not fail to **punish**
Is	1.5	**rebelling**? Do you want to be **punished**
Hos	13.16	Samaria must be **punished** for **rebelling**

Refuse see Stubborn

Sin

Lev	16.21	all the evils, **sins**, and **rebellions**
	26.41	penalty for their **sin** and **rebellion**,
Num	14.18	and forgive **sin** and **rebellion**
1 Kgs	8.50	all their **sins** and their **rebellion**
Job	34.37	To his **sins** he adds **rebellion**
Ps	5.10	their many **sins** and their **rebellion**
Is	1.28	crush everyone who **sins** and **rebels**
Jer	33.8	forgive their **sins** and their **rebellion**
Lam	3.42	"We have **sinned** and **rebelled**,
Ezek	20.38	those who are **rebellious** and **sinful**.
Mic	1.5	have **sinned** and **rebelled** against God.

Stubborn, Refuse

Deut	2.30	had made him **stubborn** and **rebellious**,
	21.18	a son who is **stubborn** and **rebellious**
	21.20	Our son is **stubborn** and **rebellious**
	31.27	how **stubborn** and **rebellious** they are
Josh	22.18	**refuse** to follow him now? If you **rebel**
2 Kgs	18.7	**rebelled** against the emperor...and **refused**
Job	15.26	proud and **rebellious**; he **stubbornly**
Is	30.9	**rebelling** against God...always **refusing**
	59.13	have **rebelled** against you...and **refused**
Jer	5.23	You are **stubborn** and **rebellious**;
	6.28	They are all **stubborn rebels**,
	7.26	became more **stubborn** and **rebellious**
Heb	3.8	**stubborn**...when they **rebelled**

Heb	3.15	**stubborn**...when they **rebelled**

REFUGE

Num	35.6 – 28			x7
Josh	21.13 – 38			x5

City

Num	35.6	give the Levites six **cities** of **refuge**
	35.11	you are to choose **cities** of **refuge**
	35.15	These will serve as **cities** of **refuge**
	35.25	return him to the **city** of **refuge**
	35.26	leaves the **city** of **refuge**
	35.28	must remain in the **city** of **refuge**
	35.32	has fled to a **city** of **refuge**,
Josh	20.2	Choose the **cities** of **refuge**
	20.9	These were the **cities** of **refuge**
	21.13	(one of the **cities** of **refuge**),
	21.21	(one of the **cities** of **refuge**)
	21.27	(one of the **cities** of **refuge**)
	21.32	(one of the **cities** of **refuge**)
	21.38	(one of the **cities** of **refuge**)
1 Chr	6.57	Hebron, a **city** of **refuge**,
	6.67	Shechem, the **city** of **refuge**

God, Lord

2 Sam	22.33	This **God** is my strong **refuge**;
Ps	9.9	The **Lord** is a **refuge** for the oppressed,
	19.14	O **Lord**, my **refuge** and my redeemer!
	46.7	the **God** of Jacob is our **refuge**.
	46.11	the **God** of Jacob is our **refuge**.
	59.9	you are my **refuge**, O **God**.
	59.17	My **refuge** is **God**,

REFUSE

Ex	7.14	—	11.9	x9
Jer	5.3	—	8.5	x5
Heb	11.24	—	12.25	x5
Lev	26.15 – 31			x4
1 Kgs	2.16 – 20			x4
1 Kgs	20.35	—	22.49	x4
Num	14.11 – 43			x3
Num	22.13	—	23.25	x3
Deut	15.7 – 9			x3
Deut	25.7 – 9			x3
Neh	9.16 – 29			x3
Esth	1.12 – 17			x3
Job	22.7 – 9			x3
Prov	21.7 – 25			x3
Lam	1.19	—	3.8	x3
Zech	14.17 – 18			x3

Command see Obey

Help

Deut	15.7	not be selfish and **refuse** to **help** him.
	31.18	And I will **refuse** to **help** them then,
	8.15	when you **refused** to **help** me?
Judg	22.9	You not only **refused** to **help** widows,
Job	31.16	I have never **refused** to **help** the poor;
Ps	74.11	Why have you **refused** to **help** us?
Is	58.7	not **refuse** to **help** your own relatives.
Lam	1.19	but they **refused** to **help** me.
	2.3	**refused** to **help** us when the enemy
	3.8	for **help**, but God **refuses** to listen;
Mt	25.45	**refused** to **help** one of these least

Obey, Command, Law

Ex	16.28	people **refuse** to **obey** my **commands**?
Lev	26.15	If you **refuse** to **obey** my **laws**
	26.21	to resist me and **refuse** to **obey** me,
	26.27	to defy me and **refuse** to **obey** me,
Num	14.22	and have **refused** to **obey** me.
Deut	18.19	will punish anyone who **refuses** to **obey**
	21.20	rebellious and **refuses** to **obey** us;
Josh	22.20	Achan son of Zerah **refused** to **obey**
2 Kgs	17.15	They **refused** to **obey** his instructions

Neh	9.16	and **refused** to **obey** your **commands**.
	9.17	They **refused** to **obey**
	9.29	stubborn, they **refused** to **obey**.
Esth	1.12	king's **command**, she **refused** to come.
	1.15	and she **refused** to **obey** it!
Ps	78.10	they **refused** to **obey** his **law**.
	95.10	They **refuse** to **obey** my **commands**.
Prov	1.29	always **refused** to **obey** the Lord.
	3.7	**obey** the Lord and **refuse** to do wrong.
Jer	2.20	**refused** to **obey** me and worship me.
	5.5	and **refuse** to **obey** him.
	13.10	evil people have **refused** to **obey** me.
	35.12	you **refuse** to listen to me and to **obey**
Ezek	5.6	**commands** and **refused** to keep my **laws**.
Dan	9.11	broke your **laws** and **refused** to listen
Acts	7.39	But our ancestors **refused** to **obey** him
Heb	3.10	and **refuse** to **obey** my **commands**.

Punish

Ex	8.2	If you **refuse**, I will **punish** your country
	8.21	if you **refuse**, I will **punish** you
Deut	18.19	will **punish** anyone who **refuses** to obey
Jer	11.8	they **refused**. So I brought...**punishments**

Worship

Num	25.11	**refused** to tolerate the **worship** of any
Deut	30.17	**refuse** to listen, and...**worship** other
Judg	2.19	**worship** other gods, and **refused** to give
Jer	11.10	**refused** to do what I said...**worshipped**
Dan	3.14	you **refuse** to **worship** my god

REGULATION

Lev	11.1	—	20.18	x16
Lev	5.10	—	7.37	x14
Lev	22.9	—	25.2	x11
Num	15.2 – 29			x6
Num	8.26	—	9.14	x4
Neh	11.23	—	13.30	x3
Ezek	43.11	—	44.24	x3

Observe

Lev	16.29	following **regulations** are to be **observed**
	16.31	These **regulations** are to be **observed**
	16.34	These **regulations** are to be **observed**
	22.9	All priests shall **observe** the **regulations**
	23.14	This **regulation** is to be **observed**
	23.21	are to **observe** this **regulation**
	23.44	**regulations** for **observing** the religious
	24.3	This **regulation** is to be **observed**
Num	9.12	**Observe** the Passover according to all the **regulations**.
	9.14	**observe** it according to all the rules and **regulations**.
	15.2	**regulations** for the people of Israel to **observe**
	15.14	he is to **observe** the same **regulations**.
	15.18	**regulations** for the people of Israel to **observe**

REJECT

Jer	4.30	–	10.25	x8
Num	14.11	—	16.30	x5
1 Sam	15.23	—	16.7	x5
Deut	31.20	—	32.19	x4
Mk	6.3	—	9.12	x4
Rom	11.1 – 28			x4
Lev	18.25 – 28			x3
2 Kgs	21.22	—	23.27	x3
Ezek'	20.13 – 24			x3
Hos	8.3	—	9.17	x3
Lk	9.22	—	10.16	x3

Choose

2 Kgs	23.27	I will **reject** Jerusalem, the city I **chose**,
2 Chr	6.42	do not **reject** the king you have **chosen**.
Ps	89.38	your **chosen** king...and **rejected** him.

Ps	132.10	do not **reject** your **chosen** king,
Is	41.9	I did not **reject** you, but **chose** you.
Jer	12.7	I have **rejected** my **chosen** nation.
Rom	11.2	not **rejected** his people, whom he **chose**
1 Pet	2.4	stone **rejected** by man...but **chosen**

Command see Law

God

2 Kgs	21.22	He **rejected**...the **God** of his ancestors,
2 Chr	6.42	**Lord God**, do not **reject** the king
Job	22.17	These are the men who **rejected God**
Ps	9.17	of all those who **reject God**.
	15.4	He despises those whom **God rejects**,
	36.1	he **rejects God** and has no reverence
	53.5	**God** has **rejected** them,
	60.1	You have **rejected** us, **God**,
Is	1.4	You have **rejected**...the holy **God**
Hos	9.17	The **God** I serve will **reject** his people,
Mk	7.9	a clever way of **rejecting God's** law
Lk	7.30	**rejected God's** purpose for themselves
Rom	11.1	Did **God reject** his own people?
	11.2	**God** has not **rejected** his people,
Gal	2.21	I **refuse** to **reject** the grace of **God**.
1 Thes	4.8	is not **rejecting** man, but **God**,
2 Thes	1.8	to punish those who **reject God**

Law, Command

Lev	20.22	**laws**...so that you will not be **rejected**
	26.43	full penalty for having **rejected** my **laws**
1 Sam	15.23	you **rejected** the Lord's **command**,
	15.26	You **rejected** the Lord's **command**,
Neh	9.29	but in pride they **rejected** your **laws**,
Ps	50.17	you **reject** my **commands**.
	107.11	the **commands** of...God and had **rejected**
	119.118	**reject** everyone who disobeys your **laws**;
Ezek	5.6	**rejected** my **commands** and refused to keep my **laws**.
	20.13	my **laws** and **rejected** my **commands**,
	20.16	**rejected** my **commands**, broken my **laws**,
	20.24	**rejected** my **commands**, broken my **laws**,
Dan	9.5	We have **rejected** what you **commanded**
Mk	7.9	a clever way of **rejecting God's** law

Lord

see also **God**

Num	11.20	because you have **rejected the Lord**
	15.31	he has **rejected** what the **Lord** said
	16.30	these men have **rejected the Lord**.
Deut	28.20	If you do evil and **reject the Lord**,
	32.19	**Lord** saw this, he...**rejected**
1 Sam	12.12	you **rejected the Lord** as your king
	15.23	you **rejected** the **Lord's** command,
	15.26	You **rejected** the **Lord's** command,
2 Kgs	17.20	The **Lord rejected** all the Israelites,
Ps	10.3	the greedy man...**rejects the Lord**.
	77.7	Will the **Lord** always **reject** us?
	88.14	Why do you **reject** me, **Lord**?
	132.0	Do not **reject** your chosen king, **Lord**.
Is	5.24	you have **rejected** what the **Lord**
Jer	2.37	I, the **Lord**, have **rejected** those
	5.5	have **rejected** the **Lord's** authority
	6.30	I, the **Lord**, have **rejected** them.
	7.29	I, the **Lord**...have **rejected** my people.
	9.5	The **Lord** says that his people **reject**
	14.19	**Lord**, have you...**rejected** Judah?
Lam	2.7	The **Lord rejected** his altar
	3.31	The **Lord**...will not **reject** us for ever.
1 Pet	2.4	the **Lord**...**rejected** by man

Refuse

Num	14.11	**reject** me? How much longer...**refuse**
Ps	50.17	**refuse** to let me correct you; you **reject**
Is	59.13	**rejected** you, and **refused** to follow
Jer	2.20	**rejected** my authority; you **refused**

Jer	5.5	rejected the Lord's authority and refuse
Ezek	5.6	rejected my commands and refused to
Hos	4.6	refused to acknowledge me and...rejected
Lk	7.30	rejected God's purpose...and refused
Gal	2.21	I refuse to reject the grace of God

Teaching

Deut	31.29	and reject what I have taught them.
Neh	9.29	teachings, but in pride they rejected
Jer	6.19	because they have rejected my teaching
Hos	4.6	and have rejected my teaching,
	8.12	teachings for the people, but they reject
1 Thes	4.8	rejects this teaching is not rejecting

Worthless

Ps	118.22	which the builders rejected as worthless
Jer	6.30	worthless dross, because I...have rejected
Mt	21.42	which the builders rejected as worthless
Mk	12.10	which the builders rejected as worthless
Lk	20.17	which the builders rejected as worthless
1 Pet	2.4	living stone rejected by man as worthless
	2.7	which the builders rejected as worthless

REJOICE

	Is	65.18 — 66.10	x4

Joy, Glad, Happy

2 Sam	1.20	glad; do not let...pagans rejoice.
Ps	5.11	rejoice; they can always sing for joy.
	31.7	I will be glad and rejoice
	32.11	be glad and rejoice
	68.3	But the righteous are glad and rejoice
	97.1	glad! Rejoice, you islands of the seas!
	97.8	are glad, and the cities of Judah rejoice
	149.2	glad...because of your Creator; rejoice,
	149.5	rejoice in their triumph and sing joyfully
Is	9.3	them great joy, Lord...They rejoice
	12.3	joy to the thirsty...God's people rejoice
	65.18	Be glad and rejoice for ever in what
	66.10	Rejoice with Jerusalem; be glad for her,
Jer	31.13	and be happy, and men...will rejoice.
Joel	2.23	Be glad, people of Zion, rejoice at what
Zeph	3.14	shout for joy, people of Israel! Rejoice
Zech	9.9	rejoice, people of Zion! Shout for joy,
1 Pet	1.8	rejoice with a great and glorious joy
Rev	19.7	Let us rejoice and be glad;

REMEMBER

Deut	4.39 —	9.27	x11
Prov	3.1 —	4.21	x6
2 Tim	1.3 —	3.15	x6
Ps	74.2 – 22		x5
Lk	1.36 —	2.19	x5
Lk	21.32 —	24.8	x5
Ex	32.13 —	33.13	x4
Deut	24.9 —	25.19	x4
Neh	4.14 —	6.14	x4
Neh	13.14 – 31		x4
Ps	137.1 – 7		x4
Prov	21.2 —	23.35	x4
Jer	14.10 —	15.15	x4
Jn	2.17 —	4.53	x4
Jn	14.26 —	16.4	x4
Heb	13.2 – 7		x4
Gen	30.22 —	32.12	x3
Deut	11.2 —	12.12	x3
Judg	8.15 —	9.17	x3
Ps	106.4 – 45		x3
Ps	119.49 – 55		x3
Ecc	1.11 —	2.16	x3
Ecc	11.8 —	12.1	x3
Ezek	2.7 —	3.20	x3
Ezek	16.22 – 63		x3
Hos	7.2 —	9.9	x3
Mic	6.5		x3

Mt	26.75 —	28.7	x3
Lk	16.25 —	18.17	x3
Jude	.6 – 17		x3

Choose

Ex	33.13	Remember...you have chosen this nation
Deut	30.1	you will remember the choice I gave
2 Chr	6.42	do not reject the...chosen. Remember
Ps	4.3	Remember that the Lord has chosen
	74.2	Remember your people, whom you chose

Covenant see Promise

Evil, Wicked

Ps	9.5	wicked; they will be remembered no
	109.14	Lord remember the evil of his ancestors
Prov	10.7	remembered as a blessing, but the wicked
Ezek	36.31	You will remember your evil conduct
Hos	7.2	I will remember all this evil;
Heb	10.17	not remember their sins and evil deeds
Rev	18.5	God remembers her wicked ways.

Forget

Deut	4.39	So remember today and never forget
	25.19	no one will remember them any longer. Do not forget!
1 Sam	1.11	and remember me! Don't forget me!
Ps	9.12	God remembers those who suffer; he does not forget
Prov	3.1	forget what I teach you...remember
	4.4	Remember what I say and never forget
	7.1	Remember what I say...never forget

Heart

Ps	42.4	heart breaks when I remember the past,
Prov	4.21	Remember...keep them in your heart.

Help, Needy

Judg	8.15	Remember when you refused to help
Ps	106.4	Remember me, Lord, when you help
Jer	15.15	Remember me and help me.
Acts	20.35	help the weak, remembering the words
Gal	2.10	was that we should remember the needy

Holy

Ps	30.4	Remember what the Holy One has done,
	97.12	Remember what the holy God has done,
Is	8.13	Remember that I, the Lord...am holy;

Judge

Ps	119.52	remember your judgements of long ago,
Prov	21.2	remember that the Lord judges your
Ecc	11.9	remember that God is going to judge

Life

Ex	30.16	lives, and I will remember to protect
Deut	29.16	remember what life was like in Egypt
Job	7.7	Remember, O God, my life is only a
Ps	89.47	Remember how short my life is;
Prov	22.6	and he will remember it all his life.
Ezek	16.22	life...you never once remembered

Love

2 Chr	6.42	Remember the love you had for your
Ps	25.7	love and goodness, remember me,
2 Cor	7.15	love...grows stronger, as he remembers

Needy see Help

Power

Job	36.22	Remember how great is God's power;
Dan	9.15	your power is still remembered.

Promise, Covenant

Gen	9.15	I will remember my promise to you
	9.16	and remember the everlasting covenant
	32.12	Remember that you promised to make
Ex	2.24	remembered his covenant with Abraham,
	6.5	and I have remembered my covenant.
	32.13	Remember the solemn promise you made

Lev	26.42	I will **remember** my **covenant** with Jacob
Ps	74.20	**Remember** the **covenant** you made
	105.42	He **remembered** his sacred **promise**
	106.45	he **remembered** his **covenant**,
	119.49	**Remember** your **promise** to me, your
	132.2	**Remember**, Lord, what he **promised**,
Jer	14.21	**Remember** your **promises** and do not
Lk	1.72	and **remember** his sacred **covenant**.

Punish

Josh	22.17	**Remember** our sin at Peor, when the Lord **punished**
Neh	6.14	**remember** what Tobiah and Sanballat have done and **punish**
Ps	10.12	**punish** those wicked men! **Remember**
Is	26.14	have **punished** them...No one **remembers**
Jer	14.10	I will **remember** the wrongs they have done and **punish**
Ezek	6.9	**remember** me...that I have **punished**
Hos	8.13	will **remember** their sin and **punish** them
	9.9	will **remember** their sin and **punish** them

Raise

Lk	24.6	been **raised**. **Remember** what he said
Jn	2.22	he was **raised**...his disciples **remembered**
	12.16	been **raised** to glory, they **remembered**
2 Tim	2.8	**Remember** Jesus Christ, who was **raised**

Servants

Ex	32.13	**Remember** your **servants** Abraham,
Deut	9.27	**Remember** your **servants**
Josh	1.13	**Remember** how Moses, the...**servant**,
1 Sam	1.11	**servant**! See my trouble and **remember**
2 Chr	6.42	**Remember** the love...for your **servant**
Ps	119.49	**Remember** your **promise** to...your **servant**;
Is	44.21	**remember** that you are my **servant**.
	63.11	**remembered** the past, the days of Moses, the **servant**
Mal	4.4	**Remember** the teachings of my **servant**
Lk	1.48	has **remembered** me, his lowly **servant**!

Slaves

Ex	6.5	enslaved, and I have **remembered** my
Deut	5.15	**Remember** that you were **slaves** in
	15.15	**Remember** that you were **slaves** in
	24.18	**Remember** that you were **slaves** in
Ps	74.2	**Remember** your people...whom you brought out of **slavery**
Eph	6.9	**Remember** that you and your **slaves**
Col	4.1	treat your **slaves** that you

Suffering

Neh	9.32	**Remember** how much we have **suffered**!
Ps	9.12	God **remembers** those who **suffer**;
	10.12	**Remember** those who are **suffering**!
Heb	13.3	**Remember** those who are **suffering**,

Wicked see Evil

Words

Job	19.23	that someone would **remember** my **words**
Lk	24.8	Then the women **remembered** his **words**
Acts	20.35	**remembering** the **words** that the Lord
2 Pet	3.2	**remember** the **words** that were spoken

Wrong

Prov	17.9	**wrong** you. **Remembering wrongs** can
Jer	14.10	**remember** the **wrongs** they have done
	31.34	I will no longer **remember** their **wrongs**.
Ezek	16.63	the **wrongs**...but you will **remember**
	36.31	You will **remember**...the **wrongs**
Heb	8.12	will no longer **remember** their **wrongs**.

AV REMISSION see FORGIVE

REPENT

2 Chr	6.26	—	7.14	x4
1 Kgs	8.35	—	48	x3
Lk	15.7	—	10	x3

Sin

1 Kgs	8.47	**repent**...confessing how **sinful**
2 Chr	6.37	**repent**...confessing how **sinful**
	33.19	**sins** he committed before he **repented**
Lk	15.7	over one **sinner** who **repents**
	15.10	rejoice over one **sinner** who **repents**.
	17.3	**sins**, rebuke him, and if he **repents**,
	24.47	**repentance** and the forgiveness of **sins**
Acts	5.31	**repent** and have their **sins** forgiven.
	26.20	that they must **repent** of their **sins**,
Rev	2.21	given her time to **repent** of her **sins**,

RESCUE

1 Sam	9.16	—	12.11	x7
Is	34.8	—	38.14	x7
Judg	6.9	—	7.7	x6
2 Kgs	16.7	—	20.6	x6
Deut	4.20	—	6.21	x5
Ex	2.17	—	3.8	x4
1 Chr	16.35	—	17.21	x4
Dan	6.14—27			x4
Ps	71.2—11			x3
Ps	144.7—11			x3
Is	62.11	—	63.16	x3
2 Tim	3.11	—	4.18	x3

Evil, Wicked

Ps	37.40	and **rescues** them...from the **wicked**,
	59.2	Save me from those **evil** men; **rescue** me
	71.4	**rescue** me from **wicked** men,
	82.4	**Rescue** them from the power of **evil**
	97.10	he **rescues** them from...the **wicked**.
Jer	15.21	**rescue** you from the power of **wicked**
	20.13	**rescues** the oppressed from...**evil** men.
2 Thes	3.2	**rescue** us from **wicked** and **evil** people;
2 Tim	4.18	the Lord will **rescue** me from all **evil**
Tit	2.14	to **rescue** us from all **wickedness**

God

Ex	13.19	When **God rescues** you,
Deut	5.6	your **God**, who **rescued** you from Egypt,
	5.15	I, the Lord your **God**, **rescued** you
	8.14	your **God** who **rescued** you from Egypt,
	13.10	your **God**, who **rescued** you from Egypt,
	20.1	your **God**, who **rescued** you from Egypt,
1 Sam	10.19	your **God**, the one who **rescues** you
2 Kgs	17.7	their **God**, who had **rescued** them
	17.39	Lord your **God**, and I will **rescue** you
	19.19	**God**, **rescue** us from the Assyrians,
2 Chr	18.31	and the **Lord God rescued** him
Job	5.21	**God** will **rescue** you from slander;
Ps	49.15	But **God** will **rescue** me;
	71.4	My **God**, **rescue** me from wicked men,
Is	29.22	**God** of Israel, who **rescued** Abraham
	35.4	**God** is coming to your **rescue**,
	37.20	**God**, **rescue** us from the Assyrians,
1 Thes	1.10	and who **rescues** us from **God**'s anger
2 Thes	3.2	Pray also that **God** will **rescue** us from

Lord

see also **God**

Deut	6.12	the **Lord** who **rescued** you from Egypt,
	6.21	the **Lord rescued** us by his great power.
	13.5	the **Lord**, who **rescued** you from Egypt,
	21.8	**Lord**, forgive...Israel, whom you **rescued**
	32.36	The **Lord** will **rescue** his people
1 Sam	11.13	this is the day the **Lord rescued** Israel.
1 Kgs	1.29	the living **Lord**, who has **rescued** me
2 Kgs	18.32	thinking that the **Lord** will **rescue** you.
2 Chr	32.22	the **Lord rescued** King Hezekiah
Ps	9.13	**Rescue** me from death, O **Lord**,
	68.20	our **Lord**, who **rescues** us from death.

194

Ps	106.43	Many times the **Lord rescued** his people,
	143.11	**Rescue** me, **Lord**, as you have promised;
Is	29.6	the **Lord** Almighty will **rescue** you
	34.8	when the **Lord** will **rescue** Zion
	35.9	Those whom the **Lord** has **rescued**
	36.18	thinking that the **Lord** will **rescue** you.
	38.14	**Lord**, **rescue** me from all this trouble.
	45.25	I, the **Lord**, will **rescue** all
	52.9	The **Lord** will **rescue** his city
	63.16	**Lord**...who has always **rescued** us.
Lam	3.58	You came to my **rescue**, **Lord**,
Hos	12.13	The **Lord** sent a prophet to **rescue**
Acts	12.11	**Lord** sent his angel to **rescue** me
2 Tim	3.11	the **Lord rescued** me from them all.
	4.18	the **Lord** will **rescue** me from all evil
2 Pet	2.9	**Lord** knows how to **rescue** godly people
Jude	.5	how the **Lord** once **rescued** the people

Might see **Strength**

Oppressed, Slaves

Ex	6.6	I will **rescue** you...from your **slavery**
Deut	5.6	who **rescued** you from Egypt, where you were **slaves.**
	6.12	who **rescued** you from Egypt, where you were **slaves.**
	6.21	**slaves** of...Egypt, and the Lord **rescued**
	8.14	who **rescued** you from Egypt, where you were **slaves.**
	13.5	who **rescued** you from Egypt, where you were **slaves.**
	13.10	who **rescued** you from Egypt, where you were **slaves.**
2 Sam	7.23	**rescued** from **slavery** to make them your
1 Chr	17.21	**rescued** from **slavery** to make them your
Ps	72.14	He **rescues** them from **oppression**
Is	59.16	**oppressed**. So he will use his own power to **rescue**
Jer	20.13	He **rescues** the **oppressed**
Hos	12.13	**rescue** the people of Israel from **slavery**
Mic	6.4	I **rescued** you from **slavery;**
Zeph	3.19	punish your **oppressors;** I will **rescue**

Safe, Protect, Save

Job	5.21	**rescue** you from slander; he will **save**
Ps	6.4	**save** me, Lord; in your mercy **rescue** me
	7.1	I come to you for **protection; rescue** me
	35.17	**Rescue** me from their attacks; **save** my
	37.40	and **rescues** them; he **saves** them
	49.15	God will **rescue** me; he will **save** me
	59.2	**Save** me from those evil men; **rescue** me
	68.20	**saves;** he is the Lord...who **rescues**
	69.18	Come to me and **save** me; **rescue** me
	71.2	**rescue** me. Listen to me and **save** me!
	79.9	**save** us; **rescue** us and forgive
	97.10	he **protects**...his people; he **rescues** them
	106.10	He **saved** them...he **rescued**
	107.2	whom he has **saved.** He has **rescued** you
	143.9	to you for **protection**, Lord; **rescue** me
	144.7	**rescue** me; **save** me from the power of
	144.11	**Save** me from my cruel enemies; **rescue**
Is	17.10	who **rescues** you and who **protects** you
	63.9	**saved** them. In his love...he **rescued**
Jer	17.14	**rescue** me and I will be perfectly **safe.**
	31.7	has **saved** his people; he has **rescued**
	33.16	**rescued** and will live in **safety.**
Lam	3.58	came to my **rescue**, Lord, and **saved**
Dan	6.27	He **saves** and **rescues;**
2 Tim	4.18	**rescue** me from...evil and take me **safely**

Slaves see **Oppressed**

Strength, Might

Ex	15.13	**rescued;** by your **strength** you guided
	32.11	**rescued** from Egypt with great **might**
Deut	5.15	**rescued** you by my great...**strength.**

Deut	26.8	power and **strength** he **rescued** us
	32.36	**rescue** his people when...their **strength**
Judg	6.14	your great **strength** and **rescue** Israel
Neh	1.10	**rescued** them by your great...**strength.**
Is	17.10	**rescues** you and who protects you like a **mighty rock.**
Jer	50.34	will **rescue** them is **strong** — his name
Zech	10.6	Judah **strong;** I will **rescue** the people

Wicked see **Evil**

RESPECT

Mal	1.6	—	3.16	x6
1 Pet	2.17	—	3.16	x5
Prov	13.15	—	14.22	x3
Ezek	22.8 – 26			x3
Lk	18.2 – 20			x3
1 Thes	4.12	—	5.13	x3

Bow

1 Sam	24.8	**bowed** down to the ground in **respect**
	28.14	and he **bowed** to the ground in **respect.**
2 Sam	1.2	and **bowed** to the ground in **respect.**
	9.6	he **bowed** down before David in **respect.**
	14.4	**bowed** down to the ground in **respect,**
Esth	3.2	their **respect** for Haman by kneeling and **bowing**
Is	60.14	And **bow** low to show their **respect.**

REST

Heb	3.11	—	4.11	x15
Lev	25.4	—	26.43	x5
Ex	16.23 – 29			x4
Ex	31.13 – 17			x4
Lev	23.3 – 39			x4
Deut	5.14	—	6.7	x3
Job	3.13 – 26			x3
Ezek	31.6	—	32.32	x3
Mt	11.28	—	12.43	x3

Dedicated

Ex	16.23	a holy day of **rest**, **dedicated** to him.
	16.25	a day of **rest dedicated** to the Lord,
	20.10	a day of **rest dedicated** to me.
	31.15	a solemn day of **rest dedicated** to me,
	35.2	a solemn day of **rest dedicated** to me,
Lev	25.4	**rest** for the land, a year **dedicated**
Deut	5.14	a day of **rest dedicated** to me

Sabbath, Solemn

Ex	16.25	today is the **Sabbath**, a day of **rest**
	31.13	Keep the **Sabbath**, my day of **rest**,
	31.15	seventh day is a **solemn** day of **rest**
	35.2	a **solemn** day of **rest dedicated** to me,
Lev	23.3	the **Sabbath**, is a day of **rest.**
2 Chr	36.21	to make up for the **Sabbath rest**
Lk	23.56	On the **Sabbath** they **rested,**

REVEAL

Jn	12.38	—	16.13	x10
Dan	2.19 – 47			x6
Eph	3.3	—	5.32	x6
Rom	7.13	—	9.23	x5
1 Pet	1.5 – 20			x5
Rom	1.17	—	3.21	x4
Gal	1.12	—	3.23	x4
Rev	1.1 – 9			x4
Hab	1.1	—	2.19	x3
Tit	1.3	—	3.4	x3
Rev	19.10	—	20.4	x3

Glory

Lev	10.3	I will **reveal** my **glory** to my people.
Ps	19.1	How clearly the sky **reveals** God's **glory!**
Is	40.5	the **glory** of the Lord will be **revealed,**
Jn	2.11	**revealed** his **glory**, and his disciples

Jn	13.31	the Son of Man's **glory** is **revealed**;
	13.32	if God's **glory** is **revealed** through him,
Rom	8.18	**glory** that is going to be **revealed** to us.
	9.4	them his sons and **revealed** his **glory**
	9.23	also wanted to **reveal** his abundant **glory**
1 Pet	4.13	be full of joy when his **glory** is **revealed**.
	5.1	share in the **glory** that will be **revealed**.

God

Gen	35.7	**God** had **revealed** himself to him there
Ex	3.18	**God**...has **revealed** himself to us.
	5.3	**God**...has **revealed** himself to us.
2 Sam	7.17	everything that **God** had **revealed**
1 Chr	17.15	everything that **God** had **revealed**
	17.25	my **God**, because you have **revealed**
Ps	19.1	How clearly the sky **reveals God's** glory!
Is	1.1	which **God revealed** to Isaiah
Dan	2.28	**God** in heaven, who **reveals** mysteries.
Amos	1.1	**God revealed** to Amos all these things
Jn	13.31	**God's** glory is **revealed** through him.
	13.32	if **God's** glory is **revealed** through him,
	13.32	**God** will **reveal** the glory of the Son
	14.17	Spirit who **reveals** the truth about **God**
	15.26	Spirit, who **reveals** the truth about **God**
	16.13	Spirit...who **reveals** the truth about **God**,
Rom	1.17	For the gospel **reveals** how **God**
	1.18	**God's** anger is **revealed** from heaven
	2.5	when **God's** anger...will be **revealed**.
	8.19	longing for **God** to **reveal** his sons.
1 Cor	14.6	bring you some **revelation** from **God**
	14.26	another a **revelation** from **God**,
Gal	2.2	**God revealed** to me that I should go.
Eph	1.17	make you wise and **reveal God** to you,
	3.3	**God revealed** his secret plan
	3.5	**God** has **revealed** it now by the Spirit
Tit	2.11	**God** has **revealed** his grace
	3.4	love of **God** our Saviour was **revealed**,
1 Pet	1.12	**God revealed** to these prophets that
Rev	1.1	**God** gave him this **revelation**

God's People

Lev	10.3	I will **reveal** my glory to **my people**.
Is	5.16	and he **reveals** his holiness by judging **his people**.
Rom	9.4	They are **God's people**; he...**revealed**
Col	1.26	but has now **revealed** to **his people**.

Jesus

1 Cor	1.7	our Lord **Jesus** Christ to be **revealed**.
Gal	1.12	**Jesus** Christ himself who **revealed** it
1 Pet	1.7	Day when **Jesus** Christ is **revealed**.
	1.13	when **Jesus** Christ is **revealed**.
Rev	1.1	events that **Jesus** Christ **revealed**.
	1.2	the truth **revealed** by **Jesus**
	1.9	the truth that **Jesus revealed**.
	12.17	the truth **revealed** by **Jesus**.
	19.10	the truth that **Jesus revealed**.
	19.10	For the truth that **Jesus revealed**
	20.4	the truth that **Jesus revealed**

Lord

Deut	33.8	You, **Lord**, **reveal** your will
1 Sam	3.21	The **Lord** continued to **reveal** himself
2 Kgs	8.10	The **Lord** has **revealed** to me that
Ps	9.16	The **Lord** has **revealed** himself
	102.16	the **Lord**...will **reveal** his greatness.
Is	19.21	The **Lord** will **reveal** himself to
	40.5	glory of the **Lord** will be **revealed**,
Amos	3.7	**Lord** never...without **revealing** his plan
Mic	1.1	**Lord revealed** to Micah all these things
Hab	1.1	the **Lord revealed** to the prophet
Jn	12.38	did the **Lord reveal** his power?
1 Cor	1.7	our **Lord** Jesus Christ to be **revealed**.
2 Cor	12.1	and **revelations** given me by the **Lord**.

Prophet

Num	12.6	**prophets** among you, I **reveal** myself
Ezek	7.26	You will beg the **prophets** to **reveal**
Amos	3.7	**revealing** his plan to...the **prophets**.
Mic	3.11	**prophets** give their **revelations** for money
Hab	1.1	**Lord revealed** to the **prophet** Habakkuk.
1 Pet	1.12	God **revealed** to these **prophets**
Rev	19.10	**revealed** is what inspires the **prophets**.

Truth

Jn	14.17	Spirit who **reveals** the **truth** about God
	15.26	who **reveals** the **truth** about God
	16.13	who **reveals** the **truth** about God,
Rom	7.13	its **true** nature as sin might be **revealed**.
	16.25	the **revelation** of the secret **truth**
Eph	4.24	and **reveals** itself in the **true** life
	5.13	their **true** nature is clearly **revealed**;
	5.32	secret **truth revealed** in this scripture,
1 Tim	3.9	they should hold to the **revealed truth**
Rev	1.2	the **truth revealed** by Jesus Christ.
	1.9	the **truth** that Jesus **revealed**.
	12.17	faithful to the **truth revealed** by Jesus.
	19.10	hold to the **truth** that Jesus **revealed**.
	20.4	proclaimed the **truth** that Jesus **revealed**

Vision

Num	12.6	I **reveal** myself to them in **visions**
Dan	2.19	was **revealed** to Daniel in a **vision**,
2 Cor	12.1	now talk about **visions** and **revelations**

REVENGE

	Ezek	24.8	—	25.17	x7
	Jer	50.15	—	51.11	x5
	1 Sam	25.26 – 39			x4
	Num	35.12 – 27			x3
	Deut	32.35 – 43			x3
	Josh	20.3 – 9			x3
	2 Sam	3.30	—	4.11	x3

Anger

Prov	6.34	**angrier** than when...jealous; his **revenge**
Ezek	24.8	where it demands **angry revenge**.
	25.17	full **revenge**...They will feel my **anger**.
Mic	5.15	in my great **anger** I will take **revenge**
Rom	12.19	**revenge**...but instead let God's **anger** do

Punish

Deut	32.35	Lord will take **revenge** and **punish** them;
	32.41	take **revenge** on my enemies and **punish**
	32.43	**punishes** all who kill...He takes **revenge**
Jer	5.9	I **punish** them...and take **revenge**
	5.29	will **punish** them...I will take **revenge**
	46.10	will take **revenge**; today he will **punish**
	51.6	now taking my **revenge** and **punishing** it
Ezek	25.17	**punish** them severely and take...**revenge**

REVERENCE

	Prov	14.2	—	15.33	x4

God

Gen	20.11	no one here who has **reverence** for **God**
Ps	36.1	rejects **God** and has no **reverence**
Ecc	7.18	If you have **reverence** for **God**,
	12.13	Have **reverence** for **God**,
Rom	3.18	nor have they learnt **reverence** for **God**.
1 Tim	2.2	with all **reverence** towards **God**
Heb	12.28	worship **God**...with **reverence**

Lord

2 Chr	19.9	your duties in **reverence** for the **Lord**.
Job	28.28	you must have **reverence** for the **Lord**.
Ps	19.9	**Reverence** for the **Lord** is good;
	25.12	who have **reverence** for the **Lord**
Prov	1.7	must first have **reverence** for the **Lord**.
	9.10	must first have **reverence** for the **Lord**.
	14.2	that you have **reverence** for the **Lord**;

Prov	14.26	**Reverence** for the **Lord** gives confidence
	14.27	**Reverence** for the **Lord** is a fountain
	15.33	**Reverence** for the **Lord** is an education
	23.17	let **reverence** for the **Lord** be
	24.21	Have **reverence** for the **Lord**, my son,
Is	11.2	know the **Lord's** will and have **reverence**
	33.6	is their **reverence** for the **Lord**.
Acts	9.31	as it lived in **reverence** for the **Lord**.
Col	3.22	because of your **reverence** for the **Lord**.

REWARD

Prov	10.16	—	14.24	x9
Mt	5.12	—	6.18	x6
Heb	10.35	—	12.11	x4
Esth	6.3 – 11			x3
Mt	10.41 – 42			x3

God, Lord

Gen	30.18	**God** has given me my **reward**,
	15.2	**Lord**, what good will your **reward** do
Num	24.11	**Lord** has kept you from...the **reward**.
Ruth	2.12	a full **reward** from the **Lord God**
1 Sam	26.23	**Lord rewards** those who are faithful
2 Sam	22.21	The **Lord rewards** me because
Ps	18.20	The **Lord rewards** me because
	62.12	You yourself, O **Lord**, **reward** everyone
Prov	25.22	and the **Lord** will **reward** you.
Mt	5.46	Why should **God reward** you if
Rom	2.6	For **God** will **reward** every person
1 Cor	3.8	**God** will **reward** each one
Eph	6.8	that the **Lord** will **reward** everyone,
2 Tim	4.14	the **Lord** will **reward** him
Heb	11.6	that **God** exists and **rewards** those
Jas	1.12	as his **reward** the life which **God** has

Right

2 Sam	22.21	**rewards** me because I do what is **right**;
	22.25	**rewards** me because I do what is **right**,
Ps	18.20	**rewards** me because I do what is **right**,
	18.24	**rewards** me because I do what is **right**,
Prov	11.18	is **right**, you are certain to be **rewarded**.

RICH

Lk	16.1 – 30			x8
Prov	21.17	—	23.31	x7
Jas	1.10	—	2.6	x6
Deut	26.9	—	28.56	x5
Deut	31.20	—	33.24	x5
2 Sam	12.1 – 5			x5
Prov	10.4	—	11.24	x5
Prov	28.6 – 22			x5
2 Cor	8.7	—	9.11	x5
1 Tim	6.5 – 18			x5
Prov	13.7	—	15.16	x4
Ecc	5.10 – 12			x4
Lk	18.23	—	19.2	x4
Deut	6.3	—	8.18	x3
Ruth	2.1	—	4.11	x3
Prov	18.11	—	19.4	x3
Ecc	9.11	—	10.20	x3
Dan	10.3	—	11.38	x3
Mt	19.22 – 24			x3
Mk	10.22 – 25			x3
Lk	12.15 – 21			x3
Rom	10.12	—	11.12	x3
Rev	2.9	—	3.18	x3
Rev	18.3 – 19			x3

Generous

2 Cor	9.10	a **rich** harvest from your **generosity**.
	9.11	make you **rich** enough to be **generous**
1 Tim	6.18	be **rich** in good works, to be **generous**

Heaven

Mt	6.20	**riches** for yourselves in **heaven**,
	19.21	and you will have **riches** in **heaven**;
Mk	10.21	and you will have **riches** in **heaven**;
Lk	12.33	and save your **riches** in **heaven**,
	18.22	and you will have **riches** in **heaven**;

Kingdom

Mt	19.23	**rich** people to enter the **Kingdom**
	19.24	**rich** person to enter the **Kingdom**
Mk	10.23	**rich** people to enter the **Kingdom**
	10.25	**rich** person to enter the **Kingdom**
Lk	18.24	**rich** people to enter the **Kingdom**
	18.25	**rich** person to enter the **Kingdom**
Jas	2.5	**rich** in faith and to possess the **kingdom**

Need

Ps	132.15	**richly** provide Zion with all she **needs**;
Jer	31.14	the **richest** food and satisfy all the **needs**
Ezek	27.33	the **needs** of every nation. Kings were made **rich**
1 Cor	4.8	you **need**? Are you already **rich**
2 Cor	9.10	**need** and will make it grow and produce a **rich**
1 Jn	3.17	a **rich** person sees his brother in **need**,
Rev	3.17	am **rich** and well off; I have all I **need**.

Poor

Ex	30.15	The **rich** man is not to pay more, nor the **poor** man less,
Lev	19.15	favouritism to the **poor** or fear the **rich**.
	25.47	**rich**...a fellow-Israelite becomes **poor**
Ruth	3.10	either **rich** or **poor**, but you didn't.
1 Sam	2.7	makes some men **poor** and others **rich**;
2 Sam	12.1	one was **rich** and the other **poor**.
2 Kgs	23.2	**rich** and **poor** alike.
	25.26	**rich** and **poor** alike,
2 Chr	34.30	**rich** and **poor** alike.
Esth	1.5	**rich** and **poor** alike.
	1.20	whether he's **rich** or **poor**.
Job	34.19	nor favour the **rich** against the **poor**,
Ps	49.2	**rich** and **poor** together.
Prov	10.4	**poor**, but hard work will make you **rich**.
	10.15	the **rich**; poverty destroys the **poor**.
	11.24	still grow **richer**. Others...grow **poorer**.
	14.20	**poor** man, but the **rich** have many
	15.16	be **poor** and fear the Lord than...be **rich**
	22.2	**rich** and the **poor** have this in common
	22.7	**Poor** people are the **rich** man's slaves
	22.16	or oppress the **poor** to get **rich**,
	28.6	**poor** and honest than **rich** and
	28.22	**rich**...they do not know when **poverty**
	30.8	let me be neither **rich** nor **poor**.
Is	19.15	**rich** or **poor**, important or unknown,
	24.2	**rich** and **poor**.
Jer	16.6	**rich** and the **poor** will die in this land
Mic	6.12	Your **rich** men exploit the **poor**,
Mt	19.21	**poor**, and you will have **riches** in
Mk	10.21	**poor**, and you will have **riches** in
	12.44	their **riches**; but she, **poor** as she is,
Lk	18.22	**poor**, and you will have **riches** in
	21.4	their **riches**; but she, **poor** as she is,
Rom	11.12	spiritual **poverty** brought **rich** blessings
2 Cor	6.10	**poor**, but we make many people **rich**;
	8.9	**rich** as he was, he made himself **poor**
Jas	2.5	**poor** people of this world to be **rich** in
Rev	2.9	you are **poor** — but really you are **rich**!
	13.16	**rich** and **poor**,

RIGHT (RIGHTEOUS)

Prov	14.12	—	18.17	x11
Ezek	18.19 – 29			x10
Prov	20.4	—	22.21	x8
Ezek	33.14	—	34.16	x7
Rom	2.2	—	3.12	x6
Job	31.7	—	33.32	x5
Prov	2.9	—	4.27	x5
Is	59.14	—	61.3	x5

Mal	2.6	—	3.8	x5
1 Jn	1.9	—	3.12	x5
Job	10.3	—	11.13	x4
Prov	11.18	—	12.15	x4
Dan	9.5 – 18			x4
Mk	5.15	—	7.27	x4
Jn	7.6	—	8.48	x4
Heb	11.33	—	13.18	x4
Gen	16.5	—	18.19	x3
Ex	8.26	—	10.29	x3
Ex	18.16 – 19			x3
Deut	32.4	—	33.19	x3
2 Chr	19.2	—	20.32	x3
Ecc	2.21	—	3.16	x3
Is	30.10 – 18			x3
Is	32.8	—	33.15	x3
Amos	5.14	—	6.12	x3
Mt	14.4	—	15.26	x3

Christ, Jesus

Rom	3.22	God puts people **right** through...**Jesus**
	3.24	put **right** with **him** through...**Jesus**,
	3.25	puts **right** everyone who believes in **Jesus**.
	5.17	put **right**...will rule...through **Christ**.
1 Cor	1.30	**Christ**...our wisdom...we are put **right**
	6.11	put **right** with **God** by...**Jesus**
Gal	2.16	put **right** with God only through...**Jesus**
	2.17	put **right** with God by our union with **Christ**,
Phil	3.9	**righteousness**...through faith in **Christ**,
2 Pet	1.1	**righteousness** of our...**Saviour Jesus**
1 Jn	2.1	**Jesus Christ**, the **righteous** one.
	2.29	You know that **Christ** is **righteous**
	3.7	**righteous**, just as **Christ** is **righteous**.

Command see Law

Evil, Wicked

2 Chr	19.2	**right** to help those who are **wicked**
Job	27.7	punished like **wicked**, **unrighteous** men.
	31.7	from the **right** path or let myself be attracted to **evil**,
Ps	7.11	a **righteous** judge...condemns the **wicked**.
	9.16	**righteous** judgements, and the **wicked**
	34.21	**wicked**; those who hate the **righteous**
	45.7	love what is **right** and hate what is **evil**.
	51.4	what you consider **evil**. So you are **right**
	75.10	**wicked**, but the power of the **righteous**
	125.3	the **righteous** themselves might do **evil**.
Prov	3.32	who do **evil**, but he takes **righteous** men
	3.33	**wicked** men, but blesses...the **righteous**.
	10.24	The **righteous** get what they want, but the **wicked**
	11.20	hates **evil-minded** people, but loves those who do **right**.
	11.21	**evil** men will be punished, but **righteous**
	12.3	**Wickedness** does not give security, but **righteous** people
	12.12	**evil** things to do, but the **righteous**
	12.21	to **righteous** people, but the **wicked**
	12.28	**Righteousness** is...life; **wickedness**
	13.6	**Righteousness** protects the innocent; **wickedness** is the downfall
	13.25	**righteous** have enough...but the **wicked**
	14.19	**Evil** people will have to bow down to the **righteous**
	15.6	**Righteous** men keep...wealth, but **wicked**
	15.9	**evil** people, but loves those who do ...**right**.
	29.27	The **righteous** hate the **wicked**
Ecc	3.16	find **wickedness** where justice and **right**
	3.17	to judge the **righteous** and the **evil**
	8.14	**righteous** men get the punishment of the **wicked**,

Ecc	9.2	comes to the **righteous** and the **wicked**,
Is	26.10	**wicked** men...never learn to do...**right**.
Jer	13.23	but **evil** could learn to do what is **right**.
	35.15	your **evil** ways and to do what is **right**
Ezek	18.27	When an **evil** man...does what is **right**
	33.19	When an **evil** man...does what is **right**
Amos	5.14	to do what is **right**, not what is **evil**
	5.15	Hate what is **evil**, love what is **right**
Hab	1.4	**Evil** men get the better of the **righteous**,
	2.4	**evil** will not survive, but...**righteous**
Mal	3.18	to the **righteous** and to the **wicked**,

Glad see Joy

God

Job	4.17	anyone be **righteous** in the sight of **God**
	25.4	anyone be **righteous**...in **God's** sight?
	34.17	Are you condemning the **righteous God**?
	35.7	Do you help **God** by being so **righteous**?
Ps	7.9	You are a **righteous God**
	7.11	**God** is a **righteous** judge
	31.1	You are a **righteous God**;
	50.6	heavens proclaim that **God** is **righteous**,
	71.19	Your **righteousness**, **God**,
	72.1	with your **righteousness**, O **God**;
	85.11	**God's righteousness** will look down
Prov	21.12	**God**, the **righteous** one, knows
Lk	7.29	had obeyed **God's righteous** demands
Rom	2.5	**God's** anger and **righteous** judgements
	3.25	**God**...is **righteous**.
	3.25	**God** shows that he himself is **righteous**
2 Cor	5.21	might share the **righteousness** of **God**.
Phil	3.9	the **righteousness** that comes from **God**
Heb	11.4	won **God's** approval as a **righteous** man,
Jas	1.20	not achieve **God's righteous** purpose.
1 Pet	2.23	his hopes in **God**, the **righteous** Judge.
2 Pet	1.1	through the **righteousness** of our **God**

Happy see Joy

Help

2 Chr	19.2	it is **right** to **help** those who are wicked
Job	22.3	doing **right** benefit God, or...**help** him
	32.9	or **helps** them to know what is **right**.
Ps	41.12	**help** me, because I do what is **right**;
Is	1.17	**right**. See that justice is done — **help**
Mal	2.6	**right** themselves, but they also **helped**

Jesus see Christ

Joy, Glad, Happy

Job	33.26	**God** with joy; God will set things **right**
Ps	19.8	**right**...those who obey them are **happy**.
	32.11	that are **righteous**, be **glad** and rejoice
	48.11	give **right** judgements; let there be **joy**
	51.14	will **gladly** proclaim your **righteousness**.
	58.10	**righteous** will be **glad** when they see
	68.3	But the **righteous** are **glad** and rejoice
	97.11	shines on the **righteous**, and **gladness**
	97.12	All you that are **righteous** be **glad**
	107.42	The **righteous** see this and are **glad**,
	132.9	is **right**; may your people shout for **joy**!
Prov	15.23	a **joy** it is to find just the **right** word
	29.2	a **righteous** ruler and...a **happy** people.
Is	3.10	**Righteous** men will be **happy**
	64.5	who find **joy** in doing what is **right**,
Rom	4.6	**happiness** of the person whom God accepts as **righteous**,
1 Pet	3.14	doing what is **right**, how **happy** you are!

Justice, Judge

Gen	16.5	the Lord **judge** which of us is **right**,
	18.19	and to do what is **right** and **just**.
Job	8.3	never twists **justice**; he never fails to do what is **right**.
	37.23	he is **righteous** and **just** in his dealings
Ps	7.9	a **righteous** God and **judge** our thoughts

Ps	7.11	God is a **righteous judge**
	9.8	**righteousness**; he **judges**...with **justice**.
	9.16	himself by his **righteous judgements**,
	33.5	Lord loves what is **righteous** and **just**;
	48.11	You give **right judgements**;
	50.6	is **righteous**, that he himself is **judge**.
	51.4	So you are **right** in **judging** me;
	72.1	king to **judge** with your **righteousness**
	72.2	**justice** and govern...with **righteousness**.
	89.14	is founded on **righteousness** and **justice**;
	97.2	he rules with **righteousness** and **justice**.
	99.4	**justice**...you have brought **righteousness**
	119.7	As I learn your **righteous judgements**,
	119.62	you for your **righteous judgements**.
	119.75	know that your **judgements** are **righteous**
	119.137	**righteous**, Lord, and your laws are **just**.
	119.160	your **righteous judgements** are eternal.
	119.164	for your **righteous judgements**.
Prov	2.9	will know what is **right**, **just**, and fair.
	8.20	the way of **righteousness**...follow the paths of **justice**,
	16.2	you do is **right**, but the Lord **judges**
	21.2	do is **right**, but...the Lord **judges**
	31.9	for them and be a **righteous judge**.
Ecc	3.16	where **justice** and **right** ought to be.
	3.17	to **judge** the **righteous** and the evil
Is	1.17	to do **right**. See that **justice** is done
	5.7	**right**, but their victims cried...for **justice**.
	5.16	**right**...he reveals his holiness by **judging**
	9.7	basing his power on **right** and **justice**,
	16.5	is **right**, and he will see that **justice**
	32.16	**righteousness** and **justice** will be done.
	54.14	**Justice** and **right** will make you strong.
	56.1	Do what is **just** and **right**,
	59.14	**Justice** is driven away, and **right** cannot
Jer	9.24	and I do what is **just** and **right**.
	22.3	you to do what is **just** and **right**.
	23.5	wisely and do what is **right** and **just**
	33.15	That king will do what is **right** and **just**
Ezek	33.20	do isn't **right**. I am going to **judge** you
	45.9	Do what is **just** and **right**.
Dan	4.37	Everything he does is **right** and **just**,
Amos	5.15	love what is **right**, and see that **justice**
	5.24	let **justice** flow...and **righteousness**
	6.12	**justice** into poison, and **right** into
Mic	3.9	hate **justice** and turn **right** into wrong.
Hab	1.4	better of the **righteous**, and so **justice**
Lk	12.57	not **judge** for yourselves the **right** thing
Jn	5.30	so my **judgement** is **right**,
	16.8	is **right** and about God's **judgement**.
Acts	4.19	**judge** which is **right** in God's sight
Rom	2.2	God is **right** when he **judges** the people
	2.5	**righteous judgements** will be revealed.
	14.22	he does something he **judges** is **right**!
1 Cor	4.5	**judgement** on anyone before the **right**
2 Tim	4.8	which the Lord, the **righteous Judge**,
1 Pet	2.23	hopes in God, the **righteous Judge**.

Law, Command

Ex	15.26	**right** and by keeping my **commands**,
	18.16	**right**, and I tell them God's **commands**
Ps	19.8	The **laws** of the Lord are **right**,
	106.3	obey his **commands**...do what is **right**.
	119.137	You are **righteous**, Lord, and your **laws**
	119.142	**righteousness** will last...and your **law**
	119.160	your **law** is truth, and all your **righteous**
Jer	22.3	**command** you to do what is **just** and **right**.
Ezek	18.9	carefully keeps my **laws**. He is **righteous**,
	18.19	was **right** and good. He kept my **laws**
	18.21	keeps my **laws**, if he does what is **right**
Zeph	2.3	obey his **commands**. Do what is **right**,
Rom	2.13	the **Law** that people are put **right**
	2.18	from the **Law** to choose what is **right**;

Rom	3.20	**right**...by doing what the **Law** requires;
	7.16	that I agree that the **Law** is **right**.
	8.4	that the **righteous** demands of the **Law**
	9.31	seeking a **law** that would put them **right**
	10.5	put **right with God** by obeying the **Law**:
Gal	2.16	put **right**...never by doing what the **Law**
	2.21	is put **right with God** through the **Law**,
	3.11	**right with God** by means of the **Law**,
	5.4	put **right with God** by obeying the **Law**
Phil	3.6	be **righteous** by obeying...the **Law**,
	3.9	**righteousness**...gained by obeying the **Law**.
Jas	2.8	the **right** thing if you obey the **law**

Lord

Ps	1.6	The **righteous** are guided...by the **Lord**,
	4.3	the **Lord** has chosen the **righteous**
	11.7	The **Lord** is **righteous**
	25.8	Because the **Lord** is **righteous**
	33.5	The **Lord** loves what is **righteous**
	34.15	The **Lord** watches over the **righteous**
	34.17	The **righteous** call to the **Lord**,
	35.24	You are **righteous**, O **Lord**,
	37.39	The **Lord** saves **righteous** men
	85.13	**Righteousness** will go before the **Lord**
	119.137	You are **righteous**, **Lord**,
	129.4	But the **Lord**, the **righteous** one,
	145.17	The **Lord** is **righteous** in all he does,
Is	1.27	Because the **Lord** is **righteous**,
2 Tim	4.8	the **Lord**, the **righteous Judge**,
1 Pet	3.12	the **Lord** watches over the **righteous**

Mercy

Ps	26.11	I do what is **right**; be **merciful** to me
	102.13	**mercy** on her; this is the **right** time.
Dan	4.27	is **right**, and be **merciful** to the poor.
	9.18	**merciful**, not because we have done **right**.

Please

Deut	12.28	what is **right** and what **pleases** the Lord
2 Chr	14.20	what was **right** and what was **pleasing**
Prov	21.3	is **right** and fair; that **pleases** the Lord

Praise

Ps	35.28	**righteousness**, and I will **praise** you
	65.1	it is **right** for us to **praise** you
	119.7	**righteous judgements**, I will **praise** you
	119.62	**praise** you for your **righteous**
	140.13	The **righteous** will **praise** you indeed;
	147.1	pleasant and **right** to **praise** him.
Is	24.16	**praise** of Israel, the **righteous** nation.
	61.3	what is **right**, And God will be **praised**
Phil	4.8	**praise**: things that are true, noble, **right**,

Save

Ps	26.11	**right**; be **merciful** to me and **save**
	31.1	You are a **righteous** God; **save** me,
	37.39	The **Lord saves righteous** men
	51.14	**save** me, and I will gladly proclaim your **righteousness**.
Prov	11.9	wisdom of the **righteous** can **save** you.
Is	1.27	Lord is **righteous**, he will **save** Jerusalem
	56.1	just and **right**, for soon I will **save**
Ezek	18.27	is **right** and good, he **saves** his life.
	33.19	**right** and good, he has **saved** his life.
1 Tim	2.6	the **right** time that God wants everyone to be **saved**,
2 Pet	2.5	the only ones he **saved** were Noah, who preached **righteousness**,

Sight

1 Kgs	22.43	what was **right** in the **sight** of the Lord;
2 Chr	20.32	what was **right** in the **sight** of the Lord;
Lk	16.15	look **right** in other people's **sight**,
Acts	4.19	which is **right** in God's **sight** — to obey
	8.21	your heart is not **right** in God's **sight**.

2 Cor   8.21   **right**, not only in the **sight** of the Lord,

True

Deut	32.4	faithful and **true**; he does what is **right**
Ps	15.2	what is **right**, whose words are **true**
	105.19	came **true**. The word of the Lord proved him **right**.
Lk	1.20	will come **true** at the **right** time.
Phil	4.8	things that are **true**, noble, **right**,
Rev	15.3	how **right** and **true** are your ways!

Wicked see **Evil**

World

Ps	9.8	rules the **world** with **righteousness**;
Ecc	8.14	in the **world**: sometimes **righteous** men

RIGHTS

1 Cor	9.4 – 18			x10
Mt	20.15	—	21.27	x7
Lev	25.24 – 48			x6
Mk	10.40	—	11.33	x6
Gen	25.31 – 34			x5
Lk	20.2 – 8			x4
2 Sam	19.28 – 41			x3
Prov	31.5 – 9			x3
Jon	4.4 – 9			x3

Justice, Judge

Ecc	5.8	denies them **justice** and their **rights**.
Is	1.17	**justice** is done ...give orphans their **rights**,
	10.2	their **rights** and from getting **justice**.
	11.4	**judge** the poor fairly...defend the **rights**
Jer	5.28	give orphans their **rights** or show **justice**
Amos	5.7	twist **justice** and cheat people out of their **rights**!
Lk	12.14	**right** to **judge** or to divide the property
Jn	5.22	given his Son the full **right** to **judge**,
	5.27	he has given the Son the **right** to **judge**,

Needy see **Poor**

Orphans

Deut	24.17	foreigners and **orphans** of their **rights**
	27.19	**orphans**, and widows of their **rights**.
Ps	82.3	the **rights** of the poor and the **orphans**;
Is	1.17	give **orphans** their **rights**,
Jer	5.28	They do not give **orphans** their **rights**

Poor, Needy

Job	24.4	the **poor** from getting their **rights**
Ps	82.3	Defend the **rights** of the **poor**
	140.12	of the **poor** and the **rights** of the **needy**.
Prov	29.7	person knows the **rights** of the **poor**
	29.14	If a king defends the **rights** of the **poor**
	31.5	and ignore the **rights** of people in **need**.
	31.9	Protect the **rights** of the **poor**
Ecc	5.8	the **poor** and denies them...their **rights**.
Is	10.2	the **poor** from having their **rights**
	11.4	the **poor** fairly and defend the **rights**

Widows

Deut	24.17	**rights**; and do not take a **widow's**
	27.19	and **widows** of their **rights**.
Is	1.17	orphans their **rights**, and defend **widows**.

RITUAL

Lev	14.2	—	16.34	x17
Num	5.8	—	6.13	x4
Num	15.25	—	16.47	x4
Num	28.22	—	29.11	x4
Ex	29.4	—	30.10	x3
2 Chr	29.18	—	30.24	x3

Offerings

Lev   12.7   **offering** to the Lord and perform the **ritual**

Lev	14.19	the **sin-offering** and perform the **ritual**
	15.15	a **burnt-offering**. In this way he will perform the **ritual**
Num	6.11	a **burnt-offering**, to perform the **ritual**
	8.12	a **burnt-offering**, in order to perform the **ritual**
	28.22	a **sin-offering**, and in this way perform the **ritual**
	28.30	a **sin-offering**, and in this way perform the **ritual**
	29.5	a **sin-offering**, and in this way perform the **ritual**
	29.11	offered in the **ritual** of purification

Take Away (sin)

Lev	6.30	in the **ritual** to **take away sin**,
	12.7	**ritual** to **take away** her impurity,
	12.8	**ritual** to **take away** her impurity,
	23.26	**ritual** is to be performed to **take away**
	23.28	performing the **ritual** to **take away sin**.
Heb	9.13	**taking away** their **ritual** impurity.

RIVAL

Deut	4.24	—	6.15	x3

Tolerate

Ex	20.5	I **tolerate** no **rivals**.
	34.14	**tolerate** no **rivals**.
Num	25.13	did not **tolerate** any **rivals** to me
Deut	4.24	he **tolerates** no **rivals**.
	5.9	I **tolerate** no **rivals**.
	6.15	**tolerates** no **rivals**.
Josh	24.19	He will **tolerate** no **rivals**,
Nah	1.2	The Lord God **tolerates** no **rivals**;

SABBATH

Neh	13.15 – 22			x10
Lk	13.10	—	14.5	x9
Mt	12.1 – 12			x8
Mk	1.21	—	3.4	x8
Lev	23.3	—	24.8	x7
Jer	17.21 – 27			x6
Ezek	20.12 – 24			x6
Ezek	44.24	—	46.12	x6
Lk	6.1 – 9			x6
Jn	5.9 – 18			x4
Acts	13.14 – 44			x4
Acts	15.21	—	18.4	x4
2 Kgs	11.5 – 9			x3
Neh	9.14	—	10.33	x3
Is	56.2 – 6			x3
Ezek	22.8	—	23.38	x3
Jn	7.22 – 23			x3
Jn	19.31 – 42			x3

Command see **Law**

Holy, Sacred

Ex	20.8	Observe the **Sabbath** and keep it **holy**
	20.11	blessed the **Sabbath** and made it **holy**.
Deut	5.12	Observe the **Sabbath** and keep it **holy**
1 Chr	9.32	the **sacred** bread...every **Sabbath**.
2 Chr	2.4	on **Sabbaths**...and other **holy** days
	8.13	of Moses for each **holy** day: **Sabbaths**,
Neh	9.14	them to keep your **Sabbaths holy**,
	10.31	the **Sabbath** or on any other **holy** day,
	10.33	the **sacred** offerings for **Sabbaths**,
	13.22	sure that the **Sabbath** was kept **holy**
Is	58.13	If you treat the **Sabbath** as **sacred**
Jer	17.22	**Sabbath**; they must observe it as...**sacred**
	17.24	observe the **Sabbath** as a **sacred** day
	17.27	observe the **Sabbath** as a **sacred** day.
Lam	2.6	put an end to **holy** days and **Sabbaths**.
Ezek	20.20	Make the **Sabbath** a **holy** day
	44.24	and they are to keep the **Sabbaths holy**.
Jn	19.31	the coming **Sabbath** was especially **holy**.

Col   2.16 about **holy** days...or the **Sabbath**.

Law, Command

Lev	19.3	the **Sabbath**, as I have **commanded**.
Deut	5.15	I **command** you to observe the **Sabbath**.
2 Chr	8.13	the **Law**...for each holy day: **Sabbaths**,
Ezek	20.16	my **laws**, and profaned the **Sabbath**
	20.24	broken my **laws**, profaned the **Sabbath**,
Mt	12.2	our **Law**...to do this on the **Sabbath**!
	12.5	actually break the **Sabbath** law,
	12.10	our **Law** to heal on the **Sabbath**?
	12.12	**Law**...to help someone on the **Sabbath**.
Mk	2.24	**Law**...to do that on the **Sabbath**!
	3.4	**Law** allow us to do on the **Sabbath**?
Lk	6.2	what our **Law** says you cannot do on the **Sabbath**?
	6.9	**Law** allow us to do on the **Sabbath**?
	14.3	our **Law** allow healing on the **Sabbath**
	23.56	**Sabbath** they rested, as the **Law**
Jn	5.10	is a **Sabbath**, and it is against our **Law**
	5.18	only had he broken the **Sabbath** law,
	7.23	on the **Sabbath** so that Moses' **Law**
	9.16	for he does not obey the **Sabbath law**.

Observe

Ex	20.8	**Observe** the **Sabbath** and keep it holy
Deut	5.12	**Observe** the **Sabbath** and keep it holy
	5.15	I command you to **observe** the **Sabbath**.
2 Chr	36.21	**Sabbath** rest that has not been **observed**.
Is	56.2	those who always **observe** the **Sabbath**
	56.4	honour me by **observing** the **Sabbath**
	56.6	who **observe** the **Sabbath** and faithfully
Jer	17.22	on the **Sabbath**; they must **observe** it
	17.24	**observe** the **Sabbath** as a sacred day.
	17.27	**observe** the **Sabbath** as a sacred day.

Profane

Neh	13.18	by **profaning** the **Sabbath**.
Ezek	20.13	They completely **profaned** the **Sabbath**.
	20.16	**profaned** the **Sabbath** — they preferred
	20.21	They **profaned** the **Sabbath**.
	20.24	they had...**profaned** the **Sabbath**,
	23.38	**profaned** my Temple and...the **Sabbath**,

Sacred see **Holy**

Teach

Neh	9.14	**taught** them to keep your **Sabbaths**
Mk	6.2	On the **Sabbath** he began to **teach**
Lk	4.31	he **taught** the people on the **Sabbath**.
	6.6	On another **Sabbath** Jesus...**taught**
	13.10	One **Sabbath** Jesus was **teaching**

Worship

Lev	19.30	**Sabbath**, and honour the place where I am **worshipped**.
	23.3	the **Sabbath**, is a day...for **worship**.

SACKCLOTH

	1 Kgs	20.31 —	21.27	x4
	Esth	4.1 – 4		x4
	Jon	3.5 – 8		x3

Ashes

Esth	4.1	**sackcloth**, covered his head with **ashes**,
	4.3	them put on **sackcloth** and lay in **ashes**.
Is	58.5	and spread out **sackcloth** and **ashes**
Jer	6.26	Put on **sackcloth** and roll in **ashes**.
Dan	9.3	wearing **sackcloth**, and sitting in **ashes**.
Jon	3.6	on **sackcloth**, and sat down in **ashes**.
Mt	11.21	put on **sackcloth** and sprinkled **ashes**
Lk	10.13	put on **sackcloth**, and sprinkled **ashes**

SACRED

	Ex	33.7 —	40.9	x14
	Lev	20.3 —	22.15	x13
	Is	64.10 —	66.20	x7

	1 Sam	20.8 —	21.6	x6
	Ex	29.6 —	31.14	x5
	Num	18.3 – 32		x5
	Num	4.15 – 20		x4
	Joel	2.1 —	3.17	x4
	Gen	12.6 —	14.13	x3
	Ex	25.8 —	26.1	x3
	Lev	10.4 – 18		x3
	Lev	25.12 —	27.9	x3
	2 Kgs	10.22 – 27		x3
	1 Chr	22.19 —	23.28	x3
	Neh	10.33		x3
	Is	56.7 —	58.13	x3
	Jer	17.22 – 27		x3
	Ezek	43.12 —	44.19	x3

Dedicate see **Offering**

Gift see **Offering**

Holy

Gen	12.6	the **sacred** tree of Moreh, the **holy** place
Ex	40.9	with the **sacred** oil, and it will be **holy**.
Lev	10.17	in a **sacred** place? It is very **holy**,
	12.4	that is **holy** or enter the **sacred** Tent
Jer	31.23	**sacred** hill of Jerusalem, the **holy** place
Ezek	43.12	top of the mountain is **sacred** and **holy**.

Offering, Dedicate, Gift, Sacrifice

Ex	25.30	the **sacred** bread **offered** to me.
	29.6	the **sacred** sign of **dedication**
	35.2	**sacred**, a solemn day of rest **dedicated**
	38.24	**dedicated** to the Lord for the **sacred**
	39.30	the **sacred** sign of **dedication**,
Lev	8.9	the **sacred** sign of **dedication**,
	22.2	treat with respect the **sacred offerings**
	22.3	comes near the **sacred offerings**
	22.4	may eat any of the **sacred offerings**
	22.6	may not eat any of the **sacred offerings**
	22.7	then he may eat the **sacred offerings**,
	22.10	may eat any of the **sacred offerings**;
	22.12	may not eat any of the **sacred offerings**.
	22.14	eats any of the **sacred offerings**
	22.15	shall not profane the **sacred offerings**
	27.9	every **gift** made to the Lord is **sacred**,
Num	6.20	a **sacred offering** for the priest,
	18.9	the most **sacred offerings** not burnt
	18.32	the **sacred gifts** of the Israelites
2 Chr	2.4	we will present **offerings** of **sacred** bread
	35.13	boiled the **sacred offerings** in pots,
Neh	12.47	The people gave a **sacred offering**
Is	65.3	**offer** pagan **sacrifices** in **sacred** gardens
Hos	3.4	without **sacrifices** or **sacred** stone pillars,
Eph	2.21	a **sacred** temple **dedicated** to the Lord.

SACRIFICE

see also **OFFER**

	Heb	7.27 —	11.17	x27
	Ezek	42.13 —	46.24	x22
	Lev	4.3 —	7.15	x19
	2 Chr	28.3 —	30.22	x18
	1 Sam	1.3 —	3.14	x12
	2 Kgs	14.4 —	17.36	x12
	2 Chr	33.6 —	35.14	x10
	Jer	44.3 – 24		x10
	Ezek	20.26 —	23.39	x10
	Deut	12.6 – 31		x9
	1 Sam	15.15 —	16.11	x9
	Ezek	39.17 —	40.43	x8
	Ex	8.8 – 29		x7
	1 Kgs	10.5 —	13.2	x7
	2 Chr	7.1 —	9.4	x7
	Dan	8.11 —	9.27	x7
	Hos	3.4 —	6.6	x7

Ex	29.3	—	30.10	x6
2 Kgs	21.6	—	23.10	x6
Ezra	3.2	—	4.2	x6
Lev	1.2 – 13			x5
Lev	16.6	—	17.8	x5
Josh	22.23 – 29			x5
Ezra	6.3 – 21			x5
Jer	6.20	—	7.31	x5
Heb	13.10 – 20			x5
Gen	22.2 – 7			x4
Num	15.3 – 10			x4
1 Kgs	1.9 – 25			x4
1 Kgs	8.5 – 64			x4
Ps	50.5 – 23			x4
Ps	51.16 – 19			x4
Jer	11.12 – 17			x4
Ezek	16.19 – 36			x4
1 Cor	9.13	—	10.20	x4
Ex	5.3 – 17			x3
2 Sam	6.13 – 18			x3
1 Kgs	3.2 – 4			x3
2 Kgs	12.3 – 4			x3
1 Chr	21.26 – 29			x3
Ezek	18.6 – 15			x3

Command see **Law**

Covenant see **Promise**

Death

Is	53.10	**death** was a **sacrifice** to bring
Acts	20.28	his own through the **sacrificial death**
Rom	3.25	by his **sacrificial death** he should become
	5.9	**sacrificial death** we are now put right
Eph	1.7	by the **sacrificial death** of Christ
	2.13	by the **sacrificial death** of Christ.
Col	1.20	through his Son's **sacrificial death**
Heb	13.20	as the result of his **sacrificial death**,
Rev	1.5	by his **sacrificial death** he has freed us
	5.9	**sacrificial death** you bought for God

Dedicate

| 1 Chr | 29.21 | **sacrifices**, **dedicating** them to the Lord, |
| Ezek | 43.18 | **dedicate** it by burning **sacrifices** on it |

Festival, Feast

Ex	23.18	**sacrificed** to me during these **festivals**
Num	25.2	women invited them to **sacrificial feasts**,
1 Sam	20.29	celebrating the **sacrificial feast** in town,
1 Kgs	1.9	Judah to come to this **sacrificial feast**,
	12.33	**sacrifice**...in celebration of the **festival**
2 Chr	35.8	bulls for **sacrifices** during the **festival**.
Ezek	36.38	were offered as **sacrifices** at a **festival**.
	45.23	the **festival** he is to **sacrifice** to the Lord
Acts	7.41	offered **sacrifice** to it, and had a **feast**

Gods, Idols

Ex	22.20	who offers **sacrifices** to any **god** except
Judg	16.23	offer a great **sacrifice** to their **god**
1 Kgs	11.8	and offer **sacrifices** to their own **gods**.
2 Kgs	5.17	not offer **sacrifices**...to any **god**
	22.17	have offered **sacrifices** to other **gods**,
2 Chr	34.25	have offered **sacrifices** to other **gods**,
Ps	106.28	ate **sacrifices** offered to lifeless **gods**.
	106.37	as **sacrifices** to the **idols** of Canaan.
Jer	1.16	**sacrifices** to other **gods**, and...made **idols**
	7.9	offer **sacrifices** to Baal, and worship **gods**
	11.12	the **gods** to whom they offer **sacrifices**
	19.4	by offering **sacrifices** here to other **gods**
	44.3	offered **sacrifices** to other **gods**
	44.8	**idols** and by **sacrificing** to other **gods**
	44.15	wives offered **sacrifices** to other **gods**,
	44.23	offered **sacrifices** to other **gods**
	48.35	from offering **sacrifices** to their **gods**.
Ezek	6.13	they burnt **sacrifices** to their **idols**.
	16.19	as a **sacrifice** to win the favour of **idols**.
	16.20	and offered them as **sacrifices** to **idols**.

Ezek	16.21	children and **sacrificing** them to **idols**?
	16.36	killed your children as **sacrifices** to **idols**.
	18.6	**idols** of the Israelites or eat the **sacrifices**
	18.15	**idols** of the Israelites or eat the **sacrifices**
	20.31	same **idols** by **sacrificing** your children
	22.9	of them eat **sacrifices** offered to **idols**.
	23.37	They **sacrificed** my sons to their **idols**.
	23.39	killed my children as **sacrifices** to **idols**,
Hos	11.2	**sacrificed** to Baal...burnt incense to **idols**.

High Priest see **Priest**

Honour see **Please**

Idols see **Gods**

Joy see **Praise**

Law, Command, Regulation

Ex	8.27	**sacrifices**...just as he **commanded** us.
Lev	10.18	the **sacrifice** there, as I **commanded**.
Deut	33.10	obey your **Law**; They will offer **sacrifices**
2 Chr	35.13	**sacrifices**...according to the **regulations**,
Ezra	3.4	**regulations**...they offered the **sacrifices**
Jer	19.5	as **sacrifices**. I never **commanded** them
Heb	10.1	**Law**, then, by means of these **sacrifices**
	10.8	**sacrifices**...offered according to the **Law**.

Love

| Hos | 6.6 | constant **love**, not your animal **sacrifices**. |
| Rev | 1.5 | He **loves** us, and by his **sacrificial** death |

Obey

| Deut | 33.10 | **obey** your Law; They will offer **sacrifices** |
| 1 Sam | 15.22 | better to **obey** him than to **sacrifice** |

Please, Honour

Gen	8.21	odour of the **sacrifice pleased** the Lord
Ex	12.27	**sacrifice** of Passover to **honour** the
Num	15.7	The smell of these **sacrifices** is **pleasing**
	15.10	The smell of this **sacrifice** is **pleasing**
Ps	20.3	be **pleased** with all your **sacrifices**.
	50.23	thanks is the **sacrifice** that **honours** me,
	51.19	will be **pleased** with proper **sacrifices**
Prov	15.8	**pleased** when good men pray, but hates the **sacrifices**
	21.3	**pleases** the Lord more than bringing him **sacrifices**.
Is	43.23	did not **honour** me with your **sacrifices**.
	60.7	**sacrifices**...offered on the altar to **please**
Jer	6.20	or be **pleased** with their **sacrifices**.
Hos	8.13	**sacrifices**. But I...am not **pleased**
Mal	1.11	**sacrifices**. All of them **honour** me!
Acts	7.41	**sacrifice** to it, and had a feast in **honour**
Eph	5.2	and **sacrifice** that **pleases** God.
Phil	4.18	**sacrifice** which is acceptable and **pleasing**
Heb	10.8	**pleased** with **sacrifices** and offerings
	13.16	the **sacrifices** that **please** God.

Praise, Joy, Thanks

Lev	22.29	you offer a **sacrifice** of **thanksgiving**
2 Chr	29.31	**sacrifices** as offerings of **thanksgiving**
	30.22	they offered **sacrifices** in **praise**
Ps	27.6	With shouts of **joy** I will offer **sacrifices**
	50.14	the giving of **thanks** be your **sacrifice**
	50.23	Giving **thanks** is the **sacrifice**
	54.6	**sacrifice**, O Lord; I will give you **thanks**
	107.22	They must **thank** him with **sacrifices**, and with songs of **joy**
	116.17	will give you a **sacrifice** of **thanksgiving**
Is	56.7	give you **joy**...and accept the **sacrifices**
Jon	2.9	sing **praises** to you...offer you a **sacrifice**
Heb	13.15	offer **praise** to God as our **sacrifice**

Pray

1 Sam	7.9	**sacrifice** to the Lord. Then he **prayed**
1 Chr	21.28	his **prayer**, so he offered **sacrifices**
Ps	116.17	give you a **sacrifice**...and offer my **prayer**

| Prov | 15.8 | good men **pray**, but hates the **sacrifices** |
| Is | 56.7 | of **prayer**, and accept the **sacrifices** |

Present

| Lev | 1.13 | the priest will **present** the **sacrifice** |
| Heb | 8.3 | to **present** offerings and animal **sacrifices** |

Priest, High Priest

Lev	1.9	**priest** will burn the whole **sacrifice**
	1.13	the **priest** will present the **sacrifice**
	4.26	the **priest** shall offer the **sacrifice**
		Also: 4.31, 35; 5.6, 10, 13
	5.16	**priest** shall offer the animal as a **sacrifice**
	5.18	The **priest** shall offer the **sacrifice**
	6.7	The **priest** shall offer the **sacrifice**
	6.26	The **priest** who **sacrifices** the animal
	7.7	to the **priest** who offers the **sacrifice**.
	7.8	to the **priest** who offers the **sacrifice**.
Deut	18.3	**sacrificed**, the **priests** are to be given
1 Sam	2.13	offering his **sacrifice**, the **priest's** servant
2 Kgs	23.5	**priests** who offered **sacrifices** to Baal,
2 Chr	29.35	**sacrifices**...burnt whole, the **priests**
	30.15	**sacrifice**. The **priests** and Levites
	30.16	blood of the **sacrifices** to the **priests**,
Ezek	46.2	the **priests** burn his **sacrifices** whole
	46.20	the **priests** are to boil the meat offered as **sacrifices**
Heb	7.27	other **high priests**; he does not need to offer **sacrifices**
	8.3	**High Priest** is appointed to present ...animal **sacrifices**
1 Pet	2.5	holy **priests** to offer spiritual...**sacrifices**

Promise, Covenant

1 Sam	1.21	the special **sacrifice** he had **promised**
Ps	22.25	I will offer the **sacrifices** I **promised**.
	50.5	**covenant** with me by offering a **sacrifice**.
Jer	11.15	making **promises** and by offering animal **sacrifices**?
	44.24	**promised** that you would offer **sacrifices**
Jon	1.16	offered a **sacrifice** and **promised** to serve
	2.9	**sacrifice** and do what I have **promised**.
Heb	13.20	his **sacrificial** death, by which the eternal **covenant**

Regulation see Law

Require

Lev	23.37	**sacrifices**, and wine-offerings, as **required**
1 Sam	2.29	**sacrifices** and offerings which I **require**
Ezra	3.4	they offered the **sacrifices required**
Heb	9.23	**require** much better **sacrifices**.

Sin

Ex	29.36	**sacrifice**, so that **sin** may be forgiven.
	30.10	blood of the animal **sacrificed** for **sin**.
Lev	4.20	the **sacrifice** for the people's **sin**,
	4.26	the **sacrifice** for the **sin** of the ruler,
	4.31	the **sacrifice** for the man's **sin**,
	4.35	the **sacrifice** for the man's **sin**,
	5.6	the **sacrifice** for the man's **sin**,
	5.10	the **sacrifice** for the man's **sin**,
	5.13	the **sacrifice** for the man's **sin**,
	5.16	as a **sacrifice** for the man's **sin**,
	5.18	shall offer the **sacrifice** for the **sin**
	6.7	offer the **sacrifice** for the man's **sin**,
1 Chr	6.49	the **sacrifices** by which God forgives Israel's **sins**.
Ezra	10.19	a ram as a **sacrifice** for their **sins**.
Ezek	42.13	the **sacrifices** offered for **sin** or as
	43.19	bull to offer as a **sacrifice** for **sin**.
	43.21	that is offered as a **sacrifice** for **sin**
	43.22	and offer it as a **sacrifice** for **sin**.
	43.25	and a ram as **sacrifices** for **sin**.
	45.22	offer a bull as a **sacrifice** for his **sins**
	45.25	seven days the same **sacrifice** for **sin**,

Ezek	46.20	offered as **sacrifices** for **sin** or as
Heb	5.3	offer **sacrifices** not only for the **sins**
	7.27	**sacrifices** every day for his own **sins**
	9.26	to remove **sin** through the **sacrifice**
	10.2	of **sin** any more, and all **sacrifices**
	10.12	Christ...offered one **sacrifice** for **sins**,
	13.11	to offer it as a **sacrifice** for **sins**;

Take Away (sin)

Lev	1.4	be accepted as a **sacrifice** to **take away**
	16.6	offer a bull as a **sacrifice** to **take away**
2 Chr	29.24	a **sacrifice** to **take away** the **sin**
Ps	40.6	for **sacrifices** to **take away sins**.
Heb	9.28	offered in **sacrifice** once to **take away**
	10.6	**sacrifices** to **take away sins**.
	10.8	and the **sacrifices** to **take away sins**.
	10.11	these **sacrifices** can never **take away**
	10.26	any **sacrifice** that will **take away sins**

Thanks see Praise

SAD

2 Cor	6.10 —	7.11	x9
2 Cor	2.1 – 7		x7
Jn	16.6 – 22		x4
Neh	2.1 – 3		x3

Happy, Glad

Ps	90.15	as much **happiness** as the **sadness**
Prov	14.13	hide **sadness**. When **happiness** is gone,
	15.13	people are **happy**, they smile, but when they are **sad**,
Is	24.7	who was once **happy** is now **sad**,
Jn	16.20	but your **sadness** will turn into **gladness**.
2 Cor	2.3	made **sad** by the very people who should make me **glad**.
	6.10	although **saddened**, we are always **glad**
	7.9	**happy** — not because I made you **sad**
Heb	12.11	something to make us **sad**, not **glad**.
	13.17	do their work **gladly**; if not, they will do it with **sadness**,

SADDUCEES

| Mt | 16.1 – 12 | x4 |
| Acts | 23.6 – 8 | x3 |

Jesus

Mt	16.1	**Sadducees** who came to **Jesus** wanted to
	22.23	some **Sadducees** came to **Jesus**
	22.34	**Jesus** had silenced the **Sadducees**,
Mk	12.28	**Jesus** had given the **Sadducees** a good answer,

Rise

Mk	12.18	**Sadducees**, who say that people will not **rise** from death
Lk	20.27	**Sadducees**, who say that people will not **rise** from death
Acts	23.8	the **Sadducees** say that people will not **rise** from death

SAFETY

Ps	18.2 – 35		x5
Lev	25.18 —	26.25	x4
2 Sam	17.3 —	19.30	x4
2 Sam	22.3 – 34		x4
Prov	3.17 —	4.6	x4
Is	32.18 —	33.20	x4
Ezek	34.14 – 28		x4
1 Sam	20.7 – 21		x3
1 Sam	25.29 —	27.1	x3
2 Sam	3.21 – 23		x3
2 Chr	18.26 —	19.1	x3
Ps	31.4 – 20		x3
Ps	91.1 – 4		x3
Prov	28.18 —	29.25	x3

Is	23.12	—	25.4	x3
Jer	6.1	—	7.10	x3
Mic	2.2 — 10			x3
Jn	17.11 — 15			x3

Danger see Protect

Enemy
Deut	12.10	keep you **safe** from all your **enemies**
	25.19	**safe** from all your **enemies** who live
1 Sam	12.11	your **enemies**, and you lived in **safety**.
2 Sam	7.1	kept him **safe** from all his **enemies**.
	7.10	to keep you **safe** from all your **enemies**
Ps	8.2	**safe** and secure from all your **enemies**;
	17.7	your side I am **safe** from my **enemies**.
	27.11	**safe** path, because I have many **enemies**.
	69.14	keep me **safe** from my **enemies**,
	138.7	me **safe**. You oppose my angry **enemies**
Zech	8.10	and no one was **safe** from his **enemies**.

Evil
Ps	12.7	what is **evil**. Keep us always **safe**,
	140.1	**evil** men; keep me **safe** from violent
2 Tim	4.18	me from all **evil** and take me **safely**

Harm see Protect

Love
Ps	17.7	**love** and save me...I am **safe**
	40.11	**love** and loyalty will always keep me **safe**.
Prov	4.6	**love** her, and she will keep you **safe**.

Protect, Care, Danger, Harm, Shelter, Trouble, Violent
2 Sam	22.3	my **protection**, and with him I am **safe**.
2 Chr	15.5	in **safety**, because there was **trouble**
Ps	9.9	a place of **safety** in times of **trouble**.
	16.1	**Protect** me...I trust in you for **safety**.
	18.2	my **protection**, and with him I am **safe**.
	26.12	I am **safe** from all **dangers**;
	27.5	**trouble** he will **shelter** me; he will keep me **safe**
	31.20	in a **safe shelter** you hide them
	57.1	to you for **safety**...I find **protection**
	91.1	for **safety**...remains under the **protection**
	91.3	keep you **safe** from all hidden **dangers**
	91.4	be **safe**...his faithfulness will **protect**
	102.28	in **safety**, and under your **protection**
	121.7	from all **danger**; he will keep you **safe**
	138.7	by **troubles**, you keep me **safe**.
	140.1	keep me **safe** from **violent** men.
	140.4	keep me **safe** from **violent** men
	144.2	my **shelter**...in whom I trust for **safety**.
Prov	13.13	for **trouble**; follow it and you are **safe**.
	19.23	content and **safe** from **harm**.
Is	4.6	place of **safety**, **sheltered** from the rain
	25.4	**safe** in times of **trouble**. You give them **shelter**
Jer	15.20	you to **protect** you and keep you **safe**.
	17.17	my place of **safety** when **trouble** comes.
Hab	2.9	own home **safe** from **harm** and **danger**!
Acts	7.10	him **safely** through all his **troubles**.
1 Cor	10.1	**protection** of the cloud...all passed **safely**
1 Tim	6.20	keep **safe** what has been entrusted to your **care**.
1 Jn	5.18	him **safe**, and the Evil One cannot **harm**
Rev	3.10	keep you **safe** from the time of **trouble**
	12.14	she will be taken **care** of...**safe**

Save, Rescue
2 Sam	22.3	and keeps me **safe**. He is my **saviour**;
Ps	17.7	**save** me; at your side I am **safe**
	69.14	**Save** me from sinking...keep me **safe**
	138.7	**safe**. You oppose my...enemies and **save**
	140.1	**Save** me, Lord, from evil men; keep me **safe**

Jer	17.14	**rescue** me and I will be perfectly **safe**.
	33.16	**rescued** and will live in **safety**.
2 Tim	4.18	**rescue** me from...evil and take me **safely**

Secure
Num	24.21	where you live is **secure**, **Safe** as a nest
Ps	8.2	You are **safe** and **secure** from...enemies
	27.5	**safe** in his Temple and make me **secure**
	40.2	**safely** on a rock and made me **secure**.
Prov	1.33	will have **security**. He will be **safe**,
	10.9	Honest people are **safe** and **secure**
Is	33.16	you will be **safe**; you will be as **secure**
	47.8	you that think you are **safe** and **secure**.
Jer	49.31	those people that feel **safe** and **secure**!

Shelter see Protect

Temple
Ezra	9.9	rebuild your **Temple**...and to find **safety**
Ps	27.5	he will keep me **safe** in his **Temple**
Jer	7.4	We are **safe**! This is the Lord's **Temple**,
	7.10	my own **Temple**, and say, 'We are **safe**!

Trouble see Protect

Violent see Protect

SATAN
Job	1.6	—	2.7	x10
Rev	2.9	—	3.9	x5
Mk	3.23	—	4.15	x3
Rev	20.2 — 8			x3

Power
Job	1.12	said to **Satan**, "everything he has is in your **power**,
	2.6	**Satan**, "All right, he is in your **power**,
Acts	26.18	from the **power** of **Satan** to God,
2 Thes	2.9	One will come with the **power** of **Satan**
1 Tim	1.20	them over to the **power** of **Satan**;

SATISFY
Ecc	3.11	—	6.9	x4
Is	57.8	—	58.11	x3
Ezek	16.28 — 29			x3

Desire
Ezek	7.19	cannot use it to **satisfy** their **desires**
Mt	5.6	greatest **desire** is to do what God requires; God will **satisfy**
Rom	13.14	sinful nature and **satisfying** its **desires**.
Gal	5.16	**satisfy** the **desires** of the human nature.

Hunger
Job	38.39	and **satisfy** **hungry** young lions
Prov	16.26	because he wants to **satisfy** his **hunger**.
Is	9.20	but their **hunger** is never **satisfied**.
	55.2	not **satisfy**? Why...still be **hungry**?
	58.10	food to the **hungry** and **satisfy** those
Jer	31.25	**satisfy**...everyone...weak from **hunger**.
Hos	9.4	will be used only to **satisfy** their **hunger**;
Mic	6.14	be **satisfied** ...you will still be **hungry**.

Need
Ps	132.15	with all she **needs**; I will **satisfy**
	145.16	and **satisfy** the **needs** of all.
Is	58.10	and **satisfy** those who are in **need**,
Jer	31.14	and **satisfy** all the **needs** of my people.
1 Cor	7.3	each should **satisfy** the other's **needs**.

SAVE (SALVATION)
Is	41.10	—	52.10	x36
Is	56.1	—	63.19	x20
Ps	119.39 — 174			x15
2 Sam	22.1 — 49			x10
Is	36.14	—	38.17	x9
2 Kgs	18.29	—	19.12	x8
2 Chr	32.11 — 17			x8

Ps	18.3 – 48		x8
Ezek	13.22 –	14.22	x8
Rom	8.24 –	11.26	x8
Mic	4.10 –	7.9	x7
Job	5.15 –	6.23	x6
Ps	31.1 – 16		x6
Ps	69.1 – 35		x6
Ps	80.2 – 19		x6
Ps	107.2 – 28		x6
Lk	6.9 –	9.24	x6
Ps	22.4 – 31		x5
Ps	25.2 – 22		x5
Ps	106.4 – 47		x5
Ps	116.4 – 16		x5
Ex	18.4 – 10		x4
Ps	34.6 – 22		x4
Ps	86.2 – 16		x4
Mt	27.40 – 49		x4
Lk	23.35 – 39		x4
1 Sam	14.23 – 48		x3
1 Sam	17.37 – 47		x3
Job	33.17 – 30		x3
Ps	7.1 – 10		x3
Ps	17.7 – 14		x3
Ps	35.3 – 17		x3
Ps	44.6 – 26		x3
Ps	49.12 – 20		x3
Ps	50.15 – 23		x3
Ps	62.1 – 6		x3
Ps	85.7 – 9		x3
Ps	109.26 – 31		x3
Ezek	33.8 – 19		x3
Dan	6.20 – 27		x3
Acts	2.21 – 47		x3
Acts	27.20 – 43		x3

Announce, Proclaim
Ps 18.46 **Proclaim** the greatness of...God who **saves**
51.14 **save** me, and I will gladly **proclaim**
98.2 **announced** his victory...his **saving** power
Is 63.1 powerful to **save**, coming to **announce**
Acts 16.17 **announce** to you how you can be **saved**!

Believe see Faith

Care
Ps 18.35 you protect me and **save** me; your **care**
31.5 myself in your **care**. You will **save** me
31.15 I am always in your **care**; **save** me

Choose
Ps 28.8 he...**saves** his **chosen** king.
Hab 3.13 to **save** your **chosen** king.
Lk 23.35 **save** himself if he is the Messiah whom God has **chosen**!
2 Thes 2.13 God **chose** you as the first to be **saved**

Christ, Jesus, Lord
Mt 1.21 **Jesus**...will **save** his people
8.25 **Save** us, **Lord**!
14.30 **Save** me, **Lord**!
Lk 2.11 your **Saviour** was born — **Christ**
Acts 15.11 **saved** by the grace of the **Lord Jesus**,
16.31 in...**Jesus**, and you will be **saved**
Rom 5.10 more will we be **saved** by **Christ's** life!
Eph 5.23 and **Christ** is himself the **Saviour**
Phil 3.20 our **Saviour**, the **Lord Jesus Christ**,
1 Tim 1.15 **Jesus** came...to **save** sinners.
Tit 1.4 Father and **Christ Jesus** our **Saviour**
2.13 our great God and **Saviour Jesus**
3.6 **Jesus Christ** our **Saviour**,
1 Pet 3.21 It **saves** you through....**Jesus**
2 Pet 1.1 of our God and **Saviour Jesus Christ**
1.11 of our **Lord** and **Saviour Jesus Christ**.
2.20 of our **Lord** and **Saviour Jesus Christ**,

2 Pet 3.18 of our **Lord** and **Saviour Jesus Christ**.

Danger see Trouble

Defend see Protect

Distress see Trouble

Evil, Wicked
Job 13.16 will **save** me, since no **wicked** man
Ps 17.13 **Save** me from the **wicked**
37.40 he **saves** them from the **wicked**,
59.2 **Save** me from those **evil** men;
119.155 The **wicked** will not be **saved**,
140.1 **Save** me, Lord, from **evil** men;
Prov 16.17 avoids **evil**; so watch...it may **save**
Jer 4.14 wash the **evil** from your heart, so that you may be **saved**.
Ezek 13.22 giving up **evil** and **saving** their lives.

Faith, Believe, Trust
Ps 22.4 they **trusted** you, and you **saved** them.
25.5 who **saves** me. I always **trust** in you.
44.6 **trust** in my bow or in my sword to **save**
78.22 not **believe** that he would **save** them.
86.2 **save** me, for...I **trust** in you.
119.81 **save** me; I place my **trust** in your word.
146.3 **trust** in human leaders; no human being can **save**
Mk 16.16 **believes** and is baptized will be **saved**
Lk 7.50 Your **faith** has **saved** you; go in peace.
8.12 them from **believing** and being **saved**.
Acts 15.11 We **believe** and are **saved**
16.31 **Believe** in the Lord Jesus, and you will be **saved**
Rom 1.16 God's power to **save** all who **believe**,
1 Cor 1.21 God decided to **save** those who **believe**.
Eph 2.8 that you have been **saved** through **faith**.
2 Tim 3.15 **salvation** through **faith** in Christ Jesus.
Heb 10.39 we have **faith** and are **saved**.
Jas 2.14 Can that **faith save** him?
1 Pet 1.5 **faith** are kept safe...for the **salvation**

Free see Rescue

God, Lord
Ex 14.13 what the **Lord** will do to **save** you
14.30 the **Lord saved** the people of Israel
18.8 and how the **Lord** had **saved** them.
18.10 Praise the **Lord**, who **saved** you from
18.10 Praise the **Lord**, who **saved** his people
Num 10.9 **Lord** your God, will help you and **save**
Deut 32.15 God...their mighty **saviour**.
32.18 forgot their God, their mighty **saviour**,
33.29 like you, a nation **saved** by the **Lord**.
Judg 2.16 **Lord** gave the Israelites leaders who **saved**
8.34 **Lord** their God, who had **saved** them
1 Sam 7.8 to the **Lord** our God to **save** us
12.7 mighty actions the **Lord** did to **save** you
14.23 The **Lord saved** Israel that day.
17.37 The **Lord** has **saved** me from lions
17.47 **Lord** does not need swords...to **save**
2 Sam 4.9 by the living **Lord**, who has **saved** me
18.19 the **Lord** has **saved** him
22.1 When the **Lord saved** David from Saul
22.4 I call to the **Lord**, and he **saves** me
22.36 O **Lord**, you protect me and **save** me;
22.47 of the strong God who **saves** me!
2 Kgs 18.30 Don't think that the **Lord** will **save**
18.35 you think the **Lord** can **save** Jerusalem?
1 Chr 16.35 **Save** us, O God our **Saviour**;
2 Chr 32.11 the **Lord** your God will **save** you from
Job 5.15 But God **saves** the poor from death;
22.29 God brings down the proud and **saves**
Ps 3.7 **Save** me, my God!
6.4 Come and **save** me, **Lord**;

Ps	18.3	I call to the **Lord**, and he **saves** me
	18.35	O **Lord**, you protect me and **save** me;
	18.46	greatness of the **God** who **saves** me.
	22.31	The **Lord saved** his people.
	24.5	The **Lord** will bless them and **save**
	25.5	you are my **God**, who **saves** me.
	25.22	O **God**, **save** your people Israel!
	27.1	The **Lord** is my light and my **salvation**;
	27.9	don't abandon me, O **God**, my **saviour**.
	28.9	**Save** your people, **Lord**, and bless those
	30.1	**Lord**, because you have **saved** me
	31.5	You will **save** me, **Lord**;
	34.19	but the **Lord saves** him from them all;
	34.22	The **Lord saves** his people;
	37.39	The **Lord saves** righteous men
	38.22	Help me now, O **Lord** my **saviour**!
	40.9	**Lord**, I told the good news that you **save** us.
	40.13	**Save** me, **Lord**!
	40.17	You are my **saviour** and my **God**
	42.5	praise him, my **saviour** and my **God**.
	42.11	praise him, my **saviour** and my **God**.
	43.5	praise him, my **saviour** and my **God**.
	51.14	my life, O **God**, and **save** me,
	54.1	**Save** me by your power, O **God**;
	55.16	**Lord God** for help, and he will **save**
	59.1	**Save** me from my enemies, my **God**;
	62.1	I wait patiently for **God** to **save** me;
	62.7	My **salvation** and honour depend on **God**;
	68.19	he is the **God** who **saves** us.
	68.20	Our **God** is a **God** who **saves**;
	69.1	**Save** me, O **God**!
	69.29	lift me up, O **God**, and **save** me!
	70.1	**Save** me, O **God**!
	70.5	You are my **saviour**, O **Lord**
	79.9	Help us, O **God**, and **save** us;
	85.4	Bring us back, O **God** our **saviour**,
	85.7	O **Lord**, and give us your **saving** help.
	88.1	**Lord God**, my **saviour**, I cry out
	91.14	**God** says, "I will **save** those who
	106.47	**Save** us, O **Lord** our **God**, and bring us
	107.6	called to the **Lord**, and he **saved** them
	107.13	called to the **Lord**, and he **saved** them
	107.19	called to the **Lord**, and he **saved** them
	107.28	called to the **Lord**, and he **saved** them
	116.4	I beg you, **Lord**, **save** me!
	116.8	The **Lord saved** me from death;
	116.13	the **Lord**, to thank him for **saving** me.
	118.25	**Save** us, **Lord**, **save** us!
	119.41	you love me, **Lord**, and **save** me
	119.81	**Lord**, waiting for you to **save** me;
	119.166	I wait for you to **save** me, **Lord**,
	119.174	for your **saving** help, O **Lord**!
	120.2	**Save** me, **Lord**, from liars and deceivers.
	140.1	**Save** me, **Lord**, from evil men;
Is	12.2	**God** is my **saviour**;
	36.15	Don't think that the **Lord** will **save** you
	36.20	you think the **Lord** can **save** Jerusalem?"
	41.14	the holy **God** of Israel...who **saves**
	42.21	a **God** who is eager to **save**,
	43.3	the holy **God** of Israel, who **saves** you.
	43.11	the **Lord**, the only one who can **save**
	43.14	holy **God**, the **Lord** who **saves** you,
	44.23	The **Lord** has shown his greatness by **saving**
	44.24	I am the **Lord**, your **saviour**;
	45.15	The **God** of Israel, who **saves**
	45.17	But Israel is **saved** by the **Lord**,
	45.21	the **Lord**, the **God** who **saves**
	48.17	of Israel, the **Lord** who **saves** you,
	48.20	The **Lord** has **saved** his servant Israel!
	49.7	Israel's holy **God** and **saviour** says
	49.26	the **Lord**, the one who **saves** you

Is	54.5	The holy **God** of Israel will **save** you
	54.8	So says the **Lord** who **saves** you.
	59.1	the **Lord** is too weak to **save** you
	59.9	know why **God** does not **save** us
	59.11	We long for **God** to **save** us from
	60.16	that I, the **Lord**, have **saved** you,
	61.2	When the **Lord** will **save** his people
	61.10	**God** has clothed her with **salvation**
	61.11	The Sovereign **Lord** will **save** his people,
	62.11	the **Lord** is coming to **save** you,
	62.12	The People the **Lord** Has **Saved**.
	63.1	It is the **Lord**, powerful to **save**,
	63.9	but the **Lord** himself who **saved** them.
	63.11	now is the **Lord**, who **saved** the leaders
	66.5	**Lord** show his greatness and **save** you,
Jer	23.6	will be called 'The **Lord** Our **Salvation**.
	31.7	The **Lord** has **saved** his people;
	33.16	will be called 'The **Lord** Our **Salvation**.
Lam	3.58	to my rescue, **Lord**, and **saved** my life.
Dan	6.20	Was the **God** you serve...able to **save**
	12.1	are written in **God's** book will be **saved**.
Hos	1.7	the **Lord** their **God**, will **save** them,
Joel	2.32	the **Lord** for help will be **saved**.
Jon	2.9	**Salvation** comes from the **Lord**!
Mic	4.10	the **Lord** will **save** you from your
	7.7	confidently for **God**, who will **save** me.
Hab	3.18	because the **Lord God** is my **saviour**.
Zech	9.16	the **Lord** will **save** his people,
Lk	1.47	glad because of **God** my **Saviour**,
	3.6	All mankind will see **God's salvation**!
	4.19	when the **Lord** will **save** his people.
	7.16	**God** has come to **save** his people!
Acts	2.21	to the **Lord** for help will be **saved**.
	2.47	the **Lord** added...those who were being **saved**.
	4.12	whom **God** has given who can **save** us.
	13.23	whom **God** made the **Saviour**
	28.28	that **God's** message of **salvation**
Rom	3.23	is far away from **God's saving** presence.
	10.13	to the **Lord** for help will be **saved**.
1 Cor	1.21	**God** decided to **save** those
Eph	2.5	**God's** grace that you have been **saved**.
	2.8	**God's** grace that you have been **saved**
1 Tim	1.1	by order of **God** our **Saviour** and Christ
	2.3	and it pleases **God** our **Saviour**,
	2.6	**God** wants everyone to be **saved**,
	4.10	living **God**, who is the **Saviour** of all
Tit	1.3	by order of **God** our **Saviour**.
	2.10	to the teaching about **God** our **Saviour**
	2.11	**God** has revealed...for the **salvation**
	3.4	kindness and love of **God** our **Saviour**
Heb	2.3	The **Lord**...announced this **salvation**,
	5.7	to **God**, who could **save** him
	7.25	to **save** those who come to **God**
1 Pet	1.5	by **God's** power for the **salvation**
Jude	.25	to the only **God** our **Saviour**,
Rev	7.10	**Salvation** comes from our **God**,
	12.10	Now **God's salvation** has come!
	19.1	**Salvation**...belong to our **God**!

Happy, Joy

Job	33.30	**saves** a person's life...gives him the **joy**
Ps	35.9	I will be **happy** because he **saved** me.
	119.174	**saving** help, O **Lord**! I find **happiness** in
Is	25.9	**happy** and **joyful** because he has **saved**

Hope

Ps	34.18	he **saves** those who have lost all **hope**.
Is	51.5	wait with **hope** for me to **save** them.
Jer	14.8	**hope**; you are the one who **saves** us
Acts	27.20	finally gave up all **hope** of being **saved**.
	27.31	you have no **hope** of being **saved**.
Rom	8.24	For it was by **hope** that we were **saved**
2 Cor	1.10	our **hope** in him that he will **save** us
1 Tim	1.1	**Saviour** and Christ Jesus our **hope**

1 Tim   4.10   our **hope** in...God, who is the **Saviour**

Jesus see **Christ**

Joy see **Happy**

Law see **Obey**

Lord see **God, Christ**

Might see **Power**

Obey, Law
Lev	18.5	the **laws** that I give you; you will **save**
Ps	7.10	he **saves** those who **obey** him.
	50.23	I will surely **save** all who **obey** me.
	119.94	yours — **save** me! I have tried to **obey**
	119.146	**save** me, and I will keep your **laws**.
	119.153	**save** me...I have not neglected your **law**.
	119.155	**saved**, for they do not **obey** your **laws**.
Is	42.21	is eager to **save**, so he exalted his **laws**
Mal	4.2	for you who **obey** me, my **saving** power
Acts	15.1	be **saved** unless...circumcised as the **Law**

Poor
Job	5.15	But God **saves** the **poor** from death;
Ps	72.13	pity on the weak and **poor**; he **saves**
	109.31	he defends the **poor** man and **saves** him
Prov	13.8	to **save** his life, but no one threatens a **poor** man.
Ecc	9.15	**poor**, but so clever...he could have **saved**

Power, Might
Deut	7.8	is why he **saved** you by his great **might**
1 Sam	4.8	can **save** us from those **powerful** gods?
	12.7	**mighty** actions the Lord did to **save** you
2 Chr	25.15	**save** their own people from your **power**?
	32.11	God will **save** you from our **power**,
	32.17	not **saved** their people from my **power**,
Ps	49.15	will **save** me from the **power** of death.
	54.1	**Save** me by your **power**, O God;
	60.5	**Save** us by your **might**; answer our
	77.15	By your **power** you **saved** your people,
	78.42	**power** and the day when he **saved** them
	98.2	his **saving power** known to the nations.
	106.21	who had **saved** them by his **mighty** acts
	108.6	**Save** us by your **might**; answer my
	118.14	**powerful** and strong; he has **saved** me.
	138.7	and **save** me by your **power**.
	144.7	**save** me from the **power** of foreigners,
Is	51.9	Use your **power** and **save** us;
	52.10	will use his holy **power**; he will **save**
	59.17	and **saving power** like a helmet.
	60.16	have **saved** you, That the **mighty** God
	63.1	It is the Lord, **powerful** to **save**,
Jer	31.11	have **saved** them from a **mighty** nation.
Lam	5.8	no one can **save** us from their **power**.
Hos	2.10	will be able to **save** her from my **power**.
Zech	11.6	I will not **save** it from their **power**.
Mal	4.2	my **saving power** will rise on you
Lk	1.71	**save** us from...enemies, from the **power**
Rom	1.16	God's **power** to **save** all who believe,
1 Cor	1.18	who are being **saved** it is God's **power**.
2 Thes	2.13	to be **saved** by the Spirit's **power**

Pray
1 Sam	7.8	**praying** to the Lord our God to **save** us
Ps	31.1	**save** me, I **pray**!
	60.5	**Save** us...answer our **prayer**,
	64.1	listen to my **prayer**... **save** my life!
	108.6	**Save** us...answer my **prayer**,
	119.170	Listen to my **prayer**, and **save** me
Is	44.17	**prays** to it...'You are my god — **save**
	45.20	**pray** to gods that cannot **save** them
	46.7	**prays** to it, it cannot answer or **save**
Rom	10.1	might be **saved**! How I **pray** to God

Proclaim see **Announce**

Protect, Defend, Safe
Ex	15.2	**defender**; he is the one who has **saved**
1 Sam	24.15	**defend** me, and **save** me from you.
2 Sam	22.3	he **protects** me and **saves** me
	22.36	you **protect** me and **save** me;
Ps	7.1	you for **protection**; rescue me and **save**
	7.10	my **protector**; he **saves** those who obey
	17.7	**save** me; at your side I am **safe**
	18.35	you **protect** me and **save** me;
	25.20	**Protect** me and **save** me;
	28.8	**protects** his people; he **defends** and **saves**
	31.2	**Save** me now! Be my refuge to **protect**
	34.22	**save** his people; those who go to him for **protection**
	37.39	**saves** righteous men and **protects** them
	59.1	**Save** me from my enemies...**protect** me
	62.2	He alone **protects** and **saves** me;
	62.6	He alone **protects** and **saves** me;
	69.14	**Save** me from sinking...keep me **safe**
	91.14	**save** those who love me and will **protect**
	109.31	he **defends** the poor man and **saves** him
	119.154	**Defend** my cause, and set me free; **save**
	138.7	**safe**. You oppose my...enemies and **save**
	140.1	**Save** me, Lord, from evil men; keep me **safe**
Is	33.2	**Protect** us day by day and **save** us
	41.10	I will **protect** you and **save** you.
	58.8	**save** you; my presence will **protect** you
	59.20	to **defend** you and to **save** all of you
Hos	14.3	**save** us, and war-horses cannot **protect**

Rescue, Free
Deut	7.8	**saved** you by his...might and set you **free**
Job	5.21	**rescue** you from slander; he will **save**
Ps	6.4	**save** me, Lord; in your mercy **rescue** me
	7.1	**rescue** me and **save** me from all who
	35.17	**Rescue** me from their attacks; **save** my
	37.40	and **rescues** them; he **saves** them
	49.15	God will **rescue** me; he will **save** me
	54.1	**Save** me by your power...set me **free**
	59.2	**Save** me from those evil men; **rescue** me
	68.20	**saves**; he is the Lord...who **rescues**
	69.18	Come to me and **save** me; **rescue** me
	71.2	**rescue** me. Listen to me and **save** me!
	79.9	**save** us; **rescue** us and forgive
	106.10	He **saved** them...he **rescued** them
	107.2	whom he has **saved**. He has **rescued** you
	119.154	me **free**; **save** me, as you have promised.
	144.7	**rescue** me; **save** me from the power of
	144.11	**Save** me from my cruel enemies; **rescue**
Is	43.3	who **saves** you. I will...set you **free**;
	49.26	one who **saves** you and sets you **free**.
	63.9	**saved** them. In his love...he **rescued**
Jer	31.7	has **saved** his people; he has **rescued**
	31.11	Israel's people **free** and have **saved** them
Lam	3.58	came to my **rescue**, Lord, and **saved**
Dan	6.27	He **saves** and **rescues**;

Righteous
Ps	31.1	You are a **righteous** God; **save** me,
	37.39	The Lord **saves righteous** men
	51.14	**save** me, and I will gladly proclaim your **righteousness**.
Prov	11.9	wisdom of the **righteous** can **save** you.
Is	1.27	Lord is **righteous**, he will **save** Jerusalem
2 Pet	2.5	the only ones he **saved** were Noah, who preached **righteousness**,

Safe see **Protect**

Sin
Is	59.20	and to **save** all of you that turn from your **sins**.
Mt	1.21	**save** his people from their **sins**."
Lk	1.77	**saved** by having their **sins** forgiven.

Rom   3.23   everyone has **sinned** and is far away from
              God's **saving**
1 Tim 1.15   came into the world to **save sinners**.
Jas   5.20   **save** that **sinner's** soul from death

Trouble, Danger, Distress, Suffering, Violence

2 Sam 4.9   who has **saved** me from all **dangers**!
       22.3   protects me and **saves** me from **violence**.
       22.20 helped me out of **danger**; he **saved** me
Ps   18.19 helped me out of **danger**; he **saved** me
       25.17 and **save** me from all my **troubles**.
       25.22 their **troubles**, O God, **save** your people
       32.7   you will **save** me from **trouble**.
       34.6   he **saves** them from all their **troubles**.
       34.19 many **troubles**, but the Lord **saves** him
       50.15 me when **trouble** comes; I will **save** you,
       81.7   **trouble**, you called to me, and I **saved**
       107.6 **trouble** they called to the Lord, and he **saved**
              them
       107.13 **trouble** they called to the Lord, and he **saved**
              them
       107.19 **trouble** they called to the Lord, and he **saved**
              them
       107.28 **trouble** they called to the Lord, and he **saved**
              them
       116.6 when I was in **danger**, he **saved** me.
       119.153 Look at my **suffering**, and **save** me,
       143.11 goodness **save** me from my **troubles**!
Is   33.2   and **save** us in times of **trouble**.
       38.17 You **save** my life from all **danger**;
       59.11 **distressed**. We long for God to **save** us
Jer   2.27   **trouble**, you ask me to come and **save**
       2.28   When you are in **trouble**, let them **save**
Hab   1.2   before you **save** us from **violence**?
Zech   9.16   a shepherd **saves** his flock from **danger**.
2 Cor 1.10   terrible **dangers** of death he **saved** us,

Trust see Faith

Violence see Trouble

Wicked see Evil

World

Is   45.22 and be **saved**, people all over the **world**!
       49.6   so that all the **world** may be **saved**.
       52.10 **save** his people, and all the **world** will
Jn   12.47 not to judge the **world**, but to **save** it.
Acts   13.47 so that all the **world** may be **saved**.
1 Tim 1.15   Jesus came into the **world** to **save**
2 Pet 2.5   on the **world** of godless people; the only ones
              he **saved**

SCATTER

Ezek	4.13	—	6.13	x9
Jer	23.1	—	25.33	x6
Jer	29.14	—	32.37	x5
Ezek	10.2	—	12.15	x5
Ezek	28.25	—	31.17	x5
Jer	8.3	—	10.21	x4
Ezek	34.5 — 12			x4
Gen	11.4 — 9			x3
Deut	30.1 — 4			x3
Ps	68.1 — 30			x3
Jer	49.32	—	50.17	x3
Ezek	20.23 — 41			x3
Zech	1.19	—	2.6	x3
Mt	25.24	—	26.31	x3

Enemies

Num   10.35 **scatter** your **enemies** and put to flight
2 Sam 22.15 his arrows and **scattered** his **enemies**;
Ps   18.14 his arrows and **scattered** his **enemies**;
       53.5   will **scatter** the bones of the **enemies**
       68.1   God rises up and **scatters** his **enemies**.
       144.6 of lightning and **scatter** your **enemies**;
Jer   18.17 **scatter** my people before their **enemies**,

God's People, Sheep

1 Kgs 22.17 Israel **scattered** over the hills like **sheep**
2 Chr 18.16 Israel **scattered** over the hills like **sheep**
Ps   44.11 slaughtered like **sheep**; you **scattered** us
Is   49.5   bring back the **scattered people** of Israel.
Jer   18.17 **scatter my people** before their enemies,
       23.1   who destroy and **scatter his people**!
       23.2   of **my people**; you have **scattered** them
       23.3   **my people** from the countries where I have
              scattered them,
       31.10 **scattered my people**, but I will gather
       50.17 are like **sheep**, chased and **scattered**
Ezek   34.5   the **sheep**...were **scattered**,
       34.12 his **sheep** that were **scattered**
Joel   3.2   **people**. They have **scattered** the Israelites
Zech   2.6   said to **his people**, "I **scattered** you
       13.7   be **scattered**. I will attack **my people**
Mt   26.31 the **sheep** of the flock will be **scattered**.
Mk   14.27 and the **sheep** will all be **scattered**.
Jn   10.12 snatches the **sheep** and **scatters** them.
       11.52 body all the **scattered people of God**.
Jas   1.1   **people scattered** over the whole world.
1 Pet 1.1   **people** who live as refugees **scattered**

AV SCRIBE
see TEACHER OF THE LAW

SCRIPTURE

Rom	8.36	—	12.20	x15
Gal	3.6	—	4.30	x11
Rom	1.2	—	4.18	x9
1 Pet	1.16	—	5.5	x8
Mk	9.12	—	12.24	x6
Lk	4.4 — 21			x6
Jn	5.39	—	7.52	x6
Rom	14.11	—	15.21	x6
1 Cor	1.19	—	3.20	x6
1 Cor	14.21	—	15.54	x6
Heb	2.6	—	4.7	x6
Mt	21.13	—	23.5	x5
Jn	19.24	—	20.9	x5
Mt	4.4 — 10			x4
Mt	26.24 — 56			x4
Lk	19.46	—	22.37	x4
Acts	17.3	—	18.28	x4
Mk	14.21 — 49			x3
Lk	24.27 — 45			x3
Jn	12.14	—	13.18	x3
2 Cor	8.15	—	10.17	x3
Eph	4.8	—	5.32	x3

Believe

Jn   2.22   and they **believed** the **scripture**
       7.38   **scripture** says, 'Whoever **believes** in me
Rom   4.3   **scripture** says, "Abraham **believed** God
       4.9   the **scripture**, "Abraham **believed** God,
       10.11 **scripture** says, "Whoever **believes** in him
2 Cor 4.13   **scripture** says, "I spoke because I **believed**
Gal   3.6   as the **scripture** says, "He **believed** God,
Jas   2.23   **scripture** came true that said, "Abraham
              believed

Jesus

Jn   2.22   **scripture** and what **Jesus** had said.
Acts   18.28 proving from the **Scriptures** that **Jesus**

Prophets

Mt   26.56 the **prophets** wrote in the **Scriptures**
Jn   7.52   Study the **Scriptures** and you will learn that
              no **prophet**
Acts   15.15 **prophets** agree...As the **scripture** says,
Rom   1.2   **prophets**, as written in the...**Scriptures**.

Remember

Jn   2.17   disciples **remembered** that the **scripture**
       12.16 **remembered** that the **scripture** said

208

Teach

Rom	15.4	in the **Scriptures** was written to **teach**
1 Tim	4.13	**Scriptures** and to preaching and **teaching**.

True

Mt	26.54	how could the **Scriptures** come **true**
	26.56	wrote in the **Scriptures** come **true**.
Mk	14.49	But the **Scriptures** must come **true**.
Lk	4.21	This passage of **scripture** has come **true**
	21.22	all that the **Scriptures** say come **true**.
Jn	10.35	that what the **scripture** says is **true**
	13.18	But the **scripture** must come **true**.
	17.12	so that the **scripture** might come **true**.
	19.24	order to make the **scripture** come **true**:
	19.28	order to make the **scripture** come **true**,
	19.36	done to make the **scripture** come **true**:
Acts	1.16	the **scripture** had to come **true**
1 Cor	15.54	then the **scripture** will come **true**:
Jas	2.23	And the **scripture** came **true**

SECRET

Eph	3.3	−	9	x6
Col	1.26	−	2.2	x5
Deut	27.15	−	29.29	x4
1 Cor	13.2	−	15.51	x4
1 Cor	2.1	−	10	x3
Eph	5.12	−	6.19	x3

Christ, Jesus

Mt	26.4	made plans to arrest **Jesus secretly**
Mk	14.1	for a way to arrest **Jesus secretly**
Lk	22.2	of putting **Jesus** to death **secretly**.
Jn	19.38	a follower of **Jesus**, but in **secret**,
Rom	2.16	**Jesus**...will judge the **secret** thoughts
Eph	3.4	understanding of the **secret** of **Christ**.
Col	1.27	the **secret** is that **Christ** is in you,
	2.2	God's **secret**, which is **Christ**
	4.3	his message about the **secret** of **Christ**.

Message

Judg	3.19	I have a **secret message** for you.
Col	4.3	his **message** about the **secret** of Christ.

Reveal

Deut	29.29	has kept **secret**; but he has **revealed**
Prov	25.9	and do not **reveal** any **secrets**.
Is	26.21	**secretly** committed...will be **revealed**,
Dan	2.22	**reveals** things that are deep and **secret**;
Lk	2.35	and so **reveal** their **secret** thoughts
Rom	16.25	the **revelation** of the **secret** truth
Eph	3.3	God **revealed** his **secret** plan
	3.5	this **secret**, but God has **revealed** it
	5.32	**secret** truth **revealed** in this scripture,

Truth

Rom	11.25	There is a **secret truth**
	16.25	the **secret truth** which was hidden
1 Cor	2.1	to preach God's **secret truth**,
	4.1	in charge of God's **secret truths**.
	14.2	He is speaking **secret truths**
	15.51	Listen to this **secret truth**:
Eph	5.32	There is a deep **secret truth** revealed

Understand

1 Cor	13.2	all knowledge and **understand** all **secrets**;
	14.2	**understands** him. He is speaking **secret**
Eph	3.4	about my **understanding** of the **secret**

SEED

Mt	13.4 − 38		x14
Mk	4.4 − 31		x11
Lk	8.5 − 15		x8
1 Cor	15.36 − 38		x4
2 Cor	9.6 − 10		x4
Gen	47.19 − 24		x3
Lev	11.37 − 38		x3

Sow, Scatter

Gen	26.12	Isaac **sowed seed** in that land
	47.19	corn to keep us alive and **seed** to **sow**
	47.23	Here is **seed** for you to **sow**
Lev	11.37	falls on **seed** that is going to be **sown**,
	26.16	You will **sow** your **seed**,
	27.16	the amount of **seed** it takes to **sow** it,
Deut	11.10	when you **sowed seed**, you had to work
	28.38	You will **sow** plenty of **seed**
Judg	6.3	Whenever the Israelites **sowed** any **seed**,
Job	4.8	and **sow** wickedness like **seed**;
Ps	126.5	who wept as they **sowed** their **seed**,
Prov	22.8	If you **sow** the **seeds** of injustice
Is	28.25	he **sows** the **seeds** of herbs
	30.23	Whenever you **sow** your **seeds**
	55.10	and provide **seed** for **sowing** and food
Jer	4.3	do not **sow** your **seeds** among thorns.
	50.16	not let **seeds** be **sown** in that country
Ezek	36.9	again and that **seeds** are **sown** there.
Mt	6.26	they do not **sow** seeds,
	13.4	As he **scattered** the **seed** in the field,
	13.23	And the **seeds sown** in the good soil
	13.24	A man **sowed** good **seed** in his field.
	13.27	was good **seed** you **sowed** in your field;
	13.31	man takes a mustard **seed** and **sows** it
	13.37	The man who **sowed** the good **seed**
	25.24	crops where you did not **scatter seed**.
	25.26	crops where I did not **scatter seed**?
Mk	4.4	As he **scattered** the **seed** in the field,
	4.18	the **seeds sown** among the thorn bushes.
	4.20	like the **seeds sown** in good soil.
	4.26	A man **scatters seed** in his field.
Lk	8.5	to **sow** corn. As he **scattered** the **seed**
	12.24	they don't **sow seeds** or gather
	13.19	man takes a mustard **seed** and **sows** it
1 Cor	3.6	I **sowed** the **seed**
	9.11	We have **sown** spiritual **seed** among you.
	15.36	When you **sow** a **seed** in the ground,
	15.37	And what you **sow** is a bare **seed**,
2 Cor	9.6	that the person who **sows** few **seeds**
	9.10	who supplies **seed** to **sow**

SERVANT

Mt	22.3	−	26.71	x29
Gen	24.2 − 66			x18
2 Kgs	4.12	−	6.17	x18
Lk	14.17	−	17.10	x15
Is	41.8	−	45.4	x12
Gen	43.16	−	45.1	x11
1 Sam	8.16	−	10.14	x11
Lk	12.36 − 48			x11
1 Sam	25.8	−	26.18	x10
2 Kgs	16.7	−	22.9	x9
Ps	119.17 − 176			x9
Mt	18.23 − 34			x9
Gen	26.14	−	27.29	x8
1 Kgs	10.5	−	11.38	x8
Job	1.3	−	2.3	x8
Is	48.20	−	50.10	x8
Acts	2.18	−	4.30	x8
2 Sam	13.17	−	14.31	x7
1 Kgs	18.36	−	20.32	x7
Lk	19.13 − 24			x7
Gen	32.4 − 20			x6
1 Kgs	8.26 − 66			x6
Josh	1.1 − 15			x5
Judg	19.3 − 19			x5
2 Sam	9.2 − 12			x5
2 Chr	6.17 − 42			x5
Ps	89.3 − 50			x5
Ps	105.5 − 42			x5
Lk	1.38	−	2.29	x5
Esth	1.8 − 15			x4

Lk	7.2 – 10	x4	
2 Sam	19.17 – 26	x3	
Ezra	2.55 – 64	x3	
Esth	4.4 – 16	x3	
Jer	33.21 – 26	x3	
Dan	9.6 – 11	x3	
Mt	8.6 – 13	x3	
Jn	2.5 – 9	x3	
2 Cor	11.15 – 23	x3	
Col	1.7 – 25	x3	
Rev	19.2 – 10	x3	
Rev	22.3 – 9	x3	

Chosen

Gen 24.14 you have **chosen** for your **servant** Isaac.
1 Kgs 11.34 my **servant** David, whom I **chose**
1 Chr 16.12 God's **servant**...whom God **chose**,
16.22 Don't harm my **chosen servants**;
2 Chr 6.42 **chosen**...your **servant** David.
Ps 78.70 He **chose** his **servant** David;
89.3 man I **chose**...my **servant** David,
105.15 Don't harm my **chosen servants**;
105.26 his **servant** Moses, and Aaron, whom he had **chosen**.
106.23 his **chosen servant**, Moses
132.10 **servant** David; do not reject your **chosen**
Is 41.8 my **servant**...that I have **chosen**,
41.9 You are my **servant**.' I...**chose** you.
42.1 my **servant**, whom...I have **chosen**,
43.10 I **chose** you to be my **servant**,
44.1 my **servant**, my **chosen** people,
44.2 you are my **servant**, my **chosen** people
45.4 my **servant** Israel...that I have **chosen**.
49.1 the Lord **chose** me...to be his **servant**.
49.7 the Lord has **chosen** his **servant**;
Jer 33.26 my **servant** David. I will **choose**
Mt 12.18 is my **servant**, whom I have **chosen**,
Acts 3.26 And so God **chose** his **Servant**
Rom 1.1 a **servant** of Christ Jesus...**chosen**

Christ, Jesus

Acts 3.13 divine glory to his **Servant Jesus**.
4.27 against **Jesus**, your holy **Servant**,
4.30 name of your holy **Servant Jesus**.
Rom 1.1 Paul, a **servant** of **Christ Jesus**
15.16 being a **servant** of **Christ Jesus**
1 Cor 4.1 should think of us as **Christ's servants**
2 Cor 2.17 as **servants** of **Christ**.
4.5 as your **servants** for **Jesus'** sake.
11.23 Are they **Christ's servants**?
Gal 1.10 I would not be a **servant** of **Christ**.
Phil 1.1 **servants** of **Christ Jesus**
1.13 because I am a **servant** of **Christ**.
Col 1.7 **fellow-servant**, who is **Christ's** faithful
4.12 and a **servant** of **Christ Jesus**.
1 Tim 4.6 a good **servant** of **Christ Jesus**,
Jas 1.1 **servant** of God and of the Lord **Jesus**
2 Pet 1.1 a **servant** and apostle of **Jesus**
Jude .1 Jude, **servant** of **Jesus Christ**,
Rev 1.1 **Christ** made...known to his **servant**

Covenant see Promise

Faithful, Loyal

Gen 32.10 **faithfulness** that you have shown me, your **servant**.
Deut 33.8 your **faithful servants**, the Levites;
1 Kgs 3.6 your **servant**, and he was good, **loyal**,
14.8 **servant** David, who was completely **loyal**
Ps 86.2 I am **loyal** to you...I am your **servant**
89.19 you said to your **faithful servants**,
Mt 24.45 is a **faithful** and wise **servant**?
25.21 you good and **faithful servant**!
25.23 you good and **faithful servant**!
Lk 12.42 is the **faithful** and wise **servant**?
19.17 a good **servant**! Since you were **faithful**

Acts 2.27 not allow your **faithful servant** to rot
1 Cor 4.2 such a **servant** is that he be **faithful**
Eph 6.21 and **faithful servant** in the Lord's work,
Col 1.7 **fellow-servant**, who is **Christ's faithful** worker
4.7 is a **faithful** worker and **fellow-servant**
Heb 3.5 **faithful** in God's house as a **servant**,

Happy

Mt 24.46 **happy** that **servant** is if his master finds
Lk 12.37 **happy** are those **servants** whose master
12.43 **happy** that **servant** is if his master finds

Jesus see Christ

Loyal see Faithful

Obey

Gen 32.4 your **obedient servant**,
Josh 22.2 **servant** ordered you to do, and you have **obeyed**
1 Kgs 11.34 **servant** David...who **obeyed**
Ps 19.11 **servant**; I am rewarded for **obeying**
119.17 **servant**, so that I may live and **obey**
119.38 **servant** — the promise you make to those who **obey**
Is 50.10 and **obey** the words of his **servant**,
Lk 17.9 **servant** does not deserve thanks for **obeying**

Praise, Worship

Ps 22.23 **Praise** him, you **servants** of the Lord!
113.1 **servants** of the Lord, **praise** his name!
134.1 **praise** the Lord, all his **servants**,
135.1 **Praise** his name, you **servants**
Is 49.3 you are my **servant**; because of you, people will **praise** me.
Rev 19.5 **Praise** our God, all his **servants**
22.3 and his **servants** will **worship** him.

Promise, Covenant

Gen 26.24 my **promise** to my **servant** Abraham.
1 Kgs 8.26 you **promised** to...David, your **servant**.
8.56 **promises** he made through his **servant**
2 Kgs 8.19 he had **promised** his **servant** David
14.25 **promised** through his **servant**...Jonah
19.34 **promise** I made to my **servant** David.
20.6 **promise** I made to my **servant** David.
2 Chr 6.17 you **promised** to your **servant** David.
Ps 89.3 I have **promised** my **servant** David,
89.39 broken your **covenant** with your **servant**
105.42 sacred **promise** to Abraham his **servant**.
119.38 your **promise** to me, your **servant**
119.49 your **promise** to me, your **servant**;
119.65 **promise**, Lord...to me, your **servant**.
119.76 as you have **promised** me, your **servant**.
119.122 **Promise** that you will help your **servant**;
132.10 made a **promise** to your **servant** David;
Is 37.35 **promise** I made to my **servant** David.
Jer 33.21 made a **covenant** with my **servant** David
Lk 2.29 **promise**, and you may let your **servant**

Will

Ps 103.21 you **servants** of his, who do his **will**!
Is 53.2 the **will** of the Lord that his **servant**
Acts 22.14 his **will**, to see his righteous **Servant**,

Worship see Praise

SERVE

Josh	22.5	–	24.31	x15
Ezek	42.14	–	45.4	x11
2 Chr	7.17	–	13.10	x10
Ex	28.1	–	29.44	x8
1 Kgs	12.6	–	15.12	x8
Jer	27.6	–	28.14	x8
Rom	15.8	–	16.13	x8
Num	3.26	–	4.33	x7

1 Sam	2.11	—	3.1	x7
Deut	28.14	—	29.26	x6
1 Chr	7.4 – 40			x6
Gen	43.31 – 34			x5
Jer	15.11	—	17.4	x5
Jer	33.18	—	35.19	x5
Dan	6.16	—	7.27	x5
2 Cor	8.6	—	9.13	x5
Heb	7.13	—	10.3	x5
Ex	28.3	—	30.31	x4
Num	18.1 – 31			x4
Judg	2.7 – 19			x4
2 Chr	17.4 – 19			x4
Num	1.3 – 49			x3
Judg	18.4 – 30			x3
1 Sam	12.14 – 24			x3
2 Kgs	17.16 – 35			x3
2 Kgs	23.9 – 25			x3
Ezek	40.45 – 46			x3
Mal	3.14 – 18			x3
Jn	12.2 – 26			x3
Rom	7.6 – 25			x3

Christ, Jesus

Acts 15.26 in the **service** of...**Jesus Christ.**
Rom 14.18 when someone **serves Christ** in this way
15.8 I tell you that **Christ's** life of **service**
16.3 in the **service** of **Christ Jesus;**
16.9 our fellow-worker in **Christ's service,**
16.18 do such things are not **serving Christ**
Gal 2.17 mean that **Christ** is **serving**...sin?
Eph 6.5 as though you were **serving Christ.**
Phil 1.29 given the privilege of **serving Christ,**
Col 3.24 For **Christ** is the real Master you **serve.**
3 Jn 7 journey in the **service** of **Christ**

Faithfully, Loyally

Josh 22.5 be **faithful** to him, and **serve** him
24.14 and **serve** him sincerely and **faithfully.**
Judg 9.28 but why should we **serve** him? Be **loyal**
1 Sam 12.14 Obey the Lord and **serve** him **faithfully**
18.17 **serve** me as a brave and **loyal** soldier.
2 Sam 15.34 **serve** him as **faithfully** as you **served** his
1 Kgs 12.7 they will always **serve** you **loyally.**
2 Kgs 20.3 I have **served** you **faithfully** and **loyally,**
2 Chr 7.17 **serve** me **faithfully** as your father David
10.7 they will always **serve** you **loyally.**
26.5 he **served** the Lord **faithfully,**
32.1 Hezekiah **served** the Lord **faithfully,**
Ps 16.10 I have **served** you **faithfully,**
86.11 you **faithfully;** teach me to **serve** you
Is 38.3 I have **served** you **faithfully** and **loyally,**
56.6 **serve** him...and **faithfully** keep
Ezek 44.15 to **serve** me **faithfully** in the Temple
48.11 **served** me **faithfully** and did not join
Dan 6.16 whom you **serve** so **loyally,** rescue you.
6.20 you **serve** so **loyally** able to save you

Heart

Deut 10.12 **serve** him with all your **heart,**
11.13 and **serve** him with all your **heart.**
28.47 **serve** him with glad and joyful **hearts.**
Josh 22.5 **serve** him with all your **heart** and soul.
1 Sam 12.20 but **serve** him with all your **heart.**
12.24 **serve** him faithfully with all your **heart.**
2 Kgs 23.25 who **served** the Lord with all his **heart,**
1 Chr 22.19 Now **serve** the Lord...with all your **heart**
28.9 to **serve** him with an undivided **heart**
Ps 119.10 With all my **heart** I try to **serve** you;
Rom 1.9 I **serve** with all my **heart** by preaching
12.11 **Serve** the Lord with a **heart** full of
Eph 6.5 **heart,** as though you were **serving**

Jesus see **Christ**

Law see **Obey**

Loyally see **Faithfully**

Obey, Law

Josh 24.24 **serve** the Lord our God. We will **obey**
1 Sam 12.14 **serve** him, listen to him, and **obey**
12.24 **Obey** the Lord and **serve** him faithfully
2 Chr 17.4 **served** his father's God, **obeyed** God's
Job 36.11 If they **obey** God and **serve** him,
Ps 86.11 **obey** you faithfully; teach me to **serve**
119.63 **serve** you, of all who **obey** your **laws.**
Dan 7.27 all rulers on earth will **serve** and **obey**
Rom 7.6 **serve** in the old way of a written **law,**
7.25 **serve** God's **law** only with my mind,

SEX

Lev	18.6	—	20.16	x7
Lev	15.18 – 33			x3
1 Cor	5.1	—	6.18	x3

Immorality, Perversion

Lev 18.23 to have **sexual** relations with an animal; that **perversion**
Judg 19.22 some **sexual perverts** from the town
Ezek 16.43 add **sexual immorality** to all the other
Acts 15.20 keep themselves from **sexual immorality;**
15.29 keep yourselves from **sexual immorality.**
21.25 keep themselves from **sexual immorality.**
Rom 1.26 **pervert** the natural use of their **sex**
1 Cor 5.1 there is **sexual immorality** among you
6.13 is not to be used for **sexual immorality,**
6.18 man who is guilty of **sexual immorality**
10.8 must not be guilty of **sexual immorality**
Eph 5.3 of **sexual immorality** or indecency
Col 3.5 desires...such as **sexual immorality,**
1 Thes 4.3 completely free from **sexual immorality**
1 Tim 1.10 for the **immoral,** for **sexual perverts**
Jude .7 in **sexual immorality** and **perversion:**
Rev 2.14 idols and to practise **sexual immorality.**
2.20 **sexual immorality** and eating food
9.21 their **sexual immorality,** or their stealing.
17.2 of the earth practised **sexual immorality**
18.3 of the earth practised **sexual immorality**

Relations

Ex 22.19 has **sexual relations** with an animal.
Lev 18.22 is to have **sexual relations** with another
18.23 to have **sexual relations** with an animal;
19.20 man has **sexual relations** with her,
20.13 has **sexual relations** with another man,
20.15 has **sexual relations** with an animal,
20.16 a woman tries to have **sexual relations**
Deut 27.21 who has **sexual relations** with an animal.
1 Sam 21.4 haven't had **sexual relations** recently.
Mt 1.25 But he had no **sexual relations** with her
Rom 1.27 give up natural **sexual relations**
Rev 14.4 not having **sexual relations** with women;

SHARE

1 Cor	9.10	—	10.18	x7
Phil	1.7	—	4.15	x7
Num	31.36	—	32.30	x5
Josh	17.5	—	18.7	x5
1 Sam	1.4	—	2.28	x4
Acts	2.42	—	4.32	x4
Rom	8.17 – 30			x4
2 Cor	1.5 – 7			x4
Deut	18.1 – 4			x3
Deut	21.16 – 17			x3
Ezek	44.28	—	45.8	x3
Ezek	47.22 – 23			x3
Mt	24.51	—	25.23	x3
Rom	11.17	—	12.13	x3
2 Cor	5.14 – 21			x3
1 Pet	4.13	—	5.10	x3
Rev	18.4 – 15			x3

Blessings

Num	10.32	we will **share** with you all the **blessings**
Ezek	16.27	to take away your **share** of my **blessing**.
Rom	1.11	to **share** a spiritual **blessing** with you
	15.27	the Jews **shared** their spiritual **blessings**
1 Cor	9.23	in order to **share** in its **blessings**.

Christ

Rom	6.4	and **shared** his death...just as **Christ**
	8.17	for if we **share Christ's** suffering,
1 Cor	10.16	we are **sharing** in the blood of **Christ**.
2 Cor	1.5	have a **share** in **Christ's** many sufferings
Eph	5.5	a **share** in the Kingdom of **Christ**
Col	1.27	**Christ** is in you...you will **share**
1 Pet	4.13	that you are **sharing Christ's** sufferings,
	5.1	**Christ's** sufferings, and I will **share**
	5.10	**share** his eternal glory...with **Christ**,

Fate

Is	53.12	and **shared** the **fate** of evil men.
Ezek	27.36	afraid that they will **share** your **fate**.
	28.19	afraid that they will **share** your **fate**.
	32.25	**sharing** the **fate** of those killed in battle.
Mt	24.51	him **share** the **fate** of hypocrites.
Lk	12.46	him **share** the **fate** of the disobedient.
	22.37	He **shared** the **fate** of criminals,

Glad see Happiness

Glory

Is	42.8	No other god may **share** my **glory**;
	48.11	or let anyone else **share** the **glory**
Rom	5.2	hope we have of **sharing** God's **glory**!
	8.17	we will also **share** his **glory**.
	8.21	would **share** the **glorious** freedom
	8.30	and he **shared** his **glory** with them.
Col	1.27	that you will **share** in the **glory** of God.
	3.4	appear with him and **share** his **glory**!
1 Thes	2.12	to **share** in his own Kingdom and **glory**.
2 Thes	2.14	you to possess your **share** of the **glory**
Heb	2.10	to bring many sons to **share** his **glory**.
1 Pet	5.1	**share** in the **glory** that will be revealed.
	5.10	who calls you to **share** his eternal **glory**
2 Pet	1.3	to **share** in his own **glory** and goodness.

God's People

Mic	2.5	**Lord's people**, there will be no **share**
Col	1.11	**share** of what God has...for **his people**

Happiness, Glad, Joy

Neh	8.12	ate and drank **joyfully** and **shared**
Ps	106.5	**share** in the **happiness** of your nation,
Ecc	6.3	if he does not get his **share** of **happiness**
Mt	25.21	Come on in and **share** my **happiness**!
	25.23	Come on in and **share** my **happiness**!
1 Cor	12.26	all the other parts **share** its **happiness**.
Phil	2.2	**happy** by...**sharing** the same love,
	2.17	am **glad** and **share** my **joy** with you all.
	2.18	be **glad** and **share** your **joy** with me.
1 Pet	4.13	**glad** that you are **sharing** Christ's

Harvest

Mt	21.34	to receive his **share** of the **harvest**.
	21.41	will give him his **share** of the **harvest**
Mk	12.2	from them his **share** of the **harvest**.
Lk	20.10	from them his **share** of the **harvest**.
2 Tim	2.6	have the first **share** of the **harvest**.

Help, Needy

Rom	12.13	**Share** your belongings with your **needy**
2 Cor	1.5	Christ we **share** in God's great **help**.
	1.7	you also **share** in the **help** we receive.
Phil	4.15	**help** me; you were the...ones who **shared**
3 Jn	.8	**help** these people, so that we may **share**

Holiness

Heb	12.10	so that we may **share** his **holiness**.

Joy see Happiness

Life

Rom	11.17	you **share** the strong spiritual **life**
2 Cor	13.4	we shall **share** God's power in his **life**.
Rev	22.19	his **share** of the fruit of the tree of **life**

Love

Deut	28.56	**share** them with the husband she **loves**
Phil	2.2	by **sharing** the same **love**,
1 Thes	2.8	our **love** for you we were ready to **share**

Needy see Help

Offer, Sacrifice

Lev	6.18	continuing **share** of the food **offered**
Josh	13.14	**share** of the **sacrifices** burnt on the altar
	13.33	a **share** of the **offerings** to the Lord
1 Sam	1.4	**sacrifice**, he would give one **share**
	2.28	right to keep a **share** of the **sacrifices**
Hos	4.10	will eat your **share** of the **sacrifices**,
1 Cor	9.13	who **offer** the **sacrifices** on the altar get a **share**
	10.18	eat what is **offered** in **sacrifice share**

Possessions

Deut	21.17	to give a double **share** of his **possessions**
Josh	13.14	to receive as their **possession** a **share**
	13.33	their **possession** was to be a **share**
Judg	2.6	to take **possession** of his own **share**
Jer	37.12	**possession** of my **share** of the family
2 Thes	2.14	to **possess** your **share** of the glory

Power

2 Kgs	2.9	**share** of your **power** that will make me
2 Cor	13.4	we shall **share** God's **power**
Phil	3.10	**power** of his resurrection, to **share** in

Promise

Eph	3.6	**share** in the **promise** that God made

Sacrifice see Offer

Suffering

Rom	8.17	for if we **share** Christ's **suffering**,
2 Cor	1.5	have a **share** in Christ's many **sufferings**
	1.7	that just as you **share** in our **sufferings**,
Phil	3.10	I want...to **share** in his **sufferings**
Heb	2.10	**suffering**...to bring many sons to **share**
	10.34	You **shared** the **sufferings** of prisoners
1 Pet	4.13	that you are **sharing** Christ's **sufferings**,
	5.1	**sufferings**, and I will **share** in the glory
Rev	18.10	are afraid of **sharing** in her **suffering**.
	18.15	are afraid of **sharing** in her **suffering**.

SHEEP

Ezek	34.2 – 31			x20
Jn	10.2 – 27			x15
1 Sam	14.32	—	17.34	x14
Gen	29.2	—	33.13	x12
Lev	3.6	—	7.23	x10
Deut	14.4	—	18.3	x9
2 Chr	29.21	—	32.29	x9
Num	31.28	—	32.26	x8
Ex	22.1	—	23.19	x7
Zech	10.2	—	11.16	x7
1 Sam	24.3	—	25.18	x5
Deut	28.4 – 51			x4
Gen	12.16	—	13.5	x3
Gen	37.2	—	38.13	x3
Ex	9.3	—	10.24	x3
Ex	12.5 – 38			x3
Num	15.3 – 11			x3
Deut	12.6 – 21			x3
2 Sam	12.2	—	13.24	x3
1 Kgs	1.9 – 25			x3
1 Chr	4.39	—	5.21	x3
2 Chr	13.9	—	15.11	x3
2 Chr	17.11	—	18.16	x3

Jer	50.6 – 17			x3
Mt	9.36	—	10.16	x3
Mt	18.12 – 13			x3
Lk	15.4 – 6			x3

Offer, Best, Blood, First-born, Lamb, Pleased, Sacrifice

Gen	4.4	the **first lamb born** to one of his **sheep**, killed it, and gave the **best parts**
Ex	20.24	**sheep** and your cattle as **offerings**
	22.30	**first-born** of your cattle and your **sheep**.
Lev	1.10	If the man is **offering** one of his **sheep**
	3.6	a **sheep**...is used as a **fellowship-offering**
	3.7	If a man **offers** a **sheep**
	4.35	killed for the **fellowship-offerings**,
	5.6	a female **sheep** or goat as an **offering**
	5.18	as a **repayment-offering** a male **sheep**
	17.3	a **sheep** or a goat as an **offering**
	22.28	Do not **sacrifice**...a **sheep** and its **lamb** on the same day
Num	15.11	**offered** with each bull, ram, **sheep**, or
	18.17	the **first-born** of cows, **sheep**, and goats
Deut	12.6	the **first-born** of your cattle and **sheep**.
	12.17	the **first-born** of your cattle and **sheep**.
	14.23	the **first-born** of your cattle and **sheep**.
	15.19	all the **first-born** males of your cattle and **sheep**;
	17.1	**sacrifice** to the Lord...cattle or **sheep**
	18.3	Whenever cattle or **sheep** are **sacrificed**
	32.14	had the **best sheep**, goats, and cattle,
1 Sam	15.9	and did not kill the **best sheep**
	15.15	kept the **best sheep** and cattle to **offer**
	15.21	But my men did not kill the **best sheep**
	15.22	than to **sacrifice** the **best sheep** to him.
1 Kgs	1.9	Adonijah **offered** a **sacrifice** of **sheep**
	1.19	**offered** a **sacrifice** of many bulls, **sheep**,
	1.25	**offered** a **sacrifice** of many bulls, **sheep**,
	8.5	and **sacrificed** a large number of **sheep**
	8.63	**sheep** as **fellowship-offerings**.
2 Kgs	3.4	**lambs**, and the wool from 100,000 **sheep**.
1 Chr	15.26	**sacrificed** seven bulls and seven **sheep**,
2 Chr	5.6	and **sacrificed** a large number of **sheep**
	7.5	**sheep** as **fellowship-offerings**.
	29.21	**sheep**, seven **lambs**, and seven goats.
	29.22	then the **sheep**, and then the **lambs**,
	29.32	hundred **sheep**, and two hundred **lambs**
	29.33	three thousand **sheep** as **sacrifices**
	35.7	thousand **sheep**, **lambs**, and young goats,
Ezra	6.9	**sheep**, or **lambs** to be burnt as **offerings**
	6.17	two hundred **sheep**...as **sacrifices**,
Neh	5.18	six of the **best sheep**,
	10.36	**lamb** or kid born to each of our **sheep**
Ps	66.15	**offer sheep** to be burnt on the altar;
Is	1.11	of the **sheep** you burn as **sacrifices**
	1.11	tired of the **blood** of bulls and **sheep**
	43.23	bring me your **burnt-offerings** of **sheep**;
	53.7	a **lamb**...to be slaughtered, like a **sheep**
Ezek	27.21	for your merchandise with **lambs**, **sheep**,
	36.38	**sheep** which were **offered** as **sacrifices**
Hos	5.6	They take their **sheep** and cattle to **offer**
Mic	6.7	Lord be **pleased** if I bring him...**sheep**
Heb	13.20	**sheep** as the result of his **sacrificial**

SHELTER

Neh	8.14 – 17	x4
Lev	23.33 – 43	x3
Zech	14.16 – 19	x3
Acts	27.4 – 16	x3

Safe, Protect

Ps	27.5	will **shelter** me; he will keep me **safe**
	31.20	in a **safe shelter** you hide them
	62.7	my strong **protector**; he is my **shelter**.
	71.3	**shelter** and a strong fortress to **protect**
	144.2	my **shelter**...in whom I trust for **safety**.

Is	4.6	place of **safety**, **sheltered** from the rain
	25.4	**safe** in times of trouble. You give them **shelter**

SHEPHERD

Ezek	34.2 – 23			x11
Zech	11.4 – 17			x8
Lk	2.8 – 20			x5
Jn	10.2 – 16			x5
Gen	46.32	—	47.3	x3
Is	13.14	—	14.30	x3

God, Lord

Gen	49.24	Mighty **God** of Jacob, By the **Shepherd**,
Ps	23.1	The **Lord** is my **shepherd**;
Ecc	12.11	by **God**, the one **Shepherd** of us all.
Is	14.30	The **Lord** will be a **shepherd**
Mic	4.8	**God**, like a **shepherd**, watches over
	7.14	**shepherd** to your people, **Lord**

Good

Jn	10.11	I am the **good shepherd**,
	10.14	I am the **good shepherd**.

Lord see God

Sheep

Num	27.17	not be like **sheep** without a **shepherd**.
1 Kgs	22.17	the hills like **sheep** without a **shepherd**.
2 Chr	18.16	the hills like **sheep** without a **shepherd**.
Ps	49.14	**sheep**, and Death will be their **shepherd**.
Is	13.14	like **sheep** without a **shepherd**.
Jer	33.12	where **shepherds** can take their **sheep**.
	33.13	**shepherds** will...again count their **sheep**.
	50.6	people are like **sheep** whose **shepherds**
Ezek	34.5	Because the **sheep** had no **shepherd**,
	34.8	**shepherds** did not try to find the **sheep**.
	34.12	a **shepherd** takes care of his **sheep**
	34.15	will be the **shepherd** of my **sheep**,
Zech	11.4	part of the **shepherd** of a flock of **sheep**
	11.7	I became the **shepherd** of the **sheep**
Mt	9.36	like **sheep** without a **shepherd**.
	25.32	just as a **shepherd** separates the **sheep**
	26.31	will kill the **shepherd**, and the **sheep**
Mk	6.34	they were like **sheep** without a **shepherd**.
	14.27	will kill the **shepherd**, and the **sheep**
Jn	10.2	the gate is the **shepherd** of the **sheep**.
	10.11	the good **shepherd**, who is willing to die for the **sheep**
	10.12	a **shepherd** and does not own the **sheep**,
1 Cor	9.7	**shepherd** does not use the milk from his own **sheep**?
Heb	13.20	the Great **Shepherd** of the **sheep**

SIGHT

Jer	51.17	—	52.3	x5
2 Kgs	17.17 – 23			x4
2 Kgs	22.19	—	24.20	x4
Jn	9.15	—	11.37	x4
1 Kgs	21.20	—	22.43	x3
Jer	14.6	—	16.17	x3
Jer	25.9 – 18			x3
Jer	44.6 – 22			x3
Rom	3.20	—	4.17	x3
2 Cor	7.12	—	8.21	x3
Rev	12.1	—	13.13	x3

Horrifying, Horrible, Terrifying

Deut	34.12	**terrifying** things that Moses did in the **sight**
2 Kgs	22.19	I will make it a **terrifying sight**,
Jer	42.18	You will be a **horrifying sight**;
	44.6	in ruins and became a **horrifying sight**,
	44.12	They will be a **horrifying sight**;
	44.22	It has become a **horrifying sight**,
	49.13	Bozrah will become a **horrifying sight**

Jer	51.37	It will be a **horrible sight**;
	51.41	a **horrifying sight** Babylon has become
	51.43	towns have become a **horrifying sight**
Heb	12.21	The **sight** was so **terrifying**

SIN-OFFERING

Lev	4.14	—	10.19	x24
Lev	14.13	—	16.27	x14
Num	6.11	—	8.12	x7
Num	28.15	—	29.16	x6
Ezek	44.29	—	45.23	x4
Num	15.24	— 27		x3

Offer, Lamb, Present, Sacrifice

Lev	5.8	first **offer** the bird for the **sin-offering**.
	6.16	**sin-offerings** and the **repayment-offerings**.
	7.7	**sin-offering** and the **repayment-offering**:
	7.37	**sin-offerings**, the **repayment-offerings**,
	9.2	**offer** them to the Lord, the bull for a **sin-offering**
	9.7	and **offer** the **sin-offering**
	10.19	The people **presented** their **sin-offering**
	14.13	**lamb** in the place...for the **sin-offerings**
	14.19	the priest shall **offer** the **sin-offering**
	15.15	**offer** one of them as a **sin-offering**
	15.30	**offer** one of them as a **sin-offering**
	16.9	and **offer** it as a **sin-offering**
	16.11	**sacrifices** the bull as the **sin-offering**
	23.19	**offer** one male goat as a **sin-offering**
Num	6.11	shall **offer** one as a **sin-offering**
	6.14	ewe **lamb** for a **sin-offering**,
	6.16	and **offer** the **sin-offering**
	8.12	is to be **offered** as a **sin-offering**.
	15.24	to **offer** a male goat as a **sin-offering**.
	15.27	**offer** a one-year-old female goat as a **sin-offering**.
	18.9	**sin-offerings**, and the **repayment-offerings**.
	28.15	**offer** one male goat as a **sin-offering**.
		Also: 28.22, 30; 29.5, 11, 16
Ezek	44.29	**sin-offerings** and the **repayment-offerings**
	45.23	**sacrifice** a male goat...as a **sin-offering**.

SLAVE

Ex	20.2	—	23.12	x22
Gal	2.4	—	6.17	x16
Gen	15.3	—	17.27	x12
Rom	6.6	—	8.21	x12
Lev	25.6	—	26.13	x10
Deut	5.6	—	8.14	x9
Gen	29.24	—	32.5	x8
Gen	41.12	—	44.33	x8
Ex	11.5	—	15.16	x8
Jer	34.9	— 16		x8
Deut	15.12	—	16.12	x7
Eph	6.5	— 9		x6
Gen	20.14	—	21.13	x5
Gen	46.18	—	47.25	x5
Ex	5.4	—	6.9	x5
Deut	23.15	—	24.22	x5
2 Sam	18.21	— 32		x5
1 Cor	6.12	—	7.23	x5
Ezra	9.8	— 9		x4
Mk	12.2	— 5		x4
Lk	20.10	— 12		x4
Gen	9.25	— 27		x3
1 Sam	17.8	— 9		x3
Jn	8.33	— 35		x3
Jn	18.10	— 26		x3

Christ, Jesus

1 Cor	7.22	has been called by **Christ** is his **slave**.
Gal	6.17	show that I am the **slave** of **Jesus**.
Eph	6.6	do what God wants, as **slaves** of **Christ**.

| Col | 3.11 | **slaves**, and free men, but **Christ** is all, |
| Phlm | .16 | a **slave**: he is a dear brother in **Christ**. |

Obey

Rom	6.16	surrender yourselves as **slaves** to **obey**
	6.17	were **slaves** to sin, you have **obeyed**
Eph	6.5	**Slaves, obey** your human masters
Col	3.22	**Slaves, obey** your human masters

Rescue, Save

Ex	6.6	I will **rescue** you...from your **slavery**
	18.10	who **saved** his people from **slavery**!
Deut	5.6	who **rescued** you from Egypt, where you were **slaves**.
	6.12	who **rescued** you from Egypt, where you were **slaves**.
	6.21	**slaves** of...Egypt, and the Lord **rescued**
	8.14	who **rescued** you from Egypt, where you were **slaves**.
	13.5	who **rescued** you from Egypt, where you were **slaves**.
	13.10	who **rescued** you from Egypt, where you were **slaves**.
2 Sam	7.23	**rescued** from **slavery** to make them your
1 Chr	17.21	**rescued** from **slavery** to make them your
Lam	5.8	**slaves**, and no one can **save** us
Hos	12.13	**rescue** the people of Israel from **slavery**
Mic	6.4	I **rescued** you from **slavery**;

Sin

Jn	8.34	everyone who **sins** is a **slave** of sin.
Rom	6.6	no longer be the **slaves** of sin.
	6.17	at one time you were **slaves** to sin,
	6.20	When you were the **slaves** of sin,
	7.14	mortal man, sold as a **slave** to sin.

Spirit

Ex	6.9	**spirit** had been broken by their...**slavery**.
Acts	16.16	by a **slave-girl** who had an evil **spirit**
Gal	4.3	were **slaves** of the ruling **spirits**
	4.9	**spirits**? Why do you want to become their **slaves**

SON

of David

Mt	9.27	Take pity on us, **Son of David**!
	12.23	Could he be the **Son of David**?
	15.22	"**Son of David**!"
	20.30	began to shout, "**Son of David**!"
	20.31	even more loudly, "**Son of David**!
	21.9	began to shout, "Praise to **David's Son**!
	21.15	in the Temple, "Praise to **David's Son**!
Mk	10.47	**Son of David**!
	10.48	**Son of David**, take pity on me!
Lk	18.38	**Son of David**!
	18.39	even more loudly, "**Son of David**!

of God

Mt	4.3	If you are **God's Son**, order these stones
	4.6	If you are **God's Son**, throw yourself
	8.29	you want with us, you **Son of God**?
	14.33	Truly you are the **Son of God**!
	16.16	the **Son** of the living God.
	26.63	the Messiah, the **Son of God**.
	27.40	Save yourself if you are **God's Son**!
	27.43	and claims to be **God's Son**.
	27.54	He really was the **Son of God**!
Mk	1.1	about Jesus Christ, the **Son of God**.
	3.11	You are the **Son of God**!
	5.7	Jesus, **Son** of the Most High God!
	14.61	the **Son** of the Blessed God?
	15.39	This man was really the **Son of God**!
Lk	1.32	called the **Son** of the Most High God.
	1.35	will be called the **Son of God**.
	4.3	If you are **God's Son**, order this stone
	4.9	If you are **God's Son**, throw yourself

Lk	4.41	You are the **Son of God**!
	8.28	Jesus, **Son** of the Most High **God**!
	22.70	Are you, then, the **Son of God**?
Jn	1.34	I tell you that he is the **Son of God**.
	1.49	you are the **Son of God**!
	3.18	not believed in **God's** only **Son**.
	5.25	hear the voice of the **Son of God**,
	10.36	I said that I am the **Son of God**?
	11.4	the **Son of God** will receive glory
	11.27	the **Son of God**, who was to come into
	19.7	he claimed to be the **Son of God**.
	20.31	Jesus is the Messiah, the **Son of God**,
Acts	9.20	that Jesus was the **Son of God**.
Rom	1.4	great power to be the **Son of God**
2 Cor	1.19	For Jesus Christ, the **Son of God**,
Gal	2.20	I live by faith in the **Son of God**,
Eph	4.13	our knowledge of the **Son of God**;
Heb	4.14	Jesus, the **Son of God**.
	5.8	But even though he was **God's Son**,
	6.6	again crucifying the **Son of God**,
	7.3	He is like the **Son of God**; he remains
	10.29	who despises the **Son of God**?
1 Jn	3.8	The **Son of God** appeared for this very
	4.15	declares that Jesus is the **Son of God**,
	5.5	believes that Jesus is the **Son of God**.
	5.10	whoever believes in the **Son of God**
	5.12	whoever does not have the **Son of God**
	5.13	you that believe in the **Son of God**.
	5.18	for the **Son of God** keeps him safe,
	5.20	that the **Son of God** has come
2 Jn	.3	Jesus Christ, the **Father's Son**,
Rev	2.18	the message from the **Son of God**,

of Man

Mt	8.20	but the **Son of Man** has nowhere to lie
	9.6	the **Son of Man** has authority on earth
	10.23	before the **Son of Man** comes.
	11.19	When the **Son of Man** came, he ate
	12.8	**Son of Man** is Lord of the Sabbath.
	12.32	against the **Son of Man** can be forgiven;
	12.40	so will the **Son of Man** spend three
	13.37	The man who sowed the good seed is the **Son of Man**;
	13.41	the **Son of Man** will send out his angels
	16.13	Who do people say the **Son of Man**
	16.27	For the **Son of Man** is about to come
	16.28	until they have seen the **Son of Man**
	17.9	until the **Son of Man** has been raised
	17.12	will also ill-treat the **Son of Man**.
	17.22	The **Son of Man** is about to be handed
	19.28	be sure that when the **Son of Man**
	20.18	the **Son of Man** will be handed over
	20.28	the **Son of Man**, who did not come to
	24.27	the **Son of Man** will come like the
	24.30	the sign of the **Son of Man** will appear
	24.30	will weep as they see the **Son of Man**
	24.37	The coming of the **Son of Man** will be
	24.39	it will be when the **Son of Man** comes.
	24.44	the **Son of Man** will come at an hour
	25.31	When the **Son of Man** comes as King
	26.2	the **Son of Man** will be handed over
	26.24	The **Son of Man** will die as the
	26.24	man who betrays the **Son of Man**!
	26.45	The hour has come for the **Son of Man**
	26.64	you will see the **Son of Man** sitting on
Mk	2.10	that the **Son of Man** has authority
	2.28	the **Son of Man** is Lord even of the
	8.31	The **Son of Man** must suffer much
	8.38	the **Son of Man** will be ashamed of him
	9.9	until the **Son of Man** has risen
	9.12	Scriptures say that the **Son of Man** will
	9.31	The **Son of Man** will be handed over
	10.33	the **Son of Man** will be handed over
	10.45	the **Son of Man** did not come to be

Mk	13.26	Then the **Son of Man** will appear,
	14.21	**Son of Man** will die as the Scriptures
	14.21	man who betrays the **Son of Man**!
	14.41	the **Son of Man** is now being handed
	14.62	you will all see the **Son of Man**
Lk	5.24	the **Son of Man** has authority on earth
	6.5	The **Son of Man** is Lord of the
	6.22	all because of the **Son of Man**!
	7.34	The **Son of Man** came, and he ate and
	9.22	The **Son of Man** must suffer much
	9.26	the **Son of Man** will be ashamed of him
	9.44	The **Son of Man** is going to be handed
	9.58	the **Son of Man** has nowhere to lie
	11.30	the **Son of Man** will be a sign
	12.8	the **Son of Man** will do the same for
	12.9	the **Son of Man** will also reject him
	12.10	against the **Son of Man** can be forgiven;
	12.40	be ready, because the **Son of Man** will
	17.22	see one of the days of the **Son of Man**,
	17.24	so will the **Son of Man** be in his day.
	17.26	be in the days of the **Son of Man**.
	17.30	on the day the **Son of Man** is revealed.
	18.8	will the **Son of Man** find faith on earth
	18.31	prophets wrote about the **Son of Man**
	19.10	The **Son of Man** came to seek and to
	21.27	the **Son of Man** will appear,
	21.36	and to stand before the **Son of Man**.
	22.22	The **Son of Man** will die as God
	22.48	you betray the **Son of Man**?
	22.69	**Son of Man** will be seated on the right
	24.7	The **Son of Man** must be handed over
Jn	1.51	coming down on the **Son of Man**.
	3.13	the **Son of Man**, who came down from
	3.14	the same way the **Son of Man** must be
	5.27	to judge, because he is the **Son of Man**.
	6.27	food which the **Son of Man** will give
	6.53	eat the flesh of the **Son of Man**
	6.62	should see the **Son of Man** go back up
	8.28	When you lift up the **Son of Man**,
	9.35	Do you believe in the **Son of Man**?
	12.23	has now come for the **Son of Man**
	12.34	that the **Son of Man** must be lifted up?
	12.34	Who is this **Son of Man**?
	13.31	Now the **Son of Man's** glory is
	13.32	reveal the glory of the **Son of Man**
Acts	7.56	heaven opened and the **Son of Man**

SON OF GOD

1 Jn	1.3	—	5.20	x24
Jn	5.19	—	6.40	x11
Jn	3.16 – 36			x7
Col	1.13 – 22			x7
Heb	3.6	—	7.28	x7
Heb	1.2 – 8			x6
Mt	26.63	—	28.19	x5
Lk	8.28	—	10.22	x5
Rom	8.3 – 32			x5
Mt	2.15	—	4.6	x4
Lk	3.22	—	4.41	x4
Jn	1.14 – 49			x4
Mt	11.27			x3
Mk	13.32	—	15.39	x3
Jn	10.36	—	11.27	x3
Rom	1.3 – 9			x3

Believe, Faith

Jn	3.16	**Son**, so that everyone who **believes** in
	3.18	**believes** in the **Son** is not judged
	3.36	**believes** in the **Son** has eternal life
	6.40	who see the **Son** and **believe** in him
	11.27	I do **believe** that you are the Messiah, the **Son of God**,
	20.31	**believe** that Jesus is the Messiah, the **Son of God**,

H

Gal	2.20	I live by **faith** in the **Son** of God,
Eph	4.13	**faith** and in our knowledge of the **Son**
1 Jn	3.23	commands is that we **believe** in his **Son**
	5.5	**believes** that Jesus is the **Son of God**.
	5.10	So whoever **believes** in the **Son of God**
	5.13	you that **believe** in the **Son of God**.

Christ, Jesus, Messiah

Mt	16.16	the **Messiah**, the **Son** of the living **God**.
	26.63	if you are the **Messiah**, the **Son of God**.
Mk	1.1	about **Jesus Christ**, the **Son of God**.
	5.7	**Jesus, Son** of the Most High **God**!
	14.61	**Messiah**, the **Son** of the Blessed **God**?
Lk	8.28	**Jesus, Son** of the Most High **God**!
Jn	11.27	you are the **Messiah**, the **Son of God**,
	20.31	Jesus is the **Messiah**, the **Son of God**,
Acts	9.20	preach that **Jesus** was the **Son of God**.
Rom	1.3	about his **Son**, our Lord **Jesus Christ**:
1 Cor	1.9	fellowship with his **Son Jesus Christ**,
	15.28	**Christ's** rule, then he himself, the **Son**,
2 Cor	1.19	For **Jesus Christ**, the **Son of God**,
1 Thes	1.10	his **Son Jesus**, whom he raised
Heb	3.6	But **Christ** is faithful as the **Son**
	4.14	**Jesus**, the **Son of God**.
1 Jn	1.3	and with his **Son Jesus Christ**.
	1.7	blood of **Jesus**, his **Son**, purifies us
	3.23	we believe in his **Son Jesus Christ**
	4.15	declares that **Jesus** is the **Son of God**,
	5.5	believes that **Jesus** is the **Son of God**.
	5.20	in union with his **Son Jesus Christ**.
2 Jn	.3	and **Jesus Christ**, the Father's **Son**,

Dear see Love

Death

Acts	20.28	through the sacrificial **death** of his **Son**.
Rom	5.10	friends through the **death** of his **Son**.
Col	1.20	peace through his **Son's** sacrificial **death**
	1.22	means of the physical **death** of his **Son**,

Eternal see Life

Faith see Believe

Jesus see Christ

Life, Eternal, Raised

Jn	3.36	believes in the **Son** has **eternal life**
	5.21	life, in the same way the **Son** gives life.
	5.26	made his **Son** to be the source of **life**
	6.40	see the **Son**...should have **eternal life**.
Rom	1.4	to be the **Son of God** by being **raised**
Gal	2.20	This **life**...I live by faith in the **Son**
Col	1.18	the body's **life**. He is the first-born **Son**, who was **raised**
1 Thes	1.10	heaven — his **Son** Jesus, whom he **raised**
1 Jn	4.9	only **Son** into the world, so that we might have **life**
	5.11	and this **life** has its source in his **Son**.
	5.12	Whoever has the **Son** has this **life**
	5.13	eternal **life** — you that believe in the **Son**

Love, Dear

Mt	3.17	**dear Son**, with whom I am pleased.
	17.5	This is my own **dear Son**,
Mk	1.11	You are my own **dear Son**.
	9.7	is my own **dear Son** — listen to him!
Lk	3.22	You are my own **dear Son**.
Jn	3.35	**loves** his **Son** and has put everything
	5.20	Father **loves** the Son and shows him all
Gal	2.20	faith in the **Son of God**, who **loved** me
Eph	1.6	the free gift he gave us in his **dear Son**!
Col	1.13	safe into the kingdom of his **dear Son**,
2 Pet	1.17	**dear Son**, with whom I am pleased!
1 Jn	3.23	**Son** Jesus Christ and **love** one another,
	4.9	his **love** for us by sending his only **Son**
	4.10	but that he **loved** us and sent his **Son**

Messiah see Christ

Raised see Life

Spirit of God

Mt	28.19	the **Son**, and the **Holy Spirit**,
Gal	4.6	God sent the **Spirit** of his **Son**

World

Jn	3.16	loved the **world** so much that he gave his only **Son**,
	3.17	his **Son** into the **world** to be its judge,
	11.27	**Son of God**, who was to come into the **world**.
Heb	1.6	send his first-born **Son** into the **world**
1 Jn	4.9	by sending his only **Son** into the **world**,
	4.14	his **Son** to be the Saviour of the **world**.

SORROW

	Gen	44.13 – 30	x3
	Lam	1.20 — 3.32	x3

Glad see Joy

Grief, Mourning

Gen	37.34	in **sorrow** and put on sackcloth. He **mourned**
Ecc	3.4	**sorrow** and the time for joy, the time for **mourning**
Is	35.10	for ever free from **sorrow** and **grief**.
	51.11	for ever free from **sorrow** and **grief**.
	61.3	of **grief**, A song...instead of **sorrow**.
Jer	31.13	their **mourning** into joy, their **sorrow**
Mic	1.8	**mourn** and lament. To show my **sorrow**,

Heart

1 Kgs	8.38	Israel, out of **heartfelt sorrow**,
2 Chr	6.29	Israel, out of **heartfelt sorrow**,
Ps	13.2	How long will **sorrow** fill my **heart**
Jer	8.18	My **sorrow** cannot be healed; I am sick at **heart**.
Lam	1.20	**heart** is broken in **sorrow** for my sins.
Ezek	21.6	your **heart** is breaking...Groan in **sorrow**
Joel	2.13	your broken **heart** show your **sorrow**;
Mt	26.38	The **sorrow** in my **heart** is so great
Mk	14.34	The **sorrow** in my **heart** is so great
Rom	9.2	is my **sorrow**...the pain in my **heart**
1 Tim	6.10	broken their **hearts** with many **sorrows**.

Joy, Glad

Ps	30.11	my **sorrow** and surrounded me with **joy**.
Ecc	3.4	time for **sorrow** and the time for **joy**,
Jer	31.13	into **joy**, their **sorrow** into **gladness**.
Phil	2.28	will be **glad** again...and my own **sorrow**

Mourning see Grief

Trouble

Ps	13.2	I endure **trouble**? How long will **sorrow**
	90.10	all they bring us is **trouble** and **sorrow**;
Jer	20.18	only to have **trouble** and **sorrow**,
	45.3	Lord has added **sorrow** to my **troubles**.

SOURCE

	Rom	15.5 — 16.20	x4

God, Lord

Num	16.22	"O, **God**, you are the **source** of all life.
	27.16	"**Lord God, source** of all life,
Job	22.26	**God**...is the **source** of your joy.
Ps	43.4	altar, O **God**; you are the **source** of my happiness.
Is	49.5	**Lord**...is the **source** of my strength.
Rom	15.5	may **God**, the **source** of patience and
	15.13	May **God**, the **source** of hope,
	15.33	May **God**, our **source** of peace,
	16.20	And **God**, our **source** of peace,

Life

Num	16.22	**God**, you are the **source** of all **life**.

Num 27.16 Lord God, **source** of all **life**,
Ps   36.9 You are the **source** of all **life**,
Lam   4.20 They captured the **source** of our **life**
Jn   1.4   The Word was the **source** of **life**
      5.26 the Father is himself the **source** of **life**,
Col   1.18 he is the **source** of the body's **life**.
1 Jn 5.11 eternal **life**, and this **life** has its **source**

Peace
Rom 15.33 May God, our **source** of **peace**, be with
     16.20 And God, our **source** of **peace**, will
2 Thes 3.16 Lord...who is our **source** of **peace**

SOW

Mt	13.3 – 39		x10
Lev	25.3 –	27.16	x9
Is	28.24 – 25		x4
Mk	4.3 – 20		x4
Ecc	11.4 – 6		x3
1 Cor	3.6 – 8		x3
2 Cor	9.6 – 10		x3
Gal	6.7 – 8		x3

Harvest
Gen 26.12 he **harvested** a hundred times as much as he had **sown**,
Lev 25.11 not **sow** your fields or **harvest** the corn
Deut 28.38 **sow**...seed, but reap only a small **harvest**
2 Kgs 19.29 able to **sow** your corn and **harvest** it,
Job   4.8   and **sow** wickedness...now they **harvest**
Ps 126.5   they **sowed** their seed, gather the **harvest**
Ecc 11.4   never **sow** anything and never **harvest**
Is   37.30 able to **sow** your corn and **harvest** it,
     62.9   you that **sowed** and **harvested** the corn
Jer 50.16 be **sown** in that country or let a **harvest**
Mic   6.15 will **sow** corn, but not **harvest** the crop.
Hag   1.6   **sown** much corn, but have **harvested**
Mt   6.26 they do not **sow** seeds, gather a **harvest**
     13.39 **sowed**...weeds is the Devil. The **harvest**
     25.24 reap **harvests** where you did not **sow**,
     25.26 I reap **harvests** where I did not **sow**,
Lk   12.24 don't **sow** seeds or gather a **harvest**;
Gal   6.8   If he **sows**...he will gather the **harvest**

Message
Mk   4.14 The **sower** **sows** God's **message**.

Reap
Deut 28.38 **sow** plenty of seed, but **reap** only a
Ps 107.37 They **sowed** the fields...and **reaped**
Hos   8.7   **sow** the wind, they will **reap** a storm
Mt   25.24 **reap** harvests where you did not **sow**,
     25.26 I **reap** harvests where I did not **sow**.
Lk   19.21 and **reap** what you did not **sow**.
     19.22 **reaping** what I have not **sown**.
Jn   4.36 man who **sows** and the man who **reaps**
      4.37 One man **sows**, another man **reaps**.
Gal   6.7   person will **reap** exactly what he **sows**.

SPARE

Ezek	6.14 –	9.5	x5
Josh	10.30 – 40		x3
Jer	38.17 – 20		x3

Destroy
Gen 18.24 **destroy** the whole city? Won't you **spare**
Ps   26.9   **destroy** me with the sinners; **spare** me
Jer 21.10 not to **spare** this city, but to **destroy**
     51.3   Do not **spare** the young men! **Destroy**

Mercy, Save
Gen 18.24 you **spare** it in order to **save** the fifty?
2 Kgs 1.13 **merciful** to me and my men. **Spare** our
Ps   51.14 **Spare** my life, O God, and **save** me,
Jer 21.7   not **spare** any of you or show **mercy**
Ezek 7.4   not **spare** you or show you any **mercy**.
      7.9   not **spare** you or show you any **mercy**.

Ezek 8.18 **spare** them or show them any **mercy**.
      9.5   **Spare** no one; have **mercy** on no one.

SPECIAL

Lev	7.14 –	10.14	x10
Num	18.8 – 28		x9
Lev	23.11 – 39		x6
Ezek	48.8 – 23		x6
Num	15.19 – 21		x4
Ex	29.24 – 27		x3
Lev	14.12 – 24		x3
Num	5.9 –	6.20	x3
Num	8.11 – 21		x3

Offering, Contribution, Dedicate, Gift
Ex   29.24 to **dedicate** it to me as a **special gift**.
     29.26 **dedicate** it to me as a **special gift**.
     29.27 be **dedicated** to me as a **special gift**
Lev   7.14 a **special contribution** to the Lord;
      7.29 part of it as a **special gift** to the Lord
      7.30 present it as a **special gift** to the Lord
      7.32 shall be given as a **special contribution**
      7.34 breast of the animal is a **special gift**,
      7.34 right hind leg is a **special contribution**
      8.27 they presented it as a **special gift**
      8.29 presented it as a **special gift**
      9.21 **special gift** to the Lord for the priests,
     10.14 are presented as the **special gift**
     10.14 and the **special contribution**
     14.12 He shall present them as a **special gift**
     14.21 a **special gift** to the Lord for the priest.
     14.24 present them as a **special gift**
     23.11 He shall present it as a **special offering**
     23.17 to the Lord as a **special gift**.
     23.20 present the bread...as a **special gift**
Num   5.9   **special contribution** which the Israelites **offer**
      6.2   a **special vow**...and **dedicates** himself
      6.20 **special gift** to the Lord; they are a sacred **offering**
      8.11 the Levites to me as a **special gift**
      8.13 **Dedicate** the Levites as a **special gift**
      8.21 Aaron **dedicated** them as a **special gift**
     15.19 as a **special contribution** to the Lord.
     15.20 presented as a **special contribution**
     15.21 **special gift** is to be given to the Lord
     18.8   giving you all the **special contributions**
     18.11 any other **special contributions** that
     18.18 the right hind leg of the **special offering**.
     18.19 all the **special contributions** which
     18.24 present to me as a **special contribution**.
     18.26 as a **special contribution** to the Lord.
     18.27 This **special contribution**
     18.28 will present the **special contribution**
     31.29 to...the priest as a **special contribution**
     31.41 the tax as a **special contribution**
Deut 12.11 your **offerings**, and those **special gifts**
1 Cor 7.7   each one has a **special gift** from God,
Eph   3.7   of the gospel by God's **special gift**
      4.7   one of us has received a **special gift**
2 Tim 2.21 **special** purposes, because it is **dedicated**
1 Pet 4.10 for the good of others the **special gift**

SPIRIT OF GOD

Acts	4.8	–	11.28	x30
Rom	7.6	–	9.1	x24
Gal	3.2	–	6.8	x16
1 Jn	2.20	–	5.8	x16
Eph	1.13	–	6.18	x14
1 Cor	12.1 – 13			x13
Lk	1.15	–	4.18	x12
1 Cor	2.4	–	3.16	x12
Acts	1.2	–	2.38	x10
Rev	1.10	–	4.2	x9

Acts	19.2	—	21.11	x8
2 Cor	3.3 – 18			x7
Mt	10.20	—	12.32	x6
Jn	3.5	—	4.24	x6
Num	11.17 – 29			x5
Jn	14.17	—	16.15	x5
Rom	14.17	—	15.30	x5
Ezek	2.2	—	3.24	x4
Lk	10.21	—	12.12	x4
Jn	6.63	—	7.39	x4
Acts	13.2 – 52			x4
Acts	15.8	—	16.7	x4
Heb	9.8	—	10.29	x4
1 Sam	10.6	—	11.6	x3
Ezek	11.1 – 24			x3
Mt	3.11	—	4.1	x3
Mk	1.8 – 12			x3
Jn	1.32 – 33			x3
1 Cor	6.11	—	7.40	x3
1 Cor	14.2	—	15.45	x3
Phil	1.19	—	3.3	x3
2 Tim	1.7 – 14			x3
1 Pet	1.2 – 12			x3
Rev	21.10	—	22.17	x3

Angel
1 Tim	3.16	by the **Spirit**, and was seen by **angels**.
Rev	17.3	**Spirit** took control of me, and the **angel**
	21.10	**Spirit** took control of me, and the **angel**

Believe, Faith
Jn	7.39	**Spirit**, which those who **believed** in him
Acts	6.5	a man full of **faith** and the **Holy Spirit**,
	8.15	**believers** that they might receive the **Holy Spirit**.
	8.18	**Spirit** had been given to the **believers**
	11.24	full of the **Holy Spirit** and **faith**,
	19.2	**Holy Spirit** when you became **believers**?
1 Cor	12.9	One and the same **Spirit** gives **faith**
Gal	3.14	through **faith** we might receive the **Spirit**
	5.5	**God's Spirit** working through our **faith**.
1 Jn	4.1	**believe** all who claim to have the **Spirit**,

Child of God see God's People

Christ, Jesus, Son of God
Mt	4.1	the **Spirit** led **Jesus** into the desert
	28.19	the **Son**, and the **Holy Spirit**,
Jn	7.39	**Jesus** said this about the **Spirit**,
Acts	16.7	the **Spirit** of **Jesus** did not allow them.
Rom	8.9	does not have the **Spirit of Christ**
	8.10	But if **Christ** lives in you, the **Spirit**
	8.11	the **Spirit of God**, who raised **Jesus**
Gal	4.6	God sent the **Spirit** of his **Son**
Phil	1.19	which comes from the **Spirit of Jesus**
Tit	3.6	**Holy Spirit**...on us through **Jesus**
Heb	9.14	of **Christ**! Through the eternal **Spirit**
1 Pet	1.2	by his **Spirit**, to obey **Jesus Christ**
	1.11	time to which **Christ's Spirit** in them
1 Jn	2.20	**Spirit** poured out on you by **Christ**
	2.27	**Christ** has poured on us his **Spirit** on you.
	4.3	this about **Jesus** does not have the **Spirit**

Churches
Rev	2.7	to what the **Spirit** says to the **churches**!
		Also: 2.11, 17, 29; 3.6, 13, 22

Faith see Believe

Glory
2 Cor	3.18	same **glory**, coming from...the **Spirit**,
1 Pet	4.14	the **glorious Spirit**, the **Spirit of God**,

God's People, Child of God
Num	11.29	would give his **spirit** to all **his people**
Rom	8.14	led by **God's Spirit** are **God's sons**.

Rom	8.15	the **Spirit** makes you **God's children**,
	8.16	**Spirit**...declare that we are **God's children**.
	8.27	**Spirit** pleads...on behalf of **his people**
Gal	4.6	are **his sons**, God sent the **Spirit**
2 Thes	2.13	**Spirit's** power to make you **his**...**people**

Good News see Message

Hearts
Rom	5.5	our **hearts** by means of the **Holy Spirit**,
2 Cor	1.22	given us the **Holy Spirit** in our **hearts**
Gal	4.6	the **Spirit** of his Son into our **hearts**,

Heaven
Mt	3.16	**heaven** was opened...he saw the **Spirit**
Mk	1.10	**heaven** opening and the **Spirit** coming
Lk	11.13	Father in **heaven** give the **Holy Spirit**
Jn	1.32	**Spirit** come...like a dove from **heaven**
Acts	7.55	of the **Holy Spirit**, looked up to **heaven**
1 Pet	1.12	of the **Holy Spirit** sent from **heaven**.

Life
Job	33.4	**God's spirit** made me and gave me **life**.
Jn	6.63	What gives **life** is **God's Spirit**
Rom	8.2	law of the **Spirit**, which brings us **life**
	8.6	be controlled by the **Spirit** results in **life**
	8.10	**Spirit** is **life** for you because you have
1 Cor	15.45	the last Adam is the **life-giving Spirit**.
2 Cor	3.6	brings death, but the **Spirit** gives **life**.
Gal	5.16	let the **Spirit** direct your **lives**,
	5.25	**Spirit** has given us **life**; he must also
Phil	3.3	of his **Spirit** and rejoice in our **life**
Tit	3.5	the **Holy Spirit**, who gives us...new **life**

Love
Rom	5.5	**love** into our hearts by...the **Holy Spirit**,
	15.30	and by the **love** that the **Spirit** gives:
2 Cor	6.6	the **Holy Spirit**, by our true **love**,
	13.13	**love** of God, and...of the **Holy Spirit**
Gal	5.22	But the **Spirit** produces **love**
Col	1.8	of the **love** that the **Spirit** has given
2 Tim	1.7	his **Spirit** fills us with power, **love**,

Message, Good News, Word
2 Sam	23.2	**spirit of the Lord** speaks through me; his **message**
Lk	1.67	**Spirit**, and he spoke God's **message**:
Acts	4.31	**Spirit** and began to proclaim God's **message**
	16.6	**Holy Spirit** did not let them preach the **message**
1 Cor	2.13	but in **words** taught by the **Spirit**,
	12.8	The **Spirit** gives one person a **message**
Eph	6.17	and the **word** of God as the sword which the **Spirit**
1 Pet	1.12	**Good News** by the power of the...**Spirit**
2 Pet	1.21	**Holy Spirit** as they spoke the **message**

Peace
Rom	8.6	by the **Spirit** results in life and **peace**.
	14.17	**peace**, and joy which the **Holy Spirit**
Gal	5.22	the **Spirit** produces love, joy, **peace**
Eph	4.3	**Spirit** gives by means of the **peace**

Prophet
Acts	28.25	**Spirit** spoke through the **prophet** Isaiah
Eph	3.5	**Spirit** to his holy apostles and **prophets**.
Rev	22.6	gives his **Spirit** to the **prophets**,

Raise
Ezek	2.2	**God's spirit** entered me and **raised** me
	3.24	**God's spirit** entered me and **raised** me
Rom	8.11	the **Spirit of God**, who **raised** Jesus

Reveal
Jn	14.17	**Spirit** who **reveals** the truth about God

Jn	15.26	come — the **Spirit**, who **reveals** the truth
	16.13	**Spirit** comes, who **reveals** the truth
Eph	1.17	the **Spirit**, who will...**reveal** God to you,
	3.5	God has **revealed** it now by the **Spirit**

Son of God see **Christ**

Teach
Lk	12.12	the Holy **Spirit** will **teach** you
1 Cor	2.13	in words **taught** by the **Spirit**,
Heb	9.8	Holy **Spirit** clearly **teaches**
1 Jn	2.27	as his **Spirit** remains in you, you do not need anyone to **teach**

Truth
Jn	14.17	He is the **Spirit** who reveals the **truth**
	15.26	come — the **Spirit**, who reveals the **truth**
	16.13	**Spirit** comes, who reveals the **truth**
Acts	1.16	to come **true** in which the Holy **Spirit**,
1 Cor	2.13	**truths** to those who have the **Spirit**.
	14.2	secret **truths** by the power of the **Spirit**.
2 Cor	6.6	Holy **Spirit**, by our **true** love,
1 Thes	1.5	**Spirit**, and with...conviction of its **truth**.
1 Jn	2.27	his **Spirit** teaches you...what he teaches is **true**,
	4.6	**Spirit** of **truth** and the spirit of error.
	5.6	**Spirit** himself testifies that this is **true**,
	5.6	because the **Spirit** is **truth**.

Wisdom
Is	11.2	**spirit of the Lord** will give him **wisdom**,
Acts	6.3	full of the Holy **Spirit** and **wisdom**,
	6.10	the **Spirit** gave Stephen such **wisdom**
1 Cor	12.8	**Spirit** gives one person a message full of **wisdom**
Col	1.9	**wisdom** and understanding that his **Spirit**

Word see **Message**

SPIRIT(S)
	Mk	9.17 – 28		x9
	Lk	6.18	— 11.26	x9
	Mk	5.2	— 7.25	x7
	1 Sam	16.14 – 23		x5
	Dan	4.8	— 5.14	x5
	Acts	19.12 – 16		x5
	Mk	1.23 – 27		x4
	1 Cor	4.21	— 5.5	x4
	1 Cor	14.14 – 16		x4
	1 Jn	4.1 – 6		x4
	Rev	16.13 – 16		x4
	Lev	19.31	— 20.27	x3
	1 Sam	28.8 – 13		x3
	Mk	3.11 – 30		x3
	Lk	4.33 – 36		x3
	Acts	16.16 – 18		x3
	Col	2.5 – 20		x3
	1 Pet	3.4 – 20		x3
	Rev	3.1	— 5.6	x3

Christ, Jesus
Mt	8.16	**Jesus** drove out the evil **spirits**
Mk	1.25	**Jesus** ordered the **spirit**,
	3.12	**Jesus** sternly ordered the evil **spirits**
	5.12	So the **spirits** begged **Jesus**,
	9.20	As soon as the **spirit** saw **Jesus**,
Lk	4.35	**Jesus** ordered the **spirit**,
	8.29	**Jesus** had ordered the evil **spirit**
Acts	7.59	Lord **Jesus**, receive my **spirit**!
Col	2.8	ruling **spirits**...and not from **Christ**.
	2.20	with **Christ**...free from the ruling **spirits**
1 Jn	4.3	The **spirit**...is from the Enemy of **Christ**;

Consult, Dead
Lev	19.31	who **consult** the **spirits** of the dead.
	20.6	who **consult** the **spirits** of the dead,
	20.27	who **consults** the **spirits** of the dead

Deut	18.11	let them **consult** the **spirits** of the **dead**.
1 Sam	28.8	**Consult** the **spirits** for me
1 Chr	10.13	by **consulting** the **spirits** of the dead
Job	26.5	The **spirits** of the **dead** tremble
Is	8.19	from the **spirits** and **consult** the **dead**
	19.3	**consult** mediums and ask the **spirits**
	65.4	to **consult** the **spirits** of the **dead**.

Jesus see **Christ**

Spirit of God
Rom	8.16	**God's Spirit** joins himself to our **spirits**
1 Cor	2.12	world's **spirit**...the **Spirit** sent by God,
2 Cor	11.4	a **spirit**...different from the **Spirit**
1 Jn	4.1	to have the **Spirit**...find out if the **spirit**
	4.3	have the **Spirit** from God. The **spirit**
	4.4	**Spirit**...is more powerful than the **spirit**
	4.6	**Spirit** of truth and the **spirit** of error.

World
1 Cor	2.12	We have not received this **world's spirit**
1 Jn	4.4	**spirit** in those who belong to the **world**.
Rev	16.14	**spirits** go out to...the kings of the **world**,

SPIRITUAL
	1 Cor	14.1	— 15.46	x7
	1 Pet	2.2	— 4.6	x6
	Eph	1.3	— 2.5	x4
	Col	1.16	— 2.15	x4
	1 Cor	2.6 – 14		x3
	1 Cor	9.11	— 10.4	x3
	1 Tim	4.6 – 14		x3

Christ
1 Cor	15.24	**Christ** will overcome all **spiritual** rulers,
Eph	1.3	with **Christ**...every **spiritual** blessing
Col	2.15	**Christ** freed himself from...the **spiritual**

Physical
Jn	3.6	**physically** of human parents, but he is born **spiritually**
1 Cor	15.44	**physical** body; when raised, it will be a **spiritual** body.
	15.46	not the **spiritual** that comes first, but the **physical**,
1 Tim	4.8	**Physical** exercise has...value, but **spiritual**
1 Pet	3.18	**physically**, but made alive **spiritually**,

Power
1 Cor	15.24	**spiritual** rulers, authorities, and **powers**,
Eph	2.2	obeyed the ruler of the **spiritual powers**
Col	1.16	including **spiritual powers**, lords, rulers,
	2.15	the **power** of the **spiritual** rulers

World
Eph	1.3	**spiritual** blessing in the heavenly **world**.
	6.12	**spiritual** forces in the heavenly **world**,
Jas	3.15	it belongs to the **world**, it is **unspiritual**

STRENGTH (STRONG)
	Dan	8.10	— 11.23	x9
	Judg	14.6	— 16.15	x8
	Deut	3.28	— 9.26	x7
	Job	39.4	— 41.25	x7
	Prov	28.2	— 31.25	x6
	2 Sam	22.2 – 47		x5
	Dan	1.15	— 4.22	x5
	Judg	16.9 – 28		x4
	2 Sam	10.12	— 11.25	x4
	Ps	18.2 – 34		x4
	Is	7.8 – 9		x4
	Is	40.29	— 42.1	x4
	Is	49.4	— 51.12	x4
	Zech	9.17	— 10.12	x4
	Mk	3.27	— 5.4	x4
	Ex	1.7 – 20		x3
	Num	13.18 – 31		x3

Ps	59.9 – 16	x3
Ps	89.10 – 21	x3
Prov	18.10 – 19	x3

Christ, Jesus

Col	1.29	mighty **strength** which **Christ** supplies
1 Tim	1.12	**Jesus**...who has given me **strength**

Help, Defend, Protect

Ex	15.2	The Lord is my **strong defender**;
Num	21.24	Ammonite border was **strongly defended**.
Deut	1.38	But **strengthen**...your **helper**
2 Sam	22.2	my **protector**; he is my **strong** fortress.
	22.47	Praise my **defender**...the **strong** God
Job	36.19	all your **strength** can't **help** you now.
Ps	18.2	my **protector**; he is my **strong** fortress.
	35.10	You **protect** the weak from the **strong**,
	37.17	the **strength** of the wicked, but **protect**
	46.1	and **strength**, always ready to **help**
	59.11	your **strength**...O Lord, our **protector**.
	61.3	my **strong defence** against our enemies.
	62.7	he is my **strong protector**;
	71.3	a **strong** fortress to **protect** me;
	71.7	you have been my **strong defender**.
	140.7	Lord, my **strong defender**,
Prov	18.11	**protects** them like high, **strong** walls
	18.19	will **protect** you like a **strong** city wall,
	21.22	can take a city **defended** by **strong** men,
Is	26.1	Our city is **strong**! God himself **defends**
	40.31	Lord for **help** will find their **strength**
	41.10	**strong** and help you; I will **protect** you
Jer	16.19	and gives me **strength**; you **help** me
Lam	2.3	**strength** of Israel; He refused to **help** us
Dan	9.25	rebuilt with streets and **strong defences**,
Acts	9.31	**help** of the...Spirit it was **strengthened**
Rom	14.19	and that **help** to **strengthen** one another.
2 Cor	1.6	too are **helped** and given the **strength**
1 Thes	3.2	to **strengthen** you and **help** your faith,

Jesus see Christ

Mighty

Gen	49.24	**strong** By the power of the **Mighty** God
Job	24.22	in his **strength**, destroys the **mighty**;
Ps	24.8	the Lord, **strong** and **mighty**,
	103.20	you **strong** and **mighty** angels,
	65.6	**strength**, showing your **mighty** power.
	74.13	**mighty strength** you divided the sea
	89.10	with your **mighty strength** you defeated
Jer	20.11	are on my side, **strong** and **mighty**,
Ezek	17.9	take much **strength** or a **mighty** nation
Zech	4.6	military **might** or by your own **strength**,
Eph	1.19	is the same as the **mighty strength**
Col	1.29	**mighty strength** which **Christ** supplies
Heb	11.34	**strong**; they were **mighty** in battle
2 Pet	2.11	**stronger** and **mightier** than these false

Mind

2 Kgs	23.25	all his heart, **mind**, and **strength**,
Mk	12.30	your **mind**, and with all your **strength**.
	12.33	all his **mind** and with all his **strength**;
Lk	10.27	your **strength**, and with all your **mind**';

Protect see Help

Save

Job	6.13	I have no **strength** left to **save** myself;
Ps	33.17	their great **strength** cannot **save**.
	80.2	us your **strength**; come and **save** us!
	86.16	**strengthen** me and **save** me,

STUBBORN

Ex	7.3	—	11.10	x14
Jer	5.3	—	7.26	x6
Ex	13.15	—	14.17	x4
Ex	32.9	—	34.9	x4
Deut	9.6	—	10.16	x4
Jer	16.12	—	19.15	x4
Heb	3.8	—	4.7	x4
Ezek	2.4	—	3.8	x3

Evil

Ex	34.9	people are **stubborn**, but forgive our **evil**
Jer	3.17	do what their **stubborn** and **evil** hearts
	7.24	whatever their **stubborn** and **evil** hearts
	11.8	continued to be as **stubborn** and **evil**
	16.12	All of you are **stubborn** and **evil**,
	18.12	We will all be just as **stubborn** and **evil**

Proud

Lev	26.19	I will break your **stubborn pride**
Neh	9.16	our ancestors grew **proud** and **stubborn**
Job	15.26	**proud** and rebellious; he **stubbornly**
Ezek	16.50	They were **proud** and **stubborn**
Dan	5.20	because he became **proud**, **stubborn**,

Refuse

Ex	7.14	king is very **stubborn** and **refuses**
	13.15	**stubborn** and **refused** to let us go,
Deut	21.20	**stubborn** and rebellious and **refuses**
2 Chr	36.13	He **stubbornly refused** to repent
Neh	9.16	**stubborn** and **refused** to obey
	9.29	**stubborn**, they **refused** to obey.
Jer	5.3	**refused** to learn. You were **stubborn**
	6.10	are **stubborn** and **refuse** to listen
	13.10	have **refused** to obey me. They have been as **stubborn**
Zech	7.11	my people **stubbornly refused** to listen

SUFFERING

1 Pet	1.6	—	5.10	x18
Is	53.3	—	54.11	x8
Heb	9.26	—	13.3	x8
Is	47.8	—	51.21	x6
Lam	1.4	—	3.28	x6
Mt	8.2	—	11.12	x6
2 Tim	1.8	—	4.5	x6
Job	35.8	—	37.17	x5
2 Thes	1.4 – 9			x5
Neh	9.9 – 32			x4
Ps	119.50 – 153			x4
Hos	4.9	—	5.15	x4
Mt	26.6	—	27.19	x4
Acts	7.11	—	9.16	x4
2 Cor	1.5 – 7			x4
1 Thes	1.6	—	3.7	x4
Rev	1.9	—	2.22	x4
Job	2.10 – 13			x3
Ps	73.4 – 14			x3
Ps	107.10 – 39			x3
Ezek	18.19 – 20			x3
Zech	9.5 – 12			x3
Mk	14.3 – 36			x3
Jn	16.21 – 33			x3
Col	1.24			x3
Heb	2.9 – 18			x3
Rev	18.7 – 15			x3

Christ, Jesus, Messiah

Lk	24.26	necessary for the **Messiah** to **suffer**
	24.46	the **Messiah** must **suffer** and must rise
Acts	3.18	that his **Messiah** had to **suffer**;
	5.41	**suffer** disgrace for the sake of **Jesus**.
	17.3	**Messiah** had to **suffer** and rise from
	26.23	**Messiah** must **suffer** and be the first one
Rom	8.17	for if we share **Christ's suffering**,
2 Cor	1.5	have a share in **Christ's** many **sufferings**
Col	1.24	what still remains of **Christ's sufferings**
2 Tim	1.8	**Christ's** sake...take your part in **suffering**
	2.3	**suffering**, as a loyal soldier of...**Jesus**.
Heb	2.10	make **Jesus** perfect through **suffering**,
	11.26	to **suffer** scorn for the **Messiah**
1 Pet	1.11	in predicting the **sufferings** that **Christ**

1 Pet	2.21	for **Christ** himself **suffered** for you
	4.1	Since **Christ suffered** physically
	4.13	that you are sharing **Christ's sufferings**,
	4.16	you **suffer** because you are a **Christian**,
	5.1	I am a witness of **Christ's sufferings**,

Church see God's People

Cruel

Ps	42.9	I go on **suffering** from the **cruelty**
	43.2	I go on **suffering** from the **cruelty**
	107.39	by **cruel** oppression and **suffering**,
Acts	7.34	seen the **cruel suffering** of my people
	8.1	began to **suffer cruel** persecution.

Death

Ps	88.15	I have **suffered** and been near **death**;
Is	53.10	should **suffer**; his **death** was a sacrifice
Jn	12.33	kind of **death** he was going to **suffer**.
Phil	3.10	**sufferings** and become like him in...**death**,
Heb	2.9	honour because of the **death** he **suffered**.

Disaster see Trouble

Disease see Trouble

Disgrace

2 Kgs	19.3	a day of **suffering**; we are...in **disgrace**.
Is	25.8	the **disgrace** his people have **suffered**
	37.3	a day of **suffering**; we are...in **disgrace**.
	44.11	will be terrified and will **suffer disgrace**.
	45.24	but all who hate me will **suffer disgrace**.
Dan	12.2	and some will **suffer** eternal **disgrace**.
Acts	5.41	them worthy to **suffer disgrace**

Endure, Patience

Is	53.3	he **endured suffering** and pain.
	53.4	**endured** the **suffering** that should have
	64.12	us **suffer** more than we can **endure**?
Lam	3.28	**suffer**, we should sit alone in...**patience**?
2 Cor	1.6	**endure** with **patience** the...**sufferings**
2 Tim	4.5	**endure suffering**,
Heb	12.7	**Endure** what you **suffer** as being a
Jas	5.10	of **patient endurance** under **suffering**.
1 Pet	1.11	the **sufferings** that Christ would...**endure**
	2.19	**endure** the pain of undeserved **suffering**
	2.20	**endure suffering** even when you have
Rev	1.9	**enduring** the **suffering** that comes
	2.3	**patient**, you have **suffered** for my sake

Glad see Joy

Glory

Lk	24.26	**suffer** these things and...enter his **glory**?
Rom	8.17	**suffering**, we will also share his **glory**.
Heb	2.9	**glory**...because of the death he **suffered**.
1 Pet	5.1	**sufferings**, and I will share in the **glory**
Rev	18.7	as much **suffering** and grief as the **glory**

God's People, Church

Josh	22.17	his own people...We are still **suffering**
1 Sam	9.16	I have seen the **suffering** of **my people**
Is	25.8	his people have **suffered** throughout
	49.13	will have pity on **his suffering people**.
Hos	5.15	**my people** until they have **suffered**
Obad	.13	**my people** to gloat over their **suffering**
Nah	1.12	**My people**, I made you **suffer**,
Zech	1.15	the **sufferings** of **my people** worse.
	9.8	have seen how **my people** have **suffered**.
Acts	7.34	seen the cruel **suffering** of **my people**
	8.1	**church** in Jerusalem began to **suffer**
Col	1.24	**sufferings** on behalf of...the **church**.
Heb	11.25	He preferred to **suffer** with **God's people**

Good News, Message

1 Thes	1.6	**suffered** much, you received the **message**
2 Tim	1.8	part in **suffering** for the **Good News**,
	2.9	I preach the **Good News**, I **suffer**

Happy see Joy

Jesus see Christ

Joy, Glad, Happy

Job	31.29	been **glad** when my enemies **suffered**,
Ps	119.92	source of my **joy**, I would have died from my **sufferings**.
Is	53.11	life of **suffering**, he will again have **joy**;
Jn	16.21	her **suffering**, because she is **happy**
Col	1.24	I am **happy** about my **sufferings** for you
1 Pet	3.14	**suffer** for doing...right, how **happy** you
	4.13	**sufferings**, so...you may be full of **joy**

Message see Good News

Messiah see Christ

Oppression see Trouble

Patience see Endure

Punishment

Num	12.11	do not make us **suffer** this **punishment**
2 Kgs	19.3	day of **suffering**; we are being **punished**
Ps	17.14	**Punish** them with the **sufferings**
	69.26	**punished**; they talk about the **sufferings**
	73.14	**suffer** all day long...you have **punished**
Is	26.11	let them **suffer** the **punishment**
	37.3	day of **suffering**; we are being **punished**
	53.4	that his **suffering** was **punishment**
	53.5	healed by the **punishment** he **suffered**,
	59.17	to **punish** and avenge the wrongs that people **suffer**.
Hos	4.9	You will **suffer** the same **punishment**
Mic	4.6	I **punished**, those who have **suffered**
2 Thes	1.9	**suffer** the **punishment** of eternal
Heb	12.7	**suffer** as being a father's **punishment**
Jude	.7	**suffer** the **punishment** of eternal fire

Rejected

Prov	9.12	if you **reject** it, you are the one who will **suffer**.
Is	53.3	**rejected** him; he endured **suffering**
Mk	8.31	must **suffer** much and be **rejected**
	9.12	will **suffer** much and be **rejected**?
Lk	9.22	must **suffer** much and be **rejected**
	17.25	he must **suffer** much and be **rejected**

Right

2 Thes	1.6	what is **right**: he will bring **suffering**
1 Pet	2.20	**suffering** even when you have done **right**,
	3.14	should **suffer** for doing what is **right**,

Sake

Acts	5.41	to **suffer** disgrace for the **sake** of Jesus.
	9.16	him all that he must **suffer** for my **sake**.
Rev	2.3	you have **suffered** for my **sake**,

Sin

Num	9.13	**suffer** the consequences of his **sin**.
	12.11	**suffer**...for our foolish **sin**.
	14.34	**suffer** the consequences of your **sin**
Ps	25.18	and **suffering** and forgive all my **sins**.
	107.17	fools, **suffering** because of their **sins**
Lam	1.5	made her **suffer** for all her many **sins**.
	5.7	and we are **suffering** for their **sins**.
Ezek	18.19	**suffer** because of his father's **sins**?
	18.20	**suffer** because of his father's **sins**,
Hos	5.15	have **suffered** enough for their **sins**
1 Pet	4.1	whoever **suffers** physically is no longer involved with **sin**.

Terrible

2 Kgs	14.26	The Lord saw the **terrible suffering**
Ps	119.107	My **sufferings**, Lord, are **terrible**
Mt	8.6	unable to move and **suffering terribly**.
Mk	5.25	was a woman who had **suffered terribly**
Rev	2.22	will **suffer terribly**.

SUFFERING — Trouble / TEACH

Trouble, Disaster, Disease, Oppression

Deut	24.8	are **suffering** from a dreaded **skin-disease**
	29.22	**disasters** and **sufferings** that the Lord
Judg	2.18	under their **suffering** and **oppression**.
2 Sam	19.7	be the worst **disaster** you have **suffered**
2 Kgs	5.1	he **suffered** from a dreaded **skin-disease**.
	7.3	**suffering** from a dreaded **skin-disease**
2 Chr	21.15	yourself will **suffer** a painful **disease**
Job	31.29	**suffered**...when they met with **disaster**;
	37.17	**suffer** in the heat when the south wind **oppresses**
Ps	10.14	you take notice of **trouble** and **suffering**
	31.7	see my **suffering**; you know my **trouble**.
	34.19	The good man **suffers** many **troubles**,
	44.24	Don't forget our **suffering** and **trouble**!
	71.20	You have sent **troubles** and **suffering**
	107.39	by cruel **oppression** and **suffering**,
Is	16.7	weep because of the **troubles** they **suffer**.
	40.27	know your **troubles** or care if you **suffer**
Jer	2.3	I sent **suffering** and **disaster**
Lam	2.13	has ever **suffered** like this. Your **disaster**
Dan	9.18	the **trouble** we are in and the **suffering**
Hos	5.11	Israel is **suffering oppression**
Mt	4.24	**suffering** from all kinds of **diseases**
	8.2	**suffering** from a dreaded **skin-disease**
	10.8	who **suffer** from dreaded **skin-diseases**,
	11.5	who **suffer** from dreaded **skin-diseases**
	26.6	**suffered** from a dreaded **skin-disease**.
Mk	1.40	**suffering** from a dreaded **skin-disease**
	14.3	**suffered** from a dreaded **skin-disease**.
Lk	4.27	**suffering** from a dreaded **skin-disease**
	5.12	**suffering** from a dreaded **skin-disease**.
	7.22	who **suffer** from dreaded **skin-diseases**
	17.12	**suffering** from a dreaded **skin-disease**.
2 Cor	4.17	small and temporary **trouble** we **suffer**
1 Thes	3.7	in all our **trouble** and **suffering**

SYNAGOGUE

Acts	17.1	—	19.8	x11
Lk	4.15	—	44	x7
Acts	13.5	—	15.21	x6
Mk	1.21	—	39	x4
Lk	11.43	—	13.14	x4
Lk	6.6	—	8.41	x3

Discuss see **Teach**

Preach see **Teach**

Sabbath

Mk	1.21	**Sabbath** Jesus went to the **synagogue**
	6.2	On the **Sabbath** he began to teach in the **synagogue**
Lk	4.16	the **Sabbath** he went...to the **synagogue**.
	6.6	**Sabbath** Jesus went into a **synagogue**
	13.10	One **Sabbath** Jesus was teaching in a **synagogue**
Acts	13.14	**Sabbath** they went into the **synagogue**
	15.21	in the **synagogues** every **Sabbath**,
	17.2	**synagogue**. There during three **Sabbaths**
	18.4	in the **synagogue** every **Sabbath**

Teach, Discuss, Preach

Mt	4.23	**teaching** in the **synagogues**,
	9.35	He **taught** in the **synagogues**,
	13.54	He **taught** in the **synagogue**,
Mk	1.21	to the **synagogue** and began to **teach**.
	1.39	**preaching** in the **synagogues** and driving
	6.2	he began to **teach** in the **synagogue**
Lk	4.15	**taught** in the **synagogues** and was
	4.44	So he **preached** in the **synagogues**
	6.6	Jesus went into a **synagogue** and **taught**
	13.10	Jesus was **teaching** in a **synagogue**
Jn	6.59	said this as he **taught** in the **synagogue**
	18.20	my **teaching** was done in the **synagogues**

Acts	9.20	to the **synagogues** and began to **preach**
	13.5	**preached** the word...in the **synagogues**.
	15.21	**synagogues**...and his words are **preached**
	17.17	So he held **discussions** in the **synagogue**
	18.4	He held **discussions** in the **synagogue**
	18.19	into the **synagogue** and held **discussions**

AV TABERNACLE see TENT

TABLET

Deut	9.9	—	10.4	x11
Ex	24.12	—	26.33	x4
Ex	31.18	—	32.19	x4
Ex	34.1 – 28			x4
Ex	38.21	—	40.20	x3

Commandment

Ex	25.16	**tablets**...on which the **commandments**
	32.15	stone **tablets** with the **commandments**
	32.16	**tablets** and had engraved the **commandments**
	34.28	on the **tablets**...the Ten **Commandments**.
	38.21	two stone **tablets**...on which the Ten **Commandments**
Deut	4.13	**Commandments**...on two stone **tablets**.
Heb	9.4	stone **tablets** with the **commandments**

Covenant

Ex	34.28	wrote on the **tablets** the...**covenant**
Deut	9.9	**tablets** on which was written the **covenant**
	9.11	**tablets**...he had written the **covenant**.
	9.15	**tablets** on which the **covenant** was
1 Kgs	8.21	the stone **tablets** of the **covenant**
2 Chr	6.11	the stone **tablets** of the **covenant**

Covenant Box

Ex	25.16	put in the **box** the two stone **tablets**
	25.21	Put the two stone **tablets** inside the **box**
	26.33	the **Covenant Box** containing the two stone **tablets**.
	39.35	the **Covenant Box** containing the stone **tablets**,
	40.20	**tablets** and put them in the **Covenant**
Deut	10.3	made a **box** of acacia-wood and cut two stone **tablets**
1 Kgs	8.9	inside the **Covenant Box** except the two stone **tablets**
	8.21	the **Covenant Box** containing the stone **tablets**
2 Chr	5.10	inside the **Covenant Box** except the two stone **tablets**
	6.11	the **Covenant Box**, which contains the stone **tablets**

TAX COLLECTORS

Lk	18.10	—	19.2	x5
Mt	9.9	—	11.19	x4
Mk	2.14 – 16			x3
Lk	5.27 – 30			x3

Outcasts

Mt	9.10	many **tax collectors** and other **outcasts**
	11.19	of **tax collectors** and other **outcasts**!
Mk	2.15	of **tax collectors** and other **outcasts**
	2.16	with these **outcasts** and **tax collectors**,
Lk	5.30	with **tax collectors** and other **outcasts**?
	15.1	many **tax collectors** and other **outcasts**

Pharisees

Lk	18.10	a **Pharisee**, the other a **tax collector**.
	18.14	the **tax collector**, and not the **Pharisee**,

TEACH

Mk	6.2	—	14.49	x24
Ps	119.12 – 171			x20
Deut	27.3	—	33.10	x17

222

1 Tim	1.3	—	6.3	x17
Jn	6.45	—	9.34	x15
Deut	4.1	—	8.3	x11
2 Tim	1.13	—	4.2	x11
Prov	1.3	—	4.11	x10
Is	28.9	—	30.20	x8
Mt	21.23	—	24.32	x8
Lk	9.26	—	13.26	x8
Acts	13.12	—	18.25	x8
Tit	1.1	—	2.15	x8
Mt	4.19	—	5.19	x7
Acts	4.2	—	5.42	x7
Prov	6.20	—	8.33	x6
Prov	21.11	—	22.21	x6
Mt	15.2	—	16.12	x6
Mk	1.17	—	2.13	x6
Lk	4.15	—	6.6	x6
Lk	18.1	—	21.37	x6
Jn	14.23	—	15.20	x6
Rev	2.14	—	3.8	x6
Is	50.4	—	51.16	x5
Col	1.28	—	3.16	x5
Neh	8.13	—	9.29	x4
Ps	25.4–9			x4
Prov	13.14	—	16.20	x4
Jer	9.5–20			x4
Jer	31.18	—	32.33	x4
Mal	2.6–9			x4
Mt	11.1	—	13.54	x4
Acts	20.20	—	21.28	x4
1 Jn	2.27			x4
Is	1.10	—	2.3	x3
Is	42.4–24			x3
Mt	7.12–29			x3
Mt	19.8–12			x3
Rom	15.4	—	16.17	x3
1 Cor	2.4–13			x3
1 Cor	11.2–23			x3
1 Cor	14.6–26			x3
1 Thes	4.8–15			x3
Heb	5.12	—	6.2	x3
2 Jn	.9–10			x3

Amazed
Mt 7.28 was **amazed** at the way he **taught**.
   22.33 they were **amazed** at his **teaching**.
Mk 11.18 crowd was **amazed** at his **teaching**.
Lk 4.32 were all **amazed** at the way he **taught**
Acts 13.12 he was greatly **amazed** at the **teaching**

Authority, Power
Job 27.11 **teach** you how great is God's **power**,
Is 59.21 given you my **power** and my **teachings**
Mk 1.22 instead, he **taught** with **authority**.
   1.27 new **teaching**? This man has **authority**
Lk 4.32 **taught**, because he spoke with **authority**.
1 Tim 1.20 to the **power** of Satan; this will **teach**
   2.12 them to **teach** or to have **authority**
Tit 2.15 **Teach**...and use your full **authority**
Rev 3.8 **power**; you have followed my **teaching**

Believers see God's People

Christ, Jesus
Mt 4.23 **Jesus** went all over Galilee, **teaching**
   26.1 When **Jesus** had finished **teaching**
Mk 1.21 **Jesus**...began to **teach**.
   4.1 Again **Jesus** began to **teach**
   6.6 **Jesus** went...**teaching** the people.
   8.31 **Jesus** began to **teach** his disciples:
   12.35 As **Jesus** was **teaching** in the Temple,
Lk 5.3 **Jesus** sat in the boat and **taught**
   5.17 One day when **Jesus** was **teaching**,
   6.6 **Jesus** went into a synagogue and **taught**.
   13.10 **Jesus** was **teaching** in a synagogue.
   20.1 **Jesus** was in the Temple **teaching**

Lk 21.37 **Jesus** spent those days **teaching**
Jn 6.59 **Jesus** said this as he **taught**
   7.14 **Jesus**...began **teaching**.
   7.28 As **Jesus taught** in the Temple,
   18.19 questioned **Jesus**...about his **teaching**.
Acts 1.1 things that **Jesus** did and **taught**
   4.2 **teaching**...that **Jesus** had risen
   4.18 or to **teach** in the name of **Jesus**.
   18.25 **taught** correctly the facts about **Jesus**.
   28.31 **taught** about the Lord **Jesus** Christ,
Eph 4.21 were **taught** the truth that is in **Jesus**.
2 Jn .9 not stay with the **teaching** of Christ

Churches see God's People

Command see Law

Correct see Right

Forget see Remember

God's People, Believers, Churches
Is 42.21 **teachings**, and he wanted **his people** to
   51.4 **my people**, listen...I give my **teaching**
   51.16 **people**! I have given you my **teaching**,
Jer 9.13 **my people** have abandoned the **teaching**
   12.16 **taught my people** to swear by Baal
Ezek 44.23 **teach my people** the difference between
Hos 11.3 **taught** Israel to walk. I took **my people**
Mal 2.9 and when you **teach my people**,
Acts 15.1 and started **teaching** the **believers**
1 Cor 4.17 which I **teach** in all the **churches**
   7.17 is the rule I **teach** in all the **churches**.
Tit 1.1 **chosen people** and to lead them to the truth **taught**

Good News see Message

Hard
Mt 19.8 because you are so **hard** to **teach**.
Mk 10.5 because you are so **hard** to **teach**.
Jn 6.60 This **teaching** is too **hard**.

Heart
Job 22.22 **teaching**...keep his words in your **heart**.
Ps 40.8 I keep your **teaching** in my **heart**.
   119.167 **teachings**; I love them with all my **heart**.
Is 51.7 have my **teaching** fixed in your **hearts**.
Rom 6.17 **heart** the truths found in the **teaching**

Honour see Obey

Jesus see Christ

Law, Command
Ex 18.20 should **teach** them God's **commands**
Lev 10.11 **teach** the people of Israel all the **laws**
Deut 1.5 to explain God's **laws** and **teachings**
   4.1 all the **laws** that I am **teaching** you,
   4.5 I have **taught** you all the **laws**
   4.8 **laws** so just as those that I have **taught**
   4.14 to **teach** you all the **laws** that you are
   4.44 God's **laws** and **teachings** to the people
   5.31 all my **laws** and commands. **Teach** them
   6.1 **laws** that the Lord your God commanded me to **teach**
   7.11 you have been **taught**; obey all the **laws**
   17.18 the book of God's **laws** and **teachings**
   27.3 on them all these **laws** and **teachings**.
   27.26 obey all of God's **laws** and **teachings**.
   28.61 this book of God's **laws** and **teachings**,
   30.10 **laws**...written in this book of...**teachings**.
   33.10 **teach** your people to obey your **Law**;
2 Kgs 17.27 to **teach** the people the **law** of the god
2 Chr 14.4 to obey his **teachings** and **commands**.
   15.3 to **teach** them, and without a **law**.
Ezra 7.10 and to **teaching** all its **laws**
   7.25 **teach** that **Law** to anyone who does not
Neh 8.13 Ezra to study the **teachings** of the **Law**.

Neh   9.13   them good **laws** and sound **teachings**.
       9.29   **teachings**, but...they rejected your **laws**,
Ps   51.13   I will **teach** sinners your **commands**,
      78.5   our ancestors to **teach** his **laws**
      94.12   the one to whom you **teach** your **law**!
     119.27   **laws**, and I will meditate on your wonderful **teachings**.
     119.29   in your goodness **teach** me your ˙ .w.
     119.33   **Teach** me...the meaning of your **laws**,
     119.68   **Teach** me your **commands**.
     119.108 and **teach** me your **commands**.
     119.124 and **teach** me your **commands**.
     119.135 and **teach** me your **laws**.
     119.171 because you **teach** me your **laws**.
Is   42.21   so he exalted his **laws** and **teachings**,
      51.4   my **teaching** to the nations; my **laws**
Jer   32.23   **commands**...according to your **teaching**;
Lam   2.9   The **Law** is no longer **taught**,
Ezek 20.11   my commands and **taught** them my **laws**
Amos   2.4   my **teachings** and...my **commands**.
Mal   4.4   **teachings** of my servant Moses, the **laws**
Mt   5.17   the **Law** of Moses and the **teachings**
       5.19   obeys the **Law** and **teaches** others
       7.12   the **Law** of Moses and of the **teachings**
      15.3   **command** and follow your own **teaching**?
      15.6   **command**...to follow your own **teaching**.
      15.9   **teach** man-made rules as though they were my **laws**!
      22.40   whole **Law** of Moses and the **teachings**
      28.20   and **teach** them to obey everything I have **commanded**
Mk   7.8   God's **command** and obey the **teachings**
       7.9   **law** in order to uphold your...**teaching**.
      10.5   **law**...because you are so hard to **teach**.
Acts 16.21   are **teaching** customs...against our **law**

Lie

Is   9.15   is the prophets whose **teachings** are **lies**!
Jer   9.5   they have **taught** their tongues to **lie**
1 Tim 4.1   **lying** spirits and follow the **teachings**
       4.2   **teachings** are spread by deceitful **liars**

Message, Good News, Word

Deut 32.47   These **teachings** are not empty **words**;
Job   22.22   the **teaching** he gives; keep his **words**
Is   28.9   he's **teaching**? Who needs his **message**?
Jer   6.19   **teaching** and have not obeyed my **words**.
Mt   4.23   **teaching** in the synagogues, preaching the **Good News**
       9.35   He **taught** in the synagogues, preached the **Good News**
Lk   20.1   **teaching** the people and preaching the **Good News**,
Acts   5.42   to **teach** and preach the **Good News**
      15.35   they **taught** and preached the **word**
      18.11   **teaching** the people the **word** of God.
1 Cor 2.4   **teaching** and **message** were not delivered
       2.13   in **words taught** by human wisdom,
      14.6   inspired **message**, or some **teaching**.
      14.19   **words** that can be understood, in order to **teach**
1 Tim 4.6   **words** of faith and of the true **teaching**
       6.3   true **words** of our Lord...and with the **teaching**
2 Tim 1.13   firmly to the true **words** that I **taught**
       2.8   is **taught** in the **Good News** I preach.
       2.15   **teaches** the **message** of God's truth.
Heb   5.12   **teach** you the first lessons of God's **message**.

Obey, Honour

Deut   4.1   **Obey** all the laws that I am **teaching**
       4.14   **teach** you all the laws that you are to **obey**

Deut   5.31   **Teach** them to the people, so that they will **obey**
       6.1   to **teach** you. **Obey** them in the land
       7.11   **obey** what you have been **taught**;
      27.26   **obey** all of God's laws and **teachings**.
      28.58   not **obey** faithfully all God's **teachings**
      31.12   to **obey** his **teachings** faithfully.
      32.46   faithfully **obey** all God's **teachings**.
      33.10   **teach** your people to **obey** your Law;
2 Chr 14.4   to **obey** his **teachings** and commands.
Neh   9.29   warned them to **obey** your **teachings**,
Ps   34.11   I will **teach** you to **honour** the Lord.
      86.11   **Teach** me, Lord, what you want me to do, and I will **obey**
     119.17   that I may live and **obey** your **teachings**.
     119.45   because I try to **obey** your **teachings**.
     119.129 **teachings** are wonderful; I **obey** them
     119.167 I **obey** your **teachings**;
Is   42.21   **teachings**, and he wanted his people to **honour** them.
      42.24   or **obey** the **teachings** he gave us.
      59.21   to **obey** me and **teach** your children
Jer   6.19   my **teaching** and have not **obeyed**
       9.13   **teaching** that I gave them. They have not **obeyed**
      16.11   me and did not **obey** my **teachings**.
      26.4   must **obey** me by following the **teaching**
      31.18   but you **taught** us to **obey**.
Mal   2.9   not **obey** my will, and when you **teach**
Mt   5.19   **obeys** the Law and **teaches** others to
      23.23   to **obey** the really important **teachings**
      28.20   **teach** them to **obey** everything I have
Mk   7.8   and **obey** the **teachings** of men.
Jn   8.31   If you **obey** my **teaching**,
       8.51   **obeys** my **teaching** will never die.
       8.52   **obeys** your **teaching** will never die.
      14.23   loves me will **obey** my **teaching**.
      14.24   not love me does not **obey** my **teaching**
      15.20   if they **obeyed** my **teaching**,
1 Tim 4.1   **obey** lying spirits and follow the **teachings**
1 Jn   2.27   **Obey** the Spirit's **teaching**,
Rev   3.3   **taught** and what you heard; **obey** it

Power see Authority

Praise see Worship

Prophets

2 Kgs 4.38   he was **teaching** a group of **prophets**,
Is   9.15   the **prophets** whose **teachings** are lies!
Zech   7.12   **teaching**...I sent through the **prophets**
Mt   5.17   and the **teachings** of the **prophets**.
       7.12   and of the **teachings** of the **prophets**.
      22.40   the **teachings** of the **prophets** depend on

Remember, Forget

Prov   2.1   I **teach** you, my son, and **never forget**
       3.1   I **teach** you, my son. Always **remember**
       4.2   **teaching** you is good, so **remember** it
       6.20   **forget** what your mother **taught** you.
Zeph   3.7   would **never forget** the lesson I **taught**
Mal   4.4   **Remember** the **teachings** of my servant
Jn   14.26   **teach** you...and make you **remember**
1 Cor 11.2   **remember** me and follow the **teachings**
Rev   3.3   **Remember**, then, what you were **taught**

Right, Correct

1 Sam 12.23   I will **teach** you what is good and **right**
1 Kgs 8.36   **Teach** them to do what is **right**.
2 Chr 6.27   and **teach** them to do what is **right**.
Ps   25.9   humble in the **right** way and **teaches**
Prov   4.11   **taught** you wisdom and the **right** way
       6.23   correction can **teach** you how to live.
Is   51.7   what is **right**, who have my **teaching**
Dan   12.3   **taught** many people to do what is **right**

Mal	2.6	They **taught** what was **right**			
Lk	20.21	what you say and **teach** is **right**.			
Acts	18.25	**taught correctly** the facts about Jesus.			
2 Tim	2.15	one who **correctly teaches** the message			
	3.16	**teaching** the truth...**correcting** faults,			
Heb	13.9	**teachings** lead you from the **right** way.			

Temple

Is	2.3	**Temple** of Israel's God. He will **teach**
Mic	4.2	to the **Temple** of Israel's God. For he will **teach**
Mt	21.23	back to the **Temple**; and as he **taught**
	26.55	I sat down and **taught** in the **Temple**,
Mk	12.35	As Jesus was **teaching** in the **Temple**
	14.49	I was with you **teaching** in the **Temple**,
Lk	19.47	Every day Jesus **taught** in the **Temple**.
	20.1	when Jesus was in the **Temple teaching**
	21.37	spent those days **teaching** in the **Temple**
Jn	7.14	went to the **Temple** and began **teaching**.
	7.28	As Jesus **taught** in the **Temple**
	8.20	said all this as he **taught** in the **Temple**
Acts	5.21	entered the **Temple** and started **teaching**.
	5.25	are in the **Temple teaching** the people!

Truth

2 Chr	15.3	**true** God, without priests to **teach** them,
Job	15.18	Wise men have **taught** me **truths**
Ps	25.5	**Teach** me to live according to your **truth**,
Prov	22.21	will **teach** you what the **truth** really is.
Mal	2.7	of priests to **teach** the **true** knowledge
Mt	5.17	but to make their **teachings** come **true**.
	22.16	You **teach** the **truth** about God's will
Mk	12.14	but **teach** the **truth** about God's will
Lk	1.4	**truth** about everything which you have been **taught**.
	20.21	but **teach** the **truth** about God's will
Jn	8.51	**truth**: whoever obeys my **teaching** will
Rom	6.17	the **truths** found in the **teaching**
Eph	4.21	his followers you were **taught** the **truth**
2 Thes	2.15	to those **truths** which we **taught** you,
1 Tim	4.6	**true teaching** which you have followed.
2 Tim	1.13	to the **true** words that I **taught** you
	2.15	**teaches** the message of God's **truth**.
	3.16	and is useful for **teaching** the **truth**,
Tit	1.1	the **truth taught** by our religion.
	1.9	**true teaching** and also to show the error
1 Jn	2.27	what he **teaches** is **true**, not false.

Will

Ps	25.9	and **teaches** them his **will**.
	40.8	**will**, my God! I keep your **teaching**
	143.10	**teach** me to do your **will**.
Mal	2.9	not obey my **will**, and when you **teach**
Mt	22.16	You **teach** the truth about God's **will**
Mk	12.14	but **teach** the truth about God's **will**
Lk	20.21	but **teach** the truth about God's **will**

Word see Message

Worship, Praise

2 Kgs	17.28	he **taught** the people how to **worship**
Ps	40.3	He **taught** me to sing...a song of **praise**
	119.12	**praise** you, O Lord; **teach** me your
	119.171	always **praise** you, because you **teach** me
Mt	15.9	**worship** me, because they **teach**
Mk	7.7	**worship** me, because they **teach**
Lk	4.15	**taught** in...synagogues and was **praised**
1 Cor	14.26	**worship**, one person has a hymn, another a **teaching**,

TEACHERS OF THE LAW

Mk	7.1	—	12.38	x12
Mt	20.18	—	23.29	x10
Lk	9.22	—	11.53	x8
Mk	14.1	—	15.31	x5
Lk	5.17	—	7.30	x5
Lk	19.47	—	20.46	x5
Mk	1.22	—	3.22	x4
Mt	7.29	—	9.3	x3
Mt	15.1	—	17.10	x3
Lk	22.2	—	23.10	x3
Acts	4.5	—	6.12	x3

Elders

Mt	16.21	**elders**, the chief priests, and the **teachers**
	26.57	**teachers** of the Law and the **elders** had
	27.41	**teachers** of the Law and the **elders**
Mk	8.31	the **elders**...and the **teachers** of the Law
	11.27	**teachers** of the Law, and the **elders**
	14.43	the **teachers** of the Law, and the **elders**.
	14.53	the **elders**, and the **teachers** of the Law
	15.1	the **elders**, the **teachers** of the Law, and
Lk	9.22	**elders**, the chief priests, and the **teachers**
	20.1	**teachers** of the Law...with the **elders**,
	22.66	**elders**, the chief priests, and the **teachers**
Acts	4.5	the **elders**, and the **teachers** of the Law
	6.12	the **elders**, and the **teachers** of the Law.

Hypocrites

Mt	23.13	**teachers** of the Law...You **hypocrites**!
		Also: 23.15, 23, 25, 27, 29

Terrible

Mt	23.13	**terrible** for you, **teachers** of the Law
		Also: 23.15, 23, 25, 27, 29
Lk	11.46	**terrible** also for you **teachers** of the
	11.52	**terrible** for you **teachers** of the Law

TEMPLE

Ezra	1.2	—	10.9	x72
2 Chr	22.11	—	28.24	x38
2 Chr	5.11	—	9.11	x36
2 Kgs	18.15	—	25.18	x34
Neh	10.28	—	13.14	x34
1 Kgs	8.16	—	10.12	x30
2 Chr	33.4	—	36.23	x30
1 Chr	22.1	—	26.28	x25
2 Kgs	11.2	—	12.18	x19
Jer	26.2	—	29.26	x16
Ezek	7.22	—	11.1	x16
Mk	11.11	—	15.38	x13
Lk	18.10	—	24.53	x12
2 Chr	30.1	—	31.21	x11
Hag	1.2	—	2.18	x11
Jer	32.34	—	36.10	x10
1 Chr	9.2 – 33			x9
Lk	1.8	—	2.46	x9
Neh	6.10	—	8.16	x8
Jer	7.1 – 30			x8
Jer	50.28	—	52.24	x8
Dan	8.11	—	9.27	x8
Acts	21.26	—	22.17	x8
Rev	14.15	—	16.17	x8
2 Kgs	14.14	—	16.18	x7
1 Chr	16.27	—	18.8	x7
2 Chr	2.1 – 12			x7
Mt	23.16	—	24.1	x7
1 Kgs	5.3 – 18			x5
2 Chr	20.5 – 28			x5
Mt	21.12 – 23			x5
Jn	2.14 – 21			x5
2 Sam	7.5 – 13			x4
Ps	84.1 – 10			x4
Ps	74.3 – 7			x3
Is	6.1 – 4			x3
Mt	17.24 – 27			x3
1 Cor	3.16 – 17			x3
Rev	11.1 – 19			x3

Angel
Rev	14.15	another **angel** came out from the **temple**
	14.17	another **angel** come out of the **temple**
	16.1	from the **temple** to the seven **angels**:

Bow see Worship

Command
1 Chr	22.6	and **commanded** him to build a **temple**
	29.19	you **command** and to build the **Temple**
Ezra	6.3	emperor **commanded** that the **Temple**
	6.12	**command**...to destroy the **Temple** there.
	6.14	**Temple** as they had been **commanded**
Jer	26.2	the **Temple**...all I have **commanded** you
Amos	9.1	**command**: "Strike the tops of the **temple**

Consecrate see Dedicate

Contribution see Offering

Dedicate, Consecrate
1 Kgs	8.63	and all the people **dedicated** the **Temple**.
	9.3	I **consecrate** this **Temple**
	9.7	this **Temple** which I have **consecrated**
	15.15	in the **Temple** all the objects his father had **dedicated**
1 Chr	26.27	and **dedicated** it for use in the **Temple**.
	26.28	been **dedicated** for use in the **Temple**,
2 Chr	7.5	and all the people **dedicated** the **Temple**.
	7.20	this **Temple** that I have **consecrated**
Ezra	6.16	joyfully **dedicated** the **Temple**.
Neh	10.36	the **Temple** and there...**dedicate** him
Dan	9.24	and the holy **Temple** will be rededicated.
Jn	10.22	Festival of the **Dedication** of the **Temple**
Eph	2.21	a sacred **temple dedicated** to the Lord.

Defile see Profane

Duty
2 Kgs	11.18	put guards on **duty** at the **Temple**,
	12.9	**Temple**. The priests on **duty** at the
	22.4	on **duty** at the entrance to the **Temple**
	23.4	on **duty** at the entrance to the **Temple**
1 Chr	9.27	the **Temple**, because it was their **duty** ·
	9.33	the **temple** buildings and were free from other **duties**,
	24.19	**Temple** and performing the **duties**
	26.12	they were assigned **duties** in the **Temple**,
2 Chr	23.18	the **Temple**...to carry out the **duties**
	23.19	also put guards on **duty** at the **temple**
	35.2	the **duties**...to perform in the **Temple**
Neh	12.45	**temple** guards also performed their **duties**
Jer	29.26	officer in the **Temple**. It is your **duty**

Enemy see Profane

Evil see Profane

Gift see Offering

Glorious, Majestic
2 Chr	6.2	I have built a **majestic temple** for you,
Ps	29.9	in his **Temple** shouts, "Glory to God!
Is	60.7	his **Temple** more **glorious** than ever.
	60.13	my **Temple** beautiful...my city **glorious**.
Jer	17.12	Our **Temple** is like a **glorious** throne,
Rev	15.8	The **temple** was filled with...the **glory**

Happy see Joy

Heaven
2 Chr	7.3	**heaven** and the light fill the **Temple**,
Ezra	7.23	God of **Heaven** requires for his **Temple**,
Ps	11.4	**temple**; he has his throne in **heaven**.
	78.69	his **Temple** like his home in **heaven**;
Dan	8.13	will the army of **heaven** and the **Temple**
Mic	1.2	He speaks from his **heavenly temple**.
Heb	6.19	the curtain of the **heavenly temple**
Rev	11.19	God's **temple** in **heaven** was opened
	14.17	angel come out of the **temple** in **heaven**

Rev	15.5	this I saw the **temple** in **heaven** open

High Priest see Priest

Holy, Purify, Sacred
1 Chr	9.32	**sacred** bread for the **Temple** every
	29.16	a **temple** to honour your **holy** name,
2 Chr	34.8	had **purified** the land and the **Temple**
	35.3	**sacred** Covenant Box in the **Temple** that
	36.14	the **Temple**, which the Lord...made **holy**.
Neh	10.33	**temple** worship the following: the **sacred**
Ps	5.7	I can worship in your **holy Temple**
	11.4	The Lord is in his **holy temple**;
	24.3	Who may enter his **holy Temple**?
	28.2	my hands towards your **holy Temple**.
	43.3	your **sacred** hill, and to your **Temple**,
	65.4	the blessings of your **sacred Temple**.
	68.5	who lives in his **sacred Temple**,
	79.1	They have desecrated your **holy Temple**
	93.5	and your **Temple** is **holy** indeed,
	138.2	I face your **holy Temple**,
Is	64.11	**Temple**, the **sacred** and beautiful place
Jer	51.51	over the **holy** places in the **Temple**.
Lam	1.4	**Temple** now to worship on the **holy**
	2.7	his altar and deserted his **holy Temple**;
Dan	9.20	my God to restore his **holy Temple**.
	9.24	and the **holy Temple** will be rededicated.
Jon	2.4	never see your **holy Temple** again.
	2.7	and in your **holy Temple** you heard me.
Hab	2.20	The Lord is in his **holy Temple**
Zech	14.20	in the **Temple** will be as **sacred**
Mt	23.17	the **Temple** which makes the gold **holy**?
Acts	6.13	always talking against our **sacred Temple**
1 Cor	3.17	**temple** is **holy**, and you yourselves
Eph	2.21	makes it grow into a **sacred temple**
1 Pet	2.5	**temple**, where you will serve as **holy**

Honour
1 Chr	22.7	to build a **temple** to **honour** the Lord
	29.16	a **temple** to **honour** your holy name,
2 Chr	2.4	building a **temple** to **honour** the Lord
	7.21	The **Temple** is now greatly **honoured**
	20.8	and have built a **temple** to **honour** you,
Ezra	7.27	**honour** in this way the **Temple** of the
Zech	6.14	the Lord's **Temple** in **honour** of Heldai,

Idol see Profane

Joy, Happy
1 Chr	16.27	power and **joy** fill his **Temple**.
Ezra	6.16	**joyfully** dedicated the **Temple**.
Ps	27.6	**joy** I will offer sacrifices in his **Temple**;
	84.2	in the Lord's **Temple**...I sing for **joy**
	84.4	How **happy** are those who live in your **Temple**,
Ezek	24.25	**Temple** that was their pride and **joy**,
Joel	1.16	is no **joy** in the **Temple** of our God.

Majestic see Glorious

New see Restore

Offering, Contribution, Gift, Sacrifice, Tithe
1 Kgs	10.5	the **sacrifices** he **offered** in the **Temple**.
	12.26	**offer sacrifices** to the Lord in the **Temple**
2 Kgs	12.4	with the **sacrifices** in the **Temple**,
1 Chr	16.29	an **offering** and come into his **Temple**.
	23.29	weigh and measure the **temple offerings**;
	26.20	**temple**...and the storerooms for **gifts**
	26.28	the **Temple**, including the **gifts** brought
2 Chr	7.7	**Temple**, and then **offered**...the **sacrifices**
	7.12	this **Temple** as the place where **sacrifices**
	9.4	the **sacrifices** he **offered** in the **Temple**.
	24.8	box for **contributions**...at the **temple**
	24.14	**offered** regularly at the **Temple**.
	30.15	**sacrifice burnt-offerings** in the **Temple**.
	31.10	bringing their **gifts** to the **Temple**,

2 Chr	31.14	**Temple**...in charge of receiving the **gifts**
Ezra	1.4	**offerings** to present in the **Temple**
	1.6	and **offerings** for the **Temple**.
	2.68	**offerings** to help rebuild the **Temple**
	7.17	**offer** them on the altar of the **Temple**
Neh	10.35	the **Temple** each year an **offering**
	10.38	the **temple** storerooms one tenth of all the **tithes**
	12.44	where **contributions** for the **Temple** were kept, including the **tithes**
	12.47	**gifts** for the support of the **temple**
	13.12	**temple** storerooms their **tithes** of corn,
Ps	27.6	will **offer sacrifices** in his **Temple**
	68.29	your **Temple**...where kings bring **gifts**
	96.8	an **offering** and come into his **Temple**.
Is	66.20	bring **grain-offerings** to the **Temple**
Jer	17.26	**Temple burnt-offerings** and **sacrifices, grain-offerings** and incense,
	41.5	corn and incense to **offer** in the **Temple**.
Hos	9.4	as an **offering** to the Lord's **Temple**.
Joel	1.9	no corn or wine to **offer** in the **Temple**;
Mal	3.10	amount of your **tithes** to the **Temple**,
Lk	21.1	their **gifts** in the **temple** treasury,

Pagan see **Profane**

Plan

1 Kgs	8.17	David **planned** to build a **temple**
2 Chr	2.12	who now **plans** to build a **temple**
	6.7	David **planned** to build a **temple**

Power

1 Chr	16.27	**power** and joy fill his **Temple**.
2 Chr	6.41	symbol of your **power**, enter the **Temple**
Ps	96.6	**power** and beauty fill his **Temple**.
Rev	15.8	**temple** was filled with smoke from the glory and **power**

Praise see **Worship**

Pray

1 Kgs	8.29	when I face this **Temple** and **pray**.
	8.33	this **Temple**, humbly **praying** to you
	8.35	this **Temple**, humbly **praying** to you,
	8.38	hands in **prayer** towards this **Temple**,
	8.41	you and to **pray** at this **Temple**,
2 Chr	6.20	when I face this **Temple** and **pray**.
	6.24	to this **Temple**, humbly **praying** to you
	6.26	this **Temple**, humbly **praying** to you,
	6.29	hands in **prayer** towards this **Temple**,
	6.32	he comes to **pray** at this **Temple**,
	7.12	your **prayer**, and I accept this **Temple**
	7.15	this **Temple** and...hear all the **prayers**
Ezra	10.1	in **prayer** in front of the **Temple**,
Neh	11.17	the **temple** choir in singing the **prayer**
Ps	134.2	your hands in **prayer** in the **Temple**,
Is	56.7	**Temple** will be called a house of **prayer**
Dan	9.17	hear my **prayer**...Restore your **Temple**,
Joel	2.17	of the **Temple**, must weep and **pray**:
Jon	2.7	**prayed** to you, and in your holy **Temple**
Zech	3.7	**Temple**...and I will hear your **prayers**,
	7.2	**Temple** of the Lord Almighty to **pray**
Mt	21.13	**Temple** will be called a house of **prayer**.
Mk	11.17	**Temple** will be called a house of **prayer**
Lk	18.10	the **Temple** to **pray**: one was a Pharisee,
	19.46	**Temple** will be called a house of **prayer**.
Acts	22.17	while I was **praying** in the **Temple**,

Priest, High Priest

2 Kgs	22.4	the **priests** on duty at...the **Temple**
	23.2	**Temple**, accompanied by the **priests**
	23.9	**priests** were not allowed...in the **Temple**
	23.24	**High Priest**...had found in the **Temple**
1 Chr	9.2	**priests**, Levites, and **temple** workmen.
	23.28	the **priests**...with the **temple** worship,
	23.32	the **priests**...in the **temple** worship
2 Chr	5.11	As the **priests** were leaving the **Temple**,

2 Chr	7.2	the **Temple** was full of...light, the **priests**
	23.6	the **temple** buildings except the **priests**
	34.9	**Temple** was handed over to...the **High**
	34.30	the **Temple**, accompanied by the **priests**
	35.8	the **Temple** — Hilkiah, the **High Priest**,
Ezra	3.10	foundation of the **Temple**, the **priests**
	6.18	**priests** and the Levites for the **temple**
	7.6	**priests**, Levites, **temple** musicians, **temple**
	7.16	their **priests** give for the **Temple**
Neh	7.73	**priests**, the Levites, the **temple** guards
	10.28	**priests**, the Levites, the **temple** guards,
	10.36	will take to the **priests** in the **Temple**
	10.37	the **priests** in the **Temple**
	10.39	**Temple** are kept and where the **priests**
	11.3	**priests**, the Levites, the **temple** workmen,
	13.4	**priest** Eliashib...in charge of the **temple**
	13.5	the **Temple**, the offerings for the **priests**,
Joel	1.9	in the **Temple**; the **priests** mourn
Mt	12.5	every Sabbath the **priests** in the **Temple**
Lk	1.8	his work as a **priest** in the **Temple**
1 Pet	2.5	**temple**, where you will serve as...**priests**

Profane, Defile, Enemy, Evil, Idol, Pagan

2 Kgs	21.4	He built **pagan** altars in the **Temple**,
2 Chr	33.4	He built **pagan** altars in the **Temple**,
	34.8	the **Temple** by ending **pagan** worship,
	36.14	**idols**, and so they **defiled** the **Temple**,
Ps	74.3	**enemies** have destroyed everything in the **Temple**.
	74.4	**enemies** have shouted in triumph in your **Temple**;
Jer	7.30	their **idols**, which I hate, in my **Temple** and have **defiled** it.
	23.11	caught them doing **evil** in the **Temple**
	32.34	their disgusting **idols** in the **Temple** ...and they have **defiled** it.
Lam	2.7	his holy **Temple**; He allowed the **enemy**
Ezek	5.11	you **defiled** my **Temple** with all the **evil**,
	7.22	when my treasured **Temple** is **profaned**,
	8.3	the **Temple**, where there was an **idol**
	9.7	**Defile** the **Temple**.
	23.38	They **profaned** my **Temple** and broke
	23.39	came to my **Temple** and **profaned** it!
	25.3	delighted to see my **Temple profaned**,
Hos	9.8	God's **Temple**...people are the prophet's **enemies**.
Mal	2.11	They have **defiled** the **Temple**
Acts	21.28	the **Temple** and **defiled** this holy place!
	24.6	He also tried to **defile** the **Temple**,
2 Cor	6.16	**temple** come to terms with **pagan idols**?

Prophet

2 Kgs	23.2	**Temple**, accompanied by...the **prophets**
1 Chr	26.28	the **Temple**, including the gifts brought by the **prophet**
Ezra	5.2	**Temple** in Jerusalem, and the...**prophets**
	6.14	**Temple**, encouraged by the **prophets**
Jer	27.16	**prophets** who say that the **temple**
Lam	2.20	**prophets** are being killed in the **Temple**
Hos	9.8	**Temple** the people are the **prophet's**

Purify see **Holy**

Restore, New

2 Chr	24.13	**restored** the **Temple** to its original
Neh	7.70	the cost of **restoring** the **Temple**:
Dan	8.14	Then the **Temple** will be **restored**.
	9.17	**Restore** your **Temple**, which has been
	9.20	to **restore** his holy **Temple**.
Hag	2.9	The **new Temple** will be more splendid
Zech	1.16	My **Temple** will be **restored**,

Sacred see **Holy**

Sacrifice see **Offering**

Serve

2 Kgs	23.9	were not allowed to **serve** in the **Temple**
	25.14	articles used in the **temple service**.
1 Chr	6.10	(the one who **served** in the **Temple**
Ezra	6.18	the Levites for the **temple services**
	7.19	the **temple services**.
	8.17	people to **serve** God in the **Temple**.
Neh	11.12	of this clan **served** in the **Temple**.
	11.22	for the music in the **temple services**.
Ps	134.1	all who **serve** in his **Temple**
Jer	52.18	articles used in the **temple service**.
Joel	1.13	**serve** at the altar! Go into the **Temple**
Lk	1.8	in the **Temple**...in the daily **service**.
	1.23	his period of **service** in the **Temple**
1 Pet	2.5	spiritual **temple**, where you will **serve**
Rev	7.15	**serve** him day and night in his **temple**.

Spirit of God

Lk	2.27	**Spirit**, Simeon went into the **Temple**.
1 Cor	3.16	are God's **temple** and that **God's Spirit**
	6.19	body is the **temple** of the **Holy Spirit**,

Thank see **Worship**

Tithe see **Offering**

Watch

1 Kgs	8.29	**Watch** over this **Temple** day and night,
2 Chr	6.20	**Watch** over this **Temple** day and night
	7.15	I will **watch** over this **Temple**
Ezra	3.12	**watched** the foundation of this **Temple**
Mk	12.41	sat near the **temple** treasury, he **watched**

Worship, Bow, Praise, Thank

1 Kgs	5.3	not build a **temple** for the **worship**
	5.5	to build that **temple** for the **worship**
	8.16	a **temple**...where I would be **worshipped**.
	8.17	to build a **temple** for the **worship**
	8.20	the **Temple** for the **worship** of the Lord
	8.29	**Temple**...where you have chosen to be **worshipped**.
	8.41	**worship** you and to pray at this **Temple**,
2 Kgs	5.18	**temple** of Rimmon...and **worship** him.
	19.37	**worshipping** in the **temple** of his god
	21.5	**Temple** he built altars for the **worship**
	23.4	**Temple**...the objects used in the **worship**
1 Chr	16.29	offering and come into his **Temple**. **Bow**
	23.28	from Aaron with the **temple worship**.
	23.32	from Aaron, in the **temple worship**.
	25.6	to accompany the **temple worship**.
2 Chr	2.1	**temple** where the Lord would be **worshipped**,
	6.5	a **temple** where I would be **worshipped**,
	6.7	to build a **temple** for the **worship**
	6.10	a **temple** for the **worship** of the Lord
	6.20	**Temple**...where you will be **worshipped**,
	6.33	**Temple**...where you are to be **worshipped**.
	20.9	this **Temple** where you are **worshipped**.
	24.18	stopped **worshipping** in the **Temple**
	31.2	in the **temple worship**, and giving **praise** and thanks in...the **Temple**.
	33.5	**Temple** he built altars for the **worship**
	34.8	the **Temple** by ending pagan **worship**,
Ezra	8.36	to the people and the **temple worship**.
	10.1	**bowing** in prayer in front of the **Temple**,
Neh	10.33	We will provide for the **temple worship**
	11.17	**temple** choir in singing the prayer of **thanksgiving**.
	13.14	done for your **Temple** and its **worship**.
Ps	5.7	in your holy **Temple** and **bow** down
	15.1	enter your **Temple**? Who may **worship**
	27.6	in his **Temple**; I will sing, I will **praise**
	55.14	and **worshipped** together in the **Temple**.
	84.4	in your **Temple**, always singing **praise**
	100.4	the **temple** gates with **thanksgiving**,

Ps	118.19	**Temple**; I will go in and give **thanks**
	134.2	in the **Temple**, and **praise** the Lord!
	138.2	I face your holy **Temple**, **bow** down, and **praise**
	150.1	**Praise** God in his **Temple**!
Is	37.38	**worshipping** in the **temple** of his god
	38.20	Sing **praise** in your **Temple**
	57.13	and will **worship** me in my **Temple**.
Jer	7.1	**Temple** where the people of Judah went in to **worship**.
	32.34	in the **Temple** built for my **worship**,
	33.11	bring **thank-offerings** to my **Temple**;
	34.15	in the **Temple** where I am **worshipped**.
Lam	1.4	comes to the **Temple** now to **worship**
	2.6	the **Temple** where we **worshipped** him;
Hag	1.8	**Temple**; then I will be...**worshipped**
Lk	2.36	**Temple**; day and night she **worshipped**
	24.53	in the **Temple** giving **thanks** to God.
Acts	3.8	the **Temple** with them...**praising** God.
Rev	11.1	who are **worshipping** in the **temple**.

TENT

Num	1.1	—	12.10	x60
Ex	25.8	—	31.7	x34
Ex	38.8	—	40.38	x33
Num	16.9	—	20.6	x25
Ex	33.7	—	36.37	x21
Lev	14.11	—	17.9	x15
Lev	3.2	—	4.18	x11
Lev	8.2	—	10.18	x11
Heb	8.5	—	9.21	x10
1 Kgs	1.39	—	2.34	x6
2 Chr	1.3 – 13			x5
2 Sam	6.17	—	7.18	x4
1 Chr	15.1	—	17.16	x4
Lev	1.1 – 5			x3
Lev	6.16 – 30			x3
Lev	19.21	—	21.11	x3
Num	31.30 – 54			x3
Deut	31.14 – 15			x3
Josh	22.19 – 29			x3

Cloud see **Presence**

Dedicate

Ex	38.24	**dedicated**...for the sacred **Tent**
	40.9	**dedicate** the **Tent** and all its equipment
Num	7.1	he anointed and **dedicated** the **Tent**

Duty

Num	3.7	**Tent** of my presence and perform **duties**
	3.8	of the **Tent** and perform the **duties**
	8.24	shall perform his **duties** in the **Tent**
	8.26	in performing their **duties** in the **Tent**,
	18.6	can carry out their **duties** in the **Tent**.
1 Chr	6.32	**duty** at the **Tent** of the Lord's presence
Heb	9.6	**Tent** every day to perform their **duties**,

Holy, Purify, Sacred

Ex	25.8	The people must make a **sacred tent**
	26.1	Make the interior of the **sacred Tent**
	29.11	in my **holy** presence at the entrance of the **Tent**.
	29.44	I will make the **Tent** and the altar **holy**,
	33.7	Moses would take the **sacred Tent**
	36.1	needed to build the **sacred Tent**,
	36.3	brought for constructing the **sacred Tent**.
	36.6	further contribution for the **sacred Tent**;
	38.24	to the Lord for the **sacred Tent**
	38.27	hundred bases for the **sacred Tent**
Lev	6.16	a **holy** place, the courtyard of the **Tent**
	6.26	a **holy** place, the courtyard of the **Tent**
	10.4	bodies away from the **sacred Tent**
	10.18	was not brought into the **sacred tent**
	12.4	or enter the **sacred Tent**

Lev	16.20	**purify** the Most Holy Place, the rest of the **Tent**
	16.33	**purify** the Most Holy Place, the rest of the **Tent**
	20.3	and makes my **sacred Tent** unclean
	21.11	nor is he to defile my **sacred Tent**
	26.11	I will live among you in my **sacred tent**,
Josh	22.27	worship the Lord before his **sacred Tent**

Holy Place
Ex	29.30	the **Tent**...to serve in the **Holy Place**
Lev	16.20	**Most Holy Place**, the rest of the **Tent**
	16.33	**Most Holy Place**, the rest of the **Tent**
Heb	9.3	the **Tent** called the **Most Holy Place**.

Offering
Ex	35.21	**offering** to the Lord for making the **Tent**
	40.6	the **Tent** the altar for burning **offerings**.
Lev	14.11	**offerings** to the entrance of the **Tent**
	17.5	of the **Tent** and kill them as **fellowship-offerings**.
Josh	22.27	his **sacred Tent** with our **offerings**
2 Chr	1.6	**Tent** the king worshipped the Lord by **offering**

Presence, Cloud
Ex	27.21	the lamp in the **Tent** of my **presence**
	29.11	**presence** at the entrance of the **Tent**.
	29.42	entrance of the **Tent** of my **presence**.
	33.10	pillar of **cloud** at the door of the **Tent**,
	40.34	**Tent** and the dazzling light of the Lord's **presence**
	40.36	when the **cloud** lifted from the **Tent**.
	40.38	Lord's **presence** over the **Tent**
Lev	9.23	into the **Tent** of the Lord's **presence**,
Num	9.15	day the **Tent**...was set up, a **cloud** came
	9.18	long as the **cloud** stayed over the **Tent**,
	9.19	When the **cloud** stayed over the **Tent**
	9.20	the **cloud** remained over the **Tent**
	9.22	as the **cloud** remained over the **Tent**,
	10.11	the **cloud** over the **Tent**...lifted,
	12.5	**cloud**, stood at the entrance of the **Tent**,
	12.10	and the **cloud** left the **Tent**
	14.10	Lord's **presence** appear over the **tent**.
	16.42	the **Tent** and saw that the **cloud**
Deut	31.15	**cloud** that stood by the door of the **Tent**.

Priest
Ex	29.30	as **priest** and who goes into the **Tent**
Lev	3.2	the **Tent**...The Aaronite **priests**
	8.2	**Tent** of my presence and bring...**priestly**
	12.6	the **priest** at the entrance of the **Tent**
	14.23	the **priest** at the entrance of the **Tent**.
	15.29	to the **priest** at the entrance of the **Tent**
	16.23	the **Tent**, take off the **priestly** garments
	16.33	the **Tent**...the altar, the **priests**,
	17.5	to the **priest** at the entrance of the **Tent**
Num	4.16	**priest** shall be responsible for the...**Tent**
	4.20	enter the **Tent** and see the **priests**
	6.10	to the **priest** at the entrance of the **Tent**
1 Kgs	8.4	and the **priests** also moved the **Tent**
2 Chr	5.5	**priests** and the Levites...moved the **Tent**
Heb	9.6	**priests** go into the outer **Tent** every day

Purify see Holy

Sacred see Holy

Serve
Ex	29.30	the **Tent** of my presence to **serve**
	38.8	who **served** at the entrance of the **Tent**
Num	4.33	clan in their **service** in the **Tent**:
	8.26	the **Tent**, but he must not perform any **service**
	16.9	perform your **service** in the Lord's **Tent**,

Num	18.1	connected with **serving** in the **Tent**
	18.2	and your sons are **serving** at the **Tent**.
	18.4	for all the **service** in the **Tent**,
	18.21	**service** in taking care of the **Tent**
	18.31	your wages for your **service** in the **Tent**.
Heb	9.11	The **tent** in which he **serves** is greater

Unclean
Lev	20.3	and makes my **sacred Tent** unclean
	21.11	ritually **unclean** nor is he to defile my sacred **Tent**

Worship
Josh	22.27	**worship** the Lord before his sacred **Tent**
Judg	18.31	the **Tent** where God was **worshipped**
2 Chr	1.6	front of the **Tent** the king **worshipped**
Heb	9.21	**Tent** and over all the things used in **worship**.

TERRIFY
Ezek	26.15	—	28.19	x8
Is	7.2	—	8.22	x4
Jer	49.17	—	51.37	x4
Dan	7.7	—	8.17	x4
1 Sam	28.5 – 21			x3
Ezek	32.23 – 27			x3

Afraid, Fear, Tremble
Gen	15.12	and **fear** and **terror** came over him.
	28.17	**afraid** and said, "What a **terrifying** place
Ex	15.14	with **fear**; the Philistines are seized with **terror**.
	15.15	are **terrified**; Moab's...men are **trembling**;
Deut	28.66	**terror**, and you will live in constant **fear**
Josh	9.24	**terrified** of you; we were in **fear** of our
Is	7.2	were so **terrified** that they **trembled**
Jer	23.4	will no longer be **afraid** or **terrified**.
	30.5	I heard a cry of **terror**, a cry of **fear**
	30.10	do not be **afraid**...do not be **terrified**.
	46.27	do not be **afraid**...do not be **terrified**.
Ezek	26.16	**trembling** on the ground. They will be so **terrified**
	27.35	kings are **terrified**, and **fear** is written
	27.36	**terrified**, **afraid** that they will share your
	28.19	**terrified**, **afraid** that they will share your
Hab	1.7	They spread **fear** and **terror**,
Heb	12.21	so **terrifying** that Moses said, "I am **trembling**

Visions
Job	7.14	**terrify** me with dreams; you send me **visions**
Dan	4.5	saw **terrifying visions** while I was asleep.

TEST
Ex	15.25	—	17.7	x4
1 Cor	10.9 – 13			x4
Ps	78.18 – 56			x3
Rev	2.2	—	3.10	x3

God
Gen	22.1	Some time later **God tested** Abraham;
Ex	20.20	**God** has only come to **test** you
Deut	6.16	Do not put...**God** to the **test**,
	13.3	**God** is using him to **test** you,
Ps	66.10	You have put us to the **test**, **God**;
	78.18	deliberately put **God** to the **test**
	78.41	they put **God** to the **test**
	78.56	Almighty **God** and put him to the **test**.
	106.14	and put **God** to the **test**;
Ecc	3.18	I concluded that **God** is **testing** us,
Mal	3.15	but they **test God's** patience
Mt	4.7	Do not put...**God** to the **test**.
Lk	4.12	Do not put...**God** to the **test**.
Acts	15.10	want to put **God** to the **test**
1 Thes	2.4	to please **God**, who **tests** our motives.

Heb   3.9   they put me to the **test**...says **God**,
      11.17   when **God** put Abraham to the **test**.

Lord
Ex   17.7   and put the **Lord** to the **test**
Ps   26.2   Examine me and **test** me, **Lord**;
Prov 17.3   a person's heart is **tested** by the **Lord**.
Is   7.12   I refuse to put the **Lord** to the **test**.
Jer 17.10   I, the **Lord**...**test** the hearts of men.
    20.12   Almighty **Lord**, you **test** men justly;
Acts 5.9   to put the **Lord's** Spirit to the **test**?
1 Cor 10.9   We must not put the **Lord** to the **test**,

Obey
Ex 20.20   **test** you and make you keep on **obeying**
Ps 78.56   put him to the **test**. They did not **obey**
2 Cor 2.9   **test** and whether you are always ready to **obey**

AV TESTAMENT see COVENANT

THANKS

Neh	11.17	—	12.46	x8
Lk	17.9	—	19.37	x7
Col	1.3	—	4.2	x7
Ps	107.1 – 31			x6
1 Cor	14.16	—	15.57	x5
Ps	118.1 – 29			x4
Ps	136.1 – 26			x4
1 Cor	10.16	—	11.24	x4
1 Thes	1.2	—	3.9	x4
1 Chr	16.8 – 35			x3
Ps	145.1 – 10			x3
2 Cor	1.3	—	2.14	x3
2 Cor	8.16	—	9.15	x3
1 Tim	1.12	—	2.1	x3

Father see God

Glad see Joy

Glory see Praise

God, Father
Deut 8.10   give **thanks** to the **Lord** your **God**
1 Sam 25.33 **Thank God** for your good sense
1 Chr 29.13 **God**, we give you **thanks**,
Neh 12.24 praised **God**...and gave **thanks** to him,
    12.31 round the city, giving **thanks** to **God**.
    12.40 groups that were giving **thanks** to **God**
    12.46 of praise and **thanksgiving** to **God**.
Ps 30.12 my **God**, I will give you **thanks**
    50.14 the giving of **thanks**...to **God**,
    52.9 I will always **thank** you, **God**,
    75.1 We give **thanks** to you, O **God**,
    97.12 holy **God**...give **thanks** to him.
   118.28 my **God**, and I give you **thanks**;
   136.2 Give **thanks** to the greatest of all **gods**;
   136.26 Give **thanks** to the **God** of heaven;
Amos 4.5 bread in **thanksgiving** to **God**,
Mt 11.25 **Father**, **Lord** of heaven...I **thank** you
    14.19 and gave **thanks** to **God**.
    15.36 gave **thanks** to **God**, broke them,
    26.27 he took a cup, gave **thanks** to **God**,
Mk   6.41 and gave **thanks** to **God**.
    8.6 gave **thanks** to **God**, broke them,
    14.23 he took a cup, gave **thanks** to **God**,
Lk   2.28 and gave **thanks** to **God**:
    2.38 she arrived and gave **thanks** to **God**
    9.16 **thanked God** for them, broke them,
    10.21 **Father**, **Lord** of heaven...I **thank** you
    17.18 came back to give **thanks** to **God**?
    18.11 I **thank** you, **God**, that I am not
    18.43 he followed Jesus, giving **thanks** to **God**.
    19.37 his disciples began to **thank God**
    22.17 Jesus took a cup, gave **thanks** to **God**,
    22.19 a piece of bread, gave **thanks** to **God**,

Lk 24.53 in the Temple giving **thanks** to **God**.
Jn   6.11 took the bread, gave **thanks** to **God**,
    11.41 **thank** you, **Father**, that you listen
Acts 27.35 took some bread, gave **thanks** to **God**
    28.15 When Paul saw them, he **thanked God**
Rom 1.8 I **thank** my **God** through Jesus Christ
    6.17 But **thanks** be to **God**!
    7.25 **Thanks** be to **God**, who does this
    14.6 he gives **thanks** to **God** for the food.
    14.6 and he gives **thanks** to **God**.
1 Cor 1.4 I always give **thanks** to my **God**
    1.14 I **thank God** that I did not baptize
    10.16 and for which we give **thanks** to **God**:
    10.30 If I **thank God** for my food,
    11.24 gave **thanks** to **God**, broke it,
    14.16 you give **thanks** to **God** in spirit only,
    14.17 Even if your prayer of **thanks** to **God**
    14.18 I **thank God** that I speak in strange
    15.57 But **thanks** be to **God** who gives us
2 Cor 1.3 Let us give **thanks** to the **God**
    2.14 But **thanks** be to **God**!
    4.15 offer to...**God**...**thanksgiving**.
    8.16 How we **thank God** for making
    9.11 many will **thank God** for your gifts
    9.15 Let us **thank God** for his priceless gift!
Eph   1.3 give **thanks** to the **God** and **Father**
    1.16 not stopped giving **thanks** to **God**
    5.4 Rather you should give **thanks** to **God**.
    5.20 give **thanks** for everything to **God**
Phil   1.3 I **thank** my **God** for you every time
Col   1.3 We always give **thanks** to **God**,
    1.11 And with joy give **thanks** to the **Father**,
    3.16 sing to **God** with **thanksgiving**
    3.17 give **thanks** through him to **God**
    4.2 as you pray, giving **thanks** to **God**
1 Thes 1.2 We always **thank God** for you all
    2.13 why we always give **thanks** to **God**.
    3.9 we can give **thanks** to our **God** for you.
2 Thes 1.3 we must **thank God** at all times
    2.13 We must **thank God** at all times
1 Tim 2.1 and **thanksgivings** be offered to **God**
2 Tim 1.3 I give **thanks** to **God**,
Phlm .4 and give **thanks** to my **God**.
Jas   3.9 give **thanks** to our **Lord** and **Father**
1 Pet 1.3 Let us give **thanks** to the **God**
    4.16 **thank God** that you bear Christ's name.

Honour see Praise

Joy, Glad
Ps 16.9 And so I am **thankful** and **glad**,
    95.2 with **thanksgiving** and sing **joyful** songs
Col 1.11 And with **joy** give **thanks** to the Father,
1 Thes 3.9 We **thank** him for the **joy** we have

Lord
see also **God**
Lev 22.29 sacrifice of **thanksgiving** to the **Lord**,
1 Chr 16.8 Give **thanks** to the **Lord**,
    16.34 Give **thanks** to the **Lord**,
    25.3 sang praise and **thanks** to the **Lord**.
2 Chr 29.31 offerings of **thanksgiving** to the **Lord**.
Ps 7.17 I **thank** the **Lord** for his justice,
    33.2 Give **thanks** to the **Lord** with harps,
    34.1 I will always **thank** the **Lord**;
    57.9 I will **thank** you, O **Lord**,
    92.1 to give **thanks** to you, O **Lord**,
   105.1 Give **thanks** to the **Lord**,
   106.1 Give **thanks** to the **Lord**,
   107.1 Give **thanks** to the **Lord**,
   107.8 They must **thank** the **Lord**,
   107.15 They must **thank** the **Lord**
   107.2 They must **thank** the **Lord**
   107.31 They must **thank** the **Lord**

Ps	108.3	I will **thank** you, O **Lord**,	
	109.30	I will give loud **thanks** to the **Lord**;	
	111.1	With all my heart I will **thank** the **Lord**	
	116.13	wine-offering to the **Lord**, to **thank** him	
	118.1	Give **thanks** to the **Lord**,	
	118.19	I will go in and give **thanks** to the **Lord**!	
	118.29	Give **thanks** to the **Lord**,	
	119.108	Accept my prayer of **thanks**, O **Lord**,	
	122.4	to give **thanks** to the **Lord**	
	124.6	Let us **thank** the **Lord**,	
	136.1	Give **thanks** to the **Lord**,	
	136.3	Give **thanks** to the mightiest of all **lords**;	
	138.1	I **thank** you, **Lord**, with all my heart;	
Is	12.4	Give **thanks** to the **Lord**!	
Jer	33.11	Give **thanks** to the **Lord** Almighty,	
Jn	6.23	after the **Lord** had given **thanks**.	
1 Tim	1.12	I give **thanks** to Christ Jesus our **Lord**,	
Jas	3.9	We use it to give **thanks** to our **Lord**	

Offer, Sacrifice

Lev	22.29	you **offer** a **sacrifice** of thanksgiving
2 Chr	29.31	**sacrifices** as **offerings** of thanksgiving
Ps	50.14	the giving of **thanks** be your **sacrifice**
	50.23	Giving **thanks** is the **sacrifice**
	54.6	**sacrifice**, O **Lord**; I will give you **thanks**
	56.12	give your my **offering** of thanksgiving,
	107.22	They must **thank** him with **sacrifices**,
	116.17	of thanksgiving and **offer** my prayer
Amos	5.22	and **offer** your bread in thanksgiving
2 Cor	4.15	**offer**...more prayers of thanksgiving.
1 Tim	2.1	and **thanksgivings** be **offered** to God

Praise, Glory, Honour

1 Chr	16.35	**thankful** and **praise** your holy name.
	25.3	sang **praise** and **thanks** to the **Lord**.
	29.13	we give you **thanks**, and we **praise**
2 Chr	31.2	**praise** and **thanks** in the various parts
Neh	12.24	**praised** God...and gave **thanks**
	12.46	of **praise** and **thanksgiving** to God.
Ps	7.17	I **thank** the **Lord**...I sing **praises**
	34.1	**thank** the **Lord**; I...never stop **praising**
	44.8	will always **praise** you and give **thanks**
	50.23	**thanks** is the sacrifice that **honours** me,
	79.13	will **thank** you for ever and **praise** you
	92.1	give **thanks**...sing in your **honour**,
	95.2	with **thanksgiving** and...songs of **praise**.
	100.4	Give **thanks** to him and **praise** him.
	106.47	be **thankful** and **praise** your holy name.
	109.30	loud **thanks** to the Lord; I will **praise**
	138.1	I **thank** you, Lord...I sing **praise**
	145.2	I will **thank** you; I will **praise** you
Is	51.3	songs of **praise** and **thanks** to me.
Lk	19.37	**thank** God and **praise** him in loud
Rom	1.21	the **honour** that belongs to him, nor do they **thank** him.
	14.6	in **honour** of the **Lord**...he gives **thanks**
2 Cor	4.15	to the **glory** of God more...**thanksgiving**.
Rev	4.9	songs of **glory** and **honour** and **thanks**
	7.12	**Praise**, **glory**, wisdom, **thanksgiving**, **honour**,

Prayer

Neh	11.17	singing the **prayer** of **thanksgiving**.
Ps	116.17	**thanksgiving** and offer my **prayer** to
	119.108	Accept my **prayer** of **thanks**, O **Lord**,
Mt	26.26	gave a **prayer** of **thanks**, broke it,
Mk	14.22	gave a **prayer** of **thanks**, broke it,
1 Cor	14.16	Amen" to your **prayer** of **thanksgiving**?
	14.17	Even if your **prayer** of **thanks** to God
2 Cor	4.15	more **prayers** of **thanksgiving**.
Col	4.2	Be persistent in **prayer**...giving **thanks**
1 Tim	2.1	**prayers**, requests, and **thanksgivings** be
	4.3	after a **prayer** of **thanks**,
	4.4	to be received with a **prayer** of **thanks**,

2 Tim	1.3	I **thank** him...always in my **prayers**

Sacrifice see **Offer**

THRONE

Rev	1.4	—	8.3	x28
Rev	19.4	—	22.3	x9
1 Kgs	1.35	—	2.33	x5
1 Kgs	10.18 – 19			x4
2 Chr	9.17 – 19			x4
Rev	11.16	—	14.3	x4
Is	6.1	—	8.18	x3
Dan	7.9			x3

Glorious

Jer	14.21	the place of your **glorious throne**.
	17.12	Our Temple is like a **glorious throne**,
Mt	19.28	Son of Man sits on his **glorious throne**
Mk	10.37	your **throne** in your **glorious** Kingdom,

God see **Lord**

Heaven

1 Kgs	22.19	**Lord** sitting on his **throne** in **heaven**,
2 Chr	18.18	**Lord** sitting on his **throne** in **heaven**,
Ps	2.4	From his **throne** in **heaven** the **Lord**
	11.4	he has his **throne** in **heaven**.
	103.19	The **Lord** placed his **throne** in **heaven**;
Is	14.13	up to **heaven** and to place your **throne**
	66.1	**Heaven** is my **throne**,
Mt	5.34	swear by **heaven**, for it is God's **throne**;
	23.22	**heaven**, he is swearing by God's **throne**
Acts	7.49	**Heaven** is my **throne**, says the **Lord**,
Col	3.1	**heaven**, where Christ sits on his **throne**
Heb	8.1	**throne** of the Divine Majesty in **heaven**.
Rev	4.2	There in **heaven** was a **throne**

Lord, God

2 Sam	6.2	**Lord** Almighty, who is **enthroned**
1 Kgs	2.24	**Lord**...established me on the **throne**
	22.19	**Lord** sitting on his **throne** in **heaven**,
2 Kgs	19.15	**God** of Israel, **enthroned** above the
1 Chr	13.6	name of the **Lord enthroned** above the
	29.23	**throne** which the **Lord** had established.
2 Chr	18.18	**Lord** sitting on his **throne** in **heaven**,
Ps	2.4	From his **throne** in heaven the **Lord**
	47.5	**God** goes up to his **throne**
	47.8	**God** sits on his sacred **throne**;
	93.2	Your **throne**, O **Lord**, has been firm
	103.19	The **Lord** placed his **throne** in heaven;
Is	8.18	The **Lord** Almighty, whose **throne** is
	37.16	**God** of Israel, **enthroned** above the
	66.1	**Lord** says, "Heaven is my **throne**,
Jer	3.17	be called "The **Throne** of the **Lord**,
Mt	5.34	by heaven, for it is **God's throne**;
	23.22	he is swearing by **God's throne**
Acts	7.49	Heaven is my **throne**, says the **Lord**,
Col	3.1	his **throne** at the right-hand side of **God**.
Heb	4.16	and approach **God's throne**,
Rev	7.10	from our **God**, who sits on the **throne**,
	7.15	why they stand before **God's throne**
	11.16	on their **thrones** in front of **God**
	12.5	and taken to **God** and his **throne**.
	19.4	**God**, who was seated on the **throne**.
	22.1	the **throne** of **God** and of the Lamb
	22.3	The **throne** of **God** and of the Lamb

Praise see **Worship**

Right (hand)

Ps	45.9	**right** of your **throne** stands the queen,
Col	3.1	on his **throne** at the **right-hand** side
Heb	8.1	who sits at the **right** of the **throne**
	12.2	at the **right-hand** side of God's **throne**.
Rev	5.1	**right hand** of the one...on the **throne**
	5.7	**right hand** of the one...on the **throne**.

Worship, Praise

Ps	99.5	**Praise** the Lord our God; **worship** before his **throne**!
	132.7	let us **worship** before his **throne**.
Rev	4.10	sits on the **throne**, and **worship** him
	5.13	the **throne** and to the Lamb, be **praise**
	7.11	in front of the **throne** and **worshipped**
	19.4	**throne**. They said, "Amen! **Praise** God!"
	19.5	from the **throne**...a voice, saying, "**Praise**

TREMBLE

Hab	2.7	—	3.16	x5
1 Sam	13.7	—	16.4	x4
Ex	19.16	—	20.18	x3
Is	13.13	—	15.4	x3
Ezek	26.16 – 18			x3
Dan	10.10 – 16			x3
Joel	2.1	—	3.16	x3

Fear, Afraid, Terrified

Ex	15.14	and they **tremble** with **fear**;
	15.15	are **terrified**; Moab's...men are **trembling**;
	19.16	people in the camp **trembled** with **fear**.
	20.18	they **trembled** with **fear** and stood
Deut	2.25	**afraid** of you. Everyone will **tremble**
1 Sam	13.7	with him were **trembling** with **fear**.
	14.15	soldiers in the camp **trembled** with **fear**;
	15.32	**trembling** with **fear**,
Job	18.20	shudder and **tremble** with **fear**.
	23.15	I **tremble** with **fear** before him.
	26.11	they shake and **tremble** with **fear**.
Ps	4.4	**Tremble** with **fear** and stop sinning;
	55.5	I am gripped by **fear** and **trembling**;
	77.16	they were **afraid**, and...the sea **trembled**.
Is	7.2	were so **terrified** that they **trembled**
	21.4	and I am **trembling** with **fear**.
	32.11	**tremble** with **fear**!
	41.5	are frightened and **tremble** with **fear**.
Jer	5.22	you **fear** me? Why don't you **tremble**
	33.9	**fear** and **tremble** when they hear about
Ezek	12.18	**tremble**...and shake with **fear**
	12.19	They will **tremble**...and shake with **fear**
	26.16	**trembling** on the ground. They will be so **terrified**
	32.10	will **tremble** in **fear** for their own lives.
	38.20	of the earth will **tremble** for **fear** of me.
Dan	5.19	were **afraid** of him and **trembled**.
Mic	7.17	**trembling** and **afraid**.
Nah	2.10	Hearts melt with **fear**; knees **tremble**,
Hab	3.7	saw...Cushan **afraid** and...Midian **tremble**.
	3.16	and I **tremble**; my lips quiver with **fear**.
Mt	28.4	guards were so **afraid** that they **trembled**
Mk	5.33	**trembling** with **fear**,
Acts	7.32	**trembled** with **fear** and dared not look.
1 Cor	2.3	weak and **trembled** all over with **fear**,
2 Cor	7.15	welcomed him with **fear** and **trembling**.
Eph	6.5	human masters with **fear** and **trembling**;
Phil	2.12	with **fear** and **trembling** to complete
Heb	12.21	I am **trembling** and **afraid**!
Jas	2.19	also believe — and **tremble** with **fear**.

Knees

Is	35.3	to **knees** that **tremble** with weakness.
Ezek	21.7	and their **knees** will **tremble**.
Dan	10.10	hands and **knees**; I was still **trembling**.
Nah	2.10	**knees tremble**, strength is gone;
Heb	12.12	and strengthen your **trembling knees**!

Terrified see **Fear**

AV TRIBULATION see PERSECUTION, SUFFERING, TROUBLE

TROUBLE

Prov	10.10	—	17.19	x23
Prov	26.6	—	30.33	x9

Job	2.10	—	6.14	x8
Josh	6.18	—	7.26	x5
Prov	21.23	—	24.8	x5
Acts	14.22	—	17.6	x5
Gen	41.52	—	43.6	x4
Ps	107.6 – 28			x4
Jer	15.11	—	17.17	x4
2 Cor	1.4	—	2.4	x4
2 Cor	6.4	—	8.2	x4
Judg	10.14	—	11.7	x3
1 Sam	1.11	—	2.32	x3
2 Sam	12.11	—	14.10	x3
2 Chr	15.4 – 6			x3
2 Chr	28.19 – 22			x3
Job	10.15	—	12.5	x3
Job	14.1	—	15.35	x3
Job	29.16	—	30.26	x3
Ps	10.1 – 14			x3
Ps	31.7 – 10			x3
Ps	34.6 – 19			x3
Ps	55.3 – 22			x3
Prov	1.26	—	2.12	x3
Is	7.17	—	9.1	x3
Jer	2.24 – 28			x3
Mt	24.6 – 29			x3
Mk	4.17	—	5.34	x3
Mk	13.7 – 24			x3
2 Cor	4.8 – 17			x3
Rev	2.9	—	3.10	x3

Complain

Num	11.1	began to **complain**...about their **troubles**
Job	2.10	we **complain** when he sends us **trouble**?
Ps	142.2	all my **complaints**...all my **troubles**
Prov	23.29	causing **trouble** and always **complaining**.
Is	40.27	you **complain** that the Lord doesn't know your **troubles**

Darkness

Job	30.26	but **trouble** and **darkness** came instead.
Is	8.22	see nothing but **trouble** and **darkness**,
Mt	24.29	after the **trouble**...the sun will grow **dark**
Mk	13.24	time of **trouble** the sun will grow **dark**

Distress

Judg	10.16	he became **troubled** over Israel's **distress**.
2 Chr	15.6	God was bringing **trouble** and **distress**
Jer	15.11	when they were in **trouble** and **distress**.
Ezek	9.4	is **distressed** and **troubled** because of all
Zeph	1.15	a day of **trouble** and **distress**,
2 Cor	2.4	a greatly **troubled** and **distressed** heart

Happy

Job	30.26	for **happiness** and light, but **trouble**
Ps	40.14	who are **happy** because of my **troubles**
	70.2	who are **happy** because of my **troubles**
Prov	27.9	**happier**, but **trouble** shatters your peace
Ecc	7.14	God sends both **happiness** and **trouble**;
Jas	5.13	among you in **trouble**...Is anyone **happy**

Help, Protect

Gen	35.3	**helped** me in the time of my **trouble**
	42.21	the great **trouble**...he begged for **help**,
2 Sam	22.19	was in **trouble**...the Lord **protected** me.
2 Chr	28.20	of **helping** Ahaz...caused him **trouble**.
Neh	9.27	their **trouble** they called to you for **help**,
Ps	4.1	When I was in **trouble**, you **helped** me.
	18.18	was in **trouble**...the Lord **protected** me.
	20.1	**trouble**! May the God of Jacob **protect**
	22.11	**Trouble** is near...there is no one to **help**.
	37.39	**protects** them in times of **trouble**.
	41.1	will **help** them when they are in **trouble**.
	46.1	ready to **help** in times of **trouble**.
	145.14	He **helps** those who are in **trouble**;
Prov	11.8	The righteous are **protected** from **trouble**

Prov	27.10	**trouble**, don't ask your brother for **help**;
Jer	11.14	are in **trouble** and call·to me for **help**,
	16.19	you **help** me in times of **trouble**.
Nah	1.7	**protects** his people in times of **trouble**;
2 Cor	1.4	He **helps** us in all our **troubles**,
Phil	4.14	good of you to **help** me in my **troubles**
1 Tim	5.10	**helped** people in **trouble**, and devoted

Save, Rescue, Safe

Judg	10.14	**rescue** you when you get into **trouble**.
1 Sam	10.19	who **rescues** you from all your **troubles**
1 Kgs	1.29	has **rescued** me from all my **troubles**,
2 Chr	15.5	in **safety**, because there was **trouble**
	20.9	**trouble**, and you would...**rescue** them.
Ps	9.9	a place of **safety** in times of **trouble**.
	25.17	and **save** me from all my **troubles**
	25.22	their **troubles**, O God, **save** your people
	27.5	**trouble** he will shelter me; he will keep me **safe**
	32.7	you will **save** me from **trouble**.
	34.6	he **saves** them from all their **troubles**.
	34.17	he **rescues** them from all their **troubles**.
	34.19	many **troubles**, but the Lord **saves** him
	50.15	me when **trouble** comes; I will **save** you,
	54.7	have **rescued** me from all my **troubles**,
	81.7	**trouble**, you called to me, and I **saved**
	91.15	in **trouble**...I will **rescue** them
	107.6	**trouble** they called to the Lord, and he **saved** them
	107.13	**trouble** they called to the Lord, and he **saved** them
	107.19	**trouble** they called to the Lord, and he **saved** them
	107.28	**trouble** they called to the Lord, and he **saved** them
	138.7	by **troubles**, you keep me **safe**.
	143.11	goodness **save** me from my **troubles**!
Prov	13.13	for **trouble**; follow it and you are **safe**.
Is	25.4	and have been **safe** in times of **trouble**.
	29.22	who **rescued** Abraham from **trouble**,
	33.2	and **save** us in times of **trouble**.
	38.14	**rescue** me from all this **trouble**.
Jer	2.27	**trouble**, you ask me to come and **save**
	2.28	When you are in **trouble**, let them **save**
	17.17	my place of **safety** when **trouble** comes.
Acts	7.10	him **safely** through all his **troubles**.
Rev	3.10	keep you **safe** from the time of **trouble**

TRUE

see also **TRUTH**

Jn	17.3	—	19.36	x10
Dan	8.12	—	11.2	x7
Acts	10.34	—	14.22	x7
Rom	9.4	—	12.1	x7
Mt	11.19	—	15.27	x5
Jn	7.24	—	8.41	x5
Rom	1.9	—	3.4	x5
1 Cor	14.25	—	15.54	x5
1 Jn	5.6 — 20			x5
Mt	1.22	—	2.23	x4
Jn	3.21	—	5.32	x4
1 Sam	1.23	—	3.19	x3
Jer	28.6 — 9			x3
Dan	2.45	—	4.33	x3
Mt	26.54	—	27.9	x3
Lk	1.20 — 45			x3
Lk	4.21	—	5.10	x3
Lk	21.22	—	22.37	x3
Jn	12.38	—	13.18	x3
Eph	3.15	—	5.13	x3
1 Tim	3.1	—	4.9	x3
Rev	2.13	—	3.14	x3
Rev	15.3	—	17.17	x3

Rev	19.2 — 11	x3

Faith

Acts	14.22	them to remain **true** to the **faith**.
1 Tim	1.2	my **true** son in the **faith**:
	4.6	words of **faith** and of the **true** teaching
Tit	1.4	my **true** son in the **faith** that we have
Rev	2.13	**true** to me...did not abandon your **faith**

False see Lie

Grace see Love

Knowledge

Mal	2.7	to teach the **true knowledge** of God.
Rom	1.28	in mind the **true knowledge** about God,
	10.2	is not based on **true knowledge**.
Phil	1.9	**true knowledge** and perfect judgement,

Lie, False

Prov	4.24	isn't **true**. Have nothing to do with **lies**
	8.8	Everything I say is **true**; nothing is **false**
Rom	3.4	**true**, even though every man is a **liar**.
2 Cor	11.13	not **true** apostles — they are **false** apostles, who **lie**
Gal	1.20	is **true**. God knows that I am not **lying**!
1 Jn	2.27	and what he teaches is **true**, not **false**.

Life

Lk	12.15	**true life** is not made up of the things
Jn	17.3	**life** means knowing you, the only **true**
Eph	4.24	itself in the **true life** that is upright
1 Tim	6.19	able to win the **life** which is **true life**.
2 Pet	1.3	**truly** religious **life** through our
1 Jn	5.20	is the **true** God, and this is eternal **life**.

Love, Grace

Acts	14.3	their message about his **grace** was **true**
2 Cor	6.6	by our **true love**,
1 Pet	5.12	this is the **true grace** of God.
1 Jn	3.18	it must be **true love**, which shows itself
2 Jn	.1	whom I **truly love**.
3 Jn	.1	whom I **truly love**.

Prophet, Predict

2 Kgs	3.12	He is a **true prophet**.
2 Chr	36.22	through the **prophet** Jeremiah come **true**.
Ezra	1.1	through the **prophet** Jeremiah come **true**.
Ps	105.19	until what he had **predicted** came **true**.
Is	42.9	things I **predicted** have now come **true**.
	44.26	those plans and **predictions** come **true**.
Jer	28.9	that **prophet's predictions** come **true**.
Ezek	12.23	and the **predictions** are coming **true**!
	33.33	**true**...they will know that a **prophet**
Mt	1.22	said through the **prophet** come **true**,
	2.15	had said through the **prophet** come **true**,
	2.17	**prophet** Jeremiah had said came **true**,
	2.23	what the **prophets** had said came **true**:
	4.14	the **prophet** Isaiah had said come **true**,
	8.17	the **prophet** Isaiah had said come **true**,
	12.17	through the **prophet** Isaiah come **true**,
	13.35	what the **prophet** had said come **true**,
	21.4	what the **prophet** had said come **true**:
	26.56	what the **prophets** wrote...come **true**.
	27.9	the **prophet** Jeremiah had said came **true**
Lk	24.44	of the **prophets**...had to come **true**.
Jn	12.38	**prophet** Isaiah had said might come **true**:
Acts	13.27	made the **prophets'** words come **true**

Saying

Jn	4.37	The **saying** is **true**, 'One man sows,
1 Tim	1.15	This is a **true saying**
	3.1	This is a **true saying**:
	4.9	This is a **true saying**,
2 Tim	2.11	This is a **true saying**:
Tit	3.8	This is a **true saying**.

Spirit of God

Acts	1.16	to come **true** in which the **Holy Spirit**,

2 Cor 6.6 **Holy Spirit**, by our **true** love,
1 Jn 2.27 his **Spirit** teaches you...what he teaches is **true**,
5.6 **Spirit** himself testifies that this is **true**,

Worship

Jn 4.23 offering him the **true worship**
Rom 9.4 they have the **true worship**;
12.1 This is the **true worship**

TRUST

Ps	119.42 – 86		x5
Ps	25.2 – 21		x4
Ps	115.8 – 11		x4
Prov	11.3 – 13		x4
Is	25.9 —	26.4	x4
Is	30.2 – 18		x4
Jer	48.7 —	50.7	x4
Phil	2.24 —	3.4	x4
2 Kgs	17.14 —	19.10	x3
Ps	22.4 – 5		x3
Ps	27.3 – 14		x3
Ps	31.6 – 19		x3
Ps	37.3 – 9		x3
Ps	56.3 – 11		x3
Ps	78.7 – 32		x3
Prov	2.15 —	3.29	x3
Prov	13.15 —	14.22	x3
Is	48.8 —	50.10	x3
Jer	11.19 —	13.25	x3

God

2 Kgs 17.14 had not **trusted** in the Lord their **God**.
18.5 **trusted** in the Lord, the **God** of Israel;
1 Chr 5.20 They put their **trust** in **God**
2 Chr 20.20 Put your **trust** in the Lord your **God**
Ezra 8.22 **God** blesses everyone who **trusts** him,
Job 4.18 **God** does not **trust** his heavenly
15.15 **God** does not **trust** even his angels;
22.26 you will always **trust** in **God** and find
Ps 25.2 in you, my **God**, I **trust**.
27.3 attack me, I will still **trust God**.
56.4 I **trust** in **God** and am not afraid;
62.8 **Trust** in **God** at all times, my people.
78.7 put their **trust** in **God** and not forget
78.8 whose **trust** in **God** was never firm
Is 10.20 put their **trust** in the Lord, Israel's holy **God**.
Dan 6.23 hurt at all, for he **trusted God**.
Hos 12.6 **trust** in your **God** and return
Mt 27.43 He **trusts** in **God** and claims to be **God's** Son.
Acts 27.25 I **trust** in **God** that it will be just
Rom 3.2 **God trusted** his message to the Jews.
1 Cor 1.9 **God** is to be **trusted**, the **God** who
Heb 2.13 says, "I will put my **trust** in **God**.
10.23 we can **trust God** to keep his promise.
11.11 He **trusted God** to keep his promise.

Hope

Ps 62.10 **trust** in violence; don't **hope** to gain
71.5 my **hope** in you; I have **trusted** in you
Is 8.17 I **trust** him and place my **hope** in him.
Heb 10.23 **hope** we profess, because we can **trust**

Lord

see also **God**

Gen 15.6 Abram put his **trust** in the **Lord**,
Deut 1.32 you still would not **trust** the **Lord**,
Ps 4.5 to the **Lord**, and put your **trust** in him.
9.10 who know you, **Lord**, will **trust** you;
11.1 I **trust** in the **Lord** for safety.
12.6 promises of the **Lord** can be **trusted**;
20.7 but we **trust** in the power of the **Lord**
21.7 The king **trusts** in the **Lord** Almighty;

Ps 27.14 **Trust** in the **Lord**.
27.14 **Trust** in the **Lord**.
31.14 But my **trust** is in you, O **Lord**;
32.10 but those who **trust** in the **Lord** are
37.3 **Trust** in the **Lord** and do good;
37.9 Those who **trust** in the **Lord** will
38.15 But I **trust** in you, O **Lord**;
40.3 and will put their **trust** in the **Lord**.
40.4 Happy are those who **trust** the **Lord**,
56.3 O **Lord** Almighty, I put my **trust** in
69.6 those who **trust** in you, Sovereign **Lord**
84.12 **Lord**...those who **trust** in you!
112.7 and he **trusts** in the **Lord**.
115.9 **Trust** in the **Lord**, you people of Israel.
115.10 **Trust** in the **Lord**, you priests of God.
115.11 **Trust** in the **Lord**, all you that worship
118.8 It is better to **trust** in the **Lord**
118.9 It is better to **trust** in the **Lord**
125.1 Those who **trust** in the **Lord** are like
130.7 Israel, **trust** in the **Lord**,
131.3 **trust** in the **Lord** now and for ever!
141.8 But I keep **trusting** in you...Lord
Prov 3.5 **Trust** in the **Lord** with all your heart.
16.20 **trust** in the **Lord** and you will be
20.22 **Trust** the **Lord** and he will make it
22.19 to put your **trust** in the **Lord**;
28.25 are much better off to **trust** the **Lord**.
29.25 but if you **trust** the **Lord**, you are safe.
Is 26.4 **Trust** in the **Lord** for ever;
30.18 those who put their **trust** in the **Lord**.
40.31 those who **trust** in the **Lord** for help
49.4 I can **trust** the **Lord** to defend
50.10 but **trust** in the **Lord**,
Jer 50.7 Their ancestors **trusted** in the **Lord**,
Zeph 3.2 It has not put its **trust** in the **Lord**
Acts 14.23 **Lord**, in whom they had put their **trust**.
Phil 2.24 And I **trust** in the **Lord** that I myself

Promise see **Word**

Safety, Save

Ps 11.1 I **trust** in the Lord for **safety**.
16.1 I **trust** in you for **safety**.
22.4 they **trusted** you, and you **saved** them.
25.2 I **trust**. **Save** me from the shame
25.5 who **saves** me. I always **trust** in you.
44.6 **trust** in my bow or in my sword to **save**
52.7 God for **safety**, but **trusted** instead
86.2 **save** me, for...I **trust** in you.
119.81 **save** me; I place my **trust** in your word.
144.2 in whom I **trust** for **safety**.
146.3 **trust** in human leaders; no human being can **save**
Prov 29.25 but if you **trust** the Lord, you are **safe**.

Strength

Is 40.31 **trust** in the Lord for help will find their **strength**
Jer 17.5 puts his **trust** in man, in the **strength**
48.7 you **trusted** in your **strength**
Ezek 22.6 leaders **trust** in their own **strength**

Word, Promise

Ps 12.6 **promises** of the Lord can be **trusted**;
119.42 because I **trust** in your **word**.
119.74 because I **trust** in your **promise**.
119.81 I place my **trust** in your **word**.
130.5 and in his **word** I **trust**.
Jer 7.8 you put your **trust** in deceitful **words**.
12.6 Do not **trust** them, even though they speak friendly **words**.
Heb 10.23 we can **trust** God to keep his **promise**.
11.11 He **trusted** God to keep his **promise**.
Rev 21.5 these **words** are true and can be **trusted**.
22.6 **words** are true and can be **trusted**.

TRUTH

see also **TRUE**

Jn	3.3	—	10.24	x27
Jn	12.24	—	19.35	x21
1 Jn	1.8	—	5.6	x9
2 Tim	2.15	—	4.4	x8
Eph	4.15	—	6.14	x6
1 Tim	2.4	—	4.3	x6
Judg	16.10 – 18			x5
1 Cor	12.1	—	15.51	x5
3 Jn	.3 – 12			x5
Rom	1.18	—	3.7	x4
2 Thes	2.10 – 15			x4
2 Jn	.1 – 4			x4
Ps	119.18 – 160			x3
Prov	22.12	—	23.23	x3
Is	43.9	—	45.19	x3
Jer	8.6	—	9.5	x3
Jn	1.14 – 51			x3
2 Cor	6.7	—	7.14	x3
2 Cor	11.10	—	13.8	x3
Tit	1.1 – 14			x3
Jas	3.14	—	5.19	x3
Rev	19.10	—	20.4	x3

Believe

Jn 8.45 the **truth**, and that is why you do not **believe** me.

   8.46 the **truth**, then why do you not **believe**

2 Thes 2.12 that all who have not **believed** the.**truth**

2 Tim 3.14 the **truths** that you were taught and firmly **believe**.

Christ, Jesus

Jn 1.17 grace and **truth** came through **Jesus**

   14.6 **Jesus** answered him, "I am...the **truth**,

1 Cor 15.20 the **truth** is that **Christ** has been raised

2 Cor 11.10 By **Christ's truth** in me,

Eph 4.21 were taught the **truth** that is in **Jesus**.

1 Jn 2.8 because its **truth** is seen in **Christ**

   2.20 **Christ**, and so all of you know the **truth**.

Rev 1.2 and the **truth** revealed by **Jesus Christ**.

   1.9 and the **truth** that **Jesus** revealed.

   12.17 faithful to the **truth** revealed by **Jesus**.

   19.10 hold to the **truth** that **Jesus** revealed.

   19.10 For the **truth** that **Jesus** revealed

   20.4 the **truth** that **Jesus** revealed

Life

Prov 12.19 A lie has a short **life**, but **truth** lives on

   14.25 saves **lives** when he tells the **truth**

Jn 14.6 the **truth**, and the **life**;

Message see Word

Save

Prov 14.25 **saves** lives when he tells the **truth**

2 Thes 2.10 and love the **truth** so as to be **saved**.

1 Tim 2.4 **saved** and to come to know the **truth**.

Word, Message

Job 33.3 my **words** are sincere, and I am speaking the **truth**.

Prov 22.12 **truth** is kept safe by disproving the **words** of liars.

Is 43.9 to testify to the **truth** of their **words**.

Jn 3.33 his **message** confirms by this that God is **truthful**.

   17.17 means of the **truth**; your **word** is **truth**.

1 Cor 2.1 secret **truth**, I did not use big **words**

2 Cor 6.7 our **message** of **truth**, and by the power

1 Tim 2.7 proclaim the **message** of faith and **truth**.

2 Tim 2.15 teaches the **message** of God's **truth**.

Jas	1.18	us into being through the **word** of truth
Rev	1.2	**message** from God and the **truth**
	1.9	God's **word** and the **truth** that Jesus
	20.4	**truth** that Jesus revealed and the **word**

TURN

Jer	2.5	—	6.8	x21
Jer	12.8	—	18.17	x11
Job	34.15	—	39.22	x10
Acts	13.8	—	17.30	x10
Lev	13.3 – 26			x9
Ex	7.9	—	8.17	x8
Josh	18.14	—	19.34	x8
Judg	18.21	—	20.48	x8
Rev	1.12	—	3.19	x7
Rev	8.8	—	11.6	x7
Lev	26.11 – 41			x6
Ezek	38.4	—	39.29	x6
Mal	1.13	—	3.7	x6
Mt	9.22	—	13.15	x6
Acts	2.20	—	4.11	x6
Heb	10.38	—	12.25	x6
1 Kgs	11.3 – 26			x5
Josh	15.3 – 11			x4
Josh	8.5 – 21			x3
2 Chr	18.31 – 33			x3
Neh	9.26 – 35			x3
Ps	78.6 – 44			x3
Is	50.2 – 5			x3
Jer	8.4 – 5			x3
Jer	36.3 – 16			x3
Ezek	14.5 – 7			x3
Dan	11.18 – 30			x3
Rev	16.4 – 11			x3

Baptize

Mk 1.4 **Turn** away from your sins and be **baptized**,

Lk 3.3 **Turn** away from your sins and be **baptized**,

Acts 2.38 **turn** away from his sins and be **baptized**

   13.24 **turn** from their sins and be **baptized**.

   19.4 The **baptism** of John was for those who **turned** from

Believe, Trust

Ps 40.4 who **trust** the Lord, who do not **turn**

   73.10 people **turn** to them and eagerly **believe**

Jer 17.5 **turns** away from me and puts his **trust**

Mk 1.15 **Turn** away from your sins and **believe**

Acts 11.21 people **believed** and **turned** to the Lord.

   14.2 **believe** stirred up the Gentiles and **turned** them against the **believers**.

   20.21 **turn** from their sins to God and **believe**

Heb 6.1 **turning** away from useless works and **believing** in God;

   10.38 will **believe** and live; but if any of them **turns** back,

Blood

Ex 4.9 The water will **turn** into **blood**.

   7.17 and the water will be **turned** into **blood**.

   7.20 the water in it was **turned** into **blood**.

Lev 17.10 **blood** still in it, the Lord will **turn**

Ps 78.44 He **turned** the rivers into **blood**,

   105.29 He **turned** their rivers into **blood**

Joel 2.31 and the moon will **turn** red as **blood**,

Acts 2.20 and the moon will **turn** red as **blood**,

Rev 6.12 moon **turned** completely red like **blood**.

   8.8 third of the sea was **turned** into **blood**,

   11.6 to **turn** them into **blood**;

   16.4 and they **turned** into **blood**.

Darkness, Brightness, Light, Night

Job 3.4 **Turn** that day into **darkness**, God.

   30.30 My skin has **turned** dark

Ps	139.11	the light round me to turn into night,
Is	5.20	You turn darkness into light
	42.16	I will turn their darkness into light
	50.3	I can make the sky turn dark,
	58.10	darkness around you will turn to the brightness
Jer	13.16	before he turns into deep darkness
	15.9	Her daylight has turned to darkness;
Amos	5.8	He turns darkness into daylight,
Acts	26.18	turn them from the darkness to the light
Jas	1.17	change or cause darkness by turning.

Evil, Wicked

Gen	50.20	evil against me, but God turned it
Deut	9.12	evil. They have already turned away
1 Sam	12.20	an evil thing, do not turn away from
1 Kgs	13.33	Israel still did not turn from his evil
2 Chr	7.14	turn away from the evil they have been
Job	28.28	you must turn from evil.
	36.10	to turn away from evil.
	36.21	Be careful not to turn to evil;
Ps	34.14	Turn away from evil and do good;
	37.27	Turn away from evil and do good,
Prov	13.19	people refuse to turn away from evil.
Jer	2.19	evil will punish you, and your turning
	18.8	but then that nation turns from its evil,
	25.5	to turn from your wicked way of life
	33.5	turned...from this city because of the evil
	36.3	they will turn from their evil ways.
	36.7	and turn from their evil ways,
Ezek	18.30	Turn away from all the evil you are
	39.24	and their wickedness, and I turned away
Acts	3.26	of you turn away from his wicked ways.
	13.10	evil tricks, and you...keep trying to turn
	17.30	to turn away from their evil ways.
Heb	3.12	evil and unbelieving that he will turn
1 Pet	3.11	must turn away from evil and do good;
Rev	16.11	they did not turn from their evil ways.

Forgive, Mercy

Deut	13.17	will turn from his fierce anger and show you mercy.
Ps	25.16	Turn to me, Lord, and be merciful to
	86.16	Turn to me and have mercy on me;
	119.132	Turn to me and have mercy on me
Is	55.7	turn to the Lord, our God; he is merciful
Jer	36.3	turn from their evil ways...I will forgive
Hos	14.3	mercy to those who have no one else to turn to.
Mk	4.12	turn to God, and he would forgive
Acts	3.19	turn to God, so that he will forgive

Gods, Idols, Serve, Worship

Lev	19.29	turn to other gods and the land will be
Deut	8.19	or turn to other gods to worship
	11.28	turn away to worship other gods
	29.18	turns from the Lord...to worship
	31.20	will turn away and worship other gods.
Josh	24.20	foreign gods, he will turn against you
1 Sam	8.8	turned away from me and worshipped
	12.10	turned away from you, Lord, and worshipped
	12.20	turn away from the Lord, but serve him
1 Kgs	11.9	gods, Solomon did not obey...but turned
Neh	9.35	failed to turn from sin and serve you.
Ps	40.4	who do not turn to idols or join those who worship
Jer	2.5	turn away from me? They worshipped
	2.36	yourself by turning to the gods
	5.19	turned...from me and served foreign gods
	8.5	turning back? You cling to your idols
	16.11	turned away from me and worshipped
Ezek	14.5	idols have turned the Israelites away

Ezek	14.6	Turn back and leave your...idols.
	14.7	turns away from me and worships idols,
Hos	3.1	even though they turn to other gods
	4.10	turned...from me to follow other gods.
	7.16	keep on turning away from me to a god
Acts	7.42	turned away from them and gave them over to worship
1 Thes	1.9	you turned away from idols to God,

Heal

Is	6.10	they might turn to me and be healed.
	19.22	will heal them. They will turn to him,
Jer	3.22	turned...from the Lord; he will heal you
Mt	13.15	turn to me, says God, and I would heal
Jn	12.40	turn to me, says God, for me to heal
Acts	28.27	turn to me, says God, and I would heal

Heart

Deut	30.2	will turn back...and with all your heart
	30.10	have to turn to him with all your heart.
1 Sam	7.3	turn to the Lord with all your hearts,
2 Chr	20.33	not turn wholeheartedly to the worship
Ps	42.6	my heart is breaking, and so I turn
Jer	32.40	heart, so that they will never turn away
Heb	3.12	a heart so evil...that he will turn

Help

2 Chr	16.12	he did not turn to the Lord for help,
Job	6.13	there is nowhere I can turn for help.
	29.12	I helped...orphans who had nowhere to turn.
Ps	27.9	don't turn your servant away. You have been my help;
Is	17.7	will turn for help to their Creator,
Jer	18.17	turn my back on them; I will not help

Idols see Gods

Law

2 Sam	22.22	law of the Lord; I have not turned
Neh	9.26	they turned their backs on your Law.
Ps	18.21	law of the Lord; I have not turned
Mal	3.7	have turned away from my laws

Light see Darkness

Mercy see Forgive

Night see Darkness

Punish

Lev	26.24	I will turn on you and punish you
	26.28	turn on you and...make your punishment
Josh	24.20	will turn against you and punish you.
Ezra	8.22	punishes anyone who turns away from
Jer	2.19	evil will punish you, and your turning

Rebel

Neh	9.26	rebelled and disobeyed you; they turned
Is	50.5	I have not rebelled or turned away
Jer	5.23	rebellious; you have turned aside
Ezek	2.3	rebelled and turned against me

Reject

Ps	88.14	you reject me, Lord? Why do you turn
Jer	15.6	have rejected me; you have turned

Repent

2 Chr	7.14	repent and turn away from the evil
Ps	78.34	would turn to him; they would repent
Acts	3.19	Repent, then, and turn to God
	26.20	repent of their sins and turn to God

Right, Wrong

Job	31.7	If I have turned from the right path
Prov	4.26	whatever you do will turn out right.
Dan	9.5	have turned away from what...was right.
Amos	6.12	turn...right into wrong.
Mic	3.9	hate justice and turn right into wrong.
Mal	2.8	priests have turned away from the right

Rom 3.12 **turned** away from God; they have all gone **wrong;**
2 Tim 2.19 must **turn** away from **wrongdoing.**
Jas 5.20 **turns** a sinner back from his **wrong** way

Save
Job 6.13 **save** myself; there is nowhere I can **turn**
Is 45.22 **Turn** to me now and be **saved,**
59.20 **save** all of you that **turn** from your
Jas 5.20 **turns** a sinner back from his wrong way will **save**

Serve see **Gods**

Shame
Is 3.24 their beauty will be **turned** to **shame!**
Zeph 3.19 I will **turn** their **shame** to honour,

Sin
Neh 9.35 but they failed to **turn** from **sin**
Is 59.20 all of you that **turn** from your **sins.**
Jer 5.3 and would not **turn** from your **sins.**
Ezek 18.32 **Turn** away from your **sins** and live.
Mt 3.2 **Turn** away from your **sins,**" he said,
3.8 you have **turned** from your **sins.**
4.17 **Turn** away from your **sins,** because
11.20 did not **turn** from their **sins,**
11.21 that they had **turned** from their **sins!**
12.41 because they **turned** from their **sins**
Mk 1.4 **Turn** away from your **sins** and be
1.15 **Turn** away from your **sins**
6.12 should **turn** away from their **sins.**
Lk 3.3 preaching. "**Turn** away from your **sins**
3.8 that you have **turned** from your **sins,**
10.13 that they had **turned** from their **sins!**
11.32 because they **turned** from their **sins**
13.3 if you do not **turn** from your **sins,**
13.5 if you do not **turn** from your **sins,**
16.30 then they would **turn** from their **sins.**
Acts 2.38 of you must **turn** away from his **sins**
13.24 **turn** from their **sins** and be baptized.
19.4 for those who **turned** from their **sins;**
20.21 should **turn** from their **sins** to God
Jas 5.20 whoever **turns** a **sinner** back from
2 Pet 3.9 to **turn** away from their **sins.**
Rev 2.5 **Turn** from your **sins** and do what you
2.5 If you don't **turn** from your **sins,**
2.16 Now **turn** from your **sins!**
3.3 obey it and **turn** from your **sins.**
3.19 earnest, then, and **turn** from your **sins.**
16.9 they would not **turn** from their **sins**

Strengthen
Ps 86.16 **Turn** to me and...**strengthen** me
Lk 22.32 **turn** back to me, you must **strengthen**

Trouble
2 Chr 15.4 **trouble** came, they **turned** to the Lord,
Job 4.5 Now it's your **turn** to be in **trouble,**
Ps 40.14 **troubles** be **turned** back and disgraced.
70.2 **troubles** be **turned** back and disgraced.
102.2 When I am in **trouble,** don't **turn** away
Nah 1.7 **trouble;** he takes care of those who **turn**
Acts 15.19 **trouble** the Gentiles who are **turning** to

Trust see **Believe**

Wicked see **Evil**

Words
Ps 17.6 so **turn** to me and listen to my **words.**
1 Cor 9.15 **turn** my rightful boast into empty **words!**
2 Cor 9.3 may not **turn** out to be empty **words.**

Worship see **Gods**

Wrong see **Right**

UNDERSTANDING

Ps	119.27 – 169			x8
Prov	1.2	—	4.22	x8
Dan	8.15	—	10.14	x8
Mt	13.13 – 51			x6
Mt	15.10	—	17.13	x6
Mk	6.52	—	9.32	x6
Jn	12.16	—	13.28	x6
Prov	28.5	—	30.18	x4
Is	39.8	—	41.20	x4
Dan	12.4 – 10			x4
Mk	4.12 – 33			x4
Acts	7.25	—	8.31	x4
1 Cor	13.2	—	14.19	x4
Neh	8.2 – 12			x3
Job	28.12 – 28			x3
Ecc	7.3	—	8.17	x3
Is	5.12	—	6.10	x3
Is	27.11	—	29.24	x3
2 Cor	1.13			x3

Christ, Jesus
Jn 8.27 did not **understand** that **Jesus** was
13.28 **understood** why **Jesus** said this to him.
1 Cor 11.3 to **understand** that **Christ** is supreme
Eph 3.4 **understanding** of the secret of **Christ.**
5.32 I **understand** as applying to **Christ**

Commands see **Laws**

Help
Ps 119.27 **Help** me to **understand** your laws,
119.169 **help** reach you...Give me **understanding,**
Dan 9.22 to **help** you **understand** the prophecy.

Jesus see **Christ**

Laws, Commands
Ps 19.8 The **commands** of the Lord...give **understanding**
119.27 **Help** me to **understand** your **laws,**
119.32 **commands**...you will give me more **understanding.**
119.73 **understanding**...I may learn your **laws.**

Love
Jer 9.24 **understands** me, because my **love**
Eph 3.18 power to **understand**...Christ's **love.**
2 Thes 3.5 a greater **understanding** of God's **love**

Message see **Words**

Parable see **Words**

Prophets
Is 28.7 **prophets** are too drunk to **understand**
Acts 13.27 **understand** the words of the **prophets**

Scripture
Lk 24.45 their minds to **understand** the **Scriptures**
Jn 20.9 still did not **understand** the **scripture**
Eph 5.32 this **scripture,** which I **understand** as

Spirit of God
Col 1.9 and **understanding** that his **Spirit** gives.

Turn
Job 28.28 To **understand,** you must **turn** from evil.
Is 6.10 **understand.** If they did, they might **turn**
50.5 **understanding,** and I have not...**turned**
Mt 13.15 would **understand,** and they would **turn**
Mk 4.12 **understand**...if they did, they would **turn**
Jn 12.40 **understand,** and they would not **turn**
Acts 28.27 would **understand,** and they would **turn**

Wisdom
Deut 1.13 Choose some **wise, understanding,**
4.6 **wisdom** and **understanding** this great
1 Kgs 3.12 you more **wisdom** and **understanding**

2 Chr	2.12	David a **wise** son, full of **understanding**		
Job	28.12	**wisdom** be found? Where can we learn to **understand**?		
	28.20	source of **wisdom**? Where can we learn to **understand**?		
Prov	1.2	**wisdom** and good advice, and **understand**		
	2.2	to what is **wise** and try to **understand**		
	2.6	**wisdom**; from him come knowledge and **understanding**.		
	3.13	**wise** — who gains **understanding**.		
	16.21	**wise**, mature person is known for his **understanding**		
	24.3	of **wisdom** and **understanding**.		
Jer	3.15	you with **wisdom** and **understanding**.		
	9.12	Who is **wise** enough to **understand** this?		
Dan	2.21	he who gives **wisdom** and **understanding**.		
	12.10	only those who are **wise** will **understand**.		
Hos	14.9	May those who are **wise understand**		
1 Cor	1.19	**wisdom** of the **wise** and set aside the **understanding**		
Col	1.9	with all the **wisdom** and **understanding**		
Jas	3.13	you who is **wise** and **understanding**		
Rev	17.9	This calls for **wisdom** and **understanding**		

Words, Message, Parable

Jer	23.18	ever heard or **understood** his **message**,
Dan	10.1	The **message** was true but extremely hard to **understand**.
Mt	13.19	**message** about the Kingdom but do not **understand**
	13.23	who hear the **message** and **understand** it:
Mk	4.13	Don't you **understand** this **parable**?
Jn	10.6	**parable**, but they did not **understand**
Acts	13.27	**understand** the **words** of the prophets
1 Cor	14.19	five **words** that can be **understood**,
1 Tim	1.7	they do not **understand** their own **words**

UNFAITHFUL

Jer		3.6 – 20		x8
Ezek	14.13	—	18.24	x5
Deut	31.16	—	32.51	x4
Num		5.6 – 12		x3
2 Chr	29.6	—	30.7	x3
Hos	4.15	—	5.7	x3

God see Lord

Gods, Worship

Ex	34.16	**unfaithful**...and to **worship**...pagan **gods**.
Lev	20.5	**unfaithful** to me and **worshipping**
Judg	2.17	**unfaithful**...and **worshipped** other **gods**.
	8.33	again **unfaithful** to God and **worshipped**

Lord, God

Lev	17.7	no longer be **unfaithful** to the **Lord**
Num	5.6	When anyone is **unfaithful** to the **Lord**
	31.16	to be **unfaithful** to the **Lord**.
Judg	2.17	Israel was **unfaithful** to the **Lord**
	8.33	Israel were again **unfaithful** to God
1 Chr	5.25	the people were **unfaithful** to the God
	10.13	because he was **unfaithful** to the **Lord**.
2 Chr	21.13	into being **unfaithful** to God,
	29.6	Our ancestors were **unfaithful** to...God
	29.19	those years he was **unfaithful** to God,
	30.7	were **unfaithful** to the **Lord** their God.
Ps	106.39	and were **unfaithful** to God.
Jer	23.10	full of people **unfaithful** to the **Lord**;
Hos	5.7	They have been **unfaithful** to the **Lord**;
	9.1	God and have been **unfaithful** to him.

Turn

Jer	3.6	that **unfaithful** woman, has done? She has **turned**
Hos	9.1	**turned** away from your God and have been **unfaithful**

Worship see Gods

UNION

1 Jn	2.5	—	5.20	x18
Eph	1.1	—	3.12	x10
Col	1.2	—	2.11	x6
Gal	2.4	—	3.28	x5
Phil	3.1	—	4.10	x5
2 Tim	1.1	—	3.12	x4
Rom	6.3 – 23			x3
1 Cor	1.2 – 30			x3
1 Cor	4.10 – 17			x3
1 Cor	15.22 – 31			x3

Christ, Death, Jesus, Lord

Rom	6.3	baptized into **union** with **Christ**
	6.3	into **union** with his **death**
	6.23	eternal life in **union** with **Christ**
	8.1	who live in **union** with **Christ**
	8.2	brings us life in **union** with **Christ**
	12.5	we are one body in **union** with **Christ**,
	14.14	My **union** with the Lord **Jesus**
	15.17	In **union** with **Christ Jesus**,
1 Cor	1.2	belong...in **union** with **Christ**
	1.5	**union** with **Christ** you have become rich
	1.30	into **union** with **Christ Jesus**,
	4.10	but you are wise in **union** with **Christ**!
	4.15	in your life in **union** with **Christ**
	4.17	the new life in **union** with **Christ**
	9.2	your life in **union** with the **Lord**
	15.22	because of their **union** with **Christ**.
	15.31	in our life in **union** with **Christ**
2 Cor	1.21	sure of our life in **union** with **Christ**;
	2.14	in **union** with **Christ** we are...led
Gal	2.4	through our **union** with **Christ**
	2.17	by our **union** with **Christ**,
	3.26	God's sons in **union** with **Christ**
	3.27	were baptized into **union** with **Christ**
	3.28	all one in **union** with **Christ**
	5.6	when we are in **union** with **Christ**
	5.10	Our life in **union** with the **Lord**
Eph	1.1	their life in **union** with **Christ**
	1.3	in our **union** with **Christ** he has blessed
	1.4	be his through our **union** with **Christ**,
	1.11	own people in **union** with **Christ**
	2.6	In our **union** with **Christ Jesus**
	2.10	and in our **union** with **Christ Jesus**
	2.13	in **union** with **Christ Jesus**,
	3.12	**union** with **Christ** and through our faith
	6.10	strength in **union** with the **Lord**
Phil	1.1	who are in **union** with **Christ Jesus**
	1.26	in your life in **union** with **Christ**
	3.3	in our life in **union** with **Christ**
	4.7	safe in **union** with **Christ**
Col	1.2	faithful brothers in **union** with **Christ**:
	1.17	**Christ** existed before all things, and in **union** with him
	1.28	mature individual in **union** with **Christ**.
	2.6	accepted **Christ**...live in **union**
	2.11	**union** with **Christ** you were circumcised
1 Thes	5.18	your life in **union** with **Christ**
1 Tim	1.14	which are ours in **union** with **Christ**
2 Tim	1.1	which we have in **union** with **Christ**
	1.13	that are ours in **union** with **Christ**
	2.1	that is ours in **union** with **Christ**
	3.12	godly life in **union** with **Christ**
Phlm	.6	have in our life in **union** with **Christ**.
1 Pet	5.10	his eternal glory in **union** with **Christ**,
1 Jn	2.27	remain in **union** with **Christ**.
	3.6	everyone who lives in **union** with **Christ**
	5.20	in **union** with his Son **Jesus Christ**.

God

1 Jn	2.5	sure that we are in **union** with **God**;

238

1 Jn 2.6 he remains in **union** with **God**
      3.24 lives in **union** with **God**
      3.24 and **God** lives in **union** with him.
      3.24 we know that **God** lives in **union** with
      4.12 **God** lives in **union** with us,
      4.13 sure that we live in **union** with **God** and that
            he lives in **union** with us,
      4.15 he lives in **union** with **God**
      4.15 and **God** lives in **union** with him.
      4.16 lives in love lives in **union** with **God**
      4.16 and **God** lives in **union** with him.
      5.20 We live in **union** with the true **God**

God's People
1 Cor 1.2 **people**, who belong to him in **union**
Eph   1.11 be **his** own **people** in **union** with Christ
Phil   1.1 **people** in Philippi who are in **union**

Jesus see Christ

Lord see Christ

Spirit of God
Rom   8.2 **Spirit**, which brings us life in **union**
Phil   3.3 **Spirit** and rejoice in our life in **union**
1 Jn 4.13 in **union** with us, because he has given us his
            Spirit.

Sure
2 Cor 1.21 **sure** of our life in **union** with Christ;
1 Jn   2.5 **sure** that we are in **union** with **God**:
       4.13 **sure** that we live in **union** with **God**

UNIVERSE

	Gen	1.1	—	2.4	x4
	Col	1.16	—	2.20	x4

God
Gen   1.1   **God** created the **universe**,
      2.4   the Lord **God** made the **universe**,
Col 1.16   **God** created the whole **universe**
     1.20   **God** decided to bring the whole **universe**
Heb   1.2   through whom **God** created the **universe**,
      1.3   **God's** own being, sustaining the **universe**
     11.3   **universe** was created by **God's** word,

VICTORY

	Rev	2.7	—	3.21	x10
	Josh	8.1	—	11.8	x9
	Judg	1.4	—	5.11	x9
	1 Sam	14.6 – 47			x7
	2 Sam	22.40	—	23.12	x7
	Judg	11.9	—	12.3	x6
	Judg	7.2 – 15			x5
	Is	45.8	—	46.13	x5
	Is	61.10	—	63.5	x5
	Ex	14.4	—	15.21	x4
	2 Sam	18.28	—	19.24	x4
	Ps	18.39 – 50			x4
	Ps	20.5 – 9			x4
	Ps	118.15 – 24			x4
	Is	51.5	—	52.7	x4
	Judg	15.18	—	16.24	x3
	2 Sam	8.6 – 14			x3
	1 Kgs	22.6 – 15			x3
	1 Chr	18.6 – 13			x3
	2 Chr	18.5 – 14			x3
	Ps	89.17 – 42			x3
	Ps	98.1 – 3			x3
	Zech	9.9	—	10.7	x3
	1 Cor	15.54 – 57			x3

Death
1 Cor 15.54 **Death** is destroyed; **victory** is complete!
      15.55 Where, **Death**, is your **victory**?
Rev   2.11 who win the **victory** will not be hurt by the
             second **death**.

God's People
Judg   5.11 the **victories** of Israel's **people**!
1 Sam 17.47 **his people**. He is **victorious** in battle,
Ps   118.15 of **victory** in the tents of **God's people**:
     149.4   pleasure in **his people**; he honours the humble
             with **victory**.
     149.9   This is the **victory** of **God's people**.

Happy, Joy
2 Sam 19.2 **joy** of **victory** was turned into sadness
Esth 8.16 **happiness** and a sense of **victory**.
Ps   14.7 **victory** will come to Israel...How **happy**
      20.5 we will shout for **joy** over your **victory**
      53.6 **victory** will come to Israel...How **happy**
     118.24 of the Lord's **victory**; let us be **happy**,
Lam   2.17 gave our enemies **victory**, gave them **joy**
1 Thes 2.19 our **joy**, and our reason for boasting of our
             victory

Love
2 Sam 22.51 **victories** to his king; he shows...**love**
Ps   18.50 **victories** to his king; he shows...**love**
      89.17 You give us great **victories**; in your **love**
Rom   8.37 **victory** through him who **loved** us!

Power see Strength

Praise
Gen 14.20 **victory** over your enemies, be **praised**!
Judg 16.24 **praise** to their god: "Our god has given us
            victory
2 Sam 18.28 **Praise** the Lord your God, who has given you
             victory
Job 40.14 **praise** you...that you won the **victory**
Ps   20.5 your **victory** and celebrate...by **praising**

Save
1 Sam 17.47 to **save** his people. He is **victorious**
Ps   33.17 **victory**; their great strength cannot **save**.
      65.5 us **victory** and you do wonderful things to **save**
            us.
      98.2 his **victory**; he made his **saving** power
Is   45.17 is **saved** by the Lord, and her **victory**
      51.5 and **save** them; the time of my **victory**
      62.1 she is **saved**, And her **victory** shines
      63.1 to **save**, coming to announce his **victory**.

Strength, Power
2 Sam 22.40 me **strength** for the battle and **victory**
2 Chr 25.8 who has the **power** to give **victory**
Job 12.16 God is **strong** and always **victorious**;
Ps   18.39 me **strength** for the battle and **victory**
      20.6 his **power** gives him great **victories**.
      21.1 **strength**...you made him **victorious**.
      24.8 **strong** and mighty, the Lord, **victorious**
      33.17 **victory**; their great **strength** cannot save.
      45.4 **strength** will win you great **victories**!
      98.1 holy **strength** he has won the **victory**.
      98.2 **victory**; he made his saving **power**
     110.7 **strengthened**, he will stand **victorious**.
     118.16 His **power** has brought us **victory**
Is   45.24 are **victory** and **strength** to be found;
      59.16 his own **power**...to win the **victory**.
      63.1 **powerful**...coming to announce his **victory**.
      63.5 made me **strong**, and I won the **victory**
Zeph 3.17 his **power** gives you **victory**.
1 Cor 15.55 **victory**? Where, Death, is your **power**

Triumph
Ps   20.5 your **victory** and celebrate your **triumph**
      89.17 **victories**...you make us **triumphant**.
Is   41.2 **triumphant** wherever he goes? Who gives him
            victory
      46.13 the day of **victory** near ...My **triumph**
Zech   9.9 He comes **triumphant** and **victorious**,

Win

Ex	15.1	because he has **won** a glorious **victory**;
	15.21	because he has **won** a glorious **victory**;
1 Sam	14.45	who **won** this great **victory** for Israel,
	19.5	the Lord **won** a great **victory** for Israel.
2 Sam	23.10	The Lord **won** a great **victory** that day.
	23.12	The Lord **won** a great **victory** that day.
1 Kgs	22.12	**win**," they said. "The Lord will give you **victory**.
	22.15	**win**. The Lord will give you **victory**.
2 Kgs	13.17	arrow, with which he will **win victory**
	13.19	you would have **won** complete **victory**
2 Chr	18.11	**win**," they said. "The Lord will give you **victory**.
	18.14	**win**. The Lord will give you **victory**.
Job	40.14	admit that you **won** the **victory** yourself.
Ps	45.4	strength will **win** you great **victories**!
	98.1	holy strength he has **won** the **victory**.
Is	26.18	We have **won** no **victory** for our land;
	59.16	to rescue them and to **win** the **victory**.
	63.5	and I **won** the **victory** myself.
Phil	1.28	**win**, because it is God who gives you the **victory**.
1 Jn	5.4	And we **win** the **victory** over the world
Rev	2.7	who **win** the **victory** I will give
	2.11	who **win** the **victory** will not be hurt
	2.17	those who **win** the **victory** I will give
	2.26	To those who **win** the **victory**,
	3.5	who **win** the **victory** will be clothed
	3.21	those who **win** the **victory** I will give
	5.5	has **won** the **victory**,
	12.11	Our brothers **won** the **victory** over him
	15.2	who had **won** the **victory** over the beast
	21.7	Whoever **wins** the **victory** will receive

VIOLENT

Hab	1.2	—	2.17	x6
Ezek	7.10	—	8.17	x4
Ps	140.1 – 11			x3
Prov	10.6	—	11.30	x3
Is	58.4	—	60.18	x3

Deceive

Ps	5.6	and despise **violent**, **deceitful** men.
Prov	13.2	are **deceitful** are hungry for **violence**.
	16.29	**Violent** people **deceive** their friends
Is	30.12	and rely on **violence** and **deceit**.
Jer	9.5	one **violent** thing...and one **deceitful** act

Evil, Wicked

Gen	6.11	was **evil** in God's sight, and **violence**
Job	27.13	punishes **wicked**, **violent** men.
	38.15	**wicked** and restrains them from deeds of **violence**.
Ps	7.16	**evil** and are hurt by their own **violence**.
	58.2	of the **evil** you can do, and...**violence**
	139.19	**wicked**! How I wish **violent** men would
	140.1	**evil** men; keep me safe from **violent**
	140.4	**wicked**; keep me safe from **violent** men
	140.11	**evil** overtake **violent** men and destroy
Prov	4.17	**Wickedness** and **violence** are like food
	10.6	**wicked** man's words hide a **violent**
	10.11	**wicked** man's words hide a **violent**
	21.7	The **wicked** are doomed by their own **violence**
Jer	6.7	keeps its **evil** fresh. I hear **violence**
	15.21	the power of **wicked** and **violent** men
Ezek	7.11	**Violence** produces more **wickedness**.
Lk	11.39	inside you are full of **violence** and **evil**.

Oppress

Ps	72.14	them from **oppression** and **violence**;
Jer	22.17	and **violently oppress** your people.
Ezek	45.9	Stop your **violence** and **oppression**.

Protect, Safe, Save

2 Sam	22.3	**protects** me and **saves** me from **violence**.
	22.49	and **protect** me from **violent** men.
Ps	18.48	and **protect** me from **violent** men.
	140.1	keep me **safe** from **violent** men.
	140.4	keep me **safe** from **violent** men
Hab	1.2	before you **save** us from **violence**?

Wicked see Evil

VISION

Dan	7.1	—	11.14	x20
Ezek	10.13	—	13.23	x11
Acts	9.10	—	12.9	x8
Is	21.2	—	22.5	x5
Amos	7.1	—	8.1	x5
Num	24.4 – 21			x4
Dan	1.17	—	2.31	x4
Zech	1.7	—	3.1	x4
Dan	4.5 – 13			x3
2 Cor	12.1 – 3			x3

False

Ezek	12.24	there will be no more **false visions**
	13.6	Their **visions** are **false**
	13.7	Those **visions** you see are **false**,
	13.8	are **false**, and your **visions** are lies.
	13.9	**false visions** and make misleading
	13.23	now your **false visions** and misleading
	21.29	The **visions** that you see are **false**
	22.28	**false visions** and make **false** predictions.

Heaven

Dan	2.19	in a **vision**, and he praised the God of **heaven**:
	4.13	**vision**, I saw coming down from **heaven**
Acts	26.19	disobey the **vision** I had from **heaven**.
Rev	4.1	**vision** and saw an open door in **heaven**

Message, Words

1 Sam	3.1	few **messages** from the Lord, and **visions**
Is	22.1	a **message** about the Valley of **Vision**.
Ezek	13.8	Your **words** are false, and your **visions**
Nah	1.1	**message** about Nineveh, the account of a **vision**
Zech	1.7	the Lord gave me a **message** in a **vision**
Acts	2.17	**message**; your young men will see **visions**,

Predict

Ezek	13.6	**visions** are false, and their **predictions**
	13.7	**visions**...are false, and the **predictions**
	13.9	**visions** and make misleading **predictions**.
	13.23	false **visions** and misleading **predictions**
	21.29	**visions**...are false, and the **predictions**
	22.28	false **visions** and make false **predictions**.
Mic	3.6	**visions**...you will not be able to **predict**

Prophet

2 Chr	9.29	The **Visions** of Iddo the **Prophet**,
	32.32	The **Vision** of the **Prophet** Isaiah
Is	28.7	the **prophets** are too drunk to understand the **visions**
	29.11	every **prophetic vision** will be hidden
Lam	2.9	the **prophets** have no **visions**
Ezek	13.9	you **prophets** who have false **visions**
Hos	12.10	**prophets** and gave them many **visions**
Mic	3.6	will have no more **prophetic visions**,
Zech	13.4	no **prophet** will be proud of his **visions**,

Spirit of God

Ezek	8.3	in this **vision** God's **spirit** lifted me
	11.24	In the **vision** the **spirit of God**
Acts	10.19	**vision** meant, when the **Spirit** said,

Temple

Lk	1.22	he had seen a **vision** in the **Temple**.

Acts 22.17 praying in the **Temple**, I had a **vision**,

Understand

Is   28.7   too drunk to **understand** the **visions**
Dan   8.15   to **understand** what the **vision** meant
      8.17   **understand** the meaning. The **vision**
      8.27   the **vision** and could not **understand** it.
      10.1   to **understand**. It was explained to him in a **vision**.
Acts 10.19 to **understand** what the **vision** meant

Words see Message

VOW

Num	29.39	—	30.16	x20
Gen	24.2	—	26.33	x9
Heb	6.13	—	7.28	x9
Lev	27.2	— 11		x5
Num	6.2	— 21		x5
Lev	22.18	—	23.38	x4
Deut	23.18	— 22		x4
Gen	21.23	—	22.16	x3
Gen	47.29	— 31		x3
Jer	44.24	— 26		x3
Acts	23.12	— 21		x3

Fulfil

Lev   7.16   in **fulfilment** of a **vow**
      22.18 **fulfilment** of a **vow** or as a freewill
      22.21 **fulfilment** of a **vow** or as a freewill
      22.23 is not acceptable in **fulfilment** of a **vow**.
      23.38 your offerings in **fulfilment** of **vows**,
      27.2   in **fulfilment** of a special **vow**,
Num   6.21   **vow** requires him to give, he must **fulfil**
      15.3   **fulfilment** of a **vow** or as a
      15.8   **fulfilment** of a **vow** or as a
      29.39 **fulfilment** of a **vow** or as a freewill
      30.5   her father forbids her to **fulfil** the **vow**
      30.8   husband forbids her to **fulfil** the **vow**
      30.12 husband forbids her to **fulfil** the **vow**
      30.15 for the failure to **fulfil** the **vow**.
Deut 23.18 in **fulfilment** of a **vow**.

Promise, Swear

Gen   24.37 master made me **promise** with a **vow**
      26.31 his **promise** and sealed it with a **vow**.
      31.53 solemnly **vowed** to keep this **promise**.
      50.25 people to make a **vow**. "**Promise** me,
Num   6.21   Nazirite **promises**...beyond what his **vow**
      30.3   a **vow** to give something...or **promises**
      30.4   she **vowed** or **promised** unless her father
      30.6   makes a **vow**...or **promises**
      30.7   everything that she **vowed** or **promised**
      30.9   every **vow** she makes and every **promise**
      30.10 woman makes a **vow** or **promises**
      30.11 everything that she **vowed** or **promised**
      30.13 affirm or to annul any **vow** or **promise**
      30.14 that she has **vowed** or **promised**.
Deut 23.21 doing what you **promised**; the Lord will hold
             you to your **vow**
1 Sam 28.10 **vow**. "By the living Lord I **promise**
Ps   132.2 he **promised**, the **vow** he made to you,
Jer   44.24 your **promises**! Carry out your **vows**!
      44.26 to make a **vow** by saying, 'I **swear**
Ezek 20.23 another **promise** in the desert. I **vowed**
Mt   5.33   **promise**, but do what you have **vowed**
      5.34   use any **vow** when you make a **promise**.
      23.16 **swears** by the Temple, he isn't bound by his **vow**;
      23.18 **swears** by the altar, he isn't bound by his **vow**;
Mk   6.23   many **vows** he said to her, "I **swear**
Acts 2.30   **promised** him: God had made a **vow**
Heb   6.13   a **vow** to do what he had **promised**.
      6.17   so he added his **vow** to the **promise**.
      7.28   but God's **promise** made with the **vow**,

Solemn

Gen   31.53 **solemnly vowed** to keep this promise.
      47.29 and make a **solemn vow**
Acts 23.14 We have taken a **solemn vow**

Swear see Promise

WARN

Ezek	32.2	—	33.27	x9
Ezek	3.17	— 26		x6
Ezek	20.18	—	21.23	x6
2 Kgs	17.13	—	18.29	x4
Neh	9.26	— 34		x4
Num	16.38	—	17.10	x3
Jer	6.8	— 17		x3
Jer	11.7	— 11		x3
Jer	35.15	—	37.9	x3

Command

Neh   9.34   listen to your **commands** and **warnings**.
Zech 1.6   your ancestors **commands** and **warnings**,
2 Thes 3.12 **command** these people and **warn** them

Evil

2 Kgs 17.13 **warn** Israel and Judah: "Abandon...**evil**
Job   36.10 to his **warning** to turn away from **evil**.
Jer   35.15 up your **evil** ways...They **warned** you
Ezek 3.18   an **evil** man is going to die but you do not **warn** him
      3.19   **warn** an **evil** man and he doesn't stop
      33.8   an **evil** man is going to die but you do not **warn** him
      33.9   **warn** an **evil** man and he doesn't stop
      33.14 **warn** an **evil** man that he is going to
1 Cor 10.6   to **warn** us not to desire **evil** things,

God's People

2 Chr 36.15 to send prophets to **warn his people**,
Ps   81.8   **my people**, to my **warning**;
Is   56.10 who are supposed to **warn my people**,
Ezek 21.10 **people** have disregarded every **warning**
Hos   9.8   me as a prophet to **warn his people**
      12.10 the prophets I gave **my people warnings**.

Obey

Neh   9.29   **warned** them to **obey** your teachings,
Jer   11.7   I solemnly **warned** them to **obey** me,
Ezek 20.39 I **warn** you that after this you will have to **obey**

Punishment

Ex   8.21   I **warn** you...if you refuse, I will **punish**
Ezek 21.10 every **warning** and **punishment**.
Mic   7.4   **punish** the people, as he **warned** them
1 Thes 4.6   **warned** you that the Lord will **punish**
Jude .7   **punishment** of eternal fire as a...**warning**

Sin

Num   32.23 I **warn** you that you will be **sinning**
Ezek 3.19   If you do **warn** an **evil** man and he doesn't stop **sinning**,
      3.21   If you do **warn** a good man not to **sin**
      33.9   If you do **warn** an **evil** man and he doesn't stop **sinning**,

Solemn

Josh 6.26   time Joshua issued a **solemn warning**
Ps   106.26 So he gave them a **solemn warning**
Jer   11.7   I solemnly **warned** them to obey
Ezek 32.2   give a **solemn warning** to the king
      32.16 **solemn warning** will become a funeral
Amos 6.8   has given this **solemn warning**:
Acts 20.21 **solemn warning** that they should turn
2 Tim 2.14   and give them a **solemn warning**
Rev   22.18 **solemnly warn** everyone who hears

WAYS

Ps	119.3 – 128		x4
Judg	2.19 – 22		x3
Jer	35.15 –	36.7	x3

Change see Turn

Evil, Wicked

Judg	2.19	refused to give up their own **evil ways**.
1 Kgs	13.33	still did not turn from his **evil ways**
2 Kgs	8.18	the **evil ways** of the kings of Israel.
	13.2	he never gave up his **evil ways**.
	17.13	your **evil ways** and obey my commands,
Prov	8.13	I hate pride and arrogance, **evil ways**
	15.9	The Lord hates the **ways** of evil people
Jer	15.7	you did not stop your **evil ways**.
	26.3	will listen and give up their **evil ways**.
	35.15	have told you to give up your **evil ways**
	36.3	they will turn from their **evil ways**.
	36.7	and turn from their **evil ways**,
Acts	3.26	turn away from his **wicked ways**.
	17.30	to turn away from their **evil ways**.
Rom	1.18	whose **evil ways** prevent the truth
Rev	16.11	they did not turn from their **evil ways**.
	18.5	and God remembers her **wicked ways**.

Turn, Change

1 Kgs	13.33	still did not **turn** from his evil **ways**
Ps	7.12	If they do not **change** their **ways**,
Prov	20.30	experience to make us **change** our **ways**.
Jer	18.11	living sinful lives — to **change** their **ways**
	36.3	they will **turn** from their evil **ways**.
	36.7	and **turn** from their evil **ways**.
Lam	3.40	Let us examine our **ways** and **turn**
Ezek	3.18	do not warn him to **change** his **ways**
	33.8	do not warn him to **change** his **ways**
Lk	3.18	and urged them to **change** their **ways**.
Acts	3.26	**turn** away from his wicked **ways**.
	17.30	to **turn** away from their evil **ways**.
2 Cor	7.9	sadness made you **change** your **ways**.
Rev	16.11	they did not **turn** from their evil **ways**.

Wicked see Evil

WEAK

2 Cor	10.10 –	13.9	x12
1 Cor	8.7 –	9.22	x6
Is	40.29 –	41.29	x5
Judg	16.7 – 17		x4
Ezek	29.6 –	30.25	x4
1 Sam	14.24 – 31		x3
Jer	49.15 –	50.37	x3
Rom	14.1 –	15.1	x3
1 Cor	1.25 –	2.3	x3
Heb	4.15 –	5.3	x3

Faith

Rom	4.19	**faith** did not **weaken** when he thought
	14.1	the person who is **weak** in **faith**
	14.2	but the person who is **weak** in the **faith**
	15.1	**faith** ought to help the **weak** to carry
1 Cor	8.9	who are **weak** in the **faith** fall into sin.
	9.22	the **weak** in **faith** I become **weak**

Strength, Power

Judg	16.17	would lose my **strength** and be as **weak**
1 Sam	2.4	but the **weak** grow **strong**.
2 Sam	3.1	**stronger**, his opponents became **weaker**
2 Chr	14.11	a **weak** army as easily as a **powerful**
Ps	35.10	You protect the **weak** from the **strong**,
	73.26	grow **weak**, but God is my **strength**;
Ecc	12.3	your legs, now **strong**, will grow **weak**.
Is	31.3	**strong** nation will crumble, and the **weak**
	40.29	He **strengthens** those who are **weak**
	41.29	these idols are **weak** and **powerless**.
	57.10	**strength**, and so you never grow **weak**.

Lam	1.6	are **weak** from hunger, Whose **strength**
Ezek	30.25	will **weaken** him and **strengthen** the king
	34.20	you **strong** sheep and the **weak** sheep.
Dan	2.42	will be **strong** and part of it **weak**.
Zech	12.8	even the **weakest**...will become as **strong**
Rom	15.1	who are **strong**...ought to help the **weak**
1 Cor	1.25	God's **weakness** is **stronger** than human
	1.27	**weak** in order to shame the **powerful**.
	4.10	We are **weak**, but you are **strong**!
	15.43	**weak**; when raised, it will be...**strong**.
2 Cor	12.9	**power** is greatest when you are **weak**.
	12.10	For when I am **weak**, then I am **strong**.
	13.3	not **weak**; instead, he shows his **power**
	13.9	when we are **weak** but you are **strong**.
Heb	11.34	They were **weak**, but became **strong**;

WEEP

Is	15.2 –	16.9	x5
Joel	1.5 –	2.17	x4
Jn	11.31 – 35		x4
2 Sam	12.21 –	13.36	x3
Ps	6.6 – 8		x3
Jer	22.10 – 18		x3

Bitterly

2 Sam	13.36	and his officials also **wept bitterly**.
Ezra	10.1	gathered round him, **weeping bitterly**.
Is	22.4	Now leave me alone to **weep bitterly**
Jer	22.10	**weep bitterly** for Joahaz,
	31.15	the sound of **bitter weeping**.
Ezek	27.31	Their hearts are **bitter** as they **weep**.
Mt	2.18	the sound of **bitter weeping**.
	26.75	He went out and **wept bitterly**.
Lk	22.62	Peter went out and **wept bitterly**.

Jesus

Jn	11.33	**Jesus** saw her **weeping**,
	11.35	**Jesus wept**.

Mourn, Sackcloth

2 Sam	19.1	was **weeping** and **mourning** for Absalom
Neh	1.4	and **wept**. For several days I **mourned**
Esth	4.3	**mourning** among the Jews. They fasted, **wept**
Job	30.31	now I hear only **mourning** and **weeping**.
Is	22.12	calling you then to **weep** and **mourn**,
Jer	4.8	So put on **sackcloth**, and **weep**
	9.10	will **mourn** for the mountains and **weep**
	22.10	**weep** for King Josiah; do not **mourn**
Ezek	27.31	in **sackcloth**. Their hearts are bitter as they **weep**.
Joel	1.13	Put on **sackcloth** and **weep**,
	2.12	with fasting and **weeping** and **mourning**.
Lk	6.25	you will **mourn** and **weep**!

WELCOME

Lk	7.45 –	10.38	x10
Mt	10.11 – 41		x8
Lk	15.2 –	16.9	x3
Acts	28.2 – 30		x3

Stranger

Job	31.31	that I have always **welcomed strangers**.
Mt	25.38	see you a **stranger** and **welcome** you
	25.43	**stranger** but you would not **welcome** me
1 Tim	3.2	he must **welcome strangers** in his home;
Heb	13.2	to **welcome strangers** in your homes.

WICKED

Prov	10.3 –	17.15	x40
Ps	37.1 – 40		x15
Job	20.5 –	22.20	x11
Prov	2.22 –	6.16	x10
Prov	21.4 –	22.5	x9
Ps	10.2 – 15		x8
Prov	28.1 –	29.27	x7

Ecc	7.17	—	9.2		x7
Jer	12.1	—	16.18		x7
2 Thes	2.3	—	3.2		x7
Ps	119.53	—	155		x6
2 Kgs	14.24	—	15.28		x5
Job	3.17	—	5.16		x5
Job	8.22	—	11.20		x4
Job	24.6	—	24		x4
Job	27.7	—	18		x4
Ps	73.3	—	17		x4
Ps	94.3	—	23		x4
Deut	9.4	—	27		x3
2 Chr	19.2	—	21.6		x3
Ps	7.9	—	14		x3
Ps	9.5	—	17		x3
Ps	11.2	—	6		x3
Ps	36.1	—	11		x3
Ps	75.4	—	10		x3
Ps	92.7	—	11		x3
Prov	24.15	—	20		x3
Jer	23.10	—	22		x3
Jer	25.5	—	26.3		x3
Jer	30.14	—	23		x3
Ezek	20.44	—	21.29		x3
Rom	5.6	—	6.19		x3

Downfall, Disaster, Trap
Job 21.17 with disaster? Did God ever punish the wicked
Ps 9.16 wicked are trapped by their own deeds.
   94.13 until a pit is dug to trap the wicked.
  119.61 The wicked have laid a trap for me,
  119.110 Wicked men lay a trap for me,
  141.10 the wicked fall into their own traps
Prov 3.25 disasters, such as come on the wicked
   5.22 The sins of a wicked man are a trap
  11.5 wicked man will cause his own downfall.
  12.7 Wicked men meet their downfall
  12.13 wicked man is trapped by his own
  13.6 wickedness is the downfall of sinners.
  14.32 Wicked people bring...their own downfall
  22.5 from the traps that catch the wicked
  24.16 but disaster destroys the wicked.
Is 13.11 bring disaster...and punish all wicked
Zeph 1.3 bring about the downfall of the wicked.

Evil, Violent, Wrong
Gen 6.5 how wicked everyone...was and how evil
Job 3.17 In the grave wicked men stop their evil,
  4.8 plough fields of evil and sow wickedness
  27.13 punishes wicked, violent men.
  38.15 wicked and restrains them from deeds of
    violence.
Ps 7.9 Stop the wickedness of evil men
  7.14 See how wicked people think up evil;
  10.3 wicked man is proud of his evil desires;
  10.15 the power of wicked and evil men;
  26.5 of evil men and avoid the wicked.
  28.3 the wicked, with those who do evil
  34.21 Evil will kill the wicked;
  37.1 the wicked; don't be jealous of those who do
    wrong.
  64.2 of the wicked, from mobs of evil men.
  71.4 wicked men, from the power of...evil
  73.7 evil, and...are busy with wicked schemes.
  92.7 the wicked may grow like weeds, those who
    do wrong
  94.16 the wicked...against the evildoers?
  101.8 wicked in our land; I will expel all evil
  106.6 we have been wicked and evil.
  139.19 wicked! How I wish violent men would
  139.20 wicked things about you; they speak evil
  140.4 wicked; keep me safe from violent men
  141.4 joining evil men in their wickedness.
Prov 4.17 Wickedness and violence are like food

Prov 6.16 mind that thinks up wicked plans, feet that
    hurry off to do evil,
  10.6 wicked man's words hide a violent
  10.11 wicked man's words hide a violent
  12.12 wicked people want is to find evil things
  19.28 Wicked people love the taste of evil.
  21.7 The wicked are doomed by their own violence
  21.10 Wicked people are always hungry for evil
Is 9.17 wicked and everything they say is evil.
Jer 15.21 the power of wicked and violent men.
  23.22 evil lives they live and the wicked things
  25.5 wicked way of life and from the evil
  36.3 their evil ways. Then I will forgive their
    wickedness
  44.22 endure your wicked and evil practices.
Ezek 7.11 Violence produces more wickedness.
  20.44 with you as your wicked, evil actions
  21.29 You are wicked and evil,
Hos 7.1 their wickedness and the evil they do.
Jon 3.8 wicked behaviour and his evil actions.
Rom 1.29 filled with all kinds of wickedness, evil,
2 Thes 3.2 rescue us from wicked and evil people;

Protect, Rescue, Save
Job 13.16 will save me, since no wicked man
Ps 17.13 Save me from the wicked
  37.17 wicked, but protect those who are good.
  37.40 he saves them from the wicked, ...they go to
    him for protection.
  64.2 Protect me from the plots of the wicked.
  71.4 rescue me from wicked men,
  97.10 he rescues them from...the wicked.
  119.155 The wicked will not be saved,
  140.4 Protect me, Lord, from...the wicked;
Prov 11.8 righteous are protected from trouble; it comes
    to the wicked
  13.6 protects the innocent; wickedness
Jer 15.21 rescue you from the power of wicked
2 Thes 3.2 God will rescue us from wicked
Tit 2.14 to rescue us from all wickedness

Righteous
Job 27.7 punished like wicked, unrighteous men.
Ps 7.11 a righteous judge...condemns the wicked.
  9.16 righteous judgements, and the wicked
  34.21 wicked; those who hate the righteous
  75.10 wicked, but the power of the righteous
Prov 3.33 wicked men, but blesses...the righteous.
  10.24 The righteous get what they want, but the
    wicked
  12.3 Wickedness does not give security, but
    righteous people
  12.21 to righteous people, but the wicked
  12.28 Righteousness is...life; wickedness
  13.6 Righteousness protects the innocent;
    wickedness is the downfall
  13.25 righteous have enough...but the wicked
  15.6 Righteous men keep...wealth, but wicked
  29.27 The righteous hate the wicked
Ecc 8.14 righteous men get the punishment of the
    wicked,
  9.2 comes to the righteous and the wicked,
Mal 3.18 to the righteous and to the wicked,

Save see Protect

Sin
Gen 13.13 wicked and sinned against the Lord.
Deut 9.27 wickedness, and sin of this people.
1 Kgs 8.47 confessing how sinful and wicked
2 Chr 6.37 how sinful and wicked they have been,
Ps 94.23 for their wickedness and destroy them for their
    sins;
Prov 5.22 The sins of a wicked man are a trap.
  11.31 sure that wicked and sinful people

Prov	13.6	**wickedness** is the downfall of **sinners**.
Is	13.11	punish all **wicked** people for their **sins**.
Jer	16.18	double for their **sin** and **wickedness**,
	30.14	**sins** are many and your **wickedness**
	30.15	**sins** are many and your **wickedness**
	36.3	their **wickedness** and their **sins**."
Rom	6.13	to **sin** to be used for **wicked** purposes.
1 Cor	5.8	old yeast of **sin** and **wickedness**,

Trap see **Downfall**

Trouble

Ps	7.14	**wicked** people think up evil; they plan **trouble**
	55.3	the **wicked**. They bring **trouble** on me;
	94.13	of **trouble** until a pit is dug to trap the **wicked**.
Prov	11.8	**trouble**; it comes to the **wicked** instead.
	12.21	the **wicked** have nothing but **trouble**.
	16.28	**wicked** people; they stir up **trouble**
	17.11	to **wicked** people who are always stirring up **trouble**.

Violent see **Evil**

Words

Prov	10.6	**wicked** man's **words** hide a violent
	10.11	**wicked** man's **words** hide a violent
	11.11	to ruin by the **words** of the **wicked**.
	12.6	**words** of **wicked** men are murderous
	12.13	**wicked** man is trapped by his own **words**
	13.5	the **words** of **wicked** people are shameful
Rom	3.13	**words** are full of deadly deceit; **wicked**

Wrong see **Evil**

WIDOWS

	1 Tim	5.3 – 16	x11
	Deut	24.17 — 27.19	x9
	Gen	38.8 – 19	x5
	1 Kgs	17.9 – 20	x5
	Mk	12.19 – 43	x4
	Lk	20.28 — 21.3	x4

Advantage

Jer	7.6	Stop taking **advantage** of...**widows**.
Ezek	22.7	foreigners and take **advantage** of **widows**
Mal	3.5	those who take **advantage** of **widows**,
Mk	12.40	They take **advantage** of **widows**
Lk	20.47	who take **advantage** of **widows**

Poor

2 Sam	14.5	I am a **poor widow**, sir," she answered.
Job	31.16	help the **poor**; never have I let **widows**
Mk	12.42	**poor widow** came along and dropped in
	12.43	**poor widow** put more in the offering
Lk	21.2	very **poor widow** dropping in two little
	21.3	this **poor widow** put in more than all

WILL

	2 Chr	10.15 — 14.7	x6
	1 Pet	2.8 — 4.19	x5
	Rom	8.20 — 9.19	x4
	Is	52.4 — 53.10	x3
	Ezek	20.1 – 31	x3
	Jn	6.38 – 39	x3
	2 Cor	8.3 – 17	x3
	Heb	10.7 – 36	x3

Command

Josh	22.5	**commanded** you: love...God, do his **will**,
2 Chr	14.4	He **commanded**...Judah to do the **will**
	30.12	his **will** by following the **commands**
Job	23.12	what God **commands**; I follow his **will**,
	37.12	at God's **will**...all that God **commands**,

Purpose

2 Sam	7.21	It was your **will** and **purpose** to do this;

1 Chr	17.19	It was your **will** and **purpose** to do this
Rom	8.20	lose its **purpose**, not of its own **will**,
Rev	17.17	the **will** to carry out his **purpose**

Suffer

Is	53.10	It was my **will** that he should **suffer**;
Lk	22.42	if you **will**, take this cup of **suffering**
1 Pet	2.19	**suffering** because...of his **will**.
	4.19	those who **suffer** because it is God's **will**

WIN

	1 Cor	9.19 – 24	x7
	Rev	2.7 — 3.21	x6
	Gen	30.8 — 32.28	x5
	Phil	3.12 – 14	x4
	Heb	11.2 – 39	x4

Approval, Favour

1 Sam	13.12	have not tried to **win** the Lord's **favour**.
	29.4	for him to **win** back his master's **favour**
1 Kgs	11.38	**win** my **approval** by doing what I
Ezra	7.28	I have **won** the **favour** of the emperor
Esth	2.9	and she **won** his **favour**.
	2.17	any of the others she **won** his **favour**
	5.2	she **won** his **favour**,
Ps	45.12	rich people will try to **win** your **favour**.
Jer	26.19	the Lord and tried to **win** his **favour**.
Ezek	16.19	as a sacrifice to **win** the **favour** of idols.
Acts	7.46	He **won** God's **favour** and asked God
Gal	1.10	I am trying to **win** man's **approval**?
2 Tim	2.15	Do your best to **win** full **approval**
Heb	11.2	of ancient times **won** God's **approval**.
	11.4	his faith he **won** God's **approval**

Faith

1 Tim	6.12	your best in the race of **faith**, and **win**
Heb	11.2	**faith** that people of ancient times **won**
	11.4	his **faith** he **won** God's approval
	11.33	**faith** they fought...countries and **won**.
	11.39	all of these have **won** by their **faith**

Favour see **Approval**

Life

1 Sam	19.5	He risked his **life**...and the Lord **won**
Mt	16.26	**wins** the whole world but loses his **life**?
Mk	8.36	**wins** the whole world but loses his **life**?
1 Tim	6.12	and **win** eternal **life** for yourself;
	6.19	able to **win** the **life** which is true **life**.

WISDOM

	Prov	1.2 — 5.1	x19
	1 Cor	1.17 — 3.19	x17
	Prov	7.4 -- 11.9	x10
	Ecc	7.12 -- 10.1	x10
	Job	28.12 – 27	x8
	Ecc	1.16 — 2.26	x8
	1 Kgs	3.9 — 5.12	x7
	Job	11.6 — 12.20	x6
	Col	1.9 — 3.16	x6
	1 Kgs	10.4 — 11.41	x5
	Prov	23.16 — 24.14	x5
	2 Chr	9.3 – 23	x4
	Ps	119.66 – 130	x4
	Jer	49.7 — 51.57	x4
	Acts	6.3 — 7.22	x4
	Jas	3.13 – 17	x4
	2 Chr	1.10 – 12	x3
	Job	32.7 – 13	x3
	Prov	14.1 – 33	x3
	Prov	29.3 — 31.26	x3
	Jer	8.9 — 10.12	x3

Advice

Prov	12.15	**Wise** people listen to **advice**.
	13.10	It is **wiser** to ask for **advice**.
	15.12	for **advice** from those who are **wiser**.

| Is | 19.11 | Egypt's **wisest** men give stupid **advice**! |

Correct

Prov	9.8	But if you **correct a wise** man,
	13.1	A **wise** son pays attention when his father **corrects** him,
	15.5	it is **wise** to accept your **correction**.
	15.31	when you are **corrected**, you are **wise**.
	15.32	accept **correction**, you will become **wiser**.
	19.25	If you are **wise**, you will learn when you are **corrected**.

Foolish, Stupid

Job	11.12	**Stupid** men will start being **wise**
	12.17	**wisdom** of rulers and makes leaders act like **fools**.
	39.17	**foolish** and did not give her **wisdom**.
Ps	49.10	even **wise** men die, as well as **foolish**
Prov	1.7	**Stupid** people have no respect for **wisdom**
	10.1	A **wise** son makes his father proud of him; a **foolish** one
	11.29	**Foolish** men will always be servants to the **wise**.
	12.15	**Stupid** people...think they are right. **Wise**
	13.20	**wise**. If you make friends with **stupid**
	14.1	**wisdom** of women, but are destroyed by **foolishness**.
	14.3	**fool's** pride makes him talk... a **wise**
	14.17	temper do **foolish** things; **wiser** people
	14.24	**Wise** people are rewarded...but **fools**
	14.33	**fools** know nothing about **wisdom**.
	15.7	by people who are **wise**, not by **fools**.
	15.20	A **wise** son makes his father happy. Only a **fool** despises
	15.21	their **foolishness**, but the **wise** will do
	16.22	**wise**, but trying to educate **stupid** people
	17.24	at **wise** action, but a **fool** starts off
	17.28	**fool** may be thought **wise** and intelligent
	21.20	**Wise** people live in...luxury, but **stupid**
	24.7	**Wise** sayings are too deep for a **stupid**
	26.9	**fool** quoting a **wise** saying reminds you
Ecc	1.17	and **foolishness**, **wisdom** and madness.
	2.12	meant to be **wise** or reckless or **foolish**.
	2.13	**Wisdom** is better than **foolishness**.
	2.14	**Wise** men can see where they are going, and **fools** cannot.
	2.15	fate as **fools**. So what have I gained from being so **wise**?
	2.16	**wise** men, and no one remembers **fools**.
	2.19	might be **wise**, or he might be **foolish**
	6.8	is a **wise** man better off than a **fool**?
	7.4	**fool**. A **wise** person thinks about death.
	7.5	**wise** people reprimand you than to have **stupid**
	10.1	**stupidity** can cancel out...**wisdom**.
	10.2	**wise** man to do the right...and for a **fool**
	10.12	**wise** man says brings...honour, but a **fool**
Is	19.11	**fools**! Egypt's **wisest** men give stupid
	29.14	who are **wise** will turn out to be **fools**,
	44.25	show that their **wisdom** is **foolishness**.
Mt	25.2	**foolish**, and the other five were **wise**
	25.8	the **foolish** ones said to the **wise** ones
Rom	1.22	say they are **wise**, but they are **fools**;
Cor	1.20	that this world's **wisdom** is **foolishness**!
	1.25	**foolishness** is wiser than human **wisdom**.
	3.18	a **fool**, in order to be really **wise**
	4.10	sake we are **fools**; but you are **wise**
Cor	11.19	**wise**, and so you gladly tolerate **fools**!

God, Lord

Kgs	3.28	**God** had given him the **wisdom**
	4.29	**God** gave Solomon unusual **wisdom**
	5.12	The **Lord**...gave Solomon **wisdom**.
	10.24	the **wisdom** that **God** had given him.
1 Chr	22.12	**God** give you insight and **wisdom**
2 Chr	9.23	the **wisdom** that **God** had given him.
Ezra	7.25	**wisdom** which your **God** has given you,
Job	12.12	but **God** has **wisdom** and power.
	32.8	spirit of...**God**...gives them **wisdom**.
Prov	2.6	It is the **Lord** who gives **wisdom**;
	3.19	**Lord** created the earth by his **wisdom**;
Ecc	2.26	**God** gives **wisdom**, knowledge,
Is	11.2	the **Lord** will give him **wisdom**,
	28.29	All this **wisdom** comes from the **Lord**
Mt	11.19	**God's wisdom**, however, is shown
Lk	7.35	**God's wisdom**, however, is shown
	11.49	the **Wisdom** of **God** said,
1 Cor	1.20	**God** has shown that this world's **wisdom**
	1.21	**God** in his **wisdom** made it impossible
	1.24	Christ, who is...the **wisdom** of **God**.
	1.30	**God** has made Christ to be our **wisdom**.
	2.7	I proclaim is **God's** secret **wisdom**,
	3.19	to be **wisdom** is nonsense in **God's** sight.
Col	2.3	the hidden treasures of **God's wisdom**
Jas	1.5	lacks **wisdom**, he should pray to **God**,
2 Pet	3.15	using the **wisdom** that **God** gave him.
Rev	7.12	**wisdom**...belong to our **God**

Life

1 Kgs	3.11	the **wisdom** to rule...instead of long **life**
2 Chr	1.11	**life** for yourself, you...asked for **wisdom**
Ps	90.12	our **life** is, so that we may become **wise**.
Prov	3.16	**Wisdom** offers you long **life**
	3.17	**Wisdom** can make your **life** pleasant and
	3.18	**wisdom** will give them **life**.
	9.11	**Wisdom** will add years to your **life**
	13.14	of the **wise** are a fountain of **life**;
	16.22	**Wisdom** is a fountain of **life** to the wise

Lord see God

Message see Words

Obey

Prov	3.7	**wiser** than you are; simply **obey** the
Ecc	8.5	**obey** his commands, you are safe, and a **wise**
Mt	7.24	**obeys** them is like a **wise** man who built

Power

Job	9.4	God is so **wise** and **powerful**;
	12.12	but God has **wisdom** and **power**.
Jer	10.12	the earth by his **power**; by his **wisdom**
	51.15	the earth by his **power**; by his **wisdom**
Dan	2.20	God is **wise** and **powerful**!
1 Cor	1.24	**power** of God and the **wisdom** of God.
	1.26	few of you were **wise** or **powerful**
	2.4	**wisdom**, but with...proof of the **power**
	2.5	on human **wisdom** but on God's **power**.
2 Cor	1.12	by the **power** of God's grace, and not by human **wisdom**.
Rev	5.12	to receive **power**, wealth, **wisdom**,
	7.12	**wisdom**, thanksgiving, honour, **power**,

Right

Job	32.9	that makes men **wise** or helps them to know what is **right**.
Prov	15.21	the **wise** will do what is **right**.
Ecc	10.2	for a **wise** man to do the **right** thing
Jer	23.5	will rule **wisely** and do what is **right**

Sayings see Words

Strength

Prov	24.5	Being **wise** is better than being **strong**
Ecc	9.16	said that **wisdom** is better than **strength**.
Is	10.13	I am **strong** and **wise** and clever.
Jer	9.23	of their **wisdom**, nor **strong** men of their **strength**,

Dan	2.23	have given me **wisdom** and **strength**;	
Rev	5.12	**wisdom**, and **strength**,	

Stupid see **Foolish**

Teach

Job	8.10	But let the ancient **wise** men **teach** you;
	15.18	**Wise** men have **taught** me truths
	33.33	and I will **teach** you how to be **wise**.
Ps	119.130	**teachings** gives light and brings **wisdom**
Prov	4.11	I have **taught** you **wisdom**
	8.33	Listen to what you are **taught**. Be **wise**;
	13.14	The **teachings** of the **wise** are a fountain
	15.5	father **taught** you; it is **wise** to accept
	21.11	**wise** will learn from what he is **taught**.
	22.17	will **teach** you what **wise** men have said.
	28.26	follow the **teachings** of **wiser** people.
Ecc	12.9	was **wise**, he kept on **teaching**
Mt	12.42	to King Solomon's **wise teaching**;
Lk	11.31	to King Solomon's **wise teaching**;
Acts	7.22	**taught** all the **wisdom** of the Egyptians
1 Cor	2.13	in words **taught** by human **wisdom**,
Col	1.28	**wisdom** we warn and **teach** them
	2.8	**wisdom**, which comes from the **teachings**
	3.16	**Teach**...each other with all **wisdom**.

Value

Job	28.18	The **value** of **wisdom** is more
	28.19	compare with the **value** of **wisdom**.
Prov	3.15	**Wisdom** is more **valuable** than jewels;

Wise

Prov	3.18	**wise** are happy; **wisdom** will give
	16.22	**Wisdom** is a fountain of life to the **wise**
Is	44.25	**wise** I refute and show that their **wisdom**
Jer	9.23	**Wise** men should not boast of their **wisdom**,
Dan	11.33	**Wise** leaders...will share their **wisdom**
1 Cor	1.19	I will destroy the **wisdom** of the **wise**
	1.25	foolishness is **wiser** than human **wisdom**,

Words, Message, Sayings

1 Kgs	10.8	are privileged to hear your **wise sayings**!
2 Chr	9.7	are privileged to hear your **wise sayings**!
Job	16.4	head **wisely** and drown you with...**words**.
	34.3	not **wise words** when you hear them.
	38.2	question my **wisdom** with your ignorant, empty **words**?
Ps	37.30	A good man's **words** are **wise**,
	49.3	I will speak **words** of **wisdom**.
	78.2	I am going to use **wise sayings**
Prov	12.18	**words** can wound...but **wisely**
	14.3	a **wise** man's **words** protect him.
	18.4	**words** can be a source of **wisdom**
	23.16	I hear you speaking **words** of **wisdom**.
	24.7	**Wise sayings** are too deep
	26.9	A fool quoting a **wise saying**
Ecc	9.17	the quiet **words** of a **wise** man
	12.11	The **sayings** of **wise** men are like
Is	44.25	The **words** of the **wise** I refute
Jer	8.9	my **words**; what **wisdom** have they
Mt	7.24	these **words** of mine...is like a **wise**
Lk	21.15	**words** and **wisdom** that none of your
1 Cor	2.4	with skilful **words** of human **wisdom**,
	2.6	Yet I do proclaim a **message** of **wisdom**
	2.13	in **words** taught by human **wisdom**,
	12.8	one person a **message** full of **wisdom**

WITNESS

Acts	1.8	—	5.32	x6
Josh	24.22 – 27			x4
Is	43.9	—	44.8	x4
Jer	32.10 – 44			x4
Acts	22.15	—	23.11	x4
Deut	17.6 – 7			x3

Deut	30.19	—	31.28	x3
Ruth	4.9 – 11			x3
Jn	5.34 – 36			x3
Rev	1.5	—	3.14	x3

Death

Num	35.30	to **death** only on the evidence of two or more **witnesses**;
Deut	17.6	to **death** only if two or more **witnesses**
Acts	22.20	your **witness** Stephen was put to **death**

Faithful, True

Ps	89.37	that **faithful witness** in the sky.
Jer	42.5	**faithful witness** against us if we do not
Jn	8.17	**witnesses** agree, what they say is **true**
Rom	1.9	is my **witness** that what I say is **true**
Rev	1.5	the **faithful witness**,
	2.13	when Antipas, my **faithful witness**,
	3.14	the **faithful** and true **witness**,
	6.9	had been **faithful** in their **witnessing**.

WONDERFUL

	Ps	107.8 – 31		x5
	Acts	4.30	— 8.13	x5
	Ps	119.18 – 129		x4
	Acts	2.7 – 43		x4
	1 Chr	16.9	— 17.26	x3
	Jer	32.20	— 33.3	x3
	Mk	12.11	— 13.22	x3

Acts, Miracles

Ex	15.11	**wonderful** in holiness? Who can work **miracles**
Deut	4.34	worked **miracles** and **wonders**,
	7.19	the **miracles** and **wonders**,
	13.1	may promise a **miracle** or a **wonder**,
	26.8	He worked **miracles** and **wonders**,
	29.3	the **miracles**, and the great **wonders**
	34.11	has ever done **miracles** and **wonders**
Ps	66.5	his **wonderful acts** among men.
	71.17	and I still tell of your **wonderful acts**.
	106.7	not understand God's **wonderful acts**;
	107.24	his **wonderful acts** on the seas.
	135.9	he performed **miracles** and **wonders**
Jer	32.20	**miracles** and **wonders** in Egypt,
	32.21	By means of **miracles** and **wonders**
Dan	4.2	my account of the **wonders** and **miracles**
	4.3	**wonders** God shows us! How powerful are the **miracles**
	6.27	he performs **wonders** and **miracles**
Mt	24.24	will perform great **miracles** and **wonders**
Mk	13.22	They will perform **miracles** and **wonders**
Jn	4.48	unless you see **miracles** and **wonders**.
Acts	2.19	**miracles** in the sky above and **wonders**
	2.22	**miracles** and **wonders** which God
	2.43	**miracles** and **wonders** were being done
	4.30	**wonders** and **miracles** may be performed
	5.12	**miracles** and **wonders** were being
	6.8	performed great **miracles** and **wonders**
	7.36	**miracles** and **wonders** in Egypt
	8.13	the great **wonders** and **miracles**
	14.3	power to perform **miracles** and **wonders**.
	15.12	**miracles** and **wonders** that God had
Rom	15.19	by the power of **miracles** and **wonders**,
2 Cor	12.12	many **miracles** and **wonders** that prove
2 Thes	2.9	all kinds of false **miracles** and **wonders**,
Heb	2.4	all kinds of **miracles** and **wonders**
1 Pet	2.9	to proclaim the **wonderful acts** of God,

Holiness

Ex	15.11	**wonderful** in **holiness**?

Love

2 Sam	1.26	How **wonderful** was your **love** for me,
Ps	17.7	your **wonderful love** and save me;
	31.21	**wonderfully** he showed his **love** for me

Might see **Power**

Miracles see **Acts**

Power, Might

Deut	7.19	and **wonders**, and the great **power**
Ps	66.3	How **wonderful** are the things you do! Your **power**
	78.4	Lord's **power**...and the **wonderful** things
	86.10	are **mighty** and do **wonderful** things;
	98.1	**wonderful** things! By his own **power**
Is	9.6	**Wonderful** Counsellor," "**Mighty God**,
Dan	4.3	**wonders** God shows us! How **powerful**
Acts	6.8	**power**, performed...miracles and **wonders**
	14.3	**power** to perform miracles and **wonders**.
Rom	15.19	by the **power** of miracles and **wonders**,

Promise

Deut	13.1	may **promise** a miracle or a **wonder**,
2 Sam	7.28	you have made this **wonderful promise**
1 Chr	17.26	made this **wonderful promise** to me.
Eph	1.18	the **wonderful** blessings he **promises**

WORD

	Acts	11.1	— 20.35	x28
	Prov	10.6	— 16.27	x22
	Job	15.1	— 17.3	x10
	Rev	19.9	— 22.19	x10
	Prov	4.20	— 8.13	x9
	Jer	5.13	— 9.20	x8
	Jer	23.9 — 38		x7
	1 Pet	1.8	— 3.1	x7
	Job	31.35	— 34.3	x6
	Ps	119.42 — 105		x6
	Lk	3.2	— 6.49	x6
	Acts	6.2	— 9.7	x6
	Is	48.1	— 50.10	x5
	Mk	13.11	— 15.5	x5
	Jn	1.1 — 14		x5
	Jn	3.34	— 6.68	x5
	Jn	17.6	— 19.13	x5
	1 Cor	14.9	— 15.27	x5
	Eph	4.29	— 6.17	x5
	1 Jn	1.6	— 3.18	x5
	Ex	34.1 — 28		x4
	Ezek	13.2 — 8		x4
	Ezek	33.30 — 33		x4
	1 Cor	2.1 — 13		x4
	Jas	1.18 — 23		x4
	Deut	32.1 — 47		x3
	2 Sam	19.14 — 23		x3
	Job	6.3 — 26		x3
	Job	19.1 — 24		x3
	Prov	18.4 — 21		x3
	Ezek	37.4 — 16		x3
	Acts	2.22 — 40		x3
	1 Tim	1.7 — 18		x3

Believe, Trust

Ps	119.42	because I **trust** in your **word**.
	119.81	I place my **trust** in your **word**.
	130.5	and in his **word** I **trust**.
Prov	21.28	a liar is not **believed**, but the **word**
Jer	7.4	Stop **believing** those deceitful **words**
	7.8	you put your **trust** in deceitful **words**.
	12.6	Do not **trust** them, even though they speak friendly **words**.
Jn	4.50	man **believed** Jesus' **words** and went.
	5.24	whoever hears my **words** and **believes**
Acts	14.9	Paul's **words**. Paul saw that he **believed**
	28.24	his **words**, but others would not **believe**.
1 Pet	2.8	they did not **believe** in the **word**;
	3.1	any of them do not **believe** God's **word**,
Rev	21.5	these **words** are true and can be **trusted**.
	22.6	**words** are true and can be **trusted**.

Claim see **False**

Condemn

Job	15.6	**condemned** by every **word** you speak.
Lk	19.22	use your own **words** to **condemn** you!
Acts	13.27	**words** come true by **condemning** Jesus.
Jude	.9	**condemn** the Devil with insulting **words**,

False, Claim, Deceive, Lie

Ps	52.4	hurt people with your **words**, you **liar**!
	62.4	in **lies**. You speak **words** of blessing,
	78.36	But their **words** were all **lies**;
Prov	4.24	to do with **lies** and misleading **words**.
	8.13	evil ways and **false words**.
	13.5	hate **lies**, but the **words** of wicked
	21.28	a **liar** is not believed, but the **word**
	22.12	safe by disproving the **words** of **liars**.
Is	59.13	thoughts are **false**; our **words** are **lies**.
Jer	7.4	Stop believing those **deceitful words**
	7.8	you put your trust in **deceitful words**.
	9.8	tell **lies**. Everyone speaks friendly **words**
	23.31	**words** and **claim** come from me.
Ezek	13.7	**lies**. You say that they are my **words**,
	13.8	Your **words** are **false**, and your visions
	22.28	make **false** predictions. They claim to speak the **word**
Hos	10.4	empty **words** and make **false** promises
Zech	13.3	he **claimed** to speak the Lord's **word**, but spoke **lies**
Rom	3.13	**words** are full of...**deceit**; wicked **lies**
	16.18	**words** and flattering speech they **deceive**
2 Cor	4.2	nor do we **falsify** the **word** of God.
Eph	5.6	anyone **deceive** you with foolish **words**
Jas	1.22	Do not **deceive** yourselves by just listening to his **word**
1 Jn	1.6	we are **lying** both in our **words**
	1.10	to be a **liar**, and his **word** is not in us.
Rev	22.15	who are **liars** both in **words** and deeds.

God

Ex	20.1	**God** spoke, and these were his **words**:
2 Sam	16.23	it were the very **word** of **God**;
	22.31	This **God**...how dependable his **words**!
Prov	16.1	but **God** has the last **word**.
Is	40.8	the **word** of our **God** endures for ever.
Jer	23.36	perverted the **words** of their **God**,
Mt	4.4	but needs every **word** that **God** speaks.
Mk	7.13	cancels out the **word** of **God**.
Lk	3.2	the **word** of **God** came to John
	5.1	to listen to the **word** of **God**.
	8.11	the seed is the **word** of **God**.
	8.21	who hear the **word** of **God** and obey it.
	11.28	who hear the **word** of **God** and obey it!
Jn	1.2	very beginning the **Word** was with **God**.
	3.34	whom **God** has sent speaks **God's words**,
	8.47	comes from God listens to **God's words**.
Acts	6.2	neglect the preaching of **God's word**
	6.7	the **word** of **God** continued to spread.
	8.14	Samaria had received the **word** of **God**,
	11.1	Gentiles...received the **word** of **God**.
	12.24	the **word** of **God** continued to spread
	13.5	they preached the **word** of **God**
	13.7	he wanted to hear the **word** of **God**.
	13.46	the **word** of **God** should be spoken first
	17.13	Paul had preached the **word** of **God**
	18.11	teaching the people the **word** of **God**
1 Cor	14.36	that the **word** of **God** came from you?
2 Cor	4.2	nor do we falsify the **word** of **God**.
Eph	6.17	and the **word** of **God** as the sword
1 Tim	4.5	the **word** of **God** and the prayer
2 Tim	2.9	But the **word** of **God** is not in chains,
Heb	4.12	The **word** of **God** is alive and active,
	6.5	knew...that **God's word** is good,
	11.3	universe was created by **God's word**,

Heb	12.5	encouraging **words** which **God** speaks
1 Pet	1.23	the living and eternal **word** of **God**
	3.1	any of them do not believe **God's word**,
1 Jn	2.14	the **word** of **God** lives in you,
Rev	1.9	because I had proclaimed **God's word**
	6.9	they had proclaimed **God's word**
	17.17	to rule until **God's words** come true.
	19.13	His name is "The **Word** of **God**."
	19.9	These are the true **words** of **God**.
	20.4	and the **word** of **God**.

Heart

Gen	50.21	kind **words** that touched their **hearts**.
Job	22.22	keep his **words** in your **heart**.
Ps	64.4	**words** of blessing, but in your **heart**
Prov	6.21	**words** with you always...in your **heart**.
Is	29.13	**words** are meaningless, and their **hearts**
Jer	15.16	your **words** filled my **heart** with joy
Mt	15.8	me with their **words**, but their **heart**
Mk	7.6	me with their **words**, but their **heart**
Jas	1.21	the **word** that he plants in your **hearts**,

Help, Kind

Gen	50.21	So he reassured them with **kind words**
Ps	130.5	Lord's **help**, and in his **word** I trust.
Prov	12.25	but **kind words** will cheer you up.
	15.4	**Kind words** bring life
	16.24	**Kind words** are like honey — sweet to
Acts	20.35	**help** the weak, remembering the **words**
1 Cor	4.13	we answer with **kind words**.
Eph	4.29	harmful **words**, but only **helpful words**,

Honest see True

Human

Jn	1.14	The **Word** became a **human being**

Judge

Mt	12.37	Your **words** will be used to **judge** you
Jn	12.48	**words** I have spoken will be his **judge**

Kind see Help

Lie see False

Life

Deut	32.47	empty **words**; they are your very **life**.
Prov	10.11	good man's **words** are a fountain of **life**
	15.4	Kind **words** bring **life**
Jn	1.4	The **Word** was the source of **life**
	6.63	**words**...bring God's **life-giving** Spirit.
	6.68	have the **words** that give eternal **life**.
1 Jn	1.1	write to you about the **Word** of **life**

Lord

Josh	24.27	all the **words** the **Lord** has spoken
1 Kgs	13.20	the **word** of the **Lord** came to the old
	20.42	This is the **word** of the **Lord**.
2 Chr	34.21	have not obeyed the **word** of the **Lord**
	36.12	who spoke the **word** of the **Lord**.
Ps	33.4	The **words** of the **Lord** are true
	105.19	The **word** of the **Lord** proved him right.
	119.89	Your **word**, O **Lord**, will last for ever;
Ezek	5.11	this is the **word** of the Sovereign **Lord**
	6.3	Israel to hear the **word** of the **Lord**
	13.2	to listen to the **word** of the **Lord**.
	22.14	I, the **Lord**...keep my **word**.
	22.28	claim to speak the **word** of the...**Lord**,
	33.30	what **word** has come from the **Lord**
	37.4	to listen to the **word** of the **Lord**.
Zech	13.3	he claimed to speak the **Lord's word**,
Acts	13.49	**word** of the **Lord** spread everywhere
	15.35	and preached the **word** of the **Lord**.
	15.36	we preached the **word** of the **Lord**,
	16.32	they preached the **word** of the **Lord**
	19.10	heard the **word** of the **Lord**.
	19.20	the **word** of the **Lord** kept spreading
1 Tim	6.3	the true **words** of our **Lord** Jesus Christ

1 Pet	1.25	the **word** of the **Lord** remains for ever.

Love

Ps	52.4	**love** to hurt people with your **words**
Ezek	33.31	**Loving words** are on their lips,
Hos	2.14	I will win her back with **words** of **love**.
1 Jn	2.5	obeys his **word** is the one whose **love**
	3.18	**love** should not be just **words** and talk;

Obey

Deut	32.47	**words**; they are your very life. **Obey**
2 Chr	34.21	not **obeyed** the **word** of the Lord
Ps	119.67	but now I **obey** your **word**.
	119.101	because I want to **obey** your **word**.
Is	50.10	and **obey** the **words** of his servant,
Jer	6.19	and have not **obeyed** my **words**.
Ezek	33.32	listen to all your **words** and don't **obey**
Mt	7.24	these **words** of mine and **obeys** them
	7.26	**words** of mine and does not **obey** them
Lk	6.47	and listens to my **words** and **obeys**
	6.49	who hears my **words** and does not **obey**
	8.21	who hear the **word** of God and **obey**
	11.28	who hear the **word** of God and **obey** it!
Jn	8.55	and I **obey** his **word**.
	17.6	They have **obeyed** your **word**,
1 Jn	2.5	whoever **obeys** his **word** is the one
Rev	1.3	**words** of this prophetic message and **obey**
	22.7	are those who **obey** the prophetic **words**
	22.9	those who **obey** the **words** in this book.

Power

Lk	4.36	kind of **words** are these? With...**power**
Acts	19.20	this **powerful** way the **word** of the Lord
1 Cor	4.20	is not a matter of **words** but of **power**.
1 Thes	1.5	with **words** only, but also with **power**
Heb	1.3	the universe with his **powerful word**.
Rev	17.17	**power** to rule until God's **words** come

Proclaim, Preach

Jer	23.30	take each other's **words** and **proclaim**
	31.10	**proclaim** my **words** on the far-off
Acts	6.2	to neglect the **preaching** of God's **word**
	13.5	they **preached** the **word** of God
	15.21	his **words** are **preached** in every town.
	15.35	and **preached** the **word** of the Lord.
	15.36	we **preached** the **word** of the Lord,
	16.32	they **preached** the **word** of the Lord
	17.13	had **preached** the **word** of God in Berea
1 Pet	1.25	**word** is the Good News...**proclaimed**
Rev	1.9	because I had **proclaimed** God's **word**
	6.9	**proclaimed** God's **word** and had been

True, Honest, Right

Judg	13.12	When your **words** come **true**,
	13.17	you when your **words** come **true**.
Job	6.25	**Honest words** are convincing,
	17.3	am being **honest**, God. Accept my **word**.
	24.25	prove that my **words** are not **true**?
	31.35	I swear that every **word** is **true**.
	33.3	my **words** are sincere, and I am speaking the **truth**.
Ps	15.2	whose **words** are **true** and sincere,
	33.4	The **words** of the Lord are **true**
	141.6	will admit that my **words** were **true**.
Prov	8.6	**words**; all I tell you is **right**.
	12.13	by his own **words**, but an **honest**
	13.5	**Honest** people hate lies, but the **words**
	15.23	the **right word** for the **right** occasion!
	22.12	**truth** is kept safe by disproving the **words** of liars.
Ecc	12.10	but the **words** he wrote were **honest**.
Is	43.9	**right**...testify to the **truth** of their **words**.
	48.16	have always made my **words** come **true**.
Jer	1.12	to see that my **words** come **true**.
	44.28	will know whose **words** have come **true**,

248

Ezek	13.6	they expect their **words** to come **true!**
	33.33	But when all your **words** come **true**
Dan	4.33	The **words** came **true** immediately
Jn	5.24	you the **truth**: whoever hears my **words**
	17.17	means of the **truth**; your **word** is **truth**.
	18.32	to make the **words** of Jesus come **true**,
Acts	13.27	made the prophets' **words** come **true**
1 Cor	2.1	secret **truth**, I did not use big **words**
1 Tim	4.6	**words** of faith and of the **true** teaching
	6.3	the **true words** of our Lord Jesus
2 Tim	1.13	to the **true words** that I taught you
Jas	1.18	us into being through the **word** of **truth**
Rev	1.9	God's **word** and the **truth** that Jesus
	17.17	to rule until God's **words** come **true**.
	19.9	These are the **true words** of God.
	20.4	**truth** that Jesus revealed and the **word**
	21.5	because these **words** are **true**
	22.6	**words** are **true** and can be trusted.

Trust see **Believe**

World

Jn	1.1	Before the **world** was created, the **Word**
	1.10	the **Word** was in the **world**,

WORLD

Jn	6.14	—	18.37	x60
1 Cor	1.20	—	7.31	x23
1 Jn	2.15	—	5.19	x20
Ecc	1.4	—	6.12	x14
Ecc	8.9	—	11.2	x12
Gen	6.1	—	11.1	x9
Eph	1.3	—	3.10	x8
Is	23.17	—	25.8	x7
Ezek	29.12	—	32.8	x7
Dan	4.1–26			x7
Jas	1.1	—	4.4	x7
Rev	16.14	—	18.23	x7
Job	37.12	—	39.3	x6
Jer	50.23	—	51.49	x6
Jn	1.1–29			x6
2 Pet	1.4	—	3.6	x6
Mt	24.14	—	26.13	x5
Jn	3.12	—	4.42	x5
Rom	3.6	—	5.13	x5
Rom	9.17	—	12.2	x5
Heb	9.11	—	11.38	x5
1 Chr	16.14	—	17.21	x4
Mk	13.19	—	14.9	x4
Is	14.7–26			x3
Zech	1.11–19			x3

Believe see **Faith**

Blessing

Deut	7.14	in the **world** will be as richly **blessed**
Is	19.24	will be a **blessing** to all the **world**.
Rom	11.12	brought rich **blessings** to the **world**,
Eph	1.3	spiritual **blessing** in the heavenly **world**.
Col	1.6	**blessings** and is spreading throughout the **world**,

Evil, Sin

Gen	6.12	at the **world** and saw that it was **evil**
Is	24.20	The **world** is weighed down by its **sins**;
Jn	1.29	who takes away the **sin** of the **world**!
Rom	5.12	**Sin** came into the **world** through one
	5.13	There was **sin** in the **world** before
2 Cor	4.4	the dark by the **evil** god of this **world**.
Gal	3.22	whole **world** is under the power of **sin**;
Eph	2.2	you followed the **world's evil** way
Phil	2.15	a **world** of corrupt and **sinful** people.
1 Tim	1.15	came into the **world** to save **sinners**.
1 Jn	2.16	the **world** — what the **sinful** self desires,

Faith, Believe

Jn	3.12	**believe** me when I tell you about the things of this **world**;

Jn	12.46	**world** as light, so that everyone who **believes**
	17.21	the **world** will **believe** that you sent me.
Rom	1.8	whole **world** is hearing about your **faith**.
1 Tim	1.15	**believed**: Christ Jesus came into the **world**
	3.16	was **believed** in throughout the **world**,
Jas	2.5	**world** to be rich in **faith** and to possess
1 Jn	5.4	over the **world** by means of our **faith**.
	5.5	the **world**? Only the person who **believes**

Hate

Jn	7.7	The **world** cannot **hate** you
	12.25	whoever **hates** his own life in this **world**
	15.18	If the **world hates** you
	15.19	that is why the **world hates** you.
	17.14	and the **world hated** them,
1 Jn	3.13	if the people of the **world hate** you.

Justice, Judge

1 Sam	2.10	The Lord will **judge** the whole **world**;
Ps	9.8	the **world** with righteousness; he **judges**
	58.11	is indeed a God who **judges** the **world**.
	76.8	made your **judgement** known...the **world**
	82.5	**justice** has disappeared from the **world**.
	96.13	the peoples of the **world** with **justice**
	98.9	the peoples of the **world** with **justice**
Ecc	3.16	**world** you find wickedness where **justice**
Jn	3.17	his Son into the **world** to be its **judge**,
	9.39	I came to this **world** to **judge**,
	12.31	is the time for this **world** to be **judged**
	12.47	not to **judge** the **world**, but to save it.
	16.11	of this **world** has already been **judged**.
Acts	17.31	will **judge** the whole **world** with **justice**
Rom	3.6	is not **just**, how can he **judge** the **world**?
	3.19	the whole **world** under God's **judgement**.
1 Cor	6.2	God's people will **judge** the **world**

Sin see **Evil**

Suffer

Is	25.8	have **suffered** throughout the **world**.
Jn	16.33	The **world** will make you **suffer**.
1 Pet	5.9	**world** are going through the same kind of **sufferings**.

Win

Ecc	9.11	**world** fast runners do not always **win**
Mt	16.26	**wins** the whole **world** but loses his life?
Mk	8.36	**wins** the whole **world** but loses his life?
Lk	9.25	**wins** the whole **world** but is himself lost
1 Jn	5.4	we **win** the victory over the **world**

Wise

1 Kgs	4.34	all over the **world** heard of his **wisdom**
	10.24	**world** wanted to...listen to the **wisdom**
2 Chr	9.22	**wiser** than any other king in the **world**.
Ecc	2.19	**wisdom** has earned for me in this **world**.
	8.16	to become **wise** and learn what goes on in the **world**,
	9.13	how **wisdom** is regarded in this **world**.
Jer	10.12	by his **wisdom** he created the **world**
	51.15	by his **wisdom** he created the **world**
1 Cor	1.20	this **world's wisdom** is foolishness!
	1.27	**world** considers nonsense in order to shame the **wise**,
	2.6	the **wisdom** that belongs to this **world**
	2.8	rulers of this **world** knew this **wisdom**
	3.18	he is **wise** by this **world's** standards,
	3.19	what this **world** considers to be **wisdom**
Eph	3.10	**world** might learn of his **wisdom**

WORLD OF THE DEAD

Ezek	31.14	—	32.30	x14
Job	33.22–28			x3
Is	14.9–15			x3

Abandon

Ps	16.10	not **abandon** me to the **world of the dead**.
Acts	2.27	not **abandon** me in the **world of the dead**;
	2.31	not **abandoned** in the **world of the dead**;

Alive

Num	16.30	go down **alive** to the **world of the dead**,
	16.33	down **alive** to the **world of the dead**,
Job	33.28	the **world of the dead**, and I am...**alive**.
Ps	55.15	down **alive** into the **world of the dead**!

Death

Rev	1.18	have authority over **death** and the **world**
	20.13	**Death** and the **world of the dead** also
	20.14	**death** and the **world of the dead** were

Heaven

Is	7.11	the **world of the dead** or from...**heaven**.
Phil	2.10	**heaven**, on earth, and in the **world**
Rev	5.3	**heaven** or on earth or in the **world**
	5.13	in **heaven**, on earth, in the **world** below

WORSHIP
God

	2 Chr	29.11	—	35.16	x18
	Ex	7.16	—	10.26	x11
	Lev	23.2 – 37			x11
	2 Chr	5.11	—	7.20	x10
	1 Kgs	8.16	—	9.7	x8
	Jn	4.20 – 24			x8
	Heb	9.1	—	13.10	x8
	Num	28.18	—	29.35	x7
	Deut	12.4	—	14.23	x7
	2 Kgs	17.25	—	18.22	x7
	1 Chr	21.30	—	23.32	x7
	Acts	7.7	—	10.35	x7
	1 Chr	15.13	—	16.39	x6
	Is	56.3	—	60.14	x6
	Acts	16.14	—	18.13	x6
	Ex	18.12	—	20.24	x5
	Neh	8.6	—	10.33	x5
	Ezek	46.2 – 11			x5
	1 Cor	11.4 – 17			x5
	1 Kgs	18.3 – 32			x4
	Zech	14.9 – 21			x4
	Gen	24.26 – 52			x3
	Ex	12.16 – 31			x3
	Josh	22.19 – 27			x3
	1 Sam	1.3 – 28			x3
	1 Sam	15.25 – 31			x3
	1 Chr	25.1 – 6			x3
	2 Chr	15.12 – 15			x3
	2 Chr	20.9 – 33			x3
	Ps	22.23 – 27			x3
	Mt	2.2 – 11			x3
	Acts	13.16 – 50			x3
	1 Cor	14.19 – 26			x3

Idols

	Deut	11.16	—	13.13	x14
	Deut	4.3	—	8.19	x10
	Dan	3.5 – 28			x10
	Deut	27.15	—	31.20	x9
	2 Kgs	10.19 – 29			x8
	2 Kgs	17.7 – 41			x8
	2 Chr	33.3	—	34.8	x8
	Jer	1.16	—	3.24	x8
	1 Kgs	11.4	—	12.30	x7
	Ezek	20.16	—	23.49	x7
	Rev	13.4	—	14.11	x7
	Judg	2.3	—	3.7	x6
	2 Kgs	23.4 – 24			x6

	Rev	19.10	—	22.15	x6
	Lev	18.21	—	20.5	x5
	Josh	23.7	—	24.15	x5
	2 Chr	24.7	—	25.20	x5
	Is	44.9 – 17			x5
	Jer	7.6	—	9.14	x5
	Hos	8.5	—	10.8	x5
	Ex	34.14 – 17			x4
	Num	25.2 – 11			x4
	2 Kgs	21.3 – 21			x4
	Is	57.5 – 9			x4
	Ex	20.3 – 23			x3
	Judg	10.6 – 13			x3
	1 Kgs	14.9 – 23			x3
	Ps	106.19 – 36			x3
	Ezek	8.10 – 16			x3
	Ezek	16.24 – 39			x3
	Ezek	18.6 – 15			x3
	Zeph	1.4 – 9			x3

Abandon see **Unfaithful**

Claim

Is	29.13	These people **claim** to **worship** me,
	48.1	and **claim** to **worship** the God
	58.2	They **worship** me every day, **claiming**
Jer	5.2	though you **claim** to **worship** the Lord,

Command see **Law**

Disobey

Deut	11.28	**disobey** these commands and...**worship**
	28.14	**disobey** them in any way, or **worship**
1 Kgs	18.18	**disobeying** the Lord's commands and **worshipping**
2 Kgs	17.12	and **disobeyed** the Lord's command not to **worship**

Faithful

Deut	10.20	**worship** only him. Be **faithful** to him
	13.4	**worship** him and be **faithful** to him.
Job	1.1	who **worshipped** God and was **faithful**
	1.8	**faithful** and good as he is. He **worships**
	2.3	**faithful** and good as he is. He **worships**

Joy

2 Chr	29.30	**joy** as they knelt and **worshipped** God.
Job	33.26	he will **worship** God with **joy**;
Ps	100.2	**Worship** the Lord with **joy**;
Lam	2.7	had **worshipped** in **joy**.

Law, Command

Deut	10.12	**Worship**...and do all that he **commands**.
	11.28	**commands** and turn away to **worship**
	13.4	keep his **commands**; **worship** him
Josh	1.8	the **Law** is always read in your **worship**.
	23.16	God **commanded** you...if you serve and **worship**
1 Kgs	9.6	and **commands**...and **worship** other gods,
	11.9	had **commanded** him not to **worship**
	18.18	**commands** and **worshipping** the idols
2 Kgs	17.12	Lord's **command** not to **worship** idols.
	17.34	not **worship**...nor do they obey the **laws**
2 Chr	7.19	**commands**...and **worship** other gods,
	33.16	**commanded**...Judah to **worship** the Lord,
Acts	18.13	to **worship** God in a way that is against the **law**!
Rom	9.4	the **Law**; they have the true **worship**;

Offering, Present, Sacrifice

Ex	23.15	**worship** me without bringing an **offering**.
	32.8	have **worshipped** it and **offered sacrifices**
	34.15	**worship** their pagan gods and **sacrifice**
Lev	23.26	**worship**, and **present** a **food-offering**
	23.36	**worship** and **present** a **food-offering**
	23.37	**worship** and **presenting food-offerings**,
1 Sam	1.3	Ramah to **worship** and **offer sacrifices**
1 Chr	6.49	all the **worship**...and for the **sacrifices**

2 Chr	1.6	king **worshipped** the Lord by **offering**
	33.16	was **worshipped**, and he **sacrificed**
Ezra	4.2	you **worship**, and we have been **offering**
Ps	16.4	**sacrifices**; I will not **worship** their gods.
	22.25	**worship** you I will **offer** the **sacrifices**
	106.28	**worship** of Baal, and ate **sacrifices offered**
Is	19.21	**worship** him, and bring him **sacrifices** and **offerings**.
	57.6	**worship** them as gods. You pour out wine as **offerings**
Jer	7.9	**offer sacrifices** to Baal, and **worship**
	44.8	by **worshipping** idols and by **sacrificing**
Hab	1.16	**worship** their nets and **offer sacrifices**
Jn	4.23	**offering** him the true **worship**
Rom	12.1	the true **worship** that you should **offer**.
Heb	9.9	**sacrifices** presented to God cannot make the **worshipper's**
	13.10	**worship** have no right to...the **sacrifice**

Please

Deut	12.8	all been **worshipping** as you **please**,
Ezek	20.40	Israel will **worship** me. I will be **pleased**
Hag	1.8	I will be **pleased** and will be **worshipped**
Rom	12.1	**pleasing** to him. This is the true **worship**
Heb	12.28	**worship** God in a way that will **please**

Power

Neh	9.6	**powers** bow down and come...**worship** you.
Zech	8.22	**powerful** nations will come...to **worship**
Jn	4.23	by the **power** of God's Spirit people will **worship** the Father
	4.24	**power** of his Spirit can people **worship**

Pray

1 Kgs	8.41	comes to **worship** you and to **pray**
Job	33.26	**prays**, God will answer...he will **worship**
Ps	44.20	**worshipping** our God and **prayed**
	79.6	do not **worship** you, on the people who do not **pray**
Zech	8.21	to **worship** the Lord Almighty and **pray**
	8.22	**worship** the Lord Almighty, and...**pray**
Lk	2.36	**worshipped** God, fasting and **praying**.
1 Cor	11.4	a man who **prays**...in public **worship**
	11.5	woman who **prays**...in public **worship**
	11.13	to **pray** to God in public **worship**

Presence

Deut	12.5	come into his **presence** and **worship** him.
	14.23	be **worshipped**; and there in his **presence**
	26.10	the Lord's **presence** and **worship** there.
Ps	22.25	the **presence** of those who **worship** you
	42.2	can I go and **worship** in your **presence**?
Jer	34.15	my **presence**...where I am **worshipped**.

Present see Offering

Punish

Is	10.10	**punish** those kingdoms that **worship**
Ezek	11.21	**punish** the people who love to **worship**
Zeph	1.9	**punish** all who **worship** like pagans

Sacred

Ex	18.12	the **sacred** meal as an act of **worship**.
Josh	22.27	**worship** the Lord before his **sacred** Tent
1 Chr	22.19	**sacred** objects used in **worshipping** him.
Neh	10.33	**worship** the following: the **sacred** bread,
Ps	15.1	may **worship** on Zion, your **sacred** hill?
	99.9	and **worship** at his **sacred** hill!
Is	27.13	**worship** the Lord...on his **sacred** hill.

Sacrifice see Offering

Serve

Deut	4.19	to **worship** and **serve** what you see
	8.19	turn to other gods to **worship** and **serve**
	11.16	to **worship** and **serve** other gods.
	13.2	to lead you to **worship** and **serve** gods

Deut	17.3	by **worshipping** and **serving** other gods
	28.14	or **worship** and **serve** other gods.
	29.26	**served** other gods that they had never **worshipped**
Josh	23.16	if you **serve** and **worship** other gods,
	24.15	you will **serve**, the gods your ancestors **worshipped**
Judg	2.13	**worshipping** the Lord and **served** the
	2.19	would **serve** and **worship** other gods,
1 Kgs	22.53	He **worshipped** and **served** Baal,
2 Kgs	17.16	**worshipped** the stars, and **served** the god
1 Chr	23.13	**worship** of the Lord, to **serve** him,
2 Chr	11.15	**serve** at the pagan places of **worship** and to **worship**
Jer	8.2	**served**, and which they have...**worshipped**.
	13.10	have **worshipped** and **served** other gods.
	16.11	and **worshipped** and **served** other gods.
	22.9	have **worshipped** and **served** other gods.
	25.6	to **worship** and **serve** other gods
	35.15	not to **worship** and **serve** other gods,
Ezek	44.16	**serve** at my altar, and conduct the temple **worship**.
Mt	4.10	**Worship** the Lord your God and **serve**
Lk	4.8	**Worship** the Lord your God and **serve**
Rom	1.25	**worship** and **serve** what God has created
Heb	13.10	**serve** in the Jewish place of **worship**
Rev	22.3	his **servants** will **worship** him

Sin

1 Kgs	12.30	the people **sinned**, going to **worship**
	21.26	shameful **sins** by **worshipping** idols,
2 Kgs	10.29	**sin** of **worshipping** the gold bull-calves
Ezek	23.49	and your **sin** of **worshipping** idols.
Hos	13.1	people **sinned** by **worshipping** Baal,

Unfaithful, Abandon, Turn

Ex	34.16	to be **unfaithful** to me and to **worship**
Lev	19.4	Do not **abandon** me and **worship** idols
	20.5	**unfaithful** to me and **worshipping**
Deut	8.19	or **turn** to other gods to **worship**
	11.28	**turn** away to **worship** other gods
	29.18	**turns** from the Lord...to **worship**
	31.16	**abandon** me and **worship** the pagan
	31.20	will **turn** away and **worship** other gods.
Judg	2.17	**unfaithful** to the Lord and **worshipped**
	8.27	**abandoned** God...to **worship** the idol.
	8.33	again **unfaithful** to God and **worshipped**
1 Sam	8.8	**turned** away from me and **worshipped**
	12.10	**turned** away from you, Lord, and **worshipped**
Ps	40.4	**turn** to idols or join those who **worship**
Jer	2.5	**turn** away from me? They **worshipped**
	5.7	**abandoned** me and have **worshipped**
	16.11	**turned** away from me and **worshipped**
Ezek	14.7	**turns** away from me and **worships**
Acts	7.42	**turned** away from them and gave them over to **worship**

YEAST

Ex	12.8	—	13.7	x9
1 Cor	5.6 – 8			x5
Lev	2.4 – 11			x4
Deut	16.3 – 8			x4
Lev	6.16	—	7.13	x3
Mt	16.6 – 12			x3

Bread

Ex	12.8	and with **bread** made without **yeast**.
	12.15	any **bread** made with **yeast** — eat only unleavened **bread**.
	12.18	not eat any **bread** made with **yeast**.
	12.19	or foreign, eats **bread** made with **yeast**,
	13.7	not eat any **bread** made with **yeast**;
	23.15	Do not eat any **bread** made with **yeast**
	23.18	Do not offer **bread** made with **yeast**

Ex	29.2	but no **yeast**, and make some **bread**
	34.25	Do not offer **bread** made with **yeast**
Lev	6.16	be made into **bread** baked without **yeast**
	7.12	an offering of **bread** made without **yeast**:
	7.13	loaves of **bread** baked without **yeast**.
	23.6	not eat any **bread** made with **yeast**.
Num	6.15	a basket of **bread** made without **yeast**:
	28.17	**bread** prepared without **yeast** is to be
Deut	16.3	do not eat **bread** prepared with **yeast**.
	16.8	are to eat **bread** prepared without **yeast**,
Josh	5.11	grain and **bread** made without **yeast**.

Judg	6.19	flour to make **bread** without any **yeast**.
1 Sam	28.24	and baked some **bread** without **yeast**.
Ezek	45.21	will eat **bread** made without **yeast**.
Mt	16.12	**yeast** used in **bread** but from the
1 Cor	5.8	with **bread** having the old **yeast** of sin

Pharisees

Mt	16.6	guard against the **yeast** of the **Pharisees**
	16.11	from the **yeast** of the **Pharisees**
Mk	8.15	**yeast** of the **Pharisees** and the **yeast** of
Lk	12.1	guard against the **yeast** of the **Pharisees**

Names Index

The list below includes every name which appears in the *Good News Bible*. People or places that share the same name are distinguished by numbers in brackets following the name. For ease of reference, these numbers are the same as those used in the full *Concordance to the Good News Bible*. This means that in a very few cases there is no number 1. For example, you will find **Job (2)** and **Job (3)**, but not **Job (1)**, because in the full concordance **Job (1)** is not a name.

Under each name you will find a complete list of references to that name. If the same name occurs several times in a single chapter, the passage and number of occurrences are noted, rather than each individual verse, e.g. **Gen 28.4 – 13 x4**. If the name occurs several times in consecutive chapters, a total figure is given, e.g. **Gen 48 – 50 x6**.

Cross-references are provided in cases where an individual person or place is known by more than one name.

Aaron				**Abagtha**				**Abel Keramim**			
Ex	4 – 12	x 51		Esth	1.10			Judg	11.33		
	15 – 19	x 11		**Abana**				**Abel Meholah**			
	24.1 – 14	x 3		2 Kgs	5.12			Judg	7.22		
	27 – 32	x 43		**Abarim**				1 Kgs	4.12		
	34 – 35	x 3		Num	21.11				19.16		
	38 – 40	x 7			27.12			**Abel Mizraim**			
Lev	1 – 3	x 3			33.41	x 2		Gen	50.11		
	6 – 11	x 38		Deut	32.49			**Abialbon**			
	13 – 17	x 14		**Abda (1)**				2 Sam	23.24		
	21 – 22	x 8		1 Kgs	4.6			**Abiasaph**			
	24.3 – 9	x 3		**Abda (2)**				Ex	6.24		
Num	1 – 4	x 23		Neh	11.17			**Abiathar**			
	6 – 10	x 12		**Abdeel**				1 Sam	22 – 23	x 3	
	12 – 20	x 47		Jer	36.26				30.7	x 2	
	25 – 27	x 7		**Abdi (1)**				2 Sam	8.17		
	33.1 – 38	x 2		1 Chr	6.44				15.24 – 35	x 4	
Deut	9 – 10	x 3		2 Chr	29.12				17.15 – 17	x 2	
	32.50			**Abdi (2)**					19 – 20	x 2	
Josh	21.4 – 19	x 4		Ezra	10.26			1 Kgs	1 – 2	x 8	
	24.5 – 33	x 2		**Abdiel**					4.4		
Judg	20.27			1 Chr	5.15			1 Chr	15.11		
1 Sam	2.27			**Abdon (1)**					18.16		
	12.6 – 8	x 2		Judg	12.13 – 14	x 2			24.6		
1 Chr	6.3 – 57	x 6		**Abdon (2)**					27.34		
	12.23			2 Chr	34.20			Mk	2.26		
	15.4			**Abdon (3)**				**Abib**			
	23 – 24	x 9		Josh	21.30			Ex	13.4		
	27.16			1 Chr	6.74				23.15		
2 Chr	13.9 – 10	x 2		**Abdon (4)**					34.18		
	26.18			1 Chr	8 – 9	x 2		Deut	16.1		
	29.21			**Abdon (5)**				**Abida**			
	31.19			1 Chr	8.23			Gen	25.4		
	35.14			**Abednego**				1 Chr	1.33		
Ezra	7.1 – 5	x 2		see also Azariah (25)				**Abidan**			
Neh	10.38			Dan	1 – 3	x 11		Num	1 – 2	x 2	
Ps	77.20			**Abel (1)**					7.12		
	99.6			(Cain's brother)					10.24		
	105 – 106	x 2		Gen	4.2 – 25	x 7		**Abiel (1)**			
	133.2			Mt	23.35			1 Sam	9.1		
Mic	6.4			Lk	11.51				14.51		
Acts	7.40			Heb	11 – 12	x 3		**Abiel (2)**			
Heb	5.4			1 Jn	3.12			1 Chr	11.26		
	7.11			**Abel (2)**				**Abiezer (1)**			
	9.4			2 Sam	20.18			Josh	17.2		
Abaddon				**Abel Beth Maacah**				Judg	6.11 – 34	x 3	
Rev	9.11			2 Sam	20.14				8.32		
				1 Kgs	15.20			1 Chr	7.18		
				2 Kgs	15.29						
				2 Chr	16.4						

Abiezer (2)			
2 Sam	23.24		
1 Chr	11.26		
	27.2		
Abigail (1)			
1 Sam	25.2 – 43	x 8	
	27.3		
	30.5		
2 Sam	2 – 3	x 2	
1 Chr	3.1		
Abigail (2)			
2 Sam	17.25		
1 Chr	2.16 – 17	x 2	
Abihail (1)			
Num	3.35		
Abihail (2)			
1 Chr	2.29		
Abihail (3)			
1 Chr	5.14	x 2	
Abihail (4)			
2 Chr	11.18		
Abihail (5)			
Esth	2.15		
	9.29		
Abihu			
Ex	6.23		
	24.1 – 9	x 2	
	28.1		
Lev	10.1		
Num	3.2 – 4	x 2	
	26.60 – 61	x 2	
1 Chr	6.3		
	24.1 – 2	x 2	
Abihud			
1 Chr	8.3		
Abijah (1)			
1 Kgs	14 – 15	x 6	
1 Chr	3.10		
2 Chr	11 – 15	x 15	
Mt	1.6		
Abijah (2)			
1 Kgs	14.1		
Abijah (3)			
1 Chr	24.7		
Lk	1.5		
Abijah (4)			
2 Kgs	18.2		
2 Chr	29.1		

Adonijah (1) (Cont)
1 Chr 3.1
Adonijah (2)
2 Chr 17.8
Adonijah (3)
Neh 10.14
Adonikam (1)
Ezra 2.3
Neh 7.8
Adonikam (2)
Ezra 8.2
Adoniram
2 Sam 20.24
1 Kgs 4 — 5   x 2
12.18
2 Chr 10.18
Adonizedek
Josh 10.1 — 3   x 2
Adoraim
2 Chr 11.9
Adrammelech (1)
2 Kgs 17.31
Adrammelech (2)
2 Kgs 19.37
Is 37.38
Adramyttium
Acts 27.2
Adriel
1 Sam 18.19
2 Sam 21.8
Adullam
Gen 38.1 — 12   x 2
Josh 12.15
15.35
1 Sam 22.1
2 Sam 23.13
1 Chr 11.15
2 Chr 11.7
Neh 11.30
Mic 1.15
Adummim
Josh 15.7
18.17
Aeneas
Acts 9.33 — 34   x 3
Aenon
Jn 3.23
Agabus
Acts 11.28
21.10
Agag
Num 24.7
1 Sam 15.8 — 33   x 6
Esth 3.1 — 10   x 2
8 — 9   x 3
Agee
2 Sam 23.11
Agrippa
Acts 25 — 26   x 12
Agur
Prov 30.1
Ahab (1)
1 Kgs 16 — 22   x 71
2 Kgs 1.1
3.1 — 5   x 2
8 — 10   x 23
21.3 — 13   x 2
2 Chr 21 — 22   x 7
Mic 6.16
Ahab (2)
Jer 29.21 — 22   x 2
Aharah
1 Chr 8.1
Aharhel
1 Chr 4.8

Ahasbai
2 Sam 23.24
Ahava
Ezra 8.15 — 31   x 3
Ahaz (1)
2 Kgs 15 — 18   x 17
20.11
23.12
1 Chr 3.13
2 Chr 27 — 29   x 13
Is 1.1
7.1 — 12   x 4
14.28
38.8
Hos 1.1
Mic 1.1
Mt 1.6
Ahaz (2)
1 Chr 8 — 9   x 4
Ahaziah (1)
1 Kgs 22.40 — 51   x 3
2 Kgs 1.2 — 18   x 5
2 Chr 20.35 — 37   x 2
Ahaziah (2)
2 Kgs 8 — 13   x 19
1 Chr 3.11
2 Chr 21 — 22   x 14
Ahban
1 Chr 2.29
Ahi
1 Chr 5.15
Ahiah
Neh 10.14
Ahiam
2 Sam 23.24
1 Chr 11.26
Ahian
1 Chr 7.19
Ahiezer (1)
Num 1 — 2   x 2
7.12
10.25
Ahiezer (2)
1 Chr 12.3
Ahihud (1)
Num 34.19
Ahihud (2)
1 Chr 8.6
Ahijah (1)
1 Kgs 11 — 12   x 3
14 — 15   x 8
2 Chr 9 — 10   x 2
Ahijah (2)
1 Sam 14.3 — 18   x 3
Ahijah (3)
1 Kgs 4.3
Ahijah (4)
1 Kgs 15.27 — 33   x 2
21.22
Ahijah (5)
1 Chr 2.25
Ahijah (6)
1 Chr 8.6
Ahijah (7)
1 Chr 11.26
Ahikam
2 Kgs 22.12 — 14   x 2
25.22
2 Chr 34.20
Jer 26.24
39 — 40   x 2
Ahilud
2 Sam 8.16
20.24
1 Kgs 4.3 — 12   x 2

Ahilud (Cont)
1 Chr 18.15
Ahimaaz (1)
2 Sam 15.27 — 36   x 2
17 — 18   x 10
1 Chr 6.8 — 53   x 2
Ahimaaz (2)
1 Sam 14.50
Ahimaaz (3)
1 Kgs 4.15
Ahiman (1)
Num 13.22
Josh 15.14
Judg 1.10
Ahiman (2)
1 Chr 9.17
Ahimelech (1)
1 Sam 21 — 23   x 12
30.7
2 Sam 8.17
1 Chr 18.16
24.3 — 31   x 3
Ahimelech (2)
1 Sam 26.6
Ahimoth
1 Chr 6.25 — 26   x 2
Ahinadab
1 Kgs 4.14
Ahinoam (1)
1 Sam 25.43
27.3
30.5
2 Sam 2 — 3   x 2
1 Chr 3.1
Ahinoam (2)
1 Sam 14.50
Ahio (1)
2 Sam 6.3 — 4   x 2
1 Chr 13.7
Ahio (2)
1 Chr 8.14
Ahio (3)
1 Chr 8 — 9   x 2
Ahira
Num 1 — 2   x 2
7.12
10.27
Ahiram
Num 26.38
Ahisamach
Ex 31.6
35.34
38.23
Ahishahar
1 Chr 7.10
Ahishar
1 Kgs 4.6
Ahithophel
2 Sam 15 — 17   x 16
23.24
1 Chr 27.33 — 34   x 2
Ahitub (1)
1 Sam 14.3
Ahitub (2)
1 Sam 22.9
Ahitub (3)
2 Sam 8.17
1 Chr 6.7 — 52   x 2
18.16
Ezra 7.2
Ahitub (4)
1 Chr 6.11
Ahitub (5)
1 Chr 9.10
Neh 11.11

Ahlab
Judg 1.31
Ahlai (1)
1 Chr 2.31
Ahlai (2)
1 Chr 11.26
Ahoah
1 Chr 8.4
Ahoh (1)
2 Sam 23.9
1 Chr 11.12
Ahoh (2)
2 Sam 23.24
1 Chr 11.26
Ahohi
1 Chr 27.2
Ahumai
1 Chr 4.2
Ahuzzam
1 Chr 4.6
Ahuzzath
Gen 26.26
Ahzai
Neh 11.13
Ai (1)
Gen 12 — 13   x 2
Josh 7 — 10   x 27
12.9
Ezra 2.21
Neh 7.26
11.31
Jer 49.3
Ai (2)
Is 10.28
Aiah (1)
Gen 36.24
1 Chr 1.38
Aiah (2)
2 Sam 3.7
21.8 — 10   x 2
Aijalon (1)
Josh 10.12
19.42
21.24
Judg 1.35
1 Sam 14.31
1 Chr 6.69
8.13
2 Chr 11.10
28.18
Aijalon (2)
Judg 12.12
Ain (1)
Num 34.11
Ain (2)
Josh 15.32
19.7
21.16
1 Chr 4.32
Akan
Gen 36.27
Akeldama
Acts 1.19
Akkub (1)
1 Chr 3.24
Akkub (2)
1 Chr 9.17
Neh 11 — 12   x 2
Akkub (3)
Ezra 2.40
Neh 7.43
Akkub (4)
Ezra 2.43
Akkub (5)
Neh 8.7

Akrabbim
Num   34.4
Josh   15.3
Judg   1.36
Alemeth (1)
1 Chr 7.8
Alemeth (2)
1 Chr 8 − 9   x 2
Alemeth (3)
1 Chr 6.60
Alexander (1)
Mk   15.21
Alexander (2)
Acts   4.6
Alexander (3)
Acts   19.33   x 2
Alexander (4)
1 Tim 1.20
Alexander (5)
2 Tim 4.14
Alexandria
Acts   6.9
        18.24
        27 − 28   x 2
Allam Melech
Josh   19.26
Allon
1 Chr 4.34
Almodad
Gen   10.26
1 Chr 1.20
Almon
Josh   21.18
Almon Diblathaim
Num   33.41
Alphaeus (1)
Mk   2.14
Alphaeus (2)
Mt   10.3
Mk   3.18
Lk   6.15
Acts   1.13
Alush
Num   33.13
Alvah
Gen   36.40
1 Chr 1.51
Alvan
Gen   36.23
1 Chr 1.38
Amad
Josh   19.26
Amal
1 Chr 7.35
Amalek
Gen   14.7
        36.10 − 16   x 2
Ex   17.8 − 16   x 7
Num   13 − 14   x 4
        24.20   x 2
Deut   25.17 − 19 x 2
Judg   1.16
        3.13
        6 − 7   x 3
        10.12
        12.15
1 Sam 14 − 15   x 10
        27 − 28   x 2
        30.1 − 19 x 4
2 Sam 1.1 − 16   x 5
        8.12
1 Chr 1.36
        4.43
        18.11
Ps   83.7

Amam
Josh   15.26
Amana
Song   4.8
Amariah (1)
1 Chr 6.7 − 52   x 2
Ezra   7.3
Amariah (2)
1 Chr 6.11
Amariah (3)
1 Chr 23 − 24   x 2
Amariah (4)
2 Chr 19.11
Amariah (5)
2 Chr 31.15
Amariah (6)
Ezra   10.38
Amariah (7)
Neh   10.2
        12.2 − 12 x 2
Amariah (8)
Neh   11.4
Amariah (9)
Zeph   1.1
Amasa (1)
2 Sam 17.25   x 2
        19 − 20   x 8
1 Kgs 2.5 − 32   x 2
1 Chr 2.17
Amasa (2)
2 Chr 28.12
Amasai (1)
1 Chr 6.25 − 35   x 2
2 Chr 29.12
Amasai (2)
1 Chr 12.18
Amasai (3)
1 Chr 15.23
Amashsai
Neh   11.13
Amasiah
2 Chr 17.16   x 2
Amaw
Num   22.5
Amaziah (1)
2 Kgs 12 − 15   x 16
1 Chr 3.12
2 Chr 24 − 26   x 21
Amaziah (2)
Amos   7.10 − 17   x 3
Amaziah (3)
1 Chr 6.45
Amaziah (4)
1 Chr 4.34
Amen
Rev   3.14
Ami
Ezra   2.55
Amittai
2 Kgs 14.25
Jon   1.1
Amizzabad
1 Chr 27.2
Ammah
2 Sam 2.24
Ammiel (1)
Num   13.3
Ammiel (2)
2 Sam 9.4
        17.27
Ammiel (3)
1 Chr 26.5
Ammiel (4)
1 Chr 3.5

Ammihud (1)
Num   1 − 2   x 2
        7.12
        10.22
1 Chr 7.26
Ammihud (2)
Num   34.19
Ammihud (3)
Num   34.19
Ammihud (4)
2 Sam 13.37
Ammihud (5)
1 Chr 9.4
Amminadab (1)
Ex   6.23
Amminadab (2)
Num   1 − 2   x 2
        7.12
        10.14
Ruth   4.18
1 Chr 2.10
Mt   1.2
Lk   3.33
Amminadab (3)
1 Chr 6.22
Amminadab (4)
1 Chr 15.10 − 11 x 2
Ammishaddai
Num   1 − 2   x 2
        7.12
        10.25
Ammon
Gen   19.38
Num   21.24
Deut   2 − 3   x 6
        23.3
Josh   12 − 13   x 3
Judg   3.13
        10 − 12   x 23
1 Sam 11 − 12   x 3
        14.47
2 Sam 8.12
        10 − 12   x 14
        17.27
        23.24
1 Kgs 11.1 − 33   x 4
        14.21
2 Kgs 23 − 24   x 2
1 Chr 11.26
        18 − 20   x 14
2 Chr 12.13
        20.1 − 23 x 3
        24.26
        26 − 27   x 3
Ezra   9.1
Neh   2.10
        4.7
        13.1 − 23 x 3
Ps   83.7 − 8   x 2
Is   11.14
Jer   9.25
        25.19
        27.3
        40 − 41   x 4
        49.1 − 6   x 2
Ezek   21.20 − 28 x 2
        25.2 − 10 x 3
Dan   11.41
Amos   1.13
Zeph   2.8 − 10   x 3
Amnon (1)
2 Sam 3.2
        13.1 − 39 x 18
1 Chr 3.1

Amnon (2)
1 Chr 4.20
Amok
Neh   12.2 − 12   x 2
Amon (1)
2 Kgs 21.18 − 26 x 6
1 Chr 3.14
2 Chr 33.20 − 25 x 4
Jer   1.2
        25.3
Zeph   1.1
Mt   1.6
Amon (2)
1 Kgs 22.26
2 Chr 18.25
Amon (3)
Neh   7.57
Amon (3)
Jer   46.25
Amorites
Gen   10.16
        14 − 15   x 4
        48.22
Ex   3.8 − 17   x 2
        13.5
        23.23
        33 − 34   x 2
Num   13.29
        21 − 22   x 10
        32.33 − 39 x 2
Deut   1 − 4   x 12
        7.1
        20.17
        31.4
Josh   2 − 3   x 2
        5.1
        7.7
        9 − 13   x 15
        24.8 − 18   x 5
Judg   1.34 − 35   x 2
        3.5
        6.10
        10 − 11   x 6
2 Sam 21.2
1 Kgs 4.19
        9.20
        21.26
1 Chr 1.14
2 Chr 8.7
Ezra   9.1
Neh   9.8
Ps   135 − 136   x 2
Is   17.9
Ezek   16.3 − 45   x 2
Amos   2.9 − 10   x 2
Amos (1)
Amos   1.1 − 2   x 3
        7 − 8   x 5
Amos (2)
Lk   3.25
Amoz
2 Kgs 19 − 20   x 2
2 Chr 26.22
        32.20 − 32 x 2
Is   1 − 2   x 2
        13.1
        20.2
        37 − 38   x 2
Amphipolis
Acts   17.1
Ampliatus
Rom   16.8
Amram (1)
Ex   6.18 − 20   x 3
Num   3.17 − 27   x 2

Amram (1) (Cont)
Num 26.58 − 59 x 2
1 Chr 6.2 − 18 x 3
23 − 24 x 3
26.23
Amram (2)
Ezra 10.34
Amraphel
Gen 14.1
Amzi (1)
1 Chr 6.46
Amzi (2)
Neh 11.12
Anab
Josh 11.21
15.50
Anah (1)
Gen 36.2 − 29 x 7
Anah (2)
Gen 36.24 x 2
1 Chr 1.38 x 2
Anaharath
Josh 19.19
Anaiah (1)
Neh 8.4
Anaiah (2)
Neh 10.14
Anakim
Num 13.22 − 33 x 2
Deut 2.10 − 21 x 3
Josh 11.21 − 22 x 2
14 − 15 x 4
21.11
Judg 1.20
Anam
Gen 10.13
1 Chr 1.11
Anammelech
2 Kgs 17.31
Anan
Neh 10.14
Anani
1 Chr 3.24
Ananiah (1)
Neh 3.23
Ananiah (2)
Neh 11.32
Ananias (1)
Acts 5.1 − 5 x 3
Ananias (2)
Acts 9.10 − 17 x 5
22.12
Ananias (3)
Acts 23 − 24 x 2
Anath
Judg 3.31
5.6
Anathoth (1)
Josh 21.18
2 Sam 23.24
1 Kgs 2.26
1 Chr 6.60
11 − 12 x 2
27.2
Ezra 2.21
Neh 7.26
11.32
Is 10.30
Jer 1.1
11.21 − 23 x 2
29.27
32.7
Anathoth (2)
1 Chr 7.8

Anathoth (3)
Neh 10.14
Andrew
Mt 4.18
10.2
Mk 1.16 − 29 x 2
3.18
13.3
Lk 6.14
Jn 1.40 − 44 x 2
6.8
12.22
Acts 1.13
Andronicus
Rom 16.7
Anem
1 Chr 6.73
Aner (1)
Gen 14.13 − 24 x 2
Aner (2)
1 Chr 6.70
Aniam
1 Chr 7.19
Anim
Josh 15.50
Anna
Lk 2.36
Annas
Lk 3.2
Jn 18.13 − 24 x 2
Acts 4.6
Anthothijah
1 Chr 8.24
Antioch in Pisidia
Acts 13 − 14 x 4
2 Tim 3.11
Antioch in Syria
Acts 6.5
11.19 − 27 x 6
13 − 15 x 9
18.22
Gal 2.11
Antipas
Rev 2.13
Antipatris
Acts 23.31
Anub
1 Chr 4.8
Apelles
Rom 16.10
Aphek (1)
Josh 12.18
1 Sam 4.1
29.1
Aphek (2)
1 Kgs 20.26 − 30 x 2
2 Kgs 13.17
Aphek (3)
Josh 13.4
19.30
Judg 1.31
Aphekah
Josh 15.53
Aphiah
1 Sam 9.1
Apis
Jer 46.15
Apollonia
Acts 17.1
Apollos
Acts 18 − 19 x 3
1 Cor 1.12
3 − 4 x 5
16.12
Tit 3.13

Apollyon
Rev 9.11
Appaim
1 Chr 2.30 − 31 x 2
Apphia
Phlm .2
Appius
Acts 28.15
Aqaba
Ex 23.31
Num 14.25
21.4
Deut 1 − 2 x 2
Judg 11.16
1 Kgs 9.26
2 Chr 8.17
Jer 49.21
Aquila
Acts 18.2 − 26 x 4
Rom 16.3
1 Cor 16.19
2 Tim 4.19
Ar
Num 21 − 22 x 3
Deut 2.9 − 29 x 4
Is 15.1
Ara
1 Chr 7.38
Arab (1)
1 Kgs 10.15
2 Chr 9.14
17.11
21 − 22 x 2
26.7
Neh 2.19
4.7
Ps 72.15
Is 13.20
21.13 x 2
Jer 3.2
25.19
Ezek 27.21
30.5
Acts 2.11
Gal 1.17
4.25
Arab (2)
Josh 15.52
2 Sam 23.24
Arabah (1)
2 Sam 23.24
Arabah (2)
Amos 6.14
Arad (1)
1 Chr 8.15
Arad (2)
Num 21.1
33.40
Josh 12.14
Judg 1.16
Arah (1)
1 Chr 7.39
Arah (2)
Ezra 2.3
Neh 7.8
Arah (3)
Neh 6.18
Aram (1)
Gen 10.22 − 23 x 2
1 Chr 1.17
Aram (2)
Gen 22.21
Aram (3)
1 Chr 2.23

Aram (4)
1 Chr 7.34
Aramean
Gen 25.20
28.5
Deut 26.5
1 Chr 7.14
Aran
Gen 36.28
1 Chr 1.38
Ararat (1)
Gen 8.4
Ararat (2)
2 Kgs 19.37
Is 37.38
Jer 51.27
Araunah
2 Sam 24.16 − 23 x 5
1 Chr 21.15 − 28 x 7
2 Chr 3.1
Arba
Josh 14 − 15 x 3
21.11
Arbah
1 Chr 11.26
Archelaus
Mt 2.22
Archippus
Col 4.17
Phlm .2
Archite
Josh 16.2
2 Sam 15.32
1 Chr 27.33
Ard (1)
Gen 46.21
Ard (2)
Num 26.40
Ardon
1 Chr 2.18
Areli
Gen 46.16
Num 26.17
Areopagus
Acts 17.19
Aretas
2 Cor 11.32
Argob
Deut 3.4 − 14 x 3
1 Kgs 4.13
Aridai
Esth 9.7
Aridatha
Esth 9.7
Ariel
Ezra 8.16
Arimathea
Mt 27.57
Mk 15.42
Lk 23.50
Jn 19.38
Arioch (1)
Gen 14.1
Arioch (2)
Dan 2.14 − 25 x 5
Arisai
Esth 9.7
Aristarchus
Acts 19 − 20 x 2
27.2
Col 4.10
Phlm .24
Aristobulus
Rom 16.10

Arkites
Gen 10.17
1 Chr 1.15
Armageddon
Rev 16.16
Armoni
2 Sam 21.8
Arnan
1 Chr 3.21
Arni
Lk 3.33
Arnon
Num 21 — 22   x 7
Deut 2 — 4   x 6
Josh 12 — 13   x 4
Judg 11.13 — 26   x 5
2 Kgs 10.33
Is 16.2
Jer 48.20
Arod
Gen 46.16
Num 26.17
Aroer (1)
Deut 2 — 4   x 3
Josh 12 — 13   x 3
Judg 11.26 — 33   x 2
2 Kgs 10.33
1 Chr 5.8
        11.26
Jer 48.19
Aroer (2)
Num 32.34
Josh 13.25
2 Sam 24.5
Aroer (3)
1 Sam 30.28
Arpachshad
Gen 10 — 11   x 4
1 Chr 1.17 — 24   x 3
Arpad
2 Kgs 18 — 19   x 2
Is 10.9
    36 — 37   x 2
Jer 49.23
Arphaxad
Lk 3.36
Artaxerxes (1)
Ezra 7 — 8   x 5
Neh 1 — 2   x 2
     5.14
     13.6
Artaxerxes (2)
Ezra 4.7 — 23   x 4
Artaxerxes (3)
Ezra 6.14
Artemas
Tit 3.12
Artemis
Acts 19.24 — 35   x 5
Arubboth
1 Kgs 4.10
Arumah
Judg 9.31 — 41   x 2
Arvad
Ezek 27.8 — 11   x 2
Arvadites
Gen 10.18
1 Chr 1.16
Arza
1 Kgs 16.9
Asa (1)
1 Kgs 15 — 16   x 21
      22.41 — 46   x 3
1 Chr 3.10
2 Chr 14 — 17   x 28

Asa (1) (Cont)
2 Chr 20 — 21   x 2
Jer 41.9
Mt 1.6
Asa (2)
1 Chr 9.14
Asahel (1)
2 Sam 2 — 3   x 10
      23.24
1 Chr 2.16
      11.26
      27.2
Asahel (2)
2 Chr 17.8
Asahel (3)
2 Chr 31.13
Asahel (4)
Ezra 10.15
Asaiah (1)
1 Chr 4.34
Asaiah (2)
1 Chr 6.30
Asaiah (3)
1 Chr 9.4
Asaiah (4)
1 Chr 15.6 — 11   x 2
Asaiah (5)
2 Kgs 22.12 — 14   x 2
2 Chr 34.20
Asaph (1)
1 Chr 6.39   x 2
      9.14
      15 — 16   x 5
      25.1 — 9   x 5
2 Chr 5.11
      20.14
      29.12 — 30   x 2
      35.15   x 2
Ezra 2 — 3   x 2
Neh 7.43
     11 — 12   x 4
Asaph (2)
2 Kgs 18.18
Is 36.3
Asaph (3)
1 Chr 26.1
Asaph (4)
Neh 2.8
Asarel
1 Chr 4.16
Asenath
Gen 41.45 — 50   x 2
      46.20
Ashan
Josh 15.42
      19.7
1 Chr 4.32
      6.57
Asharelah
1 Chr 25.2 — 9   x 2
Ashbel
Gen 46.21
Num 26.38
1 Chr 8.1
Ashdod
Josh 11.22
      13.3
      15.46 — 47   x 2
1 Sam 5 — 6   x 5
2 Chr 26.6   x 2
Neh 4.7
      13.23 — 24   x 2
Is 20.1 — 3   x 2
Jer 25.19
Amos 1.8

Ashdod (Cont)
Amos 3.9
Zeph 2.4
Zech 9.6
Asher (1)
Gen 30.13
      35.26
      46.17
      49.20
Ex 1.4
Num 1 — 2   x 3
      7.12
      10.26
      13.3
      26.44 — 46   x 2
      34.19
Deut 27.13
      33.24   x 2
Josh 17.10 — 11   x 2
      19.24 — 34   x 3
      21.6 — 30   x 2
Judg 1.31 — 32   x 2
      5 — 7   x 3
2 Sam 2.9
1 Kgs 4.16
1 Chr 2.2
      6 — 7   x 5
      12.23
2 Chr 30.11
Ezek 48.1 — 30   x 2
Lk 2.36
Rev 7.5
Asher (2)
Josh 17.7
Asherah
Ex 34.13
Deut 7.5
      12.3
      16.21
Judg 3.7
      6.25 — 30   x 4
1 Kgs 14 — 16   x 4
      18.19
2 Kgs 13.6
      17 — 18   x 3
      21.3 — 7   x 2
      23.4 — 15   x 5
2 Chr 14 — 15   x 2
      17.6
      19.3
      24.18
      31.1
      33 — 34   x 5
Is 17.8
      27.9
Jer 17.2
Mic 5.14
Ashhur
1 Chr 2.24
      4.5 — 7   x 2
Ashima
2 Kgs 17.30
Ashkelon
Josh 13.3
Judg 1.18
      14.19
1 Sam 6.17
2 Sam 1.20
Jer 25.19
      47.5 — 7   x 2
Amos 1.8
Zeph 2.4 — 7   x 2
Zech 9.5   x 2
Ashkenaz (1)
Gen 10.3

Ashkenaz (1) (Cont)
1 Chr 1.6
Ashkenaz (2)
Jer 51.27
Ashnah (1)
Josh 15.33
Ashnah (2)
Josh 15.43
Ashpenaz
Dan 1.3 — 18   x 7
Ashtaroth (1)
Deut 1.4
Josh 9.10
      12 — 13   x 3
Ashtaroth (2)
1 Chr 6.71
Ashterah
1 Chr 11.26
Ashteroth Karnaim
Gen 14.5
Ashurbanipal
Ezra 4.10
Ashvath
1 Chr 7.33
Asia
Acts 2.9
      6.9
      16.6
      19 — 21   x 8
      24.19
      27.2
Rom 16.5
1 Cor 16.19
2 Cor 1.8
2 Tim 1.15
1 Pet 1.1
Rev 1.4
Asiel
1 Chr 4.34
Asnah
Ezra 2.43
Aspatha
Esth 9.7
Asriel (1)
Num 26.31
Josh 17.2
Asriel (2)
1 Chr 7.14
Asshur (1)
Gen 10.22
1 Chr 1.17
Asshur (2)
Ezek 27.23
Asshurim
Gen 25.3
Assir (1)
Ex 6.24
1 Chr 6.22
Assir (2)
1 Chr 6.23 — 37   x 2
Assos
Acts 20.13 — 14   x 2
Assyria
Gen 2.14
      10.11
      25.18
Num 24.22 — 24   x 2
2 Kgs 15 — 20   x 37
      23.29
1 Chr 5.4 — 26   x 2
2 Chr 28.16 — 20   x 2
      30.6
      32 — 33   x 11
Ezra 4.2
      6.22

Assyria (Cont)			Athens (Cont)			Azariah (14)			Azotus	
Neh	9.32		1 Thes	3.1		2 Chr	28.12		Acts	8.40
Ps	83.8		**Athlai**			**Azariah (15)**			**Azriel (1)**	
Is	7 − 8	x 5	Ezra	10.28		2 Chr	29.12		1 Chr	5.24
	10 − 11	x 11	**Atroth Beth Joab**			**Azariah (16)**			**Azriel (2)**	
	14.25	x 2	1 Chr	2.54		2 Chr	29.12		1 Chr	27.16
	19 − 20	x 7	**Atroth Shophan**			**Azariah (17)**			**Azriel (3)**	
	23.13		Num	32.35		2 Chr	31.10 − 13	x 2	Jer	36.26
	27.13		**Attai (1)**			**Azariah (18)**			**Azrikam (1)**	
	30 − 31	x 5	1 Chr	2.35 − 36	x 3	Ezra	7.3		1 Chr	3.23
	36 − 38	x 21	**Attai (2)**			**Azariah (19)**			**Azrikam (2)**	
	52.4		1 Chr	12.9		Neh	3.23 − 24	x 2	1 Chr	8 − 9	x 2
Jer	2.18 − 36	x 2	**Attai (3)**			**Azariah (20)**			**Azrikam (3)**	
	50.17 − 18	x 2	2 Chr	11.20		Neh	7.7		1 Chr	9.14
Lam	5.6		**Attalia**			**Azariah (21)**			Neh	11.15
Ezek	16.28		Acts	14.25		Neh	8.7		**Azrikam (4)**	
	23.5 − 23	x 6	**Augustus**			**Azariah (22)**			2 Chr	28.7
	32.22		Lk	2.1		Neh	10.2		**Azubah (1)**	
Hos	5.13		**Aven (1)**			**Azariah (23)**			1 Chr	2.18 − 19	x 2
	7 − 12	x 8	Hos	10.8		Neh	12.33		**Azubah (2)**	
	14.3		**Aven (2)**			**Azariah (24)**			1 Kgs	22.42
Mic	5.5 − 6	x 3	Amos	1.5		Jer	42 − 43	x 2	2 Chr	20.31
	7.12		**Avith**			**Azariah (25)**			**Azzan**	
Nah	1.12 − 14	x 4	Gen	36.31		see also Abednego			Num	34.19
	3.18		1 Chr	1.43		Dan	1 − 2	x 3	**Azzur (1)**	
Zeph	2.13		**Avvim (1)**			**Azariahu**			Neh	10.14
Zech	10.10 − 11	x 2	Deut	2.23		2 Chr	21.2		**Azzur (2)**	
Astarte			Josh	13.3		**Azaz**			Jer	28.1
Judg	2.13		**Avvim (2)**			1 Chr	5.8		**Azzur (3)**	
	10.6		Josh	18.23		**Azazel**			Ezek	11.1
1 Sam	7.3 − 4	x 2	**Ayyah**			Lev	16.8 − 26	x 5	**Baal (1)**	
	12.10		1 Chr	7.28		**Azaziah (1)**			Num	25.3 − 5	x 2
	31.10		**Azaliah**			1 Chr	15.17		Deut	4.3
1 Kgs	11.5 − 33	x 2	2 Kgs	22.3		**Azaziah (2)**			Judg	2 − 3	x 3
2 Kgs	23.13		2 Chr	34.8		1 Chr	27.16			6.25 − 32	x 6
Aswan			**Azaniah**			**Azaziah (3)**				8.33
Is	49.12		Neh	10.9		2 Chr	31.13			10.6 − 10	x 2
Ezek	29 − 30	x 2	**Azarel (1)**			**Azbuk**			1 Sam	7.4
Asyncritus			1 Chr	12.3		Neh	3.16			12.10
Rom	16.14		**Azarel (2)**			**Azekah**			1 Kgs	16.31 − 32	x 2
Atad			1 Chr	27.16		Josh	10.10 − 11	x 2		18 − 19	x 13
Gen	50.10 − 11	x 2	**Azarel (3)**				15.35			22.53
Atarah			Ezra	10.38		1 Sam	17.1		2 Kgs	3.2
1 Chr	2.26		**Azarel (4)**			2 Chr	11.9			10 − 11	x 12
Ataroth (1)			Neh	11.13		Neh	11.30			17.16
Num	32.3 − 34	x 2	**Azarel (5)**			Jer	34.7			21.3
Ataroth (2)			Neh	12.36		**Azel**				23.4 − 5	x 2
Josh	16.7		**Azariah (1)**			1 Chr	8 − 9	x 5	2 Chr	17.3
Ataroth Addar			1 Kgs	4.2		**Azgad (1)**				23 − 24	x 3
Josh	16.2 − 5	x 2	**Azariah (2)**			Ezra	2.3			28.2
	18.13		1 Kgs	4.5		Neh	7.8			33 − 34	x 2
Ater (1)			**Azariah (3)**			**Azgad (2)**			Ps	106.28
Ezra	2.3		1 Chr	2.8		Ezra	8.2		Jer	2 − 3	x 3
Neh	7.8		**Azariah (4)**			**Azgad (3)**				7.9
Ater (2)			1 Chr	2.38		Neh	10.14			9.14
Ezra	2.40		**Azariah (5)**			**Aziza**				11 − 12	x 3
Neh	7.43		1 Chr	6.9		Ezra	10.27			19.5
Ater (3)			**Azariah (6)**			**Azmaveth (1)**				23.13 − 27	x 2
Neh	10.14		1 Chr	6.10		2 Sam	23.24			32.29 − 35	x 2
Athach			**Azariah (7)**			1 Chr	11.26		Hos	2.8 − 17	x 4
1 Sam	30.30		1 Chr	6.13		**Azmaveth (2)**				9.1 − 10	x 2
Athaiah				9.10		1 Chr	12.3			11.2
Neh	11.4		Ezra	7.1		**Azmaveth (3)**				13.1
Athaliah (1)			**Azariah (8)**			1 Chr	27.25		Zeph	1.4
2 Kgs	8.26		1 Chr	6.36		**Azmaveth (4)**			Rom	11.4
	11.1 − 20	x 7	**Azariah (9)**			1 Chr	8 − 9	x 2	**Baal (2)**	
2 Chr	22 − 24	x 8	2 Chr	15.1 − 8	x 2	**Azmaveth (5)**			1 Chr	5.4
Athaliah (2)			**Azariah (10)**			Ezra	2.21		**Baal (3)**	
1 Chr	8.26		2 Chr	21.2		Neh	12.29		1 Chr	8 − 9	x 2
Athaliah (3)			**Azariah (11)**			**Azmon**			**Baal Hamon**	
Ezra	8.2		2 Chr	23.1		Num	34.4		Song	8.11
Atharim			**Azariah (12)**			Josh	15.4		**Baal Hanan (1)**	
Num	21.1		2 Chr	23.1		**Aznoth Tabor**			Gen	36.31
Athens			**Azariah (13)**			Josh	19.34		1 Chr	1.43
Acts	17 − 18	x 5	2 Chr	26.17 − 20	x 2	**Azor**				
						Mt	1.12			

Baal Hanan (2)
1 Chr 27.25

Baal Hazor
2 Sam 13.23

Baal Hermon
Judg 3.3
1 Chr 5.23

Baal Meon
Num 32.38
1 Chr 5.8
Ezek 25.9

Baal Perazim
2 Sam 5.20 x 2
1 Chr 14.11 x 2

Baal Shalishah
2 Kgs 4.42

Baal Zephon
Ex 14.2 – 9 x 2
Num 33.7

Baal-of-the-Covenant
Judg 8 – 9 x 3

Baalah (1)
Josh 15.9 – 10 x 2
1 Chr 13.6

Baalah (2)
Josh 15.11

Baalah (3)
Josh 15.29

Baalah (4)
2 Sam 6.2

Baalath
Josh 19.44
1 Kgs 9.18
1 Chr 4.33
2 Chr 8.6

Baalath Beer
Josh 19.8

Baalgad
Josh 11 – 13 x 3

Baalis
Jer 40.14

Baaltamar
Judg 20.33

Baalzebub
2 Kgs 1.2 – 16 x 4

Baana (1)
1 Kgs 4.12

Baana (2)
1 Kgs 4.16

Baana (3)
Neh 3.4

Baanah (1)
2 Sam 23.24
1 Chr 11.26

Baanah (2)
2 Sam 4.2 – 12 x 4

Baanah (3)
Ezra 2.2
Neh 7.7
10.14

Baara
1 Chr 8.8

Baaseiah
1 Chr 6.40

Baasha
1 Kgs 15 – 16 x 19
21.22
2 Kgs 9.9
2 Chr 16.1 – 6 x 4
Jer 41.9

Babylon
Gen 10 – 11 x 6
14 – 15 x 3
Josh 7.21
2 Kgs 17.24 – 30 x 2

Babylon (Cont)
2 Kgs 20.12 – 18 x 4
24 – 25 x 26
1 Chr 3.17
9.1
2 Chr 32 – 33 x 2
36.6 – 20 x 8
Ezra 1 – 2 x 3
4 – 8 x 12
Neh 1.2
7.6 x 2
9.7
13.6
Esth 2.6
Ps 87.4
137.1 – 8 x 2
Is 11.11
13 – 14 x 12
21.1 – 9 x 3
23.13 x 2
39.1 – 7 x 4
43.14
46 – 48 x 6
52.5 – 11 x 2
55.12
Jer 20 – 22 x 8
24 – 25 x 10
27 – 29 x 27
32 – 44 x 63
46.2 – 26 x 3
49 – 52 x 96
Ezek 1.1 – 3 x 2
11 – 12 x 2
16 – 17 x 7
19.9
21.19 – 21 x 2
23 – 24 x 5
26.7
29 – 30 x 4
32.11
Dan 1 – 5 x 16
7.1
9.1
Mic 4.10
Hab 1.6 – 15 x 3
Hag 1.12
Zech 2.6
5 – 6 x 4
Mt 1.6 – 17 x 3
Acts 7.43
1 Pet 5.13
Rev 14.8
16 – 18 x 6

Baca
Ps 84.6

Bahurim
2 Sam 3.16
16 – 17 x 2
19.16
23.24
1 Kgs 2.8

Bahurum
1 Chr 11.26

Bakbakkar
1 Chr 9.14

Bakbuk
Ezra 2.43
Neh 7.46

Bakbukiah
Neh 11 – 12 x 3

Balaam
Num 22 – 24 x 53
31.8 – 16 x 2
Deut 23.4 – 5 x 2
Josh 13.22

Balaam (Cont)
Josh 24.9 – 10 x 2
Neh 13.2
Mic 6.5
2 Pet 2.15
Jude .11
Rev 2.14

Baladan
2 Kgs 20.12
Is 39.1

Balah
Josh 19.3

Balak
Num 22 – 24 x 34
Josh 24.9 – 10 x 2
Judg 11.25
Mic 6.5
Rev 2.14

Bamoth
Num 21.19 – 20 x 2

Bamoth Baal
Num 22.41
Josh 13.17

Bani (1)
2 Sam 23.24

Bani (2)
1 Chr 6.46

Bani (3)
1 Chr 9.4

Bani (4)
Ezra 2.3
10.29

Bani (5)
Ezra 10.34

Bani (6)
Neh 3.17
8 – 9 x 3

Bani (7)
Neh 9 – 10 x 2

Bani (8)
Neh 10.14

Bani (9)
Neh 11.22

Bani (10)
Ezra 8.2

Bar-Jesus
Acts 13.6

Barabbas
Mt 27.16 – 26 x 5
Mk 15.7 – 15 x 3
Lk 23.18 – 19 x 2
Jn 18.40 x 2

Barak
Judg 4 – 5 x 13
1 Sam 12.11
Heb 11.32

Barakel
Job 32.2

Bariah
1 Chr 3.22

Barkos
Ezra 2.43
Neh 7.46

Barnabas
Acts 4.36
9.27
11 – 15 x 27
1 Cor 9.6
Gal 2.1 – 13 x 4
Col 4.10

Barsabbas (1)
Acts 1.23

Barsabbas (2)
Acts 15.22

Bartholomew
Mt 10.3
Mk 3.18
Lk 6.14
Acts 1.13

Bartimaeus
Mk 10.46

Baruch (1)
Jer 32.12 – 16 x 3
36.4 – 32 x 15
43.3 – 6 x 2
45.1 – 2 x 2

Baruch (2)
Neh 3.20
10.2

Baruch (3)
Neh 11.5

Barzillai (1)
2 Sam 17.27
19.31 – 39 x 4
1 Kgs 2.7
Ezra 2.61
Neh 7.63

Barzillai (2)
2 Sam 21.8

Barzillai (3)
Ezra 2.61 x 2
Neh 7.63 x 2

Basemath (1)
Gen 26.34

Basemath (2)
Gen 36.3 – 17 x 4

Basemath (3)
1 Kgs 4.15

Bashan
Num 21.33 x 2
32.33
Deut 1.4
3 – 4 x 9
29.7
33.22
Josh 9.10
12 – 13 x 7
17.1 – 5 x 2
20 – 21 x 2
1 Kgs 4.13 – 19 x 2
2 Kgs 10.33
1 Chr 5 – 6 x 6
Neh 9.22
Ps 22.12
68.15 – 22 x 2
135 – 136 x 2
Is 2.13
33.9
Jer 22.20
50.19
Ezek 27.6
Amos 4.1
Mic 7.14
Nah 1.4
Zech 11.2

Bathsheba
2 Sam 11 – 12 x 3
1 Kgs 1 – 2 x 8
1 Chr 3.5

Bathshua
1 Chr 2.3

Bavvai
Neh 3.18

Bazlith
Neh 7.46

Bazluth
Ezra 2.43

Bealiah
1 Chr 12.3

Bealoth
Josh 15.24
1 Kgs 4.16
Beautiful Gate
Acts 3.2 – 10   x 2
Bebai (1)
Ezra 2.3
Neh 7.8
Bebai (2)
Ezra 8.2
      10.28
Bebai (3)
Neh 10.14
Becher (1)
Gen 46.21
1 Chr 7.6 – 8   x 2
Becher (2)
Num 26.35
Becorath
1 Sam 9.1
Bedad
Gen 36.31
1 Chr 1.43
Bedan
1 Chr 7.17
Bedeiah
Ezra 10.34
Beeliada
1 Chr 14.7
Beelzebul
Mt 10.25
      12.24 – 28   x 3
Mk 3.22
Lk 11.15 – 18   x 2
Beer
Judg 9.21
Beera
1 Chr 7.37
Beerah
1 Chr 5.4   x 2
Beerelim
Is 15.8
Beeri (1)
Gen 26.34
Beeri (2)
Hos 1.1
Beeroth
Josh 9.17
      18.25
2 Sam 4.2   x 2
      23.24
1 Chr 11.26
Ezra 2.21
Neh 7.26
Beersheba
Gen 21 – 22   x 5
      26.23 – 33   x 2
      28.10
      46.1 – 5   x 2
Josh 15.28
      19.2
Judg 20.1
1 Sam 8.2
2 Sam 24.7
1 Kgs 19.3
2 Kgs 12.1
1 Chr 4.28
2 Chr 19.4
      24.1
      30.5
Neh 11.27 – 30   x 2
Amos 5.5
      8.14
Beeshterah
Josh 21.27

Behemoth
Job 40.15
Bel
Is 46.1
Jer 51.44
Bela (1)
Gen 14.2 – 8   x 2
Bela (2)
Gen 36.31
1 Chr 1.43
Bela (3)
Gen 46.21
Num 26.38 – 40   x 2
1 Chr 7 – 8   x 4
Bela (4)
1 Chr 5.8
Belshazzar
Dan 5.1 – 30   x 5
      7 – 8   x 2
Belteshazzar
see also Daniel (1)
Dan 1 – 2   x 2
      4 – 5   x 7
      10.1
Benabinadab
1 Kgs 4.11
Benaiah (1)
2 Sam 8.18
      20.23
      23.20 – 22   x 3
1 Kgs 1 – 2   x 13
      4.4
1 Chr 11.22 – 24   x 3
      18.17
      27.2
Benaiah (2)
2 Sam 23.24
1 Chr 11.26
      27.2
Benaiah (3)
1 Chr 4.34
Benaiah (4)
1 Chr 15 – 16   x 4
Benaiah (5)
1 Chr 27.34
Benaiah (6)
2 Chr 20.14
Benaiah (7)
2 Chr 31.13
Benaiah (8)
Ezra 10.25
Benaiah (9)
Ezra 10.30
Benaiah (10)
Ezra 10.34
Benaiah (11)
Ezra 10.43
Benaiah (12)
Ezek 11.1
Benammi
Gen 19.38
Bendeker
1 Kgs 4.9
Bene Jaakan
Num 33.15
Beneberak
Josh 19.45
Bengeber
1 Kgs 4.13
Benhadad (1)
1 Kgs 15.18 – 20   x 2
2 Chr 16.2 – 4   x 2
Benhadad (2)
1 Kgs 20.1 – 34   x 19
2 Kgs 6.24
      8.7 – 15   x 4

Benhadad (3)
2 Kgs 13.3 – 25   x 4
Amos 1.4
Benhadad (4)
Jer 49.27
Benhail
2 Chr 17.7
Benhanan
1 Chr 4.20
Benhesed
1 Kgs 4.10
Benhur
1 Kgs 4.8
Beninu
Neh 10.9
Benjamin (1)
Gen 35.18 – 24   x 2
      42 – 46   x 15
      49.27
Ex 1.3
Num 1 – 2   x 3
      7.12
      10.24
      13.3
      26.38
      34.19
Deut 27.12
      33.12
Josh 18.11 – 28   x 4
      21.4 – 17   x 2
Judg 1.21   x 2
      3.15
      5.14
      10.9
      19 – 21   x 40
1 Sam 4.12
      9 – 10   x 7
      13 – 14   x 4
      22.7
2 Sam 2 – 4   x 8
      16.11
      19 – 21   x 4
      23.24
1 Kgs 2.8
      4.18
      12.21 – 23   x 2
      15.22
1 Chr 2.2
      6 – 9   x 7
      11 – 12   x 5
      21.6
      27.2 – 16   x 2
2 Chr 11.1 – 23   x 5
      14 – 15   x 4
      17.17
      25.5
      31.1
      34.9 – 32   x 2
Ezra 1.5
      4.1
      10.9
Neh 11.7 – 36   x 4
Esth 2.5
Ps 68.27
      80.2
Jer 1.1
      17.26
      32 – 33   x 3
      37.12
Ezek 48.21 – 30   x 3
Hos 5.8
Obad .19
Acts 13.21
Rom 11.1

Benjamin (1) (Cont)
Phil 3.5
Rev 7.5
Benjamin (2)
1 Chr 7.10
Benjamin (3)
Ezra 10.31
Benjamin (4)
Neh 3.23
Benjamin (5)
Neh 12.33
Benjamin Gate
Jer 20.2
      37 – 38   x 2
Zech 14.10
Benoni
Gen 35.18
Benzoheth
1 Chr 4.20
Beon
Num 32.3
Beor (1)
Gen 36.31
1 Chr 1.43
Beor (2)
Num 22.5
      24.3 – 15   x 2
      31.8
Deut 23.4
Josh 13.22
      24.9
Mic 6.5
2 Pet 2.15
Bera
Gen 14.2
Beracah (1)
1 Chr 12.3
Beracah (2)
2 Chr 20.26   x 2
Berachiah
Mt 23.35
Beraiah
1 Chr 8.21
Berea
Acts 17.10 – 15   x 4
      20.4
Berechiah (1)
1 Chr 3.20
Berechiah (2)
1 Chr 6.39
      15.17
Berechiah (3)
1 Chr 9.14
Berechiah (4)
1 Chr 15.23
Berechiah (5)
2 Chr 28.12
Berechiah (6)
Neh 3.4 – 30   x 2
      6.18
Berechiah (7)
Zech 1.1
Bered (1)
Gen 16.14
Bered (2)
1 Chr 7.20
Beri
1 Chr 7.36
Beriah (1)
Gen 46.17   x 2
Num 26.44 – 45   x 2
1 Chr 7.30 – 31   x 2
Beriah (2)
1 Chr 7.23

Bigvai (4)
Neh 10.14
Bikri
2 Sam 20.1 – 21 x 3
Bildad
Job 2.11
8.1
18.1
25 – 26 x 2
42.9
Bileam
1 Chr 6.70
Bilgah (1)
1 Chr 24.7
Bilgah (2)
Neh 12.2 – 12 x 2
Bilgai
Neh 10.2
Bilhah (1)
Gen 29 – 30 x 5
35.22 – 25 x 2
37.2
46.25
1 Chr 7.13
Bilhah (2)
1 Chr 4.29
Bilhan (1)
Gen 36.27
1 Chr 1.38
Bilhan (2)
1 Chr 7.10
Bilshan
Ezra 2.2
Neh 7.7
Bimhal
1 Chr 7.33
Binea
1 Chr 8 – 9 x 2
Binnui (1)
Ezra 8.33
Binnui (2)
Ezra 10.30
Binnui (3)
Ezra 10.38
Binnui (4)
Neh 3.24
10.9
Binnui (5)
Neh 7.8
Binnui (6)
Neh 12.8 – 24 x 2
Birsha
Gen 14.2
Birzaith
1 Chr 7.31
Bishlam
Ezra 4.7
Bithiah
1 Chr 4.17
Bithynia
Acts 16.7
1 Pet 1.1
Biziothiah
Josh 15.28
Biztha
Esth 1.10
Blastus
Acts 12.20
Boanerges
Mk 3.17
Boaz (1)
Ruth 2 – 4 x 29
1 Chr 2.11
Mt 1.2
Lk 3.32

Boaz (2)
1 Kgs 7.21
2 Chr 3.17
Bocheru
1 Chr 8 – 9 x 2
Bochim
Judg 2.1 – 5 x 2
Bohan
Josh 15.6
18.17
Borashan
1 Sam 30.30
Bozez
1 Sam 14.4
Bozkath
Josh 15.39
2 Kgs 22.1
Bozrah (1)
Gen 36.31
1 Chr 1.43
Is 34.6
63.1
Jer 49.13 – 22 x 2
Amos 1.12
Bozrah (2)
Jer 48.24
Broad Wall
Neh 3.8
12.38
Bubastis
Ezek 30.17
Bukki (1)
1 Chr 6.5 – 51 x 2
Ezra 7.4
Bukki (2)
Num 34.19
Bukkiah
1 Chr 25.4 – 9 x 2
Bul
1 Kgs 6.38
Bunah
1 Chr 2.25
Bunni (1)
Neh 9.4
Bunni (2)
Neh 10.14
Bunni (3)
Neh 11.15
Buz (1)
Gen 22.21
Buz (2)
1 Chr 5.14
Buz (3)
Job 32.2
Buz (4)
Jer 25.19
Buzi
Ezek 1.1
Byblos
1 Kgs 5.18
Ezek 27.9
Cabbon
Josh 15.40
Cabul (1)
Josh 19.27
Cabul (2)
1 Kgs 9.13
Caesarea
Acts 8 – 12 x 7
18.22
21.8 – 16 x 2
23 – 25 x 8
Caesarea Philippi
Mt 16.13
Mk 8.27

Caiaphas
Mt 26.3 – 57 x 2
Lk 3.2
Jn 11.49
18.13 – 28 x 4
Acts 4.6
Cain
Gen 4.1 – 25 x 16
Heb 11.4
1 Jn 3.12 x 2
Jude .11
Cainan
Lk 3.36
Calah
Gen 10.11 – 12 x 2
Calcol
1 Kgs 4.31
1 Chr 2.6
Caleb (1)
Num 13 – 14 x 7
26.65
32.12
34.19
Deut 1.36
Josh 14 – 15 x 10
21.12
Judg 1.12 – 20 x 6
3.9
1 Sam 25.2
30.14
1 Chr 2.46 – 49 x 3
4.15
6.56
Caleb (2)
1 Chr 2.9 – 50 x 7
4.3
Caleb (3)
1 Chr 4.11
Calneh
Amos 6.2
Calno
Is 10.9
Camp of Dan
Judg 13.25
18.12
Cana
Jn 2.1 – 11 x 2
4.46
21.2
Canaan
Gen 9 – 13 x 19
15 – 17 x 3
20.1
23 – 24 x 5
28.1 – 8 x 3
31.17
33 – 38 x 9
42 – 50 x 23
Ex 3.8 – 17 x 2
6.4 – 15 x 2
13.5 – 11 x 2
15 – 16 x 2
23.23 – 28 x 2
33 – 34 x 2
Lev 14.34
18 – 20 x 3
25.38
Num 13 – 14 x 6
21.1 – 3 x 2
26.19
32 – 35 x 8
Deut 1.7
7.1
11.30
20.17

Canaan (Cont)
Deut 32.49
Josh 2 – 3 x 2
5.1 – 12 x 3
7.9
9.1
11 – 14 x 5
16 – 17 x 6
21 – 22 x 3
24.3 – 11 x 2
Judg 1.1 – 33 x 13
3 – 5 x 6
21.12
1 Sam 7.14
2 Sam 24.7
1 Kgs 9.20
2 Kgs 21.11
1 Chr 1 – 2 x 4
16.18 – 19 x 2
2 Chr 8.7
Ezra 9.1
Neh 9.8 – 24 x 3
Ps 105 – 106 x 3
135.11
Ezek 16.3
Hos 12.7
Mt 15.22
Acts 7.11
13.19
Canneh
Ezek 27.23
Capernaum
Mt 4.13
8.5
11.23
17.24
Mk 1 – 2 x 2
9.33
Lk 4.23 – 31 x 2
7.1
10.15
Jn 2.12
4.46 – 47 x 2
6.17 – 59 x 3
Cappadocia
Acts 2.9
1 Pet 1.1
Carchemish
2 Chr 35.20
Is 10.9
Jer 46.2
Carkas
Esth 1.10
Carmel (1)
Josh 12.22
19.26
1 Kgs 18.19 – 42 x 3
2 Kgs 2.25
4.25
Song 7.5
Is 33.9
35.2
Jer 46.18
50.19
Amos 1.2
9.3
Nah 1.4
Carmel (2)
Josh 15.55
1 Sam 15.12
25.2 – 40 x 5
27.3
2 Sam 2 – 3 x 2
23.24
1 Chr 3.1

East Gate
2 Chr 31.14
Neh 3.29
Ebal (1)
Gen 36.23
1 Chr 1.38
Ebal (2)
Deut 11.29
    27.4 – 13   x 2
Josh 8.30 – 33   x 2
Ebal (3)
1 Chr 1.22
Ebed (1)
Judg 9.26 – 31   x 2
Ebed (2)
Ezra 8.2
Ebedmelech
Jer 38 – 39   x 5
Ebenezer
1 Sam 4 – 5   x 2
Eber (1)
Gen 10 – 11   x 4
1 Chr 1.18 – 25   x 3
Lk 3.35
Eber (2)
Num 24.24
Eber (3)
1 Chr 5.13
Eber (4)
1 Chr 8.12
Eber (5)
1 Chr 8.22
Eber (6)
Neh 12.12
Ebez
Josh 19.20
Ebiasaph
1 Chr 6.23 – 37   x 2
    9.19
Ebron
Josh 19.28
Ecbatana
Ezra 6.2
Eden (1)
(Garden)
Gen 2 – 4   x 6
Is 51.3
Ezek 28.13
    31.9 – 18   x 4
    36.35
Joel 2.3
Eden (2)
Ezek 27.23
Eden (3)
2 Chr 31.15
Eden (4)
2 Chr 29.12
Eder (1)
Gen 35.21
Eder (2)
Josh 15.21
Eder (3)
1 Chr 23 – 24   x 2
Eder (4)
1 Chr 8.15
Edom
Gen 14.6
    25.30
    32 – 33   x 3
    36.1 – 40   x 7
Ex 15.15
Num 20 – 21   x 6
    24.18
    33 – 34   x 2
Deut 1 – 2   x 9
    23.7

Edom (Cont)
Deut 33.2
Josh 11 – 12   x 2
    15.1 – 21   x 3
    24.4
Judg 1.36
    5.4
    11.17 – 18   x 3
1 Sam 14.47
    21.7
2 Sam 8.12 – 14   x 3
1 Kgs 9.26
    11.1 – 21   x 7
    22.47
2 Kgs 3.8 – 20   x 3
    8.20 – 22   x 3
    14.7 – 10   x 2
    16.6   x 2
1 Chr 1.38 – 51   x 3
    4.42
    18.11 – 13   x 3
2 Chr 8.17
    20 – 21   x 7
    25.11 – 20   x 4
    28.16
Ps 60.8 – 9   x 2
    83.6
    108.9 – 10   x 2
    137.7
Is 11.14
    21.11   x 2
    34.5 – 9   x 3
    63.1
Jer 9.25
    25.19
    27.3
    40.11
    49.7 – 22   x 10
Lam 4.21 – 22   x 2
Ezek 16.57
    25.12 – 14   x 6
    32.29
    35 – 36   x 5
Dan 11.41
Joel 3.19
Amos 1 – 2   x 4
    9.12
Obad .1 – 21   x 8
Hab 3.3
Mal 1.4
Edrei
Num 21.33
Deut 1.4
    3.1 – 10   x 2
Josh 12 – 13   x 3
    19.37
Eglah
2 Sam 3.5
1 Chr 3.1
Eglaim
Is 15.8
Eglath Shelishiyah
Is 15.5
Jer 48.34
Eglon (1)
Judg 3.12 – 19   x 6
Eglon (2)
Josh 10.3 – 37   x 6
    12.12
    15.39
Egypt
Gen 10.6 – 13   x 2
    12 – 13   x 7
    15 – 16   x 2
    21.9 – 21   x 2

Egypt (Cont)
Gen 25 – 26   x 3
    37.25 – 36   x 3
    39 – 43   x 28
    45 – 48   x 36
    50.3 – 26   x 6
Ex 1 – 20   x 158
    22 – 23   x 3
    29.46
    32 – 34   x 10
    40.17
Lev 11.45
    18 – 19   x 3
    22 – 26   x 8
Num 1.1
    3.12
    8 – 11   x 6
    13 – 16   x 10
    20 – 24   x 9
    26.3 – 59   x 2
    32 – 34   x 7
Deut 1.3 – 30   x 3
    4 – 11   x 26
    13.5 – 10   x 2
    15 – 17   x 7
    20 – 21   x 2
    23 – 26   x 9
    28 – 29   x 6
    34.11
Josh 2.10
    5.4 – 9   x 3
    9.9
    13.3
    15.4 – 47   x 2
    24.4 – 32   x 10
Judg 2.1 – 12   x 2
    6.8 – 13   x 3
    10 – 11   x 3
    19.30
1 Sam 2.27
    4.8
    6.6   x 3
    8.8
    10.18   x 2
    12.6 – 8   x 3
    15.2 – 7   x 3
    27.8
    30.11 – 13   x 2
2 Sam 7.6 – 23   x 2
    23.21   x 2
1 Kgs 3 – 4   x 3
    6 – 12   x 21
    14.25
2 Kgs 7.6
    17 – 19   x 8
    21.15
    23 – 25   x 9
1 Chr 1 – 2   x 3
    4.17
    11.23   x 2
    13.5
    17.5 – 21   x 2
2 Chr 1.17
    5 – 10   x 7
    12.2
    20.10
    26.8
    35 – 36   x 4
Ezra 9.1
Neh 9.9 – 18   x 3
    13.2
Ps 68.30 – 31   x 2
    78.12 – 51   x 4
    80 – 81   x 3
    87.4

Egypt (Cont)
Ps 105 – 106   x 9
    114.1
    135 – 136   x 4
Prov 7.16
Is 7.18
    10 – 11   x 4
    19 – 20   x 26
    23.3 – 5   x 2
    27.12 – 13   x 2
    30 – 31   x 10
    36 – 37   x 4
    43.3
    45.14
    52.4
Jer 2.6 – 37   x 4
    7.22 – 25   x 2
    9.25
    11.4 – 7   x 2
    16.14
    23 – 26   x 6
    31 – 32   x 3
    34.13
    37.5 – 11   x 4
    41 – 44   x 26
    46 – 47   x 17
Lam 5.6
Ezek 16 – 17   x 3
    19 – 20   x 10
    23.3 – 27   x 6
    27.7
    29 – 32   x 50
    47 – 48   x 2
Dan 9.15
    11.5 – 43   x 13
Hos 2.15
    7 – 9   x 5
    11 – 13   x 7
Joel 3.19
Amos 2 – 4   x 4
    9.7
Mic 6 – 7   x 3
Nah 3.8 – 9   x 2
Hag 2.5
Zech 10.10 – 11   x 2
    14.18 – 19   x 2
Mt 2.13 – 19   x 4
Acts 2.10
    7.9 – 40   x 20
    13.17
    21.38
Rom 9.17
Heb 3.16
    8.9
    11.22 – 29   x 4
Jude .5
Rev 11.8
Ehi
Gen 46.21
Ehud (1)
Judg 3 – 4   x 12
Ehud (2)
1 Chr 7 – 8   x 2
Eker
1 Chr 2.26
Ekron
Josh 13.3   x 2
    15.11 – 46   x 3
    19.43
Judg 1.18
1 Sam 5 – 7   x 4
    17.52   x 2
2 Kgs 1.2 – 16   x 4
Jer 25.19
Amos 1.8

Gad (1) (Cont)
Num	26.15	
	32.1 – 34	x 7
	34.14	
Deut	3 – 4	x 3
	27.13	
	29.8	
	33.20	x 2
Josh	1.12	
	4.12	
	12 – 13	x 4
	18.7	
	20 – 22	x 15
Judg	5.17	
1 Sam	13.7	
2 Sam	23 – 24	x 2
2 Kgs	10.33	
1 Chr	2.2	
	5 – 6	x 5
	12.8 – 23	x 3
	26.32	
Jer	49.1	
Ezek	48.23 – 30	x 3
Rev	7.5	

Gad (2)
1 Sam	22.5	
2 Sam	24.11 – 19	x 4
1 Chr	21.9 – 19	x 5
	29.29	
2 Chr	29.25	

Gad (3)
Is	65.11

Gadara
Mt	8.28

Gaddi
Num	13.3

Gaddiel
Num	13.3

Gadi
2 Kgs	15.14 – 17	x 2

Gaham
Gen	22.24

Gahar
Ezra	2.43
Neh	7.46

Gaius (1)
Rom	16.23
1 Cor	1.14

Gaius (2)
Acts	19.29

Gaius (3)
Acts	20.4

Gaius (4)
3 Jn	.1

Galal (1)
1 Chr	9.14

Galal (2)
1 Chr	9.14
Neh	11.17

Galatia
Acts	16.6
	18.23
1 Cor	16.1
Gal	1.2
	3.1
2 Tim	4.10
1 Pet	1.1

Galeed
Gen	31.47 – 48	x 2

Galilee
see also Tiberias
Num	34.11	
Deut	3.17	
	33.23	
Josh	11 – 13	x 4
	20 – 21	x 2

Galilee (Cont)
1 Kgs	9.11	
	15.20	
2 Kgs	15.29	
1 Chr	6.76	
Is	9.1	
Mt	2 – 4	x 8
	14 – 15	x 2
	17.22	
	19.1	
	21.11	
	26 – 28	x 6
Mk	1 – 7	x 12
	9.30	
	14 – 16	x 4
Lk	1 – 5	x 7
	8 – 9	x 2
	13.1 – 2	x 3
	17.11	
	22 – 24	x 6
Jn	1 – 2	x 3
	4.3 – 54	x 6
	6 – 7	x 6
	12.21	
	21.2	
Acts	1 – 2	x 2
	5.37	
	9 – 10	x 2
	13.31	

Gallim
1 Sam	25.44
Is	10.30

Gallio
Acts	18.12 – 17	x 3

Gamad
Ezek	27.11

Gamaliel (1)
Num	1 – 2	x 2
	7.12	
	10.23	

Gamaliel (2)
Acts	5.34 – 39	x 2
	22.3	

Gamul
1 Chr	24.7

Gareb (1)
2 Sam	23.24
1 Chr	11.26

Gareb (2)
Jer	31.39

Garm
1 Chr	4.19

Gatam
Gen	36.10 – 16	x 2
1 Chr	1.36	

Gath
Josh	11.22	
	13.3	
1 Sam	5 – 7	x 4
	17.4 – 52	x 3
	21 – 22	x 2
	27.2 – 11	x 4
2 Sam	1.20	
	6.10	
	15.18	
	18.2	
	21.19 – 22	x 3
1 Kgs	2.39 – 40	x 3
2 Kgs	12.17	
1 Chr	7 – 8	x 2
	13.13	
	18.1	
	20.5 – 8	x 3
2 Chr	11.8	
	26.6	

Gath (Cont)
Amos	6.2	
Mic	1.10 – 14	x 2

Gath Hepher
Josh	19.13
2 Kgs	14.25

Gath Rimmon
1 Chr	6.69

Gathrimmon (1)
Josh	19.45

Gathrimmon (2)
Josh	21.24

Gathrimmon (3)
Josh	21.25

Gaza
Gen	10.19	
Deut	2.23	
Josh	10 – 11	x 2
	13.3	
	15.47	
Judg	1.18	
	6.4	
	16.1 – 21	x 3
1 Sam	6.17	
1 Kgs	4.24	
2 Kgs	18.8	
Jer	25.19	
	47.1 – 5	x 2
Amos	1.6 – 7	x 2
Zeph	2.4	
Zech	9.5	x 2
Acts	8.26	

Gazez (1)
1 Chr	2.46

Gazez (2)
1 Chr	2.46

Gazzam
Ezra	2.43
Neh	7.46

Geba
Josh	18.24	
	21.17	
1 Sam	13 – 14	x 3
2 Sam	5.25	
1 Kgs	15.22	
1 Chr	6.60	
	8.6	
2 Chr	16.6	
Ezra	2.21	
Neh	7.26	
	11 – 12	x 2
Is	10.29	
Zech	14.10	

Gebal
Ps	83.7

Gebalites
Josh	13.5

Geber
1 Kgs	4.19

Gebim
Is	10.31

Gedaliah (1)
2 Kgs	25.22 – 25	x 4
Jer	39 – 41	x 19
	43.6	

Gedaliah (2)
1 Chr	25.3 – 9	x 2

Gedaliah (3)
Ezra	10.18

Gedaliah (4)
Jer	38.1

Gedaliah (5)
Zeph	1.1

Geder
Josh	12.13

Geder (Cont)
1 Chr	27.25

Gederah (1)
Josh	15.36
1 Chr	12.3

Gederah (2)
1 Chr	4.23

Gederoth
Josh	15.41
2 Chr	28.18

Gederothaim
Josh	15.36

Gedor (1)
Josh	15.58

Gedor (2)
1 Chr	12.3

Gedor (3)
1 Chr	8 – 9	x 2

Gedor (4)
1 Chr	4.3 – 17	x 2

Gehazi
2 Kgs	4 – 5	x 14
	8.4 – 6	x 4

Geliloth
Josh	18.17	
	22.10 – 11	x 2

Gemalli
Num	13.3

Gemariah (1)
Jer	29.3

Gemariah (2)
Jer	36.10 – 25	x 4

Gennesaret
Mt	14.34
Mk	6.53
Lk	5.1

Genubath
1 Kgs	11.20

Gera
Gen	46.21
Judg	3.15
2 Sam	16.5
	19.16
1 Kgs	2.8
1 Chr	8.3 – 6

x 4

Gerar
Gen	10.19	
	20.1 – 2	x 2
	26.1 – 26	x 5
1 Chr	4.39 – 41	x 2
2 Chr	14.13 – 14	x 2

Gerasa
Mk	5.1
Lk	8.26

Gerizim
Deut	11.29
	27.12
Josh	8.33
Judg	9.7

Gershom (1)
Ex	2.22	
	18.3	x 2
Judg	18.30	
1 Chr	23.15 – 16	x 2
	26.24 – 25	x 2

Gershom (2)
Ezra	8.2

Gershon
Gen	46.11	
Ex	6.16 – 17	x 2
Num	3 – 4	x 8
	7.7	
	10.17	
	26.57	
Josh	21.6 – 33	x 3

Hanun (2)
Neh   3.13
Hanun (3)
Neh   3.30
Hapharaim
Josh   19.19
Happily Married
Is   62.4
Happizzez
1 Chr 24.7
Hara
1 Chr 5.26
Haradah
Num   33.15
Haran (1)
Gen   11 — 12   x 3
       27 — 29   x 3
2 Kgs 19.12
Is   37.12
Ezek   27.23
Acts   7.2 — 4   x 2
Haran (2)
Gen   11.26 — 31   x 6
Haran (3)
1 Chr 23.9
Haran (4)
1 Chr 2.46   x 2
Harar
2 Sam 23.11 — 24   x 2
1 Chr 11.26
Harbel
Num   34.11
Harbona
Esth   1.10
Harbonah
Esth   7.9
Hareph
1 Chr 2.51
Harhaiah
Neh   3.8
Harhas
2 Kgs 22.14
2 Chr 34.22
Harhur
Ezra   2.43
Neh   7.46
Harim (1)
1 Chr 24.7
Harim (2)
Ezra   2.21
       10.31
Neh   3.11
       7.26
Harim (3)
Ezra   2.36
       10.21
Neh   7.39
       12.12
Harim (4)
Neh   10.2
Harim (5)
Neh   10.14
Hariph (1)
1 Chr 12.3
Hariph (2)
Neh   7.8
Hariph (3)
Neh   10.14
Harmless Dragon
Is   30.7
Harnepher
1 Chr 7.36
Harod
Judg   7.1
2 Sam 23.24

Harod (Cont)
1 Chr 11.26
Haroeh
1 Chr 2.52
Harosheth-of-the-Gentiles
Judg   4.2 — 16   x 3
Harsha
Ezra   2.43
Neh   7.46
Harum
1 Chr 4.8
Harumaph
Neh   3.10
Haruz
2 Kgs 21.19
Hasadiah
1 Chr 3.20
Hashabiah (1)
1 Chr 6.45
Hashabiah (2)
1 Chr 9.14
Hashabiah (3)
1 Chr 25.3
Hashabiah (4)
1 Chr 25.9
Hashabiah (5)
1 Chr 26.30
Hashabiah (6)
1 Chr 27.16
Hashabiah (7)
2 Chr 35.9
Hashabiah (8)
Ezra   8.19
Hashabiah (9)
Ezra   8.24
Hashabiah (10)
Neh   3.17
Hashabiah (11)
Neh   10.9
Hashabiah (12)
Neh   11.15
Hashabiah (13)
Neh   11.22
Hashabiah (14)
Neh   12.12
Hashabiah (15)
Neh   12.24
Hashabnah
Neh   10.14
Hashabneiah (1)
Neh   3.10
Hashabneiah (2)
Neh   9.5
Hashbaddanah
Neh   8.4
Hashem
1 Chr 11.26
Hashmonah
Num   33.15
Hashubah
1 Chr 3.20
Hashum (1)
Ezra   2.3
       10.33
Neh   7.8
Hashum (2)
Neh   8.4
Hashum (3)
Neh   10.14
Hassenaah
Neh   3.3
Hassenuah (1)
1 Chr 9.7
Hassenuah (2)
Neh   11.9

Hasshub (1)
1 Chr 9.14
Neh   11.15
Hasshub (2)
Neh   3.11
Hasshub (3)
Neh   3.23
Hasshub (4)
Neh   10.14
Hassophereth
Ezra   2.55
Hasupha
Ezra   2.43
Neh   7.46
Hathach
Esth   4.5 — 9   x 4
Hathath
1 Chr 4.13
Hatipha
Ezra   2.43
Neh   7.46
Hatita
Ezra   2.40
Neh   7.43
Hattil
Ezra   2.55
Neh   7.57
Hattush (1)
1 Chr 3.22
Hattush (2)
Ezra   8.2
Hattush (3)
Neh   3.10
Hattush (4)
Neh   10.2
Hattush (5)
Neh   12.2
Hauran
Ezek   47.16 — 18   x 2
Havilah (1)
Gen   2.11
Havilah (2)
Gen   10.7
1 Chr 1.9
Havilah (3)
Gen   10.29
1 Chr 1.23
Havilah (4)
Gen   25.18
1 Sam 15.7
Hazael
1 Kgs 19.15 — 17   x 2
2 Kgs 8 — 10   x 13
       12 — 13   x 5
2 Chr 22.5
Amos   1.4
Hazaiah
Neh   11.5
Hazar Addar
Num   34.4
Hazar Enan
Num   34.9 — 10   x 2
Hazar Gaddah
Josh   15.27
Hazar Shual
Josh   15.28
       19.3
1 Chr 4.28
Neh   11.27
Hazar Susah
Josh   19.5
Hazarmaveth
Gen   10.26
1 Chr 1.20

Hazarsusim
1 Chr 4.31
Hazazon Tamar
Gen   14.7
2 Chr 20.2
Hazeroth
Num   11 — 12   x 2
       33.15
Deut   1.1
Haziel
1 Chr 23.9
Hazo
Gen   22.22
Hazor (1)
Josh   11 — 12   x 5
       19.36
Judg   4.2 — 17   x 2
1 Sam 12.9
1 Kgs 9.15
2 Kgs 15.29
Hazor (2)
Neh   11.33
Hazor (3)
Josh   15.23
Hazor (4)
Jer   49.28 — 33   x 3
Hazor (5)
Josh   15.25
Hazor Hadattah
Josh   15.25
Hazzelelponi
1 Chr 4.3
Heber (1)
Gen   46.17
Num   26.45
1 Chr 7.31 — 32   x 2
Heber (2)
Judg   4 — 5   x 4
Heber (3)
1 Chr 4.17
Heber (4)
1 Chr 8.17
Hebron (1)
Gen   13.18
       23.2
       35.27
       37.14
Num   13.22   x 2
Josh   10 — 12   x 7
       14 — 15   x 5
       20 — 21   x 3
Judg   1.10 — 20   x 2
       16.3
1 Sam 30.31
2 Sam 2 — 5   x 22
       15.7 — 10   x 4
1 Kgs 2.11
1 Chr 3.1 — 4   x 2
       6.55 — 57   x 2
       11 — 12   x 4
       29.27
2 Chr 11.10
Hebron (2)
Ex   6.18
Num   3.17 — 27   x 2
       26.58
1 Chr 6.2 — 18   x 2
       15.9
       23 — 24   x 3
       26.23 — 31   x 4
Hebron (3)
1 Chr 2.42 — 43   x 2
Hegai
Esth   2.3 — 15   x 4

Helah
1 Chr   4.5 − 7   x 2
Helam
2 Sam 10.16 − 17   x 2
Helbah
Judg   1.31
Helbon
Ezek   27.18
Heldai (1)
1 Chr   27.2
Heldai (2)
Zech   6.10 − 14   x 2
Heleb
2 Sam 23.24
Heled
1 Chr   11.26
Helek
Num   26.30
Josh   17.2
Heleph
Josh   19.33
Helez (1)
2 Sam 23.24
1 Chr   11.26
         27.2
Helez (2)
1 Chr   2.39
Heli
Lk   3.23
Heliopolis
Gen   41.45
         46.20
Jer   43.13
Ezek   30.17
Helkai
Neh   12.12
Helkath
Josh   19.25
         21.31
Helon
Num   1 − 2   x 2
         7.12
         10.16
Heman (1)
1 Kgs   4.31
1 Chr   2.6
Heman (2)
1 Chr   6.33   x 2
         15 − 16   x 3
         25.1 − 6   x 5
2 Chr   5.11
         29.12
         35.15
Heman (3)
Gen   36.22
Hemdan
Gen   36.25
Hena
2 Kgs 18 − 19   x 2
Is   37.13
Henadad
Ezra   3.9
Neh   3.18 − 24   x 2
         10.9
Hepher (1)
Num   26 − 27   x 3
Josh   17.2 − 3   x 2
Hepher (2)
1 Chr   4.6
Hepher (3)
1 Chr   11.26
Hepher (4)
Josh   12.17
1 Kgs   4.10

Hephzibah
2 Kgs 21.1
Heres (1)
Judg   1.35
Heres (2)
Judg   8.13
Heresh
1 Chr   9.14
Hereth
1 Sam 22.5
Hermas
Rom   16.14
Hermes (1)
Acts   14.12
Hermes (2)
Rom   16.14
Hermogenes
2 Tim   1.15
Hermon
Deut   3 − 4   x 3
Josh   11 − 13   x 6
1 Chr   5.23
Ps   29.6
         42.6
         89.12
         133.3
Song   4.8
Ezek   27.5
Herod (1)
Mt   2.1 − 22   x 9
Lk   1.5
Herod (2)
Mt   14.1 − 6   x 6
         22.16
Mk   3.6
         6.14 − 22   x 9
         8.15
         12.13
Lk   3.1 − 20   x 3
         8 − 9   x 3
         13.31
         23.7 − 15   x 7
Acts   4.27
         13.1
Herod (3)
Acts   12.1 − 23   x 10
Herodias
Mt   14.3 − 6   x 3
Mk   6.17 − 22   x 4
Lk   3.19
Herodion
Rom   16.11
Heshaiah
Jer   42.1
Heshbon
Num   21.25 − 34   x 6
         32.3 − 37   x 2
Deut   1 − 4   x 6
         29.7
Josh   9.10
         12 − 13   x 7
         21.39
Judg   11.19 − 26   x 2
1 Chr   6.81
Neh   9.22
Song   7.4
Is   15 − 16   x 3
Jer   48 − 49   x 4
Heshmon
Josh   15.27
Heth
Gen   10.15
1 Chr   1.13
Hethlon
Ezek   47 − 48   x 2

Hezekiah (1)
2 Kgs 16.20
         18 − 21   x 36
1 Chr   3 − 4   x 2
2 Chr   28 − 33   x 41
Prov   25.1
Is   1.1
         36 − 39   x 25
Jer   15.4
         26.18 − 19   x 3
Hos   1.1
Mic   1.1
Zeph   1.1
Mt   1.6
Hezekiah (2)
Ezra   2.3
Neh   7.8
         10.14
Hezion
1 Kgs 15.18
Hezir (1)
1 Chr   24.7
Hezir (2)
Neh   10.14
Hezro
2 Sam 23.24
1 Chr   11.26
Hezron (1)
Gen   46.9
Ex   6.14
Num   26.6
1 Chr   5.3
Hezron (2)
Josh   15.3
Hezron (3)
Gen   46.12
Num   26.19
Ruth   4.18
1 Chr   2.5 − 25   x 6
         4.1
Mt   1.2
Lk   3.33
Hiddai
2 Sam 23.24
Hiel
1 Kgs 16.34   x 2
Hierapolis
Col   4.13
Hilen
1 Chr   6.57
Hilkiah (1)
2 Kgs 22 − 23   x 9
1 Chr   6.13
         9 10
2 Chr   34 − 35   x 6
Ezra   7.1
Neh   11.11
Hilkiah (2)
2 Kgs 18.18
Is   22.20
         36.3
Hilkiah (3)
1 Chr   6.45
Hilkiah (4)
1 Chr   26.11
Hilkiah (5)
Neh   8.4
         12.2 − 12   x 2
Hilkiah (6)
Jer   1.1
Hilkiah (7)
Jer   29.3
Hillel
Judg   12.13

Hinnom
see also Topheth
Josh   15.8   x 2
         18.16   x 2
2 Kgs 23.10
2 Chr   28.3
         33.6
Neh   11.30
Jer   7.31 − 32   x 2
         19.2 − 6   x 2
         32.35
Hirah
Gen   38.1 − 20   x 4
Hiram
2 Sam 5.11
1 Kgs   5.1 − 18   x 8
         9 − 10   x 7
1 Chr   14.1
2 Chr   2.3 − 11   x 2
         8 − 9   x 4
Hittites
Gen   15.20
         23.3 − 20   x 5
         25 − 27   x 4
         36.2
         49 − 50   x 3
Ex   3.8 − 17   x 2
         13.5
         23.23 − 28   x 2
         33 − 34   x 2
Num   13.29
Deut   7.1
         20.17
Josh   1.4
         3.10
         9.1
         11 − 12   x 2
         24.11
Judg   1.26
         3.5
1 Sam 26.6
2 Sam 11.3 − 6   x 2
         23 − 24   x 2
1 Kgs   9 − 11   x 3
         15.5
2 Kgs 7.6
1 Chr   11.26
2 Chr   1.17
         8.7
Ezra   9.1
Neh   9.8
Ezek   16.3 − 45   x 2
Hivites
Gen   10.17
         34.2
         36.2
Ex   3.8 − 17   x 2
         13.5
         23.23 − 28   x 2
         33 − 34   x 2
Deut   7.1
         20.17
Josh   3.10
         9.1 − 3   x 2
         11 − 12   x 3
         24.11
Judg   3.3 − 5   x 2
2 Sam 24.7
1 Kgs   9.20
1 Chr   1.15
2 Chr   8.7
Is   17.9
Hizki
1 Chr   8.17
Hizkiah
1 Chr   3.23

Hobab
Num 10.29 – 30 x 2
Judg 4.11
Hobah
Gen 14.15
Hobaiah
Neh 7.63
Hod
1 Chr 7.37
Hodaviah (1)
1 Chr 5.24
Hodaviah (2)
1 Chr 9.7
Hodaviah (3)
1 Chr 3.24
Hodaviah (4)
Ezra 2.40
Neh 7.43
Hodaviah (5)
Ezra 3.9
Hodesh
1 Chr 8.8
Hodiah (1)
1 Chr 4.19
Hodiah (2)
Neh 8 – 10 x 4
Hodiah (3)
Neh 10.14
Hoglah
Num 26 – 27 x 2
36.10
Josh 17.3
Hoham
Josh 10.3
Holon (1)
Josh 15.51
21.15
Holon (2)
Jer 48.21
Homam
1 Chr 1.38
Hophni
1 Sam 1 – 2 x 2
4.4 – 17 x 3
Hophra
Jer 44.30
Hor (1)
Num 20 – 21 x 4
33.15 – 41 x 4
Deut 32.50
Hor (2)
Num 34.7
Hor Haggidgad
Num 33.15
Horam
Josh 10.33
Horem
Josh 19.38
Horesh
1 Sam 23.15 – 19 x 3
Hori (1)
Gen 36.22
1 Chr 1.38
Hori (2)
Num 13.3
Horite
Gen 14.6
36.20 – 29 x 2
Deut 2.12 – 22 x 2
Hormah
Num 14.45
21.3
Deut 1.44
Josh 12.14
15.30

Hormah (Cont)
Josh 19.4
Judg 1.17
1 Sam 30.30
1 Chr 4.30
Horonaim
2 Sam 13.34
Is 15.5
Jer 48.3 – 34 x 3
Horse Gate
2 Kgs 11.16
2 Chr 23.15
Neh 3.28
Jer 31.40
Hosah (1)
Josh 19.29
Hosah (2)
1 Chr 16.38
26.10 – 16 x 3
Hosea
Hos 1.1 – 9 x 7
Rom 9.25
Hoshaiah (1)
Neh 12.32
Hoshaiah (2)
Jer 43.2
Hoshama
1 Chr 3.18
Hoshea (1)
2 Kgs 15.30
17 – 18 x 8
Hoshea (2)
Num 13.3 – 16 x 2
Hoshea (3)
1 Chr 27.16
Hoshea (4)
Neh 10.14
Hotham (1)
1 Chr 7.32 – 35 x 2
Hotham (2)
1 Chr 11.26
Hothir
1 Chr 25.4 – 9 x 2
Hukkok
Josh 19.34
Hukok
1 Chr 6.75
Hul
Gen 10.23
1 Chr 1.17
Huldah
2 Kgs 22.14
2 Chr 34.22
Humtah
Josh 15.54
Hupham
Num 26.39
Huppah
1 Chr 24.7
Huppim
Gen 46.21
1 Chr 7.12 – 15 x 2
Hur (1)
Ex 17.10 – 12 x 2
24.14
Hur (2)
Ex 31.2
35.30
38.22
1 Chr 2.19 – 50 x 4
4.3 x 2
2 Chr 1.5
Hur (3)
Num 31.8
Josh 13.21

Hur (4)
1 Chr 4.1
Hur (5)
Neh 3.9
Hurai
1 Chr 11.26
Huram (1)
1 Kgs 7.13 – 40 x 9
2 Chr 2.13
4.11 x 2
Huram (2)
1 Chr 8.5
Huri
1 Chr 5.14 x 2
Hushah
2 Sam 21.18
23.24
1 Chr 4.3
11.26
20.4
27.2
Hushai
2 Sam 15 – 17 x 10
1 Kgs 4.16
1 Chr 27.33
Husham
Gen 36.31
1 Chr 1.43
Hushim (1)
Gen 46.23
1 Chr 7.12
Hushim (2)
1 Chr 8.8 – 11 x 2
Huzoth
Num 22.39
Hymenaeus
1 Tim 1.20
2 Tim 2.17
I Am
Ex 3.14
Ibhar
2 Sam 5.15
1 Chr 3.6
14.5
Ibleam
Josh 17.11
Judg 1.27
2 Kgs 9.27
15.10
Ibneiah
1 Chr 9.7
Ibnijah
1 Chr 9.7
Ibri
1 Chr 24.27
Ibsam
1 Chr 7.2
Ibzan
Judg 12.8 – 11 x 3
Ichabod
1 Sam 4.21
14.3
Iconium
Acts 13 – 14 x 4
16.2
2 Tim 3.11
Idalah
Josh 19.15
Idbash
1 Chr 4.3
Iddo (1)
1 Kgs 4.14
Iddo (2)
1 Chr 6.21

Iddo (3)
1 Chr 27.16
Iddo (4)
2 Chr 9.29
12 – 13 x 2
Iddo (5)
Ezra 5.1
Zech 1.1
Iddo (6)
Ezra 8.17
Iddo (7)
Neh 12.2 – 12 x 2
Idumea
Mk 3.8
Iezer
Num 26.30
Igal (1)
Num 13.3
Igal (2)
2 Sam 23.24
Igal (3)
1 Chr 3.22
Igdaliah
Jer 35.4
Iim
Josh 15.29
Ijon
1 Kgs 15.20
2 Kgs 15.29
2 Chr 16.4
Ikkesh
2 Sam 23.24
1 Chr 11.26
27.2
Ilai
1 Chr 11.26
Illyricum
Rom 15.19
Imlah
1 Kgs 22.8
2 Chr 18.7
Immanuel
Is 7.14
Mt 1.23
Immer (1)
1 Chr 9.10
Ezra 2.36
10.20
Neh 7.39
11.13
Immer (2)
1 Chr 24.7
Immer (3)
Ezra 2.59
Neh 7.61
Immer (4)
Neh 3.29
Immer (5)
Jer 20.1
Imna
1 Chr 7.35
Imnah (1)
Gen 46.17
Num 26.44
1 Chr 7.30
Imnah (2)
2 Chr 31.14
Imrah
1 Chr 7.36
Imri (1)
1 Chr 9.4
Imri (2)
Neh 3.2
India
Esth 1.1

Jahath (2)
1 Chr   6.20 − 43   x 2
Jahath (3)
1 Chr   23.10
Jahath (4)
1 Chr   24.22
Jahath (5)
2 Chr   34.12
Jahaz
Num   21.23
Deut   2.32
Josh   13.18
21.36
Judg   11.20
Is   15.4
Jer   48.34
Jahaziel (1)
1 Chr   12.3
Jahaziel (2)
1 Chr   16.6
Jahaziel (3)
2 Chr   20.14 − 15   x 2
Jahaziel (4)
Ezra   8.2
Jahdai
1 Chr   2.47
Jahdiel
1 Chr   5.24
Jahdo
1 Chr   5.14
Jahleel
Gen   46.14
Num   26.26
Jahmai
1 Chr   7.2
Jahzah
1 Chr   6.78
Jer   48.21
Jahzeel
Gen   46.24
Num   26.48
Jahzeiah
Ezra   10.15
Jahzerah
1 Chr   9.10
Jahziel
1 Chr   7.13
Jair (1)
Num   32.41   x 2
Deut   3.14   x 2
Josh   13.30
1 Kgs   4.13
1 Chr   2.22 − 23   x 3
Jair (2)
Judg   10.3 − 5   x 3
Jair (3)
2 Sam   21.19
1 Chr   20.5
Jair (4)
Esth   2.5
Jair (5)
2 Sam   20.26
Jairus
Mk   5.22 − 38   x 3
Lk   8.41 − 50   x 3
Jakeh
Prov   30.1
Jakim (1)
1 Chr   8.19
Jakim (2)
1 Chr   24.7
Jalam
Gen   36.5 − 18   x 3
1 Chr   1.35

Jalon
1 Chr   4.17
Jambres
2 Tim   3.8 − 9   x 2
James (1)
(Son of Zebedee)
Mt   4.21
10.2
17.1
Mk   1.19 − 29   x 2
3.17
5.37
9 − 10   x 3
13 − 14   x 2
Lk   5 − 6   x 2
8 − 9   x 3
Acts   1.13
12.2
James (2)
(Son of Alphaeus)
Mt   10.3
Mk   3.18
Lk   6.15
Acts   1.13
James (3)
Mt   27.56
Mk   15 − 16   x 2
Lk   24.10
James (4)
(Brother of Jesus)
Mt   13.55
Mk   6.3
Acts   12.17
15.13 − 19   x 2
21.18
1 Cor   15.7
Gal   1 − 2   x 3
James (5)
Lk   6.16
Acts   1.13
James (6)
Jas   1.1
James (7)
Jude   .1
Jamin (1)
Gen   46.10
Ex   6.15
Num   26.12
1 Chr   4.24
Jamin (2)
1 Chr   2.26
Jamin (3)
Neh   8.7
Jamlech
1 Chr   4.34
Jamnia (1)
Josh   15.11
Jamnia (2)
Josh   19.33
Jamnia (3)
2 Chr   26.6
Janai
1 Chr   5.12
Janim
Josh   15.53
Jannai
Lk   3.24
Jannes
2 Tim   3.8 − 9   x 2
Janoah (1)
Josh   16.6 − 7   x 2
Janoah (2)
2 Kgs   15.29
Japheth
Gen   5 − 7   x 3
9 − 10   x 8
1 Chr   1.4 − 5   x 2

Japhia (1)
Josh   10.3
Japhia (2)
Josh   19.12
Japhia (3)
2 Sam   5.15
1 Chr   3.7
14.6
Japhlet
1 Chr   7.32 − 33   x 2
Japhletites
Josh   16.3
Jarah
1 Chr   9.42
Jared
Gen   5.15 − 18   x 2
1 Chr   1.2 − 3   x 2
Lk   3.37
Jarha
1 Chr   2.34
Jarib (1)
1 Chr   4.24
Jarib (2)
Ezra   8.16
Jarib (3)
Ezra   10.18
Jarmuth (1)
Josh   10.3 − 23   x 3
12.11
15.35
Neh   11.29
Jarmuth (2)
Josh   21.29
Jaroah
1 Chr   5.14
Jashar
Josh   10.13
2 Sam   1.18
Jashen
2 Sam   23.24
Jashobeam (1)
1 Chr   11.11
Jashobeam (2)
1 Chr   12.3
Jashobeam (3)
1 Chr   27.2
Jashub (1)
Gen   46.13
Num   26.24
1 Chr   7.1
Jashub (2)
Ezra   10.29
Jason
Acts   17.5 − 9   x 4
Rom   16.21
Jathniel
1 Chr   26.2
Jattir
Josh   15.48
21.14
1 Sam   30.27
2 Sam   23.24
1 Chr   6.57
11.26
Javan
Gen   10.2 − 4   x 2
1 Chr   1.5 − 7   x 2
Jazer
Num   21.32
32.1 − 35   x 3
Josh   13.25
21.39
2 Sam   24.5
1 Chr   6.81
26.31

Jazer (Cont)
Is   16.8 − 9   x 2
Jer   48.32   x 2
Jaziz
1 Chr   27.25
Jearim (1)
Josh   15.10
Jearim (2)
Ps   132.6
Jeatherai
1 Chr   6.21
Jeberechiah
Is   8.2
Jebusites
Gen   10.16
15.21
Ex   3.8 − 17   x 2
13.5
23.23
33 − 34   x 2
Num   13.29
Deut   7.1
20.17
Josh   3.10
9.1
11 − 12   x 2
15.8 − 63   x 3
18.16 − 28   x 2
24.11
Judg   1.21   x 2
3.5
19.10 − 14   x 3
2 Sam   5.6 − 8   x 2
24.16
1 Kgs   9.20
1 Chr   1.14
11.4 − 6   x 4
21.15
2 Chr   3.1
8.7
Ezra   9.1
Neh   9.8
Zech   9.7
Jecoliah
2 Kgs   15.2
2 Chr   26.3
Jedaiah (1)
1 Chr   4.34
Jedaiah (2)
Neh   3.10
Jedaiah (3)
Zech   6.10 − 14   x 2
Jedaiah (4)
1 Chr   9.10
24.7
Jedaiah (5)
Ezra   2.36
Neh   7.39
Jedaiah (6)
Neh   11 − 12   x 3
Jedaiah (7)
Neh   12.2 − 12   x 2
Jediael (1)
1 Chr   7.6 − 10   x 2
Jediael (2)
1 Chr   11 − 12   x 2
Jediael (3)
1 Chr   26.2
Jedidah
2 Kgs   22.1
Jedidiah
see also Solomon
2 Sam   12.25
Jeduthun
1 Chr   9.14
16.38 − 42   x 4

Jeduthun (Cont)		
1 Chr	25.1 – 6	x 3
2 Chr	5.11	
	29.12	
	35.15	
Neh	11.17	
Jegar Sahadutha		
Gen	31.47	
Jehallelel (1)		
1 Chr	4.16	
Jehallelel (2)		
2 Chr	29.12	
Jehaziel		
1 Chr	23 – 24	x 2
Jehdeiah (1)		
1 Chr	24.20	
Jehdeiah (2)		
1 Chr	27.25	
Jehezkel		
1 Chr	24.7	
Jehiah		
1 Chr	15.23	
Jehiel (1)		
1 Chr	15 – 16	x 2
Jehiel (2)		
1 Chr	23.8	
Jehiel (3)		
1 Chr	26.21	
Jehiel (4)		
1 Chr	27.32	
Jehiel (5)		
1 Chr	29.8	
Jehiel (6)		
2 Chr	21.2	
Jehiel (7)		
2 Chr	31.13	
Jehiel (8)		
2 Chr	35.8	
Jehiel (9)		
Ezra	8.2	
Jehiel (10)		
Ezra	10.2	
Jehiel (11)		
Ezra	10.21	
Jehiel (12)		
Ezra	10.26	
Jehizkiah		
2 Chr	28.12	
Jehoaddah		
1 Chr	8.36	
Jehoaddin		
2 Kgs	14.2	
2 Chr	25.1	
Jehoahaz		
2 Kgs	10.35	
	13 – 14	x 8
2 Chr	25.17	
Jehoash		
2 Kgs	13 – 14	x 17
2 Chr	25.17 – 25	x 5
Hos	1.1	
Amos	1.1	
Jehohanan (1)		
1 Chr	26.3	
Jehohanan (2)		
2 Chr	28.12	
Jehohanan (3)		
Ezra	10.6	
Jehohanan (4)		
Ezra	10.28	
Jehohanan (5)		
Neh	6.18	
Jehohanan (6)		
Neh	12.12	

Jehohanan (7)		
Neh	12.42	
Jehohanan (8)		
2 Chr	17.15	
Jehohanan (9)		
2 Chr	23.1	
Jehoiachin		
2 Kgs	24 – 25	x 11
1 Chr	3.16 – 17	x 3
2 Chr	36.8 – 10	x 4
Esth	2.6	
Jer	22.24 – 28	x 2
	24.1	
	27 – 29	x 3
	37.1	
	52.31 – 33	x 3
Ezek	1.2	
Mt	1.6 – 12	x 2
Jehoiada (1)		
2 Sam	8.18	
	20.23	
	23.20	
1 Kgs	1.8	
	4.4	
1 Chr	11 – 12	x 2
	18.17	
	27.2	
Jehoiada (2)		
2 Kgs	11 – 12	x 9
2 Chr	22 – 24	x 22
Jer	29.26	
Jehoiada (3)		
1 Chr	27.34	
Jehoiakim		
2 Kgs	23 – 24	x 10
1 Chr	3.15 – 16	x 2
2 Chr	36.4 – 8	x 4
Jer	1.3	
	22.18 – 24	x 2
	24 – 28	x 8
	35 – 37	x 6
	45 – 46	x 2
	52.2	
Dan	1.1 – 2	x 2
Jehoiarib		
1 Chr	9.10	
	24.7	
Jehonathan (1)		
2 Chr	17.8	
Jehonathan (2)		
Neh	12.12	
Jehoram (1)		
1 Kgs	22.50	
2 Kgs	1.17	
	8.16 – 25	x 6
	11 – 12	x 2
1 Chr	3.11	
2 Chr	21 – 22	x 12
Mt	1.6	
Jehoram (2)		
2 Chr	17.8	
Jehoshaphat (1)		
1 Kgs	15.24	
	22.2 – 51	x 18
2 Kgs	1.17	
	3.1 – 14	x 6
	8.16	
	12.18	
1 Chr	3.10	
2 Chr	17 – 22	x 39
Mt	1.6	
Jehoshaphat (2)		
2 Sam	8.16	
	20.24	
1 Kgs	4.3	

Jehoshaphat (2) (Cont)		
1 Chr	18.15	
Jehoshaphat (3)		
1 Kgs	4.17	
Jehoshaphat (4)		
2 Kgs	9.2	
Jehosheba		
2 Kgs	11.2 – 3	x 2
2 Chr	22.11	
Jehozabad (1)		
2 Kgs	12.20	
2 Chr	24.26	
Jehozabad (2)		
1 Chr	26.4	
Jehozabad (3)		
2 Chr	17.18	
Jehozadak		
1 Chr	6.14 – 15	x 2
Ezra	3.2	
	5.2	
	10.18	
Neh	12.26	
Hag	1.1	
Zech	6.11	
Jehu (1)		
1 Kgs	19.16 – 17	x 3
2 Kgs	9 – 10	x 56
	12 – 13	x 2
	15.12	
2 Chr	22.7 – 9	x 4
	25.17	
Hos	1.4	x 2
Jehu (2)		
1 Kgs	16.1 – 12	x 3
2 Chr	19 – 20	x 2
Jehu (3)		
1 Chr	4.34	
Jehu (4)		
1 Chr	12.3	
Jehu (5)		
1 Chr	2.38	
Jehubbah		
1 Chr	7.34	
Jehucal		
Jer	37 – 38	x 2
Jehud		
Josh	19.45	
Jehudi		
Jer	36.14 – 23	x 3
Jehuel		
2 Chr	29.12	
Jeiel (1)		
1 Chr	5.7	
Jeiel (2)		
1 Chr	8 – 9	x 2
Jeiel (3)		
1 Chr	11.26	
Jeiel (4)		
1 Chr	16.5	
Jeiel (5)		
2 Chr	26.11	
Jeiel (6)		
2 Chr	35.9	
Jeiel (7)		
Ezra	10.43	
Jeiel (8)		
1 Chr	15 – 16	x 2
Jeiel (9)		
2 Chr	20.14	
Jekabzeel		
Neh	11.25	
Jekameam		
1 Chr	23 – 24	x 2
Jekamiah (1)		
1 Chr	2.41	

Jekamiah (2)		
1 Chr	3.18	
Jekuthiel		
1 Chr	4.17	
Jemimah		
Job	42.14	
Jemuel		
Gen	46.10	
Ex	6.15	
Jephthah		
Judg	11 – 12	x 23
1 Sam	12.11	
Heb	11.32	
Jephunneh (1)		
Num	13 – 14	x 2
	26.65	
	32.12	
	34.19	
Deut	1.36	
Josh	14 – 15	x 4
	21.12	
1 Chr	4.15	
	6.56	
Jephunneh (2)		
1 Chr	7.38	
Jerah		
Gen	10.26	
1 Chr	1.20	
Jerahmeel (1)		
1 Sam	27.10	
	30.29	
1 Chr	2.9 – 42	x 5
Jerahmeel (2)		
1 Chr	24.28	
Jerahmeel (3)		
Jer	36.26	
Jered		
1 Chr	4.17	
Jeremai		
Ezra	10.33	
Jeremiah (1)		
2 Chr	35 – 36	x 4
Ezra	1.1	
Jer	1.1 – 18	x 5
	5 – 7	x 5
	11 – 13	x 3
	17 – 18	x 2
	23 – 26	x 6
	29.27	
	32.36	
	35 – 36	x 5
	38 – 39	x 2
	51.64	
Dan	9.2	
Mt	2.17	
	16.14	
	27.9	
Jeremiah (2)		
2 Kgs	23 – 24	x 2
Jer	52.1	
Jeremiah (3)		
1 Chr	5.24	
Jeremiah (4)		
1 Chr	12.3	
Jeremiah (5)		
1 Chr	12.9	
Jeremiah (6)		
1 Chr	12.9	
Jeremiah (7)		
Neh	10.2	
Jeremiah (8)		
Neh	12.2	
Jeremiah (9)		
Neh	12.12	

K

Jeremiah (10)
Neh 12.33
Jeremoth (1)
1 Chr 7.8
Jeremoth (2)
1 Chr 8.14
Jeremoth (3)
1 Chr 23.23
Jeremoth (4)
1 Chr 24.30
Jeremoth (5)
1 Chr 27.16
Jeremoth (6)
Ezra 10.26
Jeremoth (7)
Ezra 10.27
Jeremoth (8)
Ezra 10.29
Jeriah
1 Chr 23 – 24   x 2
26.31 – 32   x 2
Jeribai
1 Chr 11.26
Jericho
Num 22.1
26.3 – 63   x 2
31.12
33 – 36   x 5
Deut 32.49
34.1 – 3   x 2
Josh 2 – 10   x 19
12 – 13   x 2
16.1 – 7   x 4
18.12 – 21   x 2
20.8
24.11   x 2
Judg 1.16
3.13
2 Sam 10.5
1 Kgs 16.34   x 2
2 Kgs 2.4 – 23   x 6
25.5
1 Chr 6.78
19.5
2 Chr 28.15
Ezra 2.21
Neh 3.2
7.26
Jer 39.5
52.8
Mt 20.29
Mk 10.46
Lk 10.30
18 – 19   x 2
Heb 11.30
Jeriel
1 Chr 7.2
Jerimoth (1)
1 Chr 7.7
Jerimoth (2)
1 Chr 12.3
Jerimoth (3)
1 Chr 25.4
Jerimoth (4)
1 Chr 25.9
Jerimoth (5)
2 Chr 11.18
Jerimoth (6)
2 Chr 31.13
Jerioth
1 Chr 2.18
Jeroboam (1)
1 Kgs 11 – 16   x 47
21 – 22   x 2
2 Kgs 3.3

Jeroboam (1) (Cont)
2 Kgs 9 – 10   x 3
13 – 15   x 9
17.21 – 22   x 3
23.15 – 16   x 2
2 Chr 9 – 13   x 18
Jeroboam (2)
2 Kgs 13 – 15   x 8
1 Chr 5.17
Hos 1.1
Amos 1.1
7.9 – 11   x 3
Jeroham (1)
1 Sam 1.1
Jeroham (2)
1 Chr 9.7
Jeroham (3)
1 Chr 9.10
Jeroham (4)
1 Chr 12.3
Jeroham (5)
1 Chr 27.16
Jeroham (6)
2 Chr 23.1
Jeroham (7)
Neh 11.12
Jeroham (8)
1 Chr 8.26
Jeroham (9)
1 Chr 6.27
Jeroham (10)
1 Chr 6.34
Jerubbaal
see also Gideon
Judg 6.32
Jeruel
2 Chr 20.16
Jerusalem
Josh 10.1 – 23   x 4
12.10
15.8 – 63   x 2
18.28
Judg 1.7 – 21   x 3
19.10
1 Sam 17.54
2 Sam 5 – 6   x 7
8 – 12   x 6
14 – 17   x 10
19 – 20   x 9
24.8 – 16   x 2
1 Kgs 2 – 3   x 6
8 – 12   x 16
14 – 15   x 5
22.42
2 Kgs 8 – 9   x 3
12.1 – 20   x 4
14 – 16   x 14
18 – 25   x 42
1 Chr 3.4
6.10 – 31   x 3
8 – 9   x 10
11.4
13 – 15   x 6
18 – 21   x 7
23.25
28 – 29   x 3
2 Chr 1 – 3   x 7
5 – 6   x 2
8 – 15   x 20
17.13 – 19   x 2
19 – 36   x 94
Ezra 1 – 10   x 49
Neh 1 – 4   x 12
6 – 8   x 8
11 – 13   x 17
Esth 2.6

Jerusalem (Cont)
Ps 9.14
51.18
68 – 69   x 2
76.2
79.1 – 3   x 2
87.2 – 6   x 3
102.21
116.18
122.2 – 8   x 4
125 – 126   x 2
128.5
135.21
137.5 – 7   x 2
147.2 – 12   x 2
Ecc 1 – 2   x 5
Song 1 – 3   x 4
5 – 6   x 3
8.4
Is 1 – 5   x 17
7 – 8   x 2
10.10 – 32   x 4
16.1
22.7 – 21   x 4
24.23
27 – 31   x 9
33.5 – 20   x 2
35 – 38   x 7
40 – 41   x 3
44 – 46   x 4
49.14 – 16   x 2
51 – 52   x 8
54.1 – 11   x 2
59 – 62   x 12
64 – 66   x 7
Jer 1 – 11   x 35
13 – 15   x 9
17 – 19   x 14
21 – 27   x 15
29 – 40   x 35
42.18
44.2 – 21   x 6
50 – 52   x 13
Lam 1 – 2   x 9
4.12
Ezek 4 – 5   x 9
8 – 9   x 4
11 – 17   x 13
21 – 24   x 11
26.2
33.21
36.38
40.1
43.3
48.30
Dan 1.1
5 – 6   x 2
9.2 – 25   x 7
Joel 2 – 3   x 6
Amos 1 – 2   x 2
Obad .11 – 21   x 3
Mic 1.1 – 13   x 5
3 – 5   x 8
7.11
Zeph 1.4 – 12   x 3
3.1 – 16   x 3
Zech 1 – 3   x 11
7 – 9   x 9
12 – 14   x 20
Mal 2 – 3   x 2
Mt 2 – 5   x 6
15 – 16   x 2
20 – 21   x 4
23.37
Mk 1.5

Jerusalem (Cont)
Mk 3.8 – 22   x 2
7.1
10 – 11   x 6
15.41
Lk 2.22 – 45   x 6
4 – 6   x 3
9 – 10   x 4
13.4 – 34   x 4
17 – 19   x 5
21.20 – 24   x 2
23 – 24   x 7
Jn 1 – 2   x 3
4 – 5   x 5
7.25
10 – 12   x 5
Acts 1 – 2   x 6
4 – 6   x 3
8 – 13   x 18
15 – 16   x 3
18 – 26   x 29
28.17
Rom 15.19 – 31   x 4
1 Cor 16.3
Gal 1 – 2   x 3
4.25 – 26   x 2
Heb 12.22
Rev 3.12
21.2 – 10   x 2
Jerusha
2 Kgs 15.33
Jerushah
2 Chr 27.1
Jeshaiah (1)
1 Chr 3.21   x 2
Jeshaiah (2)
Ezra 8.2
Jeshaiah (3)
Ezra 8.19
Jeshaiah (4)
Neh 11.7
Jeshaiah (5)
1 Chr 25.3
Jeshaiah (6)
1 Chr 25.9
Jeshanah
2 Chr 13.19
Jeshanah Gate
Neh 3.6
12.39
Jeshebeab
1 Chr 24.7
Jesher
1 Chr 2.18
Jeshiah
1 Chr 26.25
Jeshishai
1 Chr 5.14
Jeshohaiah
1 Chr 4.34
Jeshua (1)
Neh 11.26
Jeshua (2)
1 Chr 24.7
Jeshua (3)
Ezra 2.36
Neh 7.39
Jeshua (4)
2 Chr 31.15
Jeshua (5)
Ezra 8.33
Jeshua (6)
Ezra 2.3
Neh 7.8

Jeshua (7)
Neh 3.19
Jeshua (8)
Ezra 2 − 3   x 2
Neh 7.43
Jeshua (9)
Neh 8 − 10   x 4
12.8 − 24   x 2
Jesimiel
1 Chr 4.34
Jesse
Ruth 4.17 − 18   x 2
1 Sam 16 − 17   x 18
2 Sam 23.1
1 Chr 2.10 − 16   x 4
10.14
12.18
29.26
2 Chr 11.18
Ps 72.20
Mt 1.2
Lk 3.32
Acts 13.22
Rom 15.12
Jesus
Mt 1 − 5   x 26
7 − 28   x 272
Mk 1 − 16   x 307
Lk 1 − 24   x 342
Jn 1 − 14   x 225
16 − 21   x 93
Acts 1 − 11   x 50
13.23 − 38   x 5
15 − 22   x 22
24 − 26   x 4
28.23 − 31   x 2
Rom 1 − 8   x 24
10.9
13 − 16   x 11
1 Cor 1 − 6   x 17
8 − 9   x 2
11 − 12   x 3
15 − 16   x 4
2 Cor 1.1 − 20   x 6
4.5 − 14   x 6
8.9
11.4 − 31   x 2
13.5 − 13   x 2
Gal 1 − 6   x 17
Eph 1 − 6   x 20
Phil 1 − 4   x 21
Col 1 − 4   x 6
1 Thes 1 − 5   x 16
2 Thes 1 − 3   x 13
1 Tim 1 − 6   x 14
2 Tim 1 − 4   x 13
Tit 1 − 3   x 4
Phlm .1 − 25   x 6
Heb 2 − 8   x 15
10.10 − 19   x 2
12 − 13   x 7
Jas 1 − 2   x 2
1 Pet 1 − 4   x 9
2 Pet 1 − 3   x 9
1 Jn 1 − 5   x 13
2 Jn .3 − 7   x 2
Jude .1 − 25   x 6
Rev 1.1 − 9   x 6
12.17
14.12
17.6
19 − 20   x 3
22.7 − 21   x 5
Jether (1)
Judg 8.20

Jether (2)
2 Sam 17.25
1 Kgs 2.5
1 Chr 2.17
Jether (3)
1 Chr 2.32   x 2
Jether (4)
1 Chr 4.17
Jether (5)
1 Chr 7.38
Jetheth
Gen 36.40
1 Chr 1.51
Jethro
Ex 2 − 4   x 6
18.1 − 27   x 9
Num 10.29
Jetur
Gen 25.15
1 Chr 1.31
5.19
Jeuel (1)
1 Chr 9.4
Jeuel (2)
2 Chr 29.12
Jeuel (3)
Ezra 8.2
Jeush (1)
Gen 36.5 − 18   x 3
1 Chr 1.35
Jeush (2)
1 Chr 7.10
Jeush (3)
1 Chr 8.39
Jeush (4)
1 Chr 23.10   x 2
Jeush (5)
2 Chr 11.19
Jeuz
1 Chr 8.10
Jezaniah
2 Kgs 25.23
Jer 40.8
Jezebel (1)
1 Kgs 16.31
18 − 19   x 4
21 − 22   x 8
2 Kgs 3.2
9 − 10   x 6
Jezebel (2)
Rev 2.20
Jezer
Gen 46.24
Num 26.49
1 Chr 7.13
Jeziel
1 Chr 12.3
Jezrahiah
Neh 12.42
Jezreel (1)
(Valley)
Josh 17.16
19.18
Judg 6.33
1 Sam 25.43
27.3
29.1 − 11   x 2
31.7
2 Sam 2 − 4   x 4
1 Kgs 4.12
18.45 − 46   x 2
21.1 − 23   x 4
2 Kgs 8 − 10   x 13
1 Chr 3.1
10.7
2 Chr 22.6

Jezreel (1) (Cont)
Hos 1.4 − 11   x 3
Jezreel (2)
Josh 15.56
Jezreel (3)
1 Chr 4.3
Jezreel (4)
Hos 1.4
Jidlaph
Gen 22.22
Joab (1)
1 Sam 26.6
2 Sam 2 − 3   x 20
8.16
10 − 12   x 17
14.1 − 33   x 12
16 − 20   x 40
23 − 24   x 6
1 Kgs 1 − 2   x 21
11.15 − 21   x 2
1 Chr 2.16
11.6 − 26   x 5
18 − 21   x 12
26 − 27   x 4
Joab (2)
1 Chr 4.14
Joab (3)
Ezra 2.3
8.2
Joab (4)
Neh 7.8
Joah (1)
2 Kgs 18.18 − 37   x 3
Is 36.3 − 22   x 3
Joah (2)
1 Chr 26.4
Joah (3)
2 Chr 34.8
Joah (4)
1 Chr 6.21
Joah (5)
2 Chr 29.12   x 2
Joahaz (1)
2 Kgs 23.30 − 34   x 3
1 Chr 3.15
2 Chr 36.1 − 4   x 4
Jer 22.10 − 11   x 2
Joahaz (2)
2 Chr 34.8
Joanan
Lk 3.27
Joanna
Lk 8.3
24.10
Joash (1)
2 Kgs 11 − 14   x 20
1 Chr 3.11
7.8
27.25
2 Chr 22 − 24   x 12
Joash (2)
Judg 6 − 8   x 8
Joash (3)
1 Kgs 22.26
2 Chr 18.25
Joash (4)
1 Chr 4.22
Joash (5)
1 Chr 12.3
Job (2)
Job 1 − 5   x 23
11.3 − 13   x 2
15.1 − 17   x 2
18.1
20.1

Job (2) (Cont)
Job 22.21
29.1
31 − 35   x 20
37 − 40   x 6
42.1 − 16   x 12
Jas 5.11
Job (3)
Ezek 14.14 − 20   x 2
Jobab (1)
Gen 10.29
1 Chr 1.23
Jobab (2)
Gen 36.31
Jobab (3)
Josh 11.1
Jobab (4)
1 Chr 8.8
Jobab (5)
1 Chr 8.18
Jochebed
Ex 6.20
Num 26.59
Joda
Lk 3.26
Joed
Neh 11.7
Joel (1)
1 Chr 4.34
Joel (2)
1 Chr 5.4 − 8   x 2
Joel (3)
1 Chr 5.12
Joel (4)
1 Chr 7.3
Joel (5)
1 Chr 11.26
Joel (6)
1 Chr 27.16
Joel (7)
Ezra 10.43
Joel (8)
Neh 11.9
Joel (9)
Joel 1.1
Acts 2.16
Joel (10)
1 Chr 6.36
Joel (11)
2 Chr 29.12
Joel (12)
1 Chr 23.8
26.22
Joel (13)
1 Chr 15.7 − 11   x 2
Joel (14)
1 Chr 15.17
Joel (15)
1 Sam 8.2
1 Chr 6.28 − 33   x 3
Joelah
1 Chr 12.3
Joezer
1 Chr 12.3
Jogbehah
Num 32.35
Judg 8.11
Jogli
Num 34.19
Joha (1)
1 Chr 8.16
Joha (2)
1 Chr 11.26
Johab
1 Chr 1.43

Johanan (1)
2 Kgs 25.23
Jer   40 — 43   x 12
Johanan (2)
1 Chr 3.15
Johanan (3)
1 Chr 3.24
Johanan (4)
1 Chr 6.9
Johanan (5)
1 Chr 12.9
Johanan (6)
Ezra   8.2
Johannan
1 Chr 12.3
John (1)
(Baptist)
Mt   3 — 4   x 9
       9.14
       11.2 — 18 x 12
       14.2 — 13 x 8
       16 — 17   x 2
       21.25 — 32 x 4
Mk   1 — 2   x 7
       6.14 — 29 x 12
       8.28
       11.30 — 32 x 3
Lk   1.13 — 67 x 4
       3.2 — 20   x 8
       5.33
       7.18 — 33 x 13
       9.7 — 19   x 3
       11.1
       16.16
       20.4 — 6   x 3
Jn   1.6 — 35   x 13
       3 — 5   x 9
       10.40 — 41 x 2
Acts   1.5 — 21   x 2
       10 — 11   x 2
       13.24 — 25 x 2
       18 — 19   x 3
John (2)
(Son of Zebedee)
Mt   4.21
       10.2
       17.1
Mk   1.19 — 29 x 2
       3.17
       5.37
       9 — 10   x 4
       13 — 14   x 2
Lk   5 — 6   x 2
       8 — 9   x 4
       22.8
Acts   1.13
       3 — 4   x 8
       8.14 — 25 x 5
       12.2
Gal   2.9
John (3)
Rev   1.1 — 9   x 4
       22.8 — 18 x 2
John (4)
Mt   16.17
Jn   1.42
       21.15 — 17 x 3
John (5)
Acts   4.6
John (6)
Acts   12 — 13   x 4
       15.37
Joiada (1)
Neh   12 — 13   x 6
Joiada (2)
Neh   3.6

Joiakim
Neh   12.10 — 26 x 4
Joiarib (1)
Neh   11.5
Joiarib (2)
Neh   11 — 12   x 3
Joiarib (3)
Ezra   8.16
Jokdeam
Josh   15.56
Jokim
1 Chr 4.22
Jokmeam
1 Kgs 4.12
1 Chr 6.68
Jokneam
Josh   12.22
       19.11
       21.34
Jokshan
Gen   25.2 — 3   x 2
1 Chr 1.32   x 2
Joktan
Gen   10.25 — 29 x 3
1 Chr 1.19 — 20 x 2
Joktheel (1)
Josh   15.38
Joktheel (2)
2 Kgs 14.7
Jonadab (1)
2 Kgs 10.15 — 24 x 4
Jer   35.6 — 19 x 7
Jonadab (2)
2 Sam 13.3 — 35 x 5
Jonah
2 Kgs 14.25
Jon   1 — 4   x 20
Mt   12.39 — 41 x 4
       16.4
Lk   11.29 — 32 x 4
Jonam
Lk   3.30
Jonathan (1)
1 Sam 13 — 14   x 30
       18 — 20   x 33
       23.16 — 18 x 2
       31.2
2 Sam 1.4 — 26   x 8
       4.4   x 2
       9.1 — 7   x 4
       21.7 — 14 x 5
1 Chr 8 — 10   x 5
Jonathan (2)
Judg   18.30
Jonathan (3)
2 Sam 15.27 — 36 x 2
       17.17 — 21 x 3
1 Kgs 1.42 — 43 x 2
Jonathan (4)
2 Sam 23.24
1 Chr 11.26
Jonathan (5)
1 Chr 2.32 — 33 x 2
Jonathan (6)
1 Chr 27.25
Jonathan (7)
Ezra   8.2
Jonathan (8)
Ezra   10.15
Jonathan (9)
Neh   12.11 — 23 x 4
Jonathan (10)
Neh   12.12
Jonathan (11)
Neh   12.33

Jonathan (12)
Jer   37.15 — 20 x 2
Jonathan (13)
2 Sam 21.21
1 Chr 20.7
Jonathan (14)
1 Chr 27.32
Joppa
Josh   19.46
2 Chr 2.16
Ezra   3.7
Jon   1.3
Acts   9 — 11   x 14
Jorah
Ezra   2.3
Jorai
1 Chr 5.13
Joram (1)
2 Kgs 1.17
       3.1 — 13   x 7
       8 — 10   x 17
2 Chr 22.5 — 7   x 4
Joram (2)
2 Sam 8.10   x 2
1 Chr 18.10   x 2
Joram (3)
1 Chr 26.25
Jordan
Gen   13.10 — 11 x 2
       32.10
       26.3 — 63 x 2
Num   13.29
       31 — 36   x 17
Deut   1 — 4   x 10
       9.1
       11 — 12   x 4
       27.2 — 12 x 3
       30 — 32   x 4
Josh   1 — 5   x 23
       7 — 9   x 4
       11 — 20   x 28
       22 — 24   x 6
Judg   3.28
       6 — 8   x 4
       10 — 12   x 6
1 Sam 13.7
2 Sam 2.8 — 29   x 3
       4.7
       10.17
       16 — 20   x 13
       24.5
1 Kgs 2.8
       7.46
       17.3
2 Kgs 2.6 — 13   x 3
       5 — 7   x 5
       25.4
1 Chr 12.15
       19.17
       26.30
2 Chr 4.17
Job   40.23
Ps   42.6
       114.3 — 5 x 2
Is   9.1
Jer   12.5
       39.4
       49 — 50   x 2
       52.7
Ezek   47.8 — 18 x 2
Zech   11.3
Mt   3 — 4   x 5
       19.1
Mk   1.5 — 9   x 2
       3.8

Jordan (Cont)
Mk   10.1
Lk   3 — 4   x 2
Jn   1.28
       3.26
       10.40
Jorim
Lk   3.29
Jorkeam
1 Chr 2.44
Josech
Lk   3.26
Joseph (1)
(Son of Jacob)
Gen   30.24 — 25 x 2
       33.2 — 7   x 2
       35.24
       37.2 — 36 x 19
       39 — 50   x 144
Ex   ˙1.5 — 8   x 3
       13.19
Num   26 — 27   x 3
       36.1 — 12 x 2
Deut   27.12
       33.13 — 17 x 3
Josh   14.3
       16 — 18   x 7
       24.32   x 2
1 Chr 2.2
       5.1
       7.29
Ps   77 — 78   x 2
       105.17
Ezek   47 — 48   x 2
Obad   .18
Jn   4.5
Acts   7.9 — 18   x 7
Heb   11.21 — 22 x 2
Rev   7.5
Joseph (2)
Lk   3.30
Joseph (3)
Lk   3.24
Joseph (4)
(Husband of Mary)
Mt   1 — 2   x 11
Lk   1 — 4   x 8
Jn   1.45
       6.42
Joseph (5)
(Brother of Jesus)
Mt   13.55
Mk   6.3
Joseph (6)
(of Arimathea)
Mt   27.57 — 59 x 3
Mk   15.42 — 46 x 4
Lk   23.50 — 55 x 2
Jn   19.38 — 39 x 4
Joseph (7)
(Barnabas)
Acts   4.36
Joseph (8)
Acts   1.23
Joseph (9)
Mt   27.56
Mk   15.40 — 47 x 2
Joseph (10)
Num   13.3
Joseph (11)
1 Chr 25.2 — 9   x 2
Joseph (12)
Ezra   10.38
Joseph (13)
Neh   12.12
Joshah
1 Chr 4.34
Joshaphat (1)
1 Chr 11.26

Joshaphat (2)
1 Chr 15.23

Joshaviah
1 Chr 11.26

Joshbekashah
1 Chr 25.4 − 9   x 2

Josheb Basshebeth
2 Sam 23.8

Joshibiah
1 Chr 4.34

Joshua (1)
Ex	17.9 − 14	x 4
	24.13	
	32 − 33	x 2
Num	11.28	
	13 − 14	x 4
	26 − 27	x 5
	32.12 − 28	x 2
	34.17	
Deut	1.38	
	3.21 − 28	x 2
	31 − 32	x 6
	34.9	x 2
Josh	1 − 15	x 130
	17 − 24	x 28
Judg	1 − 2	x 7
1 Kgs	16.34	
1 Chr	7.27	
Neh	8.17	
Acts	7.45	
Heb	4.8	

Joshua (2)
Ezra	2 − 5	x 5
	10.18	
Neh	7.7	
	12.1 − 26	x 4
Hag	1 − 2	x 4
Zech	3.1 − 9	x 8
	6.11	

Joshua (3)
2 Kgs 23.8

Joshua (4)
1 Sam 6.14 − 18   x 2

Joshua (5)
Lk 3.29

Joshua (6)
Col 4.11

Josiah (1)
1 Kgs	13.2	
2 Kgs	21 − 23	x 27
1 Chr	3.14 − 15	x 2
2 Chr	33 − 36	x 19
Jer	1.2 − 3	x 3
	3.6	
	22.10 − 18	x 3
	25 − 27	x 4
	35 − 37	x 4
	45.1	
Zeph	1.1	
Mt	1.6	

Josiah (2)
Zech 6.10 − 14   x 2

Josiphiah
Ezra 8.2

Jotbah
2 Kgs 21.19

Jotbathah
Num 33.15
Deut 10.7

Jotham (1)
2 Kgs	15 − 16	x 9
1 Chr	3.12	
	5.17	
2 Chr	26 − 27	x 7
Is	1.1	

Jotham (1) (Cont)
Is	7.1	
Hos	1.1	
Mic	1.1	
Mt	1.6	

Jotham (2)
Judg 9.5 − 57   x 5

Jotham (3)
1 Chr 2.47

Jozabad (1)
1 Chr 12.3

Jozabad (2)
1 Chr 12.20

Jozabad (3)
1 Chr 12.20

Jozabad (4)
2 Chr 31.13

Jozabad (5)
2 Chr 35.9

Jozabad (6)
Ezra 8.33

Jozabad (7)
Ezra 10.22

Jozabad (8)
Ezra 10.23

Jozabad (9)
Neh 8.7

Jozabad (10)
Neh 11.16

Jozacar
2 Kgs 12.20

Jubal
Gen 4.21

Judaea
1 Sam	23.19 − 24	x 2
	26.1	
2 Kgs	16.6	
	25.23	
2 Chr	12 − 14	x 7
	17.2	
	20 − 22	x 3
	24 − 25	x 3
	28.5 − 15	x 5
Is	36.3	
Jer	40.7	
Lam	5.11	
Dan	9.7	
Mt	2 − 4	x 6
	19.1	
	24.16	
Mk	1.5	
	3.7	
	10.1	
	13.14	
Lk	1 − 3	x 5
	5 − 6	x 2
	21.21	
	23.5 − 50	x 2
Jn	3 − 4	x 4
	7.1 − 3	x 2
	11.7 − 54	x 3
Acts	1 − 2	x 2
	8 − 9	x 2
	11 − 12	x 3
	15.1	
	21.10	
	26.20	
	28.21	
Rom	15.31	
1 Cor	16.1	
2 Cor	1.16	
	8 − 9	x 2
Gal	1.22	
1 Thes	2.14	

Judah (1)
(Son of Jacob)
Gen	29.35	
	35.23	
	37 − 38	x 17
	43 − 44	x 6
	46.12 − 28	x 3
	49.8 − 10	x 3
Ex	1.2	
Num	26.19	
Josh	19.9	
Ruth	4.12	
1 Chr	2.1 − 4	x 3
	4.1 − 21	x 2
	9.4	x 3
Neh	11.4 − 5	x 2
Mt	1.2	
Lk	3.33	

Judah (2)
(Tribe)
Ex	31.2	
	35.30	
	38.22	
Num	1 − 2	x 5
	7.12	
	10.14	
	13.3	
	26.19	
	34.19	
Deut	27.12	
	33 − 34	x 3
Josh	7.1 − 17	x 3
	11.21	
	14 − 15	x 9
	18 − 21	x 9
Judg	1.2 − 18	x 10
	10.9	
	15.9 − 11	x 3
	17 − 20	x 6
Ruth	1.1 − 7	x 2
1 Sam	11.8	
	15.4	
	17 − 18	x 4
	22 − 23	x 3
	27.6 − 10	x 2
	30.1 − 27	x 5
2 Sam	1 − 3	x 9
	5 − 6	x 3
	11 − 12	x 2
	19 − 21	x 10
	24.1 − 9	x 3
1 Kgs	1 − 2	x 4
	4.20 − 25	x 2
	9 − 10	x 2
	12 − 15	x 21
	19.3	
	22.45 − 47	x 2
2 Kgs	1.17	
	3.9	
	8.19 − 23	x 4
	12.19	
	14 − 25	x 49
1 Chr	2.10	
	4 − 6	x 6
	9.1 − 4	x 3
	12 − 13	x 3
	21.5	
	27 − 28	x 5
2 Chr	2.7	
	9 − 17	x 35
	19 − 36	x 82
Ezra	1 − 2	x 4
	4 − 7	x 7
	9 − 10	x 3
Neh	1 − 2	x 3
	4 − 7	x 6
	11 − 13	x 12

Judah (2) (Cont)
Esth	2.6	
Ps	48.11	
	60.7	
	68 − 69	x 2
	76.1	
	78.68	
	97.8	
	108.8	
	114.2	
Prov	25.1	
Is	1 − 3	x 5
	5.3 − 7	x 2
	7 − 9	x 8
	11.12 − 13	x 2
	16.3 − 6	x 2
	19.17	
	22.7 − 21	x 3
	26.1	
	30.1 − 5	x 2
	36 − 37	x 5
	40.9	
	44.26	
	48.1	
	65.9	
Jer	1 − 5	x 20
	7 − 15	x 23
	17 − 40	x 90
	42 − 46	x 19
	49 − 52	x 12
Lam	1 − 2	x 3
Ezek	4.6	
	8 − 9	x 3
	17.15	
	21.20	
	25.3 − 12	x 3
	27.17	
	35.10	
	37.16 − 19	x 2
	48.1 − 30	x 3
Dan	1.1 − 6	x 2
	5 − 6	x 2
Hos	1.1 − 11	x 3
	4 − 6	x 8
	8.14	
	10 − 12	x 3
Joel	1 − 3	x 9
Amos	1 − 2	x 3
	6 − 7	x 2
Obad	.12 − 20	x 3
Mic	1.1 − 16	x 5
	5.2	
Nah	1.15	
Zeph	1 − 2	x 4
Hag	1 − 2	x 4
Zech	1 − 2	x 4
	8 − 12	x 17
	14.5 − 21	x 3
Mal	2 − 3	x 2
Mt	2.6	
Heb	7 − 8	x 2
Rev	5.5	
	7.5	

Judah (3)
Ezra 10.23

Judah (4)
Neh 11.9

Judah (5)
Neh 12.8

Judah (6)
Neh 12.36

Judah (7)
Lk 3.30

Judas (1)
(Iscariot)
Mt 10.4

Lot (Cont)
  2 Pet   2.7
Lotan
  Gen   36.20 − 29   x 4
  1 Chr   1.38   x 2
Loved-By-The-Lord
  Hos   2.1
Lucius (1)
  Acts   13.1
Lucius (2)
  Rom   16.21
Lud
  Gen   10.22
  1 Chr   1.17
Luhith
  Is   15.5
  Jer   48.5
Luke
  Col   4.14
  2 Tim   4.11
  Phlm   .24
Luz (1)
  see also Bethel (1)
  Gen   28.19
          35.6
          48.3
  Josh   16.2
          18.13
  Judg   1.22
Luz (2)
  Judg   1.26
Lycaonia
  Acts   14.6 − 11   x 2
Lycia
  Acts   27.5
Lydda
  Acts   9.32 − 38   x 4
Lydia (1)
  Gen   10.13
  1 Chr   1.11
  Is   66.19
  Jer   46.9
  Ezek   27.10
          30.5
Lydia (2)
  Acts   16.14 − 40   x 2
Lysanias
  Lk   3.1
Lysias
  Acts   23 − 24   x 2
Lystra
  Acts   14.6 − 21   x 3
          16.1 − 2   x 2
  2 Tim   3.11
Maacah (1)
  Deut   3.14
  Josh   12 − 13   x 3
  2 Sam   10.6 − 8   x 2
          23.24
  2 Kgs   25.23
  1 Chr   19.6 − 7   x 2
  Jer   40.8
Maacah (2)
  Gen   22.24
Maacah (3)
  2 Sam   3.3
  1 Chr   3.1
Maacah (4)
  1 Kgs   2.39
Maacah (5)
  1 Kgs   15.2 − 13   x 3
  2 Chr   11.20 − 21   x 2
          15.16
Maacah (6)
  1 Chr   2.48

Maacah (7)
  1 Chr   7.15
Maacah (8)
  1 Chr   7.16
Maacah (9)
  1 Chr   8 − 9   x 2
Maacah (10)
  1 Chr   11.26
Maacah (11)
  1 Chr   27.16
Maacath
  1 Chr   4.19
Maadai
  Ezra   10.34
Maadiah
  Neh   12.2
Maai
  Neh   12.36
Maarath
  Josh   15.59
Maasai
  1 Chr   9.10
Maaseiah (1)
  1 Chr   15.17
Maaseiah (2)
  2 Chr   23.1
Maaseiah (3)
  2 Chr   26.11
Maaseiah (4)
  2 Chr   28.7
Maaseiah (5)
  2 Chr   34.8
Maaseiah (6)
  Ezra   10.18
Maaseiah (7)
  Ezra   10.21
Maaseiah (8)
  Ezra   10.22
Maaseiah (9)
  Ezra   10.30
Maaseiah (10)
  Neh   3.23
Maaseiah (11)
  Neh   8.4
Maaseiah (12)
  Neh   8.7
Maaseiah (13)
  Neh   10.14
Maaseiah (14)
  Neh   11.5
Maaseiah (15)
  Neh   11.7
Maaseiah (16)
  Neh   12.41
Maaseiah (17)
  Neh   12.42
Maaseiah (18)
  Jer   21.1
          29.24
          37.3
Maaseiah (19)
  Jer   29.21
Maaseiah (20)
  Jer   35.4
Maath
  Lk   3.26
Maaz
  1 Chr   2.26
Maaziah (1)
  1 Chr   24.7
Maaziah (2)
  Neh   10.2
Macedonia
  Acts   16.9 − 12   x 4
          18 − 20   x 6

Macedonia (Cont)
  Acts   27.2
  Rom   15.26
  1 Cor   16.5   x 2
  2 Cor   1 − 2   x 2
          7 − 9   x 4
          11.9
  Phil   4.15
  1 Thes 1.7 − 8   x 2
          4.10
  1 Tim   1.3
Machbannai
  1 Chr   12.9
Machbenah
  1 Chr   2.49
Machi
  Num   13.3
Machir (1)
  Gen   50.23
  Num   26 − 27   x 2
          32.39 − 40 x 2
          36.1
  Deut   3.15
  Josh   13.31
          17.1 − 3   x 2
  Judg   5.14
  1 Chr   2.21 − 23   x 2
          7.14 − 17   x 6
Machir (2)
  2 Sam   9.4
          17.27
Machnadebai
  Ezra   10.38
Machpelah
  Gen   23.9 − 17   x 2
          25.9
          49 − 50   x 2
Madai
  Gen   10.2
  1 Chr   1.5
Madmannah (1)
  Josh   15.31
Madmannah (2)
  1 Chr   2.49
Madmen
  Jer   48.2
Madmenah
  Is   10.31
Madon
  Josh   11 − 12   x 2
Magadan
  Mt   15.39
Magbish
  Ezra   2.21
Magdiel
  Gen   36.40
  1 Chr   1.54
Magog
  Gen   10.2
  1 Chr   1.5
  Ezek   38 − 39   x 2
  Rev   20.8
Magpiash
  Neh   10.14
Mahalab
  Josh   19.29
Mahalaleel
  Lk   3.37
Mahalalel (1)
  Gen   5.12 − 15   x 2
  1 Chr   1.2
Mahalalel (2)
  Neh   11.4
Mahalath (1)
  Gen   28.9

Mahalath (2)
  2 Chr   11.18
Mahanaim
  Gen   32.2
  Josh   13.26 − 30 x 2
          21.38
  2 Sam   2.8 − 29   x 3
          17.24 − 27 x 2
          19.32
  1 Kgs   2.8
          4.14
  1 Chr   6.80
Maharai
  2 Sam   23.24
  1 Chr   11.26
          27.2
Mahath (1)
  1 Chr   6.35
Mahath (2)
  2 Chr   29.12
Mahath (3)
  2 Chr   31.13
Mahavah
  1 Chr   11.26
Mahazioth
  1 Chr   25.4 − 9   x 2
Mahlah (1)
  Num   26 − 27   x 2
          36.10
  Josh   17.3
Mahlah (2)
  1 Chr   7.18
Mahli (1)
  Ex   6.19
  Num   3.17 − 33   x 2
          26.58
  1 Chr   6.19 − 29   x 2
          23 − 24   x 4
  Ezra   8.18
Mahli (2)
  1 Chr   6.47
          23 − 24   x 2
Mahlon
  Ruth   1.1 − 5   x 2
          4.9 − 10   x 2
Mahol
  1 Kgs   4.31
Mahseiah
  Jer   32.12
          51.59
Makaz
  1 Kgs   4.9
Makheloth
  Num   33.15
Makkedah
  Josh   10.10 − 29 x 6
          12.16
          15.41
Malachi
  Mal   1.1
Malcam
  1 Chr   8.8
Malchiah (1)
  Jer   21.1
          38.1
Malchiah (2)
  Jer   38.6
Malchiel
  Gen   46.17
  Num   26.45
  1 Chr   7.31   x 2
Malchijah (1)
  1 Chr   6.40
Malchijah (2)
  1 Chr   9.10

Malchijah (2) (Cont)
Neh   11.12
Malchijah (3)
1 Chr 24.7
Malchijah (4)
Ezra   10.25
Malchijah (5)
Ezra   10.25
Malchijah (6)
Neh   3.14
Malchijah (7)
Neh   3.31
Malchijah (8)
Neh   8.4
Malchijah (9)
Neh   10.2
Malchijah (10)
Neh   12.42
Malchijah (11)
Ezra   10.31
Malchijah (12)
Neh   3.11
Malchiram
1 Chr 3.18
Malchishua
1 Sam 14.49
        31.2
1 Chr 8 — 10   x 3
Malchus
Jn   18.10
Mallothi
1 Chr 25.4 — 9   x 2
Malluch (1)
1 Chr 6.44
Malluch (2)
Ezra   10.29
Malluch (3)
Ezra   10.31
Malluch (4)
Neh   10.2
Malluch (5)
Neh   10.14
Malluch (6)
Neh   12.2
Malluchi
Neh   12.12
Malta
Acts   28.1
Mamre (1)
Gen   13.18
        18.1
        20.1
        23.17
        25.9
        35.27
        49 — 50   x 2
Mamre (2)
Gen   14.13 — 24   x 3
Manaen
Acts   13.1
Manahath (1)
Gen   36.23
1 Chr 1.38
Manahath (2)
1 Chr 2.54
Manahath (3)
Neh   8.6
Manasseh (1)
Gen   41.51
        46.20
        48.1 — 20   x 9
        50.23
Num   1 — 2   x 3
        7.12
        10.23

Manasseh (1) (Cont)
Num   13.3
        26 — 27   x 4
        32.33 — 41 x 3
        34.14 — 19 x 2
        36.1 — 12   x 3
Deut   3 — 4   x 4
        29.8
        33 — 34   x 2
Josh   1.12
        4.12
        12 — 14   x 6
        16 — 18   x 18
        20 — 22   x 14
Judg   1.22 — 35   x 4
        6 — 7   x 3
        11 — 12   x 2
1 Kgs 4.13
        11.28
2 Kgs 10.33
1 Chr 5 — 7   x 10
        9.3
        12.19 — 23 x 5
        26 — 27   x 3
2 Chr 15.9
        30 — 31   x 5
        34.6 — 9   x 2
Ps   60.7
        80.2
        108.8
Is   9.21
Ezek   48.1
Rev   7.5
Manasseh (2)
2 Kgs 20 — 21   x 10
        23 — 24   x 4
1 Chr 3.13
2 Chr 32 — 33   x 12
Jer   15.4
Mt   1.6
Manasseh (3)
Ezra   10.30
Manasseh (4)
Ezra   10.33
Manoah
Judg   13.2 — 22   x 12
        16.31
Maoch
1 Sam 27.2
Maon (1)
Josh   15.55
1 Sam 23.24 — 25 x 2
        25.2
Maon (2)
1 Chr 2.45
Maonites
Judg   10.12
Marah (1)
Ex   15.23   x 2
Num   33.8
Marah (2)
Ruth   1.20
Marduk
Jer   50.2
Mareal
Josh   19.11
Mareshah (1)
Josh   15.44
1 Chr 4.21
2 Chr 11.8
        14.9 — 10   x 2
        20.37
Mic   1.15
Mareshah (2)
1 Chr 2.42

Mark
Acts   12 — 13   x 4
        15.37 — 39 x 2
Col   4.10   x 2
2 Tim 4.11
Phlm   .24
1 Pet 5.13
Market of Appius
Acts   28.15
Maroth
Mic   1.12
Marsena
Esth   1.14
Martha
Lk   10.38 — 41 x 3
Jn   11 — 12   x 9
Mary (1)
(Mother of Jesus)
Mt   1 — 2   x 6
        13.55
Mk   6.3
Lk   1 — 2   x 15
Acts   1.14
Mary (2)
(Magdalene)
Mt   27 — 28   x 3
Mk   15 — 16   x 4
Lk   8.2
        24.10
Jn   19 — 20   x 5
Mary (3)
Mt   27 — 28   x 3
Mk   15 — 16   x 3
Lk   24.10
Mary (4)
Jn   19.25
Mary (5)
(Sister of Martha)
Lk   10.39 — 42 x 2
Jn   11 — 12   x 10
Mary (6)
Acts   12.12
Mary (7)
Rom   16.6
Mashal
1 Chr 6.74
Masrekah
Gen   36.31
1 Chr 1.43
Massa
Gen   25.14
1 Chr 1.30
Massah
Ex   17.7
Deut   6.16
        9.22
        33.8
Ps   95.8
Matred
Gen   36.31
1 Chr 1.43
Matri
1 Sam 10.21   x 2
Mattan (1)
2 Kgs 11.18
2 Chr 23.17
Mattan (2)
Jer   38.1
Mattanah
Num   21.18
Mattaniah (1)
2 Kgs 24.17
Mattaniah (2)
1 Chr 9.14
Mattaniah (3)
1 Chr 25.4 — 9   x 2
Mattaniah (4)
Neh   12.33

Mattaniah (5)
2 Chr 20.14
Mattaniah (6)
2 Chr 29.12
Mattaniah (7)
Ezra   10.26
Mattaniah (8)
Ezra   10.27
Mattaniah (9)
Ezra   10.30
Mattaniah (10)
Ezra   10.34
Mattaniah (11)
Neh   12.25
Mattaniah (12)
Neh   13.13
Mattaniah (13)
Neh   11.17   x 2
Mattaniah (14)
Neh   11.22
Mattaniah (15)
Neh   12.8
Mattatha
Lk   3.31
Mattathias (1)
Lk   3.25
Mattathias (2)
Lk   3.26
Mattattah
Ezra   10.33
Mattenai (1)
Ezra   10.33
Mattenai (2)
Ezra   10.34
Mattenai (3)
Neh   12.12
Matthan
Mt   1.12
Matthat (1)
Lk   3.24
Matthat (2)
Lk   3.29
Matthew
see also Levi (4)
Mt   9 — 10   x 4
Mk   3.18
Lk   6.15
Acts   1.13
Matthias
Acts   1.23 — 26   x 2
Mattithiah (1)
1 Chr 9.31
Mattithiah (2)
Ezra   10.43
Mattithiah (3)
Neh   8.4
Mattithiah (4)
1 Chr 15.17
Mattithiah (5)
1 Chr 16.5
Mattithiah (6)
1 Chr 25.3 — 9   x 2
Mearah
Josh   13.4
Mebunnai
2 Sam 23.24
Mecherah
1 Chr 11.26
Meconah
Neh   11.28
Medad
Num   11.26 — 27 x 2
Medan
Gen   25.2
1 Chr 1.32

287

Mibsam (1)
  Gen 25.13
  1 Chr 1.29
Mibsam (2)
  1 Chr 4.25
Mibzar
  Gen 36.40
  1 Chr 1.53
Mica (1)
  2 Sam 9.12
Mica (2)
  1 Chr 9.14
  Neh 11.17 − 22 x 2
Mica (3)
  Neh 10.9
Micah (1)
  Judg 17 − 18 x 20
Micah (2)
  Jer 26.18 − 19 x 2
  Mic 1.1 − 8 x 3
Micah (3)
  1 Chr 8 − 9 x 4
Micah (4)
  1 Chr 23 − 24 x 3
Micah (5)
  1 Chr 5.4
Micaiah (1)
  1 Kgs 22.8 − 28 x 13
  2 Chr 18.7 − 27 x 13
Micaiah (2)
  Jer 36.11 − 13 x 2
Micaiah (3)
  2 Kgs 22.12
  2 Chr 34.20
Micaiah (4)
  Neh 12.41
Micaiah (5)
  Neh 12.33
Micaiah (6)
  2 Chr 13.2
Micaiah (7)
  2 Chr 17.7
Michael (1)
(Angel)
  Dan 10.13 − 20 x 2
          12.1
  Jude .9 x 2
  Rev 12.7
Michael (2)
  Num 13.3
Michael (3)
  1 Chr 5.13
Michael (4)
  1 Chr 5.14
Michael (5)
  1 Chr 6.40
Michael (6)
  1 Chr 7.3
Michael (7)
  1 Chr 8.16
Michael (8)
  1 Chr 12.20
Michael (9)
  1 Chr 27.16
Michael (10)
  2 Chr 21.2
Michael (11)
  Ezra 8.2
Michal
  1 Sam 14.49
          18 − 19 x 7
          25.44
  2 Sam 3.13 − 14 x 2
          6.16 − 23 x 3
  1 Chr 15.29

Michmash
  1 Sam 13 − 14 x 8
  Ezra 2.21
  Neh 7.26
         11.31
  Is 10.28
Michmethath
  Josh 16 − 17 x 2
Michri
  1 Chr 9.7
Middin
  Josh 15.61
Middle Gate
  Jer 39.3
Midian
  Gen 25.2 − 4 x 2
        36 − 37 x 3
  Ex 2 − 4 x 4
        18.1
  Num 10.29
        22.4 − 7 x 2
        25.6 − 17 x 4
        31.2 − 9 x 5
  Josh 13.21
  Judg 6 − 9 x 30
  1 Kgs 11.18
  1 Chr 1.32 − 43 x 3
  Ps 83.9
  Is 9 − 10 x 2
      60.6
  Hab 3.7
  Acts 7.29
Migdalel
  Josh 19.38
Migdalgad
  Josh 15.37
Migdol
  Ex 14.2
  Num 33.7
  Jer 44.1
       46.14
  Ezek 29 − 30 x 2
Migron
  1 Sam 14.2
  Is 10.28
Mijamin (1)
  1 Chr 24.7
Mijamin (2)
  Ezra 10.25
Mijamin (3)
  Neh 10.2
Mijamin (4)
  Neh 12.2
Mikloth (1)
  1 Chr 8 − 9 x 2
Mikloth (2)
  1 Chr 27.2
Mikneiah
  1 Chr 15.17
Milalai
  Neh 12.36
Milcah (1)
  Gen 11.29
        22.20 − 23 x 2
        24.15 − 47 x 3
Milcah (2)
  Num 26 − 27 x 2
        36.10
  Josh 17.3
Miletus
  Acts 20.15 − 17 x 2
  2 Tim 4.20
Miniamin (1)
  2 Chr 31.15

Miniamin (2)
  Neh 12.12 − 41 x 2
Minni
  Jer 51.27
Minnith
  Judg 11.33
Miphkad Gate
  Neh 3.31
Miriam (1)
  Ex 15.20 − 21 x 2
  Num 12.1 − 15 x 5
        20.1
        26.59
  Deut 24.9
  1 Chr 6.3
  Mic 6.4
Miriam (2)
  1 Chr 4.17
Mirmah
  1 Chr 8.10
Mishael (1)
  Ex 6.22
  Lev 10.4
Mishael (2)
see also Meshach
  Dan 1 − 2 x 3
Mishael (3)
  Neh 8.4
Mishal
  Josh 19.26
        21.30
Misham
  1 Chr 8.12
Mishma
  Gen 25.14
  1 Chr 1.30
        4.25 − 26 x 2
Mishmannah
  1 Chr 12.9
Mishraites
  1 Chr 2.53
Mispar
  Ezra 2.2
Mispereth
  Neh 7.7
Misrephoth Maim
  Josh 11.8
        13.6
Mithan
  1 Chr 11.26
Mithkah
  Num 33.15
Mithredath (1)
  Ezra 1.8
Mithredath (2)
  Ezra 4.7
Mitylene
  Acts 20.14
Mizar
  Ps 42.6
Mizpah (1)
  Josh 18.26
  Judg 20 − 21 x 6
  1 Sam 7.5 − 16 x 7
        10.17
  1 Kgs 15.22
  2 Kgs 25.23 − 25 x 2
  2 Chr 16.6
  Neh 3.7 − 19 x 3
  Jer 40 − 41 x 10
Mizpah (2)
  Judg 10 − 11 x 4
  Hos 5.1
Mizpah (3)
  Josh 11.3 − 8 x 2

Mizpah (4)
  Gen 31.49
Mizpah (5)
  1 Sam 22.3
Mizpah (6)
  Josh 15.38
Mizzah
  Gen 36.10 − 17 x 2
  1 Chr 1.37
Mnason
  Acts 21.16
Moab
  Gen 19.37 x 2
        36.31
  Ex 15.15
  Num 21 − 26 x 23
        31.12
        33.41 − 50 x 4
        35 − 36 x 2
  Deut 1 − 2 x 7
        23.3
        29.1
        32.49
        34.1 − 8 x 4
  Josh 13.32
        24.9
  Judg 3.12 − 30 x 6
        10 − 11 x 7
  Ruth 1 − 2 x 5
        4.3 − 10 x 3
  1 Sam 12.9
        14.47
        22.3 − 4 x 3
  2 Sam 8.2 − 12 x 3
        23.20
  1 Kgs 11.1 − 33 x 3
  2 Kgs 1.1
        3.4 − 27 x 9
        13.20
        23 − 24 x 2
  1 Chr 1.43
        4.22
        8.8
        11.22 − 26 x 2
        18.2 − 11 x 2
  2 Chr 20.1 − 23 x 3
        24.26
  Ezra 9.1
  Neh 13.1 − 23 x 3
  Ps 60.8
      83.6 − 8 x 2
      108.9
  Is 11.14
      15 − 16 x 13
      25.10 − 12 x 2
  Jer 9.25
      22.20
      25.19
      27.3
      40.11
      48.1 − 47 x 40
  Ezek 25.8 − 11 x 5
  Dan 11.41
  Amos 2.1 − 3 x 4
  Mic 6.5
  Zeph 2.8 − 10 x 3
Moadiah
  Neh 12.12
Mob
  Mk 5.9 − 15 x 2
  Lk 8.30
Moladah
  Josh 15.26
        19.2
  1 Chr 4.28

Moladah (Cont)
Neh 11.26

Molech
Lev 18.21
20.2 − 5 x 3
2 Sam 12.30
1 Kgs 11.5 − 33 x 3
2 Kgs 23.10 − 13 x 2
1 Chr 20.2
Is 57.9
Jer 32.35
49.1 − 3 x 2
Zeph 1.5
Acts 7.43

Molid
1 Chr 2.29

Mordecai (1)
Esth 2 − 10 x 60

Mordecai (2)
Ezra 2.2
Neh 7.7

Moreh (1)
Gen 12.6
Deut 11.30

Moreh (2)
Judg 7.1

Moresheth
Jer 26.18
Mic 1.1

Moresheth Gath
Mic 1.14

Moriah
Gen 22.2
2 Chr 3.1

Moserah
Deut 10.6

Moseroth
Num 33.15

Moses
Ex 2 − 20 x 205
24 − 25 x 14
30 − 36 x 55
38 − 40 x 19
Lev 1.1
4 − 27 x 73
Num 1 − 21 x 155
25 − 36 x 57
Deut 1.1 − 41 x 6
4 − 5 x 7
18.14
27.1 − 11 x 3
29.1 − 2 x 2
31 − 34 x 24
Josh 1.1 − 17 x 10
3 − 4 x 4
8 − 9 x 6
11 − 14 x 27
17 − 18 x 2
20 − 24 x 10
Judg 1.16 − 20 x 2
3 − 4 x 2
18.30
1 Sam 12.6 − 8 x 2
1 Kgs 2.3
8.9 − 56 x 3
2 Kgs 14.6
18.4 − 12 x 3
21.8
23.25
1 Chr 6.3 − 49 x 2
15.15
21 − 23 x 5
26.24
2 Chr 1.3
5.10

Moses (Cont)
2 Chr 8.13
23 − 25 x 4
30.16
33 − 35 x 4
Ezra 3.2
6 − 7 x 2
Neh 1.7 − 8 x 2
8 − 10 x 4
13.1
Ps 77.20
99.6
103.7
105 − 106 x 4
Is 63.11 − 12 x 3
Jer 15.1
Dan 9.11 − 13 x 2
Mic 6.4
Mal 4.4
Mt 5.17
7 − 8 x 2
11 − 12 x 2
17.3 − 4 x 2
19.7 − 8 x 2
22 − 23 x 3
Mk 1.44
7.10
9 − 10 x 5
12.19 − 26 x 3
Lk 2.22
5.14
9.30 − 33 x 2
16.16 − 31 x 3
20.28 − 37 x 2
24.27 − 44 x 2
Jn 1.17 − 45 x 2
3.14
5 − 9 x 11
Acts 3.22
6 − 7 x 15
13.15 − 38 x 2
15.1 − 21 x 3
21.21 − 28 x 3
24.14
26.22
28.23
Rom 2 − 3 x 2
5.14
9 − 10 x 3
1 Cor 9 − 10 x 4
2 Cor 3.7 − 16 x 4
2 Tim 3.8
Heb 3.2 − 16 x 4
7 − 12 x 11
Jude .9
Rev 15.3

Moza (1)
1 Chr 2.46

Moza (2)
1 Chr 8 − 9 x 4

Mozah
Josh 18.26

Muppim
Gen 46.21

Mushi
Ex 6.19
Num 3.17 − 33 x 2
26.58
1 Chr 6.19 − 47 x 2
23 − 24 x 4

Musri
1 Kgs 10.28
2 Chr 1.16
9.28

Myra
Acts 27.5

Mysia
Acts 16.7 − 8 x 2

Naam
1 Chr 4.15

Naamah (1)
1 Kgs 14.21
2 Chr 12.13

Naamah (2)
Gen 4.22

Naamah (3)
Josh 15.41

Naamah (4)
Job 2.11

Naaman (1)
2 Kgs 5.1 − 27 x 18
Lk 4.27

Naaman (2)
Gen 46.21
Num 26.40
1 Chr 8.4 − 6 x 2

Naarah (1)
Josh 16.7

Naarah (2)
1 Chr 4.5 − 6 x 2

Naarai
1 Chr 11.26

Naaran
1 Chr 7.28

Nabal
1 Sam 25.2 − 39 x 16
27.3
2 Sam 2 − 3 x 2

Naboth
1 Kgs 21.1 − 19 x 12
2 Kgs 9.21 − 26 x 4

Nacon
2 Sam 6.6

Nadab (1)
Ex 6.23
24.1 − 9 x 2
28.1
Lev 10.1
Num 3.2 − 4 x 2
26.60 − 61 x 2
1 Chr 6.3
24.1 − 2 x 2

Nadab (2)
1 Kgs 14 − 15 x 6

Nadab (3)
1 Chr 2.28 − 30 x 2

Nadab (4)
1 Chr 8 − 9 x 2

Naggai
Lk 3.25

Nahalal
Josh 19.15
21.35
Judg 1.30

Nahaliel
Num 21.19 x 2

Naham
1 Chr 4.19

Nahamani
Neh 7.7

Naharai
2 Sam 23.24
1 Chr 11.26

Nahash (1)
1 Sam 11 − 12 x 5
2 Sam 10.1 − 2 x 2
17.27
1 Chr 19.1 − 2 x 2

Nahash (2)
2 Sam 17.25

Nahash (3)
1 Chr 4.12

Nahath (1)
Gen 36.10 − 17 x 2
1 Chr 1.37

Nahath (2)
1 Chr 6.26

Nahath (3)
2 Chr 31.13

Nahbi
Num 13.3

Nahor (1)
Gen 11.26 − 29 x 3
22.20 − 24 x 3
24.10 − 47 x 4
29.5
31.53
Josh 24.2

Nahor (2)
Gen 11.22 − 24 x 2
1 Chr 1.26
Lk 3.34

Nahshon
Ex 6.23
Num 1 − 2 x 2
7.12
10.14
Ruth 4.18
1 Chr 2.10
Mt 1.2
Lk 3.32

Nahum
Nah 1.1
Lk 3.25

Nain
Lk 7.11

Naioth
1 Sam 19 − 20 x 5

Naomi
Ruth 1 − 4 x 28

Naphish
Gen 25.15
1 Chr 1.31
5.19

Naphtali
Gen 30.8
35.25
46.24
49.21
Ex 1.4
Num 1 − 2 x 3
7.12
10.27
13.3
26.48
34.19
Deut 27.13
33 − 34 x 3
Josh 19 − 21 x 5
Judg 1.33 x 2
4 − 7 x 6
1 Kgs 4.15
7.14
15.20
2 Kgs 15.29
1 Chr 2.2
6 − 7 x 3
12.23 − 40 x 2
27.16
2 Chr 16.4
34.6
Ps 68.27
Is 9.1

Pallu
  Gen   46.9
  Ex   6.14
  Num   26.5 − 8   x 2
  1 Chr   5.3
Palmyra
  2 Chr   8.4
Palti (1)
  Num   13.3
Palti (2)
  1 Sam 25.44
Paltiel (1)
  Num   34.19
Paltiel (2)
  2 Sam 3.15 − 16   x 2
Pamphylia
  Acts   2.10
          13 − 15   x 3
          27.5
Paphos
  Acts   13.6 − 13   x 2
Parah
  Josh   18.23
Paran
  Gen   21.20
  Num   10.12
          12 − 13   x 3
  Deut   1.1
          33.2
  1 Sam 25.1
  1 Kgs 11.18
  Hab   3.3
Parmashta
  Esth   9.7
Parmenas
  Acts   6.5
Parnach
  Num   34.19
Parosh (1)
  Ezra   2.3
          8.2
          10.25
  Neh   3.25
          7.8
Parosh (2)
  Neh   10.14
Parshandatha
  Esth   9.7
Parthia
  Acts   2.9
Paruah
  1 Kgs 4.17
Parvaim
  2 Chr   3.6
Pas Dammim
  1 Chr   11.13
Pasach
  1 Chr   7.33
Paseah (1)
  1 Chr   4.12
Paseah (2)
  Ezra   2.43
  Neh   7.46
Paseah (3)
  Neh   3.6
Pashhur (1)
  Jer   20.1 − 6   x 4
Pashhur (2)
  1 Chr   9.10
  Neh   11.12
  Jer   21.1
          38.1
Pashhur (3)
  Ezra   2.36
          10.22

Pashhur (3) (Cont)
  Neh   7.39
Pashhur (4)
  Jer   38.1
Pashhur (5)
  Neh   10.2
Patara
  Acts   21.1
Pathros
  Is   11.11
Pathrus
  Gen   10.14
  1 Chr   1.12
Patmos
  Rev   1.9
Patrobas
  Rom   16.14
Pau
  Gen   36.31
  1 Chr   1.43
Paul
  see also Saul (2)
  Acts   13 − 28   x 197
  Rom   1.1
  1 Cor   1.1 − 13   x 4
          3.4 − 22   x 3
          16.21
  2 Cor   1.1
          10.1 − 10   x 2
  Gal   1.1
          5.2
  Eph   1.1
          3.1
  Phil   1.1
  Col   1.1 − 23   x 2
          4.18
  1 Thes 1.1
  2 Thes 1.1
          3.17
  1 Tim   1.1
  2 Tim   1.1
  Tit   1.1
  Phlm   .1 − 19   x 3
  2 Pet   3.15
Paulus
  see Sergius Paulus
Pedahel
  Num   34.19
Pedahzur
  Num   1 − 2   x 2
          7.12
          10.23
Pedaiah (1)
  2 Kgs 23.36
Pedaiah (2)
  1 Chr   3.18 − 19   x 2
Pedaiah (3)
  1 Chr   27.16
Pedaiah (4)
  Neh   3.25
Pedaiah (5)
  Neh   11.7
Pedaiah (6)
  Neh   8.4
Pedaiah (7)
  Neh   13.13
Pekah
  2 Kgs 15 − 16   x 9
  2 Chr 28.5
  Is   7 − 8   x 4
Pekahiah
  2 Kgs 15.22 − 26   x 5
Pekod
  Jer   50.21
  Ezek   23.23

Pelaiah (1)
  1 Chr   3.24
Pelaiah (2)
  Neh   8.7
          10.9
Pelaliah
  Neh   11.12
Pelatiah (1)
  1 Chr   3.21
Pelatiah (2)
  1 Chr   4.42
Pelatiah (3)
  Neh   10.14
Pelatiah (4)
  Ezek   11.1 − 13   x 2
Peleg
  Gen   10 − 11   x 3
  1 Chr   1.19 − 25   x 2
  Lk   3.35
Pelet (1)
  2 Sam 23.24
  1 Chr 11.26
Pelet (2)
  1 Chr   2.47
Pelet (3)
  1 Chr   12.3
Peleth (1)
  Num   16.1
Peleth (2)
  1 Chr   2.33
Pelon
  1 Chr   11.26
          27.2
Pelusium
  Ezek   30.15 − 16   x 2
Peniel
  Gen   32.30 − 31   x 2
Peninnah
  1 Sam 1.2 − 7   x 5
Penuel (1)
  Judg   8.8 − 17   x 3
  1 Kgs 12.25
Penuel (2)
  1 Chr   4.3   x 2
Penuel (3)
  1 Chr   8.25
People's Gate
  Jer   17.19
Peor
  Num   23.28
          25.3 − 18   x 4
          31.16
  Deut   4.3
  Josh   22.17
  Ps   106.28
  Hos   9.10
Perazim
  Is   28.21
Peresh
  1 Chr   7.16   x 2
Perez
  Gen   38.29
          46.12   x 2
  Num   26.19
  Ruth   4.12 − 18   x 3
  1 Chr   2.4 − 5   x 2
          4.1
          9.4
          27.2
  Neh   11.4 − 6   x 2
  Mt   1.2
  Lk   3.33
Perez Uzzah
  2 Sam 6.8
  1 Chr 13.11

Perga
  Acts   13 − 14   x 3
Pergamum
  Rev   1 − 2   x 2
Perida
  Neh   7.57
Perizzites
  Gen   13.7
          15.20
          34.30
  Ex   3.8 − 17   x 2
          23.23
          33 − 34   x 2
  Deut   7.1
          20.17
  Josh   3.10
          9.1
          11 − 12   x 2
          17.15
          24.11
  Judg   1.4
          3.5
  1 Kgs 9.20
  2 Chr 8.7
  Ezra   9.1
  Neh   9.8
Persia
  2 Chr 36.20 − 23   x 3
  Ezra   1.1 − 2   x 2
          3 − 7   x 8
          9.9
  Neh   1.1
          11 − 12   x 2
  Esth   1.1 − 19   x 5
          3.6
          8 − 10   x 4
  Ezek   27.10
          38.5
  Dan   1.21
          5 − 6   x 5
          8.20
          10 − 11   x 5
  Hag   1.1
  Zech   1.1
Persis
  Rom   16.12
Peruda
  Ezra   2.55
Peter
  see also Simon (1)
  Mt   4.18
          8.14   x 2
          10.2
          14 − 19   x 15
          26.33 − 75   x 11
  Mk   3.16
          5.37
          8 − 11   x 7
          13 − 14   x 13
          16.7 − 9   x 2
  Lk   5 − 6   x 2
          8 − 9   x 6
          12.41
          18.28
          22.8 − 62   x 12
          24.12
  Jn   1.40 − 44   x 3
          6.8 − 68   x 2
          13.6 − 37   x 6
          18.10 − 27   x 12
          20 − 21   x 14
  Acts   1 − 5   x 23
          8 − 12   x 50
          15.7
  1 Cor   1.12
          3.22

Rabbith
Josh   19.20
Racal
1 Sam   30.29
Rachel
Gen   29 — 31   x 30
        33.1 — 7   x 3
        35.16 — 25 x 6
        44.27
        46.19 — 25 x 3
        48.7
Ruth   4.11
1 Sam   10.2
Jer   31.15
Mt   2.18
Raddai
1 Chr   2.14
Rahab (1)
Josh   2.1 — 15   x 5
        6.17 — 25   x 3
Heb   11.31
Jas   2.25
Rahab (2)
Job   9.13
        26.12
Ps   89.10
Is   51.9
Rahab (3)
Mt   1.2
Raham
1 Chr   2.44
Rakem
1 Chr   7.16
Rakkath
Josh   19.35
Rakkon
Josh   19.46
Ram (2)
Ruth   4.18
1 Chr   2.9 — 10   x 3
Mt   1.2
Ram (3)
1 Chr   2.25 — 26   x 2
Ram (4)
Job   32.2
Ramah (1)
Josh   18.25
Judg   4.5
        19.12
1 Kgs   15.17 — 22 x 3
1 Chr   27.25
2 Chr   16.1 — 6   x 3
Ezra   2.21
Neh   7.26
        11.33
Is   10.29
Jer   31.15
        40.1
Hos   5.8
Mt   2.18
Ramah (2)
1 Sam   1 — 2   x 4
        7 — 8   x 3
        15 — 16   x 2
        19 — 20   x 4
        25.1
        28.3
Ramah (3)
Josh   19.29
Ramah (4)
Josh   19.36
Ramah (5)
Josh   19.8
1 Sam   30.27

Ramath Lehi
Judg   15.17
Ramath Mizpeh
Josh   13.26
Rameses
Gen   47.11
Ex   1.11
        12.37
Num   33.3 — 5   x 2
Ramiah
Ezra   10.25
Ramoth (1)
Deut   4.43
Josh   20 — 21   x 2
1 Kgs   4.13
        22.3 — 29   x 7
2 Kgs   8 — 9   x 5
1 Chr   6.80
2 Chr   18.2 — 28   x 7
        22.5
Ramoth (2)
1 Chr   6.73
Rapha
1 Chr   8.2
Raphah
1 Chr   8.37
Raphu
Num   13.3
Reaiah (1)
1 Chr   4.2
Reaiah (2)
1 Chr   5.4
Reaiah (3)
Ezra   2.43
Neh   7.46
Reba
Num   31.8
Josh   13.21
Rebecca
Gen   22.23
        24 — 29   x 26
        35.8
        49.31
Rom   9.10
Recah
1 Chr   4.12
Rechab (1)
2 Sam   4.2 — 12   x 4
Rechab (2)
2 Kgs   10.15 — 23 x 2
Jer   35.6 — 19   x 2
Rechab (3)
Neh   3.14
Rechabite
1 Chr   2.55
Jer   35.2 — 18   x 4
Red Sea
Ex   13 — 15   x 5
Num   33.8
Deut   11.4
Josh   2.10
        4.23
        24.6
Neh   9.9
Ps   106.7 — 22 x 3
        114.3
        136.13
Acts   7.36
1 Cor   10.1
Heb   11.29
Reelaiah
Ezra   2.2
Regem
1 Chr   2.47

Regemmelech
Zech   7.2
Rehabiah
1 Chr   23 — 24   x 2
        26.25
Rehob (1)
Josh   19.28 — 30 x 2
        21.31
Judg   1.31
1 Chr   6.75
Rehob (2)
Num   13.21
Rehob (3)
2 Sam   8.3
Rehob (4)
Neh   10.9
Rehoboam
1 Kgs   11 — 12   x 12
        14 — 15   x 8
1 Chr   3.10
2 Chr   9 — 13   x 27
Mt   1.6
Rehoboth Ir
Gen   10.11
Rehoboth-On-The-River
Gen   36.31
1 Chr   1.43
Rehum (1)
Ezra   4.8 — 23   x 4
Rehum (2)
Ezra   2.2
Rehum (3)
Neh   10.14
Rehum (4)
Neh   3.17
Rehum (5)
Neh   12.2
Rei
1 Kgs   1.8
Rekem (1)
Num   31.8
Josh   13.21
Rekem (2)
Josh   18.27
Rekem (3)
1 Chr   2.43 — 44   x 2
Remaliah
2 Kgs   15 — 16   x 4
2 Chr   28.5
Is   7.1
Remeth
Josh   19.21
Rephael
1 Chr   26.6
Rephah
1 Chr   7.25
Rephaiah (1)
1 Chr   3.21
Rephaiah (2)
1 Chr   4.42
Rephaiah (3)
1 Chr   7.2
Rephaiah (4)
1 Chr   9.43
Rephaiah (5)
Neh   3.9
Rephaim (1)
Gen   14 — 15   x 2
Deut   2 — 3   x 4
Josh   12 — 13   x 2
        17.15
Rephaim (2)
Josh   15.8
        18.16
2 Sam   5.18 — 22   x 2

Rephaim (2) (Cont)
2 Sam   23.13
1 Chr   11.15
        14.9
Is   17.5
Rephan
Acts   7.43
Rephidim
Ex   17.1 — 8   x 2
        19.1
Num   33.14 — 15 x 2
Resen
Gen   10.12
Resheph
1 Chr   7.25
Reu
Gen   11.18 — 20 x 2
1 Chr   1.25
Lk   3.35
Reuben
Gen   29 — 30   x 2
        35.22 — 23 x 2
        37.21 — 29 x 2
        42.22 — 37 x 2
        46.8
        48 — 49   x 2
Ex   1.2
        6.14
Num   1 — 2   x 6
        7.12
        10.18
        13.3
        16.1
        26.5
        32.1 — 37   x 7
        34.14
Deut   3 — 4   x 3
        11.6
        27.13
        29.8
        33.6   x 2
Josh   1.12
        4.12
        12 — 13   x 5
        15.6
        18.7 — 17   x 2
        20 — 22   x 15
Judg   5.15 — 16   x 2
2 Kgs   10.33
1 Chr   2.1
        5 — 6   x 9
        11 — 12   x 2
        26 — 27   x 2
Ezek   48.1 — 30   x 2
Rev   7.5
Reuel (1)
Gen   36.4 — 17   x 3
1 Chr   1.35 — 37   x 2
Reuel (2)
1 Chr   9.7
Reumah
Gen   22.24
Rezeph
2 Kgs   19.12
Is   37.12
Rezin (1)
2 Kgs   15 — 16   x 3
Is   7 — 8   x 4
Rezin (2)
Ezra   2.43
Neh   7.46
Rezon
1 Kgs   11.23 — 24 x 3
Rhegium
Acts   28.13

Rhesa
Lk   3.27
Rhoda
Acts   12.13
Rhodes
Gen   10.4
1 Chr   1.7
Ezek   27.15
Acts   21.1
Ribai
2 Sam   23.24
1 Chr   11.26
Riblah
2 Kgs   23.33
        25.6 – 20   x 2
Jer   39.5 – 6   x 2
        52.9 – 26   x 3
Ezek   6.14
Rimmon (1)
Judg   20 – 21   x 3
Rimmon (2)
2 Kgs   5.18
Rimmon (3)
2 Sam   4.2
Rimmon (4)
Josh   19.13
Rimmon (5)
Josh   15.32
        19.7
1 Chr   4.32
Rimmon (6)
Zech   14.10
Rimmon Perez
Num   33.15
Rimmono
1 Chr   6.77
Rinnah
1 Chr   4.20
Riphath
Gen   10.3
1 Chr   1.6
Rissah
Num   33.15
Rithmah
Num   33.15
Rizia
1 Chr   7.39
Rizpah
2 Sam   3.7
        21.8 – 11   x 3
Rogelim
2 Sam   17.27
        19.31
Rohgah
1 Chr   7.34
Romamti Ezer
1 Chr   25.4 – 9   x 2
Rome
Dan   11.30
Mt   8.5
        22.17
        27.2 – 15   x 3
Mk   12.14
Lk   2.1
        7.2
        20.20 – 22   x 2
Jn   11.48   •
        18.3 – 12   x 2
Acts   2.10
        10.1
        16.12 – 38   x 8
        18 – 19   x 3
        21 – 23   x 9
        25.8 – 16   x 2
        27 – 28   x 6

Rome (Cont)
Rom   1.6 – 15   x 3
2 Cor   11.25
2 Tim   1.17
Rosh
Gen   46.21
Rubbish Gate
Neh   2 – 3   x 3
        12.31
Rufus (1)
Mk   15.21
Rufus (2)
Rom   16.13
Rumah
2 Kgs   23.36
Ruth
Ruth   1 – 4   x 28
Mt   1.2
Sabeans (1)
Job   1.15
Sabeans (2)
Joel   3.8
Sabtah
Gen   10.7
1 Chr   1.9
Sabteca
Gen   10.7
1 Chr   1.9
Sachar (1)
1 Chr   11.26
Sachar (2)
1 Chr   26.4
Sachia
1 Chr   8.10
Safe Harbours
Acts   27.8
Sahar
Ezek   27.18
Sakkuth
Amos   5.26
Salamis
Acts   13.5
Salecah
Deut   3.10
Josh   12 – 13   x 2
1 Chr   5.11
Salem
Gen   14.18
Heb   7.1 – 2   x 2
Salim
Jn   3.23
Sallai (1)
Neh   12.12
Sallai (2)
Neh   11.8
Sallu (1)
1 Chr   9.7
Sallu (2)
Neh   11.7 – 8   x 2
Sallu (3)
Neh   12.2
Salma
1 Chr   2.51 – 54   x 2
Salmon
Ruth   4.18
1 Chr   2.11
Mt   1.2
Lk   3.32
Salmone
Acts   27.7
Salome
Mk   15 – 16   x 2
Salt
Josh   15.62

Salt Valley
2 Sam   8.13
2 Kgs   14.7
1 Chr   18.12
2 Chr   25.11
Salu
Num   25.14
Samaria
1 Kgs   13.32
        16.24 – 32   x 5
        18.2
        20 – 22   x 9
2 Kgs   1 – 3   x 4
        5 – 7   x 9
        10.1 – 36   x 9
        13 – 15   x 15
        17 – 18   x 12
        21.13
        23.18
2 Chr   18.2 – 9   x 2
        22.9
        25.13 – 24   x 2
        28.8 – 15   x 3
Ezra   4.10 – 17   x 2
Neh   4.2
Is   7 – 10   x 7
        36.19
Jer   23.13
        31.5
        41.5
Ezek   16.46 – 53   x 3
        23.4 – 33   x 2
Hos   8.5 – 6   x 2
        10.5
        13.16
Amos   3 – 4   x 3
        6.1
        8.14
Obad   .19
Mic   1.1 – 9   x 5
Mt   10.5
Lk   9 – 10   x 2
        17.11 – 16   x 2
Jn   4.4 – 40   x 9
        8.48
Acts   1.8
        8 – 9   x 6
        15.3
Samgar Nebo
Jer   39.3
Samlah
Gen   36.31
1 Chr   1.43
Samos
Acts   20.15
Samothrace
Acts   16.11
Samson
Judg   13 – 16   x 52
Heb   11.32
Samuel
1 Sam   1 – 3   x 25
        7 – 13   x 57
        15 – 16   x 30
        19.18 – 24   x 5
        25.1
        28.3 – 20   x 7
1 Chr   6.28 – 33   x 2
        9.22
        11.3
        26.28
        29.29
2 Chr   35.18
Ps   99.6
Jer   15.1

Samuel (Cont)
Acts   3.24
        13.20
Heb   11.32
Sanballat
Neh   2.10 – 19   x 2
        4.1 – 7   x 2
        6.1 – 14   x 5
        13.28
Sansannah
Josh   15.31
Saph
2 Sam   21.18
Sapphira
Acts   5.1
Sarah
Gen   11 – 12   x 6
        16 – 18   x 21
        20 – 21   x 11
        23 – 25   x 6
        49.31
Is   51.2
Rom   4.19
        9.9
Heb   11.11
1 Pet   3.6
Sarai
see Sarah
Saraph
1 Chr   4.22
Sardis
Obad   .20
Rev   3.1
        3.1 – 4   x 2
Sargon
Is   20.1
Sarid
Josh   19.10 – 12   x 2
Sarsechim
Jer   39.3
Satan
1 Chr   21.1
Job   1 – 2   x 10
Zech   3.1 – 2   x 2
Mt   4.10
        12.26
        16.23
Mk   1.13
        3 – 4   x 3
        8.33
Lk   10 – 11   x 2
        13.16
        22.3 – 31   x 2
Jn   13.27
Acts   5.3
        26.18
Rom   16.20
1 Cor   5.5
        7.5
2 Cor   2.11
        11 – 12   x 2
1 Thes 2.18
2 Thes 2.9
1 Tim   1.20
        5.15
Rev   2 – 3   x 5
        12.9
        20.2 – 8   x 3
Saul (1)
(King of Israel)
1 Sam   9 – 11   x 44
        13 – 29   x 217
        31.1 – 12   x 13
2 Sam   1 – 7   x 34
        9.1 – 10   x 8
        12.7

Saul (1) (Cont)
2 Sam	16.3 − 8	x 5
	19.17 − 29	x 3
	21 − 22	x 15
1 Chr	5.10	
	8 − 13	x 26
	15.29	
	17.13	
	26.28	
Is	10.29	
Acts	13.21	

Saul (2)
see also Paul
Acts	7 − 9	x 22
	11 − 13	x 8
	22.7 − 13	x 3
	26.14	x 2

Sceva
| Acts | 19.14 |

Sea
| Gen | 1.10 |

Seba
Gen	10.7
1 Chr	1.9
Ps	72.10
Is	43.3
	45.14

Secacah
| Josh | 15.61 |

Secu
| 1 Sam | 19.22 |

Secundus
| Acts | 20.4 |

Segub (1)
| 1 Kgs | 16.34 |

Segub (2)
| 1 Chr | 2.21 − 22 | x 2 |

Seir
Gen	36.20
Judg	5.4
1 Chr	1.38
Ezek	35.15

Seirah
| Judg | 3.26 |

Sela
Judg	1.36
2 Kgs	14.7
2 Chr	25.12
Is	16.1
	42.11

Seled
| 1 Chr | 2.30 | x 2 |

Seleucia
| Acts | 13.4 |

Semachiah
| 1 Chr | 26.6 |

Semein
| Lk | 3.26 |

Senaah
| Ezra | 2.21 |
| Neh | 7.26 |

Seneh
| 1 Sam | 14.4 |

Senir
Deut	3.9
1 Chr	5.23
Song	4.8

Sennacherib
2 Kgs	18 − 19	x 6
2 Chr	32.1 − 22	x 5
Is	36 − 37	x 4

Seorim
| 1 Chr | 24.7 |

Separation Hill
| 1 Sam | 23.28 |

Sephar
| Gen | 10.30 |

Sepharvaim
| 2 Kgs | 17 − 19 | x 4 |
| Is | 36 − 37 | x 2 |

Serah
Gen	46.17
Num	26.46
1 Chr	7.30

Seraiah (1)
| 2 Sam | 8.17 |
| 1 Chr | 18.16 |

Seraiah (2)
| 2 Kgs | 25.18 |
| Jer | 52.24 |

Seraiah (3)
| 1 Chr | 4.13 − 14 | x 2 |

Seraiah (4)
| 1 Chr | 4.34 |

Seraiah (5)
| 1 Chr | 6.14 |

Seraiah (6)
| Ezra | 2.2 |

Seraiah (7)
| Ezra | 7.1 |

Seraiah (8)
| Neh | 10.2 |

Seraiah (9)
| Jer | 36.26 |

Seraiah (10)
| 2 Kgs | 25.23 |
| Jer | 40.8 |

Seraiah (11)
| Jer | 51.59 − 63 | x 4 |

Seraiah (12)
| Neh | 12.2 − 12 | x 2 |

Seraiah (13)
| Neh | 11.11 |

Sered
| Gen | 46.14 |
| Num | 26.26 |

Sergius Paulus
| Acts | 13.7 |

Serug
Gen	11.20 − 22	x 2
1 Chr	1.26
Lk	3.35

Seth (1)
Gen	4 − 5	x 4
1 Chr	1.1	x 2
Lk	3.38

Seth (2)
| Num | 24.17 |

Sethur
| Num | 13.3 |

Shaalbim
Josh	19.42
Judg	1.35
1 Kgs	4.9

Shaalbon
| 2 Sam | 23.24 |
| 1 Chr | 11.26 |

Shaalim
| 1 Sam | 9.4 |

Shaaph (1)
| 1 Chr | 2.47 |

Shaaph (2)
| 1 Chr | 2.49 |

Shaaraim (1)
| Josh | 15.36 |
| 1 Sam | 17.52 |

Shaaraim (2)
| 1 Chr | 4.31 |

Shaashgaz
| Esth | 2.14 |

Shabbethai
Ezra	10.15
Neh	8.7
	11.16

Shadrach
see also Hananiah (2)
| Dan | 1 − 3 | x 11 |

Shagee
| 1 Chr | 11.26 |

Shaharaim
| 1 Chr | 8.8 |

Shahazumah
| Josh | 19.22 |

Shalishah
| 1 Sam | 9.4 |

Shallecheth Gate
| 1 Chr | 26.16 |

Shallum (1)
| 2 Kgs | 15.10 − 15 | x 4 |

Shallum (2)
| 2 Kgs | 22.14 |
| 2 Chr | 34.22 |

Shallum (3)
| 1 Chr | 2.40 |

Shallum (4)
| 1 Chr | 4.25 |

Shallum (5)
| 1 Chr | 6.12 |
| Ezra | 7.2 |

Shallum (6)
| 1 Chr | 7.13 |

Shallum (7)
| 2 Chr | 28.12 |

Shallum (8)
| Ezra | 10.24 |

Shallum (9)
| Ezra | 10.38 |

Shallum (10)
| Neh | 3.12 |

Shallum (11)
| Neh | 3.15 |

Shallum (12)
| Jer | 35.4 |

Shallum (13)
| Jer | 32.7 |

Shallum (14)
| 1 Chr | 9.17 | x 2 |

Shallum (15)
| Ezra | 2.40 |
| Neh | 7.43 |

Shallum (16)
| 1 Chr | 9.19 |

Shallum (17)
| 1 Chr | 9.31 |

Shalmai
| Neh | 7.46 |

Shalman
| Hos | 10.14 |

Shalmaneser
| 2 Kgs | 17 − 18 | x 5 |

Shamgar
| Judg | 3.31 |
| | 5.6 |

Shamhuth
| 1 Chr | 27.2 |

Shamir (1)
| Judg | 10.1 − 2 | x 2 |

Shamir (2)
| Josh | 15.48 |

Shamir (3)
| 1 Chr | 24.24 |

Shamlai
| Ezra | 2.43 |

Shamma (1)
| 1 Chr | 7.37 |

Shamma (2)
| 1 Chr | 11.26 |

Shammah (1)
1 Sam	16 − 17	x 2
2 Sam	13.3 − 32	x 2
	21.21	
1 Chr	2.13	
	20.7	

Shammah (2)
| Gen | 36.10 − 17 | x 2 |
| 1 Chr | 1.37 | |

Shammah (3)
| 2 Sam | 23.11 − 12 | x 2 |

Shammah (4)
| 2 Sam | 23.24 |

Shammah (5)
| 2 Sam | 23.24 |

Shammai (1)
| 1 Chr | 2.28 − 32 | x 3 |

Shammai (2)
| 1 Chr | 2.44 |

Shammai (3)
| 1 Chr | 4.17 |

Shammoth
| 1 Chr | 11.26 |

Shammua (1)
| 2 Sam | 5.14 |
| 1 Chr | 14.4 |

Shammua (2)
| Num | 13.3 |

Shammua (3)
| Neh | 11.17 |

Shammua (4)
| Neh | 12.12 |

Shamsherai
| 1 Chr | 8.26 |

Shapham
| 1 Chr | 5.12 |

Shaphan (1)
| 2 Kgs | 22.3 − 14 | x 5 |
| 2 Chr | 34.8 − 20 | x 5 |

Shaphan (2)
2 Kgs	22.12	
	25.22	
Jer	26.24	
	39 − 40	x 2

Shaphan (3)
| Jer | 29.3 |

Shaphan (4)
| Jer | 36.10 − 12 | x 3 |

Shaphan (5)
| Ezek | 8.11 |

Shaphat (1)
| 1 Kgs | 19.16 |
| 2 Kgs | 3.11 |

Shaphat (2)
| Num | 13.3 |

Shaphat (3)
| 1 Chr | 3.22 |

Shaphat (4)
| 1 Chr | 5.12 |

Shaphat (5)
| 1 Chr | 27.25 |

Shaphir
| Mic | 1.11 |

Sharai
| Ezra | 10.38 |

Sharar
| 2 Sam | 23.24 |

Sharezer (1)
| 2 Kgs | 19.37 |
| Is | 37.38 |

Sharezer (2)
| Zech | 7.2 |

Sharon (1)
1 Chr	27.25	x 2
Song	2.1	
Is	33.9	
	35.2	
	65.10	
Acts	9.35	

Sharon (2)
1 Chr	5.16

Sharuhen
Josh	19.6

Shashai
Ezra	10.38

Shashak
1 Chr	8.14 − 22	x 2

Shaul (1)
Gen	36.31
1 Chr	1.43

Shaul (2)
Gen	46.10	
Ex	6.15	
Num	26.13	
1 Chr	4.24 − 25	x 2

Shaul (3)
1 Chr	6.24

Shaveh
Gen	14.17

Sheal
Ezra	10.29

Shealtiel
1 Chr	3.17
Ezra	3.2
	5.2
Neh	12.1
Hag	1.1
Mt	1.12
Lk	3.27

Shear Jashub
Is	7.3

Sheariah
1 Chr	8 − 9	x 2

Sheba (1)
Gen	10.7 − 28	x 2
	25.3	
1 Kgs	10.1 − 13	x 4
1 Chr	1.9 − 32	x 3
2 Chr	9.1 − 12	x 5
Job	6.19	
Ps	72.10	
Is	60.6	
Jer	6.20	
Ezek	27.22 − 23	x 2
	38.13	
Mt	12.42	
Lk	11.31	

Sheba (2)
2 Sam	20.1 − 22	x 10

Sheba (3)
Josh	19.2

Sheba (4,
1 Chr	5.13

Shebaniah (1)
1 Chr	15.23

Shebaniah (2)
Neh	9 − 10	x 3

Shebaniah (3)
Neh	10.9

Shebaniah (4)
Neh	10.2

Shebaniah (5)
Neh	12.12

Shebat
Zech	1.7

Sheber
1 Chr	2.48

Shebna
2 Kgs	18 − 19	x 4
Is	22.15 − 20	x 2
	36 − 37	x 4

Shebuel (1)
1 Chr	23 − 24	x 2
	26.24	

Shebuel (2)
1 Chr	25.4 − 9	x 2

Shecaniah (1)
2 Chr	31.15

Shecaniah (2)
Ezra	8.2

Shecaniah (3)
Ezra	10.2 − 5	x 2

Shecaniah (4)
Neh	3.29

Shecaniah (5)
Neh	6.18

Shecaniah (6)
1 Chr	24.7

Shecaniah (7)
Neh	12.2

Shecaniah (8)
1 Chr	3.21 − 22	x 2

Shecaniah (9)
Ezra	8.2

Shechem (1)
Gen	12.6	
	33.18	
	35.4	
	37.12 − 14	x 3
	48.22	
Josh	17.7	
	20 − 21	x 2
	24.1 − 32	x 3
Judg	8 − 9	x 24
	21.19	
1 Kgs	12.1 − 25	x 2
1 Chr	6 − 7	x 2
2 Chr	10.1	
Ps	60.6	
	108.7	
Jer	41.5	
Hos	6.9	
Acts	7.16	

Shechem (2)
Gen	33 − 34	x 13
Josh	24.32	

Shechem (3)
Num	26.31
Josh	17.2
1 Chr	7.19

Shedeur
Num	1 − 2	x 2
	7.12	
	10.18	

Sheep Gate
Neh	3.1 − 32	x 2
	12.39	
Jn	5.2	

Sheerah
1 Chr	7.24

Shehariah
1 Chr	8.26

Shelah (1)
Gen	38.5 − 26	x 5
	46.12	
Num	26.19	
1 Chr	2.3	
	4.21	
	9.4	
Neh	11.5	

Shelah (2)
Gen	10 − 11	x 3

Shelah (2) (Cont)
1 Chr	1.18 − 24	x 2
Lk	3.35	

Shelah (3)
Neh	3.15

Shelemiah (1)
1 Chr	26.14

Shelemiah (2)
Ezra	10.38

Shelemiah (3)
Ezra	10.38

Shelemiah (4)
Neh	3.30

Shelemiah (5)
Neh	13.13

Shelemiah (6)
Jer	36.14

Shelemiah (7)
Jer	36.26

Shelemiah (8)
Jer	37.13

Shelemiah (9)
Jer	37 − 38	x 2

Sheleph
Gen	10.26
1 Chr	1.20

Shelesh
1 Chr	7.35

Shelomi
Num	34.19

Shelomith (1)
Lev	24.10

Shelomith (2)
1 Chr	3.19

Shelomith (3)
1 Chr	23 − 24	x 2

Shelomith (4)
1 Chr	26.25 − 28	x 4

Shelomith (5)
2 Chr	11.20

Shelomith (6)
Ezra	8.2

Shelomoth
1 Chr	23.9

Shelumiel
Num	1 − 2	x 2
	7.12	
	10.19	
	34.19	

Shem
Gen	5 − 7	x 3
	9 − 11	x 11
1 Chr	1.4 − 24	x 4
Lk	3.36	

Shema (1)
Josh	15.26

Shema (2)
1 Chr	2.43 − 44	x 3

Shema (3)
1 Chr	5.8

Shema (4)
1 Chr	8.13

Shema (5)
Neh	8.4

Shemaah
1 Chr	12.3

Shemaiah (1)
1 Kgs	12.22	
2 Chr	11 − 12	x 4

Shemaiah (2)
Jer	29.24 − 31	x 4

Shemaiah (3)
1 Chr	3.22

Shemaiah (4)
1 Chr	4.34

Shemaiah (5)
1 Chr	5.4

Shemaiah (6)
1 Chr	9.14

Shemaiah (7)
1 Chr	9.14

Shemaiah (8)
1 Chr	15.8 − 11	x 2

Shemaiah (9)
1 Chr	24.6

Shemaiah (10)
1 Chr	26.4 − 6	x 2

Shemaiah (11)
2 Chr	17.8

Shemaiah (12)
2 Chr	29.12

Shemaiah (13)
2 Chr	31.15

Shemaiah (14)
2 Chr	35.9

Shemaiah (15)
Ezra	8.2

Shemaiah (16)
Ezra	8.16

Shemaiah (17)
Ezra	10.21

Shemaiah (18)
Ezra	10.31

Shemaiah (19)
Neh	3.29

Shemaiah (20)
Neh	6.10 − 12	x 2

Shemaiah (21)
N h	10.2

Shemaiah (22)
Neh	11.15

Shemaiah (23)
Neh	12.2 − 12	x 2

Shemaiah (24)
Neh	12.33

Shemaiah (25)
Neh	12.33

Shemaiah (26)
Neh	12.36

Shemaiah (27)
Neh	12.42

Shemaiah (28)
Jer	26.20

Shemaiah (29)
Jer	36.12

Shemariah (1)
1 Chr	12.3

Shemariah (2)
2 Chr	11.19

Shemariah (3)
Ezra	10.31

Shemariah (4)
Ezra	10.38

Shemeber
Gen	14.2

Shemed
1 Chr	8.12	x 2

Shemer (1)
1 Kgs	16.24	x 2

Shemer (2)
1 Chr	6.46

Shemida
Num	26.32
Josh	17.2
1 Chr	7.19

Shemiramoth (1)
1 Chr	15 − 16	x 2

Shemiramoth (2)
2 Chr	17.8

Shemuel		
1 Chr	7.2	

Shen
1 Sam 7.12

Shenazzar
1 Chr 3.18

Shepham
Num 34.10
1 Chr 27.25

Shephatiah (1)
2 Sam 3.4
1 Chr 3.1

Shephatiah (2)
1 Chr 9.7

Shephatiah (3)
1 Chr 12.3

Shephatiah (4)
1 Chr 27.16

Shephatiah (5)
2 Chr 21.2

Shephatiah (6)
Ezra 2.3
Neh 7.8

Shephatiah (7)
Neh 11.4

Shephatiah (8)
Jer 38.1

Shephatiah (9)
Ezra 2.55
Neh 7.57

Shephatiah (10)
Ezra 8.2

Shepher
Num 33.15

Shepherds' Camp
2 Kgs 10.12

Shephi
1 Chr 1.38

Shepho
Gen 36.23

Shephupham
Num 26.39

Shephuphan
1 Chr 8.5

Sherebiah
Ezra 8.18 − 24 x 2
Neh 8 − 10 x 4
12.8 − 24 x 2

Sheresh
1 Chr 7.16

Sheshai
Num 13.22
Josh 15.14
Judg 1.10

Sheshan (1)
1 Chr 2.31 x 2

Sheshan (2)
1 Chr 2.34

Sheshbazzar
Ezra 1.8 − 11 x 2
5.14 − 16 x 2

Shethar
Esth 1.14

Shethar Bozenai
Ezra 5 − 6 x 3

Sheva
2 Sam 20.25

Shevah
1 Chr 2.49

Shihor
Josh 13.3

Shihor Libnath
Josh 19.26

Shikkeron
Josh 15.11

Shilhi
1 Kgs 22.42
2 Chr 20.31

Shilhim
Josh 15.32

Shillem
Gen 46.24
Num 26.49

Shiloah
Is 8.6

Shiloh
Josh 18 − 19 x 4
21 − 22 x 3
Judg 18.31
21.12 − 23 x 5
1 Sam 1 − 4 x 11
14.3
1 Kgs 2.27
11 − 12 x 2
14 − 15 x 3
2 Chr 9 − 10 x 2
Ps 78.60
Jer 7.12 − 14 x 3
26.6 − 9 x 2
41.5

Shilshah
1 Chr 7.37

Shimea (1)
1 Chr 3.5

Shimea (2)
1 Chr 6.30

Shimea (3)
1 Chr 6.39

Shimeah
1 Chr 8 − 9 x 2

Shimeath
2 Kgs 12.20
2 Chr 24.26

Shimeathites
1 Chr 2.55

Shimei (1)
2 Sam 16.5 − 13 x 4
19.16 − 23 x 4
1 Kgs 2.8 − 46 x 7

Shimei (2)
Ex 6.17
Num 3.17 − 21 x 2
1 Chr 6.17 − 29 x 2
23.7 − 10 x 3
Zech 12.12

Shimei (3)
1 Kgs 1.8

Shimei (4)
1 Kgs 4.18

Shimei (5)
1 Chr 3.19

Shimei (6)
1 Chr 4.26 − 27 x 2

Shimei (7)
1 Chr 5.4

Shimei (8)
1 Chr 6.42

Shimei (9)
1 Chr 25.9

Shimei (10)
1 Chr 27.25

Shimei (11)
2 Chr 29.12

Shimei (12)
2 Chr 31.12

Shimei (13)
Ezra 10.23

Shimei (14)
Ezra 10.33

Shimei (15)
Ezra 10.38

Shimei (16)
Esth 2.5

Shimei (17)
1 Chr 25.3

Shimei (18)
1 Chr 8.19

Shimeon
Ezra 10.31

Shimon
1 Chr 4.20

Shimrath
1 Chr 8.21

Shimri (1)
1 Chr 4.34

Shimri (2)
1 Chr 11.26

Shimri (3)
1 Chr 26.10

Shimri (4)
2 Chr 29.12

Shimrith
2 Chr 24.26

Shimron (1)
Gen 46.13
Num 26.24
1 Chr 7.1

Shimron (2)
Josh 11.1
19.15

Shimron Meron
Josh 12.20

Shimshai
Ezra 4.8 − 23 x 4

Shinab
Gen 14.2

Shion
Josh 19.19

Shiphi
1 Chr 4.34

Shiphrah
Ex 1.15

Shiphtan
Num 34.19

Shirtai
1 Chr 27.25

Shisha
1 Kgs 4.3

Shishak
1 Kgs 11.40
14.25
2 Chr 12.2 − 9 x 6

Shiza
1 Chr 11.26

Shoa
Ezek 23.23

Shobab (1)
2 Sam 5.14
1 Chr 3.5
14.4

Shobab (2)
1 Chr 2.18

Shobach
2 Sam 10.16 − 18 x 2
1 Chr 19.16 − 18 x 2

Shobai
Ezra 2.40
Neh 7.43

Shobal (1)
Gen 36.20 − 29 x 3
1 Chr 1.38

Shobal (2)
1 Chr 2.50 − 52 x 2

Shobal (3)
1 Chr 4.1 − 2 x 2

Shobek
Neh 10.14

Shobi
2 Sam 17.27

Shoham
1 Chr 24.27

Shomer (1)
2 Kgs 12.20

Shomer (2)
1 Chr 7.32 − 34 x 2

Shua (1)
Gen 38.2

Shua (2)
1 Chr 7.32

Shuah (1)
Gen 25.2
1 Chr 1.32

Shuah (2)
Job 2.11

Shual (1)
1 Sam 13.17

Shual (2)
1 Chr 7.36

Shuhah
1 Chr 4.11

Shuham
Num 26.42

Shulam
Song 6.13

Shumathites
1 Chr 2.53

Shunem
Josh 19.18
1 Sam 28.4
1 Kgs 1 − 2 x 3
2 Kgs 4.8 − 25 x 4
8.1

Shuni
Gen 46.16
Num 26.15

Shuppim (1)
1 Chr 7.12 − 15 x 2

Shuppim (2)
1 Chr 26.16

Shur
Gen 16.7
20.1
25.18
Ex 15.22
Num 33.8
1 Sam 15.7
27.8

Shuthelah (1)
Num 26.35 − 36 x 2
1 Chr 7.20 − 21 x 2

Shuthelah (2)
1 Chr 7.21

Sia
Neh 7.46

Siaha
Ezra 2.43

Sibbecai
2 Sam 21.18
1 Chr 11.26
20.4
27.2

Sibmah
Num 32.3 − 38 x 2
Josh 13.19
Is 16.8 − 9 x 2
Jer 48.32 x 2

Sibraim
Ezek 47.16

Siddim
Gen	14.3 − 8	x 2

Sidon (1)
Gen	10.19	
	49.13	
Deut	3.9	
Josh	11.8	
	13.4 − 6	x 2
	19.28	
Judg	1.31	
	3.3	
	10.6 − 12	x 2
	18.7 − 27	x 3
2 Sam	24.6	
1 Kgs	11.1 − 33	x 3
	16 − 17	x 2
2 Kgs	23.13	
1 Chr	22.4	
Ezra	3.7	
Is	23.2 − 12	x 3
Jer	25.19	
	27.3	
	47.4	
Ezek	27 − 28	x 3
	32.30	
Joel	3.4	
Zech	9.2	
Mt	11.21 − 22	x 2
	15.21	
Mk	3.8	
	7.31	
Lk	4.26	
	6.17	
	10.13 − 14	x 2
Acts	12.20	
	27.3	

Sidon (2)
Gen	10.15	
1 Chr	1.13	

Sihon
Num	21.21 − 34	x 6
	32.33	
Deut	1 − 4	x 10
	29.7	
	31.4	
Josh	2.10	
	9.10	
	12 − 13	x 6
Judg	11.19 − 21	x 3
1 Kgs	4.19	
Neh	9.22	
Ps	135 − 136	x 2
Jer	48.45	

Silas
Acts	15 − 18	x 21
2 Cor	1.19	
1 Thes	1.1	
2 Thes	1.1	
1 Pet	5.12	

Silla
2 Kgs	12.20	

Siloam
Lk	13.4	
Jn	9.7 − 11	x 2

Simeon (1)
Gen	29.33	
	34 − 35	x 3
	42 − 43	x 3
	46.10	
	48 − 49	x 2
Ex	1.2	
	6.15	
Num	1 − 2	x 3
	7.12	
	10.19	

Simeon (1) (Cont)
Num	13.3	
	25 − 26	x 2
	34.19	
Deut	27.12	
Josh	19.1 − 9	x 3
	21.4 − 16	x 3
Judg	1.3 − 17	x 3
1 Chr	2.1	
	4.24 − 42	x 4
	6.65	
	12.23	
	27.16	
2 Chr	15.9	
	34.6	
Ezek	48.23 − 30	x 2
Rev	7.5	

Simeon (2)
Lk	3.30	

Simeon (3)
Lk	2.25 − 34	x 5

Simeon (4)
Acts	13.1	

Simon (1)
see also Peter
Mt	4.18	
	10.2	
	16 − 17	x 3
Mk	1.16 − 36	x 4
	3.16	
	14.37	
Lk	4 − 6	x 9
	22.31 − 32	x 3
	24.34	
Jn	1.40 − 42	x 4
	6.8 − 68	x 2
	13.6 − 36	x 4
	18.10 − 15	x 2
	20 − 21	x 9
Acts	1.13	
	10 − 11	x 5
	15.14	
2 Pet	1.1	

Simon (2)
(the Patriot)
Mt	10.4	
Mk	3.18	
Lk	6.15	
Acts	1.13	

Simon (3)
(Brother of Jesus)
Mt	13.55	
Mk	6.3	

Simon (4)
(of Cyrene)
Mt	27.32	
Mk	15.21	x 2
Lk	23.26	

Simon (5)
Jn	6.71	
	13.2 − 26	x 2

Simon (6)
(the Leper)
Mt	26.6	
Mk	14.3	

Simon (7)
(the Pharisee)
Lk	7.40 − 44	x 3

Simon (8)
Acts	9 − 10	x 3

Simon (9)
Acts	8.9 − 24	x 4

Sin
Ex	16 − 17	x 2
Num	33.11	

Sinai
Ex	3.1	
	16 − 17	x 2
	19.1 − 20	x 5
	24.15	
	31.18	

Sinai (Cont)
Ex	33 − 34	x 5
Lev	7.38	
	25 − 27	x 3
Num	1.1 − 19	x 2
	3.1 − 14	x 3
	9 − 10	x 4
	26.64	
	28.6	
	33.15	
Deut	1.2 − 19	x 4
	4 − 5	x 3
	9.8	
	18.16	
	29.1	
	33.2	
Judg	5.5	
1 Kgs	8.9	
	19.8	
2 Chr	5.10	
Neh	9.13	
Ps	68.8 − 17	x 2
	106.19	
Ezek	20.36	
Mal	4.4	
Acts	7.30 − 38	x 2
Gal	4.24 − 25	x 2
Heb	12.18	

Sinites
Gen	10.17	
1 Chr	1.15	

Siphmoth
1 Sam	30.28	

Sippai
1 Chr	20.4	

Sirah
2 Sam	3.26	

Sirion
Deut	3 − 4	x 2

Sisera (1)
Judg	4 − 5	x 18
1 Sam	12.9	
Ps	83.9	

Sisera (2)
Ezra	2.43	
Neh	7.46	

Sismai
1 Chr	2.40	

Sithri
Ex	6.22	

Sivan
Esth	8.9	

Skull
Mt	27.33	
Mk	15.22	
Lk	23.33	
Jn	19.17	

Sky
Gen	1.8	

Smyrna
Rev	1 − 2	x 2

So
2 Kgs	17.4	

Soco (1)
2 Chr	11.7	
	28.18	

Soco (2)
1 Chr	4.17	

Socoh (1)
Josh	15.35	
1 Sam	17.1	x 2
1 Kgs	4.10	

Socoh (2)
Josh	15.48	

Sodi
Num	13.3	

Sodom
Gen	10.19	
	13 − 14	x 9
	18 − 19	x 10
Deut	29.23	
	32.32	
Is	1.9 − 10	x 2
	3.9	
	13.19	
Jer	23.14	
	49 − 50	x 2
Lam	4.6	
Ezek	16.46 − 56	x 4
Amos	4.11	
Zeph	2.9	
Mt	10 − 11	x 3
Lk	10.12	
	17.29	
Rom	9.29	
2 Pet	2.6	
Jude	.7	
Rev	11.8	

Solomon
see also Jedidiah
2 Sam	5.14	
	12.24	
1 Kgs	1 − 12	x 156
	14.21 − 26	x 2
2 Kgs	21.7	
	23 − 25	x 3
1 Chr	3.5 − 10	x 3
	6.10 − 32	x 2
	14.4	
	18.8	
	22 − 23	x 5
	28 − 29	x 12
2 Chr	1 − 13	x 66
	30.26	
	33.7	
	35.3 − 4	x 2
Ezra	2.55 − 58	x 2
Neh	7.57 − 60	x 2
	11 − 13	x 3
Prov	1.1	
	10.1	
	25.1	
Song	1.1 − 5	x 2
	3.7 − 11	x 3
	8.11 − 12	x 2
Jer	52.20	
Mt	1.6	
	6.29	
	12.42	x 2
Lk	11 − 12	x 3
Acts	7.47	

Solomon's Porch
Jn	10.23	
Acts	3.11	
	5.12	

Sopater
Acts	20.4	

Sophereth
Neh	7.57	

Sorek
Judg	16.4	

Sosipater
Rom	16.21	

Sosthenes (1)
Acts	18.17	

Sosthenes (2)
1 Cor	1.1	

Sotai
Ezra	2.55	
Neh	7.57	

Spain
Gen	10.4	
1 Chr	1.7	
Ps	72.10	
Is	23.6 − 10	x 2
	66.19	
Jer	10.9	
Ezek	27.12	
	38.13	
Jon	1.3	x 2
	4.2	
Rom	15.24 − 28	x 2

Stachys
Rom 16.9

Stephanas
1 Cor	1.16	
	16.15 − 17	x 2

Stephen
Acts	6 − 8	x 13
	11.19	
	22.20	

Stone of Help
1 Sam 7.12

Stone Pavement
Jn 19.13

Straight Street
Acts 9.11

Suah
1 Chr 7.36

Sucathites
1 Chr 2.55

Succoth Benoth
2 Kgs 17.30

Sudan
2 Sam	18.21 − 31	x 2
2 Kgs	19.9	
2 Chr	12.3	
	14.9 − 13	x 3
	16.8	
	21.16	
Esth	1.1	
	8.9	
Ps	68.31	
	87.4	
Is	11.11	
	18.1 − 5	x 2
	20.3 − 5	x 2
	37.9	
	43.3	
	45.14	
Jer	38 − 39	x 2
	46.9	
Ezek	29 − 30	x 4
	38.5	
Dan	11.43	
Amos	9.7	
Nah	3.9	
Zeph	2 − 3	x 2

Suez
Ex	10.19	
Num	33.10	
Is	11.15	

Sukkite
2 Chr 12.3

Sukkoth (1)
Gen	33.17	x 2
Josh	13.27	
Judg	8.5 − 16	x 7
Ps	60.6	
	108.7	

Sukkoth (2)
Ex	12 − 13	x 2
Num	33.5	

Sukkoth (3)
1 Kgs 7.46

Sukkoth (3) (Cont)
2 Chr 4.17

Suph
Deut 1.1

Suphah
Num 21.14

Sur Gate
2 Kgs 11.6

Susa
Ezra	4.9	
Neh	1.1	
Esth	1 − 4	x 9
	8 − 9	x 9
Dan	8.2	

Susanna
Lk 8.3

Susi
Num 13.3

Sychar
Jn 4.5

Syntyche
Phil 4.2

Syracuse
Acts 28.12

Syria
Num	23.7	
Judg	10.6	
2 Sam	8.3 − 5	x 2
	10.6 − 19	x 12
	15.8	
1 Kgs	10 − 11	x 3
	15.18	
	19 − 20	x 10
	22.1 − 35	x 6
2 Kgs	3.26	
	5 − 10	x 34
	12 − 13	x 11
	15 − 16	x 3
	24.2	
1 Chr	18 − 19	x 14
2 Chr	1.17	
	16.2 − 7	x 2
	18.10 − 34	x 4
	22.5	
	24.23 − 24	x 2
	28.5 − 23	x 3
Is	7.1 − 8	x 5
	9.12	
	17.2 − 3	x 2
Jer	35.11	
Ezek	27.16	
Dan	11.6 − 40	x 15
Amos	1.5	
	9.7	
Zech	9.1	
Mt	4.24	
Mk	7.26	
Lk	2.2	
	4.27	
Acts	15.23 − 41	x 2
	18.18	
	20 − 21	x 2
Gal	1.21	

Taanach
Josh	12.21	
	17.11	
	21.25	
Judg	1.27	
	5.19	
1 Kgs	4.12	
1 Chr	7.29	

Taanath Shiloh
Josh 16.6

Tabbaoth
Ezra 2.43

Tabbaoth (Cont)
Neh 7.46

Tabbath
Judg 7.22

Tabeel (1)
Ezra 4.7

Tabeel (2)
Is 7.6

Taberah
Num	11.3	
Deut	9.22	

Tabitha
Acts 9.36 − 40   x 2

Tabor (1)
1 Sam 10.3

Tabor (2)
Judg	4.6 − 14	x 3
Ps	89.12	
Jer	46.18	
Hos	5.1	

Tabor (3)
1 Chr 6.77

Tabor (4)
Josh 19.22

Tabor (5)
Judg 8.18

Tabrimmon
1 Kgs 15.18

Tachemon
2 Sam 23.8

Tahan
Num	26.35	
1 Chr	7.25	

Tahash
Gen 22.24

Tahath (1)
Num 33.15

Tahath (2)
1 Chr 6.24

Tahath (3)
1 Chr 6.37

Tahath (4)
1 Chr 7.20

Tahath (5)
1 Chr 7.20

Tahpanhes
Jer	2.16	
	43 − 44	x 2
	46.14	
Ezek	30.18	

Tahpenes
1 Kgs 11.19

Talmai (1)
Num	13.22	
Josh	15.14	
Judg	1.10	

Talmai (2)
2 Sam	3.3	
	13.37	
1 Chr	3.1	

Talmon (1)
1 Chr	9.17	
Ezra	2.40	
Neh	7.43	

Talmon (2)
Neh 11 − 12   x 2

Tamar (1)
2 Sam	13.1 − 32	x 9
1 Chr	3.9	

Tamar (2)
Gen	38.6 − 24	x 6
Ruth	4.12	
1 Chr	2.4	
Mt	1.2	

Tamar (3)
2 Sam 14.27

Tamar (4)
1 Kgs	9.18	
Ezek	47 − 48	x 3

Tammuz
Ezek 8.14

Tanhumeth
2 Kgs	25.23	
Jer	40.8	

Taphath
1 Kgs 4.11

Tappuah (1)
1 Chr 2.43

Tappuah (2)
Josh	12.17	
	15.34	

Tappuah (3)
Josh 16 − 17   x 3

Tappuah (4)
2 Kgs 15.16

Taralah
Josh 18.27

Tarea
1 Chr 8 − 9   x 2

Tarshish (1)
1 Chr 7.10

Tarshish (2)
Esth 1.14

Tarsus
Acts	9.11 − 30	x 2
	11.25	
	21 − 22	x 2

Tartak
2 Kgs 17.31

Tattenai
Ezra 5 − 6   x 3

Tebah
Gen 22.24

Tebaliah
1 Chr 26.11

Tebeth
Esth 2.16

Tehinnah
1 Chr 4.12   x 2

Tekoa
2 Sam	14.2	
	23.24	
1 Chr	2.24	
	4.5	
	11.26	
	27.2	
2 Chr	11.6	
	20.20	
Neh	3.5 − 27	x 2
Jer	6.1	
Amos	1.1	

Tel Abib
Ezek 3.15

Tel Harsha
Ezra	2.59	
Neh	7.61	

Tel Melah
Ezra	2.59	
Neh	7.61	

Telah
1 Chr 7.25

Telassar
2 Kgs	19.12	
Is	37.12	

Telem (1)
Josh	15.24	
1 Sam	15.4	

Telem (2)
Ezra 10.24

Uel
Ezra 10.34
Ulai
Dan 8.2 − 16   x 2
Ulam (1)
1 Chr 7.16 − 17   x 2
Ulam (2)
1 Chr 8.39 − 40   x 2
Ulla
1 Chr 7.39
Ummah
Josh 19.30
Unloved
Hos 1 − 2   x 2
Unni
1 Chr 15.17
Unno
Neh 12.9
Uphaz
Jer 10.9
Ur (1)
Gen 11.28 − 31   x 2
     15.7
Neh 9.7
Ur (2)
1 Chr 11.26
Urbanus
Rom 16.9
Uri (1)
Ex 31.2
     35.30
     38.22
1 Chr 2.20
2 Chr 1.5
Uri (2)
1 Kgs 4.19
Uri (3)
Ezra 10.24
Uriah (1)
2 Sam 11 − 12   x 19
     23.24
1 Kgs 15.5
1 Chr 11.26
Mt 1.6
Uriah (2)
2 Kgs 16.10 − 16   x 4
Is 8.2
Uriah (3)
Jer 26.20 − 22   x 4
Uriah (4)
Ezra 8.33
Neh 3.4 − 21   x 2
Uriah (5)
Neh 8.4
Uriel (1)
1 Chr 6.24
     15.5 − 11   x 2
Uriel (2)
2 Chr 13.2
Uthai (1)
1 Chr 9.4
Uthai (2)
Ezra 8.2
Uz (1)
Gen 10.23
1 Chr 1.17
Uz (2)
Gen 22.21
Uz (3)
Gen 36.28
1 Chr 1.38
Uz (4)
Job 1.1
Jer 25.19
Lam 4.21

Uzai
Neh 3.25
Uzal
Gen 10.27
1 Chr 1.21
Uzza (1)
2 Kgs 21.18 − 26   x 2
Uzza (2)
1 Chr 8.6
Uzza (3)
Ezra 2.43
Neh 7.46
Uzzah (1)
2 Sam 6.3 − 8   x 5
1 Chr 13.7 − 11   x 4
Uzzah (2)
1 Chr 6.29
Uzzen Sheerah
1 Chr 7.24
Uzzi (1)
1 Chr 6.5 − 51   x 2
Ezra 7.4
Uzzi (2)
Neh 11.22
Uzzi (3)
Neh 12.12 − 42   x 2
Uzzi (4)
1 Chr 7.2 − 3   x 2
Uzzi (5)
1 Chr 7.7
Uzzi (6)
1 Chr 9.7
Uzzia
1 Chr 11.26
Uzziah (1)
2 Kgs 14 − 15   x 14
1 Chr 3.12
2 Chr 26.1 − 23   x 13
Is 1.1
     6 − 7   x 2
Hos 1.1
Amos 1.1
Zech 14.5
Mt 1.6
Uzziah (2)
1 Chr 27.25
Uzziah (3)
1 Chr 6.24
Uzziah (4)
Ezra 10.21
Uzziah (5)
Neh 11.4
Uzziel (1)
Ex 6.18 − 22   x 2
Lev 10.4
Num 3.17 − 30   x 3
1 Chr 6.2 − 18   x 2
     15.10
     23 − 24   x 4
     26.23
Uzziel (2)
1 Chr 25.4
Uzziel (3)
2 Chr 29.12
Uzziel (4)
1 Chr 4.42
Uzziel (5)
Neh 3.8
Uzziel (6)
1 Chr 25.9
Uzziel (7)
1 Chr 7.7
Vaizatha
Esth 9.7

Valley Gate
2 Chr 26.9
Neh 2 − 3   x 3
Valley of Craftsmen
Neh 11.35
Valley of Gog's Army
Ezek 39.11 − 15   x 2
Valley of Judgement
Joel 3.2 − 14   x 3
Valley of Slaughter
Jer 7.32
     19.6
Valley of Vision
Is 22.1 − 5   x 2
Valley of Willows
Is 15.7
Vaniah
Ezra 10.34
Vashti
Esth 1 − 2   x 10
Vophsi
Num 13.3
Waheb
Num 21.14
Wandering
Gen 4.16
Water Gate
Neh 3.25
     8.1 − 16   x 2
     12.37
Well of The Living One
Gen 16.14
     24 − 25   x 2
Wells
Num 21.16
Wild Goat Rocks
1 Sam 24.2
Woman
Gen 2.23
Xerxes
Ezra 4.6
Esth 1 − 3   x 10
     7 − 8   x 4
     10.1 − 3   x 2
Dan 9.1
Yiron
Josh 19.38
Zaanan
Mic 1.11
Zaanannim
Josh 19.33
Zaavan
Gen 36.27
1 Chr 1.38
Zabad (1)
1 Chr 2.36
Zabad (2)
1 Chr 7.21
Zabad (3)
1 Chr 11.26
Zabad (4)
2 Chr 24.26
Zabad (5)
Ezra 10.27
Zabad (6)
Ezra 10.33
Zabad (7)
Ezra 10.43
Zabbai (1)
Ezra 10.28
Zabbai (2)
Neh 3.20
Zabdi (1)
Josh 7.1 − 18   x 4

Zabdi (2)
1 Chr 8.19
Zabdi (3)
1 Chr 27.25
Zabdi (4)
Neh 11.17
Zabdiel (1)
1 Chr 27.2
Zabdiel (2)
Neh 11.14
Zabud
1 Kgs 4.5
Zaccai
Ezra 2.3
Neh 7.8
Zacchaeus
Lk 19.2 − 8   x 4
Zaccur (1)
Num 13.3
Zaccur (2)
1 Chr 4.26
Zaccur (3)
1 Chr 24.27
Zaccur (4)
1 Chr 25.2 − 9   x 2
Neh 12.33
Zaccur (5)
Neh 10.9
Zaccur (6)
Ezra 8.2
Zaccur (7)
Neh 3.2
Zaccur (8)
Neh 13.13
Zachariah
Mt 23.35
Zadok (1)
2 Sam 8.17
     15.24 − 35   x 5
     17 − 20   x 5
1 Kgs 1 − 2   x 9
     4.2 − 4   x 2
1 Chr 6.8 − 53   x 2
     15 − 16   x 2
     18.16
     24.3 − 31   x 3
     27.16
     29.22
2 Chr 31.10
Ezra 7.2
Ezek 40.46
     43 − 44   x 2
     48.11
Zadok (2)
1 Chr 6.12
Zadok (3)
1 Chr 9.10
Neh 11.11
Zadok (4)
2 Kgs 15.33
2 Chr 27.1
Zadok (5)
Neh 3.4
Zadok (6)
Neh 3.29
Zadok (7)
Neh 10.14
Zadok (8)
Neh 13.13
Zadok (9)
1 Chr 12.23
Zadok (10)
Mt 1.12
Zaham
2 Chr 11.19

Zair
2 Kgs 8.21
Zalaph
Neh 3.30
Zalmon (1)
Judg 9.48
Ps 68.14
Zalmon (2)
2 Sam 23.24
Zalmonah
Num 33.41
Zalmunna
Judg 8.5 – 21 x 8
Ps 83.11
Zamzummim
Deut 2.20
Zanannim
Judg 4.11
Zanoah (1)
Josh 15.34
1 Chr 4.17
Neh 3.13
11.30
Zanoah (2)
Josh 15.56
Zaphenath Paneah
Gen 41.45
Zaphon
Josh 13.27
Judg 12.1
Zarephath
1 Kgs 17.9 – 10 x 2
Obad .20
Lk 4.26
Zarethan
Josh 3.16
Judg 7.22
1 Kgs 4.12
7.46
Zattu (1)
Ezra 2.3
8.2
10.27
Neh 7.8
Zattu (2)
Neh 10.14
Zaza
1 Chr 2.33
Zebadiah (1)
1 Chr 26.2
Zebadiah (2)
2 Chr 17.8
Zebadiah (3)
2 Chr 19.11
Zebadiah (4)
1 Chr 8.15
Zebadiah (5)
1 Chr 8.17
Zebadiah (6)
1 Chr 12.3
Zebadiah (7)
1 Chr 27.2
Zebadiah (8)
Ezra 8.2
Zebadiah (9)
Ezra 10.20
Zebah
Judg 8.5 – 21 x 8
Ps 83.11
Zebedee
Mt 4.21 x 2
10.2
20.20
26 – 27 x 2
Mk 1.19 – 20 x 2

Zebedee (Cont)
Mk 3.17
10.35
Lk 5.10
Jn 21.2
Zebidah
2 Kgs 23.36
Zebina
Ezra 10.43
Zeboiim
Gen 10.19
14.2 – 8 x 2
Deut 29.23
Hos 11.8
Zeboim (1)
1 Sam 13.18
Zeboim (2)
Neh 11.34
Zebul
Judg 9.28 – 41 x 6
Zebulun
Gen 30.20
35.23
46.14
49.13
Ex 1.3
Num 1 – 2 x 3
7.12
10.16
13.3
26.26
34.19
Deut 27.13
33.18 x 2
Josh 19.10 – 34 x 4
21.7 – 34 x 2
Judg 1.30
4 – 6 x 5
12.11 – 12 x 2
1 Chr 2.1
6.63 – 77 x 2
12.23 – 40 x 2
27.16
2 Chr 30.10 – 18 x 3
Ps 68.27
Is 9.1
Ezek 48.23 – 30 x 2
Mt 4.13 – 15 x 2
Rev 7.5
Zechariah (1)
Lk 1.5 – 67 x 13
3.2
Zechariah (2)
2 Kgs 14 – 15 x 4
Zechariah (3)
Lk 11.51
Zechariah (4)
Ezra 5 – 6 x 2
Neh 12.12
Zech 1.1 – 2 x 2
7 – 8 x 3
Zechariah (5)
2 Kgs 18.2
2 Chr 29.1
Zechariah (6)
Is 8.2
Zechariah (7)
1 Chr 5.7
Zechariah (8)
1 Chr 9.37
Zechariah (9)
1 Chr 27.16
Zechariah (10)
2 Chr 21.2

Zechariah (11)
2 Chr 17.7
Zechariah (12)
2 Chr 26.5
Zechariah (13)
1 Chr 15 – 16 x 2
Zechariah (14)
1 Chr 24.25
Zechariah (15)
1 Chr 9.21
26.2 – 14 x 2
Zechariah (16)
1 Chr 26.11
Zechariah (17)
2 Chr 20.14
Zechariah (18)
2 Chr 29.12
Zechariah (19)
2 Chr 34.12
Zechariah (20)
Neh 12.33
Zechariah (21)
1 Chr 15.25
Zechariah (22)
2 Chr 35.8
Zechariah (23)
2 Chr 24.20 – 22 x 6
Zechariah (24)
Neh 11.12
Zechariah (25)
Ezra 8.2
Zechariah (26)
Ezra 8.16
Zechariah (27)
Neh 8.4
Zechariah (28)
Ezra 8.2
Zechariah (29)
Ezra 10.26
Zechariah (30)
Neh 11.4
Zechariah (31)
Neh 11.5
Zechariah (32)
Neh 12.41
Zecher
1 Chr 8.31
Zedad
Num 34.8
Ezek 47.15
Zedekiah (1)
2 Kgs 24 – 25 x 10
1 Chr 3.15
2 Chr 36.10 – 13 x 3
Jer 1.3
21.1 – 4 x 3
24.8
27 – 29 x 5
32.1 – 5 x 4
34.2 – 21 x 5
37 – 39 x 18
44.30
49.34
51 – 52 x 13
Zedekiah (2)
1 Kgs 22.11 – 24 x 2
2 Chr 18.10 – 23 x 2
Zedekiah (3)
Jer 29.21 – 22 x 2
Zedekiah (4)
Jer 36.12
Zedekiah (5)
Neh 10.1
Zedekiah (6)
1 Chr 3.16

Zeeb
Judg 7 – 8 x 3
Ps 83.11
Zela
Josh 18.28
2 Sam 21.14
Zelek
2 Sam 23.24
1 Chr 11.26
Zelophehad
Num 26 – 27 x 3
36.2 – 10 x 4
Josh 17.3
1 Chr 7.15
Zelzah
1 Sam 10.2
Zemaraim (1)
Josh 18.22
Zemaraim (2)
2 Chr 13.4
Zemarites
Gen 10.18
1 Chr 1.16
Zemirah
1 Chr 7.8
Zenan
Josh 15.37
Zenas
Tit 3.13
Zephaniah (1)
2 Kgs 25.18
Jer 21.1
29.24 – 29 x 3
37.3
52.24
Zephaniah (2)
Zeph 1.1 x 2
Zephaniah (3)
Zech 6.10
Zephaniah (4)
1 Chr 6.36
Zephath
Judg 1.17
Zephathah
2 Chr 14.10
Zephi
1 Chr 1.36
Zepho
Gen 36.10 – 15 x 2
Zephon
Gen 46.16
Num 26.15
Zer
Josh 19.35
Zerah (1)
Gen 38.30
46.12
Num 26.19
Josh 7.1 – 17 x 3
22.20
1 Chr 2.4 – 7 x 3
9.4
27.2 x 2
Neh 11.24
Mt 1.2
Zerah (2)
Gen 36.10 – 17 x 2
1 Chr 1.37
Zerah (3)
Gen 36.31
1 Chr 1.43
Zerah (4)
Num 26.13
1 Chr 4.24

Zophar (Cont)
Job   27.12
       42.9
Zophim
Num   23.14
Zorah
Josh 15.33
      19.41
Judg 13.2 – 25   x 2
      16.31
      18.2 – 11   x 3

Zorah (Cont)
1 Chr 2.53 – 54   x 2
       4.2
2 Chr 11.10
Neh   11.29
Zuar
Num   1 – 2   x 2
       7.12
       10.15
Zuph (1)
1 Sam 1.1

Zuph (1) (Cont)
1 Chr 6.35
Zuph (2)
1 Sam 9.5
Zur (1)
Num   25.15
       31.8
Josh   13.21
Zur (2)
1 Chr 8 – 9   x 2

Zuriel
Num   3.35
Zurishaddai
Num   1 – 2   x 2
      7.12
      10.19
Zuzim
Gen   14.5
Num   10.19
Zuzim
Gen   14.5

Well-known passages of the Bible

Old Testament stories and events

Creation	Gen 1.1—2.4
The Garden of Eden	Gen 2.4—25
Man's disobedience	Gen 3
Cain and Abel	Gen 4
Noah and the flood	Gen 6—8
The Tower of Babel (Babylon)	Gen 11.1—9
God's call to Abraham	Gen 12
Abraham and Melchizedek	Gen 14.17—20
Hagar and Ishmael	Gen 16
Destruction of Sodom and Gomorrah	Gen 19
Birth of Isaac	Gen 21.1—8
"Sacrifice" of Isaac	Gen 22
Jacob and Esau	Gen 25.19—34
Jacob's dream	Gen 28.10—22
Joseph and his brothers	Gen 37
Joseph in prison	Gen 39—40
Pharaoh's dream	Gen 41
Moses and the princess of Egypt	Ex 2.1—10
Moses and the burning bush	Ex 3
Plagues of Egypt	Ex 7—12
Crossing the Red Sea	Ex 14
Water from the rock	Ex 17.1—7;
	Num 20.1—13
The Ten Commandments	Ex 20.1—17;
	Deut 5.6—21
Aaron and the gold bull	Ex 32
Balaam and his donkey	Num 22—24
Death of Moses	Deut 34
Rahab and the spies	Josh 2
Crossing of the Jordan	Josh 3
Fall of Jericho	Josh 6.36—40
Deborah and Barak	Judg 4
Gideon's fleece	Judg 6.36—40
Gideon's army	Judg 7—8
Birth of Samson	Judg 13
Samson and Delilah	Judg 16.4—22
Samson's last victory	Judg 16.23—31
Birth of Samuel	1 Sam 1
Samuel and Eli	1 Sam 3
David anointed King	1 Sam 16.1—13
David and Goliath	1 Sam 17
David and Jonathan	1 Sam 18—20
Saul and the "witch" at Endor	1 Sam 28.3—25
David and Bathsheba	2 Sam 11
Solomon the wise judge	1 Kgs 3.16—28
Building the Temple	1 Kgs 6
Solomon and the Queen of Sheba	1 Kgs 10.1—13;
	2 Chr 9.1—12
Elijah and the drought	1 Kgs 17.1—7
Elijah and the widow in Zarephath	1 Kgs 17.8—24
Elijah and the prophets of Baal	1 Kgs 18
Elijah and the voice of God	1 Kgs 19.1—18
Naboth's vineyard	1 Kgs 21
Elijah and the chariot of fire	2 Kgs 2.1—12
Elisha and the woman from Shunem	2 Kgs 4.8—37
Naaman's cure	2 Kgs 5
Seige of Samaria	2 Kgs 6.24—7.20
Joash the boy king	2 Kgs 12; 2 Chr 24
Fall of Samaria	2 Kgs 17.5—23
Seige of Jerusalem by the Assyrians	2 Kgs 18.13—19.37;
	2 Chr 32.1—23;
	Is 36—37
Fall of Jerusalem to Babylon	2 Kgs 25.1—21;
	2 Chr 36.13—21
Jerusalem's walls rebuilt	Neh 3—6
Ezra reads the Law	Neh 8
Call of Isaiah	Is 6
Isaiah's message to the king	Is 37
Jeremiah at the potter's house	Jer 18.1—12
Jeremiah buys a field	Jer 32
Jeremiah's scroll	Jer 36
Jeremiah's escape from the well	Jer 38.1—13
Ezekiel's vision of God	Ezek 1
Ezekiel and the valley of dry bones	Ezek 37.1—14
Ezekiel's vision of the Temple	Ezek 40—44; 47
Nebuchadnezzar's dream	Dan 2
The blazing furnace	Dan 3
Belshazzar's banquet	Dan 5
Daniel in the pit of lions	Dan 6

Well-known Bible poems and prophecies

Jacob's last words	Gen 49
Song of Moses after crossing the Red Sea	Ex 15.1—18
Song of Moses	Deut 32
Moses blesses the tribes	Deut 33
Song of Deborah and Barak	Judg 5
David's lament for Saul and Jonathan	2 Sam 1.17—27
David's song of victory	2 Sam 22; Ps 18
David's last words	2 Sam 23.1—7
Job rests his case with God	Job 19.23—27
In praise of wisdom	Job 28
The power of God	Job 36—37
God speaks out of the storm	Job 38—41
True happiness	Ps 1
"What is man?"	Ps 8
God's glory in creation	Ps 19
"The Lord is my shepherd"	Ps 23
A royal wedding song	Ps 45
"God is with us"	Ps 46
A prayer for forgiveness — "Create a pure heart in me, O God"	Ps 51
"O God, you are my God"	Ps 63
"God, be merciful to us" (Deus Misereatur)	Ps 67
"The Lord is your defender"	Ps 91
"The Lord is king"	Ps 93
"The Lord is a mighty God" (Venite)	Ps 95
A new song (Cantate Domino)	Ps 98
"We are his people" (Jubilate)	Ps 100
In praise of the Creator	Ps 104
"In their trouble they called to the Lord"	Ps 107
The Law of the Lord	Ps 119
Help from the Lord	Ps 121
In praise of Jerusalem	Ps 122
"If the Lord does not build the house"	Ps 127
"Give thanks to the Lord, because he is good; his love is eternal"	Ps 136
"By the rivers of Babylon"	Ps 137
"Lord . . . you know me"	Ps 139
"Praise God in his Temple!"	Ps 150
In praise of wisdom	Prov 8
A time for everything	Ecc 3.1—15
Everlasting peace	Is 2.1—4;
	Micah 4.1—4
Song of the vineyard	Is 5.1—7
The future king: "The people who walked in darkness"	Is 9.2—7
The peaceful kingdom: "Calves and lion cubs will feed together"	Is 11.1—9
"The desert will rejoice"	Is 35
"The glory of the Lord will be revealed"	Is 40
The Lord's servant	Is 42.1—7
The clay and the potter	Is 45
"A light to the nations"	Is 49.1—7
The suffering servant	Is 52.13—53.12
"Come, everyone who is thirsty"	Is 55
Jerusalem, city of God	Is 60
"Good news to the poor"	Is 61
"Your king is coming"	Zech 9.9—10
Mary's song of praise (Magnificat)	Lk 1.46—55
Zechariah's prophecy (Benedictus)	Lk 1.68—79
Simeon's thanksgiving (Nunc Dimittis)	Lk 2.29—32
An early Christian hymn	Phil 2.6—11

New Testament stories and events

Birth of John the Baptist	Lk 1.5—25, 57—66
Birth of Jesus	Mt 1.18—25;
	Lk 2.1—20
Wise men from the East	Mt 2.1—12
Escape to Egypt	Mt 2.13—15
Slaughter at Bethlehem	Mt 2.16—18

The boy Jesus in the Temple	Lk 2.41–51
Preaching of John the Baptist	Mt 3.1–12;
	Mk 1.1–18;
	Lk 3.1–18;
	Jn 1.19–28
Baptism of Jesus	Mt 3.13–17;
	Mk 1.9–11;
	Lk 3.21–22
Temptation of Jesus	Mt 4.1–11;
	Mk 1.12–13;
	Lk 4.1–13
Jesus calls out the twelve	Mt 10.1–4;
	Mk 3.13–19;
	Lk 6.12–16
Death of John the Baptist	Mt 14.1–12;
	Mk 6.14–29;
	Lk 9.7–9
Peter's declaration	Mt 16.13–20;
	Mk 8.27–30;
	Lk 9.18–21
The transfiguration	Mt 17.1–8;
	Mk 9.2–8;
	Lk 9.28–36
Jesus and the rich young man	Mt 19.16–30;
	Mk 10.17–31;
	Lk 18.18–30
Jesus visits Martha and Mary	Lk 10.38–42
Jesus and Zacchaeus	Lk 19.1–10
The widow's offering	Mk 12.41–44;
	Lk 21.1–4
The Word of life	Jn 1.1–18
The Lamb of God	Jn 1.29–34
The wedding in Cana	Jn 2.1–12
Jesus and Nicodemus (the new birth)	Jn 3
Jesus and the Samaritan woman (the woman at the well)	Jn 4
Death of Lazarus	Jn 11
Entry into Jerusalem	Mt 21.1–11;
	Mk 11.1–11;
	Lk 19.28–40;
	Jn 12.12–19
Jesus and the moneychangers	Mt 21.12–17;
	Mk 11.15–19;
	Lk 19.45–48;
	Jn 2.13–22
Anointing of Jesus	Mt 26.6–13;
	Mk 14.3–9;
	Jn 12.1–18
The last supper	Mt 26.26–30;
	Mk 14.22–26;
	Lk 22.14–23;
	1 Cor 11.23–25
Jesus in Gethsemane	Mt 26.36–46;
	Mk 14.32–42;
	Lk 22.39–46
The arrest of Jesus	Mt 26.47–56;
	Mk 14.43–52;
	Lk 22.47–53;
	Jn 18.1–11
Jesus before Pilate	Mt 27.11–26;
	Mk 15.1–15;
	Lk 23.1–5, 13–25;
	Jn 18.28–19.16
Death of Jesus	Mt 27.32–61;
	Mk 15.21–47;
	Lk 23.26–56;
	Jn 19.17–42
Jesus' resurrection	Mt 28.1–10;
	Mk 16.1–8;
	Lk 24.1–12;
	Jn 20.1–10
The walk to Emmaus	Lk 24.13–35
Jesus and Thomas	Jn 20.24–29
Jesus and Peter	Jn 21
"Go then, to all peoples" – the "great commission"	Mt 28.16–20
The "ascension"	Lk 24.50–53;
	Acts 1.6–11

The coming of the Holy Spirit – birth of the church	Acts 2.1–13
Peter's message	Acts 2.14–42
Ananias and Sapphira	Acts 5.1–11
The story of Stephen	Acts 6–7
Philip and the Ethiopian	Acts 8.26–40
Conversion of Saul (Paul)	Acts 9.1–19
Peter and Cornelius	Acts 10
Peter's rescue from prison	Acts 12.1–19
Paul and Barnabas commissioned	Acts 13.1–3
Jerusalem council	Acts 15
Paul at Athens	Acts 17.16–34
Paul's arrest and defence	Acts 21.27–26.32
Paul's shipwreck	Acts 27
Paul in Rome	Acts 28.16–31

Well-known passages in the Letters and Revelation

Peace with God	Rom 5
Life in God's service	Rom 12
Love	1 Cor 13
Resurrection	1 Cor 15
The one gospel	Gal 1.6–9
Fruits of the Spirit	Gal 5.22–23
Christian unity	Eph 4.1–16
The whole armour of God	Eph 6.10–17
Faith	Heb 11
God is light	1 Jn 1.5–7
God is love	1 Jn 4.7–21
The throne of God	Rev 4
The final judgement	Rev 20.11–15
The new heaven and the new earth	Rev 21

Well-known words of Jesus

"The scripture says, 'Man cannot live on bread alone' "	Mt 4.4; Lk 4.4
The Sermon on the Mount	Mt 5–7
"Beatitudes" – "happy are those . . ."	Mt 5.3–12; Lk 6.20–23
"You are like salt"	Mt 5.13
"You are like light"; "your light must shine"	Mt 5.14–16
"If anyone slaps you on the right cheek"	Mt 5.39; Lk 6.29
"Love your enemies"	Mt 5.44; Lk 6.27–28
The Lord's prayer	Mt 6.5–15; Lk 11.1–4
Riches in heaven	Mt 6.19–21; Lk 12.32–34
God and money	Mt 6.24; Lk 16.13
Why worry? "Look how the wild flowers grow"	Mt 6.25–34; Lk 12.22–31
Judging others	Mt 7.1–5; Lk 6.37–38, 41–42
Ask, seek, knock	Mt 7.7–11; Lk 11.9–13
The "golden rule"	Mt 7.12; Lk 6.31
The narrow gate	Mt 7.13–14
"I never knew you"	Mt 7.21–23
"Foxes have holes, and birds have nests . . ."	Mt 8.20; Lk 9.58
New wine, fresh wineskins	Mt 9.17; Mt 2.22; Lk 5.37–38
No pupil is greater than his teacher	Mt 10.24
Sparrows two a penny	Mt 10.29–31; Lk 12.6–7
"I did not come to bring peace but a sword"	Mt 10.34
"Whoever tries to gain his own life will lose it"	Mt 10.39; 16.25; Mk 8.35; Lk 9.24
"Come to me . . . Take my yoke . . . and you will find rest"	Mt 11.28–30
"The Son of Man is Lord of the Sabbath"	Mt 12.8; Mk 2.28; Lk 6.5
"The mouth speaks what the heart is full of "	Mt 12.34, 15.17–20; Mk 7.18–23; Lk 6.45

Blind leaders of the blind	Mt 15.14; Lk 6.39
"Peter: you are a rock, and on this rock foundation I will build my church"	Mt 16.18
"The keys of the Kingdom"	Mt 16.19
"Faith as big as a mustard seed"	Mt 17.20
Who is the greatest?	Mt 18.1–5; Mk 9.33–37; Lk 9.46–48
"Where two or three come together in my name, I am there with them"	Mt 18.20
"Let the children come to me"	Mt 19.14; Mk 10.14; Lk 18.16
"First will be last"	Mt 19.30; 20.1–16
The Son of Man who came to serve	Mt 20.28; Mk 10.45
"Many are invited, but few are chosen"	Mt 22.14
"Pay the Emperor what belongs to the Emperor, and pay God what belongs to God"	Mt 22.21; Mk 12.17; Lk 20.25
"Love your neighbour"	Mt 22.34–40; Mk 12.28–34; Lk 10.25–28
"Jerusalem! Jerusalem!"	Mt 23.37–39; Lk 13.34–35
"This is my body . . . this is my blood"	Mt 26.26–29; Mk 14.22–25; Lk 22.17–20; 1 Cor 11.23–25
"I will be with you always"	Mt 28.20

"People who are well do not need a doctor"	Mt 9.12; Mk 2.17; Lk 5.31
"God loved the world so much that he gave his only Son"	Jn 3.16
"I am the bread of life"	Jn 6.35
"I am the light of the world"	Jn 8.12
"If the Son sets you free, then you will be really free"	Jn 8.36
"I am the gate. Whoever comes in by me will be saved"	Jn 10.9
"I am the good shepherd"	Jn 10.11
"I am the resurrection and the life"	Jn 11.25
"Love one another"	Jn 13.34; 15.12–17
"In my Father's house"	Jn 14.2
"I am the way, the truth, and the life"	Jn 14.6
"Peace is what I leave with you"	Jn 14.27
"I am the vine, and you are the branches"	Jn 15.1, 5

Jesus' words from the cross:

"My God, my God, why did you abandon me?"	Mt 27.46; Mk 15.34
"Forgive them, Father!"	Lk 23.34
"Today you will be in Paradise with me"	Lk 23.43
"Father! In your hands I place my spirit!"	Lk 23.46
"He is your son . . . she is your mother"	Jn 19.26–27
"I am thirsty"	Jn 19.28
"It is finished!"	Jn 19.30

Parables of Jesus

	Matthew	Mark	Luke
Lamp under a bowl	5.14–15	4.21–22	8.16; 11.33
Houses on rock and on sand	7.24–27		6.47–49
New cloth on an old coat	9.16	2.21	5.36
New wine in used wineskins	9.17	2.22	5.37–38
Sower and soils	13.3–8	4.3–8	8.5–8
Mustard seed	13.31–32	4.30–32	13.18–19
Weeds	13.24–30		
Yeast	13.33		13.20–21
Hidden treasure	13.44		
Pearl	13.45–46		
Net	13.47–48		
Lost sheep	18.12–13		15.4–6
Unforgiving servant	18.23–34		
Workers in the vineyard	20.1–16		
Two sons	21.28–31		
Tenants	21.33–41	12.1–9	20.9–16
Wedding feast; a man without wedding clothes	22.2–14		
Lesson of the fig tree	24.32–33	13.28–29	21.29–32
Ten girls	25.1–13		
Silver coins (Matthew); gold coins (Luke)	25.14–30		19.12–27
Sheep and goats	25.31–36		
Growing seed		4.26–29	
Two debtors			7.41–43
Good Samaritan			10.30–37
Friend in need			11.5–8
Rich fool			12.16–21
Watchful servants			12.35–40
Faithful servant			12.42–48
Unfruitful fig-tree			13.6–9
Best places at a wedding feast			14.7–14
The great feast and the reluctant guests			14.16–24
Counting the cost			14.28–33
Lost coin			15.8–10
Lost son			15.11–32
Shrewd manager			16.1–8
Rich man and Lazarus			16.19–31
The master and his servant			17.7–10
The widow and the judge			18.2–5
Pharisee and tax collector			18.10–14

Miracles of Jesus

	Matthew	Mark	Luke	John
Healing				
Man with a skin disease	8.2−3	1.40−42	5.12−13	
Roman officer's servant	8.5−13		7.1−10	
Peter's mother-in-law	8.14−15	1.30−31	4.38−39	
Man (Matthew: two men) from Gadara	8.28−34	5.1−15	8.27−35	
Paralysed man	9.2−7	2.3−12	5.18−25	
Woman with a haemorrhage	9.20−22	5.25−29	8.43−48	
Two blind men	9.27−31			
Man dumb and possessed	9.32−33			
Man with a paralysed hand	12.10−13	3.1−5	6.6−10	
Man blind, dumb, and possessed	12.22		11.14	
Canaanite woman's daughter	15.21−28	7.24−30		
Boy with epilepsy	17.14−18	9.17−29	9.38−43	
Bartimaeus (blind man/men)	20.29−34	10.46−52	18.35−43	
Deaf mute		7.31−37		
Man possessed, synagogue		1.23−26	4.33−35	
Blind man at Bethsaida		8.22−26		
Crippled woman			13.11−13	
Man with swollen limbs			14.1−4	
Ten men with skin disease			17.11−19	
The High Priest's slave			22.50−51	
Official's son at Capernaum				4.46−54
Sick man, Pool of Bethzatha				5.1−9
Man born blind				9
Command over the forces of nature				
Calming of the storm	8.23−27	4.37−41	8.22−25	
Walking on the water	14.25	6.48−51		6.19−21
5,000 people fed	14.15−21	6.35−44	9.12−17	6.5−13
4,000 people fed	15.32−38	8.1−9		
Coin in the fish's mouth	17.24−27			
Fig-tree withered	21.18−22	11.12−14		
Catch of fish		11.20−25	5.1−11	
Water turned into wine				2.1−11
Another catch of fish				21.1−11
Bringing the dead back to life				
Jairus' (Matthew: a Jewish official's daughter)	9.18−19 9.23−25	5.22−34 5.38−42	8.41−42 8.49−56	
Widow's son at Nain			7.11−15	
Lazarus				11.1−44

Word Index

This index is a complete list of all the words and word-pairs included in *The GNB Topical Concordance*. It is therefore a key to the whole book.

Each word is listed alphabetically in bold type. It is followed by an alphabetical list of all the words it is paired with. So, for example, if you look up **ABANDON** you will see that the Concordance includes references for **Abandon** and **Anger**, **Abandon** and **Darkness**, and so on.

For some word-pairs there is a cross-reference, e.g. for **Abandon** and **Anger** it says **see Anger — Abandon**. This simply tells you that the verses containing that word-pair are listed under the main heading **Anger** in the Concordance, rather than **Abandon**.

Words of similar meaning are often grouped together — see **How to use the Topical Concordance** for examples. So for **Abandon** and **Lord**, the Word Index refers you to **Abandon — God**, where the two sets of verses are combined.

ABANDON
  Anger see Anger — Abandon
  Darkness
  Destroy see Destroy — Abandon
  Enemies
  Faith see Faith — Abandon
  Faithful
  God
  God's People
    see God's People — Abandon
  Lord see Abandon — God
  Obey see Obey — Abandon
  Temple
  World of the Dead
    see W of D — Abandon
  Worship
    see Worship — Unfaithful
ABOVE
  Heaven see Heaven — Above
ACCEPT
  Believe see Accept — Faith
  Bribe see Bribe — Accept
  Faith
  Gift
  God's People
  Life see Life — Faith
  Message see Accept — Word
  Offering
  Please see Please — Accept
  Prayer
  Righteous
  Sacrifice
    see Accept — Offering
  Teaching see Accept — Word
  True
  Word
ACCUSE
  Crime see Accuse — Sin
  Defend
  Evil see Accuse — Sin
  False
  God
  God's People
  Jesus
  Jews
  Lord see Accuse — God
  Sin

ACKNOWLEDGE
  God
  Jesus
  Lord see Acknowledge — God
  Power
ACTION
  Disgusting
  Evil see Action — Sinful
  Faith see Faith — Action
  Foolish see Foolish — Act
  God
  Lord see Action — God
  Mighty
  Sinful
  Wicked see Action — Sinful
  Wonderful see Action — Mighty
ADULTERY
  Commit
  Prostitute
ADVANTAGE
  Poor see Poor — Needy
  Widows
    see Widows — Advantage
ADVICE
  Wisdom see Wisdom — Advice
AFRAID
  Believe see Afraid — Trust
  Confident see Afraid — Courage
  Courage
  Danger see Danger — Afraid
  Destroy see Destroy — Afraid
  Determined
    see Afraid — Courage
  Disciple see Disciple — Afraid
  Enemy see Enemy — Afraid
  Evil see Afraid — Sin
  Fear see Fear — Afraid
  God's People
    see God's People — Afraid
  Help
  Jews
  Obey see Obey — Fear
  Power see Power — Fear
  Protect see Afraid — Help
  Punishment
    see Punishment — Fear
  Rescue see Afraid — Save

AFRAID (Cont.)
  Save
  Sin
  Suffer
  Terrify see Terrify — Afraid
  Tremble see Tremble — Fear
  Trust
  Victory
ALIVE
  Dead see Dead — Alive
  Death see Death — Alive
  World of the Dead
    see World of the Dead — Alive
ALONE
  Pray see Pray — Alone
ALTAR
  Ashes
  Blood see Altar — Offering
  Consecrate
    see Altar — Dedicate
  Dedicate
  Destroy see Destroy — Altars
  Gift see Altar — Offering
  Holy see Altar — Dedicate
  Incense see Incense — Altar
  Lamb see Altar — Offering
  Offering
  Pagan see Pagan — Altars
  Place of Worship
    see Place of Worship — Altar
  Present see Altar — Offering
  Priests see Priests — Altar
  Purify see Altar — Dedicate
  Ram see Altar — Offering
  Sacrifice see Altar — Offering
  Serve
  Sheep see Altar — Offering
  Sprinkle
  Tent
  Worship
AMAZED
  Disciple see Disciple — Amazed
  Teach see Teach — Amazed
ANGEL
  Announce
  Church
  Command

BELIEVE (Cont.)
  Spirit of God
    see Spirit of God — Believe
  Teach see Believe — Preach
  Truth see Truth — Believe
  Turn see Turn — Believe
  Word see Believe — Message
  World see World — Faith
BELIEVERS
  Apostles
    see Apostles — Believers
  Help see Help — God's People
  Love see Love — God's People
  Teach see Teach — God's People
BEST
  Offer see Offer — Best
  Sheep see Sheep — Offer
BETRAY
  Disciple see Disciple — Betray
BIRTH
  Pain see Pain — Birth
BITTER
  Anger see Anger — Bitter
  Curse see Curse — Bitter
  Mourn see Mourn — Bitterly
  Weep see Weep — Bitterly
BLESS
  Care see Bless — Love
  Choose see Choose — Blessing
  Christ
  Curse
  Gentiles
    see Gentiles — Blessings
  God
  God's People
    see God's People — Bless
  Happy
  Harvest see Harvest — Bless
  Honour
  Jesus see Bless — Christ
  Joyful see Bless — Happy
  Kindness see Bless — Love
  Life
  Lord
  Love
  Name see Bless — Lord
  Obey
  Offer
  Peace
  Praise
  Pray
  Priests see Priests — Bless
  Promise
  Prosper see Bless — Obey
  Rich
  Right see Bless — Obey
  Sacrifice see Bless — Offer
  Share see Share — Blessings
  Words
  World see World — Blessing
BLIND
  Crippled
  Cure see Blind — Sight
  Darkness
  Poor
  Sight
  Sin
BLOOD
  Altar see Altar — Offering
  Body see Blood — Flesh
  Christ see Christ — Death
  Covenant see Covenant — Blood
  Enemy see Enemy — Death
  Flesh

BLOOD (Cont.)
  God's People
    see God's People — Blood
  High Priest see Blood — Priest
  Lamb see Blood — Offer
  Life
  Offer
  Priest
  Pure see Pure — Blood
  Sacrifice see Blood — Offer
  Sheep see Blood — Offer
  Sin
  Sprinkle
  Turn see Turn — Blood
BOAST
  Pride see Pride — Arrogant
BODY
  Blood see Blood — Flesh
  Bread see Bread — Body
  Christ see Christ — Body
  Church see Christ — Body
  Dead
  Destroy see Body — Dead
  Grave
  Hang
  Heavenly
  Hell
  Jesus
  Life
  Love
  Mortal see Mortal — Body
  Raise see Body — Life
  Sin
  Spirit
  Spirit of God
  Tomb see Body — Grave
BOLD
  Message see Message — Proclaim
BOW
  Anger see Anger — Worship
  Gods
  Holy see Holy — Worship
  Idols see Bow — Gods
  Obey see Obey — Worship
  Offer see Offer — Worship
  Praise see Bow — Worship
  Respect see Respect — Bow
  Temple see Bow — Worship
  Worship
BREAD
  Body
  Cup
  Harvest see Harvest — Bread
  Heaven
  I Am see I Am — Bread
  Life
  Offer
  Present see Bread — Offer
  Sacred
  Thanks
  Unleavened
  Without Yeast
    see Bread — Unleavened
  Yeast see Yeast — Bread
BRIBE
  Accept
BRIGHTNESS
  Turn see Turn — Darkness
BRING
  Good News
    see Good News — Proclaim
BROTHER
  Love see Love — God's People

BURDEN
  Sin
CAPTIVES
  Free see Free — Prisoners
CARE
  Bless see Bless — Love
  Flock
  God
  Lord
  Protect see Protect — Love
  Safety see Safety — Protect
  Save see Save — Care
  Sheep see Care — Flock
  Shepherd see Care — Flock
CASE
  Argue see Case — Present
  Court see Judge — Case
  Judge see Judge — Case
  Law see Law — Judge
  Present
CAUSE
  Defend see Defend — Cause
CELEBRATE
  Festival
  Happy see Happy — Celebrate
  Honour
    see Celebrate — Festival
  Joy see Joy — Celebrate
  Passover
    see Celebrate — Festival
  Shelters
    see Celebrate — Festival
  Unleavened Bread
    see Celebrate — Festival
CEREMONY
  Pure see Pure — Ceremony
CHANGE
  Law see Law — Change
  Life see Life — Change
  Mind see Mind — Change
  Ways see Ways — Turn
CHEAT
  False see False — Deceive
  Poor
CHEER
  Encourage
    see Encourage — Cheer
CHIEF PRIESTS
  Arrest
  Council
  Elders
  Jesus
  Pharisees
  Teachers of the Law
CHILD OF GOD
  Father
  Love see Love — God's People
  Spirit of God
    see Sp of God — God's People
CHILDREN
  Jesus see Jesus — Children
  Love see Love — Children
CHOOSE
  Apostles see Apostles — Choose
  Blessing
  Evil
  Father see Choose — God
  God
  God's People
    see God's People — Chosen
  Good News
  Grace see Choose — Love
  Jesus
  Life

CHOOSE (Cont.)
Lord
Lot see Lot — Choose
Love
Priests
Reject see Reject — Choose
Remember
    see Remember — Choose
Right
Save see Save — Choose
Servant see Servant — Chosen
Son of God see Choose — Jesus
CHRIST
Apostles see Apostles — Jesus
Baptize see Baptize — Christ
Being see Being — Jesus
Believe see Believe — Jesus
Bless see Bless — Christ
Blood see Christ — Death
Body
Church see Christ — Body
Cross see Christ — Death
Day see Day — Jesus
Death
Enemy see Enemy — Christ
Faith see Faith — Jesus
Father see Christ — God
Forgive see Forgive — Jesus
Free see Free — Christ
Friend see Friend — Jesus
Glory see Glory — Jesus
God
Good News
    see Good News — Jesus
Gospel see Good News — Jesus
Grace see Grace — Jesus
Heart see Heart — Jesus
Hope see Hope — Jesus
Human
Judge see Judge — Jesus
Kingdom see Kingdom — Christ
Lamb see Lamb — Christ
Law see Law — Christ
Life see Life — Christ
Lord
Love see Love — Christ
Message see Message — Christ
Obey see Obey — Christ
Offer
Peace see Peace — Christ
Power see Power — Christ
Preach
Presence see Presence — Christ
Prison see Prison — Christ
Proclaim see Christ — Preach
Promise see Promise — Christ
Pure
Raise see Raise — Christ
Real
Right see Right — Christ
Right with God
    see Right — Christ
Righteous see Right — Christ
Rise see Raise — Christ
Sacrifice see Christ — Offer
Sake
Save see Save — Christ
Secret see Secret — Christ
Servant see Servant — Christ
Serve see Serve — Christ
Share see Share — Christ
Sin
Slave see Slave — Christ

CHRIST (Cont.)
Son of God
    see Son of God — Christ
Spirit of God
    see Spirit of God — Christ
Spirits see Spirit(s) — Christ
Spiritual
    see Spiritual — Christ
Strength see Strength — Christ
Suffering
    see Suffering — Christ
Teach see Teach — Christ
Truth see Truth — Christ
Understanding
    see Understanding — Christ
Union see Union — Christ
CHRISTIAN
Love see Love — God's People
CHURCH
Angel see Angel — Church
Body see Christ — Body
Christ
Elders see Elders — Church
God
Help see Help — God's People
Jesus see Church — Christ
Life see Life — God's People
Persecution
    see Persecution — Church
Spirit of God
    see Spirit of God — Churches
Suffering
    see Suffering — God's People
Teach see Teach — God's People
CIRCUMCISE
Covenant
Gentiles
Jews
Law
Obey see Circumcise — Law
CITY
Refuge see Refuge — City
CLAIM
Lie see Lie — False
Word see Word — False
Worship see Worship — Claim
CLEAN
Disease see Disease — Heal
Priests see Priests — Pure
Pure see Pure — Holy
Sin
Unclean
CLEAR
Conscience
    see Conscience — Clear
CLOUD
Dark
Heaven
Power see Cloud — Heaven
Son of Man
    see Cloud — Heaven
Tent see Tent — Presence
COMFORT
God
God's People
    see God's People — Protect
Lord see Comfort — God
Love see Love — Help
Mourn see Mourn — Comfort
COMMAND
Angel see Angel — Command
Covenant
    see Covenant — Command
Create see Create — Command
Desire

COMMAND (Cont.)
Disobey
Faithful see Faithful — Obey
Father see Command — God
Follow see Obey — Command
Forget
    see Command — Remember
God
Happy see Happy — Obey
Heart see Heart — Obey
Honour
    see Honour — Command
Jesus
Just
Keep see Obey — Command
Law see Law — Command
Life see Life — Law
Lord
Love see Love — Command
Name see Name — Power
New
Obey see Obey — Command
Observe
Offerings
    see Command — Sacrifice
Promise see Promise — Law
Rebel see Command — Disobey
Refuse see Command — Disobey
Reject see Command — Disobey
Remember
Rest see Command — Sabbath
Right see Command — Just
Sabbath
Sacrifice
Teach see Teach — Law
Temple see Temple — Command
Turn
Understanding
    see Understanding — Laws
Warn see Warn — Command
Will see Will — Command
Worship see Worship — Law
COMMANDMENT
God
Important
Keep see Obey — Command
Lord see Commandment — God
Obey see Obey — Command
Sin
Tablet
    see Tablet — Commandment
COMMIT
Adultery see Adultery — Commit
Crime see Crime — Commit
COMPASSION
Lord
Love see Love — Mercy
Mercy see Mercy — Compassion
COMPLAIN
Trouble see Trouble — Complain
CONCEITED
Pride see Pride — Arrogant
CONDEMN
Destruction
Evil see Condemn — Sin
God
Jesus
Judge see Judge — Condemn
Lord see Condemn — God
    and Condemn — Jesus
Righteous
Sin
Wicked see Condemn — Sin
Word see Word — Condemn

CONFESS
God
Jesus
Lord
Pray see Pray — Repent
Sin

CONFIDENT
Afraid see Afraid — Courage
Determined
  see Determined — Confident

CONQUER
Enemy see Enemy — Victory

CONSCIENCE
Clear

CONSECRATE
Altar see Altar — Dedicate
Anoint see Anoint — Consecrate
Levites see Levites — Dedicate
Priests
  see Priests — Consecrate
Temple see Temple — Dedicate

CONSTANT
Love see Love — Constant

CONSULT
Fortune-teller
  see Consult — Medium
Gods
Idols see Consult — Gods
Medium
Prophet
Spirits
  see Spirit(s) — Consult

CONTRIBUTION
Levites see Levites — Offer
Priests see Priests — Gift
Special see Special — Offering
Temple see Temple — Offering

CONTROL
God
Human
Life
Lord see Control — God
Spirit of God

CONVINCE
Prophets
  see Prophets — Believe

CORRECT
Punishment
  see Punishment — Correct
Teach see Teach — Right
Wisdom see Wisdom — Correct

CORRUPT
Judge see Judge — Corrupt

COUNCIL
Chief Priests
  see Chief Priests — Council

COURAGE
Afraid see Afraid — Courage
Fail
God
Lord see Courage — God

COURT
Case see Judge — Case
Judge see Judge — Case
Justice see Justice — Court

COVENANT
Blood
Circumcise
  see Circumcise — Covenant
Command
Eternal
Everlasting
  see Covenant — Eternal

COVENANT (Cont.)
Faithful
  see Faithful — Covenant
Forget
  see Covenant — Remember
God
God's People
  see God's People — Promise
Honour see Honour — Promise
Jesus
Keep see Covenant — Obey
Last see Covenant — Eternal
Lord see Covenant — God
Love see Love — Promise
New see New — Covenant
Obey
Priests
Promise
Remember
Sacrifice see Covenant — Blood
Seal see Covenant — Blood
Servant see Servant — Promise
Sign
Tablet see Tablet — Covenant

COVENANT BOX
Holy Place
  see Covenant Box — Tent
Levites
Priests
Sacred
Tablet
  see Tablet — Covenant Box
Temple
Tent

CREATE
Being
Command
God
Heaven see Heaven — Create
Life
Lord see Create — God
New
Universe see Create — World
World

CREATURES
Elders
Holy Place
  see Holy Place — Creatures
Human
Praise
Throne

CRIME
Accuse see Accuse — Sin
Commit
Death see Death — Sin
Evil see Crime — Sin
Punish
Sin

CRIPPLED
Blind see Blind — Crippled

CROSS
Christ see Cross — Jesus
Death see Cross — Jesus
Disciple see Disciple — Cross
Jesus
Power see Power — Death

CROWN
Glory
Thorns

CRUEL
Enemy see Enemy — Cruel
Power see Power — Evil
Pride see Pride — Evil
Suffering
  see Suffering — Cruel

CRY
Grief see Grief — Weep

CUP
Anger
Bread see Bread — Cup
Punish
Suffer

CURE
Blind see Blind — Sight
Disease see Disease — Heal

CURSE
Bitter
Bless see Bless — Curse
God
Jesus
Law see Law — Anger
Lord see Curse — God
  and Curse — Jesus
Obey see Obey — Anger

CUSTOM
Jews see Jews — Custom

DANGER
Afraid
Death
Fear see Danger — Afraid
Help see Help — Danger
Life see Life — Trouble
Safety see Safety — Protect
Save see Save — Trouble

DARKNESS
Abandon
  see Abandon — Darkness
Blind see Blind — Darkness
Cloud see Cloud — Dark
Death
Gloom
Hope see Hope — Trouble
Light see Light — Darkness
Mind see Mind — Dark
Power
Trouble see Trouble — Darkness
Turn see Turn — Darkness

DAY
Christ see Day — Jesus
God
Jesus
Judgement
Last
Lord

DAZZLING
Light see Light — Dazzling
Presence see Presence — Light

DEAD
Alive
Angel see Angel — Dead
Body see Body — Dead
God
Jesus
Judge see Judge — Dead
Life
Lord see Dead — God
  and Dead — Jesus
Mourn see Mourn — Dead
Raise see Raise — Dead
Rise see Raise — Dead
Sin
Spirits
  see Spirit(s) — Consult

DEAR
Love see Love — Dear
Please see Please — Son of God
Son of God
  see Son of God — Love

DEATH
Alive
Angel see Angel — Death
Anger see Anger — Destroy
Christ see Christ — Death
Crime see Death — Sin
Cross see Christ — Death
Danger see Danger — Death
Darkness see Darkness — Death
Deserve
Destroy see Destroy — Death
Enemy see Enemy — Death
Escape see Escape — Death
Free see Death — Rescue
Grave see Grave — Death
Human see Human — Death
Hurt
Jesus see Christ — Death
Law see Law — Death
Life see Life — Death
Love see Love — Death
Mercy see Mercy — Destroy
Power see Power — Death
Punish
Rescue
Sacrifice
Save see Death — Rescue
Sentence see Death — Punish
Sin
Son of God
  see Son of God — Death
Suffering
  see Suffering — Death
Union see Union — Christ
Victory see Victory — Death
Wicked see Death — Sin
Witness see Witness — Death
World of the Dead
  see World of the Dead — Death

DECEIVE
Evil see Deceive — Sin
False see False — Deceive
God's People
  see God's People — Deceive
Lie see Lie — False
Pride see Pride — Deceive
Prophets
  see Prophets — Deceive
Sin
Violent see Violent — Deceive
Wicked see Deceive — Sin
Word see Word — False

DEDICATE
Altar see Altar — Dedicate
Anoint see Anoint — Consecrate
Festival
  see Festival — Dedication
Gift see Gift — Offer
God see Dedicate — Lord
Holy
Lamb see Lamb — Present
Levites see Levites — Dedicate
Lord
Nazirite
Priests
  see Priests — Consecrate
Pure see Dedicate — Holy
Rest see Rest — Dedicated
Sacred see Dedicate — Holy
Sacrifice
  see Sacrifice — Dedicate
Special see Special — Offering
Temple see Temple — Dedicate
Tent see Tent — Dedicate

DEEDS
Evil see Evil — Actions

DEFEND
Accuse see Accuse — Defend
Cause
Destroy see Destroy — Save
Enemy see Enemy — Help
God
God's People
  see God's People — Protect
Help see Help — Protect
Lord see Defend — God
Poor
Praise see Praise — Defender
Protect see Protect — Defend
Rights see Defend — Poor
Save see Save — Protect
Strong see Strength — Help

DEFILE
Idols
Offer see Offer — Defile
Priests see Priests — Unclean
Pure see Pure — Defile
Sin
Temple see Temple — Profane
Unclean

DEFY
God
Lord see Defy — God

DEMAND
God

DEMONS
Disease see Disease — Demons
Heal see Heal — Spirits
Name see Demons — Power
Power
Spirits

DEPEND
God
Jesus
Lord see Depend — God

DESERVE
Death see Death — Deserve
Punishment
  see Punishment — Deserve

DESIRE
Command
  see Command — Desire
Evil see Desire — Sin
God
Heart see Heart — Desire
Human
Lord see Desire — God
Natural see Desire — Human
Obey see Obey — Desire
Satisfy see Satisfy — Desire
Sin

DESOLATE
Destroy see Destroy — Abandon

DESPISE
Hate see Hate — Despise

DESTROY
Abandon
Afraid
Altars
Angel see Angel — Death
Anger
Beings
Body see Body — Dead
Condemn
  see Condemn — Destruction
Death
Defend see Destroy — Save
Desolate see Destroy — Abandon

DESTROY (Cont.)
Disaster
Doom see Destroy — Disaster
Enemy see Enemy — Destroy
Escape see Escape — Destroy
Evil see Destroy — Sin
Flood see Flood — Destroy
Fury see Destroy — Anger
God's People
Goddess see Destroy — Idols
Gods see Destroy — Idols
Grief see Destroy — Mourn
Help see Help — Destroy
Idols
Innocent
Judge see Judge — Destroy
Life see Life — Destroy
Love see Love — Destroy
Mercy see Mercy — Destroy
Mourn
Obey
Pagan
  see Destroy — Place of Worship
Place of Worship
Power see Power — Destroy
Pride
Protect see Destroy — Save
Punishment
  see Punishment — Destroy
Religion
  see Destroy — God's People
Rescue see Destroy — Save
Sacred
  see Destroy — Place of Worship
Save
Serve see Destroy — Obey
Sin
Spare see Spare — Destroy
Temple
Terrified see Destroy — Afraid
Violent
Wicked see Destroy — Sin
Wisdom
World
Worship

DETERMINE
Lot see Lot — Determine

DETERMINED
Afraid see Afraid — Courage
Confident

DEVIL
Angel see Angel — Devil

DEVOTED
God see Devoted — Lord
Lord

DISASTER
Destroy see Destroy — Disaster
Life see Life — Trouble
Punish
Strike
Suffering
  see Suffering — Trouble
Threat
Trouble
Wicked see Wicked — Downfall

DISCIPLE
Afraid
Amazed
Argue see Argue — Disciples
Baptize
  see Baptize — Disciples
Believe
Betray
Cross

DISCIPLE (Cont.)
Jesus
Love
Pharisees
   see Pharisees — Disciples
Pray
Preach
Teach
Understand
Words
   see Disciple — Understand
DISCUSS
Synagogue
   see Synagogue — Teach
DISEASE
Clean see Disease — Heal
Cure see Disease — Heal
Demons
Famine
Heal
Punish
Spirits see Disease — Demons
Strike
Suffering
   see Suffering — Trouble
Terrible
DISGRACE
Holy see Disgrace — Name
Honour
Humiliate see Disgrace — Shame
Life see Life — Disgrace
Name
Punishment
   see Punishment — Disgrace
Shame
Suffering
   see Suffering — Disgrace
DISGUSTING
Action see Action — Disgusting
Evil see Evil — Disgusting
Goddess see Gods — Disgusting
Gods see Gods — Disgusting
Idols see Idols — Disgusting
Punishment
   see Punishment — Evil
DISHONEST
Hate see Hate — Justice
Honest see Honest — Justice
DISHONOUR
Name see Name — Dishonour
DISOBEY
Command see Disobey — God
Evil see Disobey — Sin
God
Law see Disobey — God
Lord see Disobey — God
Sin
Worship see Worship — Disobey
DISPLEASE
God
Lord see Displease — God
DISPUTE
Judge see Dispute — Settle
Settle
DISTRESS
Save see Save — Trouble
Trouble see Trouble — Distress
DOOM
Destroy see Destroy — Disaster
Evil see Evil — Destroy
DOVE
Heaven
Offering
Priest see Dove — Offering

DOWNFALL
Wicked see Wicked — Downfall
DREAM
Angel see Angel — Dream
Interpret
Message see Message — Vision
Prophets see Prophets — Vision
Vision
DROWN
Flood see Flood — Destroy
DUTY
Levites see Levites — Duty
Obey
Priests see Priests — Duty
Sabbath
Temple see Temple — Duty
Tent see Tent — Duty
EAGER
Help see Help — Eager
EARNESTLY
Pray see Pray — Earnestly
ELDERS
Apostles
Chief Priests
   see Chief Priests — Elders
Church
Creatures
   see Creatures — Elders
Teachers of the Law
   see T of L — Elders
ENCOURAGE
Cheer
God
Help
Message see Message — Help
Patient
   see Patient — Encourage
Teach
ENDURE
Faith see Faith — Endurance
Love see Love — Constant
Patient see Patient — Endure
Suffering
   see Suffering — Endure
ENEMY
Abandon
   see Abandon — Enemies
Afraid
Anger see Anger — Enemies
Blood see Enemy — Death
Christ
Conquer see Enemy — Victory
Cruel
Death
Defend see Enemy — Help
Destroy
Evil see Enemy — Sinful
Exile see Exile — Enemies
Friend see Friend — Enemy
Hate see Hate — Enemies
Help
Human see Human — Enemy
Love see Love — Enemies
Oppress see Enemy — Persecute
Persecute
Plan see Enemy — Plot
Plot
Power
Protect see Enemy — Help
Punish
Rescue see Enemy — Save
Revenge see Enemy — Punish
Safety see Safety — Enemy
Save

ENEMY (Cont.)
Scatter see Scatter — Enemies
Sinful
Slaughter see Enemy — Destroy
Suffer
Temple see Temple — Profane
Terrified see Enemy — Afraid
Triumph see Enemy — Victory
Victory
Violent see Enemy — Cruel
Wicked see Enemy — Sinful
ENJOY
Life see Life — Joy
Peace see Peace — Joy
Prosperity
   see Prosperity — Happy
ENOUGH
Need see Need — Enough
ESCAPE
Anger
Death
Destroy
Punishment
Trap
ETERNAL
Believe see Believe — Life
Covenant see Eternal — Promise
Faithful
   see Faithful — Eternal
Glory
God
Kingdom
Last
Life see Life — Eternal
Light
Love see Love — Constant
Promise
Punishment
Sin
Son of God
   see Son of God — Life
Suffer
   see Eternal — Punishment
Word
EVERLASTING
Covenant
   see Eternal — Covenant
God see Eternal — God
EVIL
Accuse see Accuse — Sin
Actions
Afraid see Afraid — Sin
Anger see Anger — Evil
Choose see Choose — Evil
Condemn see Condemn — Sin
Crime see Crime — Sin
Deceive see Evil — False
Deeds see Evil — Actions
Desire see Desire — Sin
Destroy
Disgusting
Disobey see Disobey — Sin
Doom see Evil — Destroy
Enemy see Enemy — Sinful
Example
False
Foolish see Foolish — Evil
Forgive see Forgive — Sin
Free see Free — Sin
Friend see Friend — Evil
God see Evil — Lord
God's People
   see God's People — Sin
Gods see Gods — Sin

EVIL (Cont.)
Hate see Hate — Sin
Heart see Heart — Sin
Holy see Holy — Sin
Idols see Idols — Sin
Immorality
   see Immorality — Sin
Innocent see Innocent — Sin
Jealous see Jealous — Evil
Judge see Judge — Sin
Justice
Keep From see Evil — Prevent
Lie see Evil — False
Life see Life — Evil
Lord
Love see Love — Evil
Mind
Plan see Plan — Evil
Plot see Plan — Evil
Power see Power — Evil
Practices see Evil — Actions
Prevent
Pride see Pride — Evil
Prosperity
   see Prosperity — Evil
Protect see Protect — Evil
Punishment
   see Punishment — Evil
Refuse
Reject see Evil — Refuse
Remember see Remember — Evil
Rescue see Rescue — Evil
Rid
Right see Right — Evil
Righteous see Right — Evil
Safety see Safety — Evil
Save see Save — Evil
Sin
Spirit
Stubborn see Stubborn — Evil
Temple see Temple — Profane
Turn see Turn — Evil
Violent see Violent — Evil
Warn see Warn — Evil
Ways see Evil — Actions
Wicked see Wicked — Evil
World see World — Evil
EXAMPLE
Evil see Evil — Example
EXILE
Enemies
God's People
Punish
Servants
Sins see Exile — Punish
FAIL
Courage see Courage — Fail
Faith see Faith — Fail
Promise see Promise — Fail
Prosperity
   see Prosperity — Succeed
FAITH
Abandon
Accept see Accept — Faith
Action
Basis
Believe see Believe — Faith
Christ see Faith — Jesus
Endurance
Fail
Forgive
   see Faith — Right With God
Gentiles see Gentiles — Faith
Gift see Gift — Faith

FAITH (Cont.)
Give Up see Faith — Abandon
God
God's People
   see God's People — Faith
Grace
Heart see Heart — Faith
Help see Help — Faith
Hope
Jesus
Law see Law — Faith
Life see Life — Faith
Lord
Love see Love — Faith
Means see Faith — Basis
Message
Offer see Offer — Faith
Peace
Please
Power see Power — Faith
Preach see Faith — Message
Promise see Promise — Faith
Right With God
Righteous
Salvation see Save — Faith
Save see Save — Faith
Sin
Son of God see Faith — Jesus
Spirit of God
   see Spirit of God — Believe
Strong
Sure
Teaching
True see True — Faith
Truth
Weak see Weak — Faith
Win see Win — Faith
World see World — Faith
FAITHFUL
Abandon
   see Abandon — Faithful
Command see Faithful — Obey
Covenant
Eternal
God
God's People
   see God's People — Faithful
Happy see Happy — Faithful
Heart see Heart — Faithful
Holy see Holy — Faithful
Honour see Honour — Faithful
Jesus
Just
Kind see Kind — Faithful
Law see Faithful — Obey
Life
Lord
Love see Love — Faithfulness
Loyal
Obey
Praise
Proclaim
Promise see Promise — Faithful
Protect see Protect — Faithful
Punish
Right see Faithful — Just
Servant see Servant — Faithful
Serve see Serve — Faithfully
Sin
Teaching see Faithful — Obey
True see Faithful — Loyal
Witness see Witness — Faithful
Worship see Worship — Faithful

FALL
Flood see Flood — Destroy
FALSE
Accuse see Accuse — False
Cheat see False — Deceive
Deceive
Evil see Evil — False
Gods see Gods — False
Lie see False — Deceive
Predictions
Prophets
   see Prophets — Deceive
True see True — Lie
Vision see Vision — False
Word see Word — False
FAMINE
Disease see Disease — Famine
FAST
Mourn
Pray
FATE
Share see Share — Fate
FATHER
Angel see Angel — Father
Authority
   see Authority — Father
Child of God
   see Child of God — Father
Choose see Choose — God
Christ see Christ — God
Command see Command — God
Forgive see Father — Mercy
Glory see Glory — God
God
Grace
Heaven see Heaven -- God
Holy see Holy — God
Honour see Honour — God
Jesus
Kingdom see Kingdom — Father
Life
Lord
Love
Mercy
Name see Name — Father
Obey see Obey — Father
Power
Pray see Pray — Father
Presence see Presence — Father
Promise see Promise — Father
Raise see Father — Life
Son of God see Father — Jesus
Spirit of God
Thanks see Thanks — God
World
FAULT
God
Lord
Sin
FAULTLESS
Pure see Pure — Holy
FAVOUR
God see Favour — Lord
Judge see Judge — Favour
Lord
Win see Win — Approval
FEAR
Afraid
Danger see Danger — Afraid
Free see Free — Fear
God
Heart
Judgement
Lives

FEAR (Cont.)
Lord see Fear — God
Obey see Fear — Respect
Power see Power — Fear
Praise
Punish see Fear — Judgement
Respect
Terrified see Fear — Afraid
Terror see Fear — Afraid
Tremble see Fear — Afraid
FEAST
Happy
Joyful see Feast — Happy
Sacrifice
see Sacrifice — Festival
Servant
Wedding
FELLOWSHIP-OFFERING
Present
Sacrifice
FESTIVAL
Celebrate
see Celebrate — Festival
Dedication
Harvest see Harvest — Festival
Holy
Honour
Joy see Joy — Celebrate
Lamb see Festival — Offer
Law
Offer
Regulations see Festival — Law
Religious
Sacrifice see Festival — Offer
Unleavened Bread
Worship see Festival — Honour
FIRST
I Am see I Am — First
FIRST-BORN
Offer see Offer — First-born
Sheep see Sheep — Offer
FLESH
Blood see Blood — Flesh
FLOCK
Care see Care — Flock
Sheep
Shepherd see Flock — Sheep
FLOOD
Destroy
Drown see Flood — Destroy
Fall see Flood — Destroy
FOLLOW
Command see Obey — Command
Law see Law — Obey
FOOD-OFFERING
Holy
Pleasing
Present
FOOLISH
Act
Evil
Idol
Ignorant
Intelligent see Foolish — Wise
Knowledge see Foolish — Wise
Learn see Learn — Fool
Right
Sense
Sin
Stupid
Understand see Foolish — Wise
Wisdom see Wisdom — Foolish
Wise
Words

FORCE
Anger see Anger — Force
FOREHEAD
Mark see Mark — Forehead
FORGET
Commands see Forget — Law
Covenant
see Covenant — Remember
God
God's People
see God's People — Remember
Law
Lord see Forget — God
Mercy
Obey see Obey — Abandon
Remember
see Remember — Forget
Suffering
Teach see Teach — Remember
FORGIVE
Authority
see Authority — Forgive
Christ see Forgive — Jesus
Evil see Forgive — Sin
Faith
see Faith — Right With God
Father see Forgive — God
God
God's People
see God's People — Mercy
Happy see Happy — Forgiven
Heart
Heaven see Forgive — God
Jesus
Lord
Love see Love — Mercy
Mercy see Mercy — Forgive
Offer see Forgive — Sacrifice
Pray
Promise
Punishment
see Punishment — Mercy
Pure see Pure — Forgive
Rebellion see Forgive — Sin
Repent
Sacrifice
Sin
Son of Man see Forgive — Jesus
Spirit of God
Turn see Forgive — Repent
FORTUNE-TELLER
Consult see Consult — Medium
Magic
Medium
FREE
Captives see Free — Prisoners
Christ
Death see Death — Rescue
Evil see Free — Sin
Fear
Gift see Gift — Free
God's People
see God's People — Rescue
Grace see Grace — Gift
Happy
Help
Holy
Jews
Law see Law — Save
Life
Might see Free — Power
Power
Prisoners
Promise

FREE (Cont.)
Save see Save — Rescue
Sin
Slave
Spirit of God
Will
FREEWILL
Offer see Offer — Freewill
FRIEND
Christ see Friend — Jesus
Enemy
Evil
God
Jesus
Lord
Love
Loyal
Need
Neighbour
see Neighbour — Friend
Peace
Words
FULFIL
Promise see Promise — Fulfil
Vow see Vow — Fulfil
FURY
Anger see Anger — Fury
Destroy see Destroy — Anger
Punishment
see Punishment — Anger
Rage see Rage — Anger
GATE
I Am see I Am — Gate
GENEROUS
God
Need see Need — Help
Rich see Rich — Generous
GENTILES
Apostles
see Apostles — Gentiles
Believe see Gentiles — Faith
Blessings
Circumcise
see Circumcise — Gentiles
Faith
Good News
Gospel
see Gentiles — Good News
Jews see Jews — Gentiles
Law
Message
see Gentiles — Good News
Preach
see Gentiles — Good News
Salvation
Sin
Spirit of God
Worship
GENTLENESS
Love see Love — Gentleness
GIFT
Accept see Accept — Gift
Altar see Altar — Offering
Dedicate see Gift — Offer
Faith
Free
God
Grace see Grace — Gift
Levites see Levites — Offer
Lord
Message
Offer
Present see Gift — Offer
Priests see Priests — Gift

GOD'S PEOPLE (Cont.)
Evil see God's People — Sin
Exile see Exile — God's People
Faith
Faithful
Forget
  see God's People — Remember
Forgive
  see God's People — Mercy
Free see God's People — Rescue
Glory see Glory -- God's People
Heal see Heal — God's People
Heart see Heart — God's People
Help see Help — God's People
Holy
Incense
  see Incense — God's People
Joy
Judge
  see God's People — Justice
Justice
Law see Law — God's People
Lie see God's People — Deceive
Life see Life — God's People
Love see Love — God's People
Mercy
Message
Mislead
  see God's People — Deceive
Mourn
Need see Need — God's People
Obey
Oppress
  see Oppress — God's People
Peace
Poor
Power
  see Power — God's People
Praise
  see God's People — Worship
Prayer
Priests
  see Priests — God's People
Prison
  see Prison — God's People
Proclaim
  see God's People -- Message
Promise
Prosper
Protect
Punishment
  see Punishment — God's People
Rebel
  see God's People — Abandon
Reject
  see God's People — Abandon
Religion
Remember
Rescue
Reveal
  see Reveal — God's People
Rich
  see God's People — Prosper
Safety
Save see God's People — Rescue
Scatter
  see Scatter — God's People
Serve
Share see Share — God's People
Sheep
  see God's People — Shepherd
Shepherd
Sin

GOD'S PEOPLE (Cont.)
Slavery
  see God's People — Rescue
Spirit of God
  see Sp of God — God's People
Suffering
  see Suffering — God's People
Teach see Teach — God's People
Tears
  see God's People — Mourn
Turn
  see God's People — Abandon
Understand
Unfaithful
  see God's People — Abandon
Union
  see Union — God's People
Victory
  see Victory — God's People
Warn see Warn — God's People
Weep
  see God's People — Mourn
Worship
GODDESS
Destroy see Destroy — Idols
Disgusting
  see Gods — Disgusting
Image see Gods — False
Symbol see Gods — False
GODS
Anger see Anger — Gods
Bow see Bow — Gods
Consult see Consult — Gods
Destroy see Destroy — Idols
Disgusting
Evil see Gods — Sin
False
Heaven
Help see Help — Gods
Holy see Gods — Spirit
Honour
Human see Human — Gods
Idol see Gods — False
Image see Gods — False
Love
Might see Gods — Power
Obey see Obey — Gods
Offer see Offer — Gods
Pagan
Place of Worship
  see Place of Worship — Idols
Power
Pray
Priests see Priests — Gods
Punish
Real see Gods — False
Rescue see Gods — Save
Rid
Sacrifice see Sacrifice — Gods
Save
Serve
Sin
Spirit
Temple
Trust
Turn see Turn — Gods
Unfaithful
  see Unfaithful — Gods
GOOD
God
Lord see Good — God
Shepherd
GOOD NEWS
Announce
  see Good News -- Proclaim

GOOD NEWS (Cont.)
Believe see Believe — Message
Bring
  see Good News — Proclaim
Choose
  see Choose — Good News
Christ see Good News — Jesus
Gentiles
  see Gentiles — Good News
God
Jesus
Kingdom
Lord
Message
  see Message — Good News
Preach
  see Good News — Proclaim
Proclaim
Spirit of God
  see Spirit of God — Message
Suffering
  see Suffering — Good News
Teach see Teach — Message
Tell see Good News — Proclaim
GOSPEL
Christ see Good News — Jesus
Gentiles
  see Gentiles — Good News
God see Good News — God
Preach see Good News — Preach
GRACE
Choose see Choose — Love
Christ see Grace — Jesus
Faith see Faith — Grace
Father see Grace — God
Free see Grace -- Gift
Gift
Glory
God
Jesus
Law see Law — Grace
Lord
Love see Love — Mercy
Mercy see Grace — Peace
Peace
Saved
Sin
True see True — Love
Truth
GRAIN-OFFERING
Present
Proper
GRATEFUL
God
Lord see Grateful — God
GRAVE
Body see Body -- Grave
Death
Keep From
GREED
Immorality
  see Immorality — Greed
Money see Love — Money
GRIEF
Cry see Grief — Weep
Destroy see Destroy — Mourn
Mourn see Mourn — Sorrow
Sorrow see Sorrow — Grief
Weep
GUIDE
God
Lord
GUILTY
Innocent

HELP (Cont.)
Faith
Free see Free — Help
God
God's People
Gods
Happy
Heal
Heaven see Heaven — Save
Honest see Honest — Help
Idols see Help — Gods
Jesus
Joyful see Help — Happy
Law see Law — Help
Levites see Levites — Help
Lord
Love see Love — Help
Mercy see Mercy — Help
Message see Message — Help
Need see Need — Help
Offer
One Another
see Help — God's People
Oppress see Oppress — Help
Plead
Poor see Poor — Help
Pray
Prison see Prison — Help
Promise see Promise — Help
Protect
Refuse see Refuse — Help
Remember
see Remember — Help
Rescue see Help — Save
Right see Right — Help
Save
Serve
Share see Share — Help
Spirit of God
Strength
Temple
Trouble see Trouble — Help
Trust see Help — Faith
Turn see Turn — Help
Understanding
see Understanding — Help
Weak
Word see Word — Help
HELPLESS
Poor see Poor — Helpless
HIGH PRIEST
Blood see High Priest — Offer
Jews see Jews — Priest
Offer
Sacrifice
see Sacrifice — Priest
Slave
Temple see Temple — Priest
HOLY
Altar see Altar — Dedicate
Angel see Angel — Holy
Anoint see Anoint — Holy
Awe
Bow see Holy — Worship
Dedicate see Dedicate — Holy
Disgrace see Disgrace — Name
Evil see Holy — Sin
Faithful
Father see Holy — God
Festival see Festival — Holy
Food-offering
see Food-offering — Holy
Free see Free — Holy
God

HOLY (Cont.)
God's People
see God's People — Holy
Gods see Gods — Spirit
Heaven see Heaven — Holy
Honour
Jesus
Law see Law — Holy
Life see Life — Holy
Lord see Holy — God
Mighty
Name see Holy — God
Offer see Offer — Holy
Power
Praise see Holy — Worship
Presence see Presence — Holy
Priests
see Priests — Consecrate
Promise see Promise — Holy
Prophets see Prophets — Holy
Pure see Pure — Holy
Remember
see Remember — Holy
Respect see Holy — Awe
Sabbath see Sabbath — Holy
Sacred see Sacred — Holy
Share see Share — Holiness
Sin
Strength see Holy — Mighty
Temple see Temple — Holy
Tent see Tent — Holy
True
Wonderful
see Wonderful — Holiness
Worship
HOLY PLACE
Covenant Box
see Covenant Box — Tent
Creatures
Priests
see Priests — Holy Place
Pure see Pure — Holy Place
Tent see Tent — Holy Place
HONEST
Dishonest see Honest — Justice
Happy
Help
Justice
Life
Poor
Wicked
Word see Word — True
HONOUR
Bless see Bless — Honour
Celebrate
Command
Covenant see Honour — Promise
Disgrace see Disgrace — Honour
Faithful
Father see Honour — God
Festival
see Honour — Celebrate
Glory see Glory — Honour
God
Gods see Gods — Honour
Holy see Holy — Honour
Humble see Humble — Honour
Jesus
Joy see Joy — Honour
Kind see Honour — Love
Law
Lord
Love
Might see Honour — Power

HONOUR (Cont.)
Name
Obey
Offer
Passover
see Honour — Celebrate
Power
Praise see Honour — Worship
Promise
Protect
Rescue see Honour — Save
Respect see Honour — Reverence
Reverence
Sacrifice see Honour — Offer
Save
Serve
Teach see Teach — Obey
Temple see Temple — Honour
Thank see Honour — Worship
Wisdom
World
Worship
HOPE
Christ see Hope — Jesus
Darkness see Hope — Trouble
Faith see Faith — Hope
God
Jesus
Joy
Life see Life — Faith
Lord see Hope — God
and Hope — Jesus
Love see Love — Faith
Patient see Patient — Hope
Praise
Promise see Promise — Faith
Save see Save — Hope
Trouble
Trust see Trust — Hope
HORRIBLE
Sight see Sight — Horrifying
HORRIFYING
Sight see Sight — Horrifying
HORROR
Awful see Awful — Horror
HUMAN
Being
Christ see Christ — Human
Control see Control — Human
Creatures
see Creatures — Human
Death
Desire see Human — Nature
Enemy
Gods
Heart
Idols see Human — Gods
Jesus see Christ — Human
Judge see Judge — Human
Law see Law — Human
Mind
Nature
Obey
Power
Sin
Spirit of God
Wisdom
Word see Word — Human
HUMBLE
God
Honour
Lord see Humble — God
Proud
Repent

HUMBLE (Cont.)
  Turn see Humble — Repent
HUMILIATE
  Disgrace see Disgrace — Shame
HUNGER
  Jesus
  Lord
  Need
  Satisfy see Satisfy — Hunger
HURT
  Death see Death — Hurt
  Heal see Heal — Hurt
  Plan see Plan — Evil
  Power see Power — Hurt
HUSBAND
  Love see Love — Husband
HYPOCRITES
  Pharisees
    see Pharisees — Hypocrites
  Teachers of the Law
    see T of L — Hypocrites
I AM
  Bread
  First
  Gate
  God
  Life
  Light
  Shepherd
  Vine
IDOLS
  Anger see Anger — Gods
  Bow see Idols — Worship
  Consult see Consult — Gods
  Defile see Defile — Idols
  Destroy see Destroy — Idols
  Disgusting
  Evil see Idols — Sin
  Foolish see Foolish — Idol
  God
  Gods see Gods — False
  Hate see Hate — Idolatry
  Help see Help — Gods
  Human see Human — Gods
  Image see Image — Gods
  Immoral
  Incense see Incense — Idols
  Lord see Idols — God
  Offer see Offer — Gods
  Pagan
  Place of Worship
    see Place of Worship — Idols
  Priests see Priests — Gods
  Sacrifice see Sacrifice — Gods
  Save
  Serve
  Shame
  Sin
  Temple see Temple — Profane
  Trust
  Turn see Turn — Gods
  Useless
  Worship
IGNORANT
  Foolish see Foolish — Ignorant
IMAGE
  Beast see Beast — Image
  God
  Goddess see Image — Gods
  Gods
  Idols see Image — Gods
  Mark see Mark — Image
  Sin

IMMORALITY
  Evil see Immorality — Sin
  Greed
  Idols see Idols — Immoral
  Lust see Immorality — Greed
  Perversion
  Punishment
    see Punishment — Evil
  Sex see Sex — Immorality
  Sin
IMMORTAL
  Mortal see Mortal — Immortal
IMPORTANT
  Commandment
    see Commandment — Important
IMPOSSIBLE
  God
INCENSE
  Altar
  God's People
  Idols
  Offer
  Present see Incense — Offer
  Priests see Priests — Worship
  Sacrifice see Incense — Offer
  Temple
  Worship
INNOCENT
  Destroy see Destroy — Innocent
  Evil see Innocent — Sin
  God
  Guilty see Guilty — Innocent
  Lord see Innocent — God
  Right
  Sin
INSULT
  Jealous see Jealous — Insult
INTELLIGENT
  Foolish see Foolish — Wise
  Learn see Learn — Wisdom
INTERPRET
  Dream see Dream — Interpret
JEALOUS
  Anger
  Evil
  Insult
  Proud
JESUS
  Accuse see Accuse — Jesus
  Acknowledge
    see Acknowledge — Jesus
  Angel see Angel — Jesus
  Anger see Anger — Jesus
  Apostles see Apostles — Jesus
  Arrest see Arrest — Jesus
  Authority
    see Authority — Jesus
  Baptize see Baptize — Christ
  Being see Being — Jesus
  Believe see Believe — Jesus
  Bless see Bless — Christ
  Body see Body — Jesus
  Chief Priests
    see Chief Priests — Jesus
  Children
  Choose see Choose — Jesus
  Church see Church — Christ
  Command see Command — Jesus
  Condemn see Condemn — Jesus
  Confess see Confess — Jesus
  Covenant see Covenant — Jesus
  Cross see Cross — Jesus
  Curse see Curse — Jesus
  Day see Day — Jesus

JESUS (Cont.)
  Dead see Dead — Jesus
  Death see Christ — Death
  Depend see Depend — Jesus
  Disciple see Disciple — Jesus
  Faith see Faith — Jesus
  Faithful see Faithful — Jesus
  Father see Father — Jesus
  Forgive see Forgive — Jesus
  Friend see Friend — Jesus
  Glory see Glory — Jesus
  God
  Good News
    see Good News — Jesus
  Grace see Grace — Jesus
  Heal see Heal — Jesus
  Heart see Heart — Jesus
  Heaven see Heaven — Jesus
  Help see Help — Jesus
  Holy see Holy — Jesus
  Honour see Honour — Jesus
  Hope see Hope — Jesus
  Human see Christ — Human
  Hunger see Hunger — Jesus
  Joy see Joy — Jesus
  Judge see Judge — Jesus
  King see King — Jesus
  Law see Law — Christ
  Life see Life — Christ
  Lord
  Love see Love — Christ
  Mercy
  Message see Message — Christ
  Messiah
  Miracle see Miracle — Jesus
  Peace see Peace — Christ
  Persecution
    see Persecution — Jesus
  Pharisees
    see Pharisees — Jesus
  Power see Power — Christ
  Pray see Pray — Jesus
  Preach see Christ — Preach
  Presence see Presence — Christ
  Proclaim see Christ — Proclaim
  Pure see Christ — Pure
  Raise see Raise — Christ
  Reveal see Reveal — Jesus
  Right see Right — Christ
  Right with God
    see Right — Christ
  Righteous see Right — Christ
  Rise see Raise — Christ
  Sadducees
    see Sadducees — Jesus
  Sake see Christ — Sake
  Save see Save — Christ
  Scripture
    see Scripture — Jesus
  Secret see Secret — Christ
  Servant see Servant — Christ
  Serve see Serve — Christ
  Slave see Slave — Christ
  Son of God
    see Son of God — Christ
  Spirit of God
    see Spirit of God — Christ
  Spirits see Spirit(s) — Christ
  Strength see Strength — Christ
  Suffering
    see Suffering — Christ
  Teach see Teach — Christ
  Truth see Truth — Christ

JESUS (Cont.)
Understanding
  see Understanding — Christ
Union see Union — Christ
Weep see Weep — Jesus
JEWS
Accuse see Accuse — Jews
Afraid see Afraid — Jews
Apostles see Apostles — Jews
Authorities
Believe
Circumcise
  see Circumcise — Jews
Custom
Free see Free — Jews
Gentiles
High Priest see Jews — Priest
Law
Message
Peace
Plan
Preach see Jews — Message
Priest
Religion
Synagogue
Temple
Worship
JOY
Bless see Bless — Happy
Celebrate
Feast see Joy — Celebrate
Festival see Joy — Celebrate
Glad see Joy — Happy
God
God's People
  see God's People — Joy
Happy
Harvest see Harvest — Joy
Heart see Heart — Joy
Heaven see Heaven — Joy
Help see Help — Happy
Honour
Hope see Hope -- Joy
Jesus
Life see Life — Joy
Lord
Love see Love — Joy
Mourn
Peace see Peace — Joy
Power
Praise see Praise — Happy
Presence see Presence — Joy
Pride see Pride — Joy
Rejoice see Joy — Happy
Right see Right -- Joy
Sacrifice
  see Sacrifice — Praise
Save see Save — Happy
Share see Share — Happiness
Sorrow see Sorrow — Joy
Spirit of God
Suffering see Suffering — Joy
Temple see Temple — Joy
Thanks see Thanks -- Joy
Victory see Victory — Happy
World
Worship see Worship — Joy
JUDGE
Case
Christ see Judge — Jesus
Condemn
Corrupt
Court see Judge — Case
Day see Day — Judgement
Dead

JUDGE (Cont.)
Destroy
Dispute see Judge — Case
Evil see Judge — Sin
Favour
Fear see Fear — Judgement
God
God's People
  see God's People — Justice
Guilty see Guilty — Judge
Heaven
Human
Jesus
Justice
Law see Law — Judge
Lord see Judge — God
  and Judge — Jesus
Motives
Obey see Obey — Justice
Oppress see Judge — Justice
Pass
Poor see Judge — Justice
Power see Power — Justice
Punish
Remember
  see Remember — Judge
Right(eous)
  see Judge — Justice
Rights see Rights — Justice
Save
Serve
Sin
Son of God see Judge — Jesus
True see Judge — Justice
Wicked see Judge — Sin
Word see Word — Judge
World see World — Justice
JUSTICE
Command see Command — Just
Court
Evil see Evil — Justice
Faithful see Faithful — Just
God's People
  see God's People — Justice
Hate see Hate — Justice
Honest see Honest — Justice
Judge see Judge — Justice
Kingdom see Kingdom — Justice
Law see Law — Justice
Love see Love — Justice
Obey see Obey — Justice
Oppress see Oppress — Justice
Poor see Poor — Justice
Power see Power — Justice
Praise see Praise — Justice
Prevent
Right see Right — Justice
Righteous see Right — Justice
Rights see Rights — Justice
World see World — Justice
KEEP
Command see Obey — Command
Commandment
  see Obey — Command
Covenant see Covenant — Obey
Law see Law — Obey
KEEP FROM
Evil see Evil — Prevent
Grave see Grave — Keep From
KIND
Bless see Bless — Love
Faithful
God
Honour see Honour — Love

KIND (Cont.)
Lord
Love
Mercy see Mercy — Compassion
Need
Patient see Patient — Love
Word see Word — Help
KING
Anoint see Anoint — King
God
Jesus
Lord see King — God
  and King — Jesus
KINGDOM
Christ
Eternal see Eternal — Kingdom
Father
Glory
God
Good News
  see Good News — Kingdom
Happy see Happy — Kingdom
Heaven
Justice
Last
Law see Law — Kingdom
Lord see Kingdom — God
Possess
Power
Preach see Preach — Kingdom
Rich see Rich — Kingdom
Son of God
  see Kingdom — Christ
World
KNEES
Tremble see Tremble — Knees
KNOWLEDGE
Foolish see Foolish — Wise
Learn see Learn — Wisdom
Life
True see True — Knowledge
Understand
Wisdom
LAMB
Altar see Altar — Offering
Blood see Blood — Offer
Christ
Dedicate see Lamb — Present
Festival see Festival — Offer
God
Offering see Lamb — Sacrifice
Passover
Present
Priests see Priests — Offer
Sacrifice
Seal
Sheep see Sheep — Offer
Sin-offering
  see Sin-offering — Offer
Throne
LAND
Promise see Promise — Land
LAST
Covenant
  see Covenant -- Eternal
Day see Day — Last
Eternal see Eternal — Last
Heaven see Heaven — Last
Kingdom see Kingdom — Last
Life see Life — Eternal
Raise see Raise — Last
LAW
Anger
Believe see Law — Faith

LAW (Cont.)
Case see Law — Judge
Change
Christ
Circumcise
    see Circumcise — Law
Command
Curse see Law — Anger
Death
Disobey
Faith
Faithful see Law — Obey
Festival see Festival — Law
Follow see Law — Obey
Forget see Forget — Law
Free see Law — Save
Gentiles see Gentiles — Law
God see Law — Lord
God's People
Grace
Happy see Happy — Obey
Heart see Heart — Obey
Help
Holy
Honour see Honour — Law
Human
Jesus see Law — Christ
Jews see Jews — Law
Judge
Justice
Keep see Law — Obey
Kingdom
Levites see Levites — Law
Life see Life — Law
Lord
Love
Mind
Obey
Observe see Law — Obey
Perfect
Pharisees see Pharisees — Law
Priests see Priests — Law
Prison see Prison — Law
Promise see Promise — Law
Prophets
Refuse see Law — Disobey
Reject see Reject — Law
Requirement
    see Law — Command
Right see Right — Law
Right With God see Law — Save
Righteousness
    see Law — Justice
Sabbath see Sabbath — Law
Sacrifice see Sacrifice — Law
Save
Scholar
Servant
Serve
Sin
Spirit of God
Study
Teach see Teach — Law
True
Turn see Turn — Law
Understanding
    see Understanding — Laws
Wisdom
Worship see Worship — Law
LEARN
Fool
Intelligent see Learn — Wisdom
Knowledge see Learn — Wisdom
Lesson

LEARN (Cont.)
Obey
Right
Secret
Stupid see Learn — Fool
Teach
Truth
Understand
Wisdom
LESSON
Learn see Learn — Lesson
LEVITES
Consecrate
    see Levites — Dedicate
Contribute see Levites — Offer
Covenant Box
    see Covenant Box — Levites
Dedicate
Duty
Gift see Levites — Offer
Help
Law
Offer
Passover
Praise
Priests see Priests — Levites
Purify see Levites — Dedicate
Sacrifice see Levites — Offer
Separate
Serve
Tent
Tithe see Levites — Offer
LIE
Believe see Believe — Lie
Claim see Lie — False
Deceive see Lie — False
Evil see Evil — False
False
God's People
    see God's People — Deceive
Hate see Hate — Lies
Name see Name — Dishonour
Oath
Promise see Lie — Oath
Prophet
Punish
Steal
Teach see Teach — Lie
Testimony see Lie — Word
True see True — Lie
Truth
Witness see Lie — Word
Word
LIFE
Accept see Life — Faith
Believe see Life — Faith
Bless see Bless — Life
Blood see Blood — Life
Body see Body — Life
Bread see Bread — Life
Change
Choose see Choose — Life
Christ
Church see Life — God's People
Command see Life — Law
Control see Control — Life
Create see Create — Life
Danger see Life — Trouble
Dead see Dead — Life
Death
Destroy
Disaster see Life — Trouble
Disgrace
Enjoy see Life — Joy

LIFE (Cont.)
Eternal
Evil
Faith
Faithful see Faithful — Life
Father see Father — Life
Fear see Fear — Lives
Free see Free — Life
Give Up
Glad see Life — Joy
God's People
Happy see Life — Joy
Holy
Honest see Honest — Life
Hope see Life — Faith
I Am see Life — Christ
Jesus see Life — Christ
Joy
Knowledge
    see Knowledge — Life
Last see Life — Eternal
Law
Love see Love — Life
Mankind see Mankind — Life
Mercy see Life — Spare
Mortal see Mortal — Life
New see New — Life
Obey see Life — Law
Offer
Peace
Please
Pleasure
Power see Power — Life
Pray
Promise
Prosperity
    see Prosperity — Life
Protect see Life — Safe
Punishment
    see Punishment — Life
Purpose see Life — Will
Raise see Raise — Life
Remember see Remember — Life
Rescue see Life — Save
Reward
Riches
Righteous
Safe
Sake
Save
Share see Share — Life
Son of God see Life — Christ
Source see Source — Life
Spare
Spirit of God
    see Spirit of God — Life
Strong
Tree
Trouble
True see True — Life
Truth see Truth — Life
Union
Useless
Wicked see Life — Evil
Will
Win see Win — Life
Wisdom see Wisdom — Life
Word see Word — Life
World
Worry
LIGHT
Darkness
Dazzling
Eternal see Light — God

LIGHT (Cont.)
  Glory see Glory — Light
  God
  I Am see I Am — Light
  Lord see Light — God
  Presence see Light — Dazzling
  Truth
  Turn see Turn — Darkness
  World
LORD
  Abandon see Abandon — God
  Accuse see Accuse — God
  Acknowledge
    see Acknowledge — God
  Action see Action — God
  Angel see Angel — Lord
  Anger see Anger — God
  Approval see Approval — God
  Authority see Authority — Lord
  Awe see Awe — God
  Believe see Believe — Lord
  Bless see Bless — Lord
  Care see Care — Lord
  Choose see Choose — Lord
  Christ see Christ — Lord
  Comfort see Comfort — God
  Command see Command — Lord
  Commandment
    see Commandment — God
  Compassion
    see Compassion — Lord
  Condemn see Condemn — God
    and Condemn — Jesus
  Confess see Confess — Lord
  Control see Control — God
  Courage see Courage — God
  Covenant see Covenant — God
  Create see Create — God
  Curse see Curse — God
    and Curse — Jesus
  Day see Day — Lord
  Dead see Dead — God
    and Dead — Jesus
  Dedicate see Dedicate — Lord
  Defend see Defend — God
  Defy see Defy — God
  Depend see Depend — God
  Desire see Desire — God
  Devoted see Devoted — Lord
  Disobey see Disobey — God
  Displease see Displease — God
  Evil see Evil — Lord
  Faith see Faith — Lord
  Faithful see Faithful — Lord
  Father see Father — Lord
  Fault see Fault — Lord
  Favour see Favour — Lord
  Fear see Fear — God
  Forget see Forget — God
  Forgive see Forgive — Lord
  Friend see Friend — Lord
  Gift see Gift — Lord
  Glad see Glad — God
  Glory see Glory — Lord
  Good see Good — God
  Good News
    see Good News — Lord
  Grace see Grace — Lord
  Grateful see Grateful — God
  Guide see Guide — Lord
  Happy see Happy — Lord
  Hate see Hate — God
  Heal see Heal — Lord
  Heart see Heart — Lord

LORD (Cont.)
  Heaven see Heaven — Lord
  Help see Help — Lord
  Holy see Holy — God
  Honour see Honour — Lord
  Hope see Hope — God
    and Hope — Jesus
  Humble see Humble — God
  Hunger see Hunger — Lord
  Idols see Idols — God
  Innocent see Innocent — God
  Jesus see Jesus — Lord
  Joy see Joy — Lord
  Judge see Judge — God
    and Judge — Jesus
  Kind see Kind — Lord
  King see King — God
    and King — Jesus
  Kingdom see Kingdom — God
  Law see Law — Lord
  Light see Light — God
  Love see Love — Lord
  Majesty see Majesty — God
  Mankind see Mankind — God
  Mercy see Mercy — Lord
  Message see Message — Lord
  Might see Might — Lord
  Miracle see Miracle — God
  Need see Need — God
  Patient see Patient — God
  Peace see Peace — God
  Pity see Pity — Lord
  Poor see Poor — God
  Power see Power — Lord
  Protect see Protect — God
  Punishment
    see Punishment — Lord
  Purpose see Purpose — God
  Rebel see Rebel — Lord
  Refuge see Refuge — God
  Reject see Reject — Lord
  Rescue see Rescue — Lord
  Reveal see Reveal — Lord
  Reverence see Reverence — Lord
  Reward see Reward — God
  Righteous see Right — Lord
  Salvation see Save — God
  Save see Save — Christ
    and Save — God
  Shepherd see Shepherd — God
  Source see Source — God
  Test see Test — Lord
  Thanks see Thanks — Lord
  Throne see Throne — Lord
  Trust see Trust — Lord
  Unfaithful
    see Unfaithful — Lord
  Union see Union — Christ
  Wisdom see Wisdom — God
  Word see Word — Lord
LOT
  Choose
  Determine
LOVE
  Anger
  Believe see Love — Faith
  Believer
    see Love — God's People
  Bless see Bless — Love
  Body see Love — God's People
  Brother
    see Love — God's People
  Child of God
    see Love — God's People

LOVE (Cont.)
  Children
  Choose see Choose — Love
  Christ
  Christian
    see Love — God's People
  Comfort see Love — Help
  Command
  Compassion see Love — Mercy
  Constant
  Covenant see Love — Promise
  Dear
  Death
  Destroy
  Disciple see Disciple — Love
  Enduring see Love — Constant
  Enemies
  Eternal see Love — Constant
  Evil
  Faith
  Faithfulness
  Father see Father — Love
  Forgive see Love — Mercy
  Friend see Friend — Love
  Gentleness
  Glad see Love — Joy
  God
  God's People
  Gods see Gods — Love
  Grace see Love — Mercy
  Happy see Love — Joy
  Hate
  Heart
  Heaven
  Help
  Honour see Love — Respect
  Hope see Love — Faith
  Husband
  Jesus see Love — Christ
  Joy
  Justice
  Kind see Kind — Love
  Law see Law — Love
  Life
  Lord
  Loyalty
    see Love — Faithfulness
  Mercy
  Mind see Love — Heart
  Money
  Neighbour
  Obey see Obey — Love
  One Another
    see Love — God's People
  Patient see Patient — Love
  Peace
  Perfect
  Please see Please — Son of God
  Power see Power — Love
  Praise
  Pray see Pray — Love
  Promise
  Protect see Love — Help
  Punishment
    see Punishment — Love
  Purity
  Remember
    see Remember — Love
  Rescue see Love — Save
  Respect
  Right(eous) see Love — Justice
  Sacrifice see Sacrifice — Love
  Safety see Safety — Love
  Save

LOVE (Cont.)
Servant
Serve
Share see Share — Love
Sin
Slave see Love — Servant
Son of God see Love — Christ
Spirit of God
  see Spirit of God — Love
Strong
Teach
Temple
Thank see Love — Praise
True see True — Love
Trust see Love — Faith
Truth
Understanding
  see Understanding — Love
Union
Victory see Victory — Love
Wicked see Love — Evil
Wife
Wonderful
  see Wonderful — Love
Word see Word — Love
World

LOYAL
Faithful see Faithful — Loyal
Friend see Friend — Loyal
Love see Love — Faithfulness
Promise
Servant see Servant — Faithful
Serve
Swear see Loyal — Promise

LUST
Immorality
  see Immorality — Greed

MAGIC
Fortune-teller
  see Fortune-teller — Magic
Practice

MAJESTY
Glory
God
Lord see Majesty — God
Might see Majesty — Power
Power
Temple see Temple — Glorious

MANKIND
God
Life
Lord see Mankind — God
Sin
World

MANNA
Eat
Food see Manna — Eat

MARK
Beast see Beast — Mark
Forehead
Image

MASTER
Obey
Servant
Slave see Master — Servant

MEANS
Faith see Faith — Basis
Power see Power — Authority

MEDIUM
Consult see Consult — Medium
Fortune-teller
  see Fortune-teller — Medium

MERCY
Anger see Anger — Mercy

MERCY (Cont.)
Beg
Compassion
Death see Mercy — Destroy
Destroy
Father see Mercy — God
Forget see Forget — Mercy
Forgive
God
God's People
  see God's People — Mercy
Grace see Grace — Peace
Heaven see Heaven — Mercy
Help
Jesus see Jesus — Mercy
Kind see Mercy — Compassion
Life see Life — Spare
Lord
Love see Love — Mercy
Patient
Peace
Pity see Mercy — Compassion
Prosperity
  see Prosperity — Mercy
Protect see Mercy — Help
Punishment
  see Punishment — Mercy
Rescue see Mercy — Save
Right see Right — Mercy
Save
Sin
Spare see Mercy — Forgive
Turn see Turn — Forgive

MESSAGE
Accept see Message — Faith
Angel see Angel — Message
Baptize
Believe see Message — Faith
Bold see Message — Proclaim
Christ
Dream see Message — Vision
Encourage see Message — Help
Faith
Gentiles
  see Gentiles — Good News
Gift see Gift — Message
God
God's People
  see God's People — Message
Good News
Heart
Help
Jesus see Message — Christ
Jews see Jews — Message
Lord
Name
Obey
Preach see Message — Proclaim
Proclaim
Prophets
  see Prophets — Message
Revealed
Salvation
  see Message — Good News
Save see Message — Good News
Secret see Secret — Message
Sow see Sow — Message
Spirit of God
  see Spirit of God — Message
Suffering
  see Suffering — Good News
Teach see Teach — Message
Tongues
True

MESSAGE (Cont.)
Truth see Truth — Word
Understanding
  see Understanding — Words
Vision
Wisdom
World
Worship

MESSIAH
Believe
Jesus see Jesus — Messiah
Son of God
  see Son of God — Christ
Suffering
  see Suffering — Christ

MIGHT
Acts
Angel see Angel — Mighty
Free see Free — Power
Glory see Glory — Power
God
Gods see Gods — Power
Holy see Holy — Mighty
Honour see Honour — Power
Lord
Majesty see Majesty — Power
Miracles see Might — Acts
Power
Praise see Praise — Strength
Proclaim see Proclaim — Glory
Rescue see Rescue — Strength
Save see Save — Power
Strength see Strength — Mighty
Strong see Strength — Mighty
Wonderful
  see Wonderful — Power

MIND
Change
Dark
Evil see Evil — Mind
Heart see Heart — Mind
Human see Human — Mind
Law see Law — Mind
Love see Love — Heart
Peace
Punishment
  see Punishment — Mercy
Right
Strength see Strength — Mind
Understand

MIRACLE
Believe see Believe — Miracle
God
Healing
Jesus
Lord see Miracle — God
Might see Miracle — Wonder
Power see Power — Miracles
Prophet
Prove
Wonder

MISLEAD
God's People
  see God's People — Deceive

MONEY
Greed see Love — Money
Love see Love — Money

MORTAL
Body
Immortal
Life

MOTIVES
Judge see Judge — Motives

MOURN
Bitterly
Comfort
Dead
Destroy see Destroy — Mourn
Fast see Fast — Mourn
God's People
   see God's People — Mourn
Grief see Mourn — Sorrow
Joy see Mourn — Comfort
Sackcloth
Sorrow
Weep see Weep — Mourn

NAKED
Strip

NAME
Baptize see Baptize — Name
Bless see Bless — Lord
Command see Name — Power
Demons see Name — Power
Disgrace see Name — Dishonour
Dishonour
Father
Glory
Holy see Holy — God
Honour see Honour — Name
Lie see Name — Dishonour
Message see Message — Name
Oath see Name — Promise
Power
Praise see Praise — Name
Promise
Swear see Name — Promise

NATURAL
Desire see Desire — Human

NATURE
Human see Human — Nature

NAZIRITE
Dedicate
   see Dedicate — Nazirite

NEED
Enough
Friend see Friend — Need
Generous see Need — Help
God
God's People
Help
Hunger see Hunger — Need
Kind see Kind — Need
Lord see Need — God
Poor see Poor — Needy
Provide
Remember
   see Remember — Help
Rich see Rich — Need
Rights see Rights — Poor
Satisfy see Satisfy — Need
Share see Share — Help
Teach
Trouble

NEIGHBOUR
Friend
Love see Love — Neighbour

NEW
Command see Command — New
Covenant
Create see Create — New
Heart see Heart — Mind
Heaven
Jerusalem
Life
Temple see Temple — Restore

NIGHT
Turn see Turn — Darkness

OATH
Lie see Lie — Oath
Name see Name — Promise

OBEY
Abandon
Afraid see Obey — Fear
Anger
Believe see Believe — Obey
Bless see Bless — Obey
Bow see Obey — Worship
Christ
Circumcise
   see Circumcise — Law
Command
Commandment
   see Obey — Command
Covenant see Obey — Promise
Curse see Obey — Anger
Desire
Destroy see Obey — Anger
Duty see Duty — Obey
Faithful see Faithful — Obey
Father
Fear
Forget see Obey — Abandon
God's People
   see God's People — Obey
Gods
Happy see Happy — Obey
Heart see Heart — Obey
Honour see Honour — Obey
Human see Human — Obey
Judge see Obey — Justice
Justice
Law see Law — Obey
Learn see Learn — Obey
Life
Love
Master see Master — Obey
Message see Message — Obey
Power
Praise see Obey — Worship
Promise
Prophet
Proud see Obey — Stubborn
Rebellious see Obey — Stubborn
Refuse
Reject see Obey — Refuse
Right
Right With God
Righteous
   see Obey — Right With God
Sacrifice see Sacrifice — Obey
Save see Obey — Life
Servant see Servant — Obey
Serve see Serve — Obey
Slave see Slave — Obey
Spirit of God
Spirits
Stubborn
Teach see Teach — Obey
Test see Test — Obey
True
Turn
Warn see Warn — Obey
Will see Obey — Word
Wisdom see Wisdom — Obey
Word
Worship

OBSERVE
Command
   see Command — Observe
Law see Law — Obey

OBSERVE (Cont.)
Passover
   see Passover — Observe
Regulation
   see Regulation — Observe
Sabbath see Sabbath — Observe

OFFER
Accept see Accept — Offering
Altar see Altar — Offering
Anger see Anger — Offer
Best
Bless see Bless — Offer
Blood see Blood — Offer
Bow see Offer — Worship
Bread see Bread — Offer
Christ see Christ — Offer
Command
   see Command — Sacrifice
Defile
Dove see Dove — Offering
Faith
Festival see Festival — Offer
First-born
Forgive
Freewill
Gift see Gift — Offer
Gods
Harvest see Harvest — Offering
Help see Help — Offer
High Priest
   see High Priest — Offer
Holy
Honour see Honour — Offer
Idols see Offer — Gods
Incense see Incense — Offer
Lamb see Lamb — Sacrifice
Levites see Levites — Offer
Life see Life — Offer
Ordain see Ordain — Offer
Pagan see Pagan — Offer
Perfect see Offer — Best
Place of Worship
   see Place of Worship — Offer
Please see Please — Offer
Praise see Offer — Worship
Prayer
Present
Priests see Priests — Offer
Promise see Promise — Offer
Proper see Offer — Right
Regulation
Required
Right
Ritual see Ritual — Offerings
Sacred see Offer — Holy
Sacrifice
Share see Share — Offer
Sheep see Sheep — Offer
Sin-offering
   see Offer — Sacrifice
Special see Special — Offering
Take Away (sin)
   see Offer — Forgive
Temple see Temple — Offering
Tent see Tent — Offering
Thanks see Thanks — Offer
Tithes
True see Offer — Right
Unclean see Offer — Defile
Vow
Worship

ONE ANOTHER
Help see Help — God's People
Love see Love — God's People

OPPRESS
Enemy see Enemy — Persecute
God's People
Help
Judge see Oppress — Justice
Justice
Orphan see Orphan — Oppress
Poor see Poor — Needy
Protect see Oppress — Help
Rescue see Oppress — Save
Rights
Save
Suffering
   see Suffering — Trouble
Violent see Violent — Oppress

ORDAIN
Offer
Priests
   see Priests — Consecrate

ORPHAN
Oppress
Rights see Rights — Orphans
Widow

OUTCASTS
Tax Collectors
   see Tax Collectors — Outcasts

PAGAN
Altars
Destroy
   see Destroy — Place of Worship
Gods see Gods — Pagan
Idols see Idols — Pagan
Offer
Places of Worship
Priests
Sacrifice see Pagan — Offer
Temple see Temple — Profane
Worship

PAIN
Birth
Suffer

PARABLE
Understanding
   see Understanding — Words

PASS
Judge see Judge — Pass

PASSOVER
Celebrate
   see Celebrate — Festival
Honour see Honour — Celebrate
Lamb see Lamb — Passover
Levites see Levites — Passover
Observe
Regulations
Sacrifice
Unleavened Bread

PATIENT
Encourage
Endure
God
Hope
Kind see Patient — Love
Lord see Patient — God
Love
Mercy see Mercy — Patient
Promise
Suffering
   see Suffering — Endure

PEACE
Bless see Bless — Peace
Christ
Enjoy see Peace — Joy
Faith see Faith — Peace
Friend see Friend — Peace

PEACE (Cont.)
God
God's People
   see God's People — Peace
Grace see Grace — Peace
Heal
Heart
Heaven see Heaven — Peace
Jesus see Peace — Christ
Jews see Jews — Peace
Joy
Life see Life — Peace
Lord see Peace — God
Love see Love — Peace
Mercy see Mercy — Peace
Mind see Mind — Peace
Promise see Promise — Peace
Prosperity
   see Prosperity — Peace
Righteous
Safety see Peace — Security
Security
Source see Source — Peace
Spirit of God
   see Spirit of God — Peace
Trouble
World

PERFECT
Law see Law — Perfect
Love see Love — Perfect
Offer see Offer — Best

PERSECUTION
Church
Enemy see Enemy — Persecute
Jesus
Poor see Poor — Needy
Suffer

PERVERSION
Immorality
   see Immorality — Perversion
Sex see Sex — Immorality

PHARISEES
Chief Priests
   see Chief Priests — Pharisees
Disciples
Hypocrites
Jesus
Law
Sadducees
Tax Collectors
   see Tax Collectors — Pharisees
Teachers of the Law
Terrible
Trap
Yeast see Yeast — Pharisees

PHYSICAL
Spiritual
   see Spiritual — Physical

PITY
God see Pity — Lord
Heart see Heart — Pity
Lord
Mercy see Mercy — Compassion

PLACE OF WORSHIP
Altar
Destroy
   see Destroy — Place of Worship
Gods
   see Place of Worship — Idols
Idols
Offer
Pagan
   see Pagan — Places of Worship

PLACE OF WORSHIP (Cont.)
Sacrifice
   see Place of Worship — Offer
Serve
Worship

PLAGUE
Terrible

PLAN
Enemy see Enemy — Plot
Evil
Hurt see Plan — Evil
Jews see Jews — Plan
Pride see Pride — Plan
Purpose
Secret
Succeed
Temple see Temple — Plan
Trouble see Plan — Evil

PLEAD
Help see Help — Plead

PLEASE
Accept
Dear see Please — Son of God
Faith see Faith — Please
Food-offering
   see Food-offering — Pleasing
Life see Life — Please
Love see Please — Son of God
Offer
Right see Right — Please
Sacrifice see Please — Offer
Sheep see Sheep — Offer
Son of God
Worship see Worship — Please

PLEASURE
Life see Life — Pleasure

PLENTY
Harvest see Harvest — Plenty

PLOT
Enemy see Enemy — Plot
Evil see Plan — Evil

POOR
Advantage see Poor — Needy
Blind see Blind — Poor
Cheat see Cheat — Poor
Defend see Poor — Help
God
God's People
   see God's People — Poor
Happy see Happy — Poor
Help
Helpless
Honest see Honest — Poor
Judge see Poor — Justice
Justice
Lord see Poor — God
Needy
Oppress see Poor — Needy
Persecute see Poor — Needy
Protect see Poor — Help
Rich see Rich — Poor
Rights see Poor — Justice
Save see Save — Poor
Weak see Poor — Helpless
Widows see Widows — Poor

POSSESS
Kingdom
   see Kingdom — Possess
Promise see Promise — Possess
Share see Share — Possessions

POWER
Acknowledge
   see Acknowledge — Power
Afraid see Power — Fear
Angel see Angel — Power

POWER (Cont.)
Anger see Anger — Power
Apostles see Apostles — Power
Authorities
   see Authorities — Power
Authority
Believe see Power — Faith
Christ
Cloud see Cloud — Heaven
Cross see Power — Death
Cruel see Power — Evil
Darkness see Darkness — Power
Death
Demons see Demons — Power
Destroy
Enemy see Enemy — Power
Evil
Faith
Father see Father — Power
Fear
Free see Free — Power
Glory see Glory — Power
God
God's People
Gods see Gods — Power
Harm see Power — Hurt
Heal
Heaven see Heaven — Power
Holy see Holy — Power
Honour see Honour — Power
Human see Human — Power
Hurt
Jesus see Power — Christ
Joy see Joy — Power
Judge see Power — Justice
Justice
Kingdom see Kingdom — Power
Life
Lord
Love
Majesty
Means see Power — Authority
Might see Power — Strength
Miracles
Name see Power — Christ
Obey see Obey — Power
Praise
Pray see Pray — Power
Presence
   see Presence — Powerful
Proclaim see Proclaim — Glory
Protect see Power — Safe
Punishment
   see Punishment — Power
Raise see Power — Life
Remember
   see Remember — Power
Rescue
Right see Power — Justice
Safe
Satan see Satan — Power
Save see Save — Power
Share see Share — Power
Sin
Son of Man see Power — Christ
Spirit of God
Spiritual
   see Spiritual — Power
Strength
Teach see Teach — Authority
Temple see Temple — Power
Victory
Weak see Weak — Strength
Wicked see Power — Evil

POWER (Cont.)
Win see Power — Victory
Wisdom
Wonders see Power — Miracles
Word see Word — Power
World
Worship see Power — Praise
PRACTICE
Evil see Evil — Actions
Magic see Magic — Practice
PRAISE
Angel see Angel — Worship
Being see Being — Praise
Bless see Bless — Praise
Bow see Praise — Worship
Creatures
   see Creatures — Praise
Defender
Faithful see Faithful — Praise
Fear see Fear — Praise
Glad see Praise — Happy
Glory see Praise — Name
God's People
Happy
Heart see Heart — Worship
Heaven see Heaven — Worship
Holy see Praise — Name
Honour see Praise — Name
Hope see Hope — Praise
Joy see Praise — Happy
Justice
Levites see Levites — Praise
Love see Love — Praise
Might see Praise — Strength
Name
Obey see Obey — Worship
Offer see Offer — Worship
Power see Power — Praise
Priests see Priests — Worship
Proclaim
   see Proclaim — Worship
Promise see Promise — Worship
Protector
   see Praise — Defender
Rejoice see Praise — Happy
Rescue see Praise — Save
Right see Right — Praise
Righteous see Right — Praise
Sacred see Praise — Name
Sacrifice
   see Sacrifice — Praise
Save
Servants
   see Praise — God's People
Soul
Strength
Teach see Teach — Worship
Temple see Temple — Worship
Thanks see Thanks — Praise
Throne see Throne — Worship
Victory see Victory — Praise
Wonderful
World
Worship
PRAY
Accept see Accept — Prayer
Alone
Believe
Bless see Bless — Pray
Confess see Pray — Repent
Disciple see Disciple — Pray
Earnestly
Fast see Fast — Pray
Father

PRAY (Cont.)
Forgive see Forgive — Pray
God's People
   see God's People — Prayer
Gods see Gods — Pray
Heaven
Help see Help — Pray
Jesus
Life see Life — Pray
Love
Offer see Offer — Prayer
Power
Raise see Raise — Prayer
Repent
Sacrifice see Sacrifice — Pray
Save see Save — Pray
Spirit
Spirit of God
Temple see Temple — Pray
Thanks see Thanks — Prayer
Trouble
Turn see Pray — Repent
Watch
Worship see Worship — Pray
PREACH
Baptize see Baptize — Preach
Believe see Believe — Preach
Christ see Christ — Preach
Disciple see Disciple — Preach
Faith see Faith — Message
Gentiles
   see Gentiles — Good News
Good News
   see Preach — Message
Gospel see Good News — Preach
Jesus see Christ — Preach
Jews see Jews — Message
Kingdom
Message
Synagogue
   see Synagogue — Teach
Teach
Turn see Preach — Message
Word see Preach — Message
PREDICT
False see False — Predictions
Prophets
   see Prophets — Prophesy
True see True — Prophet
Vision see Vision — Predict
PRESENCE
Angel see Angel — Presence
Christ
Dazzling see Presence — Light
Father
Holy
Jesus see Presence — Christ
Joy
Light
Powerful
Spirit of God
Temple
Tent see Tent — Presence
Worship see Worship — Presence
PRESENT
Altar see Altar — Offering
Bread see Bread — Offer
Case see Case — Present
Fellowship-offering
   see F'ship-offering — Present
Food-offering
   see Food-offering — Present
Gift see Gift — Offer

PRESENT (Cont.)
Grain-offering
see Grain-offering — Present
Incense see Incense -- Offer
Lamb see Lamb — Present
Offer see Offer — Present
Priests see Priests — Offer
Sacrifice
see Sacrifice — Present
Sin-offering
see Sin-offering — Offer
Worship see Worship — Offering
PREVENT
Evil see Evil — Prevent
Justice see Justice — Prevent
PRIDE
Arrogant
Boast see Pride — Arrogant
Conceited see Pride — Arrogant
Cruel see Pride — Evil
Deceive
Destroy see Destroy — Pride
Evil
Happy see Pride — Joy
Hate
Humble see Humble -- Proud
Jealous see Jealous — Proud
Joy
Obey see Obey — Stubborn
Plan
Punishment
see Punishment — Proud
Stubborn see Stubborn — Proud
Wicked see Pride — Evil
PRIESTS
Altar
Anoint
see Priests — Consecrate
Bless
Blood see Priests — Offer
Choose see Choose -- Priests
Clean see Priests — Pure
Consecrate
Contribution
see Priests — Gift
Covenant
see Covenant — Priests
Covenant Box
see Covenant Box — Priests
Dedicate
see Priests — Consecrate
Defile see Priests — Unclean
Dove see Priests — Offer
Duty
Gift
God's People
Gods
Holy see Priests — Consecrate
Holy Place
Idols see Priests — Gods
Incense see Priests — Worship
Jews see Jews — Priest
Lamb see Priests — Offer
Law
Levites
Offer
Ordain
see Priests — Consecrate
Pagan see Pagan — Priests
Praise see Priests — Worship
Present see Priests — Offer
Pure
Regulation see Priests — Law
Ritual

PRIESTS (Cont.)
Sacred
see Priests — Consecrate
Sacrifice see Priests — Offer
Scholar see Priests — Law
Serve
Sheep see Priests — Offer
Special see Priests — Gift
Take Away (sin)
see Priests — Pure
Teach
Temple see Temple — Priest
Tent see Tent — Priest
Tithe see Priests — Gift
Unclean
Worship
PRISON
Arrest see Arrest — Prison
Christ
Free see Free — Prisoners
God's People
Help
Law
Sake
Suffer
PROCLAIM
Christ see Christ — Preach
Faithful
see Faithful — Proclaim
Gift see Gift — Message
Glory
God's People
see God's People — Message
Good News
see Good News — Proclaim
Jesus see Christ — Proclaim
Message see Message — Proclaim
Might see Proclaim — Glory
Power see Proclaim — Glory
Praise see Proclaim — Worship
Prophets
see Prophets — Proclaim
Save see Save — Announce
Spirit of God
Thank see Proclaim — Worship
Wonderful see Proclaim — Glory
Word see Word — Proclaim
Worship
PROFANE
Sabbath see Sabbath — Profane
Temple see Temple — Profane
PROMISE
Anger see Anger — Promise
Believe see Promise — Trust
Bless see Bless — Promise
Christ
Command see Promise -- Law
Covenant
see Covenant — Promise
Eternal see Eternal — Promise
Fail
Faith
Faithful
Father
Forgive see Forgive — Promise
Free see Free — Promise
Fulfil
Gift see Gift — Promise
God's People
see God's People — Promise
Heaven see Heaven — Promise
Help
Holy
Honour see Promise — Faithful
Hope see Promise – Faith

PROMISE (Cont.)
Land
Law
Lie see Lie — Oath
Life see Life — Promise
Love see Love — Promise
Loyal see Promise — Faithful
Name see Name — Promise
Obey see Obey — Promise
Offer
Patient see Patient — Promise
Peace
Possess
Praise see Promise — Worship
Protect see Promise — Help
Remember
see Remember — Promise
Rescue see Promise — Save
Rest see Promise — Peace
Sacred see Promise — Holy
Sacrifice see Promise — Offer
Save
Servant see Servant — Promise
Share see Share — Promise
Solemn
Strengthen see Promise — Help
Swear
True see Promise — Faithful
Trust
Vow see Vow — Promise
Wonderful
see Wonderful — Promise
Worship
PROPER
Grain-offering
see Grain-offering -- Proper
Offer see Offer — Right
PROPHESY
Prophets
see Prophets — Prophesy
PROPHETS
Announce
see Prophets — Proclaim
Apostles
see Apostles — Prophets
Believe
Consult see Consult — Prophet
Convince
see Prophets — Believe
Deceive
Dream see Prophets — Vision
False see Prophets — Deceive
Holy
Law see Law — Prophets
Lie see Prophets — Deceive
Message
Miracle see Miracle — Prophet
Obey see Obey -- Prophet
Predict
see Prophets — Prophesy
Proclaim
Prophesy
Reveal see Reveal — Prophet
Scripture
see Scripture — Prophets
Spirit of God
see Spirit of God — Prophet
Teach see Teach — Prophets
Teachers
Temple see Temple — Prophet
True see True — Prophet
Understanding
see Understanding — Prophets
Vision

PROPHETS (Cont.)
  Warn
  Word see Prophets — Message
PROSPERITY
  Bless see Bless — Obey
  Enjoy see Prosperity — Happy
  Evil
  Fail see Prosperity — Succeed
  God's People
    see God's People — Prosper
  Happy
  Life
  Mercy
  Peace
  Succeed
  Wicked see Prosperity — Evil
PROSTITUTE
  Adultery
    see Adultery — Prostitute
PROTECT
  Afraid see Protect — Trust
  Care see Protect — Love
  Defend
  Destroy see Destroy — Save
  Enemy see Enemy — Help
  Evil
  Faithful
  God
  God's People
    see God's People — Protect
  Help see Help — Protect
  Honour see Honour — Protect
  Life see Life — Safe
  Lord see Protect — God
  Love
  Mercy see Mercy — Help
  Oppress see Oppress — Help
  Poor see Poor — Help
  Power see Power — Safe
  Praise see Praise — Defender
  Promise see Promise — Help
  Rescue see Rescue — Safe
  Righteous
  Safety see Safety — Protect
  Save see Save — Protect
  Secure
  Shelter see Protect — Defend
  Strength see Strength — Help
  Strong see Strength — Help
  Trouble see Trouble — Help
  Trust
  Violent see Protect — Evil
  Wicked see Protect — Evil
PROVE
  Guilty see Guilty — Prove
  Miracle see Miracle — Prove
  True
PROVIDE
  Need see Need — Provide
PUNISHMENT
  Afraid see Punishment — Fear
  Anger
  Correct
  Crime see Crime — Punish
  Cup see Cup — Punish
  Death see Punishment — Destroy
  Deserve
  Destroy
  Disaster see Disaster — Punish
  Disease see Disease — Punish
  Disgrace
  Disgusting
    see Punishment — Evil
  Enemies

PUNISHMENT (Cont.)
  Enemy see Enemy — Punish
  Escape see Escape — Punishment
  Eternal
    see Eternal — Punishment
  Evil
  Exile see Exile — Punish
  Faithful see Faithful — Punish
  Fear
  Forgive see Punishment — Mercy
  Fury see Punishment — Anger
  God
  God's People
  Gods see Gods — Punish
  Guilty see Guilty — Punish
  Hate see Punishment — Enemies
  Immoral see Punishment — Evil
  Judge see Judge — Punish
  Lie see Lie — Punish
  Life
  Lord
  Love
  Mercy
  Mind see Punishment — Mercy
  Power
  Proud
  Rebel see Rebel — Punish
  Refuse see Refuse — Punish
  Remember
    see Remember — Punish
  Rescue see Punishment — Save
  Revenge see Revenge — Punish
  Righteous
  Save
  Shame
    see Punishment — Disgrace
  Sin
  Spare see Punishment — Mercy
  Suffering
    see Suffering — Punishment
  Turn see Turn — Punish
  Warn see Warn — Punishment
  Wicked see Punishment — Evil
  Worship see Worship — Punish
PURE
  Altar see Altar — Dedicate
  Blood
  Ceremony
  Christ see Christ — Pure
  Clean see Pure — Holy
  Dedicate see Dedicate — Holy
  Defile
  Faultless see Pure — Holy
  Forgive
  Heart see Heart — Pure
  Holy
  Holy Place
  Jesus see Christ — Pure
  Levites see Levites — Dedicate
  Love see Love — Purity
  Priests see Priests — Pure
  Sight
  Sin
  Sprinkle see Pure — Ceremony
  Temple see Temple — Holy
  Tent see Tent — Holy
  Unclean see Pure — Defile
PURPOSE
  God
  Life see Life — Will
  Lord see Purpose — God
  Plan see Plan — Purpose
  Will see Will — Purpose

QUARREL
  Argue see Argue — Quarrel
RAGE
  Anger
  Fury see Rage — Anger
RAISE
  Believe see Believe — Life
  Body see Body — Life
  Christ
  Dead
  Father see Father — Life
  Glory
  God
  Jesus see Raise — Christ
  Last
  Life
  Power see Power — Life
  Prayer
  Remember
    see Remember — Raise
  Right (hand)
  Son of God see Raise — Christ
  Spirit of God
    see Spirit of God — Raise
RAM
  Altar see Altar — Offering
REAL
  Christ see Christ — Real
  Gods see Gods — False
REAP
  Harvest see Harvest — Reap
  Sow see Sow — Reap
REBEL
  Command
    see Command — Disobey
  Forgive see Forgive — Sin
  God see Rebel — Lord
  God's People
    see God's People — Abandon
  Lord
  Obey see Obey — Stubborn
  Punish
  Refuse see Rebel — Stubborn
  Sin
  Stubborn
  Turn see Turn — Rebel
REFUGE
  City
  God
  Lord see Refuge — God
REFUSE
  Command see Refuse — Obey
  Evil see Evil — Refuse
  Help
  Law see Refuse — Obey
  Obey
  Punish
  Rebel see Rebel — Stubborn
  Reject see Reject — Refuse
  Stubborn see Stubborn — Refuse
  Worship
REGULATION
  Festival see Festival — Law
  Observe
  Offer see Offer — Regulation
  Passover
    see Passover — Regulations
  Priests see Priests — Law
  Sacrifice see Sacrifice — Law
REJECT
  Anger see Anger — Abandon
  Choose
  Command see Reject — Law
  Evil see Evil — Refuse

REJECT (Cont.)
God
God's People
  see God's People — Abandon
Law
Lord
Obey see Obey — Refuse
Refuse
Suffering
  see Suffering — Rejected
Teaching
Turn see Turn — Reject
Worthless

REJOICE
Glad see Rejoice — Joy
Happy see Rejoice — Joy
Joy
Praise see Praise — Happy

RELATIONS
Sex see Sex — Relations

RELIGION
Destroy
  see Destroy — God's People
Festival
  see Festival — Religious
God's People
  see God's People — Religion
Jews see Jews — Religion

REMEMBER
Choose
Command
  see Command — Remember
Covenant
  see Remember — Promise
Evil
Forget
God's People
  see God's People — Remember
Heart
Help
Holy
Judge
Life
Love
Needy see Remember — Help
Power
Promise
Punish
Raise
Scripture
  see Scripture — Remember
Servants
Slaves
Suffering
Teach see Teach — Remember
Wicked see Remember — Evil
Words
Wrong

REPENT
Forgive see Forgive — Repent
Humble see Humble — Repent
Pray see Pray — Repent
Sin
Turn see Turn — Repent

REQUIRE
Law see Law — Command
Offer see Offer — Required
Sacrifice
  see Sacrifice — Require

RESCUE
Afraid see Afraid — Save
Angel see Angel — Help
Death see Death — Rescue
Destroy see Destroy — Save

RESCUE (Cont.)
Enemy see Enemy — Save
Evil
God
God's People
  see God's People — Rescue
Gods see Gods — Save
Heaven see Heaven — Save
Help see Help — Save
Honour see Honour — Save
Life see Life — Save
Lord
Love see Love — Save
Mercy see Mercy — Save
Might see Rescue — Strength
Oppressed
Power see Power — Rescue
Praise see Praise — Save
Promise see Promise — Save
Protect see Rescue — Safe
Punishment
  see Punishment — Save
Safe
Save see Rescue — Safe
Slaves see Rescue — Oppressed
Strength
Trouble see Trouble — Save
Wicked see Rescue — Evil

RESPECT
Bow
Fear see Fear — Respect
Holy see Holy — Awe
Honour see Honour — Reverence
Love see Love — Respect

REST
Command
  see Command — Sabbath
Dedicated
Promise see Promise — Peace
Sabbath
Solemn see Rest — Sabbath

RESTORE
Temple see Temple — Restore

REVEAL
Glory
God
God's People
Jesus
Lord
Message see Message — Revealed
Prophet
Secret see Secret — Reveal
Spirit of God
  see Spirit of God — Reveal
Truth
Vision

REVENGE
Anger
Enemy see Enemy — Punish
Punish

REVERENCE
God
Honour see Honour — Reverence
Lord

REWARD
God
Life see Life — Reward
Lord see Reward — God
Right

RICH
Bless see Bless — Rich
Generous
God's People
  see God's People — Prosper

RICH (Cont.)
Harvest see Harvest — Plenty
Heaven
Kingdom
Life see Life — Riches
Need
Poor

RID
Evil see Evil — Rid
Gods see Gods — Rid

RIGHT
Bless see Bless — Obey
Choose see Choose — Right
Christ
Command see Right — Law
Evil
Faithful see Faithful — Just
Foolish see Foolish — Right
Happy see Right — Joy
Help
Innocent see Innocent — Right
Jesus see Right — Christ
Joy
Judge see Right — Justice
Justice
Law
Learn see Learn — Right
Love see Love — Justice
Mercy
Mind see Mind — Right
Obey see Obey — Right
Offer see Offer — Right
Please
Power see Power — Justice
Praise
Reward see Reward — Right
Save
Sight
Suffering
  see Suffering — Right
Teach see Teach — Right
True
Turn see Turn — Right
Wicked see Right — Evil
Wisdom see Wisdom — Right
Word see Word — True

RIGHT (HAND)
Heaven
  see Heaven — Right (hand)
Raise see Raise — Right (hand)
Throne
  see Throne — Right (hand)

RIGHT WITH GOD
Believe see Believe — Save
Christ see Right — Christ
Faith
  see Faith — Right With God
Jesus see Right — Christ
Law see Right — Law
Obey
  see Obey — Right With God

RIGHTEOUS
Accept see Accept — Righteous
Believe
  see Believe — Righteous
Christ see Right — Christ
Condemn
  see Condemn — Righteous
Evil see Right — Evil
Faith see Faith — Righteous
Glad see Right — Joy
God see Right — God
Happy see Right — Joy
Jesus see Right — Christ

RIGHTEOUS (Cont.)
  Judge see Right — Justice
  Justice see Right — Justice
  Law see Right — Law
  Life see Life — Righteous
  Lord see Right — Lord
  Love see Love — Justice
  Obey
    see Obey — Right With God
  Peace see Peace — Righteous
  Praise see Right — Praise
  Protect
    see Protect — Righteous
  Punishment
    see Punishment — Righteous
  Save see Right — Save
  Wicked see Right — Evil
  World see Right — World
RIGHTS
  Defend see Defend — Poor
  Judge see Rights — Justice
  Justice
  Needy see Rights — Poor
  Oppress see Oppress — Rights
  Orphans
  Poor
  Widows
RIPE
  Harvest see Harvest — Ripe
RISE
  Believe see Believe — Life
  Christ see Raise — Christ
  Dead see Raise — Dead
  Jesus see Raise — Christ
  Sadducees see Sadducees — Rise
RITUAL
  Offerings
  Priests see Priests — Ritual
  Take Away (sin)
RIVAL
  Tolerate
SABBATH
  Command see Sabbath — Law
  Duty see Duty — Sabbath
  Heal see Heal — Sabbath
  Holy
  Law
  Observe
  Profane
  Rest see Rest — Sabbath
  Sacred see Sabbath — Holy
  Synagogue
    see Synagogue — Sabbath
  Teach
  Worship
SACKCLOTH
  Ashes
  Mourn see Mourn — Sackcloth
  Weep see Weep — Mourn
SACRED
  Anoint see Anoint — Consecrate
  Bread see Bread — Sacred
  Covenant Box
    see Covenant Box— Sacred
  Dedicate see Sacred — Offering
  Destroy
    see Destroy — Place of Worship
  Gift see Sacred — Offering
  Holy
  Offering
  Praise see Praise — Name
  Priests
    see Priests — Consecrate
  Promise see Promise — Holy

SACRED (Cont.)
  Sabbath see Sabbath — Holy
  Sacrifice
    see Sacred — Offering
  Temple see Temple — Holy
  Tent see Tent — Holy
  Worship see Worship — Sacred
SACRIFICE
  Accept see Accept — Offering
  Altar see Altar — Offering
  Anger see Anger — Offer
  Bless see Bless — Offer
  Blood see Blood — Offer
  Christ see Christ — Offer
  Command see Sacrifice — Law
  Covenant
    see Sacrifice — Promise
  Death
  Dedicate
  Feast see Sacrifice — Festival
  Fellowship-offering
    see F'-offering — Sacrifice
  Festival
  Forgive
    see Forgive — Sacrifice
  Gods
  High Priest
    see Sacrifice — Priest
  Honour see Sacrifice — Please
  Idols see Sacrifice — Gods
  Incense see Incense — Offer
  Joy see Sacrifice — Praise
  Lamb see Lamb — Sacrifice
  Law
  Levites see Levites — Offer
  Love
  Obey
  Offer see Offer — Sacrifice
  Pagan see Pagan — Offer
  Passover
    see Passover — Sacrifice
  Place of Worship
    see Place of Worship — Offer
  Please
  Praise
  Pray
  Present
  Priest
  Promise
  Regulation see Sacrifice — Law
  Require
  Sacred see Sacred — Offering
  Share see Share — Offer
  Sheep see Sheep — Offer
  Sin
  Sin-offering
    see Sin-offering — Offer
  Take Away (sin)
  Temple see Temple — Offering
  Thanks see Sacrifice — Praise
  Worship see Worship — Offering
SAD
  Glad see Sad — Happy
  Happy
SADDUCEES
  Jesus
  Pharisees
    see Pharisees — Sadducees
  Rise
SAFETY
  Care see Safety — Protect
  Danger see Safety — Protect
  Enemy
  Evil

SAFETY (Cont.)
  God's People
    see God's People — Safety
  Harm see Safety — Protect
  Life see Life — Safe
  Love
  Peace see Peace — Security
  Power see Power — Safe
  Protect
  Rescue see Safety — Save
  Save
  Secure
  Shelter see Safety — Protect
  Temple
  Trouble see Safety — Protect
  Trust see Trust — Safety
  Violent see Safety — Protect
SAKE
  Christ see Christ — Sake
  Jesus see Christ — Sake
  Life see Life — Sake
  Prison see Prison — Sake
  Suffering see Suffering — Sake
SALVATION
  Faith see Save — Faith
  Gentiles
    see Gentiles — Salvation
  God see Save — God
  Lord see Save — God
  Message
    see Message — Good News
SATAN
  Angel see Angel — Devil
  Power
SATISFY
  Desire
  Hunger
  Need
SAVE
  Afraid see Afraid — Save
  Anger see Anger — Save
  Announce
  Believe see Save — Faith
  Care
  Choose
  Christ
  Danger see Save — Trouble
  Death see Death — Rescue
  Defend see Save — Protect
  Destroy see Destroy — Save
  Distress see Save — Trouble
  Enemy see Enemy — Save
  Evil
  Faith
  Free see Save — Rescue
  God
  God's People
    see God's People — Rescue
  Gods see Gods — Save
  Grace see Grace — Saved
  Happy
  Heaven see Heaven — Save
  Help see Help — Save
  Honour see Honour — Save
  Hope
  Idols see Idols — Save
  Jesus see Save — Christ
  Joy see Save — Happy
  Judge see Judge — Save
  Law see Save — Obey
  Life see Life — Save
  Lord see Save — Christ
    and Save — God
  Love see Love — Save

SAVE (Cont.)
Mercy see Mercy — Save
Message
 see Message — Good News
Might see Save — Power
Obey
Oppress see Oppress — Save
Poor
Power
Praise see Praise — Save
Pray
Proclaim see Save — Announce
Promise see Promise — Save
Protect
Punishment
 see Punishment — Save
Rescue
Right see Right — Save
Righteous
Safe see Save — Protect
Sin
Slave see Slave — Rescue
Spare see Spare — Mercy
Strength see Strength — Save
Suffering see Save — Trouble
Trouble
Trust see Save — Faith
Truth see Truth — Save
Turn see Turn — Save
Victory see Victory — Save
Violence see Save — Trouble
Violent see Violent — Protect
Wicked see Save — Evil
World
SAYING
True see True — Saying
Wisdom see Wisdom — Words
SCATTER
Enemies
God's People
Seed see Seed — Sow
Sheep
 see Scatter — God's People
SCHOLAR
Law see Law — Scholar
Priests see Priests — Law
SCRIPTURE
Believe
Jesus
Prophets
Remember
Teach
True
Understanding
 see Understanding — Scripture
SEAL
Covenant see Covenant — Blood
Lamb see Lamb — Seal
SECRET
Christ
Jesus see Secret — Christ
Learn see Learn — Secret
Message
Plan see Plan — Secret
Reveal
Truth
Understand
SECURE
Peace see Peace — Security
Protect see Protect — Secure
Safety see Safety — Secure
SEED
Harvest see Harvest — Seed
Scatter see Seed — Sow

SEED (Cont.)
Sow
SENSE
Foolish see Foolish — Sense
SENTENCE
Death see Death — Punish
SEPARATE
Levites see Levites — Separate
SERVANT
Angel see Angel — Servant
Announce
 see Announce — Servant
Chosen
Christ
Covenant see Servant — Promise
Exile see Exile — Servants
Faithful
Feast see Feast — Servant
Happy
Jesus see Servant — Christ
Law see Law — Servant
Love see Love — Servant
Loyal see Servant — Faithful
Master see Master — Servant
Obey
Praise
Promise
Remember
 see Remember — Servants
Will
Worship see Servant — Praise
SERVE
Altar see Altar — Serve
Christ
Destroy see Destroy — Obey
Faithfully
God's People
 see God's People — Serve
Gods see Gods — Serve
Heart
Help see Help — Serve
Honour see Honour — Serve
Idols see Idols — Serve
Jesus see Serve — Christ
Judge see Judge — Serve
Law see Serve — Obey
Levites see Levites — Serve
Love see Love — Serve
Loyally see Serve — Faithfully
Obey
Place of Worship
 see Place of Worship — Serve
Priests see Priests — Serve
Temple see Temple — Serve
Tent see Tent — Serve
Turn see Turn — Gods
Worship see Worship — Serve
SETTLE
Dispute see Dispute — Settle
SEX
Immorality
Perversion
 see Sex — Immorality
Relations
SHAME
Disgrace see Disgrace — Shame
Idols see Idols — Shame
Punishment
 see Punishment — Disgrace
Turn see Turn — Shame
SHARE
Blessings
Christ
Fate

SHARE (Cont.)
Glad see Share — Happiness
Glory
God's People
Happiness
Harvest
Help
Holiness
Joy see Share — Happiness
Life
Love
Needy see Share — Help
Offer
Possessions
Power
Promise
Sacrifice see Share — Offer
Suffering
SHEEP
Altar see Altar — Offering
Best see Sheep — Offer
Blood see Sheep — Offer
Care see Care — Flock
First-born see Sheep — Offer
Flock see Flock — Sheep
God's People
 see God's People — Shepherd
Lamb see Sheep — Offer
Offer
Pleased see Sheep — Offer
Priests see Priests — Offer
Sacrifice see Sheep — Offer
Scatter
 see Scatter — God's People
Shepherd see Shepherd — Sheep
SHELTER
Celebrate
 see Celebrate — Festival
Protect see Shelter — Safe
Safe
SHEPHERD
Care see Care — Flock
Flock see Flock — Sheep
God
God's People
 see God's People — Shepherd
Good
I Am see I Am — Shepherd
Lord see Shepherd — God
Sheep
SIGHT
Blind see Blind — Sight
Horrible
 see Sight — Horrifying
Horrifying
Pure see Pure — Sight
Right see Right — Sight
Terrifying
 see Sight — Horrifying
SIGN
Covenant see Covenant — Sign
SIN
Accuse see Accuse — Sin
Action see Action — Sinful
Afraid see Afraid — Sin
Angel see Angel — Sin
Anger see Anger — Sin
Baptize see Baptize — Sins
Believe see Believe — Sin
Blind see Blind — Sin
Blood see Blood — Sin
Body see Body — Sin
Burden see Burden — Sin
Christ see Christ — Sin

SIN (Cont.)
  Clean see Clean — Sin
  Commandment
    see Commandment — Sin
  Condemn see Condemn — Sin
  Confess see Confess — Sin
  Crime see Crime — Sin
  Dead see Dead — Sin
  Death see Death — Sin
  Deceive see Deceive — Sin
  Defile see Defile — Sin
  Desire see Desire — Sin
  Destroy see Destroy — Sin
  Disobey see Disobey — Sin
  Enemy see Enemy — Sinful
  Eternal see Eternal — Sin
  Evil see Evil — Sin
  Exile see Exile — Punish
  Faith see Faith — Sin
  Faithful see Faithful — Sin
  Fault see Fault — Sin
  Foolish see Foolish — Sin
  Forgive see Forgive — Sin
  Free see Free — Sin
  Gentiles see Gentiles — Sin
  Gift see Gift — Sin
  God's People
    see God's People — Sin
  Gods see Gods — Sin
  Grace see Grace — Sin
  Hate see Hate — Sin
  Heal see Heal — Sin
  Heart see Heart — Sin
  Heaven see Heaven — Sin
  Holy see Holy — Sin
  Human see Human — Sin
  Idols see Idols — Sin
  Image see Image — Sin
  Immorality
    see Immorality — Sin
  Innocent see Innocent — Sin
  Judge see Judge — Sin
  Law see Law — Sin
  Love see Love — Sin
  Mankind see Mankind — Sin
  Mercy see Mercy — Sin
  Power see Power — Sin
  Punishment
    see Punishment — Sin
  Pure see Pure — Sin
  Rebel see Rebel — Sin
  Repent see Repent — Sin
  Sacrifice see Sacrifice — Sin
  Save see Save — Sin
  Slave see Slave — Sin
  Suffering see Suffering — Sin
  Turn see Turn — Sin
  Warn see Warn — Sin
  Wicked see Wicked — Sin
  World see World — Evil
  Worship see Worship — Sin
SIN-OFFERING
  Lamb see Sin-offering — Offer
  Offer
  Present
    see Sin-offering — Offer
  Sacrifice
    see Sin-offering — Offer
SINCERE
  Heart see Heart — Sincere
SLAUGHTER
  Enemy see Enemy — Destroy
SLAVE
  Christ

SLAVE (Cont.)
  Free see Free — Slave
  God's People
    see God's People — Rescue
  High Priest
    see High Priest — Slave
  Jesus see Slave — Christ
  Love see Love — Servant
  Master see Master — Servant
  Obey
  Remember
    see Remember — Slaves
  Rescue
  Save see Slave — Rescue
  Sin
  Spirit
SOLEMN
  Promise see Promise — Solemn
  Rest see Rest — Sabbath
  Vow see Vow — Solemn
  Warn see Warn — Solemn
SON
  of David
  of God
  of Man
SON OF GOD
  Angel see Angel — Jesus
  Believe
  Choose see Choose — Jesus
  Christ
  Dear see Son of God — Love
  Death
  Eternal see Son of God — Life
  Faith see Son of God — Believe
  Father see Father — Jesus
  Glory see Glory — Jesus
  Heaven see Heaven — Jesus
  Jesus see Son of God — Christ
  Judge see Judge — Jesus
  Kingdom see Kingdom — Christ
  Life
  Love
  Messiah
    see Son of God — Christ
  Please see Please — Son of God
  Raised see Son of God — Life
  Spirit of God
  World
SON OF MAN
  Angel see Angel — Jesus
  Cloud see Cloud — Heaven
  Forgive see Forgive — Jesus
  Glory see Glory — Jesus
  Heaven see Heaven — Jesus
  Power see Power — Christ
SORROW
  Glad see Sorrow — Joy
  Grief
  Heart
  Joy
  Mourning see Sorrow — Grief
  Trouble
SOUL
  Heart see Heart — Soul
  Praise see Praise — Soul
SOURCE
  God
  Life
  Lord see Source — God
  Peace
SOW
  Harvest
  Message
  Reap

SOW (Cont.)
  Seed see Seed — Sow
SPARE
  Destroy
  Life see Life — Spare
  Mercy
  Punishment
    see Punishment — Mercy
  Save see Spare — Mercy
SPECIAL
  Contribution
    see Special — Offering
  Dedicate
    see Special — Offering
  Gift see Special — Offering
  Offering
  Priests see Priests — Gift
SPIRIT OF GOD
  Angel
  Baptize
    see Baptize — Spirit of God
  Believe
  Body see Body — Spirit of God
  Child of God
    see Sp of G — God's People
  Christ
  Churches
  Control
    see Control — Spirit of God
  Faith
    see Spirit of God — Believe
  Father
    see Father — Spirit of God
  Forgive
    see Forgive — Spirit of God
  Free see Free — Spirit of God
  Gentiles
    see Gentiles — Spirit of God
  Gift see Gift — Spirit of God
  Glory
  God's People
  Good News
    see Spirit of God — Message
  Hearts
  Heaven
  Help see Help — Spirit of God
  Human
    see Human — Spirit of God
  Jesus
    see Spirit of God — Christ
  Joy see Joy — Spirit of God
  Law see Law — Spirit of God
  Life
  Love
  Message
  Obey see Obey — Spirit of God
  Peace
  Power
    see Power — Spirit of God
  Pray see Pray — Spirit of God
  Presence
    see Presence — Spirit of God
  Proclaim
    see Proclaim — Spirit of God
  Prophet
  Raise
  Reveal
  Son of God
    see Spirit of God — Christ
  Spirit(s)
    see Spirit(s) — Spirit of God
  Teach
  Temple
    see Temple — Spirit of God

SPIRIT OF GOD (Cont.)
True see True — Spirit of God
Truth
Understanding
   see Understanding — Sp of G
Union
   see Union — Spirit of God
Vision
   see Vision — Spirit of God
Wisdom
Word
   see Spirit of God — Message
SPIRIT(S)
Body see Body — Spirit
Christ
Consult
Dead see Spirit(s) — Consult
Demons see Demons — Spirits
Disease see Disease — Demons
Evil see Evil — Spirit
Gods see Gods — Spirit
Heal see Heal — Spirits
Jesus see Spirit(s) — Christ
Obey see Obey — Spirits
Pray see Pray — Spirit
Slave see Slave — Spirit
Spirit of God
World
SPIRITUAL
Christ
Gift see Gift — Spiritual
Physical
Power
World
SPRINKLE
Altar see Altar — Sprinkle
Blood see Blood — Sprinkle
Pure see Pure — Ceremony
STEAL
Lie see Lie — Steal
STRANGER
Welcome
   see Welcome — Stranger
STRENGTH
Christ
Heart see Heart — Strength
Help
Holy see Holy — Mighty
Jesus see Strength — Christ
Mighty
Mind
Power see Power — Strength
Praise see Praise — Strength
Promise see Promise — Help
Protect see Strength — Help
Rescue see Rescue — Strength
Save
Trust see Trust — Strength
Turn see Turn — Strengthen
Victory see Victory — Strength
Weak see Weak — Strength
Wisdom see Wisdom — Strength
STRIKE
Disaster see Disaster — Strike
Disease see Disease — Strike
STRIP
Naked see Naked — Strip
STRONG
Angel see Angel — Mighty
Defend see Strength — Help
Faith see Faith — Strong
Life see Life — Strong
Love see Love — Strong
Mighty see Strength — Mighty

STRONG (Cont.)
Protect see Strength — Help
STUBBORN
Evil
Heart see Heart — Stubborn
Obey see Obey — Stubborn
Proud
Rebel see Rebel — Stubborn
Refuse
STUDY
Law see Law — Study
STUPID
Foolish see Foolish — Stupid
Learn see Learn — Fool
Wisdom see Wisdom — Foolish
SUCCEED
Plan see Plan — Succeed
Prosperity
   see Prosperity — Succeed
SUFFERING
Afraid see Afraid — Suffer
Christ
Church
   see Suffering — God's People
Cruel
Cup see Cup — Suffer
Death
Disaster
   see Suffering — Trouble
Disease
   see Suffering — Trouble
Disgrace
Endure
Enemy see Enemy — Suffer
Eternal
   see Eternal — Punishment
Forget see Forget — Suffering
Glad see Suffering — Joy
Glory
God's People
Good News
Guilty see Guilty — Suffer
Happy see Suffering — Joy
Heal see Heal — Suffer
Jesus see Suffering — Christ
Joy
Message
   see Suffering — Good News
Messiah see Suffering — Christ
Oppression
   see Suffering — Trouble
Pain see Pain — Suffer
Patience
   see Suffering — Endure
Persecution
   see Persecution — Suffer
Prison see Prison — Suffer
Punishment
Rejected
Remember
   see Remember — Suffering
Right
Sake
Save see Save — Trouble
Share see Share — Suffering
Sin
Terrible
Trouble
Will see Will — Suffer
World see World — Suffer
SURE
Faith see Faith — Sure
Union see Union — Sure

SWEAR
Loyal see Loyal — Promise
Name see Name — Promise
Promise see Promise — Swear
Vow see Vow — Promise
SYMBOL
Goddess see Gods — False
SYNAGOGUE
Discuss see Synagogue — Teach
Jews see Jews — Synagogue
Preach see Synagogue — Teach
Sabbath
Teach
TABLET
Commandment
Covenant
Covenant Box
TAKE AWAY (SIN)
Offer see Offer — Forgive
Priests see Priests — Pure
Ritual
   see Ritual — Take Away (sin)
Sacrifice
   see Sacrifice — Take Away (sin)
TAX COLLECTORS
Outcasts
Pharisees
TEACH
Accept see Accept — Word
Amazed
Authority
Believe see Believe — Preach
Believers
   see Teach — God's People
Christ
Churches
   see Teach — God's People
Command see Teach — Law
Correct see Teach — Right
Disciple see Disciple — Teach
Encourage
   see Encourage — Teach
Faith see Faith — Teaching
Faithful see Faithful — Obey
Forget see Teach — Remember
God's People
Good News
   see Teach — Message
Hard
Heart
Honour see Teach — Obey
Jesus see Teach — Christ
Law
Learn see Learn — Teach
Lie
Love see Love — Teach
Message
Need see Need — Teach
Obey
Power see Teach — Authority
Praise see Teach — Worship
Preach see Preach — Teach
Priests see Priests — Teach
Prophets
Reject see Reject — Teaching
Remember
Right
Sabbath see Sabbath — Teach
Scripture
   see Scripture — Teach
Spirit of God
   see Spirit of God — Teach
Synagogue
   see Synagogue — Teach

TEACH (Cont.)
  Temple
  Truth
  Will
  Wisdom see Wisdom — Teach
  Word see Teach — Message
  Worship
TEACHERS
  Apostles
    see Apostles — Teachers
  Prophets
    see Prophets — Teachers
TEACHERS OF THE LAW
  Chief Priests
    see Chief Priests — T of L
  Elders
  Hypocrites
  Pharisees
    see Pharisees — T of L
  Terrible
TEARS
  God's People
    see God's People — Mourn
TELL
  Good News
    see Good News — Proclaim
TEMPLE
  Abandon see Abandon — Temple
  Angel
  Anger see Anger — Temple
  Bow see Temple — Worship
  Command
  Consecrate
    see Temple — Dedicate
  Contribution
    see Temple — Offering
  Covenant Box
    see Covenant Box — Temple
  Dedicate
  Defile see Temple — Profane
  Destroy see Destroy — Temple
  Duty
  Enemy see Temple — Profane
  Evil see Temple — Profane
  Gift see Temple — Offering
  Glorious
  Gods see Gods — Temple
  Happy see Temple — Joy
  Heaven
  Help see Help — Temple
  High Priest
    see Temple — Priest
  Holy
  Honour
  Idol see Temple — Profane
  Incense see Incense — Temple
  Jews see Jews — Temple
  Joy
  Love see Love — Temple
  Majestic see Temple — Glorious
  New see Temple — Restore
  Offering
  Pagan see Temple — Profane
  Plan
  Power
  Praise see Temple — Worship
  Pray
  Presence see Presence — Temple
  Priest
  Profane
  Prophet
  Purify see Temple — Holy
  Restore
  Sacred see Temple — Holy

TEMPLE (Cont.)
  Sacrifice
    see Temple — Offering
  Safety see Safety — Temple
  Serve
  Spirit of God
  Teach see Teach — Temple
  Thank see Temple — Worship
  Tithe see Temple — Offering
  Vision see Vision — Temple
  Watch
  Worship
TENT
  Altar see Altar — Tent
  Anoint see Anoint — Tent
  Cloud see Tent — Presence
  Covenant Box
    see Covenant Box — Tent
  Dedicate
  Duty
  Holy
  Holy Place
  Levites see Levites — Tent
  Offering
  Presence
  Priest
  Purify see Tent — Holy
  Sacred see Tent — Holy
  Serve
  Unclean
  Worship
TERRIBLE
  Anger see Anger — Terrible
  Disease see Disease — Terrible
  Pharisees
    see Pharisees — Terrible
  Plague see Plague — Terrible
  Suffering
    see Suffering — Terrible
  Teachers of the Law
    see T of L — Terrible
TERRIFY
  Afraid
  Destroy see Destroy — Afraid
  Enemy see Enemy — Afraid
  Fear see Terrify — Afraid
  Sight see Sight — Horrifying
  Tremble see Terrify — Afraid
  Visions
TERROR
  Fear see Fear — Afraid
TEST
  God
  Heart see Heart — Test
  Lord
  Obey
TESTIMONY
  Lie see Lie — Word
THANKS
  Bread see Bread — Thanks
  Father see Thanks — God
  Glad see Thanks — Joy
  Glory see Thanks — Praise
  God
  Heart see Heart — Worship
  Heaven see Heaven — Worship
  Honour see Thanks — Praise
  Joy
  Lord
  Love see Love — Praise
  Offer
  Praise
  Prayer

THANKS (Cont.)
  Proclaim
    see Proclaim — Worship
  Sacrifice see Thanks — Offer
  Temple see Temple — Worship
THORNS
  Crown see Crown — Thorns
THREAT
  Disaster see Disaster — Threat
THRONE
  Angel see Angel — Throne
  Creatures
    see Creatures — Throne
  Glorious
  God see Throne — Lord
  Heaven
  Lamb see Lamb — Throne
  Lord
  Praise see Throne — Worship
  Right (hand)
  Worship
TITHE
  Levites see Levites — Offer
  Offer see Offer — Tithes
  Priests see Priests — Gift
  Temple see Temple — Offering
TOLERATE
  Rival see Rival — Tolerate
TOMB
  Body see Body — Grave
TONGUES
  Gift see Gift — Tongues
  Message see Message — Tongues
TRAP
  Escape see Escape — Trap
  Pharisees see Pharisees — Trap
  Wicked see Wicked — Downfall
TREE
  Life see Life — Tree
TREMBLE
  Afraid see Tremble — Fear
  Fear
  Knees
  Terrified see Tremble — Fear
TRIUMPH
  Enemy see Enemy — Victory
  Victory see Victory — Triumph
TROUBLE
  Anger see Anger — Trouble
  Complain
  Darkness
  Disaster
    see Disaster — Trouble
  Distress
  Happy
  Heart see Heart — Trouble
  Help
  Hope see Hope — Trouble
  Life see Life — Trouble
  Need see Need — Trouble
  Peace see Peace — Trouble
  Plan see Plan — Evil
  Pray see Pray — Trouble
  Protect see Trouble — Help
  Rescue see Trouble — Save
  Safe see Trouble — Save
  Save
  Sorrow see Sorrow — Trouble
  Suffering
    see Suffering — Trouble
  Turn see Turn — Trouble
  Wicked see Wicked — Trouble
TRUE
  Accept see Accept — True
  Faith

TRUE (Cont.)
Faithful see Faithful — Loyal
False see True — Lie
Grace see True — Love
Heart see Heart — Faithful
Holy see Holy — True
Judge see Judge — Justice
Knowledge
Law see Law — True
Lie
Life
Love
Message see Message — True
Obey see Obey — True
Offer see Offer — Right
Predict see True — Prophet
Promise see Promise — Faithful
Prophet
Prove see Prove — True
Right see Right — True
Saying
Scripture see Scripture — True
Spirit of God
Witness see Witness — Faithful
Word see Word — True
Worship

TRUST
Afraid see Afraid — Trust
God
Gods see Gods — Trust
Happy see Happy — Trust
Help see Help — Faith
Hope
Idols see Idols — Trust
Lord
Love see Love — Faith
Promise see Trust — Word
Protect see Protect — Trust
Safety
Save see Trust — Safety
Strength
Turn see Turn — Believe
Word

TRUTH
Believe
Christ
Faith see Faith -- Truth
Grace see Grace — Truth
Happy see Happy — Truth
Jesus see Truth — Christ
Learn see Learn — Truth
Lie see Lie — Truth
Life
Light see Light — Truth
Love see Love — Truth
Message see Truth — Word
Reveal see Reveal — Truth
Save
Secret see Secret — Truth
Spirit of God
see Spirit of God — Truth
Teach see Teach — Truth
Word

TURN
Anger see Anger — Turn
Baptize
Believe
Blood
Brightness see Turn — Darkness
Command see Command — Turn
Darkness
Evil
Forgive

TURN (Cont.)
God's People
see God's People — Abandon
Gods
Heal
Heart
Help
Humble see Humble — Repent
Idols see Turn — Gods
Law
Light see Turn — Darkness
Mercy see Turn — Forgive
Night see Turn — Darkness
Obey see Obey — Turn
Pray see Pray — Repent
Preach see Preach — Message
Punish
Rebel
Reject
Repent
Right
Save
Serve see Turn — Gods
Shame
Sin
Strengthen
Trouble
Trust see Turn — Believe
Understanding
see Understanding — Turn
Unfaithful
see Unfaithful — Turn
Ways see Ways — Turn
Wicked see Turn — Evil
Words
Worship see Turn — Gods
Wrong see Turn — Right

UNCLEAN
Clean see Clean — Unclean
Defile see Defile — Unclean
Offer see Offer — Defile
Priests see Priests — Unclean
Pure see Pure — Defile
Tent see Tent — Unclean

UNDERSTANDING
Christ
Commands
see Understanding — Laws
Disciple
see Disciple — Understand
Foolish see Foolish — Wise
God's People
see God's People — Understand
Help
Jesus
see Understanding — Christ
Knowledge
see Knowledge — Understand
Laws
Learn see Learn — Understand
Love
Message
see Understanding — Words
Mind see Mind — Understand
Parable
see Understanding — Words
Prophets
Scripture
Secret see Secret — Understand
Spirit of God
Turn
Vision see Vision — Understand
Wisdom
Words

UNFAITHFUL
God see Unfaithful — Lord
God's People
see God's People — Abandon
Gods
Lord
Turn
Worship see Unfaithful — Gods

UNION
Christ
Death see Union — Christ
God
God's People
Jesus see Union — Christ
Life see Life — Union
Lord see Union — Christ
Love see Love — Union
Spirit of God
Sure

UNIVERSE
Create see Create — World
God
Heaven see Heaven — World

UNLEAVENED
Bread see Bread — Unleavened

UNLEAVENED BREAD
Celebrate
see Celebrate — Festival
Festival
see Festival — Unl'd Bread
Passover
see Passover — Unl'd Bread

USELESS
Idols see Idols — Useless
Life see Life — Useless

VALUE
Wisdom see Wisdom — Value

VICTORY
Afraid see Afraid — Victory
Death
Enemy see Enemy — Victory
God's People
Happy
Joy see Victory — Happy
Love
Power see Victory — Strength
Praise
Save
Strength
Triumph
Win

VINE
I Am see I Am — Vine

VIOLENT
Deceive
Destroy see Destroy — Violent
Enemy see Enemy — Cruel
Evil
Oppress
Protect
Safe see Violent — Protect
Save see Violent — Protect
Wicked see Violent — Evil

VISION
Angel see Angel — Dream
Dream see Dream — Vision
False
Heaven
Message
Predict
Prophet
Reveal see Reveal — Vision
Spirit of God
Temple

VISION (Cont.)
Terrify see Terrify — Visions
Understand
Words see Vision — Message
VOW
Fulfil
Offer see Offer — Vow
Promise
Solemn
Swear see Vow — Promise
WARN
Command
Evil
God's People
Obey
Prophets see Prophets — Warn
Punishment
Sin
Solemn
WATCH
Pray see Pray — Watch
Temple see Temple — Watch
WAYS
Change see Ways — Turn
Evil
Turn
Wicked see Ways — Evil
WEAK
Faith
Help see Help — Weak
Poor see Poor — Helpless
Power see Weak — Strength
Strength
WEDDING
Feast see Feast — Wedding
WEEP
Bitterly
God's People
   see God's People — Mourn
Grief see Grief — Weep
Jesus
Mourn
Sackcloth see Weep — Mourn
WELCOME
Stranger
WICKED
Action see Action — Sinful
Anger see Anger — Evil
Condemn see Condemn — Sin
Death see Death — Sin
Deceive see Deceive — Sin
Destroy see Destroy — Sin
Disaster see Wicked — Downfall
Downfall
Enemy see Enemy — Sinful
Evil
Hate see Hate — Sin
Heart see Heart — Sin
Honest see Honest — Wicked
Judge see Judge — Sin
Life see Life — Evil
Love see Love — Evil
Power see Power — Evil
Pride see Pride — Evil
Prosperity
   see Prosperity — Evil
Protect
Punishment
   see Punishment — Evil
Remember see Remember — Evil
Rescue see Wicked — Protect
Right see Right — Evil
Righteous
Save see Wicked — Protect

WICKED (Cont.)
Sin
Trap see Wicked — Downfall
Trouble
Turn see Turn — Evil
Violent see Wicked — Evil
Ways see Ways — Evil
Words
Wrong see Wicked — Evil
WIDOWS
Advantage
Orphan see Orphan — Widow
Poor
Rights see Rights — Widows
WIFE
Love see Love — Wife
WILL
Apostles see Apostles — Choose
Command
Free see Free — Will
Life see Life — Will
Obey see Obey — Word
Purpose
Servant see Servant — Will
Suffer
Teach see Teach — Will
WIN
Approval
Faith
Favour see Win — Approval
Life
Power see Power — Victory
Victory see Victory — Win
World see World — Win
WISDOM
Advice
Correct
Destroy see Destroy — Wisdom
Foolish
God
Happy see Happy — Wise
Honour see Honour — Wisdom
Human see Human — Wisdom
Knowledge
   see Knowledge — Wisdom
Law see Law — Wisdom
Learn see Learn — Wisdom
Life
Lord see Wisdom — God
Message see Wisdom — Words
Obey
Power
Right
Sayings see Wisdom — Words
Spirit of God
   see Spirit of God — Wisdom
Strength
Stupid see Wisdom — Foolish
Teach
Understanding
   see Understanding — Wisdom
Value
Wise
Words
World see World — Wise
WISE
Wisdom see Wisdom — Wise
WITHOUT YEAST
Bread see Bread — Unleavened
WITNESS
Death
Faithful
Heaven see Heaven — Witness
Lie see Lie — Word

WITNESS (Cont.)
True see Witness — Faithful
WONDERFUL
Acts
Holiness
Love
Might see Wonderful — Power
Miracles see Wonderful — Acts
Power
Praise see Praise — Wonderful
Proclaim see Proclaim — Glory
Promise
WORD
Accept see Accept — Word
Angel see Angel — Message
Believe
Bless see Bless — Words
Claim see Word — False
Condemn
Deceive see Word — False
Disciple
   see Disciple — Understand
Eternal see Eternal — Word
False
Foolish see Foolish — Words
Friend see Friend — Words
God
Happy see Happy — Obey
Heart
Help
Honest see Word — True
Human
Judge
Kind see Word — Help
Lie see Word — False
Life
Lord
Love
Obey
Power
Preach see Word — Proclaim
Proclaim
Prophets
   see Prophets — Message
Remember
   see Remember — Words
Right see Word — True
Spirit of God
   see Spirit of God — Message
Teach see Teach — Message
True
Trust see Word — Believe
Truth see Truth — Word
Turn see Turn — Words
Understanding
   see Understanding — Words
Vision see Vision — Message
Wicked see Wicked — Words
Wisdom see Wisdom — Words
World
WORLD
Angel see Angel — World
Believe see World — Faith
Blessing
Create see Create — World
Destroy see Destroy — World
Evil
Faith
Father see Father — World
Glory see Glory — World
Hate
Heaven see Heaven — World
Honour see Honour — World
Joy see Joy — World

WORLD (Cont.)
  Judge see World — Justice
  Justice
  Kingdom see Kingdom — World
  Life see Life — World
  Light see Light — World
  Love see Love — World
  Mankind see Mankind — World
  Message see Message — World
  Peace see Peace — World
  Power see Power — World
  Praise see Praise — World
  Righteous see Right — World
  Save see Save — World
  Sin see World — Evil
  Son of God
    see Son of God — World
  Spirit(s)
    see Spirit(s) — World
  Spiritual
    see Spiritual — World
  Suffer
  Win
  Wise
  Word see Word — World
WORLD OF THE DEAD
  Abandon
  Alive
  Death
  Heaven
WORRY
  Life see Life — Worry
WORSHIP
  Abandon
    see Worship — Unfaithful

WORSHIP (Cont.)
  Altar see Altar — Worship
  Angel see Angel — Worship
  Anger see Anger — Worship
  Bow see Bow — Worship
  Claim
  Command see Worship — Law
  Destroy see Destroy — Worship
  Disobey
  Faithful
  Festival see Festival — Honour
  Gentiles
    see Gentiles — Worship
  God's People
    see God's People — Worship
  Hate see Hate — Idolatry
  Heart see Heart — Worship
  Heaven see Heaven — Worship
  Holy see Holy — Worship
  Honour see Honour — Worship
  Idols see Idols — Worship
  Incense see Incense — Worship
  Jews see Jews — Worship
  Joy
  Law
  Message see Message — Worship
  Obey see Obey — Worship
  Offering
  Pagan see Pagan — Worship
  Place of Worship
    see Pl of W — Worship
  Please
  Power
  Praise see Praise — Worship
  Pray

WORSHIP (Cont.)
  Presence
  Present see Worship — Offering
  Priests see Priests — Worship
  Proclaim
    see Proclaim — Worship
  Promise see Promise — Worship
  Punish
  Refuse see Refuse — Worship
  Sabbath see Sabbath — Worship
  Sacred
  Sacrifice
    see Worship — Offering
  Servant see Servant — Praise
  Serve
  Sin
  Teach see Teach — Worship
  Temple see Temple — Worship
  Tent see Tent — Worship
  Throne see Throne — Worship
  True see True — Worship
  Turn see Worship — Unfaithful
  Unfaithful
WORTHLESS
  Reject see Reject — Worthless
WRONG
  Hate see Hate — Justice
  Remember
    see Remember — Wrong
  Turn see Turn — Right
  Wicked see Wicked — Evil
YEAST
  Bread
  Pharisees